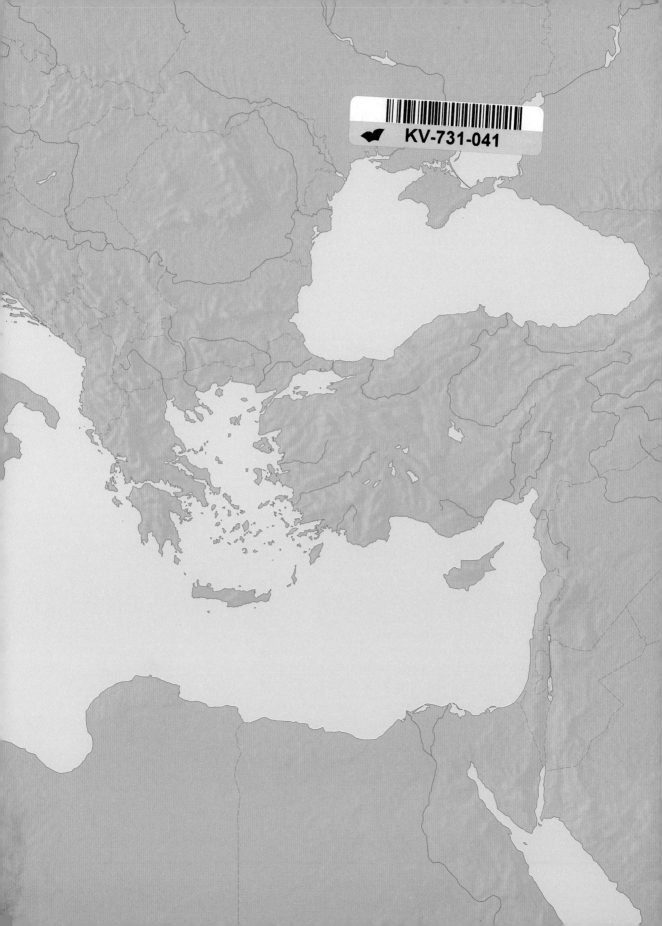

THE
MAKING
OF THE
MIDDLE
SEA

CYPRIAN BROODBANK

THE *MAKING* *OF THE* *MIDDLE* *SEA*

**A History of the Mediterranean from the Beginning
to the Emergence of the Classical World**

To Lindsay Spencer, *stella maris mea*

Frontispiece: Reconstruction of a 2nd-millennium BC eastern Mediterranean Bronze Age ship at sea, derived from the composite evidence of the Uluburun shipwreck plus Aegean and Egyptian imagery.

First published in the United Kingdom in 2013 by
Thames & Hudson Ltd, 181A High Holborn, London WC1V 7QX

First published in the United States of America in 2024 by
Thames & Hudson Inc., 500 Fifth Avenue, New York, New York 10110

This second edition published in 2024

The Making of the Middle Sea © 2013 and 2024
Thames & Hudson Ltd, London
Preface © 2024 Cyprian Broodbank
Text © 2013 Cyprian Broodbank

British Library Cataloguing-in-Publication Data
A catalogue record for this book is available from the British Library

Library of Congress Control Number 2024935121

ISBN 978-0-500-02644-1

Printed and bound in China by C & C Offset Printing Co. Ltd

Remaking *The Making,*
ten years later

A recent thought experiment of provocative scope, if unfathomable maths, claims that the amount of digital data that humanity currently generates each year would, if a single byte were equated to a drop of water, match the entire capacity of the Mediterranean and Black seas combined.[2] Regardless of the precision of this estimate of a vast, moving, imperfectly glimpsed target, the thought strikes home in an analogous sense. Despite an intervening global pandemic, enormous quantities of new information about the archaeology and deep history of the Mediterranean have continued to pour in each year since the first appearance in 2013 of *The Making of the Middle Sea,* in total volume far beyond accurate measure or comprehensive grasp. Fortunately, most are the kind of normative, vital workhorse data that contribute to the cumulative clarification, elaboration or incremental shifting of known and emergent patterns already largely captured in the 2013 synthesis. That synthesis, it should be swiftly noted, remains necessarily untouched in this second edition, as a monument to the state of knowledge and interpretation ten years ago, and equally to any errors on my part with regard to both. If even three-quarters of the edifice still stands acceptably today, let alone in another decade, the original venture might be judged to have been worthwhile. Instead, this new Preface highlights three game-changing developments of Mediterranean-wide significance, in the fields of (1) archaeologically applied science, (2) human evolution and (3) North Africa. Accompanying these are an invidiously chosen selection of others that, while more regional or local in scope, nonetheless add distinctively fresh, and sometimes spectacular, notes to our understanding of the early Mediterranean's emergence.

Since 2013, the case for acknowledging the longer historical dynamics that brought the Mediterranean into being has been resoundingly won in shallow time, for the mid-to-late 2nd and early 1st millennia BC (broadly the later Bronze and Iron Ages; Chapters 9, 10 and later parts of 8). Terms such as 'connectivity' or 'network' abound amidst recent titles pertaining to this period.[3] Books are devoted both to the Phoenicians as Mediterranean-makers and to the Mediterranean as a maker of Phoenicians,[4] while one overview regards the deed as largely done for Mediterranean Europe by the transition between these millennia.[5] For this time span, the challenge is now to integrate such expansive perspectives with the experiences of local lives,[6]

0.1 Burials at 5th-century BC Himera in northwest Sicily, interpreted as war graves.

which *The Making* sought to achieve by juxtaposing broad canvases with detailed vignettes, but certainly under-theorized. Equally in demand for this period, and finally coming within reach, thanks to scientific advances highlighted below, is some hard quantification. We still have few absolute figures, but can now make much better-educated estimates. For example, we are starting to know an extraordinary amount about the soldiers who died defending the Greek city of Himera in northwest Sicily from Carthage in 480 BC, at the terminus of *The Making*'s coverage, due to science and the excavation of a series of mass graves [**0.1**]. Unsurprisingly for a 'Greek colony', many were locally born citizen soldiers of Aegean ancestry; more surprisingly, they were outnumbered by others from a vast arc of origin north of the Mediterranean as far as the Caucasus, most of whom were recent arrivals, whether as mercenaries or people otherwise caught in the net of the Mediterranean's widening economic and demographic reach.[7]

This Preface deliberately focuses, however, on earlier times, reaching back to human origins (Chapters 3 and 4), the spread of agriculture and resultant societies around the basin (Chapters 5 and 6), and then concentrates, as in 2013, on the transformative 'long' 3rd millennium BC and its consequences (Chapters 7 and 8). There is a strong evangelizing reason for this emphasis, beyond a dash of authorial bias and what seems to be a genuine unevenness in the number and magnitude of the breakthroughs by period over the last ten years. For *The Making*'s fundamental argument was that there exist far deeper-time and gradually braiding ancestries to the Mediterranean's emergence, and from my viewpoint, at least, that message has yet to sink decisively home.

In 2013 the making of a 'middle sea' was mainly envisioned in terms of incrementally increasing connectivity and its accompanying cultures of interaction and betweenness, all embedded within the challenges and opportunities presented by cumulative environmental 'Mediterraneanization' of the basin, itself driven to varying degrees by climate change and human intervention. Understanding this process requires an acute awareness of varying scales and modes of connectivity over time, as one recent study reminds us.[8] Since 2013, further thought-provoking perspectives have come to the fore, concerning the kinds of long-term trajectories of social organization and power that preceded the Iron Age (thereby pushing beyond a clichéd, and spatially limited, contrast between earlier 'palace' societies and later city-states).

One takes its cue from the economist Thomas Piketty's dictum that regimes of low growth combined with high returns on capital tend to promote wide wealth inequalities over time.[9] It argues that the Mediterranean's low-growth environments, joined with control over patches of land (and potentially other mobile forms of capital), encouraged precisely the kinds of varied, often temporally fragile spikes of wealth and power portrayed in Chapters 7 and 8 – and, we might add, ended up with the spectrum of power-sharing arrangements, and comparatively weak state institutions, that typify the Mediterranean Iron Age onwards, up to the rival lineages that still drove Italian politics in early Roman times.[10] Another approach, likewise based on the obstacles to sustained state power under Mediterranean conditions, identifies a deep tradition of Lévi-Straussian 'house societies' evolving in niches where corporately structured households could gather and retain patrimonial wealth with impunity.[11] Physical correlates of these are convincingly visible in the grandiose, ideologically strident but non-palatial architecture attested across the Levant, Cyprus, parts of the Aegean archipelago and Sardinia by the 2nd millennium BC, then writ large across the basin by the Iron Age; textually, they accord well with the firm-like economic activities witnessed in the archives of such houses at Levantine Ugarit. In fact, both models resonate well with one final factor, namely the central presence of the sea as an anarchic space, resistive to attempts to control or extend political authority beyond it. The emergence of that sea as a cultural phenomenon remains the most crucial long-term Mediterranean story of all, and one that also now acts as a timely prompt to set out on our voyage through recent discoveries.

New science for an ancient world

Turning to the first game-changer, an increasingly fully integrated, archaeologically oriented suite of scientific methods has driven extraordinary developments over the past few years. Some derive from techniques already established long before 2013, and salient examples of such will be touched on below. But pride of place must go to the coming of age of biomolecular archaeology, deploying stable isotopes, proteins and above all ancient DNA, including whole-genome sequencing, to revolutionize our knowledge of the ancestry, relatedness, mobility, diet, health and more besides of both people and other organisms.[12] This global revolution was approaching the cusp of realization around the time that research for *The Making* was completed, but (frustratingly) with too little reliability and agreement on fundamentals to then warrant strategic inclusion, beyond the findings of a longer tradition of retrojection from modern DNA, and a few other forays – for example, into the longstanding question of the origins of the first farmers in Mediterranean Europe. Even today, ancient DNA analysis in the Mediterranean lags somewhat compared to several other parts of the world. Nonetheless, the past five to six years have witnessed a series of landmark analyses, remarkable in equal part for confirming, or amending, what we thought we knew, and for opening hitherto unimagined vistas.

These insights have tended to operate at two distinct, if mutually informing, levels. One is broad-brush, painting pictures of human ancestry over extensive regions. The other operates at the micro-level, exploring, for instance, the diversity of people within a specific settlement, or relatedness within burying groups. Globally, the former has tended to grab the scholarly limelight and wider publicity, as well as attracting the heaviest criticism for its sometimes simplistic interpretative assumptions concerning people's experienced social and cultural identities, and the material correlates of these (genetics is not cultural history).[13] In Europe north of the Mediterranean, this strand is best exemplified by the identification of a surprise major influx of eastern, steppic ancestry during the mid- to later 3rd millennium BC, alongside the anticipated mix of antecedent hunter-gatherer and broadly eastern Mediterranean genes associated with the spread of farming.[14] In certain areas, including the British Isles, this appears to have involved substantial population turnover, although the mechanisms and timescale are far less obvious than lurid popular headlines would suggest. Interestingly, in the Mediterranean, after the expected and confirmed signature of farming expansion (which laid the genetic groundwork for several ensuing millennia), the equivalent picture looks variable, and nuanced. In Iberia, the later 3rd-millennium BC transition from sophisticated Copper Age societies to differently structured, more overtly hierarchical Argaric and other contemporary communities (see Chapters 7 and 8 respectively) correlates with a substantial showing of steppe ancestry, as well as a thought-provoking bias towards, and discontinuity in, male lineages; the same strand unsurprisingly followed the first colonists into Majorca and Menorca.[15] Together with signs of a later genetic influx around the turn of the 1st millennium BC, this points to episodically much closer trans-Pyrenean links with temperate Europe than was portrayed in *The Making*. On the other hand, Aegean genomic data suggest a patchier presence of steppic ancestry, mainly in northern Greece and elsewhere on the mainland, with little among Cretan populations until the interconnected later 2nd millennium BC.[16] On Sardinia, the genetics suggest exceptional degrees of long-term population continuity from the onset of farming, with minimal influx until the start of the Iron

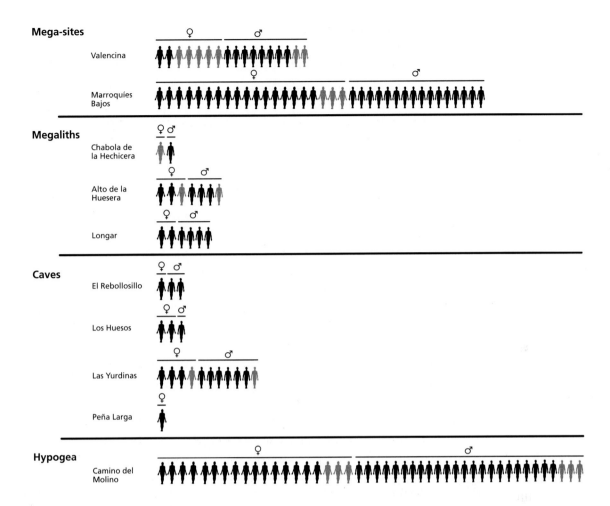

Mega-sites

Valencina

Marroquíes Bajos

Megaliths

Chabola de la Hechicera

Alto de la Huesera

Longar

Caves

El Rebollosillo

Los Huesos

Las Yurdinas

Peña Larga

Hypogea

Camino del Molino

0.2 Female and male mobility at Copper Age Iberian sites, according to strontium isotope analysis (black represents locals; grey non-locals).

Age.[17] The first analyses from the western Maghreb reveal a different picture again, with a mixture of indigenous hunter-gatherer, Mediterranean farming and Levanto-Saharan pastoral ancestries, as anticipated in Chapters 5 and 6[18] – a signature later transferred (with a little steppic derivation) to the Canary Islands, probably during Roman imperial rather than Phoenician or Punic times (cf. Chapter 10).[19]

Standing back, there are some useful points to affirm about the early Mediterranean from this marked variegation. First, and unsurprisingly, the basin's edges (especially those facing the larger Mediterranean land masses) were demographically porous, towards continental Europe, Saharan Africa and also western Asia. But secondly, communities at its maritime, insular and peninsular core were resistive to wholesale turnovers, whether thanks to buffered locations or rather because they scrambled together multiple population strands within the vortices of their own extensive interconnections, so creating individually diverse, and uniquely Mediterranean, profiles.

This brings us to the micro-level insights from the latest biomolecular archaeology. Again, it is worth emphasizing what was already known, or strongly

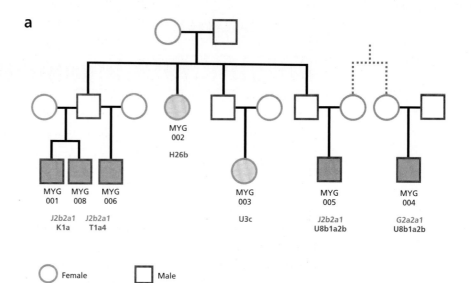

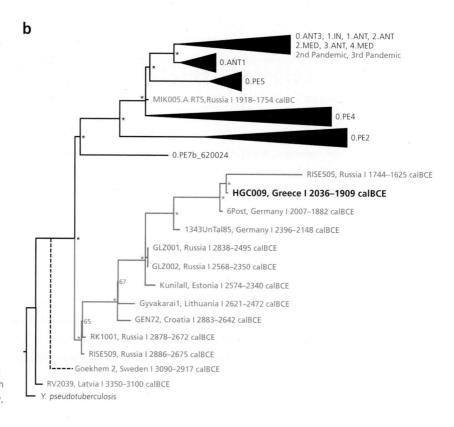

0.3 Family trees revealed by genomics (a) Aegean Late Bronze Age residents at Mygdalia in Attica; (b) bubonic plague across western Eurasia, including recent identification at Agios Charalambos in Crete (shown in bold, other ancient in grey, and modern in black).

suspected, and therefore where the new contributions really impact. While the biomolecular revolution intercepted the archaeology of temperate Europe after decades of antipathy to mobility and migrations as primary explanations of change (and therefore delivered a rude awakening), a key role for movement, from local 'Brownian motion' to long-range voyaging, has been hardwired into Mediterranean interpretation and modelling for decades, empirically on the basis of the extensive distributions of exported materials, as well as privileged insights from Levantine and Egyptian texts into people on the move – all then exalted into paradigm status by Peregrine Horden and Nicholas Purcell's *The Corrupting Sea* (2000).[20] With no revisionist case to be proven, biomolecular evidence instead brings a new granularity and human richness to the general model, helping us to get closer to answering questions of who, how, why, how many, how far, how often. Some of this pre-dated and developed in parallel to the whole-genome breakthrough. For example, stable isotope analysis from 2nd-millennium BC *terramare* villages in the Po plain (see Chapter 8) has shown that while the smaller villages drew their populations from the immediate vicinity (often with women marrying in), the largest communities stand out for the number of inhabitants who had been born further afield, including in warmer regions to the south or east (see **0.2** for a comparable example from southeast Spain a millennium earlier).[21] Meanwhile, the skills of skeletal 'osteobiography' have for some time been swelling our portfolio of individual Mediterranean life histories and experiences, including health and diet as well as movement, beyond the endlessly autopsied case of the Tyrolean Iceman (the latter discussed in Chapter 7).[22]

Illustrative of what further revelations genetics can offer are two nicely contrastive results from the latest Aegean genomic analysis.[23] The first concerns later 2nd-millennium BC Chania, a port town in western Crete already inferred from its material culture to be a modest version of the cosmopolitan, demonstrably polyglot trading cities of the Levantine coast (see Chapter 8). Gratifyingly, the genetics of Chania's burials confirm a mixture of locals, Greek mainlanders with unusually variable, Mediterranean-scrambled amounts of steppic inheritance, and possible residents from the central Mediterranean. Parenthetically, an even more recent study takes this story of port towns as genetic melting pots forward into the 1st-millennium BC central Mediterranean, which saw intense levels of mobility argued to shape patterning up to the present.[24] Iron Age coastal sites on Sardinia opened up the island's long-sequestered populace and almost half the inhabitants of the selected locations in mainland Italy boasted ancestors beyond the peninsula, while Punic Kerkouane in modern Tunisia brought together indigenous Africans and others from across the Sicilian strait – but startlingly, none from the Phoenician Levant. Returning to our second Aegean case, broadly contemporary with the first, this reflects the polar opposite tendency, in a stark revelation of Mediterranean rural priorities that pointed in a radically different direction. For among the small farming communities of Mycenaean Greece, genomic analysis has revealed an entirely unexpected degree of consanguinity, caused by close cousin intermarriage, as well as the first Aegean family tree, extracted from a pit burial of six infants at Mygdalia in Attica [**0.3a**]. This certainly enlivens the traditional picture of Mycenaean death derived from the serried ranks of standardized Mycenaean funerary goods displayed in countless museums. Prurient details apart, one intriguing suggested reason for such close intermarriage – and a profoundly Mediterranean one – is the necessity of keeping plots of slow-maturing olive trees within the family over multiple generations.

Last but not least among the recent genomic contributions to Mediterranean deep history is the identification of archaic versions of later killer pathogens. A quarter of a century ago, I speculated whether among the unseen contributing factors to the breakdown of Cycladic societies around the end of the 3rd millennium BC might lurk 'an expanding frontier of epidemic propagated in the newly integrated zone of urban communities across the Near East and their outlying regions', brought into first direct contact with the islanders around that time by the irruption into the Aegean of long-range Levantine sailing ships (a technology itself disruptive of earlier canoe-based social order).[25] I recall hesitating at the time whether to hazard such an *outré* possibility. Over the last few years, however, genetic analysis has identified an archaic version of *Yersinia pestis*, the plague bacterium, in eastern and central Europe by the 3rd millennium BC, and in 2022 the news broke of its presence by the end of the same millennium among burials at Agios Charalambos in eastern Crete.[26] These early strains may have been less lethal, perhaps not even flea-borne, and Crete is not quite the Cyclades. But for the first time a nexus of shifts in Mediterranean seafaring technology, modes of interconnection, disease vectors, demography and social organization come tantalizingly close to investigative reach, millennia before later plagues in the ages of St Cyprian, the emperor Justinian and the Black Death [**0.3b**].

As already intimated, not all the scientific game-changers of the past few years have been biomolecular. Materials science, which led the investigation of provenance during the last decades of the previous century, setting analyses of Mediterranean trade and exchange on a firm evidential footing, now offers increasingly sophisticated social insights. Microscopic analysis of sheet-gold jewelry and beads from later 3rd-millennium BC Crete reveals semi-skilled practices of sharing, fragmentation and recycling between people and contexts, with no sign of elite control over production and consumption[27] – perhaps a glimpse of the real social collectivities behind the later Minoan 'palaces' (see Chapter 8)? Again in the Aegean, clay analysis of the everyday storage, processing and cooking pots found on dozens of small family farms across the island of Kythera in the mid-2nd millennium BC document individual micro-choices made between the products of two distinct potting centres a few kilometres apart.[28] What drove such preferences, how were pots acquired and in exchange for what? As yet we have no idea, but equally, these kinds of questions are only now being asked.

New technologies of remote prospection are transforming the means of detecting and documenting archaeological sites. Above ground this has so far been effected less by the Light Detection and Ranging (LiDAR) technologies that have so

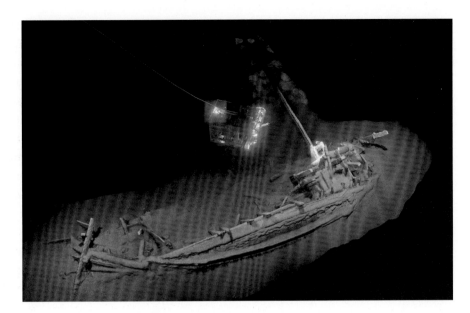

0.4 A remotely captured composite image of a 2400-year-old sailing ship preserved intact in oxygen-poor waters at the bottom of the Black Sea.

dramatically penetrated tropical forest canopies to reveal entire ancient cityscapes in Central America, Southeast Asia and elsewhere, and more by the clever deployments of drone-mounted cameras to such diverse, Mediterranean-adapted ends as spotting pottery scatters in landscape survey and patrolling ancient cemeteries to detect and deter looters in real time.[29] Beneath the waves, remotely operated vehicles offer the chance to explore far deeper than the limits not only of scuba-divers but also Mediterranean trawling, which we are gradually realizing has destroyed (as on most continental shelves) most of the underwater archaeology less than a few hundred metres in depth, largely before we even knew it was there. The first edition of this book was in time to capture the discovery, initially by a US Navy submarine, of the intact ship-shaped amphora cargoes of two Iron Age vessels that sank in some 400 m (1300 ft), cutting across the open seas between Gaza and Egypt (see p. 513). In 2018, searches in the far deeper, oxygen-starved abysses of the Black Sea off the coast of Bulgaria encountered an astonishing number of perfectly preserved ships, the oldest a 2400-year-old sail-and-oar-driven craft, 23 m (75 ft) long and of assuredly Mediterranean design, intact 2 km (1.25 miles) down in the darkness [**0.4**].[30] Back on the surface, computational simulations have meanwhile shed light on how seacraft might have been constrained or enabled in their movements by seasonal, and even daily, fluctuations in navigational conditions [**0.5**]. For canoe-based travellers, for example, some Cycladic islands are shown to be easier to reach than others of equal distance from a specific starting point,[31] and extensive knowledge was demonstrably needed to fully exploit the opportunities of wind and on/offshore breeze regimes between Cyprus, Egypt and the Levantine coast in Bronze Age sailing ships.[32]

The major breakthroughs in climate science, and their implications for the evolution of Mediterranean weather and environments over time, were already largely in place by the first decade of this century, and given a key role in *The Making* – notably the substantially wetter earlier Holocene, the crucial trend towards greater aridity over the 4th to 2nd millennia BC, and an ensuing return to slightly rainier times. Since then, a large-scale project has examined the regional patterning and interrelations of Holocene environmental change and demography around the Mediterranean, using survey and radiocarbon data as proxies for the latter.[33] This has elaborated several key points, including the rise in population with the onset of farming (staggered over time from east to west), the pan-Mediterranean demographic peak under Rome and, in between these, a mosaic of unsynchronized regional oscillations captured in large part by the narratives of Chapters 6 to 10 (although with the drop

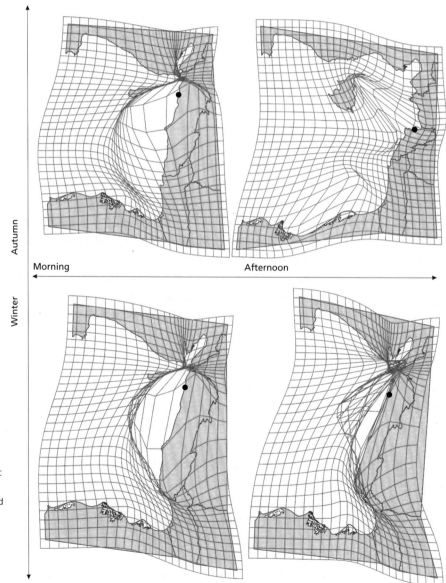

a

Autumn

Winter

Morning

Afternoon

0.5 (*right and opposite*) Two computational simulations of early Mediterranean sea travel: (a) seasonal and morning/afternoon sailing regimes between Byblos (marked) and eastern Mediterranean destinations during the Bronze Age, using cartograms that stretch or compress space to reflect sailing time under local conditions; (b) the changing accessibility of other Cycladic islands from Keros over the summer months, as modelled by navigational conditions for canoe traffic (shaded) compared to linear distances (circles) for 1- and 2-day return journeys.

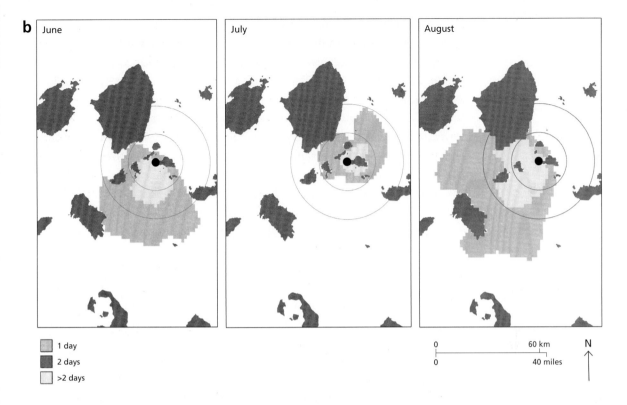

b

June | July | August

1 day
2 days
>2 days

| 0 | 60 km |
| 0 | 40 miles |

N

in southern France during the 2nd millennium BC now firmly established). The role of human activity in creating more open, 'Mediterraneanized' landscapes is apparent in most areas by the 2nd millennium BC, over and above the impact on natural vegetation of growing aridity, and in at least the Aegean a millennium or so earlier. The extent of olive cultivation, and of tree crops in general, varies hugely over time and space, from the earliest signature in the Levant (see Chapter 6) to a first southern French peak only in medieval times; tree cropping tends to correlate with both surges in population and adaptations to arid conditions. More generally, the results of this project have quantitatively substantiated one last superficially paradoxical, yet key, correlation, between the long-term drying across the basin in the 4th to 2nd millennia BC and the parallel rise in both aggregate population and complex forms of social organization (see Chapter 7, pp. 264–65). There seems little doubt that the former encouraged the development of social and agricultural mechanisms to risk-buffer food production from the vagaries of weather, as well as more intensifiable and ultimately exploitable (in scalar and social terms) forms of farming, together with investment in the networks and transport technologies needed to redistribute such resources, whether to collective or highly selective advantage.

What of the role of climate oscillations in triggering so-called social and demographic 'collapses'? Here, little overall advance has occurred since 2013, due to stubborn challenges in sufficiently refining the chronologies of both to render certain suggestive temporal correlations more causally persuasive, or even clinched (something now achieved for the Roman empire, using tight, textually derived timelines and climate data from annual ice-core laminations).[34] There is, however, one compelling exception, and it pertains to the most famous 'collapse' horizon in the early Mediterranean.[35] *The Making* was frankly sceptical that the demise of a cluster of major eastern Mediterranean Bronze Age polities around the end of the 13th century BC could be convincingly laid at the door of the weather, not least given the relatively modest climatic signature compared to earlier 'events', and the fact that this caesura came at the end of many years of experienced adaptation to surviving in an unpredictable and periodically drying world (see Chapter 9). However, it since transpires that annual tree-ring growth in Anatolia does point to precisely the kind of regional circumstance most likely to overwhelm the survival capacities of such societies, namely a short but unbroken run of drought years sufficient to exhaust inter-annual storage and resowing reserves, thereby engendering social and political turmoil. At only one juncture in the run of Anatolian tree-rings from the mid-2nd to early 1st millennium BC do three consecutive years of such drought register. It is therefore quite extraordinary that this deadly cluster falls within, or extremely close to, the narrow window of 1198–1196 BC that has long been textually established for the end of the Hittite empire. Moreover, a comparative analysis of recent Anatolian droughts reveals that they also tend to extend to the adjacent Aegean and northern Levant – in other words, exactly the neighbours most afflicted by similar political disruption around the end of the 13th century BC. As explained in Chapter 9, the eastern Mediterranean 'collapse' at that time was a socio-economic transformation long in the making, with multiple agents and knock-on effects, and not all was as it seemed to the Egyptian elites whose writings overly shape our narratives. Yet it does now appear that into that explanatory mix should be inserted one short-lived, fatal piece of climatic bad luck, whose historically serendipitous timing may have determined when the eventually inevitable wider Mediterranean paroxysm actually unfolded.

The changing shape of human evolution

The second suite of game-changing developments since 2013 returns us to the issues of hominin and human evolution and dispersal around the Mediterranean basin discussed in Chapters 3 and 4. Over the last decade or so this field has witnessed dramatic changes at a global level, thanks to new fossil finds together with ancient DNA. The upshot has been to replace a familiar picture in which a small number of discrete species evolved and spread in linear fashions across time and space (mainly out from Africa) with a mosaic comprising a larger number of species, some interacting biologically and/or culturally to create interstitial populations, and commonly engaged in complex, fluctuating expansions, often a lot earlier than anticipated. This new picture remains emergent and is currently far from agreed, but already several key finds from the circum-Mediterranean area can be highlighted and their implications drawn out. As we shall see, the lands around the Mediterranean are proving to be far more of an early hotspot at several junctures than hitherto appreciated.

The southern flank of the Mediterranean now stands out as an integral part of the broader evolution of hominins and humans in Africa, rather than a late-running sideshow. Finds of stone tools and their traces on butchered animal carcasses at Ain Boucherit in Algeria may push the earliest presence back to as much as 2.4 million years ago, well before the previous date of 1.8 million established at nearby Ain Hanech.[36] Even more crucially, Jebel Irhoud in Morocco reveals the earliest fossil anywhere of an archaic *Homo sapiens* that also displays several crucial skeletal features of later, fully anatomically modern people, together with distinctive new stone tool technologies, all dated to 315,000–300,000 years ago – twice as old as previous *Homo sapiens* remains from the site.[37] And to cap this, slightly further west, near modern Essaouira, Bizmoune Cave has produced perforated marine shell beads made at least 142,000 years ago, the oldest so far known, and thrusting back the origins of such symbolic, probably identity-marking behaviour in northwest Africa in tandem with ongoing bodily evolution.[38] Combined with a growing recognition of dynamic evolutionary developments across much of Asia, one consequence of including North Africa within the cauldron of biology and behaviour that generated our own species (and others besides) is to highlight the likely significance of the Levant, at the junction of these two continents, and itself a strategic peri-Mediterranean corridor and living space repeatedly prominent in *The Making*. To its laurels may now be added a potential status as part of the home range of that Holy Grail of human evolution, the unidentified last common ancestor of ourselves and parallel branches of the human tree.[39] Thought-provoking evidence that the later Levant was indeed a mixing place for hominins came to light in 2021 at the sinkhole of Nesher Ramla in Israel, where fossil fragments resembling Neanderthals but with unusual features suggest hybridization with another, probably Asian, species, while the accompanying stone tools hint at cross-learning from presumably nearby groups of *Homo sapiens*.[40] Cross-connectivity between human species in such (as is becoming clear) long co-inhabited regions has even been proposed as a possible driver of the ultimate explosion of Upper Palaeolithic cultures after approximately 50,000 years ago.[41]

The Nesher Ramla finds date to 140,000–120,000 years ago. Until very recently, even the youngest end of that range lay close to the oldest supportable date for a precociously early presence of *Homo sapiens* in the Levant, as known from fossils at Qafzeh and Skhul in Israel, and assumed to represent a minor, probably temporary warm-weather overspill from Africa into a similar environment (see Chapter 3). But a few years before the Nesher Ramla finds were announced, the news broke of a still earlier confirmed presence of our own species, in the form of a maxilla from Misliya, a neighbour to Skhul among the Carmel caves that have driven so much of our knowledge of human evolution and behaviour in this part of the world. At 177,000–194,000 years old, the Misliya modern human busts dramatically through the previously established horizon.[42] Together with recent indications of modern humans in China dating back 120,000–80,000 years,[43] and in Australia 65,000 years,[44] such finds permanently shatter the old paradigm that exit from Africa occurred only 55,000–50,000 years ago, hand in hand with a late, step-changing cognitive leap forward to behavioural modernity.

0.6 Panoramic view of Stelida in western Naxos, with the island of Paros (joined to Naxos at lowest sea-stands) in the background; the insets show a range of the cherts that attracted early visitors.

Both were manifestly longer-term, more gradual, probably multiple, and sometimes reversible processes that played out over vastly wider geographical theatres.

From a Mediterranean perspective, Misliya lends urgency to the previously implicit question as to how much further modern humans might have spread around the northern side of the basin, long before their traditional arrival horizon some 43,000–40,000 years ago. As yet we have no firm answer. It is unfortunate that the earliest suggestion to be proposed in the past few years, from Apidima Cave in Mani, Greece, based on a skull reconstructed as *Homo sapiens* and claimed to be a remarkable 210,000 years old, has been challenged in terms of both its anatomy and chronometry.[45] If the Apidima identification and date are correct, it would imply that even Misliya has not yet hit the chronological bottom in terms of the first modern human presence in the Levant, and we would probably need to envisage a mosaic of early expansions and potentially local extinctions in and west of the Aegean. Even if, in the final assessment, they are not, Misliya, together with the early surprises in East Asia, should nonetheless still alert us to such possibilities, as well as to the dangers of certain long-held assumptions. In terms of the possibilities, the announcement in 2022 of 54,000-year-old modern human remains and standout tool types at Grotte Mandrin in the Rhône Valley may turn out to mark one breakthrough beyond the traditional horizon[46] – chronologically more modest than Apidima yet strikingly far west – although what it implies for models of early human expansion within or around the Mediterranean basin will remain hotly debated.[47]

As for the dangers now to beware of, one is certainly the prior assumption that Middle Palaeolithic tools in Mediterranean Europe necessarily equate biologically to Neanderthals. The association of such tools, especially distinctive Levallois manufacturing techniques, with the Jebel Irhoud and first Levantine moderns should inject a permanent note of caution elsewhere, in the absence of associated fossils. In addition to this growing uncertainty as to what species were responsible for what residues around the Mediterranean over this period, there are particular implications for the interpretation of Middle Palaeolithic tools found on islands, especially those known to be insular at the time. As discussed in Chapter 3, such finds have to date reasonably been taken as indicators of the extent to which Mediterranean coastal conditions encouraged cognitive stretch, and 'behavioural plasticity',[48] among resident Neanderthals. But what, now, if at least some of these tools are instead the residues of early modern humans?

In fact, the latest review of Palaeolithic seagoing as a global phenomenon argues that the propensities of both species were initially less distinct in the Mediterranean than between moderns and others in Island Southeast Asia, the only comparably early theatre.[49] Minor Neanderthal landfalls on offshore islands are quite plausible, but a fairly slow start for modern human islanders is equally apparent (in this regard, it should be noted that since 2013 the supposedly early site of Riparo di Fontana Nuova on Sicily has been drastically down-dated to the threshold of the Holocene, and the heat taken out of early Sicilian finds in general by the likelihood of a land-bridge during parts of the last glacial).[50] Emblematic of this ambiguity is the newly explored chert-extraction site of Stelida on the modern island of Naxos [**0.6**], where it is increasingly clear both that several kinds of human visitor arrived over tens of thousands of years, far back into (and possibly before) the Middle Palaeolithic, and that the crossings involved, depending on changing sea levels and shores, ranged between the modest and effectively dry-shod.[51] Further evidence of the overall primacy of land routes is offered by genomic data from Taforalt in Morocco (nicely occupying the overlap zone between our three game-changing advances), which confirms speculation in Chapter 4 that the people emerging towards the end of the last Ice Age between the Sahara and the sea derived from an African ancestry heavily mixed with a long-distance westward expansion out of the Levant – yet zero European input from across the Gibraltar strait.[52]

While so much has changed around the Mediterranean in the field of human evolution over the last ten years, there is still no solid evidence that its maritime spaces had been breached to any significant, more than very localized degree before the final millennia preceding the Holocene.

Mediterranean Africa

New insights into the societies living along the southern shores of the Mediterranean west of Egypt during the long millennia of the Holocene prior to the Phoenicians (around 9600–800 BC) comprise our third game-changer. As was lamented in Chapter 1, information about Mediterranean Africa proved to be painfully slim, patchy and sometimes unreliable during research for the original book, especially beyond Egypt (where even the Nile Delta remains under-explored, as well as under-appreciated, as a place of alternative ways of Egyptian life and engagements with

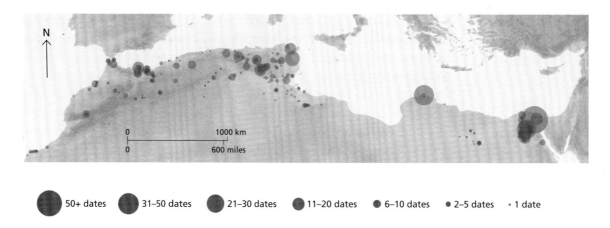

N

● 50+ dates	● 31–50 dates	● 21–30 dates	● 11–20 dates	● 6–10 dates	● 2–5 dates · 1 date

0   1000 km

0   600 miles

0.7 The spatial distribution and frequency of radiocarbon dates across Mediterranean Africa from the end of the last glacial period to the start of the Iron Age (accurate to 2019).

the Mediterranean). My disquiet over this state of affairs, and what it says about the priorities and biases of most early Mediterranean archaeology, subsequently led to a concerted path divergence in my own fieldwork and scholarship. This initially took the form of a comprehensive review and synthesis of all the radiocarbon-dated information that could be gleaned from extant publications, undertaken with Giulio Lucarini, a Saharan expert equally alarmed at the plight of this informationally doubly-orphaned area between our two worlds.[53] The exercise proved revealing, and not always in a good way [0.7]. It transpired that only a meagre 1600 or so dates exist across the entire Mediterranean zones of five modern nations for our 9000-year period – roughly half the totals for the Aegean and Italy apiece. Shockingly, about a third are devoted simply to fine-tuning the dates of pyramids and other Egyptian funerary monuments. Giza and Saqqara alone have had more radiocarbon dates lavished upon them than the entirety of Mediterranean Libya.

More positively, this review affirmed the success and resilience of hunting, gathering and foraging lifestyles across the opening three to four millennia of the Holocene, closely in line with most of the Mediterranean over much of this period, but (in contrast to the rest of the basin, as well as the Sahara) unshaken by the spike of aridity widely attested at around 6200 BC. For the Capsian, it noted the first shoots of a more ambitious social and cultural archaeology, beyond the basics of time, place and subsistence.[54] It confirmed, during the 6th millennium BC, an injection from the east of a new, gradually dominating pastoralism, mainly sheep and goat for dairy-ing, that created a second long-lasting, successful trajectory, this time discrete from the remainder of the Mediterranean, as well as the arrival of elements of a broader farming package in the northwest Maghreb, contemporary with the start of the Neolithic in Iberia. Slightly later, Saharan pastoral elements reached the Atlantic coast of Morocco at Skhirat, whose cemetery in the coastal dunes is now convinc-ingly dated to the 5th millennium BC. Most enigmatically, it identified a steep dive in the amount of available information for the 4th to early 1st millennia BC – the 'silent millennia', as we termed them.[55] This last feature turns out to have little to do with the impact of Saharan desertification – the death of a social and cultural heartland, as it was framed in 2013. Rather, it is a pragmatic product of changing archaeological visibility and research priorities, a lack of determined looking for unfamiliar signatures, and probably a shift at the time from caves (traditionally the primary targets of investigation, especially in the western Maghreb) to open dwelling places. Whatever the causes, Mediterranean Africa drops off the screen, just as other parts of the Copper and Bronze Age Mediterranean were undergoing dramatic transformations and starting to interact extensively – a circumstance that goes a long way towards explaining the former's effective exclusion from analyses of the subsequent emergence of an integrated Middle Sea. By the 1st millennium BC, and the threshold of encounters with the Iron Age progeny of social and economic changes elsewhere around the basin, our best guess was that complex pastoral societies dominated from Egypt's western desert to the Gulf of Sirte, while some form of farming of uncertain antiquity occupied the eastern Maghreb. Further west, ways of life in the central Maghreb remained entirely obscure (to which can since be added a hint of domesticated cereals from one of the Gueldaman caves in Algeria, dated to the 3rd millennium BC),[56] while a presumed but barely substantiated inheritance of earlier farming continued in the far northwest. Altogether, this is not much of an advance on the summary of tribes and ways of life sketched in Herodotus!

The challenge was to improve this situation through new fieldwork. We had already isolated the fertile northwest Maghreb (a mirror image of southwest Iberia) as a promising prospect, with its earlier domesticates and long-known hints of 3rd-millennium BC maritime exchanges across the Gibraltar strait and Mediterranean Atlantic, comprising northbound ivory and ostrich egg reciprocated by southbound beaker pottery and metalwork styles – all right at the heart of those silent millennia. Recent discoveries, moreover, had excitingly inflected this pattern.[57] From the Copper Age mega-site of Valencina de la Concepción (on which

0.8 Drone-mounted aerial photogrammetry of Oued Beht in the northwest Maghreb, with surface distribution of finds in lighter shading circled, showing the major later 4th millennium to early 3rd millennium BC focus in the north.

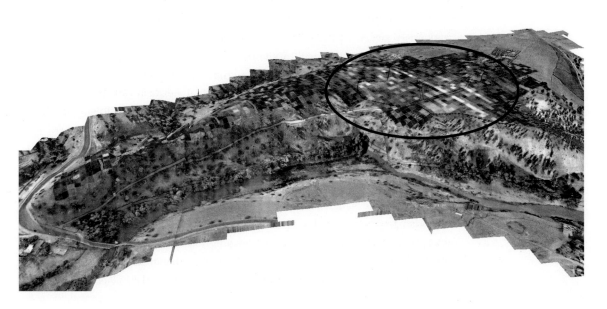

more below) came an intact elephant tusk;[58] ancient DNA revealed an Iberian input to Neolithic populations south of the strait, as well as two individuals of African descent buried in 3rd- and 2nd-millennium BC Spain;[59] and the first donkeys in Iberia now seem likely descendants of Maghrebian breeds.[60] Yet beyond such phantasmal outlines, what might west Maghrebian societies who participated in all this have actually looked like when at home? At this point, Giulio and I responded to a call from the Moroccan archaeologist Youssef Bokbot to collaborate in new archaeological investigations at the site of Oued Beht.

Oued Beht has hovered, symptomatically, on the furthest horizons of archaeological consciousness for decades. It was recognized in the 1930s under colonial French rule, when it became known as the source of thousands of polished stone axes. Reports of this lithic fecundity were encountered during research for *The Making*, but its circumstances came across as too obscure to make the final cut (a tantalizing error in retrospect). From the autumn of 2021 until the time of writing, our Anglo-Italian-Moroccan team has explored and sought to understand one of the last hitherto entirely unknown societies to have existed around the early Mediterranean, using 21st-century archaeology to enlighten a virtually 19th-century level of prior ignorance, and making every effort to interpret from the accumulating data upwards, rather than importing Mediterranean or African models and expectations that might blunt and overly smooth the raw unfamiliarity [**0.8**].[61] We now know that Oued Beht was big, with some 9–10 ha (22–25 acres) of intensive activity, arguably larger than any site of its age in Africa beyond Egypt and the Nile corridor, or indeed the iconic Early Bronze Age of Troy, and outclassed only by the vastest of the Copper Age Iberian sites (on Iberian mega-sites, see below and Chapter 7). Although the area was probably occupied by early farmers at the turn of the 6th to 5th millennia BC, and well into the 3rd (if not 2nd), its floruit dates to 3500–2900 BC, around the start of the 'long' 3rd millennium BC that was identified as such a seminal period for the Mediterranean in Chapter 7.

Oued Beht is riddled with deep, narrow-mouthed pits. One of these, excavated and finely sieved in 2022, has confirmed the presence of domesticated barley, wheat and pea, together with domesticated goats (mainly) and sheep, with cattle and pigs of perhaps diverse status, but significantly, no necessarily hunted species. In short, this single pit has confirmed a full Mediterranean-type farming package right in the midst of the silent millennia. Beyond its myriad polished axes, some of which we now know were created at the site, the material culture of Oued Beht is equally impressive, with hundreds of grinding stones for processing cereals, and a pottery industry of unparalleled technological sophistication for the early Maghreb, including an unsuspected tradition of locally made painted ceramics that outnumber similar finds in contemporary Iberia, some at least of which might now be convincingly explained as Maghrebian imports. So far, Oued Beht emerges as a major place of production, storage, consumption and exchange operating within a long-inherited farming environment. Whether that makes it an exceptionally large, populous and potentially socially complex residential village, or a regional gathering place for dispersed groups, or something entirely different, remains to be determined. Its location is thought-provoking, too; now overlooking from its heights a gritty truck-stop in the poor rural hinterland of Morocco, it lay in elephant country as late as Roman times, and was probably once far closer to the sea, via the river that flows below it, down to what was plausibly once an Atlantic inlet or estuarine wetland, today smothered by alluvial soil.

How much has all this altered the picture from *The Making*, which self-confessedly struggled at times to make sense of Mediterranean Africa beyond Egypt? In certain ways, as then posited, this southern flank of the Mediterranean was indeed different, and initially oriented more towards a greener Sahara. Yet that difference should not be timelessly essentialized, and only became amplified during the 6th millennium BC, before which farming was of restricted extent north of the sea, too. Even after that, the degree of difference varies by region, and often remains hard to gauge for lack of evidence. Places like Oued Beht, whatever its idiosyncrasies, may prove to be just as much a part of the variegated Mediterranean mainstream during the long 3rd millennium BC as equivalents in, for example, Iberia or the Aegean, and there are hints that the same may hold true for its currently all but invisible regional successors up to the start of the Iron Age.[62] Years of exciting work will be needed to delineate all this. The same may be true for the eastern Maghreb, especially in coastal areas of Tunisia such as Cape Bon, given the fact of immediately pre-Phoenician farming further inland, albeit of unknown derivation (whether west to east across the Maghreb, or trans-Mediterranean). In contrast, the 'Libyan' pastoral groups and political confederacies of eastern Mediterranean Africa do appear to represent a distinctive pathway and lineage in comparative Mediterranean terms, right up to the Iron Age.

Last but not least, what of the intriguing suggestion that the coastal landscapes of the southern shore – most of which (unlike those of much of the Mediterranean) looked out onto empty horizons devoid of enticing peninsulas and islands – discouraged people from maritime experimentation? This turns out to be true, except when it is not. The lack of early maritime initiatives from eastern Mediterranean Africa (save Egypt, and even there the first ventures developed coastwise up the Levant) and the central Maghreb make eminent sense in these terms, as does the converse orientation on a deep (peri-)desertic universe to the south. But equally, it looks increasingly likely that in the rarer cases of encouraging coastal configuration, Mediterranean Africans did go to sea. Across the narrows of the far west, it would be extremely surprising if the broad range of interactions now documented with Iberia resulted exclusively from maritime initiatives from the northern side – indeed, given how strongly the two coastlines resemble each other, and the new genetic evidence of early North Africans buried in Iberia, it would be sheer prejudice to assume so. The same may be true for the eastern Maghreb, with its corrugated shores facing the islands of the Sicilian narrows. Here, the location of Pantelleria, and the findspots of its obsidian across Tunisia (with tool production mainly at coastal sites), suggests an odds-on chance that seafaring North Africans were involved in its acquisition. Ostrich egg finds from the 3rd-millennium BC Maltese archipelago, together with preliminary reports of biologically 'African' individuals in burials there,[63] as well as in Sardinia,[64] may hint at even further-ranging seafarers from the south. The crucial distinction for understanding how a Middle Sea ultimately emerged as it did was not some innate incapacity for maritime activity on the part of Mediterranean Africa compared to the rest of the basin, so much as the segregation of its seagoing activity into widely separate zones that could not readily inter-communicate and amplify each other, and that were perhaps also only intermittently active. It was such factors that led to the drastic cumulative imbalance in connectivity relative to the rest of the Mediterranean, and all that followed from that in terms of determining patterns of abrupt change and integration during the Iron Age and subsequent centuries leading up to Rome.

From red queens to flaming grain: regional highlights from around the Middle Sea

So far, we have explored how three thematic game-changers (biomolecular and other archaeological science; the shifting picture of human evolution; and the informational rise of the southern shore) have dramatically advanced or altered the explanations set out some ten years ago. These, however, capture only a selection of the more localized breakthroughs that have taken place within particular regions, and before drawing this update to a close, we should visit a few further outstanding examples that have so far escaped the net. We start a short hop from the Maghreb, in Iberia, without doubt the area that has led the Mediterranean in terms of thought-provoking archaeology over the past ten years.

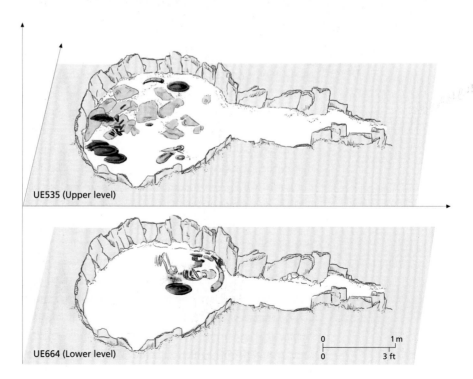

UE535 (Upper level)

UE664 (Lower level)

0   1 m
0   3 ft

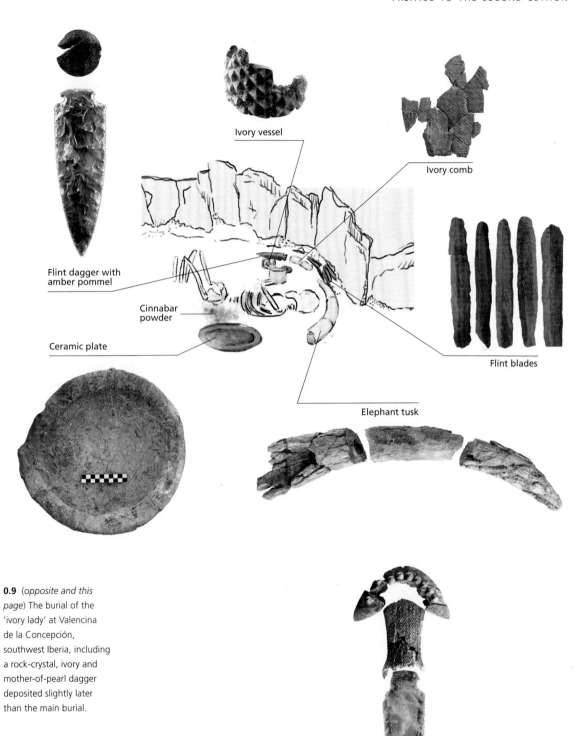

0.9 (*opposite and this page*) The burial of the 'ivory lady' at Valencina de la Concepción, southwest Iberia, including a rock-crystal, ivory and mother-of-pearl dagger deposited slightly later than the main burial.

Ivory vessel

Ivory comb

Flint dagger with amber pommel

Cinnabar powder

Ceramic plate

Flint blades

Elephant tusk

0   5 cm
0   2 in

Here, the extraordinary dynamics of the Copper Age (3200–2200 BC) continue to shake the foundations of traditional, eastern-oriented expectations. As in 2013, the lead among a number of mega-sites remains with Valencina de la Concepción, near modern Seville but then at the head of a now-lost embayment of the Guadalquivir. Valencina's vast extent of ditched enclosures variously devoted to living, ceremonial aggregation, craftworking, storage, trade in exotics and monumental burial render it by any measure the largest locale of its day anywhere in the Mediterranean save perhaps for Egyptian Memphis. Isotopic insights into how people moved around in Copper Age Iberia now suggest that on average a quarter of the people buried in one place grew up in another, but with higher proportions at such mega-sites; this mobility included both men and women (although with a preponderance of the latter; **0.1**).[65] Quite how to explain the social processes that created and sustained Valencina and its contemporaries remains a matter of debate, given the striking absence of signs of institutionalized social hierarchy, with a strong possibility of collective, charismatic or performative forms of power, status acquisition and incipient leadership. One insight comes from the recent reidentification of a single burial at Valencina as that of a young woman, between 17 and 25 years old, accompanied by unparalleled accumulations of ivory (including the entire tusk mentioned earlier), flint, amber and copper, as well as a dish containing cannabis and wine [**0.9**]. Her bones were saturated with traces of brilliant red cinnabar from the mercury mines of central Spain. Overlying this were equally extraordinary retrospective offerings, including a rock-crystal dagger with an ivory hilt adorned in mother-of-pearl, thought to be connected to a later group, again mainly of richly dressed and equipped, cinnabar-drenched women, buried at the nearby Montelirio megalithic tomb.[66]

If we move on a thousand years and a little further east, a telling contrast emerges with another remarkable find, from the Argaric Early Bronze Age, a society already highlighted in *The Making* as the most thoughtfully interpreted example anywhere in the basin of the rise in microcosm of an exploitative, dominating elite under Mediterranean conditions (see pp. 418–21). At La Almoloya in Murcia a large sunken room has been revealed, lined with benches to accommodate about fifty people, interrupted by a hearth and podium that elevated a now vanished focus of attention. Beneath its floor, hunched in a double jar burial, were found a woman with opulent gold and silver jewelry and a man with healed wounds surrounded by weapons; their baby daughter, identified from her DNA, was buried next door. In upper and adjacent rooms were quantities of grinding stones for cereals and other manufacturing tools. La Almoloya is a small place, a tiny fraction of the size of Valencina, but here, unambiguously on display, are accumulations of the means of production, right beside spaces where meetings and politics took place, and power – however engendered – was exercised [**0.10**].[67]

Before we take our leave of the western Mediterranean, it is worth asking whether it was even more extensively interconnected, especially in the 3rd millennium BC, than we have previously assumed. Valencina and Oued Beht lie about 400 km (250 miles) apart, similar to the distances that span the southern Aegean,

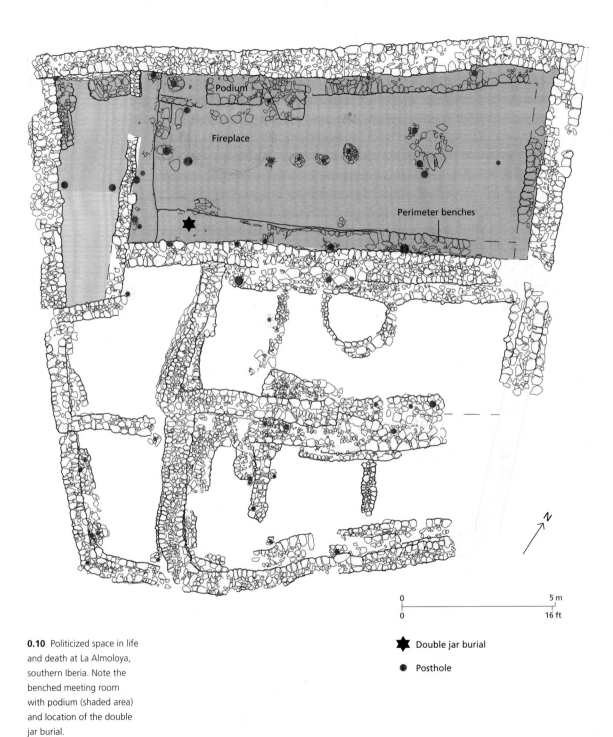

Podium

Fireplace

Perimeter benches

N

| 0 | | 5 m |
| 0 | | 16 ft |

0.10 Politicized space in life and death at La Almoloya, southern Iberia. Note the benched meeting room with podium (shaded area) and location of the double jar burial.

★ Double jar burial

● Posthole

and their extractive hinterlands for raw materials are likely to have spread somewhat further. Such distances around the 'circle of the straits' fall within reasonable range for canoe voyaging, perhaps already augmented in the west, as in the east, by overland donkey-borne portage. But two recent claims open up potentially more distant horizons. The first is the scientific identification of the earliest amber in Copper Age Iberia as Sicilian in origin, not Baltic, as previously thought.[68] Both sources are ultra-distant, but while down-the-line dispersal from the latter across temperate Europe has long been an acknowledged phenomenon, the 700–1000-km (435–600-mile) inter-island route between Sicily, Sardinia and the western Mediterranean has hitherto been judged on good grounds not to have been operating until the final centuries of the 2nd millennium BC (see Chapter 9). There is no sign of early connections around the northern continental margin, while a south-shore alternative, although intriguing in light of Mediterranean African developments, runs into a current lack of evidence in the broader Maghrebian void. The second claim, if substantiated, would turn the maritime world of the early western Mediterranean upside down. It concerns depictions of sail-and-oar-driven ships painted on the walls of the Laja Alta rockshelter, north of Gibraltar. Previously thought to reflect the recent arrival of such long-distance shipping in far western waters during the early 1st millennium BC (see Chapter 9 and fig. 9.7), some 2000 years after its invention at the other end of the Mediterranean, these images have now been argued to belong to the Copper Age or even slightly earlier.[69] Rock art is notoriously slippery to date, so the jury remains out, but if affirmed this would imply either an effectively all but instantaneous westward expansion across the Mediterranean, against the grain of intervening data, or (slightly less implausibly) an independent invention in coastal Iberia (with Valencina a prime candidate?), perhaps followed by an abeyance as Iberian societies shifted to more localized exercises of power. At the time of writing, the overall impression regarding early seafaring in the western Mediterranean is of a paradigm creaking and warping a little, but as yet unsure whether it needs to break, and if so, how completely.

South of Sicily, the remarkable archaeology of the Maltese islands has experienced a more interpretatively lively last few years than the rest of the early central Mediterranean. This has mainly circled around the dates of first settlement for the islands; the establishment of an earlier start to the monumental Temple period than hitherto known (around 3800 BC, now better aligned with comparable funerary monuments in Ozieri-phase Sardinia); and explanations for the collapse of Temple society, and its closely succeeding phases.[70] Implicit in much of this is the question of how isolated or connected the islands were at various stages, and thanks to what internal or external initiatives. An irruption of plague into a sequestered insular environment is now added to the mix of late-3rd-millennium BC doomsday scenarios, if as yet without scientific support to match the broadly contemporary identification on Crete discussed earlier.

The Making characterized the Aegean as a climax Mediterranean in terms of its maritime geography, not least for its profusion of islands. One Aegean field project is finally paying dedicated attention to the most minuscule of these.[71] The collective survey of such insular pinpricks promises to shed entirely fresh light on a special class of place, one of broad Mediterranean distribution and significance but below the threshold usually deemed worthy of investigation (exceptions in Chapter 7 include the mid-Adriatic islet of Palagruža, as well as Keros in the Cyclades).[72] At what periods were they visited, by whom, and to what ends? Were such places often truly inhabited, or inhabitable? And from a structural perspective, should we understand them as isolates on the internal margins of Mediterranean life, as fragments of larger, collectively sustainable islandscapes, or even as vibrant central places under the right conditions? Equally thought-provoking is the renewed interest in what happens when a Mediterranean island is a volcano, and blows up with colossal force within a constricted, densely inhabited archipelago. The impact of the mid-2nd-millennium BC Thera (Santorini) eruption in terms of redirecting Aegean sea-trading networks has been computationally modelled and simulated,[73] while excavations at Çeşme-Bağlararası on the east Aegean coast reveal likely victims of the resultant tsunami, buried pell-mell in the rubble.[74] Frustratingly, with one convincingly identified exception, the major Bronze Age west Anatolian polities, known from contemporary texts, that lay between such coastal centres and the Hittite uplands remain obdurately all but archaeologically invisible.[75]

Bearing in mind the current emphasis in Iberia on prominent women, it is refreshing to see this possibility renewed for the ruling groups of 2nd-millennium BC Crete by a richly interpretive reading of Minoan imagery.[76] Emphatically masculine in orientation, however, is one of the most stunning works of art ever discovered in the prehistoric Aegean [0.11], a combat scene carved on a tiny agate sealstone buried with dozens of others and an abundance of precious and other metallic wealth around 1450 BC, at the cusp of the rise of mainland palatial society, in the Tomb of the Griffin Warrior at Pylos – the richest Mycenaean tomb found since the Shaft Graves.[77] It would be churlish to end our passage through the Aegean with a wry regret that this region, which in 1972 staked its claim in Colin Renfrew's

0.11 Combat scene on an agate sealstone, just 3.4 cm (1.3 in.) across, from the grave of the 'Griffin Warrior' at Pylos in the southwest Aegean.

The Emergence of Civilisation[78] to lead the Mediterranean (nay the world) in innovative and theoretically informed interpretations of change, is back fifty years later to where it was with Heinrich Schliemann a century and a half before, headlining bling.

The easternmost parts of the Mediterranean continue to generate plentiful archaeology, often from big sites, although patterns are shifting due to the impact of war and civil strife, as well as determined rebalancings from international to nationally led initiatives on the part of several countries, the consequences of which will become clearer over the coming years. Much of this archaeology, while located in or near to the Mediterranean, has changed relatively little in our fundamental understanding of it. Two exceptions can be singled out, both revolving around crops, although ones harvested millennia apart. The first is the evidence from plant ecology and soil disturbance analysis that plant domestication was extremely gradual during the earliest phases of the Levantine Neolithic (see Chapter 5) and only accelerated later, with the increasing definition of households (thus more comparable to the timing and trajectory of animal domestication).[79] The second we owe to a conflagration that engulfed the central storage silo of Hattusa, the Hittite capital, in the early 16th century BC.[80] This catastrophe consumed 5500–7000 tonnes of cereals, enough to feed 20,000–30,000 people for a year – probably equivalent to the entire urban and inner surrounding population; it also created the largest archaeobotanical sample in the world, only a fraction of which has yet been excavated [**0.12**]. Hattusa's rulers subsequently opted for a wiser strategy of more dispersed facilities. But their loss is our informational gold mine, as analysis of the seeds reveals subtle differences in the growing conditions between subunits of the silo. Although all alike were grown on extensive ploughed fields, they appear to derive from different micro-environments and most likely reflect the taxed contributions of different villages, paid in kind to the royal centre, which was manifestly able to command and mobilize its subjects' agricultural produce on a colossal scale.

Hattusa's taxation policy is all the more convincingly reconstructed because the millions of charred seeds can be compared to surviving Hittite economic and legal writings, preserved on clay. The fruits of such combined approaches have in fact driven some of the most innovative work within the text-rich eastern Mediterranean over the last ten years. One beneficiary is the astonishingly cosmopolitan (and Mediterranean) Nile Delta city of Avaris under so-called 'Hyksos' rule, and its long legacy of connections and innovations to an Egyptian New Kingdom that ideologically excoriated its memory.[81] Beyond this, a number of pioneering studies, building beyond earlier recognition of practices of embryonic diplomacy at ancient Amarna, deploy explicitly comparative geopolitical perspectives and models drawn from modern globalization theory in order to gain new insights into Egypt and its imperial relations, hegemonic and resistive, with its neighbours, not least the precociously economically sophisticated Levantine trading city of Ugarit.[82] That ancient globalizing phenomena can be traced through material traits as well as texts is neatly shown by long-term analysis of Mediterranean 'containerization', through the changing form and distribution of that most ecumenical associated shape, the amphora, and

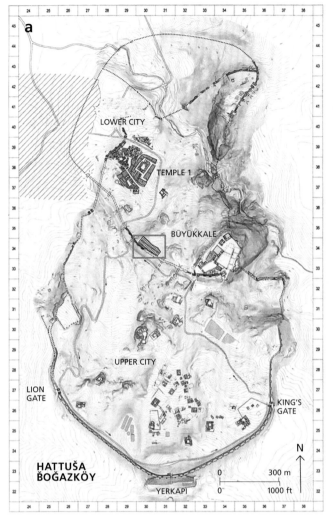

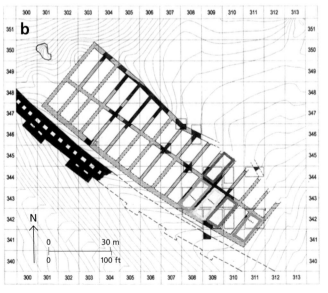

0.12 Catastrophic fire destruction of stored cereals within the central storage silo at Late Bronze Age Hattusa in central Anatolia, showing: (a) the overall plan of the Hittite capital and location of the silo; (b) plan of the silo and adjacent fortifications; (c) a silo bay full of charred cereals; and details of preserved wheat and barley.

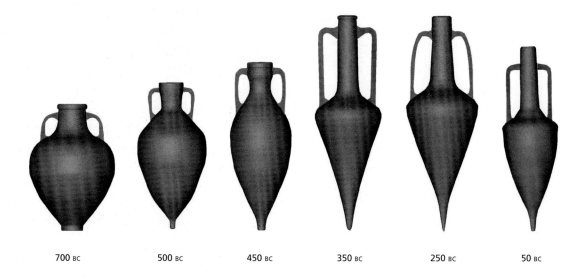

| 700 BC | 500 BC | 450 BC | 350 BC | 250 BC | 50 BC |

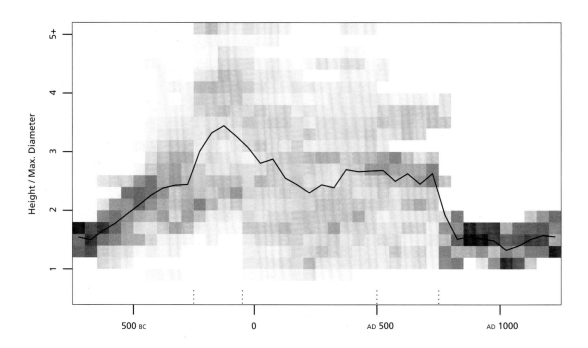

0.13 Measuring early commodification in a globalizing economy: the diversity of amphora forms from the island of Chios in the Aegean from 750 BC to AD 1250.

other specialized transport vessels for the movement of commodified liquids such as wine and oil [**0.13**].[83]

Striking new hints of the eastward spatial reach of such globalizing connections, and the porosity of the basin's boundaries, come from recently claimed traces of turmeric, soybean and possibly banana in the dental calculus of people buried in the southern Levant during the 2nd millennium BC, well before the hitherto assumed later Iron Age, Roman or later arrivals of these and other vegetal exotics of South, Southeast and (in the case of soybean) East Asian origin. If affirmed, these join earlier identifications of Indonesian peppercorns, afforded the ultimate honour of being bandaged up with Ramesses II during his mummification, and cloves from Terqa in earlier 2nd-millennium BC Mesopotamia. The most plausible explanation would be that such prized exotics arrived as small quantities of durable dried products or derived oils circulating in Indian Ocean networks and siphoned off into the east Mediterranean elite consumption sphere via the Red Sea or Persian Gulf.[84]

Archaeological apocalypse now

Mention of globalization and its victims as well as agents leads inevitably to a final glance at the present and near future. Optimism is hard to sustain, writing in the shadow of 7 October 2023 in southern Israel and its retributory sequel in Gaza. The darker side was already apparent when writing *The Making*, as the closing section of Chapter 1 indicated. Since then, the four boatmen of the Mediterranean apocalypse have been flying under full sail: war and smouldering civil strife in the east; overheating climates and out-of-control wildfires across most areas; frequently too little water, or lethally too much delivered in raging floods; a global pandemic that entered the Mediterranean via the unlikely portal of the Po plain. And driven by the boatmen and their horseman cousins to the south and east, myriad other, overburdened boatloads of desperate humanity on the move across the sea, a pulse already apparent in 2013 yet still without humane solutions on the ground, or even on the waves. The message can only be repeated: the Mediterranean has been a place of crossings, and mixings, for millennia; people have lived together in workable, heterogeneous communities, for millennia; and people beyond count have lost their lives to its darker nature and culture, for millennia. We still have much to learn from its past.

Yet the time to learn new things from the remnants that have so far survived is fast running out. Less catastrophic in terms of its human cost, but calamitous for our knowledge, the window of archaeological opportunity is rapidly and terminally closing in many parts of the Mediterranean. It will already be evident that most of the breakthroughs since 2013 that are highlighted in this Preface took place in the laboratory, through study in the storerooms of older excavations, or in the diminishing number of inaccessible locations, whether deep below the waves or far in the hinterlands. Elsewhere, the picture is increasingly bleak, due not only to the familiar factors of warfare, looting, urban sprawl, touristic development and infrastructural mega-projects, but also, to an accelerating degree, the spread of agrobusiness across the countryside. The first edition of this book opened on the Aegean island of Kythera, during fieldwork in 2001 on a 3500-year-old coastal site connected to Minoan Crete. Recently, I was out near the shores of another Mediterranean nation. A group of us were there, drawn by the report that just a few years earlier someone had brought in from the area a collection of stone tools and potsherds slightly older in date, and of types significant for wider Mediterranean interaction, yet so far never recorded in context or quantity locally, or indeed for far around. We had pictures of those finds with us; we were enthusiastic, we were free-wheeling with ideas. But what we found ourselves standing in was a mono-cropped desert of peanut fields, bulldozed in the intervening handful of years from the ancient sand-dunes, obliterated along with their fragile freight of antiquity. For an hour, five of us walked disconsolately up and down, as if in an abandoned, dys-topian open-air cinema, observing discarded peanut shells, decaying plastic and one small and singularly uninformative ceramic survival. That quantum aside, as Percy Bysshe Shelley wrote of a more durable circum-Mediterranean ruin, over two hundred years ago:

> Nothing beside remains. Round the decay
> Of that colossal Wreck, boundless and bare
> The lone and level sands stretch far away.

The fight to know the Mediterranean's past and to navigate a sustainable future is on. Now.

Cambridge
Winter 2023–24

Notes

1 Very warm thanks to the following for sharing information and thoughts with me before or during the writing of this Second Preface: Dante Abate, Hamza Benattia, Youssef Bokbot, John Cherry, David Friesem, Dylan Gaffney, Huw Groucutt, Vangelio Kiriatzi, Rafael Laoutari, Borja Legarra Herrero, Tom Leppard, Giulio Lucarini, Louise Martin, Marcos Martinón-Torres, María Martinón-Torres, Michael McCormick, Dominic Pollard, Thilo Rehren, Vasif Şahoğlu, Lindsay Spencer, Mary Anne Tafuri, Alex Weide, Toby Wilkinson and Federico Zangani. Further thanks to Ben Hayes, India Jackson, Jo Murray, Celia Falconer, Sam Clark, Anabel Navarro and Sophy Thompson at Thames & Hudson for their support and patience.
2 Pitron 2023: 79.
3 Foxhall (ed.) 2021; Knappett and Leidwanger (eds) 2018; Osborne and Hall (eds) 2022; Tartaron 2013; similarly, on the Mediterranean Iron Age as a 'globalizing' world, see Hodos 2020.
4 Respectively, López-Ruiz 2021 and Quinn 2018.
5 Iacono et al. 2022.
6 Van Dommelen 2017; Riva and Grau Mira 2022.
7 Reinberger et al. 2021; Reitsema et al. 2022.
8 Leppard and Cherry 2024.
9 Leppard 2019.
10 Terrenato 2019: Chapter 2.
11 González-Ruibal and Ruiz-Gálvez 2016.
12 Kristiansen 2014; Reich 2018.
13 Furholt 2021; Racimo et al. 2020.
14 Olalde et al. 2018; for wider recent interpretation, Kristiansen et al. (eds) 2023.
15 Olalde et al. 2019; Villalba-Mouco et al. 2021; for the Balearic islands, Fernandes et al. 2020.
16 Clemente et al. 2021; Lazaridis et al. 2017; Skourtanioti et al. 2023.
17 Marcus et al. 2020.
18 Simões et al. 2023.
19 Serrano et al. 2023.
20 Horden and Purcell 2000.
21 Cavazzuti et al. 2019.
22 Robb et al. 2019; Tafuri et al. 2023.
23 Skourtanioti et al. 2023.
24 Moots et al. 2023.
25 Broodbank 2000: 326, 338.
26 Neumann et al. 2022.
27 Legarra Herrero and Marcos Martinón-Torres 2021.
28 Kiriatzi and Broodbank 2021: fig. 6.
29 Orengo and Garcia-Molsosa 2019; Abate et al. 2023.
30 Pacheco-Ruiz et al. 2019.
31 Jarriel 2018.
32 Safadi and Sturt 2019.
33 Roberts et al. 2019.
34 For Roman and later, see Harper 2017; McCormick 2019.
35 Manning et al. 2023.
36 Sahnouni et al. 2018.
37 Hublin et al. 2017; Richter et al. 2017.
38 Sehasseh et al. 2021.
39 Martinón-Torres, María, 2022: 96–97.
40 Hershkovitz et al. 2021; Zaidner et al. 2021.
41 Greenbaum et al. 2019.
42 Hershkovitz et al. 2018.
43 Martinón-Torres, María, et al. 2017.
44 Clarkson et al. 2017.
45 Harvati et al. 2019; Harvati and Ackerman 2022; cf. Rosas and Bastir 2020.
46 Slimak et al. 2022.
47 Slimak 2023.
48 Gaffney 2021.
49 Cherry and Leppard 2025.
50 Di Maida 2022.
51 Carter et al. 2019.
52 Van de Loosdrecht et al. 2018.
53 Broodbank and Lucarini 2019.
54 Belhouchet 2008.
55 Lucarini et al. 2021.
56 Carrión Marco et al. 2022: 9.
57 Bokbot 2005; Linstädter 2016: 69–73, fig. 3.
58 Garcia Sanjuán et al. 2013.
59 Fregel et al. 2018; Olalde et al. 2019.
60 Bernáldez-Sánchez et al. 2024.
61 Broodbank et al. 2024.
62 Rodrigue 2012.
63 Malone et al. 2020: 481, table 13.3.
64 Fernandes et al. 2020.
65 Cintas-Peña and García Sanjuán 2022.
66 Cintas-Peña et al. 2023; Fernández Flores et al. (eds) 2016; García Sanjuán et al. 2023.
67 Lull et al. 2021.
68 Murillo-Barroso et al. 2018.
69 Morgado et al. 2018.
70 Groucutt et al. 2022.
71 Knodell et al. 2022.
72 For updates on these, see respectively Forenbaher 2018 and Aston 2020; Renfrew et al. (eds) 2018.
73 Knappett et al. 2011.
74 Şahoğlu et al. 2022.
75 Roosevelt and Luke 2017.
76 Shapland 2022: 216–17.
77 Davis 2022; Stocker and Davis 2017.
78 Renfrew 1972.
79 Weide 2021.
80 Diffey et al. 2020.
81 Mourad 2021.
82 Moreno García 2020; Zangani 2022.
83 Bevan 2014.
84 Scott et al. 2021.

Sources of illustrations

a = above
c = centre
b = below

ii
From Bertolino, F., Alaimo, F., & Vassallo, S. (2015), *Battles of Himera (480 and 409 B.C.): Analysis of Biological Finds and Historical Interpretation. Experiences of Restoration in the Ruins of Himera 2008–2010*

v
Marta Cintas Peña. Courtesy Research Group ATLAS, University of Seville

vi a
Reproduced by permission of Eirini Skourtanioti. From Skourtanioti *et al.* (2023), 'Ancient DNA reveals admixture history and endogamy in the prehistoric Aegean', *Nature Ecology & Evolution*

vi b
Reproduced by permission of Gunnar U. Neumann. From Neumann *et al.* (2022), 'Ancient *Yersinia pestis* and *Salmonella enterica* genomes from Bronze Age Crete', *Current Biology*, 32, 3641–3649.e8

ix
Courtesy Black Sea MAP, University of Southampton

x
Safadi & Sturt (2019)

xi
Courtesy K. Jarriel. From Jarriel, Katherine (2017), *Small Worlds After All? Landscape and Community Interaction in the Cycladic Bronze Age*, Doctoral Dissertation, Cornell University

xiv
Photo D. Depnering, inset images by N. Skarpelis. Reproduced by permission from the Stelida Naxos Archaeological Project

xvi
From Broodbank, C., & Lucarini, G. (2019), 'The Dynamics of Mediterranean Africa, *c.* 9600–1000 BC: An Interpretative Synthesis of Knowns and Unknowns', *Journal of Mediterranean Archaeology*, 32(2), 195–267

xvii
Courtesy Toby Wilkinson and the Oued Beht Archaeological Project

xx, xxi a
Miriam Luciañez Triviño. Courtesy Research Group ATLAS, University of Seville

xxi b
Photo Miguel Ángel Blanco de la Rubia. Courtesy Research Group ATLAS, University of Seville

xxiii
Courtesy Arqueoecologia Social Mediterrània Research Group, Universitat Autònoma de Barcelona

xxv
Photo J. Vanderpool. Courtesy The Palace of Nestor Excavations, University of Cincinnati, Department of Classics

xxvii a, b, c
Diffey *et al.* (2020)

xxviii
Courtesy Andrew Bevan

Contents

Preface to the Second Edition   i
Acknowledgments   6
Topographical map and chronological tables   8

CHAPTER ONE
A barbarian history   15

CHAPTER TWO
Provocative places   54

CHAPTER THREE
The speciating sea (1.8 million – 50,000 years ago)   82

CHAPTER FOUR
A cold coming we had of it (50,000 years ago – 10,000 BC)   109

CHAPTER FIVE
Brave new worlds (10,000 – 5500 BC)   148

CHAPTER SIX
How it might have been (5500 – 3500 BC)   202

CHAPTER SEVEN
The devil and the deep blue sea (3500 – 2200 BC)   257

CHAPTER EIGHT
Pomp and circumstance (2200 – 1300 BC)   345

CHAPTER NINE
From sea to shining sea (1300 – 800 BC)   445

CHAPTER TEN
The end of the beginning (800 – 500 BC)   506

CHAPTER ELEVEN
De profundis   593

Notes   611
Bibliography   630
Sources of illustrations   654
Index   656

Acknowledgments

This is a book that many people with whom I spoke insisted could, or perhaps should, not be written. Whether or not they were right the reader will judge. Regardless, I am profoundly grateful to those who thought the attempt worthwhile and backed a single author's potential coherence of vision, and the accompanying weaknesses, against the collective knowledge of the many. Whatever errors this book must contain have been greatly reduced, and its qualities substantially enhanced, by comments on the whole or parts from Carol Bell, Andrew Bevan, Denis and Hanna Broodbank, John Cherry, James Clackson, Kevan Edinborough, Borja Legarra Herrero, Vangelio Kiriatzi, Bernard Knapp, Ezra Marcus, Louise Martin, Ian Morris, Simone Mulazzani, Corinna Riva, John Robb, Stephen Shennan, Susan Sherratt, Robin Skeates, Lindsay Spencer, Mary Stiner, Jeremy Tanner, Ignacio de la Torre, Marc Vander Linden, Peter van Dommelen, David Wengrow, Ruth Whitehouse and Todd Whitelaw. Peregrine Horden and Nicholas Purcell, whose thought-provoking conception of subsequent Mediterranean history directly inspired my own effort, have been immensely supportive throughout, and without the patience and encouragement at Thames & Hudson of Colin Ridler, best of editors, together with the extraordinary talents of Ben Plumridge, Pauline Hubner, Geoff Penna, Alice Reid, Celia Falconer and Dora Kemp, I doubt whether this book would ever have appeared. To all of these, my very warmest thanks.

I am grateful for further advice, information, access to literature and all kinds of other help and kindness to Christos Agouridis, Susan Alcock, Tonyo Alcover, Michal Artzy, Ceri Ashley, Jacqueline Balen, Nick Barton, Lisa Bendall, John Bennet, Philip Betancourt, Emma Blake, Richard Bussmann, Joanne Clarke, Sue Colledge, James Conolly, Enrico Crema, Lindy Crewe, Jack Davis, Pierre Desrosiers, Ernestine Elster, Ian Freestone, Stašo Forenbaher, Lin Foxhall, Dorian Fuller, Nena Galanidou, Ehud Galili, John-Vincent Gallagher, Andrew Garrard, Michael Given, Claudia Glatz, Chris Gosden, Rafi Greenberg, Victor Guerrero Ayuso, Paul Halstead, Yannis Hamilakis, Susanna Harris, Tamar Hodos, Francesco Iacono, Valasia Isaakidou, David Jeffreys, Fernanda Kalazich, Branko Kirigin, Kostas Kotsakis, Olga Krzyszkowska, Irene Lemos, Fulvia Lo Schiavo, Simona Losi, David Lubell, Leilani Lucas, Virginia McRostie, Joseph Maran, Massimiliano Marazzi,

Marcos Martinón-Torres, Stephen Mitchell, Sarah Morris, Denitsa Nenova, Sam Nixon, Mihriban Özbaşaran, Yiannis Papadatos, Edgar Peltenburg, John Papadopoulos, Nellie Phoca-Cosmetatou, Miljana Radivojević, Lorenz Rahmstorf, Damià Ramis, Thilo Rehren, Colin Renfrew, Roberto Risch, Arlene Rosen, Curtis Runnels, Andrew Shapland, Ruth Siddall, Daniel Smail, Rachael Sparks, Simon Stoddart, Thomas Strasser, Geoffrey Tassie, Ken Thomas, Helena Tomas, Maurizio Tosi, Kathy Tubb, Sebastiano Tusa, Nick Vella, Andrea Vianello, Jean-Denis Vigne, Jaime Vives Ferrándiz, Cheryl Ward, Jennifer Wexler, Malcolm Wiener, Jamie Woodward and Karen Wright. Additional thanks to Müge Durusu-Tanriover, Tom Leppard, Clive Vella, Andrew Dufton, Pinar Durgun, Alex Knodell, Ian Randall and other members of John Cherry's graduate class at the Joukowsky Institute of Brown University, who read an advanced version of the manuscript as coursework and offered last-minute responses full of insight. Camilla Briault, Jo Cutler and Borja Legarra Herrero have all provided invaluable practical support with notes and references at different junctures, and my equal thanks go to the UCL Institute of Archaeology's unfailingly helpful librarians, Robert Kirby and Katie Meheux.

Two Directors at UCL's Institute of Archaeology, Peter Ucko and Stephen Shennan, with much appreciated advocacy from Ruth Whitehouse, granted me the initial leave to get this project underway. During parts of this I was sustained by visiting fellowships at All Souls College, Oxford, and the Classics department of Cincinnati University, a Samuel H. Kress Lectureship in Ancient Art from the Archaeological Institute of America, as well as generous grants from the Loeb Classical Library Foundation of Harvard University, Richard Bradford McConnell Trust, Dr M. Aylwin Cotton Foundation, University College London and the Cotsen Institute of Archaeology at UCLA. I thank all these for their support and apologize for the repeatedly delayed return on their investment. The final stages were greatly eased by a Mid-Career Fellowship from the British Academy, and a generous publication grant from the Institute for Aegean Prehistory.

To leave my most heartfelt acknowledgment until last, anyone familiar with Andrew Sherratt's ways of thinking will recognize the extent of his inspiration, which goes deeper than a multitude of citations can express. It was Andrew who threw down the gauntlet in 1992, observing that '"The Mediterranean in the Age of Tuthmosis III" remains to be written' and, two years later, that 'without the Bronze Age, Braudel's Mediterranean would not have existed'. I would not have had the courage to set out on this endeavour but for Andrew's example over the course of twenty years of friendship, and my trust in the assurance of his wise advice, ever-creative eye for the links I had missed, and enthusiasm for canvases on the scale that this book sets out to cover. We were all robbed of such assurances by Andrew's sudden, far too early death in 2006, when most of this book was still a mass of notes. To, and from, Andrew, *lux aeterna*.

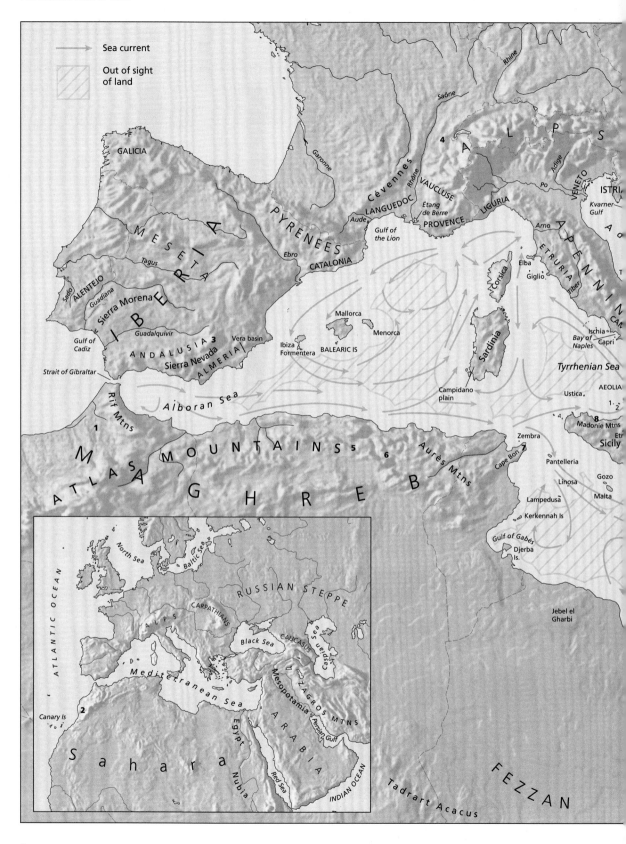

Sea current

Out of sight of land

GALICIA

Garonne

Rhine

Saône

4

A L P S

MESETA

Tagus

Cévennes
Rhône

Adige

Po

VENETO

ISTRI

Kvarner
Gulf

PYRENEES

Ebro

CATALONIA

VAUCLUSE
LANGUEDOC
Aude
Étang
de Berre
Gulf of
the Lion
PROVENCE

LIGURIA

Arno

A P E N N I N

ETRURIA

Corsica

Elba

Giglio

Tiber

I B E R I A

Sado
ALENTEJO
Guadiana
Sierra Morena

Guadalquivir

Vera basin

Mallorca

Menorca

Sardinia

Ischia
Bay of
Naples
Capri

CAM

Gulf of
Cadiz

ANDALUSIA 3
Sierra Nevada
ALMERIA

Ibiza
Formentera
BALEARIC IS

Campidano
plain

Tyrrhenian Sea

Strait of Gibraltar

Rif Mtns

Alboran Sea

Ustica

AEOLIA

1 · 2

MASAGHREB

M O U N T A I N S 5

6

Aurès Mtns

Zembra

Cape Bon 7

Madonie Mtns
Etr
Sicily

A T L A S

Pantelleria

Linosa

Gozo

Malta

Lampedusa

Kerkennah Is

Gulf of Gabes
Djerba
Is.

Jebel el
Gharbi

North Sea

Baltic Sea

RUSSIAN STEPPE

ATLANTIC OCEAN

ALPS

CARPATHIANS

Black Sea

CAUCASUS

Caspian Sea

Mediterranean Sea

Mesopotamia

ZAGROS MTNS

Persian Gulf

ARABIA

Canary Is

2

Sahara

Egypt

Nubia

Red Sea

INDIAN OCEAN

Tadrart Acacus

F E Z Z A N

Iriatic Is:
Brač
Dugi
Hvar
Korčula
Palagruža
Sušac
Vis

CARPATHIANS

CRIMEA

CAUCASUS

Black Sea

DMATIA

B A L K A N S

Danube

Stara Planina

THRACE

Bosphorus

Struma

MACEDONIA

Vardar

Sea of Marmara

ANATOLIA

ANTI-TAURUS MTNS

Tigris

APULIA

Strait
of
Otranto

EPIRUS

THESSALY

Thasos   Samothrace

Lemnos

Dardanelles

Gediz

Konya
plain

TAURUS   MTNS

Cilician
Gates

AMUQ

JAZIRA

Corfu

Pindos Mtns

Gioura

A E G E A N

Chios

Euphrates

Lefkada
Ithaca
Kefalonia

IONIAN IS

SPORADES

Euboea

Saronic
Gulf

13

Meander

Samos

Latmian
Gulf

Göksu

Gulf of
Iskenderun

Orontes

Palmyra
oasis

16

Ionian Sea

ATTICA
9

ARGOLID

PELOPONNESE

Corinthian Gulf

1

10

Aegina

8

DODECANESE

5

Kos

LYCIA

Cyprus

L E V A N T

Strait
of
Messina

eolian Is:
Alicudi
Filicudi
Lipari
Panarea
Salina
Stromboli
Vulcano

10

CYCLADES

11

12

Rhodes

Cycladic Is:
1. Andros
2. Delos
3. Ios
4. Kea
5. Keros
6. Kythnos
7. Melos
8. Siphnos
9. Syros
10. Tenos
11. Thera
12. Stelida (Naxos)

Kythera

Antikythera

11

Crete   12

Gavdos

Mesara Plain

New sites which feature in the preface:
1. Oued Beht   9. Mygdalia
2. Bizmoune   10. Apidima
3. La Almoloya   11. Chania
4. Grotte Mandrin 12. Agios Charalambos
5. Gueldaman   13. Çeşme-Bağlararası
6. Ain Boucherit 14. Misliya
7. Kerkouane   15. Nesher Ramla
8. Himera   16. Terqa

Lebanese Mtns

Beqaa Valley

Sea of
Galilee

Jezreel
Valley

Carmel

Jordan

14

15

Dead
Sea

Wadi Arabah

NEGEV

Jebel Akhdar

CYRENAICA

Gulf of Sirte

Nile
Delta

SUEZ

SINAI

Gulf of Aqaba

E G Y P T

Nile

Fayum

Gulf of Suez

Red
Sea

Wadi Hammamat

Dakhla
oasis

0   250 km

0   150 miles

9

The following chronological tables show major temporal divisions, cultural phases, other relevant archaeological information and environmental conditions. The first table (opposite) runs from 2 million to 10,000 years ago and covers the Pleistocene (Chapters 3–4); the second (pp. 12–13) runs from 12,000 to 1 BC, principally covering the Holocene (Chapters 5–10); more detailed information on the period 2500–1 BC is presented in the third table (p. 14), which correlates with the later time span of Chapter 7 and all of Chapters 8 to 10.

Years before present	2,000,000	1,500,000
CLIMATE PHASE		LOWER
MARINE ISOTOPE STAGES		
PERIOD		EAR
TECHNOLOGY	← Oldowan →	Acheuli
	←	
HUMAN EVOLUTION (simplified)	← *Homo habilis* →	*Ho*
	←	
SAHARA	? Assumed fluctuating presence ?	
MEDITERRANEAN AFRICA	● Ain Hanech	
LEVANT		● Ubeidiya
ANATOLIA		
SOUTHEAST MEDITERRANEAN EUROPE		
CENTRAL MEDITERRANEAN EUROPE		
SOUTHWEST MEDITERRANEAN EUROPE		Atapuerca (Elephante) and Or
	2,000,000	1,500,000

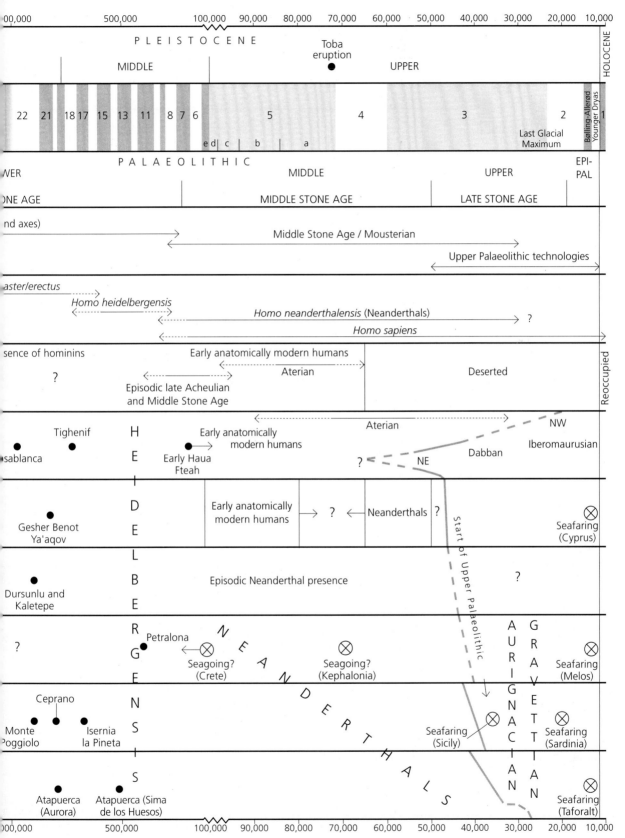

	12,000 BC	11,000	10,000	9000	8000	70
OVERALL CLIMATE	WARM BØLLING-ALLERØD INTERSTADIAL	COLD YOUNGER DRYAS		EARLY HOLOCENE WET/WARM OPTIMU		
IBERIA	TERMINAL PLEISTOCENE HUNTER-GATHERERS			HUNTER-GATHERERS (MESOLITH		
BALEARICS					U N I N H A B I T	
SOUTHERN FRANCE	TERMINAL PLEISTOCENE HUNTER-GATHERERS			HUNTER-GATHERERS (MESOLITH		
SARDINIA/CORSICA	UNINHABITED ?		?	HUNTER-GATHERERS (MESOLITH		
MALTA			U N I N H A B I T E D			
SICILY	TERMINAL PLEISTOCENE HUNTER-GATHERERS			HUNTER-GATHERERS (MESOLITHI		
SOUTHERN ITALY	TERMINAL PLEISTOCENE HUNTER-GATHERERS			HUNTER-GATHERERS (MESOLITHI		
CENTRAL/NORTH ITALY	TERMINAL PLEISTOCENE HUNTER-GATHERERS			HUNTER-GATHERERS (MESOLITHI		
EAST ADRIATIC	TERMINAL PLEISTOCENE HUNTER-GATHERERS			HUNTER-GATHERERS (MESOLITHI		
AEGEAN	TERMINAL PLEISTOCENE HUNTER-GATHERERS		HUNTER-GATHERERS (MESOLITHIC)			
ANATOLIA	TERMINAL PLEISTOCENE HUNTER-GATHERERS		HUNTER-GATHERERS		NEOLIT	
JAZIRA / NORTH MESOPOTAMIA	TERMINAL PLEISTOCENE HUNTER-GATHERERS			N E O L I T H I C		
CYPRUS	UNINHABITED?	AETO-KREM-NOS	?	PPNA	NEOLITH PPNB	
LEVANT	NATUFIAN EARLY	LATE	PPNA		PPNB C EARLY MIDDLE LA	
NILE DELTA	H U N T E R - G A T H E R E R S ?			H U N T E R - G A T H E R E R S ?		
UP-RIVER EGYPT	H U N T E R - G A T H E R E R S			H U N T E R - G A T H E R E R S		
MEDITERRANEAN NORTH AFRICA (EXCEPT EGYPT)	TERMINAL PLEISTOCENE HUNTER-GATHERERS			H U N T E R - G A T H E R E R S (C A P S I A		
SAHARA	UNINHABITED		?	HUNTER-GATHERERS SOME ANIMAL MANAGEMENT		

	12,000 BC	11,000	10,000	9000	8000	70

| 6000 | 5000 | 4000 | 3000 | 2000 | 1000 | 1 |

| OSCILLATING WETTER/DRIER | UNEVEN SHIFT TO DRIER | SLIGHTLY WETTER |
| Cold event | Saharan desertification · Aridity event | |

NEOLITHIC — EARLY MIDDLE LATE FINAL	COPPER AGE	BRONZE AGE EARLY MIDDLE LATE (ARGARIC)	IRON AGE
		BRONZE AGE EARLY MIDDLE LATE	IRON AGE
NEOLITHIC — EARLY MIDDLE (CHASSÉEN) LATE FINAL	COPPER AGE (FONTBOUISSE)	BRONZE AGE EARLY MIDDLE LATE	IRON AGE
NEOLITHIC — EARLY MIDDLE LATE (OZIERI)	COPPER AGE	BRONZE AGE EARLY MIDDLE LATE (NURAGIC)	IRON AGE
NEOLITHIC	TEMPLE PERIOD ?	? BRONZE AGE EARLY MIDDLE LATE	IRON AGE
NEOLITHIC — EARLY MIDDLE LATE	COPPER AGE	BRONZE AGE EARLY MIDDLE LATE	IRON AGE
NEOLITHIC — EARLY MIDDLE LATE	COPPER AGE	BRONZE AGE EARLY MIDDLE LATE	IRON AGE
NEOLITHIC — EARLY MIDDLE LATE	COPPER AGE	BRONZE AGE EARLY MIDDLE LATE	IRON AGE
NEOLITHIC — EARLY MIDDLE LATE	COPPER AGE	BRONZE AGE EARLY MIDDLE LATE (CETINA)	IRON AGE
NEOLITHIC — EARLY MIDDLE LATE FINAL	BRONZE AGE EARLY MIDDLE LATE	IRON AGE
COPPER AGE — EARLY LATE	BRONZE AGE EARLY MIDDLE LATE	IRON AGE
COPPER AGE — UBAID FIRST URBAN	URUK EXP.	BRONZE AGE EARLY (AKKAD) MIDDLE LATE	IRON AGE
(CERAMIC) IROKITIAN	?	? CERAMIC NEOLITHIC	COPPER AGE	BRONZE AGE EARLY MIDDLE LATE	IRON AGE
...AL LATE NEOLITHIC	COPPER AGE — EARLY LATE	BRONZE AGE EARLY MIDDLE LATE	IRON AGE
?	NEOLITHIC	MAADIAN	PRE-DYNASTIC	BRONZE AGE — EARLY DYNASTIC OLD MIDDLE NEW KINGDOMS	IRON AGE
?	BADARIAN PASTORAL	PREDYNASTIC	BRONZE AGE — EARLY DYNASTIC OLD MIDDLE NEW KINGDOMS	IRON AGE
D OTHER)	W. MAGHREB FULL NEOLITHIC?	? ? ?	IRON AGE
	'NEOLITHIC' CAPSIAN, ETC.		
?	PASTORAL — EARLY MIDDLE	PASTORAL — LATE	GARAMANTIAN

| 6000 | 5000 | 4000 | 3000 | 2000 | 1000 | 1 |

13

Time scale (BC): 2500 — 2000 — 1500 — 1000 — 500 — 1

Region	Chronological sequence (2500 BC → 1)
IBERIA	COPPER AGE · EARLY BRONZE AGE (Argaric) · MIDDLE BRONZE AGE · LATE BRONZE AGE (Early Huelva) · IRON AGE · PUNIC
BALEARICS	UNINHABITED · EARLY BRONZE AGE · MIDDLE BRONZE AGE · LATE BRONZE AGE (Talayots) · PUNIC
SOUTHERN FRANCE	COPPER AGE · EARLY BRONZE AGE · MIDDLE BRONZE AGE · LATE BRONZE AGE · IRON AGE (● Massalia)
SARDINIA / CORSICA	COPPER AGE · EARLY BRONZE AGE · MIDDLE BRONZE AGE (Early nuragic) · LATE BRONZE AGE (Nuragic climax) · IRON AGE · PUNIC
MALTA	TEMPLE PERIOD · ? ? · EARLY BRONZE AGE (Tarxien cemetery phase) · MIDDLE BRONZE AGE · LATE BRONZE AGE · IRON AGE · PUNIC
SICILY	COPPER AGE · EARLY BRONZE AGE · MIDDLE BRONZE AGE · LATE BRONZE AGE · EARLY IRON AGE · ARCHAIC–CLASSIC
SOUTHERN ITALY	COPPER AGE · EARLY BRONZE AGE · MIDDLE BRONZE AGE · LATE BRONZE AGE · EARLY IRON AGE · ARCHAIC–CLASSIC
CENTRAL / NORTH ITALY	COPPER AGE · EARLY BRONZE AGE · MIDDLE BRONZE AGE · LATE BRONZE AGE · EARLY IRON AGE · ARCHAIC–CLASSIC
EAST ADRIATIC	COPPER AGE · EARLY BRONZE AGE (Cetina) · MIDDLE BRONZE AGE · LATE BRONZE AGE · IRON AGE
AEGEAN	EARLY BRONZE AGE · MIDDLE BRONZE AGE · LATE BRONZE AGE (Thera eruption; Minoan palaces; Mycenaean palaces; Post-pal.) · EARLY IRON AGE · ARCHAIC · CLASSICAL · HELLENISTIC (⚔ Salamis ●, Alexander ●)
ANATOLIA	EARLY BRONZE AGE · MIDDLE BRONZE AGE (Kültepe archive) · LATE BRONZE AGE (Hatti; ● Uluburun) · IRON AGE (Phrygia, Lydia) · PERSIAN · HELLENISTIC
JAZIRA / NORTH MESOPOTAMIA	EARLY DYNASTIC · AKKAD · MIDDLE BRONZE AGE (Mari archive ●; BABYLONIAN) · LATE BRONZE AGE (MITANNI; MIDDLE ASSYRIAN) · IRON AGE (NEO-ASSYRIAN) · NEO-BABYLONIAN · PERSIAN · HELLENISTIC · PARTHIAN
CYPRUS	EARLY BRONZE AGE · MIDDLE BRONZE AGE · LATE BRONZE AGE · IRON AGE · ARCHAIC · PERSIAN · HELLENISTIC
LEVANT	EARLY BRONZE AGE (● Ebla archive) · MIDDLE BRONZE AGE · LATE BRONZE AGE (Qadesh ⚔ ●; Ugarit archive) · IRON AGE (David/Solomon; ● Wenamun; Israel/Judah; Assyria/Babylon) · PERSIAN · HELLENISTIC
NILE DELTA / UP-RIVER EGYPT	OLD KINGDOM · FIRST INTERMEDIATE · MIDDLE KINGDOM (12th dynasty) · SECOND INTERMEDIATE (Hyksos) · NEW KINGDOM (18th dynasty; 19th–20th Ramessid dynasties; Amarna letters ●) · THIRD INTERMEDIATE (Fragmented / United / Fragmented) · LATE 26th dynasty · PERSIAN · HELLENISTIC (Ptolemies)
MEDITERRANEAN NORTH AFRICA (EXCEPT EGYPT)	? · ? · Bates's island · ? · Carthage ● · Cyrene ● · PUNIC EXPANSION
SAHARA	SMALL-SCALE MOBILE PASTORALISTS · EXPANDING TRIBAL POLITIES · GARAMANTIAN

Right margin (vertical): **ROMAN IMPERIAL EXPANSION**

CHAPTER ONE

A barbarian history

Prelude: a Mediterranean microcosm

Out here, the only sound is the clink of wind-sculpted splinters of limestone on others half buried in the red earth. The sun has been up just a few hours, but already heat pulses in the air, all shade to shelter anything larger than a mouse has vanished, and the huge sky is bleached an unbearably brilliant white on the retina. At eye-level (the highest angle of vision that I can manage without a wince), a strip of sea, solid blue yet faintly in motion like the colours in a Rothko, half-encircles the horizon. Beyond it hovers a pallid silhouette of other, much bigger land. And in the gap between, an old Russian container ship steams up the strait, surreptitiously emptying out its tanks as it goes.

This sketch may evoke innumerable patches of land and sea around the globe, but its further particulars anchor the scene in one definite place on the east coast of the Aegean island of Kythera, in August 2001.[1] I am out there looking for a team that has been in this wilderness since dawn collecting battered lumps of 3500-year-old pottery, the surface signature of an archaeological site found a year before by another team as it swept to and fro across the peninsula, combing it for traces of this island's eventful past. Modern and medieval remains are meagre in this bleak sector, save around the old harbour at Avlemonas, twenty minutes' walk behind me. The finds are equally few from the time when the Spartans, fearful of a takeover by the all-powerful Athenian fleet, wished this island neighbour of theirs would sink beneath the waves, though a few scatters of Roman sherds among the rocks that fringe tiny, sea-filled creeks reveal small-scale comings and goings by boat several centuries later. What intrigues us, however, and brings us back to this superficially unpromising place, is the fact that as soon as we venture further back in time, to the Bronze Age and even beyond, the signal strengthens, and the landscape erupts with activity.

By now I can just make out the team, the small dark figures stationary as they count and bag their finds, their leader taller and moving, all weirdly shimmering with the heat coming off the land and horizontally striated with silver lines of mirage. A little closer I can pick out slighter actions, and sense the progress. Fieldwork here is approaching completion, although we will need to study those eloquent hunks and crumbs of pottery for days back in the shade before we reach our best assessment of what was going on. Already it is clear that most finds date to that phase of the Bronze Age when the Minoan societies of Crete were at their most powerful and influential within the Aegean. Kythera formed a part of the Minoan web of connections, and this site is just one among many contemporaries on an island commonly held to have served as a Cretan outpost. Quite what it was doing out here, how people lived in this landscape, if they did, and, if they did not, what else they were up to, are questions for later, but already from the fragments glimpsed on this visit it is clear that they had cooked food and stored something, both quite intensively to judge by the density of remains. Soil and pollen, extracted from a core drilled into a usefully located wetland near Avlemonas, inform us that this place did not look very different 3500 years ago, or indeed for some 2000 years on either side of this date. But perhaps people managed to farm this barren land nonetheless, by building terraces across the shallow folds to retain earth and moisture, as we know they did elsewhere on Kythera. Or maybe their preoccupations were quite different. For on the craggy crest of the hill that rears up behind our site, a prominent place later made sacred for a second time by the white church of Agios Georgios, an open-air shrine of the same period has just been excavated by Greek archaeologists, who found offerings of figurines, vessels and other ritual paraphernalia in metal, stone and clay, some of which came from overseas.[2] And this shrine was itself visually tied to the real fulcrum of power on Kythera, the port-town of Kastri further to the south, a place where names such as 'Knossos', 'Mycenae' and perhaps more distant locations formed part of the cultural geography of its more outward-looking inhabitants.[3]

Nor are these the earliest remains from this little patch. Tiny sherds of pottery indicate several foci 6500–4000 years ago, probably hamlets each clinging to a small patch of land. With them are shiny black flakes of obsidian, a razor-sharp volcanic glass whose nearest source lies 130 km (80 miles) distant on the Cycladic island of Melos. Even these people therefore enjoyed modest connections that reached beyond the sea, though for what now obscure reasons did they bother to try to live out here? A still older find of Neolithic date makes slightly more sense to our time-fogged perceptions: roughly 7000 years ago a visitor out hunting or fishing left a tiny arrowhead on the offshore islet to my right that now exults in the name of Antidragonera.[4] And from this vantage point in the past a speculative plunge launches off into deeper time. For the strait between Kythera and the hazy land beyond (Cape Maleas, the southeast tip of the Peloponnese) is just one segment of a corridor of sea and land that runs south towards Crete, itself occasionally (but not today, in high summer) visible beneath a long white cloud. Whatever lived on Crete in the remote past, whether elusive hunter-gatherers, as some believe, or just the bizarre creatures that we will encounter in later chapters, had to get there somehow, and Kythera lies athwart one of the most plausible routes of entry.

This scrap of Kythera, and the shifting webs of people that have tied it to other places across the sea, reflect many of the kinds of locations and activities that make up the early past of the Mediterranean, that basin of mingled sea and land whose plenitude of history and culture, both internal and world-impacting, is so vastly

1.1 A panorama over the eastern coastlands of Kythera and the small harbour of Avlemonas, taken from the heights of Agios Giorgios. Several points around the great bay have served as anchorages from the Neolithic to the present.

disproportionate to its tiny share of the planet's oceanic and terrestrial space. This book's subject is that early past, from its beginnings long before the emergence of our own species up until the formation of the Classical world, and the way in which an oecumene with the sea as its middle was forged from myriad fragments, creating a blueprint for a blue planet. In line with a number of recent broad-ranging histories it is written in the belief that if we do not understand the deeper past and its trajectories towards the present, we shall never grasp the conditions of our humanity, nor comprehend our present predicaments and impending futures.[5] As we shall see, despite some valiant starts and older studies, no such up-to-date, holistic exploration of the early Mediterranean exists, and we are all, dwellers within it (in body or mind) and others alike, very much the poorer for it. But before looking at why this immense time span and remarkable theatre are of such enduring interest, let alone how they might be effectively approached, we can linger a little longer on Kythera for a few initial insights into a few other kinds of webs, whose influence we will need to combat relentlessly. These are the webs of the mind, full of sirens and decoys, in which we ensnare the Mediterranean's past.

Three unintended visits to the nearby coast illustrate in metaphorical terms the dangers to be faced. The first, in 1802, was by the *Mentor*, wrecked off Avlemonas carrying some of the marbles taken from the Athenian acropolis by Lord Elgin, whose illustrious cargo was fished up by sponge divers, buried on the beach and completed its journey a few years later. The second, in 1843, was by the poet Gérard de Nerval. Nerval anticipated a bed of roses, primed by the tale of Aphrodite's birth off Kythera, and a flower-strewn painting by Watteau (that made no allusion to the love goddess's less polite mythic origins in the genitalia flung into the sea after Cronos castrated his father). Instead he saw black rocks with a man hung from a scaffold on the headland, and vented his spleen to Baudelaire, who re-spun the scene in *Les Fleurs du Mal*. The third visit took place a few years ago and, symptomatically, I do not know the illicit passengers' names or what became of them, but they arrived under escort on a turquoise fishing boat of Libyan lines, now impounded at a quayside further up the coast and blithely ignored by the tourists and locals pouring off the ferry from Piraeus. Each of these visits highlights desires in all too much Western thinking about the Mediterranean, the first to expropriate its antiquities and past for our own ends, the second to romance it in ways that falsify its meanings, and the third to forget the awkward bits that we do not understand or want to know about, especially if they relate to North Africa west of Egypt.

Before *Corruption*

1.2 Fernand Braudel (1902–1985), the founder and still doyen of long-term historical study of the Mediterranean.

Any new writing on Mediterranean history operates in the shadows of giants. Of these, the French historian Fernand Braudel is without doubt the most venerable, and was the first to recognize the Mediterranean's unity and distinctiveness as a field of study [**1.2**]. His massive *The Mediterranean and the Mediterranean World in the Age of Philip II* (first published in French in 1949) reconfigured space to fix the marine basin, rather than the surrounding continents, at centre stage.[6] As a leading light of the *annaliste* movement, Braudel also advocated revolutionary ideas about the aims of historical enquiry, which he saw as the pursuit of geographical, cultural and economic dynamics more than politics. Last but not least, he plumbed temporality itself, conceiving time as refracted into multiple wavelengths: the sharp oscillations of events, medium-term *conjonctures* such as social and economic structures, and the term for which he is most famous, the *longue durée* of environmental rhythms. In passing, he also added to our knowledge of the 16th-century AD Spanish monarch whose name, by a deliberate inversion of expectation, brings up the title's rear.

Ironically, and largely due to its awesome scope and rapidly acknowledged iconic status, for many years Braudel's masterpiece discouraged further comparable Mediterranean-wide studies. The last decade or so, however, has seen a resurgence of engagement with the Mediterranean as an entity, visible in a proliferation of special-ist studies,[7] several overall histories,[8] a caustically recounted circuit by Paul Theroux and the rhapsodies of the Croatian writer Predrag Matvejević, whose *Mediterranean Breviary* offers the beguiling spectacle of 'Braudel as rewritten by Walt Whitman'.[9] In part this resurgence reflects post-Cold War changes in the Mediterranean's status as a geopolitical arena. It is also connected to the troubling state of its environments and societies today. The time has clearly come, therefore, to reopen themes raised by Braudel over sixty years ago, and to explore the possibility of applying his synoptic vision to earlier parts of the Mediterranean's past.

This challenge has recently been taken up at Braudelian length and depth by a partnership between medieval and ancient historians. Peregrine Horden and Nicholas Purcell's *The Corrupting Sea: A Study of Mediterranean History* marks a sea change in our understanding, something of a paradigm shift, to invoke an abused but in this case apposite term.[10] Its themed investigation, via vignettes drawn mainly from the millennium or so before and after the birth of Christ, identifies, in a less romantic vein than Braudel, the common denominators that underlie how things have happened in the Mediterranean, give the basin's history its particular flavour, and justify its choice as a robust and rewarding frame for historical enquiry.

For Horden and Purcell a triad of fundamentals is in operation. The first is the extreme *fragmentation* of Mediterranean land- and seascapes into micro-regions that are constantly reworked and reconfigured by human agency. The unprepossessing corner of Kythera where this chapter opened is one among an all but infinite number of examples. The second is the ubiquity of *uncertainty*. This takes many forms, including the amount of rain that falls, the direction and force of the wind on a given day, and seismic or volcanic catastrophe. Uncertainty makes the Mediterranean a place of high risk yet also sudden flourishes of opportunity, and life in the basin is conditioned by efforts to survive or reduce the former while exploiting the latter. Fragmentation and uncertainty, for instance, prompt a logic of production that encourages people to diversify, overproduce and store in anticipa-tion of lean times ahead, and equally in times of glut to capitalize on their surplus by exchange, or blow it on status-enhancing displays. We take a closer look at these characteristics in the next chapter. The third common denominator is the excep-tional ease of mobility and hi-fi communication ensured primarily by the presence of the central sea, in short a propensity to *connectivity* that enables people to link the fragments, pool resources or relocate in bad times and seek gain abroad in good ones. In place of the historian Moses Finley's once orthodox vision of the ancient Mediterranean[11] as a scatter of bounded communities, rooted in agriculture, with only minor communications and accordingly little scope for markets, Horden and Purcell's Mediterranean pulses with a 'Brownian motion' made up from people's innumerable quotidian movements and small-scale interactions, as well as further-flung enterprises. The precise labels given to such activities – exploratory, extractive, reproductive, friend-making, mercantile, piratical, military, migrational, diasporic, hunting, pastoral and agricultural – are in a sense merely the superstructure above the common necessity of mobility for survival and prosperity in a Mediterranean theatre full of challenges and sudden openings.

In combination, Horden and Purcell argue, these factors create an enormously complex and highly distinctive world, whose elements operate in a way subservient to the same ground rules at many, effectively fractal, scales, from the family farm to the imperial estate, the local middleman to the merchant prince. Its unity resides not in internal uniformity, but rather in the universality and nature of exactly the opposite, a 'continuum of discontinuities', or, as the anthropologist Claude Lévi-Strauss nicely phrased it, 'not the resemblances, but the differences, which resemble each other'.[12] This Mediterranean is also constantly in flux as people reorder its fragments. Vital to the world of *The Corrupting Sea* as well as the present book, and striking a chord in our own globalizing age, is the idea of the network.[13] Mediterranean networks come in a bewildering variety of shapes, sizes and structures, and they can entangle places, people and things with equal promiscuity, helping to forge the kind of behavioural similarities we will trace in chapters to come. But equally, those entangled can often act back to modify the meshes around them. Thus while networks may remain stable for some time, they tend towards change, extending, contracting, shifting and buckling in an endless quest for the best fit with evolving circumstances. Some changes are strongly determined, some thoroughly contingent, and, critically, they commonly unfold in an undirected, self-organizing fashion rather than through any centralized control. This last fact, coupled with intrusions of exotic things, people and ideas, especially from over the sea, sooner or later undermines all effort to enforce autarkic or overarching forms of internal order, whether in the guise of dynasties, states or empires, social or ethnic formations, trade routes and centres, religious beliefs, taste, values or moralities. It is in this subversive, if strangely liberating, sense that Horden and Purcell's Mediterranean, and its sea, corrupt.

The only fly in the ointment is the time frame. The outer temporal boundaries of *The Corrupting Sea* extend from a distant point in the past to the late 19th century AD, when its Mediterranean begins to fray in the centrifuge of global connections. But it focuses between about 800 BC and AD 1300, an extended Iron Age centred on the Classical and medieval periods. By the early 1st millennium BC the relevance of a pan-Mediterranean perspective is beyond dispute, given the voyaging of people whom we know as Phoenicians between the Levant and the Pillars of Hercules (better Herakles, or, best of all, Melqart, as we will see in Chapter 9) and the explicit identification of the sea as an entity: an 'Upper Sea' for Assyrians with their other marine pole in the Persian Gulf, 'our sea' for the Greeks by the 6th century BC, and, of course, Rome's *mare nostrum*. The Mediterranean's centrality must have seemed more self-evident to its inhabitants then than it does today, given the truncated Africa and Asia shown in ancient maps, which depicted continents of comparable

1.3 Approximate map of the world as known from a Mediterranean viewpoint in about 500 BC, according to the geographical writings of Hecataeus of Miletus.

size arranged around a sea in the middle, all encircled by the bounding Ocean [**1.3**]. 'Mediterranean' was used to refer to the sea long before its extension, over the last two centuries, and initially thanks to the work of French scientific expeditions, to characterize the surrounding lands too.[14] The term appears, obscurely, around AD 200, and by the 6th century it definitely applied to the sea in the writing of Isidore of Seville, by a twist of fate resident of a city that a thousand years later helped to sponsor the Atlantic navigation that would gradually undermine the Mediterranean's place on the world stage.[15]

But what about the years preceding all this, the great expanse of time inaptly called 'prehistory' in much of the Mediterranean ('never', Braudel himself cautioned, 'say that prehistory is not history')? What of the periods that we call the Bronze and Copper ages, the Neolithic, Mesolithic, and hundreds of Palaeolithic millennia before that? This 'early Mediterranean history', a term henceforth used without apology, is our subject, and of immense significance. First, it was an intrinsically exciting period of incredible human creativity within dramatically changing physical surroundings, involving the emergence of our own species and its cognitive powers, the origins and expansion of farming, navigation and trade, the rise and fall of towns and states, the appearance of new technologies, consumption habits, ideologies and politics. Second, among this welter of developments must lie the first germs of the world portrayed in its evolved state by Horden and Purcell, which manifestly had not existed forever. Put another way, we shall see that many of the fundamentals underlying the Classical and later Mediterranean in fact emerged and proliferated earlier (often far earlier), offering the prospect of fresh and sometimes startling perspectives on the ostensibly familiar. Third, and as discussed at the end of this chapter, millions of people now living in and beyond the Mediterranean regard its early relics and their associations as things that matter powerfully today. This remote history reverberates in the present, sometimes passionately so, and getting it as right as we can is therefore a serious responsibility.

At first sight, it might seem a straightforward business to head upstream from a notional starting point around 1000 BC, and follow this world back to its source at whatever time in the past. Enterprising later historians in search of prequels to their Mediterranean have indeed launched thought-provoking forays in this direction, if not without danger of cherry-picking those traits that match later expectations to the exclusion of much that does not.[16] But this Victorian explorer's strategy will not work if the aim is to be a holistic explanation of how people living around the basin came together to create a cultural, social and ecological Mediterranean out of the initially mere geographical expression.[17] Understanding this phenomenon requires finding out how its features first emerged. To illustrate this point simply, until people could cross the sea proficiently, the Mediterranean in a real sense did not exist; a non-conveying sea could not corrupt, or in fact do much save sustain fish. Moreover, we shall need to go a stage further, for the traits finally selected as dominant, those that spread widely through the basin and shape our conception of Mediterranean ways of doing things, are initially likely to have been only a few among many options, not even necessarily the most salient ones, nor yet neatly combined. To reverse the initial riverine metaphor, we will need to begin simultaneously at the heads of many streams, of different lengths, and follow them as they meander, braid, divide, dry up, wander off and in certain cases cumulatively converge and merge. Much of the last, crucial process may have taken place at different rates in different parts of the basin, and begun on a modest, if not microcosmic scale (one feature of the world of *The Corrupting Sea* that surely can be safely retrojected). With this in mind, we would do well to keep a keen eye for what are known as 'emergent properties', as opposed to fully fledged systems, often evolving independently with little coordination amidst a wild-growth of alternatives. Equally, we shall want to spend plenty of time along streams that headed elsewhere, or eventually failed, both for their own particular interest, and if we aim to discover what brought others together to such effect.

Crucially, we also need to embrace a significant change in the nature of the principal evidence, one that should not distract from the ultimate goal, but that does demand a familiarity with alternative ways of getting to it. Ancient written sources, and likewise artistic representations, will contribute, often invaluably, to our pursuit of early Mediterranean history, but the further back we go in time, the more their quantity and distribution dwindle, eventually to vanishing point. Instead, an archaeology of the most omnivorous variety, adventurous in its remit among the social and hard sciences, and resolute in deploying its major strength – access to an unparalleled time depth – will be the key to effecting that extension of history by other means that is needed in order to explore the Mediterranean's more distant past.

The curious thing is that astonishingly little writing in this vein has come out of Mediterranean archaeology in the past few decades. Instead, the inexorable trend has been towards specialization by period, region or technique, sometimes taken to absurd extremes. To adapt one of Horden and Purcell's pithier phrases, this produces much archaeology *in* but none *of* the Mediterranean. The causes of this ghettoization are not hard to spot. Most of the blame lies with the same factor that is Mediterranean archaeology's greatest blessing, namely the floods of new information sweeping across the basin each year. It is simply no longer possible to absorb everything that one might ideally want to know even about one aspect of the Mediterranean, let alone the whole. Another factor is the unsurprising preference for local perspectives in the Mediterranean's younger nations, and other autonomously minded regions.[18] These were further favoured in the late 20th century by scholars reacting against the previous assumption that major innovations necessarily derived from Near Eastern (primarily Egyptian or Mesopotamian) precedents – a 'diffusionist' assumption with its roots in Herodotus (who believed that the Greeks learned wisdom from the east) and espoused in the late 19th and early 20th centuries by, among others, Oscar Montelius, coiner of the phrase *ex oriente lux*, Angelo Mosso, author of *The Dawn of Mediterranean Civilisation*, and Gordon Childe, the leading archaeological interpretative synthesizer of his age.[19]

At its best, a close focus encourages us to look at regional and micro-regional processes and thereby highlights the critical capacities for internal change within all Mediterranean societies – an outstanding example being Colin Renfrew's study of the Aegean in *The Emergence of Civilisation*.[20] Without such insights, large-scale history becomes suspiciously smooth, and attempts to understand commonalities and interconnections remain just so stories. At its worst, however, the result is archaeological and intellectual parochialism, a myopia that misses the linkages and parallels that give structure and explanatory coherence to the whole, that exalts what Freud condemned as the 'narcissism of small difference', with each case unique unto itself. Degrees of diversity are hardly a surprise, given that none of us is able to transmit even our genes and ideas with complete fidelity; far more striking are those instances where, despite the inevitability of difference, we find that we can in fact still connect, compare and generalize to good effect. Archaeology *in* the Mediterranean too easily finds itself in the position of a person at the bottom of a well, who can see a small patch of sky with perfect clarity, but misses the scope and constellations of the heavens.

The severity of the problem can be gauged by the fact that, notwithstanding several recent collections of valuable studies of selected themes,[21] the last two pan-Mediterranean syntheses of the basin's early past date back a generation. David Trump's *The Prehistory of the Mediterranean* provided a concise summary of what was known in 1980,[22] if one that somewhat dodged explanation and justification, and already revealed incipient data-overload when grappling with the hydra-heads of pottery style. The other is a totally different book, and an utter surprise. Entitled, with Gallic flourish, *Les Mémoires de la Méditerranée* (translated with a counter-dose of prosaic Anglo-Saxon as *The Mediterranean in the Ancient World*), its manuscript was written in 1968–69, but languished all but forgotten until 1998. The author was none other than Braudel, taking time out from the sterner stuff of *Civilization and Capitalism* to write an overview from the Palaeolithic, via Ramesses II and Philip II (of Macedon rather than Spain, as the English editor quips – though Braudel might have countered that their worlds differed less than we imagine) to the Emperor Constantine.[23] Focused on geography, culture, commerce and technology, rather than dynasts and battles, the book is vintage Braudel, and a gently magisterial voice from beyond the grave. Inevitably, it shows its age, especially in the west and centre where (as we shall discover) a dating revolution was poised to blow to smithereens the assumptions on which he depended. But it remains impressive in its vision, prescience and enticing analogies – for example between populous, supremely confident, self-proclaimingly autarkous and yet, in the final assessment, commercially vulnerable Egypt, and late imperial China. Braudel's lost masterpiece reads more excitingly over forty years on than much written on the subject today, but manifestly a work of this age can be no substitute for one informed by subsequent increases in knowledge. The closest that anyone has since come is another Frenchman, born, appropriately, in Carcassonne, namely Jean Guilaine, whose *La Mer Partagée* (1994) bears Braudel's imprimatur.[24] The title captures the ambiguously sharing and dividing aspects of the sea, and what follows is a masterly, still often up-to-date thematic exploration of societies all over the basin from the Neolithic up to 2000 BC (roughly Chapters 5 to 7 of the present book) – only to stop tantalizingly in mid-track. Given the challenges, it is little wonder that the treatments of the early Mediterranean in several recent accounts of the basin's overall history are disappointingly scanty relative to its time span and significance, though only John Julius Norwich is disarmingly frank enough to declare its 'prehistory' to be fundamentally boring – a verdict with which I hope the reader will come to disagree.[25]

Other recent syntheses that incorporate the early Mediterranean fall into one of two categories, both of which draw attention away from investigation of the basin as a whole. One dismembers the sea and its hinterlands between surveys of Europe, Africa and southwest Asia, so that Sicily rubs shoulders with Scandinavia but not Syria, Morocco with the Cape of Good Hope but not Spain. In a recent book, Barry Cunliffe (who avers that the lack of tides renders it effete beside the mighty Atlantic), portrays the Mediterranean as one of Europe's maritime boundaries.[26] In fact, such tyranny of the continents is as hoary as Herodotus. Although such divisions make some sense for the very remotest periods that will concern us, they soon become detrimental to any Mediterranean focus and cry out for counter-alignment around the sea. The other category encompasses the 'world-systems' approach, in this context advocated in its most rhetorically stimulating form by Andrew and Susan Sherratt.[27] This reworks the old diffusionist idea to argue that from about 3500 BC the Mediterranean and Europe were profoundly shaped by economic and ideological engagements with the emergent cities, states and empires of the adjacent Near East. This model will be set out more fully when the time comes, in Chapter 7. At one level its truth is beyond dispute, but regardless of the degree to which we elect to read some phases of early Mediterranean history from right to left (like cuneiform itself), or insist upon the ongoing dialogue between such wider processes and the enduring, often resistive practices of local people,[28] the basic limitation for our purpose is that it leaves huge swathes in outer darkness until ripples from the east started to reach them – places and people without history until the eve of incorporation in a wider world. A world-systems approach cannot offer an overall framework for Mediterranean history, and in fairness was never intended to do so. In contrast, the thalassocentric, Mediterranean focus offers a promising chance to write simultaneously both big and small, to locate the multiplicity of local trajectories in a wider framework that allows peculiarities and shared features alike to emerge, and thereby to avoid both the dual temptations of a steamrolling master narrative and the mere heaping up of a magpie's bricolage of local truths.

Before we turn to the materials at hand to attempt this, one last aspiration: may this book be a fundamentally *barbarian* history. This does not imply that we should ignore the grand societies that developed first in the eastern part of the basin, though a dose of scepticism concerning the approbation that we unthinkingly attribute to them thanks to the values we ascribe to their art and other remains, and greater attention to the Mediterranean's wild side, will be no bad thing. Nor does it deny that something that could be called 'Mediterranean civilization' was coalescing and spreading by interaction and convergence on shared ways of doing things by the later part of our time span.[29] Rather, 'barbarian' is intended in its original meaning, as Greece's cultural 'other', whether personified in a Persian noble or Libyan goatherd. For as one observer rightly complains, '"Mediterranean" has often been a synonym for "Greek and Roman, plus such other ancient cultures as I may happen to pay attention to"', a politically correct alternative to Classics (which should need no such fig leaf), without real commitment to basin-wide perspectives.[30] Likewise, another warns that '"Classics"…isolates the ancient world of the Mediterranean from its predecessors and contemporaries, and defines it solely in terms of its putative successors'.[31] Phenomena like Minoan Crete, or the marble figurines of the Cyclades, that for various reasons have found cultural favour in modern times, are thereby uprooted and placed in spurious ancestry to the later Greek world, while most of the rest is relegated to the shadows. In fact, although by the 14th century BC archaic Greek was being written in a syllabic script in parts of the Aegean, we have no idea how widely or for how long it had been spoken there. And we do have certain reasons to believe that Hellenic identities began to form markedly later, climaxing right at the end of this book's remit in the trauma and triumph of the Persian wars, just after a strikingly late spurt that for the first time brought the Aegean into a truly lead position within the Mediterranean.[32] The sweeping adoption across the basin of Greek-style traits came later still. To be avoided at all costs is the species of history that declares the Parthenon to be the finishing post before the athletes are even at the starting line. Naturally, the people of the Aegean will play a major part in this book, as do those of Iberia, Italy, the Levant, Africa and elsewhere, but they possess no privileged position or manifest destiny. This is an emphatically polyglot history.

An embarrassment of riches

The Mediterranean is one of the most favoured parts of the world in which to do early history through archaeology. Before we parade its strengths and the astonishing range of information on which interpretations are founded, it is well worth asking why this should be so. One reason is the duration and intensity of investigation. Curiosity about the remnants of the past is ancient in itself, especially in places like the Mediterranean where relics abounded, even if it is simplistic to equate with our idea of archaeology the clearing of older tombs at Abydos in Egypt by late 2nd-millennium BC rulers in search of Osiris, or Empedocles of Akragas's belief that the bones of fossil elephants in Sicily were those of Cyclopes.[33] More palpably ancestral were the universal savants of the Renaissance, and the antiquaries to whom they ceded place in the 17th and 18th centuries.[34] The monumental and aesthetically admired antiquities of Greek and Roman times held the greatest sway over such scholars, a dominance confirmed in the mid-18th century by the Neo-Classical doctrines of Johann Joachim Winckelmann and the first organized digging for painted vases in Etruria (roughly modern Tuscany) and at Pompeii and Herculaneum. This encouraged an adventurous southern extension of the Grand Tours undertaken by wealthy northern Europeans. Samuel Johnson affirmed that 'The grand object of travelling is to see the shores of the Mediterranean', while the Enlightenment positioned its archaeology in a glorious march towards the West's self-image, a place that it has held ever since, to the detriment of attempts at more level-headed analysis. This phase also fixed the tone, for better or worse, in one additional respect: Mediterranean archaeology to this day remains exceptionally thing-rich, and thing-focused, an archaeology of overflowing museums. Objects exist in profusion, to be counted, dated, mended, run through machines, imitated, forged, debated, fought over and still often admired for their beauty. Mediterranean artifacts are everywhere.

From an early date, pre-Classical objects can be glimpsed in scholarly writing and cabinets of curiosities. During the late 16th century Michele Mercati, a doctor at the Vatican, illustrated Neolithic or Copper Age flint arrowheads and blades, arguing that they came not from lightning strikes but were weapons and tools made before the invention of metal. Bronze figurines from Sardinia appear in the 18th-century collection of the Comte de Caylus [**1.4**], another enquiring mind who urged that antiquities needed to be explained as well as possessed.[35] And right at the end of the 18th century, the troupe of scholars attached to Napoleon Bonaparte's expeditionary force in Egypt brought an older civilization, and one from the southern side of the Mediterranean, to the attention of a Europe that had until then

1.4 An 18th-century AD engraving, easily recognizable as a record of an early 1st-millennium BC Sardinian bronze figurine, from the Caylus collection.

relied on a trickle of escaped objects, plus the Bible and Classical authors, for know-ledge in this quarter (unlike Arab scholars, incidentally, who had long engaged with the colossal ruins on their doorstep).[36]

The later 19th and early 20th centuries saw a boom in scholarly exploration of the early Mediterranean. This was part of a wider phenomenon, the very form-ation of 'prehistoric' archaeology in the wake of the demonstration of the earth's geological age, and in tandem with the idea of evolution by natural selection. In much of Europe 'prehistory' was initially grouped with palaeontology, geology or ethnography (as evidence of 'primitive' peoples) rather than the archaeology of later, literate societies. In Greece, however, the equivalent time span (at least its later phases) was regarded as the forerunner of the Classical world, fragments of whose history were thought to be preserved in Homer; Heinrich Schliemann was a pioneer in this respect. Biblical texts and the questions they prompted played an equivalent role in the Levant, though in Egypt and the Near East the time before the age of kings and writing was accorded the lowest priority, and left devoid of questions, until well into the 20th century.[37] In terms of fieldwork, Mediterranean archaeology in the late 19th and early 20th centuries was dominated, especially in the east, by 'big digs' at major sites, facilitated by cheap labour and what now seem coarse expecta-tions about the recording and retention of finds [1.5]. Some of these, for example at Troy, Knossos, Ugarit, Jericho and Thapsos in Sicily, were rediscoveries in the sense

1.5 A typical action scene from an early 20th-century big dig: the French mission at Ras Shamra (Bronze Age Ugarit), with large numbers of local workmen wielding heavy tools and foreign archaeologists striking commanding poses.

that the ancient place names were already known from written sources. Their legacy is the spectacular horizontal and vertical exposure of ancient towns and villages, plus huge numbers of tombs, but variable degrees of certainty as to what was found where, and a depressing sensation for the modern professional that vastly more data would be recoverable if the site were excavated today.

Archaeology as it emerged over the course of the 19th century was primarily a Western invention, and until the end of the Second World War its practitioners throughout the Mediterranean were predominantly Europeans, often from north of the Alps, with a smattering of American Classicists and, in the 'Holy Land', Biblical scholars and missionaries.[38] Around much of the basin, the context in which archaeology took place was explicitly or quasi-colonial. By the end of the 19th century most of North Africa (save for Libya, later to be seized by Italy), plus Malta and Cyprus, had been annexed on various pretexts to the British or French empires. At the end of the First World War this grip extended to the Levantine mandates formed after the collapse of the Ottoman empire (archaeology had been adopted as a foreign graft late in the latter's life, leading to the foundation in 1868 of the sole imperial antiquities collection more or less *within* the Mediterranean, at Istanbul). In Greece, a growing sovereign nation since the 1820s, foreign financial and diplomatic pressure could force a politics of deference, and in southern Spain the leading archaeologists of the late 19th century were two Belgian mining engineers. In the Italian peninsula, which was largely unified in the 1860s, and whose early archaeology was a primarily Italian concern from the first, Etruscan and Sicilian archaeology was in part an act of resistance against the renewed hegemony of Rome. Under such circumstances, and despite the glamour that surrounds grand colonial-age excavators such as Arthur Evans, Flinders Petrie and Leonard Woolley (all knighted), an equal glory should go to those indigenous men (and this was a chauvinist field save for a handful of foreign women, such as Kathleen Kenyon at Jericho and Harriet Boyd Hawes in Crete) who contributed to the exploration of the early Mediterranean with a fraction of the funds available to foreigners. Such figures include Christos Tsountas, the pioneer of Cycladic and Thessalian archaeology, Paolo Orsi, the discoverer of vast cemeteries around Syracuse, and Themistocles Zammit (also knighted), the father of Maltese archaeology [**1.6**]. Such people are just as emblematic in the light of current realities in the Mediterranean as the familiar heroes of the colonial story.

For since the 1950s the operating conditions have been utterly reconfigured by widespread national independence and modernizing developments. While a century ago a Mediterranean archaeologist would typically be foreign, independently funded and in pursuit of a personal agenda, today, despite a minority presence of international teams often working collaboratively with their hosts, most are nationals of the country concerned, often state employees

1.6 Themistocles Zammit (1864–1935), polymath and native founder of Maltese archaeology, served under British rule both as rector of the Royal University of Malta and as the first director of the National Museum of Archaeology.

conducting fieldwork ahead of the bulldozer. Numbers in universities, museums and governmental authorities are incomparably greater, and many are women. All this reflects the absorption of archaeology into the mainstream. It is also part and parcel of a veritable explosion of fieldwork. To give one example, in the last decade of the 20th century Israel issued permits for no fewer than 2200 excavations, some three-quarters of which were new, and mostly required by salvage efforts in advance of building to house immigrants after the collapse of the Soviet Union.[39] For all the double-edged issues associated with national sponsorship of the means to write history (to which we return at the end of this chapter), the alarming amount of rescue digs and subsequent destruction, and hand-wringing over backlogs of unpublished work, these are positive changes overall, in terms of the quantity and in most cases quality of the archaeology undertaken. No law of diminishing returns applies; on the contrary, the prospect is one of rich streams of information for creating fuller pictures of the past. Equally positive is the formulation of distinct intellectual traditions within the Mediterranean in the teeth of the Anglo-American dominance of recent archaeological thinking, which threatens to replace colonial hegemonies with new ones of the mind. Particularly notable are the left-wing tradition in Italy, and in Spain since the fall of Franco, as well as a focus on technology and its transmission in France, a nation with an impressive history of basin-wide archaeological activity.[40] All in all, Mediterranean archaeology at the start of the 21st century is more diverse than ever before, and there is exponentially more of it.

The Mediterranean is archaeologically blessed in other ways too. One under-recognized fact is its unusual wealth of freak preservation conditions – those under which a capsule of ancient reality escapes the devastating attrition (such as the rotting of organics, or dispersal and destruction of precious or recyclable goods) that afflicts most of the record and renders it, in David Clarke's resonant simile, not so much a perforated solid like a Gruyère cheese, but the finest of suspensions floating in a liquid of loss.[41] Such windows provide piercing visions of the full palette and scale of early activity, and prompt us to query the minimalist assessments of the past that degraded records tend to promote. We owe most to the Mediterranean's extraordinarily diverse environment (explored further in Chapter 2), which generates a range of preservation niches rarely matched elsewhere. Shipwrecks and drowned settlements furnish waterlogged and underwater conditions [**1.7**], while desiccation operates not only in Egypt, much of which lies beyond the Mediterranean, but also in the dry caves of Israel, southern Spain and the Balearic Islands. Volcanic eruptions bequeath two Bronze Age Pompeiis; the best known is the town of Akrotiri on the Cycladic island of Thera (modern Santorini) [**1.8**], but no less informative is Croce del Papa, near Nola, in the shadow of Vesuvius, with its almost intact huts, complete with trapped livestock. Even the famous Iceman was freeze-dried only 200 km (125 miles) from the Adriatic; he expired just on the wrong side of the watershed, but we know that he hailed from further south (see Chapter 7). Water, aridity, ash-fall and ice supplement the wealth of the standard remains in the Mediterranean in ways that challenge and force us to revise assumptions.

Extraordinary archaeological preservation by water and volcanism:

1.7 The freshwater-inundated remains of Neolithic wooden structures at La Draga in Catalonia.

1.8 Multi-storey survival of a Bronze Age town beneath tephra at Akrotiri on Thera (modern Santorini), in the Cyclades.

1.9 The prolixity of textual sources in parts of the eastern Mediterranean from a comparatively early date is illustrated by these inscribed clay tablets, found with thousands of others in the archive room of 3rd-millennium BC Ebla, in modern northwest Syria.

Another advantage is the Mediterranean's profusion of texts and images [**1.9**]. Admittedly, the former, in particular, have severe restrictions. Until the 1st millennium BC, writing was limited to the easternmost end of the Mediterranean and the Aegean. And even here, scripts only emerged well into our time span, and several scripts are undeciphered to this day (notably those of Minoan Crete and Cyprus). The breadth of written evidence also varies in terms of survival and range of subject matter. For example, the first Aegean scripts, unlike those to the east, were written principally on unfired clay tablets that only survived if a conflagration consumed the building containing them. Moreover, their largely economic remit is far narrower, and reveals a more restricted literacy than in the east, where writing soon included elite propaganda, diplomatic and other correspondence, treaties, religion, history and law codes as well as economic records. We also need to keep in the forefront of our minds the fact that people wrote not for our investigative benefit but as part of their ordering of the world, which often transgressed the categories just listed, and that writing was primarily intended for elite members of society. Certain ostensibly factual royal proclamations are highly suspect as event-historical records and tell us more about official ideology on the home front; famously, the pharaoh Ramesses II came close to losing a major battle at Qadesh in the Levant that his monuments in Egypt claimed that he won outright. But despite all this, and as long as we grasp that writing complements, rather than makes redundant, other forms of data, judicious use of text can take us to places that we otherwise could not dream of entering, revealing details as varied as long-range transfers of princesses in marriage contracts, the value of rock crystal (a big piece was worth 3000 sheep and 60 male slaves in neighbouring northern Mesopotamia some 3750 years ago) or the sheer scale of the Bronze Age cloth industry.[42] Often most telling are the unintentional insights into conventions, assumptions, priorities and orderings of places, people and things, the preoccupations taken for granted that lurk submerged under the hyperbole of royal letters or the tedious regularities of tax records. For all the limitations of early Mediterranean texts, only a fool would wish such hints away. The real challenge is to calibrate correctly those contexts that they irradiate, with those, notably in the centre and west, that they do not. The same holds true of images, with which Mediterranean archaeology abounds. Although these are more generously distributed in space and time than texts, similar cautions and opportunities apply concerning the distinction between ancient intent or ways of seeing and the information that we seek to extract, especially from the superficially more familiar narrative, naturalistic forms of representational art that developed in the eastern half of the Mediterranean during the Bronze Age.[43]

Within such a cornucopia, what are the current cutting edges of archaeological investigation of the early Mediterranean? Excavation, of course, still flourishes, but in diverse guises.[44] The big dig is now an endangered species thanks to soaring costs and higher expectations of fine-grained recovery, recording, analysis and publication – a shift from pickaxe to trowel, sieve, microscope and database that has drastically slowed the pace of work. Most such enterprises that have survived are either foreign projects with massive private or overseas state funding, or prestigious national showpieces. Examples of the former include Ashkelon in Israel and Tell el-Dab'a (ancient Avaris) in the Nile Delta, both enormous, multiperiod sites; volcanically preserved Akrotiri on Thera exemplifies the latter.[45] Although the big dig has become a white elephant, and unfashionable (a clear case of the fox and the grapes), it is worth underlining what we lose by its dwindling, for large sites hold the keys to urban life and often to interregional connections. Consider the forty-plus seasons conducted by French teams since 1929 at Ugarit, the capital of a kingdom in the 2nd millennium BC, which have yielded the early Mediterranean's broadest exposure of palaces, temples, houses and tombs, together with their contents, including imports from as far afield as Egypt, the Aegean and central Asia, as well as state and private archives that offer breathtaking prospects.[46] Under present conditions, it is typically feasible only to nibble at such sites, supplementing excavations with surface work

1.10 Rescue archaeology at Villeneuve-Tolosane, near Toulouse, reveals beneath the layout of a modern housing estate the outlines of a large Neolithic ditch-enclosed village, along with hundreds of hearths, silos and other features.

Ditch
Palisade
● Round structure
▮ Rectangular structure
▲ Other structure
◆ Pit

0   100 m
0   300 ft

N

1.11 Field survey in action: a team of archaeologists walks the uplands of Kythera in the summer of 2001. Such close combing of the surface for remnants of all periods of the past has transformed our knowledge of the ever-changing face of Mediterranean landscapes over time.

and remote probing of what lies beneath, often using new technologies. On a more positive note, the decline of the big dig correlates with a growing attention to small sites, such as rural settlements and caves, which has broadened our knowledge immensely, for small sites need not entail small questions. Finally, although much excavation currently takes place under rescue conditions, this in no way prejudices the novelty or value of results. Entire classes of extensive settlements enclosed by boundary ditches, often covering huge areas, have been discovered in Greece, southern France and Spain thanks to work in advance of building roads and housing estates [**1.10**].[47]

Increasingly, excavation shares the stage with surface surveys that analyse the long-term evidence for activity within an entire landscape, whether a valley, river drainage, massif, island, city, its hinterland or mining region.[48] Survey has deep roots in reconnoitring for ruins, but began to be systematized from the mid-20th century. In the Mediterranean, one pioneering project during the 1930s explored hundreds of sites on the Amuq plain in the northern Levant, followed soon after the Second World War by surveys of the southwest Peloponnese and the Etrurian landscapes adjacent to Rome. From the 1970s survey redesigned itself to comb smaller expanses more intensively, using closely spaced walkers. The scene with which this book opened intercepted one of almost a hundred surveys that have collectively covered thousands of square kilometres in the Aegean, with comparable coverage in Italy and parts of the Levant [**1.11**]. It also reveals this technique's ability to turn terra incognita into landscapes swarming with life, indeed one contribution has been to expose the unimagined extent to which Mediterranean countrysides could be peppered with small communities and other activity areas, almost all of which escaped earlier notice. Surveys also build intellectual bridges, for its landscape focus encourages an engagement with scientists, historians and anthropologists with parallel interests (often inspired by Braudelian *annales* traditions), as well as the adoption of methods ranging from aerial and satellite image analysis to empathetic exploration of the sensual perceptions of ancient men and women.[49] Lastly, survey is critical to reconstructions of past demography, and the tendencies of populations to expand under favourable conditions, and crash if these altered. At a fundamental level it is difficult to think about the past and the actions of people in it without some notional grasp of orders of magnitude. To take two extreme cases, the population of the Mediterranean under the Roman empire at its peak is thought to have been 35–50 million people, while 20,000 years earlier, at the height of the last glaciation, it may have been a mere 45,000, roughly a thousandth of the later figure (further discussed in Chapters 4 and 10, respectively). The first estimate comes from fiscal and other records, the latter from analogy with ethnographically studied hunter-gatherers, but for most of the periods in between and, just as importantly, for the distributions of people in different parts of the basin at any given time, we are primarily reliant on the numbers, size and nature of the numerous dots on the maps that survey has generated.

Another frontier lies underwater, from the shoreline down to the inkiest depths. The Mediterranean was one of the birthplaces of maritime archaeology. The 1960s dives on a 3200-year-old boat that sank off Cape Gelidonya, a cruel stretch of the Turkish coast, remain a landmark, though the title of the world's earliest shipwreck is now held by a slightly older neighbour at Uluburun [**1.12**], more recently excavated, and there are potential challengers elsewhere in the form of hull-less debris scatters up to a thousand years older (seafaring, as we shall see, long pre-dates all of these sites, but its earliest indications are indirect proxies such as traces of human

1.12 The submarine frontier of Mediterranean archaeology. At Uluburun, off the southern coast of Turkey, a diver some 45 m (150 ft) down prepares to raise a 14th-century BC copper ingot, with pottery transport jars in the background.

presence on islands).[50] State-of-the-art deep-sea exploration technology is currently breaking the prior restriction to shallow coastal waters, opening up the revolutionary prospect of investigating early open-sea crossings and finding cargos free from the depredations of sports divers and other disturbance – though the damage wreaked by bottom-trawling turns out to be chronic even several hundred metres down.[51] On the Skerki Bank between North Africa and Sicily, remotely operated vehicles far below the waves have located wrecks of Roman or later date. The search for a vanished submarine off southern Israel encountered two 8th-century BC cargo ships 400 m (1300 ft) down, and a 3rd-century BC merchantman has been found at the eerie depth of 3 km (2 miles) off Cyprus. The discovery of older deep-sea wrecks is surely only a matter of time. In the meantime, Mediterranean maritime archaeology is far from being limited to shipwrecks, fascinating as these time capsules are in terms of cargos, trade routes and shipbuilding techniques. Additional underwater research, especially along the intensely investigated coasts of southern France and northern Israel, have encountered Neolithic villages drowned by sea level rise.[52] The ancient harbours at Tyre and Sidon in Lebanon have been delineated by coring the sediments that later choked them.[53] Most dramatically, in 1991 an intrepid diver, drawn to a cave entrance now 37 m (120 ft) underwater off Marseilles, swam in darkness for 150 m (490 ft) along a sinuous tunnel to emerge in a painted cavern last entered dry-shod 9000 years ago, and which now bears his name: Grotte Cosquer.[54] Less courageous, but no less informative, is armchair study of maritime culture, through the evaluation of early navigational capabilities (based on ancient depictions of ships, ethnographic reports of similar craft and experimental replicas), sailing conditions (from practical experience, both modern and ancient data on winds and currents and early navigators' descriptions of seamarks and travel times), as well as the nature of supporting coastal landscapes and the vital intangibles of seagoing ideology.[55]

Archaeological science constitutes a final cutting-edge activity, with the basin a favoured zone of application for global developments liable to generate possibilities over the coming decades that we can at present hardly imagine. Five areas stand out. The first is the quest for provenance, or the identification of where raw materials and objects came from.[56] This deploys a range of chemical isotope and geologically based techniques. Its clearest successes are associated with materials of restricted natural occurrence. One example is the research on distinctive stones like obsidian, which is found in fewer than a dozen major outcrops in the circum-Mediterranean region, and whose superb cutting qualities ensured that it was in wide demand.[57] Analysis of the clays and minerals in pottery is equally insightful; extraordinarily, we know, for instance, that a particular type of container for oil or wine on the Uluburun shipwreck was made in the Mesara region of Crete and that very similar pots, perhaps made by the same potters, ended up in a royal palace on mainland Greece and at a settlement on Sardinia, the latter some 2000 km (1250 miles) from Uluburun.[58] More controversial, if vitally important, results come from the analysis of metal artifacts, ores and the by-products of metallurgy; not only are the techniques complex and less self-evidently lucid, but metals are highly prone to mixing through recycling.[59] The second area is the investigation of ancient technologies, for instance the temperatures reached, recipes used, degree of standardization and fidelity of knowledge transmission.[60] A third developing field is analysis of organic residues, mainly of lipids, acids and other traces that can pick up the presence of oils, resins, alcohols or narcotics in the pores of pottery, as well as hints of diet and cuisine from cooking pots.[61] A suite of approaches usually bundled together as 'environmental archaeology' represents a fourth realm of application that includes analysis of animal bones, seeds, pollen, charcoal and phytoliths (microscopic silicates in plant cells), in pursuit of questions about domestication, diet and consumption, economy and landscape reconstruction.[62] The last advance is in the extraction of information from human beings. Here the high-profile strand is mitochrondrial DNA inherited via the female line, and male Y-chromosome lineages.[63] Despite exciting claims and counter-claims it must be stressed that, due to the difficulties in extracting ancient DNA, most of the patterns generated derive from analysis of people alive today, and we must guard against a host of simplistic assumptions when trying to make links to the deeper past. Less trumpeted but at least as promising is the reconstruction of life histories from the physical and chemical information contained in ancient bones and teeth.[64] This includes health and diet, status, the timing and nature of traumas or violence, marks of heavy muscular activities like spear-throwing or seed-grinding, and the difference in such respects between men, women and children.

The ambiguous results from some scientific techniques prompt a cautionary note that, while applicable to all archaeological inference, is particularly relevant when archaeology engages with the magic box of science. This is simply that the answers obtained will only be as sophisticated as the questions asked, and many of the questions that we are interested in cannot be solved in this way. It is one thing to establish that something moved from A to B, but quite another to explain the desires or 'needs' that made it worth making the transfer in the first place, the social milieux and means of procurement that effected this (direct collection from source, raiding, profit-oriented trade or gift-giving, to mention just a few options), the value of the substance transferred, the timing of the transfer within the artifact's overall cultural biography, and the way in which it was ultimately consumed. These questions return the ball firmly to archaeology's court, and must tax both our ingenuity and grasp of past human action if they, and others like them, are to be convincingly addressed.

North Africa, the great lacuna

So much for the present strengths of Mediterranean archaeology. But the riches also embarrass in their uneven distribution. Some of this is inevitable; we cannot wish literacy into being in Neolithic France, or hope for icemen in Malta. But there are imbalances in exploration too. Many of these are minor. To take islands as examples, we know a lot more about those in the southern Adriatic than those in the north, while the first proper survey on Corsica is only recently underway. A few lacunae in time or space are larger and more troubling. Until recently, the Palaeolithic of

Turkey and the southern Balkans was thinly attested. Again in Turkey, rescue work along the eastern river valleys doomed by dam-building, coupled with the overlay of later cities, long discouraged work on much of the Mediterranean coast. Albania, parts of the former Yugoslavia and Lebanon are likewise still catching up.

But only a single imbalance is so devastating that it threatens to undermine the integrity of the overall study of the Mediterranean. This is the dearth of information on the early societies of Mediterranean North Africa. A comparable problem faced Braudel in the 1940s. Then, the archives of the Ottoman empire, which controlled over half the circumference of the basin, were still a closed book to Western scholars. Otherwise, Philip II would surely have shared Braudel's title with his contemporary, Suleiman the Magnificent. Yet Braudel, who confessed that as a young teacher on his first posting to Constantine in Algeria, the 'spectacle of the Mediterranean as seen from the opposite shore, upside down',[65] stimulated his vision of history, could at least hazard a fair guess, the accuracy of which was later confirmed, that the Ottoman Mediterranean 'lived and breathed with the same rhythms' as the Christian. In the case of early North Africa, we cannot be so sure that a similar statement would hold good, and indeed exasperatingly inconclusive indications hint that it would not.

In the Nile Delta, some 17,000 sq. km (6500 sq. miles) in its present form and accounting for roughly half Egypt's arable land, the problem is only moderately severe; we do know a certain amount, even if we suspect that it may be misleadingly little. In the remainder of Mediterranean Africa, however, it is chronic, despite a nearness measured by dust from the Sahara that falls as red rain across southern Europe [1.13].

1.13 The proximity of Africa. During a seasonal reversal of the prevailing winds, a plume of red Saharan dust is blown north across the mid-Mediterranean narrows, smothering Sicily, parts of Italy and reaching towards Greece.

In fact, it has become standard practice in most writing on the early Mediterranean to tacitly more or less ignore most of the southern flank from the end of the Palaeolithic until the arrival of Phoenician and Greek settlers.[66] Nor can the blame be laid entirely at the door of Mediterranean scholars, for most African archaeologists equally ignore this sector of the continent's rim. From a Mediterranean viewpoint, this is a disaster. For the fertile zone between Tunisia and the Atlantic (whose Arabic name, the Jazirat al-Maghreb, means 'the islands of the west', an interesting way of conceptualizing this in-between region) contributes around a quarter of all the land in the basin, while the coast from Alexandria to Ceuta (Africa's Gibraltar) claims a sizeable proportion of its shoreline. Whatever did or did not happen here, we can hardly afford to simply avoid its history.

What accounts for this dearth of information? Part of the answer may be a lack of looking. But despite the prejudices of some Classicizing thinkers (the Swiss writer Emil Ludwig notoriously claimed in 1942 that 'to the life of the Mediterranean, the Acropolis is more important than the whole history of Morocco'),[67] under colonial rule a good deal of archaeology of the early periods was undertaken in the Maghreb. The Frenchman Gabriel Camps, in particular, became a staunch advocate of North African archaeology and Berber culture.[68] In Cyrenaica (currently better known as the hinterland of Benghazi), a British team excavated the huge Haua Fteah cavern in the 1950s, documenting 14 m (46 ft) of deposit that still represent North Africa's master sequence from the Palaeolithic to the Greeks [1.14]; the cave has recently

1.14 Haua Fteah ('great cavern') lives up to its name in this image from the 1950s excavation by a British team.

been re-excavated.[69] There was also great interest, albeit based on flawed premises, in trans-Mediterranean contact across lost land-bridges. One relic of this is the hybrid term 'Iberomaurusian' for the Maghreb's last Upper Palaeolithic phase (see Chapter 4). Moreover, some of these connections were thought to run from south to north; for instance, various early scholars considered the Capsian phenomenon in the Maghreb (see Chapter 5) to be a progenitor of the French Upper Palaeolithic or Iberian Neolithic. The debunking of such proposals in the 1930s heralded a new, much-needed chronological rigour, but also hastened an investigative divorce between south and north.[70]

The next major shift came with the political independence of the North African nations, mainly in the 1950s but only in 1962 in bloodily contested Algeria. Numbers of active foreign archaeologists fell, most dramatically in Algeria, which embraces the largest share of the Maghreb facing the Mediterranean. Many of those who continued pursued external agendas, either early matters of human origins, or later ones such as Roman imperium. With its origins as a colonial practice, and the grand Greek, Roman and early Christian remains felt to be emblematic of alien rule, archaeology struggled to put down local roots and to claim funding in nations with other priorities.[71] Apart from the touristic asset of Roman ruins, the antiquities favoured since independence have tended, understandably, to be representative of non-European achievements, especially Carthaginian, Numidian and Islamic monuments. Recent initiatives in Tunisia, Libya and Morocco are encouraging, but the fact remains that in comparison to the meteoric advances elsewhere in the Mediterranean over the last few decades, our knowledge of the early history of the southern flank west of Egypt has virtually stood still. Our reaction to this parlous state of affairs should, of course, be to try harder rather than to avert our gaze, and at least to offer some heuristic interpretative options.

Yet the low archaeological profile of much of Mediterranean North Africa may not be entirely due to a lack of prospection. Perhaps, at certain periods, its history was differently constituted from that of the remainder of the basin; if so, to explore it with European or Levantine preconceptions would be misleading. In the coming chapters we shall encounter several indications that this was indeed the case. For the present, two indications from Tunisia must suffice. Had this book opened there, rather than in Kythera, the story would have been radically different. On Djerba, an offshore island twice the size of Kythera, no definite prehistoric sites were found by a recent survey, while the total number of sites older than the 1st millennium BC discovered by recent surveys in this, by North African standards, well-prospected country, amounts to just fifteen.[72] Even allowing for biases in detection, this is a minute figure compared with those from the northern or eastern flanks of the Mediterranean, or the 1500 Roman sites located by the same Tunisian projects. Something different surely was going on.

One intriguing hypothesis is that for long periods much of the North African littoral was oriented not on the Mediterranean, but the great continental expanse to its south.[73] Its inhabitants concentrated on hunting and gathering of wild resources, and later mobile pastoralism, with little interest in the maritime interactions building up in the remainder of the basin. There are, as we shall see, good reasons to favour this line of thought. Far from implying that history in this part of the world was a conqueror's prerogative, or that the Maghreb, Cyrenaica and the rest were not in some sense part of the Mediterranean, we shall need to be alert to the idea that the basin's early history could follow other trajectories than those prescribed in the Levantine and European flanks. But even this begs the question as to *why* Mediterranean North Africa followed a path less trodden (if we decide that it indeed did). As we shall see, societies in most other parts of the basin seldom rooted themselves so exclusively in the land masses behind them. One suggestion is that geography played an isolating role, notably the combination of a rugged 'mountain exoskeleton' facing the sea, adverse currents, and a vast desert to the south that also thrust between the Maghreb, Cyrenaica and other habitable areas, breaking up the coastal strip into a series of widely separated virtual islands.[74] This undoubtedly captures part of the truth, but under certain conditions we shall need to recognize a more positive pull from Saharan environments and societies – so much so that we cannot grasp what happened in Mediterranean Africa without venturing far to its south. To answer the paradoxes of early history west of the Delta we shall require more Africa, not less, in our Mediterranean.

In the Nile Delta the problem is different in its nature and causes.[75] Egypt, of course, is no poor relation abandoned by African and Mediterranean archaeologists, but a cultural trophy claimed by both. Here, too, we shall gain much by embedding its developments within northeast Africa. But our Mediterranean perspective focuses particular attention on the great fertile triangle where the Nile intercepts the sea. The problem is that the archaeology of this crucial deltaic interface lies under a thick blanket of river silt and much of it beneath the water table, creating problems first of detection and then logistical ones for excavation. As a result, as late as 1988 one expert could complain that 'our idea of the history of Egypt is therefore the history of the region starting with Heliopolis [at the triangle's southern vertex] and stretching further south deep down into the Sudan'.[76] He might have underlined too the danger of imposing a misleadingly uniform version of Egyptian history, derived from the Nile Valley, onto the potentially different world of the Delta. Since the 1980s a few windows have started to open up (the largest, at Avaris, has been mentioned already), though to this day most of the exposed areas remain limited. Even these reveal that long before the foundation of Alexandria in 331 BC, a coastal city tellingly described in Roman times as 'towards' rather than 'in' Egypt, Delta communities could look strikingly different from those of the Nile Valley, and display closer affiliations to their Mediterranean neighbours. One challenging but rewarding task will be to include Egypt in our Mediterranean history, but in a manner that filters it through the lens of this deltaic junction point.

New frameworks:
time and climate change

Thirty years ago, the greatest structural revolution underway in early Mediterranean archaeology was a chronological one. Radiocarbon dating offered the first chance to establish stand-alone time frames for every corner of the basin, and to place relative sequences, established by changes over time in styles of pottery and other artifacts, within an absolute temporal grid.[77] This was a huge advance on the previous scheme, based on the reigns of Egyptian pharaohs, tied in through Egyptian records to datable astronomical events, and extrapolated across the basin by a cat's cradle of exports or precarious stylistic parallels. The overall impact, especially after the calibration of radiocarbon dates to achieve accurate calendrical ones, was to lengthen chronologies and alter key synchronisms. Phenomena like the huge stone temples of Malta and the first megalithic tombs in Western Europe, which had often been assumed to be echoes of Egyptian architecture refracted via Mycenae, turned out to be centuries earlier than the pyramids, and proof of independent evolution, thereby liberating the central and west Mediterranean from a presumption of eastern priority. Radiocarbon dating also enabled a massive extension of accurate timescales, for while no pharaoh ruled much before 3000 BC, its limits lie some 50,000 years ago. Half a century of advances in radiocarbon, augmented by complementary or stand-alone techniques like tree-ring dating and others for the still deeper past, now place us in the happy position (aside from such significant fine-tuning as the grand conflict over a discrepancy of a century or so in the 2nd-millennium BC Aegean between advocates of Egyptian-derived versus scientific dates) of being able to employ calendrical dates BC throughout the period on which this book, save Chapter 3, concentrates. A salutary indication of what this advance means, and an ironic one given the seminal status of Braudel's thoughts on the nature of historical time, is the fact that the major errors, especially in the centre and west, that render parts of his *The Mediterranean in the Ancient World* obsolete today stem directly from the unfortunate fact that he was writing slightly too early to benefit from its insights; the continued use of wildly erroneous dates garnered from older literature by later historians is less forgivable. One final and invaluable benefit of our secure time frame is that we can begin to liberate ourselves from the artificial period labels that have dominated and cramped our interpretations for too long.

Today, the biggest incipient and future revolution in Mediterranean and indeed global frameworks is a quite different one. For a long time it has been obvious that before the last glaciers retreated, and for much of the earth's last two-and-a-bit million ice-age haunted years known as the Pleistocene, the Mediterranean looked very different from today. Equally, there are indications of fluctuations even within the ensuing Holocene, the present interglacial (starting around 9600 BC) that we so optimistically designate as a separate phase of world climate – the best known being the so-called Little Ice Age. Indeed several trailblazing projects in the Mediterranean have centred their efforts on the relationship between environmental changes and

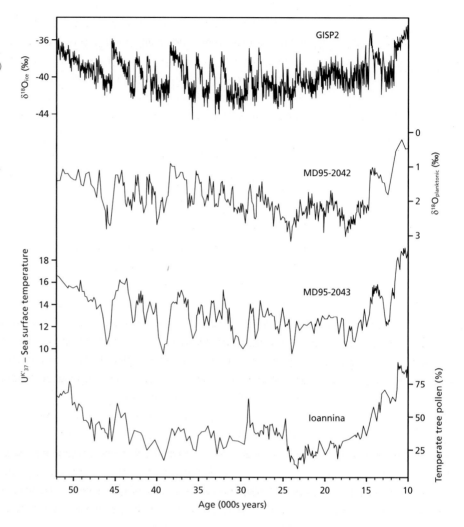

1.15 Measures of climate change from 50,000+ to 10,000 years ago, from cores taken in (from top to bottom) the Greenland ice sheet, offshore Portugal, the far western Mediterranean, and Lake Ioannina in northwest Greece. The close similarity between all these is notable, as is the jagged nature of the changes witnessed.

those seen in the archaeological record, notably a UNESCO-sponsored study of former sustainability in the arid zone south of Tripoli, analyses of desertification in the Vera basin in southern Spain, and most recently investigation of the links between water and human society in southern Jordan.[78] Thanks to current alarm over global warming (which will have a dire impact on the fragile Mediterranean), we now know immeasurably more about past climate change, as well as its solar and orbital triggers, and enjoy a good standard of resolution within the basin itself [1.15].[79] Earth's master records come from cores bored into the bed of the Pacific Ocean, refined by others extracted from the Greenland and Antarctic ice. Thanks to similar preservation conditions to those that so enrich its archaeology, as well as its avoidance of the kinds of glacial erasure of the long-term record suffered at higher latitudes, the Mediterranean supplements the overall picture with a rich array of local data. Seabed cores give information on marine temperatures, salinity, ecology, sediments washed off land and freshwater run-off, shoreline data plot the rises and falls of sea level, while lakes and other wetlands reveal comparable insights as well as long pollen records. Tree rings, species of beetle and other fauna, calcitic accretions in caves, stream flows and sedimentation rates increase the data spectrum. South of the basin, cores drilled into now-vanished Saharan lakes prove that although Atlantic weather has always been the principal influence on Mediterranean climate, tropical monsoons also exerted some, perhaps indirect, influence on the southern-most fringes of the basin during the warmest and wettest phases of the past.[80] All these proxy sources have their issues, and share the general problem of distinguishing climate-related impact from the signatures of human activity, especially once farming developed on an ambitious scale, but combined they provide many insights into an ever-changing Mediterranean.

Some strategic conclusions of this research need to be highlighted before we touch on specific details in the coming chapters. Over the long term, climate change in the Mediterranean, as elsewhere, has been the norm not the exception (indeed the only constant is inconstancy), and its tempo could be rapid.[81] Even the Holocene, on whose relative quiescence most human achievement has been predicated, has been far from uniform, with shifts between markedly wetter and drier conditions, sharper medium-term oscillations, and a few severe short-term 'events'.[82] One crucial consequence is that the environmental conditions underpinning Horden and Purcell's thesis are not natural or eternal to the Mediterranean, but a 5000–6000-year phase (with its own sub-phases), nested between a different preceding regime and a future that we can only start to discern. Further back in time, the changes become more dramatic, and continue for as long as we or our ancestors have lived around the basin. None of this in itself turns coincidences between climatic changes and historical processes into proof of a causal connection, but it does engineer a real change of perspective and demand that we give serious attention to such possibilities. Though Braudel mused that climate might be the ultimate source of change, and Childe popularized an 'oasis' theory of agricultural origins (by which drought squeezed hunter-gatherers into well-watered niches where they altered their means of food acquisition to survive), the role of climatic factors in the interpretation of Mediterranean archaeology has traditionally been the preserve of a fringe ranging from the speculative to the lunatic, too often used to explain allegedly lurid collapses and consequently studiously ignored by the mainstream. The time has come to bring climate change into the heart of Mediterranean history, and not merely to depict a variably bosky, parched or chilly backdrop, but as an active element in the shaping of life all around the basin.

To do this well, however, we must avoid the naiveties of determinism. After all, we deal with a double translation, from climate (temperature, rainfall and the like) to environments and ecologies, and from these to cultural perceptions of affordances and limits in a temporarily stable or changing land- (or sea-) scape. As one champion of climate-informed perspectives observes, 'climate is not destiny. It reveals human ingenuity and creativity'; another reminds us that deteriorating conditions can have a galvanizing effect, encouraging innovation as an alternative to conservatism, flight or collapse – a subtler version of Arnold Toynbee's challenge and response model, whose excesses Braudel once lampooned as reducing the role of environment to 'that attributed to the cane in some English public schools: a severe but effective moral tutor'.[83] In fact, circumstances are everything. The impact of environmental change on people typically depends on its rapidity, magnitude, duration and frequency. Frequent short fluctuations, even if severe or sudden, are predictable risks that encourage built-in resilient responses to enable them to be ridden out. Rare, unprecedented or massive ones are far more likely to be unanticipated, overwhelming and a trigger for social change. Moreover, individuals and communities confronted with similar phenomena might react very differently. This is partly a matter of perceived advantages and threats; for controllers of the food supply a drought could initially be seen as an opportunity to accrue power, only becoming the disaster it already seemed to less fortunate people if it became prolonged. But it also depends on how threats to ways of doing things, and measures to combat these, relate to the strategies of leading people as well as wider ideology. A climate-induced threat might be attributed, for example, to divine wrath, stimulating a greater investment in religious activities and thus accelerating the consumption of resources. Neighbouring groups can also be differentially locked in or flexible in this respect, and variably survive, transform or fail. None of this should come as a surprise, given the current inability of governments and citizens to substantially alter behaviour that is advantageous in the short term, in the face of overwhelming signs of global warming, even when the evidence comes from science, one of the most persuasive ideational frameworks in the contemporary world.

There is one final inverse rider to add: while appreciation of the influences of environmental change upon human societies is growing in sophistication, the accusation of catastrophic human impact on past environments is receiving more sceptical treatment, despite recent popularization; we shall encounter very few cases in which only Mediterranean people managed to inflict really serious damage in this respect.[84]

The present danger

Last but far from least, we must consider how the Mediterranean's early past relates to the basin's troubled present. What threats does its archaeology face today, and how might better understanding of the past help, if not to solve current problems, at least to place them in perspective, and encourage the creation of a more tolerant, viable future? To start with the first question, the Mediterranean's archaeology is certainly in dire need of effective defenders, thanks to the cruel coincidence that places one of the world's hotspots of archaeological riches over a cluster of economically modest to poor nations often swamped by the challenge. Among the physical threats the most universal are consequences of development. Modern farming, mainly in lowlands densely occupied for millennia, must have destroyed tens of thousands of archaeological sites over the last few decades, frequently without any record. Headlong urbanization, often over ancient centres, continues apace; a third of Greek nationals live in Athens. Added to this are the exponential demands of mass tourism, both global and internal, which have encouraged unfettered building in places such

1.16 The threat to the archaeology and broader environment of the Mediterranean coastal zone from large-scale development and mass tourism is inescapable at Torremolinos in southern Spain.

as the south of Spain [**1.16**] and coastal Turkey, and leave huge swathes of other landscape bungaloid. Mediterranean tourism began in Roman times, and Edward Lear already grumbled about a trickle of tourists to Paliokastritsa, his favourite beach on Corfu, in the 1860s, the decade that saw the first Thomas Cook tours to Egypt. But today the Mediterranean attracts, for the notorious four esses of sun, sea, sand and sex, more annual visitors than its standing population, and unsustainable multiples of this ratio on the most popular islands.[85]

All these factors impact disproportionately heavily on the coast and immediate hinterland, the membrane between sea and land where the battle for environmental sustainability and against pollution will also largely be fought (where it is not already lost), and where archaeology urgently needs to forge common cause with the wider conservation movement.[86] According to one estimate, almost a fifth of the Mediterranean coastline lies under concrete or tarmac, with this proportion approaching half on Mallorca. It is easy to criticize, and to forget that there is little alternative to intensification in places where population densities have climbed to planet-leading spikes of over 1000 people per sq. km (or more than 2500 per sq. mile),

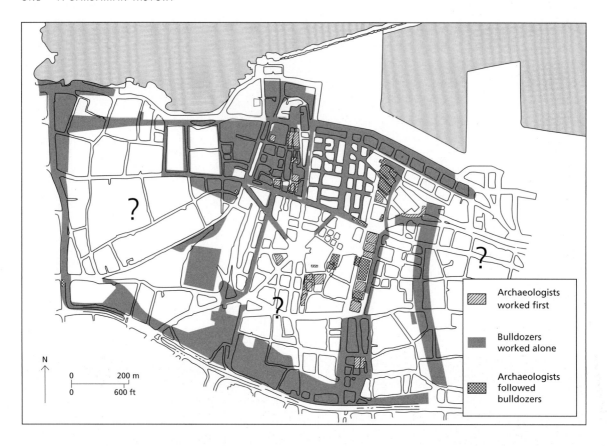

Archaeologists
worked first

Bulldozers
worked alone

Archaeologists
followed
bulldozers

N

0   200 m

0   600 ft

1.17 Map of central Beirut, showing the extent of archaeological excavation and of destruction without such documentation during rebuilding in the wake of the last civil war.

as in the Nile Delta and tiny, overloaded Malta (the very highest densities, in Gaza and Monaco, reflect freak conditions, one tragic, the other ludic, while at only 20–30 people per sq. km (or 50–75 per sq. mile), coastal Libya and Corsica represent the other extreme).[87] Equally, even if tourism eventually proves fickle as monocrop, its income prevents abandonment on many of the islands, encourages well-managed interior landscapes, and contributes heavily to the incomes of Cyprus, Malta, Israel and most of the North African states. Yet the impending crisis cannot be ignored; the current generation may, according to one seasoned observer, prove to be the last to witness a reasonable archaeological record in the Mediterranean.[88] To give two dismal examples, on the Croatian tourist island of Hvar, 30 per cent of all pre-historic to Roman sites have been destroyed or damaged (including those within protected areas) and 65 per cent of its shipwrecks looted,[89] while during post-civil war reconstruction in Beirut, a city atop precursors going back millennia, 90–95 per cent of the area cleared in advance of building was bulldozed without archaeological supervision, a disastrous 'memorycide' for a nation learning how to live with itself [**1.17**]. In the chilling phrase of one of the bravest chroniclers of Beirut's travails at the hands of the developers, the new city rising from the ashes is a 'lobotomized phoenix'.[90]

These multiple pressures mean that archaeology bids for its place and share of resources against stiff, sometimes invincible, competition from other local, national and multinational interests. This is hard enough when a well-known site is concerned. Examples of popular sites whose visitation has been planned to enable their survival as well as public access include the subterranean labyrinth of Hal Saflieni on Malta [**1.18**], and the modern walkways around the above-ground maze of Knossos, where some 600,000 visitors each year were trampling the soft gypsum pavements and stairs to oblivion.[91] In the more common circumstance where the site is barely known to the public, or newly discovered and of unexceptional potential, the battle to achieve even basic documentation before destruction can be far tougher. Hardest of all is the effort to preserve coherent landscapes that might present, for example, an ancient city and its cemeteries, or a sacred site in its setting, as an integrated whole. Overall, the most successful and ethically resolved attempts have engaged hearts, minds and interests at diverse levels, starting with local people, and shown the remains of the past to be an asset to all parties rather than a burden, and that have presented a site accessibly, preferably with finds in a nearby museum rather than a national, let alone, foreign, capital.[92] All this, of course, costs far more than is normally available; a protective shelter may cost as much as an excavation. But the consequences of failed dialogue are seen in the ongoing tide of destruction, even if they are seldom as well studied as the case of the Maltese temple at Mnajdra,

1.18 State-of-the-art visitor management at the vulnerable underground burial complex of Hal Saflieni on Malta, one of the island's World Heritage Sites. Educational spaces, walkways and the upper levels of the archaeological monument are visible; below this, small groups are guided through a network of chambers and tunnels carved out of the rock some 5000 years ago.

1.19 Fragments of marble figurines of the 3rd millennium BC, part of a still larger number said to have been looted from the small Cycladic island of Keros and now largely dispersed into private collections. Subsequent archaeological fieldwork at the site has confirmed the unique frequency of such finds there, but the contextual integrity of these examples has been destroyed forever.

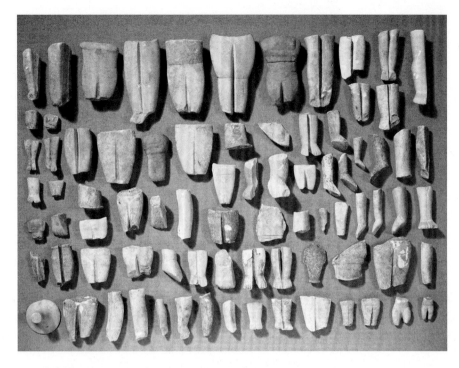

where a brief communication breakdown in 2001 created a pretext for one disgruntled interest group to spray-paint and dynamite the giant stones.[93]

A different physical threat, for which the battle for hearts, minds and interests is equally engaged, comes from the looting of objects to be sold on the international art market.[94] Classical remains have generally been worst affected, but hard-hit older categories include the marble Cycladic figurines hailed by Moore, Brancusi and their like as inspirational [**1.19**] or the Sardinian bronzes already known to the Comte de Caylus. Increasingly, almost anything that fetches a few dollars is fair game in a rapidly growing market. Like tourism, looting is nothing new. As the vast holdings of antiquities in north European and American museums attest, the Mediterranean has been haemorrhaging its material past for several centuries, through means variously illegal, illicit yet tacitly sanctioned, imperially decreed and occasionally even locally permitted. But none of this excuses the present tidal wave, which is explicitly illegal by national and international laws, destructive of a finite resource, tied to sleazy big business measured in hundreds of millions of dollars (second only to the drugs and arms trades), and often operates as an outrider of war and its aftermath. Moreover, we are now aware exactly the degree to which looting kills history by generating objects that can only be appreciated in isolated terms, stripped of their associations, and leaving in its wake sites so ransacked that often little sense can be made of them. Part of the battle involves engagement at the source, with picaresque characters like Angelos Batsalis, nicknamed 'Niotis' ('of Ios'), a cobbler, folk poet, drug-dealer, forger and looter in the Cyclades, or an Italian equivalent who boasted of robbing 4000 Etruscan tombs.[95] But while rural poverty endures this will never be enough. During a depression in the late 1980s and following the first Gulf War, Jordanian farmers dug countless ancient cemeteries 'as if they were tomato farms', simply as a source of income and without a thought for the future benefits that abstinence might bring.[96] Real breakthroughs will need to come at the demand as well as supply end, with legal strictures on marketing antiquities of dubious origin by dealers and auction houses, and a change on the part of the collectors (both individuals and museums) whose desires, however laudable in their own minds, sustain the tragedy.

And what of the manipulation of the Mediterranean's past for political ends, to create docile subjects, fervent patriots or sectarian zealots?[97] Again, the darker side of the present offers a searing riposte to the patronizing complacency of those outsiders who persist in viewing the Mediterranean as simply a nice place in which to holiday. Lebanon's penultimate war killed 5 per cent of its population (equivalent to 3 million Britons or 16 million Americans); the conflict continues, hot and cold, in the disputed 'Holy Land' to its south; wounds in the former Yugoslavia close too slowly; Cyprus is still divided by its drab Green Line; Picasso's *Guernica* returned relatively recently to a democratic Spain; and at the time of writing the Arab Spring hangs in the balance, while four economies north of the sea hover on the critical list, and African refugees risk their lives to reach the Italian island of Lampedusa, along a route opened some 8000 years ago in boats at least as seaworthy [**1.20**]. Just slightly

1.20 North African economic and political refugees crowd a small boat brought to land at the tiny outlying Italian island of Lampedusa in 2011; in recent years, many others have not survived the crossing in unseaworthy craft.

further back in generational time lurk other memories of civil wars, the commonly violent birth of over a dozen sovereign states, and torture, exile and 'ethnic cleansing' at the hands of authoritarian regimes all around the basin. Moreover, history is sure to stay very much alive in a theatre whose population has plateaued in the north but is predicted to grow fivefold between 1950 and 2025 in the south, where African nations' GDPs are barely an eleventh of those in the north, which contains two resident nuclear powers, which is running out of fresh water even before global warming hits home, through which passes a third of the world's oil and thousands of its economic migrants and refugees, and which is shared between Christian, Islamic and Jewish communities among all of whom exist militant groups whose rhetoric asserts the impossibility of cohabitation.[98]

The manipulation of the Mediterranean's past has long been standard practice at the imperial, national and provincial scales, indeed it is the very distance of the past from the present that tempts people to treat it flexibly. Xerxes, Alexander and Sultan Mehmet II all visited what they believed to be Troy to declare vengeance for the East or victory for the West, a tradition reworked into a pleasanter vein by the plans for an international peace park linking the battlefields of Gallipoli and Troy across the Dardanelles.[99] Under colonial rule, supposed archaeological affirmation of localized identities might be deliberately fostered to distract from more dangerous affiliations, hence the concept of an indigenous 'Eteocypriot' as opposed to Hellenic archaeology during British rule on Cyprus, and the implied equation between ancient Phoenicians and modern Maronites during the Mandate period in Lebanon.[100] But such sentiments can also evolve internally, against resented nation states. Intriguing instances come from several large Mediterranean islands. In 1979, 30,000 inhabitants of Heraklion in Crete blockaded the town's museum in order to prevent Minoan objects leaving for an exhibition in New York and Paris, a loan brokered by an unpopular government in Athens.[101] Members of the Sardinian independence party are known as 'nuraghisti', a nickname taken from the island's distinctive Bronze Age towers. Unsurprisingly for a theatre vibrant with recent nation building, the pressing into service of archaeology as an underpinning of national identities has been commonest of all, although attitudes to the earlier past vary from Greece, where it is invested with such symbolic capital that it verges on archaeolatry, to countries where its association with vanished inhabitants (in Spain popularly thought to be 'Moors') renders it of less consequence.[102] Some of these tendencies seem insidious, others enabling, and the distinction between use and abuse is partly a matter of opinion. But we perpetrate a '*trahison des archéologues*' if we decline to engage with such debates, challenge how the past is deployed in the present or show how subtler, more accurate archaeological interpretations open up different perspectives from the typically crude visions of the political imagination.[103] With such thoughts in mind, what can a pan-Mediterranean approach to the basin's early history contribute to its present and future, and of what dangers should it be wary?

Certainly, we need to recognize that the in fact only relatively recent usage of 'Mediterranean' as an ascription for people is freighted with contentious issues.[104] Ever since the decline of Mediterranean economies against those of northern Europe, a trend beginning in the 18th and 19th centuries AD and still relevant today, the term has held ambivalent connotations as an outsider's stereotype, both of the romantic kind (the land of blue skies and lemon blossom, of spontaneity, hospitality, blood feuds and olive oil, as often caricatured in word, and also paint)[105] and pejoratively, to vindicate external domination as the only solution for lands declared to be sunk into corruption and drained of former vigour. Even the unfettered love that Braudel professed for the Mediterranean can seem suspect to a jaundiced postmodern eye.[106] Equally, we need to be aware of the nuances that the term can imply among people living there today.[107] Often, it denotes a cosmopolitanism opposed to nationalist loyalties, popular among such minorities as Catalans, Berbers, Turks repelled alike by the legacy of Atatürk and the prospect of political Islam, and Maltese intellectuals seeking wider horizons for their island nation. Another use seeks distance from continental neighbours. Thus Israel asserts Mediterranean credentials relative to the surrounding Arab world (and the original homes of many of its people). For certain Egyptians a window on the sea is more defining than the line of the Nile, and for other Africans, both northern and southern, the Sahara rather than the central sea marks the border between Europe and Africa (Napoleon, conversely, allegedly declared Africa to begin at the Pyrenees). None of these views is ultimately right or wrong, but collectively they reveal a desire for more open ways of thinking about political and cultural associations, a need ever more urgent in the light of the basin's geopolitics now and for the foreseeable future. Here, the big question, as starkly phrased by Joschka Fischer, Germany's former foreign minister, is whether the Mediterranean in the 21st century will become a sea of cooperation or one of conflict.[108] The former, infinitely preferable, option develops the 1995 Barcelona Declaration (followed in 2008 by the Union pour la Méditerranée), signed by the European Union and most other Mediterranean states; this is dedicated to neighbourly relations, pluralism, minority rights, democracy and dialogue over trade, tariffs, immigration, the environment and terrorism. But if conflict prevails, the Mediterranean Sea, to quote *The Times* of 1992, is set to become for Europe 'what the Rio Grande is to the United States', a closed frontier fortified by isolationist European origin myths grounded in Celts or Carolingians, and embittered on both sides by self-fulfilling 'clash of civilizations' polemic.

Several specific ways in which the Mediterranean's early history might help to enlighten the present and future for people both in and beyond it suggest themselves. One is by presenting a portrait of the basin before it became a cockpit of monotheistic world religions, and with the imposed gridiron of national identities and peoples also wrenched off. This portrait would reveal, in the words of one advocate of a more self-aware archaeology in the Aegean, a 'tapestry of traditions' rather than the 'platter of simplistic models of culture history…that has passed as common table fare in much popular archaeological prose'.[109] Of course, as soon as the curtain lifts on texts and their accompanying images, we

1.21 An example of ancient ethnic stereotyping: Levantines, Nubians and Libyans held down by Ramesses II, as portrayed in Egyptian art of the 13th century BC.

find people on the Nile being defined by their leaders as distinct from, and superior to, those living elsewhere, to the degree that one way of expressing Egyptian kingship was to dominate Levantines, Nubians and others held to be different and illustrated as such [**1.21**].¹¹⁰ But while this reveals the antiquity of attitudes that remain all too alive and well today it in no way demonstrates that such categories were solid, archetypal or of agreed validity beyond Egypt, which may well be a special and, as we shall see, actually quite complex case in this respect. Without denying the likelihood of various constellations of social, cultural and other identities, early Mediterranean history instead comprises an ever-shifting kaleidoscope of webs of people and practices changing within and between places. It was out of such webs, not as formative, adamantine nodes within them, that the solid groups and boundaries we have inherited and reified arose, gradually and generally late, through a mixture of self-identification and categorization by others. Even these stereotypes were regularly reworked, as they are to this day. The reality instead resembles that expressed in an eloquent sand painting by Yukinori Yanagi, of the flags of all the Pacific nations and their surrounding and colonial powers, into which was then released a multitude of ants. As the ants burrowed, the sand grains shifted, blurring the colours and forms, creating fresh patterns and interpenetrations that subverted the sharp rectilinear order of the original.

Our task, at one level, is to release the Mediterranean's ancient ants and map and interpret their activities with as few preconceptions as possible.

However, it must be acknowledged that even this alternative, interactionist, anti-nationalist and more self-aware vision of the Mediterranean's past, with its clear analogies to current globalization and consequent 'glocalization', is not itself an entirely innocent model to guide the future of the Mediterranean basin, or indeed the planet.[111] Already we have implied that the ancient Mediterranean as a human world was not a given, but came into being as a consequence of actions over time, that in this sense it was long in the process of becoming. If such 'mediterraneanization' was therefore a dynamic process, it necessarily involved change, often conflictual, and so produced winners and losers, the latter people who, from the former's perspective, were surely often seen as within, but not 'of' the Mediterranean.[112] Examples of victims are legion in the context of the relations between Iron Age enclaves and indigenous people that we will explore towards the end of this book, but such issues of gain and loss are sure to have been played out in the deeper past too. To ignore this would create a history as crassly triumphalist, and deceptive, as the worst excesses of nationalism. Overall, as a place of mobility, encounter and flux, the early Mediterranean constitutes a good, instructive, even guardedly hopeful place to study the world. We ignore its past to our poverty and arguably at our peril. But its darker sides will be equally relevant to how its present and future are made, both by people living there and the rest of us.

CHAPTER TWO

Provocative places

Mediterranean centres and edges

'There are places', wrote the poet Joseph Brodsky, 'that, when you examine them on a map, make you feel for a brief moment akin to Providence, places where history is inescapable...places where geography provokes history.'[1] The Mediterranean is full of such places and, while avoiding the simplicities of determinism and acknowledging that culture reworks physical spaces, it is manifest that over time these have tended to encourage or discourage certain kinds of activities and decisions by people in their vicinity. The role of the basin's physical attributes in fashioning its history has been recognized since Herodotus and Strabo. Braudelian geography was a way of getting historical answers, while Horden and Purcell focus on environments and ecologies; in fact, all three help to define a genuinely distinctive theatre. So far, we have looked at the Mediterranean as an idea and a place in which archaeologists and historians work, but we can no longer neglect its physical face. Given the basin's diversity, such an exploration is no easy matter. But without some grasp of the kinds of places in which people lived, Mediterranean history becomes meaningless, whether its concern is the routines of villagers, rhythms of navigation, policies of rulers or fortunes of battle.

This chapter is an interpretative description of physical land- and seascapes. Our ultimate aim is a cultural one and will demand that we ask how people engaged with the Mediterranean's waters, mountains, animals, plants and minerals, how they exploited its opportunities, modified or adapted to its constraints, and made its dangers bearable. But across the many millennia that will concern us, there were huge changes in all these respects, that need to be traced phase by phase in future chapters, and defy prior summary. Even the physical Mediterranean only gradually reached its current form over our time span, and alters to this day. As alluded to in Chapter 1, the present climate and ecology, that underpin the world of *The Corrupting Sea*, are only 5000–6000 years old. The outlines of the basin would have been familiar in detail about twice as far back, while despite oscillations in the remoter past between cold periods that shrank the sea and reduced much of the land to tundra or steppe, and wet, warm periods lusher than today, a few elements have a longer ancestry measured in hundreds of thousands of years. Even when, over the next four chapters, we encounter marked differences from the portrait that is sketched here, it will be helpful to have this benchmark for comparison.

To start with, we need a working definition of the Mediterranean's centre and edges. The former is readily offered by the sea in the middle, a 'peninsula in reverse', as Trump memorably called it, a 'liquid continent' for Horden and Purcell.[2] The Mediterranean Sea extends some 3800 km (2350 miles) east to west and between 750 and 400 km (460 and 250 miles) north to south. At 2.5 million sq. km (965,000 sq. miles), it makes up less than one per cent of the world's marine space. Whether this inclines us to concur with the self-styled Mediterranean islomane Lawrence Durrell that 'the Mediterranean is an absurdly small sea' will be decided over the course of this book, from viewpoints as diverse as the Neanderthal and Phoenician, though we can already concur with his continuation that 'the length and greatness of its history make us dream it larger than it is'.[3] From the perspective of our own age, when it has been reduced to a minor gulf of the Atlantic traversable by plane in an hour or two, the challenge will more often be to magnify it; even in the 16th century AD the Mediterranean, as measured by travelled time, was typically two to three months long, and what we would regard as delays and inefficiencies were the standard operating conditions.[4] Returning to practicalities, however, even the sea's extent is somewhat negotiable. Should the Black Sea be included, another 461,000 sq. km (178,000 sq. miles) connected via the slender Bosphorus and Dardanelles? Plato, writing when Greek towns ringed its shores, certainly thought so. But although a close neighbour, and far more than the Mediterranean's backyard, the Black Sea has a notably more equable, continental environment, a totally contrastive maritime aspect (it is effectively islandless, for a start) and, partly as a result, a different early history from the larger basin.[5] What, too, of the 'Mediterranean Atlantic' beyond another long, if broader, strait at Gibraltar?[6] This was later a key zone in the conversion of Indian Ocean-derived sailing technology and holy war for the conquest of the western ocean and the Americas. Pragmatism offers a solution here, for apart from tendrils extending along the coasts of Iberia and Morocco, maritime ventures in this arena only began at the very end of our time span. To summarize, then, the expanse of sea from Gibraltar to the Levant, and the Gulf of Sirte to the head of the Adriatic, sets our central stage.

Edges are not so easily decided, save perhaps in the furthest west. Elsewhere, they need to be sought within the surrounding land masses, dividing *terre marine* (in Boccaccio's eloquent oxymoron) from the non-Mediterranean.[7] Intuitively, we sense that they should fall somewhere short of temperate Europe, the Sahara and the north Arabian desert, but at a finer grain various options present themselves, none of which is entirely satisfactory and applicable in all directions. Braudel wrestled with this and came up with the famously elusive answer that the Mediterranean had a hundred frontiers. As critics have remarked, however, we need a firmer idea of when we are, and are not, in the Mediterranean, if the basin is to have much meaning as a focus of analysis. Several options remain even if we exclude more ideational definitions (Braudel's economic frontier that embraced Spain's American

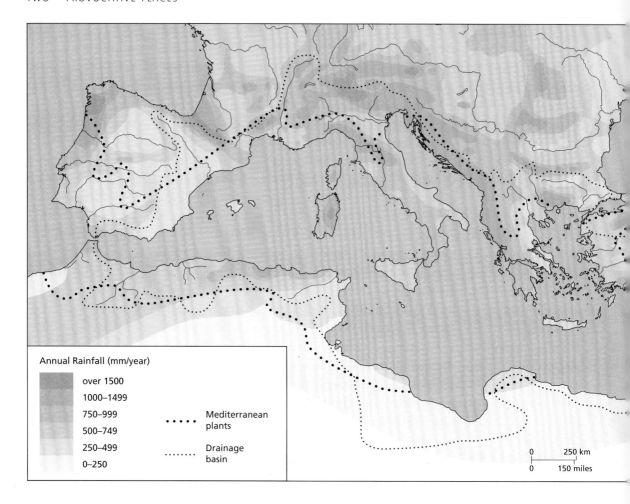

Annual Rainfall (mm/year)

over 1500
1000–1499
750–999
500–749
250–499
0–250

····· Mediterranean plants

········ Drainage basin

0   250 km
0   150 miles

2.1 Braiding Mediterranean boundaries explored by rainfall, plant life and river drainages.

colonies, for example, or the intellectual one that had Goethe already there before he left Frankfurt), and ignore such modern political conundrums as the case for Portugal and the consequences of Yugoslavian disintegration.[8]

The most popular approaches invoke climate, vegetation and topography.[9] A look at their strengths and weaknesses proves none better than the other, but it does reveal an encouraging tendency to braid and overlap [**2.1**]. The technical definition of a Mediterranean climate is a particular variety of semi-arid regime in which winter rainfall predominates (ideally threefold) over summer levels, and where summers are hot, and winters mild to cool. In the present case, and including the sea, this describes an area of 6 million sq. km (2.3 million sq. miles), certainly centred on the basin, but extending west to the Canaries and east to the Caspian, near Tehran. Similar, but more tightly defined, is a Mediterranean delineated by plants. Various species have been recruited to this end; the most iconic is the olive, a frost-sensitive tree that needs the summer drought to produce its oil-rich fruit, and which for some possesses a mystical potency. Witness Durrell in purple torrent: 'The whole Mediterranean – the sculptures, the palms, the gold beads, the bearded heroes, the wine, the ideas, the ships, the moonlight, the winged gorgons, the bronze men, the

philosophers – all of it seems to rise in the sour, pungent taste of these black olives between the teeth'; or more gnomically, Aldous Huxley vaunting this tree as 'symbol of a classicism enclosed in a romanticism'.[10] Climate and olives produce some plausible results, but cut off the head of the Adriatic and exclude drier stretches of the African shore as far as the Levantine border. Such definitions are also vertically challenged, for they omit Mediterranean mountain tops; olives grow up to just 300 m (1000 ft) above sea level in northern Italy, even if somewhat higher at around 1300 m (4250 ft) in southern Spain. Edges of this kind are also susceptible to redrawing by quite minor shifts in climate; during the 2nd millennium BC, for example, people on the Anatolian plateau relished local pig fat in place of olive oil, but by Roman times olives grew only a little further south in the upland city of Sagalassos, where, however, they cannot thrive today,[11] and an olive is currently in fruit outside the window of the room in London in which I write.

What about the limits of what Australian Aborigines would call the 'saltwater country'?[12] A circum-marine definition is attractive, and serves better than climate and vegetation along the African coast. But how broad a strip should we include? Modern writers plump somewhat randomly for between 50 and 150 km (30 and 90 miles). Under Greek and Roman communication conditions, distances in the lower part of this range are cited by ancient sources in relation to the legal writ of decrees connected with the sea and coast.[13] Another informative approach is to delineate the land that trends towards the sea, defined by the watersheds of rivers and streams flowing into it, though this hits trouble where climate and olives did too: in eastern and central North Africa, not least at the terminus of the Nile.[14] The Mediterranean can undoubtedly claim the great coastal oasis of the Nile Delta on grounds of adjacency and seasonality, though barely rainfall, which is less than 200 mm (8 in.) per year in Alexandria and down to 25–30 mm (around 1 in.) at Cairo. Yet the remainder of the river, at 6650 km (4130 miles) the world's longest, belongs to an utterly different African world, fed by lakes and summer monsoons far to the south.[15] Hence the marked dissonance between the Nile's seasonal rhythm and that of the rest of the basin. Until modern damming, the surge of revitalizing Nile floodwaters and nutrients reached the Delta in September, having taken a month to traverse Egypt, then slowly receded until the start of a dry season early in the year.

The search for edges finds no single answer, but rather a distinct if fuzzy zone of transition. For Horden and Purcell this creates a gradient as common denominators cease to combine in full strength,[16] something intuitively obvious from plentiful hints to those travelling into or out of the basin. One corollary is that entering or leaving the Mediterranean can result from incremental movements as well as conscious journeys. A best fit for the various edges in fig. 2.1 suggests a terrestrial Mediterranean of some 2.3 million sq. km (900,000 sq. miles), a coincidentally close match with the extent of the sea, plus perhaps around 10 per cent more if we include the zone of fall-off. Over a quarter lies in the Maghreb, a fifth in the Iberian peninsula, slightly less apiece in Italy and the Aegean, and the rest comprises coastal strips of varying width in the south of France, Dalmatia, southern Turkey, the Levant and northeast Africa, as well as the islands set in the sea.[17]

This flexible solution has the further advantage, as we turn to contact zones between the Mediterranean and regions beyond, of easing the transition and stressing a distinction between edges (blurred but real) and barriers (much rarer). The basin has never been a sealed space, and several key elements in its development are external in origin, if subsequently localized in their application and adaptation, a truth illustrated by the non-trivial fact that numerous ingredients of what we think of as Mediterranean cuisine derive from the Americas or South Asia, and bear little relation to the suite of foods available a thousand years ago, let alone further back in time. 'The edges', as Purcell says, 'alter the contents', a maxim that will hold true from the beginning.[18]

The maritime contact zones between the Mediterranean and its neighbours are few and marked by straits and swift currents that require skilled seamanship to exploit effectively, but those on land vary much more. On the European side the boundary is porous. This is particularly true of the swathe of uplands across Iberia and southern France, though a few river valleys do concentrate movement: those of the Ebro, Aude and its Atlantic partner, the Garonne, and above all the turbulent Rhône, a river hard to navigate, but that slices a lowland corridor through the massif dividing southern from temperate France. Further east, the serried walls of the Alps form a belt 100–200 km (60–120 miles) thick that wraps around the head of Italy, here sharply dividing the Mediterranean from central Europe. This can be bypassed along the corniche of Liguria and coastal Provence, or to the east via the Friuli–Ljubljana gap, which gives access to the central Balkans. But even the Alpine wall is perforated by some twenty seasonal high passes. Given favourable circumstances and incentives, Mediterranean trans-Alpine links are perfectly achievable. Moving further east again, the lower but extensive ranges of the southern Balkans and western Anatolia create another broad edge-zone. Here too, we can pick out corridors and impediments. The dearth of passages through the southern Balkans, save for those carved by the Vardar and Struma, might deflect connections towards a circuitous route via the Black Sea and up the Danube, which also opens up the Russian steppe and the Caucasus. By contrast, the uplifted rectangle of Anatolia (equivalent to the Iberian Meseta at the other end of the basin), with its westward and southward flowing rivers, is often invoked as a land-bridge between the Levant and Europe, an isthmus between the Mediterranean and the Black and Caspian seas, and, inside the basin, an alternative to the sea-route between the Levant and Aegean. We should, however, beware a tendency to think of such regions just as places of passage – few people live on bridges, and we shall see that Anatolia heaved with activity.[19]

On the African flank east of the Maghreb the land is generally low lying and countless small seasonal wadis run seaward. Here, the pattern of routes in and out of the basin is controlled not by physical relief, but conditions in the Sahara. In its present state, as 9 million sq. km (3.5 million sq. miles) of hyper-aridity, dune-rippled *ergs* (sand-seas), hard desert and high mountains, the Sahara constricts movement to routes marked by strings of oases, and to people and animals able to tolerate intervening conditions. But as we shall see, the Sahara has not always worn this aspect. Kinder climates open up an immense front along the southern side of the Mediterranean, that could engulf the coastal fringe in a different, continental universe. And in the northeast corner of Africa, the Nile provides the longest corridor of all, and one at least semi-resilient to changing conditions in the Sahara. As a conduit of movement in and out of the basin, the Nile enjoys a fortuitous combination of qualities.[20] Even at its lowest, the river runs north at 1.8 km per hour (slightly more than 1 mile per hour), a speed that quadruples at the annual flood. In antiquity the 900-km (560-mile) river voyage from Thebes to Memphis took under two weeks with the current. The prevailing winds, moreover, blow from the north, so that once sails had been introduced, journeys upstream were equally straightforward. Furthermore, the Nile is fringed by a strip of valley land between 2 and 17 km (roughly 1.3 and 10 miles) wide, a food-producing cornucopia. Small wonder that the Nile proved a more favourable axis of movement, until late in our history, than the similarly aligned Red Sea, with its winds, shoals and dangerous shores, or the overland route along the Hejaz, the dry west coast of Arabia.

Between the Nile Delta and highland Anatolia lies one last vital contact zone. The Levant constitutes a derisory 3.3 per cent of the land in the basin, but thanks to its wider connections this scrap has repeatedly been of disproportionate significance on the Mediterranean, and indeed global, stage.[21] Much of it is hemmed in by a deep belt of arid land, currently desert, that was often used as a marginal hinterland, but (unlike the Sahara) never, until the end of our time span, as a point of access to other regions. Yet at both ends lie slim but vital passages. One runs over the Suez isthmus and plugs into Africa via the Nile corridor. The other, in the north, lies across the Jazira (another 'island' in Arabic), a low saddle of grassland south of the Anatolian highlands and a part of the continental, extended lobe of Mediterranean climate. In the west it grades into the Levant, just where major passes ascend into Anatolia. But a mere 200 km (125 miles) from the coast the Jazira crosses the Euphrates, which swings west to lie closer to the sea than, say, Madrid, and enters Mesopotamia. Thence it rolls on to the Tigris, melding to its south into the Mesopotamian alluvium, the boundary being conventionally set where the rains fail and farming depends on riverine irrigation. The Jazira forms a keystone in the great arch of the Fertile Crescent, one of whose horns runs down the Levant, the other into Mesopotamia and the piedmont of the Zagros mountains. While every connection in and out of the Mediterranean influenced its history, these two in the east alone brought contacts with, and eventually combined, radically more potent agents of change. By the later 4th millennium BC a newly pharaonic Egypt was turning the Nile into the central chamber of a civilization, while equivalent developments in Mesopotamia began slightly earlier and then spread across the Jazira. From this time we can no more exclude Egyptian Thebes or the cities of Sumer from our Mediterranean history than Braudel could keep Antwerp out of his. But as we will see, the Levantine exceptionalism that resulted from this mixture of Mediterranean conditions and unrivalled strategic location can in fact be identified far earlier, in this tiny region's role in the global expansion of humans and their ancestors, followed by the emergence of farming, as well as later, with the rise of several world religions.

Mediterraneans and mediterraneoids

In 1943, at the turning point of the last major imperial war that the Mediterranean has suffered to date, the historian, archaeologist and geographer John Myres delivered the annual Frazer lecture at Cambridge on the subject of 'Mediterranean Culture'.[22] His translation of the Mediterranean as the 'Midland sea', although accurate, seems an oddly terrestrial inversion to an English reader (he was, after all, born in Preston, Lancashire). That apart, his lecture still contains much relevant sense, not least in the attention paid to the 'little men'. 'What', he asked 'are the permanent features of their mode of life, without which nothing could have been achieved, either by gods or by heroes; upon which have been erected noble superstructures; into which, in evil times, Mediterranean man withdraws to recuperate?' And what justified Myres's choice of the Mediterranean, if not the gods, heroes and noble superstructures of the standard panegyric? His answer is a simple one, yet arresting; the Mediterranean, he believed, is a 'geographical region unique as a home for man'. Unfortunately he never set out the grounds for this exalted status and few of the many others who echo this verdict on the Mediterranean as a portion of the earth's surface have done so either. Those that try to typically fall back on its intercontinental position between Europe, Asia and Africa, a rare distinction but most relevant in later periods, or on the concept of the Mediterranean as a natural crossroads, which it is for birds (many millions migrate over it each year),[23] and latterly people, but not to a degree unparalleled on the planet. How, as an initial step in our endeavour to explain the Mediterranean's remarkable history, might we affirm Myres's bold assertion more precisely and cogently?

One effective approach is to compare the Mediterranean with those other parts of the world that share its most distinctive characteristics, the inland 'middle sea' and the specific climate regime [**2.2**]. Each draws out the unusual status of the Mediterranean at a global level, and between them they do indeed identify a unique space. Beginning with inland seas, the Mediterranean beats all rivals in terms of size, by more than fivefold the neighbouring Black and Red seas as well as more distant associates in the Persian Gulf, Caspian Sea and Baltic (commonly known as the 'Mediterranean of the north', a compliment that is tellingly never reversed).[24] It is twice the size of icy Hudson Bay and comfortably exceeds the empty expanse of the Gulf of Mexico. Despite its greater size, moreover, its east–west alignment fosters broadly comparable conditions throughout, which eases the transfer of everything from crops to perfumes, seafaring techniques to landscape know-how, while at the same time including, as we shall see, enough vertical variation to match the advantageous complementarities of, for example, the north–south aligned Baltic.[25] A handful of less fully enclosed marine theatres, defined by continental coastlines and strings

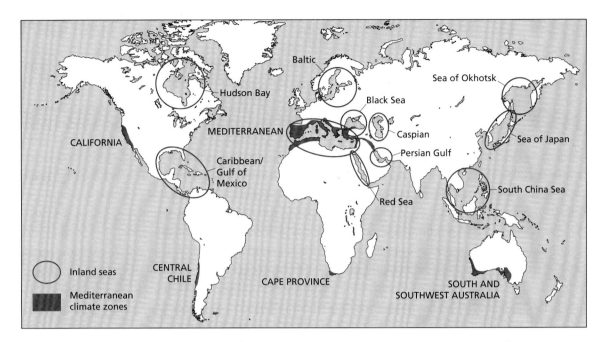

Baltic

Sea of Okhotsk

Hudson Bay

Black Sea

MEDITERRANEAN

Caspian

Sea of Japan

CALIFORNIA

Caribbean/
Gulf of
Mexico

Persian Gulf

South China Sea

Red Sea

Inland seas

CENTRAL
CHILE

Mediterranean
climate zones

CAPE PROVINCE

SOUTH AND
SOUTHWEST AUSTRALIA

2.2 The world's
five environmentally
mediterraneoid regions
(shaded in grey) and its other
major inland seas.

of offshore islands as a bulwark against the open ocean, are comparable in size, if mostly somewhat smaller, notably the Caribbean, Europe's Atlantic facade and the South China, Japanese and Bering seas.[26] To these we might add the fantastic interplays of sea and land between big islands and small archipelagos in island Southeast Asia and the southwest Pacific. Admittedly, vastly larger quasi-Mediterranean spaces can be identified, too, as the world's great oceans are themselves surrounded by land. Thought-provoking as it is, however, to consider the Indian Ocean before or after European intrusion, or the circum-Pacific of today and tomorrow, as supersized Mediterraneans, such analogies make little sense until the last few thousand years, or considerably less in the latter case, before the present.[27]

The Mediterranean is equally unusual in its climate (which we defined earlier as semi-arid, summer-hot and winter-wet) and thence environment. It is, in fact, one of just five 'mediterraneoid' areas in the world. The others lie in southern California, central Chile, south and southwest Australia, and Cape Province in South Africa [2.2] – a group for which the provenances of wine offer the best mnemonic, thanks to the friendliness of all to viticulture.[28] In aggregate, mediterraneoids make up only 2 per cent of all land on the planet, and owe their existence to highly specific conditions created by oceanic winds and currents off the west coasts of continents between about 30 and 45 degrees north or south of the equator. The Mediterranean is larger than all the rest combined, thanks to the absence of an intercepting north–south mountain barrier near the ocean, coupled with the elongated inlet of the sea, which allow the climate zone to penetrate far inland. Despite the distances between them, evolutionary parallels over the last few million years have produced astonishingly similar kinds of plant life in all the mediterraneoid zones, in particular drought-tolerant, fire-adapted and tough-leaved species. In the Mediterranean proper, this takes the form today of high, dense growth known as macchia or matorral, scrubby garrigue, low, aromatic phrygana, grassy steppe, and evergreen trees such as holm and prickly oak, olive and pine, with deciduous species confined to well-watered areas.[29] The fynbos flora of South Africa, the mallee of south Australia and the American chapparal are fundamentally similar.

Intriguingly, the Mediterranean seems to have raced ahead in terms of social complexity and intensity of interaction relative to inland seas and mediterraneoids in other parts of the world. Starting with comparative thalassology,[30] a slower clock for the Caribbean is inevitable given the later colonization of the Americas, but even in AD 1492 it remained less impressive than most of the Mediterranean at the equivalent date BC.[31] Despite early seafaring by hunter-gatherers in the Sea of Japan, the take-off came later here, too, coeval with the Classical world and first Islamic empires,[32] and similar observations hold true for the Baltic as well as, with a backward stretch of a millennium or so, much of Europe's Atlantic facade.[33] The Red Sea's navigation appears to have been tied to a pharaonic timetable, although more is surely to be revealed there. The closest matches are the Persian Gulf, where long-range sea trade began in the 6th millennium BC,[34] if with less consolidated follow-through than in the Mediterranean, and perhaps the South China Sea, whose earliest maritime contacts remain shadowy.[35] In relation to the other mediterraneoids, the contrast is starker. All sustained unusually dense populations of hunters and gatherers, but farming was locally taken up only in one (central Chile, gradually, over the 1st millennia BC and AD), and lapped round another (Cape Province, itself unsuitable for crops needing summer rain, but turned into grazing land by Khoisan pastoralists).[36] Well after the birth of Christ, minor chiefs may have arisen in Chile, and large villages of sedentary hunter-gatherers in California provide good analogues for Levantine societies 12,000 years earlier.[37] In all other mediterraneoids, state-level organizations appeared recently and in colonial guise, starting in Chile with the Inca around AD 1480 and elsewhere in the context of European imperialism. That all were absorbed by European empires indicates their relative vulnerability as well as the prospects of transferring techniques from the true Mediterranean, and in all cases heavy environmental impact dates back only to these last exploitative centuries.

What made the Mediterranean unique was its combination of these already individually unusual characteristics.[38] Coastal California and its offshore Channel Islands are the only parallel, in a very minor key, for coexistence of a mediterraneoid climate and maritime theatre (hardly an inland sea), and it is intriguing that here, from about AD 800 and especially after AD 1150 dense, ideologically charged canoe-borne networks between chiefly communities arose that look similar to formations in parts of the Mediterranean four millennia earlier.[39] Add in a third factor, matched only in the non-mediterraneoid Persian Gulf and the seas off East Asia, namely proximity to the cores of two of the world's earliest civilizations, which emerged just beyond the basin and first communicated through it…and if Brodsky is right, we might anticipate some truly exceptional, and provocative, developments in the Mediterranean's early history.

A basin is born

The Mediterranean's form and many of its properties are legacies of plate tectonics, and therefore a temporary conjunction in *la très longue durée*.[40] There is no real beginning to its geological history. In the age of the dinosaurs (250 to 65 million years ago) a warm primordial sea, christened Tethys after the consort of Oceanos in Greek myth, extended over the entire area, linking the proto-Atlantic and Indian oceans, but dividing the African and attached Arabian plates from Eurasia [**2.3**]. Tethys is still with us: the raw material for the Mediterranean's gaunt limestone landscapes (recall that in which this book opened), with their red soils and capacity to swallow water and spew it out elsewhere, fashioning caves, springs and *poljes*, formed as the seabed of this gerontic ocean. There are still Tethyian relics among Mediterranean plant life today. But the defining stages in the basin's shaping came after the passing of the dinosaurs, when Africa and Arabia (variously joined or divided at Suez or the Bab-el-Mandeb, the two termini of the Red Sea) drifted north towards Eurasia, squeezing the sea between them. They collided in the area of modern Iraq some 15–20 million years ago, severing Tethys into a proto-Mediterranean fragment in the west, and an eastern half that has since shrivelled into the Black, Caspian and Aral seas. Atlantic and Indian ocean waters remained divided here until 1869, when the Suez Canal opened.

The clash of plates, which continues today as Africa muscles 2 cm (0.8 in.) a year into Europe, accounts for the fundamentals of the Mediterranean's outline. At the point of contact the heavier African plate slides under the Eurasian, raising and shattering it into fragments, each gyrating independently. From this derives the glaring distinction between the Mediterranean's generally straight, smooth southern shore (the diving plate) and the phenomenal complexity of its centre and north (the up-thrust, broken plate). The consequent bucklings of the Tethys seabed created the dramatic mountain ranges that run along the Mediterranean's entire length, whose sharpness and height (regularly 2000–3000 m (6500–10,000 ft), sometimes over 4000 m (13,000 ft)) reveal their youth: on the African side the great line of the High Atlas, Rif and a few outliers further east, in the north the Sierra Nevada, Pyrenees, Alps, Apennines, Dinarics, Pindos and Taurus, the last grading into the Anti-Taurus (with a small spur into Lebanon), the Caucasus, Zagros and onward in a continuous gigantic wrinkle that culminates in the Himalayas. Much of the remaining land is uplifted too. Two-thirds of Greece and three-quarters of Italy are hill or mountain country. The central plateau of the Iberian Meseta lies above 500 m (1600 ft), and much of the interior of the Maghreb east of the

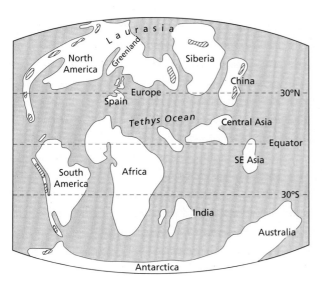

2.3 Before the Mediterranean: an approximate geography of the Tethys ocean and surrounding continents during the Cretaceous.

Rif comprises high plains. Any sailor approaching the sheer walls of Mallorca's Tramontana, the White Mountains of Crete or the sabre-line range hanging over Kyrenia on Cyprus soon realizes that most islands are the tips of other, sometimes towering, submarine massifs. Except along the eastern stretches of the North African coast, wisps of high land always hover in clear weather on Mediterranean horizons. No wonder, then, that for one enthusiast of high altitudes, the Mediterranean is not simply the sea between the lands, but that between the mountains.[41] We shall see profound changes over time in the extent to which this elevated Mediterranean was visited, exploited or even inhabited by hunters, farmers, pastoralists, traders, lumberjacks and others engaged on ritual journeys.

Conversely, caught between uplifted high ground and the sea, large lowland plains are at a premium, especially on the northern side. Notable examples are those of Languedoc in France, in Italy the Po Valley (carved by Alpine meltwaters), Campania and the Tavoliere, in Greece Thessaly and much of Macedonia, and the Turkish Amuq. Subsidence where plates pull apart or run alongside each other creates many of the most dramatic valleys, or deep inlets of the sea. The longest is that running from the Red Sea through the Wadi Arabah, Dead Sea (the lowest terrestrial place on earth), Jordan Valley, Sea of Galilee, and sky-high Beqaa Valley between the Lebanon and Anti-Lebanon mountains, finally to peter out in the Amuq. This traces the contact line between the African and Arabian plates and forms the northern extension of Africa's Great Rift Valley. Most lowlands, however, are more modest affairs, typically small basins among the hills, or thin ribbons that string out inhabitants along the coasts [PL. II].

Needless to say, the tectonic clash also explains why the Mediterranean is so prone to earthquakes and punctuated by active, dormant and extinct volcanoes [2.4].[42] The northeast and central parts of the basin are worst afflicted, and the Aegean, in particular, is one of the most active parts of the world's crust, with a fault in the Gulf of Corinth that in aeons to come will rival the Californian San Andreas in its menace. Volcanoes erupt both on land and from the sea, creating havoc, wonder, useful stones and, in time, rich soils. Alongside rapid episodes of climate change, earthquakes and volcanoes testify that natural events can operate on a faster, more devastating timetable than Braudel's

2.4 An eruption of Vesuvius, one of the youngest but most violent volcanoes in the Mediterranean, as witnessed by William Hamilton and the artist Pietro Fabris from across the Bay of Naples on the lit-up night of 8 August 1779.

longue durée, and test Mediterranean people's response and recovery skills to the limit. More positively, along with the impact of limestone (jagged peaks, caves and springs in particular), volcanic craters and fumaroles created strange features in the landscape whose wondrous properties attracted ritual visits from an early date.[43]

From a geological perspective, the rest is mere details. By the period known as the Miocene (22 to 5 million years ago), which is also notable for a superabundance of apes that include our ancestors among them,[44] the Mediterranean would have been readily recognizable from space. Many of the islands and peninsulas were starting to emerge, if still with unfamiliar forms and connections; Crete, for example, broke off from Turkey some 9 million years ago, carrying with it horses, deer and crocodiles, then disintegrated and foundered, before arising again looking more like its modern self some 2–3 million years ago.[45] The blindingly white, soft marl landscapes of many Mediterranean lowlands, so favoured by farmers, are the remnants of more recently uplifted sea- and lake-beds than those earlier petrified into hard limestone. And while volcanism has a long history (the Troodos mountains in Cyprus, for example, are the debris from submarine eruptions as old as *Tyrannosaurus rex*, later thrust above the surface), most of the now-recognizable volcanoes between Turkey and Italy emerged relatively late, and overlap with the arrival of our close ancestors, or sometimes even our own species, around the shores of the sea. Chapter 3 will pick up the story from here.

Five tectonic consequences

In the meantime, how has tectonic history shaped the Mediterranean lands as places in which to live? We can identify at least five major consequences. Most stem from the first, the astonishingly broken-up nature of the basin's landscapes. Braudel knew that there were 'ten, twenty, or a hundred Mediterraneans, each one subdivided in turn',[46] and fragmentation is elevated to a defining property by Horden and Purcell. The basin is even richer in 'habitat islands' than real ones, areas of similarity surrounded by seas of difference that range from the 'island' of the Maghreb down to minuscule patches. An afternoon walk on Crete can take one from surroundings reminiscent of Wales to ones more like North Africa.[47] Some of this fragmentation operates fractally in a manner that matches the social fractal noted in Chapter 1, revealing similar patterning on the grand through to microcosmic scales.[48] Maps display the horizontal fragmentation well, but there are vertical versions too. Around much of the coast, for instance in Spain, where the Sierra Nevada rear over the Costa del Sol, Provence, Liguria, Dalmatia, parts of the Aegean, southern Turkey and Lebanon, environments are stacked one above the other, so that a day or two's walk from the coast will traverse a ribbon of (in summer) sweltering lowland, then hill country and finally soaring peaks flecked with snow [PL. I]. An experiment conducted to establish areas within reach of early communities in southern Spain discovered that the average change of altitude in a two-hour walk from each was over 700 m (2300 ft).[49] In such corrugated landscapes, water seldom

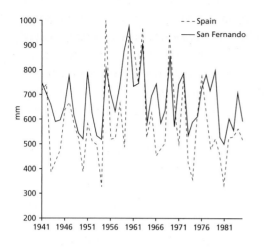

mm

1000
900
800
700
600
500
400
300
200
1941 1946 1951 1956 1961 1966 1971 1976 1981

- - - Spain
—— San Fernando

2.5 The extreme inter-annual variation in rainfall in many parts of the basin is illustrated in this graph of precipitation for the whole of Spain and for San Fernando, near Cadiz. The unusually close correlation between the general and local plots is attributable to the latter's location on the path of incoming Atlantic weather; once within the basin the relationship breaks down.

travels far; rivers are typically short, rushing and often of little use for boats far inland;[50] some never reach the sea but drain into lakes, evaporation pans, marshes or sinkholes. Of course, this fragmentation is not equally intense everywhere. Macedonia, the Negev or the high plains of the Maghreb are less minutely broken up than, say, the Abruzzi or most of the islands. Quantifying such phenomena is challenging, but one approach will be suggested when we turn to examine the Mediterranean's shores.

Both the overall tectonic history of the Mediterranean and its shattered details influence our second consequence, namely the pattern of Mediterranean weather and especially rainfall [**2.5**].[51] We have seen that the very existence in this part of the world of a semi-arid Mediterranean climate owes everything to the placements of ocean, inner sea and mountains at an appropriate latitude. Unsurprisingly, therefore, the Atlantic dominates Mediterranean weather, with a Saharan input in the south, and another from the Russian steppe in winter, though mountains protect the basin from the worst continental conditions. Most rain clouds enter from the west, which is why the eastern parts of the basin are drier, and the western flanks of each major peninsula tend to be more lush. Coupled with a marked offset in mid-basin (such that, against intuition, coastal Algeria, Sicily, southern Greece and Turkey lie on the same latitude), which places the southeast in a hotter, drier band, this accounts for the general pattern of the basin's climate. For instance, it explains why the Maghreb enjoys a clement regime, while most of the eastern half of coastal North Africa, as well as Sinai and the Negev, are semi-desert or steppe, with Saharan dunes lapping up to the coast along the Gulf of Sirte. Annual rainfall averages 400–700 mm (16–28 in.) in the northern Mediterranean, and often at least twice as much in the mountains, but it drops to a mere 50–100 mm (2–4 in.) for most of coastal northeast Africa, a level prohibitive to rain-fed cultivation.

But this being the Mediterranean, complexity plays havoc with generalization. Much of this is thanks to the rain-snaring proclivities of mountains. Unlucky Crkvice in Montenegro, where Atlantic and Russian weather meet, is the wettest place in the basin. Mountains can act, in Braudel's simile, as water towers for lands around their base.[52] Without the Sierra Nevada and Atlas, the plains of Granada and Marrakesh would parch,[53] but even more striking is Cyrenaica, an uplifted block similar in size to Crete (directly to its north) that catches what rain there is, creating a verdant habitat island amidst the harshest stretch of African coast, known in Arabic as the Jebel Akhdar ('green mountain'; a miniature version lies further west, in the Jebel el Gharbi near Tripoli).[54] Elsewhere, however, mountains can block the rain. Hence the odd fact that the driest sector on the northern side of the Mediterranean is Spanish Almería, close to the Atlantic, but cut off by surrounding peaks. Several of the major lowland plains are also surprisingly arid. Elsewhere, the limestone swallows up water, and it is this, as much as its serrated ridges, that renders the Dinaric range of the eastern

Adriatic so daunting. Other limestone uplands, such as the Grands Causses in France and many in the Aegean, have also probably never presented a much friendlier aspect than they do today. The upshot of all this variation is a patchy distribution of rain, often over tiny distances, that nuances or counters the overall trends. And rainfall is equally variable from year to year, with small clouds easily deflected by one place to the detriment of others. Some areas are certainly favoured, but what will actually happen in any given year is very hard to guess. Long-term averages rarely reflect yearly reality, with most locations seeing much more, or alarmingly less, rain fall on the thirsty soil. Drought bites home every few years, and a major deluge might devastate the landscape every ten, twenty or a hundred years. Mediterranean people live in the shadow of this uncertainty, and take precautions accordingly. It is interesting to compare the situation with that along the course of our equatorial interloper, the Nile. This itself is no stranger to fluctuating floods, but these impact uniformly along its length, are dampened in the Delta by a high water table, and compared with the rest of the basin seems a paragon of stability. In later antiquity Egypt's grain harvest was one of the most reliable elements in the supply strategies of cities.

A third legacy of tectonics generates complexity too, but this time relating to movement. The map of the Mediterranean is full of potential attractors and nodes of communication: islands, capes, gateways between sea and hinterland, passes, straits, and isthmuses for overland travel and transfer from sea to sea, all at a range of scales. It reveals apparent obstacles, too: expanses of open sea, deserts and high mountains that appear to shut off coastlands from the interior, or ring off each plain into cell-like isolation. In all cases, the reality is more intriguing. Geography mattered, but it rarely determined, and although certain points came to the fore often, and others seldom if at all, there were few if any eternal central places even at a local level – a point that chimes in with the interplay and mutual constitution of shifting networks, places and societies (outlined in the previous chapter), which regularly reworked geography's meaning and significance.[55] We should be sceptical of such proclamations as 'Sicily is the crossroads of the Mediterranean', or 'Iberia turns its back on the Mediterranean and faces the Atlantic'.[56] However resonant these initially seem, they invariably prove false over the medium or long term. And concerning division, even the mountains, open seas and deserts can serve as highways rather than barriers if the technology and incentives are sufficient; the self-contained Mediterranean terrestrial cell is usually an illusion, a prison only for interpretations.

Under such conditions, few routes are really dictated by nature and proximity need not equate with close relations. There are usually multiple solutions to the issue of travel between points, as the young Theseus knew when planning to visit his father in Athens: by land, sea or both, and by straight line or roundabout route? In this sense geography may provide a multitude of nodes but it also offers chances to short-circuit them. Which wins out in a given situation is decided by the comparative advantages of transport (human portage, pack animals, wheeled vehicles or seacraft of different capabilities), the bulk and value of carried goods, any number of social factors, and a good dose of serendipity. Choices favoured at a given period owed their popularity to specific circumstances, some prominent again today, but many forgotten. Of course, we shall see in the coming chapters that a few routes do figure repeatedly. The cliffs above the Dog River in Lebanon are carved with inscriptions from passing armies [PL. III], from those of New Kingdom pharaohs to Napoleon III's troops, but even here there are other possibilities by land or sea for travel between the northern and southern Levant. Likewise, a few key straits stand out, but the intensity of activity across them was far from constant. It is striking that the few really consistent funnels of movement over time tend to lie on the basin's fringes rather than in the thick of its topographic melee – for example the Nile Valley, the Jazira, and the great defile of the Cilician Gates via which highland Anatolia and the Levant communicate. We return to the subject of routes when we start to look at the sea and how people have moved across it.

The fourth legacy of tectonic history is the profligate existence of desirable minerals [2.6]. On geological maps the Mediterranean parades peacock colours and forms the western end of a long mineral-rich belt extending into the Himalayas.[57] Uplifted lumps of seabed are especially rich in rare stones and metal ores, and support unusual plants once broken down into soils.[58] The basin's tectonic formation explains the uneven spread of this bounty, giving advantage to certain regions, and stretching the 'taskscapes' of those wanting to acquire them through expeditions or exchange.[59] In terms of minerals the major distinction is between their abundance in the north and east as far as Egypt, in contrast to the dearth in the rest of the African Mediterranean. At a more detailed level, the link between mineral formation and intense geological activity places most sources in rugged, upland and often insular landscapes, usually far from the best agricultural land and so again requiring movement to acquire them (ancient Etruria is an exception, blessed with rich volcanic soils as well as abundant ores). Stones and metals recur throughout the chapters that follow, but before some are introduced here, it is worth noting a few other minerals used, or suspected to have been used, in our time span, such as the alum of the Aeolian Islands, bitumen from the Dead Sea, cinnabar in the Aegean, and sulphur from Sicily, let alone clays for potting.

Humdrum stones outcrop everywhere, and even marbles are fairly widespread, but those with special properties, whether hardness, smoothness, colour, gleam or translucency, are much rarer.[60] Fine flints and dense stones that take a high polish are mainly found in the mountains, in particular the Alps. In contrast to the plumage and pelts of the tropics, Mediterranean archaeology is fortunate in that many brightly hued substances are durable; one concentration of brilliantly coloured and patterned rocks runs along the lines of the Nile, Red Sea fault and intervening desert (providing red granite, alabaster, amethyst and Sinai turquoise, to list but a few). Volcanism creates hard basalts and other stones for grinding, as well as occasionally obsidian, the ultra-hard, darkly gleaming glass that we have already come across as a calling-card of early seagoers on Kythera and a success story in provenance analysis. All sources of obsidian [2.6] in the basin occur on volcanic islands: primarily Melos and (for speckled varieties) Giali in the Aegean, Lipari in the Aeolian Islands,

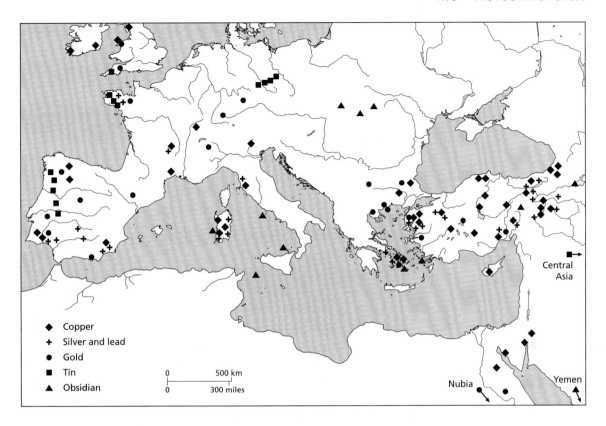

2.6 The major sources of metals and obsidian in and around the Mediterranean; note the extremely uneven distribution, both overall and of specific minerals, as well as the greater dependency on external sources in the case of tin.

Palmarola off the Campanian coast, a group of outcrops at Monte Arci on Sardinia and (for a distinctive green variety) Pantelleria, between Sicily and Tunisia. Other sources lie just beyond the basin, on the Anatolian plateau, in the Carpathians and, more distantly, Ethiopia and Yemen.

Mediterranean metals are concentrated too.[61] Zones with several ores or native metals, many used in antiquity, occur in Iberia, Sardinia, Etruria and Anatolia, the last blending into the Aegean and southern Balkans. Other areas are well endowed with a single metal, notably Cyprus, which, as its Greek name implies, is a major source of copper. Some metals are more widespread than others. Copper is broadly available, with medium or small occurrences even in places like the south of France, southern Levant and Sinai, that are otherwise devoid. Iron, though used only occasionally and in precious meteoric form until the final centuries covered in this book, is widespread too. Silver and gold, however, are more restricted. The former, extracted from silver-rich lead, came mainly from Anatolia, the Aegean source of Lavrio at the southern tip of Attica, and Iberia, with minor possibilities in Sardinia. Gold was collected in its native form and was generally rare, if less so in Anatolia, the Balkans and Iberia. The only prolific gold source lay well beyond the Mediterranean, in Egypt's eastern desert and further south in Nubia (modern Sudan). External sources are again relevant in the case of one last metal, namely tin, the second ingredient (with copper) of bronze. Small deposits exist in all the basin's polymetallic regions, often in natural alloys, but there is ferocious disagreement as to whether any were used in early times. Once the Bronze Age began the Mediterranean's major sources of tin lay in granitic massifs well outside the basin, principally far-off central Asia, and probably the Erzgebirge (Ore Mountains) of Bohemia, as well as Cornwall and Brittany.

The fifth and final influence of tectonics is on biodiversity.[62] Mediterraneoids all harbour very large numbers of species, especially plants, many of them endemics that exist nowhere else in the world. The smallest, Cape Province, is richest relative to its size. But the true Mediterranean benefits from lying at a junction of continents and boasts the largest absolute tally, some 25,000 plant species, half of which are endemic – four times the number in the rest of Europe, 10 per cent of those on the planet and including half the world's aromatics and oil-bearers, all of which helps to place the basin in the top eighteen hotspots of biodiversity on Earth. Tectonics provide the background explanation once again, for over geological time the writhing land and reconfigured seas have repeatedly subdivided ranges, thereby hastening genetic and behavioural divergence. Unsurprisingly, therefore, many of the endemics are found on mountains and islands. On Crete, several plants' entire global distribution consists of a few hundred square kilometres in the mountainous interior.[63] Turning to animals, Corsica has an endemic trout, which it must have retained since it and Sardinia split off from Italy 30 million years ago, while in 2004 DNA analysis confirmed a 'living fossil' native mouse on Cyprus.[64] Such creatures are survivors of a once larger and stranger Mediterranean island fauna.[65] All over the world, encircling seas and confined territory have selected for a slim portfolio of land animals on islands. Good swimmers are disproportionately common, in particular hippopotamus, elephant and deer, whose water-crossing prowess runs to 100 km (60 miles), 50 km (30 miles) and 5–10 km (3–6 miles) respectively, and whose herding habits help a breeding pool to make the transit. Carnivores, at the precarious tip of the food chain, and usually landlubbers, are notably rare. When an island is reached, the meagre pickings encourage bigger species to shrink, sometimes leading to dwarfism. On the other hand, the absence or rarity of predators encourages smaller ones to grow. Other changes save energy, for instance slowness, or flightlessness in birds, and a further acquired trait is naivety, in other words the non-recognition of external killers. At various periods over the last few million years, over a dozen Mediterranean islands sported bizarre morphed bestiaries variously composed of dwarf elephants, hippopotami and deer, giant rodents, flightless birds and other idiosyncratic creatures, in the main swimmers, rafters or (once) fliers, but in a few cases relicts from expansion via since submerged land-bridges [2.7]. As expected, there were few carnivores: a fox-sized canid on Sardinia and a genet on Cyprus.

What, we might ask, do such weird and wonderful characteristics have to do with early Mediterranean history? The fates of the now almost entirely extinct island animals in several cases dovetail with the earliest human occupancy of their homes, as set out in coming chapters. In botanical terms the answer is of wider currency, for the mosaic of variation across small distances created incentives for people to bind habitats together into integrated landscapes, while rarer scents, resins, fine woods

2.7 An artist's impression of the dwarfed or outsized fauna created by insularity on certain Mediterranean islands, in this case Malta, and featuring flightless swans and giant tortoises alongside miniature elephants.

and other vegetal products, with properties ranging from the mouth-watering to mind-blowing, joined the distribution of minerals as a further incentive to draw people into longer-range movement.

This partial portrait of the Mediterranean, built up from overlapping tectonic consequences, reveals in sum a highly distinctive ecology, created out of the forms and properties of land and sea, climate and environment, minerals, plants, animals, and of the interplays between these and one last crucial set of players – the basin's human inhabitants. On one matter there is universal agreement: the appearance of practically every square metre of the Mediterranean today, save a few remote fastnesses, has been altered, directly or indirectly, by the past activities of people.[66] Beyond this, opinions part company.[67] Many travellers, artists and environmentalists have concluded that the early inhabitants of the Mediterranean were a disaster, despoilers of an earthly paradise. In opposition to this 'ruined landscape' theory, however, an increasing number of modern experts take a cooler look and reply that, whatever the undeniable delinquencies of the present, the actual evidence for such past enormities as mass deforestation and land degradation leading to catastrophic erosion has been exaggerated. Instead, they argue for unconscious yet intimate coevolution over the millennia, with people learning to manage the Mediterranean sustainably for growing numbers of inhabitants, even in periods of substantial climate change, and in response its ecology becoming more resilient than that of other mediterraneoid regions and in fact even more diverse thanks to human manipulation and injection of new species. Without denying specific cases of overexploitation, even quite early, there is much to be said for this latter, historically accretional view of the evolution of Mediterranean landscapes.[68] Moreover, unlike most plants and animals, people were not passively divided by the Mediterranean; they actively brought it together. But we have looked long enough at the land; it is time we turned to the sea, to the basin's central fact.

Periplous: *exploring the sea*

Just as deserts are far from uniform, so the sea too is variegated. In ancient Greek a *periplous* entailed the extended navigation of coasts, and description of such journeys; its interminable lists of land- and seamarks, anchorages and travel times, all mentally compiled during our time period and first written down around its end, were means of creating what Braudel, recalling flights in small seaplanes across the basin, called maps 'made up of memories laid end to end' [**2.8**].[69] We shall likewise pass high over the sea, and dive beneath it, but must never forget that its main significance lies in movements across its surface. From the earliest days of navigation, these opened up land that was otherwise out of reach or only attainable circuitously, and once efficient, powered seacraft emerged, travel by sea would outstrip that by land in terms of speed and bulk, a lead sustained until the age of steam. The Mediterranean Sea therefore held out the prospect of rolling back the 'tyranny of distance',[70] or at least of rendering it of very variable significance for sailors and landlubbers. Ultimately, the sea formed a multi-directional, low-friction highway for fast, direct communications (if fraught with risks and hazards of its own), increasingly not just in-between space, but a maritime place and participant in its own right.

We can start with several suggestive facts.[71] Just as the basin gets most of its weather from the Atlantic, so the sea relies upon the ocean to its west for survival. The summer heat creates not only a roasting pan for millions of tourists, but also one for gargantuan evaporation. Rainfall cannot make good the deficit. Nor can rivers;

2.8 A small modern *gulet* approaches the line of distinctive islets strung off Cape Gelidonya (the 'Cape of the Swallows' in ancient Greek) in southern Turkey, one of the innumerable land- and seamarks that articulate Mediterranean journeys by sea.

only the Nile, Rhône and Po are of substantial size, and they inject just a quarter of the input needed to keep the Mediterranean alive, with a further trickle via the Black Sea from the meandering giants of the Russian steppe. The rest comes from a colder, less saline inrush from the Atlantic. Past Gibraltar the tides that syncopate life on the Atlantic coast fail, save in a few shallow gulfs where rises and falls are detectable – as anyone who has sloshed along a causeway of planks in Venice, or got caught by 3-m (10-ft) oscillations in the gulfs of Gabès and Sirte, will know. The lack of a tidal range gives many Mediterranean shorelines an accessible, vertically compressed aspect.

One consequence of tidelessness, as well as the meagre continental shelf (only a fifth of the Mediterranean is less than 200 m (650 ft) deep, in contrast to almost the entire Baltic and North seas), is that coastal marine life is comparatively poor, save where lagoons or river mouths inject nutrients, and around Gibraltar and the Dardanelles, where the Atlantic and Black Sea pour in.[72] This picture changes little as we move into deeper waters, where the seabed is commonly 2–3 km (1–2 miles) down, and as much as 5 km (3 miles) off Cape Matapan, the central tip of the Peloponnese – further from the surface than the peak of any Mediterranean mountain, and recently found to be home to a reclusive population of sperm whales. As early as 1860 an encrusted cable recovered from the seabed off Sardinia furnished proof of life in the abyss,[73] but it is again relatively narrowly based because high evaporation makes for a salty sea and salt water sinks, accumulating in concentrations too high for many marine animals. Most fish inhabit the upper levels of the open sea, where they are notoriously hard to catch unless, as in the case of the famous tunny drives off Sicily and its satellites, they come inshore to feed or during annual migrations. As a result fishing, like so much else in the Mediterranean, is an unpredictable business, often shore-based, small-scale and seldom a reliable mainstay, if a useful supplement and from time to time prodigiously rewarded in terms of catch.[74]

Moving from beneath the waves to glide high above them enables us to appreciate that the Mediterranean Sea is an agglomeration of sub-basins separated by islands and gigantic peninsulas that thrust seaward. Braudel distinguished between a smaller western and a larger eastern half, divided at the channel between Sicily and Africa, where the gap between northern and southern shores shrinks to 145 km (90 miles); Cape Bon in Tunisia is occasionally visible from high ground in Sicily. This primary division works well for Mediterranean Africa, where it separates the Maghreb from the generally dry, low land stretching east to the Nile. But in the north it exacerbates an embarrassing tendency to omit the Adriatic, which is never considered part of the east (and whose archaeology, as we saw in Chapter 1, has suffered from a similarly low profile until recently).[75] Preferable is a triple division into a west Mediterranean extending from Gibraltar to Sardinia and Corsica, a central Mediterranean embracing the seas around Italy (a peninsula that can be thought of as a strip of land, or as the parallel coasts of two sub-basins), and an east Mediterranean starting in the Aegean and Cyrenaica.

We can focus in further. Three almost landlocked sub-basins stand out, with narrow passages that lead to open sea: the Aegean, Adriatic and Tyrrhenian. Each of these miniature Mediterraneans differs from the others: the Aegean and Adriatic are similar in size and multitude of islands, but the latter is elongated, with most islands hugging one shore, while the Tyrrhenian is larger, enclosed by island giants as much as continental land, but empty save for a few volcanic specks. These sub-basins will emerge as places where the Mediterranean soon became 'a sea of close neighbours'.[76] But to put them in perspective, they make up only a fifth of the basin's marine space. Half as much again comprises two semi-enclosed regions, the Alboran Sea in the far west, where Iberia and Africa converge to within 160–70 km (100–5 miles), and the waters between Cyprus, the northern Levant and Anatolia. The majority is very different, with long coasts looking out on empty horizons, the start of the extensive sea deserts beyond sight of land that lurk at several points in the Mediterranean. To give an inkling of the response that such a geography could prompt, the sea on the margins of later pharaonic Egypt was known as 'the Great Green', an uninviting empty plain that vanished into the haze save where the low line of homeland curved away in the distance.[77]

How do the currents and winds swirling between the convoluted masses of land influence movement across these seas? Naturally, much of the answer lies in the changing capabilities of seacraft, but we can offer some preliminary observations.[78] The Atlantic injection circulates anticlockwise in sweeping longshore currents and internal eddies (see map on pp. 8–9). Beaches in Gaza and Israel are made of redeposited African sand. Currents are typically sluggish, though at narrows they accelerate, at Gibraltar to 6 knots (11 km or 7 miles per hour), a serious obstacle to ships departing the Mediterranean until recently. In the Strait of Messina between Sicily and peninsular Italy, surges create the whirlpools that inspired the *Odyssey*'s Charybdis, and attract spawning swordfish from the open seas, as palisades of their decapitated heads in the Catania fish market testify. Save under such circumstances, currents are only a modest help or hindrance to Mediterranean mariners. Far more relevant are the winds, whose names – *mistral, bora, tramontana, meltemi, levanter, scirocco, khamsin* and many more – conjure up as romantic a response in northern sensibilities as they do a practical respect among Mediterranean navigators. A strong blast can neutralize or reverse the surface current. Moreover, wind direction and intensity fluctuate wildly and unpredictably. True, the prevailing pattern consists of winds from the north, most violent between October and March. But as ever, Mediterranean generalizations are of limited validity. Endless travellers' tales of frustrated plans and surprise landfalls, bolstered by meteorological data, reveal that the wind can spring surprises pleasant and unpleasant from any point of the compass and at any time. Daily cycles of on- and offshore breezes offer further possibilities for short hops. Atmospheric equivalents of Charybdis concentrate where mountains meet the sea, in the perilous Gulf of the Lion south of Marseilles, where winds hurtling down the Rhône Valley spew out, roaring, and similarly off the coasts of Malaga, Dalmatia, the Aegean and southern Turkey, the last of which boasts the world's earliest demonstrable shipwreck at Uluburun. On the other hand, in any season the sea can assume a lake-like innocence, with the so-called halcyon days falling in the middle of winter. And these are just the extremes among a spectrum of conditions best insured against, and exploited, by practical knowledge, and those prepared to wait. As a rule of thumb, a safe place to be is far enough offshore to avoid coastal squalls, reefs and cliffs, but close enough to avoid getting lost, and to run for shelter should one of the terrible storms of the open sea gather to seaward. In a small boat, the horizon at sea level lies 5–7 km (3–4 miles) away, but in the final assessment, judging whether this hedging position wastes chances or courts disaster is the mark of an experienced Mediterranean navigator.

These conditions have fostered two theories about the impact of the wind on Mediterranean movement by sea. One argues that prevailing winds, configurations of land and sea, and boat technology combined to encourage specific sea-paths and trunk routes. Certain areas did well, and others were disadvantaged, an acute example of the latter being the African coast, a lee shore onto which boats were easily driven and also fraught with sandbanks and reefs.[79] The other instead stresses flexibility of destination within a fickle environment, with expedient goals rather than preordained plans, and points to evidence for this in the eclecticism of early cargos.[80] In fact, both options can be sensibly accommodated. For an individual sailing the freedom of choice could be considerable, especially if distances were small and the purpose not tied to a specific place and time. But equally, prevailing winds would, over time, select for particular axes of movement, especially for long crossings reliant on runs of steady weather, as well as choices of seasonally sheltered anchorages, with accumulating knowledge of successful runs encouraging convergence upon them and so the emergence over time, and under specific social conditions, of regular routes and hubs.

To integrate our portraits of land and sea, we need to concentrate where these realms converge, first at the coast and then those special, wraparound coasts known as islands. Coasts are always interesting as places of opportunity, danger, and cultural as well as literal liminality and promiscuity. The Mediterranean's do not disappoint. Unravelled like the intestine of a blue whale, they are 46,000 km (28,500 miles) in length, more than the Earth's circumference and a higher proportion of global coastline than the basin's share of planetary space.[81] The northern shore accounts for the vast majority, and the lion's share goes to the Aegean, one small sub-basin that accounts for an astonishing third of the total, followed by peninsular Italy and Dalmatia. We can usefully quantify and map the coastal indentation that helps to create this [2.9].[82] Indented zones of coast occur in most parts of the basin, but the longest and most intricate mass in a few stretches. The greatest concentration is the fantastically convoluted Aegean, though Dalmatia and parts of southern and central Tyrrhenian Italy are also prominent and there are smaller but significant foci in the Gulf of İskenderun, where the Levant swings west into Anatolia, at Gibraltar, and, in North Africa, along the Nile Delta (an unstable shore, however, as we shall soon discover) and coastal Tunisia. In contrast, relatively featureless coasts predominate along the remainder of North Africa, but also in Adriatic Italy, the Levant and to a lesser degree southern France and Spain. What might we learn from this? Rather as the configurations of various tracts of sea allowed preliminary ideas to form

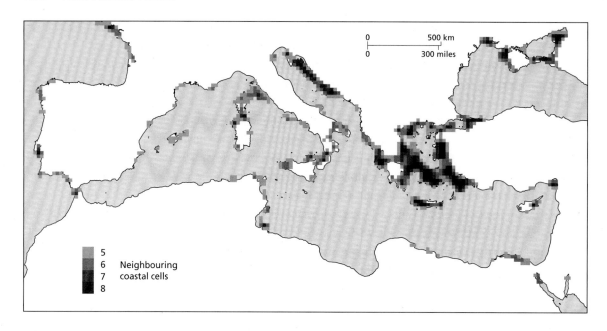

5
6
7   Neighbouring
8   coastal cells

2.9 An exploration of relative indentation around the coast of the Mediterranean by dividing the coastal zone into equally sized cells and assessing how many surrounding cells also contain a coastal element, thereby creating a proxy for areas in which coastal topography might encourage maritime activity.

about likely kinds of connection across them, the lie of the coasts provides clues as to where land and sea mingle closely enough to prompt and reward maritime over terrestrial travel, in short likely hotspots for early seagoing.[83] Conversely, long, straight shores suggest conditions where terrestrial and maritime coastwise movement might remain closely comparable, and competitive, as options.

Coasts vary in appearance too.[84] High coasts in uplifted regions create sea-marks and marine vistas, captured by names like 'Panorama' and 'Mirabello', that might entice people into them.[85] Low-lying shore is harder to spot from a boat, poorer in navigational marks, and often coupled with treacherous shoals. The longest stretch of the latter is eastern North Africa (save for the Cyrenaican interlude), then swinging north to where the Carmel ridge meets the sea near Haifa. Rocky shores occupy about three-quarters of the coast. Their appearance can be forbidding, but unbroken stretches without sheltering fissures or larger inlets and other interruptions are rare. Soft shores are more variable in nature and more changeable over time. In addition to beaches and dunes, two other varieties deserve attention, one more common in the past than today, the other quite the contrary, and both, as we shall discover, hiding a disproportionate number of our best-preserved archaeological surprises. The first are coastal marshes and lagoons, exceptionally rich in fish and birdlife, as well as natural salt pans that created a substance of likely importance throughout the past, but whose now visible residue is next to zero.[86] In the past century many have been condemned as malarial swamps by 'progressive' governments and drained to create farmland; an area larger than Cyprus has been lost in the last fifty years. Their survival in Albania and Sardinia, both spared this aspect of modernization, and to a lesser degree in Languedoc, offers an idea of their former extent. Other major wetlands, we might note, pepper the interior, for instance the crater-lakes of central Italy, the internally draining basins of the southern Balkans and Anatolia, the Ghab depression in Syria, a string of Levantine rift valley lakes from Galilee to the Dead Sea, and the seasonal saline *chotts* and *sebkhas* of North Africa.

The second, rarer species of ancient coastal wetland is the alluvial river delta.[87] Mediterranean rivers can create deltas largely thanks to slow currents and lack of tide. That they have done so in the past is proven by large underwater cones of sometimes perilously unstable mud rising from the seabed, on which deltas such as that of the Rhône rest today. But this does not mean that deltas have always existed. In their present form, most are relatively young reflections of stable sea levels and high rates of erosion (both natural and human-induced) that provide their raw material; global warming allied with reduced input due to damming will soon spell their death knell. Many are in retreat already, even that of the mighty Nile, which until recent damming was fed by more than 100 million tonnes of river-borne silt each year. When the latest round of delta-building began is a question with many answers. Some in Iberia and most in the east Adriatic date after the end of the Roman empire, but the shifting locations of ancient Priene plot an older seaward march by the Meander in western Turkey, whose delta has advanced 20 km (12 miles) in the past 2500 years, at an average of 8 m (26 ft) a year [**2.10**].[88] Most of the Rhône's advance was over by Classical times, since when it has subsided as fast as it grew.[89] The Nile has performed even more prodigiously. The northern limit of Egypt, where marshy lagoons gave way to coastal dunes and then the sea, was known in antiquity as 'Reed-thicket', a name surely ever on the move, and indeed in the last 10,000 years the Nile Delta has grown from a vestigial stub to a fertile triangle 17,000 sq. km

2.10 The march of the Meander delta over several millennia, and its consequences for coastal topography.

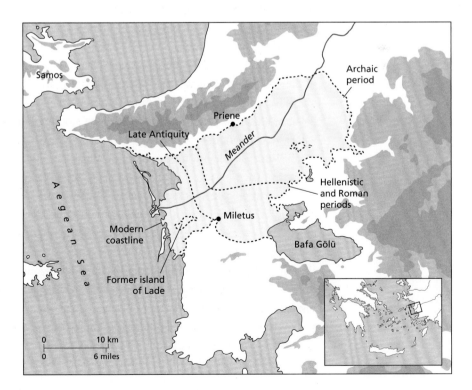

(6500 sq. miles) in extent, rivalling the cultivatable land in the valley to its south by the time of the pharaohs, and larger than all but two Mediterranean islands [PL. V].[90] Within our time frame, the overall point is that to envision coastal landscapes involves subtracting much current deltaic land. This results in fewer, smaller coastal plains, but also more unclogged creeks and embayments, offshore islets and navigable river mouths than are visible along the smothered modern coast, and therefore far more anchorages for early mariners [2.11].[91] Furthermore, a surprising number of currently landlocked sites were once coastal or easily accessible from the sea. Walking the banks of the Guadalquivir in Seville, just beyond the Mediterranean proper, it is hard to grasp that they stand just 11 m (36 ft) above sea level, and close to the point where once salt and fresh water met.

As we have seen, certain stretches of mainland coast are so marine as to be almost islands (the Latin etymology of 'peninsula'). But what of those fragments of genuinely sea-surrounded land on which navigators kept so close an eye?[92] By virtue of their location in the midst of the sea, and the startling fact that they enjoy over a third of the total coastline, islands play a dramatically greater role in Mediterranean history than their size (in sum less than 5 per cent of the basin's land area) would lead us to anticipate [PL. IV]. Even the largest fall outside the Earth's top thirty – a rare respect in which the Mediterranean must concede to other enclosed seas, notably the Caribbean and those of the East Asian rim. The big five (Sicily and Sardinia roughly tied in first place, then Cyprus, Corsica and Crete), followed at a distance by Euboea, Mallorca, Lesbos and Rhodes, often operated as miniature continents, too large to be comprehended as islands by the eye, and internally highly diverse. Taking 0.1 sq. km (0.04 sq. miles) as a cut-off point, there are about 360 smaller islands, most under 100 sq. km (40 sq. miles), and after this trail thousands of islets and reefs. Diminutive scale need not, however, imply insignificance; while some substantial islands, such as Malta, are low-lying, volcanic Alicudi, at 5.2 sq. km (2 sq. miles) one of the smallest of the Aeolian cluster centred on Lipari, thrusts its triangular peak 675 m (2215 ft) into the sky, catching rain clouds and acting as a seamark from afar. Palagruža, a mid-Adriatic scrap that fails the aforementioned qualifying threshold, will nonetheless figure repeatedly in this book.

Because islands are products of the forces that uplift and fracture the edges of the Eurasian plate, or sea-born products of the associated volcanism, the vast majority congregate in the northern Mediterranean, especially the Aegean and Adriatic, whose intricate shores they further embellish. North African islands are few and, save for a few islets off Morocco, concentrate off Tunisia: flat, barely insular Djerba, the Kerkennahs, tiny La Galite and Zembra, plus Pantelleria and the Pelagies (Lampedusa, Linosa and Lampione), which today belong to Italy but are physically closer to Africa. Most islands lie fairly close to the mainland, each other or both. The remotest are the aptly named Pelagies (from the Greek meaning 'open sea'), at 140–165 km (85–100 miles) uniquely out of sight of major land, their distant neighbours Malta and Gozo, and the Balearics (Mallorca, Menorca, smaller Ibiza and Formentera, the latter two also known as the Pitiusics, and which also lie unusually far from each other). At the other extreme are islands so close to the main-land that they barely qualify at all, including two of the largest, Sicily and Euboea. Places such as these, set beside the Mediterranean's long, slender peninsulas, blur the division between island and mainland, and raise questions such as whether Sicily is so different from Calabria or Apulia (the toe and the heel of Italy), or indeed the Peloponnese, another compromised almost-island facing different seas and split up by a mountainous heart. Lovely Istria, protruding into the northern Adriatic, has been described as island, peninsula and hinterland all in one. Lastly, the multi-tude of small islands creates all kinds of patterns: rare singletons, satellites of bigger islands, and archipelagos either dispersed or cheek by jowl, some strung out along the coast, others in discrete clusters, others again festooned between larger land. The last is well illustrated by the coastal Dalmatian islands, Sušac, Palagruža (Italian Pelagosa, which gives a better idea of its open-sea location) and the Tremiti Islands off Italy's Gargano peninsula, which create a line of stepping stones over the other-wise open Adriatic. In short, most Mediterranean islands are the opposite of insular, at least by stereotypical perceptions of the term, and seldom usefully regarded as isolates.[93] Highly diverse, fragmented and linked into wider patchworks of land and sea, islands are accentuated variants of all Mediterranean environments.

We shall return to many of the questions raised about sea, coast and islands in relation to specific developments in the chapters that follow. But standing back, can we discern any useful overall Mediterranean distinctions? Some tendencies certainly emerge, even if they are less than absolute, and the fractal tendency creates mini-ature replicas in unlikely places of traits witnessed on a grander scale elsewhere. The most salient conclusion is the disadvantaged maritime status of much of the African shore. Save for a few stretches, it is less indented, bereft of alluring islands, poorer in both anchorages and navigational marks, and the prevailing winds beat against it, a suite of factors to add to the other possible reasons for divergence in much of Mediterranean Africa that were proposed in Chapter 1. However, such factors are not unique to the southern shore. Several apply in less acute forms to parts of the Levant, Adriatic Italy and the northwest Mediterranean. For now it is an open question whether we should anticipate less precocious seagoing in such places, or simply more linear, coastwise movement in contrast to the multidirectional networks of, for example, the Aegean.[94]

The voyage ahead

The Mediterranean is, of course, more than a convoluted mass of land between which shimmers a central sea. It is a place full of people, and the rest of this book asks how this human world came into being, how the changing potential of every-thing we have reviewed in this chapter – sea, mountains, lowlands, minerals, plants, animals, climate and the rest – was learned, lived and turned to advantage. A broadly chronological approach to this question runs the risk of any narrative, namely a runaway entrainment in pursuit of the rise of this, the acme of that, as well as an exaltation of the new at the expense of enduring practices, but without a sequent framework the staggering range of developments within our remit could never be understood coherently. My hope is that this book's framework will allow the ways in which deep structuring elements of life in the Mediterranean first coalesced and expanded to be traced, while at the same time sampling the sheer diversity of trajectories, all at as many scales as information allows. Analogies for such an approach come less from writing than orchestral music, in which, within a coherent whole, themes interweave over time, coming and going in various keys or picked up by different instruments, or such paintings as the avowedly symphonic later canvases of Kandinsky and the creations of *pointillisme*, in which innumerable dots glow in miniature, while combining to create patchworks of related colours and, when we step far enough back, a grander overall image.

The breaks that define the chapters that follow reflect major transition points in early Mediterranean life, some of which, it will come as no surprise, coincide with climate shifts. Naturally, they do not always work equally well in all parts of the basin (it would be rather suspicious if they did), but they do offer a better fit with what was going on than the traditional Palaeolithic, Mesolithic, Neolithic, Copper, Bronze and Iron labels, which were helpful as first approximations in their day, but connote confusingly different time periods in each part of the basin, often fail to capture the overall structure of developments even in a given region, and are sometimes imposed wholly inappropriately. The sooner this antiquated system is replaced by reference to centuries and millennia BC, the better. For the present, however, we will still need to genuflect periodically to the traditional terms. The chronological tables on pages 10–14 offer a guide to the nightmare of terminologies, and each chapter will rehearse as painlessly as possible those names of convenience still used to refer to particular periods in specific regions. The time spans covered by each chapter shrink progressively from tens of thousands of generations, to thousands, hundreds, tens and finally a mere twelve to fifteen generations in the penultimate chapter, a reflection only in part of the ever finer-grained, more abundant information at our disposal, and more fundamentally of the accelerating pace of overall change.

Chapters 3 and 4 explore how the predecessors of modern humans filtered into the basin, and the activities of our own species up to the end of the last severe glaciation. Chapter 5 covers the huge changes associated with the run-up to, and first millennia of, the present Holocene phase of Earth's climatic history, especially the expansion of maritime activities and agricultural communities around the basin, plus the seeds of divergent trajectories in North Africa. Chapter 6 is interstitial; it traces the elaboration of such ways of life, which, but for subsequent momentous interventions, might have set the pattern for much of later Mediterranean history. Chapter 7 takes on a series of fundamental changes between 3500 and 2200 BC, and marks a crux. This time span witnessed the drying of the Mediterranean's climate, and the beginnings of the regime familiar to us today. It also saw the rise of large-scale societies in Mesopotamia and Egypt, and their first impact on parts of the Mediterranean. Many features of later Mediterranean life first become visible in

2.11 Early photograph of small sailing craft near the mouth of the Yarkon River in modern Israel; even modest rivers might often be navigable or at least offer shelter for the seacraft of antiquity.

embryonic form at this stage. Dividing Chapter 7 from Chapter 8 is the last climate crunch to hit the Mediterranean, around 2200 BC, but otherwise the division is artificial, because the ensuing and, in the east, extremely glitzy phase (think Mycenae, or Tutankhamun) in many senses represents simply the growth and proliferation of things set in train in the preceding millennium. Chapter 9 explores the new social, economic and connective developments on either side of 1200 BC that enabled the first truly pan-Mediterranean networks to arise. Chapter 10 completes the story, and examines how this world powered up and spread to almost every corner of the basin, quickly and often aggressively. The end-date of 500 BC is chosen not for any deep significance, and in historical terms marks an arbitrary point within a continuum of Mediterranean developments. Rather it aims to dovetail with the ostensibly familiar Classical world, and to invite an onward exploration into that world of the deeper patterns set out in the preceding chapters. Chapter 11 summarizes those patterns as we have seen them coalesce, and formulates a few new questions for the centuries that followed.

CHAPTER THREE

The speciating sea

(1.8 million – 50,000 years ago)

Beginning in deep time

3.1 Reconstruction of the dried-out Mediterranean basin during the Messinian Salinity Crisis.

Africa is the natural starting point for any long-term history of the Mediterranean. As we saw in Chapter 2, it was movement of the African plate and its Arabian annex that created the basin's first recognizable precursors. And what Africa gave, it could also take away, by the tiniest tectonic twitch. About 5.9 million years ago, close to the transition from the Miocene to Pliocene, when the bipedal ancestors of ourselves and others were restricted to a zone well to the south, one such geological spasm propelled Africa into Iberia and a then conjoined Morocco. This shut down two straits along the present lines of the Guadalquivir and western Rif that until then had channelled in the Atlantic. The result was the Messinian Salinity Crisis [**3.1**].[1] Deprived of oceanic inflow, sea levels plummeted by as much as 1300 m (4250 ft), until the Mediterranean Sea was reduced to saline pockets in a glittering desert of evaporites, down to which the Nile and Rhône carved gorges to rival the Grand Canyon, one with its waters plunging some 700 m

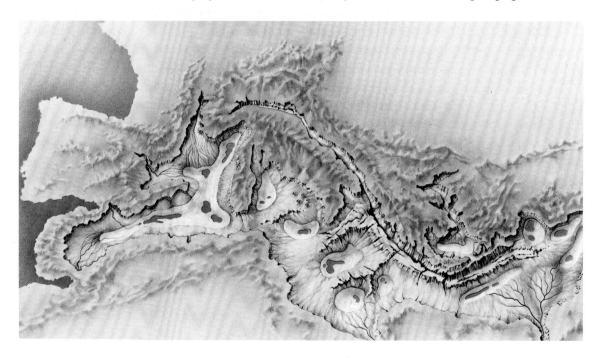

(2300 ft) over a sill beneath modern Cairo, the other still present underwater in the Gulf of the Lion. The sea's return when the barrier was breached at Gibraltar, a few hundred thousand years later, was equally dramatic. An estimated 65 cu. km (15.5 cu. miles) of water surged into the desiccated basin every day for a century. Traces of this nightmarish Messinian abyssal desert can still be seen in deep-sea cores. While the basin was dry, North Africa and Europe swapped animal species freely by land for the last time. More poignantly, the sea's retreat enabled ancestors of the now-extinct goat-antelope *Myotragus balearicus* to walk out between the salt deserts to Mallorca and Menorca, where they evolved in isolation for over 5 million years, only to be annihilated in the last instants of evolutionary time by the arrival of seafaring people a few thousand years ago.[2]

It was also from the African side that hominins (the bipedal, generally bigger-brained scions of the hominid family) first reached the margins of the Mediterranean. To the best of our knowledge, though this is exceptionally provisional, the earliest to glimpse the sea did so from some point now geologically deformed past recognition on the high plateau of northeast Algeria, near Ain Hanech (the 'Spring of the Snake').[3] The sedimentary bluffs around Ain Hanech were first put on the map for their wealth of animal fossils rather than traces of hominins, but investigations since 1992 have documented three layers containing limestone choppers and other flint tools [**3.2**]. The excavators argue that these can be dated to approximately 1.8 million years ago, through a combination of scientific techniques, the associated animal species and parallels with artifacts from Olduvai Gorge in East Africa. This places them early in the Pleistocene, the last great geological age in the earth's history, whose severe climatic shifts will soon demand our attention. The positions of the tools suggest that they were slowly covered by silt on the margins of a river, or its residual oxbow lake, as it wound through open savannah. Nearby lay the bones of hippopotami, horses, gazelle and others, whose carcasses the tool-users scavenged. From which branch of the fairly young genus *Homo* the tool-users came is unknown, as no skeletal parts have been found, and as many as five different candidate hominins coexisted in Africa around this time. The Ain Hanech team opt for *Homo habilis*, but equally plausible is an early appearance of *Homo ergaster* (better known by its name in Asia, *Homo erectus*), our direct anatomical and, in a generic sense, behavioural ancestor: upstanding, rangy, clever and well-adapted to tree-studded grasslands, where it added tubers to the diet of a scavenger and small-prey hunter.[4]

3.2 One of the oldest artifacts in the Mediterranean: a chopping tool from Ain Hanech, with parallels at Olduvai Gorge in East Africa.

3.3 Map of sites mentioned in this chapter, also showing the Pleistocene natural refugia (shaded in grey), approximate limits of enduring snow during maximal glacial phases and, as insets, (*bottom left*) long-term sea level fluctuations and (*top right*) the gradual tectonic formation of the Mediterranean as illustrated by the outline of later Pliocene Italy, some 3.5–2.5 million years ago.

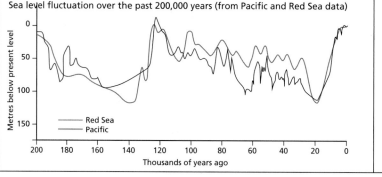

Snow cover 6–12 months per year
Snow cover 2–6 months per year

Vaufrey

Atapuerca

Torralba

Abric Romaní

Orce

Mugharet el 'Aliya
Salé
Kebibat
Dar es Sultan
Casablanca

Gorham's Cave,
Vanguard Cave

Tighenif

Ain Hanech

Taforalt

Oued Djebbana

Jebel Irhoud

Bir el Ater

Sea level fluctuation over the past 200,000 years (from Pacific and Red Sea data)

Metres below present level

Red Sea
Pacific

Thousands of years ago

3.4 (*below*) A basalt hand axe from Ubeidiya. Both around the Mediterranean and more widely, the early presence or absence of these distinctive, in several senses multifaceted objects can be variously explained in terms of differences in chronology, connectivity, materials or cognition.

In fact, exactly where and when hominins first encountered the Mediterranean is likely to remain an elusive question for the foreseeable future. In the Jordan Valley, beside a precursor of the Sea of Galilee, and slightly younger than Ain Hanech, is the site of Ubeidiya [**3.4**, **3.5**].[5] Here, among the thousands of tools, are early examples of hand axes, an enduring form whose proposed functions range from all-round penknife to emblem of potency in mating displays, and that characterizes a new phase in tool production, known as the Acheulian, that began more than 1.5 million years ago and lasted for well over a million years.[6] Some intervening presence can be predicted in northeast Africa, especially where the African Rift Valley merges

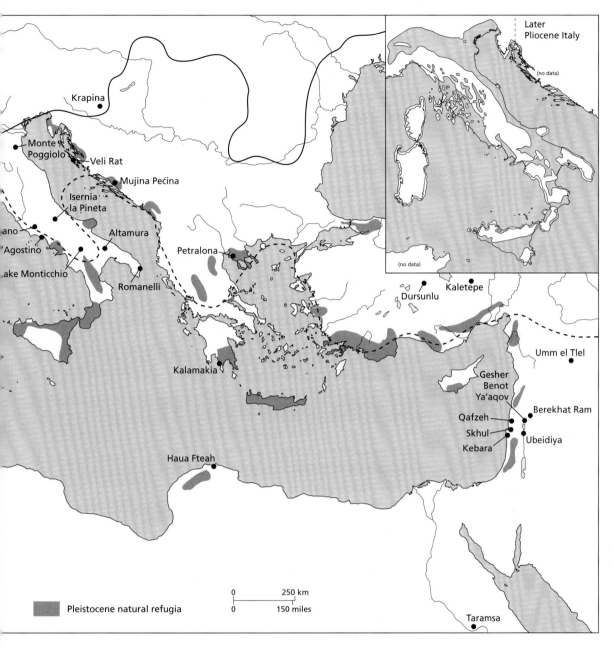

Later Pliocene Italy

(no data)

(no data)

Krapina

Monte Poggiolo

Veli Rat

Mujina Pećina

Isernia la Pineta

ano

Altamura

Agostino

Petralona

Dursunlu

Kaletepe

ake Monticchio

Romanelli

Umm el Tlel

Kalamakia

Gesher Benot Ya'aqov

Berekhat Ram

Qafzeh

Skhul

Kebara

Ubeidiya

Haua Fteah

Taramsa

Pleistocene natural refugia

0   250 km
0   150 miles

with the gateway to the Levant. Still older dates might be anticipated, too, perhaps towards the end of the Pliocene, when a continuous belt of savannah still ran from Africa to the Asian Pacific coast, inviting widespread dispersal across and beyond Africa.[7] This is lent some credence by recent surprises such as 1.8 million-year-old hominins at Dmanisi in the Caucasus, and the strange hobbit-like creatures that survived until 18,000 years ago on Flores in island Southeast Asia, which may hint at earlier exits from Africa and complex subsequent flows and evolution.[8]

Regardless of the details, what significance should we attribute to places like Ain Hanech and Ubeidiya within overall patterns of hominin expansion across Africa and

Asia? The number of African animals at Ubeidiya suggests that its hominins, too, were a minor overspill of African *ergaster*, from which tinier numbers percolated east into Asia. Indeed, these first appearances on the southern margin of the Mediterranean reflect not so much the giant steps of a pioneering species, but sporadic pulses of small-scale expansion from core populations in East Africa, and perhaps elsewhere, followed by retreats and local extinctions.[9] *Ergaster*'s flexibility and intelligence had its limits in the face of the increasingly dry, unstable conditions that we shall see were starting to become established, cyclically uniting and dividing the ecological niches that early hominins could exploit. After Ain Hanech the record in northwest Africa is silent until about a million years ago, when intermittent traces begin in the caves and modern quarries excavated early in the 20th century to build a new port at Casablanca, followed by 700,000-year-old *ergaster* fossils at Tighenif in Algeria.[10] A comparable silence divides Ubeidiya from its 800,000 year old neighbour Gesher Benot Ya'aqov, where waterlogging preserves remarkably early smoothed wooden objects and plant remains alongside traces of fire.[11] These silences may in part be due to non-survival or failure of detection, but in the well-explored Levant they lend weight to the suggestion of an ephemeral initial presence, punctuated by long gaps.

3.5 Part of the Ubeidiya formation, whose tilted geology exposes multiple early strata to investigation, seen here in its landscape setting of the Jordan Rift Valley, with the Sea of Galilee in the distance.

An equally minimal assessment can be made of the degree to which the arrival from time to time of hominins in North Africa and the Levant led to any engagement with the sea. Even allowing for our ignorance of *ergaster*'s precise cognitive powers, it can be safely hazarded that, unlike the European discovery of the Pacific (at least as immortalized by Keats), there was no Cortesian visual climax on the final ridge. As we shall discover, in clement periods the region of the Sahara through which hominin groups expanded would have been studded with extensive bodies of water, of which the Mediterranean's margins probably seemed just a saltier variant. At most, the river mouths and coastal lagoons may have offered good scavenging and hunting. Overall, the conclusion in this chapter concerning early maritime activity and use of marine resources will be that the encounter between hominins and the sea was far from a case of love at first sight. For a very long time indeed, the Mediterranean Sea remained a forbidding expanse, a barrier circuitously circumvented, whose resources were only gradually learned and exploited, initially with both feet on dry ground. Plato, putting words into the mouth of Socrates in the *Phaedo*, famously likened the coast-dwelling inhabitants of Classical Greece to ants or frogs round a pond.[12] His simile offers more scope for distinction than is commonly recognized. For while the bulk of this book chronicles and analyses the emergence of ever more centripetally oriented, culturally amphibious Mediterranean societies, this first historical chapter, save for a few rather evidentially problematic frog-hops, highlights an immense centrifugal period, one of rootedness in continental hinterlands, that instead lives under the sign of the ant.[13] In this specific sense, this was a pre-Mediterranean world, and provides a deep-time counterpoint to the maritime orientations that subsequently developed with increasing velocity.

The palaeo-Mediterranean

What did the Pleistocene Mediterranean actually look like? This is more than a matter of idle curiosity, for the basin underwent repeated transformations during this epoch, and these fashioned the shifting theatre in which its inhabitants lived. The last geological events of pan-Mediterranean significance were the restoration of the oceanic connection at the end of the Messinian Salinity Crisis, and the opening of the Red Sea to the Indian Ocean at the Bab-el-Mandeb, which determined that the sole remaining overland exit from Africa would brush the Mediterranean at Suez. It would be wrong, however, to ignore later tectonic activity, not only because its infinitesimal torture of the Mediterranean's landscapes continues to this day, but also because over this chapter's timescale it substantially resculpted the basin's physiognomy. Italy and its islands are a case in point [**3.3**].[14] About a million years ago (when hominins were about to arrive there) much of the current peninsula had already been thrust up from the sea, but the Apennines were still lower, Apulia and the Monte Gargano massif remained islands quite recently divorced from Dalmatia, and Calabria would hide underwater for another 200,000–300,000 years. Proto-Sicily comprised two islands separated by a shallow sea until 700,000 years ago;

these were then united by a colossal eruption that spawned Etna, at about 3330 m (10,925 ft) in current altitude the Mediterranean's largest volcano, and the sight of which, in 1828, helped to persuade the geologist Charles Lyell of the earth's immense age. Etna's birth was one of many such cataclysms in the Tyrrhenian region, and comparable processes of uplift, subsidence, contortion and volcanism were at work more widely across the Mediterranean within the same expanse of time.

While the land's bones were being reshaped, global climates were trending towards generally cooler, drier conditions, which brought an end to the subtropical world of Tethys and its immediate descendants, and prompted here and in the other mediterraneoids the evolution of distinctively Mediterranean-type floras – the first olive pollen, for example, comes from a seabed core in the west Mediterranean that dates back slightly over 3.2 million years.[15] This crystallized into a new, Pleistocene, regime around 2.5 million years ago, marked by oscillations between colder and warmer phases, ultimately driven by long-term fluctuations in the earth's orbit, its relatively faster-paced wobbles and tilts, feedback effects between ocean water, ice and greenhouse gases, and the sheer chance that a continent had drifted to the South Pole, where it allowed a mass of ice to accumulate.[16] The last time such factors had coincided was 290 million years ago, and the consequent Permo-Carboniferous age lasted for 10 to 20 million years. Such durations are a cruel reminder of the fact that our busy bubble of warmer times, which we bravely distinguish as the Holocene, is in the natural course of things merely a short blip in a much longer chill.

As our knowledge of Pleistocene climate improves, particularly with regard to more recent phases, a complex picture has emerged that defies categorization into the discrete 'ice ages' of traditional climate history, a term in fact doubly inappropriate in the Mediterranean, where, as we shall see, aridity, not ice, posed the main challenge. Major long-term fluctuations are designated by a sequence of Marine Isotope Stages (MIS), identified by the oxygen isotope ratios preserved in microfauna found in deep-sea cores. These relate to the proportion of the planet's seawater that was locked up in ice caps, and so provide a crude proxy for global climate. The MIS sequence marked a revolutionary advance when first delineated four decades ago, but ice caps take millennia to melt, and tens of millennia to accumulate. Fresh data from cores drilled into the Greenland ice sheet (a superb, annually updated repository of data for the northern hemisphere), and most recently Antarctica, coupled with other sources such as pollen in lake cores, are more sensitive to shorter-term conditions and reveal a much spikier pattern nested within the MIS cycles. This tendency for rapid, drastic alteration is sinisterly known as the 'flickering switch' of climate behaviour.[17] Some flickers comprised cold or warm stages a few millennia in duration apiece, but major shifts are detectable over much shorter, even decadal, time spans. Clearly, the climatic playing field has never stayed level for very long.

For the first million and a half years of the Pleistocene, the incoming regime was fairly mild. But from slightly less than a million years ago, and more markedly over the last 450,000 years, both the overall cooling and the amplitude of oscillations increased. Regular peaks of cold occurred every 100,000 years, correlated with drier conditions (an important generalization), and each short, warm interglacial witnessed an increase in the rains. This drove the cyclic opening and closing of corridors across Africa and the Levant alluded to earlier, as well as phases of population extension and subdivision further south, and elsewhere in Eurasia, that accelerated human genetic and cognitive development.[18] Although this Pleistocene drying is commonly held to be responsible for creating a hyper-arid desert across the Sahara, this was only fully realized under certain conditions.[19] Over time, dry periods were punctuated by interglacials when the Indian and Atlantic ocean monsoon belts shifted northward, nourishing in the Sahara a semi-arid, seasonal patchwork of savannah, grassy steppe, running wadis and huge shallow reedy lakes. This lured animals, plants and the hominins and later humans who fed on them to expand into it and towards the Mediterranean, of course ignorant of the threat of isolation and local extinction in the coastal strip should the cold and desert return. This dual process has been likened to a colossal demographic pump that alternately drew in and expelled entire communities of plants and animals (including bipedal ones) in a manner that profoundly influenced the long-term pattern of history in Mediterranean Africa.[20]

What wider impact did such Pleistocene conditions have on the Mediterranean basin itself?[21] There were two major transformations, one on land, the other marine. Starting with the former, even in full glacial periods the basin was shielded from the worst of the weather by mountains along its northern edge, and its environments therefore enjoyed greater stability than those beyond the mountains and, as just seen, in the Sahara. Moreover, although large expanses of the Mediterranean were reduced in the north to cold steppe and in the south to milder, dry steppe grading into desert, with perennial snow and even glaciers on high ground, the fragmentation identified in Chapter 1 as a fundamental Mediterranean characteristic ensured that a large amount of environmental diversity survived. A critical role was played by sheltered pockets known as refugia, over fifty of which can be identified in botanical terms, covering a sizeable minority of the Mediterranean, including several of the larger islands.[22] For many Mediterranean species, refugia spelt survival, though the bolt-hole sometimes proved too small eventually to sustain a self-regenerating population. Combined with the role of the sea as a midway barrier to species shifting south to escape the cold, or north to escape desertification, this made parts of the basin a peculiar catchment for animals and plants, often in bizarre juxtapositions without analogue today.

At the start of each major warm phase, including the last interglacial, unromantically known as MIS 5e (127,000–117,000 years ago), and the present Holocene, floral survivors would break out to recolonize the Mediterranean, temperate Europe and parts of the Sahara, creating landscapes of grassland and trees, dominated in optimal conditions by deciduous woods. Concurrently, as we saw at Ubeidiya, a bridgehead of African climates, plants and animals often extended into the southern Levant. This summary smoothes a more complicated reality, with environments and climates occupying all kinds of intermediate positions between the extremes. Moreover, although certain regularities permit cautious deployment of recent phases to shed light on older ones, complex specific interplays ensured that each phase evolved uniquely in its details. We shall investigate several key phases in this and the following chapter, culminating in the well-investigated Last Glacial Maximum (dated by radiocarbon to 21,000–18,000 BC) and the ensuing warming that led up to the start of the Holocene.

Meanwhile, fluctuations in sea levels caused by the waxing and waning of ice caps affected the Mediterranean's immense coastline.[23] At the Last Glacial Maximum global stands lay 120–30 m (400–25 ft) lower than today, a drop at least matched by equivalent dips further back in time. During such periods, as well as shorter phases of mass iceberg calving in the Atlantic known as Heinrich events, cold water flooded into the Mediterranean, altering the composition of its marine life and chilling the atmosphere. At the opposite extreme, the last interglacial is immortalized in stable sectors of the coast by fossil beaches and wave-carved caves 3–6 m (10–20 ft) above the modern shore. Some contain remains of molluscs that are now only found off West Africa, revealing warmer waters than have ever existed during the Holocene. For most of the time, however, sea levels rose and fell between these outer brackets, in delayed concert with climate fluctuation, and with substantially lower stands than today's over most of the Pleistocene.

How much sea level change altered the coastline depended on the local lie of the land and the extent of the sea's drop; if the former was steep and the latter modest, shorelines remained similar, though not identical, to those of modern times and a fair number of ancient sites situated close to former shores should survive. But in gently sloping areas, the glacial maxima in particular substantially augmented the Mediterranean's lowlands, to the approximate tune of 300,000–400,000 sq. km (115,000–155,000 sq. miles). These drowned, archaeologically all but inaccessible plains, well watered, probably grazed by game animals and close to the softer climatic influence of the sea as well as the rich diversity of foods in coastal and estuarine landscapes, are widely held to have been magnets for early occupation.[24] In addition, they created new corridors between regions, and ones that benefited from fairly consistent conditions along their length. Under some circumstances, lower sea levels forged another kind of terrestrial link in the form of land-bridges between places otherwise divided by water. The survival of the Mediterranean Sea confirms that the Strait of Gibraltar and the Sicilian narrows remained open, but, in contrast, the shallow Dardanelles and Bosphorus have acted as often as isthmuses as straits during the course of the Pleistocene.

Most intriguing of all is the impact of lower sea level on islands. Particularly in the Aegean, Adriatic and central Mediterranean, many became joined to each other or the mainland, though the insular status of others, such as Cyprus and the Balearics, has not been compromised in recent geological time. Which islands were connected when depends on details that can be hard to pin down decisively, especially given the countering or exacerbating effects of vertical tectonic movement. A question mark therefore hangs over fine-grained reconstructions beyond roughly 100,000 years ago, and in a few cases even later. Sicily provides a cautionary tale.[25]

Today, the Messina strait dividing it from peninsular Italy is a minimum of just 3 km (2 miles) wide and 72 m (235 ft) in depth at its shallowest point. On the face of it, therefore, Sicily and mainland Italy should have fused under full glacial conditions. Yet this spot lies on a plate boundary and has already risen several metres over the last 150 years for which accurate measurements exist. Add a 127,000–71,000-year-old beach now elevated 90 m (300 ft) above the sea near the strait, and we might start to wonder whether Sicily was ever solidly attached to other land. The most likely solution, for reasons set out below, is that it fluctuated between genuine insularity and one compromised by stepping-stone islets and shallows.

Another way of investigating whether a given patch of land was once an island is by taking a look at its fossil terrestrial animals. In particular, the presence, absence and (given fluctuating sea levels) date of the strange island creatures introduced in the previous chapter allow an independent check. Again, Sicily illustrates the point.[26] Its earlier Pleistocene fossils display strong endemic traits indicative of a true island (or islands, given Sicily's multiple origins), but in the later Pleistocene, part of which broadly matches the date of the elevated beach just cited as evidence against a solid land-bridge, the faunal portfolio becomes merely imbalanced, with certain continental types present, but not others that are poor swimmers, such as ibex. Endemics equally betray the existence of former islands in unexpected places. Dwarf elephants and deer lived in southern Calabria perhaps as late as the last interglacial, while *Hoplitomeryx*, a weird five-horned creature, evolved and died out alongside giant owls on Monte Gargano, now the spur of the Italian boot, when it was still an island in the Adriatic.[27]

The first peoplings of the northern Mediterranean

The intermittent presence of hominins along the southern flanks of the Mediterranean well over a million years ago has been suggested above to be a by-product of changes in natural environments and hominin behaviours across the African continent. Africa's leading role in the generation of hominins over the immense period known there as the Early Stone Age (starting with the first tools and ending 250,000 years before the present), ensures that the same holds partly true for the lands around the northern side of the Mediterranean, where the equivalent period is known as the Lower Palaeolithic. The question as to when, where, how and how often these lands were frequented has been hotly debated between the partisans of longer and shorter chronologies.[28] It holds a special importance for us, because it determines the point at which a circum-Mediterranean theatre began to emerge.

There is widespread agreement that around 500,000 years ago, the visibility of archaeological sites increases dramatically in Mediterranean and temperate Europe, signalling the establishment of substantial, fairly permanent occupation. Assemblages of Acheulian tools with improved formal symmetry can be convincingly linked to the presence of *Homo heidelbergensis*, a new, larger-brained, probably more carnivorous archaic human, standing tall at an average 1.75 m (5 ft 9 in.) and weighing a muscular

90 kg (200 lbs) [**3.6**].[29] *Heidelbergensis* is considered on grounds of fossil evidence and analysis of its descendants' ancient DNA to be a common ancestor of both Neanderthals and ourselves. Its residues are commonly found beside ancient waterholes, good places for scavenging carcasses or finishing off a trapped animal. At Torralba in northern Spain, for instance, tools mingle with the bones of an extinct kind of elephant. Some sites lie close to ancient beaches, but there is no sign that the sea had become a source of food; rather, the attraction was probably more open coastal landscapes, abundant fresh water and therefore large animals, in contrast to an interior heavily wooded in warmer phases. A glimpse into one such place is offered by the damage on the tusks of elephants from their fighting during summer droughts around coastal lagoons near Rome some 334,000–301,000 years ago.[30] The complex, if expedient and still narrowly focused, engagements of *heidelbergensis* with the world are indicated by evidence of the transport of useful stones over 30 km (20 miles), controlled use of fire, application of stoneworking know-how to elephant bone, and the rare survival of wooden artifacts, notably untipped spears at Schöningen in Germany[31] (though, interestingly, fire and wooden items are attested markedly earlier in the Levant, at Gesher Benot Ya'aqov).[32] Larger brain size argues for bigger social groups and communication through simple language, an advance on the grooming-based social habits inferred for their predecessors. In effect, we are in the presence of early people.

Heidelbergensis emerged as a species roughly 600,000 years ago, although precisely where in Africa or western Eurasia is unknown. Its expansion within Europe took place during a warm interglacial window open some 528,000–478,000 years ago, and may have been quite rapid and smooth, to judge from the close parallels between skeletons and hand axes found north and south of the Mediterranean. Apart from their bigger brains, more flexible social systems and so greater adaptive capacity in the face tougher climatic times, further reasons behind the sustainability of this expansion may have been the reduction to eventual extinction of a daunting mix of large hyenas and sabre-toothed cats in Europe, whose carcass-destroying habits left slim pickings for scavenging humans, as well as improved weapons to fend such competitors off.

Until a few years ago, this horizon might have been taken to mark the genuine first arrival of people north of the Alps. But the Lower Palaeolithic is a fast-moving field. New finds in East Anglia push back the first arrivals in the British Isles to more than 780,000 years ago.[33] And in Mediterranean Europe long-contested clues pointing with variable reliability towards earlier occupancy have solidified into certainties at a few key sites. The most rigorously excavated is a giant honeycomb of sinkholes and caves at Atapuerca in northern Spain [PL. VI], where the evocatively named Aurora Bed, itself 860,000–790,000 years old, has now been trumped by the nearby Sima del

3.6 Skull of *Homo heidelbergensis* from Petralona in northern Greece, possibly already with some incipient Neanderthal traits.

Elephante, which boasts tools and hominin fossils dated to 1.1–1.2 million years ago, comparable to claims made on slighter grounds for finds in deep gullies near Orce in Andalusia.[34] In Italy several sites fall just shy of a million years in age, notably Monte Poggiolo on the edge of the Po plain, Ceprano near Rome, and possibly the scatter of tools and elephant, deer and bison bones at Isernia la Pineta in Molise.[35]

As the residue from over half a million years of presence, these early sites are still thin on the ground. Although in some regions, most plausibly Iberia, they could reflect the remnants of a slender continuum of occupation, most can be interpreted in a manner similar to early finds on the southern side of the Mediterranean, and in Asia, namely as the traces of sporadic cycles of expansion and contraction by groups on the margins of a core *ergaster* population. Further support for the latter hypothesis comes from good evidence for the absence of hominins in numerous rich fossil beds across Europe, and the skeletal remains at Atapuerca, which represent an isolated offshoot of *ergaster*, defined as *Homo antecessor*.[36] If this interpretation of the earliest data from Mediterranean Europe is right, both long and short chronologies are valid in different senses. The earliest presence does indeed date well before 500,000 years ago, but the surge in overall, sustained occupancy came long after.

From a Mediterranean perspective one of the most intriguing issues raised by the earliest horizons in southern Europe is the route by which hominins reached Iberia and peninsular Italy. There are two possibilities. The more parsimonious in terms of its implications for hominin abilities is that they expanded overland on the same long anticlockwise axis via the Levant that would be taken by several of their successors – this itself, of course, a cumulative outcome of countless minor extensions, rather than any conscious intent to settle the subcontinent. Given the tendency of the glacial cycles to periodically degrade parts of the narrow Levant to steppe and desert, even this option would not always have been straightforward, and we might expect a staccato pattern, with the Levant serially playing the role of conduit, filter and barrier. The alternative axis is a maritime frog-hop across the Mediterranean Sea at one of its narrow points, the implications of which would be manifest for our history.

Let us look first at the evidence from Europe itself. Unless an extremely early dispersal is envisaged (before 1.7 million years ago), the overland option is favoured by a peculiar paucity of hand axes at many of the earliest sites, which could indicate attenuated transmission over very long distances, and the consequent loss of this manufacturing tradition.[37] The appearance of new horse and caprine species alongside artifacts in Iberia is also suggestive, as neither are swimmers and thus bear witness to other overland expansions around this time. Ostensibly ranged against these points are the location of the earliest sites at the western end of Europe, and the lack of equally early intervening sites in Anatolia, the southern Balkans and the Aegean. Yet neither is quite what it seems. Iberia harboured an atypical suite of carnivores whose habits left substantial carcasses; the focus there may reflect greater success at maintaining a scavenging foothold, thereby increasing visibility for us today but creating an optical illusion as far as arrival route is concerned.[38] In much the same way, the fact that the earliest lion bones in Europe derive from Pakefield in Suffolk is somewhat unlikely to identify an actual point of entry.[39] Moreover, the lack of intervening sites may simply reflect a lack of prospection until the last few years.[40] Fresh discoveries at Dursunlu and Kaletepe are in fact pushing the earliest known traces in Anatolia back to 1 million–800,000 years ago, double the previous age of the first finds. Sites older than a million years are surely now extremely likely in this part of the world.

The maritime alternative only enters the picture if some form of sea crossing was feasible at such an early date.[41] Here, we need to tread a delicate path between a 'temporal chauvinism'[42] that denies this possibility before the emergence of modern humans, and a credulity that abandons critical faculties in the face of the first scrap of purported evidence. As explained in Chapter 1, theories of early trans-Mediterranean movement initially arose over a century ago in the first flush of colonial archaeology, based on apparent similarities between tools on either side of the sea, coupled with an enthusiasm for antediluvian land-bridges. Since the 1920s, these notions have been eroded by the refinement of synchronisms, awareness of the potential for independent convergence on similar solutions for making tools (which might explain, for example, similarities between late Acheulian 'cleavers' in Iberia and Africa), a realization that the Gibraltar strait and Sicilian channel have remained open throughout the last few million years, and fossil testimony that the Pleistocene sea was an effective barrier for most land animals. However, the maritime option has recently returned to tentative favour in the minds of some Palaeolithic experts.[43] In Mediterranean terms this is in part due to those Iberian sites located suggestively (if not, as discussed, necessarily significantly) near the shortest crossing from Africa, in part to the confirmed sporadic presence on the southern shore, and in part, as we shall see, to several claims from the Mediterranean islands. But this revival equally owes much to a potential analogy from the again surprise-springing Indonesian island of Flores, where stone tool discoveries seem to imply that 800,000 years ago hominins crossed 20–30 km (12–20 miles) of sea between Bali (then joined to Java and thence mainland Asia) and Lombok (attached to other islands extending eastward to Flores).[44] The persistence of a water-gap here gains some credibility despite the great age of the finds and location on an active fault because it lies athwart Wallace's Line, a biogeographical barrier that for millions of years has blocked the expansion of Asian animals towards Australia, even swimmers as proficient as deer. Apart from hominins, only elephant-like stegadonts, komodos and giant tortoises among the larger land animals have crossed it by their own efforts.

In the light of the Floresian phenomenon, plus the obvious point that overall hominin expansion must have included crossing broad rivers, it would be foolish to deny categorically the possibility that some hominins dispersed into southern Europe by sea. Given the first Iberian dates, this could potentially have occurred even earlier than in island Southeast Asia. But how compelling is this scenario? The most likely crossing is at the Gibraltar strait, which, as one Palaeolithic archaeologist wryly puts it, is 'crossed continuously nowadays by windsurfers from Spain and illegal immigrants from Morocco'.[45] Under the severest Pleistocene conditions the strait shrunk from its present 14 km (9 miles) to two 5-km (3-mile) hops between midway islands, and the currents slackened.[46] However, there are objections to this intriguing possibility. First, save for aquatic hippopotami, there is little sign in the fossil record of other animal transfers after the Messinian land-bridge was submerged.[47] Second, as will become apparent, strong negative evidence from later periods suggests that even more sophisticated early people did not make the crossing to any noticeable degree; indeed the first undeniable evidence dates to the very end of the Pleistocene. Without finds of stone tools made of materials only available on the other side, or parallel technologies not explicable by convergence of ideas, the Gibraltar option hovers short of confirmation or refutation.[48] The possibility in the broader Sicilian channel, though, can be confidently rejected. Sicily is devoid of clear anthropogenic material until 40,000–35,000 years ago, when, as we will discuss in Chapter 4, its affinities lie with Europe, while its idiosyncratic earlier fauna imply isolation from predators, and the dates of early sites in peninsular Italy tend to point to an expansion from north to south.[49]

This leaves the purported evidence for sea crossings to other Mediterranean islands. Most candidates were either in fact not insular at the time, for instance Capri was attached to peninsular Italy when Acheulian tools were left there, or rely upon evidence whose nature and date is questionable, and at worst (for example on Cyprus and Sardinia) rejected by expert opinion.[50] The most recent claims come from Crete, where a fanfare of publicity has announced the finding of artifacts claimed to be at least 107,000–130,000 years old on the basis of their redeposited geological context and several times more ancient on grounds of technological parallels, although some caution is required given the lack of securely dated contexts and battered nature of the finds.[51] Sea-crossing distances to Crete over much of the last half million years seem to have been much shorter than at present and, interestingly, in contrast to Crete's earlier dwarf hippopotami and mammoths, by 150,000–100,000 years ago fossils of normal-sized elephants and mice, as well as several varieties of deer, show that endemism was declining.[52] Potentially, the latter could reflect shoreline changes that eased access for all comers, including hominins, or the ghostly presence of a (hominin?) predator, either way at a comparatively late date.

Even if we acknowledge the possibility of a few freak crossings over the more than 1 million years during which hominins lived round a shifting mosaic of windy coasts, the ultimately important question is what wider conclusions should, or should not, derive from this. We have already cast doubt on significant early population transfers out of Africa by sea. Similarly, it is entirely unwarranted to regard any such events as marking the birth of a true seagoing tradition, or equally as indices of precocious cognitive sophistication. In the case of Flores, the presence of Wallace's Line implies that options open to other animals, such as unassisted drifting on one of the tropics' natural vegetation rafts, should not alone have sufficed to effect a successful transfer. In situ experiments, however, have shown that rudimentary paddled manipulation of a floating platform made all the difference.[53] The basic requirement was only the slightest modification of nature's sweepstakes – minimally culturally enhanced floating – plus a good run of luck for a few people, set against potentially huge numbers of fatal failures. In the Mediterranean, vegetation rafts are unlikely (another impediment to animal crossings), but the shortest necessary crossing distances to places such as Crete are quite small enough to fall within range of assisted drifting, and the degree of intentionality could have been equivalently modest. The wider implication seems to be that if a few hominins did make such island landfalls, they had arrived at what constituted for them a cul-de-sac rather than a stepping stone across the sea.

Two species both alike in dignity

If even the Strait of Gibraltar acted more as a barrier than a bridge, we must imagine a Mediterranean that in terms of connections for hominins and their successors worked very differently from that familiar to us. The northwest Maghreb and southern Spain were not all but touching neighbours, but effectively as distant apart as either is from China or California. The role of the sea as a separator of early circum-Mediterranean populations (in reality a more enduring one than the Sahara), is driven home by the separate evolutionary paths witnessed to its north and south over most of the half a million years after the first appearance of *heidelbergensis* in Europe.[54] In time the differences became so entrenched that when the end products finally overlapped and met in Europe less than 45,000 years ago, as Neanderthals and our direct ancestors, modern *Homo sapiens*, they present a strange reality: human beings of what can be considered, in effect, to be two different species.[55] The proof of divergence comes partly from their skeletons, but the clinching case is made by mitochondrial DNA, which reveals that these northern and southern Mediterranean populations last shared an ancestor between 700,000 and 400,000 years ago, and that subsequent segregation allowed genetic differences to accumulate. In biological terms this makes for a straightforward case of allopatric speciation, the process by which new species arise from genetic shifts after expansion and separation from the region inhabited by their common ancestor. This has no parallel among people alive today, as it needs vastly more isolated generations to take effect; in the case of the twin descendants of *heidelbergensis*, the elapsed time is at least ten times that since the final modern human exodus from Africa. That the Mediterranean Sea enabled such evolutionary divergence to take place is a powerful testimony to the severity and duration of the sea's role as an obstacle for early people.

On the northern side of the Mediterranean, the physical 'Neanderthalization' of *heidelbergensis* people can be plotted through skeletal evidence and DNA.[56] In part of the Atapuerca cave complex known as the Sima de los Huesos ('Pit of the Bones'), the remains of at least thirty-two men, women and children lie crammed at the base of a narrow shaft, into which their corpses had been thrown, probably for reasons of hygiene and discouragement of carnivores rather than early ritual [3.7]. Over 500,000 years old, they already display a few incipient Neanderthal traits. From Altamura in southeast Italy comes another skeleton, of a man who fell 8 m (26 ft)

3.7 Members of the Atapuerca team with the rich finds of hominin skeletons from the Sima de los Huesos, or 'Pit of the Bones'.

into a cave mouth and groped his way into its depths before he died.[57] DNA analysis indicates that the Neanderthal genome was largely complete by 230,000 years ago, and skeletons displaying full Neanderthal traits appear by 150,000 years ago. Physical changes continued towards what are usually considered the 'classic' thickset, muscular and broad-nosed Neanderthals of 70,000 years ago onward, though in fact this simply denotes a late stage in an evolutionary continuum subsequently cut short by extinction.

Switching to the southern side of the Mediterranean, a parallel process was at work over much of Africa.[58] Archaic versions of *Homo sapiens* appeared by 300,000–250,000 years ago, and anatomically modern humans by 200,000–160,000 years ago; evidence from mitochondrial DNA indicates that most key genetic characteristics had coalesced by around 200,000 years ago, with a bottleneck moment at some point around this time, during which the global population of modern humans collapsed to a few thousand. The southern flank of the Mediterranean played a part in this evolution, if somewhat on the periphery, to judge by the later dates for a surprisingly rich suite of fossils.[59] Those from Salé and Kebibat in Morocco date to between 450,000 and 250,000 years ago and still belong to *heidelbergensis*, if with possible *sapiens* traits. More substantially *sapiens* is another Moroccan find from Jebel Irhoud, about 160,000 years old, while definitely anatomically modern are a skeleton 70,000 years old from Dar es Sultan, a similarly dated child buried facing the sky at Taramsa in Egypt and maybe somewhat older mandibles from Haua Fteah in Libya [**1.14**]. Most intriguingly, anatomically modern people not dissimilar to the Irhoud individual were also buried in the Skhul and Qafzeh caves in Israel between 130,000 and 80,000 years ago.[60] Presumably, the warm conditions of the last interglacial and its aftermath had again turned the southern Levant into a little tongue of Africa, encouraging such people to extend their range. Whether these intruders moved into a vacuum, or lived side-by-side with whatever kind of humans lie behind the preceding stone tools, is impossible to determine, but as so often in the Levant the moment was transitory, for these anatomically modern humans disappeared again from the region as the climate deteriorated, only returning less than 50,000 years ago in a very different guise. In the interim, Neanderthals filtered in from the north. This multiple turnover of occupancy, with or without overlaps, speaks volumes about the fragility of life for all early humans in this slender strip as the climate altered.

There are striking similarities between the two kinds of humans coming into being around the perimeter of the Mediterranean.[61] Some of the physical distinctions can be overplayed, and simply reflect climate-selected traits. Thus the Neanderthals' large sinuses took the edge off freezing, dry air, whereas the gracile figures of modern humans were a response to hotter climes. Skin colour presumably differed, too, with the eventual modern human expansion into Europe bringing initially dark southerners into contact with apparently pale, ginger-haired Neanderthals. More significantly, on both sides of the sea the size difference between the sexes became less pronounced, a sure sign of growing cooperation between them.

At the deeper level of behaviour the parallels for a long time at least matched the differences. Brain size increased to modern levels all around the Mediterranean by 200,000 years ago; indeed Neanderthal crania were slightly larger, though we cannot vouch for the mental links within. Developments in tools display comparable trends, starting with the replacement of hand axes by flake-based 'Mousterian' traditions that denote the start of the African Middle Stone Age and the equivalent Levantine and European Middle Palaeolithics around 250,000 years ago. This did not imply long-distance contacts or movements around the basin, but a convergence on similar technological solutions in different kinds of human mind. The Levallois technique, which struck flakes from preformed cores, was employed on both sides of the sea and indicates deeper learning and more anticipation than anything witnessed before. Composite spears with hafted stone points, and the first blade-like tools, were more common among moderns but also made by Neanderthals. The latter's composite spears are mainly a feature of the Levant, where, exceptionally, they may hint at an

3.8 Fragment of a Middle Palaeolithic stone point embedded in the neck bone of a wild ass at Umm el Tlel, where other examples retain traces of the bitumen adhesive that once mounted them to wooden spears.

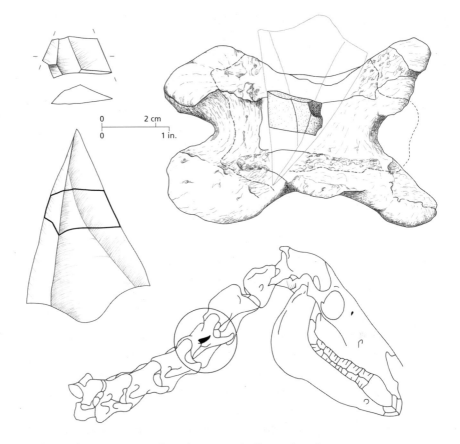

overlap and interaction with early anatomically modern humans; some were even bonded with bitumen. One such was found impaled in a wild ass's neck-bone at Umm el Tlel in Syria [**3.8**],[62] and by this time preferential hunting of large, prime-age game (an unusual carnivore tactic) is in fact visible in the animal bones from archaeological sites all over the basin. Hunting was cooperatively executed, with forward planning evident in butchery that selected certain body parts for transport and later consumption, while scraping tools indicate that skins were processed and put to use.[63] Gradually, the fires to which meat had long been brought to soften it for eating became formalized into hearths where concepts of food sharing and other socializing forms of behaviour took shape.[64] All round the basin the endurance of such ways of doing things for over 100,000 years does not demonstrate torpid brains so much as the sheer success of this low-density lifestyle for small groups of hunters.[65]

The principal distinction between the two species lay in the greater propensity for symbolic expression among early modern humans – although even this domain admits some common ground. Both Neanderthals and anatomically modern humans used pigments as ephemeral forms of decoration, mainly red ochres, and both sometimes deliberately buried their dead, the former occasionally at times and in places that exclude any possibility of learning via the latter.[66] The biological affinity of the person who made deliberate cuts across a tiny pebble at Berekhat Ram in Israel 280,000–250,000 years ago, in order to increase its resemblance to a woman, is unknown.[67] But the incidence of more complex symbolism begins to accumulate differentially in areas occupied by anatomically modern people. The best evidence comes from the furthest tip of Africa, at Blombos Cave on the southern Cape coast, where carved designs on lumps of ochre as well as ornaments made from seashells date back over 70,000 years.[68] But contributions come from the true Mediterranean too: the burials at Skhul and Qafzeh differed from Neanderthal interments in their formalization and inclusion of fallow deer antlers, a wild boar's jaw and seashells. Such shells, pierced and ochre-stained, appeared at Taforalt Cave (also known as the Grotte des Pigeons) in Morocco 82,000 years ago, 40 km (25 miles) from the coast; one at Oued Djebbana in Algeria had even been transported 200 km (125 miles) inland.[69] Exactly what weight to place on these durable yet elliptical hints of symbolism, ritual and bodily ornament is hard to gauge, and behind this imponderable lies a further one concerning language.[70] Both kinds of human certainly spoke, but there is no agreement as to the comparative complexity of syntax and expression. Early modern humans probably did differ from Neanderthals in terms of symbolic and affective thought, and its reification in art and speech, but how significantly we shall probably never know.

That in many respects very similar trajectories should be witnessed among the separated offspring of *heidelbergensis* is not surprising, given a common ancestry and the comparable experience of Pleistocene climatic turbulence and its consequences for environments on both sides of the Mediterranean. Both kinds of people expanded and contracted their ranges, endured, evolved and learned, or locally failed to do so and died out, through several major glacial-interglacial cycles and, just as importantly, the innumerable shorter fluctuations that selected for flexible minds that could respond to, and effectively exploit, the potential of shifting surroundings. We shall spend most of the remainder of this chapter among the Mediterranean Neanderthals, whose lives are richly illuminated by a huge amount of archaeological research. But first, what more can be said of contemporary developments on the African side of the basin?

In North Africa the state of the Sahara was, as ever, the critical factor.[71] A long glacial from about 300,000 to 250,000 years ago swept the Sahara and probably also Mediterranean Africa of people, which explains why there is no trace of the transition from the Early to Middle Stone Age throughout this great region. This transition was effected further south, and when people returned during the next warming they were probably already anatomically close to modern, and certainly using the new range of tools. Among their sites, one represents a limit of expansion, the newly investigated Benzú rockshelter near Ceuta, opposite Gibraltar.[72] Interestingly, when drier times returned, these groups held out for a while even in the Fezzan area of the central Sahara, maybe because the transition back to desert was gradual, but perhaps also because their adaptive abilities were slightly better honed. Eventually the desert won once again, but the pattern of human return and resilience is yet more impressive in the last interglacial, the wettest period attested in the Sahara over the last 350,000 years, and especially in its immediate aftermath.

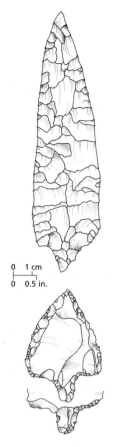

0   1 cm
0   0.5 in.

3.9 Tanged Aterian points, some probably for attachment to missile weapons, from sites in North Africa.

This time the distinguishing trait is a suite of tools known as Aterian, after the Algerian site of Bir el Ater.[73] This added small projectile tips with attachment tangs to the standard earlier Middle Stone Age toolkit, creating light missile weapons ideal for bringing down fast game like gazelle in open landscapes with little cover for stalking [**3.9**]. The Aterian seems to have emerged out of a movement into Nubia and the eastern Sahara during the last interglacial that was itself unusual because its associated tool types remained distinguishable from the products of the pre-existing inhabitants (though new dates suggest that tanged points occur slightly earlier in the Maghreb).[74] The Aterian heyday began over 80,000 years ago and continued for more than 20,000 years, as this complex dispersed across the slowly drying Sahara, the Maghreb (but notably never beyond, into Iberia), the Jebel el Gharbi south of Tripoli, and perhaps Cyrenaica, where enigmatic early levels at Haua Fteah contain blades, possibly reflecting the arrival of modern humans, with Aterian traces in the overlying levels. This innovative Aterian is an arresting development in one further respect. Its location athwart the approaches to the exit from Africa in the millennia preceding the expansion of modern humans across the globe, as well as the previously noted association with symbolic shell ornaments, give its makers a fair chance of being some of our direct forebears.

The end of this North African world was brought on by a double blow some 70,000–74,000 years ago, in the form of the onset of a new glacial phase (MIS 4, the penultimate in the planet's history to date), on top of which was mapped a nuclear winter triggered by a cataclysmic eruption of the Toba supervolcano, which sent 1000 cu. km (240 cu. miles) of Indonesia into the atmosphere.[75] This double setback may have been responsible for a further bottleneck in human demography, and the temporary eclipse of evidence for symbolic behaviour in Africa.[76] It probably brought about the end, too, of the first incursion of modern humans in the Levant. Certainly, by 60,000 years ago, after a period of shifting efforts to avoid the worst conditions, the Sahara was once again a vast, empty swathe of aridity, as it would remain for almost 50,000 years. People using Aterian toolkits were cut off in the Maghreb. There they hung on, but for how long, and whether any thread of continuity into more recent times can be traced there, or in the smaller habitat islands of the Jebel el Gharbi and Cyrenaica, is questionable. We will pick up this strange trail again after 50,000 years ago in Chapter 4, but we would do well to linger for a little longer on the further side of this temporal divide, and north of the marine one formed by the sea.

Neanderthals in the sun?

What of the Mediterranean Neanderthals? We can begin by admitting the randomness of the name given to the Middle Palaeolithic inhabitants of Europe, which goes back to a fossil find in 1856 from the Neander Valley in Germany.[77] In combination with the cold-combating features of Neanderthal physiognomy, the choice of name creates an image of these people as hardy northerners adapted to harsh conditions beyond the Alps. Yet this impression is misleading. Even the priority of discovery is illusory, for a Neanderthal skull had in fact already been unearthed at Gibraltar in 1848. Unfortunately, Europe had other matters on its mind in 1848, a year of revolutions in politics rather than human origins, and the fossil languished until the chance to claim the species as *gibraltarensis* was irretrievably lost. Concerning adaptation to cold, while features like wide sinuses show that the Neanderthals underwent evolutionary selection and probable bottlenecks during glacial phases (a likelihood supported by new research on the Neanderthal genome),[78] it is more accurate to think of them as periodically and perforce cold-enduring, rather than cold-loving, people. Their distributions tended to shift southward towards the Mediterranean and Black Sea at each glacial advance, and many of those who could not escape from truly harsh tundra conditions surely reached the limits to their capacity to adapt and so died out, time and again.[79]

In addition to open Neanderthal locations, cave sites become common for the first time, whether due to better survival as we approach the present, or more skilful use of fire to clear hyena dens and eject the huge, vegetarian cave bears hibernating in their depths. Krapina Cave in Croatia, well excavated for its time back in 1899–1905, still provides our largest group of skeletons.[80] Neanderthal sites continue to be found in profusion. There is a sharp rise in numbers in the basin, especially in the east, after 65,000 years ago, thanks to the penultimate glaciation and its aftermath.[81] But the Mediterranean story is not simply one of periodic inflows by northern refugees. Southern Neanderthals are attested well before 100,000 years ago, in balmy interglacial landscapes. Coastal and lakeside areas blessed with milder maritime climates, plenty of fresh water, a range of foods and easy connections along the shore display lengthy, intensive occupation, notably in the long-known haunts of Iberia, southern France and Dalmatia, as well as more recently explored parts of the Neanderthal world in Italy, the Aegean and the Black Sea.[82] To this we can now add the startling fact of Neanderthals in the Levant.[83] Neanderthal skeletons 60,000–50,000 years old come from Kebara Cave in the Carmel ridge [**3.10**]. These Neanderthals moved south to avoid the cold of Anatolia or western Russia in the penultimate glacial, perhaps as early anatomically modern humans were vacating the Levant. What are presumably their tools (though, interestingly, they are in effect indistinguishable from those of the previous inhabitants belonging to another species) extend all over the Levant as far as the edge of the Negev and the Gulf of Aqaba, defining a range limit at the very threshold of Africa. Altogether, we might hazard a guess that Neanderthals lived in greater numbers and more continuously in the Mediterranean basin than in any other part of their range. We have already seen that in evolutionary terms Neanderthals are unthinkable without the existence of the Mediterranean Sea as a barrier, and can now affirm that some of the basin's land also formed an enduring home. As will transpire, Neanderthals were among the first to eat the sea's products and possibly to travel over its surface; the next chapter reveals that the last of them died on its shores. From its evolutionary beginnings to its final whimper, the history of the Neanderthals, people in many ways our haunting, ultimate 'other',[84] is a tale with profoundly Mediterranean twists.

3.10 Kebara Cave, set in the rugged limestone escarpment of the Carmel ridge, where Neanderthals once roamed 60,000–50,000 years ago.

To understand how Neanderthal lives meshed with the world around them, we need to take a closer look at environmental developments as the exceptionally lush penultimate interglacial receded. We can do so with startling accuracy, thanks to the finer-grained picture created as local pollen cores come into play to augment oceanic and ice-cap data (for example, within the 102,000 years of the Italian Lake Monticchio core, vegetation shifts over time spans as short as a couple of centuries can be discerned).[85] The MIS 4 glacial (71,000–58,000 years ago), whose start was exacerbated by Toba's eruption, has already been introduced in the context of its hand in the demise of the Saharan Aterian. Further north, Mediterranean Neanderthals rode it out with marked success. In fact, much more challenging were the ensuing wild fluctuations (within a middling range) during an exceptionally climatically jagged MIS 3 (58,000–24,000), a phase that has been the focus of impressively detailed environmental reconstruction.[86] A complex mosaic of ecologies coexisted in the basin, whose patterning altered with shifts in temperature and rainfall. During milder phases, the Levant was covered with a temperate grassy steppe dotted with trees. Chillier steppe extended over Iberia save for a strip of grassland with stands of pine and oak along the southern coast; grassland and cool forest predominated in northern Italy and southern France, with deciduous woods in those parts of southern Italy and the Aegean not claimed by steppe. During the harsher phases, grassland, steppe and tundra expanded everywhere, but retreating trees held out in pockets, buffered against annihilation by the sea's ameliorating effect and the wealth of hideaways afforded by folds in the land. A particularly sharp image emerges from the environs of Gibraltar [PL. VII], a protected coastal niche in the south, whose pattern can be extrapolated along the Malaga coast.[87] Here a patchwork of savannah, wetland, matorral and scrub endured, studded with oak, pine, juniper and olive, and supported a wide range of land animals as well as 145 varieties of bird. Such windows warn us that we should expect considerable diversity within each environmental zone.

Climate fluctuations also brought changes in the animals available for hunting, with colder phases often creating ideal open conditions for grazing herds, and warmer ones (as well as more buffered refugia) patchier landscapes, with multiple ecological zones and diverse resources in close proximity. Even at the glacial maxima true arctic fauna such as reindeer, saiga antelopes, mammoths, woolly rhinoceroses and arctic foxes penetrated no further into the basin than the Iberian Meseta, southern France, northern Italy and Croatia.[88] A more significant long-term impact of climate fluctuations was the cumulative winnowing of Mediterranean Europe's more exotic earlier Pleistocene animals, and the promotion of increasingly familiar ones, save on certain islands where archaic endemics survived until much later. This process was a drawn-out one, thanks to the number of refuges, and extinctions probably came about more from the demographic collapse of small populations than total eradication of suitable environments. Peninsular Italy is a well-studied example, and a striking one because its north–south alignment allowed mammoths and bison to wander the Po steppes while the last elephants, rhinoceroses and fallow deer shared southern Apulia with horses, ibexes and others.[89] By 250,000 years ago monkeys had vanished from Italy, and 150,000 years later hippopotami, the most temperature-sensitive of the pachyderms, were on the brink, though pockets of elephants and rhinoceroses held out, as in Iberia, into MIS 3 (elephants survived longer on the eastern and southern flanks of the basin, in Syria until their final slaughter by Assyrian hunters in the early 1st millennium BC, and in Morocco until less than 1000 years ago). The last lions roamed Tuscany at the start of the Holocene, and a few residual hyenas haunted Salento's first Neolithic. Apart from these dwindling species, the animals that lived alongside Mediterranean Neanderthals are mostly still known in the basin today, albeit with altered ranges or in domesticated form: red and roe deer, boars, aurochs, horses (plus their extinct cousin the steppe ass), ibexes, chamoix, rabbits, hares and, for predators, wolves, brown bears and red foxes. Two were especially important. Red deer proved the supreme adapters of the later Pleistocene and beyond, happy to form large herds in the grassland, tundra and steppe, or to disperse in open woodland. Ibexes colonized craggy open spaces and even sea cliffs, their descendants in Europe's mountains today being the meagre remnant of a once physically larger and much more widespread species.

Mediterranean Neanderthals therefore inhabited a different world from those in the 'mammoth steppe'[90] and coniferous woods north of the Alps. As Neanderthal sites appear to display slight regional variations in terms of technologies and other ways of doing things, it is interesting to ask whether any recognizably Mediterranean practices can be detected among them. In most respects Mediterranean Neanderthals were unexceptional. They were relatively thin on the ground, and therefore as prone to local crashes as any other predator at the apex of the food chain. Estimates for the entire, neatly defined Levantine arena envisage a population of below a thousand, and one recent genetic study even concludes that the total west Eurasian pool of breeding-age Neanderthal women may have been as low as 3500.[91] Nowhere did the animals they preyed on, even the most vulnerable species, exhibit signs of over-kill.[92] Like all Neanderthals, they led hard, brief lives and enjoyed social interactions of uncertain cognitive depth.[93] They made hearths, carried their tools with them, were attracted to pigments, occasionally buried each other deliberately, if without demonstrable burial goods, from France to Israel, and fashioned artifacts in antler, bone, shell and wood as well as stone; the fourth rarely survives but there are sug-gestive fragments at Abric Romaní in Catalonia.[94] Social worlds were fairly small and territories often extremely localized. Neanderthals in the Grotte Vaufrey, south of the Dordogne, found most of what they needed within a day or so's walk; those living in the caves of the Ligurian coast obtained most stones nearby, with only a few choice flints coming from longer distances, and the local stones' properties resulted in different working techniques at each site.[95] Up on the Anatolian plateau, obsidian was used near to its sources, but seldom travelled far, while at Kalamakia on the Mani peninsula Neanderthals knapped *lapis lacedaemonius*, a hard, speckled green andesite from a unique source just 30 km (19 miles) to the north (later used for Minoan seals and in medieval mosaics from Constantinople and Palermo to Santiago de Compostela).[96]

Although not above occasional scavenging, like all Neanderthals, those in the Mediterranean were impressive big-game hunters, targeting prime specimens even of aurochs that stood 2 m (6 ft 6 in.) at the shoulder.[97] Where possible, they concentrated on one or two particularly rewarding species. From their massive musculature and handheld weapons, we can deduce that their killing style involved short-range ambushes from cover, probably cooperative and involving both sexes, a highly effective if dangerous technique. The fairly static habits, or short, vertical migrations, of most Mediterranean animals encouraged the localization of south-ern Neanderthals' lives, a tendency that deepened in food-rich niches like those in the Carmel range in Israel and the caverns running along the base of the ibex-tra-versed Rock of Gibraltar, where Neanderthals congregated in unusual numbers for much of the year.[98] But elsewhere, ranges may have been stretched by Mediterranean seasonality and the different foods available at a distance.[99] In the drier far south of the Levant, Neanderthals seem to have alternated seasonally between upland and lowland, and in the Pyrenees, Alps and Apennines tools found at higher altitudes than in earlier times may reveal similar practices. Mujina Pećina Cave near Trogir in Croatia provides a well-focused picture; in the spring and autumn Neanderthals hunted bison, aurochs, deer, ibexes and chamois from this base, but over the summer and winter they abandoned it to the cave bears and moved elsewhere, in all probability down to the now-drowned coast.[100]

But the most significant distinction between the Mediterranean Neanderthals and their northern contemporaries is the extent to which they supplemented hunting and scavenging with a spectrum of gathered foods. Northern Neanderthal diets were almost entirely carnivorous, for lack of alternatives, and in common with high-latitude hunter-gatherers to this day. But although isotopic analyses of Neanderthal skeletons confirm a meat-dominated diet in the Mediterranean too, several of their sites extend the picture.[101] Botanical remains prove that as a supplement, maybe to tide over hard times, Neanderthals at Kebara Cave also ate wild peas, pistachios, acorns and possibly grasses (if these were not introduced as bedding); at Gorham's Cave at Gibraltar they consumed pine nuts, gathered from stone pines dotting the landscape around the base of the Rock.[102] Tortoises were a favourite at both sites, and people from Kebara stole ostrich eggs. These omnivorous facets of southern Neanderthal diet admittedly pale in terms of range and relative importance beside those of later hunters and gatherers in the Mediterranean, and more challenging prey was mostly spurned in favour of lethargic or immobile targets.[103] Nonetheless, a growing awareness of the spectrum of foods that Mediterranean environments might yield is apparent.

Mediterranean Neanderthals extended this gathering to include seashores and estuaries. Marine shells found in still earlier cave deposits in southwest France probably arrived in seaweed gathered, perhaps like the grasses at Kebara, for bedding, or were brought by birds. But the big, juicy mussels deposited by a hearth of lentisk and juniper wood in the Vanguard Cave at Gibraltar, some 49,000–45,000 years ago, had manifestly been picked out and carried from a former estuary that lay 3–4 km (2–2.5 miles) away when the sea was lower, heated over the flames and eaten [3.11].[104] A child's burnt, shell-rich faeces preserve the aftermath. Lower strata at Vanguard, almost 100,000 years old, yield shell fragments too, as do other sites in the Bay of Malaga, and round the coast of France to southern Italy, mainly in the form of food debris but sometimes converted into scraping tools.[105] Larger coastal denizens appear as well: monk seal bones with butchery cuts at Vanguard and Grotta di Sant'Agostino in Latium, as well as dolphin from Gibraltar.[106] Neanderthals displayed less interest, however, in fish. A few flatfish bones are known from the Middle Palaeolithic levels at Grotta Romanelli in Italy and Iberian coastal sites; if not transported by roosting birds, as is quite likely, they could imply occasional spearing in shallow, estuarine water.[107]

Overall, the restriction of seafood consumption to Neanderthals living near the coast, and to slow or immobile shoreline species plus presumably stranded windfalls, argues for expedient exploitation when circumstances favoured or necessity impelled it, rather than a thorough embrace of marine lifestyles. This pattern finds parallels in broadly contemporary sites associated with anatomically modern humans in southern Africa, which yield shells and sea mammals. But a noticeable difference is the regular evidence for fishing, including deep-water species at Blombos Cave and, at

Katanda in the Congo, the world's oldest harpoons.[108] The coasts of Mediterranean Africa and Atlantic Morocco, which were occupied by modern humans rather than Neanderthals, also produce signs of fishing, as well as consumption of shellfish and sea mammals, in particular at Mugharet el 'Aliya in Morocco and Haua Fteah. We return to this in the following chapter.

In the meantime, the obvious question is whether any of these strand-walking Mediterranean Neanderthals went a stage further and travelled across the sea. To put this in perspective, the modern humans soon to expand again out of Africa on their path to global hegemony certainly would possess this capacity. Such abilities are commonly assumed to be the exclusive property of modern humans, and raise questions of cognitive sophistication and the skills needed to build reliable craft, plan maritime ventures and navigate.[109] As in the case of the Lower Palaeolithic, the arguments for and against Neanderthal seafaring are bedevilled by poor data and contentious claims. In itself, some of this obscurity argues against the likelihood. For example, not a single definite Middle Palaeolithic find is known from Sicily, Sardinia or Corsica, whose combined area is a fifth that of mainland Italy, which has hundreds of uncontroversial sites.[110] All these big Mediterranean islands had enough resources to allow long-term habitation, but appear to have lain empty. The lack of contact between Neanderthals in Iberia and early modern humans in the Maghreb is equally suggestive, and on both accounts. There are, however, tantalizing hints that a

3.11 Conjectural reconstruction of a group of Mediterranean Neanderthals at Gibraltar. Note the documented consumption of mussels and tortoises.

few Mediterranean Neanderthals may have undertaken short movements across the sea. Middle Palaeolithic tools from several Greek islands are reasonably documented, if still not scientifically dated. The best case is Kefalonia, opposite the southern end of a long mainland coast running south from Dalmatia that has abundant evidence for Neanderthal presence.[111] Other now insular find-spots off this coast were probably then joined to the mainland, including Corfu and Lefkada and the site of Veli Rat on Dugi in the Adriatic,[112] but sea depths and an up-thrusting major fault argue that Kefalonia was always cut off by a few kilometres (or at least a mile) of sea. In the Aegean, near another Neanderthal hotspot in Thessaly, there are plausible finds on the northern Sporades, but more surprising are reports of tools on Melos (not made from obsidian), for this island was never divided by less than 10 km (6 miles) from the rest of the Cyclades, many of which merged at lower sea levels.[113] The chronology is frustratingly open, but later dates within the Middle Palaeolithic would make the best sense in terms of lower seas and increasing activity on adjacent mainlands as glacial conditions intensified.

If (and that qualification should be firmly retained for the present) the island Middle Palaeolithic sites are genuine, and if Neanderthals made the tools (the alternative of otherwise invisible early modern humans is a long stretch), then at least a few such people must have developed limited water-crossing abilities. Use of tree trunks and crude paddles lay within Neanderthals' woodworking skills, to judge from the remains of trunks, flattened planks and fashioned sticks among the finds at Abric Romaní.[114] The fact that all the islands concerned are modest in size would favour brief visits, maybe in response to shifts in local environments and demography, rather than permanent residence. Equally striking is the emphasis on the Greek archipelago, an area whose intricate configuration we drew attention to in Chapter 2, and whose role as a focus of nascent seafaring will be further affirmed in Chapter 5. As with the breadth of foods at Mediterranean Neanderthal sites, such potential relics of short-range seagoing may imply that the basin had begun to fashion behaviour and encourage certain kinds of innovation, despite vast differences between its Pleistocene and later environments. In this narrow sense, Mediterranean societies could have started to come into being from a very early date, and outside our own species.

CHAPTER FOUR

A cold coming we had of it

(50,000 years ago – 10,000 BC)

The modernization of the Mediterranean

Some 50,000 years ago, the Mediterranean was shared by two kinds of humans, the Neanderthals and anatomically modern *Homo sapiens*, who divided it at Gibraltar and Sinai. Over the ensuing few thousand years the latter expanded into the Levant and then Europe.[1] By happy coincidence this diaspora unfolded over a period that now falls within the range of calibrated radiocarbon dates. This greatly sharpens our chronological resolution and enables dates to be given in ranges of years 'BC', in accord with the remainder of this book – if spanning still mind-boggling durations compared to later history.[2] This Upper Palaeolithic expansion is plotted by toolkits of finer blades, distinctive scrapers, carving burins and greater use of bone, as well as a crescendo of symbolic and artistic activity, and was part of the process by which they (or rather *we*, as these people were in their essentials like us, in brain as well as body) spread across Eurasia, on the path towards global saturation. In Europe these people are often called Cro-Magnons, after the southern French rockshelter where their bones were first found, but this term expropriates a phenomenon of utterly non-European origin, and we shall refer to them simply as 'moderns' for as long as others remained in the Mediterranean from whom they need to be distinguished.

When and where our minds attained their present structure, and in particular the capacity for expressive, symbolic and creative thought, is one of the grail quests of human evolution. Until recently, the most popular hypothesis proposed an abrupt, genetic mutation or neural rewiring of the brain among one subset of anatomically modern humans around 50,000 years ago.[3] As the location of this cerebral revolution would not be detectable in skull shape, and because it also proved peculiarly hard to identify via immediately visible cultural fireworks, this theory's supporters had ample scope for speculation. One favourite arena was the old evolutionary engine of East Africa, but others implicated areas further up the Great Rift Valley, in the continent's northeast, or even that ancient corridor, pressure point between the desert and sea, and home to early symbolism, the Levant itself.[4] For a glorious interpretative moment, this small Mediterranean fragment became a contender for the cradle of the modern mind.

Sadly for the Mediterranean, the tide is turning in favour of a more gradual, widespread development of cognition among the soup of populations within Africa,

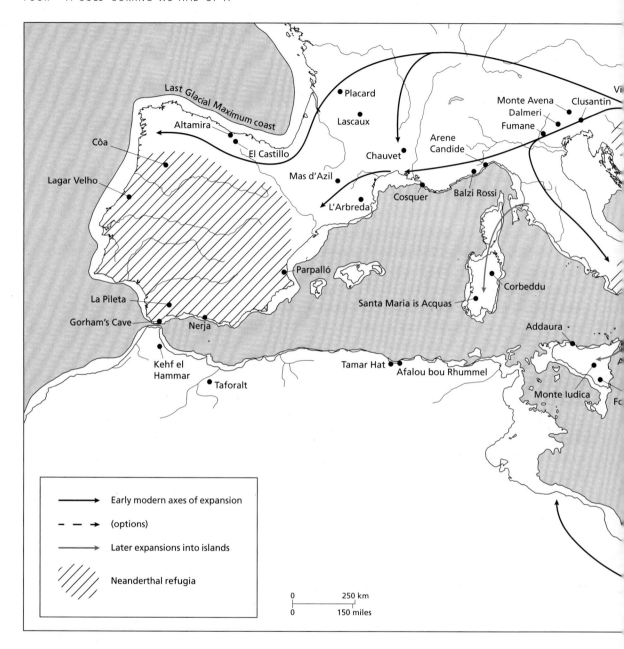

4.1 Map of sites mentioned in this chapter, also showing the coastline at the Last Glacial Maximum, approximate avenues of expansion by modern humans, and main likely Neanderthal refugia.

stretching well back into the ancestry of anatomically modern humans and perhaps shifting its spatial focus over time.[5] As we saw in the previous chapter, incised ochre and shell beads at Blombos Cave, similar beads transported over the Maghreb, and the funerary accompaniments of the escapees buried in the southern Levant all testify to sporadic flashes of symbolic activity at a considerably earlier date, some notably close to the southern edges of the Mediterranean. One proposal is that such precocious spikes, the ensuing quiescence between 70,000 and 50,000 years ago, and finally the resurgence over the following 5000 years and onward, reflect an initial cumulative build-up among growing, interacting and largely African populations,

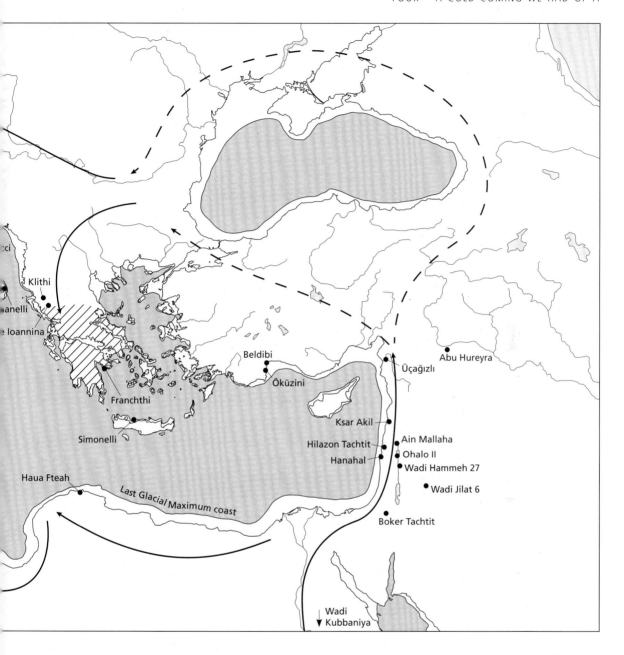

followed by subsidence during the setback of the MIS 4 glacial and Toba's eruption, then succeeded by recovery and global expansion in the Upper Palaeolithic, which enabled concentrations of creative humanity to emerge all over the planet.[6] In short, what we detect is not so much the origin of modern cognition (which remains shrouded in the early days of our species), but the subsequent florescences that resulted from the meetings of many such minds, first in Africa and the Levant and then ever more widely.

Relative to the rest of the continent, most of Mediterranean Africa was by now something of a sideshow, if nevertheless an intriguing one. We left it in Chapter 3 as the return of a hyper-arid Sahara cut people off in the habitat islands along the coast. How long they held out there is a serious question. In terms of survival prospects the Maghreb, today containing about a quarter of the land in the entire basin, was easily the largest refuge, even as its high plains dried and desert invaded in the south, but its westerly location rendered it also the most isolated. Its initially plentiful Aterian sites had fallen silent by 40,000–30,000 BC, with only a few enigmatic blips over the next 10,000 years.[7] A population that at first could have run into the thousands drastically declined, perhaps to partial extinction. The picture further east, in Cyrenaica, is quite different.[8] At Haua Fteah, above the Middle Stone Age lies a typical Late Stone Age (the African equivalent of the Upper Palaeolithic) known as the Dabban, which emits mixed messages of either local development from its predecessor or derivation along a considerable distance of inhospitable coastal strip from the Levant. The latter possibility would match the surprising hints from DNA analysis of an early inflow of Levantine people to North Africa.[9] Some ten millennia after it appeared in Cyrenaica, the Dabban took advantage of a milder climatic interlude to gain a foothold further west, around the long-abandoned springs of the Jebel el Gharbi. But from here the last jump to the Maghreb was apparently a bridge too far; and even the repeopling of the Jebel el Gharbi would eventually succumb in the teeth of deteriorating conditions to a combination of small numbers, great distances and attenuated links between annexes of inhabitable land.

How did modern humans expand around the remainder of the Mediterranean? From a comparative perspective, the greatest surprise is that the sea initially acted as a barrier for them just as much as it had for their predecessors. Archaeologists working on both sides of the Gibraltar strait are adamant that even *in extremis* the last Aterian groups in the Maghreb made no attempt to cross into Neanderthal Europe, while as we have just seen, the people responsible for the Dabban did not penetrate far enough west, perhaps leaving the southern side of the narrows empty for a long time.[10] The latter groups are unlikely to have realized that a further shore existed, or conceived of the open sea to their north as an escape route. All this is superficially strange, because at a global level modern expansion was impressively aquatic in contrast to its hominin predecessors.[11] From an early date, sea crossings, and by inference reliable seacraft, brought hitherto inaccessible places into range, Australia across 60–100 km (35–60 miles) of ocean by at least 45,000 BC and maybe a lot earlier, the archipelagos of western Melanesia and Japan over the next 5000–10,000 years.[12] These maritime thrusts from the eastern Eurasian rim may owe much to dispositions acquired along a southerly, coastal route eastward across Asia, maybe exiting Africa across the Red Sea at the Bab-el-Mandeb some 60,000 years ago – well before any circum-Mediterranean movement began.[13] Whatever the precise dates, the contrast between this eastward route along tidal shores rich in marine resources and headed into a gigantic patchwork of outsized, accessible islands, and the separate, later and dry-shod exit across the Suez isthmus up through the island-poor Levant into Europe (or in the case of the Dabban along North Africa) could explain why the initial expansion around the Mediterranean was so obdurately non-aquatic in character. Mediterranean moderns had to generate a seafaring orientation and technology from scratch, and that required time. If this distinction is valid, fervent faith in widespread and proficient Mediterranean seagoing from dates comparable to those far to the east is a victim of misleadingly uniform expectations, and also belittles the significance of the later passages of maritime thresholds that do stand out in the Mediterranean.

The overland expansion stemmed from northeast Africa, although we possess frustratingly little information about this staging area and the main routes across it at the relevant time, save for a few ineloquent tool sites and quarries.[14] The return to the Levant had begun by 47,000–45,000 BC, signalled by Boker Tachtit on the edge of the Negev, Ksar Akil in Lebanon and slightly later Üçağızlı in the north, with its early finds of shell beads [4.2].[15] In all probability the small outpost of Neanderthals that had filled the vacuum left by the failure of the previous excursion of *Homo sapiens* from Africa had in turn already been eradicated by hard times, and it speaks volumes for the adaptability of the moderns now filtering in that they could take over under such circumstances – the first time, indeed, that a human group had penetrated the Levant against the climatic trend. Beyond the Levant, the trail goes cold at the mountains of Anatolia, and we do not know whether the first moderns entered Europe directly via the Bosphorus and Dardanelles (then reduced by lower sea levels, if not dry) or at the end of a long loop around the Black Sea and thence from the southern Russian steppe. Either way, the marine theatre of the Aegean seems to have been bypassed.[16]

Sites appear in the Danube basin around 44,000 BC, from where groups leapfrogged through a swathe of land north of the Alps and south of the European plains as far as the El Castillo and L'Arbreda caves of northeast Spain, taking advantage of a well-documented climatic amelioration.[17] The first demonstrable reforging of contact with the Mediterranean basin since Üçağızlı occurs at Grotta di Fumane in the Po Valley, where moderns arrived about 41,000–40,000 BC. The grazing of the northern edge of the basin here, and in southern France, could be interpreted as the sequel to a separate, archaeologically invisible axis of advance through the east and central Mediterranean, but the evidence is non-existent, and such sites are more convincingly understood as offshoots of continental expansion.[18] Out of this web of places and people within mid-latitude Europe arose the nexus of traits known

4.2 Perforated shell ornaments, probably once strung as beads, made from marine gastropods at Üçağızlı.

as the Aurignacian.[19] In contrast to the elaborate later Upper Palaeolithic culture of Europe, the Aurignacian is characterized by simple, flexible toolkits, if ones commonly made from better, often more distant flints, some from remote quarries such as Monte Avena, 1450 m (4750 ft) high in the Dolomites. But other Upper Palaeolithic hallmarks appear too. Inland Grotta di Fumane yielded roughly 500 shell ornaments from thirty species, many of them perforated for wearing. It also boasts painted designs on fallen fragments of the cave wall, the putatively early date of which is now supported by the dramatic demonstration that the first red discs and hand stencils in caves in northeast Spain were created by at least 38,800–35,300 BC.[20] Figural cave art appears to have taken off a short few thousand years later in the Aurignacian, as spectacularly exhibited by the paintings of Chauvet Cave in the Ardèche, a densely populated part of southern France hemmed in at the time by tundra-steppe, mountains and the Atlantic [**4.3**].[21]

In contrast to this rapid spread, movement south into the rugged peninsulas of the Mediterranean was sluggish and uneven.[22] Until recently the Aurignacian was all but absent in the Aegean; a few finds now plug the gap, but still fall relatively late. In Iberia, the swift arrival in the northeast was followed by an immense delay in progress south and west. South of the Po the Aurignacian is mainly found along the Tyrrhenian coast, though one site much further south is of unquestionably wider importance. This is Riparo di Fontana Nuova in southeast Sicily, where a bunch of pioneers hunted red deer and scouted out the land widely enough to find flint about 100 km (60 miles) further north at Monte Iudica.[23] As established in Chapter 3, Sicily was probably often reachable via islets in a diminished Strait of Messina. Such a crossing was therefore hardly a giant leap, and furthermore it was a temporary incursion, to judge by the lack of subsequent evidence for some 20,000 years. But it does possess one advantage over earlier claims of island occupation in the Mediterranean: it indisputably happened.

4.3 Closely observed animal depictions at Chauvet Cave, such as these lions and bison, reveal an apparently startlingly early date to fully fledged figural art around the northwest margins of the Mediterranean.

Why did moderns take such a strangely long time to reach even the continental extremities of Mediterranean Europe? Of course they faced environmental challenges, and the typically broken landscapes may have seemed unattractive until spaces further north had filled up. But it is hard to imagine that people of the kind that had expanded from Africa through the Levant and Eurasian plains would have been daunted by these for an appreciable amount of time. In one instance the dangers were admittedly more dramatic, for from a volcanological point of view southward-bound moderns in Italy could not have timed it worse.[24] Ischia blew up three times in 10,000 years, and around 37,000 BC the Phlegraean Fields near Naples suffered the basin's most colossal convulsion of the last 200,000 years, which smothered huge areas up to 50 m (165 ft) deep in ash and generated a plume borne on the winds as far as the Volga. Eruptions on this scale must have disrupted if not destroyed life throughout southern Italy, and the first Sicilians whom we have just encountered could plausibly have been displaced people fleeing this devastation. But such special instances apart, it seems inescapable that, in contrast to the genuine natural obstacles to settling and holding the habitat islands of Mediterranean Africa, delays around the northern shores owe little to nature and much more to prior occupancy.

For the major reason for the slow, patchy progress southward in all the great peninsulas of the northern Mediterranean was surely the continuing existence there of longstanding refugia for Neanderthals. The correlation between advancing moderns and Neanderthal retraction has attracted different, not always incompatible, explanations.[25] For some, the former caused the latter. Scenarios of genocide may be groundless, but over many generations differences in hunting efficiency, reliability of social connections and child survival rates arguably allowed moderns to out-compete and overwhelm Neanderthals. However, the priority can equally be reversed to argue that Neanderthals were by this time already under exceptional stress, a marked species like so much of the Mediterranean's early fauna.[26] As humans highly optimized for a specific spectrum of conditions, in contrast to our own more generalized species, their reaction to change outside this envelope was to retreat (where possible) rather than adapt in situ.[27] But each time the cold intensified, such pull-backs into refuge pockets split up by the sea and mountains increased the risk of local eliminations, eroding the overall viability of Neanderthals as a species, while the chaotic oscillations of MIS 3 added a further challenge just as the presence of moderns further north made it harder to regain land, connections and therefore numbers during warmer phases. In this sense Mediterranean refugia offered respite, but in the long term could turn into deathtraps for people lacking the flexibility to transform their potential, or adequate sea-crossing skills to sustain links between them. From this perspective, the intrusion of moderns into the southern Neanderthal realms was no victorious advance but an infiltration of emptied land. Behind both scenarios, and intermediate possibilities, lurks a profound uncertainty as to how often moderns and Neanderthals met within the thinly peopled landscapes of Europe, and what transpired if or when they did. There appears to be a very minor (if thought-provoking) Neanderthal element in the DNA of modern Eurasians, but above this bottom line of potential sporadic sexual encounters all kinds of possibilities for interaction, or its absence, remain.[28]

Along the northwest edge of the Mediterranean, the final Neanderthal collapse came quite swiftly, probably during a severe cold spike around 38,500 BC, and after a brief overlap in southwest France and northeast Spain, where hybrid toolkits known as Châtelperronian may hint at a little Neanderthal learning from moderns.[29] Evidence from Vindija Cave in inland Croatia suggests that Neanderthals survived somewhat later in the forested tracts of the northern Balkan interior, again with hints of adopted Aurignacian practices, but as we move further south into the Mediterranean proper, the realities behind the archaeological traces of the last Neanderthals become more intriguing.[30] In the coastal Balkans and the Aegean firm dates for their final demise are lacking, but we do know that it took a long time for moderns to establish themselves; for millennia this area could have been either a Neanderthal redoubt, or something of a no-man's-land.[31] The Italian Neanderthals vanished well before 30,000 BC, but in the far south a mixed tool tradition seems to parallel the Châtelperronian; moreover, some unusual features in the subsequent south Italian Aurignacian toolkit may even reveal a unique counterflow from Neanderthal woodworking traditions.[32]

Iberia presents the most striking picture.[33] There is no trace of cross-learning, though later Lagar Velho in Portugal offers a potential case of human hybridity, in the form of a child with a purportedly partly Neanderthal skeletal inheritance, but interred with typically modern accoutrements.[34] Iberia's distinction instead lies in the fact that Neanderthals lived on in parts of the peninsula for hundreds of generations after moderns took over in the northeast. Some of the last Neanderthals on the planet were those at Gibraltar, and their final death on the rock may have come as late as 32,500–30,000 BC, or even 27,000–26,500 BC, in isolation to judge by the markedly later arrival of modern groups to reuse their dwellings.[35] Two factors contributed to this resilience. One was the Iberian peninsula's superb qualities as an environmental refuge (as set out in Chapter 3, with particularly easy conditions in the vicinity of Gibraltar), and the other its unparalleled combination of a constricted, mountain-barred entrance and a swelling interior, which in demographic terms allowed a relatively big Neanderthal battalion to survive longer than elsewhere. It is a thought-provoking geographical coincidence, or no coincidence at all, that Iberia was both a focus for the earliest hominins in Mediterranean Europe, and the place from where the last who were not us walked out forever into the night.

Cultured hunter-gatherers

By the time the Neanderthals had vanished, the world was heading towards a new full glacial phase. This (to date) Last Glacial Maximum (21,000–18,000 BC) is the best investigated and therefore most amenable to detailed reconstruction. Whether or not it was marginally less bad than other late Pleistocene glaciations is academic;

it was certainly quite severe enough and, more importantly, the only one to have tested the survival mechanisms of modern people throughout the Mediterranean. This last point underscores the fact that with the advent of such people, we need to embrace a more nuanced relationship between environmental change and human activity than hitherto, with people now developing sophisticated ways of insulating or buffering themselves from the worst, and of exploiting whatever openings the shifting conditions brought. Some insulation was literal, in the forms of new, tailored leather clothing implied by the widespread use of bone needles, shoes detectable in the detailed morphology of foot bones, and lightly built or transportable shelters, all of which enabled people of recent African descent to expand and endure in the teeth of conditions that even cold-adapted Neanderthals could not tolerate.[36] But physical insulation was only one of the strategies now pitted against adversity. Before we turn to the struggle for survival through the long millennia of the Last Glacial Maximum, we should therefore take a closer look at the unprecedented Mediterranean societies already emerging.

Mediterranean Neanderthals had begun to explore the potential diet breadth of the basin's environments, but modern hunter-gatherers were the first to realize their full potential, in certain areas tracing an acceleration right from the start, and universally by the Last Glacial Maximum. From the advent of the Levantine Upper Palaeolithic onward, the bones at archaeological sites reveal increasing pressure on prey, a trend that followed the bow wave of expansion irrespective of climate conditions, and that later humanity has sometimes held in check but never definitively reversed.[37] It may appear bizarre to trace modernity by measuring tortoises, but the outcome is telling: after millennia of low-level consumption by Neanderthals, the declining size and age of these vulnerable, slowly reproducing animals once moderns arrived betrays quickly unsustainable levels of attrition. Similar patterns of progressive depletion are seen for most of the optimal large game, forcing successive shifts to smaller, faster ungulates, as well as targets such as game-birds, hares and rabbits that required more energy or skill to catch but bred fast enough to sustain high losses. The diversity and rapid turnover in tool types that erupts in the Upper Palaeolithic reflects an ever-inventive response to the need for more efficient means to kill and process all kinds of quarry. It was also probably at around this time that traps, snares and nets were first deployed to turn the tables on nimble prey, and collecting baskets first woven. Such inventions enabled the young and elderly to be more effectively recruited to the food-quest, and in contrast to the slight gender distinctions inferred for Neanderthals, women may have started to become differentiated by an association with lower-risk forms of meat acquisition, tailoring of clothes and shelters and, as we shall see shortly, plant-related activities. Specialized roles within the community, as well as more intricate seasonal schedules, were gradually beginning to emerge.

The concept of communities reminds us that these hunter-gatherers were, for all their apparent strangeness and distance, people with families, kin, social lives and personae marked by distinctions of age, status and role as well as sex, cultural beings who inhabited landscapes assuredly invested with symbolic meaning and myth.[38] Like many recent hunter-gatherers they would have lived for most of the year in bands of one or two dozen people, sharing food and much else in common, with only a limited sense of personal ownership. But each band would have been connected to others via larger social affiliations numbering hundreds of people. These connections increased the flow of information, skills and materials, as well as the choice of mating and other partners. Furthermore, they fostered long-term stability by reducing the risks facing each individual band in adversity; should conditions improve they equally facilitated a swift and coordinated response. These aggregate groups may only have met on special occasions, but the critical distinction from Neanderthal societies was that they stayed immanent in the mind, and could be drawn on even when their constituent members were scattered in space, or even over ancestral time. The result was the creation of the first recognizable Mediterranean networks – ones that often, due to the low densities at which these hunter-gatherers lived, delineated connections over distances rivalling those of far later times, despite the fact that all overland mobility remained pedestrian.

This 'release from proximity'[39] and capability for notional communion while far apart was intimately connected with an explosion of symbols and other designators of social relations and identity. Many were gleaming, colourful, seductively smooth, skilfully fashioned or otherwise enchanting things.[40] The shell ornaments of North Africa and the Levant are good early examples, but as deteriorating conditions broke down groups in the former and disrupted connections in the latter, Europe came to the fore, late in the Aurignacian and among the 'Gravettian' societies that followed from 30,000–31,000 BC. Glossy beads made from marine shell, mammal or fish bone, deer teeth, steatite or mammoth ivory, figurines carved into the inaptly named 'Venus' or werebeast forms, and the artistic representations in painted meeting caves across the northwest, all played a part in maintaining relations over long distances. Mediterranean shells travelled inland as far as the Rhine, and one distinctive suite of Aurignacian beads is attested right across Italy and the Aegean.[41] Beads, strung or sewn onto garments, became particularly popular, thanks to their lightness, visibility and aesthetic as well as durable properties, and they gradually outstripped pigments as a medium of personal adornment.[42] The additional fact that they were readily quantifiable and of naturally standardized shapes (in the case of the popular tusk shells, neatly segmentable), made them also early forms of valuables and status markers. This in turn raises a further question: did long-range transport simply reflect direct access to sources over great distances, and individual high mobility and ostentation, or had things begun to be exchanged from person to person (or region to region – coastal shells for northern ivory?), and if so, was this entirely embedded in reciprocal social etiquette such as gift-giving, or had concepts of equivalence, and even advantage, already begun to emerge?[43]

The things, practices and networks that make up the Gravettian first coalesced north of the Alps, and indeed one of the Gravettian's impressive features in contrast to earlier periods is the maintenance of life at these latitudes right up to the Last Glacial

Maximum.[44] But the Gravettian enjoys high visibility in Mediterranean Europe too. In Epirus and at Franchthi Cave in the Peloponnese, the Upper Palaeolithic in Greece comes briefly into focus before a period of virtual desertion.[45] Peninsular Italy was well occupied, or reoccupied from southern France after a possible collapse within the Aurignacian. Mobile groups penetrated the Iberian interior from their earlier focus around the coast. One residue of this criss-crossing infiltration is the open-air rock art of the Côa Valley in Portugal, which started with images of horses, aurochs and ibexes, and is surely but the remnant of a widespread tradition obliterated by rain and wind.[46] Back in Italy, art again hints at long-range movement. The handprints and skilfully depicted horses in Grotta Paglicci in Apulia are unique in Italy, yet find close parallels in Provence and the Rhône Valley. Given their fixture on cave walls, a far-travelled visitor from France is the only likely explanation.[47]

Occasionally, a particular locality comes into sharper focus. Gravettian levels at the cluster of sites variously known as the Balzi Rossi, Grimaldi or Menton caves, on the Ligurian coast close to the modern Italian–French border, reveal a band's base camp or perhaps a meeting point for wider gatherings.[48] Much of their stratigraphy was destroyed by Prince Albert I of Monaco and other late 19th-century excavators, but enough can be reconstructed to confirm an exceptional status. In addition to thick layers of occupation debris, the caves produced many symbolic and exotic finds, not least fifteen out of the nineteen early figurines known from Italy (and a third of all those from Western Europe), eight of which have recently re-emerged in Canada after disappearing shortly after their discovery [PL. VIII]. Stylistic details indicate ties as far away as the Russian steppe. Equally arresting is the number of burials. Together with a few from Grotta Paglicci and elsewhere in southern Italy, these offer insights into some of the people living at this time [4.4]. Most of the skeletons belong to adolescent or adult men, several outstandingly tall at 180–90 cm (5 ft 11 in.–6 ft 3 in.), with massive musculature, especially on the legs, that speaks

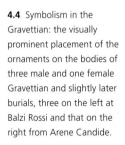

4.4 Symbolism in the Gravettian: the visually prominent placement of the ornaments on the bodies of three male and one female Gravettian and slightly later burials, three on the left at Balzi Rossi and that on the right from Arene Candide.

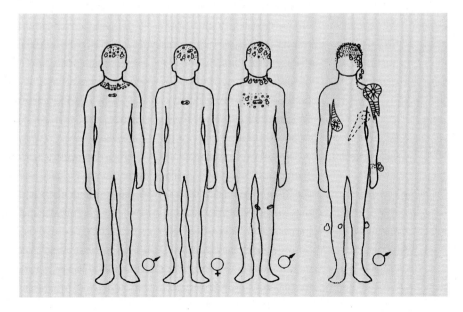

of active lives in rough or far-flung lands. Bodies were laid out singly, in pairs or in one instance as a triple inhumation, in an extended posture that drew attention to their adornment with strings of beads, some of mammoth ivory, at the wrists, chest, neck and forehead, the last relics of elaborate headdresses. Such rare yet spectacular special treatment surely reflected exceptional, powerful qualities, whether in terms of physical prowess, social prestige or leadership. One explanation for this accentuation in a part of the basin that would never achieve such prominence again until the post-Roman foundation of Genoa is the gentle climate in the lee of the Alps, which under incipient glacial conditions offered major advantages. But another possibility is of deeper interest. Astride a communication bottleneck between France and Italy, under conditions that made long-range mobility essential, overwhelmingly terrestrial, and impossible via the Alps, do these caves provide a precursor of the kind of contingent, context-specific nodes and central places that we shall encounter again and again at the heart of later Mediterranean networks?

Enduring the Last Glacial Maximum

From such glimpses of hunter-gatherers on the northern fringes of the Mediterranean, we can turn to the reconstruction of conditions during the Last Glacial Maximum, into which these people were headed.[49] The nadir lasted for some 3000 years, but climates had begun to deteriorate from an already poor, unstable state several millennia before 21,000 BC, and even after 18,000 BC there would be little improvement for several thousand years. Sea temperatures in the centre of the basin averaged 5–9°C (41–48°F) in summer and a chilly 2–6°C (36–43°F) in winter, and icebergs drifted west of Gibraltar. Year-round snow lay as low as 1500 m (4900 ft), with three to six month cover over much of the remainder in southern Europe, huge glaciers ground through the Alps, and small ones formed in the Atlas, Pyrenees and Apennines, the Balkan, Anatolian and Lebanese mountains, and even on Crete, Corsica and Sicily. Steppe speckled with low, dry scrub spread over great areas, merging inland into tundra in the north and temperate desert in the Levant and North Africa. Along the driest stretches of African coast the Sahara lapped close to the shore, while the Nile meandered or lay stagnant for parts of the year. Such landscapes owed as much to dryness and constant winds as to actual cold. They reflect global conditions under which tundra and polar steppe tripled their grip on the planet, with temperate steppe and desert likewise on the march.

As with previous glacials, however, we must qualify this bleak portrait. Once again, sheltered, often coastal microclimates ensured the survival of Mediterranean plants and animals, as well as refugees from further north. Pollen and charcoal show that the Po Valley was reduced to a dusty plain with a gallery of trees along the river, but oak, elm, walnut, birch and pine rallied around the mouth of the Arno, while holly and laurel grew in the Madonie mountains of Sicily.[50] Liguria was a veritable glacial riviera in which even olives hung on, accompanied by a mixture of red deer, ibexes and a few reindeer intruding from the north. Such pockets, some large, others smaller but locally crucial, dotted the basin; the subsequent genetics of the olive, which shows at least one major separation phase in the past, may preserve a relic of their dividing and preserving role.[51] Two of the biggest refugia lay in the west, predictably one in Iberia, south of a Meseta roamed by tundra fauna, another (but how populous?) on the seaward flank of the Atlas, where grassy savannah dotted with pine and oak stretched to the shore, and cedar held out on higher ground. Charcoal and pollen from Cosquer Cave, the now-submerged, painted cavern near Marseilles mentioned in Chapter 1, reveal a finer-grained picture. The blazing torches by which people drew and gazed at the images on its walls were made of Scots pine, now gone from lowland Provence, while the pollen, though dominated by steppe plants, also reveals juniper and clumps of birch.[52] On Crete, cosseted by the sea, a native palm may have survived.[53] And one further set of refugia deserves special mention, given subsequent history. In a steppe- and grassland-dominated Levant, olive, evergreen oak, almond and terebinth clung on in the hills, while the declivity of the Jordan Valley sheltered patches of woodland. Perversely, a few major Levantine lakes survived or even expanded, because the low evaporation generated by cooler conditions more than counterbalanced the reduced rainfall. Lake Lisan, an expanded version of the Dead Sea that at its maximum extent stretched from the Galilee to Wadi Arabah, held out in the Jordan Valley, and around Azraq in the eastern steppe-desert huge, ephemeral sheets of water appeared, magnets in winter and spring for migratory herds of gazelle and their human hunters.[54] Of equal interest are the enduringly mosaic-like character of such environments and the very varied composition of their individual tesserae, which in certain cases preserved resilient microcosms of typical warm-weather Mediterranean ecologies, and in others created radically different compositions from less familiar constituents.

The coastline of the Mediterranean was likewise unfamiliar [4.1].[55] Two or three times more of the planet's water was frozen than is the case today, mainly in the gargantuan ice sheets that sprawled over northern Eurasia and America. This drove sea level down to 120–30 m (390–425 ft) below the present stand. The dramatic consequences can be reconstructed in detail, alongside the pattern of later rises. The principal straits looked quite different, with Gibraltar and the Sicilian narrows reduced to some 8 km (5 miles) and 60 km (35 miles) respectively, while the Bosphorus and Dardanelles stood dry, causing the level of a thus isolated Black Sea to plummet. Sea-gaps between islands shrank or vanished altogether. Corsica and Sardinia fused to create 'Corsardinia', at 35,000 sq. km (13,500 sq. miles) the largest insular land mass to have existed in the basin in the history of modern humans. Sicily, whether or not linked to Italy, stretched south to absorb Malta. Many Aegean and Adriatic islands fused with the mainland or each other, with losses offset by newcomers arising in shallower seas, especially the Aegean and Sicilian narrows. Along the coast, the area exposed varied with the lie of the land. Shorelines typically moved 5–15 km (3–10 miles) from the modern stand, but in steeper zones much less – for example, the lack of change in the shells used for ornaments at Riparo Mochi (one of the Balzi Rossi caves, in Liguria) before, during and after the glacial climax testifies to a fairly stable coast and ecology as well as cultural continuity.[56] In areas of low relief, however, the gain could be substantial, some 50 km (30 miles) seaward along much of southwest France and in parts of the Aegean, for example. In two cases great plains emerged, one in the northern Adriatic, the other in the Gulf of Gabès, each some 40,000–50,000 sq. km (15,000–20,000 sq. miles) in area, or double the size of Sicily. Altogether, the Mediterranean gained some 300,000 sq. km (115,000 sq. miles) of land, the equivalent of a second peninsular Italy.

How did changing shores shape life round the edges of the sea? Much is often made of the possibility that shrinking inter-island distances encouraged sea crossings, but in fact short-range opportunities existed at every sea level stand, and, as we shall see, it would take more specific conditions to draw people into the maritime world to any great degree. More promising is the suggestion, also made for previous glacials, that most hunter-gatherers followed the herds to live out on extended coastal plains, where their archaeology is largely lost to us.[57] Daring exploration of now-submarine caves off Marseilles confirms that an apparent lack of people in Provence is due to the fact that most lived in landscapes currently beneath the sea, and in rugged regions like the Aegean such exposed tracts comprised a high proportion of all usable lowland.[58] Not all the gains were necessarily attractive, however. There are rival visions of the great plain at the head of the Adriatic: one a rich vista dotted with game animals and hunter-gatherer base camps, the other a brutal wind-blasted heath of mudflats, bogs, gravel banks and clumps of pine, a haunt of the lonesome elk.[59] On balance the rosier view is likely to have at least some truth to it, and neatly explains the draining at this time of human traces from the inland Trieste karst, as well as the handful of outposts overlooking the plain around Pula in Istria and current islands in the Kvarner Gulf. But the verdict remains out for the other exposure, whether a scrubby inhabitable steppe or barren desert, now inundated off Tunisia.

As the Last Glacial Maximum tightened its hold on the Mediterranean, people congregated in more sheltered areas. For all the survival skills of humans living further north in Europe, it is likely that numbers of these moved south into the basin too, not as strangers but drawing on contacts long sustained by social networks and circulating objects. Both locals and newcomers became gradually stockier in physique as glacial conditions winnowed much of the gracile African inheritance from their bodies.[60] But before we explore what else transpired in these Mediterranean refuges, it is well worth asking approximately how many people were attempting to live round the basin during the Last Glacial Maximum, and with what consequences. The answer will be speculative, and overly simplified given the tendency for hunter-gatherer numbers to fluctuate under unstable conditions, but even the order of magnitude proves salutary. Hunter-gatherers, past and present, exist at almost universally very low densities. The best estimates for Western Europe and Iberia at that time are an average of less than one person per 60 sq. km (or slightly less than 25 sq. miles), although with huge differences between relatively packed pockets and expanses barren of humanity.[61] Allowing for land won as the sea shrank, this implies a mere 45,000 or so inhabitants for the entire basin, and given the tracts of snowbound upland and desert, even this errs on the optimistic side. This shockingly small figure, equivalent to a single large city of the 5th century BC, compares with guesses of a global population of 1–2 million at the Last Glacial Maximum.[62] If this total is broken down, it becomes apparent that most regions only supported a few thousand people, and smaller refuges must have had a perilously fragile demography in the low hundreds, right at the brink in terms of long-term viability, unless they could maintain effective links with pools of people in neighbouring parts of the basin.

That people often experienced chronic difficulties in maintaining such linkage may be indicated by the break-up of the Gravettian during the Last Glacial Maximum, with disparate 'Epigravettian' traditions developing in Italy and areas further east, and Solutrean followed by early Magdalenian ones in Iberia and France.[63] Certain regional populations may have dwindled to vanishing point. Much of southern Dalmatia, the Aegean and upland Anatolia lay empty, and turnovers would have been likely, as ever, in parts of the Levant.[64] But as during earlier crises, the African habitat islands offer the most compelling doom scenarios.[65] Dabban occupation held on in Cyrenaica but collapsed at or slightly before the onset of the Last Glacial Maximum in the Jebel el Gharbi, a vulnerable, hemmed-in spot even with the benefit of territorial gains as sea level fell.[66] It is therefore all the stranger that in the later part of this inauspicious phase signs of activity reappear in the Maghreb, in the guise of barbary sheep hunters at Taforalt and Tamar Hat. Their signature is known as the Iberomaurusian, a tradition that continued in Mediterranean Africa long after the Last Glacial Maximum (as well as a misnomer that reflects early credence in trans-Gibraltar connections).[67] Whether or not its initial materialization is truly this early – and it must be confessed that the first Maghrebian dates are not unproblematic – the emergence of the Iberomaurusian poses interesting questions.[68] For with the Sahara closed, the Jebel el Gharbi empty and no discernable maritime contacts with Europe, the earliest Iberomaurusian can only be explained by a westward venture from distant Cyrenaica, or a resurgence, despite the almost total intervening silence, and marked skeletal dissimilarities between the two horizons, of populations descended from Aterian survivors in the Maghreb, with all that this would imply in terms of physical, genetic and linguistic distinctions from other moderns around the basin. In support of the latter possibility are the few blips of an ongoing presence noted earlier, as well as a later signal at the recently investigated Kehf el Hammar Cave in Morocco, from a basal stratum pre-dating the Last Glacial Maximum, below Iberomaurusian tools, dry-land plants and rodents that date to the end of the glacial climax.[69] Anyone emerging from the Maghreb as conditions improved after the Last Glacial Maximum must have felt like, and been viewed as, a visitor from another planet.

Circumstances elsewhere around the Mediterranean were seldom this extreme. A few favoured areas even saw a rise in population. One such region was the southern Iberian coast, protected from the cold blasts of the Meseta by the Sierra Nevada, and still enjoying the vestiges of a seaside climate.[70] Sites here are numerous and closely packed, and at the merest hint of a relenting in the climate regime, the wielders of superb Solutrean spearheads would expand into southern France [4.5]. Under

4.5 A finely crafted Solutrean spearhead from Placard Cave in southwest France.

such abnormally dense conditions conflict is inherently likely, and the distinctive portable art of this region, known from the stone plaques found at Parpalló Cave, may reflect efforts to negotiate such tensions.[71] Confined territory, together with the extreme local ecological diversity created by the abrupt transitions between sea and mountains, had other significant consequences too. For it encouraged a relatively tethered lifestyle in southern Iberia, involving lengthy periods of residence at a single place, with a high proportion of nourishment obtained quite close at hand. In short, by reducing mobility it marked a noticeable shift towards more sedentary lifestyles.

Elsewhere around the edges of the Mediterranean, other examples of this trend can be discerned, each time associated with unusually rich, concentrated resources, as well as a degree of circumscription. At Wadi Kubbaniya, on what survived of the Nile upstream near Aswan, people lived for at least half the year off catfish, aquatic plants, waterbirds and desert animals, a way of life that probably resembled that in a then far lower-lying Nile Delta that has since been lost to the sea or scoured to oblivion by the resurgent river.[72] Neighbours on the Nile again lived cheek by jowl and tensions may have run high, to judge by the alleged killing of one young man with projectile points in his chest. A final well-preserved example in the basin itself comes from the upper Jordan Valley, then occupied by groups using tool types known as the Kebaran. One of their dwelling areas, identified as Ohalo II, has been obligingly exposed by recent droughts in the Sea of Galilee, then part of Lake Lisan [**4.6**].[73] Around 20,000–19,000 BC, people occupied huts made of tamarisk, oak and willow at least during the spring and autumn, to judge by the seasonality of animals and plants, and occasionally buried their dead. From a surrounding mosaic of savannah, steppe, woods and upland they obtained a range of animals, including three species of gazelle, each with its own preferred environment, goats, steppe ass, woodland-loving aurochs and boars, as well as waterfowl and fish from the lake. In addition, they gathered forty varieties of seeds, nuts, berries and roots, including

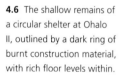

4.6 The shallow remains of a circular shelter at Ohalo II, outlined by a dark ring of burnt construction material, with rich floor levels within.

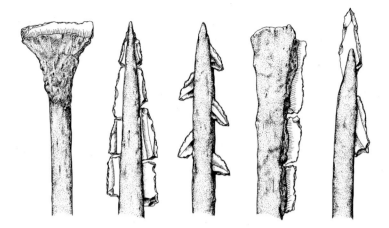

4.7 Options for flexible mounting of microliths to create light missile weapons, including arrowheads, as well as skinning, fine cutting and reaping tools.

from Mediterranean plants such as wild barley, wheat, olives and grapes, all of which were riding out the glacial climax in this little niche. Some of the cereals were even ground and roasted.

Projectiles and grinding introduce two final developments that can be detected in unrelated regions all over the basin, both of which reflect the drive to squeeze food resources ever harder, and loosely associated with the Last Glacial Maximum, if with sporadic earlier beginnings. The first is a shift in weapon and tool technology towards small, 'microlithic' products. This produced more cutting edge per unit of flint (a real advantage with montane sources under snow and ice) and enabled easily maintained 'plug-in/pull-out' composites [4.7]. At first the main use was for light projectiles such as throwing spears, harpoons and arrows, an evolution given impetus by hunters' concentration in refuges of limited size but highly diverse potential targets. Harpoons and projectile points had been developed earlier in Africa, but atlatls (spear-throwing devices) are first attested during the Gravettian, and Mediterranean bows and arrows, though not provable until the end of the Pleistocene, are strongly implied by a proliferation of tiny stone tips during and just after the Last Glacial Maximum.[74] These refinements were accompanied by efforts to extract more from kills: tiny tools were useful for small carcasses, and the numbers of fire-cracked stones reveal stone-boiling of meat to render its nutritious fats.

Processing was also the key to efficient and intensive use of wild plants. These had already served Mediterranean Neanderthals as a supplement, and their successors probably expanded on this earlier and more ambitiously than we can detect – and not just for sustenance, given impressions of simple woven items found in central Europe, and 35,000-year-old flaxen cords, some dyed, that have recently been identified in the Caucasus.[75] Microliths would later help to construct the first harvesting sickles, but before this came heavy grinding stones for seeds and nuts.[76] Groups all over the basin gradually began to manufacture these, sometimes millennia before the Last Glacial Maximum. Finds at Ohalo II (where such stones bear traces of starch grains), Grotta Paglicci in southern Italy and late Dabban sites in North Africa illustrate this trend. While the Mediterranean stayed relatively chilly and arid, plants remained in dietary terms second fiddle to meat, but even so (and equally with respect to the new hunting technologies) the basin stood far ahead of the continent to its north, where the equivalent broadening of the food spectrum would not begin until the ice was in full retreat.

Sea-fishing and Corsardinia

The harvest of lake fish at Ohalo II prompts questions about sea-fishing, and whether conditions at the Last Glacial Maximum encouraged ventures onto the Mediterranean Sea for other reasons too. As established in Chapter 3, Neanderthals had recognized the shore as a source of food and this was never forgotten. Later people ate sea molluscs and adorned themselves with the most alluring of their shells. Sea mammals remained a minor dietary element along the coast, now with the addition of the great auk, a fat-rich, flightless bird resembling a penguin, that inhabited vast colonies in the north Atlantic until it was eaten to extinction in the 19th century AD – these birds spread as far as the central Mediterranean during glacial phases, as evidenced at Archi on the Messina strait.[77] More novel is the appearance of such creatures in art.[78] In the northwest, seal images appear during the Solutrean, peaking later in the Magdalenian. Most are carved and portable; a few inland finds offer glimpses of mobile items or people. At Mas d'Azil in southwest France the incisor of a possibly Atlantic and presumably beached sperm whale was also found, engraved with the image of an ibex in a nice juxtaposing of sea and cliff.

But the most exciting discoveries are those from the inundated Cosquer Cave off Marseilles, dated to 21,500–20,000 BC, and so right at the heart of the Last Glacial Maximum [4.8].[79] Marine creatures make up 11 per cent of the figural images that survive where the cave wall is still above sea level, ranking after horse, ibex and aurochs. The roll call is eight incised seals shot by projectiles, three painted auks [PL. IX], one or more fish, and some questionable jellyfish, almost all demonstrating deep familiarity with the animals' appearance and behaviour, down to observations

4.8 A cross-section through the present submarine entrance, approach passage and principal caverns of Cosquer Cave. During the Last Glacial Maximum the cave mouth stood 80–90 m (260–295 ft) above sea level and some distance inland.

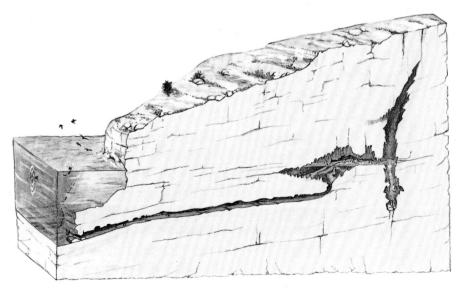

0	20 m
0	60 ft

like the two male auks fighting over a female in early summer. Cosquer, together with a few Iberian coastal caves, breathes new life into the old idea of a Mediterranean zone in Palaeolithic art, distinct in its subject matter and style from inland representations. The one frustration is that because the cave was never used for habitation, we cannot compare this image-world with the bones of animals actually consumed in coastal Provence at this time.

As mentioned, at least one fish, of unascertainable species, appears in the art of Cosquer. Nearly 150 other fish images are known from some thirty Upper Palaeolithic caves, a total almost equal to that for mammoths.[80] They concentrate in France and Iberia, with a focus at La Pileta, now 55 km (35 miles) inland in southwest Spain, but extend as far as Grotta Romanelli in southern Italy. Most belong several millennia after the Last Glacial Maximum, and the earliest images tend to be of riverine or migrant species, especially trout and salmon, or portable carvings of flatfish. Bones of sea-fish have been recovered from before the Last Glacial Maximum at a few sites in North Africa (see Chapter 3), in upper levels at Üçağızlı and in questionable context at Gorham's Cave at Gibraltar. At its height a remarkable total of thirty species appear at Nerja Cave on the Bay of Malaga (then 4 km or 2.5 miles from the shore), mainly small inshore denizens, but also big sturgeon as well as Atlantic cod, haddock and pollock that came through the Gibraltar strait to feed.[81] Quite what to infer from this is less obvious, as few if any of these species were necessarily intercepted far from shore. The central significance of early sea-fish finds is therefore not that they furnish definite evidence for extensive seagoing, but rather that they add a further marine element to the widening spectrum of foods consumed in the Mediterranean. The stronger signature in the west is due to the Atlantic influx of ocean fish (which created a marine profile in the Alboran Sea just as strange to modern eyes as some of its terrestrial contemporaries) as well as the migration of freshwater-spawning species such as salmon and sturgeon.

Clinching proof for seagoing around the Last Glacial Maximum instead comes from the same kinds of evidence that pertained earlier, both negatively and positively, namely signs of movement between places that required the crossing of sea-gaps. As we saw, one extremely short-range event definitely occurred between mainland Italy and Sicily in the Aurignacian, while before this Neanderthal and possibly even earlier short hops may have occurred sporadically in the Aegean. To these we may now add, from the Simonelli Cave in western Crete, a poorly dated modern human skull with fossils of extinct deer in its surrounding breccia.[82] But the secure lead is taken over by another large island, Sardinia, or, rather, the fused insular land mass of Corsardinia. From the Corsican end of this, the Italian mainland, which then reached as far as Elba and its satellites, lay across 15 km (10 miles) of sea that is nowadays swept by swift currents. Corsardinia's larger fauna comprised an endemic triumvirate: the fast-breeding hare-like *Prolagus sardus*, a native deer and a small dog-like predator, all now extinct.[83] Until recently, the case for Palaeolithic presence was mired in the usual controversies engendered by excited claims, sceptical reactions and shaky data, most notoriously in the case of the so-called Venus of Macomer, an enigmatic, unprovenanced figurine made of volcanic rock that combines a woman's body with – to the eye of faith – a *Prolagus* head.[84] For the earlier Palaeolithic nothing has altered, but excavations at Corbeddu Cave in eastern Sardinia have yielded a scrap of human bone associated with cold-weather plant pollen suggestive of the Last Glacial Maximum, bracketed by underlying strata 30,000 years old and overlying ones dated to 16,800 BC onward.[85] This lends credence to previous less secure hints from the cave, mainly a few artifacts in levels presumed to be early, and peculiar accumulations of deer bones that, though bearing no incontrovertible traces of human intervention, are hard to attribute to the local canid.[86] Soon after the Corbeddu find, roadworks at Santa Maria is Acquas on the Campidano plain in the south exposed Upper Palaeolithic tools in a soil horizon is thought to date before the end of the Last Glacial Maximum.[87]

What exactly can we infer from the Corsardinian evidence? Certainly, it gives an idea of the minimum water-crossing capabilities of some Mediterranean people by the Last Glacial Maximum, though the distance is hardly more than an optimist might attribute to a fortune-favoured crossing by earlier human species. It is unlikely to have been a unique event, but equally it does not clinch the case for widespread or longer-range sea travel of an intensity that might start to qualify the overwhelmingly land-based character of the networks linking people together. There is no sign of contact across the Gibraltar strait between users of Solutrean and Iberomaurusian tools, and although low sea levels offered easier access to obsidian sources on islands, which do indeed act as excellent tracers of seagoing at least this early in Melanesia and Japan,[88] the bald fact is that no Mediterranean island obsidian (including even Sardinian) has yet been found at any site securely dated to this juncture or the immediately following millennia.

So in a world of apparently still reluctant seagoers, why did people cross to a place like Corsardinia? One clue may be the fact that despite the glaciers crowning Corsica's peaks, Corsardinian climate would have been milder than that of mainland Italy, especially in the southern half where the finds concentrate.[89] Hunter-gatherers may have relocated to this land mass that offered better conditions, was big enough to live off and just happened to necessitate a sea crossing – not that different from hops between habitat islands in North Africa or countless other, less visible shifts round the basin's rim as climate deteriorated. Corsardinia's role as a refuge during the worst of times might also explain the lack of traces of subsequent activity until millennia later, at the start of the Holocene. Sea-crossing skills could, after all, just as easily effect a reversal once conditions improved, and the manifold attractions of mainland life outweighed the weather. Alternatively, the first islanders may have remained too few to become truly established. Either way, a later abandonment could explain the fact that, uniquely among larger Mediterranean endemics, the native deer and canid survived at Corbeddu well after this first influx of people, until the very end of the Pleistocene.[90] In all likelihood they were granted a temporary reprieve by the limited number of hunters, the island's large recesses and arguably the temporary nature of the first incursion.

A false dawn

The pitiless climatic clamp began to relax episodically from about 18,000–17,000 BC, heralding the start of the first return to interglacial conditions for a hundred thousand years, and this time with the unprecedented difference that moderns were spread all round the Mediterranean.[91] Within a relatively few millennia, a combination of radical climate amelioration and the actions of these clever, dynamic people would transform the basin and indeed the planet [4.9].[92] It took roughly 9000 years for the major ice sheets to melt and longer for sea level to reach its modern

4.9 A transforming Mediterranean: (*right*) the jagged record of climate change after the Last Glacial Maximum, showing the Bølling-Allerød interstadial, reversion to a cold Younger Dryas, abruptly warming transition to the Holocene, and subsequent developments; (*below*) the impact of rising seas on coasts and islands in the southern Aegean (white areas represent land at the time; sea depths of 50 m (165 ft) and 100 m (330 ft) are shown in lighter grey).

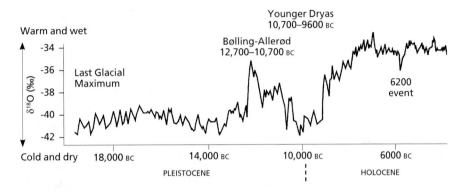

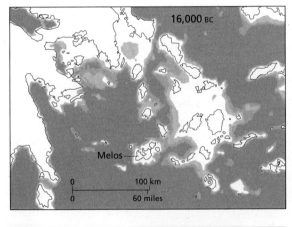

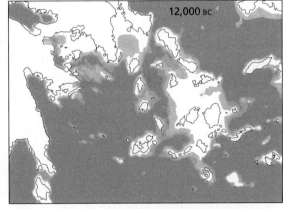

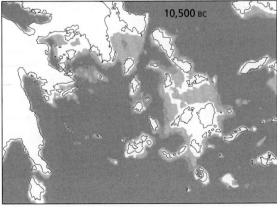

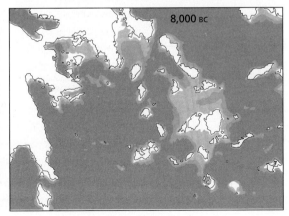

stand, though in the Mediterranean most mountains were released from the grip of year-round ice and snow by 14,000–13,000 BC. The first marked acceleration in temperature rise and the return of the rains dates to 12,700–10,700 BC, a phase known as the Bølling-Allerød interstadial, during which temperatures were similar to today's and rainfall greater. In North Africa, the northward shift in the monsoon belt typical of interglacials brought increased precipitation and a more even seasonal incidence, with summer monsoons and Mediterranean winter rain. The Nile revived with a vengeance, in an alarmingly wild form for hunter-gatherers caught between its turbulence and the desert. Predictably, the Bølling-Allerød witnessed a surge in the pace of sea level recovery, peaking at 1.5–2.0 cm (0.6–0.8 in.) per year, enough to be noticeable in the lifetime of a coastal dweller, and to drown plains near the shore within generational memory. By the end of this phase sea level was just over halfway to its current level, though with many current islands still conjoined or welded to the mainland, and the Pleistocene coastal plains going but not yet gone.[93]

As so many times before, plants burst from their refugia to retake the basin, describing an overall trend of expansion from southeast to northwest that reflects the general climatic cline, but at a finer resolution a chaos of local breakouts, determined by generous rainfall more than temperature.[94] Birch, pine and fir were common early recolonizers in the north, followed by deciduous trees. In the Levant as far east as the Jordan Valley, woodland was on the increase, mainly oak and terebinth, and beyond this a vast warm grassy steppe developed, a now-vanished landscape with swathes of wild cereals and other grasses, speckled with stands of trees.[95] Other parts of the basin took longer to recover. The Anatolian plateau remained a dry, bare steppe and in the Sahara lakes had yet to form.[96] In this fast-changing world the whereabouts of animals were equally fluid. Cold-weather species retreated, eventually to vanishing point, and in the north and east there was a resurgence of forest-loving aurochs, boars and roe deer. Much of this substituted the conveniently herding species of the open plains, and their hunters' dreams of mass kills, for elusive or solitary prey. Red deer, those arch-adapters, dispersed and maintained their hold, as did the similarly resilient gazelle and barbary sheep on the basin's eastern and southern fringes, respectively. Other species of sheep and goat flourished in the Taurus, Levantine uplands and, further east, in the Zagros. Ibexes and chamois, however, both denizens of exposed rocky terrain, fought a long retreat against encroaching trees. One finale is signalled by the crash in counts of ibex bones after 14,500 BC at Grotta Paglicci, on the flanks of Monte Gargano in southeast Italy, as the forest smothered the mountain's peak and extinguished its crag-dwelling fauna.[97] Meanwhile, equids most at home in open landscapes underwent a decline towards local elimination over most of Mediterranean Europe and the Levant, though a few European steppe asses eluded their species' extinction for some time in southern Italy, Asian onagers survived in the Levantine interior and horses never quite vanished from the Meseta.[98] South of the equid-dividing sea, African wild asses, the progenitors of the domestic donkey, continued to thrive in the more open landscapes of North Africa.

4.10 Human and animal figures incised on the wall of Addaura Cave.

But the most explosive and dazzling response to the end of the Last Glacial Maximum was by the Mediterranean's Epipalaeolithic people. Unlike Neanderthals, they did not passively await the return of warmer times, but scouted, probed and leapfrogged ahead of shifting eco-frontiers, already educated by experiences in refugia for what the now-emerging environments of the wider Mediterranean had to offer.[99] The bewildering variety of pathways they pursued can be explained in part by antecedent traditions, long-nurtured in regional redoubts, in part by the specific opportunities and niches that opened up in each area, and in part by the rapid turnover of such openings under the cumulative impact of warming. Mediterranean fragmentation ensured that within a day's walk diverse, evolving resources were available, resources that in more homogeneous areas of the world lay further apart in space or over the passage of time. For instance, patterns of food acquisition at Franchthi Cave, which was reoccupied in the Bølling-Allerød, described a shift from ibex, chamois, steppe ass and aurochs to a later, more diversified reliance on deer, pig, huge amounts of land snails as well as plentiful marine molluscs and some inshore fish, shadowing a transition from more open to more wooded surroundings interspersed with scrub.[100]

Normally we can only infer these hunter-gatherers' activities and appearance from their garbage and rare shell-decorated burials, but occasionally we are treated to a better insight. One such is offered by the poorly dated but roughly contemporary incised images at Addaura Cave on Monte Pellegrino above Palermo, at a time when people were returning to Sicily in strength [**4.10**].[101] Here, lithe, striding women and bearded men hunt, transport bundles and join in group dances. Some sport bird beaks or penis sheaths, and one much debated depiction shows contorted floating figures, maybe shamans on their dream-quest, or trussed-up victims. Whether they represent mythic events or everyday life, these images reveal a world of constant movement, rich in symbols and ritual. Different insights into contemporary world-views come from pebbles and other objects scored in a way that appears to mark the passage of time.[102] These are widespread in Iberia, southern France and Italy, with outliers as far as the Levant. Beyond revealing the challenges of scheduling activities in an ever-changing world, they may hint at deeper emergent ideas about time and the cosmos.

The most generalized initial response to the waning of the cold was a wave of expansion into hitherto empty or thinly inhabited regions, part of a global population boom that amply demonstrates hunter-gatherers' capacity to multiply fast when the going is good. The Magdalenian and its post-Kebaran contemporaries in the Levant represented bow waves of pioneer reclamation that maintained remarkable uniformity over extensive areas, the former from the northwest Mediterranean as far as Britain and Russia by 12,000 BC, the latter signalled by a rash of tiny sites spreading deep into the grassy parkland coming into being all the way from Sinai to the Euphrates.[103] The late efflorescence of cave and portable art in the Magdalenian, immortalized by Lascaux and Altamira, as well as the ongoing circulation of seashell far inland, make sense in terms of ritual integration and sharing of knowledge in a rapidly changing natural and social world. Although most of the Sahara remained empty, and the perilously rushing banks of the Nile were sparsely occupied, Iberomaurusian groups in Mediterranean North Africa blossomed and began to move south, inland, as conditions improved.[104]

Repeopling also entailed smaller-scale infilling. On the south Turkish coast the hinterland of the Gulf of Antalya filled up with sites, such as Öküzini and Beldibi caves, set against increasingly wooded backdrops.[105] It was from such bridgeheads, or ones further east in the Taurus foothills, that people began to infiltrate the southern Anatolian plateau.[106] This process is poorly understood, but one consequence was the appearance in the Levant of tiny quantities of central Anatolian obsidian by 14,000 BC, its earliest arrival in the Mediterranean proper.[107] Similar infilling and radiation to take over very different kinds of landscapes took place in the southern Balkans, along the wooded coastline of Dalmatia and in the wider Adriatic, where an estimated several thousand hunter-gatherers appeared swiftly between the hills and the sea, presumably an archaeological optical illusion created by their retreat from the drowning Adriatic plain.[108] Sicily was certainly an island (just) when people began to re-enter it, though Aegean Lemnos and Adriatic Brač were still probably joined to their nearest mainland when the first hunter-gatherers arrived.[109]

Given the diversity of environments and foods in the midst of which bands of hunter-gatherers lived, it is unsurprising that forms of mobility varied considerably. Residential mobility, whereby the entire group and its base camp moved periodically through the cycle of the year, seems to have been the norm in certain cases, notably the immediately postglacial Levant, where sites were small and undifferentiated save for a few large seasonal aggregation points around the basin of the Azraq lake [**4.11**].[110] But under certain circumstances, fixed base camps can be identified by the wider range of finds, depths of deposits and occasional burials, and mobility instead took a 'logistical' form, by which specific task groups spread out seasonally, or on shorter expeditions. Two good examples of the latter are the Taforalt and Afalou bou Rhummel caves in the Maghreb, both of which reveal plentiful human remains (up to 183 individuals, with skeletal peculiarities that support the idea of a long-isolated population in Africa's northwest), an early effort at trepanation, a distinctive cultural marker in the pulling of incisors at puberty, and a symbolic efflorescence of animal and human figures and carved ostrich eggshell.[111] The distinction between the fixed base camp

4.11 The large seasonal aggregation site of Wadi Jilat 6 in the Azraq basin, seen in the foreground with a subsequently incised wadi beyond, was a magnet for gazelle hunters in the late-glacial Levant.

kind of mobility and residence patterns that were in effect sedentary is a matter of degree. Indeed, as we have seen, a partly sedentary way of life had occasionally been practised during the Last Glacial Maximum, where localized resources and spatial constraints encouraged it. In addition, ways of living could change over time within a region, and not always describing a neat evolutionary sequence towards fixed abodes. The thin strip between the Jordan Valley and the Mediterranean Sea provides a good illustration. Here, the residential mobility just alluded to was replaced early in the Bølling-Allerød by what we shall soon see was the most sophisticated semi-sedentary society yet to emerge in the Mediterranean, but which would itself revert to higher mobility in its final phase.

The shifting patchwork of new environments also had a profound impact on hunting tactics. The ever greater reliance on killing and carefully processing small or solitary game explains the increasing prevalence of microlithic projectile points and cutting or scraping tools, many now in tiny 'geometric' forms. It may cast light, too, on the incipient domestication of dogs, for symbiosis with a smell-sensitive predator offered obvious advantages in detecting camouflaged, elusive prey in overgrown landscapes. The timings of the surely multiple occasions around the world when dogs split genetically from wolves are controversial, but signs of canine incorporation into human culture date to the last few thousand years of the Pleistocene in Europe and the Levant.[112] More generally, early postglacial millennia saw the rise of ultra-specialized hunting, best documented in north-central parts of the basin, though comparable wild goat hunters also start to appear in the Taurus at this time.[113] Much of this entailed seasonal ventures into the mountains, to heights seldom frequented

133

4.12 Seasonal activity in the Mediterranean highlands as climate ameliorated is well illustrated by excavations at Klithi rockshelter, seen at centre right amidst the cliffs and gorges of the Pindos mountains.

before. Each window of opportunity was sandwiched between the retreat of one line (snow) and advance of another (timber). A telling example is Klithi rockshelter in the cliffs of the dramatic Vikos Gorge, which slices through the Pindos mountains of northwest Greece [**4.12**].[114] Between 16,500 and 12,500 BC, Klithi was one point in a web of locations that enabled summer access by task groups based on the now half-inundated coastal plain to the west, or beside Lake Ioannina. Klithi was visited for a few days each year by a handful of hunters, who used it to process carcasses brought in from expeditions in the surrounding highlands. The precisely targeted nature of such activity is revealed by the bones, over 99 per cent of which come from ibexes and chamois, both difficult targets mainly killed in their prime. Meanwhile, at Grotta del Clusantin in the foothills of the Italian Alps, marmots were the almost exclusive victim during summer visits around 12,000 BC, in all likelihood valued for fur and fat as much as their meat.[115]

Not all activity in the now increasingly accessible uplands was this focused, however. A veritable scramble to exploit the southeastern Alps erupted as they began to open up after 12,500 BC, with frequent traces of people at altitudes over 1000 m (3250 ft).[116] Finds of children's milk teeth suggest residential mobility, with whole families who wintered below in the Po or Adige valleys moving to the highlands for the summer. At Riparo Dalmeri, on the Asiago plateau, at an altitude of 1240 m (4070 ft), ibexes dominate the animal bones, but the hundreds of ochre-drawn depictions on stone slabs illustrate other animals as well, including red deer, beavers, marmots, hares and squirrels, in addition to local lake fish.[117] The truly special-purpose sites in this part of the mountains are found almost twice as high, while the movement of flints suggests the crossing of passes over 2600 m (8500 ft) in altitude.

Along some, but certainly not all, of the coast, seafoods became increasingly important as coastal plains shrank, though the famous calculation that one would need to eat 150,000 cockles to gain the calorific equivalent of one red deer should never be forgotten.[118] Two zones of particularly thorough exploitation stand out. One is in the Tyrrhenian region, where coastal middens of discarded shells are a regular feature by 12,000 BC. The shrinking size of shells over time in the abundant middens around the shores of northwest Sicily reveals a familiar story of steady depletion, in this case by people moving into a hitherto more or less virgin island.[119] The other zone is Iberia, partly under Atlantic influence, where fish bones and art reveal an intensification of the earlier fishing habit late in the Magdalenian (13,000–10,000 BC), with open-water fish now more common, as well as tiny species like sardines most plausibly taken in nets.[120] Bone harpoons are ubiquitous in southern Iberia and France, but one comes from an altogether more arresting location: an Iberomaurusian stratum at Taforalt Cave in Morocco, where it dates to the 12th millennium BC, and stands out as an alien, trans-Mediterranean intrusion [**4.13**].[121] Whether it arrived in Africa as hafted flotsam, embedded in a fish that got away, or finally bears witness to linkage across the Gibraltar strait is impossible to determine. If the last of these options (as is tempting to assume), it should be stressed that this find is the first, but for this period still singular, definite sign of interaction between Iberia and the Maghreb, two regions with still nothing else of significance in common among their cultural repertoires.

By now there is good evidence that people were eating plants in a minor way around much of the basin, with especially well-documented remains of wild legumes and cereals at Franchthi.[122] But the engagement with this floral potential was led by the Levant, at one end of a Fertile Crescent uniquely rich in large-seeded grasses, including wild stands of wheat and barley, as well as abundant legumes.[123] Here, exploitation of a broad spectrum of plants went back to Ohalo II at the Last Glacial

4.13 The first trans-Mediterranean object? Fragment of a harpoon tip of Iberian type discovered in the Maghrebian cave of Taforalt.

Maximum, accompanied by grinding stones and, at an indeterminate point, simple microlithic knives for reaping food- or fibre-rich plants – a few of which, as also in North Africa around the same time, start to preserve traces of polish from slicing stems.[124] The ample rain of the Bølling-Allerød, together with rising populations in this ecologically diverse yet condensed zone of wooded hills, grassland and lakes, now began to effect a more thoroughgoing, active and culturally embracing use of plants.[125] Natural stands of cereals and other species were nurtured and encouraged (by controlled burning, for example), creating in effect wild gardens. Evidence comes from plant finds (which number 150 species at contemporary Abu Hureyra on the Euphrates),[126] the first true sickles assembled from mounted flints, and a boom in grinding gear, including deep mortars, some with incised designs and others carved into bedrock as an ultimate testimony to sedentary ways [PL. XI]. Human teeth reveal the damage done by carbohydrates while bone chemistry confirms a more vegetal diet.[127] Such wild plant tending and consumption was simply one element of a broader cluster of traits that collectively delineate the Early Natufian (12,500–10,800 BC), without doubt the most unusual and elaborate societies existent in the Mediterranean at this time, and for which the conventional Epipalaeolithic label seems entirely inappropriate.[128]

The core Natufian zone lay in the northern part of modern Israel, at ecological hotspots in the lush country between the Jordan Valley lakes and Mediterranean coast, though elements of Natufian culture and activity can also be found, mainly associated with more mobile hunter-gatherers, as far south as the Negev and as far north, inland, as the Euphrates. Within the focal area, sedentary occupation at the same spot over much of the year can be deduced from three kinds of evidence, beyond the small, round, hut-like structures encountered. One is the first presence of modest stone- or mud-lined storage pits; their contents are unknown, but wild cereals or legumes are obvious candidates. Such pits indicate a shift in emphasis towards delayed, seasonal, rather than immediate returns from the food-quest.[129] The origins and antiquity of food storage are obscure (as are those for meat preservation by smoking, salting or drying, all alternatives to the natural freezers of northern glacial climes). Like so much else, it probably had minor, episodic beginnings further back in time, but the Natufian marks its coming of age and the start of the accession to social and economic prominence of what later became a crucial element of Mediterranean lifestyles. A second indication of sedentism is the appearance of the earliest 'commensals', or behaviourally and genetically altered animals, such as house mice and sparrows, that became entirely dependent on stable human residence.[130] Third, tooth eruption stages among the animals hunted appear to suggest that virtually year-round kills were brought back to the same location, by hunting parties that had manifestly been absent from what we might now call 'home' for some time, often in quite distant habitats.[131] This last point reminds us that for all their prowess with plants, the Natufian people were proficient hunters too, mainly of gazelle but also aurochs, boar, deer, sheep, goat and onager, and adept to an unprecedented degree in netting and snaring of birds and other small, fast game.[132]

I (*previous page*) The often spectacular
vertical stacking of Mediterranean
environments is a product of the basin's
violent tectonic history. Here, snow-capped
Mount Ida in central Crete towers over
its wooded foothills, the coastal end of
the fertile Mesara plain, and the island's
southern shore near the Bronze and Iron
Age port of Kommos.

II (*opposite*) Cellular lowland plains ringed
by mountains, and often with an outlet on
the sea, have acted as foci of settlement
for millennia. This Cretan view shows the
Bronze Age palace of Knossos, aligned on
the sacred peak of Mount Iouktas. Under the
fields beyond the palace lies a big, largely
unexcavated town.

III Egyptian and Mesopotamian royal
inscriptions side by side at the mouth of the
Dog River in Lebanon, where the mountains
and sea squeeze the options for travel on
foot and create a long-lasting terrestrial
conduit.

IV This satellite view of the Cyclades, Dodecanese, Crete, and more northerly Aegean islands, including Samos, Chios and Lesbos, demonstrates the huge diversity of Mediterranean islands in terms of size, shape, constellation and relationship to a sometimes almost-insular coastline.

V The Nile Delta, greatest in the Mediterranean, has created a massive verdant triangular oasis, seen here in its modern form, on the otherwise arid northeast African coast. Beyond, the coast curves away to the Levant, while the Gulf of Suez gives access to the Red Sea; in the far distance, the rugged marches of Sinai.

VI (*opposite*) Archaeologists at work on one of the great exposures of Palaeolithic levels at Atapuerca in northern Spain, which were initially revealed by the late 19th-century construction of a mining railroad.

140

VII (*opposite*) The rock of Gibraltar, as it looks today and as it might have appeared during phases of lower sea level to the Neanderthals occupying large caverns along its base.

VIII (*right*) Two Upper Palaeolithic female figurines long ago excavated from the Balzi Rossi caves, near Menton in France, that have recently resurfaced in Canada: (*left*) a small serpentine dual-headed pendant; (*right*) a more typical mammoth ivory figurine.

IX (*below*) Among the creatures depicted by Upper Palaeolithic people during the Last Glacial Maximum on the walls of the Cosquer Cave, now entered underwater off Marseille, is the great auk, a penguin-like flightless bird only recently driven to ultimate extinction in the north Atlantic, and once a harbinger of glacial conditions and influxes of cold oceanic water in the Mediterranean.

X Natufian bone sickle haft from Hanahal Cave in the Carmel escarpment in modern northern Israel, with what can be identified as a young gazelle carved on its tip, in an intriguing juxtaposing of the spheres of plant-gathering and hunting.

XI These heavy, well-crafted mortars and pestles from the Natufian site of Wadi Hammeh 27 in modern Jordan testify in exceptionally elaborated form to an increasing investment in grinding equipment for processing grass seeds and other initially wild crops in several parts of the Mediterranean after the Last Glacial Maximum.

Gazelle bones provide an eloquent testimony to contemporary hunting skills, for the ages of the animals killed shows that even these swift creatures came under greater pressure than ever before. Many were intercepted and slaughtered en masse in their seasonal migrations through the steppe, while other gazelle species were taken individually by hunting among the crags of the Lebanon, at altitudes of up to 2000 m (6500 ft).

The number of people in these Natufian communities can only be estimated from the extent of the sites and counts of the huts among which either nuclear families or more extended, maybe polygamous, groups were distributed. For larger places like Ain Mallaha (or Eynan to use its Israeli name), beside Lake Hula, some 200 people is the realistic upper limit [**4.14**]. Skeletal and cultural distinctions between communities in the core area indicate several distinct groups, and could imply a link between residential territory and social identity, though, interestingly, the artifacts tentatively associated with women's activities (plant-related) are more localized in style than those male-affiliated (hunting gear), which could hint at gendered distinctions in terms of labour and mobility.[133] Indeed, to characterize the Natufian merely in terms of food and size of communities, unique as these were, is to miss out on the sheer sophistication of its symbolic world. Most of its components find parallels earlier and elsewhere: burial, figural art, body ornaments (now of stone as well as animal products), and long-range exotics, mainly shells from the Mediterranean, Red Sea and even the Nile,[134] plus tiny amounts of Anatolian obsidian. What is new is the intensity of their deployment and their combination in unprecedented ways, for example in a carved bone sickle handle carved into a gazelle [PL. X].[135] The burials, of which some 400 are known, are more frequent than elsewhere in the Mediterranean, and bodies more richly ornamented, perhaps denoting kinship position, social role or status achieved in life. Natufian sedentism owed its

4.14 Plan of the living structures, burials, hearths, grinding equipment and storage facilities at the major Natufian settlement of Ain Mallaha, and cumulatively indicative of a growing investment in sedentary life.

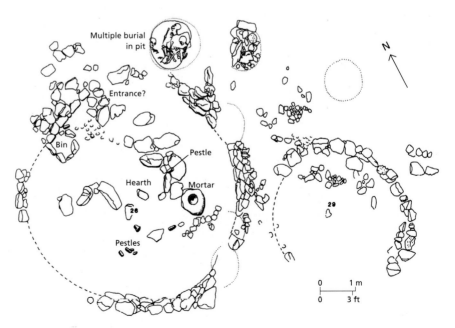

145

success not just to its viability in an unusually favourable window, but its compelling attractiveness in terms of social opportunities and the excitement of participation in such congregations of people. Big Natufian communities were complex places, in effect unfamiliar hunter-gatherer villages, and while they certainly drew upon deeper Mediterranean traditions, they also looked to a very different future.

The sting in the tail

It would be too beguilingly simple to depict the Mediterranean in the Bølling-Allerød interstadial as a hunter-gatherer demi-paradise. If indices of violence are sought, they can be found, not least in the form of arrowheads embedded in human victims.[136] But against this must be weighed the overall picture from the skeletons of the basin's now-record numbers of inhabitants, for example the healthy, if grit-worn Natufian teeth, which reveal few episodes of childhood or adult stress, similar data from Italy, and instances where the injured, toothless and even dwarf had been cared for enough to survive.[137] At the very least, there was a notable reduction in external stresses and, as elsewhere on the planet, the conclusion is irresistible that humanity in its modern guise had never had it so good. No less significantly, the manners in which Mediterranean people lived were more diverse than ever before. To crudely caricature these as a vegetable-led diet in the Levant, hunting domination in the north and south, and marine exploitation in the coastal west is far too simple, as all three of these mainstays were combined with differing central tendencies right across the basin. Yet inherent in such distinctions of degree was the potential for very different kinds of futures should any of these tendencies intensify.

Around 10,700 BC this halcyon age was rudely interrupted by a swing back to glacial conditions that lasted for roughly 1100 years – a duration often referred to as a cold snap by climatologists, but nearly as protracted as the span of time from Charlemagne (or his great contemporary the Abbasid Caliph Harun al-Rashid) until the present. This bleak if critical phase is known as the Younger Dryas, after the tundra plant that first helped to identify its existence.[138] This was the last joker in the Pleistocene pack, and similar in impact and duration to the earlier Heinrich events associated with spates of Atlantic iceberg calving. The Younger Dryas itself was triggered, in an illustration of the paradoxical feedbacks in the world's climate system, by icy meltwaters from the shrinking North American ice sheets spewing into the north Atlantic, where they shut down the conveyor currents of warm water and precipitated an abrupt return to cold, dry times. It was harshly felt across the Mediterranean, and in parts of the Aegean and Levant may have brought even worse aridity than the Last Glacial Maximum. The advance of the trees halted and was then reversed. Sea level rise petered out globally, and Lake Lisan dropped by some 200 m (650 ft) to below the level of the Dead Sea today.

For Natufian communities, the Younger Dryas had disastrous consequences. Caught between a rapidly deteriorating climate and a population that had peaked at exceptional densities during a boom time, the time-honoured refuges must have been

4.15 Reconstruction of the remarkable Late Natufian burial of an elderly woman, accompanied by a range of animal parts, recently found at Hilazon Tachtit.

overwhelmed and the southern Levant probably experienced substantial mortality.[139] The often physically smaller, less well-nourished Late Natufian survivors reverted to residential mobility (back in essence to the Kebaran), with the old sedentary bases still used for burials in a poignant display of remembrance of things past. After burial the new practice of skull removal and curation initiated a long Levantine tradition and probably began as a way of reconciling an ancestral sense of place with the realities of a life again on the move. The most ritually charged Natufian burial dates to this late phase: the recent find at Hilazon Tachtit Cave in Galilee of the shells of fifty tortoises consumed in a funerary meal, a golden eagle's wing-tip, a leopard's pelvis, martens' skulls, an aurochs's tail, a boar's leg, and last but not least a severed human foot, all buried with a small, elderly disabled woman, who has been interpreted as a shaman [**4.15**].[140] Elsewhere there was less far to fall, but effects were still marked. Istrian sites ceased to be frequented, while in northwest Greece Klithi, abandoned since 12,700 BC when the forest reached the area and drove off the ibexes, enjoyed a converse return to favour as the arboreal tide temporarily ebbed.[141] In North Africa a gap in dated horizons in the Maghreb looks suspicious, and further east Haua Fteah stood empty.[142] Archaeologists elsewhere in the Mediterranean have been slow to identify the Younger Dryas's chilly signature, but the signs are often there; for instance, at Grotta Romanelli on the sea cliffs of Apulia, between coastal lagoons and the inland plain, the first occupation was accompanied by the remains of dry-land horses, steppe asses and bustards, as well as that harbinger of cold, the great auk.[143] And in one further realm of activity there is a clear correlation with the Younger Dryas. This, as we shall learn in Chapter 5, is the start of proficient Mediterranean seafaring, a crucial stage in the creation of the Middle Sea.

CHAPTER FIVE

Brave new worlds

(10,000 – 5500 BC)

Pigmy hippopotami and the island of black glass

Cyprus, the solitary insular giant of the far eastern Mediterranean, has yet to enter our history. Like other islands, it has its claimed Palaeolithic finds, but it stands out for the thoroughness with which they have been found wanting. The cramped rockshelter that does yield the earliest definite evidence for the arrival of people, right at the end of the Pleistocene, was first discovered back in 1961 by the son of an RAF officer, out fossil-hunting on the cliffs of the Akrotiri peninsula in the south of the island – an area still encompassed by one of the few foreign bases to outlive the waning of imperialism. Aetokremnos, 'the eagle's cliff', was relocated and excavated in the late 1980s [**5.1**].[1] Its upper stratum, dated to the 11th millennium BC, had abundant signs of people, including hearths, stone tools, and a few shell and stone ornaments. With these were thousands of sea-shells, bones of bustards and many other birds, a few wild boar toe fragments (once attached to skins?) and, last but far from least, almost 4000 bones of the extinct Cypriot pigmy hippopotamus, whose full-sized ancestors had swum over from the

5.1 Aerial view of the steep Akrotiri peninsula in Cyprus, with the Aetokremnos rockshelter about one quarter of the way down on the left. Lighter sea tones below indicate a different, lagoonal coastline at the end of the Pleistocene.

mainland far back in the Pleistocene, and which glories in the Linnaean name of *Phanourios minutus*. Changes to its leg structure and the placement of nostrils and eyes reveal that this stocky grazing beast the size of a pig had adapted on Cyprus to rough terrain as much as wetland.[2] Aetokremnos's lower stratum, however, had a very different character. A few artifacts were found there too, but most of the finds comprised 218,000 densely packed hippopotamus bones, from at least 500 animals, plus a few hundred more from dwarfed elephants; a third of the bones bore traces of fire.

The excavators offer the following reconstruction. The first people to venture out to Cyprus from the mainland found it stocked with pigmy hippopotami. Unused as these were to predators, they made easy targets, and from time to time hunting bands would settle in to exploit this vulnerability. They explored the island thoroughly, to judge by local cherts and blue picrolite used for tools and beads. Hippopotami killed elsewhere were transported to Aetokremnos to be butchered and eaten, creating a thick bone midden. But the rate of slaughter eventually proved too much for a species already under pressure from the environmental changes at the end of the Pleistocene. The hippopotami dwindled to extinction, and the hunters shifted for a while to smaller prey, mainly birds, before abandoning the effort and perhaps the island too.

This makes a compelling narrative, consonant with the huge accumulation of bone and its mid-slope location, neither of which are features of natural hippopotamus bone beds at sinkhole traps or birthing and dying sites. But it remains controversial nonetheless.[3] The lack of cutmarks, marrow extraction or skeletal articulation are all puzzling, as is the practice of lugging heavy carcasses to the site intact (for all body parts are present). Others point to the shelter's low roof and argue that it was merely a cache, smoking-space or dump for activities carried out in the open air. Most troubling of all is the differing composition of the two strata, and the possibility that what little overlap there is between them reflects churning over once people moved in. Sceptics contend that the hunters post-date the hippopotami and instead lived mainly off birds and molluscs. Further traces of such visitors, probably summer encampments to judge by their exposed locations, are in fact currently emerging from coastal sand-dunes and river mouths elsewhere on the island, some now submerged; their signature too is one of birds, shells and stone tools.[4] On the other hand, the hippopotami certainly did vanish around this time. Elsewhere on Cyprus, their last well-dated bones belong to the start of the Bølling-Allerød warming, and are absent from Holocene sites, thereby defining a window of some 4000 years during part of which people were present and potentially cohabiting with a meat prospect hard to ignore. Given this smoking gun, even if the ambiguities of Aetokremnos cannot clinch the case, other finds might well do so in the future. A tantalizing report of hippopotamus bones with tools at Arkhangelos Mikhail, in the underexplored north should, for example, raise a speculative eyebrow.[5]

Aetokremnos therefore constitutes a question mark in the debate over human responsibility (whether by direct overkill or attrition through habitat destruction,

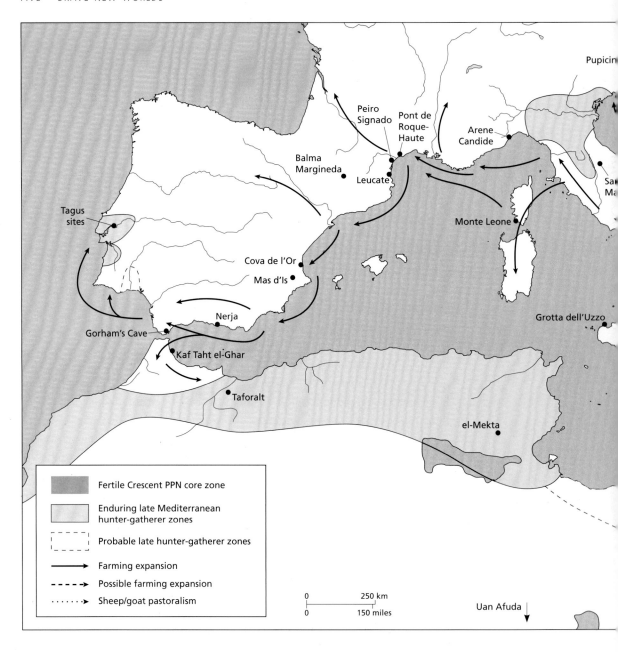

5.2 Map of sites mentioned in this chapter, also showing high North African lake stands, the initial core zone of farming, subsequent main axes of expansion, and some of the principal residual Mesolithic enclaves.

disease and competition from other introduced animals) for a crescendo of extinctions among the Mediterranean's island endemics from the end of the Pleistocene onward.[6] The larger insular mammals were worst hit and the cumulative loss was almost total. Of all those that had evolved over hundreds of millennia, today just two shrew species remain, one (like many a resistance movement) in the Cretan mountains, the other on Sicily and Gozo, plus a Cypriot mouse newly elevated to endemic status on the basis of its genes.[7] Keeping a low profile has obviously been advantageous, as is apparent from the better survival rate of reptiles, too. The largest mammal to hang on into later times was the hare-like, fast-breeding *Prolagus sardus.*

These endured on Sardinia until the boom years of the Iron Age, and in Corsican obscurity into Roman times, when Pliny the Elder and Polybius mistook them for rabbits; sheltered from the predations of black rats, one redoubt even held out on an islet off Sardinia until the 18th century AD.[8] The Balearic goat-antelope, *Myotragus balearicus*, vanished during the 3rd millennium BC, under suspicious circumstances addressed in Chapter 7. Aside from far earlier losses, everything larger – hippopotami, elephants, deer and a few carnivores – died out just before, during or after the end of the Pleistocene, admittedly during a phase of climatic turbulence (if no more so than earlier oscillations), but also close to the times of human arrival. Indeed, save for the arguably temporary intrusion of people into Corsardinia at the Last Glacial Maximum, there is no solid example of lasting coexistence between large island mammals and humans. The corollary is worth noting too: excepting the few tiny endemic survivors, all the Mediterranean island mammals seen today are domestic or feral descendants of continental fauna purposefully or accidentally introduced by people – even the wild goats and mouflons touted as curiosities on and beyond islands, whose elegant horns betray recessive ancestral characteristics that returned once they were no longer being deliberately bred for other traits.[9] This anthropogenic process has boosted the species count on islands, yet banalized their hitherto unique compositions.

An archaeological site as tiny as Aetokremnos would have earned its place in the hall of fame had it demonstrated just one potential 'first'. Yet it and its newly found contemporaries announce a further practice of even more fundamental importance for Mediterranean history. As we have seen, by the Last Glacial Maximum certain people commanded seagoing abilities sufficient to cross modest stretches of open water, and there are sporadic signals of earlier short-range activity going back to the Aurignacian, and perhaps Neanderthal or even older culturally enhanced forms of floating. Such intermittent, tentative false starts and messing about with prototypical boats manifestly had a long, if thoroughly obscure, history, and forms the background and baseline for subsequent Mediterranean developments. But a presence of people on Cyprus denotes something that on present evidence is entirely new: substantially longer-range, actively navigated and probably more regular maritime movement. The deep seas surrounding Cyprus ensured that the distances were little different from modern ones, namely 65–70 km (40–45 miles) from Turkey and 100 km (60 miles) from the northern Levant, both crossings entirely without intervening stepping stones, and therefore giant leaps by the Mediterranean standards of their time. Moreover, the fact that early sites encircle the island could imply further cruising along the shore after initial landfall, searching for suitable campsites.

In this respect Cyprus is not quite alone. Before Aetokremnos was excavated, tiny amounts of obsidian from Melos had been detected in levels of comparable age (and all subsequent phases) at Franchthi Cave in the northeast Peloponnese, two places 120 km (75 miles) apart as the crow flies, and never linked by land in recent geological times.[10] Once again two Mediterranean firsts can be identified, the maritime one now sharing the prize with Cyprus, the other marking the earliest access to island obsidian – some 20,000 years later, it might be noted, than in Japan and 10,000 years after Melanesia.[11] Over the last few years, our resolution on this exploit's context has greatly improved.[12] Obsidian first appears at Franchthi in levels characterized by a diet almost as parlous as that of a hippopotamus-less Aetokremnos, with decreases in land mammals and fish, vast numbers of snails and shifts in marine molluscs. Crossing distances to Melos from Attica, the nearest mainland, via hops through the western Cyclades, were 15–20 km (10–12 miles) apiece (plus intervening coastwise travel), again similar to the present [5.3].[13] A more direct but

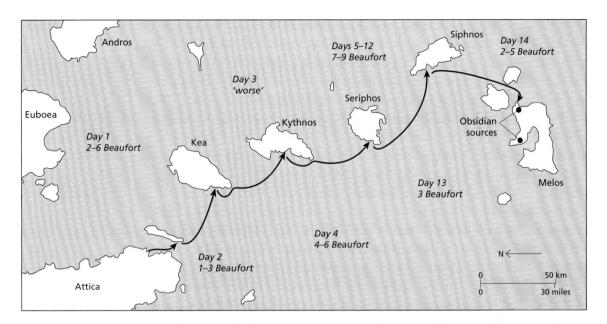

5.3 Experimental travel in a hypothetical reed boat and its journey time between Attica and Melos, mapped with notes on changing weather conditions.

hazardous open-sea route with jumps of up to 35 km (22 miles) ran southeast from Franchthi via then shrinking or drowning islets west of the Cyclades, though the tiny quantities of obsidian cast doubt on whether Franchthi was procuring directly or from undiscovered intermediaries. The individual crossing distances on neither route rival those to Cyprus, but the sum totals are higher, as much as 250–300 km (150–185 miles) via Attica, with return journeys to be considered. Moreover, as was long ago pointed out, we are surely only spotting the tip of an iceberg, for this discovery of the two Melian outcrops of obsidian in the midst of a complex archipelago

153

only makes sense as the outcome of a more thoroughgoing maritime exploration of the Aegean that has otherwise left almost no trace.[14]

Such maritime distances become more impressive and thought-provoking when translated into travel time. No boat remains or depictions are known this early, or for several more millennia, so it is impossible to ascertain whether seacraft improved at this juncture, but on balance it is more likely that the same kind of craft that must have existed by the Last Glacial Maximum, if not before, remained in use. After all, a boat afloat after 10 km (6 miles) should, all things being equal, still be so after 100 km (60 miles). Simple vessels still, or until very recently, in use provide a good idea of the general options and performance.[15] Reed-built, skin-and-frame and fire-hollowed dugout craft were all feasible with the toolkits of the time. Each might carry a few people and a light load in moderate seas over some 20 km (12 miles) a day as the crow flies. An experimental journey from Attica to Melos in a 6-m (20-ft) reed boat with six paddlers managed this in good conditions, but once days lost to bad weather are taken into account it took two weeks to complete a one-way journey, implying trips of a month if time for quarrying and return against prevailing winds is added in [5.3].[16] Certain people (probably men) must have been away at sea for a long time. Even the shortest crossing to Cyprus from coastal Turkey, from where the island presents the easiest, lengthways target, would have required a couple of days and the intervening night, and the journey from the Levant is longer, with all sight of land lost in mid-crossing. These are skilful exploits in comparison to anything that can be clearly demonstrated to have taken place substantially earlier. As such, they mark the inception of true *seafaring* in the Mediterranean, and the point at which the basin begins to rival the earlier foci of activity along the west Pacific rim – though the Pacific retained its lead, with a daring crossing to the island of Manus in Melanesia, shortly before 12,000 BC, that traversed 200–20 km (125–35 miles) of open ocean, 60–90 km (35–55 miles) of which lay out of sight of land.[17] In both these theatres, it should be underscored, seafaring was an emphatically hunter-gatherer invention.

So why did true seafaring emerge in the Mediterranean at this time and in such places?[18] For many years, limitations on radiocarbon dating and climate reconstruction precluded more than a general correlation with the rosy effects of postglacial warming and rising seas. Now, however, we know that the earliest Melian obsidian was obtained in the 11th millennium BC, and perhaps slightly earlier within that millennium than at Aetokremnos. It is a shock to realize that both these fall in the depths of the Younger Dryas (10,700–9600 BC), that drastic return to cold, arid conditions and a chilly sea no longer encroaching on coastal territory. If this correlation is broadly sustained – and slightly earlier finds cannot be ruled out[19] – Mediterranean seafaring began in hard not halcyon times, and this in turn forces a rethink as to why people started to practise it. Humans as much as hippopotami were under stress, and one likely answer is a search for refuges that would enable members of a recently booming population to survive as prospects deteriorated. Episodic visits to Cyprus (climatically buffered by its maritime location) neatly parallel the contemporary Late Natufian reversion to mobile lifestyles, and a further association between the two might be discerned in the fact that the first sea-fish at inland Hatoula, in Israel, date to the Late Natufian.[20] Similarly desperate adaptations can be envisaged in the Aegean, with the discovery of obsidian a non-commensurate compensation for other losses less visible to us. There are points of comparison with the move to Corsardinia at the Last Glacial Maximum, but this time there was a crucial difference: seagoing became more than a means of hopping across marine moats, and started to become an activity that reaped additional dividends. What began as a short-term response to crisis conditions became locked in as a longer-term practice, as amply revealed by ongoing acquisition of Melian obsidian long after the Younger Dryas had faded into memory, plus a crescendo of seafaring from early in the Holocene that built upon the cumulative legacy of maritime know-ledge. From this juncture, we no longer need to ask whether seafaring existed to any serious degree in the Mediterranean, and instead can begin to enquire where it was being practised, by whom, and to what ends and effects.

Are the points in Mediterranean space where we first witness seafaring equally significant? There are sure to be plenty of surprises in store, but before we succumb to the pessimistic assumption that our pattern of discoveries is random, let us return to the properties of Mediterranean coasts analyzed in Chapter 2, and particularly the extent to which likely natural hotspots of early maritime activity are identifiable, in the present context as seafaring 'nurseries'.[21] The most promising candidates are, first of all, the Aegean, followed by Dalmatia and its southward extension, as well as south-ern Italy, Sicily and the arc from Tuscany through Elba to Corsica and Sardinia, plus several smaller foci, including at Gibraltar and the Gulf of İskenderun, where Anatolia and the Levant meet. Late Pleistocene conditions would not have altered this greatly, although some regions might have been enhanced, notably the Gulf of İskenderun, which was probably larger and studded with islands now turned into hills mired by river-borne silt, while parts of the Aegean were being gradually re-insularized, poten-tially creating islanders in situ from any inhabitants who did not retreat.[22] It is striking how well this list correlates with the most reliable traces of early maritime activity, from the possible Neanderthal or earlier experiments in and around the Aegean, via the Aurignacian of Sicily, the Corsardinians of the Last Glacial Maximum, and the Iberian harpoon found in Morocco, to the quantum leap in the Younger Dryas rep-resented by ventures in the Aegean and out to Cyprus. That the final breakthroughs occurred in the east is no surprise, given the Aegean's qualities as a maritime nursery, the particularly ghastly Younger Dryas endured in this sector of the Mediterranean, and arguably also the exceptional dynamics of the Natufian Levant.

Just as we will shortly find was the case for another epochal development in the opening phases of the Holocene, the emergence of true seafaring in the Mediterranean was a result of processes specific to unusual places at an unusual time. Once triggered in one or more parts of the basin, however, its expansion to others had the potential to revolutionize the logic of Mediterranean space and erode the nearly 2 million-year-old tyranny of the basin's 'negative geography', a world of sea-barriers, peninsular cul-de-sacs, waterlocked islands, constricted isthmuses and habitat islands cut off by desert. Elements of the world of a Middle Sea could start to appear, very faintly at first, and mainly in favourable areas, but in time gaining clarity, reach and dynamism. The sea's margin was no longer merely a source of food and materials, but a potential portal to maritime connections that could bind together patches of land hitherto cut off from each other, or separated by immense overland distances. This is most obvious in the case of islands. The distance required to reach Cyprus from Anatolia (which was of an order that typically kept seafarers within sight of land, given decent visibility and high ground at both ends) would bring Crete, Corsica, Sardinia and a host of smaller islands into range; in fact it omits only a few remote outliers, mainly the Balearics and a few specks south of Sicily. From now on, islands' qualities such as their size, distance, place amidst wider configurations, and rare resources would exert increasing influence over activity on and around them, whether seasonal visits or long-term settlement and the inception of island life. But such crossing distances also span several of the basin's key narrows, notably across the Aegean and, perhaps most importantly, the 72 km (45 miles) of the Strait of Otranto between the Balkan coast and heel of Italy. Such links could start to break down the barriers between people living in the sequence of peninsulas and sub-basins along the northern side of the Mediterranean, whose only connection until now had been their far-distant northern roots in continental Europe. In the case of the African Mediterranean, geography and culture would prompt radically different results, as we shall see at the end of this chapter, but this exception should not detract from the wider observation that the advent of seafaring raised the prospect of a Mediterranean turned inside out, an arena more fittingly understood from its centre than its edges.

Paradise regained?

The end of the Younger Dryas came swiftly around 9600 BC, with temperature rises of as much as 7°C (12.5°F) in a few decades. This marked the beginning of the Holocene, the most recent 11,600 years of the planet's life into which most human achievement has been crammed and during which, without our interventions, Earth would broadly resemble its state in the previous interglacial over 100,000 years ago.[23] In the Mediterranean the overall trends in climate and environment continued those of the Bølling-Allerød until about 5500 BC, with a peak around 8000–7000 BC, when temperatures averaged 2°C (3.5°F) above present.[24] In other respects, too, the early Holocene echoes a litany familiar from earlier warmings. Rainfall was higher, albeit to varying degrees. Estimates of 20 per cent above current levels (a welcome extra 50–200 mm (2–8 in.) in most areas) are a reasonable minimum, but in the south the incursion of the tropical monsoon belt made for greater differences, as much as doubling modern levels in the southern Levant and multiplying those in the Sahara ten- to twentyfold.[25] For the first 4000 years the rains also fell more evenly through the year and were more reliable in incidence – a vital distinction from later, including modern, times. Rain-filled aquifers and raised water tables brought springs to life, created or amplified lakes and other wetlands and fed countless steadily flowing streams and rivers. Most of the human initiatives witnessed in this chapter are directly or indirectly predicated on the relative abundance of fresh water.[26]

A deciduous, humid wildwood expanded with its attendant ecologies, including elusive, dispersed animals, particularly on the northern fringe of the Mediterranean and in temperate Europe.[27] The succession as climate improved and plant ranges expanded was initially chaotic, but ultimately resolved in many areas to large tracts of mixed oak forest, with conifers in the mountains and open scrub across poorer limestone country. Further south, especially in the drier parts of Iberia, the Aegean and the Levant, tree cover was patchier and alternated with prickly scrub or great tracts of savannah dotted with almond, pistachio and terebinth. What we regard as typically Mediterranean shrubs and herbs, as well as olive and other evergreens, maintained a rather modest profile, while on Crete trees like hazel, alder and lime, all unknown there today, appear in the pollen record.[28] In parts of the Levant and southern Anatolia, woodland took a strangely long time to advance, its climax on the Anatolian plateau falling as late as 6300–4300 BC. One reason may have been that the expansion of the trees was being retarded through deliberate burning to maintain open landscapes of greater benefit to the unprecedented, ever-growing numbers of people by now living there, as we shall see, in a new cultural universe and an increasingly interventionist relationship with nature.[29]

Spectacular natural changes were wrought in North Africa [5.4].[30] A northward shift of 600–700 km (375–435 miles) brought summer monsoons over the Saharan watershed, allowing their run-off to head into the Mediterranean. In the south the Sahel frontier advanced into what had been the heart of hyper-aridity. Combined with winter rainfall from the north, this nurtured within the Sahara verdant massifs, running wadis and vast shallow lakes that covered a tenth of modern Libya. At 340,000 sq. km (130,000 sq. miles), Lake Mega-Chad was as big as Italy, and over ten times the size of its modern rump. Between lay savannah, steppe and stretches of residual semi- or true desert. The proof of this transformation lies in pollen cores, relics of high lake stands, finds of freshwater molluscs in the desert and a rolling invasion from the south of aquatic or savannah animals – mainly giraffes, elephants, hippopotami, rhinoceroses, buffalo, gazelle and crocodiles. These last are attested by their bone remains, the rock art of hunters who followed them, and isolated populations that survived in the Maghreb to entertain Roman audiences in the Colosseum, or in the case of a cluster of crocodiles recently stumbled upon in Mauretania, even to this day.[31] The arrival of such animals in a Maghreb long isolated by desert explains the extinction at this time of local giant buffalo, camel, gazelle and deer, a relatively rare phenomenon within Africa but typical, as we have seen, of the Mediterranean's true islands, if for somewhat different reasons.[32] Otherwise, the early Holocene's environmental impact in the Maghreb and Cyrenaica was less dramatic, and in line with other southerly parts of the basin. One new feature, however, was a long coastal corridor of vegetated land between the two areas, and running on to the mouth of

5.4 Northern Africa, showing the boundary between the desert and Sahel today and at the Last Glacial Maximum, the approximate northern limit of the early Holocene monsoon and the location of major early Holocene lakes; (*inset*) detail of the flowing wadi system in the area of modern Libya.

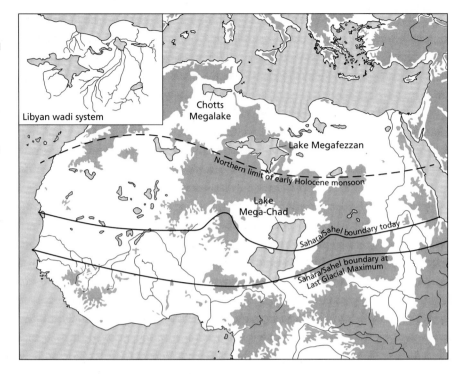

Libyan wadi system

Chotts Megalake

Lake Megafezzan

Northern limit of early Holocene monsoon

Lake Mega-Chad

Sahara/Sahel boundary today

Sahara/Sahel boundary at Last Glacial Maximum

the Nile, which relieved the former isolation. Much of Mediterranean North Africa also gained a belt of peridesert savannah to its south. Comparable changes took place on a smaller scale in the Negev and Sinai, and all along the eastern margins of the Levantine corridor.

The end of the Younger Dryas reinitiated sea level rise, with a peak rate of 2.3–4.0 cm (0.9–1.6 in.) per year, or up to 4 m (13 ft) a century, at about 7500 BC.[33] The sea still stood 55 m (180 ft) below its present level in 9600 BC; by 8000 BC it lay at −35 m (−115 ft), at which stage most coastal outlines resembled today's, and by 5500 BC at only −10 m (−30 ft), after which the rate of rise petered out to reach approximately current levels a millennium and a half later. It became warmer, too, as revealed by seabed cores, warm-water shells and (the most bizarre proxy) finds at archaeological sites lying at latitudes of 35–40 degrees of a broad size range of dusky grouper, a fish that starts its life as female but undergoes a sex change to male at about 80 cm (30 in.) in length, and mixed sizes of which indicate waters warm enough to breed.[34] The Mediterranean as a whole became richer in marine life. Over this time span many sites across the basin see high, if uneven, quantities of fish bones that hint at bonanza years and perhaps shifting shoals as marine conditions evolved. It has even been argued that a milder climate created a more navigation-friendly sea, although we can be fairly sure that the early Holocene Mediterranean was still no mill-pond.[35]

Encroachment on the remnants of glacial plains was largely over by 8000–7000 BC, bringing the sea in certain areas right back to the feet of the mountain facade. The generation of islands from land hitherto joined to the mainland continued for longer – even the British Isles only became such again around 6200 BC.

In combination, the result was to drown some of the best lowland and often leave only upland above water, with exceptionally gaunt effects still visible in the karstic islandscapes of Dalmatia. At some time, and in a manner much disputed, sea level rise brought the Mediterranean to the brim of the Sea of Marmara and then a Black Sea that had once been greatly shrunk by Pleistocene evaporation. Disappointingly, the dramatic proposal that this triggered a catastrophic deluge as the Mediterranean's waters thundered into the exposed lowlands (a reprise of the Messinian event that opened this history) is now largely discredited in favour of a more gradual merging.[36]

Equally important were developments at the mouths of the rivers and streams flowing into the Mediterranean.[37] Lower seas had forced them to incise channels down to their outlets, ranging from little gullies to elongated valleys and veritable canyons. The Holocene has witnessed a tug of war between the invasion of these by rising seas, and their infilling by soils washed down from the interior. Until about 5500 BC, the speed of sea level rise and low rates of erosion thanks to a gentler climate, stability of wooded slopes and modest levels of human activity, ensured that marine invasion won hands down. Mediterranean coasts would have been more indented than today, riddled with creeks and occasional deep fjords; the Latmian Gulf in western Turkey, for example, thrust 50 km (30 miles) further inland, and the now trout-stocked, idyllic lake of Bafa Gölü near Didyma was an arm of the sea [2.10].[38] Conversely, there was normally little chance for growth of river deltas, thanks to the flooding of any build-up not flushed out by the gradients of the rivers themselves. The same may hold true for many of the lagoons that became a common feature of later shallow, soft shorelines until modern drainage, though great salt marshes must have flourished in low-lying areas as the sea lapped in, insinuating itself into the slightest fold in the land. Franchthi casts light on one such turnover: there, mud-loving molluscs were replaced by sand and rocky shore species around 7000 BC, as the sea flooded the coastal plain and drew close to steeper slopes near the cave.[39]

The only significant climatic blip within this ecological, if (as we shall see) not unambiguously social golden age has only recently been confirmed by environmental records, and is christened by its approximate date the '6200 event'.[40] Like the Younger Dryas, it was caused by North American cold-water discharge into the Atlantic, in this case the final demise of the ice sheet and a sudden redirection of its meltwaters as the last ice dams broke. The cooling was sharp, in the order of 6°C (11°F) on land, with a mix of drier weather in the south and east and flash-flooding deluges in the north, but this time it was mercifully short, with 150–200 years of overall impact and a much briefer spike of maximum incidence. Even so, it can be aligned with a horizon of changes all over the Mediterranean, some of decisive significance.

Another serpent may have lurked in the garden, though its presence is uncertain and certainly heavily camouflaged. The warming and humidity could have loosed into the basin diseases hitherto kept south of the Sahara, including high- and low-mortality infections as well as ancestors of epidemic diseases that later developed more virulent strains under greater population densities.[41] Even if their advent

159

came substantially later, a general association between higher levels of disease and warmth, humidity and (for reasons we now come to) transfers to humans resulting from closer coexistence with animals is likely to be correct. This provides a counter-trend to the resumption of sharp demographic growth in the early Holocene, and opens our eyes to the multiplicity of vectors that we need to consider in this brave new Mediterranean world.

The nuclear explosion of the Levantine Neolithic

The early Holocene Levant combined a propitious ecology, a strongly forcing topography, a superlative window of opportunity and, last but not least, an exceptional cumulative build-up in cognitive and practical terms since the Last Glacial Maximum (after all, the last time *Homo sapiens* occupied the Levant during an interglacial, 100,000 years earlier, nothing comparable occurred). Out of this arose the first farming communities of the Neolithic, a new age indeed (if only tangentially in regard to stone) that heralded transformations of society, culture, economy and relations between people and nature that would, as they spread and diversified, irreversibly alter western Eurasia and parts of North Africa.[42] In fact, the Levant is simply the best-investigated segment of a larger nucleus of change that extended east across the Jazira into northern Mesopotamia and the Zagros piedmont, encompassing much of the Fertile Crescent.[43] Over half this overall arc lay beyond the Mediterranean basin (the vast majority of which was, conversely, excluded), but most still fell within the eastward-thrust lobe of Mediterranean climates mapped in Chapter 2, whose pronounced seasonality accounts for the unusual abundance of large-seeded wild cereals in the region. The global tally of hotspots of early farming is growing,[44] but still remains limited, and the fact that one, and on current information the earliest, overlapped with the Mediterranean is one of the great formative factors (the second, after the location of the sole land route out of Africa) that has shaped the course of its history and rendered this so dynamic from such an early date. Semi-Mediterranean in origin, this western Eurasian brand of farming would over time be further reworked by the challenges and opportunities of a maritime basin, and in turn become the greatest sculptor of Mediterranean landscapes and ecologies since the end of the Pleistocene.

The Levant and wider Fertile Crescent were unusually fortunate in the range of plants and animals susceptible to domestication [5.5].[45] Initially most significant among the former were three cereals (emmer wheat, einkorn wheat and barley), four pulses (pea, lentil, chickpea and bitter vetch) and flax. The last of these, a source of fibre for cords and consequently woven linen cloth, as well as oil, reminds us that domestication was not all about staples, and, indeed, sugar-rich figs may have been an early target too.[46] Domestication marked the final stage in a coevolution of plants and people. It built upon far older hunter-gatherer plant lore, and more specifically the gathering, grinding, roasting or baking and consumption of wild cereals and pulses

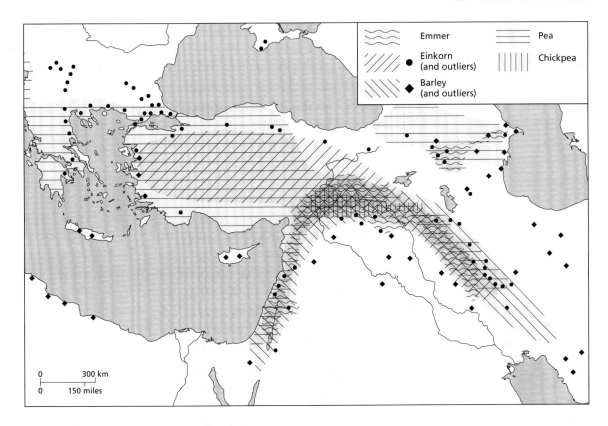

Emmer

Einkorn
(and outliers) ●

Barley
(and outliers) ◆

Pea

Chickpea

0   300 km
0   150 miles

5.5 The distribution of the wild progenitors of plant domesticates in the Levant, wider Fertile Crescent and surrounding regions.

by the Last Glacial Maximum, graduating in the Levant to the wild cultivation of the Early Natufian. Such practices survived the Younger Dryas, to judge by the numbers of Late Natufian grinding stones and a vegetal signature in the chemistry of human skeletons.[47] Indeed, one isolated flash in the pan at Abu Hureyra on the Euphrates, shortly before it was abandoned to drought, hints that some of the rye seeds (not again a regular crop for many millennia) may have been in effect domesticated.[48]

The faunal situation was just as propitious. Out of 148 large herbivores on the planet today, fewer than a tenth have ever been domesticated.[49] The rest are unwilling to breed in captivity or simply too behaviourally intractable – cases in point being the skittishness and aggression during their ruts of deer and gazelle, two favourite quarries of Mediterranean hunters. In addition to the dog, which acquired new roles as a guardian and herder, the Fertile Crescent boasted four of this select club in the wild: sheep, goat, boar/pig and aurochs/cattle. Their domestication created a 'walking larder' (effectively storage on the hoof), and again was the culmination of a longer process.[50] Sheep and goat, both naturally herding creatures, had attracted scant attention while better hunting targets abounded, but became of greater interest as the preferred prey species declined, the number of mouths to feed grew, and alternative approaches to animal exploitation came to the fore.[51] Conversely, images and figurines stretching back into the Pleistocene suggest that people had long attributed a sacred power to that hulking, dangerous mass of meat, the aurochs, and its taming might be partly understood in this symbolic light.[52] The initial contribution

161

from domesticated fauna came, like that of hunted game, in the form of meat, hides, and other body parts that demanded the animal's death. Exploitation of renewable, or as commonly termed 'secondary', animal products[53] – milk-based from sheep, goats and cattle, wool once sheep and goats had been bred for shaggy outer coats, and traction by cattle and later additional species – followed at staggered junctures, sometimes considerably later.

From such perspectives farming was simply one more intensification of food production (admittedly with gigantic potential), the ultimate in a delayed-returns way of life, and, in the Fertile Crescent, an accident waiting to happen.[54] Once we focus on the details, however, questions of timing and incidence are less apparent, and for good reason. The latest generation of archaeological analyses and reconstructions of genetic lineages reveal a pattern of multiple foci and lengthy experimentation (therefore also potentially very varied motives over time and space) around the core zone.[55] Some of this resulted from practices intended to preserve as much as subvert existing societies, as the continuation rather than nemesis of inventive hunter-gatherer strategies that had already lighted upon efficient food extraction, storage and probably exchange as ways of surviving in a diverse world. Several of the foci overlap in the northern Levant and southeast Anatolia, but there were important extensions into the Crescent's extremities, notably for cereals and sheep in the southern Levant and goat and sheep on the flanks of the Zagros. Only slowly did this web of activities converge into something readily identifiable as farming. Given all this, the timing of domestication events has become something of a semantic distraction. Technically these are defined by the genetic shifts that reduce or nullify a species' ability to survive and reproduce naturally, or in visible terms traditionally identified by traits such as size reduction in animals, and in cereals a tougher junction between the seeds and stalk, a rare anomaly in the wild that militates against natural resowing by shattering when ripe, but greatly eases the reaper's task by holding the ear together (Natufian harvesters of wild cereals got around this by reaping while still green). Yet well before such changes are attested, plant and animal remains at archaeological sites betray hints of management in such details as the accompanying weeds and patterns of slaughter, respectively. Cultivation of cereals still largely wild in form continued for the first thousand years of the Holocene, until progressive selection and isolation from wild stands made easy-reaping variants both numerically dominant and reliant on human hands for resowing.[56] Likewise, the faunal protagonists in their wild guises were being corralled, culled, selectively bred and even (as we shall see in the case of Cyprus) moved over substantial distances by the 9th millennium BC, if not even earlier in a few cases, with full domestication following only a millennium or so later.[57]

There was, however, far more to Neolithic origins than domestication. Equally central were the formation and spread of village communities, which tied more people to a more place-based lifestyle than ever before, and a range of symbolic practices that enabled people to engage with plants, animals and increasing numbers of each other in new ways, and to negotiate the complicated entanglements that ensued.[58] In this sense, too, the Levant had a flying start with the Natufian, to which we might now add further hunter-gatherer groups riding out the Younger Dryas beyond our immediate purview in southeast Anatolia, who also experimented with sedentary life and sought to enculture the wild.[59] A final vital ingredient for the cumulative spread and pooling of fresh ways of doing things was widespread networks of contact. All hunter-gatherers maintained these of necessity, but those in the Levant were unusual in their habit of converging on corridors like the Jordan Valley, where novelties were juxtaposed and reinforced each other, as well as in the recent extension of such networks across the sea. Individually, none of the above factors was decisive; but together they created dynamite attached to a fuse lit as soon as people were released from the grip of glacial aridity.

The societies of the early Holocene Levant and adjacent regions are collectively known as the Pre-Pottery Neolithic (PPN). The opening PPNA phase (9600–8500 BC), was a volatile time of rising populations as the climate warmed and new environments opened up.[60] Under its umbrella lurks a range of societies united by little more than the use of Khiam points, distinctive arrowheads found from Sinai to the northern Fertile Crescent. Although a good indicator of long-range interaction, further affirmed by the circulation of Anatolian obsidian, Mediterranean and Red Sea shells, brightly hued minerals and Dead Sea bitumen, the spread of Khiam points should not disguise major distinctions between their users in different areas. Many small stone tool scatters mark no more than ongoing, ever more intensive hunting, especially of gazelle. Meanwhile, the northern Fertile Crescent experienced a hunter-gatherer climax of astonishing ritual elaboration, exemplified at Göbekli Tepe in southeast Anatolia by massive monoliths carved with wild animals and male symbols, one unfinished pillar weighing 50 tonnes [5.6].[61]

Yet in a short stretch of the Jordan Valley north of the Dead Sea, and perhaps in the Damascus basin and additional patches further afield, some groups took a different course. As in the Early Natufian, rising populations hemmed in by sea and steppe faced acute challenges that were best solved in situ. The Early Natufian solution had been to settle down in places within range of diverse, rich wild resources. This time, however, certain crops, especially wild cereals, were themselves transported to augment such sweet patches, and tended there outside their normal habitats.[62] This deceptively simple practice is the most likely mechanism by which easy-reaping strains were isolated and their domestication accelerated. Ecological micro-diversity in the fully Mediterranean segment of the Fertile Crescent served as a major enabler in this respect, shortening distances so much that many transfers must have lain within the territory of a single community.[63] The receiving

5.6 One of the decorated monoliths carved by early Holocene hunter-gatherers at Göbekli Tepe, outside the Mediterranean basin itself but within the eastward extension of its climate zone across the northern Fertile Crescent.

environments were new to the age too: seasonally flooded fans of light soils along the valley margins, deposited by streams and springs fed by the new rains.[64] Plants used to drier savannah or hill soils responded to the abundant water and greenhouse climate in the Jordan Valley and similar environments with burgeoning yields, spurring ongoing manipulation by their tenders, and by some point in the PPNA there is little doubt that a few crop stands had been in effect domesticated. The upshot was a turning point in history: the lifting of the lid imposed by natural abundance on population numbers, density and aggregation. By the end of the PPNA, settlements of unprecedented size had arisen in such places – at Jericho, Netiv Hagdud and Gilgal in the Jordan Valley, and Tell Aswad near Damascus.[65] Jericho, the largest at 2.5 ha (6 acres), may have numbered as many as 500 people, almost certainly more than had ever lived in a single spot on the planet until then, and the first human community substantial enough to reproduce itself, if it chose to, within its own boundaries [5.7].

The culture of these communities blended new features with reworked ancient traditions. Proclamations of permanence were prominent among the former. Dwellings continued to be circular, like Natufian huts, but were made of more durable mud-brick, and between them in several cases stood free-standing, well-sealed silos for crops [5.8].[66] When these eventually decayed they were rebuilt in much the same place, so that over time the debris rose as a mound, or tell, above the land, a monumental statement of the community's attachment to a specific place, and a deeper sense of time.[67] Jericho's inhabitants laboured for collectively thousands of hours to construct a sturdy stone wall and tower-like structure threaded by an internal stairway, the first to divert floodwater from the copious nearby spring, the second of unknown purpose [PL. XII].[68] As among certain other groups in the Fertile Crescent, ritual took on an immense importance at such places; its surviving gear and locales

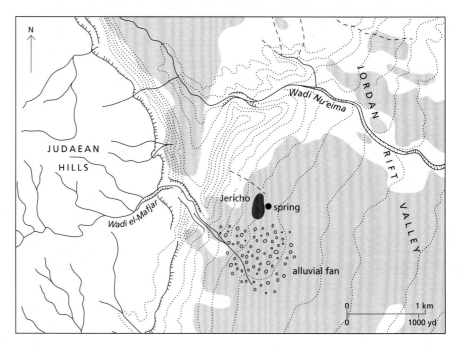

5.7 The propitious early Holocene environs of Jericho and its adjacent oasis on the abundantly spring-fed lowlands at the edge of the Jordan Rift Valley. The shaded area shows the approximate extent of the area under cultivation today.

5.8 Reconstruction of one of the large cylindrical grain silos recently discovered at Dhra', on the eastern flank of the Rift Valley, near the Dead Sea. Note the suspension of the raised floor to improve air circulation and deter rodents.

hint at ceremonies that exercised a magnetic effect on the viewer, drawing people in, and helping to resolve the literally unspeakable problems created by the physical adjacency of such multitudes. Some of these ritual markers reflect emergent concerns, for instance the first embellishment of dwellings with wall-paintings, at Ja'de on the Euphrates, and the growing popularity of figurines of women, as opposed to animals during the Natufian, which may testify to women's prominence as the nurturers of incipient plant domestication.[69] Equally new, and emblematic as well as practical, were polished stone axes, tools for digging or clearing that affirm increased environmental reworking. Others, however, had a deeper history, notably the caches of human skulls and numerous burials. This dialogue with the dead, whether as generic ancestors or specific individuals and the relationships that they had embodied, drew on clear antecedents in Natufian practice.

The Levantine PPNA was just the initial stage in an extraordinary trajectory, never envisaged by the first agents of change, that accelerated in the following PPNB (8500–6700 BC), as growing numbers of people, accumulations of domesticates and evolving cultural practices fed back on each other within a zone of interaction about 1000 km (600 miles) across.[70] Many PPNB traits were accentuations of PPNA trends, but there were also substantial modifications and divergences whose longer-term repercussions lead many to regard this, rather than the PPNA, as the defining phase for the western Eurasian Neolithic and all that followed from it.

It was only now that farming came together as an integrated, widely applicable practice based on full domesticates (if initially still accompanied by plenty of hunting), with regular cross-breeding consolidating the initial suite and generating improved new variants – notably easier, free-threshing bread wheat and barley.[71] In the pioneering PPNA, floodwater cultivation appears to have been the norm, on the basis of the major sites' proximity to spring-fed or other seasonal wetlands, and the marsh plants mixed in with the cereals.[72] Seeds were scattered during the spring onto waterlogged soils as the spate subsided, and needed little tending save for protection from birds and animals until the harvest. Although easy in terms of labour, this system restricted cultivation to the niches where these precise conditions reigned. In the PPNB it was supplemented and gradually replaced by a type of farming still different from that practised over the past few thousand years in the Mediterranean, but

5.9 Pre-Pottery Neolithic B rectangular houses at Beidha in southern Jordan: (*above*) plan showing densely packed comparable household modules and one larger, possibly ritual-oriented structure; (*below*) reconstruction of a house showing its arrangement over two storeys.

recognizable in certain elements and extremely enduring in its own right. This was the horticulture of winter-sown crops in small, garden-like dry-land fields, productive, readily created artificial environments maintained by a back-breaking cycle of hoeing, weeding and, where possible, human watering from nearby springs, probably also dug wells, or other sources to supplement rainfall.[73] Domesticated animals pastured nearby played a critical part too, beyond supplementary food and materials, thanks to their manure, which maintained nutrient levels in the soil. The combination of sheep, goats, cattle and pigs, each with their own grazing preferences, offered a balanced, flexible portfolio as well as meat packages of conveniently differing sizes. By such mixed farming, a group of five people deriving most of their food from cereals could subsist from a few hectares of fields and the immediately surrounding grazing land, in contrast to the far greater expanses typically required by an equivalent number of hunter-gatherers – a first indication, along with the invitation to a shorter spacing between births once people ceased to be on the move so frequently, of farming's potentially dramatic impact over time on Mediterranean demography.

The accompanying labour regime dominated everyday life, culture and ideology, and prompted new ideas about ownership of its fruits as well as hereditary rights over the land itself, concepts typically less accentuated among hunter-gatherers. Farming reflected an entrapment as much as triumph, and by boosting populations to levels that could not be sustained in any other way, it raised the spectre of future crises should conditions ever deteriorate. Its spread also reflects a victory for big demographic battalions rather than health. Early farmers' skeletons show them to be hard-working, disease-ridden, prone to toothache from a carbohydrate-rich diet and harrowed by 40–50 per cent mortality among the young, with higher stress levels among the survivors compared with their hunter-gatherer forebears.[74] Just like their domesticated animals, Mediterranean farmers became smaller and less rugged in build, evolving 'utility model' physiques adapted to sedentism and routinized but less physically extreme work.[75] Last but not least, farming further entrenched divisions of labour by gender.[76] Plants had probably already become a female domain in hunter-gatherer and incipient agricultural communities, and skeletal

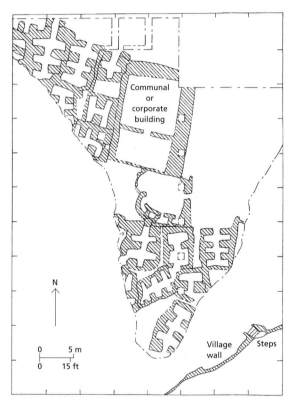

Communal or corporate building

N

0   5 m

0   15 ft

Village wall   Steps

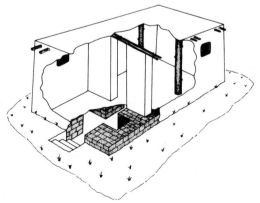

studies of early farmers demonstrate that their processing was certainly women's work, probably for a couple of hours each day, followed by the preparation of gruels or oven-baking of simple flatbreads.[77] It was an arduous task to judge by pathologies derived from prolonged kneeling and grinding. If women tended the nearby garden plots too, a responsibility compatible with lower mobility during pregnancy and nursing, the inner realm of home and fields may have started to be thought of as female space, with men's status tied to the still significant realms of hunting, other long-range provisioning, and presumably fighting.

Closely linked is growing evidence for the household as the primary social and productive unit.[78] Unsurprisingly, much of this comes from identifications of structures that we can consider discrete houses. At a general level, the most obvious shift is from the circular structures of the PPNA and earlier times to substantial rectangular, and often tightly compartmentalized buildings, sometimes with two storeys plus a flat rooftop working area, though this trend was far from uniform or irreversible [**5.9**].[79] The autarky of households is revealed by replications of food production, storage and tool manufacture areas in each structure, and their increasing transference indoors and away from prying eyes. The size of houses and numbers of burials under floors or benches (a further sign of the significance of residential definition) suggest that these households consisted of nuclear families, typically an adult couple and about two to four surviving parents or children. It is unclear whether we should read the architecture at face value, and infer the emergence only now of this classic building block of later societies, with the PPNA, Natufian and other late hunter-gatherer groups having more communal, fluid or polygamous arrangements.[80] But regardless of the nuclear family's precise antiquity, its prominence by the PPNB had repercussions for logics of economic production. Among societies that shared food and other resources (most, or all, of those hitherto existent), incentives to work harder were slight, given the lack of preferential reward. But once farming households emerged, increased labour leading to a degree of overproduction in terms of food helped to smooth over likely fluctuations in the number of hands that this tiny workforce could muster.[81] Looking ahead, overproduction and the storage of its fruits beyond the yearly cycle would take on a far greater importance in the future, by enabling households to tide over bad years as farming expanded into unpredictable environments and as local conditions deteriorated (see Chapter 7) – still tiny clouds on the horizons of the PPNB, but of thunderhead proportions in millennia to come.

Families might fail with a run of bad luck or poor management, but conversely they might prosper from good land, better fortune or sheer hard work. If the gains were cumulative and heritable this might translate into long-term gradations of wealth more easily than among hunter-gatherers, where such distinctions seldom outlived an individual's achievements. The greater privacy of households at one level proclaims autarky, but it might also hint at the endurance of an older levelling ideology inimical to the outward flaunting of whatever differences existed. The emergence of groups of community leaders is, as we shall see, likely within the largest PPNB communities, but whether they were selected on grounds of age and experience (in other words as elders), seniority within lineages of families, wealth, specific skills, or combinations of these is unknown.[82] Their long-assumed orchestration of activity in the ritual buildings that now became common, and the by now well-attested feasts in which large amounts of meat were consumed, is ambiguous in this respect, for such practices might equally serve to bind a community together by affirming shared membership, or accentuate the status of a minority able to participate prominently. Possible signals of people regarded as outstanding come from rare special treatments in burial, the growing quantities of accompanying objects in the later PPNB, as well as the curation of skulls and their plastic, flesh-like modelling with layers of lime-plaster, finished off by painted details, eyes picked out in cowrie or obsidian and strange, net-like headgear rendered in bitumen [5.10].[83]

These fundamentals help to give meaning to a series of astonishing phenomena that we can now explore sequentially. With hindsight, the Early PPNB (8500–8100 BC) was fairly muted.[84] Nonetheless, it witnessed the start of a critical merging of innovations that had originated bottom-up in separate niches into an integrated zone encompassing the entire Levant and beyond. Within this, and building upon PPNA activities, raw materials, crafted goods, plants, animals and people were on the move. Whatever social realities lay behind the displacement of objects among earlier hunter-gatherers around the Mediterranean, by now much of this movement undoubtedly consisted of exchanges between people, in effect early forms of trade, certainly influenced by personal, familial or community relationships, as well as ideas of reciprocity, but probably already bringing with it a sense of desirousness, gain or good value, in whatever terms this was perceived.[85] Thanks to obsidian, seashell, coral, carved chlorite bowls, highland cedar, bitumen and other durables, some of these flows can be traced, but otherwise we rely on inference, for example from the proliferation of small clay and other incised tokens whose precise meaning is lost, but that collectively mark a growing consciousness of exchanges between people and their consequences.[86] Much of this involved goods that were presumably regarded as valuable (surely at this stage including domesticated plant and animal stock), though mundane, everyday exchanges must have taken place too, however invisibly to us, and are likely to have equally, if unfathomably, ancient roots.

By the Middle PPNB (8100–7200 BC) the standard farming suite of domesticates was well established, and snowballing effects become more evident.[87] In one core zone in and around the Jordan Valley, settlements at 'Ain Ghazal and Basta outgrew Jericho to become tells of 4–5 ha (10–12 acres), though smaller communities remained the norm here and the rule elsewhere. Large sites in particular display an explosion of ritual activity. Caches of human figures, shorter busts and heads shaped from pale clay or lime-plaster on an armature of reeds appeared at 'Ain Ghazal [PL. XIII] and Jericho, and there was a proliferation of elaborately decorated skulls [5.10].[88]

5.10 Pre-Pottery Neolithic B decorated skull from Jericho with inset cowrie eyes.

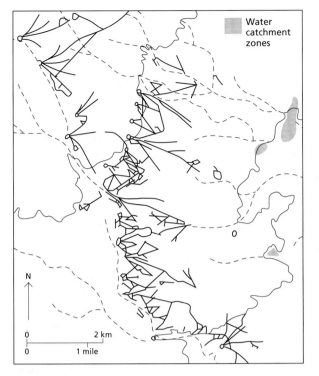

5.11 Long lines of low stone walls create kite-like patterns in profusion across the dry steppe near Jawa in northern Jordan. Used by hunters to funnel gazelle into convenient killing zones, such structures date to various junctures in different parts of the Levant, but these are of relatively early Holocene date.

Such communities appear to have controlled the flow of exchanged goods, becoming central places in regional networks, and were also probably the bases for long-range expeditions to acquire prized materials. For example, Mediterranean and Red Sea shells were acquired in different regions of the Levant, but 'Ain Ghazal and Basta are unusual in enjoying good access to both.[89]

The Late PPNB (7200–6700 BC) saw a further acceleration of these trends and a veritable population boom.[90] 'Ain Ghazal, Basta and a few other sites in the same area mushroomed into mega-sites of 10–14 ha (25–35 acres), probably with several thousand inhabitants. This was driven by both internal growth and the pulling power of heightened social and ritual engagement. Impressively, it did not depopulate surrounding regions. For numbers of small settlements were sharply on the rise too, in parallel with a marked outward drive, whether through out-migration by bands of farmers (often young people, we can assume, given burgeoning populations) with their seeds and herds, or the adoption of domesticates by already partly implicated hunter-gatherer neighbours. Among the regions brought more fully into the farming zone was the Mediterranean coastal strip, as attested by the lowest level at Ras Shamra (later the famous trading city of Ugarit).[91] Also infiltrated were the fringes of the inland steppe, until now still a land of roundhouse-dwelling hunter-gatherers preying on gazelle and wild ass with the aid of immense wall lines converging on a killing zone, the 'desert kites' best known in the Wadi as-Sirhan [5.11].[92] Boundaries between hunters and farmers often shifted and blurred, with wild meat crossing in one direction, and cereals, pulses, sheep and goats in the other. From one such internal boundary on the edge of the dry Judaean hills, and perhaps marking it in ways obscure to us, come the miraculously surviving plastered skulls, stone masks, headdresses, basketry, mats, knotted and semi-sewn linen and range of seeds and fruits deposited in the Nahal Hemar Cave [5.12; PL. XIV].[93]

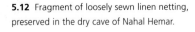

5.12 Fragment of loosely sewn linen netting, preserved in the dry cave of Nahal Hemar.

Towards a sustainable Levantine future

The immediate sequel to the Late PPNB climax in the Levant is a confusing but, for our purposes, informative period from 6700 to 6200 BC. Conventionally, it marks the Final PPNB or PPNC, and the transition to a Late, or Pottery, Neolithic (6200–5500 BC).[94] The last of these labels is best avoided.[95] Heat-alteration of materials, whether lime extraction for plaster, softening of metals or hardening of clay, was widespread during the PPN, with open fires and bread ovens providing chances to experiment at moderate temperatures. Fire-hardened clay objects date to as early as the 10th–9th millennia BC at Mureybet on the Euphrates, and from the 8th millennium in the Levant. Some already took the form of containers, alongside wares made of lime and ashes, woven baskets and presumably also wooden vessels. The shift to regular use of fired pottery took place in the early 7th millennium BC in the north and the late 7th in the south, incidentally long after its earliest global appearance among East Asian hunter-gatherers,[96] and also, as we shall see, post-dating African innovations. By 6500 BC potting skill had improved greatly. Its products were used for boiling, stewing and serving food, leading to improvements in taste and nutrition. Another crucial function, proved by the extraction of fatty acids from potsherds of this date, was processing of milk, perhaps initially to create readily digestible yoghurts even before full lactose intolerance had developed among adults, as well as more durable cheeses and other milk-based foodstuffs – in short, the first attested secondary products.[97] Pottery and its ramifications aside, two other Levantine trends stand out at this time. One is the eclipse and eventual unsynchronized abandonment of the PPNB mega-sites and networks by around 6300–6200 BC. The other was further expansion into hitherto thinly peopled lands, coupled with further changes that presage a more diversified future for Mediterranean farming.

How did the collapse of the giant inland PPNB communities come about?[98] The widening mesh of communities throughout the Levant might have rendered the hubs in the Jordan Valley less central in terms of ritual power and control of exotic valuables. Perhaps, therefore, they just faded away. But other processes may have been at work too. One possibility is that tensions between the priorities of the individual family and the vastly larger community proved in the end insuperable within the limited structuring mechanisms that such societies created, and precipitated fissioning. At 'Ain Ghazal, we may even possess the first demonstrable instance of real environmental degradation as a result of Neolithic activity, in the form of soil loss triggered by tree-felling to open arable land and fuel production of lime-plaster, as well as overgrazing by sheep and goats (remains of which increased markedly over hunted gazelle in the final levels).[99] Another contributing factor by the end could have been abrupt climate change.[100] The 6200 event fell decisively too late to explain the overall pattern, but may have hastened the end by dispersing people and discrediting a leadership unable to avert disaster. The last two suggestions point to an interesting possibility. Although large PPNB communities lived in intimate contact with their ancestral past, they may have been enjoying their present as if there were no tomorrow. Given the overall balmy conditions of the early Holocene, this would be understandable. But such a way of living would also become unsustainable in the Mediterranean as soon as the climate began to oscillate or the consequences of unfettered exploitation took effect.

In this light, several 7th millennium BC Levantine developments can be seen as attempts to structure Neolithic life in more sustainable ways. By the Late PPNB, domestic animals had begun to show up on the inland steppe, and during the mid-7th millennium BC mobile herding of sheep and later goats became established there, replacing hunting in most areas by 6000–5500 BC, a final reprieve for the long-harried gazelle.[101] In the coastal zone, different trends came to the fore. In the north, plentiful villages appear in Cilicia and the Amuq plain around 7000 BC, that at Mersin (Yumuktepe) with wattle-and-daub houses, domesticates and dark-surfaced, incised pots reminiscent of wooden prototypes.[102] What lifestyle these farming villages replaced is unknown. Possibly this wooded shore was a late hunter-gatherer enclave, like others we will encounter around the basin, but alternatively we are missing its first farmers, a real possibility given Ras Shamra just to the south, and one to which we return in the context of nearby Cyprus. The coast comes alive all the way down to Ashkelon in the far south, nowhere more so than at Atlit-Yam, now thanks to sea level rise 8–12 m (25–40 ft) underwater and 200–400 m (650–1300 ft) off the Carmel shore.[103] Here, the sand-smothered structures, wells and burials extend over 4 ha (10 acres) [**5.13**], but even more interesting are the clues concerning marine activity. Cases of an ear pathology caused by diving into cold, deep water have been identified in the skeletons, and 97 per cent of the fish bones belong to grey

5.13 An early well, dug to tap fresh water by the coastal villagers of Atlit-Yam, and now itself preserved underwater thanks to subsequent sea level rise.

trigger fish, the adults of which prefer to live at some depth and therefore, on this shallow-sloping coast, imply capture from boats. Whether fishing by farmers began in response to crisis conditions is an open question. Inland Hatoula got plenty of coastal fish back in the PPNA, and a few slightly earlier,[104] so Atlit-Yam may instead reflect the growing visibility of coastal life as rising seas drove settlements closer to the modern shore, coupled with the surge in natural marine abundance seen in many parts of the basin around this time.

With such thoughts in mind, we should approach the Levantine Late Neolithic as much more than the dustcart after the PPNB parade. Its culture was more regionally variegated, less eye-catching and less interconnected, its settlements generally small (under 0.5 ha or 1.25 acres), dispersed and short-lived – mere hamlets or farmsteads.[105] But they materialize in a strikingly broad range of ecological niches and hint at major shifts in the farming portfolio. Continuing the terminal PPNB trend, hunting dwindled into insignificance, with sheep and goats on the rise as arrowheads declined. As mentioned, the first secondary products came into play, and although northwest Anatolia emits the strongest signal of milking at this time, people in parts of the Levant are likely to have practised this at least as early. The new way of life in dry-land landscapes based on mobile herding now also penetrated the Negev and Sinai. Turning to new crops, Mersin yields the first evidence of regular olive exploitation, around 6000 BC.[106] Thousands of crushed olive stones in pits at marginally later Kfar Samir, another underwater site off Carmel, confirm the extraction of oil, a nutritious food with a long shelf life, as well as a fuel and later unguent (curing the intact fruit to remove their bitterness, on the other hand, only started in the late 1st millennium BC).[107] Initially, wild trees would have been harvested, but their selection and pruning marked the first steps towards domestication. Accompanying these shifts are hints of reformulated social relations. Elaborate ancestral rituals and skull manipulations were superseded by small, flexibly deployed female figurines and different approaches to time and descent.[108] To the east, beyond the Mediterranean basin, among small communities on the Jazira, a separate revolution was underway: the reassignment of carved stamp seals from their initial role as decorators of human bodies and cloth, to their impression on clay pellets, and deployment of the resultant 'sealings' to assert ownership and track exchanges over time and distance far beyond the potential of face-to-face meetings.[109]

Several observations should be made about this cluster of features. First, as we shall discover in future chapters, they anticipate a startling number of key elements of later Mediterranean life. Second, although many were subsequently realigned to serve the interests of large-scale economies, they appear first in the context of the transition to a small-scale world of little villages, hamlets and farmsteads. Nearly two millennia of experimentation in an ever more unreliable environment would elapse before they crystallized into a suite of strategies capable of supporting cycles of new, differently structured large-scale societies in the Levant. But third, and in contrast to previous population collapses in the fragile Levantine corridor, going back to the first hominin infiltrations, the new demographics enabled by farming, allied to the notable resilience and adaptive inventiveness of these generations of Mediterranean farmers, ensured that this time around the Levant, even in apparent recession, remained in play, both in its own right, and as a potential conduit of connections between the regions around it.

Beyond the mountains and across the sea

In pursuing Levantine farming from its origins to its settling in as a broadly balanced Mediterranean practice by the 7th–6th millennia BC, we have left the remainder of the basin behind. We can now set the clock back and examine what happened elsewhere, first among the Levant's neighbours in Anatolia and Cyprus. Both areas were vital to subsequent expansion of this new way of life to the rest of the Mediterranean, and the way in which it came to them can also shed light on the early Holocene Levant's role as an exporter of people. Strictly speaking, the Anatolian plateau lies outside the environmental bounds of the Mediterranean, but it matters as a land connection to the Aegean and because within it, 150 km (90 miles) from the coast, emerged Çatalhöyük, the most famous of all the mega-sites and one whose radius of activity certainly encompassed the Mediterranean hinterland.

The earliest Neolithic of the Anatolian plateau had a mixed ancestry.[110] Farmers moving up from the Fertile Crescent constituted one element, but hunter-gatherers had already resettled the edges of the plateau by the final millennia of the Pleistocene, and their descendants played a part too. Other pioneers were also implicated. Obsidian was now coveted for more than razor-sharp tools; its dark gleam shone from figurines' eyes and polished mirrors, ranking it with other enchanting and exotic materials like marine shell and coral, and by 8300 BC a workshop at Kaletepe, beside the central Anatolian Göllü Dağ source, was turning out products typical of the Levant but unparalleled in its immediate environs.[111] The likeliest explanation is that this workshop was run by long-range expeditionary groups from the south – the first instance of operations mounted by lowlanders to extract mineral wealth in highland Anatolia, a major, typically state-sponsored practice in later times. On the plateau, Aşıklı Höyük had domesticated crops and managed sheep and goats by 8400 BC.[112] Its claustrophobic, tightly packed mass of houses foreshadows later Çatalhöyük, and may have been a response to harsh upland winters – one of the new challenges facing farmers at these altitudes. Aşıklı Höyük reveals that another, initially minor innovation was getting closer to the Mediterranean, for from it come a few tiny items made from copper. The epicentre of experimentation with metals lay in copper-rich southeast Anatolia, where the site of Çayönü has yielded thousands of little beads, pins and awls, made from malachite or native copper cold-hammered as a malleable stone in the 9th millennium BC, but later heat-treated.[113] Such techniques had spread to lead-rich galena by 7000 BC. Sporadic objects and, rarely, metalworking knowledge percolated across the plateau and into the Fertile Crescent, where a few nuggets of raw Jordanian copper also circulated in the PPNB.

5.14 A detail of the closely packed houses and yards of Çatalhöyük, seen in this reconstruction from above, with their roof-top activity areas and walkways.

Çatalhöyük began to coalesce from 7400 BC on a large fan of river-borne soil splayed across the Konya plain [**5.14**].[114] At first, it lay in the midst of hunter-gatherer land, and the intake of the plain's indigenous people contributed to the site's meteoric growth to a 13.5-ha (33-acre) mound, occupied by 3000–8000 people in the 7th millennium BC. A hunter-gatherer legacy is visible in the microliths of the lowest levels, and their myths must lie behind the atavistic paintings on the walls of otherwise impeccably Neolithic household dwellings, full of vultures, leopards, spectacular, still-wild aurochs and other fierce beasts [PL. XV], all at odds with a meat diet dominated, according to the bone remains, by domestic sheep. Such images and accompanying rituals drew people in and helped to bind the swollen, potentially fissile community together. For how much of the year this warren of abutting houses and middens was in fact occupied to full capacity is open to question, and there is some evidence for a seasonally fluid pattern. The spring-flooded wetland surrounding Çatalhöyük was not farmed but used for roofing material, aquatic food and aurochs hunts; cereals, sheep and goats were tended some kilometres away on drier land.[115] Obsidian was acquired 170 km (105 miles) to the east from Göllü Dağ and a little copper trickled in from further afield. The forests of the Taurus mountains provided deer, boar, timber, berries and acorns, as well as distant vistas of the Mediterranean, whence came seashells and date palm fronds, the last most probably arriving in the form of baskets of organic goods lost to us.

West of the Konya plain there still lies virtual terra incognita before the mid-7th millennium BC, although tantalizing hints from current excavations, for example of red plaster floors underlying levels dated to 7000 BC near the coast at Ulucak, near Izmir, imply that the borders of this earliest Neolithic world lie closer to the Aegean than we knew.[116] By the mid-7th millennium, farming had appeared in strength in the southwest Anatolian lake district. Small communities like Hacılar and Bademağacı compare with their modest Levantine contemporaries. They too are referred to as Late Neolithic until 6100 BC, but thenceforth as Copper Age (or 'Chalcolithic' – 'Copper-stone'),[117] the first of a series of antiquated and ill-correlated metal-based labels for time periods with which we will henceforth have to contend – recall that copper had begun to show up millennia earlier. As in the Levant, this expansion was accompanied by the break-up of the mega-sites.[118] By 6350 BC Çatalhöyük was shrinking and streets began to divide its houses, replacing the former rooftop walkways and entrances. In the final layers structural timbers became rarer and various marks of drier times connote the 6200 event. By 6000 BC an adjacent Copper Age community half its predecessor's size had taken over, elaborate painted decoration had shifted from house walls to pots, and a ripple of small villages and hamlets repopulated the Konya plain as the mega-site went down. To the south, on the coast, hunter-gatherers survived in the Gulf of Antalya until the early 7th millennium. Finds there, at Öküzini, of a few polished axes indicate interaction with farmers – maybe, as we will see, including those moving west along the coast into the Aegean by this time.[119]

Further south again across the now-inviting sea lies Cyprus, where this chapter opened. Here, a series of dramatic further discoveries have engendered a heady state of rolling interpretative revolution, and an insular microscope that reveals startling views as to how the Neolithic must have come together and spread across the neighbouring mainland too.[120] Until roughly twenty years ago, the consensus was that the Cypriot Neolithic began around 7000 BC with the Khirokitia phase, a puzzling isolate characterized by an anachronistic combination of roundhouses, carved stone vessels and the absence of pottery and cattle.[121] Between this and earlier Aetokremnos lay a gap of over 2500 years. That gap is now riddled with new finds. The newest, identified both inland and on the coast, is an early 9th millennium BC horizon contemporary with the later PPNA and the start of the PPNB.[122] Its most striking features are a roundhouse at Klimonas, now much more of its age and emblematic of long-term presence, plus the hunting (with dogs) of wild pig. Whether or not these pigs were descended locally from the earlier boars faintly attested at Aetokremnos, they had manifestly been introduced at some time to stock the island with game after the hippopotami had vanished, and cast indirect light on how people in the Levant were managing animals that to us still look undomesticated. Continuity in human occupancy is equally hard to gauge, but it does begin to look as if Cyprus, once visited, was never quite forgotten; the temporal gap has reduced almost to a three-figure duration over which progressively lengthier visits are extremely plausible.

Regardless, this opening phase of the 'Cypro-PPN' undoubtedly did grade into a further phase of roundhouse settlements, notably Mylouthkia and Shillourokambos in the south and Arkosyko in the north, that span the late 9th and entire 8th millennia BC, synchronizing with the end of the Early PPNB and the entire Middle PPNB in

5.15 The loose collection of roundhouses constituting the early Cypriot village of Shillourokambos, set in this reconstruction within a savannah-like landscape with semi-free-ranging yet carefully managed herds.

5.16 The faunal record for early Holocene Cyprus reveals repeated injections of new species, and fresh stock among existing ones, both of which indicate regular comings and goings by people between the island and mainland. The PPNB dates here refer to the Cypriot variant of the sequence. (Grey bars show overall probable date ranges. Black arrows indicate the earliest evidence for the arrival of new species. Grey arrows indicate the probable introduction of new lineages of animals.)

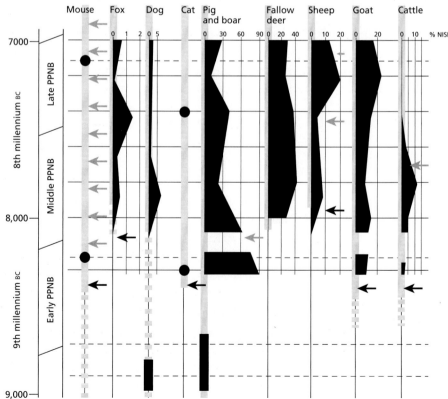

the Levant [**5.15**].[123] These contain domesticated cereals and pulses, none of which, save possibly barley, was native to the island. New animals were introduced, some at early stages of domestication, others still wild in appearance, plus a few commensals dependent on the environments of settled communities.[124] At Shillourokambos traces of their stockades have been unearthed. First to join the managed pigs were initially semi-wild goats and cattle, plus cats, whether mousers to combat that other fellow traveller of grain-storing farmers or, on the basis of one accompanying a human burial, of symbolic resonance, like the animals occasionally found in Levantine funerary contexts [**5.16**]. Sheep and a few foxes followed soon afterwards, but the most unexpected major arrivals were wild fallow deer, which to judge by the bones from kills, were released into the still understocked island and hunted as game without any effort at control. Other traces of a consciously transported mainland world include burials, stone bowls, PPNB-type tools, Anatolian obsidian and the human skulls and goat skeletons ritually deposited in deep water wells (themselves the earliest known in the eastern Mediterranean) at Mylouthkia.

Cypro-PPN farming was palpably of off-island origin and unveils the reach and potential of maritime movement by early farmers, with implications as crucial for early Mediterranean history as the prior achievements of seafaring hunter-gatherers. Slightly different crop profiles at each site, and parallels with diverse localities on the mainland on the part of the animals, argue against a single point of origin, but strong suspects for a primary role must be the archaeologically invisible people of the Gulf of İskenderun before the appearance there of pot-using villages, whose hinterland embraced a zone of roundhouse architecture stretching to the Euphrates.[125] This maritime nursery has already been highlighted in the context of Aetokremnos; one key to the Cypro-PPN is surely a continued tradition of seafaring there, while another must have been the loss of its coastal lands to rising seas, just as regional populations were also on the rise.

This peopling of an island with farmers and their way of life is as emblematic of the logistical abilities and scalar ambitions of early Holocene people in this part of the world as Jericho's tower or Göbekli Tepe's colossal carved pillars. Viable numbers of people and five species of sizeable animals, plus a suite of crops, had to be shuttled over sea-gaps of at least 65–70 km (40–45 miles). Although we still lack physical remains or images, the most likely seacraft by this time are no longer permeable reed boats but watertight dugout canoes made out of great trees from the nearby mountains – as we shall see in coming chapters, there is no sign of any more powerful seagoing technology for almost another five millennia, and such craft would still be lucky to make the crossing in less than a couple of days. Moreover, this was not a one-off event. Three intriguing strands of evidence demonstrate that for a long time Cypriot farmers remained in close touch with mainlanders.[126] First, the animal bones reveal periodic influxes of new stock [**5.16**], with at least eight episodes of introduction at Shillourokambos, most clustered in the earlier part of its 1400-year life, and some of them responses to local failures that underscore the advantages of a continental back-up for island-based life; these injections, incidentally, also cast light on likely levels of less visible animal transfers on the mainland. Second, measurements on the molars of the house mice that presumably smuggled aboard capacious canoes reveal no divergence over time from Levantine norms, thereby arguing for a steady trickle of new mice to the island. Third, obsidian kept coming, particularly to Arkosyko (a natural entry-point facing the Taurus passes into upland Anatolia), which obtained raw nodules and dispersed blades across the island.[127] Fish hooks, as well as remains of deep-water hake and shark, at Arkosyko leave little doubt that it was in part Cypriot canoes that plied the seas to maintain lines of contact. Seafaring, fishing, trading, tending of plants and animals and hunting were united in a cooperative endeavour essential for initial success and long-term survival. This nexus of confident social groups, microcosms of sustenance and robust seafaring technology operating over medium-range distances marked a distinctive Neolithic way of life that would bring radical changes to the ways in which people lived along the coasts, islands and hinterlands of the entire northern flank of the Mediterranean.

But before exploring further west, what happened in the longer term to Cypriot Neolithic societies? Several peculiarities of the Khirokitia phase now make better sense as Cypro-PPN derivatives, but the persistence of the increasingly archaic round-houses and continued lack of pottery, a loss of cattle in the early 7th millennium BC for (as we shall see) some 4000 years, the adherence to deer hunting as a mainstay for almost as long and the gradual disappearance of obsidian, all suggest a steady decline in external contacts. It is a moot point whether this reflected the deliberate rejection of an outside world of which islanders remained aware, but whose innovations they considered to be irrelevant or inimical in comparison to insular ways of doing things, or an unconscious drift towards parochialism similar to the reduction of horizons all over the Levant after the break-up of the PPNB sphere.[128] One little community perched on the rocky tip of the Karpass peninsula switched, like Atlit-Yam, to fishing, with catches including large tunny, while Khirokitia, the biggest community on the island, shifted to a heavier reliance on sheep and goat just before it finally fizzled out; both look like sporadic efforts to reconnect to mainstream ways of life, but if so, neither survived.[129] Cyprus now completes its hat-trick of early Holocene firsts by illustrating just how odd the lives of Mediterranean islanders might become. Once a target for pioneering seafarers and farming settlers, the island slowly slipped into an internal rut, and over the horizon of continental concerns, where it stayed until the surrounding world had altered beyond recognition.

The last hunter-gatherers of the northern Mediterranean

The intuitively hardest point to grasp about the Mediterranean in the early Holocene is that for most of the immense time span of the Levantine Neolithic and its immediate offshoots, farming remained east of a line running from the Negev to Cyprus and up a shifting axis through Anatolia. To the west, hunter-gatherer lifestyles continued until far later. Farming began in the Aegean around 7000–6500 BC, contemporary with the Late PPNB boom and its aftermath; at the other end of the basin, it only reached Iberia around 5500 BC, by which time the Levantine Neolithic was drawing to a close. North Africa also remained free of farming until the mid-6th millennium BC, as we shall see at the end of this chapter. On the European side of the basin, the last hunter-gatherers are known as Mesolithic, a sandwich-filler of a term (post-Palaeolithic, pre-Neolithic) that disguises the fact that their microlithic tools, and the practices behind them, were essentially Holocene continuations of themes developed by the warm-weather hunter-gatherers of the postglacial Pleistocene that we encountered in Chapter 4.[130]

It is hard to put flesh on the bones (or stones) of these people, largely thanks to our patchy knowledge of their sites, many of which were open air and low key in their archaeological signature.[131] Despite a common preference for aquatic locations, also lacking so far are waterlogged find-spots like those that have preserved basketry, wooden implements, nets, traps and even entire canoes in contemporary temperate and northern Europe. Stone tools, food debris, ornaments, burials, rock art and markings on incised or painted pebbles afford strictly limited views into this cultural universe. People were generally well nourished and typically, if not always, mobile, although often over less distance than many of their cold-weather predecessors. Their numbers were probably volatile, with a tendency to boom as local conditions peaked but also to overshoot and crash or disperse, the aftermath of which presumably casts light on several hints of population redistributions between regions, sometimes seemingly rapid and extensive.[132] Certain individuals clearly mattered, as they always had done; at Grotta dell'Uzzo in Sicily a few of the dead may even have been founder burials laid in the natural soil beneath the midden.[133] Others in southern France died violently, bearing traces of scalping or headhunting, maybe as a result of heightened stresses around the 6200 event.[134] There is nothing to suggest communities as complex as the Early Natufian, but beyond this, the paucity reflects our loss, not their poverty. To reflect on the potential extent of that loss, in Australia, where hunter-gatherer traditions continue up to the present, this same age of greening land and rising seas is thought to have been that in which the Rainbow Serpent myths were first formulated, an age of ancestral creation.[135]

In terms of the food-quest it is an exaggeration, but a pardonably illuminating one, to characterize the Mesolithic as the age of the snail, and of molluscs in general.[136] Of course this was not the whole story in terms of diet breadth and, equally, in terms of social prowess, no rock artist painted snail collecting. But early Holocene conditions typically made for difficult hunter-gatherer arcadias, in which small foodstuffs of fixed location balanced the challenges of foraging for larger but unpredictable prizes. Thick deciduous woodland dispersed the browsing deer, aurochs and boars to a degree only partly offset by seasonal hauls of nuts, acorns, fungi and berries (and caries in human teeth from the Grotta dell'Uzzo do indeed betray sweeter-toothed hunter-gatherers).[137] The ideal niches were varied and provided year-round possibilities; many were prime Mediterranean micro-ecologies combining in close proximity unforested mountains, wooded or more open lowland and coasts. One such was the

Sorrentine peninsula on the southern side of the Bay of Naples, where the land rises to 1500 m (4900 ft) only 2 km (1.25 miles) from the sea, and the meat intake was a mixture of ibex, boar and shellfish.[138] A larger zone of this description lay in an arc of steep relief from the Pyrenees via southern France, northern and Apennine Italy, to the Trieste karst and Istria.[139] Here thrived a rich Mesolithic tradition known as the Sauveterrian (9000–6500 BC). Two sites at the extremities of this arc provide some flavour. Balma Margineda, a cave 970 m (3180 ft) high in the Andorran Pyrenees and by this time used for several millennia, now served as a highland summer camp for people coming up from the Aude Valley to hunt and catch trout in the streams.[140] Meanwhile, off in the uplands of Istria, a cluster of sites focused on Pupicina Cave, a base rich in shell ornaments, where bone chemistry suggests a diet mainly of plants, but that also served as a venue for autumn boar feasts.[141]

Elsewhere, rich concentrations of marine foods played a bigger role. Even if the popularity of coastal life is partly an optical illusion created by the loss of comparable earlier sites to rising seas, the pattern is sustained across enough coastal topographies to inspire general confidence. At Grotta dell'Uzzo analysis of human skeletons reveals a diet rich in sea and plant foods, and the molluscs eaten tell us that at first people used the cave only in winter, but later frequented it year-round as they took more to fishing during the 8th–7th-millennium BC pan-Mediterranean burgeoning of sea life.[142] A similar pattern is evident on the east Adriatic coast; highlights are a base camp at Vela Spilja on Korčula, with thick layers full of the remains of small fish and rarely big ones, as well as dolphins, molluscs and land animals, a string of newly identified sites from Albania to northwest Greece, and the long-known midden above Sidari beach on Corfu.[143] But two areas stand out in terms of marine lifestyles, albeit in different ways, one showing how these could tether people and make them relatively sedentary, the other, in quite different circumstances, connected with widespread travel across the sea.

5.17 Close-up of the accumulations of marine shells, discarded after consumption by coastal and estuarine hunter-gatherers, that created huge white middens along the coast of Atlantic Portugal and parts of the Mediterranean proper.

The first lies formally just outside Mediterranean waters, in southern Portugal, where Atlantic tides flooding in and out of the long, winding channels cut by the Tagus and other rivers running off the Meseta nourished an inexhaustible cornucopia of molluscs, crustaceans, fish, sea mammals, seabirds and local as well as migratory waterfowl.[144] On the inner sections of such estuaries, hunter-gatherers settled down, creating middens of shells up to 100 m (330 ft) long and up to 2–3 m (6–10 ft) high [5.17]. The differing proportions of oysters, cockles and limpets reflect not so much local preferences (however attractive the idea) but the muddy, sandy or rocky beds in the immediate surroundings. Within middens, finds of acorns, nuts, berries and game still reveal trips to the wooded interior, but the lure of the shore was overwhelming. By the later Mesolithic, and perhaps hastened by the 6200 event, most Iberian people were living on the coast all round the peninsula – the culmination of a long and remarkably consistent trend going back to Solutrean and Magdalenian times.[145] The extent to which the white, shell-built middens of southern Portugal in particular created monuments rooting people in their locality is clear from the fact that storage pits and striking numbers of burials were dug into them.

Our second, very different, example of seaward orientation lies in the intensely coastal and insular landscapes of the Aegean. Even allowing for site losses to sea level rise, and uneven prospection (with a startling proportion of all known sites identified by a single scholar with a good eye),[146] the last Aegean hunter-gatherers manifestly did concentrate in certain areas, mostly though not all coastal. Just outside the Aegean, we have just noted one such focus in northwest Greece; another has recently come to light around the Sea of Marmara and the Dardanelles.[147] Others must lie undetected along further well-watered, estuarine stretches of coast, such as the west Anatolian seaboard. But it is Franchthi Cave that continues, as it did during the first obsidian procurement, to raise the standard in every sense, and to offer a superb window into how changeable the lifestyles of these hunter-gatherers

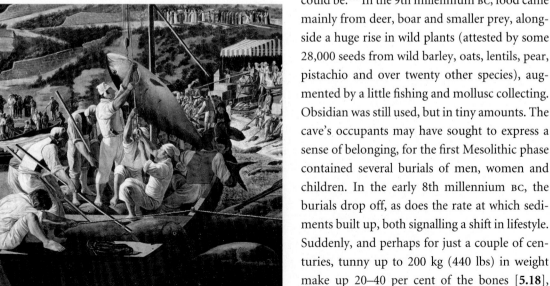

5.18 Large tunny make a spectacular catch, as illustrated by this detail from an early 19th-century painting of one such moment in southern Italy. But precisely what does the discovery of their bones in early Holocene sites imply for fishing practices and seagoing more generally?

could be.[148] In the 9th millennium BC, food came mainly from deer, boar and smaller prey, alongside a huge rise in wild plants (attested by some 28,000 seeds from wild barley, oats, lentils, pear, pistachio and over twenty other species), augmented by a little fishing and mollusc collecting. Obsidian was still used, but in tiny amounts. The cave's occupants may have sought to express a sense of belonging, for the first Mesolithic phase contained several burials of men, women and children. In the early 8th millennium BC, the burials drop off, as does the rate at which sediments built up, both signalling a shift in lifestyle. Suddenly, and perhaps for just a couple of centuries, tunny up to 200 kg (440 lbs) in weight make up 20–40 per cent of the bones [5.18], specialized tools for fish processing appear, and obsidian increases thirtyfold relative to other stones. Here and elsewhere in the Mediterranean (save for a dubious showing in Gorham's Cave, at Gibraltar, before the Last Glacial Maximum), tunny are a new, Holocene, catch. Being fast-moving, primarily open-water fish, their presence is often taken as proof of deep-sea fishing, and so a surrogate for seagoing, but they also shoal around promontories where the oxygenated water attracts prey, and during their annual migrations they swarm into coastal bays and along narrow straits, in which constricted locations they can be netted or speared from the shore. As at Grotta dell'Uzzo, people spotted a new marine opportunity and altered tack to exploit it, maybe investing in nets and canoes, and going seasonally mobile along the coast and between islands.

Other Aegean evidence complements the picture of growing maritime activity. Two well-documented sites are open-air Maroulas on Kythnos in the Cyclades and the Cyclops Cave on minuscule Gioura in the outermost Sporades, both sea-girt at the time.[149] Reports are coming out of similar activity elsewhere, not least a Mesolithic on Crete, hitherto an anomaly as the only one of the Mediterranean's big five devoid of such finds.[150] Kythnos and Gioura were too small and poor to sustain hunter-gatherers year-round, but were repeatedly visited. The former lies on the inter-island passage to Melos, dates to roughly the time of the maritime surge at Franchthi, and has abundant obsidian, as well as round huts and burials suggestive of seasonal occupancy. Gioura obtained a little obsidian too; the Cyclops Cave's fauna include deer, small wild boars (if their mineralized bones do not point to an older, Pleistocene walk-on, followed by insular dwarfing),[151] various birds, both coastal and semi-open sea-fish, and the hooks with which to catch them [5.19]. Tunny, mackerel and bonito, all mainly denizens of open water, had been decapitated elsewhere and maybe salted for transportation from the catching grounds.[152] Missing fish heads, island burials and more obsidian are all parts of a picture that is largely lost to us, but that if visible in its entirety would surely reveal a network of seasonal sea-paths paddled by the practitioners of a dynamic maritime culture. The sea-children of the Aegean nursery were coming of age.

5.19 Fish-hooks from the Cyclops Cave on the north Aegean islet of Gioura.

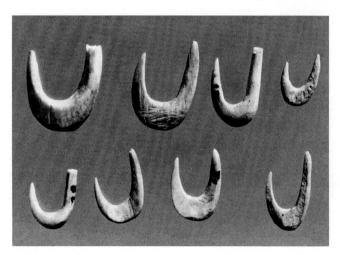

But how widespread was the phenomenon of island-based hunter-gatherers, beyond the Aegean, Cyprus and quasi-continental Sicily? Sardinia and Corsica, now sundered from each other and roughly modern in form, can certainly be added to the roll call.[153] After acting as a refuge in the Last Glacial Maximum, followed by likely subsequent abandonment, they were repeopled during the 9th to 8th millennia, via a sea crossing now tripled to 50 km (30 miles), and with the squeeze on mainland territories by rising sea levels arguably

5.20 The staple meat supply on Mesolithic Sardinia: a skeleton of little *Prolagus sardus*.

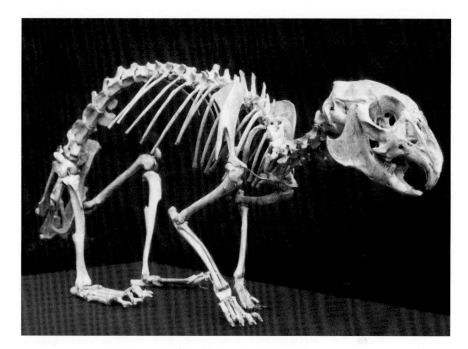

the motivation. Although as on Cyprus, and we might now add, Crete, there is no cast-iron proof of human culpability, it is an otherwise extraordinary coincidence that the native deer and canid vanished around this time. Their departure left only *Prolagus sardus*, a dreary dietary prospect indeed [**5.20**]. Exactly how monotonous is brought home by careful analysis of the Monte Leone rockshelter, at the southern tip of Corsica.[154] Here, *Prolagus* comprised three-quarters of the bones; an estimated 75,000–150,000 of these hare-like creatures were devoured over five centuries of sporadic occupation – a tribute to their breeding rate, given *Prolagus*'s survival into later times. The rest of the menu comprised sardines and eels, spiced up with the occasional vole, mouse, bird, mollusc, seal or beached dolphin. Most people were trappers and inshore fishers who moved up and down the coast as they depleted a given area, perhaps seasonal visitors but more plausibly permanent residents; a crippled skeleton from Araguina-Sennola implies one individual who had been on Corsica for some time.

People on islands prompt us to ask how much real seafaring, as opposed to just strand-line activity, was going on in the Mesolithic sphere. The attractive concept has recently been proposed of early Holocene 'foraging seascapes' in the Mediterranean,[155] but how widely does it apply? In the Aegean, and earlier in the seas around Cyprus, it resonates well with the visible tip of the iceberg, though even here most food was still taken on land. Further west, however, it is worth enquiring to what extent the iceberg actually existed. Of course, the presence of people on Corsica and Sardinia proves seafaring, and a further hint comes from Dalmatia. Here, most islands with Mesolithic finds were still joined to the mainland or so close as to make no odds. But one find from Vela Spilja is more telling: a pestle made from an igneous pebble whose source is one of several volcanic islets already well out to sea by this time.[156] The prime candidate is mid-Adriatic Palagruža, whose tiny size belies its significance as a maritime stopover (and also a source of fine chert on its satellite, Mala Palagruža), and from which comes a reciprocally suggestive possibly Mesolithic shell bead. This pebble aside, however, central Mediterranean island stones reveal a very different picture from the east. Most remarkably, there was virtually no use of obsidian – just one potentially secure find apiece from Sicily and Apulia, a dubious candidate from Liguria and a few of unknown origin from northwest Greece and Albania.[157] In the case of the Lipari source, part of the explanation is that the main flow quarried in antiquity was only created during a volcanic eruption in the 9th millennium BC (most of what is visible today was formed in medieval times). Possibly the minor sources on remote Palmarola and Pantelleria had not yet been discovered (itself good negative evidence), while the total absence of obsidian from Sardinian sources in the interior furnishes additional proof of the coastal orientation of the island's hunter-gatherers. Further west, we lose both the convenient tracer of obsidian sources and easily accessible islands, but on the basis of what we do see, there is no sign of sea crossings between the 12th-millennium BC Iberian harpoon at Taforalt in the western Maghreb, and the start of the Neolithic. Despite the time-honoured penchant for seafood in the west and central Mediterranean, a tentative case might be made that true hunter-gatherer seafaring was rarer than in the east, especially in regions less endowed with indented coasts and islands. Any such distinction would, of course, have ramifications for understanding the subsequent expansion of farming.

The neolithicization of Mediterranean Europe

Neolithic farming communities replaced this Mesolithic world in the northern half of the Mediterranean basin at different times between 7000 and 5500 BC, save for a few enclaves that held out slightly longer [5.21]. Overall, the trend was strongly from east to west, if with informative variations. The start date in the east was conditioned by the acceleration towards full domestication, followed by the Late PPNB boom in farming settlements. Over the course of its 3500-km (2175-mile) expansion beyond central Anatolia and Cyprus, the Neolithic displayed impressive consistency in its core features, principally the suite of domestic animals and plants, pottery and other objects like polished stone axes, often collectively known as the Neolithic 'package'. One great facilitator was the basin's latitudinal orientation, which offered comparable environments from the Jordan to the Atlantic; another, the robustness and amenity to transport of most Mediterranean domesticates. Sheep, for example, were popular right across the basin, thanks to their modest size, propensity to store fat on the hoof, and provision of meat and milk – and residue analysis affirms that small-scale, if sometimes quite intensive, milking played a major role in sustaining the spread of the Neolithic.[158] But a lot of remodelling also occurred en route,[159] so that the Iberian Neolithic, while bearing a distinct family resemblance to the Levantine PPNB, could never be mistaken for its identical twin. Some of this may

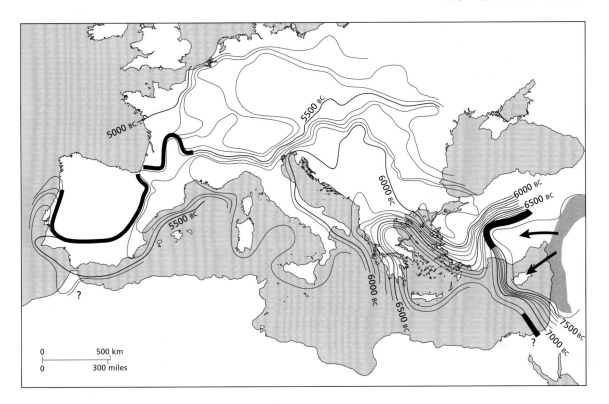

5.21 The changing speed of the spread of farming around the Mediterranean basin and deeper into Europe, as represented by one-century isobars. The long pause in western Anatolia may reflect lack of investigation, which is also a problem at entry points to North Africa, but elsewhere the pattern is well determined.

reflect genuine losses at several bottlenecks in transmission, but these changes represent more than simply a cumulative cultural impoverishment, or, as one expert puts it, the discarding of heavy luggage on the long journey west.[160] From nuances of crop choice to matters of pottery style, they also reflect accommodations with specific conditions in each area, continual honing with experience and creation of local meanings within the inherited framework.

The mechanisms behind this transformation have been heavily contested.[161] For a long time, one hypothesis was that local hunter-gatherers independently domesticated plants and animals, as in the Fertile Crescent.[162] With boars and aurochs roaming the basin's woods and stands of wild cereals and legumes between these in several regions, this seemed a genuine possibility, though the absence of native wild sheep and goats already placed limits on the scope. But stringent analyses of bones, seeds, the cave strata that contribute much of our information and most recently genetics, today testify beyond doubt that no such in situ transition to farming in fact took place on this flank of the Mediterranean before exogenous domesticates arrived from further east.[163] Why this should have been so, and what alternative, counterfactual histories of indigenous management and domestication might have transpired if this swathe of the basin had been more isolated, or given extra time, remain interesting issues – and in the case of pigs (but only these) there is intriguing genetic evidence that people living in southern Europe soon *after* the advent of farming substituted the eastern breeds for ones derived from locally domesticated boars, which over time swamped the intruders.[164] Sticking to history as it actually

185

played out, however, the conclusion is inescapable that only the critical overlap between one sliver of the eastern Mediterranean and the core of early farming in the Fertile Crescent enabled a drastic, irreversible and strategic change of this kind to emerge and spread so early over so much of the remainder of the basin.

With the elimination of local domestication, the quest for an active Mesolithic contribution has shifted to the proposal that hunter-gatherers adopted domesticates and other traits through contact with farmers, slotting them into their lifestyles until they in effect became Neolithic.[165] The possible incentives range from the social (for example, the incorporation of Neolithic traits in hunter-gatherer exchange networks or feasts) to the pragmatic (maybe sedentary propensities and plant management skills predisposed hunter-gatherers to appreciate the advantages of domestic strains?). The jury concerning this possibility still remains out, and the arguments for and against will be best evaluated on a case by case basis.

The alternative to Mesolithic-focused scenarios is, of course, that the Neolithic spread primarily by the actual movement of people who lived by farming and its range of associated cultural practices – in other words, an extension of the same process that had filled in the Levant, Anatolia and Cyprus. As farming, once established, sustained far higher densities of people than hunting and gathering, it swamped or absorbed pre-existing populations.[166] To illustrate this contrast, it is quite plausible that the number of hunter-gatherer inhabitants of a region as large as Sicily (some 25,000 sq. km or 10,000 sq. miles) was comparable to the population of a single mega-site such as 'Ain Ghazal or Çatalhöyük. Alongside demic turnover would surely have come a redrawing of the linguistic map, though there are philological obstacles to the proposal that it was farming that first dispersed Indo-European languages.[167] Early versions of this migratory scenario in the Mediterranean and further north envisaged a broad wave of advance, in aggregate a slow rolling frontier,[168] but more favoured now are punctuated, leapfrogging jumps by small founder groups from one suitable patch directly to the next, each creating a little enclave that propagated local expansion and further onward leaps.[169] The timing of the next jump depended on when the best niches had been claimed, or among these fission-prone, post-mega-site groups, when social tensions made moving on preferable to in situ negotiation. This did not need to wait for a local saturation point to be reached.[170] Expansion could therefore be rapid, and might in time evolve a distinctive ethos and impetus. Over the last two decades an impressive amount of archaeological evidence has accumulated to suggest that this mechanism was a, or perhaps the, major means by which the Neolithic dispersed. Genetic data are harder to interpret, but seem to indicate that at least 15 per cent of modern European DNA derives from Near Eastern immigrants of plausibly Neolithic age, a substantial figure given that plenty of local genes must have been picked up via intermarriage with native people as farming spread west.[171] Most such analyses imply higher immigration in the Mediterranean than temperate Europe, and in the east than the west, possibly up to 85 per cent in the Aegean, according to one study of Y-chromosomes, which reflect arguably more mobile men.[172] Such east–west clines, underpinned by older generations of archaeological data, long sustained a conventional compromise and contrast, with primacy awarded in the east to an influx of farmers and in the west to local hunter-gatherer 'neolithicization', the dividing line typically falling somewhere in central Italy.

Before we ask whether recent archaeological investigations sustain or alter this received wisdom, one increasingly uncontroversial feature of Neolithic expansion must be spotlit, as it represents something fundamentally new in Mediterranean history. For whatever the social and economic processes involved in the spread of farming, there is no doubt that maritime mobility was a major medium for its dissemination. The marine short-cuts of Mediterranean geography and the sea's wider connecting potential began to come more fully into play, and to demolish the barriers to contact between opposing shores, sub-basins and islands. The Neolithic expanded from the east to west Aegean, across the Adriatic and via the Tyrrhenian Sea to the Atlantic. The big islands figured prominently, from 9th-millennium BC Cyprus, to (as we will see) Crete, Sicily, Corsica and Sardinia, all of whose place in the flow of the Neolithic stream is proven by their earliest dates for sheep and goat (two convenient proxies), which fully kept pace with the adjacent mainlands.[173] The fact that overland expansion in temperate Europe, and in particular 6th-millennium BC 'Linearbandkeramik' dispersal from Hungary to the Paris basin, could be equally rapid underscores the point that the advantage of Mediterranean maritime movement was not yet speed, but directness and accessibility.[174] Viewed from the perspective of the deeper past, the shift from a circum- to trans-Mediterranean axis announces an inversion of the Palaeolithic regime, in which most novelties had entered from the continental edges and the basin's peninsular extremities served as refuges for doomed creatures and ways of life. Now, a place such as southern Italy was a cul-de-sac no longer, and rather a stepping stone and accelerator of innovations, while refugia for older practices began to coalesce instead on the basin's northern margins.

This provokes two further observations. First, if much transmission was by sea, we will have lost a disproportionate number of early farming sites to the last millennia of sea level rise, for low coastal shelves are likely to have been as attractive to farmers as to hunter-gatherers. At Franchthi, the cave was used from early in the Neolithic as a peripheral activity area for a now partially drowned open settlement, while at Leucate in southwest France an inundated Neolithic settlement was found during the dredging of the lagoon.[175] Second, the Mediterranean Neolithic's spread represents the fusion of two initially separate developments: maritime hunter-gatherer seafaring and terrestrial farming, first in the context of Cyprus and then repeated all over the basin. The rapidity and success with which these were combined must have varied, speeding or retarding events in different theatres. Moreover, the local players cannot be reduced to a simple dichotomy between hunter-gatherer seafarers playing ferryman to landlubber farmers. We have seen that in the western half of the basin the Mesolithic fishing folk were not necessarily adept seafarers, while equally, dietary evidence reveals that many maritime farmers had an aversion to seafood;[176] in short, all manner of cross-overs was possible. With these thoughts in mind, we can take a closer look at the Neolithic as it expanded from the eastern Mediterranean to the Atlantic.

Leapfroggers around the pond

We left Mediterranean farming as it was spreading overland across Anatolia, and with a maritime branch long established on Cyprus. The former pathway implied a twofold adaptation, from Mediterranean conditions to those of the Anatolian plateau, then back again as it entered the Aegean. This may have exerted a brake on progress westward. It also fashioned the Neolithic as it would look in and beyond the Aegean, for it was now that hitherto minor traits such as little figurines of plump, ample-buttocked women and seals with geometric designs for stamping skin or cloth became popular.[177] The earliest Neolithic to reach the east Aegean coast may eventually prove to date just before 7000 BC, with pioneers filtering in overland or via the southern coastal passage.[178] But from about 6500 BC an increasing number of small, low tells appear, especially where the east–west river corridors debouch. Meanwhile, in the northwest, at the gateway to the Balkans, hunter-gatherer concentrations around the Sea of Marmara, Dardanelles and entrance to the Black Sea delayed the start of the Neolithic.[179] Here, the Fikirtepe phase is as late as 6100 BC (an approximate date that will repeatedly emerge as significant), for instance at Ilıpınar, a ring-shaped farming village beside Lake Iznik, and Hoca Çeşme on the Evros River, now the border between Turkey and Greece. Along the south coast the record is non-existent save for the waning of hunter-gatherer activity at Öküzini in the 7th millennium BC though, as we shall see, finds from Crete suggest that at the start of that millennium, and maybe occasionally even earlier, seafaring farmers leapfrogged from Cilicia, the Amuq or just possibly Cyprus past stretches of savage coast from one fertile embayment to the next.

The Neolithic in the west and south Aegean began between 7000 and 6500 BC, first and foremost in the great plain of Thessaly and its northward extension to where the coast swings east near later Thessaloniki.[180] Franchthi may provide insights into the interface with hunter-gatherers, and on Crete the lowest levels of the tell above which rose the Bronze Age palace of Knossos boast some of the earliest dates of all. The first expansion appears not to have been terrestrial, via the northern Aegean, largely due to the hunter-gatherer block in the Sea of Marmara and maybe others in the estuaries and woods of Macedonia, a current blind spot. Rather, it seems to have crossed the Aegean via chains of islands, albeit leaving little impress on the latter en route.[181] This implies maritime proficiency on a par with the advent of farming on Cyprus over a millennium earlier, and neatly illustrates the tendency to target desirable areas, even at a distance, rather than crawling from one scrap of land to the next. A coastal route along the south Anatolian coast would have provided experience in this respect, and most probably led to the farming settlement of Crete (plus, we might suspect, Rhodes); there are striking similarities between the dark-surfaced pottery with incised designs at Knossos and Mersin, both belonging to the early 7th millennium BC. In the rest of the Aegean, pre-existent hunter-gatherer maritime knowledge must have played a vital role. It also left another telling mark on the first Neolithic communities, for their early strata in western Turkey, Greece and even Knossos contain obsidian from Melos, in the last case 170 km (105 miles) from its source across the open sea, and in other cases twice as far via coastal and island-hopping routes. Obsidian's recondite Aegean origin was surely learned from hunter-gatherers, some of whose descendants possibly specialized in supplying it – in turn perhaps explaining the fact that the early Neolithic's microlithic arrowheads reveal Mesolithic antecedents.

Such particular legacies apart, the Aegean Neolithic was exogenous, introduced by small groups of migrants into a region only patchily inhabited by hunter-gatherers who were swiftly assimilated.[182] Even at Franchthi, where Mesolithic people had gathered wild barley and oats, the case for local adoption is at best partial.[183] An initial level with sheep, goats, later pigs, possibly domestic cereals and new kinds of blades could reflect acquisitions from nearby farmers. But this was a false start, for a temporal gap separates this from the ensuing layer, which had the full Neolithic package without substantial Mesolithic traits. Elsewhere, the Neolithic was associated with open spaces rather than caves (notably expanses of arable plain and rolling hills that seemingly had been lightly inhabited, if at all, by hunter-gatherers), intensive horticulture of the kind developed in the PPNB and a preponderance of sheep augmented by smaller numbers of the other standard domesticates, with little wild fauna or hunting gear. We now know, thanks to the new Mesolithic finds on Crete, that the people who followed a babbling brook up to its lush confluence with a smaller stream and there set up a farming community just after 7000 BC were not the first to make landfall on the island, but Knossos still furnishes unusually clear insights into these newcomers.[184] The lowest stratum covered a quarter of a hectare (two-thirds of an acre) and implies a founding nucleus of just a few families. Nonetheless, except for the initial absence of pots it contained the full farming and cultural package, none of which was local to the island. Everything had to be carefully shuttled across the sea to replicate a way of life familiar wherever the arrivals had departed from – as with the earlier Cypriot farmers, a conveniently visible microcosm on the move, that must have had numerous parallels across the Aegean and elsewhere.[185]

Thessaly emerged as the main attractor, with the greatest accumulation of people at this time west of the Konya plain.[186] Following a poorly known early 7th-millennium phase in which pottery, as at Knossos, was missing or extremely rare, some 120 tells began to mushroom up in the east Thessalian plain during the Early Neolithic (6500–5800 BC). Each was a small village of some 50–250 people, typically less than an hour's walk from its neighbours. The most fully excavated lies further north at Nea Nikomedeia, with free-standing, squarish wattle-and-daub houses and at first monochrome, then red- or white-painted pots [5.22].[187] Each house is assumed to have

5.22 The Neolithic reaches the Greek mainland at Nea Nikomedeia: (*above*) figurine of a woman; (*below*) the village's loosely arranged square-to-rectangular houses.

belonged to a family, but cooking took place in communal spaces and implies sharing too. One bigger structure with either female, frog-like or birthing figurines, large polished axes, caches of well-knapped flint blades, and clay tokens may be a meeting-house, home to a successful family or just possibly a shrine. In contrast, the broken-up, drier lands south of Thessaly stayed sparsely inhabited in the Early and ensuing Middle Neolithic (5800–5500 BC), and most of the archipelago was empty of permanent residents.[188] In the far south, after the initial newcomers, Crete's Neolithic evolved along its own lines, with limited external contacts.[189] Its secluded pathway, and the more southerly origins of its farmers, may provide some context for the mysterious language(s) revealed 5000 years later in the undeciphered Minoan scripts, which are unrelated to the speech of mainland Greece, and have no surviving parallels elsewhere.

Farming took several more centuries to reach western Greece and the southern end of the Adriatic, and once again the well-known clusters of hunter-gatherers in this region may have acted as a retardant. Sheep, goats and poorly fired pots infiltrated the Sidari midden on Corfu by 6500 BC (a genuine case of Mesolithic adoption?), but for the first full farming horizons there and elsewhere in Albania, southern Dalmatia and the Apulian heel of Italy, we wait until a century or so on either side of 6000 BC.[190] Thereafter, expansion during the Early Neolithic (in the Adriatic roughly coterminous with the 6th millennium BC) described two principal axes, one up the Dalmatian coast, the other across the Adriatic at Otranto into southern Apulia, or via a longer (140-km or 85-mile) island-hopping route further north, straight to the Tavoliere plain. The second option compares closely to previous trans-Aegean routes towards Thessaly. Traces of its passage or the aftermath have survived in the form of pottery on little Sušac, the Tremiti Islands and even Palagruža.[191] The last of these, some 20 ha (50 acres) of lacerating rock, with no fresh water source and on average only 290 mm (11.4 in.) of rain per year, was impossible to farm, and must owe the passing honour to its midway location, which as we learned had already been discovered by hunter-gatherers.

The first Adriatic farming communities retained the same package of animals and plants as used further east, particularly in northern Greece.[192] They targeted similar areas of arable land, notably in Apulia, the Tavoliere, and a rare break in the towering maritime facade of the eastern Adriatic between Šibenik and Zadar. Neolithic culture in this theatre departed in certain respects, however, from Aegean models, an index of further reworking, albeit with little traceable to hunter-gatherer traditions, nor across the barrier of the Dinaric range to the Balkan Neolithic of the Starčevo culture, which was expanding northward on the inland side of the mountains. As in the Aegean, most Adriatic settlements were open. Gone are the tells, due to the use of wood rather than mud-brick or wattle-and-daub for building in this well-forested zone, and in their place are extensive ditch-enclosed settlements with houses widely spaced within. The most famous are some 780 in the Tavoliere, many of whose outlines were detected by aerial photographs taken in the Second World War [**5.23**].[193] Asfaka in northwest Greece, Smilčić near Zadar, and others in Sicily

5.23 A typical Neolithic settlement in the Tavoliere, identified in this 1940s aerial photograph by its encircling ditches and the small internal C-shaped cuttings assumed to delineate individual household plots.

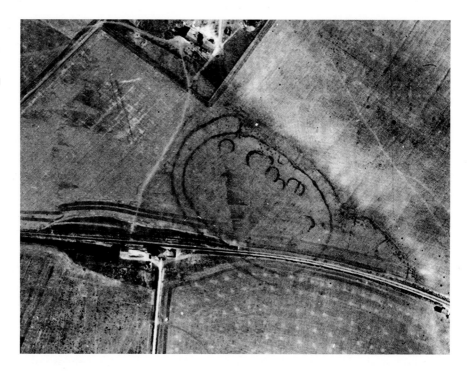

5.24 An exceptionally elaborate Cardial-impressed pot from Cova de l'Or near Valencia, showing a figure with upraised arms. The surface appearance and rounded bottom indicate the close relationship to basketry.

and northeast Italy define the overall zone. Another trait is impressed decoration on pottery, a minor feature in the east but the principal way of decorating pots in the Early Neolithic of the central and west Mediterranean, where it counters the demise of painted patterns beyond southern Italy.[194] The designs imitate basketry, an old hunter-gatherer medium, but also plausible for a Neolithic transported in canoes. Regional varieties include a circum-Adriatic type, the 'Stentinello' styles of Calabria and Sicily, and several Tyrrhenian, Ligurian and Provençal-to-Iberian Cardial (cockleshell-impressed) traditions that describe a notably coastal distribution, the last evolving by 5600 BC into the so-called classic Cardial [**5.24**]. Behind these extensive trans-maritime zones of stylistic similarity must lie a mixture of genealogies of descent among farming potters, as well as widespread webs of connection, with individual pots in the west known to have moved over distances of 50–100 km (30–60 miles).[195]

Neolithic expansion up both coasts of the northern Adriatic was slow, taking about half a millennium to reach the head of the sub-basin.[196] Farming appeared in Istria by 5700 BC, and near Trieste around 200 years later, where a potsherd from Edera Cave offers one of the few unambiguous Adriatic instances of hunter-gatherer contact with farmers.[197] On the Italian side it breached a previously static front beyond the Tavoliere about 5500 BC and advanced to the centre and northeast of the peninsula.[198] Along the coast and in parts of the interior the

191

sites reflect fully Neolithic communities, those at the head of the Adriatic cultivating different strands of wheat and evincing other traits that betray a conjunction at last, north of the mountains, with the Balkan interior and central Europe.[199] Elsewhere, however, it was a different matter.[200] Mesolithic groups survived for several centuries in the Dinarics and Apennines, and as late as 5300–5200 BC in the eastern Alps. Mesolithic resilience also accounts for the delay in settling the water meadows, marshes and woods of the Po plain, where salvage work is starting to encounter long-anticipated hunter-gatherers beneath as much as 6 m (20 ft) of mud, followed by hybrid communities that grew crops but still hunted their meat.[201] At other inland Italian settlements, such as little San Marco near Gubbio in the Biferno Valley, hunting remained prominent and other older traditions were maintained.[202] This persistence of hunting, and in certain areas overall Mesolithic lifestyles, contrasts markedly with the pattern further east.[203]

Compared to the Adriatic situation, expansion in and beyond Tyrrhenian Italy was astonishingly fast [**5.21, 5.25**].[204] The Neolithic materializes almost instantaneously in both south and north, during the first two centuries of the 6th millennium BC, then only fractionally later in Mediterranean France, and reached the Atlantic by 5500 BC. One axis took in Calabria, where wattle-and-daub houses clustered amidst the coastal sand-dunes, and Sicily, whose eastern plains were dotted with ditched Stentinello villages.[205] In western Sicily Grotta dell'Uzzo shifted from a year-round hunter-gatherer base to its eventual demotion as a farmer's shelter [**5.26**]. The other route is delineated by the roughly simultaneous appearance of most Neolithic traits on Corsica and Sardinia by 5700 BC, and a century or two earlier due north on the western Ligurian mainland, most notably at the cave of Arene Candide. Differences in impressed pottery styles between Sicily and the northern Tyrrhenian trace divergent pathways out of southern Italy, the latter's via Tuscany and offshore settlements on the little island of Giglio. This division, like the

5.25 Leap-frogging expansion of farming nuclei between the Tyrrhennian region, southern France and further west can be demonstrated by cladistic analysis of differences in the morphology of sheep bones seen at a range of sites. While one axis of advance spread incrementally westward along the coast, another sprang directly from the northern Tyrrhenian into southwest France.

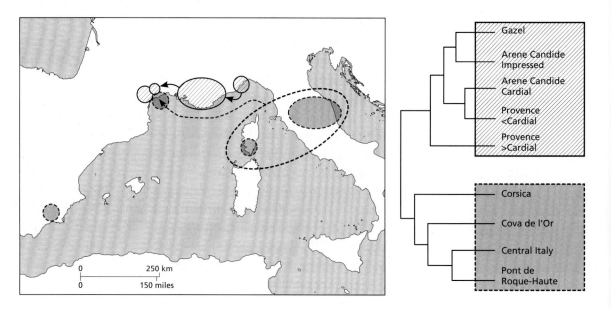

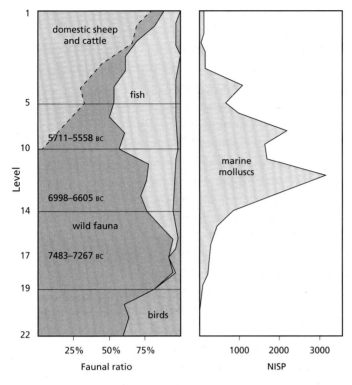

5.26 Patterns of meat and sea mollusc consumption at Uzzo Cave show complex fluctuations over time, with only gradual if eventually decisive takeover by domesticated animals. In contrast to the rapid appearance of Neolithic traits elsewhere, this is surely due to the fairly remote, cul-de-sac location of this west Sicilian site, and the consequent resilience of older ways of life.

earlier bifurcation around the mouth of the Adriatic, was a reflection of the coastal and island geography in this part of the Mediterranean, with Sicily and Sardinia remaining insulated from each other by 280 km (175 miles) of unbroken sea.

More controversial are the mechanisms behind this suddenly galloping pace. For some, the speed itself argues for dispersal and uptake through indigenous hunter-gatherer networks, with the villages of eastern Sicily marking the high-water mark for migrant farmers. This conviction was long fortified by the ubiquity of caves rather than open sites as the principal find-spots from the Tyrrhenian westward, and the wild animals often found in the first levels with Neolithic traits. Moreover, the initial suite of domesticates was sometimes incomplete. Corsica only gained cattle after 5000 BC, while Arene Candide started with plentiful domestic sheep for eating and milking, then cattle possibly a little later, and its first swine were wild boars.[206] The paucity of plants (either wild or domestic) simply reflected, however, the absence of evidence, as older excavations seldom sieved the soil to recover their remains; new investigations at the Pendimoun rock-shelter on the Italian–French border soon found wheat and barley.[207]

But serious objections attend the idea that farming spread from the Tyrrhenian to the Atlantic primarily through native hunter-gatherers gradually becoming Neolithic. One is the point that the incoming Neolithic was more demonstrably maritime than the local Mesolithic. Another is whether caves tell the whole story. Newly discovered open sites reveal a different picture, and, as we shall learn in Chapter 6, two only marginally later waterlogged villages in France and Iberia preserve, thanks to their subsequent submergence, ample domesticates and other remains that prompt questions as to what sea level rise might have deprived us of a few centuries earlier. Finally, as chronology becomes more refined, the sparseness of the later, 'Castelnovian' Mesolithic between the Alps and the Rhône is becoming apparent; by the time the Neolithic reached here, something had already winnowed parts of this once rich hunter-gatherer landscape, and the first farming sites commonly show up in places where hunter-gatherer occupancy was not just thin, but entirely absent.[208] Arene Candide was one such vacant niche, for its Neolithic directly overlies much older levels, and the same holds true for most of western Liguria, flanked by late hunter-gatherer redoubts at the root of the Apennines and in rugged Provence.[209] The same hiatus is observed on Corsica.[210] In other words, reports of the death beyond

Italy of maritime expansion by farmers are exaggerated, however stripped down and adapted the package sometimes became, and the principal reason for exceptionally rapid westward expansion may have been not vibrant hunter-gatherer populations, but their prior decimation, a matter to which we must return.

We have slightly anticipated developments west of the Tyrrhenian Sea in order to make a revisionist case for the western half of the Mediterranean in general. In fact, there are growing indications that expansion along the alternately forbiddingly sheer and welcoming, lowland coast of southern France and Spain took exactly the form that has just been outlined (and might indeed give insights into how farming spread along the similar, still unexplored, south Turkish coast 1500 years earlier).[211] In Languedoc, west of the Rhône estuary (itself a likely Mesolithic enclave), the Neolithic open site of Pont de Roque-Haute now confirms abundant sheep, few wild animals, three kinds of wheat, and pottery styles and obsidian from the distant central Tyrrhenian.[212] Just how discrete, as well as distant, the founding groups that targeted such places might be is startlingly demonstrated by its close neighbour at Peiro Signado, just 3 km (2 miles) away, which instead had strong Ligurian connections [5.25].[213] These sites begin around 5700 BC; a mere a century or so later the process had extended far along the Iberian coast, again often with substantial gaps in time and space between first farmers and last hunter-gatherers, and an impressive retention of the range of crops and animals witnessed further east.[214] Mas d'Is in Alicante offers a rare view of an open community with built houses and a nearby ditched enclosure.[215] Harder to explain are the functions of some upland caves, such as the Cova de l'Or, 650 m (2150 ft) up in the hills behind Valencia, with wheat, barley, sheep and goats.[216] Did farmers so rapidly penetrate these uplands for cultivation, herding or hunting, is this a rare case of genuine adoption by hunter-gatherers hanging on to their traditional lands, or does the abundance of elaborately decorated pottery, its parallels with a contemporary local horizon of rock art and other ritual-associated finds, suggest a more arcane role for such places?[217]

From here to the ocean, the paths lay along the wild Andalusian coast, where the Nerja Cave had domesticates by 5500 BC, or via inland basins north of the Sierra Nevada, either way converging on the mouth of the Guadalquivir and thence up the Atlantic coast. As we saw earlier, there were certainly still ample hunter-gatherers in Atlantic southern Iberia, most of them now living and dying around the focus of the huge shell middens along the Tagus, Sado and other estuaries. Their retrenchment left plenty of intervening areas for farmers, and two segregated parallel lifestyles came into being here, with a few hunter-gatherer estuarine strongholds operating as late as 4500–4300 BC, eventually surrounded by farming communities.[218] Pots occasionally appear in the upper levels of the shell middens, but not domesticated animals, and the bone chemistry of southwest Iberians at this time affirms a division between a land-based Neolithic diet and the more aquatic one maintained until the end by hunter-gatherers.

To complete this outline of Neolithic expansion from the Jordan to the Tagus, what happened in parts of the Mediterranean zone far from the coast, particularly in the west, where large expanses of interior lie within our remit, and long river valleys open the way? In the tightly bounded basin of the lower Rhône, Neolithic groups multiplied locally for generations before pushing inland and finally uphill, where in the late 6th millennium they ran into the last hunter-gatherers of the interior.[219] In the Pyrenees and Cantabrian mountains too, hunter-gatherers held on, into the later 5th millennium BC in the latter case, where they only gradually merged into the world of the Neolithic.[220] The unique language, genes and blood-group signatures of the Basque country may well be a testimony to the resilience of such people in mountainous, out-of-the-way places. In the remote limestone plateau of the Alentejo in southern Portugal, the first menhirs are arguably translations of Mesolithic wooden equivalents erected by the last hunter-gatherers in transition.[221] But on both sides of the Pyrenees lay inviting valley corridors along the Aude and Garonne, and up the Ebro. Only in the last few years has it become apparent how soon farmers exploited these, in the first case bringing impressed pottery to the Bay of Biscay, and in the second a swift repopulation of parts of inland Iberia, which for millennia had been haemorrhaging people to the coast.[222] The Mediterranean Neolithic had lost none of the capacity it had shown in Thessaly and the Tavoliere for switching to large-scale terrestrial settlement when the opportunity arose.

Standing back, and acknowledging the variety of circumstances that spread the Neolithic throughout the northern half of the Mediterranean, three main conclusions are abundantly clear. One is that migration by farming groups remained a mechanism, and probably the dominant one, not just in the east and centre but also the west, much of it in the form of jumps from one favourable spot to the next. Second, some hunter-gatherer contribution to this process is indisputable, particularly through transmission of seafaring knowledge, starting in the Gulf of İskenderun, with a later supercharging phase in the Aegean and perhaps another at the mouth of the Adriatic. Interestingly, this is best attested in the eastern half of the basin, not the west, where hunter-gatherers have traditionally held the interpretative upper hand. But instances of hunter-gatherers becoming even partly Neolithic are rare along the main axes of expansion and no less so in the west – indeed the shell-midden dwellers of Atlantic Iberia exemplify exactly the opposite tendency. Instead, this process belongs mainly to a twilight phase leading to the extinction of hunter-gatherer lifestyles in bypassed redoubts or on the basin's margins, for instance the Sea of Marmara, the Po Valley, the uplands of northern Italy, southern France and Iberia and eventually the Atlantic estuaries. Hunter-gatherers and farmers alike were superbly attuned to Mediterranean conditions, yet in different ways and in different niches that made conversions and cross-overs rarely viable until the future lay manifestly with the new way of life. This should hardly surprise us. Their seasonal schedules differed, the hard labour and indifferent health of the Neolithic is unlikely to have appealed to hunter-gatherers with access to good hunting, foraging and fishing, and the two probably had quite different concepts of nature (in terms of relations with plants and animals as well as land) and the supernatural (for example, contrast the Neolithic obsession with ancestors and fertility with the likely animistic spirit worlds of hunter-gatherers). In the Levant one had gradually transformed into the other over millennia, via floodwater cultivation, but this remained unique within the Mediterranean. Further west a pre-evolved farming package and its attendant ideology was juxtaposed with hunter-gatherers nowhere near the brink of opting for farming by themselves.

Third, something changed drastically towards the end of the 7th millennium BC. As we have seen, evidence for late hunter-gatherer sites reduces sharply across broad areas, sometimes earlier but always by about 6000 BC, leaving voids, especially in the central and western Mediterranean, into which farmers later expanded. Local boom and bust cycles may have played a part, but responsibility for the overall horizon can surely be placed on the climate deterioration of the 6200 event, which hit hard and fast at the end of a long optimum.[223] From a pan-Mediterranean perspective, the pace of Neolithic advance surged immediately after this. It had taken most of a millennium for farming to spread from western Anatolia to the bottom of the Adriatic, and (depending on one's starting date) at least as long again to emerge from the Levant, implying expansion rates of a kilometre or so a year or a day's walk per generation (in practice most moves will have been shorter, for instance to a new village nucleus in Thessaly, or longer but infrequent, for example across the sea to Crete). Much of this is attributable to the need for ongoing tweaking of the 'package' and its integration with seafaring, as well as a few hunter-gatherer blocks at potential conduits of advance.[224] But thereafter, save for the strangely slow movement up the Adriatic, farming spread extremely fast to the western end of the basin, taking only 300–500 years to cover 1500 km (900 miles) as the crow flies, at an average of 3–5 km (2–3 miles) per year or a leapfrog each generation of 75–125 km (50–80 miles).[225] Farmers would have been affected by the 6200 BC event too, but their numbers enabled faster recovery, and renewed advance before surviving hunter-gatherers had found a chance to recuperate. In this respect, the delay in the Adriatic could have something to do with exceptional hunter-gatherer resilience to the event in the north, in turn thanks to the Po Valley or because the Adriatic's attenuated form concentrated survivors – either way making the Adriatic operate as Mediterranean peninsulas had during the Palaeolithic, as a refuge whose effect intensified at its far end, but this time in reverse.

Saharan super-attractor and deltaic dam

The early Holocene history of Mediterranean Africa could not be more different from that of the Levant or southern Europe, and some of the roots of subsequent divergence undoubtedly go back to this period. Few North African plants were susceptible to domestication, save for some wild barley and oats in the Maghreb comparable to the stands of southern Europe (which were not domesticated either), and sorghum in the southeast Sahara and Sudan, still-wild sprays of which were placed in Tutankhamun's tomb.[226] Pearl millet, Africa's first native floral domesticate, emerged in the 2nd millennium BC, south of the Sahara. In contrast, the faunal options were relatively promising: widespread aurochs and, in the Maghreb, wild boars (both deep-time Eurasian intruders long gone native), as well as truculent African barbary sheep and, in northeast Africa, wild asses. Beyond this distinction, however, little is gained by measuring North Africa against the Levantine or European Neolithics and finding it wanting, nor, as will be affirmed in Chapter 6, by applying 'Neolithic' to all things African associated with pottery or stone axes. On the contrary, there is much to be lost, for it distracts us from an intrinsic exploration of the trajectories that actually did emerge in North Africa, few of which resemble those of farming societies elsewhere in the Mediterranean.

The paramount early Holocene development was the repeopling of the Sahara for the first time in 50,000 years. Descendants of Iberomaurusian hunter-gatherers filtered into this vast region from the Mediterranean coast, but the earliest and largest influx came from the south, shadowing the monsoon's desert-greening advance and the accompanying bow wave of Sahel fauna.[227] This was underway by the start of the 9th millennium BC on the southern fringes and the banks of the Nile. Soon it reached the central Saharan massifs, mountain-islands taken over as year-round bases from which people ventured out seasonally into drier lands. These pioneers were black Africans who presumably spoke early versions of the Nilo-Saharan languages that still survive in parts of the region. We glimpse them in the engraved and painted rock art of the Sahara, an open-air treasury of information preserved by the arid climate of later times, and which starts with a phase characterized by images of buffalo, giraffes and elephants, followed by a 'round head' style preoccupied with hunter-gatherer activities and a realm of spirits, masks and animal-headed people [5.27].[228] Other sources of information expand our insights. Harpoons, nets

5.27 Among the vibrant but often loosely dated rock art of the Sahara, this 'round head' style appears to date primarily to the early Holocene repeopling of this vast region, largely by populations moving in from the south.

5.28 Capsian sickle, needle, mask and beads, carved in bone, shell and ostrich egg. Not to scale.

and fine stone tools garnered abundant animals and plants from lakes and wadis. A 9000-year-old, 8-m- (26-ft-) long mahogany dugout canoe at Dafuna in Nigeria, then on the edge of Lake Mega-Chad, attests to watercraft probably on a par with Mediterranean seacraft.[229] Such traits once earned these people the sobriquet 'Aqualithic',[230] whose oddity reflects a distinctive way of life but overlooks terrestrial hunting and gathering activities. Finally, these people made pots long before anyone in the Mediterranean, a further measure of at least semi-sedentism, and probably used mainly for boiling plant foods.[231] As later in the central and west of the basin, their impressed surfaces imitated baskets and perhaps nets.

Two parts of the Sahara may have seen experiments in the husbandry of wild animals. In the Tadrart Acacus massif, part of the southwest Libyan Fezzan, the case is fairly compelling.[232] There, the huge Uan Afuda Cave was occupied from 9000 BC, initially by mobile groups hunting barbary sheep. But from about 8000 BC, and associated after 7000 BC with slightly drier conditions blurring into the severe aridity of the 6200 event (which finally triggered an abrupt hiatus in activity), residence became more fixed and foodstuffs broader-based. The latter embraced a range of land animals, birds and fish, as well as wild millet, sorghum and tubers. Numerous grinding stones and preserved gathering or storage baskets parallel this shift. Most interestingly of all, layers of trampled barbary sheep dung within the cave appear to indicate human corralling and feeding, an interpretation supported by injuries on the animals' bones presumably caused by efforts to escape, as well as rock art depictions elsewhere of pregnant or suckling sheep. In the end, barbary sheep were never domesticated, either because time ran out when the 6200 event hit, or because they were behaviourally too boisterous. But their corralling implies constrained, delayed-returns storage on the hoof, to be drawn upon when needed. Moreover, such practices could have predisposed people later on to integrate externally introduced domesticates into their way of life.

The second potential instance of animal husbandry concerns cattle and is hotly disputed.[233] Exhaustive genetic research points to an early division between Eurasian and African cattle, and therefore independent domestication of the latter within North Africa. But approximately when? The focus lies in the southeast Saharan borderlands between Egypt and Sudan, where claims for management of wild beasts during the 9th millennium BC in the Nabta Playa basin rest on an inconclusive combination of habitat reconstruction and the nuances of the bones themselves. The argument strengthens in the early 7th millennium, when walk-in wells were dug to enable animals to drink, and by 6000–5500 BC the genesis of Africa's grand tradition of cattle herding for meat, blood and potentially already milk was certainly underway, with wider North African repercussions that will become apparent in Chapter 6.[234]

The Tadrart Acacus and Nabta Playa are about as far from the Mediterranean as London, so what do developments this far south have to do with the North African coastal region? Satisfactory answers are hard to come by, for the interface between these two worlds in the northern Sahara, the driest residual band, is poorly explored. But we can hazard a guess from what we know about patterns in the Mediterranean

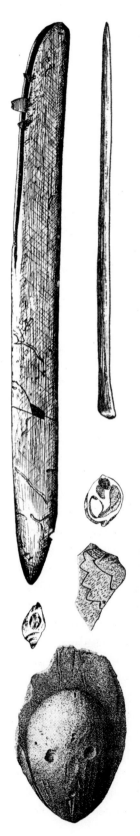

zone. At the start of the Holocene, hunter-gatherers occupied most of Mediterranean Africa, or, as in the case of Haua Fteah, reoccupied it after the Younger Dryas. They were descended from local Iberomaurusian groups and continued their predecessors' burial and other skeletal rituals, shaping skulls into masks, as well as carving ostrich egg, used intact for containers and in fragments for beads.[235] In the later 7th millennium BC a few groups in the Maghreb may have picked up pottery use from further south.[236] The best known of these people are the Capsian groups of Tunisia and eastern Algeria, named after their site of el-Mekta near the Roman town of Capsa [**5.28**].[237] Their presence is marked by massive middens that rival those of coastal Portugal, dense masses of fired and burnt stones, animal bone and colossal quantities of land snails, hence their name in French, *escargotières*, as well as the Arabic *rammadiya*, or ashy place. Up until the late 7th millennium BC these people were fairly sedentary, clumping in the richest patches and sometimes burying within their middens. They lived off the local big game (hartebeest, aurochs and zebra) and untold numbers of large, juicy snails, to which the charred wild onions discovered in one midden give a suitably Mediterranean culinary twist. But in the late 7th millennium, these hunter-gatherers switched sharply to smaller species (gazelle, hares, and even with the snail spectrum), proliferations of microliths (some mounted in sickles), and higher mobility, all adaptations that related, we might suspect, to the drier conditions brought on by the 6200 event.

Beyond the local details, what is telling for wider Mediterranean patterning is where these people elected to live. Before the end of the Pleistocene, hunter-gatherers were already moving out of the North African coastal zone into the interior as climate improved. In the Capsian this tendency solidified, as symbolized by the preference for ostrich egg over seashell as a decorated medium. Such people seem to have avoided the coast in favour of the lush savannah or open woodland then widespread across the interior and high plains, often setting up near springs. Further east at Haua Fteah, one of the few sites occupied (perhaps seasonally) near the sea, very few fish and molluscs augmented the barbary sheep, gazelle, pine nuts and wild legumes (preliminary reports of early domestic cereals have been dashed by the confirmation that they are Classical intrusions), and there is no sign of maritime ventures comparable to those elsewhere in the Mediterranean.[238] A few late Capsian hunter-gatherers moved to the Tunisian coast, where they ate more significant amounts of fish and shellfish, but most headed south to seasonal winter lakes in the northern Sahara.[239] In short, the strong gravitational pull of the coast witnessed elsewhere in the basin was inverted in Mediterranean Africa. One negative reason, as noted in Chapter 1, may have been the unfriendliness of much of this long shore to maritime experiments, but such an aversion implies the existence of a positive alternative too. This was the enormous, patchily verdant, game-rich Sahara of the early Holocene, which for North Africans acted as a much more powerful super-attractor than the sea. But the strategic impact on long-term Mediterranean history of a once greener Sahara was not limited to the tug it exerted at this time on human activity along the southern shore. Devoid of domesticated plants, yet with virtually limitless space for hunting and potentially herding, and with placid rather than turbulent bodies of water, the Sahara encouraged radically different lifestyles and cultural values. Its influence on the inhabitants of Mediterranean Africa promoted trajectories that were utterly different from, and in some respects antithetical to, those in the rest of the basin.

This indifference to Mediterranean Neolithic lifestyles also helps us to explain farming's conspicuous lack of headway in Egypt for thousands of years after it became established a mere 250 km (150 miles) away in the Jordan Valley. The early Holocene Nile Valley was in effect just one more North African aquatic environment, grading into the main Saharan zone via lake basins whose remnants make up the modern oases and playas of Egypt's Western Desert. We have a good grasp of the settled fishing, hunting, water-plant-gathering and pottery-using people who flourished along its upper corridor once the river had got over its roiling postglacial spate.[240] Frustratingly, the same cannot be said of the zone around the mouths of the Nile, which for us is more relevant.[241] As we saw earlier, the apogee of sea level rise was not a propitious time for deltas, but inner fragments of this mightiest Mediterranean example did survive, though with a bight of the sea thrust 50 km (30 miles) inland, scattered with drowning relics of Pleistocene beaches and turtle-backs of wind-blown sand. Once the pace of sea level rise abated after 7500 BC, the Nile quickly gained ground. Silt accumulated between sandbanks, perhaps a metre (3 ft) of it by 5500 BC, creating marshes, lagoons, raised levees along the river branches and eventually terra firma, the opening stages of an advance that continued, with a few setbacks, until the construction of the Aswan High Dam in the 1960s (disastrously a trap for silt as much as water). No traces of the first inhabitants of this waterworld have yet emerged from beneath the subsequent metres of silt laid down by the river, but there is little doubt that as the Delta swelled into the most ecologically stupendous wetland in the basin, it became home to substantial numbers of sedentary hunter-gatherers with a strong aquatic streak. One legacy of such invisible populations may be later Egyptian adeptness with the papyrus reed, a palpably hunter-gatherer technology that was turned to make everything from boats, sandals, mats and food to, finally, a writing surface. More immediately, such people and the delta environment itself are likely to have been a major barrier to any coherent expansion of the Levantine Neolithic package via the Mediterranean coastal zone.

One expert on farming expansion writes that 'Early Holocene Egyptians did not need agriculture and did not seek it, until the tables turned and agriculture sought them'.[242] This makes good sense for the first millennia of the Holocene, but they, and other North Africans, would be quick to take up and adapt elements of what it offered when their own world began to change. With regard to crops, current data suggest that this moment falls within the time span of the next chapter, though Deltaic mud could smother some slightly earlier surprises. But by 5800 BC, domestic sheep and goats of indubitably Levantine origin appeared in the hills along the African shore of the Red Sea.[243] Soon they reached the lake basins west of the Nile, by 5700 BC at Dahkla and 5500 BC at Nabta Playa, where they slotted into the already established cattle herding. If our previous surmises are correct, this infiltration circumvented the Delta, instead passing through Sinai and across the narrow Gulf of Suez. The circumstances bring us full circle back to the Levant, where the PPNB collapse had been followed in the later 7th and 6th millennia by a spread of small-scale sheep and goat herding into the desert-steppe margin.[244] From there, once the 6200 event had abated, sheep and goats were well placed to expand into northeast Africa (and northern Arabia), either accompanied by their herders or taken up by local people. Either way, on present knowledge these creatures were the first foreign domesticates to enter Africa.

But only just, for a couple of centuries after sheep and goats first materialized in northeast Africa, a separate enclave, this time of full mixed farming, appeared 3500 km (2175 miles) further west at the tip of the Maghreb. The caves within a small triangle described by modern Tangier, Ceuta and Tétouan, just south of Gibraltar, have long been known to contain pottery, including some Cardial sherds, as well as sheep, goats, cattle and pigs,[245] though in a shocking illustration of the paucity of modern fieldwork in Mediterranean Africa, until recently not a single domesticated plant pre-dating the Iron Age had been detected beyond Egypt. In the past few years this picture has radically improved. New investigations at Kaf Taht el-Ghar, near Tétouan, confirm wheat and barley by 5400 BC, according to pollen analysis grown in newly opened glades among the woodland,[246] while discoveries near Melilla expand the key zone eastward and push the earliest date for domesticated plants and animals back to around 5600 BC.[247] There is little scope for local domestication (even putatively, only from aurochs and boar), and the early date, far-off location and overall signature affirm an independent injection to that of sheep and goat via the Red Sea. In fact, this demonstrably full farming enclave is only superficially incongruous in the western Maghreb. If we recall the maritime leapfrogging proclivities of Neolithic groups in southern France and especially nearby Iberia, it becomes obvious that this Maghrebian Neolithic originated as an integral part of the same process – to those involved simply the intake of one further coastal niche, perhaps by now partly vacated, like those on the opposite side of the sea, rather than a portentous footstep in a new continent. This trans-Gibraltan expansion may even have enabled a few Maghrebian hunter-gatherer technological and cultural traits to enter the mix in the Iberian deep south and Atlantic regions.[248] It says a lot for maritime transmission all along the northern side of the Mediterranean, and equally for the obdurate resistance of Egyptian hunter-gatherers, that derivatives of the Levantine suite of domesticates could reach the western Maghreb, almost 4000 km (2500 miles) from their original source, before most had managed to infiltrate the blockage on the nearby Nile.

CHAPTER SIX

How it might have been

(5500 – 3500 BC)

A hundred Mediterranean flowers bloom

The years between 5500 and 3500 BC are the Mediterranean's forgotten age. This may seem an outrageous statement to those archaeologists bringing to light and interpreting its remains. Certainly, it is anything but dull; indeed, over its duration societies around the basin developed in arguably more diverse directions than at any other time in the Mediterranean's past. It is also an age of major innovations, not least the widespread use by its end of metals. So why forgotten? Primarily because these years stubbornly and intriguingly refuse to fit into any neat, overall narrative. Earlier, the expansion of farming offered a common thread, with burgeoning life in the semi-green desert as its southern equivalent. After 3500 BC, give or take a generous few centuries, sweeping changes across and beyond the basin created fundamentally new vectors that presage the better-known Mediterranean of later times. Between these lies an unsynchronized wild-growth legacy of the initial Neolithic in the north, variations on the hunting and pastoral themes in the south, and in the east precocious initiatives with deep Levantine roots as well as discernible links to the broader Near East. Viewed with hindsight, this age was the last pan-Mediterranean anarchy, the last time when local ways of doing things enjoyed an all but universal primacy throughout the basin, before larger-scale logics slowly began to reshape Mediterranean history over the next three millennia.

In climatic terms the years covered in this chapter are also interstitial, and flicker back and forth.[1] The early Holocene optimum, ultimate sponsor of the transformations explored in the previous chapter, was coming to an end. Ahead, starting at an indeterminate time between 4000 and 3500 BC and continuing to this day, lay a tougher regime that would engineer a drier basin and the rebirth of a hyper-arid Sahara. Separating these lay a phase of oscillations. These had little impact in clement areas, but swings were felt acutely in the more sensitive Levant and North Africa, which experienced marked wetter and drier phases, as well as other southerly parts of the basin.[2] In the meantime, sea level rise slowed to a halt, as the last of the Pleistocene ice caps joined the oceans. By the early 4th millennium BC it had reached the level it occupies today, which it has never substantially transgressed, as is neatly demonstrated by Palaeolithic paintings at Cosquer Cave, which run right down to the current waterline.[3] From now on, shifts in the relative stands of land and sea, of the kind attested all over the later Mediterranean by drowned buildings and dry harbours, have to be laid at the door of tectonic action. The tables slowly began to turn, too, in the struggle at river mouths between marine incursion and deltaic reconquest. The prodigious Nile had begun to win earlier, as we saw in Chapter 5, and the locations of archaeological sites and sand-bars in the Rhône delta reveal the land beginning to push out around 3700 BC, though (as alluded to in Chapter 2) in most cases growth took a lot longer, and the heavily silted, straight or out-bowing lowland coasts of modern times are a relatively recent, and largely post-Roman, creation.[4] Other coastal wetlands also began to stabilize. In 5000 BC the land on which Venice now stands was dry and 20 km (12 miles) from the coast, but by 4000–3500 BC the world's most illustrious lagoon had begun to take shape.[5]

It is symptomatic that these 2000 years are afflicted by an appalling tangle of regional terms for each phase within them, often inconsistently applied and connoting differing start and end-dates within a general trend from east to west. In Europe, the Levant and Turkey these reflect early efforts to establish and subdivide phases on a regional basis with reference to their dominant technology, stone for the Neolithic and metal for the Copper Age. This has long been undermined by metal finds in Neolithic contexts, and the terms must be taken simply as conventional labels that can disguise as much as highlight the true rhythms of change as we now understand them. We also need to guard against the prejudices attached to each; for example, the span from 4500 to 3200 BC in the Aegean is referred to both as a (conservative) Final Neolithic and as a (progressive) Copper Age. To summarize as painlessly as possible, this chapter equates to the entire Levantine Copper Age (divided between Early and Late at 4500 BC), the Anatolian Middle and Late Copper Age (again divided at 4500 BC), and the Aegean Late (5500–4500 BC) and Final Neolithic or Copper Age (4500–3200 BC); in the Adriatic, Italy and Tyrrhenian it covers the end of the Early, and all of the Middle and Late Neolithics, and in France and Iberia most of the Early plus all of the Middle Neolithic. Across much of North Africa these labels are meaningless. Instead, a sequence of Pastoral phases has been defined for the Sahara, and along the Nile a series of names is borrowed from exemplary sites (such as 'Badarian' and 'Maadian'), with 'Neolithic' applied to northern Egypt before 4000 BC.[6] A variably appropriate Neolithic sequence is deployed over the Maghreb and coastal regions to its east.

This witch's brew of terms must not distract us from investigating what people were actually up to around different parts of the Mediterranean basin, and now also in the midst of the sea. Between 5500 and 3500 BC this question enjoys a provocative counterfactual potential, for what we shall encounter are long-extinct societies, many without close later Mediterranean analogies, which nonetheless could have become prototypes for later ways of life had subsequent circumstances not extinguished them. How these societies might otherwise have evolved – what, to indulge a fantasy, some Aztec-sponsored Caribbean Columbus or Chinese Marco Polo might eventually have blundered into – remains guesswork. Recent analogues such as Sudanese pastoralists for North Africa, Papuan villages for Neolithic southern

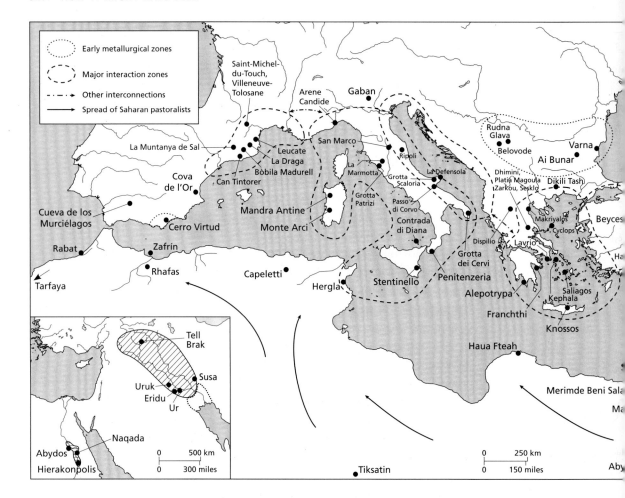

6.1 Map of sites mentioned in this chapter, also showing the principal interaction zones within the Mediterranean during the late 6th to early 4th millennia BC and connections between them, Saharan pastoral expansion, the principal early foci of metallurgy and (inset at left) the main Ubaid zone centred on Mesopotamia, and the early 4th-millennium BC accumulation of power along the Nile.

Europe, American Southwest pueblos for the Levant and Anatolia, Caribbean islanders in the archipelagos, and the hunter-gatherer villages of the American Pacific Northwest for the Nile Delta are all plausible suggestions, but it is equally possible that Mediterranean histories would have veered down pathways that have no parallel in the ethnographic present. But we can be sure of one thing: the ancient Mediterranean as we know it to have evolved over the last few millennia, with all its enduring impact on our lives today, would not have existed in anything like its present form. Exploring the Mediterranean from 5500 to 3500 BC is therefore not merely a sterile exercise in reconstructing a confusing heap of long-dead societies, but a strange window into how it might have been.

Pastoral symphony with noises off

We can open the first window where we ended Chapter 5, in North Africa. There the Sahara had been reclaimed by hunter-gatherers, with others of local ancestry in the Mediterranean zone, and, we guessed, a populous, aquatic variant in the Nile Delta. Cattle-based herding had emerged in northeast Africa's Four Corners region, where

Egypt, Sudan, Chad and Libya meet, and early in the 6th millennium BC Levantine sheep and goats filtered in across the Red Sea. Save for a small enclave of Levanto-European mixed farming at the western end of the Maghreb, crop cultivation was apparently absent. Much would soon change, making North Africa host to at least five fundamentally different kinds of society, while along the Nile Valley by 3500 BC the foundations of pharaonic rule were becoming established. In order to understand the Mediterranean's southern flank at this time, and the northeast African roots of later Egyptian exceptionalism, we need to start at the heart of the matter, in the Sahara.

Before the end of the 6th millennium BC cattle pastoralism, with a graft of sheep and goats, started to expand westward from its initial epicentre.[7] This percolating tide of animals and their herders, flowing along wadis and pooling around lakes and grazing land, created a new lifestyle that would dominate the Sahara for nearly 2000 years, and which we know as the Middle Pastoral. Similar groups moved east to the edge of the Nile Valley, with longer-term consequences that would be quite different. Ostensibly, this expansion could have been triggered by the resumption of a wetter regime in the wake of the 6200 event, but introducing an alternative to wild game also makes sense as a strategy to ensure a reliable food source, and so survival, in a still viable, but less predictable, environment of fluctuating lakes and intervening dry phases.[8] New analysis of residues in pottery confirm that Saharan cattle were being milked by 5000 BC,[9] and if later African pastoralism is any guide, they may also have been bled for human consumption, but were probably too valuable on the hoof for their meat to be often on the menu. It is unlikely, moreover, that the spread of cattle pastoralism was a result of uptake by earlier Saharan hunter-gatherers. For one thing, it is not at all clear that many of the latter had made it through the harsh end of the 7th millennium BC; cave occupation histories suggest the opposite.[10] In addition, pastoralism correlates with a switch in Saharan rock art to a new 'bovidian' style, no longer preoccupied with hunting and ritual, but instead with cattle herding, milking and men [6.2; PL. XVII].[11] It is likely that this fresh influx of people spread Afro-Asiatic languages (which include ancient Egyptian, modern Berber and Chadic, all affiliated, probably since the Pleistocene, with the Semitic tongues of the Near East), which had hitherto been confined to northeast Africa.[12] If so, the romantic notion that the Capsian groups of the Mediterranean zone were proto-Berbers is sadly unlikely.[13]

The most frequent relics of these pastoralists are scatters near former lakes or swamps of pottery, tools and perforated boulders used to hobble cattle and (according to rock art) trap savannah creatures such as giraffes, ostriches and, in one vainglorious instance, a lion.[14] At these seasonally occupied sites, people still hunted, fished and gathered, processed and stored wild plant food. But between these places and seasons, entire communities and their herds were on the move from one grazing range to the next, creating a truly nomadic lifestyle. Indeed, if the movement of brightly coloured stones and pigments over immense distances is any guide, such pastoralists were more mobile than the hunter-gatherers whom they replaced. This lifestyle created societies structured in profoundly different ways from those of Neolithic farmers in the eastern and northern Mediterranean.[15] In place of the

0   30 cm

0   12 in.

6.2 Rendition of a rock-painted Saharan pastoral scene showing herded cattle and processing of milk products in pots, from the Tadrart Acacus.

household, the human body and cattle became subjects of cultural preoccupation. Status, probably more concentrated in men than in heavily plant-oriented Neolithic communities, would have been attained by amassing animals as the principal token of wealth. In this mobile world the referents that became fixed and ritually elaborated at seasonal aggregation points were not so much dwellings, which were only transitorily used, but the tombs where humans and animals were laid to rest at the end of their travels. Tumuli built over both people and cattle become a prominent feature in the eastern and central Sahara in the late 6th and 5th millennia BC, as do other ceremonial structures associated with the remains of sacrificed cattle. This 'primary pastoralism' was far more spatially extensive than the marginal variant, based on sheep and goats, that was forming around the same time on the drier fringes of the Levant, and a world entirely sufficient unto itself compared to the secondary types that would later emerge elsewhere in the basin, in tight symbiosis with sedentary, urban societies, whose upland and steppic borders they haunted.

The 5th-millennium BC Badarian societies of the Nile Valley, known for their encampments and burial grounds of bodies decked out with bright stone, copper, gold and Red Sea shell beads, pigment-grinding palettes and combs for lost coiffures, were an offshoot of this world, if one whose importance would be retrospectively amplified by its contribution to the formation of later Egyptian culture around sanctified bodies, tombs and arguably cattle.[16] To understand how farming came to Egypt, we need to look closer to the Mediterranean. The Delta itself, an ever-growing patchwork of solidified land, ponds and marshes among which flowed seven major branches of the Nile and a maze of minor channels, retains almost all of its secrets until after 4000 BC, under 7–8 m (23–26 ft) of mud. Almost, for a few years ago a small sounding beneath the later town of Sais hit a sandy basal stratum with pots, catfish and deep-channel species, but also Levantine pigs and other domesticates, overlain by another with the four main domestic animals as well as wheat and barley, though still plenty of fish.[17] This matches long-known sites further inland, dating to a century or two on either side of 5000 BC, at Merimde Beni Salame near Cairo, and in the Fayum basin, the latter fairly short-lived ventures enabled by a southward shift

6.3 Well-preserved basket-lined pits for cereal storage on the edge of the Fayum basin.

in Mediterranean winter rains and a now-extinct conduit from the Nile, which fed a sheet of water far larger than the Fayum's current residual lake.[18] The inhabitants of such places grew Levantine domesticated cereals and flax, raised cattle, sheep, goats and pigs (the last external injection completing a local reassembly from diverse beginnings of the Levantine farming package, possibly with some new Levantine breeds of the earlier faunal arrivals), and made pottery, including models of watercraft.[19] At the same time, however, they carried on exploiting the wild cornucopia of river and lake, as well as the desert margins. Indeed, the basket-lined, tightly sealed grain silos dug into ridges overlooking the Fayum may indicate that storable cereals were mainly used as a back-up in the event of a dearth of wild foods – a vegetal equivalent to the logic of cattle pastoralism, if in this instance almost certainly adopted by the descendants of invisible earlier hunter-gatherers rather than brought by farmers from the Levant [**6.3**].[20] In other respects, this Neolithic is peculiar. At Merimde the accumulation created by a thousand years' collapse of the flimsy oval huts, and the burial of children within the settlement, encourage us to infer relatively sedentary village life, especially after 4600 BC, but well-defined houses are hard to discern.[21] Despite Levantine contacts revealed by the incoming domesticates, as well as new spinning and weaving gear, arrows and mace-heads, further connections to the south testified by desert stones and possibly cattle, sheep and goats, plus (as we shall see) a two-way trickle via northern Egypt of exotic seashells, Levantine copper and southern gold, communities at the Nile's junction with the Mediterranean were still rooted on their own deep, and to us archaeologically inaccessible, local past.[22]

Over the course of the 5th millennium BC, wheat and barley spread far up the Nile, beyond even the then-greater reach of Mediterranean rains and instead cultivated by a distinctive regime of riverine flood-basin irrigation anchored in the Nilotic cycle of inundation and retreat, which dictated autumn sowing and an early spring harvest, a calendar different from that in the Mediterranean.[23] Even then, and perhaps in part due to the need to adapt their growing seasons, cereals were initially adjuncts and back-ups to diverse herding and hunting lifestyles, a combination reminiscent of the mix of floodwater farming and hunting in the first Levantine Neolithic five millennia earlier. Finally, around 3900 BC, and significantly close to the onset of desertification across North Africa, a massive and relatively sudden switch-over to a reliance on barley and wheat as the staples of existence (cultivated in a 2:1 ratio that would remain stable until the Iron Age) took place throughout the Egyptian stretch of the Nile.[24] The demographic consequences in an environment of immensely rich, irrigable soils were electric and irreversible. The years around 4000–3900 BC are an Egyptian watershed, the start of a Predynastic age that culminated with astonishing rapidity in sacred rule over a unified riverine kingdom, by about 3000 BC.[25] We defer a closer look at this until Chapter 7, because until mid-millennium the key transformations were confined to a 200–300 km (125–85 miles) ribbon far upriver, where a string of vying nodal communities arose at places such as Hierakonpolis, Naqada and Abydos, with a ruling group at the head of each. This slender crucible of destiny lies well south of the Mediterranean basin, and the formative phases of later royal culture reveal little debt to Mediterranean, or even specifically Deltaic, traditions. Instead, the preoccupation with richly furnished death monuments (soon coupled with early efforts to preserve the body), attractive desert rocks carved into body ornaments but now also superb stone vessels, and the long-range circulation of copper and gold all derive from the Saharan pastoral world, strangely grafted onto farming and consequent sedentism within the Nile Valley.

What was going on during these fateful years in northern Egypt? For the first time the archaeology of the Delta itself comes into real focus, especially in the east. Here, the countless sandbanks rising above the high-water mark of inundation offered locations for occupation and burial close enough to the modern land surface to be regularly detected, and in time to rise up as Africa's first tells.[26] According to one estimate, by 4000 BC the Deltaic triangle became home to as many as 80,000 people, already a major concentration of Mediterranean humanity.[27] The principal site we know about is Maadi, a sprawling 18-ha (45-acre) settlement near the southern vertex.[28] Its houses retained earlier traditions of light, wattle-and-daub construction, augmented by underground chambers of uncertain function, and burials were simple affairs compared with their most lavish upriver contemporaries. Moreover, pottery styles, a common tradition of ponderous basalt vessels and small inflows of copper point to stronger affiliations with the nearby Levant than the Nile Valley stretching away to the south, a link that we revisit at the close of this chapter. From a circum-Mediterranean perspective, the native societies of the Nile Delta, while exceptionally populous, evince no signs of complexity prior to the mid-4th millennium BC that are not at least matched in other parts of the basin that we shall visit. The one significant distinction for the future was the prospect of revolutionary change if the Delta came within reach of the radically differently constituted and aggressively expansive societies arising to its south, deep in Nilotic Africa.

Thus, by unusual paths, the elements of Levantine farming consolidated their second African bridgehead, in a vast riverine ribbon oasis from which the surrounding environment precluded further expansion, save by the faunal component in an already realized pastoral guise. What, by way of comparison, was the consequence of the first bridgehead on the continent, gained several centuries earlier, right at the opposite end of the basin, in the western Maghreb? The impact of this Neolithic enclave on ways of life in the rest of the Maghreb, and its long-term cultural and, we might add, linguistic and genetic legacies, are still to be resolved.[29] As in northeast Africa, there were limits to the potential cultivation of Mediterranean crops, but in theory no reason why they, and the people and animals accompanying them, should not have spread back east by land or sea to take over the fully Mediterranean realm of the Maghreb. Maybe they did, but if so, and notwithstanding a lack of looking in the key landscapes of Algeria, no visible, sustained surge matches the unmissable signature on the other flanks of the basin. Perhaps, on the other hand, the founding groups in an initial toe-hold no larger than the coastal rim of the Gulf of the Lion never built up their critical mass, arguably because the prohibitively open expanses of the Alboran Sea channelled connections through the slender conduit at Gibraltar. Later divergences in pottery style do indicate that contact was gradually lost with groups across the sea, though this could argue as persuasively for the successful attainment of demographic independence as isolation. Some expansion clearly did take place during the early 5th millennium BC, down the Atlantic coast of Morocco, and eastward between the mountains and the sea. Whether the descendants of immigrant farmers or local hunter-gatherer uptake lie behind this is an open question, given the sparse information to hand, as is the degree to which the package held together as it spread. Along the Atlantic, a loosely defined Neolithic is attested at Rabat by the early 5th millennium, and some traits continue to Tarfaya in the far south of Morocco, but most of the Atlantic Saharan shore stayed the domain of shellfish-harvesting hunter-gatherers for much of the Holocene.[30] To the east, on the Chafarinas Islands, close to the Moroccan–Algerian border and today still owned by Spain, but then the tip of a cape thrusting out from the Maghreb, a state-of-the-art excavation at Zafrín has uncovered the outline of a hut containing a peculiar reper-toire: pottery (some of it impressed), grinding stones and other tools, ostrich eggs, sheep and goats (only), along with the remains of seals, fish and shellfish, plus possible traces of cereal pollen [6.4].[31] But to the south, even modest distances inland, farming seems to have gained little or no foothold.[32]

6.4 This artist's impression of activities within the structures at Zafrín evokes a Neolithic scene only partly familiar to eyes acclimatized to Europe.

A Tellian or Oranian 'Neolithic' spread as far as eastern Tunisia, exemplified by Rhafas Cave near Oujda, where the bones are mainly from sheep, goats and hunted game, and, apart from a single Cardial sherd, pottery has only vague parallels to the west and north.[33] Regardless of such labels, limits to the spread of domestic crops and animals are hinted at by a few reliable beacons in the archaeological obscurity. One is Capeletti Cave, 1540 m (5050 ft) up in the Aurès mountains of east Algeria, overlooking the Roman town of Timgad.[34] The cave lies so close to the snowline that it must only have been used seasonally, which itself tends to imply a mobile way of life for at least some of its occupants. Sheep and goats are present in the lowest levels around 5300 BC, but here, halfway across Africa, they could as easily have arrived via the Sahara, while the boars and a few cattle appear to have been wild. Plant remains were found, but all of wild species, mostly acorns and grapevines. The absence of crops is hardly decisive at this altitude, but might hint that people here were out of touch with cereal-growers.

Meanwhile, clustered around shallow, saline lakes in lowland Tunisia, the 'Neolithic of Capsian Tradition', a palpable misnomer, appeared around 5000 BC.[35] Most of the introductions that mark the shift from earlier Capsian lifestyles, notably pottery (occasionally earlier, and for snail cooking and milk boiling?) and patchily represented domestic sheep and goats, are as likely to have arrived from the south via interactions with Saharan groups, with only polished stone axes definitely pointing to Mediterranean origins. Sites often comprise the upper levels of earlier *escargotières*, hunting continued and, again unusually for this sector of the basin, there is positive evidence for the ongoing gathering of wild grasses, nuts, fruits and bulbs, and against domesticated crops. On the far side of the Gulf of Sirte, at Haua Fteah, sheep and goats, smaller than the wild barbary sheep and slaughtered at different ages, appear slightly earlier, along with pots and hoe-like implements of uncertain use; domesticated crops remain completely absent.[36] Any of these might have reached Cyrenaica along the slender coastal corridors from west or east, but once again the most likely axis is from the south, via Saharan pastoralists.

On present evidence, therefore, the west Maghrebian offshoot of the northwest Mediterranean Neolithic was a fairly restricted phenomenon and in the end peripheral to African ways of life. To its east, as far as the edge of the Nile Delta, Mediterranean Africa was inhabited from 5500–5000 BC by people living by various combinations of herding, gathering and hunting, but not crop cultivation. Such ways of life based on the selective uptake of domesticates alongside wild foods only enjoyed only a brief, very patchy currency on the northern side of the Mediterranean, and a fairly marginal if longer-lasting status in the Levant. In much of Mediterranean Africa, however, they became the norm, primarily thanks to the wider orientation on pastoral practices, decoupled from crop cultivation, that had arisen in the Saharan heart of North Africa. As we shall see in future chapters, this lifestyle survived for millennia along Africa's Mediterranean fringe, even as that heart was ripped out by the return of the desert.

Such divergence, however, did not always entail absolute isolation from other Mediterranean currents, and one detail is significant in this respect. Pieces of

6.5 The lagoon-edge escargotière at Hergla in coastal Tunisia, under excavation.

greenish obsidian from the Sicilian channel island of Pantelleria have been detected in coastal Tunisia and eastern Algeria, including on the islet of Zembra, 12 km (8 miles) off Cape Bon, and also transported along with seashells far in the interior [PL. XVI].[37] A few fragments indicate local knapping. Such obsidian appears in upper levels at the superbly analyzed site of Hergla, a big late 7th- and 6th-millennia BC midden beside the salty Halk en Menjel lagoon on the Hammamet Gulf, a place of exceptional interest for its unusual littoral location, abundant marine molluscs and fish bones, total absence of domesticates, and square, house-like structures that suggest a surprisingly village-like aspect [6.5].[38] Such a profile counters occasional suggestions that the entire Neolithic package might have jumped the wider sea-passage from Sicily into the eastern end of the Maghreb,[39] but the obsidian remains and pots at Hergla also show ambivalent North African and south-central Mediterranean affinities. Pantelleria was one of four obsidian islands supplying the central Mediterranean at this time, but the find-spots of its own variety describe a concentration in the eastern Maghreb, western Sicily and other islands in between, notably Malta and Lampedusa. Usually it is assumed that this distribution reflects the activities of Neolithic seafarers from the northern side of the channel, with the African finds simply overspill. This could be partly right, for this period was, as we shall shortly see, a heyday of small-island settlement and maritime circulation of obsidian in the northern Mediterranean's sub-basins. Yet there are certain indications that Pantelleria may not have been permanently inhabited at this juncture, and lain open to all manner of visitors, while the first contexts at Hergla date at least as early as any with such obsidian outside Africa.[40] Throw in the further facts that Pantelleria lies closer to Africa (70 km or 45 miles) than Sicily (100 km or 60 miles), that the cliffs with its green variety face south, and that the nearest, in this case clearly inhabited sector of North African coast is the only one where a topography of deep bays, headlands and offshore islands provides an enticing maritime prospect (the selfsame shore on which Carthage later arose),[41] and it is well worth asking whether we in fact possess here, at last, a hint of indigenous North African seafaring. But regardless as to who brought obsidian to the Maghreb, we should not overlook one indisputable, and equally significant truth. The Mediterranean Sea's slender waist was finally coming to life as a crossing point, and people from either side are likely to have met, however fleetingly, for the first time in history.

A proliferation of islanders

The black pearl of the Sicilian channel may or may not have been inhabited as people came and went for its obsidian, but even if Pantelleria still lay empty, its neighbours and many other modest islands across the basin were certainly becoming long-term homes to farming communities. Hitherto, although islands were familiar places, often visible from the mainland and well-reconnoitred, relatively few had been permanently settled,[42] principally the big five (arguably less as islands per se than coast-rich land masses), some medium-sized inshore examples (in the Aegean Chios, Thasos and possibly Rhodes; Brač, Hvar and Korčula in the Adriatic), plus a handful of small islands close to population hubs, like the Tremiti group east of the Tavoliere, and the Sporades off Thessaly – though the Neolithic at the Cyclops Cave on tiny Gioura is so rich in painted pots that the cave may well have become a ritual place, still only visited seasonally.[43] During the 5th and 4th millennia BC all this changed [**6.6**]. Islands witnessed a greater influx at this time than any other environment in the basin, even if in absolute terms the numbers must have been small, often in the hundreds even once population had built up, and no more than a few families in certain cases.[44] Crossings to Pantelleria testify to people's abilities to navigate to scraps of land well out to sea, and similar efforts elsewhere in the channel brought the Neolithic package across 80 km (50 miles) from Sicily to Malta before 5000 BC, as well as pottery, sheep, goats and pigs to Lampedusa. The last of these, at 120 km (75 miles) from other land, must define the remotest community in the Mediterranean, close to the limit to what was attempted by sea at this time. North of Sicily the roll call continues. Peopling of the Aeolian cluster began on the largest, obsidian-rich island of Lipari, from where it spread to Salina, Filicudi and the rugged speck of Panarea, although settlers avoided the sharp cone of tiny, outlying Alicudi, and visits to regularly erupting Stromboli and Vulcano appear to have been brief, perhaps ritual adventures. Others lived on Elba and Giglio, off Tuscany, though visitation rather than inhabitation remained the order of the day on Palmarola, another obsidian island. In the Adriatic many newly inhabited islands lay so close to the mainland as to make little odds, and what stands out is the persistence at a few more fully maritime locations after the initial trans-Adriatic passage of farming. On the tiny Tremiti Islands and Sušac sheep and goat bones, harvesting gloss on sickle blades, grinding stones and ruined houses affirm that people had come to stay.[45] Finally, this was a great age of Aegean island settlement, building on a long tradition of seafaring, exploration, visits and pioneer habitation. Most of the densely packed Dodecanese and other eastern islands

6.6 After the initial spread of farming came numerous expansions of Neolithic settlement into the smaller islands of the Aegean and central Mediterranean.

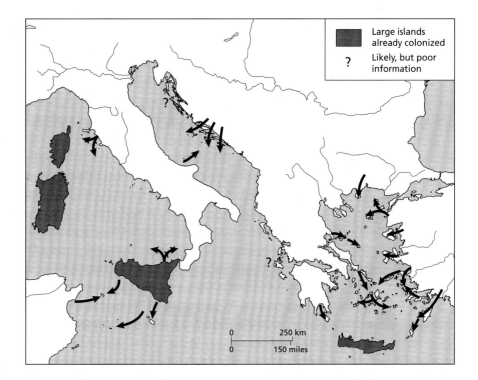

were settled, and springing from there, some of the Cyclades were occupied during the 5th millennium BC [**6.6**]. Over the 4th millennium further influxes filled in many other islands in the archipelago. It is now that we find the first traces where this book opened, on Kythera.

Few islands of any substance remained uninhabited after about 3500 BC. Most that did were extremely small, unusually far from other land, or both; some, indeed, could not sustain life for any length of time, such as the tiny, waterless stopover of Palagruža.[46] During the late 4th and 3rd millennia BC, the smallest Cyclades would finally be taken in, down to little Delos, as would Ustica, just 50 km (30 miles) north of Palermo but hidden in a sea desert and until then seldom frequented.[47] When the handful of islands off Tunisia came into play remains a mystery. Zembra has Pantellerian obsidian, and mouflon that descend from goats introduced at some stage, but nothing else until it was stocked with rabbits and, inadvertently, black rats in Roman times. Almost landlocked Djerba has been searched, more or less fruitlessly until the Iron Age, and the Kerkennahs and the Galite Islands remain blanks.[48] The only really distinguished members of the latecomers' club are the Balearics. As will be explained in Chapter 7, it is well-nigh certain that these big but remote islands lay empty until the late 3rd millennium BC, winning the distinction of being the last land masses in the Mediterranean to become peopled, and maybe even to feel the impress of a visiting human foot.[49]

For the first time we also possess solid evidence concerning the boats in which people crossed the sea. There are still no depictions, save for a dubiously interpreted scribble on a sherd from Hvar,[50] but ample compensation is the splendidly

213

preserved remains of one craft, admittedly not from an island, nor indeed the sea itself, but the waterlogged Neolithic village of La Marmotta on Lake Bracciano, north of Rome [6.7].[51] Discovered in 1994 and dated to 5450 BC, the La Marmotta boat was a dugout canoe 10 m (33 ft) long and with a beam of just over 1 m (3 ft), all carved from a single oak. It would have taken hundreds of person-hours of labour to construct, and along with the Neolithic house must have been one of the most ambitious creations of its age. Travel around the Mediterranean in a near-identical replica powered with short paddles by a crew of eleven shows the design to be sea-worthy.[52] It averaged 3–4 km (2–2.5 miles) per hour at sea, or 32 km (20 miles) per day, although this should be reduced to 20–25 km (12–15 miles) for a laden craft and distances measured as the crow flies. This kind of performance would bring Lipari in range from Sicily in a single day, and tie many Aegean islands together by one-day crossings, but it implies two or three days and intervening nights to reach a place like Malta. Such ventures could easily exploit short windows of navigational opportunity, rather than being dependent on prevailing weather patterns, though runs to and from Malta and other Sicilian channel islands pushed the envelope in this respect, and may often have made better headway heading south with summer winds behind them.

6.7 The La Marmotta dugout canoe: (*below*) the original vessel as preserved; (*right*) an approximate replica sets out to sea.

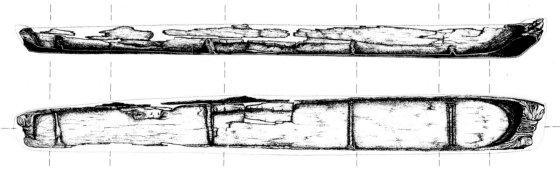

It is all too easy to assume, simply because we possess it, that the La Marmotta boat represents a breakthrough in waterborne technology, and thereby explains the parallel spurt in island life. But its replica's performance confirms rather than extends the ranges proposed in Chapter 5 for earlier times, on the basis of the ethnography of simple seacraft and other experiments. Boats hollowed out by fire-setting and (in the Neolithic) polished stone axes surely had considerably earlier invisible origins, and altogether there seems no doubt that the La Marmotta craft was built to a basic design known at least since the first farmers set out for Cyprus several millennia earlier. So if islands were no easier to reach from the standpoint of nautical technology, why did more people go to live on them?[53] Equally wanting are indications of any broadening of subsistence to facilitate survival on these often relatively impoverished patches of land. Bones and seeds demonstrate that island farmers transported the Neolithic world of animal husbandry and crops with them, implanting capsules of familiarity amidst the sea. Hunting was in sharp decline, and only the occasional deer bone echoes the earlier game-stocking strategies practised on Cyprus. Conversely, while communities such as Saliagos in the Cyclades enjoyed bonanza hauls of tunny and other fish, this remained a sideline, and was also hardly an insular monopoly. In fact, on all except the largest islands, wholesale introduction of the Neolithic package, tweaked in favour of hardier crops and breeds, was the only means by which people could hope to get beyond seasonal visits, and bring the Mediterranean's archipelagos into the realm of permanently settled space. Lastly, even repeat visits to collect desirable stones would not have easily elided into habitation, for the simple reason that lengthy expeditions were probably single-sex operations. Palmarola and maybe Pantelleria are examples of islands visited for a very long time without anyone electing to live there, but the best illustration is Melos in the Cyclades, whose obsidian had been obtained since the 11th millennium BC, but whose first inhabitants only arrived in the 5th or 4th millennia[54] – strangely enough, later than Lipari, where obsidian collection and occupancy began broadly simultaneously in the early 6th millennium BC.

The likely answer as to why people now started to live more on islands is a very prosaic one.[55] People simply moved out to them as populations on the mainlands rose, the best niches became ancestrally held by others, and as communities periodically split and went their separate ways. In short, much island life began as an infilling of second-best but, with farming, now tolerable places, comparable to what we shall see in other outlying parts of the Mediterranean lowlands. In those areas of the Aegean, Adriatic and to a lesser extent Tyrrhenian where mainland and islands are inextricably interwoven, the initial decisions can hardly have been radical, and in this respect the answer to the conundrum of Melos versus Lipari is simply that the latter was closer to long-inhabited Sicily than the former was to anywhere save other equally long-empty islands. Melos and most of the Cyclades owed their eventual peopling to the fact that where scatters of islands extended far out to sea, the island-living habit once learned could be repeatedly applied, encouraging little inter-island settlement cascades, and also enabling mutually sustaining networks of islanders to form – along with back-up from the mainland, a vital factor in overcoming the setbacks and local failures that must have dogged such processes more than our coarse resolution allows us to see.[56] The end points of such incremental expansions are the kinds of events that do stand out as extraordinary and slightly hubristic, or desperate, if viewed in isolation, such as the attempt to settle distant Lampedusa, assuredly the end of the line in every sense.

The birth of regular small-island life should not distract us from developments on the handful of already settled far larger islands. We saw in Chapter 5 how Cyprus described a trajectory from initial close connections with the outside world to virtual closure by the 7th–6th millennia BC. Over a span of some centuries after the end of the bizarrely pottery-free, deer-rich Khirokitia phase, running well into the 5th millennium BC, it then evinces no definite signs of life at all.[57] This gap could reflect a genuine population collapse or, as has been intriguingly argued, a reversion to low-visibility, mobile ways of life by a never large population of islanders able to essentially reject the Neolithic.[58] When Cypriots do become visible again, in the local Late Neolithic (4800–4000 BC) and Early Copper Age (4000–3500 BC), there is still little sign of external input or other catching up, save for the extremely tardy uptake of pottery.[59] Communities chose similar locations and scales of occupation to their predecessors. Houses were closely packed and implausibly small for family households, as at earlier Khirokitia, though now more squared-off and followed by a switch to subterranean dwellings at the start of the Copper Age. Hunted fallow deer supplied if anything more of the meat than before, while cattle remained conspicuously absent. Despite Cyprus's wealth in this material, the Early Copper Age barely earns its name from the few hammered native copper artifacts made after 4000 BC, a very late date by east Mediterranean standards and, along with the popularity of blue picrolite for beads and figurines [6.8], reminiscent of the PPNB rather than the contemporary Levant and Anatolia. The causes of this deepening time warp and insular idiosyncrasy need to be sought in internal Cypriot perceptions and indifference to alternative ways of life, coupled with a decline in westward and seaward engagement by people on the Levantine mainland at this juncture, to which we shall return.

6.8 Cypriot Copper Age cruciform figurine carved from blue picrolite, reflecting a local island style and material. An identical item hangs from the figurine's own neck.

Crete, Sardinia and Corsica experienced more orthodox Neolithics, and plenty of contacts with the outside world. Crete had been relatively sequestered until 5500 BC, but then took off.[60] Knossos spread over 4–5 ha (10–12 acres) and was divided between wealthier and poorer farming families, pottery styles began to follow the rest of the Aegean, and new weaving technology was introduced. After 4500 BC, settlements become visible all over the island for the first time. A similar pattern can be seen on Sardinia and Corsica.[61] During the 5th millennium BC open settlements eclipsed caves, and grew in size and numbers, both on the coasts and in the interior. Even before the end of that millennium there are signs of inter-island movement. Sardinian obsidian appears to have been discovered as soon as farmers moved inland; it soon reached Corsica (and, as we shall see, much of the north Tyrrhenian region), while serpentine bracelets from Corsica appear on Sardinia. Island culture became more elaborate too, as illustrated by figurines on Sardinia and smartly outlined bowls on Corsica with parallels in France. All this reached a climax on Sardinia from around 4000–3400 BC with the start of the Ozieri phase. Settlement numbers tripled to as many as 200, particularly around the great Campidano plain in the south. Most were small hamlets, but others grew into agglomerations of up to 100 houses, some with added porticos, matched by a closely associated tradition of elaborate rock-cut tombs. Pottery became better fired and fancier, with swirls and lines of dancers, its exports unearthed as far off as the Piazza della Signoria in Florence; even cooking pots sprang tripod legs. And as we shall see, Ozieri-phase use of metals is among the earliest in the central Mediterranean. From now on larger, more fertile and mineralogically better-endowed Sardinia started to pull away from its rougher Corsican neighbour, opening up a gap in relative social complexity that would widen over the millennia.

In the long term, the impact of countless individually minor moves further out to sea, or deeper into the larger islands' landscapes, was anything but peripheral to Mediterranean history. We saw in Chapter 5 how the maritime axis of initial Neolithic expansion reflected a seismic reordering of Mediterranean connections towards the coastal and maritime core of the basin, in contrast to the pull of the continental edges that dominated the Pleistocene. Now the connecting webs grew denser and stronger in the island-studded sub-basins, as groups of islanders forged links with each other, the mainlanders they had left behind and others on the opposing coasts before them. We shall encounter excellent examples when we take a wider look at Neolithic trade, and an additional tracer is the large number of wild animal species that invaded island ecosystems in the 5th and 4th millennia BC, the smaller hidden in the bilges or cargos of frequent canoe traffic.[62] In the Aegean, and the narrower parts of the Adriatic and Tyrrhenian, the sea in the middle was slowly promoted from being simply something crossable to becoming the focus of newly emergent social constellations. Over time and under favourable circumstances, the islanders in such places, originally marginal people on the internal frontiers of the inhabited Mediterranean, would start to play disproportionately prominent roles in regional and eventually further-flung patterns of contact and trade.

Even by the end of the time span covered in this chapter, most of this still lay in the future, but a couple of premonitions can be detected. In the Aegean, the setting up of farming villages on some of the Cyclades in the 5th millennium BC coincided with more profligate obsidian use across the southern Aegean, as these consolidated communities in the middle of the sea transformed conditions of access for islanders and mainlanders alike.[63] But the best example at this juncture is Lipari. [64] The earliest settlers of the 6th millennium BC lived in farming plots scattered over its countryside. Around 5000 BC, however, a new, village-level community of 100–200 people arose on the island's later acropolis and current capital, a defensible point overlooking the best harbour [**6.9**]. While Lipari's obsidian was flowing out over the central Mediterranean, the acropolis site obtained a remarkable number of fine stone axes

6.9 View across Lipari to the coastal acropolis, beneath which lie deep layers of Neolithic and later occupation; further off in this small cluster of islands lie Panarea and Stromboli.

and flints from overseas, as well as exceptional quantities of painted pots, normally reserved for ritual use by their closest Calabrian neighbours, and only more readily available 150–200 km (90–125 miles) away. Potting clay was also brought in, hardly a standard item of exchange at this time, and an important hint that some of these imports were acquired abroad by the islanders themselves. By the end of the 5th millennium BC, copper ores were being imported for local smelting, and on the plain of Contrada di Diana, just below the acropolis, a further hub of activity came into being. It consisted of an extensive spread of large open-air earth ovens, masses of debris from obsidian production, numerous fine axes, and grinding stones stained with ochre. One attractive interpretation of this strange accumulation is that it reflects the residues of seasonal gatherings of strangers as well as locals, drawn by the magnet of obsidian but also the chance to trade, feast, socialize and swap news in the midst of the sea with people from far away.[65] Such scenarios were unthinkable a millennium earlier, and symbolize the start of the Mediterranean islands' coming of age.

The myopic Mediterranean

From the emerging societies of the Mediterranean islands we turn to their progenitors among mainland Neolithic societies on the northern flank of the basin. Here, hunter-gatherers held out in a few secluded spots until the late 5th millennium BC, especially in northern Iberia, inland parts of the Midi and the Po plain.[66] They succumbed in the end to the Neolithic's big battalions, probably through a mixture of eventual local adoption, appropriation of their hunting land, violent endings, and intermarriage, perhaps of the former's women to the latter's men, as argued by bone chemistry and DNA analyses in central Europe.[67] This was a transformation with no going back once the population rose to levels unsustainable by reversion to wild foods. Yet the triumph of farming should not lull us into the cosy belief that we now face a familiar world. To portray Neolithic farmers as Mediterranean 'peasants', and their communities as ancestral to the rural villages of yesteryear, is void of meaning in a world with no urban antithesis, and distracts from its enduring strangeness.[68] Across Mediterranean Europe, blurring into temperate regions to the north and Copper Age western Anatolia, lay a mosaic of myopically local villages, replete with an intricate symbolic culture, crammed into the fertile plains with thinner scatters between. Here, farming still meant more or less what it did as it expanded, women laid claim to the inner space of village and fields by tending plants and children, making pots and deploying figurines, while the men staked out wild spaces beyond by vestigial hunting, as well as trade and rituals in the secret recesses of painted caves. A normal death ended with one's bones mingled in the garbage of a boundary ditch, and a woman could reveal her identity to a stranger (whose speech she might not grasp if he came from more than a few dozen kilometres away) by a smile or grimace from which several front teeth had been deliberately removed.

6.10 Fragments of basketry and their methods of construction from La Draga.

This sketch is, of course, a simplified caricature, drawing heavily on Italian data,[69] and does little justice to subtler distinctions. But it does intimate how vastly better informed we are about such societies compared to their local predecessors. In addition to a century of normal excavation and survey, a series of recently discovered waterlogged Neolithic villages strung out along the Mediterranean are revolutionizing our understanding. We had reason to appreciate Atlit-Yam in Israel in Chapter 5, and earlier in this chapter La Marmotta on Lake Bracciano for its dugout canoe. Similar conditions exist at Dispilio near Kastoria in northern Greece, while a submerged site in the Leucate lagoon near Perpignan is notable among other things for its remains of swordfish (a true open-sea catch save at its breeding grounds in the Messina strait).[70] Most remarkable of all is La Draga, half-inundated by Lake Banyoles in Catalonia, where excavations above and below water have uncovered a village dating to 5300–5150 BC [**1.7, 6.11**].[71] It comprised two rows of eight to ten rectangular wooden houses, rebuilt several times from deciduous oak and poplar, infilled by willow and hazel wattle and lashed together by clematis and linden cords, all from the nearby woods and lakeside. There were granaries on the better-drained slopes and cobble-filled earth ovens for cooking meat, with tripod stands alongside to suspend vessels for roasting or boiling grain. From the lake come the normally decayed paraphernalia of Neolithic life – wooden bowls, ladles, scoops, spindles, sickles, digging sticks and javelins, yew bows and willow or dogwood arrows, and of course baskets [**6.10**]. Half a million grains of wheat, diverse other cereals, broad beans, peas, fruits and nuts also survive.[72] Flint arrived from Narbonne, and a few marble vessels, bracelets and beads are heirlooms or trade objects from as far as

6.11 The Neolithic village at La Draga: waterlogged levels under excavation.

the Tyrrhenian. It is hard to know how to compare such a site with the contrastive preservation of the tiers of mud-built houses encased in a Thessalian tell, or the diffuse, flat Tavoliere settlements from which later ploughing has stripped even the house floors. Behind this difficulty, and exacerbated by the otherwise stimulatingly divergent approaches taken by archaeologists in each region, lies the unanswered question as to how much Neolithic communities in each region fundamentally resembled each other beyond the distinctions imposed by local cultural expression, current preservation and modern interpretation.[73]

We can start our exploration with what happened to farming. In contrast to the further round of developments nascent in the Levant before the end of Chapter 5, the answer is relatively little, beyond the selection and introduction of strains and breeds better suited to local conditions.[74] Household-based intensive horticulture mixed with some animal husbandry remained the norm. Waterlogged La Marmotta, surrounded by deciduous woods, provides a long list of cereals and legumes that were eaten, we assume, as gruels and flatbreads cheered by herbs, salt or honey (this last identified in a pot on the southern Meseta), along with wild grapes, figs, hazelnuts, berries and other seeds.[75] All the evidence points to an overwhelmingly vegetarian daily diet, with meat-eating mainly syncopated by periodic feasts. [76] In light of their size, even slaughtered sheep and goats must have been shared beyond the family, and cattle with entire communities and perhaps their neighbours.[77] Testimony to such events are the great earth ovens encountered at Contrada di Diana and La Draga, and popular across southern France and mainland Italy too. To provide some idea of the scale of consumption, after one event at Makriyalos in northern Greece the remains of several hundred animals and vast numbers of pots were discarded in a large pit.[78] At many villages, especially in the primary foci of farming-based life, wild animals were rare, if not quite taboo. They were more common on the margins of regions cleared for farming or areas of hunter-gatherer resilience, though for upland caves with wild animal bones it is often impossible to distinguish between hunting parties of farmers and residual Mesolithic folk. They also appear as totems and art in south Italian men's ritual sites out in the wilds, as exemplified by the red and roe deer skulls piled up underground in the rock-cut Ipogeo Manfredi, or the hundreds of deer images executed in bat-dung paint at the Grotta dei Cervi at Porto Badisco [**6.20**].[79] Fish and shellfish were popular at a few coastal, lagoonal and island settlements, with mussels prized enough at La Draga to be brought 50 km (30 miles) inland, but in general seafood was seldom eaten in quantity.[80]

In addition to ongoing milking, a few lesions on cow thigh bones, for example at Knossos by 5800–5300 BC, indicate that cattle were starting to pull heavy loads, though whether yet ploughs, as often assumed, or rather sleds and other contraptions is uncertain.[81] Cattle became particularly prominent in the larger settlements of southern France, Italy, Sardinia, Corsica and Crete.[82] In terms of pasture they were far more extravagant to maintain than sheep or goats (cows less so than massive oxen, but still a viable herd of thirty head needed as much land as would support a Neolithic village on cereals – though woodland browse around many settlements might mitigate this), but in return they provided high milk and meat yields, now traction power, and last but far from least copious manure. In the Rhône Valley their husbandry entailed the artificial encouragement of large tracts of a savannah-like grassland studded with oaks, similar to the Iberian *dehesa* ecologies, whose origins remain more elusive.[83] Bigger villages and bigger animals may therefore go together, their farming a kind of 'gardening with cows'.[84] Although embedded in quite different societies from those of North African pastoralists, here, too, cattle ownership may have correlated with wealth, not so much through accumulation of larger herds as the control of lusher pasture for their grazing and access to their muscle power within the farming world.

Milking and traction leave only wool outstanding among the major secondary products of the Mediterranean's faunal suite. As we shall see, in the Levant the first steps in this direction were certainly underway, but the rest of the basin still remained devoid of wool and largely linen-, grass- and hide-dependent for garments and other gear. Concerning textiles, the salient innovation of this time in Europe and Anatolia was instead the spread of vertical looms, attested by durable clay or stone weights, which set up a long-term antithesis with the presumably older and less visible ground-looms that remained the norm in the Levant and Egypt for millennia to come.[85]

The only entirely new, native domestications of significance had nothing to do with survival, and everything to do with mind altering. Experiments with sugar-rich fruits opened perceptions and taste buds to yeast-based fermentation and intoxication. As in the remainder of Neolithic Europe, people drank a range of sweetened, resinated or spiced alcoholic beverages fermented from fruits and grains.[86] Wild grapevines prefer the woodland margins but are fairly resilient to other environments, and flourished widely in the Mediterranean and neighbouring regions, including the great highland massif comprising the Caucasus, south Caspian mountains and northern Zagros, the warmer stretches of the Black Sea littoral and the major river valleys of temperate Europe.[87] Cultivation, probably for wine, may have begun as early as the 6th millennium BC in and around the Caucasus; wine production is confirmed there from the late 5th millennium BC by the recent find of a grape press, fermentation vats and other equipment (as well as the planet's first surviving leather shoe) at the Areni Cave in Armenia.[88] But this does not preclude independent efforts elsewhere – indeed the DNA of modern vines appears to point to both a major eastern event and much later cross-breeding with local varieties.[89] On Mediterranean sites of this age grape pips are common, but usually too small in size or number to clinch domestication. We shall encounter one possible exception in the Levant, and another definite one stands out in northern Greece where, around 4000 BC, pressed residues are found at Dikili Tash and the pip sizes at Dimitra suggest domesticated plants.[90] Equally intriguing is the case of the opium poppy.[91] This probably originated in Iberia, where sap-rich heads, stored in baskets woven from esparto grass and brightly painted with geometric designs, were discovered at the end of the 19th century along with burials and further preserved shoes, this time of plaited grass, in the dry recesses of Cueva de los Murciélagos, almost a kilometre (half a mile) up in the Cordoba mountains [**6.12**, **6.13**]. Opium compounds are also detectable in the

6.12 Exceptionally well-preserved esparto grass basket from the Cueva de los Murciélagos.

6.13 The fortuitous discovery of the Cueva de los Murciélagos burials, as imagined in an early engraving.

Neolithic burials from a disused mine at Can Tintorer near Barcelona, and the seeds occur at La Marmotta. Opium poppies only reached the Aegean after the Neolithic, an interesting counter to the westward spread of the agricultural domesticates. It is intriguing to speculate how much the exuberant swirls on Neolithic material culture owe to visions triggered by opium-based or other natural hallucinogenic substances.

Returning to pragmatics, how were these European Mediterranean landscapes inhabited?[92] Most farmers targeted the fertile lowlands, patchily clearing woodland from around the houses, and these remained the vortices of life in most regions until at least 4500–4000 BC. In addition to Thessaly and the Tavoliere, which throbbed with some 10,000–20,000 people each, other concentrations of Neolithic humanity arose in the plains of western Macedonia, eastern Sicily, parts of northeast Italy, the Rhône, Aude and Garonne valleys and lowland Catalonia. Beyond, smaller and more broken up lowland areas were also settled, occasionally at village level but often at the scale of hamlets or single homesteads. In the Aegean, small groups expanded on the margins of Thessaly and into the Peloponnese and similar microcosms dotted peninsular Italy, for instance the handful of families living at Penitenzeria at the tip of rough Calabria, or San Marco near Gubbio in Umbria.[93] Even the Vera basin in southeast Spain, less arid than today but never an easy prospect for farming, attracted pioneer settlers from about 5000 BC.[94] Such communities, typically surrounded by wild land rather than packed cheek by jowl in the few extensive plains, and more heavily reliant on outside contacts for survival, were the terrestrial equivalents of those moving into the smaller islands at the same time, with the great difference compared to certain islands being that their chances of later achieving unanticipated centrality were much slimmer.

Lastly, what of the rearing masses of more mountainous land? In general, the Neolithic remained a low-altitude phenomenon, ultimately the easiest way to average the environmental tolerances of its constituent domesticates. It therefore signified a marked retreat from high ground in comparison to the age of warm-weather hunter-gatherers.[95] But there are some interesting finer distinctions. At one extreme, farming only began in the clefts of the northern Pindos mountains as late as the 1st millennium BC.[96] On the other hand, the uplifted plateaux at both ends of the basin were already seeing plenty of action. Anatolia was examined in Chapter 5, and now Iberia comes into focus, with a penchant for mobile, cave-based sheep and goat herding perhaps linked to late hunter-gatherer adoption in remote areas (a feature also of the wild Velebit in Dalmatia),[97] but also wheat and barley alongside the poppies at Cueva de los Murciélagos, which formed part of a landscape of upland farmers.[98] Typically, however, Mediterranean uplands had to wait until the 4th and 3rd millennia BC to receive resident communities, and then under changed circumstances (see Chapter 7). In the meantime, vast areas lay empty – liberating or frightening land for settled people, only traversed by tiny numbers of traders, stone procurers, hunters or initiates, hastening onward towards the nearest houses or remote places of ritual.

Three of the greatest concentrations of people yield rich social insights. Each enjoyed a boom phase in the size, number and cultural elaboration of its communities, but the timings differ. In Thessaly this falls in the Aegean Middle and Late Neolithic (5800–4500 BC); in the Tavoliere, in the Italian late Early and early Middle Neolithic (5500–4800 BC); and in the river valleys of southern France in the Middle Neolithic, or Chasséen (4700–3600 BC). Given the strong local character in each case, the east–west trend in date cannot reflect transmission from one to the next (unlike earlier and later processes encountered in the course of our history). Instead it reflects the differing time lags between the arrival of farming and build-up of a sufficient number of people. To emphasize the independence of each boom, we start late and in the west.

Braudel, in patriotic mode, once proclaimed the Chasséen to be his country's 'civilisation néolithique nationale', but although indeed unusual from our perspective in that it extends over much of non-Mediterranean France too, new work has stressed the distinctiveness of the southern version and also drawn attention to parallels on the other side of the Pyrenees, in Catalonia.[99] The Mediterranean Chasséen communities concentrated in the farmland and pasture along the Rhône, Aude and Garonne, where we have seen that they encouraged a landscape of oak-studded grassland for their cattle (here and elsewhere the abundant acorns could feed pigs and, as a back-up food, people). At Villeneuve-Tolosane, near Toulouse, an area of 30 ha (75 acres) under a housing estate is peppered with some 700 circular and rectangular hearths, cobbled areas and grain silos, almost half enclosed by ditches and palisades [1.10].[100] At Saint-Michel-du-Touch the concentration covers 20 ha (50 acres), and about the same at Bòbila Madurell in Catalonia.[101] Poor preservation of houses makes it hard to tell how many people lived in such villages, and numbers may have fluctuated seasonally, but occupation was certainly loosely clustered compared to the crowded tells of the Aegean and Levant.

Further east, the great gift of the Tavoliere is its remarkable information about settlement numbers, size and layout, primarily obtained in the Second World War from aerial photographs that captured the ghosts of cumulatively incised encircling ditches and the small, inner c-shaped ditches believed to surround each dwelling, just before the disastrous advent of tractor-drawn deep ploughing.[102] Of 566 sites thereby identified within the 3200 sq. km (1200 sq. miles) of the Tavoliere, 95 per cent occupy 7 ha (17 acres) or less and, on the basis of their c-ditch counts, each comprised only a handful of houses. The few larger villages are Middle Neolithic creations of internal growth or the coalescing of smaller communities. Passo di Corvo is the largest, 28 ha (69 acres) as defined by its inner zone or 172 ha (425 acres) as measured by a 3-km- (2-mile-) long outer ditch. Despite the enormous latter extent, only a hundred or so c-ditches can be counted within, implying a substantial yet still village-scale population of some 500 people (a cautionary tale for the diffuse Chasséen). The outer ditches clearly demarcated a more inclusive concept of community boundaries than the inner concentration of housing, probably enclosing cultivated or grazed areas and perhaps defining the transition between spaces dominated by women and men.[103] Against a recent proposal that Tavoliere sites were not farming settlements at all, but occasional aggregation or ritual centres,[104] we can cite

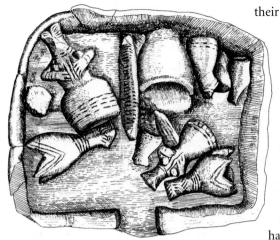

6.14 Model Thessalian household from Platia Magoula Zarkou.

6.15 The core of the later Neolithic settlement at Dhimini, showing households divided by courtyard walls and, on the central elevation, a large porched 'megaron'.

0 10 m
0 30 ft

their vast numbers, the debris in their ditches and the decapitation of living-floor levels by ploughing, as well as the fact that at comparable Stentinello sites in eastern Sicily, where cuttings were made into bedrock rather than soil, rows of postholes outline large rectangular houses.[105]

Traditionally, the extensive, loosely occupied flat sites of the west and central Mediterranean are contrasted with the compact, elevated tells of Thessaly, which, at 1–2 ha (2.5–5 acres), were far smaller, if nonetheless crowded with between fifty and a few hundred people.[106] This remains an instructive comparison. But over the last couple of decades, archaeologists in Thessaly and adjacent parts of Macedonia have realized that large flat sites existed there too. Makriyalos, the most fully excavated (in advance of a new road and rail route between Athens and Thessaloniki), comprised rubbish-filled ditches and thinly scattered houses like those further west, with strikingly little difference in farming activities from the nearby tells.[107] Their very existence makes us wonder under what circumstances the vertical tells literally arose. Building material is one factor (accumulating mud and earth versus rotting wood), but as with the PPN in the east, tells also indicate a close association over many years between households and specific plots of land, built on time and again until an inhabited monument lifted high above the fields.[108] That this distinction was self-conscious is proven by Middle Neolithic Sesklo, which comprised both a tell community of large, well-built houses furnished with elaborate pots, and a surrounding lower settlement of flimsier, simply equipped abodes.[109] Successful Thessalian households' quests for segregation are further illuminated by a late proliferation of dividing compound walls on the tells, a tendency for cooking and eating to take place inside these rather than, as earlier, in shared open space, and the popularity of house models, one from Platia Magoula Zarkou with the members of a notably large family within [**6.14**].[110] In the final phase, between 4800 and 4500 BC, a single large-porched house known as a 'megaron', access to which was controlled by walls and gates, came to dominate the tops of several Thessalian tells, notably Sesklo and the younger coastal site of Dhimini [**6.15**].[111]

These large houses may signal that 2000 years into Mediterranean Europe's longest Neolithic sequence, some form of institutionalized village leadership had emerged in Thessaly. If so, this is an exception that proves the rule, for equivalents have not emerged elsewhere. This should not really surprise us. For as already

225

hinted, it is unlikely that any Neolithic settlement on the northern flanks of the Mediterranean held more than a few hundred people, far less than the eastern mega-sites of the Late PPNB two to three millennia earlier. They therefore fall within the range of what are slightly misleadingly termed 'egalitarian' communities, in which authority and status are spread diffusely, often on the basis of personal attributes, between diverse kinds of people and realms of action, rather than concentrated in a leading individual, family or kin group.[112] In such highly tangled communities a ritual expert might not be the same person as an experienced elder (in this context anyone alive at forty), a war-band leader, a skilled crafter, or the head of a family grown wealthy thanks to its stake in the best land, making it very hard for linked-up, let alone inherited, forms of power to become established. The tensions inherent in this system may have something to do with the endemic violence attested by frequent cranial wounds on men and women in Italy. Its ambiguities also make sense of the odd treatments of a few individuals after death.[113] Until a late date, the Neolithic dead are at best sporadically visible, and when we do see them the settings imply one-off circumstances rather than straightforward leadership. Good examples are the old man trepanned and then buried with a mass of ritual objects in the Grotta Patrizi in southern Italy, and the reconstitution within a 7.4 × 5.0 m (24 × 16 ft) wood-lined pit at Saint-Michel-du-Touch of two skeletons from bodies that had decomposed elsewhere, accompanied by decorated pots, stone beads and pierced sandstone plaques, over which a pebble mound was raised.[114]

It goes without saying that against this kind of background, structured power relations between communities were unlikely to evolve. Big communities were just larger than their neighbours, not their territorial overlords, and a village's authority probably extended little further than its fields, a kilometre or so beyond the houses. To what extent even this might be challenged is uncertain. Cases have been made for and against a Hobbesian state of endemic 'warre' between villages in Thessaly,[115] but although ditches and palisades can fulfil peaceful functions like drainage, corralling and boundary delineation, it is suggestive that at Stentinello in Sicily a wall ran along the inner rim of the deep perimeter ditch, while the level of violence seen on Italian skeletons is unlikely to relate entirely to internal fracas.[116] Yet however peacefully or otherwise each community got on with things, they still needed their neighbours on a variety of levels. Even the largest were barely populous enough for internal inter-marriage to suffice, and every smaller hamlet and farm would have had to marry out, cross-breed its small flocks with other herds, and draw upon a wider pool of expertise for specialized needs, including ceremonial rites and long-range trade. The wider ties and identities fashioned by such interdependence between hundreds if not thousands of people profoundly shaped Neolithic social landscapes, whether compressed into a cluster of big plains villages, or spread over thinly peopled country.

Such observations make sense of Neolithic culture's dense variegation. Some of this has vanished into the realm of informed speculation, notable the divergence of speech and formation of local dialects and languages that we can envisage after the initial spread of whatever language(s) the first farmers spoke and some creolization

6.17 The Levante-style rock art of southern Iberia is hard to date, but much of it appears to belong to Neolithic or slightly later times; in the selection here, female harvesters, some wielding sickles, are juxtaposed with an adventure in hive-robbing, a reminder that honey offered a rare source of sweetness.

6.16 (*above*) Elaborately painted Neolithic cup in the Serro d'Alto style of southern Italy, with echoes of textile designs in its decoration and an ornate handle.

with hunter-gatherer tongues.[117] To the rescue comes pottery, which now enjoyed its first peak of technological and stylistic sophistication.[118] As intimated for the Levant and Africa, the function of early pots varied, in the Aegean beginning with a minor social role, in the centre and west with a one-suits-all approach. It then diversified almost everywhere on the northern side of the Mediterranean to embrace coarser cooking and storage (taste-enhancing and parasite-proof respectively), as well as technically highly ambitious, smartly shaped and intricately decorated vessels for formalized eating and drinking, some with elevated pedestals, flat bases suggestive of table use, and handles on the first clear drinking cups [**6.16**]. Elaborate 'salt pots' in the Aegean and the Danilo phase of Dalmatia further remind us that eating entailed far more than simply survival.[119] Turning to the designs that covered pots, the broad early zones of stylistic similarity seen in, for example, impressed wares, broke up into localized traditions as people settled in and multiplied. This reached extremes around 5500 BC in Thessaly and southern Italy. The former boasts fourteen to sixteen distinct styles of confined, overlapping distribution, many spectacularly painted bichrome and trichrome creations, with in the latter region a similar profusion of painted and impressed wares, in both cases often imitating basketry or textiles (oddly square-mouthed pottery in northern Italy instead mimicked wooden vessels). Clay analysis informs us that few pots now moved far from where they were made, and we can extract from this stylistic localism a glimpse of the narrow horizons of the skilled women who probably made them.[120] Likewise, the coexistence of multiple styles within a single community hints at complicated social relations. Conversely, where settlements were thinly scattered, and so in more acute need of each other, such as among the Aegean islands, uniform styles extended over much broader areas.[121]

Similar trends can be discerned in ritual places and practices. We encountered the Cova de l'Or in the hill country now divided between Valencia and Alicante in the context of the spread of farming, and raised the possibility of a sacred function. One of its ornate Cardial pots depicts a human figure with hands upheld, an image also found in the local rock art but further paralleled on a carved pig bone at the Gaban

rockshelter in the Adige Valley of northern Italy, as well as earlier on the walls of Çatalhöyük.[122] Such widespread horizons soon shrank. In the landscapes around the Cova de l'Or, and the well-studied Serpis basin, a distinctive rock art tradition continued, with contrasting styles used to map and maybe contest symbolic space, and haunting images of farming in areas where no farmers yet lived, as well as depictions of wilderness activities such as thieving honey from wild beehives [**6.17**].[123] Figurines multiplied in a bewildering range of styles and genders that quite refute the traditional effort

6.18 Remnants of cult in the lower cavern of Grotta Scaloria, where Neolithic pots, tools and bones were found clustered around stalagmites, stalactites and a pool of still water.

6.19 (*below*) Bono Ighinu-style figurine with elaborate headdress, from Sardinia.

to lump them together as 'mother goddesses'. Hundreds of examples come from the Aegean, with the Sardinian Bono Ighinu figurines one of the first and largest traditions in the central Mediterranean [**6.19**].[124] Astonishingly, one figurine in use at La Marmotta was in fact an Upper Palaeolithic object carved at least 20,000 years earlier.[125] The same preference for highly local ways of doing things can be seen within as confined a region as Apulia, where the ceremonial cave of Grotta Scaloria [**6.18**], sealed by an ancient collapse that preserved painted pots still placed to capture water droplets falling from the stalactites (and incidentally some of Europe's last wild ass bones), contrasts with Grotta dei Cervi's paintings of deer, men and women, trending in the deeper recesses towards male exclusivity, and children's handprints [**6.20**].[126]

6.20 Male hunters, stags and geometric motifs, part of a world of symbols and wildland ritual, in the Grotta dei Cervi at Porto Badisco.

Longer-range vision

The real surprise is that these myriad, self-absorbed little communities dotted around the plains, valleys and islands of Mediterranean Europe had just as much access to desirable far-off materials and objects as others around the basin with more obvious outward orientations. As seen in previous chapters, people had been collecting things and depositing them elsewhere even prior to the emergence of modern humans; well before the Last Glacial Maximum some transfers of gleaming seashells encompassed distances of 1000 km (600 miles). And, as also noted, among mobile hunter-gatherers it is hard to ascertain whether this reflects simply co-transport of things on the move with their original users (for instance a tool or necklace), or sometimes transfers between people, with all that then follows in terms of concepts of exchange within the social and economic mindsets and motives of the people involved. Even once we can be fairly certain that exchange was happening, further questions arise. In addition to ideational profundities, to what extent were the often extensive final distributions that we document today the creations of individually short down-the-line transfers of ever-diminishing amounts of material from A to B, then B to C, then C to D, or did a few people move things over substantially longer ranges, and if so who were they? All these are manifestly vital questions given the centrality of trade to so much later Mediterranean history. Yet despite a firm intuition that transfers between people had begun by the first millennia of the Holocene, and probably well before in the Upper Palaeolithic, such questions remain hard to crack until surprisingly late. In Africa this is due to continued mobility and scanty data, in earlier Holocene Mediterranean Europe to a mixture of ongoing hunter-gatherer lifestyles and leapfrogging farmers, and in the PPN Levant, the most promising early arena, to mobile groups embedded in, and also regionally encircling, the cores of village life – for example, recall the likelihood that access to Anatolian obsidian began not by long-range exchange, but procuring expeditions that went to the highlands to bring it back. With the settling in of locally rooted communities on the northern flanks of the Mediterranean and in the contemporary Levant, we now get the first really good chance to look at these issues in more interesting ways, and with the additional advantage that growing numbers of people, and their relations to each other, triggered a take-off in the amount and variety of things set in motion.[127]

The vast majority of materials and objects used in most places were locally sourced, even if local quality was poor. We have already seen that, in contrast to its later performance, Neolithic pottery seldom moved very far – though a few trans-Adriatic instances stand out.[128] Certain prized things were regularly displaced over 50–100 km (30–60 miles), notably hard volcanic grinding stones, ochre for pigments, cinnabar or the green variscite used in Iberia for ornaments, as well as fine flints, such as those of the Vaucluse, Alpine foothills, Gargano, and Hyblaean massif of southeast Sicily (the last producing blades up to 20 cm or 8 in. long).[129] Beyond this, a few materials show up radically further from home. One is obsidian, to which we return below. But equally far-travelled were lustrous polished axes and amulets of greenish-blue meta-morphic or igneous rocks, in particular those of southern Italy, the Aegean and above all 'jadeite', actually eclogite, from the western Alps.[130] Bracelets made of the spiny oyster *Spondylus gaederopus* percolated deep into the Balkans and central Europe, mainly but not exclusively from the northern Aegean.[131] The imports to regions poor in such materials, including the populous lowland plains and many islands, could be extensive. Malta obtained grey flints, dark basalt axes and red ochre from Sicily, black obsidian from Lipari and green from Pantelleria, greenstone axes from Calabria, and a pendant of Alpine jadeite, a list that reveals how much of the colour palette that relieved the drab hues of everyday material came from far away.[132] We sometimes know quite a lot about the places from where such materials were extracted. Obsidian quarries are obvious point sources that have been closely investigated, but they are not alone. The flint mine at La Defensola on the Gargano peninsula, next to the Tavoliere, consisted of deep galleries worked by lamplight with antler picks.[133] Neolithic mines are known in Catalonia, one at Can Tintorer with shafts 50 m (165 ft) long and 14 m (45 ft) deep dug in search of variscite (touched on earlier in the context of the opium detected in skeletons buried in its disused sections), another for salt at the appositely named La Muntanya de Sal.[134] We are less informed about where such materials were worked, although shell-bead manufacturing locales have been identified as far apart as Franchthi and Arene Candide.[135]

Such information allows us to plot patterns of connection with some accuracy. Naturally, we need to pay attention to the quantities involved. Over half the axes in Liguria and southern France were made from nearby west Alpine stone, some superb items over 35 cm (14 in.) in length [6.21], but further afield Alpine axes were much rarer and smaller, with the few beyond the Pyrenees, and in southern Italy, delineat-ing the western and southern limits of a spread whose northern edge runs through Scotland.[136] With these warnings in mind, the major exchange arenas that emerge are the Aegean, parts of the Adriatic and Tyrrhenian sub-basins (the last two only feebly linked across peninsular Italy), and a corridor centred on southern France, extending west into Catalonia and east towards the Po. The maritime nature of most of these zones is striking, and testimony to the integrative role of populated islands. But the degree of overland or coastwise linkage between the Rhône and Ebro is also marked, in fact more so than at any subsequent time until the 1st millennium BC. In contrast, the now less frequented mountains formed impediments to such reciprocal contacts, cutting off Dalmatia and southern France from their continental hinterlands, and nudging connections inward to the central sea. Exactly how these objects and materi-als moved, however, is not entirely clear. The different ranges argue that many were exchanged for social reasons within the dense relationships that tied neighbouring households and villages together, occasionally escaping the vortex of one such system to be captured by the next; others worth the effort came in from a few days' walking or paddling away, and a minority came as prized or otherwise special-purpose exotics over longer distances, often across the sea.[137] The link between maritime and longer-range movement is striking. Beyond the obvious fact that island-free stretches of sea

6.21 The distribution of fine southwest Alpine axes in and well beyond the Mediterranean, with the earliest distribution zone at 5500–4900 BC highlighted. The diameter of the circles is proportional to the number of axes at each location. Note the rapid fall-off beyond southern France and northern Italy, save for a far-off accumulation among the megalithic monuments of Brittany.

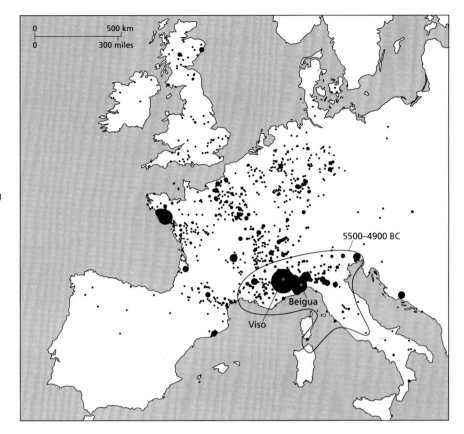

necessitated longer transfers, if transfer there was to be, this suggests that the less encumbered sea facilitated dispersal more than overland travel, whose impediments were social as well as physical, involving repeated negotiation of the niceties of local customs at each village along the route.[138]

In terms of sheer resolution, however, nothing rivals the information provided by obsidian, whose Mediterranean heyday in terms of amounts in circulation roughly coincides with this chapter.[139] Quite why it travelled is not evident in all cases; near its sources it was expediently employed for most sharp edges, but further off it became a rarity whose role was restricted to cutting soft tissues (butchery, human scarification, or the cutting and shaving of hair?); clearly its meaning shifted with distance from its points of origin.[140] The regions supplied from each source were fairly discrete, which points to an unsurprising decline in ease of access and transport as distance increased. Melos was predominant in the Aegean, overlapping with the Anatolian sources on the eastern seaboard and Carpathian ones at the Balkan interface.[141] Almost no Melian obsidian crossed into the Adriatic, which was supplied meagrely from the Carpathians and central Mediterranean. From peninsular Italy westward to southern France, plus a few finds in Catalonia and the Pantellerian obsidian in the eastern Maghreb, central Mediterranean sources enjoyed a complete dominance.[142] Access to sources seems not to have been closely controlled by people living near them, but remained open to local islanders and such others as had the means to reach them.

231

With four separate sources and over 3000 objects tested for their provenance, the central Mediterranean provides a unique opportunity to compare shifting obsidian preferences and circulation patterns over time [**6.22**].[143] In the earlier 6th millennium BC, all the sources supplied constricted, largely coastal constituencies: Lipari (whose obsidian is particularly high quality and translucent) in Sicily, Calabria and Malta; the Monte Arci quarries of Sardinia the islanders' own considerable needs, plus Corsica, Elba and northern Italy; the minor Palmarola source in nearby Campania and other parts of central Italy; and, as we saw earlier, Pantellerian obsidian covered western Sicily, other Sicilian channel islands and the eastern Maghreb. Subsequently, Sardinian obsidian penetrated southern France, especially Provence and occasionally Chasséen sites beyond the Rhône, while obsidian from Lipari starts to be found all over coastal and inland Italy south of Tuscany, and well into the Adriatic. By the end of the 5th millennium BC, Lipari's dominance had extended further north to the Po, ousting Sardinian products from first place even at Arene Candide in Liguria. Sardinia was now the principal supplier only to itself, Corsica and southern France. Significant details also shed light on the condition in which obsidian travelled, and thence how it circulated. As in the contemporary Aegean, areas up to 100–200 km (60–125 miles) or so from the source (southern Calabria, for example, where Lipari obsidian was the material of preference) reveal not only the final blades, but remnants of cores from which blades were struck, and sometimes

6.22 The dispersal pattern from each of the sources of obsidian in the central Mediterranean, aggregated over time.

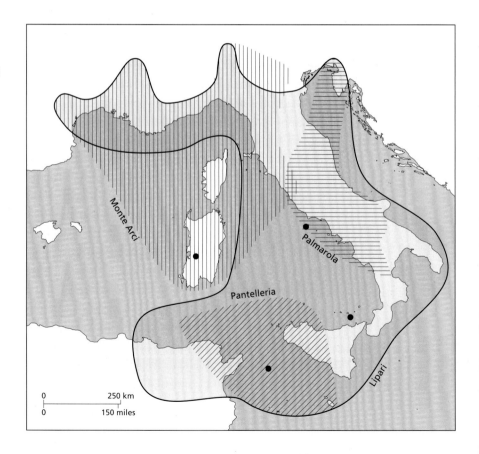

detritus from preparing the core itself. In contrast, more distant sites often have only finished blades.[144] Within the former zone, either local people went to the source and brought raw material home to work, or travelling knappers from the source brought obsidian to them, working it locally or en route. But in more distant regions obsidian typically comprised only 1 per cent of the stone used, and finished blades were obtained through exchange, a conclusion borne out by occasional finds of caches of pre-prepared tools in central and northern Italy, and equally rare 'middleman' sites for entire regions, such as Passo di Corvo for the Tavoliere. Behind such observations we sense the ghosts of unusual specialist individuals or groups moving over much longer distances than most of their contemporaries.[145]

With the interesting exception of its deep penetration of the interior Maghreb (a reflection of more generalized long-range terrestrial mobility across North Africa), Mediterranean obsidian circulation is strongly associated with movement by sea, well beyond the requirement of getting off its islands. It is tempting to wonder whether its cultural value lay partly in this maritime association. Transport of Lipari's obsidian to Calabria implied the ability not merely to cross the Strait of Messina, no challenge since the Aurignacian, but the skilled business of navigating its length, which demanded knowledge of its racing, treacherous currents, and the later transport of such obsidian round the heel of Italy and into the Adriatic was manifestly maritime.[146] In one other fascinating instance, logistical implications in the data enable us to define the route and guess at the people involved in some detail. In southern France almost all the obsidian comes from just one of several Sardinian outcrops, whose visually identical products otherwise circulated promiscuously around the northern Tyrrhenian.[147] This exclusivity effectively rules out an indirect acquisition by French consumers from the general Tyrrhenian network, in favour of a direct connection between coastal France and one specific Sardinian source 400 km (250 miles) away, including an open-sea journey of 150 km (90 miles) between France and Corsica, which in terms of likely canoe speeds and lost time translates into a return journey of a couple of months. These bold travellers must have been Sardinians closely connected to one source on their home island, or parties from southern France to whom only one outcrop was known or accessible, which would be unsurprising in view of the inland, scattered locations of outcrops in the Monte Arci region. Obsidian distributions equally help to confirm those stretches of sea that were not yet open; the absence of Sardinian material in Sicily and elsewhere in the southern Tyrrhenian, in particular, is silent witness to one still unbridged expanse of big blue.

An intimation of things to come in Mediterranean Europe

As we shall see in Chapter 7, during the 4th and 3rd millennia BC communities around the Mediterranean altered fundamentally, forming new social structures and networks in conjunction with changing environmental conditions. In most parts of the basin, the crux of change lay around or after 3500 BC. But premonitions can be spotted earlier. We saw in Africa how the Nile Valley was turning into a hotbed of dynamic political culture that would soon follow the floodwaters downstream to engulf the Delta. In the northern half of the Mediterranean the changes would not come from the outside but from within, even if they share commonalities with parallel shifts over the remainder of Europe. And their roots become apparent by the late 5th and early 4th millennia BC, especially in the Italian Late and Aegean Final Neolithics, both of which align more convincingly with the future than the past.[148] In order to do least chronological violence to the integrity of our history, these harbingers of change need to be explored briefly at this juncture, for the moment without too much speculation about their wider significance, to which we return, adding further vectors over a wider canvas, in Chapter 7, which covers one of the most decisive ages in Mediterranean history. Four changes are evident before 3500 BC, all of which, we may suspect, were loosely interlinked but started off locally in different areas, and only gradually coalesced.

The first is a gradual transformation of landscapes of settlement. The earliest manifestation is the abandonment soon after 5000 BC of hundreds of loci in the Tavoliere, which was thereafter sparsely occupied until the Iron Age. This was followed several centuries later by a similar trend over much of Italy.[149] Processes in Thessaly were less dramatic, but, as elsewhere in the Aegean, the Final Neolithic saw the slow break-up, after 2000 years, of the old primary agricultural communities, the emptying of many established villages and the end of megaron houses.[150] The demise of Neolithic villages in Italy and the Aegean was not universal, but exceptions tend to come from areas slower to take off and sometimes environmentally favoured – for example, Ripoli and other sites in central and northern Italy, the Ozieri villages of Sardinia and Final Neolithic Knossos.[151] Over well-surveyed parts of the basin the typical scale of settlement shrank to hamlets or single farmsteads, widely dispersed across the landscape, with a partial reversion to cave occupation.[152] Accompanying this was a centrifugal push into marginal land, including uplands and tiny islands. A rash of little sites spread across hitherto empty tracts of the Peloponnese and Crete, the smaller Cyclades, the hills overlooking the emptied Tavoliere, upland Calabria and the hinterlands of Liguria and Tuscany.[153] The deeper environmental and social reasons for this landscape inversion are explored in Chapter 7, when further examples after 3500 BC strengthen the case for a sweeping if imperfectly correlated process.

Second, as living places became smaller and more ephemeral, places of burial became more prominent.[154] Earlier treatments of the dead were often archaeologically elusive, with human remains found in ditches or pits between or under houses, so that the dead became reincorporated into the community, or strikingly exceptional in their circumstances. Defined burial grounds were rare, save for cremation cemeteries next to some Thessalian tells (another affirmation of distinction by tell-dwelling families?), the first cist graves and rock-cut tombs in southern Italy and Sardinia, and the earliest tumuli over burials in the later 5th-millennium BC Tavertet tombs of Catalonia (plus versions of this type, including the construction at Saint-Michel-du-Touch, in southwest France).[155] For all the publicity given to a very few richly endowed burials, in most cases no objects were left with people in death. But at the end of the 5th millennium BC all this began to change, with the regular appearance of formal cemeteries, some with massive above-ground architecture, or no less impressive subterranean features, and often containing gravegoods. In the Aegean, southern Italy and Sicily this initially took the form of modest clusters of cist graves, in the Tavoliere sometimes dug into the abandoned villages to assert a link to the ancestral past.[156] Impressive rock-cut tombs for communal burials (known as hypogea) appeared on two central Mediterranean islands. On Ozieri-phase Sardinia, one of the few places where village-scale life survived, the most impressive of several thousand *domus de janas* ('witches' houses') were large, multiroom tombs and ritual arenas that imitated houses down to their carved, red-painted beams and roofs, with bull heads in relief on the walls, all furnished with decorated pots and figurines [**6.23**].[157] In the Maltese archipelago tombs with kidney-shaped lobes appear from 4100 BC; one at Xaghra on Gozo contained sixty-five burials.[158] And from the far west, a megalithic tradition of above-ground tombs constructed from massive blocks of stone covered by an earthen mound began to spread out from the Alentejo upland of southern Portugal, home to more than 2000 such tombs, the earliest dating to the 5th millennium BC and making this region, along with Brittany, an epicentre of megalith construction along the Atlantic facade.[159] The Tavertet tumuli already expressed an awareness of such monuments, but after 4000 BC true megalithic dolmens appear in Catalonia, with an influx up the Tagus into the southern Meseta.[160] This initial zone would explode after 3500 BC into a 'véritable dolmenisme' in the western half of the Mediterranean.[161]

Our third change is the opening up of social interaction, most obviously in the Aegean and Tyrrhenian.[162] In both regions, the centuries between 4500 and 4000 BC witnessed the demise of the multitude of local decorated pottery styles and their replacement, through convergence rather than emission from a single source, by

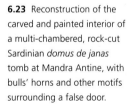

6.23 Reconstruction of the carved and painted interior of a multi-chambered, rock-cut Sardinian *domus de janas* tomb at Mandra Antine, with bulls' horns and other motifs surrounding a false door.

plain varieties, more or less uniform over extensive areas. These must have helped small groups taking in new landscapes to establish flexible relations with each other, free from the weight of past social boundaries. In the Aegean this took the form of simple pattern-burnished and red-crusted surfaces.[163] In southern and central Italy the part was played by shiny monochrome Diana-Bellavista pottery (the first half of whose name derives from the meeting place for travellers below the Lipari acropolis).[164] It was paralleled in Malta by Red Skorba wares, in Sardinia by Ozieri styles and further north by Lagozza pottery, which in turn links to the dark, burnished and incised pottery of the Chasséen and its Iberian cousins – the paradoxical correlation with the Chasséen acme of village life further west nicely underlining the imperfectly coordinated initial incidence of each change across the northern Mediterranean. This shift was paralleled in the Aegean by a marked de-skilling of pottery production, attested by the demise of finely made vessels at the expense of coarser, lower-fired products.[165] In conjunction with the rise of utilitarian, mass-produced plain pottery in the Levant during its own Copper Age, as well shall see, we might conclude that the opening phase in the social life of Mediterranean pottery was essentially over. More open social networks help to explain, too, a general increase in the amount of material in circulation. In the central Mediterranean, the Late Neolithic was obsidian's high noon, especially in the case of widely connected Lipari.[166] It now regularly reached even the persistently out-of-the-way Abruzzo-Marche region of east-central Italy.[167] Aegean marble beakers and other fine creations also describe surprisingly wide connections.[168]

Our fourth and final new development is the emergence of the first metallurgy in Mediterranean Europe.[169] This side of the basin is richly endowed with ores, both in uplifted parts of the mainland and on the increasingly settled islands. Nearby Balkan regions led the way during the late 6th millennium BC, as in Anatolia with beads and other simple forms fashioned from native, sometimes heat-treated copper, but quickly followed by the first casting in open moulds. Early in the 5th millennium BC, pit-like copper mines were dug at Ai Bunar in Bulgaria and Rudna Glava in Serbia, just a few days' walk from the Mediterranean, the first smelting to extract copper from its ore took place at Belovode near Belgrade (currently dated as early as anything equivalent further east), and native gold was panned in streams.[170] Metal items become heavier, technically more sophisticated and more numerous, reaching a temporary peak around 4000 BC. Two-piece moulds for axes with an integral shaft-hole hint at a degree of learning from Anatolia, but the final products circulated in a manner indistinguishable from stone axes west of the Alps, and the contexts in which gold was used also argue for a deep embeddedness in local culture. The great Varna cemetery on the Black Sea contained 6 kg (13 lbs) of gold, a quarter (roughly 900 objects) in a single grave; it covered bodies and sheet-wrapped stone with glitter.[171] Gold paint was even employed to decorate pots.

As in Anatolia and the Levant, metal goods quickly slotted into longer-range trade. By 5000–4500 BC, Balkan copper and gold items, mostly 'trinkets' rather than tools, were filtering into the Aegean.[172] The first local Aegean metallurgy, in copper,

6.24 The early 4th-millennium BC settlement of Kephala on Kea in the northern Cyclades, a windswept location between the metal ores of Lavrio to the north and those of other Cycladic islands to the south, which may explain the traces of metallurgy found across it.

gold, silver and lead, dates to the Final Neolithic (4500–3200 BC), stimulated by the Balkan connection, proximity to Anatolia (where, unlike the Balkans, silverworking also began early, around 4500 BC) and the discovery of ores in the Cyclades as these became fully settled. Copper from Lavrio in Attica was smelted just after 4000 BC at Kephala on nearby Kea in the Cyclades [**6.24**], and green or blue ore-derived pigments start to adorn figurines.[173] The first objects manufactured in the Aegean were simple tools, jewelry and flat ring-idols in silver and gold [**6.25**]. A similar pattern prevailed in the central Mediterranean, where a trickle of mid-5th-millennium BC Balkan imports into the Adriatic was followed by local metallurgy

6.25 Silver jewelry of 4th-millennium BC date from the impressive Alepotrypa Cave in the Mani peninsula of the southern Peloponnese.

both there and in the Tyrrhenian by 4000 BC.[174] In northern Italy the commonest product was a simple copper awl, for tattooing or as a punch for pressure-flaking elaborate flints, both classic examples of the application of new technology to traditional ends.[175] Metallurgy is also prominent on islands, notably ore-rich Sardinia (which produced the earliest silver west of the Aegean) and Lipari, which imported ores from across the sea. In southern Italy, Sicily and France, metals were more or less absent until 3500 BC. Until a few years ago, it looked as if this horizon extended to Iberia. But an independent origin for metallurgy in this prodigally metalliferous peninsula now seems to be affirmed by the discovery, at Cerro Virtud in the Vera basin, of a potsherd with copper smelting slag attached, dated to 5000–4500 BC, and so decisively earlier than anything west of the Balkans.[176] If this lonely datum is upheld, Cerro Virtud stands at the head of a long tradition of Iberian metal extraction and working that only became fully integrated with the wider Mediterranean some three-and-a-half millennia later, on the threshold of the Iron Age.

A dazzling Levant

All that remains for us to investigate of this forgotten age in the Mediterranean is its Levantine dimension. In many senses the best, or at least most strikingly precocious, has been left to last. When we departed from the Levant in Chapter 5, it lay in a kind of creative recession following the end of the PPNB mega-sites, its people scattered into little communities but ones increasingly experimenting with sustainable ways of living within Mediterranean conditions. This Late Neolithic pattern continues into the Early Copper Age, but by the Late Copper Age of the later 5th and early 4th millennia BC, first in the north and then in the drier south, where it was encouraged after 4500 BC by a millennium-long spell of weather substantially wetter than today's, a second cycle of large, dynamic communities arose, quite different from those of the PPNB. Moreover, the Levant was acquiring interesting neighbours. We noted its links to the Nile Delta earlier, and return to these at the end of this chapter. In western Anatolia, the assertion that 'the [Copper Age] people are the real Neolithic'[177] rings true from a European viewpoint, with a village like Beycesultan on the Meander, or Hacılar in the lake district reminiscent of the northern as much as eastern Mediterranean. At Ilıpınar in the northwest, the pottery resembles Balkan Vinča traditions, while from village to village across this broad interface Melian and Anatolian obsidian mingled. Even here, however, surprising facets flash out. Kulaksızlar near Izmir, a 6th-millennium BC production centre for marble figurines of the 'Kilia' type [6.26] contained some 900 faulty rejects, a chastening number higher than the total of known finished examples; its products dispersed up to 400 km (250 miles) across western Anatolia, while the marble beakers also made at the site spread across the Aegean and into the Black Sea.[178]

Moreover, much as the Nile Delta lay downstream of a river corridor in which momentous events were underway from 4000 BC, so, too, the northern Levant graded east into a distant world between two rivers, whose transformation began even earlier, and was the source of ripple effects felt to its west, in the Mediterranean basin, and its north, in central and eastern Anatolia. Farming had spread earlier into the rain-fed zone of northern Mesopotamia, and partly in response to the arid 6200 event, it had evolved small-scale river-tapping channel and canal irrigation.[179] The unintended but revolutionary consequence was to open up to farming the vast and fertile yet rain-poor alluvium further south. This unleashed a population explosion between 5400 and 4000 BC, rather earlier than in Egypt. A swathe of Ubaid villages appeared (named after a type-site in southern Iraq), first in the south and then spreading back north, not without signs of

6.26 Kilia figurine of a type manufactured and distributed in large numbers across western Anatolia.

conflict, to establish an unprecedented level of cultural and symbolic homogeneity throughout Mesopotamia.[180] Large, dense villages of 9–10 ha (22–25 acres) like Ur and Eridu, with populations of a couple of thousand, became socially complex places that exercised a degree of administrative surveillance over flows of goods and materials through clay sealings and tokens, maybe controlling in this way smaller communities in their vicinity. They also erected small, free-standing temples. As on the northern side of the Mediterranean towards the end of the Neolithic, richly decorated pottery and other media gave way to plainer, more uniform material, but in this context not to ease communications between small-scale communities, so much as to standardize and order the material world – it is in this light, as well as a drive to boost output, that we should see the first use of a slow wheel to mechanize pottery production.[181] The Ubaid's potential was realized from around 4000 BC in the emergence of the world's first cities, at Uruk and Susa on the southern alluvium (the former covering 70–100 ha or 170–250 acres), and in the north at Tell Brak, possible ancient Nagar.[182]

As in the case of Egypt, the main impact of these game-altering developments on the nearest, Levantine segment of the Mediterranean came after 3500 BC; and even then relations with Mesopotamia were less direct, and differently structured from those with the Nile. Well before that, however, the alluvium's lack of metals, stones and wood drove Ubaid communities to look to their peripheries, much as did the inhabitants of the plains of Thessaly and the Tavoliere, but on a larger scale and with the critical distinction that their outlying networks engaged radically different ecologies, whose combined contribution further fired up the emergent properties at the centre.[183] To the south, the shallow, subtropical Persian Gulf thrust 200 km (125 miles) inland from its current marshy limit (after having been almost entirely dry at the Last Glacial Maximum), and we can assume inspiring oral versions of the flood legends later committed to writing.[184] Finds of Ubaid pots all the way down the Gulf, together with lumps of barnacle-covered, reed-impressed bitumen coating, are all that survive of a vigorous sea trade in reed boats for Omani copper and maybe dates.[185] In the north, contact was established with metalworkers in highland southeast Anatolia as well as north Levantine groups with access both to metals in the Taurus and (as we shall learn) copper from the southern Levant.[186] These routes acted in reverse as conduits for the outward transmission of Mesopotamian innovations. Later, after 3500 BC, as the Mesopotamian sphere expanded and a unified kingdom arose along the Nile, the Levant's role would gradually alter – still highly inventive, economically superbly connected and sometimes politically powerful in its own right, but dominated for long periods by its giant new neighbours. Between this future and its glory years as part of the Neolithic nuclear zone lies the Levantine Late Copper Age, a time of societies that were both remarkably innovative in a Mediterranean context and open to outside ideas on their own terms. This potent combination forged what can be seen, at least in the south, as the Levant's last flourishing of truly indigenous societies and, from our perspective, practices that prefigure many features of later Mediterranean life.

In the northern Levant the best insights come from the plains of the Amuq and Cilicia.[187] Superficially, surveys of the former reveal something akin to Thessaly, a landscape densely dotted with modest villages. But a few places were larger and more complex in appearance and functions, even if the precise structure of their societies still eludes us. At the large site of Tell Kurdu, goods were marked with seals impressed into clay, and a 90-sq.-m (970-sq.-ft) structure with grill-like foundations to enable underfloor air circulation may have served as a central granary, if so indicating the accumulation of cereals on a considerable scale, whether via some kind of voluntary or enforced tithe on produce, or starkly unequal landholding. At Mersin on the western shore of the Gulf of İskenderun, and below the metal-rich Bolkardag mountains, a remarkable fortification wall with a gate guarded by towers was built around 5000–4800 BC, and the overlying level saw a tripartite building with storage magazines added; a slight frisson is engendered by the fact that horizons of destruction become frequent [6.27].[188] These constitute the first probable examples in the Mediterranean basin of grain storage beyond household levels, and of large-scale defence walls. Sites like Kurdu and Mersin exploited rich farmland in their surrounding plains, but while such niches were fairly widespread in the basin, their architecture and its social implications were not. The explanation must be sought in a wider framework, specifically the advantage that these places enjoyed at the junction between metal-rich Anatolia, the southern Levant, and connections eastward

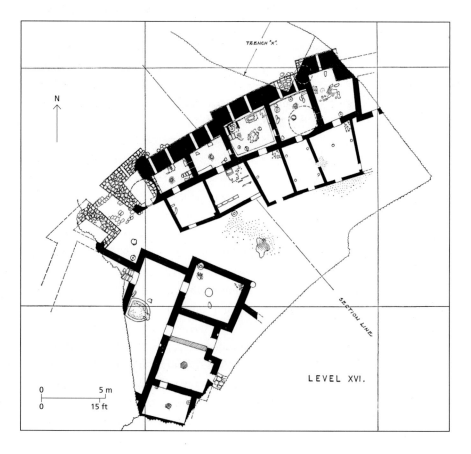

6.27 Plan of Mersin in the early 5th millennium BC, showing heavy fortifications, gateway and structures within.

along the grassy saddle of the Jazira into Mesopotamia. In cultural terms, Copper Age Cilicia and the Amuq faced east and south, with their backs to the rugged hinterland from which they obtained metals.[189] Ubaid influence is detectable in pottery shapes as far south as Hama on the Orontes, and still further through the adoption of slow wheel technology and eclipse of painted pots at the expense of plain, mass-produced chaff-tempered wares.[190] Mersin's imposing public architecture may also find its precedents back in Mesopotamia. Such developments prefigure in embryonic form the kinds of circumstances and responses that would become increasingly central to Mediterranean history as long-range relations and consumer demands for distant resources strengthened.

In the more fully explored southern Levant, Mesopotamian influence is all but non-existent, save for adoption of the slow wheel indirectly via potters further north. Instead, we encounter a more or less pristine Mediterranean phenomenon.[191] Building upon the pioneering Late Neolithic, habitation spread to all the major environmental zones suitable for farming, including not only the Jordan Valley and coastal plain, but stone longhouses on the Golan Heights and, as the rains increased and revived now-vanished perennial rivers, a string of settlements along the currently arid Beersheba Valley on the northern margins of today's Negev desert. Pastoralists extended further south into Sinai and well to the east of the Jordan. Population surged, and with this came the return of major communities. The largest we know of is Tuleilat Ghassul, east of Jericho at the currently landmine-sown, northern terminus of the Dead Sea, a settlement of 20 ha (50 acres) with scraps of wall-paintings that allow us to snatch frustratingly fragmentary glimpses in blue, green, yellow, red, brown and black of angular people in brightly patterned clothes, sun rays, animals, plants and enigmatic 'spook masks' [PL. XVIII].[192] Slightly later, other large communities arose along a vibrant 60-km (35-mile) stretch of the Beersheba Valley, notably at Shiqmim [6.28].[193] One idiosyncrasy there was a troglodytic penchant for digging chambers and tunnels under (and sometimes prior to) houses, like ant farms, in the words of Shiqmim's excavator.[194] These were adaptations to the overwhelming heat of the Negev, as well as secure storage spaces, and maybe bolt-holes from trouble. Overall, the abundance of local traits resembles Mediterranean Europe's Neolithic rather than the conformity of Ubaid Mesopotamia. Thus representations of people were common yet extremely variable; from violin-like schematics to ivory figurines of great verisimilitude at Bir es-Safadi in Beersheba, and basalt pillars with beaky human features and receptacles for offerings in the Golan.[195] Likewise, and mirroring the late 5th and 4th millennium BC trend across the northern flank, places of burial are found in profusion. They range from artificially extended, labyrinthine caves such as Peqi'in in Galilee and Nahal Qana in Samaria, full of clay bone-boxes adorned with human faces, to small dolmens in the Golan, to tumulus fields for the mobile herders of the Negev and the excitably christened 'Cave of the Warrior'.[196] This last was found in 1993, in parched canyonland 10 km (6 miles) west of Tuleilat Ghassul; it held a man buried in a foetal position on a twill-woven reed mat, wrapped in 7 m (23 ft) of linen of elaborate weave and coloured trimming, accompanied by further textiles, a basket, wooden bowl, leather sandals, bow and arrows and (in case we felt we had left the deeper past behind) a large flint blade, the whole lot saturated in red ochre.[197]

As in the north, the social structure behind this second spike of complexity is hard to fathom. One hypothesis is that larger communities were the centres of early chiefdoms that controlled territories tens of kilometres across and smaller subordinate settlements within them.[198] If so, this would constitute a milestone for Mediterranean social organization, but there is in fact little decisive support, save the questionable assumption from evolutionary anthropology that chiefs are a necessary stage between egalitarian societies and urban states of the kind that arose later, in the Bronze Age. Settlements provide if anything less evidence of central power within the community than the Thessalian villages with their megaron houses, and in the south storage still ran at household level. The overwhelming message from the burial realm is of communal ideologies, with little scope for individual aggrandizement – the Cave of the Warrior (as peculiar an outlier as the one-off ritual burials further west) is outstanding for its preservation but not its wealth. In all likelihood big communities, if less 'egalitarian' than those of Mediterranean Europe, were dominated by groups of elders, lineage heads or ritual specialists, not that unlike the earlier PPNB mega-sites, if differently expressed in material terms.

The intriguing fact is that signs of wider regional integration, beyond the usual circulation of flints, valued goods and a local specialism in heavy, well-crafted basalt bowls, are found less in political organization than a series of big, free-standing, well-furnished shrine buildings and their altars and walled precincts. These drew people and things from far-flung parts of the southern Levant.[199] Three examples are known, one constructed after an earlier phase of household ritual at Tuleilat Ghassul, another on a soaring rock shelf at Ein Gedi, overlooking the Dead Sea and a verdant spring-fed wilderness oasis [PL. XX], and a third at Gilat on the border

6.28 Diagrammatic cross-section of an 'ants' nest' of underground complexes at Shiqmim.

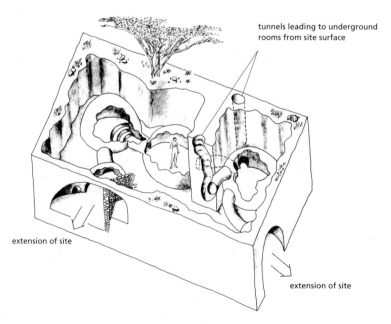

tunnels leading to underground rooms from site surface

extension of site

extension of site

6.29 Figurine of a ram from the Gilat shrine, bearing models of three drinking cornets on its back.

of the northern Negev; in different ways all were nodal points in their landscapes. Such sacred places displayed close similarities, and arguably direct interconnections, beyond their architecture. These include masses of conical drinking horns, known as cornets, bowls with fenestrated pedestals, violin figurines, and exotic objects, one at Ein Gedi probably an Egyptian stone vessel. The provenances of clay and stone prove that many pots and figurines arrived from diverse points of origin, suggesting that people travelled from far and wide to make offerings, and perhaps to participate in ceremonial eating and drinking. For one further aspect of these sites that is now coming to light is their connection to agricultural produce. The Gilat shrine is famous for two figurines, one of a ram with cornets on its back [**6.29**], the other of an explicitly sexed, seated woman balancing a churn-like object on her head [PL. XXI]. Full-sized churns can be confidently associated with processed milk products.[200] Similar research has identified olive oil as the contents of a hundred torpedo-shaped pots that uncannily presage the later amphora form.[201] They came to Gilat, according to clay analysis, from several locations in the uplands to the north. The shrine at Tuleilat Ghassul instead stored olives intact, in a local environment in which the trees would not naturally grow.[202] Plentiful spindle whorls reveal textile production to be another major activity at Gilat. Whatever the nature of the cult, its beliefs and religious personnel, shrines were clearly implicated in the movement and accumulation of a range of crops and animal products. One interpretation views the entire phenomenon in terms of the sacred and pragmatic management of risk; another might emphasize instead the exchange and sometimes sacrifice of a fresh suite of highly desirable agricultural products.[203]

Such cult sites echo in ritual form the integration, ecological complementarity and widening portfolio of Copper Age Levantine farming. Building on and adapting primary horticulture, the salient principles were diversification, flexibility and tuning to the variegation of the land. For example, crops in Beersheba were almost certainly irrigated by construction of check dams to divert stream floodwaters into their fields, a practice little different in principle from the larger-scale basin inundation developed at much the same time (coincidentally or not) on the Nile.[204] Without this it is unlikely that communities like Shiqmim could have flourished in what was still marginal land for farming, and indeed the archaeologically shadowy origins of this technique may go back to final PPNB and subsequent experimentation, as farmers moved into drier areas.[205] Another novelty was the big vermin-proof ceramic container (widely known as a pithos, from the later Greek) for long-term storage of produce, while no less significantly one archaic variety of wheat was rejected, signalling the first stage in its path towards global extinction a few millennia later.[206] As will be recalled, olives had been gathered and pressed to extract oil substantially earlier, initially in wild form. By now, generations of artificial propagation (and perhaps grafting, which was certainly known by the Bronze Age) in pursuit of greater yields had led to their domestication, ahead of the rest of the Mediterranean by two to four millennia. Aside from Tuleilat Ghassul, the best evidence comes from the uplands, notably a cache of 1200 stones at Modi'in west of Jerusalem, an extraction vat at Rasm Harbush in the Golan and further new finds from Jordan.[207] Evidence of grape cultivation and wine production is numerically less impressive, but fortified by the useful fact that after the Last Glacial Maximum (when wild examples were gathered at Ohalo II), the grapevine's natural range retreated north, with the result that any pips found in the Copper Age south should imply introduced, cultivated plants.[208] Cornets may have been used for drinking wine, though their mounting on the Gilat ram argues rather for milk-based liquids. Among potential sweeteners, the fig was local and long cultivated, but the date palm and pomegranate were neither, even if the latter would become so closely tied to the Levant via its association with a later Phoenician love goddess that its Linnaean name means the 'Punic fruit'. Copper Age dates and pomegranates have been found in dry caves in the Judaean hills, including one whose additional treasures (to be revealed shortly) argue that eating exotic fruits was a high-status or ceremonial practice.[209]

An equivalent range of animal secondary products were by now in use too, if probably still on a small scale. Milk and its derivatives were nothing new, but the cultural emphasis on churns hints at a new prominence, maybe connected to hard, more transportable cheeses.[210] Lesions on cattle bones suggest, as at several other places across the basin, that some dragged heavy loads, but, as elsewhere, quite what is uncertain, and there is as yet no unambiguous sign of ploughing.[211] Last but not least, sheep or goat wool began to be sheared, spun and woven, probably for the first time. Sheep in particular are today inextricably linked to wool, but the first domesticates had short outer coats, like their wild progenitors. It took selective breeding, maybe initially for other goals in the chilly highland margins of the Fertile Crescent, to produce fleecy outer coats.[212] Once available, the great advantages of wool over linen were its easier processing for plain products, and (as soon as white rather than the original brown hair was bred for) superior retention of colour dyes for fancier ones.[213] Its coming enabled a polychrome, patterned world of textiles to develop, of which the brightly garbed painted figures at Tuleilat Ghassul are a premonition. The first Copper Age evidence comes from dry Levantine caves: preserved scraps dyed to a colour palette similar to the Tuleilat Ghassul murals and, as an unlooked-for bonus, fragments of a wooden ground-pegged flat loom of the kind that long remained standard in the Levant and Egypt, in distinction to the vertical looms by now becoming characteristic of Europe and Anatolia.[214]

Adopting a broader perspective, this expanded suite of Levantine Late Copper Age farming activities was of unique sophistication for its time in the Mediterranean, preceding by millennia anything equivalent elsewhere in the basin, and establishing practices that would remain central to agrarian life there until recent times. Why was the Levant so advanced in this respect? The answers lie in a rare set of circumstances. One was the advantage of being first. By 5000 BC elements of farming were 4000 or more years old in the Levant, while in the west and Egypt they had only arrived a few centuries earlier. Over those four millennia the Levant had experienced an entire cycle of trial and error with ways of getting the most out of plants and animals, including the vital low-profile efforts of its Late Neolithic – for example, the kind of long-term investment implied in cultivating olives, which can take a decade to mature and only fruit every second year, is manifestly not a first-generation farmer's strategy.[215] By the time this complex had crystallized, large-scale expansion of farmers with their way of life was a thing of the past in the east, and the alternatives, namely diffusion or local uptake, would take a lot longer to disseminate. In fact, looking ahead to Chapters 9 and 10, only when generalized mobility returned to the Mediterranean as a major dispersal mechanism in the Iron Age would this suite of practices spread to every corner of the basin. Another factor was the Levant's adjacency to other, non-Mediterranean regions themselves generating transferrable innovations, notably woolly sheep and vines to the northeast. This increased the pool of options to an unusual degree. Crucial, too, was the fact that some of the new approaches improved chances of survival in an uncertain climate, lessening the risk by spreading it over more crops, improving storage and easing transport, and it is extremely relevant in this respect that the end of the early Holocene optimum hit the relatively dry Levant sooner, and harder, than most other parts of the basin. Lastly, in the Late Copper Age these forms of farming were operated by some of the most complex communities in the Mediterranean, and it is therefore worth asking whether some had begun to harness them for ends beyond the household level. As was alluded to in Chapter 5, the enormous potential of such practices was their applicability at any scale from a modest and prudently diversified household economy to the stupendous wealth generation of a landed elite. At this early stage the jury is out, but on balance any incipient shift towards more optimized zoning of activities (with olive and vine cultivation in the hills, cereals in the plains and sheep and goat herding in the uplands and steppe fringes) is more likely to reflect community-level selection of the best combination and emphasis for their particular niche, plus the circulation of specialized products through social and, as we have seen, cultic networks, rather than any overarching regional economic management.

So far, our portrait of the Late Copper Age Levant has been rather lacking in the medium that gives its name to the age. There are advantages to this, as excessive enthusiasm on the part of archaeologists for metals from too early a date can distort interpretation of the societies that they only later helped to transform. But we can now complete our exploration by highlighting this last realm of Levantine (and Anatolian) dynamism. For the Levant and Anatolia comprised the most advanced of the several foci of metalcrafting arising around the basin. We saw in Chapter 5 that copper even preceded pottery at central and southeast Anatolian sites near the ores. In the 6th millennium BC, Anatolia continued to set the pace, with the casting of small objects, simple axes and chisels.[216] The mid-5th millennium start of the Late Copper Age saw further advances, such as larger tools, two-piece moulds for fully three-dimensional forms like shaft-hole axes, multifaceted moulds for the flexible casting of any one among a selection of small objects, the first silver, and, now if not earlier, deliberate alloying (a technique hard to prove given the often naturally mixed Taurus sources), especially in the form of arsenical additions to copper.[217] Somewhere between Anatolia, the Balkans and the remaining circum-Pontic regions, the dagger first appeared as a new special-purpose, two-edged fighting weapon with no stone precedent and a great future ahead of it.[218] The best evidence derives from Arslantepe and Değirmentepe, the latter close to the ores of southeast Anatolia, and both outside the Mediterranean basin, but similar activities took place in Cilicia and the Amuq. It is hard to deny a link between this growth in proficiency and Ubaid Mesopotamia's interest in acquiring and consuming metals.

Of more immediate concern is the emergence during the 5th millennium BC of a new centre of extraction and production in the southern Levant.[219] This was mainly based on copper from Wadi Arabah, especially Feinan in Jordan [PL. XXVII], though arsenical copper, not a naturally occurring alloy in the south, also reveals imported Anatolian or Caucasian metal. One striking organizational feature, apparently shared with Anatolia, is that smelting to liberate the metal from the ore took place at the consuming villages rather than the mines themselves, the two 100 km (60 miles) apart in the case of the Beersheba settlements, which were notably active in this respect.[220] This ostensibly bizarre habit argues that the first ores were extremely copper-rich relative to their weight, that the amounts of metal produced were modest (a supposition backed up by the fact that at Shiqmim stone axes outnumber copper ones at a ratio of 250:1), and that control over the transformational mysteries of metallurgy was guarded by village authorities, perhaps behind the compound walls of wealthier households (the secrecy surrounding imported arsenical alloys was even greater, and extends to their virtual invisibility at the working stage to this day).[221]

The most spectacular metal finds in the southern Levant were discovered in 1961 in a remote cave high in the sheer cliffs of the Nahal Mishmar Gorge, which cuts through the Judaean hills close to the southern end of the Dead Sea [6.30].[222] Like the Cave of the Warrior, they were a happy by-product of the search for further Dead Sea Scrolls, and of derdoing worthy of Indiana Jones. Over 400 metal items weighing 140 kg (310 lbs) were hidden here, alongside 6 of hematite (iron ore), 6

6.30 The Nahal Mishmar hoard as found, following the intrepid exploration of small caves high in the cliff face.

of hippopotamus ivory, several pots and a wealth of organic goods, notably the wool-related remnants mentioned earlier, along with linens, olives, nuts and pomegranates [PL. XXII]. The timing is controversial, maybe about 4000–3500 BC, though the (antique?) reed mat used to wrap the objects offers a somewhat earlier date.[223] The surrounding circumstances are equally obscure. Corpses in the adjacent chambers could intimate a funerary rite, but a dramatic alternative is that the items belonged to the Ein Gedi shrine, and were hidden away at the end of Copper Age.[224] Such imponderables aside, what can be said for certain is exciting enough. Among the contents are 10 cylindrical crowns sprouting animal totems, over 100 standards with fluted, incised or knobbed designs, some surmounted by ibexes (maybe together with gazelle taking the place of deer further west, as symbols of wild, male domains), 260 maceheads, a very widespread weapon before the rage for daggers, several drinking horns and 4 small jars, altogether an utterly undreamt of demonstration of metallic wealth and technical virtuosity. Pure copper was used for simple tools but arsenical copper for more complex, cast items. The latter, although of imported metals, were made in the south at several locations, for their stone cores are of local rocks, including Wadi Arabah chalk.[225] The most ambitious were cast by the lost-wax technique, in which the metal is poured into a closed mould shaped around an original of the object made in wax, which melts away. At first glance the Nahal Mishmar treasure might prompt us to revise our scepticism concerning the rise of chiefly rulers, but a cooler appraisal reveals that though obviously intended to invest certain people with glitter and authority, its components have not been found in their original context of use, and the repetition of a limited number of insignia indicates a considerable number of eligible users – while 'crown', of course, is our term for objects whose symbolic connotations at the time may have been entirely different.[226]

How the northern component of Nahal Mishmar's metals arrived is unknown. In contrast to the robust maritime networks emerging in other parts of the basin, there is surprisingly little evidence of sea traffic in the easternmost Mediterranean at this juncture, with a gulf between the watchers on Mersin's battlements and the reticent islanders of Cyprus that is far wider than the sea-gap between them. It is tempting to explain this as an index of the degree to which the rise of Mesopotamia temporarily shifted the gaze of coastal dwellers at the northern end of the Levant to the east, and inland. An intriguing argument for one exception around 5500–4500 BC involves the large nodules of Anatolian obsidian (one weighing 22 kg or 48 lbs) found on the coast at Tell Arqa in northern Lebanon and Tel Kabri in northern Israel.[227] These might indeed be relics of a canoe traffic between such natural entry-points to the interior, but overland transport cannot be ruled out. Furthermore, even if movement by sea was responsible, was this the last hurrah of the ancient obsidian trade before its eclipse by metals, or the germ of a new kind of coastal, middleman activity with a long future ahead of it?

Such northern connections are matched by no less significant finds entering the Levant from further south. Egypt is the only plausible source for eight rings of gold or electrum, a natural silver-gold alloy, found in the Nahal Qana burial cave [PL. XIX]. Their size (4.3–5 cm (1.7–2 in.) in diameter) and much later Egyptian parallels raise the thought-provoking possibility that they served as early ingots of standard weight and value.[228] Nile shells and even fish remains show up in the southern Levant, as well as the first turquoise from southern Sinai and a few Egyptian stone bowls.[229] The ivory at Nahal Mishmar and elsewhere may hail from the Nile too, though herds of hippopotami still wallowed in Levantine swamps. In return, and following the inflow of domesticates, the copper found at Maadi and further up the Nile is likely to be of south Levantine extraction, probably routed via the Beersheba Valley. These flows represent only a trickle over roughly a millennium, and in this case there is little doubt that they passed overland along the dry shores of northern Sinai, which is studded with the remains of small pastoral encampments at this time.[230] With this return to Egypt our investigation comes full circle, and to the threshold of a new age in the Mediterranean.

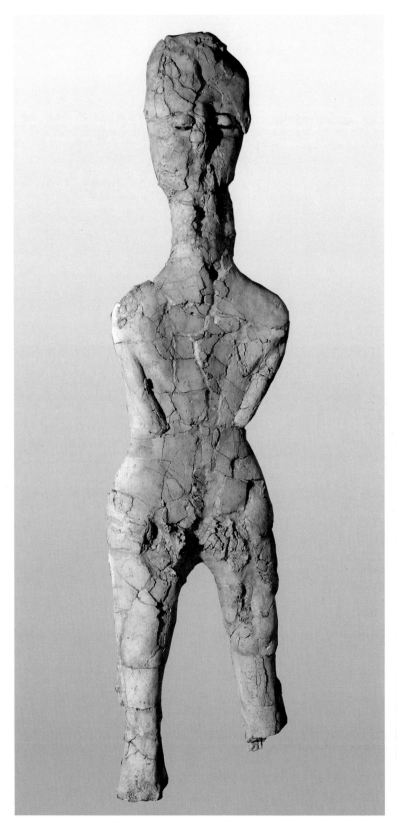

XII (*previous page*) The tell site of Jericho, showing the decayed condition today of the great trenches dug through it in the 1950s, with the functionally enigmatic Pre-Pottery Neolithic A circular stone tower in the foreground, and a glimpse of the surrounding green oasis and its Rift Valley margins beyond.

XIII (*left*) One among many of the large human figures discovered at the Pre-Pottery Neolithic B megasite of 'Ain Ghazal in modern Jordan; plaster construction on a reed core, with bituminous mastic outlines for the eyes.

XIV (*right*) This stone mask, with its traces of green and red paint, as well as asphalt adhesive for attached hair, is one of the many remarkably preserved finds from Pre-Pottery Neolithic B storage of ritual apparatus at the dry cave of Nahal Hemar, southwest of the Dead Sea.

XV (*below*) Among the famous wall-paintings at Çatalhöyük, the great Neolithic megasite high on the Anatolian plateau, are prominent images of still-wild aurochs, the ancestors of domestic cattle, surrounded by frenetically active human figures.

XVI (*opposite*) The towering southern cliffs of the little island of Pantelleria, in the Sicilian strait, face towards North Africa and contain seams of a distinctive greenish obsidian that was widely used over the south-central Mediterranean. Above, the later intensive agricultural terracing so typical of many Mediterranean islands has obliterated much of the island's early archaeological record.

XVII (*right*) Early rock engraving of cattle being milked at Tiksatin, Libyan Sahara.

XVIII (*below*) Restored design of brightly coloured wall-paintings from the south Levantine Copper Age site of Tuleilat Ghassul, just north of the Dead Sea, offering glimpses of contemporary ritual and symbolism, as well as the advent of richly woven polychrome textiles.

XIX Eight gold and electrum rings, up to 5 cm (2 in.) in diameter, from the Copper Age use of Nahal Qana Cave, today in northern Israel. The metal is probably Egyptian, and the approximately standardized ring-form and rough finish may suggest an early variety of ingot.

XX (*below*) The Copper Age shrine complex at Ein Gedi, located on a high bluff near a copious spring, overlooking the dry country immediately west of the Dead Sea. The outlines of an enclosure, gateway and ritual buildings, plus a central circular structure, are clearly visible. Such prominent places acted as magnets for regional interaction and possibly 'pilgrimage'.

XXI From another Copper Age sacred complex, that of Gilat on the fringe of the Negev, today in southern Israel's arid zone, comes this remarkable figurine of a seated woman with prominent sexual features, tattoos and, balanced on her head, a milk-processing churn characteristic of this period in the southern Levant.

XXII (*overleaf*) A selection from among the hundreds of finds from an exceptionally rich Copper Age hoard hidden in the Nahal Mishmar Cave, among the tall cliffs of Judea, seen here after restoration (compare with fig. 6.30). These include so-called 'crowns', standards, maceheads and various vessels, made of pure or alloyed copper, as well as a large perforated item carved from hippopotamus ivory.

CHAPTER SEVEN

The devil and the deep blue sea

(3500 – 2200 BC)

Flights of fancy

Imagine two series of flights around the Mediterranean in one of the slow, low-flying seaplanes that Braudel delighted in over half a century ago. The first takes place in the time span of the previous chapter, around 5000 BC. Then 2500 years later the journey is repeated. By the mid-3rd millennium BC, an aerial traveller would find the Mediterranean profoundly altered. The most obvious difference would be the colours and textures of its landscapes. Despite the basin's eternal variegation, the later flights, especially if undertaken in summer, would have passed over a generally drier, more dun-coloured land, with fewer solid expanses of trees. Along the southern shore the tawny desert has crept closer to the sea. A sharp eye for wisps of smoke or the twinkle of fires at dusk would reveal marked changes in the places and aggregates in which people lived. The earlier flights would have detected a predictable pattern of lowland clusters and much intervening wilderness on the northern and eastern flanks, with the traces thinner but widespread across North Africa. But two-and-a-half millennia later, all this has altered. Settlement has spread over far more of the northern side of the basin, even to unprepossessing areas. By contrast, populated zones have shrunk drastically in North Africa. Heading east, unprecedented concentrations of people would start to be sighted, first (and in stark contrast to the sparseness elsewhere on this side of the Mediterranean) a mass of habitations in the verdant triangle of the Nile Delta, with a vast smudge vaguely glimpsed just to its south, and then, as the pilot swings up the coast and the sun sinks, imparting to the sea a metallic sheen, a few large, dense pools of firelight north of the Lebanese mountains. Our traveller's hunch might well be that there were more people living around the Mediterranean as a whole than ever before, and if tempted to speculate, a guess of 5 to 10 million might come to mind.[1] Less open to question would be the fact that many of these millions have started to live in quite different ways from their ancestors.

Further reconnaissance would help to pinpoint some of these differences. Most astonishing would be the sheer scale of activity in certain regions. A return in daylight to the northern Levant, for example, would reveal the great pools of firelight to emanate from large towns, ringed with great walls and centred on a grand building with courtyards, columns and multiple tiers of rooms. On closer inspection, some

7.1 Map of principal sites mentioned in this chapter, also showing the four major maritime networks of the 3rd millennium BC, the main axes of connections beyond the basin and (inset) the rise of consolidated states in Egypt and Mesopotamia.

of the occupation in the Nile Delta would resolve into extensive regular compounds with cellular mud-brick buildings, set in large, neatly ploughed fields and vineyards. From the Jordan Valley to Iberia, small- to medium-sized fortified settlements, a few dominated by one or more outsized houses, would attract attention. A sweep over Malta, on the other hand, would find an island studded with strange half-roofed, cloverleaf-shaped structures built of colossal, well-fitted blocks of stone, and from here westward great masses of stones and earth, many burial monuments half-sunk

Main zones of maritime and associated long-range interaction

Main links in/out of the Mediterranean

Possible sail/canoe link

Velika Gruda, Mala Gruda

-RIATIC

Troy
Poliochni
Manika
Thebes
Strophylas
Chalandriani
Kastri
Nemea
Tiryns
Kolonna
Lerna
Dhaskalio-
Kavos
Kastri
Knossos
Malia
AEGEAN
Mochlos
Phaistos
Myrtos

Alacahöyük
Mahmatlar
Küllüoba
Kestel/Göltepe
Tarsus
Arslantepe
Hammam
Habuba Kebira
Tell Brak
Ebla
Umm el-Marra
Hama
Mari
Vounous
Lapithos
Vasilia
Ras
Shamra/
Ugarit
Qatna
Mosphilia
Byblos
Sidon
Tyre
Tel Dan
Hazor
Khirbet Umbashi
Beth Yerah
Jawa
EGYPTIAN-
LEVANTINE
Megiddo
Ai
Tell esh-Shuna
Tel Yarmouth
Tel Erani
Tell Ibrahim Awad
Mendes
Ashkelon
Arad
Tell el-Fara'in/Buto
Tell el-Sakan
En Besor
Haua Fteah
Minshat Abu
Omar
Wadi Feinan
Sais
Marsa Matruh
Tell el-Farkha
Maadi
Bubastis
Memphis,
Saqqara, Giza

in the landscape, would be a common sight. The sea itself would seem more alive, on a lucky day with a white flash of a sail catching the light in the eastern seas, or a long, slender, paddled canoe surging its way over the waves, perhaps far out to sea between France and the peaks of Mallorca. Only in Africa west of the Nile would signatures be subdued compared with the earlier passage, the plumes of dust from animals and herders on the move rarer than before, and often resolving, as the plane dives down to inspect, into a scrambling troupe of goats. And to the traveller's frustration, over the Maghreb a mysteriously persistent veil of Atlantic fog obscures much of the view day after day, leaving nobody any the wiser.

Had our curious explorer been able to touch down close to habitation, perhaps not always a wise idea, unless well armed, one additional distinction would soon have become obvious. The Mediterranean had always been home to diverse groups of people, but until now most of the variation had been horizontal, between regions or, at the community scale, between members who performed different roles within broadly egalitarian societies. By 2500 BC, however, and indeed several centuries before this, vertical gradations of status and wealth have emerged to a dramatic degree in widely separate parts of the basin, so much so that Mediterranean individuals might now be far apart not only in terms of space and ways of life, but also their power over others and the elaboration of the cultural universe around them. Much of this archaeologists can infer from the kinds of remains routinely available. We are fortunate, however, in the survival of two particular people, men born within a couple of centuries of each other near the close of the 4th millennium BC, both of whom achieved an elevated position (if in very different ways), and, although strictly speaking interlopers in the basin, both exemplary nonetheless of the growing distinctions within it.

The first, an experienced man of about forty-five at time of death, had been forgotten for over five millennia when his frozen body emerged from the ice 3200 m (10,500 ft) up in the Tyrolese Alps in the summer of 1991, a gift of global warming abetted by the nicely trans-Mediterranean event of a fall of Saharan dust.[2] Tattooed, 1.65 m (5 ft 5 in.) tall, probably brown-eyed and accompanied by the remnants of high-altitude clothing and other gear [**7.2**, **7.3**], this 'Iceman' and the circumstances of his death have attracted an inordinate amount of forensic, not to say prurient, attention. X-rays have detected a flint arrowhead embedded in his shoulder, and the blood of four people is said to have been spattered over his possessions. Yet, despite the exceptional and cruelly undignified manner in which he came to our attention, the Iceman's way of life is likely to have been typical of many people living around the mountainous borders of Mediterranean Europe at this time. He was, for example, no stranger to metals or frequent illness. A copper axe hafted in yew was found beside him, and his hair retained traces of metalworking; less happily, he suffered from arthritis,

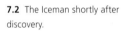
7.2 The Iceman shortly after discovery.

7.3 A reconstruction of the Iceman on the move, including cold-weather grass cape, knapsack, bow and other equipment.

diarrhoea and sundry other complaints. He was also highly mobile, whether as a herder, hunter, trader or fugitive, a conclusion drawn from the backpack and self-sufficient survival kit he carried, with its fire-lighting equipment, medicinal substances, knife, bow and arrows, as well as hints from pollen analysis that he had recently spent time in farmland further south.

The physical body of our second man has never been rediscovered, or at least re-identified, and one later tradition has it that he was killed by a hippopotamus. But its idealized, muscular form has been immortalized in art, and his name, written with the signs of a catfish and a chisel, was proclaimed all along the Nile, his home river, on desert rocks between it and the Red Sea and on pots in the southern Levant.[3] The surviving depictions, which he commissioned, announce that he too was a fighter (or a leader of fighters and mass decapitators of prisoners), as well as a man on the move over long distances. Here, however, the similarities end. For while the Iceman's body was clad in leather, fur and grass, riddled with disease and probably stank, this second body, we can surmise, was dressed in fine linens, crowned, perfumed, flushed with wine, shaded from the sun and elevated above the ground – and even its footwear was carried with ceremony by an attendant. And while the Iceman may have been widely known among small communities along the Adige, his counterpart claimed authority beneath new gods over at least a million people, a third of whom dwelt within the Mediterranean basin. This second individual is the pharaoh Narmer, best known for a carved stone ceremonial palette that ranks among the most evocative, if disturbing, icons of early kingship [**7.4**]. Even allowing for the manifest self-glorification, Narmer was one of a brief sequence of Egyptian rulers

7.4 The two faces of the Narmer palette, with their rich imagery of royal power and cosmological order.

who forged a unified Egyptian kingdom extending right to the mouths of the Nile, as well as an ideology of divine kingship and cosmic order that underpinned this and infused it with spiritual significance. His name was in all likelihood more widely renowned than any other up to this point in world history. Between these two near-contemporaries lies a yawning chasm, whose span measures the distinctions in the scale and scope of power now emerging in the Mediterranean.

This chapter investigates what we can usefully conceptualize as the 'long' 3rd millennium BC, a critical time span extending back into the later 4th millennium, and that witnessed four epochal developments. The first was the onset of a drier climate, and so the gradual formation of the Mediterranean environment as we know it today. Twinned with this from birth was the resurgence of desert in the Sahara. The second was the expansion of the first large-scale societies, Egyptian and Mesopotamian, into the easternmost parts of the basin, and their impact on people living there, a turn of events that will require us to consider the role of such influences over a widening area for the remainder of this book. Egypt and Mesopotamia, along with the Indus Valley in Pakistan and China's Yellow River, comprise the four early foci of such societies over the entirety of Eurasia and Africa, and their proximity to the Mediterranean is a decisive coincidence whose importance for the basin's subsequent history is hard to exaggerate. Our third development is the appearance of smaller, but no less novel, societies over the northern half of the basin, a phenomenon anticipated in Chapter 6 and now examined in full. The fourth dimension of this crux in Mediterranean history is a boom in long-range activity, especially by sea. Individually vital as each of these undoubtedly was, the ultimate key to understanding the overall transformation of the Mediterranean over the 'long' 3rd millennium BC lies in evaluating the relatedness, or autonomy, of each of these developments relative to the others.

Environmental mediterraneanization

Major environmental changes played out across the Mediterranean basin during the 4th and 3rd millennia BC.[4] Some of the first hints came from shifts among dominant plant communities: at the risk of over-simplification, from deciduous trees and lowland woods to greatly reduced, typically dry-leaf or coniferous tree cover and the spread of tough, often thorny, scrub (prickly oak, wild olive, pistachio and other hardy plants), interspersed with low, herb-rich growth, open savannah sparsely dotted with trees, or steppe, blending into semi- or full desert in the driest areas. In a theatre as varied as the Mediterranean, such shifts were neither simultaneous nor uniform in incidence and degree. Many thinly soiled limestone uplands had long been cloaked with nothing more than scrub, while in certain relatively well-watered areas, including rain-snaring mountain ranges, the broadleaf woods survived in strength until Roman or later times, and sometimes are still with us.[5] Thousands more years were needed to create in full the remarkable ecology seen today, but individually significant details cannot mask a fundamental truth: the 'long' 3rd millennium's transition denotes the end of the earlier Holocene Mediterranean, and the emergence of a familiar regime, ancestral to that of modern times.

One school of thought holds that the triggers of this momentous change were primarily anthropogenic and signify the stage at which Mediterranean people's impact first becomes widely detectable, as communities expanded out of their initial farming zones to clear and exploit more of the landscape, in growing numbers and utilizing a widening panoply of agricultural techniques. There is definitely some truth to this.[6] Broadleaf oaks grew best on the same soils that farmers sought to cultivate, and the reduction of their woodland was accordingly only a matter of time.[7] Traces in certain areas of growing soil erosion and more frequent fires accompanying the vegetational changes are themselves causally ambiguous, but today, at least, it is a combination of freshly exposed, sun-parched earth (burnt, bulldozed, ploughed up or overgrazed – though the last less often than the goat's many detractors would have us believe) and violent summer rainstorms that results in the worst soil loss.[8] Moreover, in a telling parallel, sediments from the Río Tinto, and downstream in the Gulf of Cadiz, reveal that metal extraction in the great ore-belt of southwest Spain was certainly starting to contaminate waterways – some of the earliest industrial pollution in the world.[9]

Yet despite this contributing human factor, new research has now established beyond doubt that a cumulative shift towards drier climates and environments was a central fact of the 4th- and 3rd-millennia BC Mediterranean, itself part of a worldwide pattern triggered by changing solar radiation levels, associated with a southward drift of the monsoon belt, and arguably the last major alteration in the Earth's climate until that of the present day.[10] The case for the Mediterranean is clinched by a convergence of data. Several clues derive from botanical details. For example, vegetation changed in Tunisia, which was inhabited at low intensity, and even in the Balearics when these were still devoid of people.[11] Species of trees that once flourished in the basin but now grow only in or beyond its northern margins vanished even from the most inaccessible cliffs, where they would have been safe from grazing animals.[12] Meanwhile, eastern Mediterranean seabed cores reveal the end of the last organic-rich layers indicative of abundant freshwater run-off, while those drilled into lake-beds document permanent drops in water levels from southern Spain to Turkey, as well as in much of North Africa.[13] In the most severe cases, coastal lagoons turned into salt flats, notably that bordering the Tavoliere, whose desertion during the later Neolithic we witnessed in the last chapter.[14] Of course, as hinted by the pattern of vegetation change, drying was typically gradual and staggered in time and space. At a crude level it began in the hotter, more arid south and east, sometimes before 4000 BC, and spread as a rolling frontier that only reached the wettest parts of the north (if ever) after the end of this chapter's time span, and with the usual regional anomalies – the southern Levant, for example, enjoyed a significant wet spell around 3000 BC within a wildly see-sawing long-term decline, while Lake Tigalmamine in Atlantic Morocco, a maverick counter-case attributable to its high altitude and oceanic climate, actually expanded.[15]

This slow but profound transformation of the Mediterranean's environments is crucial to our history for two related reasons. One consequence of drier times would have been increasingly unpredictable rainfall, variously bringing drought, flash-floods or, with luck, something in between. In other words, what was underway was not just the mediterraneanization of a natural environment, but the emergence of the regime of risk and opportunity identified in Chapters 1 and 2 as decisive to the shaping of later Mediterranean societies. Even if the incidence of disaster or bonanza was sporadic – crop-threatening droughts occur every five to ten years in many parts of the modern basin, or several times in the lifetime of someone who survives to adulthood – it was now frequent enough for coping strategies to make sense for human actors, and to be put permanently in place precisely because the call upon them was so unpredictable. As alluded to in Chapter 1, one key to surviving and flourishing under such conditions was to invest in storage, both of water by retention mechanisms, and foods by ancient preservation tricks such as salting, drying and smoking, newer ones like conversion of milk into cheese, 'storage on the hoof', by which animals fattened during a good year could be eaten in a lean one, and, for farmers, primarily overproduction of crops and retention of surplus beyond that needed as seed, at a household or community level.[16] In contrast to the seasonal nature of most hunter-gatherer storage this encompassed inter-annual timescales, up to two years for cereals, whose shelf life began to matter more than previously. Another option was to diversify, spreading eggs between baskets. And a third was to go mobile. For farmers, the limits to this last in terms of residence were narrower than for pastoralists, and their mobility would mainly entail movement of foodstuffs to respond effectively to dearth or glut, as well as a massively enhanced investment in networks of association and reciprocal assistance between communities, a form of 'social' rather than physical storage that buffered collectively for far longer than even durable foods could survive.[17] As Horden and Purcell put it, such a suite of practices is 'extraordinarily resilient; it cushions against sudden disaster; it absorbs pressures and defuses stresses; it is malleable and ductile, hard to snap under strain'.[18] What archaeologists have been slow to recognize, however, is the fact that this highly anti-autarkous, connective kind of behaviour, far from being intrinsic to Mediterranean life since the spread of farming, would have started to become radically more prominent in the 'long' 3rd millennium BC, as the new environmental regime bit home among a population overwhelmingly committed to agriculture. Initially imperceptibly, but ingrained year after year, century after century, this would slowly but remorselessly reshape, within each micro-region, many of the essentials of life around the basin.

And that leads us to the second reason why all this matters so much. For it is otherwise the strangest of coincidences that the Mediterranean should have witnessed its first widespread, sustained signs of rising social inequalities just as its environment was altering in this way. In the trusting days of the 1970s, such emergent elites were argued to have played a beneficial role in managing and pooling the resources of a patchwork ecology for the general good, a 'friendly bank manager model' that grows more implausible with each passing year.[19] If such altruistic motives figured at all, they faded quickly. Cooperative survival networks were in fact chronically susceptible to the accumulation of imbalances over time that would create build-ups of social debt and obligation to the fortunate few, unless strong mechanisms were in place to counter them. A further unpalatable truth is that in adversity cooperation may not always be the most advantageous strategy. It can be impractical, for instance, if the harvesting season is so abbreviated that everyone has to look to their own in the same few weeks.[20] Moreover, competition or naked aggression might prove more attractive to those able to muster the force for it, and such rule breaking is notoriously liable to be emulated, out of cupidity or tit-for-tat necessity, if initially rewarded.[21] All this has long been recognized by those trying to explain social change in the Mediterranean, and beyond it lies the intriguing possibility that the riskier conditions in themselves promoted innovation and mental agility.[22] Yet what *is* new is the fact that the better climate and environmental data now enable us to calibrate factors once generically equated to Holocene farming conditions more decisively to a phase beginning in and around the 3rd millennium BC.[23] It would be naive to identify climate as the sole cause of the extraordinary social changes we shall witness in this chapter; several are of wider incidence than the Mediterranean, or originate beyond it, others were rooted in a deeper past, and, last but not least, we need to distinguish between meteorological statistics, the complexity of real-world environments, and people's engagements with both, the links between which involve translations in which much is altered.[24] But equally, climate change has too long been the missing element in our understanding of what happened in the Mediterranean over the 'long' 3rd millennium, and it is high time we asked how the environmental mediterraneanization it engendered meshed with other currents to reshape life throughout the basin.

The return of the Sahara

Let us start far to the south, in a region where the devastating role of desiccation has never been in doubt. Changes across North Africa go a long way towards explaining why the inhabitants of the coastal strip west of the Nile, never prominent on the radar screens of most archaeologists, dwindle almost to invisibility for the next 2000 or so years. As the monsoon belt slid southward, subtle gradations in residual rainfall over the vast area of the Sahara ensured that the desert's resurrection was far from even.[25] In the east, now one of the driest places on earth, it began with terminally falling lakes slightly before 4000 BC. In the west, nearest the ocean, it dates a thousand years later, when Saharan dust appears in Atlantic sea cores and as accumulations on Lanzarote. In the centre, an intermediate date around 3800 BC can be pinned in the Fezzan by a horizon of wind-blown sand and collapsing cave roofs.[26] By 3000 BC at the latest the Sahara had become a true desert, its former lakes reduced to salt flats and laminated silts, its wadis dry as a bone. Only where long-accumulated subterranean reservoirs breached the surface as oases, for instance at Wadi Tannezzuft west of the Acacus,[27] or in mountainous regions that still snagged the occasional rain cloud (nowadays 5–12 mm (0.2–0.5 in.) of rain falls in a good year), could people continue to operate. Those who did stay substituted hardier goats for cattle, and it was in this Late Pastoral phase (3800 BC until well into the 2nd millennium BC) that an ultra-mobile nomadic pattern, of people and animals constantly on the move between small, dispersed patches of grazing, began to shape.[28] Unsurprisingly, the relics of these stopovers are ephemeral, often no more than stone tumuli and layers of animal dung, though something of the varied groups inhabiting the desert is hinted by notable differences among the skeletons of those buried beneath the piled-up stones. However, most of the population departed the lost heartland of North Africa, whether to the south (where pastoralism eventually reached the Cape of Good Hope, another mediterraneoid land, beyond the intervening tsetse fly belt, around the start of the 1st millennium AD), to the west, where cattle, sheep and goats appear at Dhar Tichitt in Mauritania by 1500 BC, or to the Mediterranean coast and the Nile, areas that concern us more closely.[29]

For Mediterranean Africa beyond the Nile Delta, the rebirth of the Sahara spelt a return to the conditions its inhabitants had endured during the Last Glacial Maximum, when the Maghreb, Jebel el Gharbi and Cyrenaica were cut off by a combination of desert and sea, although this time their isolation would be lessened by slightly better survival abilities in the former and sporadic maritime contacts across the latter. The Maghreb remained a Mediterranean environment from the coast to the summits of the Atlas, with deciduous trees and stands of cedar at high altitudes.[30] Immediately to the south, here and elsewhere, lay a semi-desert of sparse scrub and achabs, plants that sprout only after a rare fall of winter rain, and whose presence would be well known to seasonal visitors.[31] Cyrenaica's 'green mountain' formed a smaller, drier equivalent far to the east. Between these, a speck of wooded hills held out in the Jebel el Gharbi, and juniper grew on offshore Djerba,[32] but most of the intervening coast along the Gulf of Sirte became, as it has remained to this day, a dry land interspersed with salt flats, where rainfall was too low to permit farming until water-harvesting techniques were developed, probably through local initiatives, in Roman times. Communications along this stretch ran inland, well back from the sea, via a chain of oases that connected with those west of the Nile Valley.[33]

From now until the early 1st millennium BC, these habitat islands were doubly orphaned. Formerly on the periphery of a Saharan world that revolved around cattle pastoralism rather than Mediterranean agriculture, and thereby probably routed even in areas suitable for the latter along a different course from the rest of the basin, they were now bereft of that defining focus. Refugees from the south must have percolated into Mediterranean Africa, but there is no indication that the core elements of Saharan pastoral culture outlived the loss of its heartland. The demise of the Saharan world has rendered these regions academic orphans, too, neither at home in mainstream African archaeology, nor (with a few exceptions) in that of the Mediterranean until the arrival of Phoenicians and Greeks, save when occasional contacts across the sea demand a footnote. Egyptian experts, likewise, tend to engage west of the Nile only

7.5 Among the weaponry depicted in the rock art from the High Atlas is that associated with this male figure, surrounded by other diverse symbols, and probably of approximately 3rd millennium BC date.

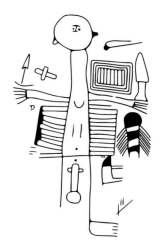

when drawn by texts mentioning encounters between cultivators on the alluvium and other people beyond its limits. All this makes it hard to evaluate whether the lack of self-evident developments in Mediterranean Africa west of the Nile in, and after, the 'long' 3rd millennium BC was a consequence of genuine quasi-isolation, or simply reflects a lack of dedicated looking. At present, the best guess is a substantial element of the former, obfuscated by a lot of the latter.

Starting with the Maghreb, a predominantly pastoral lifestyle is commonly assumed, but we in fact have no idea if, or how widely, agricultural enclaves existed in the west by this time. Given this ignorance, we cannot even begin to decide whether the Maghreb was a full and busy place, as its size, if under cultivation, would lead us to anticipate, a sparsely inhabited landscape of herders, or a mix of the two. A recent survey in the Rif encountered little except tumuli and a few cave occupations, and the best evidence instead comes from Atlantic Morocco.[34] Close to the ocean in the vicinities of Casablanca and Rabat, two later 4th- or 3rd-millennium BC cemeteries at El-Kiffen and Skhirat held the remains of people whose way of life is unknown but who were buried with pots, polished stone axes, flints, beads of ostrich egg, bracelets and small cups carved in elephant ivory, and a stone vessel. Two of these materials – ostrich egg and ivory – first reached Iberia in small amounts in the 3rd millennium BC.[35] In return, the western Maghreb as far as Algiers received a few Iberian objects, mainly decorated pots, copper tools and weapons.[36] Indigenous exchanges distributed these inland. Several of the metal forms appear in rock art high in the Atlas, at heights of 2500 m (8200 ft) that imply seasonal visitation [**7.5**].[37] Whether any local metallurgy was inspired by such imports is more a matter of faith or scepticism than proof either way, although copper may have been produced in West Africa south of the Sahara by this time.[38] Lastly, most of the megalithic tombs built in the Maghreb seem to date to the 2nd millennium BC, but one or two, and in particular an impressive enclosure with a more than 5-m- (16-ft-) high menhir at M'zora near Tangier [**7.6**], as well as cists in the vicinity, may be offshoots of earlier Iberian traditions.[39] They beg the question as to what else might lie beneath Tangier, known from Phoenician times as Tingi but, as the only

7.6 A North African megalith: the M'zora menhir near Tangier.

sheltered anchorage on the African side of the strait, presumably an older gateway. As before, the western end of the Maghreb displays closer contacts with other parts of the basin than anywhere else along the African shore until we reach the Nile Delta.

Further east, information is exceptionally thin. In Algeria there is a hint of growing numbers of sites, and an increase in cattle at Capeletti Cave shortly before its abandonment in the early 3rd millennium BC, both of which might reflect a Saharan influx.[40] Pottery around the gulfs of Gabès and Sirte ceased to be decorated, as it had been in accordance with Saharan conventions. At Haua Fteah the only sign of external contact is an Egyptian shell bracelet, traded between oases or along the coastal strip before this key cave site, too, went out of use, leaving it empty from about 3500 BC until the Iron Age.[41] A few Egyptian basalt vessels at Marsa Matruh, about a third of the way along the shoreline passage to Cyrenaica, support the latter route.[42] Elsewhere in Cyrenaica there are only scatters of stone tools and pottery, plus small tumuli and other burial sites.[43] In the mid-1st millennium BC, Herodotus stated that the indigenous people here had lived by sheep and goat herding, a standard derogatory colonial claim that we would normally wish to interrogate via the lens of archaeology, but in this case at least compatible with what little we know.[44]

The final direction open to those abandoning the Sahara was towards the slim oasis of the Nile. Even the Nile's flow reduced substantially around this time, but it remained a magnet nonetheless.[45] Indeed, as argued in the previous chapter, such influxes, resultant population pressure and aggregation may in part explain the switch to cereals, grown in annually inundated basins on the flanks of the river, as the main source of food by 3900 BC. Elements of the pastoral world had exerted a formative influence on the ritual preoccupations of Nile Valley society from an earlier date, notably the fixation on tombs and the sanctity of the body.[46] But despite this legacy, as sedentary farmers in the valley multiplied explosively over the course of the 4th and 3rd millennia BC, they differentiated themselves from residual pastoralists to the west. This, coupled with the physical barriers imposed by the Sahara, would make sense of the split between ancient Egyptian and the Berber languages, whose antecedents were presumably forming across the Sahara at this time.[47] A consciousness of 'them' versus 'us' is exemplified in the 3rd millennium BC by Egyptian contrasts between dwellers in the 'black land' of Nile silt, and those in the 'red land' of the desert. In fact, by this time Egyptian activity in the Western Desert was restricted to gazelle hunts and stone-quarrying operations, with few of the textual inscriptions that begin to pepper the Nile corridor incised more than 20 km (12 miles) from the valley's rim.[48] Skirmishes with 'Tjehenu' (usually translated as 'Libyans') are recorded, and an iconography of these people as vanquished enemies had evolved by 3000 BC.[49] Tjehenu also served as some of the earliest mercenary soldiers in Egypt, and others, probably those from the oases closest to the Nile, provided a fine oil of uncertain identity (but almost certainly not olive-based), and apparently lived in settled communities. Beyond this, Egyptian ignorance was only marginally less total than ours; the desert was too broad, and the coastal route to the west by land or sea too long, perilous and unrewarding. The same cannot be said, however, for the upriver Egyptian elites' view to the north.

The first superpowers:
Egypt and Mesopotamia

Along the upper Egyptian reaches of the Nile, and beside the rivers of Mesopotamia, ultimately world-impacting initiatives were afoot by the early 4th millennium BC, as we glimpsed offstage in Chapter 6. Their pace accelerated through the later 4th and 3rd millennia. The full reasons for this genesis lie beyond our remit, as does the question of whether a climatic common denominator underlaid social transformations here as well as in the Mediterranean (though a case can definitely be made).[50] Certainly, in both Egypt and Mesopotamia a dual riverine effect operated: the river as creator of alluvial lands made populous by farming, within which minor shifts in how things were done could amplify spectacularly, and the river as a conduit between zones with very different environments, resources and culture: highland Anatolia and the Persian Gulf for Mesopotamia, northeast Africa and the Levant for Egypt.[51] From the former perspective, the results were 'pristine' events, from the latter, far from virgin births.

Quite what we should call the political entities that emerged, typically focused on towns or cities, and ruling over a multitude of subjects spread over sometimes extremely extensive hinterlands, is an open question.[52] In their own day, the terms of reference were the land, its symbolic limits and its ruler, and it is not by chance that while most of the Mediterranean proceeds into Copper and Bronze ages, Egyptian and Mesopotamian chronology, as described by contemporaries and in our own day, shifts to a sequence defined by royal lifetimes or ruling places. Popular generic terms are 'polities', 'states' (later 'empires') and 'complex societies'. Each has advantages and drawbacks. The first is neutral and flexible enough to deal with the many smaller-scale and often politically fissile entities that would arise over the next 3000 years around the Mediterranean, though its mildness fails to convey the true grandeur and sanctity immanent in, for example, pharaonic Egypt. 'State', with its emphasis on organizational power, sets the bar appropriately high; as one expert puts it, 'If you can argue whether a society is a state or isn't, then it isn't.'[53] Nervousness of modernizing implications sometimes encourages the prefix 'archaic', or 'early', but this loses as much as it gains by disguising the sheer dynamism of these creations, as well as some disturbing parallels between ways of exerting power in their day and ours. 'Complex societies' opens up an interpretative vipers' nest. Such formations clearly did entangle very diverse kinds of people and groups, and supervised huge flows of material and information. But smaller social units could be 'complicated' in their own way (recall the Neolithic villages of Mediterranean Europe, or earlier Çatalhöyük),[54] and in fact one distinctive feature of the new regimes was a drive in certain sectors to simplify and thereby better control – for example by mass production, standardized weights and measures, and certain uses of the early writing associated with them.[55] All these terms, and others such as 'kingdom', will be deployed interchangeably henceforth, as seems intuitively appropriate. However we decide to name them, over the long term the economic impact of their spread across the Mediterranean lifted populations and aggregate wealth there to levels otherwise unattainable. Yet this, and the fact that their fabulous creations now fill the world's museums, should never disguise the other truth that, as one Iberian archaeologist puts it, their rise entailed 'success for the few and oppression, exploitation and coercion for the many'.[56] The wealth of the few came from many sources, but undoubtedly among them were taxes creamed off farmers reduced to peasantry, and the proceeds from sweated labour of the unfree in agrarian estates or manufactories. The proliferation of such institutions would bring new splendour, but also new dangers, toil and inequities, to many aspects of Mediterranean life.

The Egyptian and Mesopotamian paths to statehood were different and the outcomes distinctive. Although, as intimated in Chapter 6, the latter has chronological precedence, the desiccation of North Africa has already brought us to the banks of the Nile, and it is there that we accordingly begin, by tracing the expansion of a society that had only fully embraced farming a few centuries earlier, and never quite shaken off the cultural trappings of a pastoral ancestry (so, no lengthy economic or cultural Neolithic gestation here). Meteoric changes culminated by 3000 BC in the creation of the largest territorial state, and the most theocratic, then in existence.[57] At first, the cockpits of power accumulation and strife remained far upriver, circumscribed by the desert and thereby accentuated. The exact sequence of events is lost to us, but was assuredly less smooth than later Egyptian sources would have us believe. The players are no less shadowy, probably initially ritually sanctioned chiefs, each controlling the people, key resources and trade along a sector of the Nile corridor. Among the early winners were rulers at Hierakonpolis in the deep south, a sprawling expanse of houses in the shadow of a grand, decoratively indented, mud-brick facade. Hierakonpolis boasted some ostentatiously rich as well as numerous poor tombs, and was a city of the dead as much as the living. By the end of the 4th millennium BC, however, the consolidating crown had gone to Abydos, best known for its colossal burial monuments, which are associated with the early kings later grouped into a 1st Dynasty and their hazier precursors, known as Dynasty 0. In one of these (Tomb U-j, maybe that of the so-called 'Scorpion king'), the earliest Egyptian writing has been discovered, painted on pots and incised on labels attached to goods for the deceased [7.7]. The context is as redolent of royal ceremonial associations as of incipient bureaucracy.[58]

Meanwhile, the process of political expansion and spread of upriver African culture burst the bounds of the initial nuclear area, heading both upstream to subdue the territories of similarly emergent elites as far as what became known as Nubia and, of more interest to us, downstream into the Delta and the Mediterranean rim. Indeed, one of the many insights from Tomb U-j is the inclusion among the names written on the labels of Buto and Bubastis, both later known as major Delta towns.[59] This joins a mass of evidence, derived from later traditions, allusions on art objects sponsored by the early kings (not least to martial triumph there on Narmer's palette), and recently archaeology, that points to the Delta's incorporation in an emerging Egyptian state in the last centuries before 3000 BC.[60] There were compelling reasons to control this region. The ever-growing Delta was by now

7.7 Tomb U-j at Abydos: (*left*) pierced bone label showing a heron perched on a building, which can be read to denote a town name, possibly in the Delta, and arguably as a reference to the shrine of Djebaut at Buto; (*right*) view of the cellular architecture, with most of the finds removed.

7000–8000 sq. km (2700–3100 sq. miles) in extent, already comprised only slightly less than half the cultivatable land along the Egyptian Nile, and was home to several hundred thousand people.[61] In addition, although in many respects so far a sequestered area, it could potentially serve as a springboard to the Levant, with which it had long-term connections that gave access to desirable materials and technologies. Finally, it defined a natural boundary for a river-kingdom, even if its inhabitants and customs must have appeared foreign, even quasi-Levantine, to upriver eyes. What happened when these hitherto different worlds, that of the Nile Valley and the peri-Mediterranean land of the Delta, became integrated? To explore this, we need to take a closer look at the latter's archaeology, as it emerges from the enveloping silt.

Two sites, Buto itself (modern Tell el-Fara'in) and the cemetery of Minshat Abu Omar, are particularly informative.[62] The existence of both is a testimony to the Delta's expansion. The location of Buto still lay beneath the sea in 5000 BC, became divided from it by a belt of swamps a thousand years later, and by 3300 BC, a few centuries after the site was first occupied, already lay several kilometres inland amidst fertile mud a metre thick. Minshat Abu Omar's environs underwent a similar change from marsh to arable. In contrast to the tenor of later, reconciliatory Egyptian sources, which present the merger with the Nile Valley on equal terms, as the union of two crowns, archaeological indications of major indigenous hierarchies in the Delta are conspicuous by their absence.[63] Instead, all the signs point to a unilateral direction of influence, from south to north. At Buto, a typical Delta village of reed and daub huts, using local types of pottery was replaced a little after 3500 BC by mud-brick houses, matched by a leap in the amount of pottery of upriver style. At Minshat Abu Omar and other Delta cemeteries, funerary customs and rituals from the Nile Valley spring up suddenly in an area with apparently no previous commitment to elaborate burial. In these tombs, wealth and power claims are manifest; for example, the largest 2 per cent of the graves at Minshat Abu Omar contained 25 per cent of all the copper goods, and, intriguingly, the largest of all – graced with an indented interior facade similar to that at Hierakonpolis – held a nine-year-old child, whose status could have been hereditary, rather than due to its own efforts, given the age at death.[64] Whether these abrupt shifts in Delta life- and death-styles resulted from colonizing groups intruding from the valley, piecemeal conquest and pacification from that quarter, emulation of upriver ways of doing things by local people, or, most likely, a combination of all these, is secondary in the final assessment to the strident message of political and cultural annexation from the African interior over this corner of the Mediterranean.

The consolidation of a unified territorial state along the Nile continued into the 3rd millennium BC. During the Old Kingdom (27th to 22nd centuries BC) between 1 and 1.5 million Egyptians of diverse ancestry were ruled by a pharaoh as all-caring, perfect and terrible, at least in royal ideology, as only an incarnation of the god Horus could be.[65] Spanning the vertiginous gulf between king and commoner was an elite of officials, many members of the extended royal family. Some were present around the king, others governed the provinces into which Egypt became divided, or served as priests at the proliferating royal and regional temples, or in the mortuary cults that consolidated coevally with techniques of mummification. Living kings may have been peripatetic, a fitting strategy in a land linked by a single artery, but by 2800 BC, if not earlier, a capital was forming at Memphis (anciently known, among other names, as Ineb-hedj, or 'White Walls'), at the balance point between the Nile corridor and Delta. Because it was located on the valley floor (a popular choice as the annual inundations reduced) and is now deeply buried, we know absurdly little about this city hovering on the edge of the Mediterranean, save that it was enormous – estimates of 100–200 ha (250–500 acres), plus as much as 1100 ha (2700 acres) for a wider metropolitan area, have been hazarded.[66] On the low escarpment above Memphis stood Saqqara, Giza and their neighbours [7.8], a string of necropoleis in the midst of which arose the royal pyramids, manifestations of colossal labour in pursuit of the cosmic and salvational, on a scale inconceivable in the age of Narmer – whose palette, incidentally, was laid to rest around this time, already a relic of a bygone age, at the now-provincial town of Hierakonpolis.

Moving from Memphis towards the Mediterranean, how did its incorporation in this Egyptian state affect the Delta, home to roughly half a million people, or between one in two and one in three Nile-dwellers? [7.9] Many of its inhabitants continued to live in villages perched on turtle-backs, and a few aquatic communities survived on the water margins (the emblem of one northwestern province was the harpoon; scenes of elite sportfishing and hunting in reed swamps also abound in early Egyptian art).[67] But a radically new element had appeared in the landscape by 3000 BC, and arguably a century or two earlier. This was the royal or otherwise elite estate, planted on vast holdings of prime agricultural land that had been either seized or reclaimed from wilderness in the hitherto less populous western Delta.[68] Several such establishments have been excavated, revealing large, planned rectilinear complexes of buildings, and mass-produced coarse clay bread moulds and jars holding

7.8 The step pyramid of the pharaoh Djoser (roughly 2667–2648 BC) at Saqqara is one of the earliest in a long line of pyramids surmounting the desert-edge escarpment west of Memphis.

fermented beer slurry, both for labourers' rations. Many of the animal bones come from cattle, which matches the remains of clover grown as a fodder crop to feed great herds of beasts.[69] In addition to providing meat and milk, some of the cattle were by this time undoubtedly bred as plough oxen. Indeed, the number of weed seeds found among the cereals hints at open fields worked by plough teams and seasonal gangs of harvesters rather than the traditional household plots.[70] Grape pips, texts and images reveal the introduction of vines from the Levant, tended in trellised vineyards, often on the well-drained gravels of the Delta's margins.[71] Here was the home, too, of papyrus, which became the Delta's emblem in Egyptian art, as well as the material for

7.9 The Nile Delta in the 'long' 3rd millennium BC: (*top*) map of its extent and river branches by 3000 BC; (*centre left*) wooden label from Abydos commemorating a royal visit by the pharaoh Aha; (*centre right*) plan of a large, complex building of early 3rd millennium BC date at Buto; (*bottom*) detail from a generic scene of aquatic life in the Old Kingdom tomb of Kagemni at Saqqara.

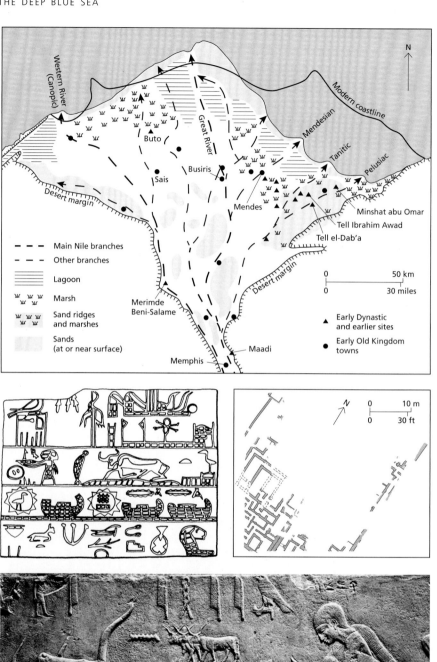

a new writing surface. All this is a far cry from village-based horticulture. Spatially extensive, costly in outlay, and profligate in the labour needed to tend and process crops and animals, as well as to turn out mass-produced linen garments, stone vessels and other goods, these estates were wealth-generating enterprises, often run by literate overseers (much more than 'scribes'). They exploited the cornucopia of the Delta, improved through select Levantine additions, for the sumptuary and accumulative advantage of the living and, thanks to the rise of voracious mortuary cults, deceased members of the Memphite royal court and its upriver antecedents.

The tensions in this exploitative relationship may help to explain the assiduous attention paid by Egypt's rulers to treating the Delta as an indissoluble element of a unified kingdom. Symbolically this was propagated by a binding imagery of knotted or interwoven papyrus and reed (the latter standing for upriver Egypt) that overtly expressed unity and, obliquely, captivity.[72] Administrators of provinces were rotated, so that in theory they could not put down local roots. Associations between prominent Delta communities and the royal house were proclaimed.[73] Rulers recorded visits to shrines erected to Delta divinities, such as the cobra goddess Wadjet at Buto (symbolized by a heron on top of her shrine) and Neith at Sais; both divinities also appear in royal names and titles. Only in death were there limits, for these pharaohs baulked at burial north of Memphis. In contrast, and casting doubt on the long-term success of royal policy, at Mendes – an eastern Delta centre that experienced most of the trends outlined above – burial monuments built in the mid-3rd millennium BC around a new local temple indicate that one provincial elite was starting to see itself as native to the area, perhaps as a result of ultimately counterproductive royal grants of land in the vicinity as rewards for loyal service.[74] Arguably equally subversive was the construction of a Levantine-style shrine building at Tell Ibrahim Awad.[75] What the multitude of less illustrious people, especially those with ancestries in another past, thought of this involuntary integration, which brought them within the bounds of a numinous land of the gods but reduced many to labourer status, we can only guess, for they remain voiceless to posterity. This was merely the first round in a long tug of war over the Delta's affiliations, and indeed the evolving identity of Egypt itself.

Contemporary Mesopotamia can be covered more briefly because, however critical its indirect impact via the development and dispersal of key innovations, to which we will shortly turn, the two rivers lay more distant from the Mediterranean, some 200 km (125 miles) off at the nearest point. As we saw in Chapter 6, organized village-level craft production, regulation of the flow of goods by sealings, and small community temples all preceded the state in Mesopotamia, and by the early 4th millennium BC supernova cities had arisen at Uruk and Susa in the irrigation-farmed south and at Tell Brak in the rain-fed north. Uruk, which has lent its name to the period spanning much of the 4th millennium BC, grew further later in that millennium, to 250 ha (620 acres), of which 9 ha (22 acres) alone belonged to the Eanna temple's precinct.[76] Its population probably numbered roughly 20,000 people. Production underwent leaps in scale and standardization, especially of pottery containers (now thrown on a fast hand-propelled wheel) and textiles.[77] Much of this was organized by temple workshops that transplanted large amounts of labour from the household into a growing industrial sphere. A good deal of the weaving was female work, to judge by depictions on seals of women with their hair practically braided into pigtails. In the south, writing appeared earlier than in Egypt, in the guise of cuneiform signs impressed into clay tablets, initially for the detailed enumeration and grading of goods, rations and personnel.[78] Only gradually did it accrue the phonetic equivalences to speech that would allow its roles to diversify. Another long-lasting innovation was the cylinder seal, whose image-carved surface rolled in damp clay served, like other seals, to denote ownership, verify transactions or authenticate goods, but in addition broadcast elaborate messages about new forms of power through scenes depicting control over bestial or human enemies, the high life in manifestations ranging from the sumptuary to the sexual, and the world of the gods and the favours they bestowed on the luckiest mortals.[79]

Although manifestly urban in focus, we know little about political structure in Mesopotamia during this formative time. However, by the 3rd millennium BC vying urban polities with territories of several thousand square kilometres apiece had crystallized from southern Mesopotamia to the Jazira – a quite different outcome from that along the Nile.[80] At the head of each stood a king and royal family resident in a palace, linked to tutelary city gods and surrounded by a council of elders, as well as exalted temple officials. A superficial political unification of the entire region was realized between 2350 and 2200 BC by the conquest of these polities by Sargon of Akkad (whose name connoted true kingship, and whose grandson Naram-Sin was depicted wearing the horns of a god), but the 'empire', infrastructure and new capital that he created fell apart after a few generations.[81] The next cycle of inklings of an imperial future for Mesopotamia would not return for several centuries to come.

Civilizing processes

The early states of Egypt and Mesopotamia are not just remarkable political creations. New kinds of elite culture and large-scale economy arose inextricably with them, and these reveal much common ground despite separate origins and enduringly different stylistic 'looks'. Some elements were genuine innovations under the prevailing hothouse conditions – for instance, writing, the fast potter's wheel and others soon to be discussed. More, however, were expropriations, refinements and redeployments, in the pursuit of ambitious new goals, of practices developed earlier, at a smaller scale, within, or often beyond, their domains. Examples abound in the realms of metallurgy and other craft skills (including the bow-driven drill, a distant descendant of hunter-gatherer weaponry), viticulture and probably the wider use of fermentation to make leavened bread and beer, woollen textiles, administrative use of seals and, last but not least, increasingly elaborate ritual observances to supernatural beings.[82] In certain cases, we simply cannot establish precedence. This is unfortunately true of one key breakthrough, that of animal traction hitched to both ploughs and wagons (the latter another deployment of rotary motion in parallel to the potter's wheel). The first reliable later 4th-millennium BC dates are tied between Mesopotamia and Europe,[83] with hints from the Mediterranean, as we saw in Chapter 6, that cattle were pulling loads of some kind substantially earlier. Much the same goes for a new generation of metal weaponry. Daggers, as we saw in Chapter 6, originated on either side of 4000 BC, in Anatolia, the Balkans or the Pontic region, but their elongation into swords and mounting on poles as thrusting spears could well be Mesopotamian.[84] Of course, the uptake was not entirely uniform. Egypt's long-lasting aversion to carts and wool sheep reflects, respectively, the role of riverine transport and lack of extensive steppe or upland pasture along the Nile. But overall the sums were far more than the disparate parts: what made the real difference was the pooling and integration of elements, each with an ascribed place. Packages of behaviour began to be formulated that can be regarded as 'civilizational' in that they represented ways of doing things that, if far from sealed and immutable, were more long-lasting and overarching than the rule of dynasties, though we shall need to keep the term firmly separate from the uncritically approbatory connotations that tend to attach to it.[85]

To start at the top, the primary role of elite culture was to legitimize and enjoy the fruits of an unequal social order, and in this sense it complemented a threat of violence that was seldom far from the surface.[86] It radiated in all directions. Laterally, it affirmed, by shared experience, membership of the inner circle within and beyond each polity that benefited most from the system. Downward, it was deployed in public pageants, such as royal ceremonies, funerals or religious festivals, that syncopated the lives of the majority (maybe 90 per cent of people at an informed guess), who had no normal access to high-status goods, for whom the new order brought meagre if any rewards and whose daily lives had become routinized by organized labour and aesthetically impoverished by the replacement of traditional styles with the drab uniformity of mass-produced goods (Uruk and Old Kingdom pottery is notoriously plain).[87] Arguably most vitally of all, much of it was directed upward, to perpetuate the well-being and stability of its earthly sponsors and their subjects through sacrifice to the gods as the ultimate arbiters of cosmic order – beings themselves experiencing a transformation from the legions of local spirits or ancestral figures presumably rife among village farmers to the slimmed-down ranks of formal deities of particular dynasties and cities.

Such culture was intended to draw gasps. Eye-catching brilliance derived from many mineral and organic sources, but above all radiant metals, led by non-corroding gold, an ideal symbol of eternity and the gods. Resins and scented oils charmed the nose, food and rarefied drinks the tongue, complex musical instruments the ears, and smoothly finished objects surprised the touch. Alcohol, aptly described as 'the most effective drug of all time' for its mixture of convivial and mind-altering properties, became central to this lifestyle, in the forms of both wine and beer, the latter long predominant in Mesopotamia and among less privileged groups in Egypt [7.10].[88] The very act of pouring such liquids could take on erotic overtones. The scale and subtlety of consumption is indicated by the discovery in Tomb U-j at Abydos of 4500 litres

7.10 Mesopotamian banqueting scene from a seal found in the royal cemetery at Ur; note the beer drunk through straws.

(1200 gallons) of wine, some flavoured with figs and terebinth resin, and bottled in 700 jars, some probably imports but many local imitations of Levantine types, perhaps in an effort to allude to a more exotic origin for the vintages than was in fact the case.[89]

Elite culture's definition was made easier by the simplification of its opposite, but still required further strategies that explain many of its details.[90] Use of materials far beyond the ability of ordinary people to obtain was one option. Lapis lazuli, whose source lay in the distant highlands straddling the borders of Afghanistan and Pakistan, is an excellent example. Its deep blue became synonymous in Mesopotamia with fabulous riches, gods, royal heroes like Gilgamesh, and lustrous dark hair (in a distant echo of this, the curly locks of Homer's gods were still true blue), and in Egypt with regeneration and the night sky.[91] The queen's name in one Jazira town translates as 'lapis lazuli girl'.[92] But there were other means of distinction. One was quantitative, evident in gargantuan buildings scaled up from humble predecessors, or staggering repetition: tens of thousands of stone vessels were buried with certain early pharaohs. Another explored the qualitative axis, through the virtuoso crafting of one-off, unique works. New fine metalworking techniques such as granulation, filigree, soldering and riveting embellished ornate jewelry, weapons, drinking, dining and liquid container vessels and other status symbols. An allied approach was the combination of precious substances, each with their symbolic resonances, to create multimedia, polychrome objects distinct from the typically single-medium status objects of earlier times, and flaunting an ability to acquire and pool materials of different origins until the time came to bring them together. Two sheet-gold statues with inlaid lapis lazuli eyes, once covering a wooden core, from Tell el-Farkha in the Nile Delta, illustrate this nicely [PL. XXIV]; they also capture a local aesthetic of the human figure shortly before pharaonic codified poses and proportions (themselves projections of legitimate order) eradicated it, and they further underscore how often such combined materials were committed to divine or royal images.[93] Creations such as these were beyond the wildest dreams of earlier craftspeople, however expert. The most skilled practitioners, especially those working in the media of most interest, became permanently attached to royal or other elite households or temples, were fed and supplied from their stores, and their persons and products, in effect, owned by others. By the 3rd millennium BC, Mesopotamian texts listed such artisans and their tools as war booty.[94] This marked the birth of a tradition of royal-sponsored hyper-crafting that continued unbroken to the Fabergé eggs of Tsarist Russia, and beyond.

7.11 A 3rd-millennium BC clay model of a solid-wheeled, covered wagon, from Hammam in the central Jazira, today in eastern Syria.

Fundamental economic transformations, meanwhile, were altering the manner and scale in which resources were exploited, wealth acquired and raw materials and goods produced and exchanged. As already illustrated by the estates of the Nile Delta, some of this entailed investment of accumulated wealth in capital-intensive projects of a scope hitherto unimaginable, and often involving mass workforces, whether free, dependant or enslaved captives. In addition to human sweat, it was now that the potential of animal secondary products was finally exploited to the full.[95] One decisive element was traction. Regardless of where and when load-pulling and light ploughing initially evolved, teams of hulking male draft oxen, the state-of-the-art tractors of their age, came into their own on the immense, flat, ruralized hinterlands around the new towns and estates of Mesopotamia and Egypt.[96] With ample labour available to bring in the harvest, these could be farmed extensively in large ploughed fields that yielded less per unit area than closely tended household plots, but higher absolute returns for the landowner. The same goes for four-wheeled wagons in Mesopotamia [**7.11**]. Over gentle ground and short distances these enormously eased the transport of crops and other bulk products. Satellite imagery of the Jazira reveals hollow ways radiating out from the towns, in part entrenched by the passage of such vehicles.[97] Crop processing itself could be mechanized; an Uruk-period sealing from Arslantepe in central Anatolia illustrates a threshing sledge, the underside lined with cutting flints, maybe a widely distributed type known as 'Canaanean blades', also used for sickles [**7.12**].[98] On the steppic fringes of Mesopotamia, herding of vast numbers of sheep and to a lesser extent goats for wool and milk products became feasible, too. There were ample hands to weave on an industrial scale, and woollen textiles, often coloured, patterned or otherwise decorated, came into their own. The milk-based products of large-scale dairying likewise now

7.12 Among the less familiar deployments of traction today is this animal-drawn threshing sledge, illustrated on a clay sealing from Arslantepe.

found a ready urban market, Under these circumstances, just as the processed products of olives, vines and other fruits had less to do with subsistence than sumptuary extravagance, so such exploitation of animals allied with other forms of wealth creation and display as much as the prosaic daily realities of nutrition.[99]

Terms such as 'market' and 'capital' bring us to arguably the most profound development associated with the emergence of the early Egyptian and Mesopotamian states and their urban populations. For within them, the socially instigated desires for lifestyle markers, driven by a conspicuous elite in this respect, led to the birth of the first consumer societies, while a parallel obsession with establishing gradations of quality, plus perhaps the branding of goods with standard packaging containers and seals of authentication, created what were, in effect, commodities.[100] Unsurprisingly, the creation of measures of capacity in the 4th millennium BC was followed in the 3rd millennium by full-blown metrology.[101] And crucially, aspirations, materials, weights and measures became articulated by the rudiments of a market operation and its modes of calculation, in which the value of things, which fluctuated with supply and demand, was pegged against certain standards, both at the level of exchange between rulers and internally between private people.[102] If the essence of a market could develop millennia before the layout of marketplaces, so proto-currencies could emerge long before coinage, and indeed without such a medium of value equivalence it is hard to imagine how multilateral exchange of any complexity could have flourished. It was in this context that metals became of revolutionary significance, and differentiated from other attractive or rare materials and traditional status goods.

That metals became selected as the medium for proto-currencies was due not only to their glitter, relative rarity, portability, durability or even apparently universal appreciation, all of which contributed to their roles in elite culture, as we have seen, but were shared to varying degrees with rival materials. The decisive factor was their liquid convertibility, the fact that they could move to and fro between raw material, crafted object, and standard of value or, in effect, bullion.[103] Henceforth, a metal item, no matter how costly in terms of the labour invested in it (the 'added value' of skilled crafting), or the social lustre gained by association with particular personalities or events, held the potential for an alternative life due to its 'prime value' as a lump of known quantity. Metal might be used to buy and sell, to pay taxes, even to finance a loan or repay a debt.[104] The metal initially selected was copper. In Mesopotamia this had been reduced to utilitarian status by the later 3rd millennium BC and its role taken over by silver.[105] In Egypt, however, copper retained this role for longer; silver was much rarer, likened to the moon, and only became a currency a thousand years later. Gold was allotted values relative to other metals, but remained universally above the level of currency, the precious metal par excellence, imbued with exalted symbolism. In the Akkadian period, ten shekels of silver, at that time about 110 g (3.9 oz), would buy one or two bulls, five or six rams, between two- and one-third of a slave (an unpleasant index of the fact that people had variable 'added' value according to their skills), 20 kg (45 lbs) of wool or 100 litres (25 gallons) of oil.[106] Metal-based price structures enabled local equivalences to operate even at the village level, in grain, wool or slaves, and, of course, for transactions to occur without the presence of the metals themselves.

A cascade of consequences followed for metals.[107] The written records attest to a surge in the amount of copper, silver and gold available in Mesopotamia and Egypt. This necessitated better extraction techniques, for example of copper from much richer but less easily smelted sulphide ores,[108] and, as we shall see, the reorganization of metal-yielding landscapes around specialized communities resident permanently or seasonally at mines, often in remote locations. The commodification inherent in the use of metals as currencies encouraged production of standardized units, in other words ingots, while their abundance led to a growing preoccupation with control over access and the protection of values against inflation. Inflows and outflows in payments, gifts to courtiers or trade were monitored closely. The scarcity of precious metals outside elite circles was encouraged (even if contemporaries did not see it quite that way) by their lavish display in settings that put them permanently or temporarily out of reach, for example in the furnishing of temples, or royal burials. Ironically, however, the overwhelming importance of metal circulation helps to explain a growing problem in terms of archaeological visibility. For as metal objects acquired bullion value, the temptation to melt them down if damaged or simply of more use in another form grew rapidly. Analysis of silver items from late 4th-millennium BC Egypt and Levantine Tell esh-Shuna, for instance, has identified admixtures of gold that indicate the recycling of alloyed or gilt silver artifacts.[109] Metal concentrations also made prime targets in warfare; the asset-stripped, burnt palace, whose archives enumerate the abundance of metals present just before disaster struck, becomes a regular archaeological frustration. The greatest accumulations that have survived to the present, and therefore exert a disproportionate effect on our understanding, did so thanks to freak circumstances: the few royal tombs that eluded ancient or modern robbers, notably at 3rd-millennium BC Ur, mid-2nd-millennium Mycenae and later that of Tutankhamun (soberingly, all quite minor from an archival perspective), hoards either ritually interred or buried in a panic but never recovered, the occasional building that burnt too fast to be emptied, and later a handful of shipwrecks. Such random troves apart, we are largely dependent on texts and the occasional image for our insights into the astonishing lost world of ancient metalwork.

The construction of value equivalences triggered ripples of emulation. Part of this occurred within the domain of metallic classification. One clue is the proliferation of alloys. While sometimes an unintended consequence of working with polymetallic ores, certain alloys were deliberate, including arsenic-rich coppers and the tin-copper bronzes that, as we will see later in this chapter, first appear regularly from the later 3rd millennium BC, after earlier sporadic instances. The assumption that these sought to improve mechanical and casting properties sometimes stands up to scrutiny of the functions to which the products were put, but not always, and an intriguing alternative is that alloys attempted to imitate the surface effects of precious metals, a silvery sheen in the case of arsenical copper, and a red-gold one in the

281

case of bronze.[110] Likewise, while a tendency towards skeuomorphism, the emulation of characteristics of one medium in another, was itself nothing new (recall the echoes of basketry, wood and textiles in Neolithic pot decoration), and even now was hardly restricted to metal originals (consider the newly explosive popularity of artificial, vitreous blue faience in the light of both lapis lazuli and Sinai turquoise), metallic features, such as gleam, angularity of contours, and construction features such as rivets, becomes a feature of production in other media from as early as the start of the Old Kingdom in Egypt.[111]

First Mediterranean repercussions

Why does much of the above matter, besides a neighbourly curiosity, to the history of the Mediterranean beyond the Nile Delta? First, many of the materials implicated did not occur naturally in Mesopotamia or Egypt and could only be acquired outside their borders, towards all points of the compass and including those that necessitated an engagement with the Mediterranean proper. Pragmatically, this was a function of the geology and ecology of alluvial plains, but it also owed much to an esteem for things brought from the ends of the known world as affirmations of the cultural centrality of the places where they were consumed, and the cosmic centrality of their rulers and gods.[112] Such materials had to be procured in increasing amounts as consumption spirals took off. One means of doing so was trade, sometimes over extremely long ranges, and at first in valuable but low-bulk substances, as is witnessed in both respects by lapis lazuli.[113] Alternatives flexed the first states' man-mobilizing muscles, whether in the form of expeditions to extract directly from source,[114] or booty raids to take from those living there, the latter easiest in the dawn years before other polities consolidated, and tempting because they directed violence outward against people deemed 'foreigners'. From around 3500 BC all these means of acquisition irrupted into the southeast corner of the Mediterranean, and over the coming millennia their tentacles would feel their way cumulatively deeper into the basin.

A second reason is that many of the objects, technologies, economic practices, aesthetics, values and beliefs developing in Egypt and Mesopotamia were picked up by neighbouring Mediterranean societies, and thence spread widely, either overtly or in sometimes thick disguise.[115] Those with a propensity to be deliberately transferred or to escape with ease were adopted swiftly and piecemeal. Others required wholesale social or economic reorganization, and so took longer or were rejected. Furthermore, such adoptions were catalysts that began to influence local aspirations and strategies. We shall find many examples in this and coming chapters of the enormous benefit of being the first to define the nature of the good life, its attributes and values, and conversely of the dependencies that this generated elsewhere.

The final reason to take a long look at Mesopotamia and Egypt at this stage is the suggestion, building on the first and second points, that in fact such interventions, demands and uptakes became the driving forces of change across the Mediterranean as a whole over the following millennia. This brings us back to 'world-systems' as a way of understanding the growth of large-scale societies and interregional economies in the Mediterranean (and the rest of Europe) from the 4th to 1st millennia BC, as raised in Chapter 1.[116] This identifies a 'core' of urban societies with advanced agriculture and manufacture (initially Mesopotamia and Egypt), a 'periphery' of smaller societies (for our purposes initially in adjacent parts of the Mediterranean) engaged in unequal economic and ideological relations with the core, which they supplied with materials, receiving in return trappings of elite culture that bolstered nascent leaders, and a vast outer 'margin' of independent societies in which any escaping scraps of core culture lost their original meaning. Expansion was driven by burgeoning consumption at the centre and the tendency for peripheries to be structurally altered by interaction with the core, until they fused with it, driving peripheries and margins ever outward. There is much to recommend this as a schematic way of conceptualizing *one* of the principal emerging vectors of change in the Mediterranean, albeit in a way different from that in which its participants rationalized their actions, with often much reworking at the receiving ends, and havoc played by the connective possibilities of a central sea on any expectation of concentric zoning. But equally, this and the coming chapters will furnish ample evidence for other quite different and equally formative processes at work in the basin. We do best to conceptualize an emergent world-system in the east as a further newcomer among the many networks by now criss-crossing parts of the Mediterranean, even if one of exceptional extent and sometimes gigantic gravitational pull.

The 'Uruk expansion' between about 3600 and 3100 BC is a spectacular early example of such dynamics in operation.[117] From the Zagros to Anatolia and west to the Syrian reaches of the Euphrates, clusters of south Mesopotamian features appear, including architecture, writing, cylinder seals, wine-jars and other pottery, notably the mass-produced bevelled-rim bowls used as bread moulds or ration units. Some were embedded in existing communities, others announce new foundations and a few overlie a destruction horizon. This spread has been variously attributed to colonies from the south running an extractive operation that siphoned off key resources (especially metals) to the advantage of their home cities, trading enclaves integrated in local interaction spheres and host societies, or refugees from faction-fights or overpopulation on the southern alluvium seeking a fresh start. Whatever its explanation, the Uruk expansion had a dramatic effect on its neighbours. In the metal-rich highlands of Anatolia, for example, the already relatively complex Copper Age community at Arslantepe was succeeded by one with thousands of Uruk-type sealings, public buildings including temples with wall-paintings, and rich metal finds, including spearheads and swords 60 cm (2 ft) long, one with silver inlay.[118]

For our purposes the key issue is how far Uruk connections spread towards the Mediterranean. At the westernmost swing of the great Euphrates bend, some 200 km (125 miles) from the Mediterranean coast, one of the most impressive new foundations of all was established around 3400 BC, on empty land. Habuba Kebira was a planned town of 18 ha (45 acres), defended by a thick wall covered by towers, with

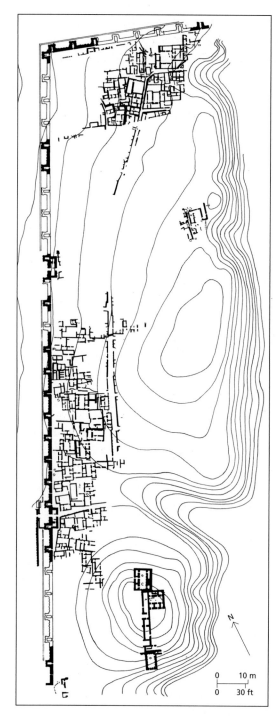

7.13 Plan of the large Uruk foundation at Habuba Kebira, as revealed by rescue excavation in advance of dam construction and flooding.

pottery typical of southern Mesopotamia, a dearth of agricultural tools that suggests that it obtained its food by other means, and residues of silver extraction [**7.13**].[119] On the nearby heights of Jebel Aruda stood temples and grand houses. It is odd, therefore, that Uruk-related finds drop off sharply between here and the coast, with only a few bevelled-rim bowls reaching as far as the Amuq and Hama – little more, in fact, than was attested in the preceding Ubaid period.[120] On these grounds it is commonly assumed that Habuba operated entirely upriver towards Anatolia. Yet its location lies too far south for this to make complete sense, while it averages the requirements for a western as well as northern gateway admirably. Most significantly, moreover, a few ultra-high status objects of Mesopotamian origin or association did get through to Egypt at this time, in particular cylinder seals, which were locally copied and help to explain fleeting Mesopotamian borrowings in early Egyptian elite art (notably motifs of entwined monsters and men mastering lions), and pieces of lapis lazuli in richly appointed tombs, some 4000 km (2500 miles) away from their source and, tellingly, cached en route as raw lumps of immense value at Jebel Aruda.[121] A transfer less easy to understand in terms of its mechanism is that of the indented facade design, already encountered in Deltaic as well as upriver Egypt but with a deeper ancestry in Mesopotamia. Routes across the intervening deserts can be ruled out, as probably can direct circum-Arabian connections (though hints of intervening activities here are growing), leaving indirect linkage via the Levant as the most likely option. In short, what happened west of the Euphrates was a shift in articulation and actors, which enabled a few Mesopotamian objects to percolate to the Mediterranean seaboard, where their exalted value and associations ensured that they eventually gravitated into elite hands within Egypt. This flow marks the start of a new role for the Levantine sliver of the Mediterranean, as the sole conduit of interaction between these superpowers, whose awareness of each other's existence surely remained at this stage dim and refracted.

Early in the 3rd millennium BC, Mesopotamia's focus shifted to the south, via the Persian Gulf to copper sources in Oman and a sea-route to the emergent Harappan cities of the Indus Valley.[122] Currently landlocked Ur, with its famous royal tombs, was a port for this trade, on a coastline that then thrust far inland. Levantine contacts carried on via intermediaries on the Euphrates, but only with the late 3rd-millennium BC hegemony of Akkad did the west again figure prominently in Mesopotamian geopolitics. The desire to establish access to metal sources, and now also cedar wood, was the stimulus, and cities in northern Syria were devastated along the way.[123] The 'silver mountain' referred to in Akkadian texts denotes the Taurus. The 'cedar forests' also claimed as conquests may have been those of the Amanus range rather than more distant Lebanon; either way, they appear in the exploits of Gilgamesh, who killed their guardian, the monster Humbaba, and returned with their felled timbers. Earlier kings had found long, fragrant beams to span their buildings in the nearby Zagros, and this extension, to what in later times was reckoned as a half-year trek, argues for impressive transport logistics, even with the flow of the Euphrates to help the return journey.[124] Not for nothing did Naram-Sin title himself King of the Four Quarters, and the cedar raid episode in the Epic of Gilgamesh, a work compiled from diverse traditions around or slightly after this time, likewise expresses an urge to dominate the uttermost ends of the world.[125] It is in this context that we find the earliest Mesopotamian reference to the Mediterranean, or the small fragment of it that Akkadian expeditions encountered and named an Upper Sea, juxtaposed with their Lower Sea of the Persian Gulf, and facing which Sargon claimed to have erected images of himself.[126] No trace of these has ever been found, but surviving Akkadian monuments in this genre give some idea of what may have once looked out over the lapis-blue waters of the Gulf of İskenderun [7.14].

7.14 Akkadian kings as divine world-conquerors: Naram-Sin, wearing the horns of a god, ascends a mountain above his victorious soldiers on this stele found at Susa, on the southeast borders of Mesopotamia. Similar monuments may once have been erected on the Mediterranean fringes of Akkad.

From an Egyptian viewpoint, there could be no such momentous discovery of the Mediterranean, for incorporation of the Nile Delta was an integral part of Egypt's unification as a territorial state. But that state shared with Mesopotamia the problem that many of the materials it desired only existed outside its boundaries, even if these were relaxed to include the adjoining deserts and their manifold stones. Two routes lay south, one up the Nile to Nubia and its gold, the other, by about 2500 BC, via the Wadi Hammamat to the Red Sea and thence Punt (roughly Eritrea and the northern Horn of Africa), a source of tropical exotics.[127] Egypt also engaged extensively with the Levant, as already attested by the transplantation of vines, and Uruk-type imports. Again, metals were critical, principally copper from Sinai and the southern Levant, and indirectly silver from more distant sources. But equally coveted were the woods, resins, aromatics, fruits and oils that flourished in

7.15 Schematic map of the main Egyptian modes of interaction with the southern Levant, showing the older overland axis with its concentration of finds at the terminus of the Ways of Horus, and the more northerly emphasis of its seaborne alternative.

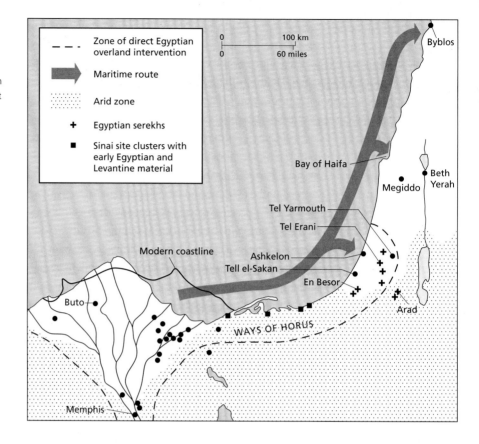

Mediterranean environments, and above all cedar, in this case truly of Lebanon, whose hard, scented, decay-resistant red wood Egypt began to import a thousand years before Akkad, at first in tiny, but then ever-growing amounts.[128] Flinders Petrie, excavating tombs at Abydos, found the sand so drenched in cedar oil that he could still detect its heady tang.[129] Along this axis, several modes of acquisition coexisted, all exploiting the constricted entry- and exit points of the Nile to enforce a cosmological quarantine between the ordered kingdom along the river and the allegedly chaotic world beyond [**7.15**]. This also nicely facilitated royal oversight of the inflow of goods, and hence their use and dispersal within Egypt. In Sinai, state-organized quasi-military expeditions were mining copper and turquoise before the mid-3rd millennium BC, in a landscape formerly the exclusive preserve of pastoralists; juniper, with its piquant leaves and berries, may also have been transplanted from there to Egypt.[130] In addition, however dubious the veracity of certain of the episodes of 'smiting the Asiatic' and raiding the 'sand-dwellers' proclaimed by Egypt's rulers, there is no doubt that along the southern fringe of the Levant, attacks by the world's largest state on its closest neighbours were often an effective means of obtaining materials or temporary obedience. An ivory handle from Abydos shows Levantine captives carrying jars [**7.16**], while a late 3rd-millennium BC text even refers to a marine raid at the 'Antelope's nose', possibly a reference to the Carmel peninsula.[131] Finally, there was trade and other forms of non-violent acquisition

7.16 Ivory handle from Abydos, showing people in Levantine dress bringing jars and other goods, possibly as captives.

from Levantine people, ambiguously represented within Egypt as a form of 'tribute', and whose changing pattern over time rewards exploration in detail.

Small-scale overland contact and transmission across northern Sinai, along a dry, briny coastal passage backed by dunes and rocks, had to date been effected by a patchy scatter of Copper Age groups between the Levant and the Delta. This pattern lasted until the climax of state formation in Egypt (roughly 3100–3000 BC), when the Egyptian presence intensified in the southern Levant and began to display a logistical structure indicative of official intervention.[132] The Sinai passage became formalized as a 10-day, 250-km (150-mile) route known as the Ways of Horus. Around the Levantine terminus large stations were established, whose outfitting was strongly Egyptian, but made on the spot. Seals and sealings testify to controlling procedures, while 'serekhs' (royal monograms equivalent to later cartouches) of Narmer may connect to estates back in the Delta. Fortified Tel Erani, at 24 ha (60 acres), is one impressive example; another at En Besor, located at the best spring at the trailhead of the Ways, was organized around a big mud-brick building in Egyptian style with numerous bread moulds and beer jars for provisioning caravans; at newly discovered Tell el-Sakan, it is estimated that 90 per cent of the pottery is Egyptian in style or origin.[133] Such stations managed a system that extended as far north as modern Tel Aviv, and through which Egyptian officials and their intermediaries extracted goods for export to Egypt, notably copper, oils and initially wine in the distinctive Levantine jars commonly found as imports (or local imitations) in Egypt itself. How much extraction was conducted by command, and how much through reciprocal trade, is hard to discern. Such state-led initiatives, or their less formal antecedents, were presumably also the means by which vines and Eurasian plough-traction were introduced to the Nile.

Around 2700–2600 BC this overland system fell into abeyance, replaced in the southern Levant by a less intrusive Old Kingdom network of contacts with rising local centres, plotted by a smattering of Egyptian prestige goods and a hub of connections at Beth Yerah in Galilee.[134] Under the Old Kingdom contacts intensified by sea, following the inception of a minor maritime route in the late 4th millennium BC.[135] In particular, the central Levantine coast, now northern Israel and Lebanon, was targeted for bulk imports of cedar, whose use, in a classic illustration

7.17 Detail of the massive cedar-wood planking brought from Lebanon to make the solar boat of Khufu; note the shell- rather than frame-first construction.

of sky-rocketing consumer demand, had spread to coffins, architecture and water-craft in Egypt (the superbly preserved 26th-century BC, 43-m- (141-ft-) long royal barge of Khufu, or Cheops, he of the Great Pyramid, used 12 tonnes of cedar, with the shortest single hull plank 7 m (23 ft) long and 12 cm (almost 5 in.) thick) [**7.17**; PL. XXIII].[136] Alongside this and other fragrant woods went oils and resins, Anatolian metals, rare stones, including a second pulse of lapis lazuli, and other goods. There was a clear logic to this shift. As Egypt established direct control over the Sinai mines, the need to obtain copper from presumably locally contested south Levantine sources evaporated, much as the inception of a home wine industry reduced, at least temporarily, the need for substantial imports. Attention switched to materials and substances that were only accessible further to the north.

The donkey and the sail

Two revolutionary innovations in transportation, sponsored by Egypt's capital wealth and accumulated know-how, lent decisive impetus to these sequent initiatives, and remained of lasting importance long after this exemplary opening exercise in the large-scale extraction of the basin's mineral and vegetal wealth was

7.18 Clay model of a donkey carrying capacious panniers or jars, from Azor.

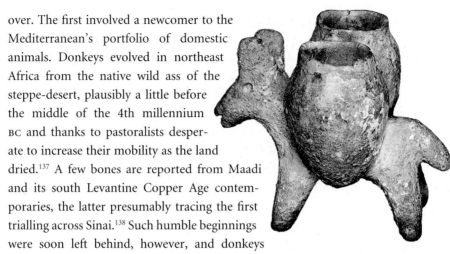

7.19 Fragment of the so-called 'Libyan palette', once similar in scale to that of Narmer's, and of unknown provenance within Egypt. Between the bands of cattle and gazelle or goats runs a sequence of donkeys; more problematic in terms of the dry-land theme are the fruit-trees below, and walled settlements depicted on the reverse side.

over. The first involved a newcomer to the Mediterranean's portfolio of domestic animals. Donkeys evolved in northeast Africa from the native wild ass of the steppe-desert, plausibly a little before the middle of the 4th millennium BC and thanks to pastoralists desperate to increase their mobility as the land dried.[137] A few bones are reported from Maadi and its south Levantine Copper Age contemporaries, the latter presumably tracing the first trialling across Sinai.[138] Such humble beginnings were soon left behind, however, and donkeys became coveted possessions [7.19]. Ten in their prime were buried around 3000 BC beside a royal enclosure at Abydos, in a manner otherwise reserved for lions (and, as we shall see, river-craft), in Akkadian texts a donkey cost two to four times as much as a bull, and four times the price of a standard slave, and by the later 2nd millennium they fetched some $468 in today's value, a sum that falls neatly midway within their current price range.[139] It is not hard to see why. Donkeys can pull loads or be ridden, but it is as beasts of burden that their qualities truly shine. This was quickly appreciated, to judge by the spinal pathologies on those from Abydos, as well as a donkey figurine of similar date from south Levantine Azor, which sports two panniers [7.18]. They are able to carry some 50–90 kg (110–200 lbs) over 30–50 km (20–30 miles) a day, survive on the roughest of diets, and their adaptation to hot steppe conditions enables them to drink enough to go without water for several days, and endure extremes of dehydration and heat.[140] Although lacking the dromedary's ability to cross expanses of true desert, donkeys are more usefully flexible in the Mediterranean and its semi-arid surrounds. For long-range transport over uneven terrain they represented the first marked improvement on human portage, and when grouped into logistically well-supported caravans, such as those we can imagine plodding along the Ways of Horus, they could shift substantial aggregate bulk. As their use percolated into humbler communities, donkeys would prove no less useful for shuttling smaller loads over the short, hard, often vertical distances between Mediterranean micro-ecologies, thereby integrating dispersed landholdings and, on an intermediate scale, local central places with their hinterlands.

The second innovation was the introduction of the sail, which had momentous repercussions.[141] Up to this point, locomotion over water had relied on paddler-power, which imposed modest ceilings on size, speed and cargo comparable to overland travel in the last two respects. The harnessing of the wind changed this forever, and ushered in prototypes of the kinds of ships that would tie the Mediterranean, and indeed the world, together until the age of steam. By Classical times an average single day and night's sail would cover some 100–50 km (60–90 miles),[142] and although averages were rarely the reality at sea, and the first sailing ships assuredly slower and clumsier, even they represented a mighty blow against the 'tyranny of distance', and the advent of a new age of low-friction maritime bulk transport. For example, the ten days spent traversing the overland Ways of Horus compare reasonably with the time that would be needed for a parallel sea journey in a laden canoe, but an early sailing ship moving at an estimated 2–5 knots (4–9 km per hour) would cover the distance in one or two days.[143] In the involuted geography of the Mediterranean, such straightforward land versus sea comparisons were rare, and all kinds of other factors often impinged, so the donkey's future in long-range transport remained assured, but no wonder that in this specific case, a state-sponsored effort to establish efficient, direct connections, the overland route withered once sea traffic took off.

Where sailing was invented is uncertain, and several epicentres may have risen across the planet.[144] One possibility is the Persian Gulf, with its shallow tongue then protruding into southern Mesopotamia. As we found in Chapter 6, this was travelled in reed boats by the late 6th and early 5th millennia BC, but a contemporary image of a purportedly masted craft is sadly inconclusive.[145] A 4th-millennium BC start shuttling between the coastal cities of Mesopotamia and Susa is also plausible, and sails must certainly have been used on 3rd-millennium BC voyages to the Indus, in which context their competitive edge explains the switch in long-range eastern trade from overland to sea-routes.[146] The best evidence, however, comes from the Nile. There can be no doubt that boats had been part of life on the river for millennia; deep-channel fishing and riverboat models had a long history, while the Egyptian language contains over eighty words for watercraft.[147] Moreover, unlike the rivers of Mesopotamia, the Nile was a perfect experimental laboratory, in which the current conveyed boats downstream, while the prevailing winds from the north, with something to catch on, could propel them back up against the flow.[148] About 3500 BC, large angular boats appear in upriver imagery, with deck cabins, long steering oars at the rear and bristling with paddlers.[149] Plank-built construction is proven by the discovery of fourteen such craft buried at Abydos in around 3050 BC, one over 17 m (55 ft) long. The Abydos boats were oddly held together by cross-hull lashings, a relic of reed-bundle craft, or possibly connected to the need to dismantle ships for desert carriage to the Red Sea or around Nile cataracts. Their wood was poor, mainly local sycamore, acacia and tamarisk. Although such boats are depicted and excavated in association with royal ceremony and fighting, they surely also played a less glamorous role in shifting goods, tribute and grain up and down the river. A few of the images sport palm fronds or banners mounted in the bows, and after 3200 BC these quasi-sails

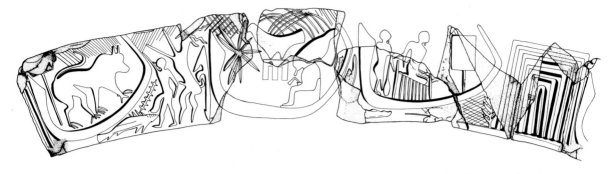

7.20 Roll-out of the images on a cylindrical incense burner from Qustul in Nubia, modern Sudan, showing several rivercraft, that on the right with a partially preserved, forward-mounted square sail and approaching a large structure with indented facade.

were replaced by depictions of the real thing: square, forward-mounted and presumably linen, the most unimpeachable from an aspiring elite burial at Qustul far upriver in Nubia [**7.20**] (another, better known example is unprovenanced and unfortunately may number among fakes made for the early 20th-century AD antiquities market).[150] The adaptation of a riverine vessel into a seagoing craft able to handle the Mediterranean's changeable winds and rough waves was far from straightforward. Nile craft had a shallow freeboard (which encouraged the retention of paddled locomotion), low manoeuvrability with the sail placed so far forward, and no keel. Quite where and when the conversion to marine conditions was effected is guesswork, but the likeliest answer is the Delta early in the 3rd millennium BC, just as Egyptian *wadj wer*, or 'the Great Green', began to connote the sea as opposed to Deltaic marshes.[151] For over 2000 years sea traffic was received at river-ports inside the Delta, similar to others further up the Nile (as well as the Mesopotamian *karum*, originally a river quay), but thanks to the sea's influx able to operate year-round, even when the river was at its lowest. Only in the 1st millennium BC were harbours finally built out on the marshy, shifting coast itself.[152]

The mist lifts with a suite of Old Kingdom texts and images.[153] An inscription of the pharaoh Sneferu (2613–2589 BC), a major builder himself and father of Khufu, the greatest of all, records a convoy of forty ships filled with wood, a neat revelation of the feedback cycle between growing access to foreign timber and a take-off in the scale of shipping. Trade by sea is mentioned on the so-called Palermo Stone, but the funerary monuments of Sahure (2487–2475 BC) and Unas (2375–2345 BC) are the first to illustrate the vessels involved [**7.21**]. They depict solid, seagoing ships with bipod or tripod masts, long oars for manoeuvring or ancillary travel, a truss from stem to stern holding the ship together (another relic of reed-built techniques), heavy stone anchors, a mixture of stereotypical Egyptians and Levantine people, the latter including children and so probably captives rather than emissaries or crew, all performing onboard obeisance to pharaoh, plus a cargo of jugs and, less predictably, bears, the last a reminder of the kinds of exotics that we tend to forget. The sail was supported by a yard above and boom below, as would remain standard for a thousand years. This rig, and the stepping of the mast further back, may have allowed headway as much as 30 degrees off the wind.[154] In combination with some tacking or jibing ability, the on- and offshore coastal breezes and, as a last resort, the leverage of long oars, this permitted progress up the Levantine coast even against prevailing

7.21 Well-preserved illustration of an Old Kingdom seagoing ship from the mortuary temple of Sahure at Abusir.

winds.[155] The overwhelming impression is of the sheer scale of these machines, their complexity and the intricacies of wood, linen, rope, joinery and rigging, handling know-how, and even the bodily discipline of rowing backwards. In later times they could still cost a fortune; in 2nd-millennium Egypt a tall mainmast alone, typically 16 m (52 ft) high, was priced similarly to a slave.[156] All this argues that the first sailing ships represented an acme of state-level endeavour. For now, the image of one such prototype nudging free of the last mud-shoals and reed-banks into the choppy, still silt-stained waters of the open sea offers as evocative a symbol as one could desire of the changing face of the Mediterranean.

The Levant at the crossroads

The position of the Levant, once part of the Neolithic nucleus, and subsequently home to the most diversified farming and spectacular metallurgy in the Mediterranean, was changed forever during the Early Bronze Age (3500–2000 BC). So far in this chapter we have encountered it as a periphery of newly giant neighbours, at the start of a long, if interestingly discontinuous, path that would lead to political dependency and, by the middle of the 1st millennium BC, provincial incorporation. But there is another, less negative, viewpoint: that from within. How did people there react to and reap advantage from the fluke of geography that rendered them the sole intermediaries between Egypt and Mesopotamia, and purveyors of substances in demand in both? Equally, how did internal Levantine traditions and conditions, themselves shifting as climates became drier, shape local lifestyles and alter the rules of wider engagement? Such issues force us to investigate bottom-up as well as top-down. This is a matter of vital importance, both because the over-assumption of world-systemic stimulus has had an unfortunate tendency to dampen efforts to explore how local and wider Mediterranean conditions contributed to the creation of societies in the Levant that were far from simulacra of their alluvial neighbours, and because it enables us to examine the Levant alongside the rest of the basin, as well as against a looming eastern and southern backdrop.[157] The lessons learned here will prove repeatedly significant in coming chapters, as the kinds of large-scale connections in which the Levant was already enmeshed spread further into the Mediterranean.

Different ecologies, traditions and exposure to external influences ensured that late 4th and 3rd millennia BC Levantine societies were far from homogeneous. A major division lay between north and south, with larger-scale developments in the former, and more obvious loss around 3500 BC of the Copper Age spike of complexity in the latter, possibly hastened by a short arid snap, and including the demise of farming and a switch to pastoralism in the Beersheba Valley. How much this owed to the differing nature of outside contacts, and how much to the less constricted and better-watered landscapes in the north, remains an instructively open question. Distinctions can also be picked out between the interior and Mediterranean coast. For all this, however, we can make certain generalizations. Although settlements fluctuated in population, and were sometimes abandoned, especially in the south, the overall growth of large tells is a testimony to community organization, stable landholding, reliable connections and robust agriculture.[158] Concerning the last of these, the legacy of the later Neolithic and Copper Age was a complex, superbly flexible range of options, pre-adapted not only to the environmental conditions now becoming prevalent, but also to the new market for its products, the demand for which now began to encourage a concentration on particular optimal crops or animal yields in certain regions, as well as more explicit integration of these regions' specialized products into a wider economic network.[159]

Beyond the original farming base, this comprised vines, olives and other tree crops, as well as routine use of animals for traction, carriage, dairy foods and wool, recently supplemented, thanks to widening connections, by mechanized ploughing, threshing and wheeled transport.[160] Water management, suspected in the Copper Age if not earlier, becomes indisputably visible. Early Bronze Age Wadi Feinan in Jordan was criss-crossed with small check dams, water-diverters and receiving fields,[161] while at Khirbet Umbashi and Jawa in the eastern borderlands of Jordan and Syria, channels and reservoirs harvested run-off from a large area of undulating volcanic steppe-desert, enabling the herding of vast flocks of sheep and goat, together with back-up cereal crops, by pastoralists geared to provide large quantities of dairy products to emergent urban markets further west [7.22].[162] Similarly specialized pastoralism, probably on a smaller scale, flourished in the Negev.[163] A parallel boom in upland settlement is often taken to reflect growing demand for vines and olives, although different explanations for a similar trend across much of Mediterranean Europe, as we shall see, urge caution and the association may be most valid for specific micro-ecologies, such as the rain-catching, rugged hills of northwest Israel and Lebanon, that offered the best prospects in this respect.[164] Terrace walls are notoriously hard to date, and the first appearance of the extensive, contour-wrapping versions characteristic of much the Mediterranean today definitely falls much later (in most regions around or after the end-date of this book), but simple cross-slope efforts to retain soil and moisture may also date this far back in the Levantine hills, and indeed differ little in principle from the check dams being

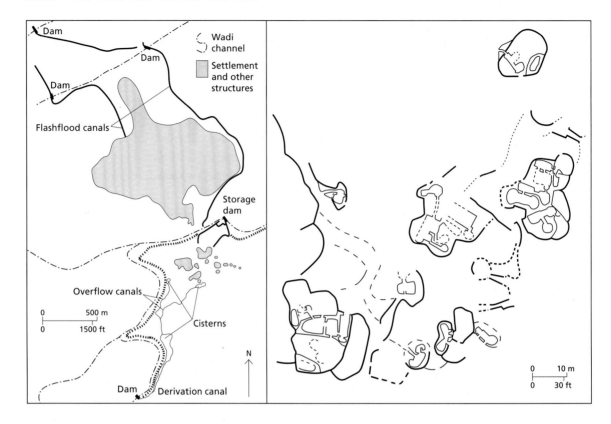

7.22 Complex installations for water management and animal penning sustained the large-scale exploitation of sheep and goat for their secondary products at the steppic site of Khirbet Umbashi in modern-day southern Syria: (*left*) map of the system of channels, dams and pools; (*right*) corrals and other structures in the southwest built area.

built in dry-land areas.[165] Lastly, where the mountains rose higher, above farms and orchards alike towered great silent forests, rich in aromatic, resinous species such as pine, juniper, box and cedar.

Let us look first at the north, where the cessation of Uruk contacts left behind a landscape of small centres, widespread contacts and enduring legacies, such as the cylinder seal and the fast potter's wheel, used to churn out masses of drinking goblets. Exactly how the sequel to this phase came about is frustratingly obscure, and would undoubtedly benefit from closer comparison with what we shall find further west in the Mediterranean as well as what we have seen further east in Mesopotamia.[166] But fast changes must have occurred over the middle centuries of the 3rd millennium, because by 2400 BC at least one urban, literate polity was in full swing less than 80 km (50 miles) from the shores of the Mediterranean. This is Ebla, today Tell Mardikh, situated on a prominent hilltop settled since 3500 BC in the rolling country southwest of Aleppo, in a classic Mediterranean micro-region of arable, hills and wetland mapped onto an increasingly strategic crossroads where the Levantine corridor met the route from the Euphrates and passages into Anatolia – an auspicious location at every level [PL. XXV].[167]

Even by the most cautious readings, the evidence from Ebla blazes across our horizons like a comet. The later 3rd-millennium site was a town of 55 ha (135 acres), surrounded by a 6-m- (20-ft-) thick fortification wall, and dominated by a multi-storey palace building. Only part of the latter has been exposed, mainly a grand staircase clad in fine wood with a shell-inlaid flower design, and an archive room that held a staggering 17,000 cuneiform tablets [**1.9**]. Many of the tablets are written in a local west Semitic tongue with borrowings from the Sumerian language of southern Mesopotamia, but there are also texts in Akkadian, which had started to become a shared language of communication over long distances. The tablets contain records of the administration of the palace's economy, exchanges of letters concerning trade, politics and elite intermarriage with other powers in the east, royal decrees, and the hymns and myths of already ancient Mesopotamian divinities, as well as east Mediterranean ones like the sea god Dagan, who survived to be excoriated in the Old Testament. From the tablets, we learn that Ebla ruled a kingdom of at least 10,000 sq. km (3850 sq. miles; larger than Cyprus, Crete, Corsica or indeed the contemporary Nile Delta), delimited to the west by a line of small coastal polities, to the south by others along the Orontes, and to the north and east by major powers on the Euphrates of whom we will hear again, notably the already booming entrepôt of Mari.[168] This domain was constructed from a mosaic of formerly autonomous smaller towns and villages, now ruralized by their subordination to an urban-centred state (entire villages were bought and sold), and their inhabitants effectively reduced, like those of the Delta, to the status of peasants.[169] The mechanisms of territorial aggrandizement were warfare interspersed with diplomatically, often nuptially, brokered outbreaks of peace – other decorative cut-out inlays show Ebla's enemies put to the sword and their severed heads counted, in grisly contrast to the flowery royal stairway [**7.23**]. The last king of this phase in Ebla's life was one Ishar-Damu, and we are reasonably confident that his own city and palace were in turn sacked and torched by Sargon or Naram-Sin of Akkad.

7.23 A darker side to palatial power: fine limestone inlay from Ebla, once set in a large wooden beam, showing the collection of severed heads of enemies.

This was no reincarnation further west of Uruk-period Habuba Kebira, and for all its Mesopotamian cultural trappings, Ebla differs in intriguing details suggestive of local Levantine traditions. For one thing, the apex of the social pyramid was broader and blunter than appears to have been the case by now in Mesopotamia. Ebla's kings were less powerful and self-glorifying in art and literature, and the presence of decision-making councils and assemblies was unusually strong.[170] Moreover, the size and role of temples, although imposing in local terms, was modest by Mesopotamian standards. Although the basic idea of a town focused on a royal palace that served as the king's house and ceremonial focus, a hub of economic and administrative activity, place of storage and hotspot of craft production, was ultimately of Mesopotamian and probably Egyptian origin (if not in fact generic to most early states), specific practices at Ebla were idiosyncratic: the administration was simpler, for example, and access to the palace's courts less constricted. Altogether, Ebla provides the earliest attested example of a species of palace-based economy, adapted to

Mediterranean conditions, that would thrive in parts of the eastern half of the basin for more than a millennium, and come to dominate much of its life.

The archives reveal marvellous vignettes of capital-intensive farming methods in a Mediterranean environment.[171] The palace engaged in cereals mainly for the sake of labour rations, and vines and olives for wine and oil, both to supply the palace and as cash crops for market circulation. In what seem to be locations on higher ground, olives often predominate – one queen, for example, granted a priestess land with 16,320 units of olives, 8800 of 'sowable', and a compact 630 of vineyard. Royal and other elite holdings consisted not only of estates (some worked by the oxen and wagons recorded as stabled at the palace), but also scattered holdings among the kingdom's villages. A man by the name of Irniba owned 30,600 units spread over twenty-one locations, a portfolio that may reflect his canny approach to risk spreading, conscious cherry-picking of the best plots, sporadic royal munificence, complex inheritance patterns, or a combination of any or all of these. In addition, sheep flocks numbered in the tens of thousands, and fed a textile industry in which the royal family held a considerable stake. This was a palace economy geared to wealth extraction and the mobilization of surplus on a huge scale, a system tilted to the elite's advantage with little besides ceremonial panaceas and security-at-a-price given in return to the mass of small-scale farmers.

Fine crafting and trade comprised the other major wealth-generating activities, although Akkadian ransacking has ensured that the material residues are thinner than the textual in this respect. Surviving hints include Egyptian stone bowls, some bearing royal cartouches, 22 kg (almost 50 lbs) of raw lapis lazuli (surely an oversight, given that the palace's archive lovingly detailed dozens of varieties among its prized possessions), and fragments of multimedia figures and furniture in stone, metal, wood, ivory, bone and shell [7.24].[172] But it is from the archive that we learn of the 800 women weaving, grinding corn and cooking, the 500 smiths, 140–60 carpenters, 30–40 physicians, 26–30 musicians and 14 barbers – several thousand people by most estimates – supported (if the term is not too charitable; these people were dependants, and mostly unfree) by rations or payments from the palace.[173] The tablets also tell us something of the palace's priorities: lists of goods and raw materials are largely restricted to metals, lapis lazuli and richly patterned, coloured woollen cloth. Many of the products of industry were used internally by the elite (apparently a few hundred people) during celebrations of births, marriages and victories, or offered to the gods. Others were given out to lower officials and other retainers as gifts or reward for services (creating a palace-affiliated 'look' in, for example, jewelry and costume). And large amounts were committed to external trade with other entrepôts, notably Mari, some 400 km (250 miles) away to the east.

Metals had infiltrated the Eblaite economy to an astonishing degree, in both quantitative and qualitative terms, and they were regularly on the move.[174] Silver was the value standard by this time, with gold at Ebla two-and-a-half to five times as valuable but copper only a twentieth its cost. An annual average of as much as 45 kg (100 lbs) of gold and five to ten times this weight in silver passed through the

7.24 Elite material culture at Ebla: (*left*) small multimedia figure of a man-headed bull familiar from Mesopotamia, with golden body over a wooden core and steatite beard; (*right*) Egyptian import in the form of the lid of a stone perfume jar carved with the name of the late Old Kingdom pharaoh Pepi I.

palace in the fifty years of activity revealed by the archive, with individual transactions that varied from a few grams to almost 1.5 tonnes (the former underlining the penetration of the economy at the micro-level, the latter the staggering maxima). Most metal was obtained for the palace through trade, or from officials granted the right to tax-farm the peasantry in kind, with the expectation that they pay their own dues in metallic form (a clear sign of smooth convertibility). With respect to trade, Ebla's intermediate location between Mesopotamia, Egypt and the Anatolian metal zone was highly propitious, for while in late 3rd-millennium BC Mesopotamia the value of silver to gold was 10:1, in Egypt (where gold was easily obtained) it was as high as 1:2–1:3.5. Ebla's ratio reflects a middleman position, further brought out by its interest in silver-gold alloys. There is little doubt that it played these early, and as yet unintegrated, exchange rates to the full.

The wonders of Ebla should not blind us to other probably comparable polities in the north, along the Orontes Valley at Hama and the huge tell of Qatna, as well as substantial dependent towns such as 25-ha (60-acre) Umm el-Marra, in the Jabbul plain east of Aleppo, where a prominent free-standing funerary monument contained the burials of high-status women, their babies, several men, donkey skulls, wooden coffins and the familiar litany of gold, silver and lapis lazuli.[175] But as we track southward, the scale of settlement and social organization tends to contract.[176] Several communities in northern Israel fell into the 20–30 ha (50–75 acre) range at certain times in their oscillating histories and can lay claim with some credibility to urban status, notably the well-known later sites of Dan, Hazor and above all Megiddo, the last of which boasted several shrines and a circular altar. But

7.25 View of Arad, showing houses and the bastioned fortification wall in a dry landscape.

surrounding them, and further south, settlement size shrinks until we run into the Egyptian outposts on the marches of Sinai. Neatly fortified Arad, a heavily excavated site on the edge of the Negev, covered only 6 ha (15 acres), divided into clusters of housing and small shrines [**7.25**]; Ai, equally interesting as the earliest large settlement to emerge in the relatively recently settled hill country, was barely double this. Moreover, southern communities were often unstable; Megiddo virtually vanishes for the first centuries of the 3rd millennium BC, despite an apparently short wet spell in the south around this time, and several sites on hilltops seem to have imitated tells to grace themselves with a false antiquity.

Some south Levantine settlements possessed facilities for bulk storage of grain or olive oil, for instance an impressive multi-siloed granary at Beth Yerah [**7.26**], while later 3rd-millennium BC Tel Yarmouth sported a modest 'palace' also with ample provision of storerooms.[177] Whether these reflect an elite's tax on family production, the proceeds of capital-intensive farming by such people, or stores set aside by the community as a whole against a bad harvest is anyone's guess. The overall impression is that households maintained much of their autonomy, and that despite efforts to identify chiefs or kings (and thence states), the reality, at least south of Megiddo, was still a landscape of large and small villages, run by quite self-effacing groups

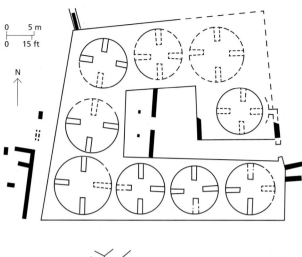

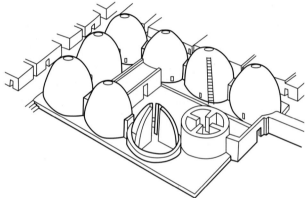

7.26 Large-scale storage for cereals at the multi-siloed granary of Beth Yerah, shown in plan and conjectural domed reconstruction.

of powerful individuals or families – much as in the Copper Age, if culturally with a different aspect.[178] Communal charnel houses for the remains of the dead, and other scatters of modest built graves outside settlements, likewise point to relatively small-scale inequalities, as does the fact that, despite connections to Egypt and the north, no form of writing, little power imagery and only sporadic bureaucratic use of seals were at this stage adopted.[179] Trade patterns were also lively but mainly regional, stitching together the variegated landscape as they had for millennia.

The potential exceptions to this last assessment are wine and copper, both of which were at some stage exported to Egypt, albeit not always through mechanisms that fall under the category of 'trade' (oil exports, to judge by the clay provenance of the containers, came primarily from further north).[180] These showed striking resilience in the face of changing Egyptian strategies. South Levantine wine exports declined once Egypt established its own vineyards, but with tellingly little effect on local levels of production and consumption.[181] Copper production intensified to an industrial scale, now focused at special-purpose installations near the ore sources, all remote places on the edge of the dry zone. Those at Wadi Feinan are mercifully undamaged by later mining and provide a sharp picture of the chain of operations from mine galleries to smelting, casting of standardized objects and recycling of waste droplets and artifacts [**7.27**; PL. XXVII], all overseen by a village-level community amidst a populous landscape neatly divided between metallurgy, farming and pastoralism.[182] Hundreds if not thousands of tonnes of slag accumulated, and the resultant pure copper was cast into small bar-shaped ingots for ease of transport. On the coastal plain at Kfar Monash, hundreds of the 800 copper sheets discovered with a hoard of tools and weapons also seem to be units for trade.[183] Certainly, much of this copper was siphoned off south until Egypt had enforced its monopoly over the Sinai ores and pulled back its Levantine outposts. But again it is striking that the climax at Feinan, and at Arad, which handled transport west, actually occurred after this switch. This implies that local consumption more than buoyed up local production, or that copper exports were redirected to other parts of the Levant, perhaps via the growing coastal sea-route.

A consequent question is whether or not the overbearing proximity of Egypt had a suppressing impact on south Levantine societies. Was this, in recent economic parlance, a case of the 'development of under-development'?[184] The limited size and

7.27 The abundant evidence for 3rd-millennium BC copper metalworking at Wadi Feinan includes: (*top*) moulds for casting objects and slender ingots; (*below left*) the crescentic ingots themselves; (*below right*) items re-melted in a bowl-shaped crucible.

often interrupted lives of even major settlements, as well as (less open to alternative environmental explanation) Egypt's intermittent 'smiting' claims, could hint that this was indeed so. In addition, there is a strange paucity of wealth goods in the south, especially precious metals, relative to the Copper Age and contemporary societies further north. If the theory is correct, the heaviest impact fell early, during the rapacious phase of Egyptian outposts, when imports and exports do seem exceptionally skewed. The partial disengagement of Egypt and its shift towards maritime destinations further north, which is sometimes claimed to have brought about a crisis in the south, seems on the contrary to have eased conditions and opened up local opportunities. In addition to continuity in viticulture and a surge in copper production, it was at this stage, too, that major southern settlements began to construct fortifications, ever more ambitiously as the millennium continued, and arguably more reflective of internal rivalries during a phase of regional prosperity than fear of the odd Egyptian raid.[185] The lesson for us is that becoming a backwater in world-systemic terms could have compensating advantages at a local level.

The maritime Levant comes of age

Before we take our leave of the Levant, what of its coasts and seas, which were being plied during the 3rd millennium BC by Egyptian sailing ships? This relatively straight shore, with few embayments larger than a river mouth and a feeble smatter of islets, mostly sandstone remnants of Pleistocene beach dunes, played little part in the genesis of Mediterranean seafaring, save at its northern terminus in the embracing curve of the Gulf of İskenderun. Nor is there much indication of later Neolithic and Copper Age sea traffic along its length. All this changed during the later 4th and especially the 3rd millennia BC, which mark the start of a fundamental Levantine realignment towards the maritime world, whose significance becomes clear if we consider that within 2000 years it would culminate in the Phoenician connections that encompassed the entire length of the basin. This volte-face, without which the Levant might have stayed as terrestrial in orientation as much of North Africa, was highly contingent on the region's recently acquired role as middleman between Mesopotamia and Egypt (as well as metal-rich Anatolia, and soon additional players further west), combined with the desirability abroad of its own products, decisively consolidated by the invention of a propulsion device that suddenly made bulk sea transport fast and efficient.

Yet, as with Ebla, whatever the initial debt to external circumstances, the new conditions were quickly seized upon and transformed by those Mediterranean people in the right place at the right time. Indeed, although Egypt's first seagoing ships take the limelight in terms of the formalization of maritime routes and explosion in scale, a few late 4th-millennium BC stirrings of sea connections pre-date them.[186] These take the form of crude boat images at Megiddo and Tel Erani, and a few pots netted from the seabed off Israel, one of Egyptian clay and still holding freshwater Nile molluscs, perhaps bait or a seafarer's snack. And in one stretch of the central Levant where the plain between the sea and mountains narrows to just 4–5 km (2.5–3 miles), rendering alternatives to agriculture especially attractive, on a small cliff-girt promontory below the cedar-clad peaks of Lebanon, a few of the thousands of jar burials in the cemetery of one coastal village clustered around a spring became peculiarly rich in silver and other exotic imports.[187] That community was Gebal, better known by its Greek name of Byblos (a suggestive reference to papyrus, and only thence to books), and its rise surely began as a local entrepôt and instigator of sea traffic up and down the coast [7.28]. In the early 3rd millennium BC, as Egypt's appetite for the timber in Byblos's immediate hinterland intensified, a special relationship began to blossom. A late 2nd-Dynasty royal stone bowl has been found there, and from the nearby mouth of the Adonis River (named for a Levantine deity and now the Nahr Ibrahim), which runs blood-red with iron-rich soils each spring, comes the lucky find of an axe engraved with the name of a 4th-Dynasty lumberjack gang or ship's crew, one of several Egyptian formalized work groups that acquired nautical links.[188] From now on, Byblos appears disproportionately often relative to other Levantine places in Egyptian records, and was accorded a special role in Egyptian cosmology. The very sailing craft that tied this economic, political and sacred knot became known in time as 'Byblos ships'.[189]

A closer look at this striking community as it evolved over the 3rd millennium BC proves rewarding.[190] Just like Ebla, Byblos resulted from a fusion of the local and external, but with radically different results. It stands as a prototype of a distinct kind of maritime community that would materialize all over the Mediterranean in

7.28 Aerial view of the coastal site of Byblos, overlooked by its Crusader castle and hemmed in by the modern town. The surprisingly small, densely packed nature of the ancient settlement is readily apparent.

the years to come – extending further and later, indeed, than the palatial system. The principal structures were a probable ruler's residence, the temple to Ba'alat Gebal (the 'Lady of Byblos'), and a ritual enclosure close to the 'sacred lake' conjured out of the former waterhole. Local culture predominated, but Egyptian elements existed in profusion too, particularly in the vicinity of the temple, where the Lady's cult blended with a montane manifestation of Egyptian Hathor. Egyptian votives are intriguing in their variety, for they include socially modest gifts, including cosmetic pots with female associations, as well as vessels engraved with royal names, including that of Pepi I (2321–2287 BC), who celebrated his jubilee with offerings at the twin poles of his world, at Byblos and Elephantine, above the Nile's First Cataract – a cautionary illustration of the symbolic significance behind some of what we often uniformly gloss as trade.[191] The stone vessels dedicated at the temple differed from those in the ruler's residence, for while most of the former were ritual items, the latter comprised tableware similar to Egyptian gifts at the palace of Ebla.[192] From its fame, far-flung contacts and the quantity of cedar and other goods passing through it by this stage, one might imagine that Byblos had grown into a mighty city. In fact, as far as we can determine, it remained remarkably small, slightly more than 5 ha (12 acres), with a population of 1000–2000. It is hard to call this a kingdom with a straight face, and 'state' is quite absurd, yet it was a place of considerable wealth, and one that conducted relations at least partly on its own terms with some of the most powerful kings of its day. Herein lies Byblos's long-term significance, for the later Mediterranean would see many more small, rich and dynamic sea-trader polities (here the looser term is definitely helpful) effloresce at key junctures and places in subsequent history. Many arose, like Byblos, bottom-up from local entrepôts, routes and networks; a few, notably Tyre and Aegina, would finally challenge in wealth and influence the greatest territorial powers of their day.

Mention of Tyre encourages us to look beyond the admittedly exceptional case of Byblos. Despite difficulties in digging down to the deepest levels of subsequently burgeoning cities on the sea, there is little doubt that a string of other maritime centres emerged at propitious points on the Levantine coast. The previously insignificant offshore islet of Tyre, which offered sheltered anchorages and some insulation from the tergiversations of mainland life, was first occupied in the 3rd millennium BC.[193] Its later priests told Herodotus that they believed that rites began there 2300 years earlier, a close enough stab to hint at accurate dynastic or temple-based year counts; another intriguing Tyrian legend connects its origins to canoe traffic.[194] Sidon, also a future Phoenician city, moved closer to the shore and traded up and down the coast, as did the ancestor of Beirut.[195] In the north, newly fortified Ras Shamra may be identifiable in the archive of Ebla by its ancient name of Ugarit, and in the south Ashkelon began to emerge.[196] Several features of Levantine pottery also reveal the growing importance of maritime connections, increasingly to the north as well as south. In particular, the trade in olive oil, resinous liquids and wine (the last less often destined for Egypt) that was taking off in the central stretch, now comprising northern Israel and stretching into Lebanon, stimulated the design of the first jars for bulk transportation of liquids by sea (torpedo-shaped Copper Age vessels for oil reflected a false start earlier and slightly further south, in the context of overland movement).[197] Hard-fired, tough, 'metallic ware' jars with highly recognizable combed decoration were ancestral to the amphorae of the 2nd millennium BC, while a range of red-polished or painted jars and jugs accentuated their appearance to advertise the product contained or point of origin – in short the rudiments of a potentially competitive marketing ploy.[198]

The growth of maritime trade along the Levant raises an inevitable question. Egyptian priority in the introduction of sail technology to the Mediterranean is not in doubt, nor is the reality of royal convoys from the Nile during the 3rd millennium BC. But can we take pharaonic decrees as a complete reflection of who controlled traffic up and down the coast? Were all Levantine people depicted in the Egyptian ships on Old Kingdom monuments in reality captives, and how soon did Levantine maritime communities with easy access to high-quality timber invest in construction of sailing ships themselves, perhaps further customizing them for Mediterranean conditions? In short, when did 'Byblos ships' start to have a Byblite or otherwise Levantine element in their ownership as well as design and route? The answer is likely to be increasingly so as the 3rd millennium BC rolled on, and certainly by the late 3rd-millennium replica stone anchors were being dedicated at a new, thoroughly un-Egyptian tower temple at Byblos.[199]

Over the same time span, maritime interaction spread up the northern Levant, past the Amanus forests and glimpses or even landfalls at Cyprus, to Early Bronze Age Tarsus, fortified, widely connected to north and east, and itself contributor of a pot to a 4th-Dynasty tomb at Giza in Egypt.[200] Just 80 km (50 miles) beyond Tarsus, but 1800 m (5900 ft) up in the 'silver mountain' via the Cilician Gates, huge volumes of diverse ores were being extracted at the labyrinthine Kestel mine and turned into metal at a nearby miners' village at Göltepe, a rough place of wattle-and-daub pit houses and industrial smelting gear, surrounded by carefully managed woodland fuel supplies.[201] This was conveyed down to the coast and into the maritime sphere, or overland towards Ebla and further east, or north into the Anatolian interior, which was occupied as far as the Caucasus by gradually urbanizing societies extravagant in their deposition of metal wealth, and themselves foci of metallurgical experimentation, fired by trade and technological interplay with the lowland cities to their south, both of which tempted military bids at overlordship by the Akkadian kings.[202] Post-Uruk Arslantepe boasted a tomb crammed with seventy-five items in silver, copper and various alloys, topped off with four teenage sacrifices, a boy and three girls.[203] Accumulations of metalwork with Pontic parallels were buried in around 2300 BC at Alacahöyük, including an ultra-rare meteoric iron dagger with a gold handle, while hoards at Mahmatlar and the rising site of Troy in the far northwest contained silver ingots among other glitzier finds, and reflect an uneasy position between the world of metal equivalences to the southeast and a quite different approach to metals beyond, in Mediterranean Europe.[204] Most such places lay beyond the reach of sea traffic, but Troy, at least, faced a Mediterranean shore as well as the interior. Did a few 'Byblos ships' (in any sense) probe tentatively further on, towards the Aegean? Here we cross the junction between the Mediterranean we have explored so far in this chapter, and another crystallizing independently to the west.

Prickly leaves and brazen men

People along the northern side of the Mediterranean during the 'long' 3rd millennium BC also began to forge different kinds of lives from their Neolithic predecessors, but removed from direct contact with Egypt and Mesopotamia. In world-systems parlance most inhabited an obscure margin that refracted beyond recognition the meanings of any eastern objects or ideas that attained the escape velocity to reach it. From our point of view, however, the advantage of this distance is that it renders these parts of the basin the best in which to explore how Mediterranean societies could transform themselves bottom-up, largely or wholly without eastern input, and in concert with the basin's shifting environments. We already suspect that such processes played a larger role in the Levant than can easily be isolated from the sound and fury to the south and east. In west Anatolia and parts of the Aegean, where interfaces with the Levant began in turn to inject a boost by the later 3rd millennium, untangling trajectories still requires care, though eastern echoes grow rapidly fainter and more selective with distance. But further west, as far as the Atlantic, what happened did so independently, embedded in Mediterranean circumstances, and with striking resemblances across the basin.

Compared with the tangle of period names in Chapter 6, the late 4th and entire 3rd millennia BC are straightforward. Following various terminal Neolithics that ended between 3500 and 3000 BC come the Copper ages of the west and centre, and the Early Bronze Age of the Aegean, with Italy and Dalmatia shifting from Copper to Early Bronze ages shortly after the mid-3rd millennium. But what is in these names? Strictly speaking, the latter is a misnomer, because true bronze, an alloy of copper and much rarer tin, only regularly appeared even in the Aegean around 2500 BC, thanks to connections explored near the end of this chapter.[205] Copper remained the basic metal for tools and weapons, to varying degrees accidentally or deliberately alloyed with arsenic. Gold and also now silver were used for jewelry where available, save in Iberia, where metalwork remained narrowly focused on tools and weapons – one aspect of this peninsula's distinctive, and relatively isolated metallurgical trajectory.[206] At a deeper level, though, these metal-derived terms reflect a belt of increasingly 'flashy' communities right across Mediterranean Europe, ancestral to the Bronze Age societies of the following millennium. This was matched by increased production and the first use of less tractable copper sulphide as opposed to copper oxide ores.[207] As further east, mine galleries and segregated smelting sites are found in Iberia, northern and central Italy, the Aegean and even the late-starting south of France.[208] We saw earlier that the effluent from activity in southwest Spain was sufficient to create an environmental fingerprint detectable as far as the Gulf of Cadiz.

Metallic terminologies also nicely capture the new social roles performed by metal goods, as status symbols to be acquired, displayed and disposed of conspicuously in lavish burials. Metal forms and aesthetics shaped what was deemed desirable and unleashed a cascade of consequences for other materials. It was now, rather than when metals first appeared, that chipped stones began to retreat, whether to extinction (as in the case of Tyrrhenian obsidian beyond Sardinia, where the local material hung on until the early 1st millennium BC) or into such specialized niches as virtuoso arrowheads exquisitely produced from fine flints, or obsidian razors in the Aegean.[209] In southern Italy, and rarely elsewhere, flint daggers were even knapped in imitation of metal ones. Of course, the ubiquity and status of metals were far from uniform. In regions of abundance, copper tools quickly became utilitarian – a good example of the triumph of function over flashiness is the fact that almost three-quarters of the Iceman's copper axe was hidden by its haft.[210] Meanwhile, in ore-poor Valencia, southern Italy and Sicily, metal goods remained uncommon until well into the 3rd millennium. The glaring contrast, however, is with Mesopotamia, Egypt and the Levant, for further west, metals did not yet operate as proto-currencies, nor were they stockpiled as bullion, save in interstitial Anatolia, where there was a definite awareness of the value equivalences being established further east.[211]

The social pre-eminence of metals is emblematic of a wider suite of trends that accelerated through the later 4th and 3rd millennia BC, metamorphosing the

Neolithic world beyond recognition, and creating fresh resemblances across the northern half of the Mediterranean – a 'great simplification' according to one archaeologist viewing this from a Neolithic perspective.[212] We came across premonitions of this in Chapter 6, in failing traditional villages, increasing funerary activity and opened-up social and economic networks. All these now reward closer attention. But first, they too were inextricably associated with broader changes in social behaviour. For one thing, the spectrum of prestige and wealth markers in metal, stone, textiles and now again well-manufactured, highly decorated pottery (after a lapse at the end of the Neolithic, also noted in Chapter 6) expanded and converged on a similar vocabulary over extensive areas. In addition, compared with the, to us, anonymous lives of most Neolithic people, a new assertiveness on the part of individuals leaps out, an emphasis on personae with lives differentiated from the group, and similar to those of others engaged in the same kinds of striving. Form and decoration in human figurines become immensely varied. Witness, for example, the variety among some 2000 stone, plaque-like images from southwest Iberia, which may reflect details of genealogy and identity.[213] Facial details on figurines also became more prominent, and grooming and adornment of real bodies extremely popular, as reflected by finds of razors, tattooing needles, colourants, jewelry and hair- or dress-pins, as well as allusions to patterned clothing.[214] Men's and women's roles were more vehemently distinguished, and gradually became entrenched into distinctions in power.[215] Celebrations of masculinity were strident. One reason why daggers spread like wildfire was their adoption as the predominant male emblem, the first codification of an emergent warrior identity, alongside older ways of being a man in the wider world, notably hunting.[216] In contrast, female referents in contemporary Italian imagery (created for whose benefit and viewpoint?) became their sex and clothing.[217] The nexus between prestige possessions, individual identities, physical appearance and gender is beautifully illustrated by statue stelae, standing stones carved into flat portrayals of men and women in a patchy band running from the Black Sea via the north Aegean (including Troy) and Alps to France and Iberia [7.29]. Battered and reused over time, their original positions are poorly preserved and their meaning uncertain. Some stood over graves, but others out in the landscape, perhaps marking points within the wider social webs that their creators were bringing into being.[218]

Where and how were these new people living? The break-up of villages into dispersed farms or hamlets, which we detected in parts of Italy and the Aegean late in Chapter 6, became generalized from about 3500 BC.[219] A richly studied case in point is southern France, a landscape of coastal plains and lagoons backed by dry, scrubby limestone plateaux (the Garrigues) and then the high Grands Causses and Cévennes, neatly zoned in Languedoc but crumpled together in Provence.[220] Through this roiled the Rhône, a divider rather than a unifying focus like the Nile. Here, Chasséen villages were replaced by swarms of settlements using a welter of local, short-lived pottery styles. Their raw numbers need not imply more people, for Copper Age settlements typically comprised one or a handful of families apiece and many probably lasted for only a few generations. Unlike the abandonment of the Tavoliere, the French lowland

7.29 More than life-size anthropomorphic stele from Arco, north of Lake Garda in Alpine Italy, gendered male on the strength of the multiple daggers, halberds and axes; note also the elaborate festoon belt and necklace.

was not emptied. The Étang de Berre, a lush, coastal lagoon, became a focus for small communities living off fish and molluscs as well as farming; others dotted the interior plains.[221] Most striking, however, was the move into the hitherto all but uninhabited Garrigues. The best-studied pioneers are known from their pottery's type-name as 'Fontbouisse'. Hundreds of their stone longhouses (timber buildings were not an option in this land) have been found beside small patches of soil amidst the limestone; ten or more, for instance, ringed the little arable basin of Viols-le-Fort in the Aude [7.30].[222] Such movement into agriculturally marginal landscapes is widely paralleled from Iberia to Crete, and indeed onward into parts of the Levantine hill country.[223]

Small islands were microcosms of such environments. Some that have hardly been inhabited since became homes at this stage, including Lavazzo, at 0.6 sq km (0.25 sq. miles) the largest of a cluster of islets between Corsica and Sardinia, and several Cycladic scraps that are today deserted save for the occasional goat.[224] Archipelago conditions and differing geologies within the Cyclades enable us to detect with exceptional clarity one further consequence of living in such 'exploded' communities that must in fact have been universal across their range.[225] This is the ubiquity and necessity of interaction, beyond anything in the Neolithic, and mapped not in the grand sweep of connections we have traced elsewhere (and to which we return towards the end of this chapter), but by ceaseless small-scale contacts between neighbours, what Horden and Purcell conceptualize as a form of Brownian motion. Tiny settlements, especially those in risk-prone landscapes, were heavily dependent on mutual comings and goings, whether for help in times of need, bringing together workforces larger than a family, viable marriage partners, breeding of flocks, or access to materials, craft and ritual skills, let alone anything coveted from further

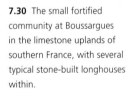

7.30 The small fortified community at Boussargues in the limestone uplands of southern France, with several typical stone-built longhouses within.

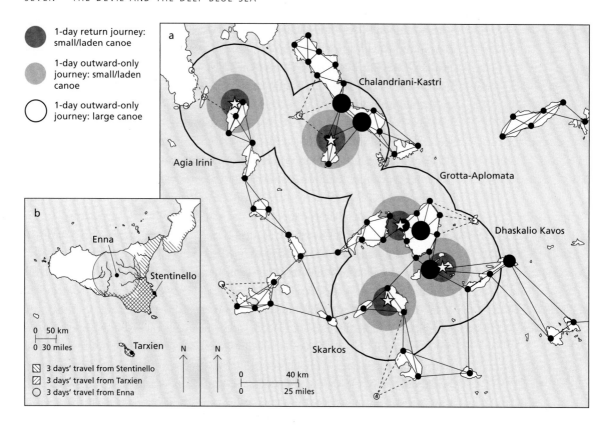

7.31 Connections and experiences of distance among island societies during the 'long' 3rd millennium BC: (a) modelled networks in the Cyclades, by joining evenly distibuted points to their closest neighbours, with well-connected loci indicated by larger dots, shaded travel ranges from five major centres of a 1-day return and outward-only journey in a small or laden canoe, plus (in outline) the more extensive reach of a 1-day journey in a large canoe; (b) the range of a 3-day journey under similar conditions from Stentinello in southeast Sicily, Tarxien in Malta and modern Enna in the Sicilian interior.

afield [**7.31**]. As we know from non-local clays the amounts of pottery and other goods that Cycladic islanders now shuttled to and fro over modest distances were part of the fabric by which they held their world together, and ensured collective social and economic survival in the long term. Comparable micro-patterns are starting to emerge from mapping the movements of pottery and stone in Iberia,[226] and surely lie behind the multiplicity of regional styles seen in southern France and elsewhere.

Over much of the northern flank of the Mediterranean, an equally striking axis of movement into marginal land was vertical, a return in strength to the higher ground for the first time since the up-rush of warm-weather hunter-gatherers, and presaged at an unusually dizzy altitude by the Iceman going on his fatal way, and more typically by peopling of the Garrigues. Some of this in fact had little to do with settlement. Most high-grade ores and stones around the Alps had to be sought high up. Moreover, several extraordinary concentrations of Copper Age (and later) rock art, sometimes as high as 1000–1500 m (3250–5000 ft), announce that a few montane areas were becoming invested with ritual power.[227] The largest of these galleries of images lie well inland at Valcamonica and Valtellina, two river defiles carved through the southern Alps to the Po plain. Much closer to the sea, only 30 km (20 miles) as the crow flies from the French Riviera, are the estimated 37,000 images pecked into soaring glacier-smoothed sandstones high beneath the sky on Mont Bégo [**PL. XXVI**]. Once thought to be graffiti left by Hannibal's soldiers, the geometric patterns, daggers and halberds (a short-lived European variant on the spear, with the blade mounted transversely, like an axe), long-horned cattle heads, oxen yoked to ploughs, outlines of enclosed fields (indicative of newly staked out land as people expanded into hitherto empty zones), and rare aureolated males, afford a superb insight into the preoccupations of Copper Age men, who probably sought this remote wilderness as a place of initiation.

But for every rock art spectacle there were scores of humdrum sites, often at altitudes of between 500 and 1000 m (1600 and 3250 ft), and occasionally associated with a pulse of upland erosion.[228] A good example is the opening up of wild east Liguria by groups ascending the steep gullies from the coast, and punctuating the mantle of silver fir in the process.[229] What were people up to in such places? One popular explanation is that they were Mediterranean Europe's first pastoralists, not of the truly nomadic Saharan variety, nor the Levantine steppic version (once small in scale but now established as a specialized supplier of new towns and palatial industries), but rather a vertically 'transhumant' kind in which herders with their sheep and goats oscillated seasonally between upland summer grazing and lowland winter pasture, zones often juxtaposed in the Mediterranean.[230] From Classical times to the recent past dramatic transhumant movements are well attested, sometimes operating over hundreds of kilometres, with thousands of animals.[231] But whether this makes sense in the Copper and Early Bronze ages of the northern Mediterranean is another matter.[232] For a start, it is a mystery how the even seasonal upland populations revealed by site numbers far higher than in Africa or on the Levantine steppe could hope to survive by pastoralism without urban markets in which to exchange their products for other foodstuffs. Moreover, analysis of places like Troina, a pioneering settlement cluster 650 m (2100 ft) up in the lovely hills of inland Sicily, or comparable open and cave sites in the Aegean, affirm that most are a short walk from patches of arable good enough to sustain a few families.[233] Equally, where examined, the ages of animals at death demonstrate year-round, rather than seasonal, occupation, and other evidence suggests beasts kept for a mixture of meat and secondary products, less herdable pigs (as well as cattle) accompanying the predominant sheep and goats, and no sign of herding on the scale needed for an animal-based diet. As a *coup de grâce*, in the few instances where experts have looked, cereal and pulse remains suggest that crops were cultivated too. In short, although it would be wise to allow for a degree of behavioural latitude in particular circumstances and some elasticity in the envelope of possibilities (recall the early herders of the Velebit mountains mentioned in Chapter 6), it seems that most of the new uplanders were mixed farmers, and that pastoralism as a discrete practice of any magnitude remained a thing of the future in this part of the basin.

In fact, a broader look at how people were farming on this flank of the basin confirms relatively few changes compared with the Levant, most of them inflections of established practices. The staples remained the same, with an enhanced role for drought-resistant barley in drier areas, and a few new variants (such as Celtic bean) filtering into the north from temperate Europe.[234] A key difference in the Aegean is that domestic olives and vines were widely cultivated.[235] At Myrtos, a hamlet in southern Crete, storage jars held resinated wine.[236] Elsewhere, however, the case is tendentious, with little agreement as to what constitutes proof. Concerning the central Mediterranean, olives and vines are said to be present at Tufariello in southern Italy in the later 3rd millennium BC, but if so, this is an anomaly, as parallels in Italy, Dalmatia and indeed France are lacking.[237] In southern Iberia signs of vine cultivation remain ambiguous, although analysis of the morphology of olive stones could argue for an independent domestication, again by the later 3rd millennium BC, a possibility supported by the genetics of the olive, which indicates more than one focus of early cultivation.[238] Patchy local initiatives would be unsurprising, as both plants grew widely in their wild form, and the principles of fermentation were long understood (well documented in Copper Age Iberia by a range of beers, meads and hallucinogen-spiked beverages that provide an alternative explanation for the marked increase in liquid-holding vessels among the pottery repertoire).[239] What is notable by its absence, however, is the scalar revolution in production seen in the Levant and (for vines) the Nile Delta. Stepping back from specific crops, there is no trace of irrigation or terracing either,[240] and while the Iberian *dehesa*, a landscape of savannah and scattered oaks browsed by herds and interspersed with fields (similar to the Chasséen landscape outlined in Chapter 6), may have formed around this time, it is hard to tell whether this was due to human management, or nature's response to drier times.[241] One feature that is, however, decidedly striking at settlements in very different niches is the first serious investment in storing large amounts of food over long periods, either in the capacious jars that become popular from this time, or pits and other forms of underground silos. In a good year, the surplus grain, pulses and perhaps, in the Aegean, olive oil produced at household level were being carefully held over for the future.

Smaller settlements created chances to expand animals' contribution within a mixed farming package, further augmented by a resurgence of hunting.[242] This meant more meat on the table, as well as more storage on the hoof. Most of both now came from sheep and especially sturdy goats. Along with drier times and upland life, their smaller size explains why these now ousted cattle into distant third place in most bone counts, if emphatically not in muscular and symbolic potency. Moreover, and in tardy equivalence to the Levant, a full range of secondary products came into play in most areas. Milking was as old as farming in this part of the Mediterranean, but expansion into marginal lands may have prompted more emphasis on durable dairy products, if a wide horizon of coarse pots with perforations around the rim, in southern France, Sardinia, Corsica, Italy and the Aegean, is correctly attributed to such practices.[243] Wool was a genuine novelty, whether thanks to crossing with fleecy breeds from further east, or local selection.[244] In addition to depictions of patterned clothing and a new abundance of spinning equipment, the date of wool's appearance rests on two significant Alpine absences. First, the well-insulated Iceman would assuredly have worn woollens had they been available in the late 4th millennium BC, yet no trace was found on him. Second, a few centuries later, in the waterlogged lake villages of the northern Alps, which preserve plant- but not animal-based organics, linen suddenly vanishes, and the most logical explanation is its replacement by non-surviving wool. Another freak of preservation does, however, cast doubt on how swiftly it spread to the west; at Cueva Sagrada near Lorca in southern Spain, a later 3rd-millennium BC burial accompanied by a linen tunic, painted leather bag and esparto mat, has a potentially archaic feel.[245] Lastly, along with a new interest in equids, to be explored when we look at the rise of long-range connections, traction was taking off, again raising questions of indigenous development from earlier cattle haulage versus external introduction, in this case as plausibly from central or Eastern Europe as the Levant. Ploughing motifs appear in southern Alpine rock art, associated with men, presumably those coming up from suitable lowland soils [**7.32**], Nemea in the Peloponnese contributes a model of a yoked ox, and by the end of the 3rd millennium BC waterlogged Ledro in northern Italy preserves a simple wooden plough.[246]

After looking at ways of life, what of the new ways of death that we began to detect in Chapter 6, from the start of the 4th millennium, and which intensified after 3500 BC? It is no coincidence that the ephemeral settlements in which most people lived find their inverse in the formalized nature of the places where they were buried – both the stone and earth pimples in the landscape so obvious to our aerial traveller at the start of this chapter, which in fact loomed over more earthbound travellers, and subterranean places that eluded the former, but spoke volumes to the latter. A visible cemetery was an excellent means of asserting rights to land at a time when the demise of traditional villages and the settling of new areas played havoc with ways of regulating claims. Moreover, real or fictional descent from the buried dead provided a usefully flexible means of anchoring people's place in the emergent new world.

7.32 Images of early traction in Mediterranean Europe: (*above*) fragmentary ox figurine bearing a yoke, from Nemea in the Peloponnese; (*below*) rock-art of a ploughing scene from Mont Bégo.

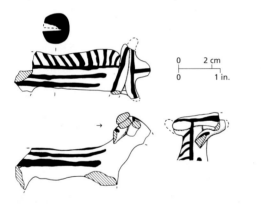

0   2 cm
0   1 in.

Over time, the hitherto relatively rare practice of depositing objects with the dead also gathered pace. By placing things in tombs, the living celebrated or altered the persona and status of the deceased, while competing with others through the extravagance of their giving.

In southern Iberia and France most of the tombs were collective repositories. One newly discovered burial cave at Camino del Molino in Murcia (southern Spain) contained the skeletons of no fewer than 1300 people, apparently most of those who died in a nearby community over several centuries in the later 3rd millennium BC.[247] Tombs also varied greatly in form. Megalithic structures with overlying mounds, ultimately derived from Atlantic traditions but losing some of their sacred aura, were common in the west, both rectangular 'corridor' graves and simple dolmens holding ten to fifty burials. The latter were erected by the thousand on the newly tamed uplands of the Midi, much as they had been under similar circumstances in the Golan Heights a millennium or so earlier.[248]

7.33 Interior of the main chamber and entrance passage of the Cueva del Romeral at Antequera, which blends dry-stone corbelling and megalith traditions.

Architecturally refined monuments with shaped blocks or adroit dry-stone masonry are also a feature of the 3rd millennium. Over eighty round tombs with a corbelled roof of smaller stones pepper the approaches to the settlement of Los Millares in Almería, to which we shall return, but the most awe-inspiring is the Cueva del Romeral, further west at Antequera, close to the hulking megalithic mass of its predecessor, with its 30-m (100-ft) underground passage to two beehive-shaped chambers [**7.33**].[249] Meanwhile, as already exemplified by Sardinian 'witches' houses', people around the Tyrrhenian Sea tended to prefer a subtractive approach, digging away soft rock to create single chambers or warren-like hypogea. But this division belies a more complex reality. Dolmens sprang up even on Sardinia during the later 3rd millennium BC, while hypogea with hundreds of burials at Roaix and elsewhere in the Vaucluse create a complementary counter-pocket along the Rhône.[250] Probably the largest of all such funerary monuments, the 42-m- (138-ft-) long, splendidly named Epée de Roland, dominates a cluster of rock-cut, megalith-roofed hybrids on a hilltop near Arles [**7.34**].[251] Long ago ransacked, enough nonetheless survives from these last tombs to date their start to 3300–2800 BC. Further east, in Dalmatia and around the head of the Adriatic, a tradition of stone tumuli arose during the 3rd millennium BC.[252] The Aegean continued a local preference for cist or rock-hewn graves holding single and multiple burials, save on Crete, parts of which opted instead for overground, highly visible circular and rectilinear collective tombs.[253] In western Anatolia, by contrast, jar burials predominate, if the dead are visible at all.[254]

Two observations stand out from this parade of funerary expressions. First, its sheer variety reflects independent responses to common underlying social conditions. Second, in a thought-provoking reversal of the too-easy assumption that innovations in the Mediterranean started in the east, the largest tombs demanding most investment of effort lie far to the west. In their time such tombs must have been one of the most effective ways of expressing individual or collective power and achievement west of Italy; for us they are also the first premonition of audacious social trajectories in the centre and west that were quite unconnected to those in the east.

Before we investigate this key issue further, we need to stand back from this tapestry of ways of life and death around the northern side of the Mediterranean, and ask how it came about. Most of the generic changes were unrelated to Mesopotamia and Egypt. Even in the case of the Levant, parallels rooted in Mediterranean conditions are as common as specific borrowings. Potentially strong arguments for a direct debt and east-to-west sequence of adoption at this juncture can only be made

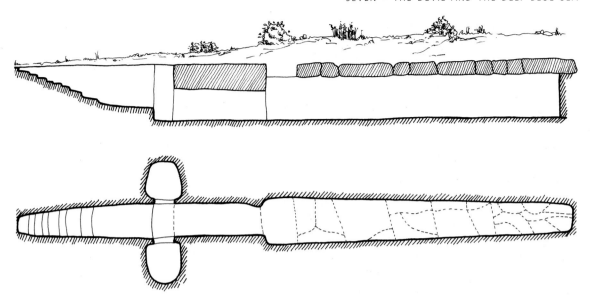

7.34 Cross-section and plan of the enormous underground burial monument known as the Epée de Roland.

for wool, ploughs (for which temperate Europe is an alternative source) and (in the Aegean) olives, but even these are not incontrovertible, and it is as refreshing to reverse the gaze and look, for instance, at the pulse of activity in the upland Levant as part of a basin-wide phenomenon. Additional eastern connections specific to west Anatolia and the Aegean are enumerated later, but the fundamental point is that the basic ways of living being forged in the European Mediterranean, which would underpin history there for a long time to come, evolved (unlike farming) in situ, and in patchy synchrony. In fact, there are also many parallels, if as yet few direct connections, with the temperate remainder of Europe, with some of the changes in how and where people lived, interacted and were buried, forming part of a broader picture that extends north of the bordering mountains.[255] Yet one final factor lent a distinct edge and character to developments in the south. This brings us back to environmental mediterraneanization and its consequences.

It is not hard to envisage how such changing conditions would have prompted some of the changes we have seen, and cast light on their uneven timing within the broad horizon. Several of the lowlands that had nurtured masses of Neolithic villages were surprisingly close to the limit of viability once rainfall reduced and became less reliable. The Tavoliere, abandoned by the later Neolithic, as we saw in Chapter 6, only needed slight shifts to move from breadbasket to minor dust bowl, and the demise of the southern Chasséen has been similarly explained.[256] Many Neolithic villages may have slowly faded, their inhabitants dispersing into surrounding areas as a skein of smaller communities, their cultural traditions transformed along the way. Even where older ways of life remained sustainable in most years, a run of droughts, perhaps allied to the allure of alternative, arguably less restrictive, lifestyles in neighbouring areas that had already undergone the transition, would have slowly eroded adherence. Viewed more positively than as a mere reaction, the combination of spreading out, storing more and building stronger ties between communities is a classic package for risk-buffered farming. It can help to explain the

313

apparent paradox that people moved into, rather than away from, poorer places for farming just as climate change was rendering them even less inviting, and without any fundamental shift in the means of subsisting there.[257] This simple fact, combined with the occasional wefts of older traditions woven into new ways of life, is an eloquent testimony to the manner in which the promptings of climate change might be thoroughly reworked by human ingenuity to unexpected ends.

Lilliputian lords

More dramatic consequences of the altered social and environmental conditions were also springing up along the northern flanks of the Mediterranean by the middle of the 3rd millennium BC. Out of the landscape of scattered, interconnected farmsteads and hamlets new centres begun to emerge, including large villages quite unlike their Neolithic predecessors in form and location, accompanied by unmissable signs of aggrandizing individuals or groups equally without good local precedent. Explaining such spikes of aspiring power and authority has become a central challenge for archaeologists – witness the full title of Colin Renfrew's influential *The Emergence of Civilisation: The Cyclades and the Aegean in the Third Millennium BC*.[258] In fact, it is not too hard to understand how, out of the background just sketched, small nuclei of social power started to emerge, and such explanations may have more currency in the Levant, too, than is commonly acknowledged. Their growth and entrenchment over time, let alone their coalescing into anything recognizable as 'civilization', admittedly constitute a taller explanatory order. Yet, as in Egypt and Mesopotamia, even the most grandiose outcomes started from, and were decisively shaped by, small beginnings, and it is on the specific forms these took in Mediterranean Europe that we now need to focus.

It would actually be surprising if the networks of communities now evolving under environmentally mediterraneanizing conditions did not generate inequalities, and quite rapidly in areas where the selective pressures were greatest and Neolithic traditions most swiftly lost.[259] As intimated early in this chapter, one possible route of advancement exploited the very interconnections intended to ensure mutual survival, whose weakness was the fact that things seldom did stay in equilibrium for long, given the unequal niches that people occupied, the differential skills, foresight and risk-taking propensities of participants, and pure random good or bad luck, for instance in runs of rainfall or births of children. Initially mutual exchanges could easily become lopsided, generating net winners and losers over time, as some called on help more than others, leading the less fortunate to accrue debts redeemable only by offering food, goods or labour to those better favoured. Such people could then deploy accumulations of these to sponsor status-reinforcing largesse or compete for, and commission, further marks of distinction. Some kinds of successful place and people are in this sense predictable, for instance those in micro-environments that sustained slightly more reliable crops or perhaps a plough team. That this train of consequences is more than mere speculation is strongly supported by the fact that the most impressive spikes of aggrandizement shot up, as we shall see, in challenging areas where famine versus feast were starkly opposed, and the relatively advantaged could most easily establish a hold over their neighbours, and begin to compete with other winners in the next arena over the hills. Conversely, more clement regions are revealingly thinner on such indices of change.[260] A second, sometimes complementary, possibility of equal significance was to exploit a central place in local or regional webs of communication.[261] We have come across this kind of phenomenon from time to time before, most recently in Lipari and the coastal Levant, and as networks became more vital to everyday social and economic life, the opportunities increased exponentially. In a gradually drying theatre whose natural resources were unevenly allocated, power commonly went to those best placed and equipped to move things around and to control movement itself, thereby determining connections and distributions between surrounding communities, as well as access to distant things. As ever, geography in certain parts of the basin was more conducive to this than in others.

Such means of accruing power were as unpleasant for those at the receiving end as in Mesopotamia, Egypt or indeed the territory of Ebla. Contestation, resistance, outright seizure and defence of gains, together with the endemic insecurity created by an unpredictable environment and the dissolution of traditional order, all lie behind increasing signs of conflict in the 3rd millennium BC. In contrast to indiscriminate minor violence in the Neolithic, the skeletons of people killed are now almost entirely male, sometimes apparently mutilated, and hit by arrows. More than forty arrow injuries are known in Iberia, some 12 among the 289 bodies buried at the sonorously named San Juan ante Portam Latinam in the Basque country, and the lethal nature of missile-based fighting compared to the posturing of dagger duels is further borne out by a late phase of Iberian rock art, which depicts all-out combat between groups of archers [7.35].[262] The casualties seem modest relative to those we can envisage in and around Mesopotamia and Egypt by this time, but such attrition, if continued for any length of time, would have a serious impact on small communities.[263] Unsurprisingly, a rash of fortifications (strikingly similar to the contemporary horizon in the Levant) added a largely new form of monument to this part of the basin. These typically had stout stone walls, protruding bastions and occasionally elaborate gateways or outlying ditches or satellite forts. Their size and complexity varies from major constructions implying more than 100,000 worker-days, albeit spread over many years, to tiny fortified farmsteads whose investment implies a galvanizing level of fear.[264]

Two exceptionally environmentally challenging regions, southern Iberia and the southern Aegean grading into western Anatolia, experienced the most sustained

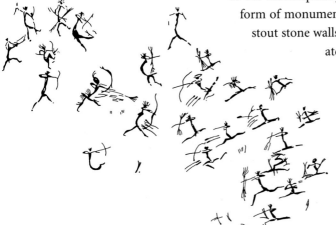

7.35 Two bands of probably Copper Age skirmishing archers exchange fire in this depiction on the walls of the Los Dogues rockshelter, north of Valencia.

315

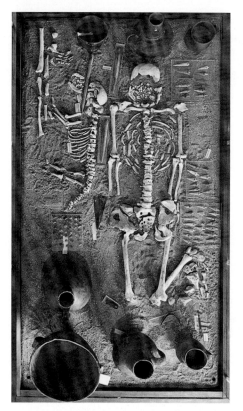

7.36 This richly furnished single burial of a man at Mirabella Eclano, surrounded by an assortment of weaponry, pots and his dog, is typical of many assertive small-scale statements of status and power around the flanks of the European Mediterranean during the 3rd millennium BC.

take-offs. They make a thought-provoking pair, the latter in fingertip touch with the peripheries of Mesopotamia and Egypt, but the former at the furthest Mediterranean point from such contacts, in a location where even the diffusionist Gordon Childe entertained independent development, and we can now affirm from the extreme paucity of imports that 'bottom-up' was indeed the only way in which things would change for a long time to come.[265] A close look at these hotspots is our obvious priority. But in order to appreciate the emergent properties and propensities of much of the northern flank of the Mediterranean, it is worth drawing attention to a few signals elsewhere. Several tombs stand out in terms of size or number of goods. We have already admired the huge examples above Arles, whose location at the junction between the Rhône corridor and Mediterranean coastwise routes was decidedly privileged. At a less extreme level, the rich tumuli of Velika and Mala Gruda occupied a similar position within communications along the Adriatic and through the Dalmatian mountains.[266] More remarkable for wealth than size are several burials in southern Italy. At Mirabella Eclano in Campania, in the midst of a landscape of small settlements, most with no sign of metals, a man was interred alone save for his dog, three copper daggers and two flint ones, a copper axe, numerous flint arrowheads and other shapes, several pots and a stone rod [**7.36**].[267] Italy also produced a few unusually big communities, including one not far from Mirabella Eclano at Tufariello, which was fortified, and noted earlier as an anomalous candidate for olive and vine cultivation.[268] In France, the Fontbouisse farms were overshadowed in the end by a village of forty to fifty longhouses at Cambous, and further west another girdled by ditches watched over the Aude at Carsac.[269] The use of a copper mine at Cabrières likewise correlated with a local spike of social differentiation.[270] In France, Corsica and Sardinia, modest defences were built, for instance little, bastioned Boussargues on a high point in the Garrigues, sheltering five Fontbouisse houses and barely 30 m (100 ft) across, or Monte Baranta near Olmedo in Sardinia [**7.30**].[271] Such flashes in the pan compare tolerably well with plenty of manifestations in Iberia and the Aegean, though not the most spectacular instances.

In Iberia, the density and combination of manifestations is of a different order of magnitude, unmatched west of the Aegean until the end of the 2nd millennium BC.[272] One major arena was Almería and eastern Granada, stretching towards Murcia, rugged country dissected by rivers and dotted with small coastal and inland basins. Even Almería was less desperately arid than it is today, as it withers at the demands of thirsty cities, tourists and tomatoes (exacerbated by global warming), but already a landscape of dry maquis and thin galleries of trees along seasonal river courses.[273] The background was a typical one of small dispersed sites, most recently

7.37 A reconstruction of Los Millares, showing the concentric bastioned defence walls, scatter of circular huts (with conjectural roof form), and some of the tumuli clustered along the approaches.

established. Since the late 19th century AD, the most famous site has been Los Millares, which assertively rides the cliff-girt tip of a high plateau at the confluence of the Andarax River and a smaller torrent [**7.37**].[274] Los Millares deserves far more respect outside Iberian circles than it receives, for it represents a remarkable spike of local social power, palpably neither the Aegean colony once claimed by diffusionists nor, as recently argued, a vague gathering place for mobile people.[275] Comparable sites existed 50–70 km (30–45 miles) away, to the north at Cerro de la Virgen and El Malagón, to the east at Las Pilas, and further off under modern Lorca, though an intriguing lack of parallels in Valencia may hint at an area where inequality was held in check (in contrast to the 'backwater' status often attributed to such places).[276] Given the mass of intervening mountains, each Millaran major site may have been pre-eminent within a few hundred square kilometres of landscape, though there is no definite proof that these hinterlands became formal territories or their inhabitants dependent subjects.

Los Millares grew larger and more elaborate through the 3rd millennium BC, with enough of its interior occupied by round huts to infer a population of as much as a thousand people.[277] One of more than a hundred fortified Copper Age sites in Iberia, it was defined by several lines of walls, the outermost sporting regular bastions and a complex gate whose layout reflects a brutal military logic.[278] Compact, heavily defended fortlets were built on the skyline or along access routes towards the end of the site's life, whether as part of the wider defences, or reflective of a community fragmenting into sparring factions. The inner approach across the plateau was dotted with round, above-ground corbelled tombs, of which eighty-three survive.[279] These were communal, containing on average twenty burials, many of whose bones

317

had been carefully grouped. The minimum total of 1140 interments is so much lower than the number of people who must have lived and died at Los Millares over the centuries that it implies a high-status burial area from which most people were excluded. Even within this privileged ground, some tombs are richer than others in copper and gold, fancy flint and marble, pottery decorated with symbolic eyes, and rare materials such as green variscite, yellow amber, black jet and white ivory and ostrich egg, the last two of African origin, and overall a list of desirables strikingly distinct from 'core' culture far to the east – notably in the absence of blue. The quantity of goods dwarfs that in other cemeteries along the Andarax. Before leaving this remarkable and, as an emergent Mediterranean central place, paradigmatic location, a few salient points deserve note: there is no trace of any large residential or public building, food storage was in pits outside the huts, with no evidence for control or concentration, and while metallurgy and flint-knapping both took place, the degree of dependence or freedom on the part of craft specialists is unfathomable, as it is, indeed, throughout the northern flank of the Mediterranean at this time.[280]

Panning out from southeast Spain, a few Portuguese sites, such as Zambujal and Vila Nova de São Pedro, resemble Los Millares in miniature, with concentrations of copper, gold, decorated pottery and other trade goods in a fortified centre.[281] More excitingly, however, a spate of recent discoveries, often during rescue excavations, in southern Portugal and above all along the valleys of the Guadalquivir and Guadiana, has brought to light an extraordinary new class of supersites in open ground [7.38].[282] These effectively extend the zone of large communities and emergent elites over large parts of the southern Iberian peninsula. Three of the largest are La Pijotilla near Badajoz, Marroquíes Bajos near Jaén and Valencina de la Concepción near Seville (it is tempting to speculate that a similar site lies undetected near the magnificent tombs of Antequera). There is much still to learn about these unexpected places, as only tiny fractions have been exposed and their populations and social structures remain largely guesswork. Inner zones of as much as 20–40 ha (50–100 acres) were studded with huts, some dug in so that thatched or rush roofs were almost flush with the ground, and pockmarked with storage pits, the latter at Valencina apparently concentrated within a quarter protected by a ditch 7 m (23 ft) wide and 4 m (13 ft) deep (a notable difference from Los Millares). Beyond lay up to five concentric circles of ditches, oddly reminiscent of the Neolithic in otherwise vehemently Copper Age communities, and some palisaded or walled. The outermost enclosed huge areas (300-400 ha or 750–1000 acres at Valencina), presumably used for fields and pasture as well as richly appointed, typically collective, burials in grand megalithic or dry-stone tombs. Patterns among smaller surrounding sites suggest that each centre did exercise real power at a distance, over agricultural produce and flows of materials and craft goods.[283] Several acquired, and in some cases demonstrably made, plentiful objects in copper, gold, marble, quartz, rock crystal, variscite, flint, volcanics, pottery and ivory. Valencina again stands out for a zone, no less than 9 ha (22 acres) in extent, devoted to metalworking.[284] Furthermore it established close relations with mining communities such as Cabezo Juré, dozens of kilometres

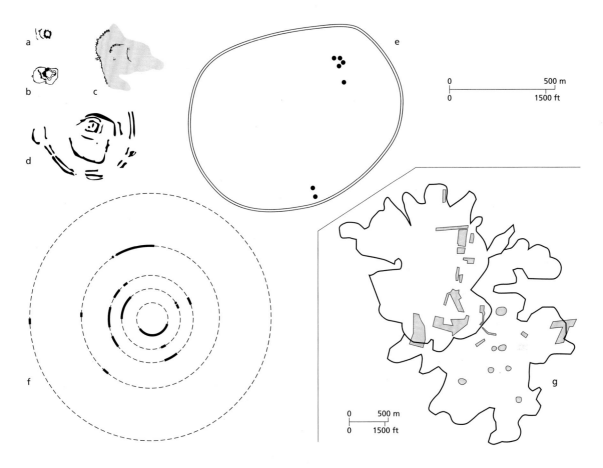

7.38 Recent discoveries have transformed our knowledge of major settlements in Copper Age Iberia. At top left, three long-known centres: (a) Vila Nova de São Pedro, (b) Zambujal, (c) Los Millares. Contrast now with (d) Perdigões, (e) La Pijotilla (with burials marked), (f) Marroquíes Bajos, and (g) Valencina de la Concepción, in the last case showing excavated areas and possible division between habitation and funerary zones.

away in the mountains and itself an eye-opening place unmatched west of Anatolia, where powerful, well-fed and fancily accoutred people in a fortified hilltop enclave controlled the production and circulation of copper, once the ore had been dug out by others less fortunate than themselves.[285]

Before we take our leave of Copper Age Iberia, it is worth drawing attention to one often overlooked feature of particular interest from a Mediterranean viewpoint. Most of the major sites lie inland, often high up, and this terrestrial focus dovetails neatly with the vigorously Marxist approaches to social inequality and the means of production that dominate much of their interpretation. But what of coastal equivalents and their activities? The most often cited is Zambujal, which lay on a then unsilted sinuous estuary. But Valencina, the most impressive of all and now land-locked west of Seville, likewise lay at the head of a great estuarine inlet where the Guadalquivir flowed into an enlarged Gulf of Cadiz, a superb gateway between the arable wealth of a major river valley and an aquatic realm that led first to the mining belt parallel with the coast, and then to further Iberian and northwest African horizons.[286] Just off this the spindly little islands of the Cadiz archipelago are famed from Phoenician times, but a much ignored fact is the presence of scraps of Copper Age pottery beneath later strata.[287] While the comparatively straight, island-poor coast of Iberia cannot compete overall as a natural seafaring theatre with the Aegean,

319

7.40 (*opposite*) An early photograph of the spectacularly preserved 'great treasure' of Troy, one among several such accumulations discovered by Schliemann in later 3rd-millennium BC contexts, and containing an eclectic range of metalwork and other prestige goods, to this day unmatched for its time in the Mediterranean.

7.39 (*below*) Lerna: (*right*) plan of the Early Bronze Age structures, including the House of the Tiles, its predecessor on a different alignment and the fortification wall, plus the circular outline of a large tumulus erected after the House's destruction; (*left*) examples of clay sealings, an innovation in the Aegean at this stage.

the mouths of the Tagus and Guadalquivir, the Cadiz archipelago and long throat of the Gibraltar strait presented locally outstanding opportunities. Coastal traffic and points of origin for crossings to North Africa that, as we have now established from both sides, traded Iberian for African products, must have concentrated in this maritime zone, where seagoing was surely more prominent in the lives of powerful people than we have appreciated.

The Early Bronze Age Aegean is one of the most exhaustively scrutinized parts of the Mediterranean during the 'long' 3rd millennium BC, largely because it is widely believed to hold the secret as to why urban, palatial 'Minoan' society emerged on Crete in the centuries around 2000 BC – an early case of the impact on our priorities of an assumed manifest destiny.[288] In fact, with one critical distinction in relation to potential linkages to the east, to which we return in the next section, the major centres and manifestations of social power here were more or less on a par with southern Iberia, as well as much of the southern Levant (whose strategic placement, of course, was different again). Rather than explore the Aegean for Minoan roots, or purely as a child of an eastern world-system (which certainly shaped later trajectories but did not trigger them in the first place), it is refreshing to look at it instead as one further variant on themes variably accentuated in several parts of the basin. Here, the Aegean will be generously construed to include west Anatolia, which itself formed an intermediate zone between the northern and eastern Mediterranean.

The initial aftermath of the decline of Neolithic tell communities was, as ever, dispersal and small-scale settlement of the drier south at densities comparable to those in Iberia. It was there, in southern mainland Greece, the Cyclades and Crete, as well as west Anatolia, that the next round of developments took place, mainly after 2700 BC. As in Iberia, the new foci arose in different places from earlier ones, with

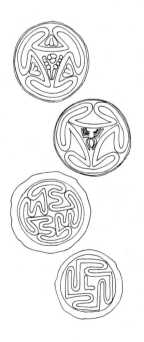

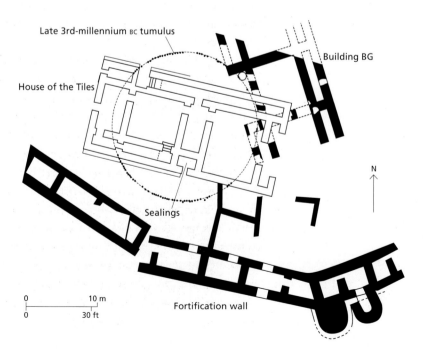

Late 3rd-millennium BC tumulus

Building BG

House of the Tiles

Sealings

N

0   10 m
0   30 ft

Fortification wall

the exception of Knossos, whose venerable site was occupied more or less continuously from the first days of farming to Roman times. A further similarity with Iberia is the variety of forms that social ascendancy took. In mainland Greece, large, sometimes fortified communities several hectares in extent, such as Lerna, Tiryns and Thebes, compare reasonably well with Los Millares and its peers, and dominated equivalent hinterlands; that at Tiryns built what may have been a colossal granary.[289] The coastal mega-site at Manika on the Euripos strait is a diffuse enigma equivalent to Iberian ditched communities.[290] Debris from metal production and other materials reveal that such sites served as hubs of craftworking, as did their Iberian equivalents. So far, so similar, the major differences being that a few sites were dominated by a grander two-storeyed building, most famously the so-called 'House of the Tiles' at Lerna, and that a rudimentary practice of sealing goods furnishes stronger proof of tributary territories [**7.39**].[291] Generically similar places arose in west Anatolia. Troy, a 9-ha (22-acre) settlement with a heavily fortified citadel entered via imposing ramps and gates that gave onto huge cavernous longhouses and storage structures, has too long stood alone, but as work in western Turkey accelerates, comparable sites are being uncovered, inland at Küllüoba and down the coast at Limantepe, an isthmian location obviating the long haul around the Karaburun peninsula.[292] With surprisingly few cemeteries in these parts of the Aegean, save at Manika and in Attica, aspiring people and their vocabularies of prestige are hard to discern, with the glaring exception of Troy, where the famous treasure hoards of intricate jewelry, vessels, figurines, weapons and tools variously wrought in gold, silver, copper, diverse alloys and meteoric iron, as well as scraps of textiles, rock crystal and lustrous stone battle-axes of Black Sea type, one carved in lapis lazuli, provide in an extreme form something of the flavour [**7.40, 7.41**].[293] We shall return to these depositions when we look at Troy from another perspective, as an interface and interpreter between different worlds.

The preference for coastal locations on the part of these mainland sites is more obvious

7.41 Polished lapis lazuli battle axe with traces of gold leaf on the band of studs, from Troy.

7.42 Marble head of a Cycladic figurine, unusual both for its size and the degree of preservation of painted facial markings and diadem.

than in Iberia, and although each drew upon its agricultural hinterland, most also engaged in maritime trade. Being on the sea was vital for some, notably Troy on the Dardanelles (to which it was connected by a sheltered inlet, later an alluvial plain and eventually a battlefield in the imaginations of Homerically inspired visitors) and Manika on the north–south trunk route of the western Aegean. Once we enter the archipelago, seaward orientation becomes paramount and the fortunes of those islands that made it into midstream abundantly apparent. Cycladic communities with all-round maritime connectivity emerged at nodal points among the webs of short inter-island hops.[294] Similar centres arose elsewhere, in the north at Poliochni on Lemnos and, in the south, Kastri on Kythera and Kolonna on Aegina, the latter embarking on a long career as a hub of sea trade.[295] None is a match in size for the largest mainland sites and, except at offshore Kolonna, the big buildings vanish. But these places were often fortified, and always rich in prestige goods and other imports, as well as signs of production in metals and other media, including the well-crafted, and now iconic, marble figurines of the Cyclades, whose once tattooed naked bodies seem jarringly primitive in a world obsessed with clothing [**7.42**].[296] In the Cyclades our insights into prestige culture and society are boosted by a rich if – thanks to the price fetched by figurines today on the art market – disastrously looted burial record consisting of cramped little graves, most with a single incumbent, yet several outstandingly rich in metal, marble, and decorated pottery.[297] One good example of a Cycladic island trader community is Chalandriani-Kastri on the wild coast of northern Syros.[298] A still more extreme case is Dhaskalio Kavos at the tip of the small, rocky island of Keros, where a large community prospered at a nodal position

for inter-island trade and arguably ritual [**1.19, 7.43**].[299] It is likely that both gained control over maritime movement in their vicinity. For devotees of Cycladic figurines, Dhaskalio Kavos's claim to fame is that it captured and held more of these (many deliberately smashed during or after their deposition) than anywhere else in the islands. For archaeologists, no less important is the spider's web of connections with surrounding islands, best traced by the fact that almost all its pottery was imported.[300] From a Mediterranean perspective, Dhaskalio Kavos may be the earliest known case, perhaps along with contemporary Tyre, of an island community that could not feed itself off its own barren little patch of land, and instead traded for its food, and far more besides: a maritime specialization indeed.

This leaves only the giant island, or mini-continent, of Crete. Here, several of the features met elsewhere are juxtaposed. In the northeast a small peninsular trading settlement, now on the islet of Mochlos, with a cemetery rich in stone vessels and gold jewelry, would have been at home in the Cyclades.[301] Other north coast sites maintained Cycladic links associated with metals, in which Crete is notably poor.[302] Yet the built tombs of Mochlos are communal, like most of those on Crete, including many circular ones in and around the Mesara plain in the south, so in this sense more akin to Iberian practice.[303] Meanwhile, the largest centres lay elsewhere, at Knossos, Malia and Phaistos, none, incidentally, as large as Los Millares.[304] Because these sites expanded into palatial towns a few centuries later, their Early Bronze Age levels are often truncated or inaccessible, which reduces knowledge of their layouts to glimpses and guesses. Malia and Knossos provide hints of big buildings or terraces by the later 3rd millennium BC. For whatever reason, however, no cemeteries have been found for these primary settlements, though they abound elsewhere. To put it mildly, with the evidence to hand, it takes a massive dose of hindsight to identify Crete as the sole area along the length of Mediterranean Europe whose societies would shortly accelerate into something comparable to Ebla.

Compared to the pharaohs or the kings of Ebla, leading people in such Iberian, Aegean and other societies were, in Jean Guilaine's words, mere 'petits seigneurs'.[305] For all the optimistically christened 'chiefly' graves, and the real inequality, scales of operation and the reach of power remained limited, and although the greatest centres were more populous than the Neolithic villages they succeeded, they were still only on a par with the PPNB Levantine mega-sites – if radically different in organization. Tribute from surrounding communities was imposed in a few instances in the Aegean and probably Iberia, as we have seen, but most political economies fit comfortably in the 'prestige goods' type delineated by anthropologists, in which status and power are defined by the ability to acquire, control and ration a suite of small goods of high, if competitively negotiable value.[306] As in Mesopotamia and Egypt, where after the shift to capital-oriented economies such goods still mattered immensely, these were chosen for their natural or enforced scarcity, whether in terms of distant origin (such as ivory and ostrich egg in Iberia), association with a specific source (the burials of the miners at Can Tintorer were never adorned with the green variscite extracted for the benefit of far-off, more successful people),[307] or

7.43 (*opposite*) An island central place of the 3rd millennium BC: the islet of Dhaskalio and adjacent shore of Kavos, at the western extremity of the small Cycladic island of Keros, command an extensive panaorama over the surrounding 'islandscape'. The islet was densely overbuilt with houses, and the Kavos shore witnessed large-scale deposition of marble and other status goods.

level of required crafting expertise. Metals typically qualified on all counts, but they did more than this for the powerful. To be decked out in them probably denoted not simply wealth, but shining or sharp qualities to be admired, feared, followed or resisted. In contemporary rock art, the fiery solar disc acted as an attractor for images of metal objects, especially daggers, and when it aureolated the human figure, we glimpse something of how 'brilliant' people wished to be seen.[308]

Probing further, what kinds of prominent people might this chapter's aerial explorer have run into should he or she have touched down at, say, the House of the Tiles, or at a funeral in a massive or richly appointed tomb? Plenty were men, unless we are quite misled by the strenuous claims of this sex at the time, and power was more all-round, concentrated and visible than in the Neolithic. In contrast to Egypt (but arguably to a much lesser extent the Levant) leadership looks a surprisingly secular business, not without its rituals, but lacking a noticeably sacred tinge. Beyond this, the fact of local, bottom-up growth ensured ample variation. Some leading people appear to be sharply individualized, perhaps tolerably analogous to the 'big men' of classic anthropology: dynamic, entrepreneurial and when necessary aggressive figures mobilizing labour and retinues by feasting, gift-giving or other largesse, while pursuing competitions for status played out through widely agreed rules with rivals elsewhere and involving the accumulation of prestigious goods and materials via trade or sponsored production.[309] Where rich single tombs stand out, as for example in the Cyclades, the fit can be quite compelling. But in other cases high personal status may have been subordinated to the corporate authority of powerful lineages, factions or other groups.[310] As seen earlier, the south Levant may have taken this path too, and although social realities can be masked by the presentation at a funeral, and individual leaders can lurk behind deceptively collective ideologies, some of the richest multi-burial tombs point in this direction, for example at Los Millares (with each group's tomb ranked against others) and on Crete. Even where great houses were erected, as in parts of the Aegean, how many had access? In the repeatedly remodelled citadel of Troy, several stood side-by-side at certain times, and the regalia among the treasures include repeats, as if several people wore or wielded them.[311] Finally, certain forms of leading role might be effectively extinct and so quite alien to our repertoire of expectations. Over time, a few would win out at the expense of others, through emulation of those that worked best and elimination of those that proved to be less robust in an unforgiving world, but in this sense the 'long' 3rd millennium BC was an extended period indeed, and still early days.

This portrait of the people behind Schliemann's 'jewels of Helen' or buried in the echoing recesses of great tombs in the west, is a harsh one, in which power was a pragmatic, often coercive business, and where distinctions between models of leadership in the end mattered less than the common aim of cornering resources, connections and people. As in the emergent states south and east of the Mediterranean, an element of persuasion and charisma, whether initially truly altruistic, merely bamboozling, or a bit of both, must also lie behind the embryonic stages of this new social order.[312] Even once established, there will have been benefits for some outside the charmed circle – gifts, trickle-down gains and basking in reflected glory for members of a retinue, lineage or other hangers-on – while sponsored communal events sought the loyalty as well as labour of the wider group. Such benefits help to explain one last feature. In as fickle an arena as the mediterraneanized basin, holding on to gains for long would never be easy, and big man structures are chronically frail in these terms, because no framework exists to maintain a hereditary lead if descendants prove less adept at the game. It is therefore unsurprising that Mediterranean Europe, not unlike the southern Levant, was strewn with mini-Ozymandian relics. Isolated wealthy graves may reflect efforts without issue in the next generation, and even funerary monuments still in use centuries after their construction could be hijacked by different groups over time. The few skeletons accompanied by wealth goods that have been studied argue that a better diet was seldom guaranteed from birth.[313] And yet, though almost every efflorescence of gathered power between Troy and Zambujal imploded eventually, with new ones thrusting to take their place, many in the Aegean and Iberia did manage to survive and expand for several centuries. We do not really know whether this was because their locations repeatedly favoured ambitious individuals, because corporate leadership facilitated passing on of power, or because hereditary principles and other structures had been formulated that allowed minor dynasties to emerge. Whatever the answer, such sustained ascendancies of individuals, places or social groups point to a future in which their successors would spring up ever more often, in more parts of the Mediterranean, and in ever larger, more structured and durable forms.

Far horizons and the call of voyaging

So far, we have explored the Mediterranean during the 'long' 3rd millennium BC as a patchwork of regions, highlighting how societies were changing in each. But this was a new age for connectivity too, not only the ubiquitous Brownian motion now so vital to keeping local life ticking over, or the bulk goods passing up and down the Levant, but also truly long-range contacts by land, and especially sea. Earlier archaeologists took the kinds of cultural changes we have witnessed in the northern Mediterranean, along with this fresh signature of long-distance associations across the subcontinent as a whole, as the combined markers of a massive westward thrust of Indo-European language speakers, often thought to originate north of the Black Sea.[314] This has now been rejected on good archaeological grounds, at least beyond the Carpathian basin, but there are also philological objections to the counter-proposal of a prior spread of Indo-European as the principal language(s) spoken by the first farmers moving west several millennia earlier (see Chapter 5).[315] Early Mediterranean linguistic geography is highly speculative, given that hard evidence even by the 3rd millennium BC extends no further than the writings of one north Levantine polity and a handful of towns in the Nile Delta. The most likely scenario is a mosaic of wildly differing languages of variable antiquity, plus widespread multilingualism, with the extremes of variegation so plausible during the climax of the Neolithic starting to be winnowed in parts of the basin during the 3rd millennium BC by widening connections, and in the southeast by state-approved speech.[316] In this mix Indo-European speakers must already have been embedded, yet the spread of these speech communities was probably not an event, but a drawn-out, partly serendipitous process, still ongoing throughout the 1st millennium BC, when the first central and west Mediterranean writing catches the last gasps of a welter of indigenous languages, many unrelated to Indo-European or even each other. In all probability Indo-European languages were favoured at different junctures by their adoption and emulation as prestige, gender-specific or trade languages, along with modest migratory expansions from time to time, of the kind we shall witness in future chapters.[317] For far-flung ties in the 'long' 3rd millennium BC were undoubtedly articulated by precisely the kinds of aggrandizing people and places just encountered on the northern side of the basin, and indeed ensured a gradual, if uneven, increase in linkage and learning between the flashes of display that flared up in different regions. Men, perhaps footloose, younger men in particular, were already the principal agents of activity away from home (hunting, fighting, trade and other kinds of procurement), and they retained their control of this domain as it burgeoned in cultural and spatial terms beyond its rather secondary Neolithic significance.[318] In this sense the return to hunting, growing signs of warfare and explosion of long-distance trade were mutually implicated male strategies. Interaction at a distance could certainly involve violence as well as peaceful exchange. We saw earlier how Egypt launched seaborne attacks against the Levant, and smaller raids on far-off targets must equally lie behind part of the widening circulation of desirable, exotic things, and the growing propensity to fortify, both so widely attested elsewhere in the Mediterranean.

As in Egypt and the Levant, new means were found to conquer distances more effectively. In the northern Mediterranean these drew on options potentially available since the Neolithic, thereby emphasizing that social demands triggered innovations in transport, rather than vice versa. Donkeys got as far as the Aegean during the later 3rd millennium, presumably after being pressed into overland service across Anatolia, but they only percolated further west considerably later.[319] Because Europe's steppe ass, a cousin of the African variety domesticated as the donkey, was already extinct, the sole available native equid was the horse, which survived the end of the Pleistocene in a giant reservoir centred in the grassy steppes north and east of the Black Sea but also extending towards the lower Danube and Caucasus, and in pockets further west, including one on the Iberian Meseta.[320] In the first of these, from about 3500 BC, people began to manage horses for milking, riding and hunting their wild relatives for meat, a different suite of tasks to those inflicted simultaneously on the donkey, and inseparable from the genesis there of nomadic societies, pastoralists with attitude comparable to those of the now-lost mid-Holocene Sahara, and with famous descendants in the form of the Scythians.[321] From here, horses had spread by the end of the 3rd millennium BC into Anatolia, Mesopotamia (where they were known as 'donkeys of the mountain', a reference to

7.44 These scenes of horse-taming from several locations within Iberia are poorly dated, but may add to the increasing evidence for indigenous domestication during the 3rd or early 2nd millennia BC.

their acquisition via the Caucasian and east Anatolian massif), the Levant and the Aegean, occasionally still ridden, as we know from depictions on Akkadian seals, but mainly as a means of pulling wheeled vehicles at speed.[322] Meanwhile, a separate domestication was underway in Iberia. To judge by an enclosure full of bones at Cerro de la Encina, Iberian horses were eaten at the end of long lives. They were ridden, as demonstrated by figurines at Cabezo Juré, and probably carried loads – the ships of the Iberian interior [**7.44**].[323] The first horses in the middle of the basin, identified at Maccarese near Rome, could just as easily derive from such Mediterranean stock, or other pools of wild animals in central Europe, as from the east, and either way they pre-date the arrival of the, in local terms, more exotic donkey.[324]

At sea, we might initially imagine the equivalent to be a rapid adoption of the sail. But this was emphatically not the case. The expansion of sailing ship technology west across the Mediterranean was a stadial, staggered process that, as we shall see in Chapters 8 and 9, took the entire 2nd millennium BC to reach Gibraltar – a reminder of the fact that such ships demanded a totally fresh approach to boatbuilding (simply mounting a canoe with a sail small enough to prevent capsizal made little difference to speed, while the Indo-Pacific outrigger solution was apparently never tried), as well as different operating disciplines, and capital investment that could as yet seldom be brought to bear.[325] Instead, paddle-driven canoe technology was pushed to its technical and performative limits. How do we know this? Despite a number of seabed finds either lost overboard or from sunken cargos,[326] true shipwrecks with hull remains still elude us, but we do for the first time possess clues of another kind, in the form of a sudden swathe of boat images that runs from the Levant and Egypt, as we have already seen, west to the Aegean and Malta [**7.45**].

The Aegean repertoire mainly consists of Cycladic images and clay models at Mochlos, both prominent foci of sea-trading.[327] Small craft are represented at Cretan Mochlos but the Cyclades portrayed large, slender canoes with a fish totem at the high end (probably the stern) and long lines of paddles. First found at Chalandriani-Kastri on Syros, incised on ritual pots of the mid-3rd millennium BC, the start of this horizon has recently been pushed back 1000 years by the discovery of rock peckings showing similar craft, interspersed with other symbols, at the terminal Neolithic settlement of Strophylas on Andros.[328] On Malta, a mass of such boats, one sporting a central cabin, was scratched on a great slab in the megalithic 'temple' of Tarxien (a place that we will soon revisit), during or after its main phase of use, and either way in the mid- to late 3rd millennium.[329] Even a parsimonious reading suggests that such craft were 15–20-m- (50–65-ft-) long and crewed by at least twenty-four paddlers.[330] Whether plank-extended dugouts or fully plank-built, they clearly

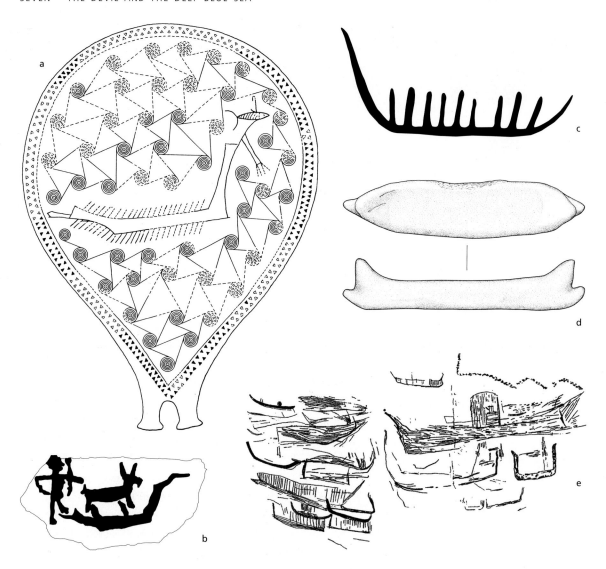

7.45 Canoe imagery of the 'long' 3rd millennium BC: (a) large canoe on a Cycladic pottery 'frying pan' from Chalandriani-Kastri on Syros; (b) small canoe with quadruped, rock-pecked at Korphi t'Aroniou on Naxos, also in the Cyclades; (c) earlier rock-carved Cycladic variant newly documented at Strophylas on Andros; (d) clay model of a small craft from Mochlos on Crete; (e) multiple carvings on a megalith at Tarxien, Malta. Not to scale.

descended from earlier Neolithic canoes. Physical remains of boats constructed by lashing the planks together survive from the 2nd millennium BC in British estuaries,[331] and such 'sewn' craft are also known from later wrecks and art in the west and central Mediterranean, where they may represent the epilogue to an older, more widespread tradition (indeed lashing may be indicated by zigzags on the hulls of a few Cycladic depictions).[332] While the dearth of earlier images makes it impossible to prove categorically or deny that such outsized canoes plied Mediterranean waters prior to roughly 3500 BC, the overall horizon of depictions, the introduction of facilitating (if not strictly essential) metal tools, including saws, and the simultaneous rise in maritime activity converge to argue for a genuine innovation. Where this began we cannot say. The date of the Andros boats, and the distinctive design, rule out any debt to Byblos ships and also prove an Aegean contribution, but other foci further west are likely too. Last but not least, a comparison with the great paddled canoes of New Zealand, California and the Pacific Northwest before and at the time of European contact offers further insights. Such craft were liable to have been used in warfare and ceremonial as well as trade, could carry a modest cargo of about a tonne, and covered at least 40–50 km (25–30 miles) per day, at double the speed of a smaller canoe – but less than half that of a sailing ship with a fair wind.[333]

Yet to restrict our investigation to nautical technology is to miss something of deeper importance for the maritime history of the Mediterranean. For in addition to asking why bigger seacraft were thought worth building at this juncture, we need to consider why, after millennia of invisibility, boats suddenly spring into view. It was, of course, certainly not for our informational advantage. In fact, most of the contexts are ritually charged: decorated pots on which canoes are juxtaposed with vulvas, fish and stars or sunbursts, rock images accompanied by rich symbolism, and colossal sacred buildings in Malta and Egypt.[334] They suggest that, unlike every-day activity in smaller canoes, which continued unabated, travel in the new craft was ideologically charged, imbued with power, status and cosmological overtones. Among the Cycladic islands, only the largest communities and most powerful men commanded enough people to crew such craft, which substituted for the mainland-ers' great houses as the foci of organization and investment.[335] Outsized canoes were the means by which such places and people exerted control over sea communica-tions, in practical and symbolic terms. Over short distances, such craft rendered sea-raiding far more devastating, and could perform awe-inspiring ceremonial roles. But their additional symbolic potency, and a source of glory for navigators and crews, lay in the realm of long-range sea travel, a spatial equivalent to terrestrial ascents into the high mountains.[336]

Ventures over distances that pushed the envelope of what paddled propulsion could achieve demand a separate term – *voyaging* – to distinguish them from the merely competent and only rarely long-range seafaring of preceding millennia. Part of the reward and prowess resided in the exotic goods and news brought from far off to impress those at home, as well as engagement with illustrious people beyond the sea; that the voyagers were a tiny, exclusive minority is particularly clear in the Cyclades, where, out of a population in the thousands, only a few hundred probably crewed the big canoes, while most other people probably never travelled beyond their nearest neighbouring islands.[337] Part also lay in the act of travel itself, as a triumph over dangers and proof of esoteric knowledge of seamarks and the heavens, the mental maps accompanying the birth of long-range navigation, some of neces-sity by night, and reliant on astral observation. The 'long' 3rd millennium BC begat the warrior ideal, as we have seen, but on certain coasts and islands this was matched and combined with an Argonautic and Odyssean one: the elite male seafarer as far-travelled, brave, enduring and wealthy through his deeds. Summer voyages timed to mesh with likely runs of favourable conditions will have clashed with the demands of the agricultural calendar at home, a mismatch that must have encouraged the great-est mariners to turn specialist, possibly at the level of entire communities at places like Tyre, Keros, Mochlos and the faintly suggested case of the Cadiz archipelago.[338]

Recalling, too, the stone anchors dedicated in sacred precincts at Byblos, there is no doubt that a new maritime culture was coming into being, more charged in its attitudes to the marine universe and the craft that crossed it than pragmatic earlier engagements – and one, we might hazard, that populated the sea with gods. Coupled with the invention of the sail, this was the first major maritime development in the basin since the Younger Dryas and the early Holocene expansion of seafaring.

It is time to experience this in action. We look at three manifestations, first a great jump in maximum crossing distances across open sea, second a surge of activity on consciously remote small islands, and third the creation of sea-woven interaction networks of unprecedented extent. All of these, with the partial exception of the third, were effected not by the distance-shrinking sailing ships of the east, but by canoes.

Previously unattempted crossings mark the conquest of two of the central and west Mediterranean's uninterrupted sea deserts, potentially lethal places with midway expanses completely out of sight of land, and with nowhere to run to if a storm blew up. One of these was the 250 km (150 miles) of open sea between Sardinia and Sicily, five to six days of exhilaration or terror even in a fast canoe with a modest freeboard. We know this was crossed because Sardinian styles of pottery, megalithic tombs and a western custom of trepanning skulls materialize in the far west of Sicily halfway through the 3rd millennium BC.[339] Interestingly, from now on the facing, southern end of Sardinia, hitherto the back of beyond, displays many more signs of social dynamism.

The other was a descent on Mallorca and Menorca, which hold the honour of being the last sizeable tracts of land to be settled in the entire Mediterranean. Their remoteness is underscored by the fact that they were the only major islands to have experienced no influx of land vertebrates since the reflooding after the Messinian event, 5 million years earlier. As noted at the start of Chapter 3, this left a walk-on colonist from that remote period as their undisputed master until the last instants of evolutionary time: the corpulent goat-antelope *Myotragus balearicus*, whose hoof-prints are preserved in the islands' sandstones, scraps of whose pelts may survive in dry caves where they went to cool off, and whose occasionally preserved turds reveal a voracious stomach adapted to digest even poisonous boxwood [**7.46**].[340] The end for this engaging relic of another age came thousands of years after that of the basin's larger endemics. It still thrived around the mid-4th millennium BC, but by 2000 BC it was gone.[341] For years archaeologists argued, on skimpy grounds, for an earlier human frequentation of *Myotragus*'s home, and therefore an extended coexistence, including its corralling in caves.[342] While the occasional prior visit can never be ruled out, rigorous analysis has demolished the foundation for these claims in favour of an incredibly delayed arrival in the later 3rd millennium BC – a marked exception to the trend for ever earlier dates of people on islands.[343] To islands heavily browsed (like others millennia earlier) by their endemic herbivore, the first settlers introduced a mainland culture of intriguingly boat-shaped longhouses, metals, sheep, goats, cattle, pigs and dogs, along with stowaway wood- and dormice. Their impact

7.46 *Myotragus balearicus*, the last of the larger Pleistocene island bestiary to survive, thanks to the long-retained isolation of the Balearic archipelago.

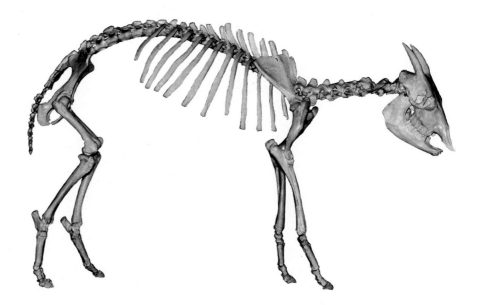

can be seen in the environmental record; *Myotragus*'s nemesis came swiftly, through habitat devastation, devouring by hungry settlers, or some goat-borne pathogen to which it had no resistance. One further telling detail rewards our attention. These two Balearics were peopled before Ibiza and Formentera, their small westerly neighbours that break down the crossing distance from Iberia to two 85-km (50-mile) jumps. This, plus the close resemblance of a later megalithic tomb at Ca Na Costa on Formentera to others in southeast Iberia, argues that these stepping stones played no part in initial settlement.[344] Instead, Mallorca and Menorca were reached directly, by a minimum crossing of 170 km (105 miles) from Catalonia, or much more if, as good parallels with Fontbouisse societies imply, these pioneers of yet another marginal niche had actually derived from southern France.[345] Even with a tailwind whistling down from the Ebro or the Rhône, and island-clinging cloud masses or migrant birds to navigate by, this was an intrepid deed bearing a founder cargo of crops, animals and other gear. Note a last codicil, however: one great sea-barrier in this part of the Mediterranean remained unbreached, that between Menorca and Sardinia, ensuring that direct contact between the central Mediterranean and Iberia remained a thing of the future.

Turning to our second manifestation, peaks of activity on remote little islands, often lying close to longer sea connections, are a peculiar characteristic of this phase of ambitious canoe-borne travel, before the spread of sailing ships that would tend to bypass such rocky isolates, relegating them again to emptiness, and later sea-shrines, hermits, fishermen or lighthouse keepers. The first regular settlement of lonely Ustica, far out in the sea just north of the route between Sardinia and Sicily, makes sense in this light, as, in the Aegean, does that of Antikythera, and the finds on Parapola, an obscure rock between the Peloponnese and Cyclades.[346] But the strangest phenomenon of all is minuscule Palagruža, almost the only place from which

7.47 Tiny Palagruža, in the midst of the open Adriatic sea, lives up to its Italian name of Pelagosa. Today it sports a lone lighthouse to warn ships of its existence, but in the later 3rd millennium BC it was a magnet for long-range voyaging.

both shores of the Adriatic can be seen [**7.47**].[347] After slight traces of passage during the expansion of farming came three millennia of silence, abruptly broken in the later 3rd millennium BC by thousands of stone arrowheads, one discovered by a early modern visitor embedded in a buried skeleton, alongside plentiful stone blades and decorated Dalmatian bowls. Many of the stone objects were made of chert from nextdoor Mala Palagruža, but this hardly explains the whole phenomenon. It very much looks as if armed men came to this scrap of rock, as a test in itself or as part of longer voyages, and engaged in combat with each other or the crews of passing seacraft, perhaps even leaving many of the arrows as part of a maritime warrior cult otherwise lost to us.

Concerning the third manifestation, certain kinds of objects now circulated further than ever before by sea (as well as overland, where they equally benefited from the opening up of networks). Those most spectacularly displaced are not always the most informative, as they tend to be outlying escapees that prove the cumulative superconductivity and interlocked nature of a sequence of trading circuits, but tell us little about the reality inside each. Supreme examples are two carnelian beads, etched on the Indus or in Mesopotamia, that ended up in a hoard on Aegina in the Aegean by the end of the 3rd millennium BC [7.48], and a gold dagger from the Mala Gruda tumulus in Montenegro that matches central Anatolian forms in baser metal.[348] Other immensely long-range displacements show more structure, but only grazed the edge of the basin, notably the trickle of lapis lazuli down the Levantine coast to Egypt (one small segment of its 4000-km (2500-mile) journey from central Asia),[349] and the overland spread down the Levant, from 2700 to 2300 BC, of red or black polished pottery derived from wares in the Caucasian, Iranian and east Anatolian highlands, and variously explained by a wine-drinking, metal-working or migratory, pastoral connection.[350]

Instead, we focus on three networks, principally of the mid- to later 3rd millennium, that stretched over large expanses like sprawling octopi, overspilling sub-basins to erase Neolithic boundaries, and yet different, too, from the targeted Byblos route, as well as earlier Uruk and Egyptian expeditions.[351] They were expressed through dissemination of suites of small but valued symbols of a shared way of life among prominent people, mainly metalwork, figurines, items carved or chipped from high-quality stone, and – a newcomer to long-range trade in Mediterranean Europe – pottery drinking vessels covered with designs whose subtle distinctions those in the know would appreciate. Alongside, less visibly, flowed small quantities of the raw materials implicated in this interaction, and the skills to work them. In each case, the veneer of uniformity over great distances dissolves if we focus on individual contexts, which were usually embedded in local culture. For participants in such voyages culti-vated dual identities and affiliations, one rooted in specific places, the second shared with trading partners and other social equals living at a distance, so creating a virtual elite community recognizable by its emblems. In this sense mobility became institu-tionalized not through the kinds of royal cosmologies seen further east, but by social alliances and contacts between peers. Where such people were thick on the ground, fierce little vortices formed, and where the travel costs or transport modes shifted gear, accumulations and other anomalies tend to cluster.

We begin in the west, with the Mediterranean version of the 'beaker' network, a wider universe also involving central Europe, the lower Rhine, south Baltic, British Isles and temperate France over the mid- to late 3rd millennium BC.[352] Beakers were capacious drinking vessels (probably for beer, fermented punches or mead sweet-ened with honey), incised or combed with a bewildering range of patterns, some notably 'international', but others, often later in date, that went native, and whose intricacies have absorbed modern archaeologists just as much as they presumably did the social-decoding skills of drinkers in the 3rd millennium [7.49]. Associated, more or less loosely, were archery gear, especially wrist-guards, sometimes shifts in metalwork and additional features such as amber, mainly northern, but perhaps occasionally inferior material from Sicily.[353] The warrior connotation is apparent, and isotopic analysis of the skeletons from beaker burials in central Europe and Amesbury in southern England confirms the mobility of these people, some of whom were first-generation immigrants to the regions where they died.[354]

7.48 (*opposite*) A far-travelled object: carnelian bead decorated in a style typical of the Indus Valley or southern Mesopotamia, discovered on the Aegean island of Aegina, today just opposite Athens.

7.49 Shared styles in distinctive drinking vessels are a marked feature over much of the Mediterranean in the 3rd millennium BC. This beaker with corded and impressed decoration accompanied a burial at Forcalquier-La Fare in southeast France; it shares its particularities with others in the same region, and generic parallels over much of the western half of the Mediterranean and parts of temperate Europe.

Huge numbers of beakers and related objects are found in parts of Iberia and southern France, especially at the mouth of the Tagus, where dates well before 2500 BC confirm an early point of origin, and from about 2500 BC in Almería, the Aude and lower Rhône, all regions with already evident signs of social aggrandizing.[355] The southern French sequence begins at coastal and riverine sites with 'international' beakers of the maritime type prevalent in Atlantic Europe, later replaced by spreading local styles.[356] Lower density beaker use extended into the western Maghreb, Mallorca, northern Italy and Sardinia (but significantly not Corsica, an early instance of this island being cut out from the connections enjoyed by its polymetallic neighbour), from where a few reached western Sicily, providing part of the earlier case for voyaging but quickly morphing to suit the local preference for painted pottery.[357] The articulating routes were mostly coastal or riverine, the Rhône providing important links with beaker-using people in temperate Europe. But open-sea connections also blossomed. In addition to those involving big islands, an entirely new maritime zone emerged in the 'Mediterranean Atlantic' just beyond Gibraltar, based on tidal estuary-head sites such as Valencina and Zambujal. North along the Atlantic facade, this lobe of beaker associations reached Galicia and cut across the Bay of Biscay to reach Brittany.[358] Indeed, all along the seaways as far as Scandinavia, where boat imagery peppered the rocks of fjords and islets, the later 3rd millennium was a time of new maritime confidence and ambition, if mainly prestige-oriented, with much less implication in everyday networks of survival. Further south, Mediterranean Atlantic connections brought Iberian metalwork, fancy flints, wrist-guards and beakers to the oceanic coast of Morocco, from where some filtered inland, as we saw earlier in this chapter.[359] In return, ivory and ostrich egg, both known as tomb goods in Atlantic Morocco, trickled into Iberia in raw form, where they were carved into local styles.[360] Whether beakers or metal goods were also made in the western Maghreb is unclear, though it raises interesting questions of adoption, or of people on the move, between these extremities of Europe and Africa, that have been in abeyance since the dispersal of farming. We might equally wonder whether any Iberian voyagers paddled further east along Mediterranean Africa, and even speculate whether this ebullient maritime activity might have possibly encountered the Canaries.

There is a surprising dearth of tracers of long-range Tyrrhenian trade, save in Sardinia, and a low profile in the Aeolian islands compared to the Neolithic.[361] Only an increase in seafaring among the so-called 'Gaudo' communities around the Bay of Naples, perhaps a displacement of earlier Aeolian centrality, catches the eye as a hint of things to come.[362] This quiescence, and the more fragmented nature of Tyrrhenian culture at this time, reminds us that networks could diminish as well as burgeon, but what caused this temporary eclipse is unclear. One possibility is the realignment of the western and northern edges of the Tyrrhenian sub-basin towards the beaker zone, combined with the paucity of desirable metals in southerly regions. Over in the Adriatic, more was astir, with even a few archery-related elements of the beaker complex filtering in.[363] The acme here, which would tie together seas and coasts from the head of the Adriatic as far south as Malta and the Gulf of Corinth, came right at the end of the 3rd millennium BC, under peculiar conditions that we shall encounter at the start of Chapter 8. But the internal roots of this lie a few centuries further back.[364] In contrast to the low level of Neolithic traffic, trans-Adriatic crossings became more frequent, as witnessed not least by the popularity of visits to Palagruža. On the same latitude, it was the great tumulus of Mala Gruda on the deep, sheltered Bay of Kotor that snagged from circulation, alongside other wealth goods, that golden Anatolian dagger, while the types of gold rings buried here and in the profligately metal-rich Vučedol communities of the Danubian interior materialize as far south as a similar cluster of tumuli on the Ionian island of Lefkada.[365]

Long-range interaction was intensifying in the Aegean by 2800–2700 BC.[366] It operated between the vibrant sea-trading sites of the Cyclades and other islands and coasts, which circulated metals, figurines, drinking and pouring vessels, including the 'sauceboat' and first jugs (in this region often for wine), as well as a liquid transport bottle and other markers of the good life. Many were locally copied, spreading a way of looking and living. If the cyclic journeys down to Crete and their long return clawed back against prevailing winds via the east or west Aegean seaboard, and those around the north Aegean, are unravelled, they easily qualify as voyages.[367] Different stages in the transformation of metals took place at separate points along the way, the mining in often remote locations, smelting on windswept headlands, and casting into objects at settlements.[368] Initially, extra-Aegean contacts were scanty, save for a piece of eastern hippopotamus ivory tusk at Knossos, a sneaking suspicion that the folded-arm pose of Cycladic figurines aped Anatolian metal originals, and ties in the northeast, around Troy, to southeast Europe and a metal-rich interaction zone around the Black Sea.[369] But after 2500 BC, as big buildings arose at several Aegean centres, this interaction sphere started to overlap increasingly with others to the east [7.50]. A new set of ceramic drinking vessels derived from metal prototypes, their gloss still retaining the latter's aesthetic, coalesced along routes through western Anatolia and was adopted by sea-trading circuits in the central and eastern Aegean, ousting older island rituals surrounding trade, status and burial.[370] One type, the depas (so named by Schliemann after what he saw as a match with a cup described by Homer nearly 2000 years later), is an elegant two-handled form whose frequent lack of a base hints that its contents were downed in one, or passed round, a subtle reminder of the social performances that accompanied drinking. With these came the tentative use of a fast wheel for potting at a few larger sites.[371] In Crete, drink was instead sipped from handleless little goblets, similar to those of Ebla. North Levantine or Mesopotamian metal and pottery flasks for scented oils percolated or were copied further west (Troy boasts a gold example and an ornate pin crowned by a row of six miniatures) [7.51].[372] And as noted already, administrative use of seals spread to the Aegean, as one part of a range expansion that advanced its other frontier to the Indus; most were stamp seals of the kind prevalent in Anatolia, though a few imported Levantine cylinder seals or their impressions survive, notably at the trading hubs of Poliochni and Mochlos.[373] It can even be argued that the Aegean began to use similar ponderal units to those of the Levant.[374] On Crete, a smattering of Egyptian stone vessels appeared, soon locally copied, as did beads made of blue faience, that vitreous ersatz echo of lapis lazuli and turquoise already popular in the east, and a symptom of how the Aegean colour palette might realign under external influence.[375]

Meanwhile, by the later 3rd millennium BC the world of Aegean metals was being stirred up in a manner unparalleled further west. Complex moulds and ornate decorating techniques invented in Anatolia or Mesopotamia appeared, including fine granulation in gold, which lent jewelry at Troy a look analogous to that from royal burials at Ur.[376] And while hitherto most metals had been mined within the Aegean, fresh sources and alloys now came into play, the most significant combining tin and copper to create true bronze.[377] Tin and its alloy appeared in Mesopotamia,

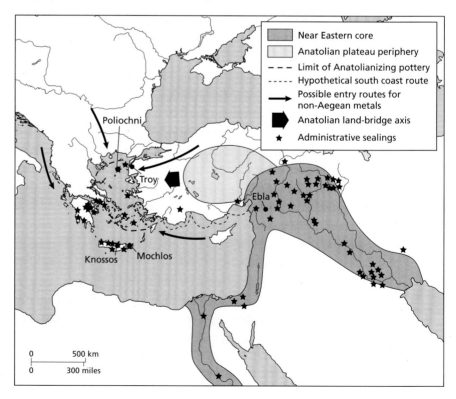

7.50 By the mid-to-late 3rd millennium BC, the Aegean was more exposed than other sub-basins further west to the positive and negative effects of indirect contacts with the larger-scale world of the Near East and its outliers.

7.51 The metallic, cosmetic and sumptuary combine on this gold pin from Troy, with spiral decoration and six attached miniature flask-like jugs, the latter alluding to scented oils or other rarefied liquids.

Anatolia and rarely Egypt (which waged a lengthy resistance to it) early in the 3rd millennium, but quantities rose rapidly after 2500 BC, and spread to the north Levant and Aegean, much probably in pre-alloyed form.[378] At Ebla, tin's value equalled that of silver, and bronze ranked above copper.[379] The first usage of bronze, as suggested earlier, may have owed as much to its rich colour, and (if not pre-alloyed) control over initially arcane knowledge of its recipe and access to its discretely sourced ingredients, as to greater strength and lower casting temperature. The early sources of tin, which is thirty times rarer than copper in the earth's crust, are fiercely disputed.[380] It exists in Western and central Europe (both Mediterranean and temperate), but save for a few finds, some of which may be chance alloys, on the Balkan interface there is little sign of deliberate use there until the end of the 3rd millennium BC.[381] Traces of tin in Iberian artifacts are definitely considered accidents of the peninsula's polymetallic soup. The same has been argued for putative tin-working at the Kestel mine in the Taurus mountains, but the number of early tin-rich finds at nearby Tarsus and Tell Judaidah does in this case lend support to some local extraction from low-grade ores at this time.[382] Though the verdict remains out, here and elsewhere in and beyond Anatolia, the majority of the tin deliberately used at this juncture seems to have come from far to the east, primarily in central Asia, and reached the Mediterranean by two routes. One, also travelled by lapis lazuli obtained from the same rugged part of the world, ran down the Indus and by sea to Mesopotamia, from where it dispersed westward. The other lay to the north, via the Caspian and Caucasus to the Black Sea and Anatolia. Finds of the oil-rich seeds of Caucasian *Lallemantia* plants in northern Greece suggest that the tin on this northern route also picked up fellow travellers.[383] The first Aegean tin bronzes reflect a modest trickle at the end of immense roads, along which metal often changed hands and forms. Yet despite this attenuation, the Mediterranean moral of the tale is that despite being 3000 km (1850 miles) away from the principal source, Aegean people picked up on this circulating novelty before southern Iberians, in many respects their most comparable rivals, had learned to exploit the supplies on their own doorstep.

This observation, extended further to embrace other imports and emulations of eastern goods, raises several intertwined issues. Did the wider networks in which the Aegean was becoming enmeshed exert a more directional and gravitational pull than those that existed further west? In other words, did a Near Eastern world-system start to tug and distort patterns first forged locally, and socially? To a modest degree this may well have been the case, especially with regard to silver, which by 2500 BC was a proto-currency further east, and recorded in huge amounts at Ebla a century or two later. The Aegean and west Anatolia are rich in this metal, and at Troy silver was cast into ingots, a suggestive index of engagement with eastern economies. Speculatively, the scarcity of silver as opposed to gold in Cretan tombs could possibly be explained by the former's higher exchange than symbolic value, which encouraged its passage straight through the island, heading east. A related issue is fidelity of transmission. Save for the additional Pontic axis, the options in terms of connecting routes had not changed since the expansion of farming: overland via the high, non-Mediterranean plateau of Anatolia, or by sea along the south coast. The Anatolian interior was criss-crossed by webs of interaction that blurred seamlessly into the Aegean and the Balkans at one end and the Levant at the other, with places such as Küllüoba acting as repositories and passers-on of all kinds of goods and information.[384] This potentially allowed innovations put to use in Anatolia in something like their eastern manner to be faithfully transmitted west, for example sealing, the potter's wheel and advanced metallurgical techniques. However, knowledge of the heartlands of Mesopotamia must have been refracted to a mythic level, and things passed on but not employed along the way probably likewise arrived with their meaning garbled by transfer from one community to the next. Troy, which faced the Near Eastern, Pontic, Balkan and Aegean worlds, experienced all the advantages and tensions that stemmed from its promiscuous cultural connections. The wealth and variety of its treasures, from amber to lapis lazuli, plus the metals galore, is unique in the Aegean, and the obsession with buried hoards, which included even ingots designed for trade, is symptomatic of an ambivalent desire to consume wealth by committing it to the ground, while retaining the option to reuse it, or in other words of a vacillation between the strategies of Mediterranean funerals further west, and the accumulative priorities witnessed to the east.[385]

Turning to maritime connections, many of these may also have been effected by down-the-line activity and so had the same quality as their terrestrial counterparts, though the archaeological blind spot of the southern Turkish coast afflicts us again. Mochlos was one plausible terminus, where rowlocks shown on in its small clay boat models hint that the idea of oars to replace paddles escaped west ahead of the sail,[386] though other intermediaries must have existed, including on Rhodes, the gateway to and from the Aegean. Yet the sea-route offered the alternative possibility of direct communication without intervening participants, one that might convey objects and ideas associated with 'civilized' behaviour faithfully over great distances. A residue of such hi-fi transmission may be preserved in a few Egyptian bowls made of grey-white mottled anorthosite gneiss, found unstratified at Knossos.[387] If these arrived near the time of their manufacture (2600–2200 BC), this would be of great interest, for such bowls were associated in Egypt with royalty and its immediate circle, and in the Levant concentrate at the palace of Ebla, where they are thought to be pharaonic gifts. Such meaning-rich, prestigious trophies would be precisely the kind of things sought by aspiring Aegean elites, or granted them as tokens of recognition. Direct contacts with Egypt are unlikely, and unnecessary given that these things could be found closer to hand in the Levant. Perhaps occasional Aegean canoes did voyage east, to Tarsus or beyond. Or perhaps a few voyagers on Byblos ships (the two terms strictly and broadly construed, respectively) probed far to the west of their normal cruising range to intercept Aegean silver, a metal in which they had long traded. After all, the mid-3rd-millennium BC date at which the Byblos run consolidated is precisely when eastern objects begin to increase to a modest degree in the Aegean, and also when Cretan groups broke off cultural contacts with their Cycladic trading neighbours and started to search more exotic horizons.[388]

This leaves one final question. Did access to the great world to the east give aspiring people in the Aegean a decisive advantage over their equivalents in Iberia and elsewhere in the Mediterranean?[389] To put it another way, Egypt, Mesopotamia and the Levant are manifestly unnecessary to explain stirrings of social and political change all over the basin, but did they subsequently help to reinforce this trend in the Aegean, enabling more successful take-offs both now and in the ensuing millennium? Here the answer must surely be affirmative. The pool of economic, technological and ideological possibilities in the east, not least those already adapted to Mediterranean conditions by people in the Levant and parts of Anatolia, provided blueprints that obviated the need to reinvent the wheel (literally, and metaphorically for much else besides). They offered pointers as to how power could be institution- ally entrenched, beyond its assertion in extravagant competitive tournaments – even if these means, too, had to be converted to fit local circumstances and would never be straightforward to maintain in a precarious, ever-shifting social and natural environment. Likewise, even if, as is perfectly feasible in each case, such practices as ploughing, weaving of wool and olive and vine cultivation did arise independently, or at least at arm's length from the 'core', the east proffered pre-formulated templates for fitting them together into defined lifestyles and effective packages for wealth generation. And finally, this larger eastern world could stimulate local leaders in neighbouring regions to intensify production of the materials it required, and offer desirable goods in return. Much of what unfolded could notionally have happened unaided, in isolation from the east, as the first Iberian florescence amply indicates, but given that in terms of (variously) ecology, resource diversity, constriction, scale and prior history the Guadalquivir was not the Nile, the Meseta not Nubia, and the Mediterranean Atlantic and western Maghreb not the Levant, it would have taken far longer for breakthroughs to consolidate, with more failures along the way. By the late 3rd millennium BC the Aegean therefore did stand in a position exceptionally pregnant with possibilities, as its locally grown elite began tentatively to engage with a larger-scale world.

Calypso's isles

It may seem perverse to close a chapter that has traced a boom in contact across much of the Mediterranean with two islands that lay far out of the stream. But their extraordinary societies are very much exceptions that prove the rule, as demon- strated not least by the manner of their eventual demise, and as exceptions they are also quite intrinsically strange enough to attract our attention. They may in fact be less unusual than we think; the Mediterranean of the 'long' 3rd millennium BC must have retained more obscure corners than archaeologists have yet plumbed, and in particular certain island conditions allowed trajectories to diverge for longer and

7.52 Monte d'Accoddi on Sardinia is one of the most impressive and least widely known monuments in the early Mediterranean. Here, a view along the axial ascent ramp to the summit of the massive pyramidal structure.

more deeply than was often possible on the mainland.[390] Corsicans, for instance, were erecting their granite menhirs in exceptional numbers.[391] In the interior even of better-connected Sardinia, fat figurines and Ozieri-type traditions were long clung to, and a massive pyramidical platform with a processional approach ramp and red-plastered building on its summit arose at Monte d'Accoddi, over the ruins of an earlier village, burial ground and overthrown menhir.[392] The second version of this monument, constructed around 2800 BC after its predecessor had burnt, was 9 m (30 ft) tall, 30 × 40 m (100 × 130 ft) in ground plan and was ascended by a 40-m- (130-ft-) long ramp culminating in a steep flight of steps – a unique structure that, cloaked in spring verdure, has a peculiarly Maya aspect [**7.52**]. What went on there is unknown, but around it pottery and figurines cluster thickly.

But it is on Malta and Gozo that construction of stone ritual structures reached its most regularly spectacular form.[393] These islands are only 315 sq. km (120 sq. miles) in combined area, and realistic estimates of sustainable densities suggest that there can never have been more than a few thousand islanders.[394] Yet from roughly 3600 BC, through a crescendo of activity that climaxed in the first half of the 3rd millennium, these people erected an unparalleled series of some twenty-five megalithic buildings that we call 'temples', for want of a better grasp of their functions [PL. XXVIII]. These were among the largest free-standing buildings in the world until the pyramids in Egypt. The curving, multilobed ground plans of the basic temple unit resemble earlier rock-cut tombs, but the dead continued to be placed underground in no less fantastic rock-cut hypogea [**1.18**]. The most extensive of these, at Hal Saflieni, was paired with the greatest temple complex at Tarxien and, although almost completely emptied before archaeologists learned of it, is thought to have held the remains of some 9000 people, crammed into several dark, resonant storeys of ochre-painted labyrinthine chambers, passages and hollowed-out simulacra of temple architecture that burrowed deep underground.[395] The

7.53 'Sleeping lady' figurine from Hal Saflieni, surely associated with this site's elaborate death rituals. Note the enduring fidelity to earlier ideals of bodily form, one of the many respects in which societies on Malta eschewed wider developments during much of the 'long' 3rd millennium BC.

vignettes of death-rituals at a recently excavated hypogeum at Xaghra, near the Ggantija temple on Gozo, partly compensate for this loss: ancestral individuals were buried first, sometimes intact and one wearing a headdress of cowries, followed by thousands of disarticulated remains, whose skulls and long bones were moved about and clustered for viewing.[396] Both temples and burial sites yield a wealth of symbolic objects, including obese and other figures of women and men, typically dressed in a skirt-like garment and ranging from one more than life-size colossus to tiny sleeping miniatures, as well as carved reliefs of swirling designs and animals (plus bones from their sacrifice), models of temples, astral aids (several temples align on the risings of celestial bodies, or other features in the land- or seascape), stone axes and masses of elaborate pottery [**7.53**].[397] In contrast, the remains of where people lived have been largely obliterated or buried by later erosion and terracing, save for some postholes around the temples and a few scraps preserved under later field walls.[398] We are thus left to reconstruct society from the exceptional rather than the quotidian. The local group associated with each temple was probably modest, perhaps 100–200 people living off the little arable basins on the edges of which most temples stood, though there must have been ritual mechanisms for engaging more islanders in major building projects. A growing investment in screens, barriers and secret voice-holes in the later, most grandiose temples suggests that access and ritual participation became concentrated in a minority of people who thereby wielded authority, but there is no hint of individual leadership. Instead, everything points to an ultra-corporate society, with competition channelled into intergroup rivalry in building. Art and skeletons indicate, moreover, that women held more powerful positions than seems to have been normal at this time. To round off the strange flavour, the record of these chronologically 'Copper Age' people is entirely devoid of metals.

Explanations of this incredible phenomenon have been sought in numberless theories, from the New Age to the soberly archaeological. One of the most initially appealing, namely that the islands' location comparatively far from other land led to their isolation and cumulative divergence in way of life ('esoteric efflorescence', in a memorable phrase also applied to Easter Island), is undermined by two facts.[399] One is that for the first 1500 years following their arrival in about 5000 BC, these islanders displayed no difficulty in maintaining outside contacts, as indicated by pottery styles that evolve in parallel with Sicily, and imports of stone and other materials.[400] Etna looms on the northern horizon, visible on a clear day. The other is that imports in the temple period itself are not as rare as was once thought: greenstone axes, flint, ochre and a few exotic pots got through, and, as we have seen, the concept of the hypogeum itself had a wider currency.[401] What may instead have happened was a greater channelling and control of links to the world over the sea by the temple authorities, such that an artificial sense of separation and difference was created where none had previously been perceived.[402] This chimes well with the fact that a striking number of temples lie close to access points from the coast, as well as the boat images noted earlier (if these do not date to the following phase).[403] The scope offered by physical insularity was thus manipulated to create a cultural island. But why? One reason could be that this encouraged attention to focus on a frenzy of construction and ritual, to the advantage of those invested in it. Another, maybe related, was that influential islanders wished to reject the social norms developing to the north, specifically the more open, male, martial and metal-associated way of life, in favour of an ultimately Neolithic-derived tradition and differently structured relations between the sexes.[404] The drive to affirm these conservative values led to

7.54 The Copper Age acme of the long Cypriot roundhouse tradition, in the form of the large 'pithos house' at Mosphilia, reconstructed here with its contents.

a spiral of ritual assertion, perhaps with Tarxien-Hal Saflieni and Ggantija-Xaghra acting as island-wide foci by the end. Either way, the relative weakness of contemporary long-range activity in the central Mediterranean made such self-imposed quasi-isolation more feasible than elsewhere; it is very hard to imagine temple-period Malta surviving long in the Early Bronze Age Aegean.

Our other hidden island is Cyprus, thirty times larger than the Maltese cluster, and with a history of divergence from the surrounding mainland that began as early as the 7th millennium BC. Here, a few dozen kilometres from a northern Levant well on its way to the rise of urban, literate palace-based states, the archaic tradition of roundhouses, the heterodox portfolio of pig, sheep, goat and fallow deer, and a younger but equally idiosyncratic style of cruciform figurines in blue-green picrolite, reached its climax in the local Cypriot Middle Copper Age (3500–2700 BC), a phase that in fact evinces only a minor, tardy start to production from the island's copper ores, using by now primitive techniques, and equally slim indices of off-island contacts.[405] Cyprus has no buildings of a weirdness to compare with Malta's temples, but at the village of Mosphilia the circular houses became more

imposing and strictly zoned internally; one was converted into a segregated ceremonial space for depositions, including a set of figurines contained in a house-shaped
bowl [**7.54**].[406] This was again a society committed to different practices from those
current in the world around it. Cyprus's size makes a sustained, conscious strategy
of differentiation harder to envisage than on Malta and Gozo. The long sleep-walk
may instead reflect a sense of self-sufficiency on a large, fertile island for a modest
population living by traditional means that still worked well enough, abetted by a
lack of interest, so far, from people living over the water.

Regardless, both capsules of lifestyles differentiated from the mainstream fell
apart amidst widespread signs of penetration by the outside world before the end
of the 3rd millennium BC. Maltese temple culture ended between about 2400 and
2200 BC, leaving many of the great structures derelict.[407] After an apparent hiatus,
several were reused as living places or cemeteries by people with extensive central
Mediterranean affiliations (as we shall see at the start of Chapter 8), who introduced
the first metal items, and probably the first horses, to the Maltese islands.[408] One
scenario is that temple society overstepped the limits of sustainability in pursuit of
ever more hands to fuel a competitive crescendo of temple construction, and collapsed, perhaps with devastating population loss, although, admittedly, burials at
Xaghra show no signs of stress.[409] Another is that a sharp drying phase that, as we
will see in the next chapter, affected parts of the Mediterranean late in the 3rd millennium BC, pushed it over the edge, though this too runs up against lack of proof.
A third option is revolt against the temple-based leaders (who, despite their grounding in Neolithic tradition, were in fact forging a highly divided society in terms of
access to ritual power), with an ensuing embrace of alternative, off-island customs.
A final scenario, potentially in the aftermath of any of the preceding ones, is an
incursion of newcomers. Whatever the truth, something that remains to this day
hauntingly unusual passed utterly beyond memory, leaving only enigmatic ruins,
and henceforth Malta and Gozo would produce unexceptional variants of central
Mediterranean societies until the arrival of the Phoenicians.

In the case of Cyprus, by 2700–2500 BC Copper Age society was beginning to
show signs of internal disruption and new external connections.[410] Shortly afterwards a suite of indisputably off-island features and surge in settlement numbers,
including big villages, denote a late start to the Early Bronze Age.[411] These include
rectangular architecture, burials in chamber tombs, red-polished pottery drinking
ware and flasks similar to those at Tarsus, changes in cooking, a cluster of shifts
in animal husbandry that brought secondary products to the island with for once
truly revolutionary speed and coherence (including a reintroduction of cattle after
almost 5000 years, as well as ploughs, new breeds of goat, donkeys, slightly later
horses, and upright, warp-weighted looms of Anatolian type), plus new cereals and
wine production (though olive cultivation had begun before the end of the Copper
Age). Many of these activities are illustrated by models of ploughing, milking, grape-
crushing and cult offerings at a tall cattle-shrine, some on huge zoomorphic jugs and
flasks, with an ebullience that celebrates the newness of this way of life on the island

7.55 Clay model of a ploughing scene from the northern Cypriot site of Vounous, one of many indices of rapid cultural and economic turnover during the later 3rd millennium BC on this island.

[**7.55**]. The sheer sweep of these changes, the paucity of convincing internal roots, and the fact that many initially appear in the north and east, especially at Vounous and Lapithos opposite the Anatolian coast, make some influx of people from this quarter one plausible explanation, although aspiring locals may well have established contact with outsiders and emulated their ways too.[412] Certainly, sailing ships passing close to the island must have infringed Cyprus's seclusion. Their stop-offs register in a trickle of imports, at first faience beads but soon Egyptian stone vessels, along with scraps of gold, silver and other metals. But what really galvanized Cyprus's external relations was the realization of the island's potentially vast copper resources, coupled with acquisition of the skills needed to smelt its sulphide ores.[413] Copper began to appear in quantity in rich burials on the island. Much of its presumed outflow was initially controlled by a north-coast entrepôt at Vasilia, which received weaponry, other bronzes and ingots from Anatolia in return.[414] The upshot was a strategic shift: Cyprus, if never entirely relinquishing a distinctive cultural profile, became abruptly 'normalized' relative to its neighbours, and within a few centuries was a major player in east Mediterranean trade. As in the Maltese islands, the victory for connectivity, and the emerging world of the Bronze Age, was complete.

CHAPTER EIGHT

Pomp and circumstance

(2200 – 1300 BC)

All that glitters

If asked to name the most spectacular discoveries from the early Mediterranean, most people's answers would gravitate to the 2nd millennium BC. Take, just in the Aegean, the 'Palace of Minos' at Knossos, the treasures of Mycenae, the frescoed interiors of Akrotiri, buried by the Thera volcano, and the Homeric resonance of Troy. Or further east, the cosmopolitan city of Ugarit, the time capsule of the Uluburun shipwreck off the wild southern coast of Turkey, and the urban giant of Tell el-Dab'a, now rising again from the Delta's mud to challenge us as in its heyday it did the kings of the Nile Valley – including the founder of a line that fizzled to its end with the teenage Tutankhamun, whose tomb furnishes another marvel, beyond the basin itself but tracing connections far into it. Even setting iconic finds aside, the 2nd millennium BC is without earlier parallel in terms of quantity and quality of evidence. Beyond the normal staples of archaeology, troves of written records illuminate their surroundings like starbursts, while the increase in representational imagery reveals undreamt-of vistas. Of course, text and image must be understood as expressions of preoccupations often quite different from the answers that we seek from them. But notwithstanding this, the 2nd-millennium BC Mediterranean offers a convergence of data that is rare and privileged on a global scale for its time, and long afterwards.

Admittedly, this is not the whole picture. Much of the above applies mainly to that part of the basin between the Nile Delta, Levant and Aegean, during their Middle and Late Bronze ages. In the contemporary Early and Middle Bronze age central and west Mediterranean, different, smaller-scale, if no less interesting societies flourished, whose characteristics and engagements (if any) with people to the east we will need to explore, too, in order to obtain a balanced view of how Mediterranean lives were evolving. Unfortunately, the information about Africa's coastal belt west of the Nile reaches its nadir at this point.[1] Slight relics of contact with people from other shores shed a glimmer of light on tentative trans-Mediterranean connections, but little on the indigenous people themselves, about whom we remain ignorant until things heated up on Egypt's western, 'Libyan' desert marches in the final centuries of the millennium. Equally, even in the east a few areas buck the trend, revealing very different ways of living on the edges of a big world. Last but not least, even at the heart of that world, the underpinnings of its grandeur and authority were still

345

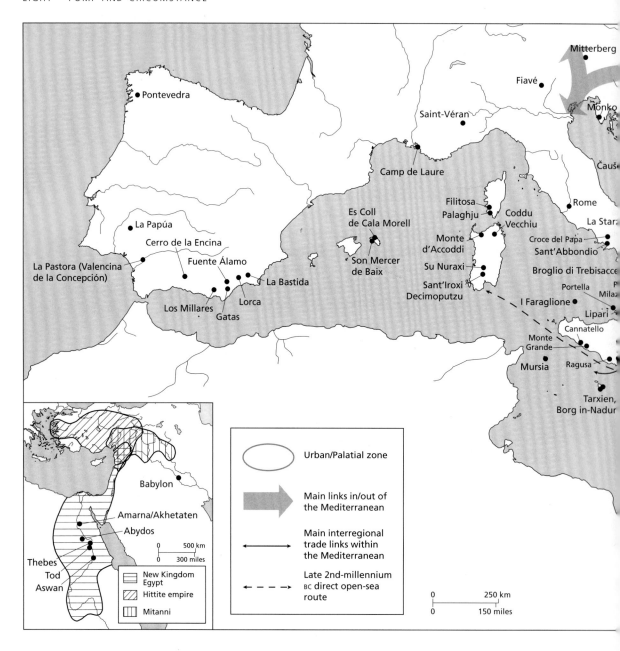

8.1 Map of principal sites mentioned in this chapter, also showing the extent of the urban and palatial world during the 2nd millennium BC, significant connections within and beyond the basin and (inset) the extent of the principal later 2nd millennium BC eastern proto-empires, and their zones of overlap.

in part grounded in modest, humdrum practices, across the countryside, in towns and at sea, that remained highly sensitized to the scope of the possible within a Mediterranean environment. Demands from the top shaped behaviour lower down, commonly influencing what was grown, manufactured or traded, but, equally, there were enough gaps in the vision and reach from the summit to ensure that all kinds of separate localized priorities continued to operate. Braudel once astutely surmised that 'the dazzling civilizations we have glimpsed may have been no deeper than a layer of gold leaf'.[2] We need not feel guilty at being drawn to that dazzle, for it signals some of the most decisive (if not always palatable) developments in Mediterranean

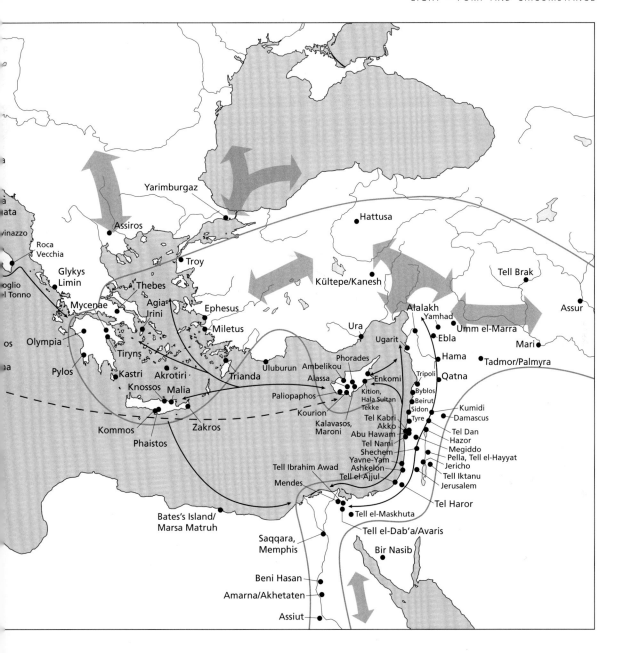

history at this time, but its brightness must not blind us to other ways of living within the shadows it cast, and beyond its range.

The previous chapter introduced the idea that these 2nd-millennium societies, so often enthusiastically seized upon by archaeologists and historians of later periods as ancestral to the Classical world, themselves had their origins back in the 'long' 3rd millennium BC, among the seismic shifts that Mediterranean lives and environments underwent over that time span. Accordingly, this chapter's theme is no longer why such ways of living first emerged. Instead, it asks how they coevolved, expanded and interacted within Mediterranean conditions, to create a patchwork of similar cultural practices and realms of engagement that embraced a growing proportion of the land and sea, and one ultimately distinct from the original civilizations of Mesopotamia and upriver Egypt. If we can understand, for example, why certain people were tuning to a wavelength more akin to their equivalents' across the sea than to those of close neighbours beyond the basin, we will have laid promising foundations for the final stages of our history. For if a puzzle hangs over this period, it concerns legacies rather than origins, and the transition from the Bronze Age to the ostensibly different, and for the first time truly pan-Mediterranean, Iron Age of the 1st millennium BC. To allow a proper interpretative run-up towards this final question, the present chapter stops unconventionally early, at around 1300 BC (allowing for some local flexibility), with the Bronze Age system in the east still running on full throttle, and therefore well before a notorious, traditionally epoch-ending horizon of destructions there a century later.

A testing time

For now, however, the end of the Bronze Age lies in the future. More compellingly urgent is a marked hiatus towards the close of the 3rd millennium BC. For although strong underlying similarities link the societies of this and the ensuing millennium, in the short term the transition was often anything but smooth. The nature and causes of this disruption furnish one last instance of climatic perturbation and its impacts on early Mediterranean history. Over parts of southwest Asia, the drying trend that we have tracked for more than a millennium underwent a jagged acceleration after 2500 BC, culminating from approximately 2200 BC in two spikes of severe aridity, before a levelling off at the start of the 2nd millennium.[3] Windborne Mesopotamian dust shows up in unprecedented Holocene quantities in cores from the Persian Gulf, sand layers accumulated at coastal sites, lakes fell in the Levant, streams down-cut as their gradients steepened and rainfall grew more intermittent and prone to flash-flooding deluges, while a drought-tolerant, humped breed of cattle, the zebu, was introduced to the Jazira, and at Saqqara an ultra-dry-loving beetle species makes its first appearance.[4] Across the rest of the Mediterranean, complementary climatic evidence is tardily, if patchily, starting to emerge from the Aegean to the Atlantic.[5]

Archaeological signatures of abrupt change extend, albeit unevenly, across the basin. The downturn intersected with Mediterranean history at a busy time of diverse, unprecedented developments. This, and the varied nature of micro-ecologies, ensured that both the climatic impact and people's responses varied immensely, though with some association between drier areas and greater dislocation. A closer look at several examples proves rewarding, for as ever in the study of so-called 'collapse', we learn a lot about societies from how they fall apart, endure or adapt.[6] In fact, even this drawn-out disaster, whose magnitude exceeded anything that people could predict or prepare against, reveals impressive resilience on the part of many of the new kinds of societies that had been evolving around the basin in the preceding thousand-plus years. We can even discern a few exceptional cases where, thanks to protection from the worst, the implosion of pre-existing centres and interconnections, or the stimulus of adversity itself, fresh initiatives were fostered in previously obscure parts of the basin.

In general, the most elaborate and rigid social structures of trade were most susceptible to collapse, both because the reputation of those at the top for effective organization and intercession with the gods was compromised, and because their investment in the status quo gave them less incentive to initiate change.[7] Though a long-claimed run of low Nile floods is proving harder to affirm than once thought, Old Kingdom Egypt, perhaps intrinsically prone to disintegration after centuries of centralized rule and the growing local embeddedness of powerful families, broke up into local dominions around 2160 BC.[8] Contemporary sources refer to militias and crises, while a later literature, manifestly rhetorical and obsessed with the benefits of royal order, but also surely reflecting an admixture of real memories, lamented recurrent famines and cannibalism. Archaeological testimony comes from Mendes in the eastern Delta, where late Old Kingdom burials were poor and cramped, with skeletal markers of nutritional stress; subsequently, the cemetery was desecrated, a nearby temple razed and dozens of massacre victims left lying amidst the marks of conflagration.[9] But even in Egypt there was another side to the story, for the ending of central taxes, royal prerogatives and toiling on monument construction brought dividends to people beyond the traditional elite, whose cultural and spiritual worlds were enhanced by modest, localized forms of status goods (often garbled versions of Old Kingdom types), as well as widening access to the sacred paraphernalia and texts that ensured access to the afterlife. Among the numerous survivors, not least in the Delta, this release from the pharaonic straitjacket created vibrant opportunities for new people and forms, including the soon-ubiquitous scarab seal,[10] to take hold. These would continue to influence society and culture long after the return of the kings.

The demise by 2150 BC of the Akkadian hegemony in Mesopotamia, which had displayed its fragility at each royal succession, is unsurprising.[11] More striking is a waning of many towns across the Jazira, save Brak and irrigation-based Mari on the Euphrates, a blow from which urban life there took centuries to recover.[12] In neighbouring regions the picture is uneven.[13] Ebla and Hama hung on in a reduced form, but Ugarit was abandoned, as apparently were Tyre and Sidon.[14] While Byblos survived, it lost its special relationship with the pharaohs – 'none sail north to Byblos today' as was bemoaned, from an Egyptian perspective, in the hazily dated *Admonitions of Ipuwer*.[15] Further south the picture is especially bleak.[16] According to one estimate south Levantine population crashed to a tenth or twentieth of its previous level. Most large settlements emptied, to be replaced by a scatter of tiny, short-lived sites, often marked by burial tumuli or dolmens. All over the Jazira and Levant, this dislocation enabled expansion and penetration by the tribal pastoral groups that, during the 3rd millennium BC, had been coalescing in the steppic fringes, stimulated not least by the growing urban market for their products. Such people were known as known as 'Amorites' and often viewed with trepidation by villagers and town-dwellers – the last king of Akkad allegedly battled some of them northeast of the Palmyra oasis, itself an island of connections in a drying steppe.[17] The subsequent distribution of Amorite names argues for the infiltration of many settled communities, sometimes at the very highest, dynastic levels.

Elsewhere in the basin the evidence is patchy. Most of the ambitious Aegean societies of the previous centuries, including the great houses of southern Greece, the canoe-based maritime circuits of the Cyclades and the rash of settlements that had swept out across the landscape, came to an end.[18] The timing around 2200 BC is highly suggestive. Los Millares and most of its Iberian contemporaries likewise went into terminal decline, though the chronology suggests a more drawn-out process, and one grounded in a transition from supersites controlling trade in prestige goods to a more robust pattern of multiple, smaller controlling sites based on localized power relations.[19] As noted in Chapter 7, the end-date of the Maltese temples stands open between 2400 and 2200 BC, making this most enigmatic of island societies potentially another casualty. Coincidentally or not, the close of the 3rd millennium BC also witnessed the demise of other megalithic climaxes in the west, from Antequera to Arles, and a sharp reduction in social complexity also on Sardinia.[20]

So much for the doom and gloom, the grim reality of which is hardly in doubt. But as we saw in the Nile Delta (and, from an Amorite point of view, elsewhere), the inverse can be equally striking. Three more examples highlight further subtleties and affirm that plenty of Mediterranean societies survived, and even flourished. Our first comes from the southern Levant, one of the worst-hit regions and today renowned for unrivalled research into the impact of aridity.[21] Among the ranks of villages and towns that failed, a minority in fact survived. Some of these carried on cultivating olives and grapes, which implies regular water supply and confirms that these crops had become part of the local fabric of survival. Such places may reflect more flexible communities where adjustments were easier to effect (especially among non-hierarchical villages east of the Jordan), although it must be admitted that many simply lay close to the few springs or streams that survived the desiccation, for instance at Tell Iktanu in Jordan. But equally, it is becoming clear that the surviving former inhabitants of settlements deprived of such a lifeline did not simply abandon farming for pastoralism – actually a more romantic than practical response to Mediterranean adversity. Rather, in place of a firm division between complex agricultural communities and specialized herders, the pattern blurred as these ends of the spectrum converged on an oscillating middle, creating a shifting combination of low-density, small-scale farming and herding able to respond and relocate as necessary.[22] At least for some groups, this resilient strategy of rolling with the environmental punches appears to have worked fairly well.

A second positive response could not be more different and focuses, surely not coincidentally, on a region blessed with the highest rainfall in the Mediterranean. We saw in Chapter 7 how trans-Adriatic networks strengthened in the 3rd millennium BC, while rich tumuli along the eastern seaboard attested to the rise of sporadic metal-rich elites, all rather on the fringes of the far-flung beaker and Aegean connections to

8.2 Necklaces and pendants in faience, ostrich egg, large fish-bones and pebbles, one of the last inlaid with mother-of-pearl, are among the finds from the cemetery within the former temple at Tarxien that testify to a new emphasis on off-island culture and connections.

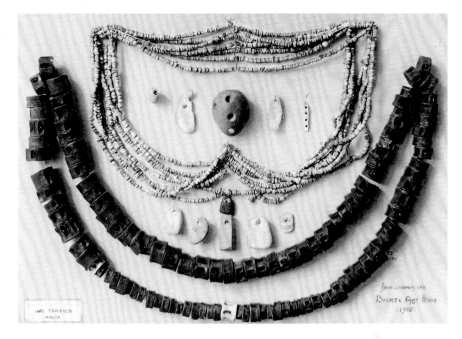

the west and east. One cluster of tumuli with inhumations and cremations, ornately impressed drinking and eating vessels, daggers and archery kit is known as the Cetina culture, after a brimming river that flows out from the rain-gathering mountains and their ore-rich hinterland into the Adriatic near Split, opposite an enticing prospect of islands spreading out towards southeast Italy.[23] These modest beginnings offer little warning of its eruption over the last two centuries of the 3rd millennium BC all over the coastal Adriatic, from the Trieste karst and Veneto to Apulia and Campania, and out through the Strait of Otranto into the wider central Mediterranean.[24] It took the end of the Cold War for the penny to drop that Cetina is the common denominator behind a long-noted set of parallels in pottery, cremations, figurines and other finds as far apart as post-temple Malta, Sicily and western Greece, including a site beneath the altar of Zeus at Olympia. At one end of this distribution, necklaces of faience (by this time a widely distributed technology), ostrich egg and fish bone, copper daggers and axes, and a strange blue and gold bead, accompanying the cremation urns in the ruined temple at Tarxien on Malta, as well as Pantellerian obsidian on contemporary Gozo, proclaim a wide and eclectic range of marine connections [**8.2**].[25] It is possible, too, that the Tarxien boat images (see Chapter 7) date to this, rather than the temple, phase; if so, they join one more from the Ionian island of Ithaca of similar date – an apposite find for the legendary home of Odysseus.[26] At the other end, in the Gulf of Corinth, the cross-over of Cetina expansion with the surviving elements of Aegean networks explains a trail of bossed bone plaques, carved in Sicily and found not only in Apulia and at Tarxien, but as far east as Lerna and Troy [**8.3**].[27] Behind part of this Cetina expansion lay the circulation of Alpine and Balkan metals, maybe now including tin, but the intrusive flavour abroad is also strongly suggestive of maritime groups on the move from Dalmatia.[28] Regardless, the expansion's timing and

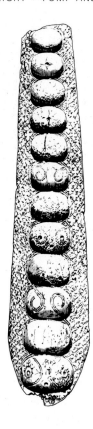

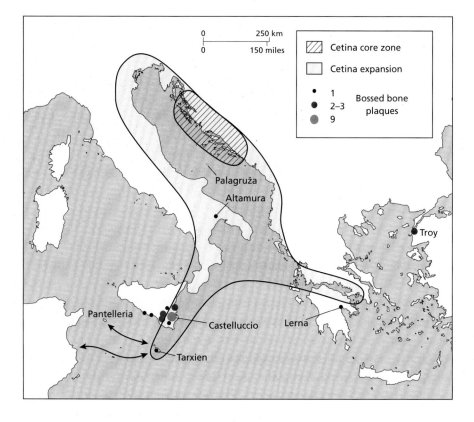

8.3 Cetina expansion temporarily brought the Adriatic into wider Mediterranean prominence, arguably for the first time. The networks it forged enabled the functionally enigmatic bossed bone plaques of Sicily (example pictured *left*) to reach destinations as far apart as Malta, where Sicilian strait connections were also expanding, and the Aegean sites of Lerna and Troy, long before regular contacts were established between the Aegean and central Mediterranean in the mid-to-late 2nd millennium BC.

abrupt evaporation at the start of the 2nd millennium closely associates it with the climatic crunch around 2200 BC. As this disrupted neighbouring societies and hubs of trade, a sudden window of opportunity opened for the seafarers based in between, in a region largely impervious to drought. Looking far into the future, it is decidedly thought-provoking that the next time Adriatic seafarers broke out into the wider Mediterranean would also be the next time that Aegean societies imploded, 1000 years later, at the end of the Bronze Age.[29]

Our final example of interesting times is Crete. There, the centuries after 2200 BC, which saw widespread disruption elsewhere in the Aegean, are a time of dramatic social change that culminated in the construction of the first Minoan palaces around 1950–1900 BC.[30] In Chapter 7 we concluded that over most of the 3rd millennium BC Iberia and the Aegean were fairly comparable in terms of the bottom-up growth of minor foci of wealth and power, with the crucial difference that the Aegean enjoyed links, however filtered, to larger societies further east, from which Iberia was cut off. A broadly world-systemic perspective therefore holds good for the Aegean earlier in the 3rd millennium and subsequently for much of the 2nd, but the truth is that the initial take-off was restricted to Crete, and took place exactly when the principal core zones to the east were in decline.[31] Whether this patchily lush mini-continent out to sea was better buffered from climatic hardship, or whether the latter destabilized communities sufficiently to allow a few advantaged groups to expand, are unresolved matters. Add to this a fascination ever since Sir Arthur Evans with the culture of palatial Crete

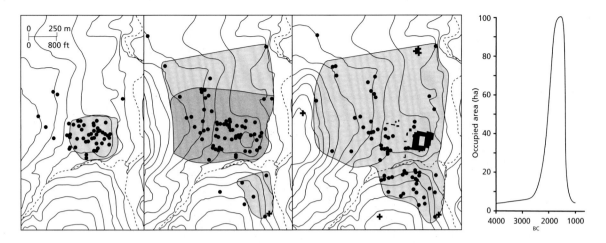

8.4 Knossos takes off: from mid-3rd millennium BC village, to expanding proto-urban centre around 2000 BC, to an exceptionally large early 2nd millennium BC palatial town. Plotted against a longer duration, the urban spike appears particularly dramatic.

8.5 The earliest definite Aegean image of a sailing ship is on this seal-stone from a tomb at Platanos in southern Crete, dated stylistically to within a century or so of 2000 BC. Note the accompaniment of large, pelagic fish.

and its mythic legacy, and it is no surprise that 'Minoan state formation' remains one of the more alluring, if intractable, questions in Mediterranean archaeology.

One stumbling block is the fact that we are still not sure precisely what we are trying to explain. As we shall see, at a schematic level the Minoan palaces and towns represent one western extremity of a fluctuating continuum of Bronze Age palatial states that stretched deep into Asia, yet they display peculiarities in significant details that equally hint at stranger places, and ambiguous ancestries. The other problem is the poor archaeological record just preceding their emergence, not least thanks to the great levelling and overbuilding operations that followed. In spite of this, scraps of evidence reveal an island in ferment. Knossos, the oldest continuously inhabited place on Crete (a fact that might have mattered if recognized at the time), offers tantalizing hints. In around 2200 BC a massive wall and court were built on the same alignment as the later palace facade, and by the end of the millennium the surrounding settlement had grown prodigiously from 5–6 to around 40 ha (12–15 to 100 acres) – in other words, from a village to one of the Mediterranean's larger communities in at most ten generations [**8.4**].[32] Here and elsewhere extensive territories began to be staked out; new wheeled vehicles allowed bulk goods to be conveyed to emergent towns (the other, pot-throwing, use of rotary technology entered the island roughly simultaneously), while the rise of peak-top sanctuaries, open-air shrines at highly visible points in the uplands, ritually unified the lowland communities around them.[33] Early experiments with writing indicate other emergent forms of symbolic control.[34]

Crete's relations with the wider Mediterranean underwent restructuring too. In Chapter 7 we saw that by the mid-3rd millennium BC Cretan groups were occasionally obtaining exotics from further east, perhaps in return for Aegean silver. From around 2000 BC Cretan seals start to depict the first sailing ships known in the Aegean [**8.5**].[35] The generic similarity to the Byblos ships of the preceding millennium militates against independent invention, but this still raises questions. Were these eastern ships? If so, from where? Or do the images imply Cretan adoption of a technology picked up abroad, like uses of the wheel? If the latter – and by soon afterwards

8.6 Clay model of a sistrum, a musical instrument associated in Egypt with the goddess Hathor, and found in an early 2nd-millennium BC funerary context at Archanes, south of Knossos. The precise significance of this link remains elusive, but hints at the widening cosmological ambit of an emergent Crete, perhaps mediated via Byblos.

Aegean people were certainly building such vessels – the depictions imply that the eastern contacts, which such ships themselves greatly facilitated, were now direct enough to transmit construction details, and much else besides. Either way, the trans-Anatolian overland route to the Aegean, which had dominated the 3rd millennium BC, was superseded.[36] From this point on, eastern imports focus on Crete, their numbers rise sharply and for the first time Aegean exports become visible too, the earliest on Cyprus.[37] Several of the early imports on Crete are Egyptian, notably scarabs, amulets and cosmetic pots, mainly derived from the provincial culture of the Nile Delta and further upriver, plus several clay imitations of the sistrum, a symbol of Hathor [**8.6**].[38] We should, however, resist the urge to assume that direct contacts had opened up with the Nile, for such goods could well have been obtained from the intervening Levant, perhaps at Byblos, a focus of silver and other distant trade, itself soon to take up writing in the guise, unlike Crete, of adapted Egyptian hieroglyphs. From an only slightly later context at Byblos, similar scarabs and amulets were interred with a promiscuous range of Egyptian, Levantine and broader Near Eastern metalwork, seals and beads in a jar dedicated, perhaps after a voyage, over the ruins of the temple to Ba'alat Gebal – the Lady of Byblos synonymous with Egyptian Hathor, herself a protectress of travellers [**8.7**].[39] This find, combined with the flavour of imports on Crete, casts an unexpected light on the opening stage of Crete's direct engagement with the east Mediterranean, in terms of locations, the likelihood of non-royal

8.7 A selection of the highly diverse contents of the Montet jar (named after its excavator), dedicated at Byblos and including examples of an ape figurine, early Egyptian scarabs and toggle pins of a type most popular further north.

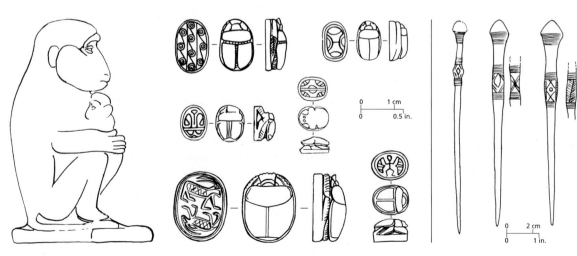

players, and a persistent association with women, ritual, or both.[40] Just as patterns of change within Crete imply something more specific than simply a culmination of processes common to much of the 3rd-millennium BC Aegean, so the early eastern contacts confound expectations. We may never know precisely why Minoan palatial society arose as and when it did, but our best hope is to appreciate the peculiarities of its internal structure and the unusual Mediterranean circumstances within which they emerged.

The east Mediterranean palatial polity in outline

After 2000 BC, communities and landscapes all over the east Mediterranean began to regenerate swiftly. The details varied, but we can pick out common trends over the 2nd millennium that reveal convergence on broadly similar practices and ways of life. Landscapes, though as diverse as ever, and still with large areas of small-scale mixed farming interspersed with upland, steppe, wetland and tracts of surviving woodland, began to take on a more anthropogenic, zoned and (as donkeys and carts percolated into wider use) integrated and complementary aspect. This reflected the impact of palatial and other urban economies, which led the way in large-scale cereal farming to feed themselves and their dependent labourers, plus in cash-cropping of olives and vines both for internal consumption and, increasingly, export. People in the plains and surrounding, patchily olive-silvered hills were most closely embroiled with such power-centres, but the latters' feelers reached into mountains and steppe as well, reaffirming the uneasy symbiosis with the pastoral communities multiplying there in response to burgeoning markets for milk products and wool. Many of the shrines to the gods that would become such a regular feature of the east Mediterranean in the 2nd millennium BC were situated in settlements, but others (like the Cretan peak sanctuaries) sprang up at high elevations, which often became the seats of deities and so visually bound towns and their hinterlands into sacred as well as economic units, these two spheres being intimately connected.[41]

The towns and the palaces at their hearts represent a common module that we first encountered at Ebla in Chapter 7, but one that as it proliferated adapted to a wide range of scales. A few giant communities reached 100 ha (250 acres) or more, with populations well into five figures and multi-storey palaces as extensive as a sizeable village. More frequent were medium to small towns of a few thousand inhabitants, focused on less grandiose, though still imposing, central buildings. Although it is often assumed that the early Mediterranean was overwhelmingly rural, in equivalent Mesopotamia it is thought that up to 80 per cent of people were town-dwellers,[42] and even though east Mediterranean proportions are more elusive, and surely varied, there is little doubt that here, too, towns held concentrations of producers and consumers that sometimes at least matched numbers in the surrounding countryside.[43] This should not disguise a marked boom-to-bust tendency in the life histories of individual urban communities. At first glance this seems belied by the solidity of the tells that they often generated, which certainly do indicate durable beliefs about residence and community, but closer inspection reveals a bewildering pattern of urban foundation, abandonment, expansion and shrinkage, as local or wider opportunities and adversity dictated.

Palaces as they evolved in their east Mediterranean form were central to most urban communities and, beyond, to an entire economic system.[44] As witnessed at Ebla, 'palace' connotes far more than the residence and household of a ruler, even if most never quite relinquished this patrimonial aspect, at least at a symbolic level.[45] It serves as the shorthand for a physical and organizational structure dedicated to large-scale farming, storage and processing, skilled multimedia manufacture, technological know-how and innovation in hothouse conditions, literate supervision of the complex flows of materials and labour demanded by such tasks, as well as trade and gift-giving (often deploying its own high-value products), both internally and with peers beyond the palace's rule. Gone are the days when food storage in the palatial system was interpreted in primarily benevolent terms as a form of managerial 'redistribution' necessary in an uncertain environment, taking a tithe in good times and dispensing aid in bad ones; people could survive perfectly well in the Mediterranean without palaces, and texts suggest that bailing out subjects (as opposed to affirming the debts of the less fortunate) rarely figured in palatial agendas.[46] Instead, palaces were extractive institutions that mobilized wealth from taxes, estates, share-cropping, compulsory labour, trade or other means in the interests of those near the top of the hierarchy, whose position was validated by traditions of deference, kinship and other social alliances, association with the gods to whom they sacrificed and judicious rewards to loyal retainers, backed if necessary by coercion, over which palaces jealously guarded a military monopoly.[47] The proportion of the agricultural, manufacturing and trading activity that palaces controlled via such 'command economies' was far less than the total amount going on in their territories, leaving plenty of room for independent activity, some of which they taxed but much of which operated at a level below their reach.[48] But this does not imply that palaces were weak; rather, they were selective, targeting sectors with maximal potential for wealth generation, calculated displays of largesse and status definition. In addition to the universal focus on oil, wine, cereals and wool, care was taken to stockpile costly materials, especially those obtained from afar, and to ensure control of craftspeople with the skill to turn these into yet more valued objects; fleeing craft experts could be recovered by force, while their agreed transfer between palaces became a conduit for the transmission of cutting-edge skills. In fact, the greatest, most long-established palaces must have been extraordinary repositories of knowledge, not just in practical terms, but of recondite information about the worlds of people and gods, distant times and places, and the deeper meanings and histories of the intricate objects and images with which they were filled. Within these generalizations there was room for a lot of variation in time and space, but the Bronze Age palace loomed over 2nd-millennium BC east Mediterranean society and economy as it towered over its subjects' houses, and we accordingly need to retain a generic model of its workings in our minds.

Ports were an equally key element in such east Mediterranean landscapes or, in this instance, coast-scapes. They might be towns in their own right, but the locally paramount urban palatial settlement usually lay a little distance inland. Some smaller ports arose independently, perhaps run by consortia of sea-trading families, and accumulated a degree of wealth belied by their diminutive size. Byblos, which never grew substantially, already furnished an example of this highly Mediterranean phenomenon in Chapter 7, and we shall encounter others below. Harbour facilities still mainly comprised those offered by nature: bays, coves, the lee of coastal islets or headlands, lagoons and lastly rivers, at their mouth or further upstream.[49] This entailed offshore mooring for large or laden ships, unloading by smaller lighters, and perhaps applications of pitch to hulls to avoid the attentions of marine worms.[50] Faint hints of artificial improvement can be picked up at a few Levantine ports, for instance poorly dated cuttings in a long sandstone ridge at Sidon, a breakwater of boulders at Yavne-Yam, and a reference in the Ugarit archives to a ship colliding with a quay.[51] Sadly, in the Mediterranean nothing has been found to rival Marsa Gawasis, ancient Sawaw, Egypt's early 2nd-millennium BC Red Sea port, with its ship timbers, still-coiled ropes, stone anchors, votive shrines, workshops, storerooms and discarded storage chests from the Punt trade.[52] A wall-painting from Akrotiri does, however, afford us one glimpse of an Aegean harbour, set amidst a cluster of coves, in sprinting range of a coastal town [PL. XXX], while a later, 14th-century BC painting from the tomb of Kenamun in upriver Egyptian Thebes shows a quayside scene on the Nile with docked Levantine ships [8.8].[53] Both underscore that there was more to ports than their facilities. They were gateways, places of encounter between different people (note the formalized greetings and demarcating dress codes) and knowledge hubs, where news and ideas as much as goods were sought and exchanged. Even though commonly under palatial supervision, not least due to the lucrative harbour dues surely generated by their comings and goings, such melting pots slowly encouraged the rise of personae and practices less susceptible to control by terrestrial authority. The term 'port power' nicely summarizes this phenomenon, which would intensify steadily over the millennium.[54]

8.8 Cross-cultural encounter at a river-port somewhere along the Nile during the 14th century BC, as portrayed at Egyptian Thebes in the tomb of Kenamun. Levantine merchants dock their ships and unload goods, while Egyptian men and at least one woman await them with a balance-scale and other equipment at the ready. Formalized greeting gestures and rituals are much in evidence.

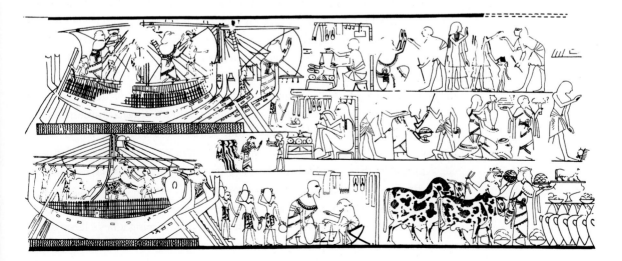

Towns, palaces and coastal ports, together with expanses of land dotted with their subordinate villages, farms and occasional elite estates, are the main components of the regional power structures we know as 'states' or 'polities'. As discussed in the previous chapter, the utility of such terms is sometimes greater or less, but semantics aside, the political units into which much of the east Mediterranean became divided display vast variations in scale, from a few dominions of well over 10,000 sq. km (3850 sq. miles) to numerous examples comprising a single town with a surrounding territory hardly a tenth that size – Crete, an island of 8260 sq. km (3190 sq. miles), was divided up at one point into perhaps a dozen or so such units.[55] Moreover, these entities grew and shrank as they subsumed their neighbours, themselves were swallowed, or simply fell apart. How authority within them was distributed is another matter again. The model of a king with an encircling court of relatives and other high officials is a decent norm, but confounded by several cases where leadership is strangely low-profile and may have been quite differently constituted, and others where royal power barely exceeded that of a wider elite group.[56] In Mesopotamia and Egypt, too, power was more widely shared than once believed, but the Mediterranean provides unusually insistent clues of heterogeneous forms of rule. If there is a common feature to these early Mediterranean states it lies less in how they were governed than in their alignment across micro-environments. A remarkable number of those encountered in this and the following chapters occupied a lateral cross section of landscape, typically defined by a river's course, with one foot in the sea, the main body set back slightly in a coastal plain, and the other foot planted in a rugged hinterland, typically giving access to routes reaching far into the interior.[57] This combination was favoured over time, thanks to its unrivalled ability to harness and integrate the food-mobilizing and wealth-acquiring openings of both land and sea. Its mesh with the typical scales of Mediterranean landscapes also goes some way to explaining the modest size of many polities.

Evaluating such palatial polities requires striking a balance between uncritical adulation of their artistic creations and an excessively mordant concentration on their exploitative, unequal and sometimes blatantly brutal faces. Somewhere in the middle lies the crucial truth that for better or worse these were radically successful entities in their own terms, ones that transformed substantial parts of the basin. Demography and aggregate wealth surged in their spheres of operation. Pan-Mediterranean population probably pushed towards 15 million people over the course of the 2nd millennium BC, with perhaps a quarter of the whole in the 10–15 per cent in the east that came under palatial sway.[58] Within this, some places experienced peaks that would remain locally unrivalled for the rest of this book's time span.[59] Only some of this dramatic growth can be explained by the nutritional edge enjoyed by those, similarly distributed, areas most invested in large-scale olive oil production. Likewise, this chapter plots massive overall distinctions in total wealth between the east and the rest, regardless of internal distribution. However rapacious elites might be, they had an interest in encouraging a large labour pool and tax base, and whatever the involuntary Faustian bargains struck by subjects in terms of their personal security within states, there is no doubt that the essentially new economic security created by state-level structures vastly stimulated production, exchange and consumption, with the palaces themselves leading the way.

Finally, we need to clarify what these polities were not. The new abundance of writing and images reveals a number of name labels and visual stereotypes for locals and foreigners, beyond those already noted in Egypt in Chapter 7. While these inform us about how those at the top defined themselves and their subjects relative to others considered to be different, as early efforts at ethnic ascription they were crude and tell us practically nothing about any senses of identity felt by those people on whom such categories were imposed, which we may suspect were subtler amalgams of a localized sense of place or kinship and broader affiliations (a rare known example being the self-ascriptive 'Canaanite' for much of the Levant),[60] to be negotiated and played up or down as the occasion required. Moreover, beyond an Egyptian idealization of a cosmically central Nile Valley as the true dwelling place for Egyptian people, there is nothing to suggest that these categories mapped closely onto the geopolitics of the age.[61] Much the same can be said of language, where states hastened the selection of a few winners over a likely multitude of losers, but again with multilingualism, formal trade languages and mosaics of speech communities within each region still very much the norm. Early east Mediterranean polities were thus quite different creatures from later nation states. Not until well into the Iron Age, and then only in certain cases, can strongly constituted ethnic groups be taken as even semi-reliable building blocks for major dimensions of Mediterranean history – a matter to which we return in Chapters 9 and 10.

Palaces around the pond

So much by way of introduction. What of the actual texture of developments around the east Mediterranean? For now we shall restrict ourselves to the first half of the 2nd millennium, as after 1500 BC considerable alterations took place within the general framework. We begin on the Nile, where the start of the Middle Kingdom in the final decades of the preceding millennium denotes reunification, again originating upriver, and, under a strong 12th Dynasty based near el-Lisht (south of Memphis), the resurgence of royal power at home and abroad.[62] This regime lasted for two centuries, after which the fissioning tendencies resumed. Despite a self-conscious back-referencing to Old Kingdom and still earlier pharaohs, the reality was more complex, due in part to the enduring legacy of widened social access and more caring forms of lordship derived from the years of fragmentation, and in part to fresh initiatives such as the conquest of Nubia, which boosted the gold supply, and widespread irrigation in the Fayum, which augmented Egypt's already vast areas of farmland.

At the Mediterranean interface two features stand out. One was the resumption of the Old Kingdom tradition of royally sponsored sea-trading and raiding, especially to the central and north Levant. A discovery at Memphis provides superb insights into such expeditions. Inscribed on a granite block later reused as a statue base are sections of the annals of the great Amenemhat II (1911–1877 BC), dating to early in his reign, during a spate of largesse perhaps intended to solidify a contentious succession.[63] The Mit Rahina inscription, as it is known, records among other projects two overseas ventures. One, to uncertain northerly destinations, possibly including Cyprus, brought back 1554 captives alongside raw and worked metals, precious stones and other fine goods, including furniture. The second, in two ships, targeted the central Levant and returned with a precisely documented cargo of 231 lengths of Lebanese cedar, 65 captives or otherwise human chattels, 23 kg (50 lbs) silver, 133 kg (293 lbs) bronze, 435 kg (959 lbs) copper, 19 kg (42 lbs) white lead, 37 bronze daggers decorated with gold, silver and ivory, 225 kg (496 lbs) emery and 537 kg (1184 lbs) of other grinding sand, diverse other stones, quantities of oils and resins, spices such as coriander and cinnamon, 73 fig trees and other less identifiable vegetal products. The cargo's diversity is as striking as the presence of substances we would otherwise hardly imagine. The king's annals also listed gifts to temples, notables and soldiers. Another lucky strike bears the first of these out. Under the temple of Montu at Tod, well up the Nile, the selfsame pharaoh dedicated four copper chests filled with gold ingots, cups and flowers, silver ingots and 150 carefully folded silver cups and other vessels decorated in styles reminiscent of the Aegean or Anatolia, plus lapis lazuli and other fine stones, seals and scarabs [PL. XXIX].[64] The Tod 'treasure' confirms where some of the wealth acquired via Mediterranean expeditions ended up, and reminds us that, especially in Egypt, temples too were consumers on a grand scale.

The other salient feature of Egypt's Mediterranean connections concerns the Delta itself and nearby parts of the southern Levant. The green triangle continued to extend seaward, and its proportion of Egypt's still growing population increased accordingly throughout the 2nd millennium BC, at the expense of the Nile Valley.[65] In the east a now-vanished strand of the Nile known as the Pelusiac branch became established as a major waterway, bringing the river and expanses of verdant farmland far closer to Sinai. Pollen reveals a virtually treeless landscape of cereals grown on well-drained land, with grasses and marsh plants interspersed, while animal bones affirm a superabundance of birds, fish and other waterlife.[66] As for the teeming numbers of people living in this other Egypt, by now heading towards a million, their composition, identities and degree of assimilation to the resurgent Egyptian state are hard to gauge.[67] Certainly, the Middle Kingdom made efforts to affirm uniformity. Offerings to the shrine at Tell Ibrahim Awad in the Delta resemble those at Elephantine far to the south on the First Cataract, and further east forts were erected, just as in Nubia, to guard the gateway to Siniatic copper and turquoise.[68] But despite this, the contemporary *Tale of Sinuhe*, a reflection on what it meant to be Egyptian written from the perspective of a scribe in Levantine exile, still expressed strangeness through the feelings of a 'marsh-man' in Nubia.[69] Moreover, material remains, human skeletons and personal names among the upper echelons of society reveal, alongside the hundreds of thousands of parochial farmers living in the Delta's maze of fields, swamps and river channels, a substantial element with unmistakably Levantine connections.[70]

8.9 Brightly garbed south Levantine men and women, accompanied by children and laden donkeys, approach the margins of Egypt in this tomb painting from Beni Hasan on the Nile.

Even upstream at Beni Hasan, tomb paintings show the arrival in Egypt of donkey caravans driven by people whose colourful robes, weaponry and hairstyles distinguish them as Levantine [**8.9**], and the intervening northern Sinai was peppered with tiny ephemeral sites at this time.[71] A steady donkey-borne coming and going tied together the southern Levant, Sinai and eastern Delta, driven by a combination of pastoralism, commerce, mining and flight from periodic droughts, some of which led to permanent infiltration, settlement and mingling (a long-term pattern echoed in the Biblical story of Joseph and his notably Mediterranean prescience in matters of storage). Other newcomers contributed less voluntarily to Egypt's voracious labour pool: the captives listed at Mit Rahina alone swelled Egypt's population by about 0.1 per cent – a drop in the ocean, but the only drop that we happen to know about. Given that this was an age in which the official ideology proclaimed being Egyptian to be synonymous with adherence to specific cultural norms, in which Sinuhe defined his exile in terms of things alien to Egyptian ideals of bodily comfort, physical appearance and language, it is also possible that in the Delta, something that for upriver Egyptians (and many modern archaeologists) could only be explained in terms of foreign influx, was in fact partly an unmentionable ancestral element of the indigenous population, going back hundreds if not thousands of years.

8.10 Gridded town plans preceded later Classical practice by at least 2000 years, and some of the earliest are royal foundations in Egypt, in this case the initial settlement of Tell el-Dab'a in the eastern Nile Delta.

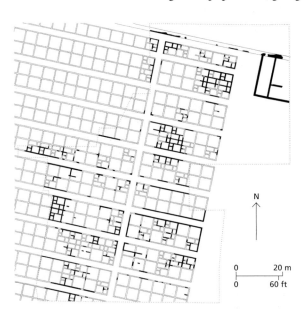

0   20 m
0   60 ft

These cultural currents swirled most strongly around a place known today as Tell el-Dab'a, where the seaward flow of the Pelusiac Nile intersected the head of the Wadi Tumilat, the land corridor to Sinai and beyond.[72] Here, an impeccably canonical royal estate and grid-planned town were laid out at the start of the 12th Dynasty [**8.10**]. Their initial name translates as 'Royal Settlement of Amenemhat I, Justified, At the Door of the Two Roads', the last epithet redolent with locational destiny. Some 200 years later this Delta settlement had rocketed to 75 ha (185 acres), making it one of the biggest places in the Mediterranean and a magnet for consumption in its own right rather than a mere cog in the royal machinery of Nilotic redistribution and transhipment. As the grip of the late Middle Kingdom

8.11 Mixed messages from a mud-brick tomb at Tell el-Dab'a identified, from a scarab, as that of a deputy treasurer known as Amu, who was laid out in a typically Levantine posture, with a Levantine dagger but mainly Egyptian pots. In front of the chamber, five or six donkeys have been interred.

pharaohs began to loosen it swiftly became itself a seat of local dynasts. And as the settlement grew, it also shook off its official guise and revealed a radically different, thoroughly hybrid life- and death-style. Houses and burials bore Levantine as well as Egyptian characteristics; metalworkers employed techniques unfamiliar to the Nile; and Levantine temples arose, one with palpably un-Egyptian charred acorns at the altar before it, probably all that remains of a foreign goddess's sacred tree.[73] Within the garden of a palace of impeccable Egyptian design, the tombs of high officials had a palm placed in front, in deference to Deltaic traditions, while their chambers were stuffed with foreign goods. These included Levantine weapons, a scarab inscribed in faulty Egyptian to the 'overseer of foreign lands', and sacrificed pairs of donkeys, the last a Canaanite practice connoting the caravan trade [**8.11**]. Nor did all Tell el-Dab'a's connections point to terrestrial routes. Pottery and jewelry with ties to Cyprus and Crete, as well as a locally carved cylinder seal portraying a sailing ship accompanied by Baal-Zephon, a north Levantine deity associated with the maritime world [**8.12**], confirm that the sea-paths were equally well-travelled.[74] Some time between 1800 and 1650 BC this vortex of people and networks acquired its better-known ancient name of Avaris, in which form we shall visit it again.

Levantine society's bounce-back after 2000 BC was just as impressive, and in the south closely tied to the rise of the Middle Kingdom. This was the fourth round in a cycle of ever more experienced building of big communities in a fickle environment since the Neolithic, and it proved the most ambitious, an acme until well into the 1st millennium BC.[75] In contrast to the preceding millennium, when the north completely outstripped the south, towns with grand entrance gates and massive ramparts to deter battering rams, cuneiform literacy, tin-bronze, and wheel-thrown pots are encountered throughout the Levant, ruled by powerful, if never divine, kings. Both maritime and inland trade routes striated the region, most running north–south

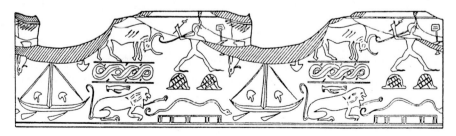

8.12 Roll-out of the design carved on a cylinder seal from Tell el-Dab'a, showing a ship, sea-and-storm god astride twin mountains, plus bull and snake that probably signify other Levantine deities.

8.13 Redolent of both combat and the felling of aromatic trees, the fenestrated axe became a distinctive power symbol in the early 2nd-millennium BC Levant. This exceptionally elaborate example, intricately decorated with granulation and other elaborate techniques, and with figures from the Epic of Gilgamesh visible in the fenestrations, was found beneath a major temple at Byblos.

as before, but with a cross-over in the Jezreel Valley between the southern coastal trail and a northern one running inland east of Lebanon between the Galilee and Orontes Valley. The robustness of long-haul routes through the interior in the face of maritime competition illustrates the fact that the choice of sea versus land transport depended on a subtly varying calculus involving not just speed and bulk, but also value, security and intervening markets, which could tip the balance either way, especially for lighter or valuable goods.

From this time, as already noted, Levantine communities (save in the extreme north) are also known as Canaanite, a contemporary term loosely denoting the land, its people, products and traditions.[76] Levantine culture demonstrates strongly recurrent themes at this time, including distinctive metal weaponry and wealthy tombs. One combination of these that resonates with the *Tale of Sinuhe*'s account of one-on-one combat as means of asserting Canaanite male status are the male 'warrior' burials at places such as Sidon and a resurgent Jericho, accompanied by daggers, spears and perforated bronze axes – the last emblematic of tree-felling as well as fighting, and taken up as a symbol as far off as Crete [**8.13**].[77] But equally, the Levant was turning into a cultural melting pot of traits from Egypt, Mesopotamia, Anatolia, Cyprus and occasionally the distant Aegean. Egyptianizing emblems and deities, in particular, appeared on seals, ivories and, at Tell Sakka near Damascus, even wall-paintings.[78] This openness extended to personal names, which display a mix of Canaanite, Amorite, Hurrian (highland Anatolian) and, at the titular level, Egyptian derivations. A further striking feature was the prominence of sizeable shrines, now often of tower-like form or situated in open high places.[79] Unlike Mesopotamia and Egypt, where temples were usually permanently endowed, the maintenance of the gods' homes in the Levant was a private, palatial or communal responsibility and commonly reflected the concerns of specific groups of worshippers. In this sense, the boat models, anchors and gilt-bronze men dedicated amidst the diminutive pseudo-Egyptian erections at Byblos's 'Obelisk temple' [**8.14**], when compared to the figs, and bones from sheep, goats, plus a few pigs and costly cattle, at the local shrine of a farming village at Tell el-Hayyat in the Jordan Valley, speak volumes about the dominant preoccupations at different points within the Mediterranean landscape.[80]

Focusing in, the explosion of urban life in the south is startling after the less complex settlements of the previous millennium and the desertification with which it ended. Sites near springs, year-round rivers or other lush pockets were unsurprisingly popular, and irrigation probably underwrote the massive populations that accumulated in the Hula and Galilee basins.[81] Evidence for the distribution of polities comes from archaeology and Egypt's Execration Texts, the latter ritual incantations listing Egypt's foes, many of whom lay, luckily for us, in the southern Levant (among them the first mention of Jerusalem, a highland settlement whose physical remnants at this stage are mere scraps on the bedrock).[82] Archaeology confirms that the recovery began earliest on the coast, especially at a string of burgeoning ports between Ashkelon, at this time the largest coastal town anywhere in the Levant [**8.15**], and Akko (Crusader

Acre). Some of these only make sense in terms of sea traffic.[83] Little Tel Nami, for instance, on the Carmel coast, was tightly sandwiched between wetlands and the waves.[84] Only later did urbanism spread inland, where a true giant arose at Hazor in Galilee, near the junction between the interior north–south trail and the Jezreel Valley corridor to the sea. Hazor, whose ramparts enclosed 75–80 ha (185–200 acres) and contain 1 million cu. m (35 million cu. ft) of soil, numbers among the handful of true supersites around the east Mediterranean.[85] Its palace has been located, though not yet the archive that would clarify the extent of its sway, which according to most estimates

reached over several thousand sq. km in the Galilee basin, Golan Heights and southern Lebanon, swallowing in the process a polity in the Hula basin based on Tel Dan. In general, the southern pattern was of a patchwork of polities of variable size and authority, many aligned in typically Mediterranean fashion as slivers of coast and hinterland, several more in the highlands or segmenting the Jordan Valley, and all alike tugged in economic and perhaps political terms between the gravitational pulls of Hazor, Ashkelon and the Levant's real southern terminus at this time, Avaris in the Nile Delta.[86]

8.14 (*opposite*) Diminutive obelisks at the eponymous shrine at Byblos, probably dedicated to a Levantine deity but indicative of revived connections with Egypt. Some bear hieroglyphic inscriptions, and the temple as a whole acted as a focus for dedications, including of the axe illustrated in fig. 8.13, as well as model boats and huge numbers of gilt bronze figurines.

So much for the overall scene, but the intensity of investigation in the southern Levant gives us a rare chance to explore the texture of these emergent Mediterranean landscapes at a finer grain of resolution. For beneath the urban pinnacles lay tiers and networks of villages, hamlets and farms, many integrated with urban economies and thence the wider world, to whose shifting rhythms their agriculture and craft goods both contributed and responded. Huge numbers of rural sites cover the hill country of Israel, especially the wetter north and the western slopes most dedicated to tree crops, by now certainly enhanced by painstakingly built little terraces and rock-cut cisterns.[87] East of the Jordan one of the best explored is Tell el-Hayyat, which we just visited in the context of its modest temple.[88] It was a village of a couple of hundred people in the hinterland of a medium-sized town known in later antiquity as Pella and today as Tabaqat Fahr, itself perched on the edge of the Jordan Valley and uncomfortably close to Hazor. Potters at Tell el-Hayyat made a lot of the vessels used by its urban neighbour, and the amount of olive remains tells us that the community had also invested heavily in oil production, much of which was probably consumed locally, but some donkeyed down the Jezreel Valley (where its final bottling may have taken place)[89] to the coastal towns and from there off across the sea. The micro- and the macro-scales in this part of the Mediterranean, just like the hinterland and coast, had become more intimately linked than ever.

Further north the parallels with the 3rd millennium BC are stronger. Small, rich ports clung to the Lebanese coast.[90] Byblos regained some of its special relationship with the pharaohs, but although its rulers flaunted coveted Egyptian titles and royal gifts (as we know from their lavish tombs), in a now more multilateral web of connections they struggled to prevent rivals from provisioning Egypt with timber too. Sea traffic at Tyre, Sidon, Beirut and Tripoli flourished in the lee of offshore islands or peninsulas. Montane communities bloomed high in the Beqaa Valley, and further inland the ramparts of Qatna delineate a city of 100 ha (250 acres).[91] In the far north, beyond the Levant's mountain-pinched waist, Ebla remained substantial but had yielded to Yamhad as the paramount territorial state and regional power.[92] Inconveniently, the latter's capital is encased in the hulking tell, crowned by an Arab castle, in the middle of modern Aleppo, and we know it almost entirely from what contemporaries wrote [PL. XXXI]. Yamhad ruled over some 20,000 sq. km (7700 sq. miles), a major holding by any standard of the time, and its western dependencies, each with their own dynasties, included two trading centres renowned in their own right. One was Ugarit, now apparently a fortified town, the other Alalakh (Tell Atchana), Antioch's predecessor as the hub of the Amuq, which has produced a small archive and a hoard of tusks from still not exterminated local Asian elephants.[93] By now a more modest place than when we visited its elite cemetery in Chapter 7, Umm el-Marra still honoured its royal dead from the previous millennium but had adapted to a drier present by concentrating on a leather industry supplied by hunting the wild onagers of the endless dun steppe to its east.[94]

Away to the east, two or three days' journey by land followed by a descent of the busy Euphrates by barge, lay Mari, a 100-ha (250-acre) caravan city with strongly

8.15 (*opposite*) The great Levantine town and seaport of Ashkelon, the closest major stop to the Nile Delta on the southern coastal route, with its massive arc of ramparts. Less obvious today is the location of the anchorage for the numerous ships that made landfall here.

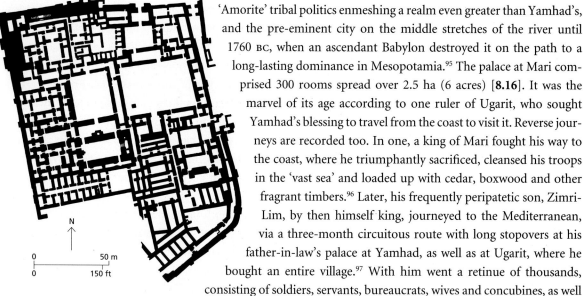

8.16 Plan of the vast early
2nd-millennium BC palace at
Mari on the Euphrates, in its
own time an acknowledged
wonder. Note the several
large courtyards, big royal
audience chambers and
ample provision for storage
and other activities.

'Amorite' tribal politics enmeshing a realm even greater than Yamhad's, and the pre-eminent city on the middle stretches of the river until 1760 BC, when an ascendant Babylon destroyed it on the path to a long-lasting dominance in Mesopotamia.[95] The palace at Mari comprised 300 rooms spread over 2.5 ha (6 acres) [**8.16**]. It was the marvel of its age according to one ruler of Ugarit, who sought Yamhad's blessing to travel from the coast to visit it. Reverse journeys are recorded too. In one, a king of Mari fought his way to the coast, where he triumphantly sacrificed, cleansed his troops in the 'vast sea' and loaded up with cedar, boxwood and other fragrant timbers.[96] Later, his frequently peripatetic son, Zimri-Lim, by then himself king, journeyed to the Mediterranean, via a three-month circuitous route with long stopovers at his father-in-law's palace at Yamhad, as well as at Ugarit, where he bought an entire village.[97] With him went a retinue of thousands, consisting of soldiers, servants, bureaucrats, wives and concubines, as well as huge quantities of metal and other gifts dispensed and received along the way – altogether quite a pageant for Mediterranean eyes. We owe such details to Mari's modern treasure, its archive of 20,000 tablets, including 6000 letters, dating mainly to the reign of Zimri-Lim, its last king, that lay bare the scope and detail of this far-reaching palace economy just across the Mediterranean's eastern border.[98] The insights from this archive exceed any hope of summary here. Among those most relevant to us are the interstate alliances involving Yamhad and Qatna, the latter still directly reachable, even for large, if lightly burdened expeditions, across the desertifying and dangerously lawless steppe via Tadmor, later Palmyra, without the detour along the otherwise preferred northern route through Yamhad.[99] Equally revelatory are the emissaries of Babylon reported as present as far south as Hazor, and last but not least Mari's key role as a dispenser of central Asian tin, which it traded on into the Mediterranean.[100] Tin consignments went from Mari to Hazor, Qatna, Yamhad and Ugarit, in the last case including small amounts destined for a man of 'Kaptara', and the interpreter working for this place's chief trader at Ugarit.[101] Kaptara further appears at Mari in the context of gold-embellished weapons, metal vessels, textiles and leather. Like its Egyptian cognate 'Keftiu' (first encountered in the early Middle Kingdom), this term denotes Crete, or the generic southern Aegean – the first external textual acknowledgment of the region's existence.[102]

But before we take the great Cilician bend and head west for Cyprus and the Aegean, an Anatolian detour is essential. We know little about coastal Turkey at this time, but inland, on the plateau, processes of great significance for our history were underway. As seen in Chapter 7, the communities of 3rd-millennium BC Anatolia, and the status of the rulers whom the kings of Akkad claimed to have fought, are hard to pin down. Out of these, however, a set of large, evenly matched towns dominated by palaces had arisen by 2000 BC, several of which enjoyed links with the northern Levant and Mesopotamia.[103] From the lower town of one such centre, Kanesh (modern Kültepe), comes another remarkable set of documents. Most belonged to an enclave of Mesopotamian merchants, one of more than twenty spread over central Anatolia, whose families operated from Assur on the Tigris, 775 km (480 miles) away as the crow flies.[104] These merchants ran donkey caravans between the alluvium and highland towns, trading Anatolian gold and silver for Mesopotamian textiles and eastern tin (the import of tin a sign that any Anatolian tin mines were far from meeting current demand).[105] The surprises from this archive are threefold, though all probably reflect practices that had begun, less visibly to us, considerably earlier. First, the foreign merchants and their trade in organic or recyclable goods would be undetectable without textual revelation. Second, the scale was enormous. The caravans engaged 200–50 donkeys, each laden with 60 kg (130 lbs) of metal or cloth, travelling for 35–40 days; it has been calculated that well over 100 kg (220 lbs) of silver and a thousand large, heavy textiles were moved annually over the period from 1920 to 1850 BC that the archives illuminate. Treaties, security agreements and tolls en route regulated their passage. Third, the trade was operated by families and consortia or 'companies' under little palatial scrutiny, and these undoubtedly aspired to and obtained a lucrative profit – in a nice inversion of expectations, 200 per cent gross on textiles and 100 per cent on tin before transport costs. The Akkadian word *tamkarum* used to denote these entrepreneurial figures so familiar with profit margins, loans, taxes, smuggling and coping with local royal monopolies, can be justifiably translated as 'merchant'.[106]

This intricately balanced phase of interconnections was closed by the rise of Babylon in the south and interstate warfare in the north from which emerged, in the late 17th century BC, a parallel, and in this case first, supra-regional power in Anatolia, the Hittite kingdom of Hatti, with its capital at Hattusa (modern Boğazköy) in the north-central highlands of modern Turkey.[107] While the Kanesh archive hangs beyond the basin's edges as a hint of what we might be missing elsewhere within it, Hatti's first intervention in the Mediterranean was brutally direct and went after booty and tribute, a strategy that entailed the sacking of Yamhad, Alalakh and Ebla, in the last case the final blow to a venerable city. By 1500 BC the outline of a new power structure was starting to crystallize in this part of the Mediterranean.

Cyprus remained buffered from such events, yet increasingly engaged in off-island interaction after the decisive end, around 2500 BC, of its long isolation on the internal margin of the east Mediterranean system. The key, as suggested at the end of the previous chapter, was copper, for which Cyprus is one of the largest sources in the world, and the timing related to the introduction of techniques to work its previously intractable sulphide ores – plus, we can now add, the decline of Omani copper sources, which had hitherto served as the bulk supplier to Mesopotamia [8.17].[108] Mine galleries are visible by the 19th century BC at Ambelikou, and by the 18th–17th centuries the export of copper is attested archaeologically and textually, the latter mainly from Mari, where we encounter the name Alashiya, long to be associated with the island.[109] A century later a smelting installation at Phorades confirms industrial-scale production in the mining zones of the interior, among the colourful

8.17 Copper-rich parts of the Troodos foothills have remained mining landscapes for much of the time span from the Bronze Age to the present, as seen here near Skouriotissa. Modern mines often obscure or destroy traces of ancient activity.

ore gossans of the Troodos piedmont.[110] Allied with equally recently introduced state-of-the-art farming techniques, the impact on the island's societies was electric. Initially, and reflecting the Anatolian axis that had broken Cyprus's isolation, as well as easy access to major mining regions, the main anchorages lay along the north coast, where they helped to stitch together an inshore route between the Aegean and Levant during the centuries on either side of 2000 BC.[111] Increasingly, however, metal-rich tombs, a series of forts in the centre and east, and frequent destructions signal an island in ferment, as other communities competed for advantage in controlling routes from the ore sources to the coast, and over the sea to mainland markets.[112] Out of this rose one particular winner, which coalesced at a lagoonal river mouth on the hitherto sparsely settled southeast shore facing the Levant, only a day's sail from Ugarit, whose partial twin it would later become.[113] Early Enkomi was a heterogeneous boom-town community, and from almost the first stage it stands out for its involvement in copper production and trade. In addition to copper, Cyprus diversified to export its pots to the Levant, Egypt and occasionally the Aegean, while imports increased in the form of seals, metalwork, liquids and an adapted 'Cypro-Minoan' version of a script used on Crete.[114] It is odd that Cyprus, so close to the Levant and rich in copper, arose as a major player notably later than more distant, resource-poor Crete. Nonetheless, by 1500 BC a turnaround that must have been variously exhilarating or alarming for its inhabitants was well on the way to establishing it in a centre-stream position within Mediterranean trade.

Our tour ends in the Aegean, where by 2000 BC Crete was already on the cusp of dramatic changes. Soon afterwards, towns with labyrinthine Minoan palaces at their heart emerged, first at Knossos, Phaistos and Malia in the fertile centre, and all over the island in the next few centuries [**8.18**; PL. II].[115] The palaces were places of public ceremony, sacred rituals, fine craft production, and, in the first and largest examples, agricultural storage on a grand scale.[116] They segmented the island into small- to medium-sized polities of typical form, with their palatial towns set among the arable lowlands on or near the coast, surrounded by smaller communities that grew grain, vines and olives (now sometimes on gently terraced fields), and soon grading into a pastoral montane interior. Knossos's disproportionate size and cultural pre-eminence encourage speculation that it played Hazor or Yamhad to its neighbours and gradually established a hegemony over the island.[117] Administration was exercised through writing, mainly in Linear A, a native script that remains undeciphered, in part because it surely records an extinct, arguably non-Indo-European language originating far back in the island's past. Palatial Crete is, in addition, renowned for a veritable explosion of intricate artistic creations, the best known of which are Kamares and Marine-style painted pottery, carved stone vessels, work in faience, ivory and (rarely surviving) metal, as well as pictorial wall-paintings.[118]

Superficially, Crete resembles much of the east Mediterranean at this time. But scratch the surface and one begins to doubt whether it can be pigeonholed so easily, glimpsing instead alternative ancestries in the vying societies emerging in the 3rd

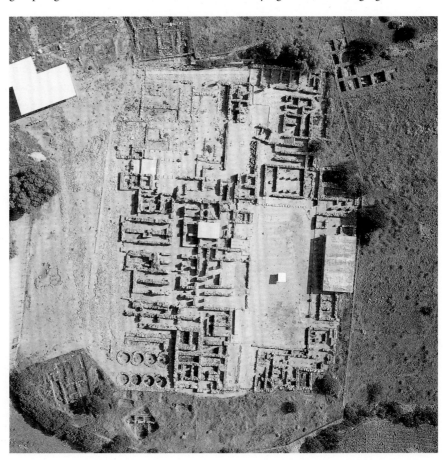

8.18 This aerial view of the Minoan palace at Malia in north-central Crete reveals the focus on a central courtyard of communicative and ritual significance, as well as large high-status rooms, long storage magazines, probable workshop areas and a pod of eight circular silos.

millennium BC across much of the northern Mediterranean, or (among the club of insular oddities) even as temple-period Malta writ large. Peculiar features include the strikingly urban character of the island for its size, which is under half the territory ruled by Yamhad, or a quarter the area of the southern Levant. Crete was studded with small towns, a handful of larger ones, and last but not least Knossos, which at 100 ha (250 acres) exceeded most cities west of Mari.[119] Towns must have accounted for at least half the island's population, and average urban house size reached a peak that would not be seen again on Crete until the threshold of Classical times.[120] At Knossos the scale of the palace too is outstanding: 1.3 ha (3.2 acres) in ground-plan, extended over several storeys, and able to hold over 5000 people in its central court.[121] Also unusual, though not unique, is the absence of clear advertisement of rulers, which could imply corporate rather than individual, dynastic leadership.[122] If we take the imagery at face value, this consisted in part of elite women. Finally, the ubiquitous emulation of palatial styles between and, vertically, within polities, together with the staggering investment and fast fashion turnovers in individualistically decorated drinking and serving pottery (a medium that under most states became uniform, if not drab), suggests a competitive, volatile society that never quite settled down into an established order.[123] This suspicion is fortified by the frenetically performative and theatrical aspect of palatial rituals, from public processions to bull-leaping.

The emergence of palatial Crete reconfigured the Aegean islands and much of the coastal rim into a lively periphery, with each area interacting with Crete in its own way.[124] Behind this lay acquisition of metals, in which Crete was deficient and which encouraged its entry into Mediterranean trade networks, notably involving silver from Lavrio (control over which is less often considered than it should be) and more distant metals obtained via intermediaries in the east and maybe west Aegean. In the Cyclades, the east Aegean's islands and peninsulas and on Kythera, where this book opened amidst a surge of new settlements supplying a booming port at Kastri, nodes of maritime trade flourished at key points. Over time their relationship with

8.19 The handful of well-appointed houses and other buildings crowded within a tight, heavily fortified perimeter on the promontory of Agia Irini, situated on the Cycladic approaches to the silver lodes of Lavrio.

8.20 Finds from the Mycenae Shaft Graves number among the most iconic objects in archaeology, but in fact represent extremely diverse origins and meanings. The silver and gold bull's head pouring vessel (*above left*) is almost certainly a Cretan religious item redeployed in a Peloponnesian death-ritual, while the lion-hunt scene on the dagger (*above right*) is of a wider visual currency localized through its choice of equipment, and executed in a skilled *niello* 'painting in metal' technique of uncertain eastern Mediterranean origin.

Crete deepened into ties of cultural affiliation. Several kinds of activities could lie behind this 'minoanization', from emulation by socially aspiring locals, to influxes of Cretans, to political control from one or more Cretan palaces, notably Knossos.[125] A few island centres grew as large as some of the Cretan towns, notably Trianda on Rhodes and probably Akrotiri as well, the latter uniquely preserved to the height of two- or three-storey buildings thanks to a huge eruption of the Thera volcano ([**1.8**]; discussed below). On the other hand, Agia Irini, a small, heavily fortified silver- and textile-manufacturing cluster of rich houses, probably each for a family 'firm', on the agriculturally poor island of Kea (the last staging post for passage via the Cyclades to Lavrio in Attica), is more reminiscent of Tel Nami in Israel and other tiny, yet precocious port communities [**8.19**]. Still closer to the Greek mainland, Aegina established a key trading role independent of Crete, at first as a hub for the Saronic Gulf. It soon accumulated enough wealth to obtain jewelry paralleled at Avaris, and to furnish a rich warrior burial in a deep shaft-like grave – the prototype of a death-style soon taken up by its mainland neighbours.[126]

Initially the Greek mainland was less integrated, and parts robustly indifferent to Crete, full of resilient, relatively self-sufficient village communities.[127] By the 17th and 16th centuries BC, resistance began to crumble, led by parts of the Peloponnese that enjoyed easy maritime links to the south, as well as potentially further north and west, with people and materials in southeast Europe and the central Mediterranean.[128] At Mycenae and a few other places, shaft graves and other burials plot a crescendo in deposition of gold, silver, bronze, fine stones, faience, ostrich egg and other exotica [**8.20**; PL. XXXIII].[129] The diverse, often distant origins of raw materials and finished objects mapped the Aegean, wider east Mediterranean and Europe from a point on their edges where they intersected.[130] Many items, such as the individually decorated swords and daggers, must have featured in lost tales of heroic warriors and their possessions. Others, such as the famous libation vessel in the form of a bull's head, recall Crete, while links to the Cyclades are particularly abundant. A model balance scale in sheet gold, once thought to have weighed the souls of the dead, may instead hint at how much of this wealth was acquired. Here we shall pause for the moment, on the verge of later Aegean developments, and contacts further west in the Mediterranean.

We cannot, however, leave the Aegean without a look at the most devastating natural event in the 2nd-millennium Mediterranean, one contemporary with the peak of expansion on Crete and the Mycenae shaft graves. The eruption of the Thera volcano bequeathed to us at Akrotiri a Bronze Age Pompeii without the bodies, and conditions of preservation we have to thank repeatedly in the course of this

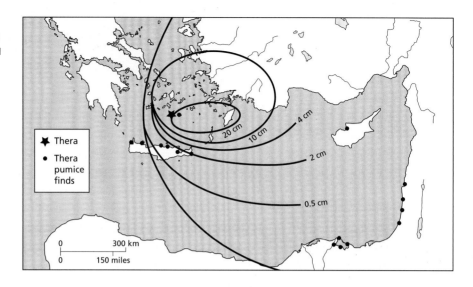

8.21 Extrapolation from known residues in cores and terrestrial sites of the ash-fall from the Theran eruption.

chapter.[131] Beyond lies an entire Bronze Age landscape sealed under metres of ash. The volcano threw up an ash plume whose eastward drift on the wind is detectable in sea and lake cores across the Aegean and into Turkey, while a 6–11-m- (20–36-ft-) high tsunami left its mark at coastal sites in north Crete, and pumice floated far and wide on the currents [**8.21**].[132] Once blamed for the final, fiery demise of palatial settlements on Crete in the early 15th century BC, we now know from finer examination of the pottery styles caught in both events that the two catastrophes were separated by several generations – a discovery that throws us back on human causes for events on Crete, and underscores the resilience of these Mediterranean societies, which survived an event often likened to the AD 1883 eruption of Krakatoa in Indonesia, which killed more than 30,000 people.[133] The bone of contention is now instead the exact date of the eruption. This is of much more than arcane interest because it connects with cultural phases across the Aegean and affects how these align with the independently dated histories of Egypt and adjoining parts of the east Mediterranean, as well as European sequences. A traditional date in the late 16th century BC is challenged by radiocarbon, and by signatures of an event that may, or may not, be attributable to Thera in the Greenland ice and tree-ring growth across the northern hemisphere, which are collectively argued to support a date a century earlier, perhaps as precise as 1628/7 BC (though each has its attendant problems).[134] Around this controversy battalions of archaeologists, radiocarbon experts, volcanologists and climate scientists have converged, generating countless papers and oceans of vitriol, yet no agreed verdict. Recently, the all but miraculous find of sprays from olive trees killed by the eruption have become symbols of neither peace nor victory, due to issues in sequencing their contorted rings and matching them to those from other tree species in Turkey.[135] With any luck this debate may be close to resolution, but in turning now to explore contacts between communities sitting round the east Mediterranean pond, we must for the moment bear in mind a disconcerting uncertainty as to precisely how the acme on Crete and contemporary Aegean societies fit with the wider pattern.

An east Mediterranean
trading system crystallizes

If we want to understand how these regions in the east Mediterranean coevolved and converged to create a greater whole, we need to investigate this part of the basin as a theatre of interaction. On land the options in terms of how to get around had changed little since the 3rd millennium BC: travel on foot, in drawn carts for short hauls or by donkey over short and long distances alike, the last exemplified by the Kanesh traffic. Horses were still rarely ridden at this stage, a situation that continued perhaps until larger animals had been bred or obtained from the Russian steppe. Sea travel around the east Mediterranean was now entirely the preserve of sailing ships, still among the most complex and capital-intensive machines of their day (though prices for donkeys reveal that caravans were not cheap either). Sadly, despite several underwater cargo scatters, including one off northeast Crete,[136] and finds of stone anchors, actual remains of ships elude us until the 14th century BC. Partial exceptions are two Middle Kingdom votive masthead finials, now in Athens but surely modern arrivals to the Aegean.[137] The dedication on one, to 'the one whom the land-bringer, the Lord of the Winds and Hathor, Mistress of the North Wind shall love', should evoke the sympathy of any mariner. Egyptian images from the first half of the 2nd millennium are also frustratingly lacking. Thankfully, we have the Akrotiri wall-paintings, which depict masted ships raiding a coastline and participating in a short-range nautical procession [**8.22**; PL. XXX].[138] The latter, clearly engaged in a ritual event, were elaborately painted and propelled, save for one hastening ahead with its sail hoisted, by hordes of paddlers in an archaizing style reminiscent of older canoes. As on the earlier Cretan seals that announced the arrival of new shipping in the Aegean, the mast was single rather than bipod and had migrated back to mid-ships since the Old Kingdom depictions, allowing the boat to steer a useful 90–100

8.22 An Aegean ship a-sail around the middle of the 2nd millennium BC, with its mast mid-ships, sail supported by booms above and below, and steering oars in the stern. Similar but heavily festooned craft follow, driven by paddlers, in this image of a nautical festival from the West House of Akrotiri on Thera.

degrees off the wind.[139] Keels for better direction-holding only appeared in imagery in mid-millennium, but may have been invented earlier in the seas of the Levant or between these and the Aegean.[140] Hardest to gauge is maximum ship size. One minimalist analysis avers that no seagoing ships substantially exceeded 20 tonnes in terms of cargo and 15 m (50 ft) in length.[141] Yet, even accepting the unreliability of allusion to vessels several times this volume in the Middle Kingdom's *Tale of the Shipwrecked Sailor* (a Red Sea saga that also featured fantastical giant lapis serpents),[142] a brilliant interpretation of the Mit Rahina ship inventories as the world's earliest bills of lading deduces vessels of at least 25 and possibly almost 70 tonnes in capacity.[143] Wherever we set the limit, the abundance of small boats in the Akrotiri paintings, and as models at Byblos's Obelisk temple, suggest that large ships were in fact heavily outnumbered by little, mundane craft. Even in 16th-century AD Genoa, arguably the Ugarit of its day, only 2 per cent of the ships recorded in customs registers exceeded 30 tonnes.[144]

We saw in the previous chapter that fast new sailing ships could short-circuit the terrestrial Ways of Horus between Egypt and the southern Levant. As they opened up the rest of the eastern basin, they effectively shrank it: travel from the Nile Delta to Cyprus required two to three days, with maybe a week to ten days between the north Levant and the Aegean, where the archipelago's resultant diminution demolished the world-view of the last canoe-based voyagers.[145] Of course, this assumes a perfect run; actual journey times will often have been substantially slower due to adverse winds, with much involuntary lingering in port. At least equal amounts of time also passed in conduct of negotiations, where the social and business aspects seamlessly melded, as well as in physically obtaining the cargo. The Mit Rahina boats departed from Egypt in early summer and returned in the autumn, a period embracing the entire traditional sailing season, and all for a short run up the Levantine coast.[146]

If such journeys could be cumulatively plotted they would reveal the emergent lineaments of long-range routes, at least as tendencies, from out of the constant tangle of local to-and-fro movement, diversions due to weather and sheer range of options in the Aegean. The oldest trunk route ran along the Levant; another that lasted until well into the present millennium linked the Levant and Aegean via Cyprus and the coast of south Turkey. On certain long journeys reliant on consistent weather, the prevailing winds encouraged different sea-paths out and back. One example raises the issue of direct contact between Egypt and the Aegean across the open seas south of Crete.[147] This trans-Mediterranean voyage, which figures in the *Odyssey* as a five-day crossing with a fair wind and necessitates travel over 200 km (125 miles) out of sight of land, demanded sterner stuff of mariners than coast-hugging traffic, although the much faster, safer craft now available meant that it may have been no more dangerous or glory-gaining than feats performed in canoes throughout the Mediterranean a millennium earlier.[148] But while a following wind was very likely heading south, the reverse was a rare prospect. This argues that Egyptian-initiated contact with the Aegean was uncommon, and that any Aegean-sponsored ventures returned by a circuitous route up the Levant and along Anatolia, ensuring that return cargos were mixed in origin. Add in the fact that most Egyptian finds on Crete (and vice versa) were of types readily available at Levantine ports, and the deduction must be that the Levant, once again, frequently acted as the intermediary. Some direct contacts between Egypt and the Aegean may be likely, but are hard to verify until well into the 2nd millennium, and even then retain an exotic 'edge-of-our-world' quality, often fantastical or mythic,[149] distinct from cosy connections in the Aegean or across Levantine and Cypriot seas, as well as more attenuated but fairly faithful transmission between the Aegean and both the Levant and Cyprus.

We therefore have a decent idea of the physical means by which long-range connections were effected and the kinds of directional links and durations involved. Much harder to demonstrate at this stage are the motives of producers, transporters and consumers, let alone the identity of the people in the middle who did the actual moving, and the frequency of their operations. We might wish to take our cue from the emergence across the broader Near East over the previous thousand or so years of consumer groups, metal-based currencies, value equivalences and market mechanisms alongside an etiquette of gift-giving, all confirmed early in the new millennium by the testimonies of Kanesh and Mari – though neither is strictly speaking Mediterranean nor maritime, and we have to wait until the later 2nd millennium BC for equivalent textual insights within the basin. But we should be aware of complementary possibilities, too. Thinking about voyages between the Aegean and Egypt has encouraged us to ponder the impact of distance and travel on how people imagined each other and their lands. Although the capital-based economies of east Mediterranean palatial polities differed in kind as well as scale from the fixation on prestige goods or (as we shall see) short-term tribute in smaller-scale societies elsewhere, we still need to be alert to conditions under which the exotic qualities of foreign objects, or the voyages by which they were obtained, enhanced the political legitimacy, sacral authority or social affiliations of the people who ultimately controlled them.[150]

People with different statuses and roles could in fact have moved around for a bewildering number of reasons, of their own volition, following instruction, or under compulsion (recall the captives bound for Egypt in the Mit Rahina annals; war, along with conviction of criminals, seems at this juncture to have been a far more significant means of obtaining slaves than trade). Goods travelling with them might be personal possessions, items to be traded, formal tribute or plain booty.[151] Skilled craftspeople might move by royal transfer, marriage (a vector for high-status women as weavers in particular) or, at a humbler level, through independent quests for an opening for their talents.[152] Moreover, sometimes the talent on the move left no archaeological trace. Take music: from its archive we know that the court at Mari listened to Mediterranean performers from Hazor, Qatna and Yamhad.[153] Certain forms of writing may also have been more mobile than static clay archives suggest; the first proof of mobile jotters comes later in the millennium, as we shall see, but the adoption of an Aegean-related script on Cyprus, plus a scrap of linear writing at Tel Haror in Israel, could indicate fluid, mongrel scripts transferred between people on the move, quite distinct from the scribal schools and formal literacy of Mesopotamia and Egypt.[154] And last, after many centuries of urban life in this part of the planet, and growth of wetland with stabilizing sea levels, it would be rather surprising if one accompaniment to mobility were not microscopic and entirely involuntary. Later 2nd-millennium texts refer to transfers of epidemic diseases (one called the 'Asiatic disease' in Egypt), but already in the 18th century BC crude communal graves at Tell el-Dab'a, that cauldron of people in the pullulating, damp Nile Delta, have been interpreted as plague pits.[155] A town in this kind of environment may have bred death as much as it encouraged life, negating any increase in well-being and needing a constant influx to sustain itself.[156]

For all these possibilities and hints, the fact is that prior to the archives of the later millennium it is difficult to detect the personae involved in and benefiting from east Mediterranean trade, beyond the expectation that most of the latter belonged to the upper echelons. It is therefore to the materials and objects themselves that we turn for further insights. Nor is this straightforward, thanks to the wildly varying degree to which these are visible in the ground, images and texts.[157] The typical archaeological signature of contact is a smattering of smallish items, such as scarabs, seals, jewelry and pots, to which we can add uptake of foreign symbols such as the Egyptianizing ones common in the Levant, or the monstrous griffins and versions of a minor Nilotic hippopotamoid deity, Tawaret, found in the Aegean.[158] But while these offer thought-provoking clues, not least as to the regal or sub-regal flavour of such connections, it would be naive to assume that they indicate the full measure of contacts. We have in fact every reason to believe that much trade concerned materials that archaeologists seldom find in anything like their true original quantities. And in the exploration that follows, not every occurrence of such things necessarily denotes connections over great distances; much circulated internally or over short ranges, but collectively they define a maturing, and often long-lasting, basic repertoire for Mediterranean trade.

Movement of metals remained, as in the 3rd and 4th millennia BC, one of the major reasons for long-range connections, and their original quantities survive only in texts, the occasional pictures and such troves as the Tod and Mycenae shaft grave depositions.[159] For the precious metals much the same sources prevailed: Anatolia and the Aegean for silver (still the principal proto-currency save in Egypt), and Nubia for most of the gold. As we have seen, the decline of Omani copper output was the stimulus for Cyprus to take over as main supplier of this utilitarian metal, which was needed in vast amounts. A few other copper-producing areas survived, mainly in Anatolia and at Egyptian mines in Sinai; by the later millennium that at Bir Nasib had generated roughly 100,000 tonnes of slag.[160] Faced with such abundance and economies of scale, however, the incentive for smaller operations collapsed in the Aegean, which relied mainly on imported Cypriot and Anatolian copper, as did the Levant, where the old mines in the south lay idle, their dry landscapes abandoned to grazing.[161] Ingots themselves dated as far back as the twin births of the metal trade and metrology. But new at this time was the so-called oxhide form [**8.23**].[162] Misleadingly named for its resemblance to the flayed skin of an ox, at 25–30 kg (55–65 lbs) (normally of copper) this would be a lousy rate of

8.23 Typical oxhide ingot of pure copper, one of the standardized commodities of eastern Mediterranean trade from about the middle of the 2nd millennium BC. This example, from a transitional 13th- to 12th-century BC hoard at Enkomi on Cyprus, bears a chiselled identifying mark.

exchange, and the explanation lies instead in ease of handling, with the 'legs' acting as grips or for lashing to donkeys, which could carry two such ingots – later in the millennium between them worth in bronze the same price as the beast itself, which simplified cashing in, when necessary, at the end of a caravan run.[163] The origins of the oxhide ingot are mysterious; the earliest examples are found in the Aegean, in the 17th–15th centuries BC, yet analyses suggest that these, unlike numerous later ones, were not made from Cypriot or other Mediterranean metal.[164] Tin still came mainly via extended supply routes from central Asia. Karnab mine in the Zeravshan Valley of Uzbekistan and Tajikistan gives us pause for thought about the exploitation, often in faraway places, that lies behind the lustre of Bronze Age trade.[165] Excavations at one of thirty mines in the vicinity exposed a fissure 30 m (100 ft) long that had generated a tonne of tin and was so narrow that the extractors must have been women or children. As we know from other early mining contexts, it is unlikely that those who put in the hard labour reaped its profits.[166] This casts something of a shadow over the generosity of the king of Mari, whose archive records that he gave away half Karnab's weight in tin as gifts to fellow rulers in the Levant.[167] Such inversions of the glamorous face of Mediterranean trade were the everyday experience of miners, weavers, farmers, lumberjacks and many others besides, in and increasingly beyond the basin.

Textiles match metals in textual prominence and archaeological elusiveness.[168] Despite much overlap at the local level, an overall division emerged at the finer end of production and trade between Egypt's linen industry and the wool-based ones on the sheep-rearing steppe and uplands of the Levant, Anatolia and Aegean.[169] The former strove for purity of whiteness and fineness of weave, eventually up to 80 threads per cm (200 per in.). The latter, thanks to the better dye-taking propensity of wool, promoted colours, brilliant, jazzy patterns and perhaps, as in Mesopotamia, tapestry, to judge by the details of certain wall-paintings, which may echo lost wall-hangings.[170] Egypt's fascination with foreign woollens is apparent in the 'coats of many colours' worn by Canaanites in Egyptian depictions, and by designs painted as canopies on the ceilings of Egyptian tombs from the Middle Kingdom onward, some of which find precise matches in the elaborate red, white and blue garments seen in later Aegean wall-paintings [8.24].[171] The Aegean may have pioneered two additional desirable fabrics that helped it to break into east Mediterranean markets. Purple dye demanded intensive, nauseatingly smelly extraction from the murex, a marine mollusc fished up from some depth in the spring (so before the sailing season), and

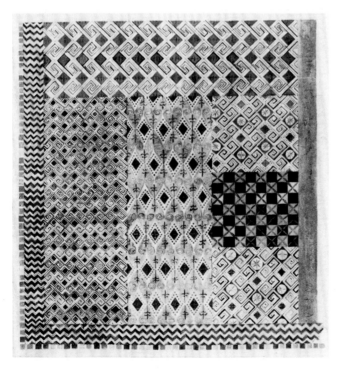

8.24 This imitation of a fine multi-coloured woollen textile was painted on the ceiling of a Middle Kingdom tomb at Assiut on the Nile. The woven originals of such designs can most plausibly be sought in the Aegean or other leading wool-producing regions in the eastern Mediterranean.

each of which could tint, after processing, between 0.05 and 1 g (0.002 and 0.04 oz) of wool.[172] Purple cloth is attested in the 14th–13th-century BC central and north Levant, famously the home of superior molluscs, by dye works, texts and a surviving scrap from Qatna.[173] Decisively earlier, however, are the middens of crushed shells at 19th–18th-century BC sites in east Crete, which may reflect an early initiative subsequently swamped by Levantine quality and quantity.[174] Even more tantalizing is a case made at Akrotiri from a preserved cocoon, together with the diaphanous clothing illustrated on the walls, for wild silk production from a moth native to the Aegean, Cyprus and southern Adriatic.[175] Remnants from later, Iron Age cemeteries (in central Anatolia and Germany) support the existence of a western industry later eclipsed when Chinese degummed silk from domesticated moths reached the Mediterranean under the Roman empire.[176]

Crushed shells and insect cocoons remind us that significant trade items may lurk in unexpected places, particularly within the almost infinite spectrum of seldom recovered organics (though, equally, surprises spring up among durable materials that we tend to undervalue: as alluded to in Chapter 1, Mari recorded a large piece of rock crystal traded between kings for 3000 sheep and 60 slaves).[177] We saw earlier that the most voluminous element of the Mit Rihana shipment from Lebanon to Egypt was cedar wood. Charcoal from non-local cedar, beech and yew has also been identified at Akrotiri,[178] whose wall-paintings furthermore illustrate the gathering of saffron, as a dye or medicine, plus, as on Crete, exotic monkeys and gazelle disporting themselves with such verve and behavioural accuracy that their presence in Aegean menageries is the only plausible solution[179] – such collections were a widespread elite affectation, and we can recall that Lebanese bears were already depicted in transit to Egypt by the Old Kingdom. From Tel Nami in Israel come charred remains of Spanish vetchling, a plant whose natural range does not extend east of the Aegean, and which (tellingly, in terms of the transmission of information) has to be heavily processed to avoid causing illness; could this be the 'Keftiu bean' named in a Egyptian medical tract as a remedy for bowel problems?[180] Other Egyptian texts list a staggering number of oils, resins and other liquids, minutely qualified by their origin or base material.[181] Many are impossible to identify definitively today, and as the most plausible matches date to later in the 2nd millennium, we can defer for now in favour of two vegetal products that undoubtedly did move in quantities to match if not exceed metals and textiles.

These are wine and olive oil, by now trade liquids par excellence. Both had a long storage life, greater in the case of wine than beer and other fermented drinks, and were simple to transport. They also offered great scope for creating more exclusive or simply differentiated products through refinement, wine by *terroir*, superior cultivars, vintages, blends or additives, oil by adding scent to render it a perfume, fancy soap or ritual ointment.[182] Now, if not before, both accrued a wide range of sacred, sacrificial, erotic, medicinal and other connotations. Moreover, their base plants could be intensively cultivated on a grand scale or left in abeyance as the need arose. Both were widely and regularly consumed in their east Mediterranean and Anatolian areas of production, if more rarely beyond. Viticulture was exceptionally profitable.[183] Later Anatolian texts mention prices for prime vineyards forty times higher than other farmland, and wine tripled in price between Carchemish and Mari, where (as in most of Mesopotamia proper) beer remained the principal brew. One wine-bearing caravan from Yamhad arrived at Mari with the equivalent of 4000 modern bottles. Egypt had introduced vines from the Levant in the 3rd millennium BC, but local production was repeatedly outstripped by demand, ensuring a steady flow of imported wine. Olive oil, similarly, was prized in Mesopotamia and Egypt, where a bewildering range of local alternatives derived from other plants and clarified animal fat remained standard.[184] In Egypt, where the olive would not naturally grow, the first transplanted trees began to put down irrigated roots as late as the 17th–16th centuries BC.[185]

The trade in these and other liquids brings us to a major development that is, for once, highly visible in the mainstream archaeological record. In Chapters 6 and 7 we remarked on several early Levantine experiments in the design of specialized ceramic containers for the transport of liquids. After 2000 BC this consolidated into standardized types in the Levant and neighbouring regions, often made in places like the Jezreel Valley, midway between the oil- or wine-producing hinterland and coastal ports.[186] For bulk transport, a plain, collared, pointed-base form that held up to 25–30 litres (7–8 gallons) (or a similar weight to that other commodity, the oxhide ingot) evolved out of earlier prototypes [8.25].[187] Known as the Canaanite jar, it was in effect an amphora, and stands at the head of a lineage of vessels that would dominate trade in liquids in and beyond the Mediterranean until less than a thousand years ago.[188] The pointed base aided lifting, embedding in beach sand

8.25 Canaanite jars perfected the basic form of the amphora as a tough, stackable liquid transport jar (*below*), and were produced to several standard capacities. At the later 2nd-millennium BC Ugaritic port at Minet el-Beida this batch (*right*) of some eighty was discovered lined up in a warehouse ready for shipment.

8.26 The visual advertisement of provenance and probably contents on the surface of certain classes of containers for desirable liquids took diverse forms: (*top*) a spectrum of small Cypriot juglets; (*above*) bulky stirrup jar of a widely exported later 2nd-millennium BC type made on Crete and bearing a stylized octopus.

and multilevel stacking shipboard. For small volumes of more precious liquids, a range of attractive little juglets was created in the Levant, Nile Delta and Cyprus.[189] Each region had its own instantly recognizable shape and shiny, painted or incised surface [**8.26**]. This enables us to trace exports, and soon their imitations, with gratifying accuracy. More importantly, and again with a few premonitions back in the 3rd millennium BC, it manifests a phenomenon that is still with us: visual branding of luxury goods. Towards the middle of the millennium Cypriots made a successful push to take over this market with new 'base-ring' types.[190] The Aegean, which displayed a decidedly sporadic record in this respect in the early centuries of the 2nd millennium BC (implying a later start for its export trade in liquids?), and which vehemently rejected the canonical amphora form until the Bronze Age was over, began around the same time to circulate its own side-spouted shape, known due to its peculiar handle as a 'stirrup jar' [**8.26**].[191] This versatile form could act, dependent on size or decoration, in either bulk or bijou capacities, and would become one of the most widespread trade forms in the Bronze Age Mediterranean.

Ceramic transport vessels are just one dimension of a new phase in the history of Mediterranean pottery. The preceding chapter discussed how skeuomorphism, the copying of the traits of one medium in another, was encouraged by the proliferation of sheet-metal vessels and growing intricacy of cross-media values. The status of pottery in particular was compromised as the low value of clay squeezed it out of elite circles and mass-produced wheel-made wares relegated it to the mundane. Skeuomorphing became part of the search for a new niche for this ancient craft, sometimes imitating designs on textiles, but above all in reference to metal.[192] Echoes of metallic features became more apparent in the ebullient, sharply finished, thin-walled or brilliantly polished forms of Levantine and Anatolian pottery and the comparable, occasionally even arcaded or crinkly rimmed pottery of the Aegean. But some potters maintained the status of their wares by an entirely different strategy. Earlier, we noted that more Cretan pottery was richly decorated than that of east Mediterranean contemporaries, and that this contrast to the plain surfaces or simpler patterns prevalent in established polities might imply a less stable, overtly competitive social order in Crete. But in addition it proclaims a desire to give 'added value' through skilful artistry to a lowly material, both in an internal context, where there was probably never enough metal to triumph outright (especially if silver drained eastward), and in long-range trade, where in this respect it was fairly successful. A strikingly large proportion of the moderate numbers of Cretan pots to reach Cyprus, the Levant and Egypt, accompanying

8.27 Selection of the grave goods in a medium-ranking tomb at Abydos on the Nile, as photographically arranged by Sir Arthur Evans. Among the typical Egyptian items, an elaborately decorated Cretan Kamares ware pottery pouring vessel stands out. Such semi-open vessels were traded on their own merits rather than thanks to any contents.

other less archaeologically visible cargos (and possibly some less instantly recognizable pots, as evidence from Tell el-Dab'a suggests), were gorgeously patterned cups and pouring vessels that moved not as containers but in their own right.[193] One, recently found at Sidon, was a cup probably made near Phaistos shortly after 1900 BC, another an extraordinary vessel with floral sprouts discovered long ago near Aswan, far up the Nile. Such pots sometimes ended up in the graves of well-to-do people in Egypt [**8.27**], and as an ultimate compliment, were occasionally locally imitated.[194]

From this observation we can venture a more general proposal about the way in which young Aegean polities, first on Crete and later the islands and mainland too, managed to participate against the odds, and with a semblance of parity, within an east Mediterranean world in which the rules of the game and values of most cards had been determined long before by other players, in which the only high card that some Aegean people held was silver, and in which the Aegean sat so far from the table that the bidding was barely audible. For the finer realms of Aegean production focused ruthlessly on increasing the value of humble local raw materials, not just from clay to decorated pottery, but wool to dazzling textiles and grapes and olives to wine and perfumed oil.[195] Even in metal, virtuoso embellishment is extraordinarily apparent. Of course, the Levant (which sat practically on the card table itself), as well as Cyprus, pursued similar approaches, and the texts, images and surviving masterpieces of the east deny any claim that fine crafting was an Aegean monopoly. Yet nowhere else did so much depend on it. Not for nothing did later Ugaritic myth place the god of crafts not in any random exotic location, but specifically in Crete.[196]

Equally, nowhere else betrays such fascination with the flexible valencies of things. Pots imitated metal, but also stone, textiles, leather and basketry; stone quoted metal; wall-paintings cited textiles; even metal highlighted its own syntax. The most telling example concerns a number of Egyptian Old Kingdom stone vessels in mid-2nd-millennium BC Crete [**8.28**].[197] Most if not all reached the island nearly a thousand years after their manufacture, as antiques recirculated thanks to tomb looting during the breakdown of authority late in the Middle Kingdom. Their association with the most venerable fount of power in the Mediterranean may have lent legitimacy to Crete's more shallow-rooted elite; if so, we might infer that their age was understood. Furthermore, some were cleverly converted into Cretan forms, by subtracting or adding parts, and local 'fakes' also exist, both of straightforwardly Egyptian vessels and, bizarrely, of the Cretan conversions from such vessels. Whether these, any more than skeuomorphs, were meant to truly delude is questionable; more significant is the

8.28 The intricacies of reception, emulation and relative knowledge involved in east Mediterranean cross-cultural exchange are intriguingly drawn out by the varied and creative Cretan responses to imported Egyptian antique stone vessels.

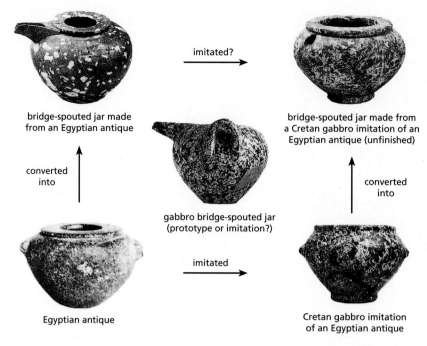

bridge-spouted jar made from an Egyptian antique

imitated?

bridge-spouted jar made from a Cretan gabbro imitation of an Egyptian antique (unfinished)

converted into

converted into

gabbro bridge-spouted jar (prototype or imitation?)

Egyptian antique

imitated

Cretan gabbro imitation of an Egyptian antique

consciousness of illusion and ambiguity, and knowledge, verging on connoisseurship, needed to appreciate what was going on. Standing back, the exceptional investment in crafting of base materials, the plays on illusion, the desire to strut on the larger east Mediterranean stage, and the agonistic nature of Aegean societies on the home fronts where most objects were deployed, may in combination shed light on a phenomenon too often accepted without question, namely why the Aegean both now and again in the 1st millennium BC created painted pottery of a mesmerizing intricacy and visual power without parallel in the Mediterranean. Setting aside claims of innate Hellenic genius, this may bring us some way towards a cultural, economic and interaction-based framework for understanding the emergence of what we call 'Greek art'.

Returning to pragmatics, so far this portrait of a web of interconnected polities risks underplaying the internal barriers to be overcome, and so giving the impression of a smoother process than is likely for anything save pathogens. Cases of resistance or indifference on practical or ideological grounds abound. Wheels made it to Poland over a thousand years before their uptake on Crete.[198] Cyprus long consumed more venison relative to lamb than anywhere else in the east Mediterranean.[199] Apart from Crete (often an intriguing anomaly), nowhere else committed to stone vessel aesthetics as deeply as Egypt, no matter how many sacred oils or other pharaonic wonders came with them.[200] In a multitude of ways Egypt, or at least the upstream version defined by ancestral pieties and cosmologies aligned on the Nile, proved the most obdurate in the rejection of external ideas. In the Middle Kingdom tin-bronze was proportionately far rarer than in temperate Europe, wheeled vehicles were seldom depicted and olive cultivation was yet to begin, while flat looms staked to the ground excluded the upright machines used elsewhere, and such ostensibly uncontroversial bodily props to gesture and appearance as vessels with handles,

8.29 Chariot-borne archer-pharaohs were a new element in Egyptian iconography from around the mid-2nd millennium BC, and lag slightly behind comparable imagery elsewhere. Here, the 15th-century pharaoh Amenhotep II reveals his strength by shooting arrows through the 4–5 cm (1.5–2 in.) of copper in an oxhide ingot. As seen in Chapter 9, such royal treatment of an emblem of Mediterranean maritime trade could be a case of hitting the target but missing the point.

and earrings, remained unpopular.[201] But given the propensity for military innovations to diffuse rapidly, the most telling instance is the combination of chariot, horse and high-velocity composite bow as a mobile, fast-careering firing platform.[202] Horse-drawn chariots were invented between 2300 and 1900 BC, either in the Russian steppe or north Mesopotamia.[203] Within a century or two they had become a coveted accoutrement of status across Anatolia, the Levant and, immortalized on crude grave markers and tiny gold rings, as far as the Aegean, in whose broken topography they made more symbolic than practical sense. Yet the first horse bones in Egypt date as late as 1680–1640 BC and upriver kings rejected chariotry for another century [**8.29**].[204] The vector that altered all this came from the Delta, and the wider circumstances bring us to one of the most extraordinary, if profoundly misunderstood, episodes in early Mediterranean history, as well as the climax of developments in the eastern part of the basin over the preceding centuries.

The roads to Avaris

We last visited the Delta as centralized rule in Egypt was again foundering. On the Pelusiac branch, Avaris, that great aqueous eye on the Mediterranean, had grown into a cosmopolitan, widely connected town with a strongly Levantine flavour. Around 1650 BC a new (15th) dynasty arose there, one of several along segments of the Nile at this time. The monarchs of this dynasty had west Semitic, Levantine, names and are known to posterity as the Hyksos, from Egyptian *heqa khasut* ('rulers of foreign lands'), a title that reflects their intrusive nature in later Egyptian historiography.[205] After their eradication around 1530 BC by the Theban king Ahmose (1550–1525 BC), whose conquest of Avaris brought the Delta back under upriver rule, the Hyksos became vilified in Egyptian historical memory with a venom comparable, and based on not dissimilar paranoias, to Rome's abuse of its arch-enemy Carthage. While this speaks volumes about the ensuing New Kingdom's views on legitimacy, political unity on the Nile and the primacy of upriver cultural norms, it distracts us from the radically different version of events that archaeology in the Delta is starting to lay out for us.

Viewed dispassionately, Avaris went supernova after 1650 BC. From merely ranking as one of the biggest Mediterranean urban settlements of its day it expanded to a size estimated at 250 ha (620 acres), the largest city yet seen in the basin by a wide margin and, discounting areas set aside for the massively fortified citadel and

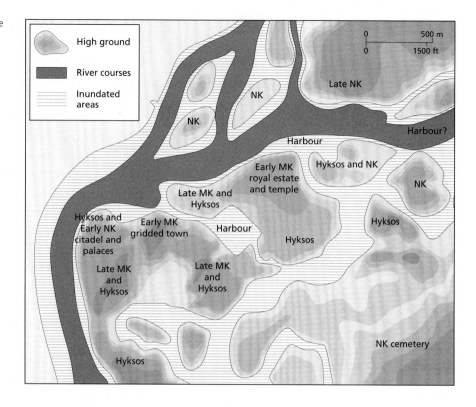

8.30 Venice on the Nile: the epithet seems particularly appropriate in this plan of Avaris, threaded with waterways, inundated areas and harbour basins. Much of this vast site remains unexcavated, despite the Herculean scale of current investigations, but the locations of major monuments and shifts in the focus and extent of the urban surrounds over time are gradually emerging (MK = Middle Kingdom; NK = New Kingdom).

palaces, implying a population of some 25,000–40,000 [**8.30**].[206] It and its successors in the eastern Delta maintained this distinction for over half a millennium. Its rule extended to vassals south of Memphis and into the Fayum, thereby controlling more than half of Egypt's farmland [**8.31**].[207] The frequency of Hyksos royal scarabs in the south Levant may denote political hegemony there too, based at a new, loosely grid-planned settlement at Tell el-Ajjul (almost certainly ancient Sharuhen) on the coast near Gaza.[208] Gifts, some of them mutilated Middle Kingdom statues, were dispatched as far as Ugarit and a now independent Nubian polity of Kush, while smaller items bearing Hyksos royal names travelled on to Hattusa and Knossos.[209] The Nubian connection operated via an oasis route that circumvented the rump of a Nile Valley state at Thebes and assured the flow of gold from the south.[210] At home, too, the culture of Avaris was mixed and tolerant, with connections all the way up the Levant, especially its centre and north, created by inflows of people plus the enduring ties of those already long locally acclimatized. There were also close links to Cyprus, as well as resident Nubian soldiery and, last but not least, strong traditional Egyptian traits in the city's later royal manifestations.[211]

Aptly christened 'Venice on the Nile' for its location on a series of turtle-backs among the braided strands of the river, and a 450 × 400-m (1475 × 1300-ft) central harbour basin linked to the main channel by canals, the analogy extends to the river-port's role as a gigantic vortex of Mediterranean trade.[212] The victory stele of Kamose, Ahmose's predecessor who commanded the first Theban assault, describes how the women of Avaris peeped out from the fortifications like fledgling creatures from within their holes, and went on to announce with relish 'I have not left a plank of the hundreds of ships of fresh cedar which were filled with gold, lapis, silver, turquoise, bronze axes without number, over and above the moringa oil, incense, fat, honey, willow, boxwood, sticks and all their fine woods – all the products of Retinu – I have confiscated all of it.'[213] Lest this be dismissed as hyperbole, extrapolated data from Avaris suggest that roughly 2 million Canaanite amphorae were imported over the 250 years preceding the city's destruction, mostly from the central and southern Levant (the latter known as 'Retinu' in Egypt, and denoting a shift from the 12th Dynasty's economic links to the centre and north).[214] This implied the average arrival of as much as 600 litres (160 gallons) of oil, wine or other fine liquids every day. This economic stimulus electrified the east Mediterranean. Cypriot pottery exports to Avaris and the Levant surged, assuredly in part tracers of consignments of copper. It was now and shortly after the Hyksos age, too, that Cretan polities reached their high-water mark and, as we shall see, instigated closer ties with Egypt. Luxury goods were consumed mainly in the city itself or traded on at a high level; a subject settlement at Tell el-Maskhuta in Wadi Tumilat, another hybrid place with Delta roots, is practically devoid of them.[215] This consuming influx applied to people as well, for Avaris's population boom was not so much a prerequisite for its seizure of the lead position in trade, which had been in the making since the Middle Kingdom, but a consequence of its status as the east Mediterranean's economic super-attractor.

8.31 The Hyksos polity and its long-range connections, mapped relative to other Nilotic, Mesopotamian and Anatolian powers.

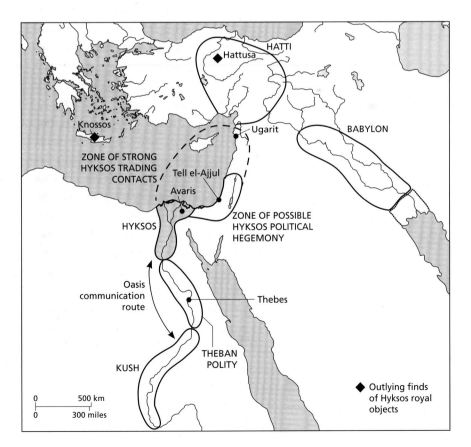

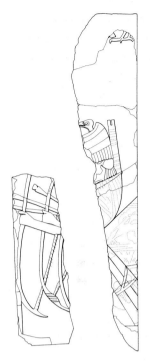

8.32 These tantalizing fragments of a painted relief from Abydos celebrate the ultimately successful Theban war against Avaris: (*left*) ranks of bowmen; (*right*) the vulture-adorned stern of a royal battle-boat on the Nile.

Hyksos Avaris was the logical culmination of an experiment in an alternative, more circum-Mediterranean and maritime configuration of space to the conventional opposition between a unitary Egyptian Nile, ruled from upriver, versus the Levant. It marked a reversion to the pattern of the Egyptian early Predynastic and Levantine Copper Age, before the coming of the kings, but now scaled up and with sea trade, spiralling consumption and geopolitics thrown in. This comparison emphasizes just how readily such an alignment might form, given the continuum of space around the Mediterranean shore, and how much political energy, assertion of divine authority and sheer force was required to deny it. From another perspective, Avaris was port power to the power of ten, and a supersized version of the general model for a successful Mediterranean polity, with one foot in the sea and the other controlling its hinterland. The difference was the huge scale and fertility of the latter, which included the Delta and regions immediately to its south (by now supporting maybe a million people),[216] arguably the orchards of the southern Levant, and indirectly the Nubian goldfields. The timing was intimately linked to the rising wealth and trading power of the Levant, plus the window of opportunity offered by the breakdown of authority on the Nile, which insubordinations in the Delta may well have hastened. No wonder the Hyksos episode was anathematized by later Egyptian kings, and its power base left, in Kamose's words, a mass of 'reddened ruin-heaps' [**8.32**].[217] The only surprise is that a Theban polity fast on the way to provincial eclipse managed by force of arms to bring this flourishing Mediterranean giant down – a turning of the tables surely largely attributable to Thebes's immediately preceding recovery of Kush and the gold supply.[218] The great unknowable remains where, otherwise, this brilliant trajectory might have ended.

Change and continuity in the east

Ahmose's sack of Avaris therefore represents a major rupture and redirecting moment in the history of the Mediterranean. Three decisions made in its aftermath by the early New Kingdom pharaohs of the 18th Dynasty presage new directions that define the centuries after 1500 BC, a period of splendour at the apex that is commonly taken, a little uncritically, as the climax of the Bronze Age. One of these was actually more reversion than novelty. From its capital upriver at Thebes the 18th Dynasty reasserted the unity of the Nile and adherence to core Egyptian cultural norms, while also subtly integrating a population, and even royal court, now manifestly of multiple origins, not least in the Delta (most of whose inhabitants remained)[219] – as well as incorporating foreign traits as diverse as upright looms, amphorae and other new vessel forms, regular cultivation of the olive (whose stones occur far upriver and leaves were woven into Tutankhamun's funerary wreath), and the first chickens, identified as 'the bird that lays every day', which arrived from the east around this time.[220] Much of Avaris was abandoned, save for the citadel. At first this housed a garrison, but then, for a few decades in the early 15th century BC, a magnificent precinct of three palaces, after which it lay empty until about 1300 BC.[221] This brief return

8.33 Wine-jar from the tomb of Tutankhamun, with its contents recorded as 'Year 4, sweet wine of the estate of Aten of the Western River. Chief vintner Aperershop'. The Western River equates to the Canopic branch of the Nile Delta.

to glory coincided with a phase of exceptional engagement with the wider east Mediterranean, and Avaris may in fact have been the famed river-port of Perunefer ('Happy Journey'), traditionally assumed to have been somewhere near Memphis. We do not know how people in the Delta viewed their 'liberation' and reunification under the Theban kings.[222] The principal context in which the region appeared over the ensuing two centuries was that of a productive royal wine industry, drawing on locally naturalized Levantine expertise – two of Tutankhamun's vintners bore Canaanite names [**8.33**].[223] Vintages were noted on amphorae sent up the Nile; the best, including *shedeh*, a red wine favoured by king and court, came from vineyards in the western Delta. A slightly later Egyptian royal vineyard measured 8.5 ha (21 acres), larger than most in France to this day, and was tended by twenty-two personnel.[224] In contrast to the age of the Hyksos, and save for the short, bright flash of a revival at Avaris, the Delta reverted to a comparatively rural backwater.

The second initiative was the 18th Dynasty's policy of taking the war to the Levant, in recognition of the fact that the Avaris phenomenon did not end with the Delta, and symptomatic of the rising prominence of soldierly values, and a standing army, in New Kingdom Egyptian society.[225] Under Ahmose this got as far as Gaza and the destruction, after a siege, of Sharuhen. Soon afterwards, Thutmose I and Thutmose III (1504–1492 BC and 1479–1425 BC, respectively) advanced as far as the Euphrates, gathering booty and submission along the way, campaigns partly responsible for the destructions attested archaeologically at south Levantine towns in the course of the 16th and early 15th centuries BC.[226] On the side, Thutmose III hunted some of the last Asian elephants in the Ghab wetlands – one of the huge shoulder blades from which was recently unearthed at Qatna.[227] We revisit this expansion and its consequences for the Levant later. For now the key point is that such interventions gradually morphed from the age-old wealth-gathering razzias and smitings of the Asiatic into the imposition of a more durable overlordship and permanently extended resource control – the genesis, in short, of a rudimentary empire. Similar vectors were encroaching on the Levant from the north and east, each hastening the others in a scramble for dominance. We witnessed earlier how the first expansion of the highland Anatolian kingdom of Hatti resulted in raids and conquests in the north Levant. Despite this polity's chronic susceptibility to fissioning and implosion, beyond its great heartland of 100,000–150,000 sq. km (40,000–60,000 sq. miles) in central Anatolia, its power periodically expanded deep into the Levant and Jazira, as well as westward towards the Aegean.[228] What with its landlocked position and covetous eye on seaports, its ring of rebellious vassals, massed ranks of chariots, mineral wealth, grain shortages, paucity of merchants, clumsy monumental art, amalgam of home-grown and foreign ideologies, and inferiority complex with regard to Egypt, the temptation to caricature Hatti as the Soviet Russia of its age is irresistible – though if the analogy is pursued, Egypt resembled imperial China rather than the United States. Another empire-building contender was a short-lived, and to us shadowy, power known as Mitanni, which ruled the Jazira during the 15th and early 14th centuries BC, at a time of Hittite contraction, and briefly inherited control over Yamhad, Alalakh and Ugarit.[229] Apart from serial annexations of the Delta by Nile Valley kings, and Akkad's late 3rd-millennium BC incursion into the north Levant, these experiments in empire mark the first attempts to establish external rule over sectors of the Mediterranean basin, a process that would accelerate swiftly over the next thousand years.

The third historically resonant decision made a few generations after the end of Hyksos Avaris was to decorate one or more of the new palaces on the citadel with wall-paintings depicting bull-leaping, undulating landscapes full of animals, and other motifs executed in a manner familiar to us from the Aegean [PL. XXXII].[230] The surviving fragments, and recognition of earlier scraps in a similar style from palaces at Alalakh and at Tel Kabri in Israel,[231] have caused a sensation in Mediterranean archaeology. At face value they are proof of exported Aegean techniques, or even craftspeople, a case strengthened by similarities in the recipes for plaster preparation, which differ from those of Egypt and Mesopotamia. Unless, however, the revisionist chronology for the Aegean proposed in the Thera eruption controversy is right, the Levantine examples are at least as early as comparable wall-paintings on Crete, Thera and elsewhere, and to Aegeanists' chagrin even bull-leaping, that spectacular Minoan emblem, finds established parallels in Levantine and Anatolian art.[232] Rather than chase the tail of origins, a more productive alternative is to understand these wall-paintings as early symptoms of a new kind of long-range interaction, radically different from those so far encountered in the east (though with much smaller-scale antecedents elsewhere, for example in the western Mediterranean beaker sphere).[233] The initiators were high-status people (maybe rulers of exceptionally ambitious polities) who sought to create a shared courtly vocabulary, and thereby forge a community of east Mediterranean coastal elites that was common to places wide apart, but excluded native inferiors. Egypt soon applied partial brakes to the internal deployment of explicitly foreign imagery. But elsewhere, as contacts and mutual knowledge grew, this 'internationalism' (in fact 'Mediterraneanism' might be more accurate in a world without nations in the modern sense) became more prominent, especially in affirmations of royal power.[234] Often convergence remained at the level of subject matter, such as the glorifying depictions of muscle-pumped kings or heroes hunting on foot or from chariots. In other cases the foreign elements slipped into compositions otherwise grounded in a specific region. But a few pieces created a genuinely merged idiom that projected universalized ideas about power and harmony, and transcended locality. Here even the symbols were hybrids, whether griffins and sphinxes, or voluted palmettes, a blend of the palm (denoting abundance in Mesopotamia), Egyptian lotus and papyrus (emblems of stable, unified rule), and Cretan lily (of ritual significance). Most of these objects were in ivory, silver, gold and faience, and associated with the inner life of the palace,

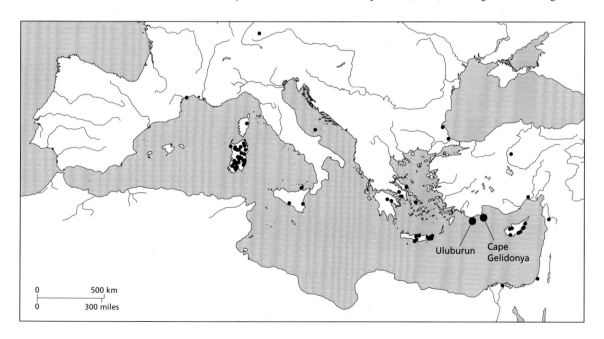

8.34 Stylistic 'internationalism' is richly illustrated by the designs on this gold bowl, one of a pair found at Ugarit. Images of men hunting lions and lions seizing other prey are interspersed with sphinxes, griffins, voluted palmettes, pomegranates, spirals and other motifs.

8.35 This map of oxhide ingot find-spots reveals their widespread currency, but is heavily skewed to areas that underwent catastrophic loss, through terrestrial destructions or shipwrecks, and so far from an accurate reflection of relative levels of consumption. Egypt, which texts and images confirm was a massive importer of copper, is barely evident, and the main source-island of Cyprus is also relatively under-represented. In addition, the finds from Sardinia and elsewhere in the west tend to be fragmentary, derived from hoards, and late in date (13th century BC onwards).

or martial display [**8.34**]. Many were portable, though the genre is nicely illustrated too by the ivory panels from a king's bed at Ugarit, and the designs on Tutankhamun's chariot gear. These developments unfolded alongside trading patterns that built to an ever greater scale upon older traditions created in or before the early 2nd millennium BC.

Among the major commodities, copper oxhide ingots feature regularly in archaeology and imagery, eventually spilling over into areas further west [**8.35**]. The growing availability of tin is apparent from plummeting prices between the Kanesh archive and those of the later 2nd millennium.[235] In a good year, Nubia generated 200–300 kg (450–650 lbs) of gold as tribute during the reign of Thutmose III, roughly as much as a quarter of the average annual quantity dispatched to Spain from the Americas in the 16th and early 17th centuries AD.[236] Mesopotamia moved to a gold standard, though silver remained the norm further west, where even in Egypt it began to share this role with long-normative copper.[237] The values of each metal across regions had tended to converge since the gross differentials of the 3rd millennium BC, the mark of a better-integrated eastern world, and a tribute not least to the activities of Levantine intermediaries – though these still found plenty of variation to play with. Oil and wine production went from strength to strength, the former boosted in the Levant by efficient new lever-arm presses [**8.36**].[238] A high-consuming wine

Uluburun Cape Gelidonya

0 500 km
0 300 miles

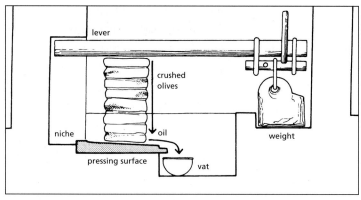

8.36 The ongoing expansion of the olive-based and wine industries in the later 2nd-millennium BC eastern Mediterranean is exemplified by (*above left*) an olive spray held up to the rays of the Aten disc by royal hands at Amarna and indicative of Nilotic cultivation; (*above right*) this reconstruction of an efficient lever-arm press from Ugarit; and (*right*) the mass-produced wine cups for large-scale participation in feasts at the palace of Pylos in the southwest Peloponnese.

culture extended all over the east Mediterranean. Ugaritic texts indicate the formalization from earlier practices of the *marzeah*, a drinking ceremony associated with social, religious or funerary occasions, later abominated by the prophets of Israel and comparable to the later Greek drinking parties known as symposia.[239] Archaeological residues of such events, as well as meatier feasts, are widespread and impressive in scale.[240]

Turning to other desirable substances, the analysis of Canaanite jars and their contents demonstrates that by this time many of those made in the north and central Levant, especially if destined for Egypt, contained terebinth or turpentine resins used as incense or in other ritual functions.[241] There are intriguing suggestions that Cypriot poppyhead-shaped juglets held opium-based substances (to label these drugs imposes puritanical modern categories), and that Egyptian Red Sea voyages had begun to obtain frankincense and myrrh from south Arabia.[242] Egypt's deeper southward reach is undoubtedly seen, moreover, in the new availability across the east Mediterranean of African elephant tusks, which substituted for those of the dwindling Asiatic elephant herds in the Levant.[243] These were also of better quality than hippopotamus ivory, which they ousted from top niches; thus the finest ivories in Ugarit's palace were carved from elephant, while hippopotamus products dominated in the rest of the town.[244] Pottery as a trade item operated within rationales identified earlier. The main branded containers, sometimes encountered far into the Anatolian highlands and up the Nile, were the Cypriot juglets, larger Cypriot and maybe Cilician red, lustrous vessels, many of elongated, arm-like form ending in a cupped dispensing hand, which initially targeted Egypt and later swung towards Anatolia (where Hattusa obtained huge numbers),[245] and arguably most successful of all by the 14th century BC, Aegean stirrup and piriform jars. Painted pots continued their fightback in the value stakes, mainly from the Aegean but with flashes elsewhere, notably a blue-painted style in Egypt and a brief explosion of exquisite floral Nuzi ware cups in the Jazira under the sway of Mitanni, just after the cessation of the most elaborate Aegean vegetal designs.[246] Even the beginning of regular glass production around 1500 BC, for brightly coloured, only mildly translucent beads, inlays, amulets and polychrome vessels, was a variation on an established theme.[247] The first glass was blue, and referenced lapis lazuli or turquoise; one of its epithets was 'stone from the kiln'. Similarly vitrified, artificial faience was in this sense its downmarket, lower-tech cousin. Production started in the experimentally inclined northern zone controlled by Mitanni, but soon spread, to Egypt perhaps thanks to a technology seizure during one of Thutmose III's campaigns, and initially as a royal monopoly. In technological terms a new invention after earlier false starts, the associations of glass were nonetheless very old indeed.

Four windows on 'trade'

The second half of the 2nd millennium BC in the east Mediterranean is renowned not only for the increasing scale of traditional activities alongside new initiatives, but also for an abundance of superlative archaeological and textual windows that provide vivid insights into the texture of specific kinds of trade and interaction, while dramatically confirming that what archaeologists typically recover is but the iceberg's tip. Before we explore the key regions of the east at this time, it is well worth taking a good look at some of these. The four selected comprise the integrated archaeology and archives of a major coastal town, the diplomatic letters of a superpower of the day, the earliest well-preserved shipwreck in the world, and an obscure islet off the coast of northeast Africa. Each time, we will move from the specifics of the case to wider, overlapping networks of connection that cumulatively start to make sense of a remarkable world.

Our first window opens on a familiar place: Ugarit, an archaeological marvel thanks to the exceptional duration and extent of modern investigations, and one where we shall extend our remit somewhat beyond this chapter's formal end-date, a liberty justified by the consistency of Ugaritic practices until the final destruction early in the 12th century BC.[248] Although we still know too little about earlier levels contemporary with, for example, Ugarit's appearance in the Mari archive, excavations

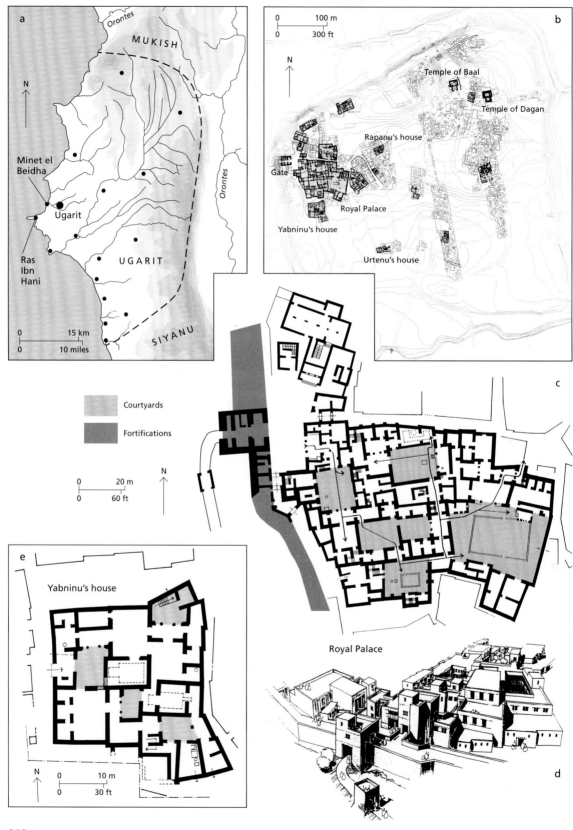

a

MUKISH

Orontes

N

Minet el
Beidha

Ugarit

Ras
Ibn
Hani

UGARIT

Orontes

SIYANU

0   15 km

0   10 miles

b

0   100 m

0   300 ft

N

Temple of Baal

Temple of Dagan

Rapanu's house

Gate

Royal Palace

Yabninu's house

Urtenu's house

c

Courtyards

Fortifications

0   20 m

0   60 ft

N

e

Yabninu's house

N

0   10 m

0   30 ft

Royal Palace

d

8.37 (*opposite*) Ugarit in the later 2nd millennium BC: (a) the extent of the kingdom, with its full range of Mediterranean environmental diversity; (b) town plan, showing investigated areas of housing and major structures; (c-d) the royal palace and main gateway through the fortifications; (e) Yabninu's house.

8.38 Stele of the god Baal, one of the principal divinities of Ugarit, found near his temple on a high point within the town. He wields a club and vegetation-sprouting spear, and the wavy lines beneath probably denote his dominion over mountains and sea. The smaller figure is likely to be a king of Ugarit.

over the last eight decades have revealed about a sixth of the later 2nd-millennium BC town, which was inhabited by 6000–8000 people [**8.37**]. Ugarit boasted a royal palace, grand mansions, residential quarters with kin groups of rich and poor families living side-by-side, wealthy tombs beneath houses, and tower temples – one of which, at the highest point and sacred to Baal, the town's principal deity, had stone anchors built in as ex-votos and probably acted as a navigational mark for shipping [**8.38**]. The thousands of unearthed tablets cover economic, diplomatic, legal, ritual, literary and mythological matters, an accumulation steeped in local and more distant literary traditions, written in four scripts and eight languages (Ugaritic, Akkadian, Sumerian, Egyptian, Hittite, Hurrian, west Anatolian Luwian, and Cypro-Minoan; conspicuously missing from this polyglot community, however, was any whisper of Aegean writing). Under loose Hittite overlordship, Ugarit ruled 2000–3000 sq. km (775–1150 sq. miles) of fertile, well-watered and populous land bordered by richly forested mountains.[249] We know little of its countryside save for allusions in the texts, which imply less than complete law and order, but the flint sickle blades common to most of the town houses, as well as oil-pressing installations in each neighbourhood, imply that although success encouraged an ever-denser urban community, most inhabitants retained their links to the fields, sometimes on a substantial scale.[250]

However, like previous centres near this junction of north–south, east–west and land–sea routes, Ugarit's wealth was pre-eminently derived from trade.[251] Residues of metalworking are widespread, as are imports, plus local copies, from other parts of the Levant, Cyprus, Egypt, Anatolia and the Aegean. The archives reel off a plethora of predictable substances, but also some that typically suffer from low visibility. One was salt, and another grain, the latter of exceptional interest because although short- and medium-range bulk movements of cereals surely became a regular feature in the topsy-turvy east Mediterranean environment as soon as sailing ships and carts became available, and certainly proved crucial to later Mediterranean urbanism, they tended to slip beneath the radar of texts and are archaeologically undetectable.[252] Before Ugarit our sole glimpse is a consignment from Yamhad heading out of the basin to Mari. Ugarit recorded shipments up and down the Levant, most of them from, but also to, the cereal cornucopia of Egypt, though even these are hard to evaluate in terms of significance and frequency.[253] Regardless, at a more general level maritime trade was clearly vibrant and crucial. Ugarit lay roughly a kilometre (half a mile) inland, but boasted five harbours. Closest to town, the exceptionally well-sheltered sandy cove of Minet el-Beida (then known as Mahadu) has produced a profusion of imports, including an ivory lid with a bare-breasted woman in hybrid style, found in a tomb with a built-in anchor, a freeze-framed snapshot of export in the form of a batch of eighty Canaanite jars lined up for loading [**8.25**], and debris from purple dye production.[254] Another harbour at Ras Ibn Hani (then Biruti) furnishes our sole example of a mould for casting oxhide ingots, located in a palace at one stage occupied by Ugarit's queen mother.[255]

A wealth of further insights into maritime culture can be gleaned from the texts.[256] One, cited earlier, mentions an artificial quay, with which a ship had collided.

Another refers to large royal musters of ships in adversity. Mahadu's overseer spent time in Cyprus buying boats for the king, but other texts establish beyond doubt the existence of private as well as royal vessels. Further tablets set out the regulations that defined the responsibility apportioned to owners, traders and crews for the safety of ships and cargo – we even learn of an unlucky ship that 'died' in a terrible storm off Tyre, whose king restored its cargo to the survivors after this had been salvaged and appropriated by a local coastguard. A few texts record specific shipments, most of which, in a healthy antidote to the tendency to gravitate towards spectacular ventures, were modest in size and destined for nearby cities on the Levantine coast; conversely, the inference from one document that giant ships of several hundred tonnes' capacity existed is flawed.[257] And lastly, although in Ugaritic mythology Baal subdued Yamm, the god of the sea, in worldly terms even a maritime power of Ugarit's stature was unable to establish a secure 'maritory' to match its territory, let alone any formal 'thalassocracy'; the sea remained an anarchic, free-for-all zone for anyone with the skill, daring and funds to set out upon it.[258]

Yet the greatest contribution made by the Ugaritic archives to our knowledge of early Mediterranean societies is their spotlight on the long-suspected, yet hitherto invisible, persona of the merchant, plus an accompanying arsenal of capital-raising, stake-sharing, risk-spreading and debt-recovery mechanisms analogous to those seen inland at Kanesh 500 years earlier, and just as commercial within the parameters of the times.[259] The palace itself was heavily involved in staging and part-funding mercantile ventures, as well as more ceremonially articulated exchanges that we come to shortly, but it did not exert overall control over trade, and raised some of its revenue by taxing others' profits in silver shekels. Thus, in an exception that proves the rule (and the sole reference to direct trade with the Aegean), one merchant won a royal favour: 'Ammishtamru, son of Niqmepa, King of Ugarit, exempts Sinaranu, son of Siginu…his grain, his beer, his oil to the palace he shall not deliver. His ship is exempt when it arrives from Crete.'[260] The person of the king, a figure of traditional, god-given authority, was screened from explicitly entrepreneurial activity, but this aversion apart, no stigma attached to trade. Indeed it was dominated by prominent insiders, who might seamlessly combine high state office at home or service as agents abroad, relations with the royal family, membership of the chariot-owning military elite, exploitation of estates cash-cropped by labour forces for internal consumption or export (witness the first stipulation in Sinaranu's deal with the palace), and mercantile trade, as well as related transport services on behalf of the palace, other interests, or both. These diversified, tentacular characteristics, together with an evident concern to own their supply and delivery chains, resemble to a certain degree the operations of a modern company.[261]

Such individuals were the incumbents of the town's most luxurious houses. Yabninu owned a multi-storey, 1000-sq.-m (35,000-sq.-ft) mansion just next to the palace, whose excavation brought to light an Egyptian stone vessel with a royal cartouche, Aegean pots, and sixty-seven tablets in several scripts, which may imply that such people were literate and multilingual.[262] His private archive lists silver, tin (in whose

8.39 The trading connections of four leading merchants at Ugarit, as documented by their own archives (or in the case of Urtenu, only the quarter of it so far available). There are marked distinctions in both overall scope and regional market preference, but all alike engaged with Cyprus.

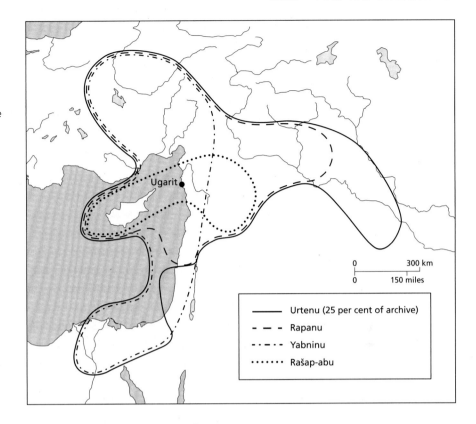

Ugarit

0   300 km
0   150 miles

——— Urtenu (25 per cent of archive)

– – – Rapanu

– · – · Yabninu

· · · · · Rašap-abu

acquisition from markets on the Euphrates he was centrally involved) and even iron, along with grain, oil, milk, wool, horses, fish, doves, tools, woods and other sylvan resources, reeds, walnuts and aromatic plants, as well as shipments and contacts with ports up and down the Levant. The less fully studied archive of Urtenu, found in another mansion until 1986 out of bounds beneath a Syrian army bunker, is eight times larger and includes correspondence between, and on behalf of, kings.[263] One striking feature of the spheres of operation of such major players, as revealed by their archives, is the extent to which these varied in range and geographical emphasis, due in all likelihood to individual merchants' webs of long-range connections, or micro-fluctuations in market conditions, otherwise too fine for us to recognize, during the slightly different time spans over which each was active [**8.39**].[264] Lesser merchants, of whom we should not lose sight despite their more modest activities, congregated at Mahadu. Being a merchant could be risky as well as lucrative, and not purely in economic terms.[265] Merchants often travelled with their goods and outside their home jurisdiction were vulnerable to lapses in protection and the frameworks of trust on which they relied; Ugaritic and other contemporary archives allude to merchants murdered or robbed at the interstices between polities, or even by unfriendly kings.

The million-dollar question is how far we should extrapolate these revelations. Foreign merchants are often mentioned at Ugarit, some of whom invested locally and wielded substantial, at times disruptive, influence in the town, as a result of which all were closely monitored.[266] This leaves no doubt that similar kinds of people existed throughout the Levant, and on Cyprus. Interestingly, merchants working with Hatti concentrated at its narrow window on the Mediterranean, particularly at Ura, a port near modern Silifke that awaits archaeological identification.[267] The situation in Egypt, where travel abroad had negative connotations, was quite different.[268] Although a term for 'merchant' does begin to appear regularly for the first time in the New Kingdom, and riverside local and regional barter-based markets had existed since at least the Old Kingdom, the confines of riverine geography and the power of the state still enabled an exceptional degree of centralized redistribution and command within this sphere. Royal or temple operators au fait with prices certainly existed, and probably accumulated profits on the side, but independent traders were modest figures, scoring minor, sometimes dubious, gains from conveying and also lending along the river, beyond the fringes of official activity and very much second fiddle in terms of access to metals to the royal tax collector. In short, they were quite unlike the fortune-makers of Ugarit. Foreign merchants, meanwhile, docked at Perunefer, wherever its exact location in the north, and perhaps further upriver. But to illustrate the spatial and economic uncertainties, we can return to the Nilotic harbour scene from the tomb of Kenamun [**8.8**], and interrogate its details.[269] Where is the setting? Kenamun was mayor of Thebes under Amenhotep III (1390–1352 BC), so a likely possibility is the latter's great river-port at nearby Birket Habu. But did foreign merchants (among them high-status women, to judge from the depiction) really get this far upriver, and with what wider implications if they did? And who were the locals (again, two men, one woman), so wisely brandishing, in this cross-cultural, all-too-easily duplicitous encounter, the only sets of balance scales depicted in Egyptian market scenes: royal officials, merchants, or both, and acting on their own or others' behalf? Without solid answers to such questions it is hard to decide how aloof Egypt remained in this respect from east Mediterranean practices, although the very depiction of such activities assumes a degree of tolerance. A similar problem, but this time raising real questions of relative economic scale and sophistication, attends the Aegean, where external and internal written evidence remains oddly silent.[270]

Our next window looks out from a royal balcony in Akhetaten, the capital temporarily established in the mid-14th century BC at Amarna, halfway between Thebes and Memphis, by Amenhotep III's son, the famous revisionist pharaoh Akhenaten (1352–1336 BC). It consists of the correspondence sent to Egypt at the zenith of its power by other major and lesser polities, independent and vassal, over the course of thirty years [**8.40**].[271] Interstate communication via emissaries and letters goes back to the early 2nd millennium BC in this part of the world, and the resultant alliances and accords had long institutionalized and facilitated flows of goods between regions. The Amarna archive reflects the formalization of such procedures into a new species of international relations that flourished over a lengthier period (from the 15th to 13th centuries BC), and arguably the world's first diplomacy.[272] The letters are formulaic documents written in versions of Akkadian, already a dead language akin in its use as a universal tongue to medieval Latin. They were read aloud in mimicry of personal conversations between kings, despite the weeks that elapsed for

8.40 An example of the Amarna correspondence: cuneiform clay tablet inscribed in Akkadian and dispatched via a merchant envoy from Cyprus to the Egyptian court, seeking closer relations and accompanying a large shipment of copper. In this case, scientific analysis of the clay has proven somewhat inconclusive as to provenance within the island.

clay letters to be conveyed in their clay envelopes, and the protracted delays while messengers were detained by courtly formalities, negotiations and seasonal closures of the route home.

Their aim was to create, maintain or subtly alter an international order based on the symbolic equivalence and fictional brotherhood between a 'great power club' of kings who ruled the superpowers of the age, and paternal relations with dependent rulers, especially in the Levant, who similarly wrote among themselves in imitation.[273] In this correspondence, rulers grappled to reconcile conflicting realities, among the Great Kings particularly their rhetoric of omnipotence and fiction of domestic autarky versus the harsher sweepstakes of power abroad, not to mention their veiled desire for things they did not possess. A nice example comes from a letter sent by Burnaburiash II of Babylon, who delicately opined 'And, as I am told, in my brother's country everything is available and my brother needs absolutely nothing; also in my country everything is available and I myself need absolutely nothing… however…'; there followed a request for a large quantity of gold.[274] Equally, cultural traditions in each region meant that a given gesture might carry different, sometimes unacceptable local connotations. For instance, in this case revealing a positive cross-cultural dovetailing, Egypt was highly averse to marrying out its princesses to other courts, though happy to receive into the pharaoh's harem foreign ones that to Egyptian eyes were symbols of subservience, while other kings found honour and political alliance in the marriage of their princesses abroad.[275] The information in the Amarna letters is virtually limitless, but for us particularly relevant is that concerning movements of people and goods, as well as other fascinating sidelights on the polities gathered around the east Mediterranean.

The Amarna correspondence reveals a different aspect of interaction from that most salient in Ugarit's archives. Instrumental were the high state officials who acted as messengers, but we glimpse other figures on the move too, and not only merchants (some of whose initiatives appear less positively as sources of diplomatic friction) and princess brides, but craftspeople, physicians, augurs and other ritual experts, given as presents or on loan; from other letters we learn that even gods could be on the move, hosted by foreign kings and acolytes.[276] With at least mortals moved huge quantities of wealth goods in raw or worked form, some as ceremonial greeting gifts to accompany exchanges of letters, others as dowry or bride-price, and a few in response to blatant importunities thinly excused by an urgent need to fulfil a pious project.[277] Commonest were gold (said by foreign rulers to be 'as plentiful as dust' in Egypt), silver, lapis lazuli, ivory, Sudanese blackwood (a bastard ebony), and bale after bale of snow-white Egyptian linen. Other textiles, woods and stones were regularly mentioned, the last often carved in Egypt to contain scented oils, as were furniture, horses, chariots and weapons, though oddly tin, cedar, glass and (save in the Cypriot correspondence) copper were rare or absent, while pottery and faience entirely failed to make the royal grade. Ostensibly these formal exchanges operated under utterly different rules from the entrepreneurial trade revealed at Ugarit, but beneath the courteous veneer of the accompanying letters lay a sharp eye for equivalence in quantities and qualities of materials (notably gold), barely veiled aspirations of advantage, and a prickly anxiety not to be demeaned, in short an economic equivalent to the endless jockeying for diplomatic position.[278] The letters reveal a further ambiguity inherent in cross-cultural exchange, insofar as Egypt tended to portray as tribute what had been volunteered as gifts to be recip-rocated, or as alliance-sealers.[279] Again, letters from Babylon are informative. The most amusing are a complaint that chariots intended as a present to a fellow Great King had been put on show at Amarna beside the tribute from vassals, a request for a princess with the codicil that should this prove impossible, any Egyptian lady who could pass as such in Babylon would do, and, in an early case of bride and preju-dice, the inverse alarm that a Babylonian princess married to pharaoh was no longer being treated as such at court.[280] Freelance mercantile trade and royal gift exchange displayed a similarly keen awareness of value; where they contrasted most was in the institutional packaging and pacing of events. The Amarna mechanism could move around unprecedented wealth in a tightly controlled, exclusionary manner that underpinned the power of royal palaces. But its great disadvantage lay in the cumbersome etiquette of correspondence between kings, which might take years to come to fruition, compared to decisions that could be swiftly brokered, often face-to-face, between independently operating merchants.

The Amarna letters focus attention on the pinnacles of society, and it is likely that gift exchange was deployed far more widely, including between merchants, when the social occasion demanded. But if we can live with this avowedly regal bias, other insights follow, for, after all, the letters acted as conduits of information, even if of a slanted kind. Some are simply striking details of which we would otherwise have no inkling, for example we glimpse Byblos (which still aspired to preferential ties with Egypt) under siege and boats forced to detour via Cyprus, Tyre's vulnerability if an enemy seized its mainland water and wood supplies, and the heirs apparent of Tyre and Jerusalem brought up as courtly hostages at Amarna to inculcate loyalty.[281] Other letters hint at deeper structural patterns. The Levantine polities caught between Egypt, Hatti and nearby friends and enemies were adroit at manipulating the situation on the ground. Even the tone of letters could shift cannily. One sent to Amarna by a king of Ugarit (in fact Hatti's, not Egypt's, vassal) opened with an unabashedly grovelling 'I fall at the feet of the king, the Sun, my lord', then switched to a greeting formula more appropriate between equals and concluded with a cheeky request to be sent some craftsmen.[282] Letters from Cyprus are revelatory in other respects, not least the inference of a resident expert in Akkadian, the fact that the sender styled himself as the pharaoh's equal, a claim reflecting a safe sea-girt distance rather than political reality, the delivery by a merchant rather than royal courier, and the exceptionally pragmatic, commercial tone, with its chasing up of transactions, requests for the exemption of Cypriot merchants from Egyptian dues, proposals for the faster, annual exchange of news, and emphasis among goods bound for Egypt on

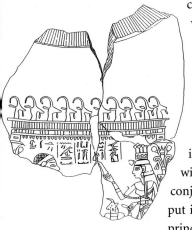

8.41 This fragment of a stone vessel celebrating the marriage of Niqmaddu II of Ugarit is thoroughly cosmopolitan in its cultural allusions, and deliberately evasive as regards the identity of the bride.

consignments of the island's copper, in return for silver, linen, oil, ivory, blackwood, chariots, horses and a gilt bed.[283] Lastly, echoing the situation at Ugarit, the entire correspondence contains only a single exchange with the Aegean, initiated by the west Anatolian polity of Arzawa under threat of conquest by Hatti, gauchely written in Hittite instead of Akkadian and peculiar for its express suspicion of the medium of written correspondence.[284] From Egypt's perspective as much as that of Ugarit, the Aegean was of fleeting interest.

Before closing our exploration of the Amarna letters, it is naturally tempting to associate the practice of international correspondence and gift-giving with the equally formulaic artistic internationalism noted earlier. After all, both conjured an imagined harmonious community of rulers and, as one advocate has put it, international objects blurred elite cultural boundaries as the movement of princesses blurred gene pools.[285] Such objects may well have numbered among the items accompanying royal letters, particularly the decorated furniture, chariots and precious metal vessels, though most such goods remained more representative of the giver's home culture in terms of raw material, style or royal inscription.[286] But another option is that international letters and international objects belonged to independent, if parallel, realms, the latter less immediately eloquent but more durable and so presenting rich opportunities for the subsequent manipulation of meaning by their owners. We saw how cleverly Ugarit's letters played off its international connections. No less ambiguous was a stone vase displayed to the select few in its royal palace, whose style mingled the Levantine and Egyptian, with an added Aegean detail in the form of a bull's-head ritual vessel [**8.41**].[287] The subject, a marriage scene involving Ugarit's king Niqmaddu II, was deliberately left open to interpretation, for the woman whom Niqmaddu weds was drawn so as to resemble an Egyptian princess, but without quite committing the diplomatic solecism, given Egypt's adamant refusal to give these away, of explicitly stating that she was in fact any such thing. Judging from this slippery piece, international art played a range of roles in the strategies of rulers and other aspiring figures in the east Mediterranean.

Our third window is a porthole 40–50 m (130–165 ft) underwater off the eastern cliffs of the savage Uluburun ('Great Cape'), which thrusts seaward from the cruel coast of Lycia in southern Turkey. Around 1325 BC, a little after the latest Amarna correspondence, a heavily laden ship foundered here, and its discovery by local sponge divers followed by a state-of-the-art underwater excavation revealed the world's earliest well-preserved shipwreck [**1.12, 8.42, 8.43**].[288] So far, we have made do with a combination of boat depictions, bills of lading, and bits and pieces recovered from the seabed. In contrast, the 15,000 artifacts (excluding some 85,000 beads) raised at Uluburun are a veritable treasure-house of information. The artifact to begin with is the ship itself, a 15-m (50-ft) vessel, the lower parts of which survive enough to reveal cedar-wood construction, joined without nails by a pegged mortise-and-tenon technique, and painstakingly built up shell-first from the keel (the frame-first method standard today was invented in the late 1st millennium AD).[289] Nothing survives of the mast, rigging and sail, so above the waterline we

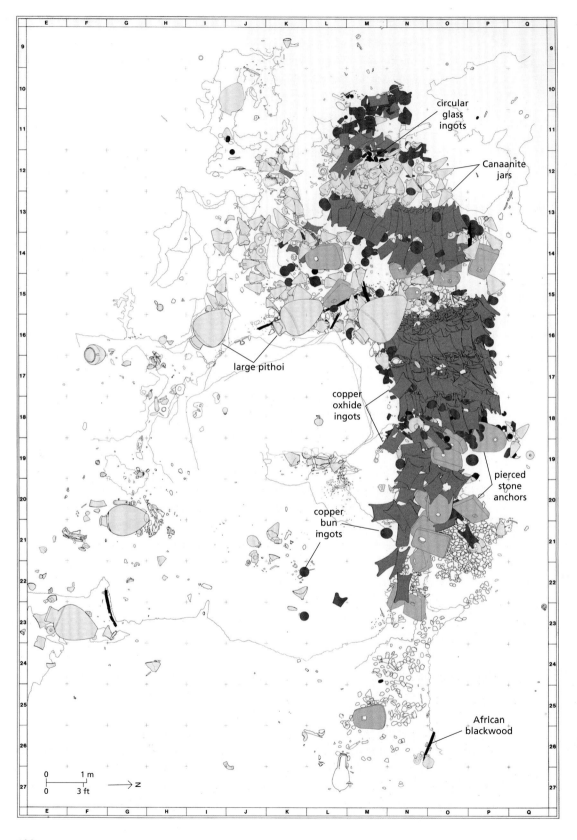

8.42 (*opposite*) Plan of the Uluburun shipwreck, showing the distribution of the main types of surviving cargo and the pierced stone anchors. The vessel's outline and pattern of lading are clearly visible, suggesting that the ship settled intact on the bottom, with subsequent spillage downslope (left), mainly of Canaanite amphorae, large jars and stone anchors.

8.43 A diver on the Uluburun wreck holds a Canaanite amphora, balanced on a stack of oxhide ingots.

must mentally splice in the Kenamun or Akrotiri images. The Uluburun ship was carrying at least 20 tonnes of cargo and shipboard gear, including twenty-four stone anchors (3 tonnes-worth) of a kind common in the Levant and occasionally found in the Aegean; this apparent superfluity served as ballast, in addition to a thousand-odd stones carried for this purpose, and enabled mooring on steep coasts, where an anchor could be simply cut away before sailing on.

The cargo, carefully packed between dense thorny plants to prevent shifting, is even more extraordinary. One or more people sustained a major blow with its loss, for the value of bulk elements alone has been calculated from prices in contemporary archives to have been enough to feed a town as large as Ugarit for a year.[290] It bears out the Mit Rahina inscription's implication that shipments were made up from a wide variety of goods, a breadth that must in part have reflected uncertainties concerning precise destinations, as well as local supply and demand, in as navigationally and economically changeable an environment as the Mediterranean.[291] On the Uluburun ship's final journey the main cargo consisted of 10 tonnes of Cypriot copper, mainly in the form of 348 oxhide ingots (a larger copper consignment than any in the Amarna letters), a tonne of tin ingots (reflecting the ideal 10:1 alloying ratio for bronze), 150 Levantine Canaanite jars, most holding half a tonne of terebinth resin and the others probably oil, 350 kg (770 lbs) of Egyptian blue glass ingots, and, often overlooked, an unknown original number of textiles, of which only tantalizing purple and red threads remain. On these piggy backed smaller, still often valuable, amounts of many other raw materials and objects, including elephant and hippopotamus tusks and carved ivories, Sudanese blackwood, ostrich eggs, gold, silver and tin both as objects and scraps for recycling, a gold-masked bronze goddess (the ship's protecting deity?) [PL. XXXIV], bronze tools and a few weapons of Levantine, Aegean and central Mediterranean types, Cypriot storage pithoi (several holding Cypriot juglets, bowls and lamps, but at least one probably a water-butt),[292] a few Aegean pots (mainly stirrup jars), faience ritual vessels, the thousands of beads, some of Baltic amber, a stone ceremonial axe from the Danube, several musical instruments (a tortoiseshell lyre, bronze finger cymbals and an ivory trumpet), basketry, matting and rope, plants for food, flavouring or sweetening such as olives, grapes, almonds, figs, pomegranates, coriander, capers and safflower, orpiment for tanning or dyeing, murex opercula (which played no part in dyeing, but was possibly a medical ingredient), bone gaming pieces, and fishing gear. Last but not least comes the apparatus of mobile trade,[293] 149 balance weights divided into sets for several different standards prevalent around the Levant and east Mediterranean,

cylinder seals and scarabs, and, stored in a pithos, a little folding wooden writing board, onto whose waxed surface no one had sadly yet inscribed [**8.44**]. Uluburun is the trading world of the east Mediterranean both in microcosm, as a moment of simultaneous conveyance, and in its widest ramifications, with the objects brought together in those few cubic metres of shipboard space originating as far apart as Afghanistan, Sudan, the Baltic and the central Mediterranean.

The circumstances of the ship's last sailing are trickier ground.[294] Plenty of items on board could have been picked up at most entrepôts around the east Mediterranean. The bulk cargo argues for one recent stop in the Levant, in the vicinity of the Carmel range to judge by the clay of most of the Canaanite jars,[295] and another at a copper-rich port on Cyprus. The minutiae of the mandible of a house mouse unlucky enough to have stowed away argue for another north Levantine stop.[296] The wreck's westerly position suggests that it had subsequently either been blown badly off course, or was heading towards the Aegean, an unusual event from Ugarit's archival perspective, with the few

8.44 Wooden folding writing tablet from Uluburun, not under an ancient stylus but instead a conservator's tool.

Aegean pots homeward-bound after circulating further east. If the latter destination holds good, this was again an important shipment, because the amount of copper on board is greater than that listed in all Aegean archives. Some would push the inferences further, using the cedar construction and best candidates for crew possessions (seals, weights, weapons and possible galley crockery) to argue for a Levantine home port and Levantine plus, more dubiously, Aegean merchants on board.[297] This is not intrinsically unlikely, but a Cypriot origin is equally possible and, as the father of modern Mediterranean underwater archaeology and initial excavator of Uluburun memorably put it, how would we define the home of a modern ship 'built in Japan but flying a Panamanian flag with a Portuguese captain and a Filipino crew...carrying Swedish automobiles and French wine to Brazil'?[298] Furthermore, we have no idea whether the ship sailed alone or in company. Its feeble armament could imply that it had an escort, and we know Egyptian ships laden with rich cargos tended to move in convoy, often with a troop of archers on board[299] – but conversely, recall Sinaranu of Ugarit's solitary ship reportedly on its way back from the Aegean. As for whether this shipment reflected a palatial or private venture, several points stand out. The size of the cargo and know-how required to work materials like glass leave little doubt that it targeted sophisticated, generically palatial markets. As for who sponsored the voyage, and whether it represented an entrepreneurial venture, one side of a royal exchange, or both, we cannot be sure, but the overall cargo composition differs in certain respects from the typical gift profiles in the Amarna letters, and the number of one-off pieces of varying value, as well as the precious metal scrap, hint at private

8.45 Fragments of a Cypriot white-slipped bowl with distinctive wishbone handle, a far-travelled piece excavated at Marsa Matruh on the North African coast.

8.46 Detail from a procession of Keftiu in the Theban tomb of Rekhmire, in this instance carrying an elephant tusk and precious metal vessels.

trade at least as an expedient sideline, if not central to the voyage.[300]

Our final window offers a less glamorous vista, onto a scruffy little islet in the calm, turquoise waters of a lagoon at Marsa Matruh on the African shore 280 km (175 miles) west of the Delta.[301] A wadi from the interior fans out to create a small plain near this protected anchorage, an uncommon combination on this dry, exposed coast. The islet is named today after Oric Bates, an early explorer of this overlooked corner of the Mediterranean and the first to recognize the islet's significance. After becoming lost again to knowledge for much of the last century, 'Bates's Island' has returned to the vanguard thanks to confirmation from new excavations that mainly Cypriot, but also Aegean and Levantine pottery [**8.45**], scraps of faience, metal and metal-casting debris were deposited here in the 14th century BC, alongside, from the African side, ostrich eggs and a few handmade local pots. The best explanation is that the islet served as a stopover, a revictualling and watering point for sea traffic, where minor goods were exchanged for the ostrich eggs so popular as curios in parts of the east Mediterranean.[302] Indeed, it makes excellent sense as a landfall for open-sea voyages from the north to Egypt on the prevailing winds, with an onward coastwise journey to the Delta and a circuitous return via the Levant to avoid contrary weather.

As we saw earlier, quite when this demanding route opened up is uncertain. A 15th-century BC pulse in the reign of that horizon-stretching pharaoh, Thutmose III, is hinted by the renewed activity at Avaris mentioned earlier, most notably the palaces decorated with Aegean-style wall-paintings. Contemporary Theban tombs show processions bringing what can be flexibly translated, in the spirit of later Amarna, as tribute or gifts, borne by Canaanites, Mesopotamians, Nubians and, most significant in the present context, 'Keftiu' with Aegean clothing and hairstyles, oxhide ingots, bolts of cloth, elephant tusks and flower-adorned metal vessels and animal-headed ritual shapes [**8.46**].[303] Do these echo Cretan expeditions to the court of a world-conquering king, just as one of Japan's early rulers dispatched a 140-strong seaborne embassy to Tang China?[304] Perhaps, but contacts remained episodic. Later Egyptian writings continue to mention Keftiu (albeit in one medical papyrus, copied from an earlier original, in the context of a curative spell purportedly in the language of Keftiu but in fact gibberish), while 'Tanaja', thought to designate the Greek mainland, and the 'Isles of the Great Green' also appear.[305] But not until the reign of Amenhotep III, another mighty ruler, do we witness the next spike of connections, roughly synchronous with activity at Bates's Island. This time it took the form of long-curated faience plaques bearing his name at Mycenae and, carved on his funerary temple in Thebes, lists of Aegean places, including Knossos and Mycenae, probably lifted from a mariner's itinerary but deployed alongside other encircling lands to affirm Egypt's cosmic centrality.[306] How infrequent such Aegean encounters with Egypt remained is underscored by another observation that takes us back to Bates's Island: the simple fact that most of the pots brought by the sailors were Cypriot rather than Aegean – a startling premonition of the rise of Cypriot maritime enterprise during the coming centuries.

In contrast, the African partners in exchange at Marsa Matruh remain obscure, beyond the likelihood that they comprised people categorized in Egypt as Libyans. A nearby indigenous cemetery noted by Bates has not been relocated.[307] If such people were seasonally mobile pastoralists, as is fairly likely, they would have sought winter grazing far inland on the desert margins and moved to the cooler coast in the summer, coincidentally when the sailing season brought most traffic from across the sea. We can only guess how these parties communicated and bartered, or whether they did so at all; silent trade with reciprocal displays of wares is a perfectly possible scenario.[308] Regardless, in such encounters at Bates's Island we sense a cross-cultural gulf utterly different from the fluent communications between kings and merchants to which we have grown accustomed. We also witness, however, an early germ of the connections that would, a few centuries later, firmly tie North Africa into the warp and weft of the maritime Mediterranean world emerging to its north.

Empires and traders

To understand how our four highlights fitted into the overall patterns around the east Mediterranean after 1500 BC we need to pan out again. As ever, a good place to start is the Levant, onto which no fewer than three of our windows afforded some view, and which was now nominally divided into spheres of external overlord-ship, the boundaries of which oscillated between the Lebanon and further north. In trying to envisage these early experiments in empire and their impact on the ground, it is best to banish later ancient, let alone recent, Old World analogies, which present a more politically and economically integrated aspect. Better parallels exist among the New World empires of the Aztecs and Incas into which the conquistadors blundered, both emergent entities still working out, with uneven success, how to control and profit from a patchwork of subject polities with antecedent traditions.[309] One top priority was acknowledgment of hegemony, for Egypt ultimately grounded in the ineffable superiority of the kingdom on the Nile, in Hatti's case in a more worldly way by the copious treaties it forced on subject polities. The other priority was the extraction of tribute or, as a last resort, booty from defeated rebel vassals. In this sense both Egypt and Hatti could be extremely successful through a mix of

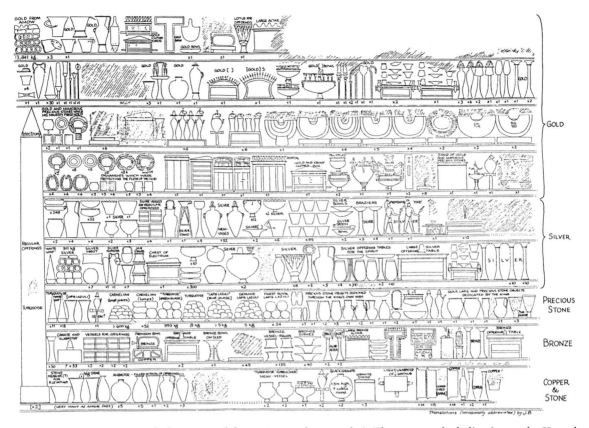

8.47 Part of Thutmose III's booty from campaigns in the Levant, as dedicated at Karnak and illustrated there, organized in tiers of relative value. Note the predominance of precious metals, and the complete absence of pottery.

diplomacy and force. A superb example is Thutmose III's dedication at the Karnak temple in Thebes after he annihilated a coalition of Levantine kings in about 1458 BC at Megiddo, the battle to which we owe the connotations of Armageddon [**8.47**].[310] The booty was displayed in tiers of value culminating in precious metals (including silver Canaanite amphorae, an otherwise unknown refinement) that confirm the economic hierarchies of the age and illustrate just how effective such coercive strategies might be. Thutmose acquired living booty, too, including 2000 horses and more thousands of captives, among them probably some expert in glass production. Hatti's approach likewise focused on metal tribute and population transfers. But a further key concern for Hatti, whose hallowed capital Hattusa lay far from the sea and the trunk routes of trade, was assured access to such arteries, to the extent of flirting with an alternative capital further south.[311] This explains a recurrent focus throughout Hatti's vicissitudes on control over the great Jazira trail through to its Mediterranean terminus at Ugarit, and over Cilicia, known as Kizzuwatna, where the Taurus passes provided its best window on the Mediterranean – a poor second to Egypt's Delta, but still a funnel up which goods from Egypt, the Levant and Cyprus could reach Hattusa. This gravitation south and seaward by one of the great powers of the day is eloquent testimony to the perceived wealth of the east Mediterranean by this time, and the consequent necessity of access to it.

But in other respects these first imperial projects in the Levant were extremely weak. For one thing, their infrastructure was thin on the ground. Hatti instituted two

8.48 The cosmopolitan court culture of the later 2nd-millennium BC Levant, with its strong Egyptianizing tinge, as illustrated by this 14th-century BC ivory carving from Megiddo.

dynastically connected viceroyships, at Aleppo and on the Euphrates at Carchemish, but elsewhere its vassals retained their local rulers, and Ugarit in particular had a very free hand as long as its king paid regular lip-service and tribute.[312] Egypt established a chain of provisioning and watering points for its armies along the Ways of Horus, and a few small governors' residences and garrisons at nodes within its sphere of influence, one of the most northerly at Kumidi (modern Kamid el-Loz) to watch over the high Beqaa Valley.[313] The accoutrements of south Levantine kingship remained suffused in loosely Egyptian motifs [**8.48**]. But otherwise neither Hatti nor Egypt invested in physical reminders or practical mechanisms of control. Equally, no effort was made to integrate conquered populations; at the height of the New Kingdom, the pharaoh claimed authority over a 2000-km- (1250-mile-) long snake of land running from Nubia to the Lebanon, but being Egyptian remained a strictly Nilotic prerogative from which inhabitants of other regions were barred. We can now better appreciate how much depended on the careful diplomatic management of relations with vassal kings, who in effect remained locally in charge, and how volatile this situation must have been, given the jostling claimants for their loyalty. The recurrence of Egyptian and Hittite military actions in the Levant is only ambiguously emblematic of strength, for it also bears witness to the frequent breakdown of alternative means of control. Lastly, and as alluded to earlier, the sea itself remained a free-for-all. Although Thutmose III's later campaigns involved naval operations and the capture of Levantine ships, 'the Great Green', as it was known in Egypt, lay beyond the control of imperial power and much of the movement across it remained in the hands of the kinds of coastal polities over whom land-based superpowers had constant difficulty in establishing enduring authority.[314]

These observations allow us to make better sense of the ambivalent face of the Levant at this time. Compared to the climax of urbanism and closely integrated rural settlements of the earlier part of the millennium, the centuries of Egyptian and Hittite hegemony represented a decline. Most of the political centres for a continuing mosaic of polities shrank, often to virtual villages clustered around their palace and temple.[315] Fortifications vanished or were slighted, to grandiose gates stripped of circuit walls. If there was no longer room in the fracture zone between Egypt and Hatti for a Hazor on a par with its mighty Middle Bronze Age peak, there was also less security and hope of prosperity for farming villages like Tell el-Hayyat. The disappearance of countless rural communities was matched by a steady drift towards alternative, more pastoral lifestyles that oscillated between dispersal into the freedom of the eastern steppes in winter, and mobile grazing in the highlands over the summer.[316] For many this offered refuge from military incursions, the burden of imperial tribute and impoverishment through the exactions of cash-cropping elites. Moreover, weaker polities meant more opportunities for preying upon the caravan trade. Urban scribes obsessed over roving, marauding bands of *hapiru* and *shashu*, terms whose usual translation as 'brigands' merely reflects their bogeyman status among town-dwellers. One Labayu was said to have taken over Shechem in upland Samaria, from where he terrorized Megiddo.[317] A more neutral analysis might conclude that aggregates of mobile people managed to establish a relatively free, sustainable, if sometimes predatory, way of life at or beyond the edges of formal polities, during a time of particularly marked inequality and exploitation.

The other side of the coin was that a few towns boomed spectacularly. The archives and archaeology of Ugarit reveal the prosperity of one Levantine town, new finds of tablets and a royal tomb at Qatna, plus a wealthy tomb at Dan, point the same way in the central Levant,[318] and in the south, even if we suspect some plagiarizing of their predecessors' conquest annals by less successful pharaohs, it is striking how often the goose could be killed and still recover to lay yet more tributary golden eggs. Goods from Cyprus and the Aegean continued to pour in to a coastal zone less affected, if at all, by depopulation than the interior,[319] and, as we have seen, the Levant's merchants commanded both their home ground and contact points with the imperial cores to north and south. Meanwhile the enduring propensity for innovation under melting-pot conditions, outside palatial control and perhaps in the context of trade, can be gauged by the appearance of no fewer than three early versions of the alphabet that adapted cuneiform or hieroglyphs, one at Ugarit, another identified at the turquoise mines of Sinai but perhaps originating earlier in the eastern Delta (possibly at Avaris?), and the third, ancestral to later alphabets, in the south Levant.[320] Levantine wealth and skill had not been drained, but concentrated at a few points in the network of trade, where they could be rapidly amassed and, when equally easily captured or bled by tribute, swiftly regenerated. Whether Egypt and Hatti explicitly recognized the cold logic of this cycle is unknown, but, either way, the economic opportunities arising from these by now highly evolved east Mediterranean conditions were proving a match in their own way for the armed muscle of the first intruding empires.

If we can draw such a partly upbeat conclusion from a strip of mainland on the very doorstep of the superpowers, it should come as no great surprise that the rise of Cyprus proceeded quite unfettered.[321] Hatti intermittently claimed it as a vassal, and offloaded political exiles there, to no discernible effect.[322] Amarna tolerated relations couched in terms of equity and mercantile pragmatism with someone writing as king of Alashiya, which is variously understood to refer to the island as a whole, Enkomi specifically, or, on the basis of the clay on which letters to Amarna were written, somewhere between the Troodos mining zone and the south coast.[323] A Ugaritic monarch received a letter couched in familial terms from one such figure, by the name of Kushmashusha, offering copper.[324] For all this, the character of political organization within the island remains intriguingly uncertain.[325] Despite the self-identification of Akhenaten's correspondent as royal, over a century

8.49 The cultural eclecticism of status goods in later 2nd-millennium BC Cyprus is apparent in this exceptionally rich assemblage from Enkomi Tomb 93, which contained local and Aegean pottery and figurines, seals and scarabs, a glass flask, silver jewelry, and abundant goldwork as well as gold scrap, the last surprising in a funerary context and indicative of the openness of the Cypriot elite to unusually pragmatic statements about wealth.

of excavations at Enkomi and the string of medium-sized towns that now sprang up along the south coast to rival it (mainly Kition, neighbouring Hala Sultan Tekke, Maroni, Kalavasos, Kourion, Alassa and Paliopaphos) has furnished no demonstrable proof of a unitary political capital, nor indeed a definite palace among their imposing public buildings. Most look rather like the foci of small independent polities. We may be missing something in terms of paramountcy, but whoever wrote to Amarna and elsewhere could have presented himself more splendidly than the domestic reality – perhaps a necessary fiction in order to correspond with kings in the first place. In some of the eastern towns in particular, Cyprus's late start and therefore poorly rooted traditions of rulership, followed by its careering economic growth, could well have led to any emergent pretensions of central authority being quashed in favour of a broader-based upper social tier engaged in copper production, cash-cropping and trade.[326] The absence of palaces, as well as large bureaucratic archives, combined with the clusters of rich family tombs at major sites, all tend to favour this scenario, which would have the latecomer in effect able to skip a step in the typical institutional sequence of east Mediterranean societies.

Whatever the realities of political culture on Cyprus, the restructuring of the island's society, economy and indeed ecology towards copper extraction and other kinds of trade is not in doubt.[327] Deep in the interior, where the original woodland was probably being fast depleted and now carefully managed to feed the furnaces, mining communities were victualled by food-growing support villages and sustained in less tangible ways by impressive shrines, under whose protection extraction and transport of copper are thought to have lain.[328] A symbolic vocabulary, focused on the oxhide ingot, was created and principally deployed in ritual settings. Thanks to such sanctions, copper was safely conveyed from a potentially lawless hinterland down to the coastal towns, where utterly different trading societies flourished, omnivorously drawing on Levantine, Anatolian, Egyptian, Aegean and indigenous traditions to create highly eclectic displays of wealth, and not above using melted scrap gold of purely bullion value as tomb goods [**8.49**]. Enkomi enjoyed a dyadic relationship across the water with Ugarit; among the tiny handful of tablets inscribed in Cypro-Minoan, half derive from Enkomi and the rest from Ugarit, all, incidentally, from merchants' houses rather than the palace; Ugarit is also a likely source of the scribe who wrote from Cyprus to Amarna in Akkadian.[329] Elite cross-residence between these two centres is entirely plausible. In addition to the trade in copper, and potentially other resources from the geologically rich, uplifted centre of Cyprus,[330] coastal communities engaged in large-scale pottery production and export, and had a marked penchant for copying and adapting traditional forms to create, and then pander to, new tastes. Another distinctive trait was the marking with abbreviated signs of newly moulded copper ingots, transhipped tin ones and pottery batches destined for external trade.[331] Cyprus may or may not have pioneered new forms of political structure, but it was definitely experimenting with fresh ways of promoting and prosecuting trade.[332]

Sailing west, along the Uluburun ship's likely intended route, we pass Rhodes, a key island between the Aegean, Cyprus and the Levant that we might suspect has a lot yet to reveal.[333] Beyond, on Crete, the early 15th century BC witnessed terminal destruction at most palaces. At Zakros, a small and only recently built palace in the east, agricultural storage had devolved to the surrounding town but the flames saved from plunderers caches of copper oxhide ingots, elephant tusks, stone vessels and other fine craft goods, a useful measure of late palatial priorities.[334] Since the Thera eruption's exoneration from direct responsibility, blame has shifted to internal crises coupled with Knossian aggrandizement, or conquest from the Peloponnese.[335] Several gutted centres were replaced by a large state based at Knossos, which itself fell apart a century later, bringing an atypically early end to Crete's palatial socie-ties.[336] From a wider perspective, the advent with this last Knossian state of flauntingly rich burials, a male-dominated hierarchy around a king and an archaic version of the Greek language (as revealed by the decipherment of Linear B, a Cretan script adapted for new sounds)[337] spelt the extinction of yet another idiosyncratically struc-tured and gendered island society.[338] Henceforth Crete, like Malta before it, would look less differ-ent from the surrounding world. This apart, the most arresting trait of the later 2nd millennium BC was the rise of a great port at Kommos, com-plete with grand public buildings and a row of six ship-sheds [**8.50**], but emphatically no palace.[339]

8.50 Plan of Building P at Kommos, whose long, parallel open-ended rooms have been interpreted as sheds for ships drawn out of the water for seasonal safety or cleaning from marine parasites. At some 38 m in length and 5.5 m each in breadth, this provision suggests substantial vessels.

N

0   20 m
0   60 ft

Unlike other Cretan harbours, it was located not on the Aegean but lay in the south, facing onto the open Mediterranean. Kommos served as a local harbour for people in its hinterland, along the Cretan coast and on satellite islands like Gavdos, but also became a magnet for long-range traffic, and as a hub of importation and tranship-ment it led the Aegean in terms of finds from the Levant, Cyprus, Egypt, Anatolia and slightly later, as will be seen in Chapter 9, places further west.[340]

The Aegean's palatial baton passed to the mainland rim, where best explored are the often heavily fortified Mycenaean centres that arose after the Shaft Grave phase, for example at Mycenae itself [PL. XXXIII], its neighbour Tiryns, Pylos in the southwest, Thebes in central Greece (at least Mycenae's equal, were it more accessible under an ugly modern city), probably the Athenian acropolis and a brand-new find south of Sparta.[341] In typical Mediterranean fashion such polities combined an extensive territory with a window on the sea. This combination eclipsed hitherto flourishing small-island traders such as those on Aegina, which lost out as Mycenae encroached on its Saronic Gulf sphere.[342] Despite their fame, these palaces and their towns were smaller than the largest of the preceding Minoan examples, and lasted for just ten generations or so. The Mycenaean leadership's addiction to fighting and ostenta-tious burial (the shaft graves now largely replaced by round, corbelled tholos tombs) argues for an up-scaled version of the small, competitive elites common over much of Mediterranean Europe since the 3rd millennium BC, legitimized and entrenched thanks to cultural drapery and economic practices borrowed with varying degrees of fidelity from Crete and further east, and given some procedural gravitas by a basic level of literacy, again externally acquired.[343] One advantage is that Linear B can be read, but the fact that the fire-preserved tablets for the entire kingdom of Pylos amount to just twice the number from the largest private merchant's archive at Ugarit reins in expectations. Linear B tablets focused narrowly on internal palatial matters.[344] They reveal command economies well-attuned, within a limited remit, to Mediterranean conditions, and concentrated on large-scale production of woollen and linen textiles, perfumed oil, wine and, to a lesser degree, bronze.[345]

As usual, many of these goods circulated internally, but plenty were also for export, and the archives allude to a wider world through reference to exotic materials, Semitic loanwords for gold, ivory, cumin and sesame, and people or things described as Tyrian, of Beirut, Cypriot or Egyptian.[346] Otherwise, however, a resounding textual silence surrounds trade. Combined with the infrequent, tangential nature of external mentions of the Aegean (which leave some doubt as to how often its rulers attained the wider acknowledgment they seemed to yearn for),[347] this leaves us overwhelmingly in the realm of archaeology when it comes to discerning patterns of contacts between the Aegean and regions further east. That such connections still existed is manifest. When a king of Pylos sat on one of the items of furniture minutely described in his archive as made of blackwood inlaid with ivory, glass and gold, his posterior rested on imported materials paralleled at Uluburun and in a smattering of survivals across Aegean sites.[348] Something had to pay for such exotica, as well as inflows of copper and tin. In addition to the presumed export of textiles and silver, the period of the

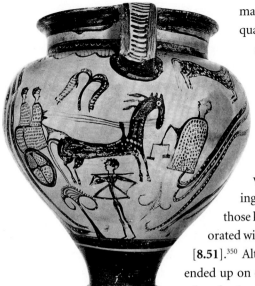

8.51 Large krater, or wine-mixing vessel, of probable Aegean manufacture but buried on Cyprus, with a scene of chariot-riding, less typically juxtaposed with a figure wielding a balance-scale and flanked by large octopi.

mainland palaces was characterized by an exceptional surge in the quantities of Aegean painted pottery sent east, most of which is traceable to manufacture in the Argolid, often near Mycenae.[349]

Thousands of pieces of decorated Aegean pottery have been found on Cyprus, particularly at the port of Hala Sultan Tekke. Ugarit and Abu Hawam, near Akko on the Bay of Haifa, yielded hundreds more, and many other communities acquired a few pieces. Most were closed pots for transporting oil, maybe wine and, in other less constricted-mouthed forms, viscous unguents or honey, but a substantial number were drinking or serving vessels. Particularly interesting among the latter are those known as kraters, big, deep-bellied wine-mixing vessels, often decorated with chariots, in one case with a facing figure holding a balance scale [**8.51**].[350] Although made in the Argolid, they were rarely used there. Most ended up on or beyond Cyprus, making them the first open shape to be produced primarily for export. The krater form had a prior history in Levantine and Cypriot conviviality, and the Aegean's painted versions played up the allusions to elite lifestyles. In fact, the status of Mycenaean pottery abroad varied; one krater was interred with Yabninu at Ugarit, but other Mycenaean pottery is found in middling contexts, and it faced stiff competition from Egyptian-style bronze drinking sets and Cypriot goods.[351] People at Tell el-Ajjul harnessed it to local Egyptianizing practices.[352] As for who conveyed it, east of Cyprus counts of Aegean pottery dropped off sharply, while Cypriot pots outnumbered Aegean ones at Uluburun and Marsa Matruh and a 3:1 ratio typified the Levant.[353] Perversely, therefore, the explosion in Aegean pottery exports, at least beyond Cyprus, may be an index of growing Cypriot rather than Aegean activity. Aegean knowledge of the east Mediterranean may have remained partial, with a reasonable acquaintance with Cypriot and a few Levantine ports contrasting with much slighter knowledge of other coastal regions.

So much for the Aegean societies of the textbooks, but others reward a closer look too. Some comprise the ghost-polities of its eastern seaboard. Hatti faced south, in the main, but it was also embroiled in tussles and deals with a shifting mosaic of polities to its west, over whom it enforced fleeting supremacies.[354] This entanglement reached as far as the Aegean, where troubles with freebooting maritime aggrandizers on the west Anatolian coast provide some idea of how effortlessly the sea liquidated imperial writ.[355] Writings at Hattusa reveal the names of several polities and their towns. Arzawa was the largest, with its capital Apasa, possibly to be equated with later Ephesus; as we saw earlier, it was the only one to write to Amarna, and a century before it had supplied shipwrights for Perunefer on the Nile.[356] Others included Ahhiyawa (arguably 'Achaea', and denoting one or more Mycenaean polities of uncertain location that exploited the haze of distance to bid for Great King status),[357] Millawanda (probably coastal Miletus, previously a minoanized community)[358] and maybe Troy, with unquenchable optimists discerning cross-references to Homeric politics.[359] In material terms Troy was now a grand fortified acropolis surrounded by a large town and extensive hinterland that included the island of Samothrace; it was in contact with Mycenaean polities across the Aegean, Cyprus and the Levant, and in all likelihood other places around the Black Sea.[360] But – apart from Troy, another sizeable town at Panaztepe on an islet in the mouth of the Gediz River, tiny windows at Miletus and Ephesus, a few rock carvings in Hittitesque style, and a swathe of Mycenaean-type tombs in the southwest, extending to Rhodes and Kos – we know absurdly little on the ground about this crucial zone, where names in the texts still drift across virtual terra incognita.[361] Once again, Turkey's archaeological wild west has a lot still to tell us about life within it, as well as links over and around the Anatolian peninsula.

One part of west Anatolia that cropped up regularly in royal archives is Lukka, which corresponds to Lycia, the mountain massif hanging over Turkey's south coast, and off whose cliffs the Uluburun ship met its doom.[362] Lukka is intriguing because it does not comply with expectations. External references to it named neither kings nor capital, referred to no treaties, and portrayed it as an ungoverned space that bred trouble for others on land and sea. An Amarna letter complained of Lukka raids on the Delta, with the intriguing insinuation of Cypriot encouragement – peevishly denied by whoever replied from Cyprus, complaining of similar attacks.[363] Lycian archaeology proves similarly elusive, for the excavations at later Iron Age to Roman towns such as Tlos and Xanthos (Lycian Arñna), whose names correspond to places mentioned at Hattusa, have drawn an almost complete Bronze Age blank. However we populate Lukka in our imagination, with sturdy mountaineers, sea-raiders, or both and more, the point is that it represented a substantial capsule of non-palatial, maybe non-urban and presumably rudely non-Akkadian-conversant people within the polite circle of the east Mediterranean, and one that survived very well on its own terms, if the frequency with which it bothered the literate world is anything to go by.

In the Aegean proper, interstitial areas like this grow in density until, on its western and northern fringes, they fill the frame. On the eastern side of the Greek peninsula, modest palaces reached only as far north as coastal Thessaly; in the west no further than the Peloponnese. Images on the walls of Pylos of fleece-clad rustics slaughtered by palatial soldiery surely refer to near neighbours, as well as this most westerly and peripheral of all Mediterranean palaces' cultural anxieties.[364] Beyond lay differently structured, smaller-scale societies; another, often well-watered zone that underscores the specificity and non-inevitability of palatial regimes. We know too little about such unglamorous communities. For the Pindos mountains, all we can say is that they were thinly dotted with hamlets, which could have supplied cheese or timber to southern markets.[365] But in one case we are better off, thanks to a handful of archaeologists admirably indifferent to the blandishments of the palatial south. At the great 'toumba', or tell, enveloped by modern Thessaloniki, and slightly further north at Assiros, a distinct pattern of elevated villages emerged, each with a perimeter wall and storage facilities for grain and pulses far beyond immediate needs [8.52].[366] Analysis of their seeds identified few weeds, indicative of crops still carefully tended in small plots rather than plough-farmed open fields.[367] Here we may, at last, have identified a genuine example of communal food reserves, created by clusters of villages without

8.52 The charred remains from large baskets and jars in this storeroom at Assiros represent some of the best-preserved evidence for harvested crops and their storage known in the early Mediterranean.

emphatic leaders. It is equally interesting that these places gave a very guarded reception to such potentially socially destabilizing southern imports as Mycenaean drinking pottery and the local variants of it soon turned out by entrepôts elsewhere on the coast.[368] Glimpses like these reveal robust, sometimes resistive as much as engaging or desirous, ways of Mediterranean life, independent of the palatial world.

From here it is but the tiniest of steps into the central and west Mediterranean, which this chapter has too long neglected and with which it ends. But before we cross over this locally faint divide, we can take brief stock of the economic and interactive structures in the east that we leave behind. At a rough guess (supported by the number of substantial consumers of that convenient tracer, Aegean painted pottery),[369] by the later 2nd millennium BC a network of some forty to fifty principal producing, trading and consuming centres existed around the east Mediterranean, from the Nile Delta to the Peloponnese, typically if not always centred on palaces, and most definable as urban. Beyond, innumerable further communities fed into the system; these received trickle-down benefits to varying degrees, albeit in many cases reaching zero and, in the most exploitative cases, negative equity. Alongside internal redistributive mechanisms, and a broader culture of socially embedded exchange, market-like conditions flourished, building on the 'long' 3rd millennium's establishment of proto-currencies, and with a number of the major trade products now standardized and commodified. Widespread interaction went hand in hand with a growing convergence of cultural practices at the more exalted levels. But while this created a broad consensus in terms of the relative esteem in which overall categories of materials and objects were held, and while the smoother flows of goods did quite a lot to reduce distinctions in the exchange values of the same thing in different places, on-the-spot prices across space and time clearly continued to vary and offer ample opportunities for profit. The reasons lie in familiar Mediterranean conditions: the uneven distribution of coveted resources, fluctuations in harvests and other conditions within each micro-region, and the fickle navigational and other transport conditions controlling access to each, as well as the general speed of movement between them.[370] To this we might add the unsynchronized cycles of consumption at each centre, which guaranteed frequent swings in localized supply and demand. Finally, the palatial strategy of stockpiling a spectrum of desirable materials and goods as a form of capital accumulation, and the exchange value of such things when put into circulation, ensured that the pathways along which each moved when re-injected into the network described patterns far more complex than simply transfer from points of natural occurrence to ones of absence; Keftiu carrying elephant tusks to Egypt are just one Bronze Age version of coals-to-Newcastle, and made perfect sense.[371]

Initially more perplexing is the degree to which certain regions specialized in the production of objects or substances whose raw materials were widely available in the basin, notably textiles, wine, oil and painted pots. One reason, taking the cue from the political economist David Ricardo's law of comparative advantage,[372] could be that growing ease of seaborne movement facilitated importation to such a degree that it made better sense to acquire finished versions of certain things that in the past had been locally manufactured, and to concentrate instead on locally optimal products for trade, determined by a combination of materials and skills – the catch being that not all could benefit equally from the growth thereby generated, as certain regions would gradually discover. Another is that many places invested in detailing of their products (particular weaves, patterns, flavours, scents or, failing these, branded packaging), to ensure a specific cachet within generic demand. A third factor was the idiosyncrasies of cultural preference in the consuming regions with which each production zone was in easiest contact.[373] Overall, this suite of developments was fundamental to the formation of an increasingly widespread kind of east Mediterranean economy, culture and lifestyle. Initially sponsored by the great palaces of the Bronze Age, it would long outlive and outgrow them.

For even at this high noon of the palatial system, potential future problems are not hard to spot. Most involve the growing challenges faced by palaces in maintaining their controlling grip. The connecting sea, as we have noted, remained an essentially anarchic space. In some areas, the complexity of coasts, seas and islands over which trade networks shifted and flickered made it hard for any point to maintain a nodal position, particularly if the means of doing so was a territorially embedded institution like a palace and dynasty. In social terms, too, problems lay on the horizon. For all the cordial relations between the palace and successful merchants at Ugarit, the priorities of each were not in complete harmony, and tensions were even more likely where political authority was less amenable to mercantile practices.[374] In addition, more people were getting in on the cultural and economic act. The nature of our data encourages us to pay a lot of attention to the exclusive, often socially incestuous life of people at the top, and not without reason, for their evolving definitions of an apex lifestyle were major drivers of growth. Certain forms were so closely entwined with pharaonic ideals that they were described as 'after the king's own heart'.[375] But by the later 2nd millennium BC we start to discern some rather different participants. One group consisted of a more open, less traditional, and thoroughly international elite.[376] The great merchants of Ugarit and some extraordinarily eclectically furnished wealthy tombs on Cyprus stand out in this respect, but the phenomenon was more widespread – consider, for example, the grand, keel-vaulted masonry tombs not only at Ugarit and Enkomi, but also Knossos and Mycenae.

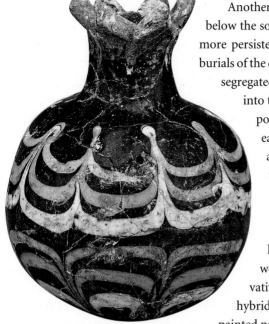

8.53 Among the potentially subversive materials widely disseminated by the later 2nd millennium BC in the eastern Mediterranean was glass. As shown by this polychrome flask from Enkomi, formed around a subsequently removed core into the symbolically fecund shape of a pomegranate, plasticity and brilliant colours were more important than transparency, and allowed early glass to emulate and compete with more traditional media.

Another group was bigger and potentially equally subversive. For below the social stratosphere, the course of the millennium reveals ever more persistent clues in architecture, goods and moderately appointed burials of the consolidation of a broader sub-elite group, sometimes firmly segregated from those at the top, in others grading imperceptibly into them, and yet distinct too from the mass of rural and urban poor.[377] This group may have comprised 10–20 per cent of the east Mediterranean population, a formidable cohort that on any reckoning numbered several hundred thousand people, whose satisfaction required increases of labour input and manufacturing output across the system as a whole. Such people were not averse to possessing high-status luxury objects if available, or to state-sponsored feasts and other largesse – in this sense the trickle-down effect was alive and well. But less recherché products, some technologically innovative, some avowedly imitative and many prone to stylistically hybridizing tendencies, also started to target this market, including painted pottery, mass-produced faience cylinder seals, and the simple mould-made glass objects that followed the bow wave of royal innovation, soon to be followed by younger materials of even less predictable future impact and cultural affordance [**8.53**].[378] This high turnover of fashions was in itself indicative of increasingly open social mobility and aspirations. We might well wonder whether, faced with these ever-expanding, diversifying cohorts of products, practices and consumers, the sway of the palaces over east Mediterranean life might start to become somewhat precarious.

All not so quiet on the western front

But for the moment such questions must wait, and instead we double back in time to explore what had happened since the start of the 2nd millennium BC in the west and central parts of the basin during their Early and Middle Bronze ages – labels that reflect an unevenly increasing use of tin-bronze, drawing, with much of Europe, on tin sources in Cornwall, Brittany, Bohemia and perhaps some of the Mediterranean occurrences in Iberia, Tuscany and Sardinia.[379] We shall encounter glaring social and cultural differences within and between Iberia, France, the Tyrrhenian and Adriatic, which render the kinds of narratives of convergence so evident in the east premature, interpretations more fragmented, and discrete take-off trajectories harder to compare. Yet despite all this, and the blurred boundary with the Aegean, at a strategic level an overall contrast with the areas under palatial or otherwise urban control further east is worth drawing in order to highlight chastening distinctions of kind and scale that too often pass unnoticed.

Take, for instance, demography. On Sardinia, the durability of the thousands of stone towers in which we shall discover that most islanders lived by the mid-2nd millennium BC lends credence to order-of-magnitude estimates of island population. One calculation of 35,000 people may be too low,[380] given an unknown degree of attrition of towers and uncertainties about the size of the family groups inhabiting each, but even if we double this, the average density was unlikely to greatly exceed a meagre 3 inhabitants per sq. km (or about 8 per sq. mile) – still comfortably within the range for all the European, and parts of the easternmost, Mediterranean a millennium earlier. In contrast, on Crete by 1500 BC, Knossos alone held 25,000–30,000 people, overall urban population must have been at least three times higher, and the total with country-dwellers thrown in can hardly have been less than 150,000–200,000, all on an island a third the size of Sardinia.[381] In other words, the Cretan density was at least five or six times higher (probably more) than that on Sardinia, and similar arguments could be made elsewhere.[382] Meanwhile, in the unique context of the Nile Delta, something approaching a million people crowded into an area still smaller than Sardinia, and until recently ruled from a capital (Avaris) housing perhaps half the number of people on the latter entire island. To nuance these figures, approximately 10,000 of those denizens of the Delta were probably literate and five to ten times as many were members of the social elite and sub-elite groups (so straddling the figure for all Sardinians).[383] Crude as these figures are, they ram home the real distinctions wrought by two millennia of differential economic growth, urbanism and intensified, mobilized production of food and just about everything else.

As Sardinia demonstrates, most landscapes west of the Aegean remained far more sparsely occupied than those in the east. Signs of human intervention were more limited, and separated by extensive wilderness. The consolidating patchworks of olive groves and vineyards characteristic of the cash-cropping east find no parallel, nor do the latter's agricultural terraces. As before, there are only a few, largely unconfirmed hints of olive and vine cultivation, and analogues for the east's efficient apparatus for extracting, refining, storing and transporting the resultant liquids are conspicuously absent.[384] The only late exception, as we shall see, is southeast Italy, a region in close touch with the Aegean. As argued in Chapter 6, sobriety need not have followed from the lack of extensive viticulture, indeed a sharp rise in fruit seeds at Italian sites, and a proliferation of drinking vessels, from the chalices of southern Spain to flamboyantly handled cups in peninsular Italy, point to a range of other fermented drinks.[385]

Another major contrast was in speed of movement, and the experienced scale of Mediterranean space. On land there was by now little difference around the basin, save for those parts of North Africa that had yet to resound to a horse's hoof; remains of a cartwheel from Pontevedra in northwest Iberia, dated to around 1700 BC,[386] are a only a few centuries later than the cart model from Crete. But at sea things were quite different. The Aegean adopted sailing ships early in the 2nd millennium BC and within a few centuries these began to probe the Tyrrhenian. But local adoption in the central and west Mediterranean came substantially later.[387] Just how much later is a matter of guesswork, but from Italy to Iberia the first images date to the transition from Bronze to Iron Age. Early in the millennium incised canoes decorated a pot on Filicudi in the Aeolian islands, and as late as the 14th century BC a sail-less longboat was depicted at Thapsos in Sicily, a well-connected coastal site to which we shall return. Although ostensibly a swiftly roving sailing ship should have been its own best advocate, there were clearly long delays in uptake, presumably due to the investment needed for their construction, the learning curves involved in building and handling, and probably (as earlier in the Aegean) the resistance of canoe-focused groups. Until at least 1300 BC, the speed and transport capabilities associated with sailing ships were a prerogative of eastern interlopers. The 2nd-millennium BC east Mediterranean is commonly portrayed as a vast expanse compared to a more parochial west, but the latter's seas, by geographical measures alone more open in several sectors than those further east, in fact remained more awe-inspiring for people travelling across their distances than the shrunken frog-ponds that the sail had created off the Nile, Levant, Cyprus and coastal Aegean [**8.54**].

This paradox helps us to explain why, although the 3rd-millennium BC beaker interaction sphere had amply proven the potential for voyaging to stitch together long-range connections in the west when such practices enjoyed commensurate social status, the aftermath once this abated early in the 2nd millennium was a still bafflingly diverse, scantily interconnected set of societies and ways of doing things. This even included the survival, and indeed 'baroque' climax, of neo-megalithic burial in parts of France and a few of the more sequestered major islands.[388] For however much we quibble over the finer details subsumed in the east under 'palace', no comparable common denominator in terms of social structure can even be tendered for the centre and west. The nearest we get is the ongoing rise and fall of accumulating, craft-sponsoring, if now often less extensively networked, minor leaders and their entourages, a widespread propensity to fortify even tiny settlements (a sure sign of endemic insecurity, and absent in the state-dominated east beyond a few small, wealthy trading hubs), and a notably 'secular' flavour to many societies, reflected in a strange dearth of sacred sites compared to earlier and later

8.54 This differentially scaled map of the Mediterranean suggests the contrasting experiences of local maritime space around the middle of the 2nd millennium BC, with distance-shrinking sailing ships commonplace in the east, incipient as visitors in the centre, and effectively unknown in the west. The inevitable accompanying distortion of terrestrial space is obviously to be ignored.

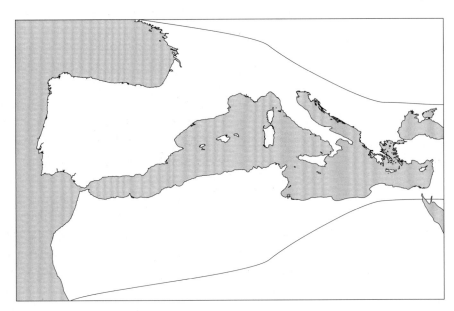

8.55 Most of the richest Argaric tombs were excavated and illustrated by the Siret brothers in the late 19th century AD. This funerary assemblage from Fuente Alamo illustrates the typical copas, or drinking vessels, one with a metal ring around the stem, as well as daggers, a comparatively rare sword, tools, silver and copper jewelry including a simple diadem, as well as faience and ivory beads.

phases, as well as the contemporary east. Even generous definitions must preclude the realistic identification of towns or states west of Pylos,[389] but there was still plenty of variability in the prevailing kinds of community, from scattered farms and hamlets to others clumped into villages or hillforts, and from egalitarian social orders to a few with palpable inequalities. Concerning the latter, southern Iberia again furnishes one of the most thoughtfully investigated areas in the entire basin in terms of how social and economic exploitation actually operated, in microcosm, within the potentials and constraints of production and control in a Mediterranean environment. Building on the testimony of Chapter 7, and given the number and variety of attempts over the course of the 2nd millennium BC (even those that imploded), there is little doubt that larger, more durable social formations would have eventually arisen independently, here and elsewhere west of the Aegean, had indigenous history not so soon collided with that of the east. But rather than view societies in the centre and west in terms of what they failed to become in time for the eastern stopwatch, we do better to explore them in their own terms, as the outcomes of distinctive, and by their own lights fairly successful, ways of Mediterranean life.

We can start in the far west, in a region that, as in the previous millennium, produces the most compelling evidence for social hierarchies anywhere outside the east Mediterranean. Also in common with the previous cycle during the Copper Age is the fact that Iberia remained a self-contained experiment, a peninsula containing a fifth of the Mediterranean's land, yet in common with the neighbouring Maghreb only tenuously connected beyond its maritime and montane boundaries. We see this in the idiosyncrasies of its metal industry, which continued to draw on the wealth of internal sources but was slow to shed archaic technologies and adopt locally available tin for deliberate alloying [8.55].[390] Daggers evolved into swords, halberds and finally spears, as elsewhere, but the amount of weapons and other metal finds, especially in locally available silver, is modest compared to other parts of the Mediterranean and Europe.[391] Signs of external contacts include occasional foreign weapons, a handful of faience beads on the edge of the European and Mediterranean distribution, and a few tusks' worth of raw ivory from the Maghreb, where art in the Atlas mountains still depicted Iberian-type weapons, though there is less evidence than in the preceding millennium for activity across and around the strait.[392] More mysterious is a bunch of twenty-seven copper javelin heads of an ostensibly Levantine type variously dated between 2200 and 1600 BC, found back in AD 1860 in the outer flank of the La Pastora burial mound at Valencina de la Concepción, near Seville.[393] These could conceivably be another instance of eastern objects that escaped into the margins beyond the reach of direct contacts, but it is more probable that, as with a handful of other Bronze Age east Mediterranean goods, they arrived as antiques as a result of Phoenician traffic on the younger side of 1000 BC.[394] How much Iberian people really knew about the outside world during the 2nd millennium BC is a speculative matter, but all the signs are that they seldom ventured far afield or received travellers from across the sea.

These considerations underscore local and regional factors as renewed spikes of social power began to emerge. The most emphatic were the Argaric communities, dating to 2200–1550 BC and named after El Argar in the Vera basin of Almería.[395] This unprepossessing coastal valley, semi-arid, hemmed in by gaunt uplands and little more than 1000 sq. km (385 sq. miles) in extent, is one of the best explored landscapes in the Mediterranean, thanks to exemplary excavations at Gatas and Fuente Álamo, wider survey of its settlements and pioneering efforts to investigate the relationship between human activity, degradation and desertification of its fragile environment.[396] From the end of the 3rd millennium BC the Vera basin doubled or tripled its population over a few centuries to 1700–3400 people, which seems to have strained the valley's envelope of environmental tolerance. This closely followed the

8.56 The lower courses of substantial Argaric houses, their associated tombs and cisterns jostling for space on the constricted summit of Fuente Alamo, from where they dominate the surrounding settlements and landscape.

decline of Copper Age Los Millares a few valleys to the west, encouraging us to think in terms of shifting foci as much as overall Iberian growth. However, although the Vera basin was a hotspot, Argaric sites can be seen over much of southeast Spain, defining a zone as broad as that of the mainland palaces in the Aegean. Loosely comparable sites extended further still, triggered by either emulation of, or resistance to, Argaric activity. The major Argaric sites were rocky eyries surrounded by cliffs or artificial fortifications. Spread unevenly over 10–12 ha (25–30 acres), the largest, such as Lorca and La Bastida in Murcia, and Cerro de la Encina near Granada, approximately matched the Copper Age apex, as well as, more thought-provokingly, some of the more modestly sized coastal or island centres in the east Mediterranean.[397]

What makes these Argaric communities so fascinating is the detailed picture they provide of a rising elite of powerful families located at the physical pinnacle of the settlements, and its consequences [**8.56**].[398] These occupied large rectangular, two-storey houses that towered over the community and sheltered private storage jars and rich, sharply gender-distinguished individual or paired burials under the floors, in contrast to the communal

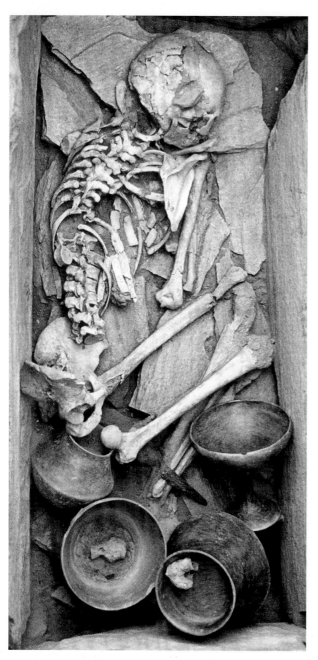

8.57 A typical Argaric burial, inhumed alone in a slab-built grave in the settlement of Cerro de la Encina, near Granada, accompanied by drinking vessels and a small dagger.

storage pits and collective tombs of the Copper Age [**8.57**]. Feasting on cattle was associated with the wealthier households' funerals, while others made good with sheep and goat.[399] Human skeletons are just as informative. At Cerro de la Encina they testify to the healthier, less strenuous life enjoyed by the wealthy. This became entrenched from childhood. In the Vera basin high physical diversity among the male skeletons argues that men married into communities, and a wider integration may be hinted at by the deficiency of male burials of fighting age on the margins of the basin compared with the central community at El Argar.[400] The latter also cornered weapons, metal tools and jewelry. In general, although metals circulated further than in the Copper Age, access was more controlled, with smelting into ingots near mines in the Sierra Morena, casting at the central sites and display by the lucky few.[401] The inequality within and between communities was not based on agricultural or other innovations, as claims for irrigation farming and polyculture have been dismissed, but rather in control of human labour and the extraction of surplus as tribute.[402] Particularly telling is the fact that Argaric centres were often poorly placed in terms of farmland but nonetheless had efficient grinding and storage installations concentrated in their elite quarters, to which less fortunate members of society must have trudged up to mill, or weave on the many looms, whether under obligation or in return for food and other goods.[403] Over time, and unlike the situation in lowlier farmsteads, barley came to eclipse other crops at these places, revealing a growing monoculture or requisitioning that selectively targeted grain.[404] Combined with monotonously plain pottery, ubiquitous drinking chalices, eradication of alternative avenues of symbolic expression (such as the previously rich repertoire of figurines), and a clear concentration of swords in the Argaric heartland, this smacks of a grim, exploitative social order in which powerful people strove to establish an ascendancy locally and at a distance, to drive home their advantage and to maximize economic gains over others within the sweepstakes of a harsh and constricted corner of the Mediterranean. In unadorned fashion, the Argaric lays bare relations of power surely fundamentally similar to those hidden beneath the attractive fig leaves of 'civilized' culture over much of the eastern Mediterranean.[405]

Around 1550 BC these Argaric societies fell apart. Just as the outside world can take no credit or blame for their emergence, so too the end was a strictly internal affair. Indeed, overall the Argaric trajectory's lack of synchrony with wider patterns in other parts of the Mediterranean underscores Iberia's relative isolation. Given the absence of any trace of socially beneficial activities on the part of powerful people, or even efforts to drape themselves in some form of sacred legitimacy, their demise is at one level unsurprising and was surely a relief to those on the receiving end; declining health and a flight to pitifully marginal land characterized the latest Argaric.[406] Further responsibility can be shared, as with the demise of the Copper Age, between Iberia's location, which offered little scope for external engagement and no access to a broader currency of ideas and mechanisms for maintaining power, and the exigencies of a harsh environment. Concerning the latter, this time excessive human intervention rather than climatic events seems to be to blame. In their drive to intensify yields, Argaric elites inflicted real damage on parts of southern Spain, where erosion became serious and the last deciduous woods along the streams vanished, to be replaced by hardy tamarisk, which thrived in saline conditions.[407] Post-Argaric communities were smaller and less spectacular, but they relied on sustainable farming practices, and with the demise of this predatory elite, metals also materialized more frequently in the former Argaric lands and all over southern Iberia.[408]

Adjoining regions offer contrastive insights. The rain-poor high savannahs of the southeast Meseta were densely settled for the first time, especially close to rivers and wetlands, with the emphasis on cattle (for milk, meat and traction) and horses, the latter also popular at a few Argaric sites.[409] Many settlements took the distinctive form of a small circular enceinte with concentric walls up to 11 m (36 ft) high, known as a *motilla*. These reflected a need for protection among rolling open spaces, and counter the tendency to consider unusual monumental structures to be an exclusively insular trait in the west and central Mediterranean. Stabling and manufacture clustered within the walls, while houses extended beyond. Motilla communities were smaller, socially more cohesive, and (like most places outside the acquisitive Argaric zone) modest in metals and other wealth goods, although a little ivory did penetrate this far inland. Further west, long-distance Atlantic connections had temporarily declined, leaving the Copper Age hubs on the Tagus without successors.[410] But close to the lower reaches of the Guadalquivir, in the Huelva mountains, a zone that a few centuries latter would achieve Mediterranean-wide importance due to its fecundity in ores, there are striking hints of an increase in mining and metal circulation from about 1700 BC, associated with changes in the local vegetation and the establishment of fortified communities, in the case of La Papúa a rival, at 14 ha (35 acres) of enclosed area, for the largest Argaric sites.[411]

Looking further afield, there were few if any ripples from Argaric initiatives. The arrival of people on the major Balearics in the 3rd millennium BC, and peopling

8.58 A boat-shaped house at Es Coll de Cala Morell on Menorca, mid-2nd millennium BC in date and still broadly similar to those occupied by the first generations of Balearic islanders.

of smaller Ibiza and Formentera at the start of the next millennium, barely altered these islands' marginal position, which would only end when sailing ships and pan-Mediterranean networks broke in with the Iron Age.[412] Places like Son Mercer de Baix on Menorca and some thirty tiny sites identified on Formentera numbered only a few families apiece, in the former still living in ship-shaped longhouses [**8.58**].[413] They were reliant on sheep, goats and barley, with slight access to copper, but seldom tin or other imports. In these secluded conditions most innovations came in the architecture of death.[414] Dolmens and other megalithic tombs stayed popular until mid-millennium, as did rock-cut tombs, which pepper the Menorcan cliffs [**8.59**]. Symptomatically, extreme localism then triumphed, as each island went its own way. On Menorca this involved a move away from dolmens and experimentally towards the rectangular, keel-vaulted and masonry-built funerary *navetas* that, along with ongoing cave burial, typify the late 2nd and early 1st millennia BC.

Further east, from Catalonia to Mediterranean France, among a patchwork of coastal lagoons, cleared lowlands, surviving woods and limestone uplands, the social and economic profile remained modest among the communities living by farming plus, in France, still a substantial amount of hunting.[415] Near the mouth of the Rhône, as before a favoured point at the convergence of coastal and interior routes, a sizeable defended enclosure arose at Camp de Laure,[416] but otherwise communities remained small and simple, indeed even less noticeable in the second half of the millennium than the first, with few striking finds save for a handful of pieces of faience and amber percolating in from the north. Copper mining actually declined in

8.59 The cliffs of Menorca are riddled with rock-cut tombs mainly dating to the 2nd millennium BC.

the Midi, as local mineralizations were eclipsed by larger, more organized extraction of the high Alpine ores, in the west notably at Saint-Véran.[417] Throughout the 2nd millennium BC southern France kept its back to the sea and maintained an introverted way of life, largely sufficient unto itself in an unusually clement Mediterranean niche. Together with the open seas of the west, this created a substantial buffer between Argaric developments and others in the central Mediterranean.

An island of towers

Heading southeast from France over the apparently largely empty sea, we bear down on another archaeologically prominent zone that rivals the Argaric in its demand for our attention. Corsica was in this respect secondary to its larger neighbour, and more cut off. Corsican dolmens and especially menhirs retained great local significance; over 250 of the latter were aligned in attenuated rows at Palaghju [**8.60**], while at Filitosa a strange complex of towers, menhirs, huts and perimeter wall was erected from around 1600 BC.[418] Meanwhile, in the south a few stone towers (*torres*) mirrored on a stubbier scale a new way of life across the Strait of Bonifacio. For in Sardinia an extraordinary new template for the standard living unit emerged, one that thrust 15–20 m (50–65 ft) skyward in a thick granite- or basalt-walled,

8.60 The enduring megaliths of an island far out of the stream: the alignment of menhirs at Palaghju on Corsica.

multi-storey conical tower topped with a balcony, dark and pokey on the inside but out in the landscape prominent from afar [PL. XXXV].[419] We have already come across these *nuraghi* (a name traceable to Roman times, and surely Bronze Age in origin) in Chapter 1 as identity symbols for modern separatists, and in this chapter as robust ruins that encourage population estimates.

A preceding phase on either side of 2000 BC saw experimental constructions and the inception of water cults that later became an important element in Sardinian rituals.[420] It also coincided with dereliction of the great platform pyramid of Monte d'Accoddi and the last burials in earlier rock-cut 'witches' houses', that at Sant'Iroxi Decimoputzu ending on a spectacular note with 200 bodies and an accumulation of swords, one of which was an extremely rare Argaric escapee that somehow jumped the formidable barriers between these regions. From 1800–1600 BC true nuraghi multiplied across the landscape at a prodigious rate, initially to the virtual exclusion of other forms of settlement; some 7000 survive today, with a further 1000 known to have fallen victim to land clearance over the last two centuries alone. The thickest clusters, approaching 1 structure per sq. km (or about 3 per sq. mile),[421] occur in the broken upland zone of the interior, close to patches of farmland, rather than on the lowland plains, though coastal clusters are attested too, and nuraghi spread onto the poorer land as good niches filled up. In parallel, burial monuments adopted an elongated, smartened-up megalithic design, with an elaborate ceremonial forecourt [8.61].[422] These 'giants' tombs' hark back to the Neolithic in terms of their corridor-like form, and make odd partners for the very contemporary stress on territorial claims inherent in the nuraghi. Most giants' tombs related to a specific group of nuraghi. Yet their numbers are less than a tenth of the latter, prompting queries as to which members of living society they contained. One possibility is that in death people were altitudinally stratified (as possibly on Menorca too); most went to low-profile caves in the sides of valleys, while a minority rested higher, in the enormous tombs riding the plateaux.[423]

Such matters invite further questions about the societies behind the island's monuments. This was in origin very much an internal phenomenon; only later would nuragic Sardinia become embroiled in Mediterranean connections. The first proto-nuraghi arose in the Sardinian interior, the subsequent canonical tower form barely escaped the island's confines to southern Corsica, and although dolmens survived patchily over much of the central Mediterranean, nothing compared in size or elaboration with the giants' tombs. Aside from differential access to these tombs, which could be read in various ways, there is no evidence of social hierarchies; nuraghi were far too ubiquitous to be emblematic of an elite, and although individually defensive in stance their overall distribution in no way delineated more regional lines of protection.[424] The establishment of wider political territories came decisively later, at the turn of the 1st millennium BC. We are thus left with the conundrum as to why farming families otherwise apparently comparable to countless others around the Mediterranean felt the necessity to invest in homes whose labour requirements undoubtedly exceeded their own means and implied the help of the

8.61 The theatrically imposing facade of this Sardinian 'giant's tomb' at Coddu Vecchiu contrasts with the constricted access to the interior of the burial monument behind it.

selfsame neighbours in whom trust is belied by the form of the structures erected. Perhaps nuraghi reflected that quintessentially Mediterranean tension between mutual reliance and vying for advantage, driven to extremes by the unstable conditions of an expanding, fissioning, internally infilling population, and surely also by more specific competitive aspects of Sardinian social structure that will probably elude us forever.

Stirrings in the centre

The remainder of the central Mediterranean can be conceptually divided at this stage into three zones, one of unusually wide connections in north Italy and the head of the Adriatic, another of similar connective dynamism among the peninsulas and islands of the south Tyrrhenian, with a quieter pair of regions between them in central Italy and Dalmatia, across parts of which interesting trends can nonetheless be spotted.

We start in the first of these, which enjoyed strong connections to temperate Europe.[425] Ties to the metal-rich societies clustered around the Alps explain the rise of metalwork in burials (in the vicinity of Verona 10–20 per cent of the dead were armed men or richly adorned women), the hoards lost or sacrificed in watery places, and the doubling up of local flanged axes as ingots and exchange standards.[426] Other links ran east from Friuli, via the lowland corridor of Slovenia towards the chiefly Otomani societies of the Danube plain and its upland fringes, known for their regularly planned fortified settlements, ambitious trade to all points of the compass and an ideology that flaunted metal, horses and chariots.[427] In the northwest corner of the Adriatic, running up the Po and into the southern Alps, many communities lived in or beside wetlands. Some were genuine lake dwellings in a broader Alpine tradition

– places such as Fiavé, built out over the water on 9–10-m (30–33-ft) pinewood piles driven into the lake-bed.[428] Such sites have yielded wooden artifacts, including a plough and a yoke for oxen, as well as the first possible evidence for gnocchi.[429] Following a wanton pioneer clearing phase that left burnt trees where they fell,[430] other farming, cattle-rearing communities moved from about 1700 BC onto the rich, heavy, damp soils along the southern tributaries of the Po, which were rendered viable by a drying environment and heavy-duty ploughs. The numerous remains of these *terramare* settlements consist of large villages defined by banks and ditches laid out in a rectangular form suggestive of the orderly intake of a freshly opened ecological niche.[431] Both in settlement form and metalwork there are resemblances to Otomani traditions, though, as in Macedonia, some kind of levelling ideology in a clement environment seems to have worked against the rise of social inequalities. The *terramare* phenomenon appears alien to the Mediterranean as we normally imagine it, and the closest parallels for its wetland farming way of life may well lie in the rural backwaters of the Nile Delta and a few other even less well-known fluvial zones. Further east the plains give way to the limestone of Istria and the Trieste karst, and a less earthen archaeology.[432] The main feature here is a rash of small hillforts beginning around 1800–1600 BC, the earliest dense concentration in Europe and attributable to a combination of local tensions in a quasi-insular setting, not unlike Sardinia, and proximity to Otomani forts. Monkodonja, an exceptionally impressive example of the 300 hillforts in Istria alone, was girded with concentric stone-built circuit walls and an elaborately planned defensive gate [**8.62**].[433] The eye of faith has discerned Aegean inspiration in a nearby round tomb, but common sense instead a local grounding in the time-honoured Adriatic tumulus tradition.

Further down both sides of the Adriatic and in Tyrrhenian Italy, between the northern networks just outlined and others in the deep south, societies remained low key and broadly unchanged from the previous millennium, if with a few brilliantly preserved windows into the kinds of unexceptional community with which we need to much more broadly populate the Mediterranean than the archaeological targeting of glamorous sites usually enables us to do. In Dalmatia, hillforts were rare until late in the Bronze Age. However, the now-abandoned limestone

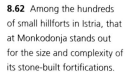

8.62 Among the hundreds of small hillforts in Istria, that at Monkodonja stands out for the size and complexity of its stone-built fortifications.

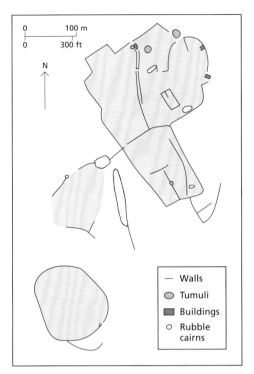

—	Walls
⬭	Tumuli
▪	Buildings
○	Rubble cairns

8.63 Remarkably clear traces of 2nd-millennium BC farmsteads, with their field walls, trackways, tumuli and other features, can still be seen on the surface of Dalmatia's abandoned limestone landscapes, in this case at Čauševića, near modern Zadar.

landscapes are littered with 2nd-millennium BC walls and field clearance cairns, some of the latter with skeletons beneath – a neat link between burial and territorial assertions during the intake of marginal land. The valleys and denuded uplands around Zadar offer detailed views of small farms cultivating soils then barely deeper than today.[434] At Čauševića the plan of one entire unit is discernible: buildings, enclosures, trackways, fields, cairns and tumuli, starting around 1400 BC and growing over several centuries [**8.63**]. Across the sea, in Apennine Italy, growing numbers of wattle-and-daub hamlets or villages remained the norm, and gradually contributed to the rolling back of woodland.[435] It is hard to yet attribute much supernal prescience to that located where a coastal trail switched inland to avoid the coastal marshes and cross the Tiber at its lowest ford, the later site of the Forum Boarium in what would one day become Rome.[436]

From Bronze Age Rome to a second prehistoric Pompeii, another settlement at Croce del Papa, near Nola, stands out merely for the misfortune of having lain in the path of pumice, ash and pyroclastic flows spewed out by Vesuvius in the 18th century BC, in one of many eruptions during the Holocene in this volcanically violent yet, as a consequence, exceedingly fertile and repeatedly densely settled corner of Italy [**8.64**].[437] It lay amidst a patchwork of beechwoods and narrow, neatly laid out, well drained (or irrigated), closely tended, ploughed and manured fields, several

8.64 Under the volcano: the superbly preserved remains of a small settlement at Croce del Papa emerge from under the ejecta of Vesuvius.

of whose surfaces have been excavated below the volcanic ejecta. The cart tracks criss-crossing this landscape, and the hoof-prints from herds of cattle, add to the vividness of the scene, and underscore how much more might be found on Thera, too. Within the settlement itself, the eruption preserved for posterity stockaded, thatched huts well-provisioned with grain silos and suspended joints of preserved meats, an animal pen holding nine pregnant goats, a dog sheltering in one of the huts, a threshing floor, two wells, a smart headdress of pig's teeth, pots, baskets, a wooden bucket slung on a fence, straw, foliage, cereals, ground flour, fruits and nuts, as well as the footprints of fleeing inhabitants – everyday life near the Bay of Naples nearly 2000 years before the volcano struck again, and more notoriously.

If any broader new central Italian trajectory can be singled out at this time, it is a gently growing human signature in the uplands, and tentatively even higher ground, best demonstrated in the Biferno Valley.[438] The causes of this are of some interest. One was small-scale upward seasonal movement of herds from nearby settlements (not, it should be stressed, long-range pastoralism), the other more regular communication across the peninsula. Skeletons in the Sant'Abbondio cemetery, near Pompeii, testify that men were moving and marrying over greater distances,[439] while fortified La Starza, on a pass over the Apennines, and rich 15th-century burials at Toppo Daguzzo, on a natural corridor between the Tavoliere and Campania, flourished on the strength of an increase in overland connections that, over the coming centuries, would stitch together the first coherently trans-peninsular Italian societies.[440]

Finally, the southern tip of Italy, Sicily and its small island satellites comprise a different world again, one that stands out not only for its internal characteristics but also its extensive regional connections by sea. Archaeologists coming from an eastern perspective have traditionally tended to credit this to trade with the Aegean. This zone certainly did become an interface with Aegean people by 1700–1600 BC, as we shall shortly see, and thereafter it is difficult and somewhat fruitless to unravel the relative priority of internal and external factors in driving change. But to attribute this arena's 2nd-millennium BC connections primarily to eastern activity ignores its encouraging configuration of islands, peninsulas, straits and gulfs, as well as its distinguished prior history of native maritime interaction, from the first circulation of obsidian, through Lipari as a later Neolithic island trading node, to the Gaudo societies around the Bay of Naples and its involvement at the end of the 3rd millennium BC in the Cetina phase, when Sicilian bossed plaques travelled as far as Troy, almost certainly not in Aegean craft for at least half that distance.

Along the coast of the southern mainland several large, fortified entrepôts emerged early in the 2nd millennium BC.[441] Coppa Nevigata (occupied initially at the arrival of farming) faced the Adriatic, while Roca Vecchia lay right on the pulse of the Strait of Otranto.[442] Close to both were lagoons that offered safe anchorage on this exposed shore. In Italy's instep, Broglio di Trebisacce survives but Scoglio del Tonno vanished in AD 1899, appropriately beneath the docks of Taranto.[443] While the Sicilian interior pursued ways of life with deep local traditions, including painted pottery and a boom in small settlements twinned with clusters of family tombs dug into prominent rock faces, their facades and doors carved with symbols, the coast was different.[444] Here again, more nodal communities arose, in the southeast on the almost insular promontory of Thapsos and the islet of Ognina off Syracuse, and midway along the southern shore at Monte Grande, close to a sulphur mine. The extent of the fortified agglomeration of round huts and streets at Thapsos is uncertain, but may have reached 12 ha (30 acres) by mid-millennium, larger than Shaft Grave-phase Pylos, due east across open sea.[445] A few centuries later, the dead in its cemetery of some 300 rock-cut tombs were dressed and seated on benches around elaborately decorated basins set on waist-high pedestals that tellingly scaled up Sicilian norms into something far more ambitious.

Other prominent maritime players were the inhabitants of several of the small Tyrrhenian islands, notably in the Aeolian archipelago and Vivara, a minuscule, only recently peopled, volcanic crescent in the channel between Ischia and the Campanian mainland.[446] In the Aeolians a settlement of closely packed huts on Lipari's acropolis re-established this island's leading role in regional trade, but other islanders followed suit, for example on tiny Panarea at Punta Milazzese, a village of 150–250 people on a headland overlooking twin coves that presents a classic setting for lifestyles oriented on the sea [**8.65**]. With obsidian circulation now defunct, these later generations of Aeolian traders operated as middlemen conveying goods around the Tyrrhenian Sea, especially metals, the working of which is amply attested

8.65 The village of Punta Milazzese on the Aeolian island of Panarea occupied the kind of location favoured by many early Mediterranean coastal trading communities, flanked by two small anchorages and enjoying good natural protection.

on Lipari (and likewise Vivara). Pottery production and trade between islands and further afield is also likely, in light of the identifying pot-marks on Aeolian ceramics, a seabed scatter of pots off Lipari that must reflect the relics of cargo,[447] and similarity to styles on the nearby Sicilian coast, as well as Vivara. There are compelling parallels with the canoe-borne Cycladic traders of a millennium earlier in terms of scale, goods and likely seacraft.

Of course not all small-island people were accomplished traders. Even within the Aeolians, little places such as Portella on Salina were less well connected.[448] Elsewhere the jury remains out. On Pantelleria, another former obsidian island that had become permanently settled during the 3rd millennium BC, a dense, neatly set out settlement subsequently arose at Mursia, as large as several more illustrious Aegean island contemporaries, but the islanders went their own way, creating a local tradition of burial cairns known as *sesi*.[449] Wind-battered, lonely Ustica, in the open sea 53 km (33 miles) off northwestern Sicily, was also remote to judge by its idiosyncratic pottery.[450] But in both cases the scenario of isolation may be overdrawn; Mursia's tombs contain faience, while I Faraglioni on Ustica possessed moulds for casting non-local metals, and both took part in a system of presumably notational tokens made from recycled potsherds in whole, half and quarter denominations, which connects them to the same trading practice at Vivara and Monte Grande.[451] Less ambiguous is the situation on the Maltese islands. After the demise of the temples, they briefly rejoined the wider world through Cetina-phase voyaging, and we see a startling spectrum of imports at Tarxien. Contact flourished with Ognina, off Syracuse. It was probably at this time, or in the early 2nd millennium BC, that small dolmens spread for the first time into parts of Sicily and Malta, from where at some juncture the tradition was transmitted via Cape Bon to the eastern Maghreb, initially in a style similar to its progenitors but diverging as it blended with the tumulus traditions of inland African pastoralists and further west with earlier influences across the Gibraltar strait.[452] As the 2nd millennium advanced, the modest communities on low hills or headlands across Malta and Gozo dropped away from the mainstream, with southeast Sicily remaining their last major link to the wider world.[453] The oddest feature is the deep parallel grooves that snake, occasionally for kilometres, over tracts of exposed bedrock.[454] Popularly known as 'cart ruts', they were certainly not made by wheeled vehicles, and may instead have been worn by sled-like contraptions for dragging loads (crops, or soil eroded by extravagances in the temple age?). It is entirely possible that these islands had yet to encounter the wheel.

Yet times had changed, and even remote islands with minimal external traffic were no longer safely protected by their expanses of surrounding sea. During the 2nd millennium BC practically every small-island community of any note in the southern part of the central Mediterranean ensured a location on a naturally defended hilltop or promontory, and piled up crude fortifications.[455] In the Aeolians this trend began between 1800 and 1500 BC and ended with a population nucleated on Lipari's acropolis. On Pantelleria, Mursia constructed defences 7 m (23 ft) high within the same time span, I Faraglioni on Ustica was surrounded by a bastioned wall, and a hulking line was thrown up at Borg in-Nadur on Malta.[456] These were heavy investments of labour for small island populations. The most likely explanation is that sightings of strange boats had started to spell danger as much as opportunity. Perhaps that danger was still no more than a raid by a neighbour's war canoe – the Cycladic islanders had, after all, likewise fortified their homes during their own crescendo of canoe traffic almost a thousand years earlier – but the timing among several hitherto more remote central Mediterranean islands raises the possibility that this time the cause for alarm was not merely familiar canoes but the flash of a foreign sail on the horizon.

A meeting of Mediterraneans

During the middle centuries of the 2nd millennium BC Aegean pottery began to appear in the central Mediterranean.[457] It started as a trickle at select sites but gradually grew in numbers and spread. The trading communities there were quite active and inured enough to receiving people and goods from over the sea to allow us to reject the old chauvinism that it took mariners from the east to awaken indigenous economies, and we can again recall that one precursor, the Cetina expansion, was initiated from the central part of the basin. But this does not reduce the significance of this new linkage between pre-existing networks in the Aegean and Tyrrhenian, which was soon to be extended up the Adriatic, east to Cyprus and west to Sardinia to create a bipolar 'route of the islands', closely implicated in metal trading. Despite subsequent ups and downs, and changes in the frameworks of engagement over time, this was a leap in the scope of connections, a permanent shift in Mediterranean history and a crucial stage in tying together the basin's inhabitants across a soon-to-be shrinking sea.

This westward connection is for us the most relevant axis of a more generally broadening engagement that equally reached towards the Balkans, central Europe and Black Sea, and heralded closer active ties between the Mediterranean and temperate Europe than at any time since the far-flung landscapes of mobile Pleistocene hunter-gatherers.[458] Much of this continental zone north of the Mediterranean itself saw the rise of small chiefdoms, codified warrior lifestyles, greater mobility and burgeoning metals and trade, in which copper and later bronze took on the role of a value standard played by silver in the east.[459] The first tentative indication of contact is the similarity between *ösenringe*, copper torcs used as ingots or a proto-currency in huge numbers in central and southeast Europe for two centuries on either side of 2000 BC, and a smattering of similar objects in the east Mediterranean as far south as Byblos.[460] Subsequent links are plotted by metals too, mainly weapons, drinking vessels and even an oxhide ingot fragment, as well as other east Mediterranean objects and styles that filtered north.[461] The most visible tracer, however, is amber, a strange, sun-coloured material with magical static if rubbed (hence its Greek name, *elektron*) [8.66]. This spread south into the Mediterranean from sources in the Baltic, soon ousting an inferior and sporadically locally employed Sicilian variety.[462] Some of the pieces from the Mycenae shaft graves had been carved in central Europe into

8.66 Necklace of Baltic amber found in one of the early Shaft Graves at Mycenae. Note the spacer plates between the beads, which commonly provide clues as to the location of manufacture and far-flung European trading connections.

specific forms of spacer beads that also reached the barrows of southern England; another piece, carved into a scarab, lay near the heart of Tutankhamun.[463] Changes in the routes that amber took from the Baltic illustrate how shifting regional networks within the Mediterranean shaped and altered longer-range connections beyond it, in this case drawing amber into the basin first via Carpathian communities, but later further west, towards the Tyrrhenian. For Aegean people, the latter, western point of encounter with its glowing yellow nodules may lie behind the myth of the golden apples of the Hesperides.[464]

Along all these interfaces between the Mediterranean and lands beyond, much of the pace was initially made by people north of palatial Crete, especially those well placed at the convergence of land and sea-routes in the lively corner of the Peloponnese dominated by Mycenae.[465] Indeed, the wider significance of Mycenaean societies lay less in their eventual swelling by a few modest examples of an already time-honoured roster of palatial states, than in their articulation of the core zone of palaces with non-palatial societies and materials further west and north. Only in the Aegean did chariot-horse harness designs typical of the Levant, Europe and Black Sea all coexist, and there, too, millet, another product of the Russian steppe, first percolated into the basin as a fodder crop.[466] Only there could objects as exuberantly eclectic as those in Mycenae's shaft graves have been found together; among them, a spearhead with its socket cast in the round is the first Mediterranean find of a feature invented between the Urals and Altai, and brought west by pastoralists into southeast Europe.[467] It was this interstitial role that gave Mycenaean culture its peculiar flavour, a blend of half-grasped Minoan traditions, eastern palatial tastes and values, temperate European heroic warrior ideals, and an occasional tang of the Asian steppes. Another rising power, at Troy, played a similar role in regard to Aegean links with the Black Sea, and this provides a likely context for two poorly dated ships drawn on the walls of the Yarimburgaz cave near the Sea of Marmara, one showing a slender rowed or paddled craft, the other a jaunty sailing ship.[468]

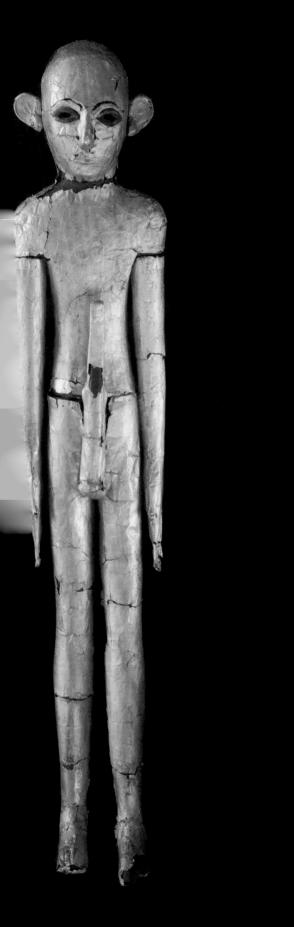

XXIII (*previous page*) The 43-m- (141-ft-) long solar boat of the Old Kingdom pharaoh Khufu (Cheops), as reassembled from thousands of parts buried beneath his great pyramid at Giza. Although a river-boat, it illustrates sturdy construction, largely from massive planks of imported Lebanese cedar, and long, efficient oars.

XXIV (*left*) One of two late 4th-millennium BC figurines recently found at Tell el-Farkha in the Nile Delta, constructed of sheet-gold pinned over a lost wooden core, and originally with inlaid lapis lazuli eyes and necklaces of other rare stones. These illustrate the multimedia combination of precious materials typical of emerging Egypt and Mesopotamia, but also an unfamiliar aesthetic relative to later Egyptian norms, possibly specific to early Deltaic culture.

XXV (*right*) Aerial view of Ebla showing the palatial acropolis, urban extent and ramparts of this great 3rd- and early 2nd-millennium BC Bronze Age centre in the fertile, well-connected northern Levant, today in northwest Syria.

XXVI (*below left*) High on the smooth rock faces of Mont Bégo in southeastern France, huge numbers of 3rd-millennium BC depictions testify to the growing engagement with upland zones, in this case in the form of seasonal visitations apparently by men, whose ritual and other preoccupations are vividly recorded.

XXVII (*below right*) The ready availability of metal-bearing lodes to early prospectors is evident in this image from an experimental reconstruction of copper extraction at Wadi Feinan in southern Jordan; note the use of donkeys for the long-range outward transport of ores or, by the Early Bronze Age, ingots and finished objects.

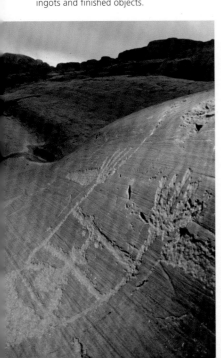

XXVIII (*above*) Set in its landscape, this cluster of trefoil-shaped 'temples' at Mnajdra on Malta illustrates the relationship between such monumental structures and access to the sea. Whoever controlled the rituals at such places also held the keys to manipulation of off-island connections. Note the huge blocks of local limestone used in construction.

XXIX (*right*) Part of the early Middle Kingdom temple foundation deposit known as the Tod treasure, discovered at the ancient town of the same name in Upper Egypt, near Thebes. Several such copper boxes held over 150 mainly silver bowls and cups, whose swirling decoration is reminiscent of contemporary Aegean painted pottery, as well as silver ingots, and quantities of raw and worked lapis lazuli. Such exotic finds testify to strong trading relations, not least by sea, with the remainder of the eastern Mediterranean.

XXX (*below*) A short-range festive procession of ships, one with sail hoisted but the others propelled in an archaizing fashion by multitudes of paddlers, approaches a natural harbour near a busy coastal town in this wall-painting preserved by a volcanic eruption at the mid-2nd-millennium BC West House of Akrotiri on Thera in the Cyclades. Note the numerous small inshore craft and diverse coastal structures, but the lack of built quays or other harbour installations.

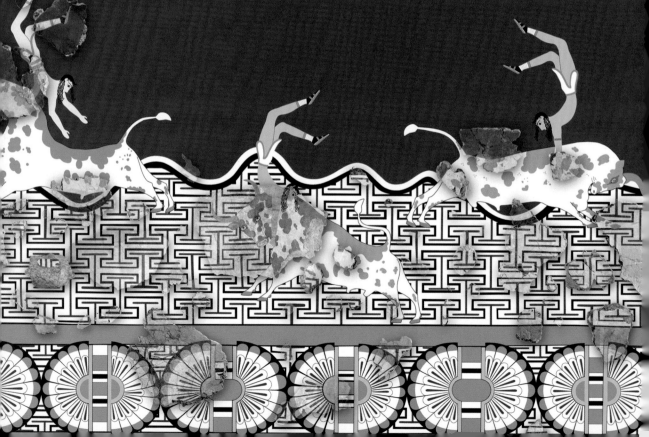

XXXI (*opposite above*) The massive, ancient and still only partly archaeologically explored citadel of Aleppo (Bronze Age Yamhad), crowned by its huge Arab castle and seen here hovering over the medieval to modern city shortly before both were engulfed in the tragic civil war that still rages at the time of writing.

XXXII (*opposite below*) Reconstruction from its fragmentary remains of one of several wall-paintings that once adorned early New Kingdom palaces at Avaris in the Nile Delta. The bull-leaping scenes, labyrinth motif and split-rosette design, as well as the style and technique of execution, strongly resemble those of Crete.

XXXIII (*right*) Behind palatial Mycenae's 'cyclopean' defence wall and famous Lion Gate lie the earlier shaft graves, found unlooted by Schliemann and remarkable for their eclectic range of wealth goods. Later incorporation of this ancestral burial ground by Mycenae's subsequent rulers is apparent in the remodelled grave circle built around them, and the outward bow of the circuit wall at that point.

439

XXXIV Among the wealth of finds from the Uluburun shipwreck, off Turkey's southern coast, is this Levantine bronze figurine of a goddess, with her head, arms and legs wrapped in gold leaf. Slightly later analogies suggest that this may have been the vessel's tutelary deity. If so, she was negligent on the day when the ship foundered in the 14th century BC.

XXXV (*below*) Sardinia as a landscape of towers, or nuraghi, extremely numerous but fairly simple in their architectural form over much of the 2nd millennium BC, but from then onwards increasingly complex in a minority of larger settlements. This evolved example from Su Nuraxi remains typical, however, of most nuraghi in its domination of a local pocket of arable land.

In schematic spatial terms, this phase of expanding networks has a world-systemic appearance.[469] As parts of the Aegean joined the urban east Mediterranean core zone of large-scale consumers and producers, the peripheries and less articulated margins relocated further north and west. Outward went the more mobile, flashy, status-enhancing and easily integrated elements of core culture and technology. Inward percolated raw metals with amber and other tracers riding on their back. Copper and gold dominated the metals (silver remaining uncommon north and west of the Aegean), but central and west European tin must also have been significant, indeed until such contacts solidified, use of tin-bronze was moderate over much of the east Mediterranean compared to later-starting but well-endowed regions such as the British Isles.[470] This process provides a context for the mid- to late 2nd-millennium BC surge in European metal production that is so evident in accumulations of scrap for recycling, uptake of bivalve moulds, compulsive, often ritualized, hoarding where routes converged and metal's sheer abundance threatened traditional values, and the direct testimony from the Alpine ore sources.[471] Estimates of output for the Mitterberg mine, which drew hundreds of labourers into the high valleys, range from 10 to 18 tonnes of copper per year,[472] comparing impressively with the 10 tonnes on the Uluburun ship, and the 54 tonnes that Amenhotep II claimed to have extorted from the Levant.[473] Conspicuously heavyweight copper- and goldwork was created in the Otomani centres, whose connections round the head of the Adriatic we encountered earlier, and which also lay athwart overland trails to the Aegean, where at Mycenae and elsewhere another chariot-riding and, in a sense, hillfort-building elite was on the make. Indigenous regimes of value subtly adjusted to eastern contacts – one example may be European people's concern to colour their faience blue by adding copper salts, in unconscious ultimate reference to lapis lazuli, and more directly its east Mediterranean substitutes.[474]

But equally, we should not exaggerate, nor anticipate, the importance of such connections at this early juncture. Not until the Iron Age did relations become close enough to fundamentally reshape the culture and economies of outlying regions. With a few exceptions in southern Italy, no defining elements of east Mediterranean ways of life and capital-accumulating economies yet took root further afield. For example, the boundaries of seal use, which had rolled out rapidly during the 3rd millennium BC to the Aegean, and the Indus, advanced no further. In fact, the first Aegean agents of contact to the north and west came from beyond the urban, palatial world of Crete. Quite who they were (entrepreneurial big men, warriors, seafarers, or all three in one?) is lost to us, but as intermediaries they were small fry compared to a leading merchant of Ugarit. Their encounters on distant ground, or modestly sized and easily stormed ships, with substantial groups of people proficient at running their own trade circuits must have been ones of effective parity that offered both sides a chance to acquire desirable things, whatever the long-term consequences of the inequities in economic scale and value regimes behind them. From these meetings between people for whom neither Akkadian nor initially silver offered any pre-agreed media for exchange, and from beginnings presumably in barter, surely eased by drinking parties of the kinds

8.67 Map of the central Mediterranean in the mid-to-later 2nd millennium BC, showing indigenous interaction zones, find-spots of Aegean-type pottery, and the main sea-routes from further east.

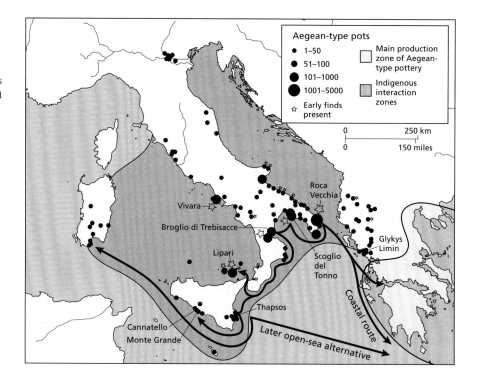

that had developed independently throughout the eastern and northern flanks of the basin, new Mediterranean and European interrelations would very gradually emerge.

The central Mediterranean dimension of this process was typical in terms of the materials involved, which, besides the Aegean imports and amber, are assumed to have comprised Sardinian and Tuscan metals, volcanic minerals like sulphur and alum (the latter used in tanning), as well as, indirectly, Alpine and Carpathian copper and gold, plus European tin, which in the south had hitherto been seldom known.[475] What made this theatre distinct (save for the still dimly understood Black Sea, maybe now experiencing its own Jason moment) was the maritime nature of the link and its realization by a bow wave of probing exploration in sailing ships [**8.67**]. In addition to the opportunity this afforded for bulk transport in and out of the central Mediterranean, this enabled routes to expand unusually fast. In Classical times it took just two weeks to reach Sicily from the Aegean, while the north–south traverse of central Europe over a similar distance remained a six-week journey in the 16th century AD.[476] Another blessing was the layout of the Tyrrhenian and Adriatic seas, which, together with the pronounced northward offset of the basin's main axis here, offered Mediterranean mariners access to latitudes close to the European interior. The opening of these sea corridors to wider Mediterranean trade, and the subsequent Iron Age extension of this process further west, help to explain why the efflorescence of the temperate European societies most actively engaged in Mediterranean trade describes a parallel westward march over time, from the Otomani hubs in the Balkans, to central European Hallstatt chiefdoms during the later Bronze Age, and ultimately the La Tène splendours of pre-Roman Gaul.[477] In the final assessment, the vital point, as ever, was that maritime travel facilitated direct, unmediated, long-range links between places far apart, and so less-garbled transmission and dialogue than overland chains of communication.

The earliest Aegean painted drinking cups, oil or unguent containers and plain pots in the central Mediterranean reveal the hands of players already prominent in the sea trade and markets of their respective home regions, namely the Argolid and Aegina in the east, and, at the receiving end, the Aeolian islands and Vivara.[478] The connecting route, braided from sea-paths intermittently travelled from far earlier times, lay up the west coast of Greece, across the Strait of Otranto, around the heel and toe of Italy and into the Tyrrhenian Sea via the Messina narrows, with their Odyssean associations, or along the straight south coast of Sicily, where Aegean pots appeared at the large settlement and sulphur-mining complex of Monte Grande, near Agrigento. The earliest find-spots signal that contacts were concentrated at, and mediated by, native trading centres, which acted as the gatekeepers as well as gateways, keeping metal-rich Sardinia and much of the rest of the Tyrrhenian (along with virtually all the Adriatic) initially outside the purview of eastern navigators.

Within a couple of centuries, however, most of the initial winners had released their grip. The rise of the Mycenaean palaces changed configurations in the east, and in Epirus new establishments such as Ephyra on the almost landlocked Glykys Limin ('Sweet Harbour') of the Acheron delta sought to intervene in traffic westward, while reshaping societies in their own hinterland.[479] In the centre of the basin, two very Mediterranean phenomena occurred: Vivara was smothered by a nearby volcanic eruption, and Aeolian traders relinquished their quasi-monopoly as the multiplicity of short-circuiting and outflanking routes around or across the southern Tyrrhenian Sea, islands and peninsulas allowed more mainlanders and Sicilians to get in on the game.[480] This was the heyday of trade with Sicilian Thapsos [**8.68**], Scoglio del Tonno at Taranto and, more enduringly, Roca Vecchia on the Strait of Otranto, which alone siphoned off half the Aegean pots in the entire central Mediterranean.[481] After 1400 BC, pottery and more rarely figurines, glass and ivory from the Aegean dispersed to scores of coastal and a few inland locations, albeit in varied quantities (often tiny, and usually fewer than

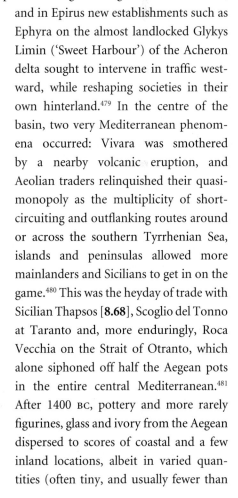

8.68 Thapsos: (*top*) plan of the sheltering peninsula, showing areas of settlement and burials; (*centre*) select Aegean and Cypriot imports; (*below*) new large-scale rectilinear architecture above and among the traditional roundhouses.

Cemeteries

0   200 m
0   600 ft

0   20 m
0   60 ft

8.69 Ivory plaque in the form of a man's head enveloped in a helmet covered with rows of boars' tusks. This example comes from Mycenae, but a fragment of a similar piece constitutes an early Aegean find in Sardinia. Such allusions to hunting and, by implication, martial prowess probably enjoyed a widespread cross-cultural currency.

internal imports) and still with precious little reaching the north Tyrrhenian or inner Adriatic. In contrast to the Argolid's dominance over exports to the east, these goods still came from all over the Aegean and western Greece, with varied preferences and reception at the receiving end too.[482] It would, of course, be naive to assume that each find-spot commemorated a visit by an Aegean trader, indeed their effective dispersal is equal testament to the vigour of indigenous networks. Outliers such as the single piece from a cup with a painted octopus discovered on Malta or the solitary Aegean fragment among 96,655 Tyrrhenian ones on Ustica surely arrived in local boats.[483] The same can be said of the painted pot deposited towards the end of interment at the great Giovinazzo dolmen, near Bari.[484] None of this detracts from the basic point that trade between the Aegean and central Mediterranean became more extensive, frequent and multidirectional at a point in time that equates further east with the Uluburun shipwreck, Amarna letters and overall peak of the palatial system.

The engagement also started to display shifts in nature that would deepen over coming centuries and so serve as harbingers of new practices and ultimately different forms of Mediterranean interaction. One was the establishment of direct linkage with Sardinia. Most of the evidence dates after 1300 BC and so awaits the coming chapter, but in the 14th century a few Aegean objects arrived, including an ivory of a warrior's head sporting a helmet sheathed, as was admired in the Aegean, with boars' tusks [**8.69**].[485] The pig-tooth headgear preserved by the eruption of Vesuvius at Croce del Papa suggests that such an object would be readily appreciated by Tyrrhenian fighters. Another new feature was the appearance of Cypriot pottery in the central Mediterranean after 1400 BC, mainly juglets and large pithoi of the kind seen on the Uluburun ship (which in return carried a sword of south Italian or Sicilian type).[486] The first Cypriot pots showed up in southern Sicily, at Thapsos and further west at Cannatello, as if the sea-traders of Cyprus were intent on cutting out circuitous routes via mainland Italy as well as south Tyrrhenian competition, in favour of a straight shot through the Sicilian narrows towards Sardinia. A last index of change was the adoption of customs from further east. At Thapsos long rectilinear buildings arose between and over the normal roundhouses [**8.68**], and tholos-like tombs were built nearby at Ragusa.[487] But it was southeast Italy that led the way in the first wheel-thrown pots, both versions of Aegean painted forms and local grey wares, whether fashioned by indigenous or migrant potters.[488] By around 1300 BC most of the visually Aegean-type pottery in the central Mediterranean was in fact produced in this part of Italy. Nor was this the only uptake. At Broglio di Trebisacce olive cultivation took off, and probably viticulture too, while Coppa Nevigata boasts the earliest donkey in Italy and possibly a purple-dyeing industry.[489] Boundaries were breaking down and wider vocabularies starting to emerge. Over a few turbulent centuries, this process would expand further, from Lebanon to Gibraltar, and the Po to Tunisia. As it culminated to embrace the entire basin, the world of the Middle Sea, so long in the making, would finally come into unified existence.

CHAPTER NINE

From sea to shining sea

(1300 – 800 BC)

A room with a view

The audience in the high room in Byblos was not going well for Wenamun, priest of Egyptian Thebes, or so the story goes in the version that has survived, as an amalgam of reportage and literary sentiment, on a slightly later papyrus, found stuffed into a pot south of Cairo and currently in the possession of the Pushkin Museum.[1] The date was around 1075 BC, and Zakar-Baal, lord of the town, sat in classic interview style with his back to the window, whose light framed his angry form. Through it Wenamun saw the roiling waves of the Mediterranean burst against the shore: the sea that sundered him from home and all that was good. His mission was a time-hallowed one, to obtain cedar to renew the sacred boat of Amun, but it had gone inauspiciously from the start. Negotiations even for passage beyond the Delta had proved time-consuming, thanks to the local potentate Smendes, and had cost Wenamun his letters of recommendation. Once en route again, a sailor on the foreign transport arranged by Smendes absconded with Wenamun's silver and gold at Dor – then already graced with a 35-m (115-ft) built quay, a century or two old when Wenamun docked, and now (in northern Israel) the oldest to survive in the Mediterranean.[2] By what chicaneries Wenamun extricated himself from this disaster is veiled by lacunae in the extant text, but they made him a marked man as he proceeded north, via Tyre and Sidon. In Byblos, shorn of his letters and gifts, he was kept waiting for a month, and when at last granted this audience, his lofty appeals to ancient custom, Egyptian overlordship and the blessings of Amun cut little ice with a self-confident local ruler impatient with rhetoric and well versed in the opposing view that his predecessors had received something more tangible, by the shipload, in return for timber. A message was dispatched to Smendes to break this impasse; three months later (making eight since Wenamun had left Thebes), he came up with the goods: a shipment of gold, silver, linen and other cloth, beef, fish, lentils and rope. The tail of this list is hardly the stuff of the Amarna letters, but the overall consignment mollified Byblite sensibilities and economic sense enough for 300 lumberjacks and as many oxen to be ordered into the mountains. As the birds migrated south, Wenamun departed with his cedar cargo, somehow evaded a vengeful squadron from Dor that patrolled offshore, and was promptly blown northwest to Cyprus. There, only intercession by an Egyptian speaker and a powerful lady saved him from

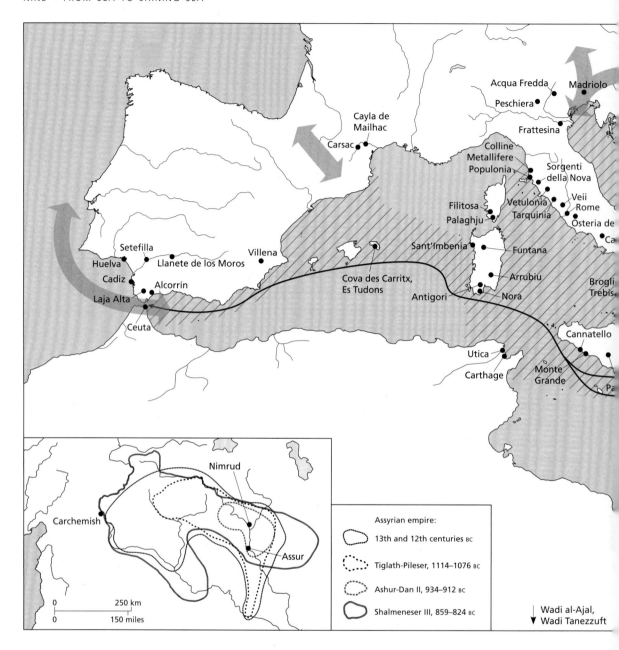

Assyrian empire:

13th and 12th centuries BC

Tiglath-Pileser, 1114–1076 BC

Ashur-Dan II, 934–912 BC

Shalmeneser III, 859–824 BC

Wadi al-Ajal,
Wadi Tanezzuft

9.1 Map of principal sites mentioned in this chapter, also showing areas of pre-existing or emergent maritime connections, the approximate 'route of the isles', using latitude sailing, the main axes of connections beyond the basin and (inset) Middle and early Neo-Assyrian territorial fluctuations.

the lynch mob gathered to meet this arrival from Byblos. 'Sleep' urged his protectress, at which juncture, pregnant with possibilities, the papyrus breaks off. That the cedar and its long-suffering guardian eventually returned to Thebes we can infer from the images at Karnak that celebrate the inauguration of Amun's new boat.

Even allowing for its mixed genres and the standard Egyptian trope of the tribulations of life abroad, the *Tale of Wenamun* is one of those treasuries of incidental detail that irradiate early Mediterranean history. We learn, for example, that the god travelled with his emissary, as Amun-on-the-road, presumably embodied in a figurine akin to that found on the Uluburun ship, and at Byblos discreetly housed in a

446

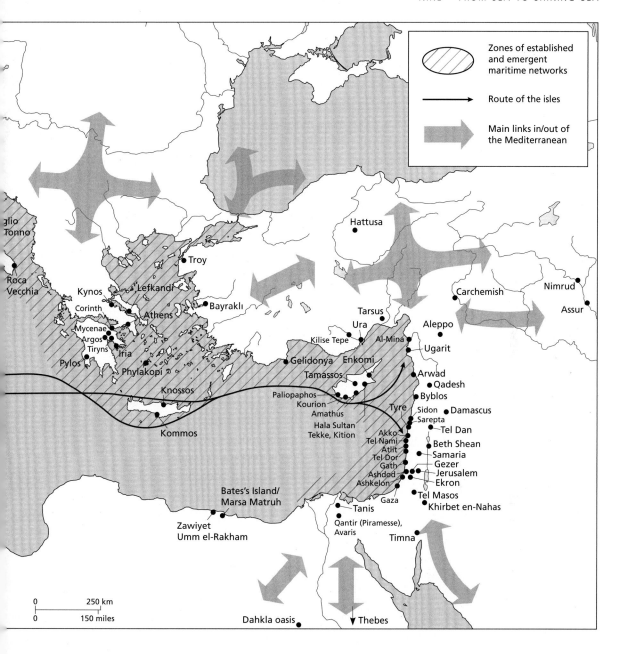

tent on the shore. Harbours stand out as refuges where seafarers lay under the protection of the local ruler, hence the delicacy of Wenamun's situation at Byblos, and perhaps Dor. Those of Lebanon were crammed with ships, of which twenty at Byblos and fifty at Sidon traded with the well-connected Smendes and others. Not one ship is specified as Egyptian in any sense except its destination – although this did not stop our anti-hero from insinuating that this rendered them Egypt's by association. In a premonition of Nausikaä's role in the *Odyssey*, women succoured Wenamun three times: with food and clothes sent by Smendes's wife with her husband's cargo, with songs by Tinetnit (a resident Egyptian entertainer, sent by Zakar-Baal along with mutton and wine to cheer the disconsolate traveller) and with protection by the enigmatic Cypriot lady. Lastly, when the lord of Byblos ordered his ancestors' records to be read out to prove the reciprocity of earlier relations with pharaoh, it is clearly implied that these were written on papyrus or leather rolls (recall the connotation of papyrus in the Greek name 'Byblos'), a shift corroborated by the disappearance of clay tablets across the Levant as cursive, informal and ultimately alphabetical scripts replaced traditional cuneiform.[3] Away from the preservation conditions of Egypt and, later, the Judaean desert, a chasm of archaeological loss suddenly gapes at our feet, one that largely explains the perversely lesser contribution of eastern archives over the coming centuries.

Behind such significant details we discern a series of profound changes since we last left the east Mediterranean. The most glaring, not least given the perspective from which the tale is told, is the diminished stature of Egypt. Abroad, Wenamun's humiliations reveal a different universe from that of Amarna diplomacy; indeed, to hurry him on his way, Zakar-Baal pointedly offered to show him the graves of previous emissaries whom he had detained until they died. No pharaoh is invoked by name, and what symbolic capital and authority Egypt retained was precariously invested in Amun's divine reputation. All this left the coast of the central Levant in a contrastingly buoyant state. Equally extraordinary is the change within Egypt itself, where again a resounding silence surrounds the matter of royalty. Local magnates controlled sectors of the Nile, in Smendes's case a Delta once again on a breakaway trajectory from upriver rule, and busy in the Levant. Less dramatic, but nonetheless surprising, is the jumpiness on cosmopolitan Cyprus at the approach of a foreign ship, and had Wenamun's misadventures propelled him still further across the seas (for all we know they did), other shocks would have been in store. For the three centuries after 1300 BC witnessed an enormous transformation in this half of the basin. In the uncritical language of earlier generations, the later part of this period saw the onset of a 'dark age', ushered in by disasters and destructions clustered around 1200

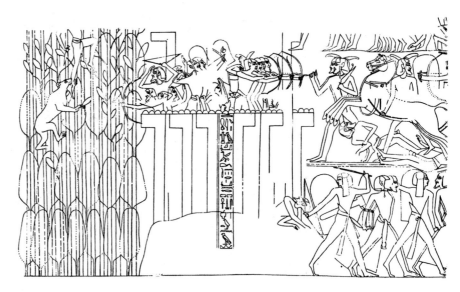

9.2 The Egyptian view of Lebanon as a land of unruly vassals in fortified towns clinging to rocks, and dense, bear-haunted woods. The missing element in this depiction from the reign of Ramesses II, and arguably the most vital, is the constant proximity of the sea.

BC and associated with a ragged region-by-region start to the Iron Age.[4] In fact, as Wenamun's tale already intimates, the reality in terms of modern knowledge and ancient trajectories was a more thought-provoking chiaroscuro. Of this we can only make sense if we straddle the paroxysms around 1200 BC with a longer, more coolly analytical time frame, from the aftermath of Amarna to the threshold of the 1st millennium BC.

The rough and the smooth in the east Mediterranean

Where better to start than at Wenamun's nemesis, the central Levantine coast? Here, all remained mercantile business as usual, powered up by the release from Egyptian authority and tribute [**9.2**]. The places identified in the Amarna letters still flourished in the 11th century BC, and recent excavations confirm smooth sequences at major sites, as well as smaller places like Sarepta, all of which maintained widespread connections.[5] From now on, this quintessentially Mediterranean landscape of bustling coastal towns and narrow, river-striated agricultural hinterlands, climbing up through forests to skyscraping peaks, is conventionally known as Phoenicia. With its invocations of purple cloth, palms, skilled crafting and mythical beasts, 'Phoenician' is a Greek collective forged later, under different circumstances, that we force upon people who identified with their individual cities (so, Sidonians, Tyrians and suchlike), and continued to see themselves more broadly as Canaanite.[6] Their Mediterranean-wide expansion still lay a few generations in the future but, free from Egyptian adjudication, the jockeying for advantage was already overt.[7] Wenamun's ship counts support other indications that Sidon had outstripped Byblos, and was the instigator of a central Levantine presence further south around the Bay of Akko. Tyre stayed a modest player until the late 11th century, as did Arwad, likewise an island town in the midst of the sea, and one that tapped its drinking water from an upwelling submarine aquifer. By way of contrast with this vein of unbroken mercantile life, to the north of Arwad, as far as Cilicia, the incidence of fiery destructions on either side of 1200 BC was greater, even if most places recovered fairly fast.[8] The permanent and textually high-decibel annihilation in about 1182 BC of Ugarit, which had remained a flourishing international player and entrepôt of the metals trade throughout the 13th century, was a dramatic exception.[9] Here, as elsewhere, however, neighbours quickly stepped in to fill the void, led by none other than Ugarit's own former port of Ras Ibn Hani.

Moving on, Wenamun's hot reception on Cyprus may reflect tensions building up towards the end of an amazing run of economic expansion and cultural inclusivity.[10] The 13th and 12th centuries BC witnessed the climax of this island's non-palatial brand of urbanism, studded with imposing houses and rich tombs, and at Enkomi oriented on a new orthogonal street grid. Alongside large-scale olive oil and textile industries, copper production blossomed under the regulation of urban shrines, reflected by large hoards at Enkomi and imagery of ingots on ornate cultic

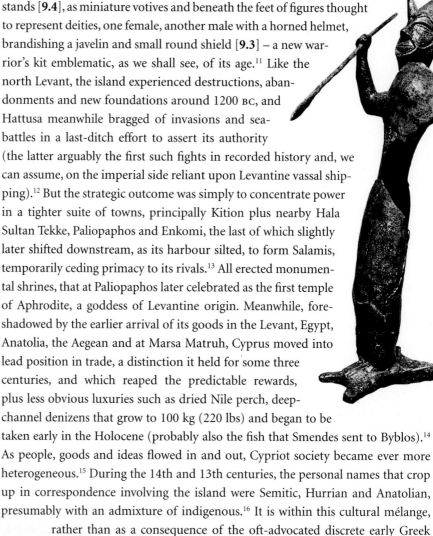

stands [**9.4**], as miniature votives and beneath the feet of figures thought to represent deities, one female, another male with a horned helmet, brandishing a javelin and small round shield [**9.3**] – a new warrior's kit emblematic, as we shall see, of its age.[11] Like the north Levant, the island experienced destructions, abandonments and new foundations around 1200 BC, and Hattusa meanwhile bragged of invasions and sea-battles in a last-ditch effort to assert its authority (the latter arguably the first such fights in recorded history and, we can assume, on the imperial side reliant upon Levantine vassal shipping).[12] But the strategic outcome was simply to concentrate power in a tighter suite of towns, principally Kition plus nearby Hala Sultan Tekke, Paliopaphos and Enkomi, the last of which slightly later shifted downstream, as its harbour silted, to form Salamis, temporarily ceding primacy to its rivals.[13] All erected monumental shrines, that at Paliopaphos later celebrated as the first temple of Aphrodite, a goddess of Levantine origin. Meanwhile, foreshadowed by the earlier arrival of its goods in the Levant, Egypt, Anatolia, the Aegean and at Marsa Matruh, Cyprus moved into lead position in trade, a distinction it held for some three centuries, and which reaped the predictable rewards, plus less obvious luxuries such as dried Nile perch, deep-channel denizens that grow to 100 kg (220 lbs) and began to be taken early in the Holocene (probably also the fish that Smendes sent to Byblos).[14] As people, goods and ideas flowed in and out, Cypriot society became ever more heterogeneous.[15] During the 14th and 13th centuries, the personal names that crop up in correspondence involving the island were Semitic, Hurrian and Anatolian, presumably with an admixture of indigenous.[16] It is within this cultural mélange, rather than as a consequence of the oft-advocated discrete early Greek migrations, that we should understand the uptake and local substitution of a range of Aegean-derived traits. Cyprus's position was won by aggressive mercantile entrepreneurship; its agents in 13th-century Tiryns seem to have intervened even in the Argolid's own specialization, incising batches of Aegean pots for their own export.[17] It also owed much to growing prowess in the realm of open-sea navigation, especially between the largest islands of the Mediterranean, which by the 13th century BC brought Cypriot products to Crete, Sicily and as far as Sardinia.[18] Only in the 11th century did this lead start to falter, symbolized by the cessation around this time of production of the iconic oxhide ingot, as Phoenicia began to compete more assertively in the same game and to penetrate the Cypriot home market.[19] This is the context, of course, for the aggressive local reception of Wenamun's Byblite ship.

9.4 The close relationship between copper production and elite ritual on Cyprus is hinted at by this ceremonial bronze stand, possibly from Kourion, showing on this face a man carrying an oxhide ingot towards a tree; on another face the figure plays a lyre.

Before we leave Cyprus, one further innovation associated with this society so fecund in metals deserves attention. This is the earliest regular production of iron.[20] We have sporadically encountered iron objects as far back as a 3rd-millennium BC dagger from Alacahöyük in central Anatolia. Most were high-value curiosities, some mounted in gold and made from meteoric metal gathered from impact craters such as one recently identified in Egypt's Western Desert. The shift to terrestrial extraction, along with smelting, carburization and tempering, dates to the 13th–12th centuries BC. To judge from textual references, Anatolian metallurgists were among the pioneers, perhaps in association with Caucasian experts,[21] but so too were the smiths of Cyprus, where small amounts of iron sometimes materialized as an unintended by-product of copper smelting. The paradox that an island superabundant in the main ingredient of bronze should have promoted the metal that gave its name to the Iron Age is only superficial, given the logics of an economy geared to marketing diverse new products, not least at sub-elite levels, and within which iron was meant to supplement rather than replace bronze.[22] Knives with iron blades and bronze hilt rivets swiftly became run-of-the-mill on Cyprus, though abroad such products remained exotic for longer [**9.5**]. The beginnings of local iron production, often (unlike on Cyprus) from rich nearby ores, were staggered over the next few centuries in different parts of the basin, each time loosely correlated with the conventional start of a regional Iron Age sequence. Iron was functionally useful, creating lighter tools and weapons easy to resharpen, but its military impact can be exaggerated, and its true significance lay in the ubiquity of its ores, which made it harder to control centrally, once the necessary know-how had diffused, than only selectively available copper and distantly sourced tin. It was this slippery, potentially subversive aspect that earned it Gordon Childe's famous sobriquet, the 'democratic metal', though 'anti-monopolistic' better captures its role among the new societies that we shall encounter across the Iron Age Mediterranean.[23]

9.5 The bronze-to-iron transition materialized in this 12th-century BC knife from Enkomi, with its iron blade and ivory handle attached with bronze rivets.

Following a practice as old as the sail itself in this part of the Mediterranean, Wenamun had skipped the southern Levant on his outward journey, and we do not know by what sea-path he returned. We, however, must stop off south of Dor. Here we pick up further reflections of Egypt's grandeur and eclipse, and the consequences of both. In the 13th century BC Egypt's grip had never been tighter.[24] Egyptian-style governors' residences and minor temples were built at key points on the coastal plain and inland, notably at Beth Shean where the valley routes from the coast and the north converged. Egyptianizing traits remained prominent in south Levantine culture, and anthropoid clay coffins, some with outlandish headdress designs, testify to the presence of Egyptians as well as the foreign soldiers they hired as garrison troops. Yet the first half of the next century saw piecemeal unravelling of this system, with a final pull-out from what remained around 1140 BC.[25] Destructions throughout the late 13th and 12th centuries accompanied, preceded and followed this. Some can be blamed on internecine warfare as imperial mediation waned, others on coastal raids of a kind becoming

451

commonplace, as we shall see, and a few on Egypt itself, notably an assault in 1207 BC by the pharaoh Merenptah against a presumably rebel Ashkelon and Gezer, which is famous today for the incidental, and manifestly exaggerated, claim in passing that it wiped out an obscure people known as 'Israel'.[26] Urban life hung on and then bounced back in the 11th century, now free from Egyptian tribute. In Galilee it stayed true to Canaanite traditions. In the southern coastal plain, however, new traits with Aegean and Cypriot affinities can be variously interpreted.[27] For some they are best explained by emulation of foreign styles, for others through the arrival of new population elements from overseas, on scales that range from minor infiltrations to mass migration of mobile people or their resettlement by Egypt (the sole power still able to move groups by edict) on land over which it was ceding control. Regardless, this evolved into the zone known as the Philistine pentapolis, infamous from an Old Testament perspective, and comprising Ashkelon and Gaza on the coast, plus Ashdod, Ekron and Gath inland among fertile fields, each with great halls and shrines, but (interestingly) nothing like a central palace structure, and according to later traditions ruled not by a king but a council of lordly *seranim*.[28]

What, we inevitably ask, of 'Israel'? With the Exodus at best a refracted folk memory of earlier expulsions of Levantine people after the fall of Hyksos Avaris, and no signs of a conquest from the desert, the most plausible candidates were already in situ, namely the inhabitants of scores of small villages and hamlets that appeared over the south Levantine highlands at this time, all politically egalitarian but articulated by open-air sacred sites.[29] This appears to have reflected the settling down as small-scale mixed farmers of motley displaced groups, and notably the mobile *hapiru* and *shashu* encountered in Chapter 8, who hitherto, under more oppressive conditions, had made a living in the hills and adjacent steppes as tribal pastoralists. It also represented the third manifestation of farming settlement in this zone since its first major peopling during the expansion of upland communities across much of the basin in the 'long' 3rd millennium BC, followed by the revival of upland agriculture to supply the great Levantine towns and markets of the earlier 2nd millennium with wine, oil and other products.[30] Upland farmers reappeared east of the Jordan too, in thoroughly un-'Israelite' regions, yet one marked distinction in the west was the absence of pig bones, a taboo that contrasted sharply with their frequency at Philistine sites,[31] and marks one of the earliest indices of a nascent desire to assert behavioural differentiation and self-definition among certain groups around the Iron Age Mediterranean.

The agendas of Biblical archaeology have unfortunately distracted attention from the kinds of economic insight within a Mediterranean framework that have been so fruitfully pursued further north and on Cyprus. In fact, despite the Old Testament's emphasis on bloody conflict, the lowland towns and upland communities must have been symbiotic, as in the Middle Bronze Age. The movement across both of massive collar-rimmed jars may indicate the conveyance as well as storage of oil and wine destined for urban and coastal markets (they surely served as water-butts too).[32] It is hard to credit that Philistine towns on the coastal plain

9.6 The early 1st-millennium BC fort at Khirbet en-Nahas in Edom, today in southern Jordan, surrounded by large slag heaps from copper production.

were as focused on subsistence and innocent of trading links as has been argued, given their close tracking of foreign pottery styles and the region's long history of oil and wine trade with Egypt.[33] Equally noteworthy was the return to Levantine copper extraction after a millennium of abandonment. At Timna this began in the 13th century BC under Egyptian royal auspices, circumstances that suggest a bid for self-sufficiency at a time of spiralling consumption and harder Cypriot bargaining as the decorum of interregional trade began to fray.[34] At Feinan, the resurgence post-dated Egypt's retreat, and played a later part in the rise of the Iron Age polity of Edom [**9.6**].[35] In the by now long-marginal Beersheba Valley, a vibrant community with widespread connections at Tel Masos may indicate, in an echo of 4th- and 3rd-millennium patterns, the path by which this copper moved west.[36] More shadowy was the inception of an arduous overland trail up the Arabian coast of the Red Sea, debouching into the Mediterranean between the Wadi Arabah and Sinai or further north, and bringing incense, myrrh and other fragrances from south Arabia that until now only Egyptian maritime expeditions had enjoyed the potential to obtain.[37] This monopoly-busting route, for most of its length in the hands of indigenous groups entirely beyond state control, became feasible largely thanks to the south Arabian domestication a few centuries before of the ultra-hardy dromedary, a camel at home in low, hot deserts, unlike its highland Bactrian cousin.[38] Dromedary bones appeared around the Levantine terminus during the 14th and 13th centuries BC, to be followed by northwest Arabian pottery finds at Tel Masos, though neither in amounts indicative of regular caravan traffic until substantially later.

Egypt itself is, as already intimated, our first case of long-term contraction. It took the form not of violent yet temporary destructions, but a sustained diminution of internal and external authority.[39] Although it remained vastly populous, a byword for wealth, fertility and awesome antiquity, Egypt during the 1st millennium BC would experience few phases of political resurgence comparable to those of the past, and from the 7th century BC onward it suffered a series of unprecedented conquests and absorptions by rivals based in, and finally beyond, Mesopotamia. By the mid-12th century control over the Levant was gone, monument building had virtually ground to a halt and tombs were being emptied to recirculate their bullion value, in a subaltern, internal version of the injections effected by earlier pharaohs by foreign plunder and tribute.[40] Later in the same century came sharp price rises in grain and oil.[41] By 1069 BC, a few decades but several reigns later, and just after Wenamun's journey, the last New Kingdom pharaoh, so invisible in the *Tale*, was dead. Egypt openly split into an upriver polity, ruled by Wenamun's superiors, the high priests of Amun at Thebes, which had benefited from colossal land donations under the Ramessids, and another in the Delta, whose first king was none other than Smendes, that mixed blessing as a sponsor. A comparison with the situation in the 13th century BC brings out the relatively abrupt and precipitous nature of these changes. Then, the monument building and foreign-power projections of the Amarna age were revitalized by a new Ramessid dynasty, reliant as much on armed might as numinous authority.[42] Sabre-rattling in the Levant against the superpower of Hatti had culminated in 1275 BC in a chaotic, nail-biting yet ultimately inconclusive clash at Qadesh between the core and confederate infantry and chariotry of each, numbering ten of thousands of troops and thousands of chariots on each side, and very probably the largest mass of soldiery yet brought together on the planet [**9.7**].[43] News of the battle must have rippled through the east Mediterranean as it did in the aftermath of the battle of Lepanto, almost 3000 years later. No less emblematic of the

9.7 The Egyptian official version of the gigantic battle that unfolded around the central Levantine town of Qadesh on the Orontes river in 1275 BC, as repeatedly portrayed on Ramesses II's temples and other buildings. An heroically outsized pharaoh routs the threatening mass of enemy chariotry all but single-handedly.

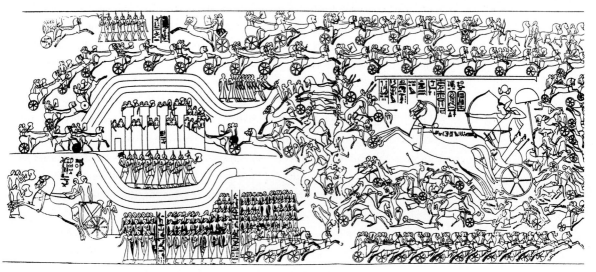

age was the ensuing peace treaty and marriage between Ramesses II (1279–1213 BC) and a daughter of the king of Hatti, all replete with impeccable 'brotherly' sentiments – if recorded with sharply differing interpretative glosses, as indeed was the result of the battle itself, on temples in Egypt and a silver tablet (of which we possess the clay copy) at Hattusa.[44]

From our perspective one connecting thread between these glory days and the political nadir of the 11th century was the return to prominence of Deltaic Egypt, after several centuries of subordination. Unlike the preceding Hyksos ascendancy and the coming phase of secession, this resurgence began in the context of a strongly unified state, even if, as the contemporary Papyrus Anastasi averred, people at either end of this could still barely understand each other.[45] Horemheb (1323–1295 BC), the last king of the 18th Dynasty, constructed a massive fortress over the ruins of the earlier palaces at Avaris, in recognition of the need to be closer than was sacred Thebes to the jump-off point for operations against Hatti or recalcitrant Levantine vassals, as well as to the vibrant Mediterranean maritime interface.[46] His protégé and brief royal heir, the first Ramesses, hailed from Avaris and had commanded a strongpoint on the marches to its east. Ramesses II formalized this investment in the Delta by founding a new capital and military base just north of Avaris. Known as Piramesse ('House of Ramesses'), and identified as the site of Qantir, this latest giant of the Delta may have spread over as much as a breathtaking 10 sq. km (4 sq. miles), larger even than Avaris in its prime.[47] It had quarters devoted to industrial production, especially bronzeworking for weaponry on a colossal scale (foreign iron was long resisted), and some of the last glass-making before this skill was strangely abandoned, to be later restarted with quite different, natron-based techniques in the 1st millennium BC.[48] There were great barracks, stables for chariot horses, granaries, palaces and temples. Nearby, on an adjacent branch of the Nile, lay the similarly new town of Tanis, its port and, thanks to ongoing alluviation, successor by Smendes's and Wenamun's day. Mediterranean penetration is evident in the worship of Levantine gods at Piramesse and further upriver. The increasingly popular Levantine deity Astarte appeared, now sometimes shown riding on horseback [**9.8**], and new popularity was enjoyed by a syncretism going back to pre-Hyksos times, between Baal-Zephon and Egyptian Seth, the patron god of the Ramessids.[49] These deities claimed two of the four principal temples at Piramesse, the third being that of Wadjet, a Delta goddess from time immemorial, and only Amun's, the fourth, with solid Theban associations. The embrace of Seth, a god of disorder and sea-conqueror seen as the antithesis of upriver divinity during the Hyksos wars, speaks volumes about efforts to incorporate the Delta in Ramessid cosmology as something more than a part of the Nile. Indeed, a stele commemorating the '400th year of his reign', reaching back to the 17th century BC,[50] looks suspiciously like

9.8 This fragment of painted limestone from Egyptian Thebes illustrates two phenomena of increasing significance during the closing centuries of the 2nd millennium BC: the growing penetration of Egypt by foreign cults, in this case that of Levantine Astarte, here depicted nude, probably brandishing a bow, and the rise of horseback riding, initially bareback and hitherto an apparently uncommon practice.

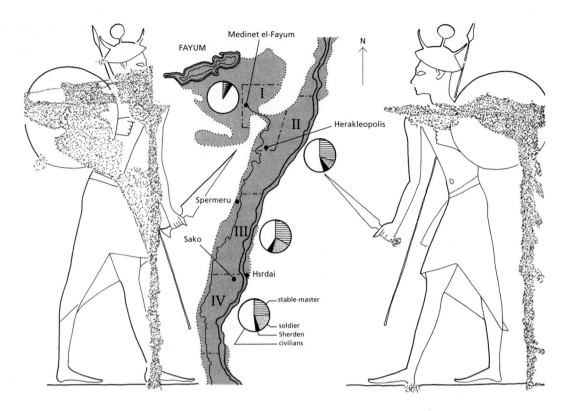

9.9 War and peace for Egypt's Mediterranean mercenaries, in this case Shardana depicted left and right as royal bodyguards but also settled, along with other military personnel, in the Fayum and stretches of the Nile immediately to its south, according to the mid-12th-century BC Wilbour Papyrus.

the nearest thing to a tacit rehabilitation of the Hyksos world-view, if not its dynasty, that a later pharaoh could concede.

Mortal foreigners were abundant in the Delta too, and nowhere more so than in the army. Following the peace after Qadesh, a friendly Hittite unit was stationed at Piramesse, and while foreign mercenaries were nothing new in Egypt, these now started to be recruited from the Mediterranean sphere.[51] Fragments of a papyrus from Amarna depicting soldiers in vaguely Aegean gear may imply that this practice began slightly earlier, but it certainly took off in the 13th century BC.[52] Royal texts and images stereotyped such people with attributes and labels, a few of which will reappear in different contexts later in this chapter, notably the 'Shardana', shown with horned helmets and effective-looking swords, who served as pharaoh's body-guard, fought at Qadesh and by the 12th century BC were renting land in small groups of ten to twenty in the Fayum and further south [**9.9**].[53] In reality, the popu-lation element from the wider Mediterranean was probably a very fluid amalgam of mercenaries, traders and other characters of more varying backgrounds than Egyptian officialdom was able to discern or ready to admit. The picture of Tanis in Wenamun's day, with its multitude of foreign ships coming and going, argues that this permeability survived the broader changes around it.

One other group of people who were increasingly drawn by the magnet of the Delta brings us back, after over a millennium of ignorance, to some of the inhab-itants of Mediterranean Africa west of the Nile. After a quiescent phase in Egyptian texts, incursions by Libyan groups stud the royal annals of the later 13th and 12th

centuries BC [**9.10**].[54] Three points stand out, reading between the Egyptian lines that gloated at wholesale slaughter and the booty recovered from tented encampments, including metal vessels, weapons and linen sent as gifts or acquired from Libyans in service on the Nile. First, among the desert oases a tribal political process had been building up.[55] We can detect this in the archaeology of Wadi Tanezzuft and Wadi al-Ajal, where the availability of water drew people in and encouraged greater attachment to place, as indicated by megalithic tombs and other ceremonial structures.[56] Above the minor lineages, paramount leaders arose, marked out in Egyptian depictions, beyond the usual tattoos, hairstyles, cloaks and penis sheaths, by ostrich plumes and swords. Date palm cultivation, horses and perhaps metalworking appeared in the oases around this time, though the first cereals came slightly later, and the entire families and vast heads of cattle, sheep and goats that Egypt's armies captured argue for a fairly mobile pastoral society.

9.10 High-status Libyans depicted in a late New Kingdom Egyptian artistic idiom, sporting ostrich feathers, animal-hide garments and tattoos. Such depictions and textual references increase sharply towards the end of the 2nd millennium BC.

Egypt had, in short, unwittingly nurtured on its desert periphery one of the earliest known nomadic confederacies, one with a predatory, expansive interest in its sedentary neighbour's resources. Second, despite the gruesome defeats that late New Kingdom pharaohs claimed to have inflicted, Libyan infiltration of the western Delta was successful, permanent and tacitly acknowledged as such by the 12th century BC. Third, these groups were in touch with people from over the sea, presumably thanks to summer encounters similar to those envisaged at Marsa Matruh in Chapter 8. We glimpse this in Egyptian allusions to combined raids from the desert and sea, in a rock carving from Dahkla oasis, showing Libyans with huge genitals swarming over a ship (in point of fact the first seacraft depicted in North Africa west of the Nile) [**9.11**],[57] and in the soon-overrun military response: namely, a line of Ramessid control points along the coast, one at Zawiyet Umm el-Rakham, 320 km (200 miles)

9.11 The pastoral and maritime worlds meet in this vibrant image from Dakhla oasis. In addition to the large vessel, several of the explicitly male figures seem to carry smaller models of boats.

457

west of the Delta, with Canaanite jars and Aegean stirrup jars from passing ships still in the storerooms of its fort, overlain by a layer of Libyan occupation.[58]

If Egypt seems diminished, the loose empire ruled by the pharaohs' arch-rivals and brother-kings in Anatolia had, in the meantime, disintegrated completely. The 13th century BC again began well here, with a slight edge over Egypt at and after Qadesh, and an ambitious extension of the fortifications coupled with copious temple building at Hattusa [**9.12**].[59] But investments in bombast, defence and piety could not avert inroads by less traditional enemies. Just as Egypt unintentionally engendered tribal confederacies beyond its borders, Hatti stimulated 'Kaska' groups in the northern Pontic mountains, one of whose incursions was probably responsible for the eventual sack of Hattusa at the start of the 12th century.[60] By the time Hattusa fell, however, it was half-deserted and its kings departed.[61] More lethal in the long term had proven a major new power based at Assur on the Tigris, which swallowed the remnants of Mitanni, chewed off Hatti's metal-rich southeastern territories and then reached towards the sea.[62] A flurry of contemporary royal rock-monuments imply that internal rivalries and secessions accompanied Hittite political collapse; in the mid-13th century BC one royal prince, Kurunta, was already claiming an independent Great Kingship in Cilicia.[63] For us, the divergent sequels on the plateau and further south are informative. While the plateau reverted to non-urban lifestyles,

9.12 Hattusa's version of a Lion Gate was one of several entrances through the grandiose 13th-century BC extension of the city's defences, but such displays did little to avert the dissolution of central power on the Anatolian plateau within a few generations.

with influxes from the Balkans, southern towns from the Jazira to Tarsus survived and new ones were founded, initially under a Great King at Carchemish, later as independent polities[64] – a strong hint that rule from Hatti's ancestral home in the highlands had been a distorting imposition on its Mediterranean territories and their trading imperatives. Further west, life carried on at Kilise Tepe, above the passage carved by the Göksu River to the sea, and presumably in the fastnesses of Lycia.[65]

The new power based at Assur is known as 'Middle Assyrian' to distinguish it from the Assur of the earlier Anatolian caravan trade and the Neo-Assyrian empire that looms over the end of this chapter and much of the next. Unlike Hatti, it survived as a regional power long enough for its monarch Tiglath-Pileser I (1115–1077 BC)to spring a tribute- and cedar-extracting visit on the Phoenician ports a decade or so before Wenamun's journey.[66] There he indulged in a boat cruise to Arwad and boasted of killing a *nahiru* – almost certainly a sperm whale based in the deeps between Cyprus and the Levant, given this sea-creature's association elsewhere with ivory (Mediterranean scrimshaw, in other words). Even Middle Assyria shrank back to its north Mesopotamian core in the later 11th century, but nonetheless it displayed certain unusual features for its time that may have given it a decisive edge, and look, with hindsight, rather like the germs of a more integrated model of empire building (in short, more the Great Game than happy families).[67] Its letters to Amarna revealed the pushiness of upstart rulers to join the 'great power club', as well as bald rationales at odds with prevailing etiquette – one complained, for instance, that the rewards of gift exchange did not cover the costs of transfer.[68] Moreover, Middle Assyria's presence seems to be more visible on the ground, in restructured settlement patterns and culture, than anything in the domain of Hatti.[69]

The starkest political collapse around the 13th–12th-century transition lay, however, on the fragile edge of the Bronze Age palatial zone, in the Aegean.[70] Here, arguments for continuity versus change are rendered emotive by their implications for the antiquity of what would later be known as Greek civilization. It is undeniable that several strands of earlier ways of doing things were transmitted with varying fidelity across the intervening centuries, including the full spectrum of cereal, olive and vine farming, seafaring practices, elements of religion and the Greek language itself, along with its tradition of oral poetry.[71] In Crete, where palatial organization had been on the wane for some time and social transition was therefore easier to manage, continuities are exceptionally strong, not least in worship at the great cave and mountain shrines of the interior.[72] But it is equally manifest that the final destructions of the palaces at Mycenae, Tiryns, Pylos, Aegean Thebes and elsewhere on either side of 1200 BC represented a real political and economic rupture, entailing territorial dissolution, the extinction of a narrowly palatial literacy (a unique kind of loss at this time) and the dispersal of formerly attached craft specialists. Unlike the picture further east, there were abundant signs of trouble in the Aegean's palatial societies over the 13th century BC, in the form of unremedied destructions, accelerating investments in fortification, hints that prestige symbols were slipping from palatial control, growing penetration of Aegean trading activity by Cypriot interests

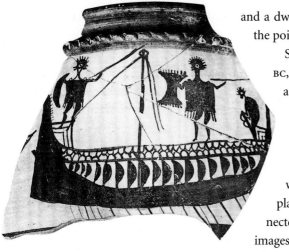

9.13 Part of a post-palatial pot from Kynos in central Greece, showing javelin-wielding warriors with peculiar shields on board on a galley-like ship.

and a dwindling presence of Aegean goods in eastern markets, to the point of virtual disappearance from Egypt.[73]

Several communities flourished during the 12th century BC, at a traditional coastal location in the case of Tiryns, where a modest ruler's hall rose over the ruins of the palace, but more often in new sites that prospered along maritime routes freed up by the demise of palatial power, notably in the Dodecanese, the Cyclades and the tangles of sea-paths around Euboea, Attica and the northeast Peloponnese, as well as the western mainland and Ionian Islands.[74] In such places, a distinct post-palatial culture emerged, still well connected but differently so from its predecessors, with vigorous images of fighting on land and sea on its pottery [**9.13**]. This was surely an age of epic tales involving new kinds of warrior bands, while the memories and physical ruins of fallen citadels were still fresh.[75] Among these was Troy, destroyed twice within little more than a century and probably just one celebrated casualty sung about at the time [PL. XXXVI].[76] The immediately post-palatial Aegean was equally typified by keen flirtation with Adriatic metalwork and Cypriot ironware, and a growing preference for consigning the dead to the flames before the ground, in line with the rise of cremation in southern Europe and its long-standing popularity in Anatolia.[77] However, as the Aegean entered its Iron Age in the 11th century, the reduction in scale and return to backwater status could not be disguised. Signs of external connections more or less dried up for two to three generations, a mere handful of communities (most plausibly Knossos, Athens and Argos) retained any claim to be more than small villages and regional populations slumped by between half and three-quarters, to levels last seen in the 3rd millennium BC.[78] A pollen core taken not far from the former palace of Pylos registers the lowest human impact on the landscape over the last 4000 years.[79] Life among the clusters of thatched houses spread across the Aegean stayed as well attuned as ever to the basic rhythms of the Mediterranean environment, but it was on average briefer than before, and its parallels in terms of practices, values and horizons lay more with the centre and west than the world through which Wenamun wheedled his way further east.[80]

Catastrophe or sea change… into something rich and strange?

The explanation of this horizon of turbulence, and the intriguingly diverse trajectories heading into and out of it, have exercised Mediterranean scholars for over a century. In contrast to earlier transformations, climate played no significant part; only in the 8th century BC may we see an appreciable shift from conditions prevailing since the start of the 2nd millennium. Unfortunately, the wrong kind of message tends to be extracted from the Ugaritic references to grain shipments mentioned in Chapter 8, several of which involved Egyptian consignments dispatched to alleviate dearth in Anatolia, or in another case couched as a demand from Hattusa (which boasted huge granaries) to Ugarit for 450 tonnes to be transported urgently to Ura in Cilicia.[81] As noted already, these snippets, far from indicating that drought was bringing this world to its knees, instead point to a 2nd-millennium BC origin for the practice of shipping grain, often but not always the bountiful, exceptionally reliable harvests of Egypt, in bulk over substantial distances – a further role for sailing ships that would regularly keep later Mediterranean towns and cities alive through lean years. They are, in short, an index of robust precocity, rather than weakness. Equally, there is no evidence that Bronze Age palatial societies brought doom upon themselves by overexploiting the landscapes around them. This transformation began and ended with human actions.

Two basic interpretations have held the stage.[82] The traditional one regards the sum changes we have explored as a straightforward catastrophe, descending out of a clear Late Bronze Age sky to destroy states and empires in their prime, perpetrated by people at or beyond the edges of the east Mediterranean, and over the rubble of which Iron Age societies would painstakingly rebuild.[83] It rests upon a largely unquestioning reading of proclamations by 13th- and early 12th-century BC pharaohs of resounding victories against sea and land assaults on the Delta, several coordinated with Libyan incursions. As ever, the Egyptian version of events deployed ethnic labels and visual stereotypes, principally feathered headgear and horned helmets (which coincidentally also fed visceral phobias in the 19th and 20th centuries AD), to identify a shifting suite of enemies said to come from the vaguely comprehended maritime world to the north and west. Of these, Shardana had confusingly already served Egypt as mercenaries; others, such as Peleset and Shekelesh, were hitherto less familiar, while a few flashed so briefly in and out of the textual limelight that we may well doubt whether the royal annalists really understood whom they were describing. One famously self-glorifying rendition [**9.14**], on Ramesses III's mortuary temple at Medinet Habu in Thebes, portrayed inter-ship

9.14 Detail of the (in)famous depiction of overseas ship-borne raiders defeated in the Nile Delta by the forces of Ramesses III. The ships on both sides by now lack a lower boom, allowing for more flexible navigation, and several of the bird-headed non-Egyptian craft are notably symmetrical from bow to stern.

fighting at the mouth of the Delta around 1179 BC, at the end point of a purported trail of mayhem down the Levant and as far inland as the Euphrates.[84] Add to this the reports from Ugarit's terminal years of sea raids by flotillas of anonymous enemies, its own ship deployments off Lycia, and attacks on Cyprus embarrassingly launched from Ugaritic territory,[85] and a cat's cradle of possibilities becomes woven into a narrative of invasion and migration by that notorious modern invention: 'The Sea Peoples'.[86] Several of the Egyptian namings sound with varying degrees of plausibility as if they might relate to specific parts of the Mediterranean, notably Shardana (Sardinia?), Shekelesh (Sicily?) and Peleset (the Philistine zone, whether as intruders there, or, like Israel at this time, an identity crystallizing in situ to mark it off from its neighbours?). The eye of faith even spots Achaeans and Danaans from the Aegean in the obscure Ekwesh and Denyen. Insofar as any cause for this deluge of war-bands and migrants is offered, the apparent geography of names is typically used to argue that a crisis in the Aegean (itself underexplicated) opened the floodgates there and further west to a surge of gathering momentum.[87]

It is only too easy to spot the weaknesses in this explanation, which at its best may describe real events, without explaining their deeper roots, and at its worst puts a naive trust in the royal propaganda and analytical acumen of an Egypt on the cusp of disintegration itself.[88] But before turning to its alternative, we must acknowledge three crucial respects in which the Sea Peoples model does highlight significant features of the time, if ones better understood in more systemic terms than those preferred by its advocates. First, however fast the bounce-back in favoured regions, the reality of violence, presumably slaughter, dislocation and, in certain cases, longer-lasting demographic and economic diminution, along with a recession of elite power and culture, is too evident in the archaeological record to be wished away; measured in terms of aggregate social development over the short-term, this horizon can indeed plausibly be seen as a major, if temporary, step backwards.[89] Among the permanent social and regional losers were the Aegean palatial elites, plus those parts of their hinterlands most integrated into their political economy, as well as the royal houses of places such as Ugarit. Perceptions of safety plummeted in certain areas, too: in 12th–11th-century Crete over a hundred highland fastnesses emerged, set back from the coast and easily defended.[90] Whether warfare was more lethal than in earlier or later times is hard to gauge, but on a small scale it surely became more endemic, and fighting styles shifted away from massed infantry and chariots to skirmishing with thrown javelins, new slashing swords, small shields and scant body armour, as sported by the ingot-mounted god of Enkomi [**9.4**] and comparable images elsewhere, from Medinet Habu to Mycenae and ultimately further west.[91] It is likely, too, that the breakdown of established authorities with a vested, albeit non-altruistic, interest in securing their human resource led to a sharp rise in opportunistic snatch-and-run slaving, a practice of murky but assuredly already extended ancestry.

Second, this undoubtedly was a time of high mobility. This should come as no surprise, given the growing intensity and range of movement over the 2nd millennium BC and the explosion of both in that to come. The 13th-century BC archives of Hattusa furnish us with suggestive glimpses of people on the move in quite different contexts from the Egyptian battle narratives. One letter complained of 7000 people moving into adjacent Ahhiyawan lands, an index of both official concern to husband people as a source of labour and taxation, and the grass-roots actions that undermined corralling efforts; such movements in fact make good sense of the fluctuations in settlement that are archaeologically attested in parts of the east at this time.[92] In another instance, a picaresque figure by the name of Piyamaradu flitted between west Anatolian courts, marrying off daughters and playing off kings, in a way reminiscent of Amarna-age practice, but also the cosmopolitan elites of the Iron Age.[93] That participants from the central Mediterranean became drawn into this is perfectly plausible, regardless of particular equations with Egyptian ethnonyms. As we will see, parts of the Tyrrhenian and Adriatic were burgeoning at this time and sustained close eastern connections, not least with Cyprus. Components of the new fighting kit, notably the slashing swords traded and copied as far as the Orontes River, developed earliest in central Europe and entered the Mediterranean via the Adriatic, along with distinctive knives and a taste for brooches to fasten now-lost fashions in dress [**9.15**].[94] And although most efforts to link culture change to population movement have focused on attempts to prove Aegean migrations to Cyprus and the Philistine zone, with at best equivocal results, one ceramic trait humbler than the painted pots, on which so much attention has been lavished, may well be more suggestive. This is the appearance of so-called 'barbarian ware', crudely handmade jars, bowls and jugs found in late 13th- and 12th-century BC contexts in the Aegean, Cyprus and the Levant.[95] Though often locally made, their potting technique and style are alien to the east Mediterranean and match those of the Adriatic

9.15 Plot of a selection of the Adriatic and other central Mediterranean material in the eastern part of the basin during the 13th–12th centuries BC. Overall, this describes an axis between northwest Greece, the Gulf of Corinth, southeast Aegean islands, Cyprus and the Levant. (*Below*) handmade burnished ware vessel from Lefkandi.

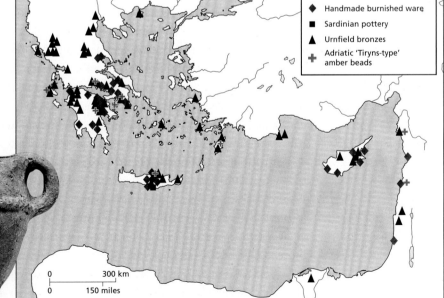

Handmade burnished ware

Sardinian pottery

Urnfield bronzes

Adriatic 'Tiryns-type' amber beads

0   300 km
0   150 miles

and south Italy. This expedient technology, which needed neither wheel nor high-firing kiln, could well correlate with the passage and stop-offs of new actors in the network. The quarrel with the Sea Peoples hypothesis in terms of mobility is not over the likelihood of frequent, multilateral and sometimes cumulatively large-scale relocation, much of it by young men – the most footloose, aggressive and armed element in most populations. It is rather with the over-simplification that results from looking at this process through Egyptian spectacles, into a sequence of ethnically organized, discrete events to be correlated with specific headgear, pots and suchlike, and which possessed the explanatory power to shut down the Bronze Age.

Third, much of this mobility was indeed seaborne. Not all of it, of course; in addition to nomads, donkey caravans and the first dromedaries, families were on the move in ox carts, if we are to believe the depictions at Medinet Habu. And around this time, as already witnessed by Astarte's iconography in Egypt [**9.8**], horses began to be ridden regularly, as sturdier breeds and better harnesses percolated from the steppes north of the Black Sea and Caspian, where mounted warfare, wielding short, powerful bows of perhaps ultimately Chinese design, was already on the rise among nomadic groups.[96] By the 9th century BC Assyria's armies, learning from encounters with such warriors on their non-Mediterranean frontiers, would be taking the lead among sedentary societies in the switch from chariots to cavalry; less dramatically, if surely causally connected, the 1st millennium BC would see new fodder crops – oats, rye and perhaps alfalfa – spread all around the Mediterranean.[97] But by the 13th century BC ships were already a preoccupation everywhere: in texts, in images ranging from official art to motifs on pottery, rock art and graffiti, and increasingly as debris on the seabed.[98] A list of rowers from the last months of Pylos reveals a muster of twelve to twenty ships, as well as personal names that translate as Swiftship, Ship-famous and Fine-harbourer;[99] a letter from Hattusa to Ugarit expressed curiosity about people 'who live on boats';[100] and well before Merenptah and Ramesses III, an inscription from Tanis lamented that 'the unruly Sharden [Shardana] whom no one had ever known how to combat, came boldly sailing in their warships from the midst of the sea, none being able to withstand them'.[101] The last two examples betray a note of baffled imperial unfamiliarity and impotence in the face of people whose life was centred on the ungovernable realm of the sea. We shall return to this promising theme, but first, what of the ships themselves?

The late 2nd millennium BC saw a surge of innovation in maritime technology. Sails lost their lower boom, becoming loose footed, and threaded with 'brail' rigging, so that their shape and angle could be more easily altered, allowing greater versatility in terms of handling to windward and so further freeing up their directions of travel.[102] We do not know where or by whom these breakthroughs were invented, but they first appeared in mid-14th-century images in Egypt and Crete, and by about 1200 BC they were ubiquitous. Some hulls became symmetrically double-prowed, often with avian figureheads, for even greater manoeuvrability at sea or in threading creeks and rivers.[103] Ships became more diverse as well as nimble. One bifurcation, as at least some merchant shipping prioritized greater bulk capacity, led to the evolution of light, slender, many-oared galleys with an ancillary sail, particularly visibly in the Aegean.[104] In effect these were more effective versions of the big canoes of earlier times in the east, and like them ideal for fast sprints (potentially repeated each day to become longer voyages), light cargos and coastal raids; they served, additionally, as platforms for sea-fights and foci of male affiliation.[105] Unlike laden sailing craft, galleys could also draw straight up on the beach. Some sailing vessels appear to have become smaller, too, as the basic technology downscaled to offer cheaper, more risk-friendly options, and maybe hulls light enough to enable haulage across isthmuses, such as that at Corinth which cut out the sea-trek around the Peloponnese. This is borne out by shipwrecks, of which several are known from the decades on either side of 1200 BC. The most illustrious, thanks to its pioneering place in underwater excavation, lies off Cape Gelidonya, on the same coast that had snared its more lavishly laden predecessor at Uluburun.[106] We cannot tell whether the Gelidonya boat was rounded or galley-like, but it was only 10–12 m (33–40 ft) long and carried a mere tonne of metal, made up of standard copper ingots, a little tin, small recycled bronze ingots and scraps for melting down (suggestive of a mobile metalsmith), plus a motley array of pots, scarabs, weaponry and other gear. Tinier still, in today's terms no more than a caique, was a boat that went down off Cape Iria, on its way to or from the Argolid with a humdrum cargo of Cretan stirrup jars, Cypriot pithoi, a cooking pot and diverse other containers.[107] Plenty of such low-profile shipping certainly existed earlier too, beneath the exalted level defined by Uluburun, but its growing prominence and the insights from its cargos offer an alternative, trade-focused perspective on the activities of contemporary seafarers to the obsession with maritime violence reflected in the writing of hostile and fearful land-ruling monarchs.

Equally, mastery of the navigational technique of latitude sailing is implied by this time (if not earlier), by the growing confidence in cutting east–west straight across expanses of open sea to a target on the far side, at this juncture best attested by ultra-long-range links between Cyprus and Sardinia, via Crete and Sicily. In the absence of compasses, this involved observing the position of the pole star, and thereby confirms nocturnal travel and a summertime rhythm to such ventures in order to maximize the views of clear skies.[108] The Mediterranean's alignment and the sequence of major sea crossings within it was a huge advantage in this respect, and the ability to sail along a given latitude therefore the key to direct passage through the basin's maritime heart (though the distance travelled along that line towards a safe anchorage or fatal shore long stayed in the realm of dead reckoning). Latitude sailing brought seafarers from Cyprus straight to southern Crete, and after minor resetting by coastwise travel, from northwest Crete to Malta (a link worth investigation), or from the western Peloponnese to Sicily (the latter recorded in Roman times as a two- to three-day run in good weather), and thence after more resetting to southern Sardinia – a passage later known as the 'route of the isles' and that closely matches the distribution of Cypriot material at this time.[109] The opportunities for interaction denied by this strategic bypassing of intervening coasts were compensated for by the fast, direct conveyance of people, merchandise and news, the relative safety from the natural and human hazards of the littoral zone, and the sometimes convenient ability to disappear into the empty deserts of the sea. Indeed, for all the vast distances, danger of high-sea storms, and sheer durations of absence, such voyages must have seemed more attractive for merchants or envoys on specific long-range missions than a politically entangled, drawn-out and in its own ways equally perilous slog along the coast, à la Wenamun.

Putting together the landlubbers' testimonies, shipwrecks, pictures, pots and navigational inferences, it transpires that 'sea people' had indeed come into being, if de-capitalized for lesser portent, shorn of their cohering definite article, and with the ethnic specificities laid aside: people 'who live on boats' in Hattusa's words, 'nomads of the sea' in a felicitous modern phrase.[110] To characterize such people as 'pirates' is rather like translating their terrestrial equivalents, the Levantine *hapiru*, as brigands; it captures the diversity of freebooting and sometimes predatory maritime lifestyles but imposes a judgment derived from the perspective of those in power who presumed to declare what constituted legality – and nobody, we can recall, had succeeded as yet in ruling the waves. If the term has value, it is in highlighting the oppositional stance to land-based authority, which distinguishes it from the otherwise similar small-boat trading and raiding that flourished all over the largely pre-state Mediterranean of the 3rd millennium BC. Whatever we call them, the rise of such people is a compliment to the scale of contemporary maritime interaction, within which they played an integral role. Indeed, on a global scale 'piracy' has tended to shadow booms in sea traffic, and Braudel observed for the later Mediterranean that peak periods for low-tonnage ships (his 'proletarians of the sea') coincided with phases of expanding trade and liberation from monopolistic, institutionally sponsored, big-ship-dominated control.[111]

Moreover, it is likely that by the late 2nd millennium BC some of the smaller ships and crews circulating in the Mediterranean had only loose, if any, affiliation to a home port or region – one reason why Egypt found them so mercurial.[112] If so, and despite the certainty of low-visibility, localized earlier origins, it is to this phase rather than the age of Amarna and Uluburun (with its directed, spatially segmented long-range traffic between at least broadly defined destinations) that we should date the coming of age of Braudel's *caboteurs*, tramps and 'travelling bazaars',[113] always on the move, their cargo in constant turnover, and often literally melting pots of things bought, sold or otherwise liberated at coastal communities or from other ships along the way. The great merchants of Ugarit seldom had cause to sail as far as the Aegean, but humbler ventures by less tethered crews of mongrel traders, fighters and metalworkers were busy tying ever more of the Mediterranean together by following coasts, short-cutting across open seas, and hauling their craft over isthmuses. If we must seek a point of origin for this essentially rootless, and often route-less activity, in which ships themselves started to become crucibles of new identities, it would be the ever-flourishing non-palatial port-towns of Cyprus, where even gods looked from the waist up like fighting sea people, while they rested their feet on the ultimate emblem of circulating metal.[114]

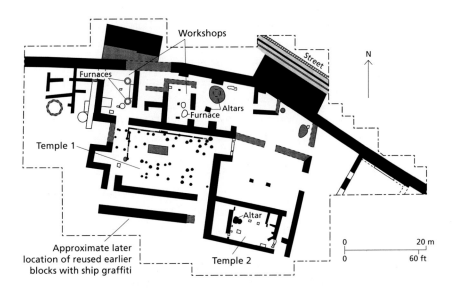

9.16 The imposing complex of temples beside the town wall at Kition in Cyprus underwent repeated modification in terms of architecture and the identity of its cults between its foundation and the later Iron Age. Initially associated with metallurgy, it later developed an explicit link with maritime activity, as evidenced by the ships incised on the long walls. This plan shows the layout at around 1200 BC, with temples, courtyards, altars and attached workshops and furnaces.

We can make one last observation about this shift in maritime life. It would be several centuries before widely connected, ostensibly politically neutral temples and their divinities fully replaced the earlier pretensions of palaces to be the protecting agencies of the world of the sea, but the years around the turn of the 1st millennium BC offer insight into the advance of this process. At the small port of Phylakopi in the Cyclades, the ruler's residence went out of use around 1200 BC but the shrine, with a mixture of Argolic, Cretan and Levantine figurines, survived in the lee of the ruined fortifications.[115] At Tel Nami, right over the sea on the Carmel coast, a place with hoards of scrap metal reminiscent of the Gelidonya cargo, and ship graffiti all over the distinctive rock pinnacle that guided sailors safely in, another well-appointed cult area has been identified.[116] A major temple at Kition (perhaps by now sacred to Astarte) was likewise incised with images of the new shipping,[117] and could be the very location of Wenamun's sanctuary from the mob (thanks to the action of its priestess?); if so, to judge by his tale, it was a kindlier one to seaborne travellers than the royal harbours of Dor and Byblos [**9.16**].

It is a short step from here to the alternative interpretation of the close of the Bronze Age in the east. This, born of dissatisfaction with the explanatory power of the overall Sea Peoples narrative, if not necessarily denying the veracity of some of its constituent elements, envisages the problem in deeper and more structural terms. A useful start is to view the political fragmentation and, in certain regions, economic abatement within the long-term sequence of boom-to-bust cycles through which the Mediterranean's and its neighbours' polities and networks have passed ever since – and by no means the opening round in the east, as previous chapters have shown.[118] Likewise, we might understand the successful infiltrations by central Mediterranean groups in terms of a paradoxical 'advantage of backwardness' that periodically favoured ambitious, less encumbered interests on the peripheral contact zone with an established but ponderous larger system, akin to the situation during the demise of the western Roman empire some 1500 years later.[119] Equally, there is

467

a certain truth to the idea that degrees of interconnection had reached an unfortunate level, sufficient to ensure that trouble could spread with alarming speed, but insufficient to enable an effective common response (even assuming that states of analytical self-awareness would have permitted this, which, as we shall see, is very much open to question).

However, we need something less generic to explain why the Iron Age resurgence would look in crucial respects so radically different from anything seen before. This requires setting aside the rhetoric of catastrophe, and instead thinking of burning palaces as problem-solving and enabling moments for certain kinds of people, the integral birth pangs of a new social and economic order, rather than a disastrous retardant to its emergence.[120] Specifically, it suggests that the crisis marked the tipping point in a long-term shift from the institutionalized, centrally organized command economies of Bronze Age palatial states and proto-empires, and the elaborate royal ideologies and culture that pervaded them, to more flexible, uncentralized and freelance trading practices, largely in the hands of private individuals or consortia, decoupled from the political sphere and explicitly motivated by profit. For the latter, the rewards would ultimately outstrip the risks that came with the destabilization of the rudimentary monitoring and arbitration provided by the great powers and their vassals. Sea people in all their varied guises were in essence as much a consequence, and manifestation, as a root cause of this profound change.

As with most apparently sudden, seismic events, pressure had been building up for some time. By the Amarna age the monumental but cumbersome edifice of the Great Kings and their imitators had established a highly coherent economy at the top, driven by centrally controlled flows of raw materials of natural scarcity, etiquette-ridden exchange of enormous, subtly valued packages of royally manufactured 'gifts' and, in the case of Egypt and Hatti, militarily enforced tribute. Yet alongside this, we glimpsed in the Levant and on Cyprus the emergence, surely from earlier roots, of a more openly mercantile and less risk-averse sector, interested in speed of response to matters of supply and demand, as well as measurable returns. Although this operated in ostensible harmony with the royal palaces, or in their interstices, fundamentally it was in tension with their fixation on legitimacy and social order.[121] We also identified a further challenge to palatial supremacy in the growing legions of sub-elite consumers. Their tastes were only partially met by trickle-down benefits, and elements of certain industries began to address them more directly. After Amarna such trends accelerated. Too much metal was circulating for central authorities to track and control it all, not least as fresh sources and styles of goods seeped in from the central Mediterranean; accumulations of scrap at Gelidonya, Tel Nami and in other hoards attest to increasingly informal means of acquisition and stockpiling, as much as uncertain times.[122] Further technologies slipped palatial control, while subversive new ones arose, of which iron was the most defining; in the longer-term, the freed-up, mobile horizons of many skilled craftworkers that accompanied the waning of palaces was just as significant for Iron Age culture as the triumph of freelance trade.[123] And a final consumer-driven phenomenon, again with earlier stirrings, was

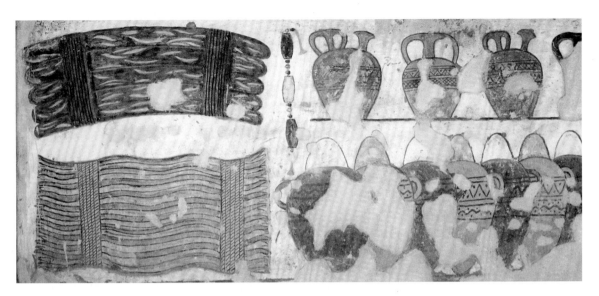

9.17 Stirrup jars portrayed with other sealed containers, stone beads, bundles of wood and cloth in the tomb of Ramesses III in the Valley of the Kings at Thebes. By this time Aegean imports in Egypt had dried up, and the jars were presumably Cypriot or Levantine. The admission of such objects to a royal tomb suggests the declining wealth of Egypt's rulers by this juncture.

the undermining by local substitution of the quasi-monopolies on niche products that certain production centres had established in distant markets – a further twist to the comparative advantages of importation versus local production.[124] A very telling example is the Aegean's painted tableware and unguent containers, which the Argolid had successfully exported to the remainder of the Aegean, the central Mediterranean and mainly sub-elite markets in the east.[125] By various junctures in the late 14th–12th centuries BC most of that in use in all three regions was no longer imported but locally made, and acquiring connotations that sheered away from Aegean associations – a trend that, incidentally, makes such pottery treacherous as a tracer of postulated Aegean migrations [**9.17**].

As the network ballooned, ever larger gaps appeared in the web of royal reach, particularly at sea, and within these, different kinds of people began to flourish. These were at best fleetingly tameable as mercenaries, and soon openly running parts of the operation, from Lukka sea-raiders, *hapiru* and *shashu* during the 14th century BC to 'sea people' in the 13th and 12th centuries. That the latter were regarded as more deadly merely indicates that by the late 13th century BC the ability of the two systems to coexist had been overwhelmed, as new modes of practice penetrated more domains of former royal prerogative or violently intercepted the interactions upon which palaces relied. The crescendo of destruction, dislocation and horror stories penned by the scribes of frantic kings around 1200 BC was but the inevitable collateral.

One strength of this revisionist interpretation is that it explains something that the traditional version cannot, namely why some kinds of people and places survived or even flourished through the crisis, while others dwindled. The Bronze Age world of controlling palatial elites was gone forever from the Mediterranean, but the reality that replaced it was more complicated than a black-and-white contrast between rising merchants and toppled kings, triumphant subalterns and cast-down elites, or dynamic cities and failing empires. A glance into the immediate and longer-term future reveals that plenty of royal houses endured, while differentials of wealth counted as much as ever (even if in some areas on a diminished scale), and empires would soon be back in more rapacious forms. At the heart of the matter, beyond the mayhem, was rather the degree to which those at the top, whoever they were and however they had got there, could extricate themselves from investment in the previous status quo, and decouple from the institutions and pretensions that had hitherto shaped political and economic values: not so much who ruled, as how, on what basis and within what remit.

Translating this into patterns across the east Mediterranean, prior history did much to shape which social groups and regions initially performed most vigorously and abjectly under changing conditions.[126] The buoyant coastal Levant and savvy trader-kings encountered by Wenamun, who both commanded local cedar like any potentate of old and bargained ruthlessly for advantage, emerged out of a long coexistence of royal houses and merchant entrepreneurs in the realms of sea trade, production and exploitation of the arable base. Something similar goes for the ascendancy of Cyprus, where Bronze Age kingship is less visible on the ground than an ebullient urban elite, and where even the messenger dispatched to Amarna had been a merchant rather than a royal envoy. At a more modest level, on Crete the early start to post-palatial society may explain another non-catastrophic transition; indeed, it is interesting to speculate whether Cyprus and Crete's successes in this respect were attributable to their buffered insular status, non-palatial politics, or the shaping of the latter by the former. At those extremities of the Levant that had felt the pressure of outside governance most keenly, the removal of overlords also created fertile ground for new orders to emerge, most clearly in the Philistine and Israelite zones, but maybe in Cilicia too. At a finer grain, lost local details must lie behind the vagaries of fate that, rather unexpectedly, saw the extinction of Ugarit, the source of so much insight into emergent entrepreneurialism, or the notably unruffled history of the Phoenician towns, which may be connected to their prior affiliations with 'sea people' networks in Cyprus and the Aegean.[127] Lastly, the resilience of Middle Assyria until a delayed severe shrinkage in the mid-11th and 10th centuries BC recalls the brash, then untimely realpolitik it had displayed in the Amarna age and its inheritance through Mitanni of several innovative industries in the Jazira, to which we might also add the last-resort option to retrench to a large, shock-absorbing riverine core.

Conversely, the regions hardest hit were those unable or unwilling to adapt to changing circumstances. The crash of the Aegean's last palatial polities was dramatic in its comprehensiveness, but otherwise small beer, given their peripheral location, modest scale and recent formation. Stunted mercantile development allowed them to be penetrated and outflanked along new routes by Cypriot and other freelance traders during the 13th century BC, and weak ideological foundations in contrast to the earlier Minoan palaces left little else to sustain them.[128] More telling was the fate of Hatti and Egypt, two principal architects of the hegemonic, universalizing order of the later 2nd millennium BC, in which both were deeply invested, and both, as we saw in Chapter 8, with weakly evolved mercantile structures. In Ramessid Egypt, an internal trade in copper, corn, utilitarian goods and the laundered proceeds of tomb looting flourished, but Wenamun's naivety illustrates the enduring dependency abroad on tradition rather than a grasp of market operations.[129] It is likely that neither superpower could really diagnose what had hit them and their regulating regime, let alone fix it, and certainly their responses were all too predictable and ineffective.[130] In the case of Hatti, the late rash of temple building in the capital looks like a devout misdirection of resources to keep the gods smiling. Likewise, a treaty with the Levantine vassal state of Amurru to ban trade between Ahhiyawa (whatever peri-Aegean polity this represented) and the Assyrian foe reeks of ponderous royal diplomacy desperately applied to the hopeless goal of managing the quicksilver operations of east Mediterranean trade.[131] In the case of Egypt, we have seen how it demonized the threat in the stereotypical form of foreign attackers whom, in those telling words from Tanis 'no one had ever known how to combat', and over whom its victories seem, in hindsight, if not purely fictional at least superficial.[132] In another 13th-century BC illustration of conceptual mismatch, a chariot-borne pharaoh showed off his might by the visual metaphor of shooting an oxhide ingot (some 5 cm or 2 in. of copper) full of arrows, as if it could be slain like a human opponent – hitting the target but missing the point? Hatti collapsed but Egypt survived, a testimony in its own view to its primordial divine foundation and the strength of kings. Yet in reality, how different were their fates at this time? Both fissioned, and in each the parts that prospered were those closest to the Mediterranean and adjacent trade routes: Carchemish and other successor states in the northern Levant, and in Egypt not the refugium around holy Thebes, but the newly independent dynasties of the Delta.

From our perspective the real victor to emerge from the changes on either side of 1200 BC was the Mediterranean, or more accurately, the hugely dynamic, volatile and potentially destabilizing, power-diffusing cultural and economic practices that people living around and in it were able to promote, once interactions over its surfaces had reached a critical scale and velocity. Terrible as the crisis undoubtedly was in the short term for many people, the Mediterranean emerged from this paroxysm to enjoy over the coming 1500 years its all-time greatest age of growth and relative ascendancy, the formative centuries of which will absorb the rest of this book. It was the Mediterranean that undid the unified Egypt of the New Kingdom, as it had almost succeeded in doing before, via Hyksos Avaris. As the Nile's window on this world, the Delta proved to be a point of access to immense wealth but also an Achilles heel for cherished visions of riverine order. In fact, this corrosive, marine effect could be generalized to encompass the overall eclipse of palace-focused economic, social and political structures, in favour of very differently constituted Iron Age polities. Nothing, incidentally, better belies the argument that centralized food storage at the palaces helped the surrounding populations to survive the Mediterranean's bad years, or better reveals beneath the gilt and heady perfume the parasitic elite-serving nature of these institutions, than the plain truth that Mediterranean economies, demography and agriculture would flourish to unprecedented degrees under quite different political regimes during the Iron Age. In fact, it is intriguing to plot the longevity of palatial institutions as a generic type across the east Mediterranean, as a perspective on how entrenched or epiphenomenal they were in the end. In the Levant, which saw the earliest Mediterranean manifestation at Ebla, this breed of palace lasted for just over a millennium, in the Nile Delta sporadically over a marginally shorter span, following political vicissitudes, on Crete (where the Minoan version was in part insular oddity too) for some six centuries, replaced by non-palatial towns well before 1200 BC, on the Greek mainland for a mere 200 years, and on Cyprus over just as brief a period, or maybe not at all, in the heart of the sea.

The centre becomes central

We have already had a taste of the contemporary central Mediterranean thanks to the presence of its products, technologies and potentially people around eastern shores. It is hard to overstress the novelty of such finds, whose sole earlier parallel lies far back in the late 3rd millennium BC Cetina expansion, which coincided with another phase of disruption. Aegean material had moved west for several centuries, and though by the 13th century BC most painted pots were locally made, Cypriot connections were now pushing to the fore, both in established zones and at fresh points of contact, marked by copper or bronze bowls, mirrors and openwork ritual stands, as well as ingots and pottery.[133] But the reverse flow belies any lazy expectations of a simple westward march of eastern ways of life. As noted earlier, Tyrrhenian or Adriatic brooches, slashing swords and tools percolated into the Aegean and further east, to become naturalized there, and handmade pots of Adriatic tradition were used and sometimes made as far off as the Levant. Moreover, not all pots of central Mediterranean type fell into this 'barbarian ware' category; in addition, bulky Sardinian jars for carrying scrap metal appeared in quantity at the Cretan port of Kommos from 1300 BC, for example.[134] To attribute all this flow to return cargos in eastern ships seems absurd; after all, the Aegean by the 12th century had reverted to a social and economic par with regions to its west, and Cyprus, though more dynamic, was too distant a player in Tyrrhenian and Adriatic waters to account for the entire pattern. Some of this eastward transfer (as well as a continued westward flow of eastern things) was very likely effected by people of central Mediterranean origin, some on the move as mercenaries or settlers, but most as tramping traders or raiders of the kind equally on the rise further east, whose networks they seamlessly expanded into – a web of coastal and island people covering two-thirds of the basin.

The fast-expanding horizons of such central Mediterranean people must have had a lot to do with local uptakes of sailing technology after several centuries of exposure to eastern designs. As noted in Chapter 8, dates for this uptake are hard to pin down; Sardinian boat models dating to the 8th, 9th and possibly 10th centuries BC show masts mounted on rounded, deckless hulls, and later wreck remains

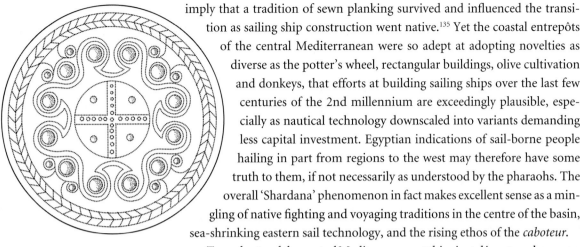

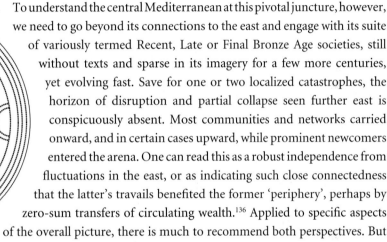

9.18 Two gold discs bearing sun-like motifs of European urnfield design, from Roca Vecchia near the strait of Otranto. Such metalwork introduced a distinctively different aesthetic to the Mediterranean.

imply that a tradition of sewn planking survived and influenced the transition as sailing ship construction went native.[135] Yet the coastal entrepôts of the central Mediterranean were so adept at adopting novelties as diverse as the potter's wheel, rectangular buildings, olive cultivation and donkeys, that efforts at building sailing ships over the last few centuries of the 2nd millennium are exceedingly plausible, especially as nautical technology downscaled into variants demanding less capital investment. Egyptian indications of sail-borne people hailing in part from regions to the west may therefore have some truth to them, if not necessarily as understood by the pharaohs. The overall 'Shardana' phenomenon in fact makes excellent sense as a mingling of native fighting and voyaging traditions in the centre of the basin, sea-shrinking eastern sail technology, and the rising ethos of the *caboteur*.

To understand the central Mediterranean at this pivotal juncture, however, we need to go beyond its connections to the east and engage with its suite of variously termed Recent, Late or Final Bronze Age societies, still without texts and sparse in its imagery for a few more centuries, yet evolving fast. Save for one or two localized catastrophes, the horizon of disruption and partial collapse seen further east is conspicuously absent. Most communities and networks carried onward, and in certain cases upward, while prominent newcomers entered the arena. One can read this as a robust independence from fluctuations in the east, or as indicating such close connectedness that the latter's travails benefited the former 'periphery', perhaps by zero-sum transfers of circulating wealth.[136] Applied to specific aspects of the overall picture, there is much to recommend both perspectives. But a further critical factor, building upon connections established earlier in the millennium, was strengthening ties to temperate Europe, in which the Tyrrhenian and Adriatic played an integral part, and served as a zone of articulation with the rest of the Mediterranean.[137] An enduring bond was forming here that would profoundly shape subsequent history on both sides of the dividing mountains. The dress and battle accoutrements that people of the central Mediterranean flaunted locally and exported east owed a great debt in terms of style, technology and raw metal to a surge in the quantity, standardization and quality of bronze production around and beyond the Alps. In reverse, eastern sheet-bronzeworking applied to body armour spread into Italy and thence further north, as did spoked chariot wheels, which in Italy spawned a fad for wheel-finialled dress-pins. At those points in the Tyrrhenian, Adriatic and Epirus where these worlds intersected, the stresses created by circulation of so much metal within partly clashing prestige-oriented and mercantile frameworks precipitated out in hoards of growing extravagance.[138] Meanwhile, northern crops such as spelt wheat and millet infiltrated parts of Mediterranean Europe,[139] and the urnfield cremation ritual that spread across much of Europe from about 1300 BC swept into north and central Italy.[140] Combined with an older, separate tradition in Anatolia, the burning of the dead gradually gained currency in a basin hitherto largely devoted to inhumation. An urnfield symbolism of boats and birds may find echoes, passed on via the central Mediterranean, among the eastern images of bird-prowed seacraft.[141]

We start our exploration of the central Mediterranean during the last centuries of the 2nd millennium BC in southeast Italy. Here settlements multiplied, and coastal entrepôts that had benefited from earlier regional and medium-range Aegean sea traffic continued to flourish even as the latter faltered, maintaining a wheel-made, commonly painted, potting tradition initially designed to substitute for Aegean imports into the 1st millennium BC, with increasing evolution into local styles.[142] Broglio di Trebisacce, an entrepôt on the Italian instep last visited as a new bridge-head of olive cultivation, peaked in the 12th century BC as a fortified, 10–15-ha (25–37-acre) settlement of perhaps 1000 people, a fifth occupying its inner acropolis.[143] Life there carried on uninterrupted into the 1st millennium BC and the site yields the earliest ironworking in southern Italy. Among the pots from Scoglio del Tonno is a Rhodian stirrup jar dating to the revival of Aegean island trading after the end of the palaces.[144] Roca Vecchia survived a murderous 14th-century sacking to be rebuilt twice, the second time with paved streets and massive wooden buildings, though here the end came before 1000 BC.[145] Such sites boasted abundant metal and plentiful other imports, at Roca Vecchia including hippopotamus tusks and an Aegean seal-stone. The key to this continued prosperity, despite shifting long-range connections, was a role within more enduring, if to us still shadowy, regional circuits. Broglio moved metal, pots and maybe agricultural produce around the Gulf of Taranto.[146] Eastern Apulia engaged across the Strait of Otranto, helping to define an interaction zone that also straddled southern Dalmatia, Albania and western Greece as far as the Ionian Islands, where shared pottery styles outlived the Bronze Age.[147] An additional advantage for communities near Otranto was the strait's role as a staging point for what we shall soon see was a fast-growing traffic into and out of the Adriatic; the hoards at Roca Vecchia contain north Italian metalwork, and even urnfield emblems of sun discs and possibly boats [**9.18**].[148]

In Sicily the picture is in some respects similar. Wealthy tombs, cosmopolitan metalwork and large structures inserted among the roundhouses show that Thapsos more than survived the partial loss of Aegean and Cypriot contacts after 1300 BC, as long-range traders switched to the more direct south-coast route to destinations further west, via Monte Grande and later Cannatello in the vicinity of Agrigento, where jars marked in Cypriot fashion were offloaded.[149] Thapsos was still lived in after 1000 BC, but by this time other communities were retreating inland, as they had done earlier on Crete. At Pantalica, among the craggy limestone gorges of the interior, the cliffs were peppered with thousands of rock-cut tombs containing inhumations, whose local roots as a way of treating the dead expressed a rejection of wider Mediterranean mortuary trends [PL. XXXVII]; the dating of a nine-room structure optimistically identified as a local palace is, however, somewhat dubious.[150] If the Sicilian retreat was a response to locally insecure coastal conditions, the

9.19 Virtual reconstruction of the multi-towered nuraghe at Arrubiu, based on the present ruins plus contemporary models that reveal the appearance of such towers' upperworks. Around such larger complexes accumulated villages of round-houses. Nothing quite like these elaborate structures existed elsewhere in the Mediterranean, underlining Sardinia's strongly indigenous cultural dynamic.

unfortunate islanders of Sicily's satellites had nowhere to hide, though their decline merely continued a trend that had set in a century or two earlier. Many small-island communities were destroyed over the 13th century BC.[151] Lipari's acropolis held on, fortified, ravaged and sharing with the adjacent areas of Sicily and Calabria a distinctive pottery that may reflect localized movements of people, or another modest zone of interaction largely ignored by the wider world.[152] Life continued apparently more uneventfully behind high walls or at promontory forts on Malta and Gozo.[153]

Sardinia was another large island that did exceptionally well at this time, and one of two central Mediterranean regions that saw a sharp rise in long-range contacts. A lack of reliable dates and abundance of recent looting for the only too 'collectable' metal votives that the islanders began to dedicate in profusion conspire to render the precise pace of change frustratingly opaque. But even at a conservative estimate, the island's population was rising fast and the formerly egalitarian nuragic landscape starting to break down.[154] In areas of better farmland, additional towers, now usually with a parapet, were joined to about a quarter of the existing nuraghi, or arose as entirely new constructions [**9.19**]. Huts clustered around such two-, three- or four-towered nuraghi, creating hamlets or small villages out of former farmsteads. For the first time in centuries, open communities of as many as 200 huts reappeared in the uplands, and occasionally on the long sparsely settled plain of Campidano in the south. The larger nuraghi imply greater control over labour, wider influence and the rise of small-scale leaders or lineages, but we remain ignorant as to the details of social structure. This is a pity, as within them must lie part of the explanation for the boom that Sardinia was experiencing. The best guess is extended families or kin groups practising intensified versions of traditional farming; a leather ox-yoke and the rarity of bones and grinding stones at Funtana near Ittireddu could hint that this prominent nuraghe controlled traction teams, and obtained its meat and flour from dependants in or outside the settlement.[155] The decline of earlier giants' tombs, the last of which received fewer, richer burials, together with the foundation of new meeting points in the landscape, both intercommunal shrine buildings and sanctuaries at wells or springs, likewise testify to dual processes of differentiation and integration.[156]

The paradox is that this tower-fixated, still internally obsidian-using society, in many ways so unlike others in the Mediterranean and retaining (unusually under such circumstances) many of its insular idiosyncrasies, also opened up spectacularly to external contacts.[157] The consequences provide the rest of the explanation for its take-off. Much of this had to do with metal. Sardinian ores had been exploited since the 4th millennium BC, but compared to Cyprus we have little idea as to how and by whom, or even which of the available range of copper, silver and possibly a little tin were extracted when.[158] What we do know is that more people, especially in the southwest and centre, now began to work local metal as a kind of cottage industry, as well as to accumulate, hoard and soon lavishly dedicate or display finished products. In addition to hundreds of copper and bronze bun-shaped ingots, oxhide types have been found at over thirty find-spots.[159] Most of the latter were of pure copper whose composition, along with markings on several, point to a Cypriot origin for all save one possibly local alloyed variant. They mainly consist of fragments, some curated for several centuries, which may imply that this eastern commodity had acquired a local social value, and in turn could explain why such ingots were accepted on a copper-rich island despite the fact that analysis of local artifacts shows them to have been seldom used to produce goods. Overall, the Sardinian pattern is impressive, for the other central Mediterranean finds amount to several pieces crammed with a mass of smashed-up local ingots into a jar under one of the largest huts on Lipari, plus singletons from Thapsos, Cannatello and Corsica.[160] Other signs of engagement with Cyprus are plentiful, building on initial contacts in the 14th century BC, swiftly eclipsing those with the Aegean, whose painted pots were soon locally imitated, and lasting until at least the 11th century, if not longer.[161] In the realm of metallurgy, parallels between heavy-duty sledgehammers, tongs and charcoal shovels employed in smelting and smithing on Cyprus (and also tellingly present on the Gelidonya ship), and those adopted on 12th-century Sardinia, demonstrate a startling techno-logical transfer between two copper-producing islands over 2000 km (1250 miles) apart.[162] Cypriot too are scraps of openwork stands, and the earliest scraps of iron.[163] This connection was partly forged by Cypriots and other eastern tramping outfits like that freeze-framed at Gelidonya; one such venture even left its characteristic stone anchor off Sardinia.[164] But Sardinia's immediately preceding seclusion and lack of later maritime reputation has engendered a strange reluctance to propose a complementary role for its own (and other Tyrrhenian) seafarers at this time. In fact, bearing in mind major changes in central Mediterranean shipping technology, the presence of Sardinian jars of the kind used to carry metals at Cannatello in Sicily, Kommos in Crete and, most recently reported, on Cyprus itself,[165] an expanding island population and maybe a 'Shardana equation', it becomes likely that Sardinians did not all simply wait for the Mediterranean to come to them, but that certain groups among them engaged it actively abroad. Prominent among the latter would have been people at major coastal settlements, such as the import-rich nuraghe of Antigori, on the Gulf of Cagliari, facing the seaways east.[166]

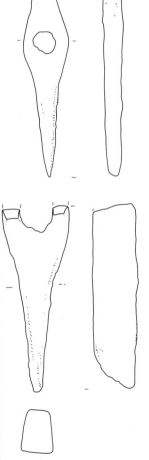

9.20 Pick-shaped ingots, seen here from the Madriolo hoard in northeast Italy, retained a close link between extraction technology and the circulation of metal as a standardized commodity.

The other fast-emerging zone lay at the other end of the central Mediterranean. Again, it was intimately tied to the expansion of sea-routes, in this case a sudden re-engagement of the Adriatic following its retirement after the dissolution of the Cetina connections.[167] The slim signs of earlier Aegean or Cypriot activity in the inner Adriatic makes an even stronger case for the priority of local initiatives than on Sardinia, and we could hazard that it was native groups that plugged the Adriatic back into the Mediterranean current, with eastern sailors slow to master this sub-basin's treacherous ways.[168] As during the Cetina expansion, the demise of a controlling economic regime in the Aegean may have provided the opportunity and incentive. An association with local adoption of distance-shrinking sailing ships is especially tempting, too, in light of something that did *not* happen: this time round, as Adriatic long-range traffic revitalized, the islet of Palagruža played no visible part, presumably because it was needed less, and offered less suitable anchorage, than in the days of canoe traffic.[169] Whatever the processes at work, the beneficiaries of these fresh connections were precisely located, and excluded not only tiny midway islets, but also most of the small hillfort communities of the Dalmatian coast and islands.[170] On the western seaboard, the well-studied Biferno Valley remained equally remote, but a few groups did gain some access to north–south sea traffic, which seems to have favoured this navigationally more friendly, island-free shore, notably around Ancona, where Aegean-type painted pots, northern metalwork and even balance weights have been found.[171]

The real winners lay as close to a source of metals as the sea could take one, as in the Cetina phase, but now further north and on a larger scale. In Chapter 8 we saw that metal production and circulation had been on the rise for some time in and beyond the Alps. Changing conditions in the east Mediterranean seem to have spurred on rather than interrupted this. Acqua Fredda, a smelting site in the southeast Alps, accumulated 800–1000 tonnes of slag.[172] Pick-shaped ingots became a standard in terms of form and weight – indeed one hoard of such objects from Madriolo, in Friuli, weighs about a talent, the eastern measure approximated by one oxhide ingot, and there is a suggestion of a wholesale shift to east Mediterranean weight denominations in the northern Adriatic at this time [**9.20**].[173] Turning to consumption, Austrian military engineers dredging Lake Garda in the 19th century initiated the discovery of Peschiera, a lake village or place of watery sacrifices that has so far yielded some 6000 items of metalwork, of types that travelled the length of Italy and on to Mycenae.[174] In between all this and wider Mediterranean networks lay the people of the eastern Po. The opening up of this area to long-range sea trade roughly coincided with the demise of many of the *terramare* villages that had settled the Po wetlands – the sole 'collapse' outside the east at this time. Whether there was a causal connection is debatable.[175] The delicate ecological management underpinning them must have been vulnerable to even mild fluctuations in the water table, and some such change may lie behind the abandonment of many around 1200 BC, especially south of the main river, where swathes of land would lie fallow for centuries. On the other hand, such villages had been notably egalitarian and poor in long-range goods, so changes in surrounding economic realities could equally have proven too much of a challenge.[176] Either way, the dissolution was a staggered process over the 14th to 12th centuries BC, comprising fall-backs, adaptation (or preferential selection for survival) and consolidation into a late cluster of larger communities along the lower Po and parallel course of the Adige.[177] These 'Valli Grandi Veronesi' villages each held 1000–2000 people, and displayed a readier engagement in trade, with finds of amber and glass and contacts with mining and smelting zones to the north. Some 30 km (20 miles) downstream, on a strand of the Po that has since abandoned it, and closer to the coast than today, a similar community emerged around 1200 BC at Frattesina.[178]

Within a century Frattesina had outpaced its local rivals and emerged as a significant entrepôt – in a sense, given its deltaic location and interstitial role, a miniature version of Avaris. Housing and manufacture spread over 20 ha (50 acres), the latter including production in bronze, iron, ivory, amber and glass, as well as humbler media. Its demonstrably local glass industry was unique outside the east Mediterranean, and it was surely to this time, when the trans-European amber trail was drawn across the east Alpine passes and down to Frattesina, that we can date a legend that sourced amber itself to the rivers flowing into the head of the Adriatic.[179] Imports at Frattesina included Aegean-type painted pots, probably made in southern Italy, ostrich eggshell and an ivory comb with a close match at Enkomi, while metal exports reached southern Italy, Sicily and the Aegean. In contrast to this wave of material imports and technical innovation, the lack of adoption of new crops and animals from further east, in contrast to southeast Italy, can be attributed to the abrupt northward displacement involved, from the heart of the basin straight to its temperate fringe. As with other Mediterranean deltas, much awaits discovery under the mud; Aegean-type pots from Torcello in the Venetian lagoon raise many questions,[180] and it has even been proposed that the feathered headdresses of certain east Mediterranean 'sea people' depictions may have their origins far away in the Veneto.[181]

Frattesina's long arm stretched out in one further direction. Much of central peninsular Italy still consisted of small villages, if ones now converging on similar ways of decorating pots, fashioning metal and consigning the body to the flames, all marks of growing coast-to-coast and north–south communication, and a precursor to the subsequent emergence of the peninsula as an integrated whole, as opposed to two coastal slivers divided by the Apennines.[182] But in Etruria more was afoot. Production from its ores intensified in the 12th century BC, driven by communities in the Colline

Metallifere and the Piombino headland opposite iron-rich, offshore Elba.[183] In the 11th century its smiths became for the first time trendsetters in fancy metalwork; their brooches spread down the coast and were copied in Sicily and Athens. From this time metal from Etruria began to oust southeast Alpine production from primacy in northern Italy, partly thanks to the ability to export pre-alloyed bronze as local tin sources were opened up; pick ingots of bronze rather than copper provided a ready-to-use product straight from the mining zone.[184] These factors interested the later residents of Frattesina, who cultivated close relations across the Apennine passes.

In parallel with this, a development of great future significance was underway. Particularly in the fertile, well-watered south of Etruria, accumulations of huts, the largest covering 15 ha (37 acres), began to coalesce on top of the steep-sided plateaux of volcanic tuff that, along with its limpid crater-lakes, render the landscape of Etruria so unmistakable.[185] From these natural acropoleis they overawed smaller places in their modest hinterlands. We have little idea how these emergent centres operated, though that at Sorgenti della Nova had a few larger buildings, and its animal bones allow us to trace the spread of donkeys up the peninsula.[186] What we do know is that within a few centuries many of these embryonic places would become hubs of well-known Etruscan polities [9.21]. Similar patterns can be detected in the extension of this landscape south of Rome, in the Alban hills, though the Eternal City itself remained a scatter of small villages, one with its cremation cemetery under the Forum Romanum.[187] The rise of Etruria and some of its neighbours still had a long way to go, but these first stirrings after millennia of placid obscurity nonetheless give us pause for

9.21 The emergence of a long-term pattern of settlement in central Italy: (*left*) the locations of major communities by the end of the 2nd millennium BC, seen here with their likely territories, noticeably anticipate the later distribution of Etruscan towns; (*right*) modest early traces of graves among the hills of Rome.

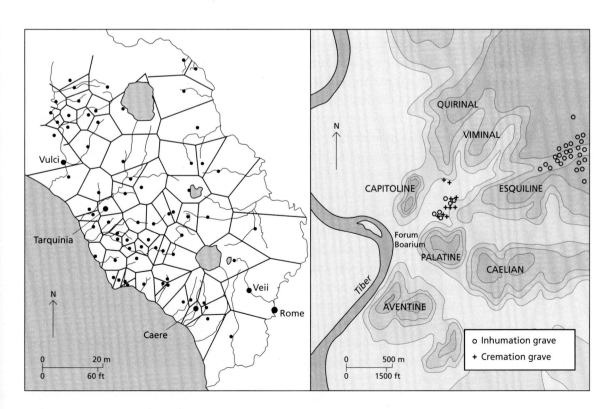

479

9.22 The enduring Corsican megalithic meets the Bronze Age, shortly before it became the Iron Age, in this anthropomorphic menhir at Filitosa sporting a prominent sword.

thought.[188] For one thing, until now, at least on the northern flank of the Mediterranean, the most obvious signs of aggrandizement have mapped onto areas of high environmental risk, and social reactions to such conditions were woven into the rise of elites within them. This may be why Etruria has detained us little before; indeed many other comparably fertile parts of the centre and west continued to happily foster small-scale societies for some time to come. A significant difference in the case of Etruria may have been the combination of agricultural fecundity, and therefore high potential population, with prodigal local metal ores, which is exceptionally rare across the basin as a whole. But even this does not explain the timing of this sleeping giant's awakening. The key to that lay rather in the new scale of connections in and around the central Mediterranean, which gave Etruria's inhabitants the incentive to realize its metallic and agricultural potential. The origins of this may go back to the south Tyrrhenian network of the mid-2nd millennium BC, with its local and Aegean participants, but if so the impact was slight, as virtually no eastern material then entered a possibly resistive Etruria,[189] and even if we assume that its metals flowed into this vortex, we have come across other examples of metalliferous regions that benefited little from supplying their neighbours closer to the pulse of trade. More immediately relevant were circumstances after 1300 BC, with Tyrrhenian maritime activity increasingly focused on Sardinia, a younger hub at the head of the Adriatic enjoying trans-Alpine connections, and, in between, Etruria, astride the Italian peninsula at a time when overland connections across and along it (now donkey-driven?) were on the rise. The emergence of Etruria illustrates the advantage of being in the right place at the right time, Mediterranean-style.

What, by way of contrast, was the picture in the west? While barriers between centre and east were coming down, the west largely remained a series of worlds apart. Corsica is an illustrative gateway, a short crossing from Etruria or Sardinia, in fact on the route connecting them, but resource-poor and still left to its own devices, to judge by the paucity of imports.[190] In a bizarre blend of Neolithic and Bronze Age practices, poorly dated around the millennium's turn, the last menhirs at Palaghju and Filitosa were anthropomorphized and endowed with swords, daggers and helmets with holes for attaching horns [**9.22**]. This last detail, soon to surface on Sardinia, too, reflects a wider European penchant for horned warriors,[191] captured in eastern depictions of sea people, though whether many Corsicans partook of their neighbours' escalating mobility seems doubtful. Beyond, little had changed in southern France since early to mid-millennium, either among the coastal lagoons and plains or in the hills.[192] Such external links as did exist ran eastward, or north, back into the continent, but even urnfield customs were slow to spread here. The Midi tells us something about what Etruria might have stayed like without mining and wider Mediterranean networks.

The central challenge is Iberia. During the 3rd and early 2nd millennia BC this westernmost peninsula of Mediterranean Europe had spawned, in effective solitude, home-grown societies of unusual scale and complexity, if ones also prone to periodic implosion. Up to the end of the 2nd millennium BC that solitude remained only faintly compromised. Ignoring a smattering of pieces that arrived as heirlooms much later, with Phoenician traders, and the continued trickle of amber, vitreous products and suchlike across the Pyrenees, the only signs of wider Mediterranean connections are two Argaric-type swords found on Sardinia some time around mid-millennium, and two 14th–13th-century BC Aegean painted fragments, plus a few other wheel-made pots, found at Llanete de los Moros, well up the Guadalquivir.[193] The latter imply that a few Cypriot, or more plausibly Tyrrhenian, traders had began to probe far to the west, and such exploratory ventures might also explain an oxhide ingot from the sea off Sète in southern France, as well as rumours of others off Formentera.[194] The thread remains, however, very thin, and even advocates employing optimistically vague chronologies find it hard to flesh out the connection more substantially until the start of the new millennium.[195] Regardless, early within that millennium Iberia's enforced aloofness would swiftly be brought to a permanent end, and we would naturally like to know with what points in indigenous cycles of growth or retrenchment, and with what sorts of people, this linking-up moment was due to intersect. Overall, Iberian societies during the late 2nd millennium BC appear to have been smaller-scale, more egalitarian and fragmented than the climaxes of the previous 1500 years, a regional 'bust' whose imminent encounter with a surge in Mediterranean long-range activity was, for all its influence upon the nature of the conjunction, entirely random and so conducive to entertainment of alternative scenarios (for example, how might things have been different if the Argaric florescence had peaked at 1000 BC?).

Compared to earlier periods, however, there is a frustrating dearth of both data and interpretative frameworks. Closest geographically to the centre and east were the Balearics and Catalonia. In the former, local ways of life continued uninterruptedly, with only a modest inflow of materials and ideas.[196] By now these islands constituted a living museum of archaic potting and metalworking techniques. On the inland plateau of Menorca, vaulted funerary *navetas*, yet another island-specific variety of monument, referenced earlier house forms and the dark burial caves still in use along gorges and sea cliffs [**9.23**]. There and on Mallorca, most islanders gathered into villages of a few hundred people, while, in contrast, a thinly inhabited Ibiza became effectively deserted for several centuries from the end of the 2nd millennium, and there may have been no one to succour or slaughter survivors of the putative ingot wreck off nearby Formentera.[197] This mixture of desertion and aggregation shares enough parallels with the slightly earlier patterning among the small central Mediterranean islands to serve as a potential register of otherwise all but invisible incursions into these waters by ships from further east. Back on the mainland, settlement was on the increase in Catalonia and up the Ebro, where modest fortified villages emerged. In the

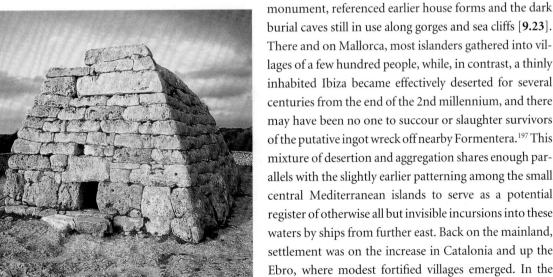

9.23 A new way of death on Menorca: the large funerary *naveta* at Es Tudons, a free-standing monument with two internal storeys.

481

9.24 The Villena hoard is unparalleled in Iberia in terms of its wealth in precious metals, but the precise dating of its contents and deposition remain very hard to determine.

11th century BC, urnfield burial rituals spread across the Pyrenees, but on the coast around Barcelona little changed until well after the start of the millennium.[198] In lands formerly dominated by the Argaric elite, ways of living were also notably lower-key. Only in the under-explored southwest, in the rich farmland of the lower Guadalquivir and the ore-rich Huelva mountains, do we detect tantalizing hints of more substantial activity, starting several centuries earlier.[199] Metal production here was considerable, and may lie behind a tardy rise in tin-bronzes across Iberia. Meanwhile, concentrated settlements were appearing in the lowlands at places, such as Setefilla, that will figure prominently in the centuries to come and the coastal zone, too, grew more active. The comparison with emergent Etruria is striking, although in Iberia evidence of external connections is far more elusive.

We can end this exploration of Iberia on the brink of its engagement with the wider Mediterranean on an appropriately enigmatic, and metallic, note: the Villena hoard [**9.24**].[200] Buried in the uplands behind Alicante, this accumulation comprises 11 gold bowls, 2 gold and 3 silver bottles, 28 gold bracelets, amber beads and a piece of iron set in gold – 10 kg (22 lbs) of metal in all. The styles are Iberian, but the deposition date fluid between the 13th and 8th centuries BC, with the truth most likely midway in between. On the one hand, hoards were still a young phenomenon in Iberia around 1000 BC, and the location, amount of precious metal and inclusion of exotic iron are all surprising. On the other hand, drinking and feasting events involving fine vessels enjoyed an Iberian ancestry going back at least two millennia. Villena's treasure does not quite fit comfortably with the Iberian past as we have seen it unfold, nor does it bear the full marks of the Iron Age world to come; its ambiguities symbolize an obscure moment of endings and new beginnings.

Of mice and Melqart

Nowhere better captures the opening of the new millennium in southern Iberia and the basin in general than the muddy environs of Huelva, today a grey industrial port at the mouth of the Odiel, a small river flowing into the Gulf of Cadiz, the great embayment just beyond Gibraltar where the Guadalquivir meets the Mediterranean Atlantic [**9.26**]. We have traced the rise of metal-extracting societies in the arc of the Sierra Morena that terminates nearby, at Río Tinto, in a fanfare of silver, gold, copper, lead and iron, as well as the growth of communities in the fertile valley of the lower Guadalquivir. But since the 3rd millennium BC we have had little cause

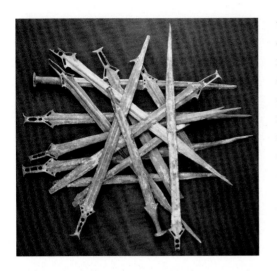

9.25 These long, distinctively hilted swords of west European and Atlantic type are but a small selection of the masses of objects and scrap metal dredged from the river at Huelva in 1923.

9.26 The Gulf of Cadiz and its metalliferous hinterland around the start of the 1st millennium BC, with a deep embayment of the Guadalquivir reaching almost to modern Seville. On the flanks of this lay Huelva (inset) and the offshore Cadiz archipelago.

to consider the coast. That now changes decisively, as an emblematic pair of discoveries at Huelva bear out. The first was made in 1923, when a river dredger struck a haul of over 400 bronzes, including nearly 200 swords, daggers and spearheads made at various points along the Atlantic facade between Ireland and western France, a few old east and central Mediterranean brooches, fragments of a 9th-century helmet from Mesopotamia and further pieces of unidentified scrap [9.25].[201] Radiocarbon dates from accompanying wood suggest that this mass of metal went to its watery grave some time between 950 and 850 BC. We can only speculate whether an accident befell a laden ship in the roadstead or, as so often along the northern flank of the Mediterranean (although less so in this sector of it), the objects were ritually sacrificed at a flashpoint of encounter and trade. Either way, this trove affirms the re-emergence of the Gulf of Cadiz as a trade hub, not least of Atlantic connections in abeyance since the end of the Copper Age.

The second, and for our purposes even more startling, discovery was made a few years ago during rescue work under the town of Huelva itself, 2.5 m (8 ft) below the water table and hidden by a layer of sterile mud.[202] Up from this depth, unfortunately in no stratified sequence, came a mass of pottery and other finds dating to the 9th, and in a few cases perhaps 10th, century BC. Over half the pots were

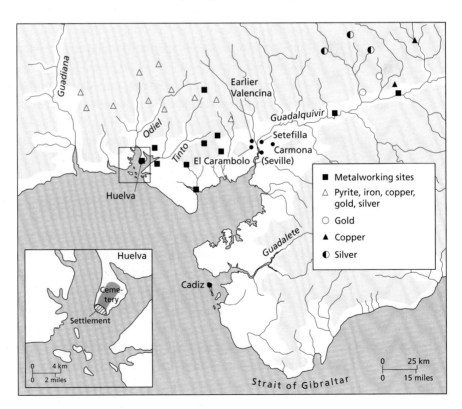

handmade Iberian products, with a few imports from Sardinia and Italy, but some 40 per cent were wheel-made plates, bowls, jugs and amphorae of completely different pedigree, with precise matches on the Phoenician coast of the central Levant [**9.27**]. Many of the latter seem to have been locally manufactured. Add to this several Cypriot and Aegean imported pots, abundant traces of silver, copper, iron and lead production, further residues from the working of ivory, ostrich eggshell, horn, wood and stone, Levantine balance weights and scraps of graffiti, as well as grape seeds, murex shells, amphora-bottled preserved fish and possible ship timbers, and the hallmarks of an east Mediterranean inrush and fusion with the far west become unmistakable.

0   10 cm

0   4 in.

9.27 These visually unprepossessing scraps of a lamp and various amphorae rims are among the thousands of pieces of pottery, many closely related to types documented at Tyre and elsewhere, that date the first Phoenician contacts at Huelva.

So how did this dramatic link-up along the entire length of the Mediterranean come to be? One set of answers lies far to the east in the opening two centuries of the 1st millennium BC, among the commercial port-towns of the central Levant, the sector of that coast best placed to dominate maritime trade when external intervention to the north and south was in abeyance, and blessed with an exceptionally smooth transition from the 2nd millennium BC. 'Phoenicia', as we noted earlier, is an externally imposed and not unproblematic flag of ancient and modern convenience. As it rockets to pan-Mediterranean prominence we encounter other impediments to balanced assessment, not least an archaeology hampered by subsequent overbuild and recent civil war, and surviving texts that, with the total loss of local records written on papyrus, reflect the views of outsiders fired up by varied cocktails of envy, fear and scorn, from Israelite prophets, Assyrian kings and Greek poets to later Roman authors traumatized by the existential threat they faced from Phoenicia's Punic offspring.[203] To savour the extent of the loss, we know that a precocious regional 'history' was composed around 1000 BC at Byblos, translated in Roman times and then vanished save for excerpts in other writings. From what does survive in the east, Phoenician communities look like evolving descendants of those mercantile, maritime, middleman societies that had transformed and helped to bring down the east Mediterranean Bronze Age – Iron Age Ugarits blended with latter-day sea people. Kings survived, but their palaces were shorn of economic centrality, their authority shared with the priests of powerful shrines and families of merchant oligarchs (described with palpable *Schadenfreude* by the prophet Isaiah after their humbling as 'princes…among the honourable of the earth'),[204] and most of their income derived from taxing the bonanza of independent wealth creation by subjects great and small, augmented by the proceeds of royal enterprises.[205] Profits were obtained from playing differential values and demands across an ever-widening

9.28 This long early Phoenician alphabetical inscription excoriated any violators of the grave and sarcophagus of Ahiram, lord of Byblos, several generations after the Zakar-Baal with whom Wenamun sparred.

9.29 The little island town of Arwad, off the Syrian coast opposite modern Tartus, overlies its larger and partially inundated Phoenician predecessor, but retains many of the features of an offshore trading community.

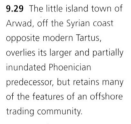

stage, with the role of capital reserves becoming more crucial as voyages grew longer and returns more delayed.[206] In material terms, too, there were links to the Canaanite past, in the emphasis on fine, often purple-dyed woollen cloth, ornate gold, silver and bronze vessels, perfumed oil flasks, exquisitely carved ivories, small faience items, and a flexible alphabetical script, as well as the indifference to decoration on the distinctive monochrome red pots used at home and now starting to show up as far away as the Gulf of Cadiz.[207] 'Phoenicians', in short, were as much the creations as creators of the evolving culture and networks associated with them.

As Wenamun discovered, by the 11th century the little harbour of Byblos was overshadowed as a shipping centre by Sidon, although one of Zakar-Baal's successors managed a last fling around 1000 BC, commissioning a great sarcophagus whose warning to any defiling enemy provides our longest known early alphabetical text [**9.28**].[208] New coring at Sidon has identified the residues of silver-lead working in harbour sediments of about this date.[209] Other minor central Levantine ports would continue to flourish, from Arwad [**9.29**] to Atlit in modern Israel, which boasts the best-preserved of the artificial quays and moles that over a few centuries on either side of 1000 BC became such a prominent feature of the Levantine coast,

9.30 Tyre from the air in the 1930s, before the expansion of modern housing. Flecks of foam mark the extent of the reef and once larger islet. The pale sandy isthmus is a late feature that has accumulated along the breakwater created by Alexander the Great's siege-works.

and unmistakable signs of investment in shipping.[210] Over the course of the 10th century BC Sidon in turn ceded its primacy to the island of Tyre (originally *Tzur*, meaning 'rock' or 'fortress'), a place occupied on and off since the 3rd millennium BC, but until now of secondary rank [**9.30**].[211] This shift may reflect the benefits of a natural sea-moat as terrestrial powers began from time to time (as we shall see) to stalk the Levant again.

Today it is almost impossible to envision this grandest, richest city of the Iron Age Mediterranean, whose wondrous beauty the Old Testament likened to a ship at sea. Its revealingly Mediterranean foundation myth evoked islets spliced together by the roots of an olive tree, but the remains of the original 50-plus ha (or more than 125 acres) of elongated reef are today densely inhabited, permitting only a single archaeological trench to reach bedrock, and in the south entire neighbourhoods and a harbour have been drowned by subsidence and the currents later diverted by Alexander the Great's siege mole, now a sandy isthmus that still robs Tyre of its insular dignity. Something of the technical feats and maritime facilities can be gauged from the sediments in cores that affirm the remodelling of Tyre's northern anchorage into a 6-ha (15-acre) *cothon*, or artificial basin,[212] tucked within the urban perimeter reputedly beside a marketplace, and linked by canal to the lost southern port to ensure shelter under shifting weather conditions, and to segregate overseas from local (soon to include naval) shipping. But the crenellated fortifications and round-arched gates famously portrayed in Assyrian images are gone [**9.31**; PL. XXXIX],[213] as

is the elaborate apparatus for provision of fresh water, and all but a few foundations of the houses for the 15,000–20,000 residents likely to have been crammed onto the island, which probably started to exhibit the high-rise tendencies seen in certain later Punic towns (still more people lived in suburbs on the opposite mainland, where the city's surprisingly plainly furnished cemeteries were also situated).[214] Maybe the greatest loss, however, is the fabled temple of Melqart, a new, specifically Tyrian god of cyclic fertility, the sea and overseas ventures, with a good claim to be true lord of the city – indeed the etymology of his name connotes precisely this.[215] Tyrian ideology conceived of his temple as a reference point for the entire Mediterranean. Its twin gold and emerald columns were balanced at the other end of the basin first by the rocks of Gibraltar and Ceuta, known as the Pillars of Melqart long before their Hellenizing reattribution to Herakles (their earliest known names, Calpe and Abyla, may also be Phoenician rather than indigenous), and later by inscribed bronze columns at a matching temple to the god at Cadiz, between the strait itself and Huelva.

Phoenician trade initially operated mainly within the old Bronze Age triangle described by the Levantine coast plus its Cypriot offset, and the access this gave to resources further afield.[216] Tyre was particularly astute at exploiting openings in the shifting map of regional power. For reasons we shall come to, the Bible's account of a 10th-century BC exchange between Tyre and Solomonic Jerusalem, of craftsmen and luxuries in return for grain, copper and Arabian exotics, building up to joint Red Sea voyages, though consonant with ambitious newcomers' efforts to snatch at the trade routes, may sadly need to be relegated to the realm of myth.[217] But similar strategies are attested a century later by Phoenician ivories in northern Israel, plus amphorae from Israel at Tyre, and before this Phoenician traders were active in the Gulf of İskenderun (the gateway to metal-rich Anatolia), on Cyprus, at Aleppo and as far east as the Euphrates. As during the preceding two millennia, some of this activity, whether specifically Tyrian, generically Phoenician or even more broadly Levantine, spilled over into the Aegean, with only the briefest caesura following the last 2nd-millennium imports, and now occasionally a little further into eastern Calabria.[218] Much of the evidence comes from Crete, notably an inscribed bronze bowl as well as possible resident eastern metalworkers at Knossos, and Phoenician pottery at a new shrine constructed at Kommos, the now reactivating anchorage on the trunk route along the island's south coast. But other contact points and way stations became enmeshed too. On Rhodes, the southeast entry-point to the Aegean, oil flasks made on Cyprus after Phoenician models were imported and themselves imitated. Prominent communities at Athens in silver-rich Attica and Lefkandi on the Euripos strait obtained small faience trinkets, metal goods (some battered antiques perhaps recently purloined from graves further east) and other Levantine or Egyptian-style imports. Unconfirmed legends hint at further calls at Kythera, later regarded as sacred to Cypro-Phoenician Aphrodite, as well as metal-rich Thasos in the north, and even the isthmus of Corinth. In all probability, it was encounters with such foreign traders within the Aegean, rather than first-hand knowledge of central Levantine realities, that initially stimulated local people in the former zone to identify such visitors, and their ways of conducting themselves, as 'Phoenician'.[219]

This attention to the traditional aspects of early Phoenician trade embeds it in longer-term Levantine practices, but also throws into sharp relief two less familiar elements whose impact began to be felt in widely separate parts of the basin. The first was a more hegemonic, sometimes territorial attitude towards geographies of trade, especially on the part of Tyre, by which political actions abroad became more overtly dictated by economic logics than in the Amarna correspondence. The spur lay in the rare circumstance of a flourishing mercantile Levant that was temporarily fairly free

9.31 (*opposite*) The temple of Melqart, with its twin pillars, rises commandingly above the battlements in this early rendering by Layard, the excavator of Nineveh, of a 7th-century BC Assyrian depiction of Tyre from the palace of Sennacherib. It shows the flight of the Tyrian king with his fleet across the sea to Cyprus.

from external intervention. This became apparent in formalized rules of engagement with terrestrial neighbours, as witnessed by Tyre's 9th-century absorption of the lands of Sidon, and its alliances with agriculturally well-endowed polities in Israel, which created grain-supplying peripheries and freed up the Phoenician zone to concentrate on lucrative cash crops and craft goods.[220] This particular house of cards would not long outlive the return of land-based superpowers to the Levant, but as an early attempt to construct a partly dispersed, discontinuous hinterland (something more formal than a web of trading connections), it was a foretaste of a strategy that Mediterranean cities on the sea would later take to far more ambitious levels.[221]

Another aspect of this approach proved more immediately durable and equally influential subsequently. It entailed the implantation at a distance of affiliate enclaves or entire communities at points that had usually already arisen as de facto nodes within a given network. This practice found parallels as far back as Uruk expansion, Egypt's recurrent interventions in the Levant and early Assur's merchant diaspora in Anatolia, but so far it had not lain within the scope of Levantine maritime polities. A first effort around the Bay of Akko may slightly pre-date Tyrian ascendancy; it gave access to the Jezreel corridor and Galilee, but its location rendered it as vulnerable as the remaining mainland edifice.[222] More promising was the 9th-century BC restoration of a by now waning Kition into a vibrant town with refurbished temples (one to Astarte, another rededicated to Melqart) and strong ties of political dependency to Tyre.[223] The overlying modern city of Larnaca takes its Greek name from sarcophagi in the orderly vaulted tombs of the Phoenician necropolis, from which come some of the earliest Phoenician inscriptions on Cyprus.[224] Considering this island's only recently diminished primacy in sea trade, plus earlier close ties between Cyprus and the central Levant, it is likely that Cypriot activities contributed a lot to the definition and spread of what are normally considered 'Phoenician' ways of doing things. Seen in this light, the regime change and urban regeneration at Kition probably reflected Tyre's drive to assert a more strictly defined ascendancy at this vital staging post for shipping, and to exclude rivals from copper mines in the nearby polity of Tamassos, which, in another innovative move, Kition would soon purchase. Kition may have been rebranded as *Qarthadasht*, or 'New Town', in the 9th century, the earliest of many new or refashioned communities, several of which bore this name in one language or another, that would soon spring up around the basin in the context of expanding mercantile initiatives.[225]

This takes us to the second decisive novelty associated with early Phoenician trade: its direct and swiftly substantial extension into and just beyond the westernmost reaches of the Mediterranean (as witnessed at Huelva), accompanied, as we shall see, by an equally striking degree of residential tenacity there on the part of certain of its agents. When this began has long been disputed. The dates around 1100 BC favoured by Classical authors could reflect sporadic visitors of unknown affiliation, like those who brought a few Aegean pots to the Guadalquivir, or the Cypriot traders whose latest visits to Sardinia are so hard to pinpoint chronologically, but they also line up suspiciously neatly with putative dispersals after the fall of

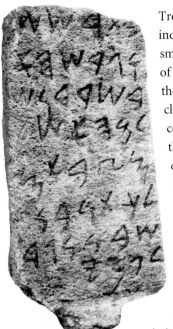

9.32 Battered stele with Phoenician writing found in secondary use built into a local house near Nora in southern Sardinia. Readings of the inscription vary, as do beliefs as to its precise dating, but it has every chance of being the earliest monumental inscription to survive in the western half of the Mediterranean, and certainly makes the first local identification of Sardinia.

9.33 The topography of early Carthage is heavily obscured by later building and substantial shore-line changes, with even the presently visible harbours of much later Punic date. This map presents the current estimate of the extent of the early town, spreading down from its acropolis (Byrsa), as well as the locations of tombs, industrial zone and tophet, and the likely initial harbour area.

Troy, a popular interpretative trope in Classical writing.[226] Several archaeological indicators along the way are likewise less than secure. For instance, a bronze smiting god, perhaps a shipboard deity, netted off Sciacca in southwest Sicily, is of so generic a type that it could equally well mark the passage of Cypriot ships at the end of the previous millennium.[227] Until very recently, the first solid evidence clustered in the 8th century BC, which was indeed a boom time for Phoenician connections (see Chapter 10). But the new finds at Huelva decisively breach this barrier, demonstrating substantial, structured contacts at least a century earlier. Confirmation of this new 9th-century horizon is starting to accumulate, especially concerning its later decades. Cadiz, by the 8th century already thriving at the opposite end of the gulf, was always a promising place to look, and in the last few years a deep trench under the modern city has discovered flimsy 9th-century structures and Phoenician pottery sandwiched between the sand-dunes and later housing.[228] On the peninsula of Nora in ore-rich southern Sardinia a stele found long ago, inscribed with Phoenician writing typical of the late 9th century, alluded to the god Pumay, as well as 'Sardinia' (the first proof of the island's name) and *tarshish*, a slippery term whose associations include metal refining [**9.32**].[229] Trumpeting and sanctifying of a landfall betrays a marking urge on the part of early Phoenician navigators, further affirmed by the naming of Melqart's pillars at Gibraltar. Other traces of a presence at this time also exist, in the form of Phoenician and a few closely dated Aegean pots at Sant'Imbenia in the northwest, a site to which we shall shortly return.[230]

Yet the African elephant in the drawing room is another *Qarthadasht*, better known as Carthage [**9.33**]. Earlier stopovers must be suspected on this indented

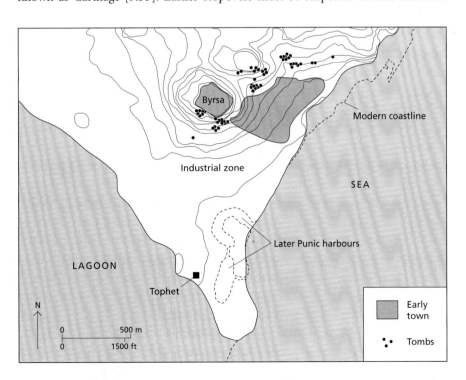

sector of North African coast, so ideally located to shelter and sponsor traffic through and around the conduit of the Sicilian narrows, and a natural destination for return shipping from Iberia, before this skirted the great navigational marker of the Cape Bon peninsula (in particular the Ras ed-Drek, or Cape Fear) and then cut out to sea to avoid the shoals and currents of the Gulf of Sirte. A Bronze Age stirrup jar is said to come from the vicinity of Carthage, as are early scraps of indigenous pottery, both reminiscent of Marsa Matruh and other late 2nd-millennium BC landfalls on the coast west of the Nile Delta, while Utica, 40 km (25 miles) up the coast and then an islet in a river mouth, was thought in Classical times to have preceded its illustrious neighbour, a claim admittedly yet to be verified archaeologically.[231] Regardless, we are surprisingly well informed about the circumstances and patently institutional nature of Carthage's foundation, thanks to a relatively credible ancient testimony that drew on the now lost annals of Tyre, and recent excavation of the earliest phases, between the beach sand and later constructions topped off by fiery Roman destruction debris.

The story began at Tyre with a factional dispute that drove Elissa, better known as Dido and both sister of King Pumayyaton (Greek Pygmalion) and wife of Melqart's high priest, to flee with members of the city's elite, picking up Astarte's priest at Kition en route. Wenamun would have recognized this blend of gods, priests, powerful women, wealth and Cyprus, and the association with Kition underscores the parallels between both these ambitious, politically motivated, elite-led takeovers of key points for maritime communications.[232] The legend's sequel in North Africa is harder to evaluate, but archaeology is unequivocal concerning the venture's ambition, and consequently the likelihood of prior familiarity with the location and its potential. Early Carthage covered 25–30 ha (60–75 acres) on and around the hill of Byrsa, which remained the citadel until the bitter end.[233] It had one or more harbours, since lost to the alluviation that has pushed the coast out half a kilometre; the harbours visible today date back no further than the battle fleets of the Punic wars. Almost from the outset its houses were imposing, stone-built structures, soon separated by a circuit wall from an industrial zone for ironworking, purple dyeing and potting. To all intents and purposes this was a Levantine merchant town transposed, at this stage the only firm candidate for urban status west of Cyprus and the Nile Delta. The main uncertainty hovers, frustratingly, over precisely when it was founded. Ancient tradition was adamant in favour of 814–813 BC, a date supported by radiocarbon against the early 8th-century BC alternative proposed on the basis of pots of Aegean type found among local and numerous Levantine, Iberian and Sardinian imported wares – one dimension of another discrepancy between ceramic and scientific dating that haunts the opening centuries of the new millennium to the tune of fifty to seventy-five years.[234]

Clearly, the burning question is what encouraged this extraordinary surge of connectivity that, after millennia of expert seafaring, finally brought the extremities of the Mediterranean face to face? It goes without saying that it signalled the definitive arrival of sail-driven shipping in the far west (and soon beyond, for a Mediterranean-type ship graffito carved on a rock face in Atlantic Galicia, and another recently identified on a potsherd from the Scilly Isles, off western Cornwall, fall within the same time span).[235] But there is no indication of breakthroughs in nautical technology or navigation since those of the late 2nd millennium BC. Pre-existing techniques brought the ends of the basin together, and principally latitude sailing of the kind that had already enabled seafarers to cover two-thirds of the basin to Sardinia, now extended to complete the route of the isles with a 400-km (250-mile) traverse to the Balearics, after which the mainland coasts converged on Gibraltar.

In the absence of any further technical revolution in shipping, the commonest answer in recent years to the causative conundrum has been Assyria.[236] However odd this suggestion might seem at first glance, there is certainly some truth to it. Chapter 7 established that the late 4th- and 3rd-millennium BC explosion of maritime trade in the Levant owed more to a new, intermediate world-systemic position between emergent Mesopotamia and Egypt, coupled with their demands for timber, oil and wine, than to the intrinsically rather unpropitious configuration of the Levantine coast. Ever since, the Levant had supplied its giant neighbours and profited by their expanding markets, while lately avoiding the recession that afflicted both. By the start of the 9th century, Assyria was on the fast track to resurgence in a fresh, expansive guise, so much so that one Neo-Assyrian king, Assurnasirpal II (883–859 BC), lubricated the opening of his vast capital at Nimrud with 10,000 skins of wine (in this instance probably non-Mediterranean).[237] This swelling consumer zone undoubtedly stimulated Phoenician and other mercantile economies. Yet this in itself does not explain why, in contrast to Cypriot long-range sea trade under not dissimilar circumstances in the 14th and 13th centuries BC, direct and well-structured interactions now flashed so readily to the furthest end of the basin. The more specific argument that rapacious Assyrian tribute demands goaded Phoenician cities to reach far to the west to obtain precious metals, especially silver, that could appease or buy resistance to their overlords has much to recommend it for the 8th and 7th centuries, by which time Assyria was reconstituted as an empire of unprecedented size, territorial integration and extractive power. But in the 9th century the reforms that would effect this had yet to translate into reality away from their Mesopotamian epicentre.[238] At the time when the first Levantine links to the far west were being forged, Assyria's own records reveal its raids and tribute to have been still essentially Bronze Age in flavour. Lists and images reel off an eclectic mixture of bullion, metal vessels, precious stones, textiles, ivory, animal skins and birds, all sporadic in incidence, with decadal gaps during the 9th century BC and a lengthier interruption at the start of the 8th century.[239] Costly as they certainly were for those at the receiving end, such extractions were no worse than prosperous cities on the sea had endured at the hands of Egypt and Hatti.

The final connecting up of the basin's seas instead requires a complementary, and more specifically Mediterranean, analytical framework. The regular appearance of Levantine shipping in the far west, as eastern markets began to expand again, was in fact primarily a capillary result of something missing during the 2nd-millennium BC climax, namely an established indigenous network of interaction and knowledge across the western as well as central Mediterranean seas. As we saw earlier, an uptake

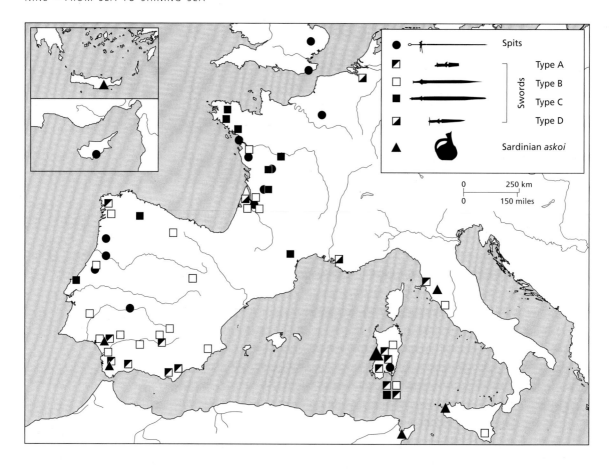

9.34 A strikingly new feature of the early 1st-millennium BC Mediterranean is its penetration by metalwork of Atlantic derivation, much of it moving within the ambit of western France, Iberia and the Tyrrhenian Sea, but with outlying parallels as far apart as the British Isles and Cyprus. Concentrations in Sardinia, and of Sardinian jug-like pottery *askoi* abroad, point to a central role for this island in long-range connections.

of sailing ships in the central Mediterranean during the terminal centuries of the 2nd millennium BC triggered there a surge in mobility and sea trade. It took some time for the isolation of the west to be broken down, but by the onset of the 1st millennium BC avidly metal-consuming Tyrrhenian communities were effecting the intake of southwest Iberia, where sailing skills they had learned from encounters with eastern sailors were in turn swiftly taken up. West and central Mediterranean metal goods and styles started to appear in each others' home areas in some quantity, hinting at both trade and travelling metalworkers.[240] At first Iberia was simply a stupendously metal-rich terminus for Tyrrhenian sailors, but as the submerged metal finds off Huelva so richly attest, it soon began to serve as a meeting point, too, with Atlantic traders drawn south by demand for their distinctive lead-rich bronzes, as well as Breton and Cornish tin.[241] Links between the Tyrrhenian and Atlantic can be traced through the spread of the latter's slashing swords well past Huelva and other Iberian find-spots to Sardinia, Sicily and Etruria, while roasting spits of a kind familiar in southeast England, western France and Atlantic Iberia ended up not just in Sardinia but also (in a further sign of eastward connections) at Amathus in Cyprus [**9.34**].[242] To complement this, a Sicilian axe arrived at Hengistbury Head on the English Channel.[243] The west and parts of the centre had been here once before, in a more attenuated manner, during the 3rd millennium BC, when the Atlantic, Iberian

9.35 Three Sardinian *bronzetti*, metal figurines made by the lost-wax technique of eastern origin. They form part of a wider Mediterranean horizon of small anthropomorphic bronzes, but remain highly local to the island in their style, attributes and preoccupations. On the left, a male authority figure with cape, staff and dagger, at centre a horned-helmeted archer, and an extravagantly armed, possibly mythic figure on the right. Many such figurines date to the 8th or 7th centuries BC, but increasingly early dates are also documented.

and French beaker interactions reached Sardinia and western Sicily, but at that stage sailing ships, the Mediterranean's real distance-shrinkers, were still confined to the Levant. This time the two meshed, and the result was electric. The 'fantastic cauldron of expanding cultures and commerces' that one astute ancient historian has described in the later Iron Age central and western Mediterranean was, we now realize, already simmering by the opening centuries of the 1st millennium BC.[244]

These connections were essentially multidirectional, but one of the hubs was certainly Sardinia, which faced all the participants, and where nuragic societies now reached their peak of hierarchical organization.[245] Few new nuraghi were being built by this time, but on the best land, especially in the south and northwest, the largest multi-towered examples had gathered over a hundred huts of client families into their shadow, and ruled small chiefdoms spread over a few hundred kilometres of tower-studded landscape. Tensions emanating from this accentuation of inequalities were mediated by ritual places of congregation, 'meeting huts' and finely built sacred wells, where the offerings included votive swords, model nuraghi and numerous bronze human figures cast by the lost-wax technique, the westward spread of which was initiated now or earlier by encounters with eastern smiths and widely travelled smiting gods. These *bronzetti* are a further index of social aspirations and anxieties, offering a gallery of mainly male role models, notably warriors with horned helmets, shields, swords or bows, and cloaked leaders or other elders with knobbly staffs [**9.35**].[246] As before, how power in Sardinia was practised is uncertain, but metals certainly mattered. The 9th-century BC destruction of a substantial nuraghe at Funtana-Ittireddu, just 10 km (6 miles) from the nearest ores, trapped 20 kg (45 lbs) of copper and bronze ingots and scrap, some of them curated fragments of oxhide type, as well as moulds and crucibles.[247] Niches in the central room, where a bench encircled a large hearth, held a piece of by now possibly local iron and two boat models. Bronze votives of masted boats, often with a stag or bull figurehead [PL. XL], point to an additional avenue for wealth accumulation through off-island ventures that, given Sardinia's location, must often have entailed voyages of some magnitude.[248] Two massive bronze bull heads recovered from a later shrine in the Balearics may once have adorned the prows of Sardinian vessels, and there are reports of a wreck off the island's west coast, facing the wild seaway to Iberia.[249] Moreover, Sardinian traders were equally drawn to northern Etruria, another metalliferous land, where their pots and bronzes, including figurines and boats, pre-date east Mediterranean objects in hoards, shrines and burials.[250] All this should make us receptive to the idea that a scatter of jug-like Sardinian pots in Iberia, Sicily, Crete and North Africa, which overlaps with Phoenician arrivals in the centre and west, may reflect the passage of Sardinian as well as eastern traders.[251]

In other words, there was no pristine Phoenician 'discovery' of the west save in terms of prior eastern ignorance. The opening up of the western seaways and tidal reaches of the Atlantic was initiated by central and then west Mediterranean sea-farers, albeit using adapted eastern nautical technology and at moderate degrees of intensity compared to Levantine activities at this time. The first eastern traders slotted into such networks and presumably benefited from local experience, possi-bly even local pilots. The scale of their activities there would in turn soon begin to transform the west, as we shall see in the following chapter, but despite the bril-liance routinely attributed to Phoenician seafarers (the pole star itself would later be named *Phoinike*), and without diminishing the prowess of their trans-Mediterranean ventures, the fact is that here, as elsewhere, they were inheritors to a mass of orally transmitted, often mythologically encoded, knowledge about navigational condi-tions and hazards, memorized sequences of land- and seamarks, significant places, people and resources, and the intricacies of local custom, all accumulated by a mul-titude of anonymous Mediterranean seafarers.

This raises the spectre that not everything we call 'Phoenician' in the centre and west had much to do with sailors from the east. If a fuzzy term even in the Levant and Cyprus, it could surely disguise a still more varied gallery of actors in and beyond the Tyrrhenian, united by maritime trading practices as much as origin (in this sense 'Phoenicians' were true descendants of 'sea people').[252] Such entangled realities are forcefully illustrated at Sant'Imbenia on Sardinia, where imitations were soon made of the early Phoenician imports, among them amphorae used within the settlement to amass metal ingots but also traded to Carthage and Iberia, arguably as wine containers – all in a community of probably mixed origins but basically nuragic layout.[253] None of this is to deny the presence of long-haul traders from the Levant, and among them from an early stage organized, strategically minded Tyrian missions, but it does make us reflect that for every such ship other crews were also at sea, hailing from different harbours and intent on journeys of differing duration and destination. And this in turn urges us to revise how we conceptualize Mediterranean networks during the opening centuries of the new millennium. Too often these are reduced to a bold Tyrian arrow thrusting west, with occasional spurs to north and south. Yet even this arterial route was stitched together from segments that could be equally travelled as self-contained journeys and all around swirled myriad other connections, especially on the northern flank, where islanders and coastal people had been forging self-sustaining webs of interaction within each sub-basin, and con-nective ones between them, for millennia. Precisely who participated in which is ultimately less interesting, and certainly far less fathomable, than the convergent, reticulate maritime world that their integration created.

More follows on the men, women and gods swept up in this, but we can end our exploration of the connecting process itself with the exemplary and only recently recognized tale of a far tinier traveller [**9.36**].[254] House mice have so far figured twice

9.36 The 1st-millennium BC advent of the house mouse in the central and western Mediterranean, after a halting maritime expansion from its initial home in the Fertile Crescent, as documented by bone and tooth identifications, including that of one unfortunate mouse that sank with the Uluburun ship.

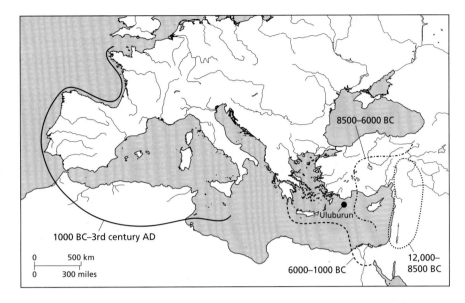

in this history, and each time as stowaways: once on the canoes bringing fresh injections to early farming on Cyprus, the second time in the guise of a north Levantine creature unlucky enough to have boarded the Uluburun ship. Until the 1st millennium BC, the house mouse was exclusively a denizen of the east, first in the sedentary, cereal-using Natufian and Neolithic Levant, where its lifestyle evolved, later spreading to Cyprus, Anatolia and northeast Africa with farming, and further afield in the 2nd millennium BC thanks to trade, as we know from that drowned in transit at Uluburun and others at the Cretan port of Kommos. The modern DNA of Cypriot mice is exceptionally diverse, as befits an island that became a maritime crossroads. Meanwhile, the native woodmouse reigned supreme in the centre and west, with the house mouse entirely absent long after suitable living conditions and canoe travel had become established there. Then, over a few centuries in the early to mid-1st millennium BC, as direct maritime links consolidated and sea traffic surged west of Italy, house mice stormed into Corsica, France, the Balearics, Spain and the western Maghreb. A few giant leaps and innumerable little scuttles: a fitting enough metaphor for the diverse tempos of Mediterranean mobility.

The rest of the Mediterranean

Mice apart, how did other areas of the basin begin to be drawn in during the first two centuries of the new millennium? We can start at the two poles of the Mediterranean, both tugged between the central sea and regions beyond, and generating later legends of fabulous wealth that veil earlier realities. The veils hang most heavily over Iberia, where the lower Guadalquivir and surroundings of Huelva must be the original behind Tartessos, a fabled argentiferous equivalent to El Dorado according to later Classical authors, and for us a key interface between connecting seas, abundant metals and rich farmland.[255] The lavish elites that thrived here from the 8th century

9.37 Ships, some with mast and rigging, painted in the Laja Alta rockshelter, including one apparently berthed in a square, artificial harbour basin.

are well known, but not their predecessors, the other participants in the earliest interactions at Huelva. A little to the east of Gibraltar, recent excavations at Alcorrín of a large, well-fortified late 9th-century settlement founded on new ground 2.5 km (1.5 miles) inland, give us some idea of what we might expect.[256] One trend that is clear, however, is the growing engagement in maritime trade on the part of coastal communities, which must have done much to prepare indigenous people for the undoubted shock of dealing with Levantine traders armed with the full mercantile paraphernalia and practices of the east Mediterranean. From the Gulf of Cadiz to the mouth of the Tagus (where west Iberian alluvial gold and other metals reached the sea), walled settlements articulated sea traffic along the coast, and stone carvings further inland displayed warriors with notched shields of a widespread Atlantic type.[257] That other eyes were turned seaward is indicated by the images at Laja Alta, one of several painted caves along routes into the uplands behind Gibraltar, where local people depicted ships fitted out with oars or mast and sail, one apparently berthed in a rectangular *cothon* harbour [**9.37**].[258]

If parts of mainland Iberia were busily opening up to seaborne visitors, people in the Balearics may well have considered their involuntary inclusion in the route of the isles, after an unbroken history of impoverished lifestyles and egalitarian values, as a more dubious honour, as well they might, so close to the end point of provision-depleting voyages and devoid of desirable resources save their own bodies, food and goods. A few hoards of off-island metalwork began to appear here, as elsewhere, but the lack of early eastern finds indicates that Levantine sailors regarded these islands at best as navigational markers and watering places.[259] Darker temptations on the part of passing crews may, however, be implied by the accelerating nucleation of dwellings, increases in weaponry and the first experimental towers, refined over the 9th century BC into fortified *talayots*, hundreds of which would sprout up on Mallorca and Menorca in the coming centuries, attracting accretions of houses rather like the Sardinian nuraghi (to which, at a modest level, they bear a generic resemblance, possibly attributable to inter-island contacts) [**9.38**]. Menorca, the first landfall for arrivals from further east, showed symptoms of social disruption in its funerary practices. The great *navetas* went out of use, and at Cova des Carritx, a

Something new, something old in the early 1st-millennium BC Balearics:

9.38 (*above*) Tower-like *talayots* became an increasingly frequent settlement type on the larger islands.

9.39 (*right*) On Menorca, the burial and ritual cave of Cova des Carritx went out of use, leaving an extraordinary range of human and other organic remains on its floors.

60-m- (200-ft-) long winding tunnel used as a burial cave since 1400 BC, exceptional preservation conditions capture a crescendo of ritual action, including deposition of wooden and horn tubes holding red-dyed human hair, followed by closure around 800 BC [**9.39**].²⁶⁰ In the Balearics we sense for one of the first times, if far from the last, that Mediterranean integration might have its losers as well as winners.

Winners and losers were increasingly obvious, too, around the opposite pole of Phoenician enterprise. We have already visited Cyprus, where Tyre's dependency at Kition extended its grip on copper and cult, triggering a combination of resistance and emulation among the island's other by now rather minor polities.²⁶¹ Meanwhile, the New Kingdom's disintegration offered elites in the Nile Delta a formal political independence to match the free hand they had exercised for some time. Many of the resultant dynasts bore Libyan names, a mark of the extent to which former pastoralists had became naturalized, joining earlier Levantine and other infiltrators to enrich a cosmopolitan society not noticeably perturbed by the breakdown of political and cosmic order on the Nile (Delta-based rulers in fact shakily re-established the former for a few generations from the middle of the 10th century BC).²⁶² The capital of this latest manifestation of a peri-Mediterranean Egypt lay at Tanis, whose monuments cannibalized carved blocks, statues and obelisks on a grand scale from its predecessors, not least the now-decaying city of Piramesse, and whose authority over other Delta towns decidedly waned over time.²⁶³

9.40 Egyptian royal statue inscribed for the late 10th-century BC pharaoh Osorkon I and sent to Byblos in revival of ancient relations, where an alphabetical inscription then dedicated it to Ba'alat Gebal, the divine Lady of Byblos.

The Delta was still agriculturally wealthy and populous enough to sponsor rare displays of old-style Egyptian power. In about 925 BC the Libyan-named pharaoh Sheshonq launched a one-off raid into the Levant to disrupt emergent polities there, a traumatic enough event to be remembered in the Bible's Book of Kings, and to leave a patch of detectable devastation north of Jerusalem.²⁶⁴ Spoils from this may have contributed to the gold and silver that his successor, Osorkon, claimed to have distributed to Egypt's gods. But the reality was less unambiguously rosy; the necropolis of Tanis contains Egypt's largest collection of intact royal burials [PL. XLI], but their wealth pales beside that of even the relatively minor Tutankhamun, and like the city's other monuments, they pressed earlier masterpieces into service.²⁶⁵ One chronic problem was penetration by Phoenician interests of the production and marketing of metalwork, glazed goods and wine.²⁶⁶ Alongside Wenamun's testimony to the Delta potentates' dependence on Levantine shipping, this plots a growing stranglehold by overseas merchants on trade with the mouth of the Nile. Add to this a longer-term decline in the export appeal of fine white

9.41 The largest surviving parts of the stele erected by Hazael of Damascus at the town of Dan, today in northern Israel. Written in Aramaic, it trumpets a victory for this expanding central Levantine polity over the House of David.

Egyptian linen against Phoenician purple-dyed woollen garments,[267] and the Delta's options for wealth generation were slipping perilously back to the agricultural. When Osorkon had his name inscribed on a possibly older royal bust that he then dispatched to Byblos in emulation of Old Kingdom practices [**9.40**], it can have done nothing to disguise the true reversal of relations with the Phoenician coast.[268]

Closer still to the Phoenician heartland, by the 9th century BC medium-sized polities had carved up the Levantine interior. In the north, several are characterized as 'Aramaean', a term as nebulous as the earlier 'Amorite' and similarly associated with infiltration by pastoralists in the aftermath of political disruption, though in this case their language would gradually become a new Levantine lingua franca, still in use at the time of Christ.[269] A few encouraged small entrepôts with well-stuffed warehouses on a coast dominated by Tyre; one serving the Amuq plain from the mouth of the Orontes was named Al-Mina ('the port') by Sir Leonard Woolley and was possibly known as *karum* ('quay', or 'trading area') in antiquity too.[270] Such polities flourished between the Mediterranean and the as yet more economically stimulating rather than politically lethal proximity of Assyria. Control over early percolation of Arabian incense and myrrh through the Levantine valleys on its way to the sea or Mesopotamia, which is registered by ritually pure chalk altars for its burning, gave a fresh boost to the interior routes, especially in the south.[271] Otherwise, free from effective external overlords, the pattern resembled the early 2nd-millennium heyday of Levantine polities, with thriving, if now somewhat smaller, towns girdled by extensive, populous and well-integrated hinterlands – what we might regard as the default setting for a Levant largely left to its own devices. Among the most prominent examples was Damascus, which under its ruler Hazael reduced the Philistine polities by land as surely as Tyrian trade was undermining them from the sea. Hazael is better known, however, for the monument erected at Tel Dan after his invasion of Galilee, in whose chilling inscription he exulted at his killing of a king of the house of David, the first contemporary proof of that line's existence [**9.41**].[272]

More elusive, not least in Jerusalem itself, is the United Monarchy that the Old Testament claims that this house's founder and his son, Solomon, established in the 10th century BC.[273] David's youth as a *hapiru* in the hills, and the struggles against the Philistine polities, fit the picture around the turn of the millennium fairly well, but the Solomonic apogee has proven archaeologically harder to authenticate, fuelling suspicions that a more modest reality was subsequently gilded, during codification of the Old Testament's narrative and divine message several centuries later. Opinion remains sharply divided, and aside from Biblical veracity, what rides on the debate for us is whether one major south Levantine polity (arguably the greatest of its day, albeit at a very low Mediterranean ebb in these terms) arose decisively before the wider 9th-century horizon, stimulated by Tyre and maritime trade on the Red

9.42 Intricately carved ivory panel of a winged sphinx, the original cherubim, almost certainly of Phoenician manufacture and once part of the furniture in the royal palace of Samaria, one of several centres that received quantities of such superb craftsmanship, variably as gifts, trade goods or tribute.

and Mediterranean seas.[274] Regardless, as in the Bronze Age, in the 9th century the hill country underwent a dual political process, creating Israel in the north and Judah in the south. Once again, the rugged south stayed initially aloof while the pace was made by the wetter north, whose suitability for orchard crops is strikingly illustrated at its capital of Samaria by sherds incised with tax receipts for oil and wine, written in early alphabetic Hebrew but referring to individuals with Canaanite and Baal-cognate names.[275] Unlike the Bronze Age, however, this time the northern upland polity also managed to snatch the grain-lands of Galilee and trail-heads towards the coast and Damascus, forming a significant presence in the Levant, and a major Phoenician satellite. This kingdom, lamented and abominated in the Old Testament, yet from our viewpoint thoroughly emblematic of the Mediterranean, with its mongrel populace, tolerance of religious diversity, aesthetic attraction to fancy ivories [**9.42**], voluted column capitals, new fashions in palace design and grand stables for chariot horses (memories of which, the sceptics assert, would later be redeployed to retrospectively drape 'Solomonic' majesty), was the Israel of the formidable King Ahab and his calumnied yet clearly dynamic consort Jezebel, daughter of none other than Ithobaal, lord of Tyre.

Between the Levant and Iberia, the regions first drawn into the web were ones where a prior tradition of indigenous networks and wider engagement was most easily tapped: mainly the Aegean and Tyrrhenian, with the latter's superior access to trans-Mediterranean routes, and the spectrum of Tuscan and Sardinian metals, gradually relegating its Adriatic neighbour to a self-contained internal circuit. Among tracers of this, at Huelva, Carthage, on Sardinia, mainland Italy and Sicily, were a few Aegean pots, still targeting their modest, if distinctive, niche of the fancily painted drinking or serving vessel.[276] Such cups and plates, often swathed in concentric semicircles, also appeared in the east, mainly around Tyre but at smaller places too, like Al-Mina, as well as on Cyprus. The focus of this style was the large offshore island of Euboea, part of a dense intra-Aegean circuit extending to Macedonia, the Cyclades and the Anatolian coast. Here lay Lefkandi, since the late 11th century BC an attractor of Levantine goods and, from the 10th century, boasting a gigantically elongated hall swiftly converted into a prominent funeral mound, in the shafts beneath which were interred a cremation with warrior gear and the gold-bedecked body of a woman, both accompanied by slightly battered eastern antiques, plus four slaughtered horses [**9.43**].[277] Around the painted pots and this spectacular, if crude, death-ritual circles an unhelpfully polarized debate over the relative priorities of Aegean and eastern mariners, muddied by Classicists intent on exploring the non-question as to how interested 'early Greeks' were in

9.43 Lefkandi on the island of Euboea: (a) reconstruction of the large yet notably simple Toumba building; (b) the cremation urn with iron weaponry, richly adorned female inhumation and sacrificed horse burials beneath its main hall; (c) pendant found on the inhumed women, suspending a damaged Near Eastern gold disc dating to the early 2nd millennium BC; (d) selection of small faience goods of Phoenician style found in later associated burials.

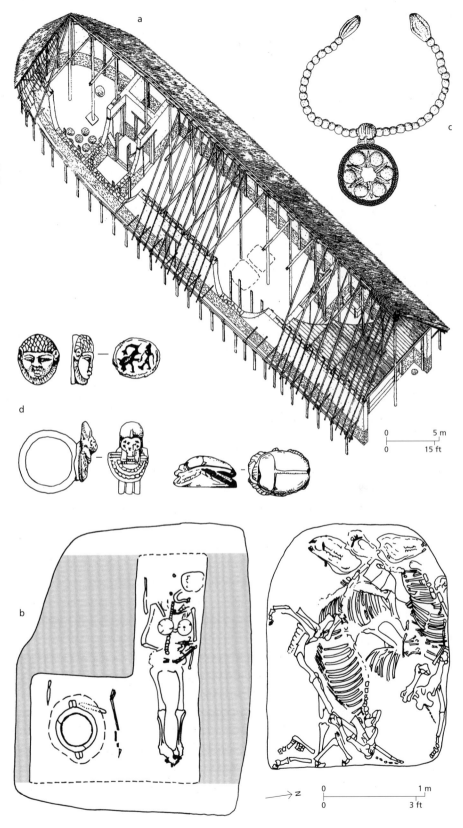

the sea and trade.[278] Many Aegean people had palpably been very interested in both for millennia and it is highly unlikely that the inhabitants of a region so conducive to maritime interaction ever lost that, especially at a place like Lefkandi, so well positioned for local traffic across the nearby strait dividing it from the mainland, and medium-range shipping up and down a sheltered corridor of communication between the south and north Aegean. There is no reason why some internal traffic should not have extended coastwise via the long-known sea-paths out from the Aegean towards the Levant and Italy, much as some far-flung Sardinian pots may denote Tyrrhenian seafarers. However, it is equally perverse to ignore the wider penetration of Levantine traders at this time. In Lefkandi's tombs, in addition to numerous finds of small, east Mediterranean trinkets, one 9th-century BC weapon-rich cremation was accompanied by a set of Levantine balance weights and imported oil flasks, raising the tantalizing possibility of a resident easterner,[279] and the concentration of Aegean pots around Tyre is suggestive concerning the origins of the shipping in which they travelled east. Neither a Hellenocentrism rooted in the Classics nor a bracingly revisionist, but equally simplifying, new phoenico-centric orthodoxy do justice to the fluid realities that were coming into being in the Aegean and more widely across the Mediterranean.

Further parallels between the Aegean and Tyrrhenian can be seen in scales of social organization over the first two centuries of the 1st millennium BC, a reminder of how deeply the former had diverged since the Bronze Age from the uninterruptedly urban world of the Levant, Cyprus and Egypt. Admittedly, in the Aegean we know far too little about the eastern seaboard save at Bayraklı in the outskirts of Izmir, a walled settlement of a few hectares in the 9th century BC.[280] But from the Peloponnese to Macedonia, including hotspots of exploration under Athens and Argos, and against a variegated backdrop of pottery and burial styles, even the largest communities of a thousand or so people still comprised loose clusters of houses and cemeteries with no vestiges of urban structure.[281] People such as the honorand at Lefkandi, or groups of similar elites at larger sites, claimed exalted status in their funerals, but the durability of their power is questionable. They were known later as *basileis*, a term derived from Linear B Greek for a minor authority, and which even after decapitation of everything higher up the social pyramid remained closer to 'big man' than the connotations of royalty it later assumed.[282] The terminal flavour of the funerary display at Lefkandi, notwithstanding associated burials in the vicinity for several generations, suggests that power was too unstable to pass on.[283] Most was probably acquired by prowess in war (a burial on the Areopagus hill of Athens, with weapons and horse gear, comes to mind), exploitation of surplus (another Athenian grave contained a model granary), trade (recall the balance weights at Lefkandi) or social arbitration – all reminiscent of the Aegean some 1500 years earlier. Maybe because of this instability, certain shrines began to adopt a more socially and regionally integrative role. Remains of offerings, rituals and feasts appeared at Olympia and Isthmia, the Peloponnese's land-bridge, a foretaste of things to come.[284] Only on Crete can a faster pace towards the revival of larger communities be discerned, notably at Knossos and, as in the previous time round, perhaps not unconnected to the island's close ties with Levantine activities – the myth of Zeus in the form of a bull abducting Europa, a princess of Sidon, from flowery meadows contains an intriguing blend of Minoan and Iron Age elements.[285]

Within an equally culturally diverse Italian peninsula, larger settlements were if anything slightly better attested, most strongly in Etruria but also among the Alban hills and at Rome, whose location where a coastal route switched inland to the lowest ford on the Tiber, avoiding the coastal marshes, became more advantageous as routes along the peninsula solidified.[286] Further south, similar trends can be seen at Capua and elsewhere in a Campania closely linked to Etruria, while in the deep south and in Sicily settlements continued to expand inland behind an enduring if thinned chain of coastal centres.[287] But under a magnifying glass the patterns become less solid. Most of the foci in Etruria were by now extensive natural hillforts crowning sheer-sided tuff plateaux, but despite influxes of people only a small proportion was actually covered by huts, in widely spaced clusters that might explain the plural forms of the names of several of the cities that later arose here. Thus the 175 ha (430 acres) of tableland at Veii reduced to 17–25 ha (40–60 acres) of habitation, and at Cerveteri (Roman Caere) eight patches of dwellings were scattered over a slightly larger plateau, suggesting in both cases populations in the low thousands.[288] Small communities dotted the farmland of Etruria, presumably typically acknowledging the authority of their nearest large neighbour.[289] Arguably, two cultural trajectories were emerging in central Italy. One manipulated the new, widely shared cremation ritual to forge social bonds and define through ornate weapons, armour, other goods and subsequent religious observances at the cemetery a vocabulary of expression for rising leaders and their retinues.[290] Further hints of a rising elite just to the south include a big, repeatedly

9.44 Cremation became widespread across Mediterranean Europe, but the pottery hut urns of early 1st-millennium BC Italy, sometimes sporting exuberant roof decoration, comprised a distinctive form of receptacle and perhaps hint that contemporary houses were more impressive than their architectural remains reveal. This 9th-century BC example is from Vetulonia in northern Etruria.

9.45 This fancy 9th-century BC bronze brooch, adorned with twisted gold wire, is a good indication of the swiftly rising skills of Italian metalsmiths and the popularity within the peninsula of distinctive forms of jewelry and dress, both highly emblematic ways of expressing cultural identity.

rebuilt hut of unknown purpose on the Palatine in Rome, rather more splendid than suggested by its floorplan (which is just a quarter the size of the hall at Lefkandi), to judge by models of such structures, whose roofs were crowned by huge animals and human figures [**9.44**].[291] A few rich burials, perhaps of the heads of descent groups, stand out in the cemetery of a smaller community at Osteria dell'Osa, a little to the east.[292] Finally, and unevenly, a central Mediterranean elite was becoming entrenched enough to attain archaeological visibility. The other trajectory continued the careering take-off of metallurgy, especially in Etruria, whose smiths now led the central and west Mediterranean in terms of innovation and skill [**9.45**; PL. XXXVIII].[293] North Etrurian centres arose amidst the coastal mines at Populonia and Vetulonia, rather different from those in the fertile south and tied in to a metal-focused belt extending via Elba to Sardinia.[294] Many of their products fed into the inflating funerary sphere, and an unknown proportion already went abroad, if Etruria's regular capture of Levantine and Aegean imports, and the links between north Etruria and Sardinia, are anything to go by. But huge amounts of metal also started to be accumulated as capital and occasionally these survive in recycling hoards, one of which at Bologna, midway between the Alpine and Tuscan mines, contained 15,000 pieces.[295]

This exploration of the Mediterranean during the opening two centuries of the 1st millennium BC has focused on those areas that initiated or, for better or worse, were swiftly drawn into the dramatic extension of connections. But what of those that remained worlds apart, in several cases for some time to come? The energetic thrust of north Adriatic trading centres into the wider Mediterranean after 1200 BC, taking advantage of altered conditions in and beyond the Aegean, was throttled a few centuries later by better-placed Tyrrhenian competition. Frattesina declined over the 9th century and was abandoned by its end.[296] On both the Italian and Dalmatian flanks, communities stayed limited in size and connections, with marked levels of internecine conflict reflected in the spread of hillforts into parts of Italy later known as Samnite territory, and a high frequency of burials with weapons.[297] Adriatic interconnections remained largely internal, although lumps of amber percolated inland to the southern Balkans, and interaction over the Strait of Otranto continued unbroken, which helps to explain the strong linguistic affinities detectable on both sides a few centuries later.[298] Another excluded sector, far from the route of the isles and lacking much tradition of maritime trade, was southern France, Catalonia, northwest Italy and Corsica.[299] In the central part of this area, however, parts of Languedoc that communicated with western France along the Aude River started to exhibit faint social stirrings in a horizon of hoards and fortified villages, such as Carsac (Carcassonne), overlooking its rich plain and river crossing, and Cayla de Mailhac. Perhaps traders in the Atlantic goods so popular in the central and west Mediterranean had started to explore an overland route into the basin with the potential to short-circuit the long haul around the Iberian peninsula. Mediterranean Africa remained almost entirely excluded, too, with so far only a pinprick of impact on life outside its immediate vicinity on the part of Carthage, still an alien marine organism clinging to the shore. The momentous implications for both the Mediterranean and Africa of such implants along their shared coast lay in the future.

For all these exceptions, the implications and consequences for Mediterranean history of the link-up revealed at Huelva possess a strategic quality that should not be lost in the detail. Previously, the sea had been becoming central to sizeable fragments of the Mediterranean basin; now it began to form the centre of the whole. In aggregate distance (if not uninterrupted crossings) the first voyages along the length of the basin stand out as global record-breakers for their time, and the culmination of a late 2nd-millennium BC outstripping of Pacific performances that had held the lead since seagoing began.[300] They also ushered in renewed symmetry to the Mediterranean, on a cultural level exemplified by the Levantine balance weights dug from Huelva's mud, which number among the first of many introduced or otherwise shared practices that would draw the basin together in coming centuries, and in terms of maritime space restoring the equality in scale first distorted by the Byblos ships of the 3rd millennium BC. In this second sense symmetry went hand in hand with drastic shrinkage. The Neolithic Mediterranean had been uniformly if unimaginably vast, that of the Copper and Bronze ages more variably so, but the Iron Age Mediterranean was simply large and, as such, potentially knowable in its entirety and so claimable, too, as 'our sea'. To illustrate the transformation, a reasonably lucky one-way passage of the basin's length in the Iron Age is thought to have taken about three months, with a biennial return often imposed by seasonal weather,[301] while the Neolithic version of this axial route took several millennia to convey farming from one end of the basin to the other, a duration beyond even collective memory. As we shall see, this shrinkage in turn powered up both centrifugal and centripetal tendencies in the basin's networks, as the entire sea turned superconductor, forging the cultural and economic conditions for a subsequent pan-Mediterranean empire that would unify the basin politically for the first (and last) time, while extending its reach also into Europe, Africa and Asia.

CHAPTER TEN

The end of the beginning

(800 – 500 BC)

Eighth Symphony (Unfinished)

If a Classical Athenian, or a contemporary from any long-established Mediterranean centre, were sent back a few centuries to 800 BC, they would find most of the general lineaments of the world around them broadly familiar. But many of the details would seem strange or undeveloped, and inhabitants of other parts of the basin with a more sheltered prior history would be in for a profound shock. In the space of three busy centuries between 800 and 500 BC the final elements in the long, complex evolution of Mediterranean ways of life slotted into place, to form the picture so familiar from what is customarily, if somewhat quaintly, known as 'ancient history'. Over this time span, criss-crossing currents render a region-by-region approach meaningless, as well as counter to the trend of connections and convergence. But two phases can still be discerned. The first, a fairly direct consequence of developments explored in the later parts of Chapter 9, and still fluid and emergent in its properties, lay in the 8th century BC, extending into the early 7th century. The participating zone remained largely as before, with southern France and its neighbours, the inner Adriatic and most of North Africa still going their own ways. Yet like Schubert's 'Unfinished' Eighth Symphony, the Mediterranean's 8th-century symphony remained incomplete. Its last movements, our second phase, overlapped with their predecessors during the 7th century but found fullest expression after 600 BC.[1] This phase saw the Mediterranean's cultural, social and economic activities intensify and its networks fill out to incorporate most of the basin, and reach well beyond. Simultaneously, rules of engagement between people and places became more codified and rationalized, in ways that would shape some of the most brilliant, as well as the most disturbing, features of the Classical and later Mediterranean.

The vitality of the 8th century BC and its immediate aftermath has long been apparent. For those with an Aegean bias, it connoted a 'Greek Renaissance'; from our perspective, rather the Aegean's active reinsertion into the wider Mediterranean, after a decidedly secondary participation since the end of the Bronze Age. Recently, it has become clear that it also ushered in a phase of wetter, cooler weather, subject as ever to vicissitudes but slightly friendlier to farming and thus a stimulus to demographic growth and expansion.[2] Estimating Mediterranean populations at this time is fraught with the usual uncertainties, but a reasonable figure for 800 BC would be 20 million, on a sharp upward curve.[3] The results were experienced most swiftly in drier regions. Numbers of people in the Aegean appear to have doubled over a century or so. In the southern Levant, population west of the Jordan almost tripled between 1000 and 750 BC, to reach its pre-Roman peak; east of the river the polities of Ammon, Moab and Edom arose within previously largely pastoral landscapes.[4] In the Levant and slightly later the Aegean, hillsides striated with terracing became an increasingly common sight, a response to both more stomachs to feed and growing markets for oil and wine. Further west, the great Tavoliere lowland of Apulia came under substantial cultivation for the first time in four millennia.[5] And at Zinkekra, in the central Saharan oasis of Wadi al-Ajal, wheat, barley, grapes and figs appeared – coupled with long-familiar domestic animals, at last a full, if temporary, outpost of agriculture in the desert.[6]

A further change in operating conditions takes us back to Assyria. During the 9th century, Neo-Assyrian kings at ever more giant capitals along the Tigris had begun to forge standing expeditionary armies and institute bureaucratic practices that would forever alter the face and reach of ancient empire, and eventually carve out and hold 1.4 million sq. km (540,000 sq. miles) of subject territory.[7] Mesopotamia, the Jazira, upland Anatolia and the Caucasus soon felt the consequences. Just after the middle of the 8th century BC, confederacies of Levantine polities, devoid of the old Bronze Age counterbalance of a super-power along the Nile, also succumbed, to a series of devastating campaigns in the aftermath of a further, drastic round of internal reforms, by the Assyrian monarch Tiglath-Pileser III (744–727). These first campaigns of conquest for many centuries by Mesopotamian kings in the Mediterranean zone annexed all the north and central Levant save for Tyre, which capitulated on terms.[8] Soon afterwards, the polity of Israel was extinguished, and 701 BC witnessed Sennacherib's mauling of Judah, from which Jerusalem fortuitously escaped after the sack of little Lachish, so notorious for the grisly depictions on the walls at Nineveh of its siege and the torture of captives [10.1]. At the other end of the Levant, Tarsus fell in 696 to the same monarch. Having secured the corridor that had linked Mesopotamia and Egypt for nearly 3000 years, his successor, Esarhaddon, took the Levant's connective properties to their logical yet unprecedented conclusion by directly

10.1 State-of-the-art Iron Age siege warfare at its grisliest: the end comes in 701 BC for the defenders of Lachish at the hands of a professional Assyrian field army, whether in combat, by later impaling or deportation. Lachish was a thankfully small town, but like many larger victims it lacked the coastal connections with which to buy clemency, even if the emergent faith and ideology of Judah had countenanced this.

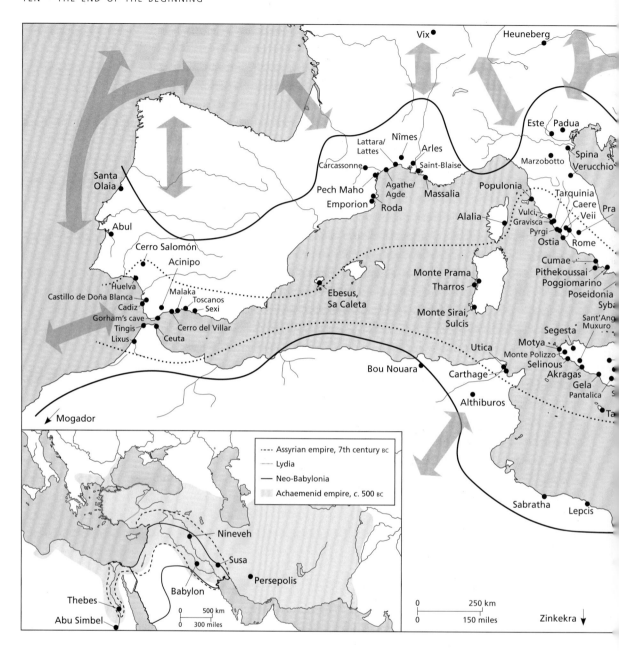

Vix
Heuneberg
Este Padua
Spina
Marzobotto Verucchio
Nîmes
Lattara/ Arles
Lattes
Carcassonne Saint-Blaise
Pech Maho Agathe/ Populonia Tarquinia
Emporion Agde Massalia Caere Pra
Roda Alalia Vulci, Veii
Gravisca
Pyrgi
Ostia Rome
Santa
Olaia
Cumae
Abul Pithekoussai
Cerro Salomón Poggiomarino
Acinipo Monte Prama Poseidonia
Tharros Syba
Ebesus, Sant'Ang
Huelva Sa Caleta Muxuro
Castillo de Doña Blanca Malaka Monte Sirai, Segesta Motya
Cadiz Toscanos Sulcis Monte Polizzo Selinous
Gorham's cave Sexi Utica Akragas
Tingis Cerro del Villar Gela
Lixus Ceuta Bou Nouara Pantalica S
Carthage Ta

Mogador
Althiburos

Assyrian empire, 7th century BC
Lydia
Neo-Babylonia
Achaemenid empire, c. 500 BC

Sabratha Lepcis

Nineveh

Susa

Persepolis

Babylon

Thebes

Abu Simbel

0   500 km
0   300 miles

0   250 km
0   150 miles

Zinkekra

10.2 Map of principal sites mentioned in this chapter, also showing the proportion of the Mediterranean integrated by 650 BC and the extension of that zone by 500 BC, the main axes of connections beyond the basin and (inset) the expansion of empires in the east.

assaulting Egypt, now politically reunified (after yet another break-up at the end of the 9th century) under a dynasty of Nubian origin that had been unwise enough to include intervention in the Levant among its restorations of tradition.[9] The Delta became for the first time a gateway for formal invasion, as opposed to demic, cultural and economic infiltration. Vassal rulers were appointed in towns that had never been reconciled to the return of upriver rule, and from this staging point Assyrian troops struck south to strip Thebes in 664 BC.

What did this entail for the Mediterranean, both those areas directly affected, and beyond? Assyrian imperial policy increasingly involved replacing client rulers

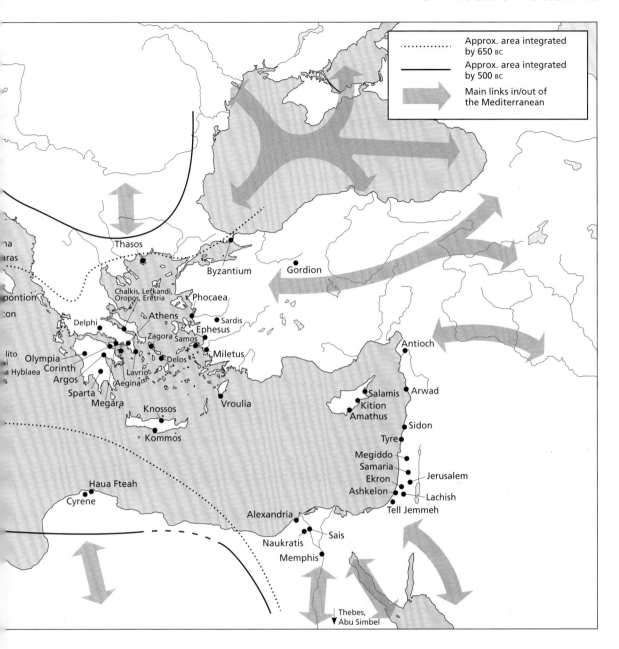

and their kingdoms with appointed governors responsible for new provinces, forced movements of people on a huge scale (by one empire-wide estimate, 4.5 million over three centuries)[10] and the return of a command economy exercised, after the extraction of war booty, via escalating tribute demands, accompanied by the intensification and reordering of regional economies. Tyre's tribute shot up several times, to the value of 4500 kg (9900 lbs) in gold by 730 BC.[11] As elsewhere, old-style broad packages of wealth goods were abandoned in favour of demands that ruthlessly targeted its optimal contribution, in Tyre's case silver, iron, purple cloth and ivory. Sidon's murex shell midden rose to an eventual height of 40 m (130 ft), and Lebanon's cedars were felled as never before.[12] Yet in productive terms Assyria needed the Mediterranean, and the economic growth of both was more symbiotic than is often recognized. Inland parts of the Levant suffered the most. It was from these that farmers and builders were deported to Mesopotamia, replaced by victims of devastation elsewhere to create an innocuous, largely rural population. But even here Assyrian policy assiduously supported, and indeed boosted, the cash-cropping of oil and wine, from upland growers to lowland processing units.[13] At Ekron in southern Israel, over a hundred early 7th-century BC installations able to churn out hundreds of tonnes of oil a year, probably by the sweat of Israelite slaves, reveals one of the biggest operations of its kind known in the ancient Mediterranean [10.3]. Drier Beersheba and tracts of Judah were turned into grain-growing support zones, a monocrop imposed against the instincts of independent farmers.[14] Edom arose on the strength of its copper mines.[15] And through all this land swelling numbers of camel caravans bore Arabian incense, myrrh and other balms, stimulated by a growing Near Eastern market.[16] The Arabian trade initially benefited the local polities at the termini of the overland trail, but with their demise, Assyria wrested control and drove one more nail into the coffin of Egyptian power, which long before had monopolized this access route's Red Sea-borne precursor. Forts and shrines in the Wadi Arabah, Negev and Gulf of Aqaba, scraps of Arabian script at Jerusalem, the Bible's curiosity concerning Arabian tribal genealogies, and the surely post-Solomonic attempt to recreate a maritime link to Arabian 'Sheba' with Tyrian help, all testify to the situation before direct Assyrian control. At Tell Jemmeh near Gaza, where caravans approached the sea, a strident Assyrian presence and masses of camel bones announced the imperial

10.3 Reconstruction of a 7th-century BC installation for industrial-scale olive oil production at Ekron.

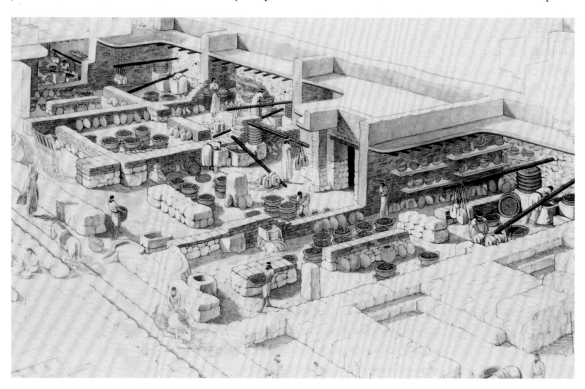

10.4 This basalt stele of the Assyrian king Sargon II, erected at Kition on Cyprus, appears imposing, but it reflected a very limited, largely symbolic maritime breach of traditional land-bound limits to the extent of Mesopotamian rule.

takeover. Camel-borne troops joined Esarhaddon's attack on Egypt, and a bronze model of a ridden camel even got as far as Rhodes.[17]

Assyria was more solicitous of pre-existing realities on the Mediterranean Sea, whose scale Mesopotamians were now beginning to appreciate.[18] This Upper Sea, of the Setting Sun, had, along with a Lower Sea in the Persian Gulf, provided the myth-tinged boundaries to Mesopotamian concepts of ideal kingship since Gilgamesh and Akkad. For all their occasional dismissal of its salty expanse as a 'Bitter River', Assyrian kings and their armies still sacrificed beside it and cleansed their weapons in its shallows. Despite its awesome might on terra firma, Assyria's writ in fact barely extended any further. A basalt stele erected at Kition on Cyprus to honour Sargon II (722–705 BC), at one extremity of the world he knew, reflected only a very tentative extension from the Assyrian viewpoint, and from a Cypriot one little more than a nominal genuflection that allowed business to be prosecuted as usual [**10.4**].[19] Likewise reminiscent of Bronze Age rulers' hollow boasts was the assertion of one Assyrian official that 'The Ionians [a term then implying islanders in general] came and attacked the cities of Samsimurana, Hasiru and…a cavalryman came to the town of Dana[bu]. I gathered available men and went. They did not get anything. When they saw my troops, they got in their boats and vanished into the midst of the sea.'[20]

Given its maritime impotence, Assyria's strategy was to tax the profits of a sea trade it could never hope to control where it came ashore, at select ports watched over by forts and imperial functionaries. For a long time this formalized version of the concentrate-and-bleed approach to Levantine sea trade, first employed by later 2nd-millennium BC Egyptian and Hittite rulers, proved highly effective. Gaza blossomed where Arabian camels met Mediterranean shipping. Owing to high overland transport costs, Levantine oil and wine were not siphoned off as direct tribute, but instead permitted to flow overseas, as before, which yielded more profit in taxes (Assyria, until recently still a beer-dominated zone like the rest of Mesopotamia, met its escalating demand for the latter from the nearby Jazira and Zagros). This swelled Ashkelon to a harbour city of 10,000–12,000 people.[21] But the supreme marriage of convenience between imperial command economies and mercantile cities on the sea was enacted at Tyre. Tyrian tribute sky-rocketed over the later 8th and early 7th centuries BC, but its wealth and power at sea grew commensurately – the association between Assyrian demands and Phoenician expansion, which we dismissed as premature in Chapter 9, now came into its own in an age of intensified activity over much of the basin. Moreover, despite repeated revolts against its overlord, the goose that laid such precious, abundant eggs was treated with a conspicuously light touch in comparison to its neighbours, and its merchants long left largely free to generate wealth as they knew best. Only after its rebellious king had fled to Kition in 701 BC was Tyre stripped of most mainland territory, only from the 670s were its ships and harbours closely monitored, and still the repeatedly besieged city itself was spared.[22] In contrast, when Sidon revolted in 677 BC it was sacked, depopulated and refounded as the 'Harbour of Esarhaddon', an explicit dependency to be deployed as a foil against its ancient rival. Not until the altered conditions of the later 7th century

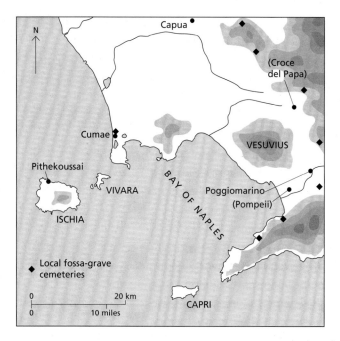

10.5 The environs of the Bay of Naples, showing the advantageous island location of Pithekoussai, and surrounding communities.

BC would this pragmatic imperial leniency towards the lynchpin of Mediterranean maritime trade run out.

Monkey business

What of the remainder of the Mediterranean? Almost every theme worth exploring in the 8th and early 7th centuries BC can be introduced via Pithekoussai, on the island of Ischia in the Bay of Naples [**10.5**].[23] This remarkable site marks a further round of seagoing activity in the inviting embrace of Campania and its offshore islets, following Copper Age Gaudo-related activity, Bronze Age Vivara, and a series of early 1st-millennium coastal communities that are only now coming to light, one at Cumae and another, with 2nd-millennium BC origins, at Poggiomarino, near Pompeii, perched on artificial islets in riverine wetland and active in the working of metals, amber and bone.[24] In every sense Pithekoussai dwarfed these antecedents. Its cemeteries and large ridge-top settlement indicate that within a few generations the community grew from obscure origins to several thousand men, women and children, one of the biggest contemporary aggregations west of Cyprus, and one of the most ambitious small-island communities so far encountered beyond Phoenicia. Its composition was staggeringly diverse. People came from Campania, Etruria and Sardinia, the Aegean (primarily Euboea and Corinth – the latter on the ascendant, as we shall see), and a range of 'Phoenician' locales, but notably without signs of formal Tyrian affiliation.[25] Burials combined eclectic traits of varied origin. Some hinted at marriages between Italian women and men from further afield, while a female finger bone with a cremated child echoed an Old Testament custom, and a young boy's cremation was accompanied by scented oil flasks from Corinth and Cyprus (the latter in Phoenician tradition). A cup made on Rhodes but later incised with a teasing hexameter verse alluding to Nestor and Aphrodite furnishes one of the first examples of the Aegean alphabet, in a Euboean version [**10.6**]. Pithekoussai had a cosmopolitan, boom-town feel, and the primary lure was trade. Despite the number of imported pots and other goods, metals stood out as pre-eminent, especially Elban iron, whose ores were so pure that they were worth shipping overseas for smelting.

An intrusive Phoenician or Aegean origin is often assumed for Pithekoussai, and the selection of an island several days' sail from the central Italian ores explained, rather anachronistically, by exclusive native control over Etruria's approaches. It is in fact more likely that Ischia, rather like Lipari in the Neolithic, was chosen by traders of disparate affiliation as a neutral insular meeting place where connections across the Tyrrhenian Sea, around Sicily and towards the east intersected. Our ignorance

10.6 'Nestor's cup' from Pithekoussai, an otherwise unexceptional Rhodian pot named for its playful allusion to the epic tradition in a Greek inscription that runs (in translation): 'I am the cup of Nestor, good to drink from. Whoever drinks from this cup, may desire of fair-crowned Aphrodite seize him.'

of the site's earliest phases could even disguise a prior history as a modest shuttler of goods and people in and out of the Bay of Naples. Its Greek name may adapt an indigenous or Phoenician original but translates as 'Monkey Island', an allusion to exotic places, whether by this time Egypt (baboons), northeast Africa in general (vervets) or the Maghreb (barbary apes), but also with connotations of imitation, persuasive chatter and encounters with creatures not quite like oneself. Its Latin name, Aenaria, referenced metals, currency and sea-travelling Aeneas.[26] This island community is a touchstone, as its names imply, for wider themes: maritime mobility, Iron Age trade, the spread of the alphabet, the consumers of an evermore interconnected Mediterranean culture, the growth of large communities in new places and, last but not least, the creation of long-term bases far from home for substantial numbers of people.

To take these in turn, Pithekoussai testifies to a continued growth in shipping, which brought countless people, goods and materials to and from Ischia, and, along with farms dotted across the island, must have kept its inhabitants fed with imported food, presumably from Campania. Boats leapt back into visibility from the 8th century BC, in media as varied as Assyrian royal reliefs, painted pottery and metal firedogs twisted into galley outlines, as if the men gathered around the hearth bonded through the crewing of such craft.[27] Wrecks further testify to an increase in both traffic and archaeologically visible commodities as well as the enduring dangrs of even a shrunken sea. The most impressive are two ships lost 50 km (30 miles) off Ashkelon around 750 BC, and detected by pioneering deep-sea techniques 400 m (1300 ft) beneath the waves, their combined total of some 800 amphorae (about 15,000 litres or 3300 gallons of liquid cargo) still delineating the hulls on the seabed [**10.7**].[28] Unless their all but exclusive focus on liquid transport is a bias

10.7 Eerily clustered on the pitch-dark sea-bed some 400 m (1300 ft) down, and imaged by deep-sea exploration technology, this mass of amphorae still plot the outline of a ship that foundered off Ashkelon in the mid-8th century BC.

10.8 The basic bifurcation in Mediterranean shipping is neatly illustrated by this scene on the so-called Aristonothos krater, found at Caere and dating to the 7th century BC, which shows a clash between a galley and round-hulled sailing ship; interestingly, in this case both seem equally heavily armed.

resulting from their incomplete, remotely controlled investigation, it contrasts with the mixed nature of earlier, and most later, cargos, and may reflect how regular the Levantine wine trade with nearby markets such as Egypt had become. Whatever the truth about maximum cargos in the Bronze Age, during the Iron Age these attained 70–80 tonnes, though there is no sign of the supersized bulk transports, of as much as 500 tonnes in capacity, reported as marvels in Roman and medieval times (an interesting, if currently unanswerable, question is the antiquity of the tendency, evident by medieval times, to deploy larger sails in the more open spaces of the western Mediterranean).[29] An early 7th-century BC pot from Caere in Etruria illustrates in simplified form, and at a moment of high tension, the two basic kinds of craft at sea – with a familiar scene of Cyclops-blinding on the reverse [**10.8**].[30] Cargo ships remained round-hulled, sail-driven craft with auxiliary oars, probably already known by their later nickname as 'tubs'. Meanwhile, in the east, the Aegean and maybe further west, slender, oared galleys grew into skinny craft 20 m (65 ft) or so long, with up to fifty rowers (hence *pentekonters* in Greek), some of a two-tiered, or bireme, design.[31] Galleys bifurcated in functional terms, too, into those designed primarily for low-to-medium-volume trade, and custom-built warships with a ram mounted on the prow and space for soldiers. Rams signalled the start of sea-battles of ship-on-ship manoeuvre as well as boarding, and the first true naval flotillas. At first these were tiny – in the 720s a mere dozen state-of-the-art Tyrian warships fought off a fleet commandeered by Assyria – and largely made up of ships in private hands, not least at Corinth, the leading Aegean maritime polity by the 7th century, which clashed at sea with its former outpost on Corfu between 680 and 644 BC.[32] As galley complements grew, drinking water requirements began to tether such craft more than their antecedents to coastal areas and quick open-sea sprints, though this still brought most of the east and central Mediterranean into range. More than sailing ships, it was such galleys passing swiftly along the coasts and between islands during the summer months that would circulate hundreds of footloose young men – traders, fighters or both – over long distances, bringing these micro-populations in contact with often initially quite different shore-dwellers.[33]

Turning from the means of mobility to the economic mechanisms and things moved, the 8th century saw extensions and departures from established practice. Most trade remained freelance and profit-oriented, still eased with timely gifts as well as a younger etiquette of guest friendship intended to safeguard people in the absence of polity-level security west of Cyprus.[34] Tyre was unusual in maintaining formalized relations with its daughter community at Carthage, which for centuries dispatched a tithe of its proceeds back to Tyrian Melqart, and it also exercised close control over another Tyrian outpost at Cadiz.[35] The inequalities inherent when relatively small-scale economies were abruptly confronted over a shrinking sea by trading regimes of great sophistication are undeniable, not least in the case of Tyre (with Assyria behind it) and a long-sheltered Iberia, and the initial profits from exchanges of the 'faience baubles for metals' type were surely commensurately immense.[36] But before we fall too readily for the stereotype of the Phoenician trader as a greedy, 'gnawing' cheat that surfaces episodically in Greek writing, we need to recall that profit-driven trade anywhere in the basin had always entailed losers as well as winners, that distance still reduced the power gap at the point of encounter, and that plenty of native societies (not least in Iberia) were no strangers to brutally asymmetrical relations themselves. Moreover, at any particular point of contact, the most blatant phase of cross-cultural exploitation can have lasted no more than a few generations, preceded by a situation in which both parties were so different that each in fact did well by its own lights, and followed by one in which all participants had become knowledgeable enough to play the same game on at least tolerable terms. In other words, even if the beginnings of this pan-Mediterranean trade network possessed a world-systemic tinge, any zoning into a core in the east versus a central and western periphery rapidly dissolved into a shifting world where exploiters and exploited existed everywhere.

As for the materials and goods on the move, a striking amount of the Bronze Age repertoire retained its appeal, if often with altered, sometimes more socially accessible meanings. In the metals trade, copper now mattered rather less, and with it tin. Silver, although mined in quantity only in Anatolia, Attica and Iberia, was widely crafted, and critically important as bullion, an exchange currency and, in the Levant, ultimately tribute by the tonne. By late Roman times, 6.6 million tonnes of waste from silver extraction had piled up at Río Tinto, the first of the two spikes that generated this lying between the 9th and mid-6th centuries BC.[37] Whatever the truth of the tale that Phoenician ships cast anchors in silver so as to carry more away with them from Iberia, the gist is obvious.[38] Iron now began to appear in bulk, too. It was smelted or worked using strikingly similar techniques in Pithekoussai, Carthage, Oropos (over the strait from Euboea) and Iberia.[39] The 160 tonnes found stockpiled in an Assyrian palace near Nineveh affirm the stupendous quantities needed for armaments and tools.[40]

Simultaneously, the basin's shared ecology encouraged the spread of purple dye industries, and above all wine and oil production. In Italy olive cultivation had been steadily advancing up the peninsula from its late 2nd-millennium BC southern bridgehead, and by the 9th century domestic grapes had got as far as Etruria, Sicily and possibly Sardinia.[41] In Iberia, whatever the ambivalent traces of earlier experiments, and despite the certainty of other alcoholic drinks (including a mead-like concoction

recently identified in an 11th-century BC pot), the definitive establishment of vine and olive cultivation came in the form of a Phoenician introduction during the 8th, or even 9th, century BC.[42] As a general rule, wine production took off faster than that of oil in the west, a reflection of local pre-adaptation thanks to a long familiarity with alcohol-fuelled rituals and hospitality, and of the roles that wine-drinking played in lubricating cross-cultural encounters, defining (as we shall see) a shared elite lifestyle, mobilizing labour through mass drinking bouts and, in certain circumstances, establishing an addictive dependency that assured the acquisition of other desirable goods in return.[43] As such practices became engrained and more regions invested in cash-cropping and export, two ceramic consequences spread wheel-thrown manufacture and the frenetic culture of brand definition, emulation and import substitution across the basin.

The first concerned transport containers [**10.9**]. Amphora production had never extended beyond the easternmost Mediterranean in the Bronze Age, but in the Iron Age it went universal.[44] The Aegean had long abandoned its peculiar stirrup jars, and by the 7th century BC its distinctive amphorae reached both ends of the Mediterranean; Italy developed its own range, and derivatives of Phoenician types were turned out in Sardinia and Iberia, the latter's sometimes for bottling piquant fish preserves ultimately derived from refined east Mediterranean cuisines. In the centre of the basin, early Carthage, despite having set up its own vineyards and olive groves on African soil from as near to the outset as we can detect, imported many amphora-loads from Sardinia, substantial numbers from Etruria and the Levant, and a few from

10.9 The marketing of precious liquids continued to shape ceramic containers: (*top*) one in a sequence of polished monochrome perfume flask designs signalling Phoenician and associated production; (*centre*) intricately painted 7th-century BC Corinthian equivalent, imitating incised metal vessels; (*bottom*) Attic-type amphora of 7th- to early 6th-century BC date for bulk liquid transport, known from its collar decoration as an 'SOS' type, with provision for standing as well as transport. Not to scale.

Iberia, Sicily, the Aegean and Pithekoussai (where both Phoenician and Aegean forms were emulated).[45] For smaller measures of perfumed oil, Phoenician flasks and their imitations, the descendants of older Bronze Age juglets, travelled widely, inspiring in Corinth an eye-catching variant known as the *aryballos*, which cheek-ily translated the images on eastern metal vessels onto clay, in black silhouette with incised details.[46] The second ceramic consequence came as potters met the demand for fine vessels for serving and drinking wine, primarily in the Aegean, where ebullient black-and-white and polychrome figural styles emerged over the 7th century.[47] Etruria produced hybrids of these, as well as its own *bucchero* tradition of gleaming, dark surfaces with the ornate handles long characteristic of Italian drinking cups.[48] Phoenician groups stayed aloof from production in this realm, however many of its fancy products they handled and circulated; they concentrated instead on fine, neatly turned plain red plates for more solid foods, largely for their own usage.[49]

The definition of a shared elite lifestyle extended well beyond wine-drinking and its accompanying paraphernalia. It was furthered by a renewed spate of luxury goods and sub-elite trinkets into the Mediterranean, many the products of work-shops in the north or central Levant, Cyprus, Egypt and Anatolia.[50] Westward percolation of eastern goods, via all manner of mechanisms, had ample Bronze Age parallels, and many of the kinds of items now circulated were also traditional, including silver, gold or bronze bowls and other beautifully decorated metalwork [**10.10**; PL. XLII], Egyptian-style faience and stone vessels, seals, ivory furniture inlays and boxes, bronze figurines and suchlike. Many bore the mon-strous motifs long favoured further east, several revived the 'international' elite imagery of the later 2nd millennium BC, and, as in the Bronze Age, a few were themselves antiques that referenced the past as much as the east.[51] The newer features all reflected improved Mediterranean connections. One was a leap in quantity, another the spatial reach that embraced Iberia and Etruria, whereas Sicily and Sardinia had been the limit during the previous millennium. The sheer size of certain objects stands out too. Massive metal cauldrons with the protruding heads of humans, lions or griffins were on the move, originating in Anatolia but coveted in the Aegean and Etruria, as were ornate chariots with heroic associations; one of the latter, made from walnut trimmed in silver and bronze was committed to the grave in far-off Huelva.[52] Lastly, a growing number of such objects were made in situ all over the basin, by mobile Levantine craftspeople no longer owned by palaces, or their skilled local emulators.[53] On Crete, votive metalwork and attempts at sizeable stone statuary betray foreign expertise; in Iberia, eastern jewellers and ivory carvers employed local and Moroccan materials respectively.[54] Outside a handful of resolutely 'Phoenician' communities – mainly Carthage, which

10.10 The size and flavour of the 'orientalizing' bronzework circulating over long distances, and also locally produced, by the 7th century BC is indicated by this reconstruction of a metre-high cauldron from Olympia.

Proto-Canaanite	Phoenician	Early Greek	Early monumental Latin	Modern English capitals
				A
				B
				C
				D
				E
				F
				H
				I
				K
				L
				M
				N
				O
				P
				Q
				R
				S
				T

10.11 A comparison of several versions of the alphabets ultimately derived from 2nd-millennium BC experiments in the easternmost Mediterranean, and then broadcast across the basin by 1st-millennium BC networks.

was intriguingly indifferent to the flashier varieties of goods – the ways in which such objects were used reveal knowledgeable local inflections and redeployments, and the onset of production in the west further strengthens the argument that most such items soon shed their eastern connotations, morphing into a flexible, if meaning-laden vocabulary of pan-Mediterranean display. This phenomenon, mis-leadingly referred to as 'orientalizing', was in fact decidedly 'mediterraneanizing' in its social intent.[55] The same is liable to be true of less tangible escapees, too, such as fragments of eastern cosmology, myth and symbolism, whether initially tied to objects on the move, or independently circulating and reconfigured in the vortices of ideas, traditions and information that places like Pithekoussai fostered. The preferential survival of such fragments in the Aegean, via Classical Greece and its posterity, offers the richest glimpses, for example of the appositely Corinthian hero Bellerophon in Lycia, fighting a hybrid monster on an equally hybrid winged charger (both with eastern antecedents), or the versions of the birth of the gods recounted by Hesiod and shown in an only superficially familiar scene on a storage jar from Tenos in the Cyclades.[56] Even the lapis-blue locks of Homeric divinities reflected a refracted Mesopotamian and Egyptian belief.[57] But the Aegean was surely not alone in this respect; central Italy's fascination with liver-divination (a Near Eastern custom already well attested at 2nd-millennium BC Ugarit) and the Mesopotamian look of its demons hint at a far wider circulation of such intangibles around the Mediterranean.[58]

With the goods and myths came writing, as seen at Pithekoussai and, earlier, at the first Phoenician stopping points mentioned in Chapter 9.[59] Alphabetical scripts originated in the later 2nd-millennium BC Levant, as merchants and other go-betweens sought to break the written word free from the limits of clay and for-malities of scribal learning enshrined in cuneiform, and to promote mobile practices, easier learning and simpler transfers [**10.11**]. Unsurprisingly, Iron Age expansion of the alphabet coincided with the decline of cylinder seals, and their rolled-out, recondite iconography, in favour of stamp seals bearing punchy, readily grasped images, which show up all over the basin. However, the pattern of adoption of the alphabet was more complex than it might at first seem. The Phoenician version cir-culated very widely and, with several consonants that were surplus to requirement in other languages switched to denote vowels in the early 8th century, an exceptionally speech-like variant emerged to write Greek and soon Italian languages. But where this began within a string of possibilities running from Euboea all the way to central Italy still remains anyone's guess. Crete, though riddled with Phoenician traits and long ago home to the first Mediterranean script beyond the Levant, was an oddly late starter, and the best bets lie further west, among polyglot communities such as Pithekoussai, where bi- or trilingualism must have been commonplace. In contrast, Cyprus enjoyed an unbroken tradition of literacy and mercantile trade, yet, outside the orbit of Kition, stuck stubbornly to local syllabic script for centuries to come.[60] Likewise, although a crude correlation between alphabets and greater, or at least more socially widespread, literacy holds good, the range of early uses that survive across the

Mediterranean is a bewildering mixture of sacred and royal proclamations, tomb curses, personal offerings and claims of ownership, poetry, exhortations to enjoy life and only rarely (as in the agricultural dues from Samaria mentioned in Chapter 9) the regulatory preoccupations standard in the Bronze Age. The scraps that survive incised into stone or pottery must be the tip of an iceberg of perhaps more cursive writing on perishable surfaces, comprising the usual archives in the Levant, but probably quite different contents elsewhere.

One further boon of the spread of writing is that its adoption finally lifts the curtain on the languages spoken in the centre and west, albeit just as their ranks were becoming thinned, as had happened earlier further east, by the linguistic repercussions of interregional contact and expanding political formations. Early texts in Italy would fossilize and preserve the last vestiges of a verbal kaleidoscope, the survivors of a mass of older, presumably occasionally even pre-Neolithic languages, several Indo-European but many not, and all nurtured, divided, merged or extinguished within a cellular topography over the millennia, until some bore no discernible relationship to anything else known to us [10.12]. Among these were Ligurian, Venetic, Etruscan, Umbrian, Oscan, Elymian, Sard and an initially tiny patch of Latin, in addition to a later Celtic influx into the Po plain, intrusive Phoenician and Greek in the south, and Messapic astride the Strait of Otranto.[61] Less of the preceding diversity was captured by the adapted Phoenician and Greek scripts of Iberia, but again 'Tartessian', 'Iberian' and other tongues can be discerned, alongside Basque, the greatest survivor of all.[62]

10.12 A traditional exercise in mapping the languages of Italy before the spread of Latin, largely from inscriptional evidence up to the 5th century BC. Even this mosaic must be a massive over-simplification, flattening the likely extent of bilingualism, blurred boundaries in speech and space, and fluidity over time.

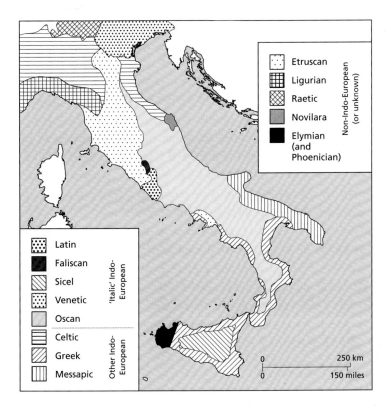

Etruscan
Ligurian
Raetic
Novilara
Elymian (and Phoenician)
Non-Indo-European (or unknown)

Latin
Faliscan
Sicel
Venetic
Oscan
'Italic' Indo-European

Celtic
Greek
Messapic
Other Indo-European

250 km
150 miles

The main beneficiaries or consumers of all this, the shining, brightly coloured or richly worked artifacts, the intoxicating wine and scented oil, the assertive or witty texts, even the handful of languages of widening currency, were an Iron Age elite, for whom they offered emblems of superiority and ways of raising labour or other resources and fashioning new political communities – defining practices and ethics for a lifestyle shared among their peers in an increasingly converging world. Many of the most conspicuous displays occurred in imposing funerary monuments, ranging from huge built tombs at Salamis on Cyprus, to large tumuli in Athens and gigantic ones up to 50 m (165 ft) across in Etruria, where funerary banquets and ancestor-venerating rituals played a

10.13 Massive stone-built tumuli, such as this series in the Banditaccia cemetery of Caere, testify to a wealthy, flaunting and internally highly competitive elite in central Italy, a phenomenon also widely encountered in other parts of the contemporary Mediterranean.

key role in community definition [**10.13**].[63] Comparable tombs sprouted up all over the lower valley of the Guadalquivir. The shared elite ethos is underlined by parallels between the prominent cremations of young armed men at the entrance gate to Eretria in Euboea – the local successor, as harbour requirements grew, to Lefkandi (whose earlier spectacular death-rituals had, incidentally, foreshadowed traits now spreading across the basin)[64] – and other examples in Etruria and Campania.[65] The insatiable desire of local leaders to acquire and customize objects and images of once eastern origin was a reflection less of any desire to emulate eastern political forms, than of the dearth of equivalent indigenous trappings of power in Iberia, Italy, and in the Aegean since the demise of the Bronze Age palaces, especially ones more subtle than simply displays of weaponry and other metalwork.[66]

Yet the term 'elite' and the acquired veneer of common practices conceal a variety of local Mediterranean truths. In the east, the power of kingship on the coast had long been waning in comparison to inland polities like Judah and, in Anatolia, the rising power of Phrygia, with its mighty royal tumulus at Gordion containing 157 bronze drinking vessels as well as well-preserved furniture and cloth (all just too early to have belonged to the fabled King Midas himself).[67] Assyrian imperial annexations hastened the demise of local kingship throughout this area. On Cyprus, not an island so far renowned for strong central authority, the royal epithet for the Salamis tombs reflects simply their splendour, and a putative palace at Amathus covered a derisory 400 sq. m (4300 sq. ft).[68] Further west, royalty was irrelevant to most outposts of eastern traders, and even Carthage soon effectively kingless. To judge from the clusters of massive tumuli, it also failed to gain much hold among local societies against rival groups of powerful individuals and lineages surrounded by their kin and other retainers drawn to their protection – the customary, if increasingly hereditary big men, now plugged into a vastly greater economy, for the second time in the Aegean but to a new degree in Italy and Iberia.[69] And sometimes escalating elite claims were themselves challenged, not surprisingly given their often shallow roots and lack of effective divine sanctification. Pithekoussai's graves project a broadly sub-elite image and suggest wide access to at least the less grandiose goods, while in the Levant, Israelite prophets poured scorn on the luxury-loving magnates of Samaria and Tyre. Last but not least, patterning in the 8th-century BC Athenian cemeteries hint at the formation there, and assuredly elsewhere, of a substantial, more inclusive 'middling' group, again muscling into archaeological visibility with an alternative ideology that was warier of dazzling imports, allusions to a glorious ancestral past and heroizing funerals – a development manifestly pregnant with possibilities for the future of Mediterranean political systems.[70]

But what were the communities to which these actors belonged actually like? Pithekoussai was remarkable for its size and rapid formation from overseas in a new location, both features that introduce two more intertwined Mediterranean-wide traits: the spread of 'urbanism' and of 'colonies' (the latter a highly unsatisfactory term, as we shall discover). Beginning with the former, Chapter 9 argued that for the first two centuries of the new millennium, towns, and the tightly surrounding or more spacious polities associated with them, remained unknown west of Cyprus and the Nile Delta, save by the very end at Carthage. Even after 800 BC, at a time of rapid population growth, developments remained variable. East of the Cyprus–Delta line, town life was initially boosted by wetter conditions and expanding trade, but Assyrian intervention exerted a heavy influence on individual urban histories; on the one hand, even the provincial governor's seat at Megiddo was a mere 6 ha (15 acres), while favoured ports like Tyre and Ashkelon boasted five-figure populations.[71] Most unexpected of all was Jerusalem, a hitherto undistinguished hill-town now transformed into a massively fortified, densely populated city of 70–90 ha (170–220 acres), ruling over a Judaean state numbering some 75,000 people [**10.14**]. Jerusalem largely owed its growth to Assyria's elimination of Samaria, its dominant northern sibling, which had triggered a flood of refugees, from skilled workers to doom-laden prophets, together with its hair's-breadth escape from an identical fate, which left it the last southern polity able to profit from the trade in oil, wine and Arabian imports – freak, exhilarating, hothouse conditions that would leave their

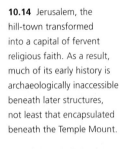

10.14 Jerusalem, the hill-town transformed into a capital of fervent religious faith. As a result, much of its early history is archaeologically inaccessible beneath later structures, not least that encapsulated beneath the Temple Mount.

10.15 A very different urban prospect, that of Tarquinia in Etruria, beneath fields save at this western edge, and surrounded by steep cliffs that show as dark shadows in this early aerial photograph. The early community was dotted around the plateau, with large open areas between.

signature on world history.[72] To the west, Carthage elaborated its already outstanding credentials, with an impressive stability in house plots and their party walls from the 8th century BC to the Roman sack in 146 BC, as well as carefully laid out cemeteries and communal shrines.[73] Yet the other early Phoenician enclaves in the centre and west that we shall encounter shortly were much smaller, and while determined to project a Levantine or Carthaginian urban aspect in their architecture, they lacked both extensive infrastructure and weight of numbers.[74]

This leaves two other pathways towards the formation of towns, both of which involved in situ coevolution across the basin, through local processes, network-based interaction, or a mixture of both, rather than wholesale massive implants from east to west, in which context Carthage remained exceptional, if not unique. One pathway followed up the earlier concentration of people at certain locations, often with plenty of farmland, in the southern Aegean, Etruria and neighbouring parts of Italy (further west, local centres, like intrusive enclaves, remained fairly small).[75] Some such places became large and populous, if still patchily occupied and loosely structured [**10.15**]. Athens numbered over 5000 people, in clumps distributed over 200 ha (500 acres). Argos, Knossos, Rome and Veii, the last now outstripping coastal Caere, were comparable, and other examples appeared at Sparta, Eretria and above all Corinth, whose widely traded products we have already noted, and whose late 8th- and 7th-century peak owed everything to its place astride an easy alternative to the circum-Peloponnesian route between the Aegean and central Mediterranean. Such places exercised some authority over territories, as the competition between Veii and Caere, nascent Rome's victories over its neighbours, and Eretria's war with rival Chalkis for the intervening Lelantine plain, all imply. Given all this, and their elite social groups, they can reasonably be thought of as emergent polities, even if their communal infrastructure remained sparse – a meagre bounding wall, inevitably known as 'Romulean', ringed the Palatine in Rome by the late 8th century BC and the principal forum was paved in the 7th century, while Corinth boasted a few shrines, and a sanctuary later sacred to Apollo offered some focus to the scattered houses of a still street-less Eretria.[76] If we deem such places to be towns, they were certainly radically different at this stage from those in the Levant, which typically packed several thousand people into sometimes as little as a dozen hectares of fortified space studded with large civic structures.

The final pathway towards urbanism was that taken by Pithekoussai, with people from far and wide aggregating, often rapidly, at niches and nodes newly favoured by networks of production and trade, a route that the case of Corinth demonstrates might overlap with the previous one.[77] Its ancestry goes back to the growth of island trading villages since the 3rd millennium BC, and to the boom towns of Hyksos Avaris in the Nile Delta and Enkomi on Cyprus. What made the Iron Age outcome so different was the rise in absolute population and the number of individuals (elite, sub-elite, artisan and, crucially, people engaged in agricultural production as well as trade) in different parts of the basin who were now able to contemplate at least semi-permanent relocation, thanks to enhanced conditions for the maritime movement of people, bulk foods, cash crops and, in fortunate cases, bullion.[78] Over time this created a voluntary equivalent at sea to the overland deportations in the east under empire, and must have equally blurred the Mediterranean's gene pool. One rough estimate suggests that the departure of a few hundred men each year led a total of 20,000–40,000 leaving the Aegean over the course of the later 8th and 7th centuries BC, maybe 2–3 per cent of all adult males and a far higher percentage in seagoing regions.[79] The motivations varied, but although 'push' factors, such as local tensions, failed harvests or excessive numbers living off a given patch, played a part in specific instances, 'pull' factors were more powerful overall. Principal among these was the opportunity to turn an arable-, mineral- or other trade-based profit (or at least to enjoy a better life), by fair means or foul, in underexploited niches all around the basin. Such niches were fairly common across the relatively thinly peopled centre and west, as well as in coastal North Africa, thereby determining the net directions of flow, but they were initially also abundant among the long underpopulated islands and valleys of the Aegean. The formation of a new community, often on fresh ground, explains the common practice of laying out streets, house plots and arable allotments in rectilinear or grid-like arrangements, witnessed alike in tiny intra-Aegean implants like Zagora on the Cycladic island of Andros and short-lived Vroulia (with its immaculately laid out housing, defences, shrine and cemetery) at the southern tip of Rhodes [10.16], and on a much more ambitious scale, as we shall see, in such transfers between sub-basins as that represented by Megara Hyblaea in Sicily.[80] Far from being a product of Greek rationalism, this grid-like layout had ample precedents in earlier Egyptian workers' towns (including Avaris's predecessor), as well as mid-2nd-millennium BC Sharuhen near Gaza, the final rebuild at Enkomi and its successor at Salamis, recent Carthage and the contemporary reconstruction of Megiddo for an Assyrian governor and transported alien populace.

10.16 The small community laid out at Vroulia on Rhodes in the later 7th century BC, with provision for the living, dead and immortal, is probably typical of many earlier and contemporary ventures as population and mobility took off.

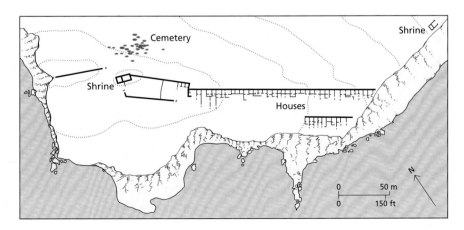

Homes away from home

At the rather arbitrary point in this continuum of mobility at which people migrated between sub-basins and over old cultural boundaries on a detectable scale, the result has become known as a 'colony'.[81] The Roman term is in fact thoroughly misleading at this juncture, given its connotations of central, imperial initiative. Greek *apoikia* (a succinct expression for 'home-away-from-home') is truer to the reality of such places, though even its differentiation from the narrowly mercantile *emporion* seems hard to police at this stage (what should we call Pithekoussai?). We do not know, besides a couple of 'New Towns', how Levantine people referred to such places, although the ancient *karum*, which wrapped up quayside, market and enclave, is a fair guess. At first these places materialized along a swathe of coast from Otranto via southern Italy, Sicily and Sardinia to southwest Iberia. This was an already mediterraneanizing zone in terms of social behaviour, agriculture and a variably deep history of maritime activity (not least due to its unusually conducive configuration),[82] with excellent arable or mining potential, and modest degrees of local political complexity. Etruria lay decisively outside it, and itself exported people to Campania, Pithekoussai and later further afield. The external inputs came from two main sources: in the newly integrated zone between the Tyrrhenian Sea and Iberia, from whatever amalgam of Tyrians, other Levantines, Carthaginians and indigenous participants lay behind the western 'Phoenicians', and along the short seaways between Italy and eastern Sicily, primarily from seafaring Euboea and Corinth, as well as nearby western Greece.[83]

Some of these new places would grow at dizzying speed, but the number of founders was typically in the low hundreds and mainly composed of young men; how could it be otherwise, at least from the Aegean, given the modest population centres there?[84] For a variety of reasons, mother cities were often retrospectively appointed, but the initial realities were less coherent and more opportunistic. Trial-and-error tales abound in the legends dealing with selection of places to settle, and the core group of specific origin was probably often no more than a shipload around an entrepreneurial leader, with accomplices and later recruits drawn from the connections that flowed in and out of such fledgling foci, and increasingly from their native neighbours, female as much as male. Pithekoussai was particularly diverse, but may still provide a reasonable idea of what many such places initially felt like – a luckily preserved glimpse that we owe to the later transfer of its activities across the bay to Cumae, on the mainland. Such hybrid places signified the westward extension of the kinds of melting-pot port communities that had long flourished in the eastern Mediterranean, and it is telling how often archaeology, or a close enough reading of later sources to penetrate their '*Mayflower* moments',[85] reveals a choice of location adjacent to, or even displacing by negotiation or force, a pre-existing centre of sea trade, whose role would then be drastically scaled up. Like eastern ports, several quickly established an economic as well as demographic symbiosis with their hinterlands. The main difference was that such transects through Mediterranean-type ecological diversity lay under the divided control of coastal dwellers and inhabitants of the interior (a swiftly more significant distinction than that between newcomers and natives). Once the coastal communities had swelled sufficiently, this was a division that many would ruthlessly overthrow.

A few highlights of this rapidly emerging world provide more texture to these observations. We start in the far west, at Cadiz (Phoenician Gadir, meaning 'Walled'), an offshore island, like Tyre, and first peopled at a similar time in the 3rd millennium BC, though with a radically different subsequent history until the Iron Age linked the two together [PL. XLIII].[86] Offshore islands were popular choices for Phoenician centres, not only because they resembled Tyre and Arwad, but also because of the liminal, in-between status they enjoyed and, in practical terms, their protective sea-moats. In Roman times Martial thought Gadir 'joyous and licentious', a judgment that without much romanticizing might apply to many Mediterranean port-towns since the Bronze Age. Thanks to an equally Tyrian combination of later overbuild and a subsiding reef that makes even its harbour channels hard to recognize, we know frustratingly little about early Gadir, save for later descriptions and some tantalizing dredged-up scraps: a voluted capital from a large shrine, with parallels at Tyre and Jerusalem, and hunks of masonry, plus bronze smiting gods cast into the sea as ex-votos, from between the southern tip of the spindly, 18-km- (11-mile-) long main island and terra firma, where a temple of Melqart greeted arrivals from the east. New excavations beneath the current city are beginning to change this, and lay bare a long adhered-to plan of houses, workshops and wide streets of 8th- and 7th-century BC date [10.17].[87] Like Huelva across the gulf, and later Marseilles and Alexandria, the choice of the as yet unsilted rocky flank of a shifting, muddy estuary offered the best prospects for a marine anchorage, and a safer option than a quay on the navigable reaches of the Guadalquivir itself.

Gadir would soon diversify to become an interface between seas, but trade in silver and other metals back into the Mediterranean was the initial reason for its existence. This explains the close involvement of Tyre in what Tyrians considered a dependency, akin to Kition and Carthage, symbolized by the twin temples of Melqart at Tyre and Gadir, as well as regular sailings between the two islands down the length of the Mediterranean. For the extraction of metal by mining communities like that at Cerro Salomón, with its remains of lamps, picks, bellow nozzles and crucibles, as well as for conveyance from the powerful inland communities to coastal outlets of mixed composition at Huelva and Castillo de Doña Blanca, Gadir was mainly dependent on indigenous power brokers and connections.[88] The most it offered to the experienced miners of the Sierra Morena were silver extraction methods gleaned elsewhere in the Mediterranean, and to a Tartessian elite already wise to manipulating metals, a flood of luxuries of the kind described earlier (cannily apportioned to perpetuate disunity), together with the injection of ritual practices suggested by shrines with Levantine traits around modern Seville, which presumably helped to ease the transit of metal, as on Cyprus centuries earlier.[89] Considering the barriers between Levantine and Iberian societies at the start of the millennium, their integration two to three centuries later, in pursuit of one of the most ambitious extractive

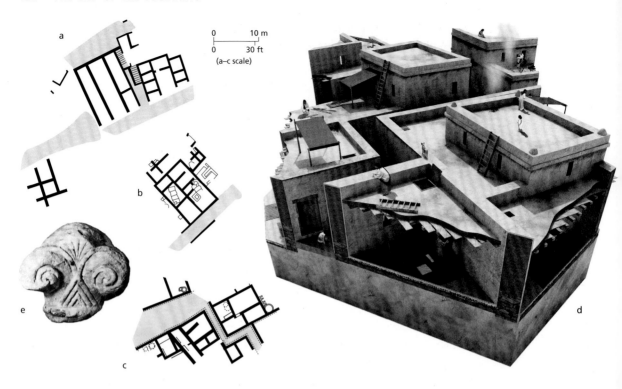

10.17 Phoenician architecture in the central and west Mediterranean: (a–c) to scale, respectively, a large warehouse and other structures at Toscanos, substantial house at Carthage, several houses plus a broad street and alleys at Cadiz; (d) reconstruction of the same neighbourhood at Cadiz; (e) voluted capital with Levantine parallels from the sea off Cadiz, close to the reputed location of an early shrine, and a rare survivor of an imposing Phoenician sacred building.

operations of its time, is a breathtaking illustration of the speed with which the Mediterranean was coming together.

More modest, but just as interesting, are a tightly spaced string of enclaves on former headlands, river mouths and islets around the Bay of Malaga and elsewhere on the Andalusian coast, well-excavated windows onto a Mediterranean landscape since altered by alluviation and destroyed by tourism.[90] Here, the coastal vista of towering forested mountains, narrow plains and short rivers was reminiscent of Phoenicia, and against it the whitened, lime-washed clusters of houses must have stood out boldly. In addition to the Phoenician pottery and balance weights, small groups of grand houses were constructed, suggestive of family firms of merchants and imported masons. This commitment to residence was further affirmed by clusters of elaborate multi-generation tombs of eastern design, located, as at Tyre, across water from the living. At the unforgettably named Sexi (the Roman version of Phoenician Sks), Egyptian stone vessels, including royal antiques, were reused as cremation urns.[91] Interestingly, however, a closer look reveals, among the carefully replicated Phoenician plates and domed bread ovens, handmade cooking pots reflective of an indigenous tradition and probably local women.[92] Moreover, in a further illustration of the precept that size and wealth did not always combine in the Mediterranean's maritime communities, most of these places remained small, with a few hundred inhabitants, their numbers probably fluctuating as ships came and went. Only Toscanos expanded to 12–15 ha (30–37 acres), flung up a defensive wall, constructed a wharf and crowned its core with a three-aisled, two-storey warehouse in impeccable Levantine tradition, overlooking its market area [**10.17**].[93]

What was the source of this wealth? With just a few kilometres between each Andalusian enclave, this was no chain of stops along a coastwise route, though most surely did pick up business during closures of the Strait of Gibraltar to Gadir-bound shipping by winter storms or Atlantic westerlies, as well as from patching up battered long-haul ships, building seacraft themselves, and benefiting, too, from an alternative land route to the head of the Guadalquivir embayment that passed through the nearby mountains.[94] Likewise, while most worked and traded metals, this was a sideshow compared to the situation at Gadir. Rather, as the remains of wine and oil amphorae, grain storage, purple dye works and fish processing imply, each enclave flourished principally by intense extraction from its little splinter of Mediterranean landscape, and circulation of the processed results through the western and central parts of the basin. For this to work, cooperation with the locals was vital. For instance, Cerro del Villar in the Guadalhorce delta, probably ancient Mainake (meaning 'Resting Place', 'Clean', or 'Empty') on the tiny 'Island of the Moon' (an allusion to Astarte?), was surrounded by fenland and woods; for its food and metal, it relied on nearby native communities.[95] For all their imposing facades, these enclaves were fragile. Several shared the shoreline with an enduring local village, or reveal hiatuses in occupation; one lost its foothold entirely.[96] None, moreover, appears to have enjoyed the political imprimatur of Tyre, nor the protection of a major shrine. Even links to Gadir were loose. Yet the lesson to be learned is that a combination of extraction, maritime and hinterland trade, transhipment, and serendipitous business with sheltering boats was profitable enough to encourage far-off people to risk all this, and make some of them rich.

A mirror image distribution of 8th century Phoenician outposts is starting to emerge on the African shore at Ceuta, opposite Gibraltar, and Lixus on the Atlantic, probably extending also east towards Oran.[97] After 700 BC, and in the wake of earlier contacts, littoral enclaves in Iberia spread northeast as far as the Segura River, with wine exports pushing ahead into the combative societies between there and the Ebro.[98] Indigenous settlements and cemeteries furnish ample insights into how such encounters generated new hybrid personae and styles, as Iberians sought to emulate incoming ways or defend traditional customs. Earlier, during the 8th century, another rash of small Phoenician settlements had taken hold further to the east, on the offshore islets and slender headlands around southern and western Sardinia, building upon 9th-century BC engagements.[99] These all faced resolutely seaward, whether due to the fractious and resistive propensities of nuragic societies, the availability of quality ores near the coast, or a greater focus on tapping into the sea trade in metals from Sardinia via Elba to Etruria than on agricultural exports. Little effort was made to engage local Sardinians and there are potential signs of conflict, including abandoned nuraghi in their vicinity, and a quickly established fort at Sulcis on the modern headland (then an offshore island) of Sant'Antioco. The gold jewels, scarabs and seals later crafted at Tharros, for example, spread far across the sea but barely registered inland, where the eastern-type goods so popular elsewhere remained uncommon.[100] Intriguingly, those native coastal communities that did survive on Sardinia adopted a guise that aligned them more with the newcomers than inland people. Behind this facade, a parallel world of towers, ritual offerings, metalworking and competition for land and retainers continued at top gear among the territories of the interior.

Sicily equals Sardinia as a huge central Mediterranean insular land mass, but its different geographical position now encouraged more diverse developments. The tricorn island with one tip nudging peninsular Italy, another looking towards Malta and a third staring at Africa over the sea's wasp-waist, always possessed the potential to be tugged in multiple directions. So far, this tendency had only been mildly visible, during the beaker network and, subsequently, the late 2nd-millennium BC shifts on the part of eastern navigators between the Messina-strait and south-coast routes (both of which, however, displayed as much desire to get past Sicily as to engage with it). Now, with the rise of Mediterranean-wide mobility, various limelights began to fall on the huge, fertile island with the convenient coasts at the centre of the basin. Under this glare, mediterraneanization swiftly bloomed, and in flowers blood-red as well as bright. Sicily's new-found importance is underscored by the fact that while in the past its relatively few maritime nodes had tended to rise or fall to each other's gain or loss, those that were now taken over, and the fresh ones being quickly imposed, flourished simultaneously and as never before. The later Greek historian Thucydides recorded a tradition of widespread early Phoenician presence in locations reminiscent of those attested in Iberia and Sardinia, but archaeology so far reveals an investment primarily in the western, hitherto backwoods, end of Sicily, where local population had been on the rise since the start of the Iron Age, and to the south, on Malta.[101] Both locations complemented Carthage on the other side of the narrows, as well as the enclaves in Sardinia. Motya, on an islet sheltered in a salty lagoon, is the only Sicilian example that has been extensively explored, and still we know nothing about how it replaced, over the later 8th century, the indigenous community underlying it.[102]

10.18 The strait of Messina and a slumbering Etna, seen from the Roman theatre at Taormina. The low peninsula in the background is the site of Sicilian Naxos, one of several Aegean-derived ventures that from the 8th century BC sought to profit along this artery of trade.

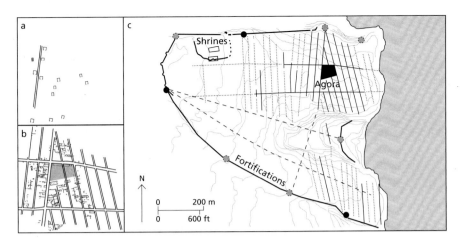

10.19 The hesitant but cooperative origins of Megara Hyblaea, with originally several grids gradually infilled with modest houses, an open communal area and arguably pre-existent roadways, later developing into a walled town with shrines and agora, but still bearing the imprint of its earliest days in the street system. The plan of the agora area is shown in (a) the 8th century BC and (b) 6th century BC; (c) is an overall plan of the later town.

Simultaneously, a rash of competitive ventures initiated from Euboea, Corinth and its neighbour and rival, Megara, sprang up at the other end of Sicily, astride the Messina-strait trunk route into the Tyrrhenian Sea [**10.18**].[103] Only once the best nodes there had been spoken for did copycat efforts spread to other niches. Again, native coastal communities haunt the tales passed down. One expedition checked out Thapsos, before opting with ostensible local approval for the site of Megara Hyblaea, further up the sheltered bay. Thanks to its only modest later success, Megara Hyblaea preserves its early gridded alignment, at first sparsely in-filled with a few dozen huts, but in a few generations accommodating several thousand people; its irregularities reflect an initial concern less with creating a coherent town than respecting native trails along the coast [**10.19**].[104] At Syracuse a group spearheaded by Corinthians expelled a local village from the islet of Ortygia, and soon began to push aggressively inland, to the detriment of nearby Pantalica – markedly faster than was normal in such situations, where a lag of one to three centuries would emerge as the norm,[105] and undoubtedly an entirely new kind of behaviour for a Sicilian coastal entrepôt.[106] Elsewhere in the interior, native hilltop villages survived, either, as at Monte Polizzo in the far west, in cultural dialogue with coastal enclaves or, like Sant'Angelo Muxaro and Lentini, for the present protected by Sicily's rugged depths.[107] Nearly a tonne of weapons and ingots found at Mendolito on the slopes of Etna are plausibly linked to the local cult of a volcano god that only later gained Hephaestian associations.[108]

Over the same time span, southern Italy was targeted by small groups across an even shorter range from the Peloponnese.[109] These had an eye for the rich farmland around the Italian instep as well as trading opportunities. In at least one case, at Incoronata near later Metapontion, they had to settle for swampy lowland that a mixed community of Greek and local inhabitants then painstakingly drained.[110] At Taranto, the indigenous entrepôt of Scoglio del Tonno was succeeded by the Spartan-led founders of Taras; Broglio de Trebisacce was likewise replaced by Sybaris. As expected of a rising star at sea, Corinth secured its presence near the Strait of Otranto, primarily through a dependency on Corfu, whose later insubordination we came across in the context of the changing face of naval engagements.

Cumulatively, the establishment of a new enclave in Sicily or southern Italy every two to three years over the last third of the 8th century BC is unmatched anywhere in the Mediterranean save, perhaps, in Andalusia.[111]

Of gods and Greeks: the rise of sanctuaries and ethnicity

So far, Pithekoussai has proved as reliable a guide as any site could be for the diverse initiatives of its time. In two respects, however, it fails us. The first concerns the role of shrines in articulating communications and trade, and in this instance the absence may simply be one of archaeological exploration in the right place on Ischia. One of the deepest contrasts between the Bronze Age and the Iron Age is the fact that in the former, religious structures in the east received less investment than palaces, and were at best modestly visible elsewhere, while in the latter they became not just holy places but visually and economically powerful elements in the Mediterranean's land- and seascapes. Reasons for this change are not hard to come by. With the demise of centralized palaces and international diplomacy, even the rudimentary protection that these provided in the east for people and goods on the move evaporated, and nothing comparable had ever existed further west. At first, the resultant freedom balanced the drawbacks, but as trade and interaction over former cultural boundaries boomed in the 8th century, the desirability of universal regulating mechanisms grew. Moreover, with the partial exception of Tyre, the Mediterranean's shallow-rooted, fissile elites were ultimately failing, for all their material glory, to secure the numinous mantle attached to earlier eastern rulers – one of the factors that would gradually split off a secular political world from the transcendent realm, and equally widen personal access to the divine.[112] The gods and their houses took on the roles of mediator and oath-binder, guarantor of qualities and quantities exchanged, secure haven for people and goods in transit, information bank and even lender of capital, reaping benefits in thanksgiving offerings and the dues from markets conducted under their protection.[113] Shrines stuck out in emerging townscapes at this time, too, but with a few exceptions, those vital to Mediterranean connections tended to be less community-specific, more inclusive, and situated in neutral areas, often stop-overs or way-finding points along sea-routes. They sacralized harbours, headlands, islands and isthmuses, replacing or adding to the local spirits, gods and monsters with which the sea had presumably always heaved.[114]

Among the Mediterranean's enormous and ever-flexible pantheon, gods on the move, or content to be blended with their equivalents elsewhere, were nothing new, as is confirmed by Wenamun's adventures and the widespread finds of metal figurines of Levantine divinities, many hitherto minor deities such as Astarte or the smiting god Reshef, whose promotion owed much to the inclusivity of their cults.[115] Similarly, maritime shrines had existed earlier, too. What was novel was the sheer popularity and proliferation of both as the mobility of mortal worshippers took off across the basin. Phoenician activity is implicated in many early examples, from Tyre to the traces of monumental shrines, unique in the west, on the Cadiz archipelago. Between these lay others, such as Gorham's Cave within the Rock of Gibraltar, last visited as a home of Neanderthals, where rituals with a marine flavour were instigated from the 8th century BC, Astarte's sanctuary at Tas-Silg on Malta, which incorporated the ruins of a Copper Age megalithic temple, and that to an unknown god at Kommos, the Cretan staging post along the route of the isles, where a Phoenician tri-pillared altar was erected around 800 BC.[116] The Phoenician figurines in native Iberian tombs could well symbolize contracts entered into by local elites under the eye of Gadir's gods,[117] while the abundance of nude female figurines may allude to the sexual rites at such sanctuaries – one place reputedly associated with such practices being Corinth.

Regardless of the details as to quite what went on at Corinth, it was there and elsewhere in the Aegean that such shrines in the end gained their greatest ascendancy, notably at Olympia in the western Peloponnese, on tiny Delos in the Cyclades, at Samos and Ephesus in the east and, of course, at oracular Delphi, recessed enough from the political map to give some credibility to its much-asserted neutrality, but conveniently placed above the Gulf of Corinth to pick up passing information and provide expert advice on overseas ventures [**10.20**].[118] At such places, wooden and mud-brick buildings were replaced by grander ones with rows of columns, carved stone highlights, Corinthian terracotta roof-tiles and lively painted designs on their interior and exterior walls.[119] The altars by which people communicated with the gods were commensurately up-scaled. Offerings prove equally informative. Among these, the wine-mixing cauldrons and tripods given as prizes in ritual games, such

10.20 This aerial view of the land- and sea-scape around Delphi, situated centre-right below the snows of Parnassus, captures both its terrestrially secluded location and its proximity to the great conduit of maritime traffic and news along the Gulf of Corinth. The oracle drew some of its power from both.

10.21 A 9th-century BC north Levantine bronze plaque inscribed in Aramaic as the booty of Hazael, but finally deposited in the late 6th century BC at the temple of Hera on Samos, with a similar find discovered at Eretria. The interpretative freedom created by the gap in time and space is typical of many such eastern finds in Aegean sanctuaries, with the identity of the dedicants and timing of their acts very much open to debate.

as those instituted at Olympia, were a recurrent feature, as were vast numbers of eastern exotica, in contrast to their mainly funerary use in the centre and west.[120] Corinth's shrine at Perachora, a short trip across the waters of the Gulf, was one magnet for these, as was Olympia, which also boasted Italian helmets among its offerings, while at Samos, two-thirds of all non-pottery finds derived from the Levant, Cyprus, Egypt or Anatolia, including a crocodile head, and mirrors that equated Egyptian Mut with Samian Hera [**10.25**].[121] Some of these imports, many of them inscribed, undoubtedly reveal non-Aegean visitors or dedicants – for example Midas of Phrygia sent a gold throne to Delphi – but they are equally a testimony to Aegean long-range trading and raiding.[122] One reason why such shrines played such an exceptionally authoritative and integrative role within the Aegean may go back to the unique circumstance of a palatial system lost without compensating continuity in urban and other civic life.

The second respect in which Pithekoussai has little to tell concerns the growth of ethnic self-awareness in certain parts of the Mediterranean. So far, this book has deliberately eschewed writing about Mediterranean people in such terms, avoiding 'Greek' and 'Etruscan' save as languages and casting doubt on 'Phoenician' unity. One reason for caution is the fact that we simply do not know how the millions of people spread over the basin across the millennia identified themselves in collective terms, beyond the pharaonic vision of Egypt, the categories Egypt projected onto its neighbours, and a few loose groupings that the latter recognized in themselves, such as 'Canaanite'. Another is the suspicion that, while ethnicities based on real or fictive descent, cohabitation or language surely must have coalesced under some conditions, these and other forms of identity were fluid and unassertive compared to those forged in later times, and radically different again, in geographical scope and constituent elements, from those trumpeted, for good or evil, in recent years. As was argued in Chapter 1, the vision of early Mediterranean history propagated in most popular accounts and modern national narratives, as a chessboard across which discrete ethnic groups have always marched, is certainly as false as it is pernicious.[123] And yet while Pithekoussai stands as a model of inclusiveness worthy of attention to this day, the fact is that a few centuries later, descendants of its Aegean-derived inhabitants were among those coining 'barbarian' as a pejorative antithesis to a Greek identity that went well beyond language. A simultaneous hardening can be discerned in other parts of the basin. Of course, it is possible that the spread of writing creates an illusion of rising ethnic self-awareness – for instance, that we only start to see Etruscans (or in their tongue 'Rasna') once Italian and Greek texts existed to identify them to us – but despite this, the sense of a real surge in ethnogenesis is strong, and indeed those forms of alphabetical writing that were adapted, as was the Greek variant, to faithfully imitate a specific spoken language may have aided in its definition.[124]

This process was inseparable from the expansion of Mediterranean networks, just like the so-called 'glocalization' that accompanies contemporary globalization.[125] Ethnic identities in the 8th and 7th centuries BC were similarly shaped by dual aggregative and differentiating impulses, often disproportionately shaped by the specific activities and characteristics of the small sub-groups of any given population that most long-range encounters actually involved.[126] Accompanying this was surely a dose of just-so accounting for the abundant signs of recent movement that travellers must have encountered, some of which filter down to us in migration tales, many with an undercurrent of ancestral justification for present realities, such as the homecoming from Troy, the wanderings of Aeneas, an invasion of the Aeolian Islands by Italian 'Ausonians', and various obscure traditions around the Otranto strait.[127] Affiliation through perceived association and common practices has been already suggested for the 'Phoenicians' in the west. In the central Mediterranean a proto-Punic variant can be detected in the highly interactive maritime triangle now described by Carthage, western Sicily and Sardinia (three areas barely in touch 500 years earlier). This was demarcated by worship of the goddess Tanit and promotion of the *tophet*, a ritual enclosure restricted (unlike the sanctuaries just visited) to locals and other initiates, in which infants were cremated and very probably sacrificed, alongside small animals, at moments of dire need or thanksgiving – the lurking Levantine background tradition of *molk*, or first-born sacrifice, brought centre stage [**10.22**].[128] Simultaneously, the adoption of Greek identities in parts of Cyprus, southern Italy and Sicily could well owe as much to the regularity of contacts with the Aegean as to substantial influxes of people.[129] Standing back a little, the conventional division of the Mediterranean at this juncture into Phoenician and Greek spheres appears to reflect not so much archetypal differences as younger ones emerging via contemporary webs of interaction.

10.22 Later memorials jostle each other above the thick layers of cinerary urns and burnt bones packed into the tophet of Carthage, whose foundation goes back to the early phases of the community.

But Greekness, in the Aegean and further afield, is an equally good example of the alternative strand of ethnic formation, via differentiation, in this case from the many other (literally) disorienting kinds of people encountered.[130] Principal among these were Phoenicians, ironically a collective that we owe to Greek, and whose Aegean connotations were deeply ambivalent. Alluring as they were to elites eager to join the wider world of exotic goods and practices, Phoenicians presented an alarming prospect for others of the middling sort, especially agrarian or less travelled people (of whom there undoubtedly remained many), for whom the explicitly mercantile, culturally deracinated practices refined in the east since the Bronze Age seemed dangerously wily (shades of the 'corrupting sea') – a defensive stance that ossified into prejudice in later Classical thought and, thanks to the latter's impact on Western elites over 2000 years later, colours attitudes to trade and stokes anti-Semitism to this day.[131] During the 8th century BC, and for some time thereafter, intimations of Greek identity were faint, ambiguous and countered by elite cosmopolitanism, although even the latter gradually evolved a Hellenic guise.[132] Such stirrings were quite widespread on the fringes of Phoenician engagement. On Cyprus, Sargon II's stele at Kition could have stirred up resentment elsewhere on this hitherto tolerant island, as evinced by its uptake of Aegean trappings and retention of indigenous syllabic scripts.[133] 'Etruscan' as both an ethnic and written phenomenon reflects similar reactions in the Tyrrhenian region, and in southwest Iberia offerings of eastern-type goods at earlier Copper Age tombs hint at attempts to control and render native the power of foreign things.[134]

In the east, and at least a match for Greek developments in terms of their long-term impact, new currents coursed through the remnant of Israel that had survived the Assyrian assault and the fall of the worldly northern kingdom, and now swirled in an unprecedented intellectual, moralizing ferment around southerly Judah's swollen, and previously remote, highland capital at Jerusalem.[135] As witnessed in Chapter 9, hints of Israelite dietary distinction had existed since the end of the 2nd millennium BC. In addition, we know from inscriptions that Yahweh had emerged by at least the 8th century as a god in both the northern and southern kingdoms, rubbing shoulders with Baal in the former and often with a consort typical of the tutelary divinities of specific Iron Age polities. Late in the 8th century BC, however, shrines to rival gods began to vanish, in favour of that encased, unexplored, within the Temple Mount in Jerusalem. Yahweh's transformation into the exclusive deity and salvation of a chosen people, whose destiny lay in a promised land and unifying city – all profoundly un-Mediterranean concepts – is hard to imagine without Judah's traditionally peripheral status, which enabled purism and disdain for the outside world to flourish, coupled with the mortal threat of Assyria and rallying efforts of a royal and priestly elite from the end of the 8th century onward. We shall probably never know whether other, no less remarkable theological and ethnic sprigs vanished under the tramp of Assyria's armies, as that at Jerusalem so nearly did.

Finally, we shall also never know whether it was unusual conditions in 8th- and 7th-century Greece and Israel that led to the formulation of two of the ancient Mediterranean's greatest literary creations, or whether the consequences of this

10.23 Lyre player seal, of a type produced in the northern Levant but most popular abroad in the late 8th-century BC Aegean. What songs the eastern sirens sang we can only occasionally glimpse from surviving hymns and epic stories in Bronze Age and later Levantine and Mesopotamian archives, but Aegean people's fondness for bardic imagery implies a growing interest in their own, as well as a more widely shared, oral poetic tradition, culminating in Homer.

exceptionalism simply preserved these examples out of a wider repertoire. The Homeric poems and the core of the Old Testament manifestly contain older elements, ranging from towns by now ruined to allusions to ancient objects and practices.[136] In the Homeric case, these were transmitted thanks to a tradition of versatile oral epic of which we possess only the latest versions, and in Israel by genealogical memories aided from the 9th century BC by northern archives. We have encountered Biblical resonances that go back to the start of the Iron Age, and maybe as far as the Hyksos. The *Iliad* preserves details from the time of Mycenae's shaft graves, while the mobile maritime ethos and figure of the flexible, aspiring seafarer, a resourceful man from a resource-poor island, so exalted in the *Odyssey*, emerged long before, alongside 3rd-millennium BC voyaging (even if, from an Aegean perspective, the creation of a freak-inhabited west as a foil was obsolete in terms of 8th-century realities and smacks of an earlier phase of exploration). But equally, alongside genuinely ancient strata and faux archaizing were clearly later elements, such as the 8th–7th-century aspect of the supposedly Solomonic golden age and of Biblical geography in general, the Homeric awareness of iron, cremation and contested domestic politics, as well as the *Odyssey*'s interlude in Phaiakia, which is portrayed as an ideal town in the west. All these observations contribute to a consensus that the Homeric poems cohered orally around 700 BC, if perhaps not frozen into writing until the 6th century, and that the Old Testament's opening books were late 8th- or 7th-century compositions, heavily edited a century or so later. In both cases, part of the motivation was political, in Judah from kings and a priesthood rebuilding a shattered polity, in Greece from a more secular elite anxious to assert its prerogatives and honour code.[137] But beyond this, such creations fostered a deeper sense of ethnic solidarity. In Israel this would survive defeat and exile. In the Aegean, which more than anywhere else struggled to resolve a local past that was glamorous yet palpably dead with the challenges of ever-widening present horizons, recitations in festivals at the great interregional sanctuaries perhaps first spun, in the blended dialects of Homer, the common stories of a war against Troy and voyaging among strange peoples, for audiences of islanders and coastal dwellers just beginning to distance themselves from their thrall to an eastern world-view [**10.23**].[138]

An Archaic end point: the burgeoning of towns and civic life

Despite the increasing symphonic strains audible by the 8th and early 7th centuries BC, the final movements in the coming together of the Mediterranean were played out slightly later, over the second half of the 7th and the entire 6th centuries. This created a world commonly known as the Archaic, although, from our perspective, it represents a culmination of much older initiatives rather than a point of origin. As explained at the start of this chapter, one of the distinctive elements was the drawing in of the rest of the basin, and even areas beyond. But before we explore this, we need to examine how a series of so far loose internal structures crystallized, rationalized and refined themselves, while at the same time growing exponentially. We will look at five developments in particular, mainly in the area stretching from the Aegean west: from large if inchoate communities and territories to true towns and states; from elite groups to formal oligarchies with codified lifestyles, their power relative to middling people negotiated, or not, within civic frameworks; from free-for-all trading patterns to more optimized, demarcated flows; from shrines to monumental temples; and from warriors and raiding galleys to patriot soldiers, mercenaries and costly naval forces.

That this cluster of processes draws our focus away from the Levant signals a major evidentiary and historical shift in the primacy of this hitherto key region. The overwhelming bias in its favour, in terms of the privileged insights offered by written records, is abruptly reversed, save for the Old Testament, by a flood of texts emanating from the Aegean. By the 6th century BC, writing was widespread there and, thanks to the later reverence for Greek culture, huge amounts survive in transmission beyond that on archaeologically durable media. In addition to poetry, dedications, laws, mathematics and philosophy – all touched upon later – Hecataeus, the first known name in a line of historians with a geographical bent, was born at Miletus around 530 BC. His works do not survive, but those of Herodotus, born a mere forty-six years later, do, and like those of his successor, Thucydides, they probed back into the centuries that concern us in this chapter. This creates the impression of a much more Hellenocentric Mediterranean than was yet the case, and drowns out, whether by ignorance or design, a multitude of other voices and memories.

But in real terms, too, the Levant underwent a drastic, if ultimately temporary, diminution at the hands of empire that gave other parts of the Mediterranean a chance to seize the lead. The immediate occasion was the replacement in the late 7th century BC of Assyrian hegemony by one deriving from further south in Mesopotamia, at Babylon, a stupendous city of roughly 80,000 people.[139] From now on, empire would cumulatively swallow empire with little dip in local impact save at the moments of transition. Babylonian policy towards the Levant stands out as exceptionally negative.[140] The last inland polities were annihilated (most notoriously Jerusalem by Nebuchadnezzar in 587 BC), spelling the demise of a brilliant tradition of urban life extending back into the Bronze Age, and the end of habitation at many ancient tells. In their place villages of surviving natives and transplanted populations, together with the estates of imperial favourites, ensured the agricultural productivity of a politically emasculated and demographically slighted landscape.[141] More surprising, in contrast to Assyria's economically motivated tolerance of mercantile cities on the sea, was the fiery sack of Ashkelon in 604 BC, followed in 572 BC, after a thirteen-year siege, by the fall of Tyre itself, whose last ruler died by the rivers of Babylon, his place taken by imperial functionaries, and the city's role usurped by a pliant Sidon.[142] The prophet Ezekiel bandwagoned on this catastrophe to extol Yahweh's wrath at Mediterranean-style excess, but the damage to Levantine commerce was real; Greek pottery, that convenient tracer of deeper flows, all but vanished from the coast.[143]

Something beyond the choler of Mesopotamian potentates must lie behind this heavy-handed treatment. One answer specific to Tyre may be that the city's success at flooding the east with Iberian silver in the end devalued this metal, triggering a shift to Egyptian and other gold that rendered Tyrian trade less vital to imperial interests.[144] This may explain Tyre's already harsher, more micromanaged treatment in the last decades of Assyrian power. But parallels between Babylonian destructiveness and the comparably drastic strategy of Egypt's Mamluk rulers – who wiped out the last of the Crusader enclaves along the same coast nearly 2000 years later – also suggest that for certain highly continental, alluvium-focused empires, the threat of disorder from the maritime realm outweighed its economic allure and benefits. On the second occasion, the world of the sea carried on flourishing elsewhere, to the advantage of other maritime powers.[145] Babylon, likewise, was utterly unable to suppress the rest of a Mediterranean whose production and consumption pumps were now fully primed for take-off, whose resources and networks were no longer being scoured and tapped off east by Tyre, and that remained free of the tribute that Levantine cities' prosperity had been forced to surmount. Wiser, surely, was the more traditional, lenient policy of Lydia, a smaller if still considerable west Anatolian empire of some 250,000 sq. km (95,000 sq. miles) by the late 7th century BC, and save (arguably) for Ramessid Egypt, the first imperial entity to be based right on the edge of the basin itself – at Sardis, just 70 km (45 miles) from the sea.[146] For Lydia, like the inland Phrygian polity it had succeeded, grew fabulously rich not only from its internal sources of gold and electrum, but also from the tribute of flourishing coastal towns in the east Aegean, which it spared after their defeat.

Let us turn to the broader picture, and first to the urban explosion around the Mediterranean's perimeter and right through its heart. Mediterranean towns were singly and collectively more fragile, vulnerable creations than is often realized[147] – witness their mid-millennium abeyance in the Levant, one of their first strongholds, as well as their rise and demise during the Aegean's Bronze Age. But the 7th and 6th centuries BC saw an immense surge in their numbers and distribution, even if most populations stayed in the four-figure range, with a few into five figures, and none attaining six figures until well after 500 BC.[148] Most arose in situ, out of pre-existing settlements drawn together in advantageous nodal positions or ecological sweet spots. They coevolved with sail-driven shipping, and in this sense both interconnections and complex communities decisively pre-dated the florescence of towns themselves. The latter represented, in the conceptualization of Horden and Purcell, demographic intensification 'congealed', and made visually as well as morally solid and coherent by investment in monuments and infrastructure.[149] Towns in turn created their own gravity fields, some strong enough to warp or supercharge the webs of interaction around them. Their territories varied greatly in size, but few were over 1000–2000 sq. km (385–770 sq. miles), in other words rarely more than a day's walk from the individual urban hub. For this reason, such units are known as 'city-states', a concept also applicable to many of the smaller one-town polities of earlier times in the east but now more widespread and invested, as we shall see, with additional social connotations.[150] Once this lifestyle became feasible on a Mediterranean-wide scale, the access it gave to everything from material goods to tutelary gods and security in an exposed world ensured its rampant popularity.[151] These advantages more than countered the social cost of cooperation and a longer tramp out to the fields from which most town-dwellers still derived their livelihood. Towns, in short, became desirable places to live in, and people voted with their feet (or oars), a conclusion eloquently borne out in the Aegean by the numerous abandonments of small earlier settlements even at a time of population growth.

Urban forms and those of the surrounding territory varied greatly, however, both between regions and in comparison to preceding examples in the east. In the west and centre, the shoreline locations of most new towns reveal their origins in earlier entrepôts, a feature still visible today among the successors constructed over many of them in Spain, Sicily, southern Italy and, as we shall discover later, France.[152] We know least about the far west. Gadir, Huelva and maybe Toscanos were urban on a modest scale, while inland medium-sized native hillforts arose, such as Acinipo near Ronda, less architecturally elaborated but sometimes adapting building methods and community layouts from their own past as well as foreign ideas, and often controlling more territory than the coastal communities.[153] Carthage, well on its way to becoming Tyre-in-the-west, was growing fast, and may have become the most populous city in the basin once Babylon had demolished the competition back in the east. We gain a clearer insight, however, from two of its maritime neighbours, Motya in Sicily and Sulcis in Sardinia, both originally small trading posts. Motya grew throughout the 7th century BC and by the 6th the entire islet was circled with defensive walls, joined by a mole to the main island of Sicily, and densely packed with warehouses, shrines, a tophet, a *cothon* harbour and housing for some 15,000 inhabitants.[154] In its industrial quarters, murex were crushed on sperm whale vertebrae, one with an iron harpoon tip embedded.[155] Sulcis did not expand so dramatically, but was more overtly territorial, staking out its metal-rich hinterland with a line of further settlements, such as Monte Sirai, which doubled up as points of interaction with surrounding native communities.[156] Urban growth and land-grabs paint an equally dramatic picture in the increasingly Greek areas of Sicily and southern Italy, confirming common underlying behaviours.[157] Established places like Syracuse continued to expand by influx and local recruitment, while younger foundations such as Selinous and Akragas on the initially ignored south Sicilian longshore were initially laid out or swiftly replanned on grandiose grids, and soon thrust inland, with the weight of their big demographic battalions, to annex great swathes of prime cereal-growing countryside. The best resolution, however, comes from Metapontion, another booming, land-seizing town on a stretch of the Italian instep so malarial from late Roman times until its 20th-century AD reclamation that it preserves an ancient pattern of small farms and drainage ditches laid out in a grid of allotments, imposed upon the landscape in a striking assertion of social ideals and the expectation of standardized production units over natural diversity [**10.24**].[158]

As in Iberia, south Italian and Sicilian native communities grew in the interior. Southern Italy saw the creation of huge, scantily occupied enclosures, such as Gravina in the uplands behind Metapontion and an extraordinary 13-km- (8-mile-)

10.24 The ancient landscape around Metapontion, showing the aerial detection of ancient land divisions and the numerous rural settlements and other sites, of later 6th-century BC date onwards, discovered within the surveyed zones.

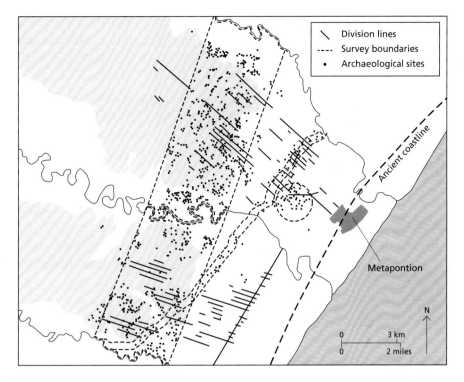

long embankment at Arpi that advertised the return of the Tavoliere.[159] Public buildings and street plans only materialized well after 500 BC, often in quite different places. In inland Sicily, internal rivalries, emulation and threats from the coastal towns triggered a coming together somewhat earlier, leading to the abandonment of promising smaller ventures such as Monte Polizzo in favour of sizeable native towns, for example at Segesta.[160] Economic relations with the new breed of coastal centres were close and could be mutually rewarding; in southern Italy indigenous hill communities fed cloth spun on Greek-style looms into the maritime lowlands and both there and in Sicily, Greek goods (mainly amphorae, drinking vessels, ornaments and weapons) penetrated deep inland.[161] But as towns hungry for land to cash-crop multiplied along the coast, the makings of conflict and mutual militarization became apparent. Early Pompeii, at a junction of local, Etruscan and Greek spheres, was a rare instance of cooperative melding; elsewhere, firmer distinctions began to reflect how people saw themselves and described others.[162] We have already come across this in the context of nascent Greek identity; the trend spread along contact zones elsewhere in the Mediterranean, as loose native affiliations solidified into territorial tribes reinforced by newly defined cultural practices, both as a local means of resistance and a newcomers' controlling strategy that streamlined negotiations with more readily identifiable local leaders.[163]

The urban pace was made, however, in two hotspots that had evolved locally throughout the earlier Iron Age: Etruria, plus its Roman appendage, and the southern Aegean. In the rich land between the Arno and Tiber, by now home to half a million people, roughly fifteen big towns with five-figure populations arose on the still

10.25 Streets and houses laid out at Marzabotto, near Bologna, a hub of expanding Etruscan-related activity beyond the Apennines.

unwalled tuff plateaux, each a substantial city-state living off as much as 1000–1500 sq. km (385–580 sq. miles) of naturally compartmentalized territory, the inner zones of which were criss-crossed by roads, studded with farms and neatly drained or watered by conduits and aqueducts.[164] Older communities like Veii, Tarquinia and Rome retained the organic imprints of the settlements out of which they emerged, but rectilinear grids characterized new starts at Doganella and a later trans-Apennine expansion to Marzobotto, near Bologna [**10.25**]. Houses became rectangular and stone-built, while burials moved off the plateaux, and shortly before 500 BC the first urban temples were erected in Veii and Rome, the two cities uneasily sharing the lower Tiber Valley, the former's temple dedicated to Etruscan Menerva, the latter's to Capitoline Jupiter [**10.26**]. This apart, we know little about the physical appearance of these central Italian mega-communities, and no less baffling are several smaller intervening centres boasting impressive architecture, such as Acquarossa and Murlo, which have been variously interpreted as minor independent players, interstate ceremonial meeting points or private elite residential mansions.[165]

The city-states of the Aegean have such a hallowed later reputation in the form of the Classical *polis* that it is hard to approach them objectively.[166] In this broken landscape, the principal players unsurprisingly arose in much the same major valleys between the sea and mountains that had sponsored earlier Bronze Age polities, but the similarities end here. At the upper end of the scale, this second cycle of Aegean urbanism bred larger towns but, with a few exceptions, smaller territories, thereby creating unusually high, often evenly balanced, ratios of town-dwellers to country-folk, and commensurately initially under-inhabited rural landscapes, even as reviving population densities broke through their previous Bronze Age records. The houses, temples and other edifices of mercantile Corinth, at this stage the only major walled town in the Aegean, extended amidst intervening fields over 400 ha (1000 acres) below the looming acropolis, but drew upon only 900 sq. km (350 sq. miles) of terrestrial hinterland.[167] To the south, Argos, Bronze Age Mycenae's heir, held less again. Athens had grown to 20,000 people by 500 BC, and provides the best examples of

10.26 This reconstruction of the frontal view of an Etruscan temple is modelled on the remains from Portonaccio at Veii.

courtyard-centred elite town houses (finally, a return for the Aegean to the standards of the Minoan palatial phase), but even so struggled to extend its grip beyond Attica towards its closest overland and island neighbours.[168] Sparta, which had a perversely ephemeral urban core, was the only outstandingly successful conquest state, acquiring approximately 8000 sq. km (3100 sq. miles) and 150,000 largely servile subjects, both totals to rival the largest polities within the Mediterranean since the late 3rd millennium BC, save for those in the Nile Delta and contemporary Lydia.[169] At the lower end of the scale the contrast with the Bronze Age was still more marked, for hundreds of small, and sometimes truly miniature, versions of this module for a polity sprouted up across the Aegean, most with populations in the hundreds or low thousands, and in several cases even partitioning minor Cycladic islands.[170] The political autonomy of such units might often be compromised by larger neighbours, but nonetheless they remained decisively more than rural villages, thanks to the self-consciously urban aspect that they shared with bigger communities and the crucial fact that, however absurd the *city*-state title may seem for such places, they remained emphatically self-constituting *citizen*-states[171] (a variant popular in western and northern Greece saw several small towns forming a territorial *ethnos* around a shared sanctuary).[172] This brings us straight to our second broader theme: the formation of civic power across this newly urbanized Mediterranean.

Here, again, our view is dominated by the Greek experience, which provides the richest data and the political vocabulary to this day. Rome, too, probably stands out more than it should from its Etruscan neighbours thanks to the transmission into modern times of its equally partial recensions of history.[173] In reality, at the apex of most later 7th- and 6th-century Mediterranean city-states in terms of wealth, authority and office stood a restricted group of powerful citizens, less formally organized and overtly hegemonic in their way of running things than the Bronze Age palatial elites. Oligarchy in various forms was therefore the rule, regardless of the niceties – after all, aristocracy (notionally rule by the best) was simply a self-regarding gloss on this basic norm, while the 'tyrants', such as Periander of Corinth, Polycrates of Samos and Athens's Peisistratids, who arose from about 650 BC, were commonly oligarchs who had broken their peers' rule of collective authority.[174] Among the few instances of kingship, Sparta's was heavily hedged, while those reported by later writers in Etruria and Rome were short-lived, hard to distinguish from tyranny and are barely visible archaeologically.[175] Rule by the few could entail power-sharing by substantial numbers of the better-off. The citizen armies that Sparta fielded shortly after 500 BC point to around 8000 full citizens, just under a quarter of all adult men in the Spartan state, though this proportion would translate into far smaller totals elsewhere.[176] Elite women played prominent, if less overtly political, roles, too. In Etruria, where high female status had long been apparent in burials, they were

10.27 Women, shown lighter-skinned, join men in this depiction of a banqueting scene in the 6th-century BC Tomb of the Leopards at Tarquinia.

literate and took part in banquets [**10.27**].[177] In Carthage, the memory of a foundress remained axiomatic. Greek priestesses were influential, too, while Sappho's poems celebrated a world of high-born female sensibility.[178] And in contrast to earlier and later artistic conventions of female nudity, the leading women of this period were depicted fully clothed in their finery.[179] Sharing of political forms was encouraged further by continued elite mobility across ethnic and state boundaries, in the forms of mercantile activity, guest friendship and, increasingly, intermarriage. Names of mixed ancestry inscribed on pots in Etruria, such as 'Rutile Hipukrates', give substance to the story recounted by the later 1st-century BC historian Dionysios of Halikarnassos of Damaratos the Corinthian, who, after making a fortune in the Tyrrhenian trade, moved to Tarquinia when his home town's politics went against him, and married into a local family.[180]

Superficially, this was a political high noon for the pan-Mediterranean urban elite. However, beneath the veneer of cultural convergence lay profound distinctions in the foundational solidity of their power. In the Levantine-derived political sphere, comprising what remained of its original homeland, parts of Cyprus, Carthage and the other Phoenician communities in the centre and west, oligarchy was deeply rooted in concepts of elite power-sharing and broader assemblies in an urban context that had matured over centuries.[181] Although the evidence to prove it does not survive, it would not be surprising if, in line with the slightly earlier initiatives of the Levantine polities facing Assyria, effective centralizing organizational tendencies had begun to reassert themselves in such polities (without a return to the ponderous economic centralization of the Bronze Age). An unusually detailed glimpse into such oligarchical structures is offered by the magistrates who governed Carthage and derived their power from a combination of land, ships and trade, given sacred sanction by ties to the priesthood – not for nothing did they promote local gods, such as Tanit and Baal Hammon, over Melqart as Tyre ran into trouble back east.[182] An interesting outlier to this distribution of stable oligarchies may well be Crete, less because of its earlier strong Phoenician connections than thanks to their abrupt cessation with the collapse of Tyrian trade at the start of the 6th century, which allowed a deeply grounded elite to establish a secluded and austere regime, not unlike that of the Sardinian interior, that removed this normally widely linked island from the map of Mediterranean connections at a critical juncture for the history of the Aegean.[183] Where thus ingrained, oligarchy was robust and endured with few signs of instability, if an equal absence of the creative political debates that erupted elsewhere.

Such debates and, as a result, virtually endemic internal conflict, instead arose where oligarchical foundations were weaker, notably across much of the Greek and Italian spheres (sadly, we know little about the constitution of the elite associated with rising native centres and ethnic self-consciousness in Iberia at this juncture, though a similarly unstable structure is likely).[184] The sources of weakness were manifold. For one thing, institutional power had few or, in most of the Aegean, ruptured roots, and the modest inequalities that had previously existed did not translate automatically into extensive authority – indeed, in terms of infrastructure the early city-states of the Aegean look decidedly flimsy alongside their Bronze Age antecedents. Furthermore, the make-up of the elite itself was now in wild flux as a new wealth and talent pushed in. In Etruria, kin-based elite lineages with their retainers (the old *gens* affiliation, descended from Bronze Age social structures) were undermined by wealth-based, narrowly family-focused claims, often by arrivistes.[185] In the poems of Theognis of Megara, the obsession with new riches, blatant competition between rivals, fickle political and personal fortunes, and the demise of customary deference, bordered on the hysterical.[186] Lastly, divine approval, the great consolidant of elite authority elsewhere, was never widely acknowledged, for reasons that are likely to go back to the strikingly secular power of the Lilliputian big men, and dearth of shrines, witnessed in Mediterranean Europe as far back as the 3rd and 2nd millennia BC (see Chapters 7 and 8).[187] This created a disconnection with the sacred realm that now, as a consequence, began to develop more independently in such regions.

Out of this precariousness at the top in the Aegean and Italy grew the impetus and necessity to engage politically with other social groups, and thence the origins of a concept of civic life that, if assuredly not wholly new, undoubtedly placed a greater emphasis than before on explicit debate and eventually constitutional frameworks of power-sharing and thought. The target was that middling group, whose outlines have surfaced several times in this and the previous two chapters, most recently in the 8th century BC. But ways of accommodating them were far from agreed upon. Those most praised by posterity and palatable today advocated measures of protection from exploitation by the rich, notably in the writings of the Athenian Solon (638–558 BC), which urged elite restraint and responsibility, opposed the rise in debt slavery among poorer farmers in a landscape of greedy estates, and called for the creation from such people of a substantial class of small-scale free landowners.[188] Positively singled out too is the widening of participation in civic life through new institutions, as exemplified by the Roman reforms of Servius Tullius (active 578–535 BC) and his predecessors.[189] Occasional signs that such ideas were gaining traction can be picked up, for instance in the laying out of open agoras as assembly areas as well as markets, or an odd wooden structure for public gathering at Metapontion.[190] In Etruria colossal tumuli were superseded by identical family-sized tombs aligned in rock-cut streets of the dead, and even drinking paraphernalia became more inclusive and impersonal.[191] Public pageants such as state religious festivals (the famous Athenian Panathenaia started in 566 BC) and Italian processional 'triumphs' played to a wider audience too.[192] However, it is easy to be carried away by hindsight. It took generations for Solonic precepts to turn the tide against ebullient Athenian oligarchs, and for all the interest in *isonomia* (equality before the law), the law codes so prominently displayed in Aegean city-states at this time reveal less interest in legality and conduct per se than in the oligarchical fixation with how power and office were shared out and regulated.[193] Moreover, just as common a means of winning hearts and minds was the populist, charismatic and levelling approach adopted by tyrants and their kingly Italian equivalents (not least Servius Tullius), whether themselves table-turning members of the charmed circle or outsiders on the make, like Servius' father-in-law and predecessor as king in Rome, Tarquinius Priscus, himself reputedly an offspring of the Corinthian Demaratos.[194] Therein lay the reason why tyranny and kingship alike became abidingly abhorrent to an elite jealously guarding its prerogatives.

Common to all these systems was a strong internal awareness of, and appeal to, the collective identity of the individual city-state, which acted as an intermediate-level affiliation (owed in earlier times in the east to ruling houses) between those of family or wider kin on the one hand, and slowly consolidating wider ethnic group-ings on the other. City-states acted, through their ruling parties, as self-conscious entities, asserting their achievements and competing with neighbours, whether in monument building, open warfare or its athletic surrogates, and creating cock-pits of fiercely local difference that was superficially at odds with the wider ethnic associations and lumped oppositions being forged at a larger scale.[195] Like pol-ities in the Levant since the Bronze Age, they forged alliances, too, often with their enemy's enemy (within and between states), but also involving looser, long-range connections, and it was in this context that the idea of a mother city for each home-away-from-home, and the cultivation of foundation stories, dates and associated founder cults, arose.

Turning from emergent political entities to their wider cultural correlates and expression, the instability and competition among the former in the Aegean and Italy sheds light on the veritable explosion of the latter, especially in the Greek case, where most leading towns became saturated with images, grandiose architecture and other forms of display, to a degree unparalleled elsewhere in the Mediterranean.[196] Much was sponsored by the wealthy, and promoted their concerns. Some grew out of pre-existing practices. The Greek symposium and its distinctive Italian versions evolved from earlier collective wine-drinking customs, now codified to insist on the reclining posture already long-standard further east, specific adornments (clothing, perfume, garlands and jewelry), accompanying music and dance, explicit emphasis on the mixing of wine with water, and various conversational as well as erotic conventions.[197] The playful, questioning imagery on symposiastic pottery reflected the preoccupations and sensibilities of participants. The literary legacy of the physically still under-investigated towns in the east Aegean reveals through their lyric poetry a continued elite addiction to sensual clothes and glittering metalwork, coupled with a dawning awareness of Arabian unguents. Writings on mathematics, philosophy and the ordering of celestial and earthly space likewise affirm a continued debt to Near Eastern erudition, gathered by tyrants like Polycrates both in the flesh, by attracting famous experts, and, in imitation of eastern tradition, through libraries of texts.[198] The immediate lodestone was nearby Lydia, a byword for luxury and just as much a part of Sappho's universe as the Greek towns along the coast, but other engagements ran along different routes.[199] For reasons that will later become clear, a direct connection emerged between the Aegean and Egypt, arguably for the first time since the 14th century BC. Along with competitive display between city-states, and tyrants' desires to flaunt their public munificence, this served to stimulate a new gigantism in Greek temple architecture.

Egyptian inspiration is also plain in the sudden eruption of large-scale Greek statuary, notably the aping of Karnak by Delos's lion-lined avenue [**10.28**] and, above all, the kouros [**10.29**], an idealized nude rendition of the young, beautiful, virtuous,

10.28 The wind-scoured Avenue of the Lions on the little Cycladic island of Delos, the religious centre of a wider island and coastal network by this time. The model for this grandiose processional way came from a very different, and much older shrine, that to the god Amun at Karnak in Egypt.

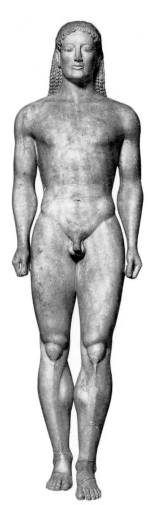

10.29 Strength, beauty, youth and virtue embodied in this kouros from Attica, the funerary monument to Kroisos, a member of the Athenian elite cut down in battle. Even in this relatively late example, the initial debt to a standard pose among Egyptian statuary can still be discerned.

authoritative and wealthy male that proved immensely popular and versatile as a grave marker, votive and victory monument for elite males, as well as its brightly coloured, heavily draped female equivalent, the kore [PL. XLIV].[200] No other Mediterranean elites invested so heavily in massive representations of the human form, although more parallels may have existed, and since been recycled, in the originally Egyptian form of hollow-cast bronze rather than stone, not least at the major Phoenician centres. Indeed, this seems the only plausible explanation for an unexpected find from Monte Prama in Sardinia, restored from thousands of later deliberately smashed-up pieces to reveal at least twenty-five stone statues of archers and pugilists in the style of native *bronzetti*, but, at 2 m (6 ft) tall, far larger and surely also skeuomorphing foreign metal sculpture.[201] These warriors once stood over a native cemetery and guarded the middle ground between Phoenician Tharros and the interior. Even native Sardinian elites had begun to engage with the wider symbolic world of the Mediterranean, and to weave it in with their own traditions.

Far-from-archaic trade

Much of what tied this world together remained commercial transactions. Except in Levantine waters, the later 7th and 6th centuries saw a further burgeoning of trade, and the final realization of a Mediterranean-wide market, already partly inter-dependent and governed by the regime of cheap maritime transport costs, specialist production and extensive importation, plus the attendant threats of short-circuiting, undercutting and substitution, that had arisen over the 2nd millennium BC in the east and survived there in a few economic refuges ever since.[202] The later 7th century BC saw the peak of the Phoenician network in the west, streamlined by internal competition towards a limited number of major operators, primarily Gadir but also new foundations such as Malaka.[203] This concentration, plus the native Iberian elite's uptake of viticulture during the 6th century BC, in their own quest for Mediterranean-style consumption, wealth and status, spelt the end for smaller Phoenician ventures in the eponymous Malaga bay. Meanwhile, connections in the Tyrrhenian region were being heavily reshaped by Etruscan sea trade, which expanded decisively throughout this period, adopting as its culture hero one Utuzte (Latin Ulysses). Its foci were Elban iron and the export to adjacent regions of the products of another now well-established local oil and wine industry, alongside those of southern Iberia, southern Italy and Sicily.[204] In both the west and central Mediterranean, a boom in marine transport is affirmed by the first tangible horizon of wrecks.[205] Best known is that of a vessel that met its end off Giglio around 600 BC, with a cargo just as diverse as those of the Bronze Age, including iron and lead ingots, Etruscan *bucchero* pottery, Corinthian perfume flasks, musical instruments and a writing tablet. Others include the remains of a ship that foundered near Gela in Sicily, most notable for a hull still built using the antiquated lashed technique (and further writing apparatus), finds off Spain and the Balearics, and an Iron Age equivalent of the Gelidonya ship, wrecked on the Rochelongue off Agde in southern

France while transporting scrap metal. To the east, the Aegean, that early nursery of seafaring whose Iron Age re-entry into the overall Mediterranean arena had partly piggybacked on Phoenician activity, now came fully into its own.[206] By the late 6th century, it ranked as one of the paramount generators of pan-Mediterranean sea trade. For a few propitious centuries the Aegean became, in fact, the new Levant: a cluster of independent, dynamic maritime trading centres at the interface between a colossal, centralized world of continental consumers in the east and an expanding mosaic of resources and markets at all other points of the compass.

To a certain degree trading circuits were becoming more spatially defined and segmented again, partly as a result of the reduction in transits across the entire Mediterranean with the eclipse of Tyre, to the gain of multiple locations around the basin, but also reflecting the maturation and growing efficiency of the networks as a whole.[207] How much this concentration, coupled with a growing self-awareness on the part of city-states and the collective projection of ethnic distinctions, eroded the free-for-all trading relations of the preceding centuries and replaced them with more discrete spheres of influence (Carthaginian, Etruscan, Greek, etc.) is a moot point. As in other domains, a good deal of 'ethnic porosity' assuredly remained.[208] Most goods and people still circulated widely, and in all manner of hulls, and those that did not seem to have fallen victim not to trade bans but out-competition, or trouble at their point of origin (naturally, east Phoenician trade went into steep pan-Mediterranean decline). Only in the later 6th century BC did Carthage endeavour to close the western seas to others, making a treaty with Rome, later its mortal enemy, that attempted to exclude all non-Carthaginian boats from the zone west of Cape Bon in Tunisia.[209] But even allowing for the bigger naval forces and well-monitored ports that we shall shortly encounter, there must be a strong suspicion that efforts to legislate over the sea were only gradually starting to gain more traction than during the Bronze Age.

Established trade goods flourished along pre-existing trajectories, notably in the realms of metals, textiles, other luxury craftwork and utilitarian goods. Wine was very widely produced, including by indigenous communities, and there are intriguing clues that living grapevines together with their ideal soils were transported around the western seas by ship.[210] In the west, the vine still far outstripped the olive, which only became established as a cash crop at various dates between the 5th century BC and Roman times.[211] For Purcell, the 7th to 6th centuries BC could be labelled the 'First Mass Sympotic Period'.[212] Glass now returned, manufactured by a new, natron-based technique.[213] And a more general feature that stands out in contrast to the intervening trickle since the 13th century BC is the Aegean's renewed role as a mass exporter to the rest of the Mediterranean.[214] Corinth led the way with small metal items as well as armour (a tribute to its excellent connections, given the lack of ores within the polity) and also vast amounts of finely decorated pottery. The latter exceeded records set at the time of the Mycenaean palaces, and some of it once again was specifically tailored to overseas tastes. By the mid-6th century Athens had taken over on the ceramic front, boasting some 200–300 resident potters and painters.[215] The initial emphasis on small perfume jars switched to drinking cups, wine-mixing vessels and display amphorae, at first in the black-figure technique and then, from about 530 BC, in red-figure, both of which echoed precious metal aesthetics [PL. XLV].²¹⁶ Although of relatively modest value and made by people whom we may wish to regard as artists but contemporaries saw as merely competent technicians, these skilful, visually intricate, narrative-rich creations manifestly were worth sending overseas, in many directions but above all to Etruria, which by the late 6th century BC was receiving several thousand each year.²¹⁷ This was far more than can be explained as a sideline accompanying other cargos, a surmise confirmed by a late 6th-century wreck off southern France, which contained 800 Athenian-made cups alongside double that number of other drinking vessels.²¹⁸ Even though nowadays elevated staggeringly beyond its original status, Greek painted pottery still stands out as emblematic of the abilities of skilled artisans to add value to clay in pursuit of a market niche. As in the Bronze Age, emulation of the simpler types soon took off beyond their core areas of production, especially in Italy and later southern France. Quite what was thereby transmitted to indigenous or Phoenician consumers is less apparent.²¹⁹ What most such people in essence desired was something aesthetically impressive from which to drink local or foreign wine, but imbalances in the mixing and drinking vessels they commonly imported suggest that many imbibed in their own customary, or newly hybrid ways, and cast doubt on how far specifically symposiastic practices spread beyond central and southern Italy. Equally, the images on pots appear to have been a less effective vector for spreading Greek myths, legends and culture in general than talking to people who already knew about them – often Corinthians, to judge from the dialect of Greek betrayed by Etruscan borrowings in this domain. In short, the export of Aegean pottery did not culturally Hellenize other Mediterranean people in any meaningful sense.

In addition, two very different bulk commodities came into their own. One was cereals [**10.30**]. In Chapters 8 and 9 we picked up from Ugarit the first mentions of sea transport of grain, much of it Egyptian, along the Levantine coast, shortly before the collapse of the palatial system. Later, several powers in the early 1st millennium BC Levant established grain-growing peripheries in order to free up core land for more profitable crops. Now, with sizeable sailing ships ubiquitous and towns sprouting up everywhere, the grain trade became a major pan-Mediterranean affair, drawing not only upon the harvests of Egypt (the eternal cornucopia in this respect), but also those of large, fertile hinterlands accessible to Sicilian powers like Syracuse, Akragas and Selinous, and newly linked-in lands in and beyond the basin, as we shall see. Pollen analysis reveals by the 6th century a sharp rise in the clearance of lowland tree cover as far apart as western Sicily and southwest Iberia.²²⁰ Yet in contrast to the annual reliance of subsequent supercities on imported grain (famously Athens by the late 5th century BC and, later, imperial Rome), few towns had yet outgrown the provisioning capacity of their surrounding countryside in a decent year, unless they chose to invest heavily in vines and olives.²²¹ The exceptions are likely to have been a handful of teeming small-island trading communities, principally those of the Levantine coast, Pithekoussai, Gadir and a resurgent community on Aegina in the Aegean, many of whose members were liable to be abroad at any given time, and

10.30 Cereals and slaves are known to have become major trading commodities by the later 7th and 6th centuries BC, but both are archaeologically hard to detect. Here an ear of grain is tellingly depicted as the emblem of one major cereal producer, the town of Metapontion in southern Italy.

where the practice of regular provisioning from a distance may in certain cases stretch back to their 3rd-millennium forebears, and long pre-date their evolution into urban centres.[222] All this leaves a slight question mark over the temporal origins of the dispersed overseas hinterlands from which many later Mediterranean towns regularly fed themselves.[223] Most 7th- and 6th-century BC movement of grain instead flexibly targeted whichever towns had suffered a poor harvest that year, thereby providing an integral buffer for the overall maintenance of a constellation of towns across the basin, while ensuring reliable profits for producers and shippers operating in an unpredictable environment blessed with swift information exchange. As a further means of turning a profit, less hardy but higher-status white wheats may have been cash-cropped for discerning consumers. In this respect it is intriguing that while wheat and, to a lesser degree, olives dominated at coastal Selinous, it was barley, fava beans and animal fat that remained the norm in the Sicilian interior, at indigenous Monte Polizzo.[224]

The other bulk commodity of growing significance had earlier beginnings, too, but appears much more disquieting today. Slaves had existed for a long time in the Mediterranean, in considerable numbers at Bronze Age palaces in the east and probably more widely at a household scale. As far as we can ascertain, most had been taken as war captives or criminals, or were the descendants of such people, although debt slavery was another downward, if redeemable route, and opportunistic coastal snatches of the kind so vividly described in the *Odyssey* must also have had a high antiquity.[225] Later, in the Iron Age, the massive scale at which Assyria organized the slave labour of its victims engendered a more commodified form of chattel slavery that slowly began to spread across the Mediterranean.[226] Disturbingly, its institution was inextricably linked to developments that now enjoy a more celebratory reception. One, most obviously in the Greek world, was broadening definitions of citizenship and the parallel stress on civic responsibility (recall Solon's injunctions against debt slavery).[227] Where effective, these ruled out a major internal source of dependent labour and formalized servile status by affirming its opposite, the freedom of citizens. Another, more general factor was the booming demand for consumer goods, among the growing middling group as well as the elite, which outpaced population growth and so threatened a shortfall that could only be averted by further mechanization of production or the drafting in of additional cheap labour. Despite an ongoing trickle of mechanical innovations, obtaining more slaves was the simpler answer in the Mediterranean for a long time to come. Some still came from the close borders of the city-state world or as spoils of war (in both cases, not least from Sicily), but ever larger numbers were obtained from the outer fringes of the basin, or beyond, and their acquisition became a significant driving force for the intake of new regions into the Mediterranean economy.

The growing volume of trade, and of trade in voluminous cargos, had several consequences for the patterning of routes around the basin, which became more defined but also subject to ever more frequent episodes of drastic redirection as the evolution of the overall network speeded up. The complexities of Mediterranean

10.31 Isthmian infrastructure: a short stretch of the paved *diolkos*, or slipway, near Corinth that facilitated haulage of cargos and entire ships between two seas, cutting out the route around the Peloponnese up to certain thresholds of bulk.

geography had long made particular nodes and networks vulnerable to being cut out as conditions changed, but never before had so much large-scale shipping operated over so much of the intricately configured parts of the basin, in particular the Aegean and central zone. Increases in scale shed interesting light on the rise and fall of seafaring centres in the Aegean. When most traffic was internal, Euboean locations on the Euripos strait connecting the northern and southern Aegean did extremely well, and it was they that began to re-establish wider connections. Their demise came in the 7th century BC, as trans-Aegean routes to the central and west Mediterranean became more important. The concomitant rise of isthmian Corinth made doubly good sense, given its position between the Aegean and the Gulf of Corinth, a sheltered seaway to the central Mediterranean, and the size of shipping, which remained moderate enough to enable the transhipment of medium bulk cargos, or transport of ships themselves over the isthmus.[228] Corinth even invested in a slipway, or *diolkos*, between its two coasts [**10.31**]. On the strength of this route, and combined with its primacy in the Saronic Gulf, nearby Aegina also took off.[229] The limitation for both lay in gradual rises in ship size, in particular for grain transport, because the solution of digging a canal across the isthmus was beyond Corinthian means (the depth of the modern cutting testifies to the challenge). The ensuing rise of Athens and Sparta marked the triumph of places nearer to the circum-Peloponnesian sea-route, and of the economic and military big battalions that a larger, and in the former case silver-rich, territory could marshal. That this sequence was far from arbitrary is underscored by Bronze Age parallels in the same part of the Aegean: from a mega-site at Manika on Euboea in the age of internal canoe traffic, to Aegina's primacy in the early 2nd millennium, to the rise of Mycenaean territorial states with their windows on the sea – the differences being the lesser role of Corinth, and the absence of truly large-scale shipping. Nor are such examples confined to the Aegean. In a clearly premeditated early 6th-century example, people from Phocaea, a seagoing city-state in the east Aegean, set out to outflank Tyrrhenian traffic by instigating trading places at Marseilles (to which we shall return) and Alalia, on the Corsican coast directly facing Elba and its iron sources.[230] Their retreat from the latter, after a close-fought engagement with Etruscan and Carthaginian ships, marked in essence the defeat of one aspiring network hub by its rivals. To underscore the fact that location still mattered at least as much as ethnicity, consider the defeat in 510 BC of Greek Sybaris, grown notoriously rich thanks to its isthmian position, where a donkey trail across Calabria to Poseidonia (Paestum), and thence on to its Etruscan trading partners short-circuited the sea-route around the Italian toe. The equally Greek assailant was the thereby bypassed town of Croton, which followed up its victory with exceptional, Babylonian-style savagery. Sybaris was wiped out, and the local river diverted to smother its site forever.[231]

Behind all this flourishing trade lies the overlooked issue of the relationship between individual enterprise and wealth on the one hand, and the economic power of the city-state on the other. The shift since the Bronze Age away from centralized forms of trade remained complete. Throughout the basin, leading merchants sprang from or created rich private families, endowed with extensive cash-cropped estates, and either still sailed themselves or sponsored ships run by their dependants, with as yet barely a flicker of the later doubts, witnessed at least in Greek quarters, about the open association of landed 'aristocrats' with trade.[232] The rural towers that sprang up in widely separate parts of the Mediterranean, around Jerusalem in the 8th–6th centuries BC, and slightly later in parts of the Aegean, are monuments to elite preoccupation with safeguarding both valuable agricultural produce for injection into the trading system, and their capital investments in the mechanical and human materiel required for its extraction.[233] Frustratingly, only the Aegean sources preserve a few names and a little of the flavour of their activities, in the tales of men like Demaratos of Corinth, whom we have met already, Kolaios of Samos, who in the later 7th century had no trouble bringing back a haul of Iberian silver straight through the ostensibly Phoenician zone, or the proverbially wealthy 6th-century trader Sostratos of Aegina.[234] We also know a fair amount, if again primarily in the Greek case, about the craftspeople who made the goods in circulation. Although sometimes hired by capital-rich entrepreneurs (Demaratos supposedly brought Corinthian experts to Tarquinia), artisans remained free in comparison to many of their Bronze Age predecessors, at least beyond the imperial Levant and probably Egypt too.[235] Most ran single- or multi-family workshops that turned modest profits in their own right. The best studied is the late 6th-century BC Athenian workshop of Nikosthenes, which employed a number of potters and decorators to manufacture elaborate black-figure vessels, each variant targeting a specific city in the Etruscan market [PL. XLV].[236] This freedom allowed real artisanal mobility, apparent in the movement to Etruria of Aegean potters, makers of architectural terracottas and perhaps mural painters – although not metalworkers, where Etruscan skills were by now second to none (the technique of gold granulation that they had recently acquired would soon be refined in their hands to produce work ten times finer than the early examples in the Troy treasures).[237]

The obvious question is: with so much independent activity going on, how did these seemingly economically weak city-states create such imposing urban landscapes and act so effectively abroad? One answer, illustrated in extreme form by the tyrants, but extending to a more general expectation of good works on the part of the elite, as a means of justifying as well as asserting their wealth, was that the private and public spheres blurred.[238] Peisistratos of Athens owned north Aegean gold mines. The riches that Samian Polycrates deployed to build wonders such as his gigantic harbour mole and a kilometre-long water tunnel derived from his own ambitious maritime raiding and trading ventures, often condemned as 'piratical' (he died, after a colourful career on the east Mediterranean stage, by crucifixion in Lydia), but that can be reasonably seen to reflect the Odyssean premise that it was not what you did at sea that mattered, so much as how you did it, and who you were. Beyond this, there were two sources of revenue.[239] One was publicly owned resources, of which the most valued were mines in the city-state's territory. Far too little attention has been devoted to the processes by which the rich silver lodes of Lavrio in southern Attica fell under Athenian control, but well before the start of the 6th century any access by strangers was surely over, and silver became a mainstay of the Athenian economy. A freak gold-strike on Siphnos in the Cyclades allowed this tiny place to walk tall on the widest stage by erecting one of the loveliest and most mathematically sophisticated monuments at Delphi [**10.32**].[240] The other main source was taxation, in the Greek case (and probably more widely) seldom directly on land or produce, but focused on transactional dues at ports or markets, which were often, of course, the same place, and a burgeoning source of revenue as interaction took off all over the basin.[241] The apparent paradox that weakly structured polities bereft of overall economic control could enjoy enormous increases in wealth is in part resolved by this critical factor. Sicilian coastal towns in particular made huge profits on the grain, oil and wine trade, not least with Carthage.

Such circumstances placed great economic and regulatory significance on the ports serving such city-states. These became, as in eastern parts of the basin centuries earlier, carefully managed if physically precarious, usually unwalled arenas through which flowed diverse characters, now injected with a further charge by the rivalries and ethnic distinctions that began to inform encounters between people at them.[242] It was probably at this stage that the term 'emporion' came into its definitional own to describe such places. The 6th-century growth of Phaleron, Piraeus's predecessor as the harbour of Athens, was accompanied by the political creation of a *metoikic* (resident foreigner) status, usually to accommodate foreign merchants at this stage – a legalism that would have been quite unnecessary a century or two earlier.[243] In southern Italy and Sicily most major towns lay right on the coast, and acted as their own ports, creating an extreme openness that may have become ultimately socially destabilizing. But in the central part of the peninsula, city-states had evolved from different origins and all the towns, save Populonia (where metal-working installations lined the shore beyond the walls and slag filled the bay), were well set back from the sea.

10.32 The Siphnian treasury at Delphi, small but perfectly formed, and paid for by the discovery of gold in the 6th century BC on an otherwise minor Cycladic island. Leading craftspeople were by now often free to move between and beyond their home polities with commissions, in a complete reversal of the situation under the palatial regimes of the 2nd millennium BC.

Portus on the navigable Tiber was located deliberately just outside the bounds of Rome; a place of foreign shrines and traders, it acted as main contact point, though an early version of Ostia also existed downstream, only to be smothered by mud and now long-lost beneath the salt pans.[244] The ports of several Etruscan city-states are better explored, notably at Gravisca, which operated for Tarquinia, and Pyrgi, which was Caere's window on the sea.[245] At both, prominent shrines presided over the harbour installations, warehouses and areas for manufacturing by both free artisans and slaves. Gravisca's shrines received offerings from the east Aegean traders and, around 500 BC, a stone anchor dedicated to Apollo of Aegina by one Sostratos – presumably a descendant to the legendary 6th-century trader. From one of the gaudily decorated shrines at Pyrgi comes the lucky find of three gold sheets, two inscribed in Etruscan and one in Phoenician [PL. XLVII].[246] The latter reads 'To Lady Astarte. This is the holy place which was made and which was given by Tiberie Velianas king over Kisry [Caere]. During the month of the sacrifice to the Sun as a gift to the temple he built a small shrine [or altar]. For Astarte raised him with her hand…and the years of the statue of the divinity in the temple [shall be] as many years as the stars above.' The Etruscan texts, as far as they can be understood, conveyed a similar message, but with deviations, notably the equation of Astarte with native Uni (Latin Juno), and a greater emphasis on the indigenous initiative for construction. Whatever the maybe hardening distinctions elsewhere, the coexistence of Aegean and Phoenician – now most often Carthaginian – people and gods on the Etruscan coast argues strongly that the world of the sea was still barely subjected to ethnic strictures.

The most remarkable emporion of all, however, lay on another navigable river far to the southeast. It went under the evocative name of 'Rule over Ships', Pi-emrôye in Egyptian, or in its better known Greek form, Naukratis. To grasp its significance, we need first to rehearse some recent events in Egypt. By now several of the Nile's older channels through the Delta were failing, and as their injections of soil ceased to balance coastal erosion and subsidence under the Delta's own weight, the sea began to encroach, flooding land in the east, where places reliant on the dwindling Pelusiac artery became doubly blighted.[247] The river's flow concentrated in three channels, in the west the Canopic and its bifurcating neighbour the Rosetta branch, and in the east the Damietta branch, the second and third of which flow to this day. When harbours first emerged on the true sea-coast of Egypt remains unknown, although recent finds affirm the tradition of an outpost by the 6th century, possibly with earlier Phoenician origins, at the mouth of the Canopic Nile, 20 km (12 miles) east of the great 4th-century BC foundation at Alexandria.[248] But for the present the political fulcrum still lay slightly upstream, and drew shipping from the Mediterranean towards it. Its capital lay at Sais in the western Delta, the capital of a 26th Dynasty that in the late 7th century BC rose from vassaldom in this hitherto provincial region to reunify the Egyptian Nile as Assyria's grip loosened, and to reimpose Egyptian state institutions after centuries of breakaway elites and quasi-tribal Libyan politics.[249] In a brief interlude before the resurgence of Mesopotamia in its Babylonian guise, this polity asserted pharaonic prestige on land all the way to the Euphrates and by sea as far as Cyprus. But it also evinced a thoroughly contemporary desire to control less ancient routes. The pharaoh Necho sought to neutralize the overland camel trail between the Levant and Arabia by initiating a canal between the Mediterranean and the Red Sea via the Nile (a variant of the modern Suez Canal whose very conception starkly illustrates the different labour pools available to Egypt and Corinth).[250] He reputedly also sponsored a Phoenician expedition to circumnavigate Africa, which would have bitten off vastly more than anticipated and whose reality is debatable.[251]

Beneath the official umbrella of Egyptian renewal and irredentism, the Deltaic core of Saite Egypt remained a mosaic of population diversity. In addition to the time-honoured presence of people with Libyan, Levantine and northwest Arabian ties, the polyglot world later reflected in the Rosetta Stone was rounded off by the arrival of Greek and southeast Aegean 'Carian' mercenaries – a striking reprise of the role of Mediterranean seagoing fighters in Egypt during the late 2nd millennium BC.[252] It was this specific connecting moment that opened Greek eyes to monumental sculpture and architecture just as the Aegean's towns were taking off, that formulated the belief in Egypt's primordial wealth and wisdom that would saturate subsequent Greek thought (and remain impervious to later Greek demonization of other parts of the Near East), and arguably that gave the Greeks their numerical system.[253] The compliment was not reciprocated, and the reasons may be readily surmised.[254] These late arrivals from a confident, increasingly self-conscious Mediterranean were not assimilators, and presented a source of cultural danger. Mercenaries on campaign got to the borders of Nubia, and incised themselves into posterity on the knees of Ramesses II's colossal statues at Abu Simbel [**10.33**], while others from Samos likened the Western Desert oases to the Isles of the Blest (a nice blend of Mediterranean and Saharan insularities), but otherwise they were confined to barracks or other remote quarters. Naukratis, as a gateway the equivalent to late imperial China's Shanghai,

10.33 A small section of the mighty leg of Ramesses II, carved in the 13th century BC at Abu Simbel, over 1000 km from the Mediterranean, graffitied by Greek mercenaries some 700 years later, and again, with neat serifs, by a 19th-century traveller.

10.34 Sensuality and savagery blend in this faience perfume flask in the form of a warrior helmeted in full Greek style, with a pharaoh's cartouche on its side. Its provenance is unknown, but this combination of features makes it a very persuasive candidate for an export made at Naukratis.

imposed similar movement restrictions on the Aegean merchants who followed in the mercenaries' wake.[255]

Naukratis was set up with pharaonic assent some 60 km (35 miles) from the then coast, on the Canopic branch.[256] A canal connected it to Sais, a convenient but safe 15 km (10 miles) away, and along this an Egyptian functionary with the sonorously antiquated title of Overseer of the Gate to the Foreign Lands of the Great Green conveyed the customs levied there back to the capital. The earliest pottery suggests a start around 620 BC, primarily involving Samians, Milesians and Aeginetans, but other east Aegean city-states quickly joined in, as did some Cypriot merchants, and a sizeable Egyptian quarter and storage facility arose alongside the Greek shrines and other structures. In a stark sign of the times, east Phoenician traders were conspicuous by their absence – a last Tyrian enclave, at Memphis, fizzled out within a decade of the foundation of Naukratis, which became the sole legitimate destination for foreign ships entering the Nile.[257] The highly profitable backbone of the trade was Aegean silver, wine and oil for Egyptian gold, grain, linen and papyrus, but much else rode on this, including locally churned out faience for the insatiable Mediterranean market in small Egyptianizing goods [**10.34**], and high-class international whores for the rich merchants passing through.[258] As a place where Greeks from many city-states lived cheek by jowl with each other and Egyptian neighbours who, at least in their official manifestation, remained resolutely different and past masters in categorizing others, Naukratis became a veritable forge for Greek identity.[259] In addition to the individual shrines built by participating city-states, nine clubbed together to erect a structure known as the 'Hellenion', one of the first allusions to this embracing term for a broader sense of Greekness. From emporic origins, Naukratis evolved over time into in effect a landless, partly pan-Hellenic city-state.[260] As ever, the Nile Delta proved to be a fertile hotbed for surprising new ways of combining things around the Mediterranean.

One final theme relating to commerce has been left until last, because its later significance and unanticipated long-term consequences risk overwhelming the pattern of its origins, and their deep roots in the past. This, of course, is the early use of coins [**10.35**]. It should be clear from the preceding chapters that coinage

10.35 Early coinage: (*left*) Lydian gold example, showing the time-honoured motif of a lion savaging a bull; (*right*) Aeginetan silver piece, dating to shortly after 500 BC and identified by this maritime polity's emblem of a sea-turtle.

was no more essential for the operation of currency and value equivalents than a marketplace was for the flourishing of markets. Both had existed in the east ever since the 'long' 3rd millennium BC, and in more recent centuries had spread throughout the basin decisively before coinage, along with ideas about commodities, standardization, financial debt and rates of exchange. Nor did coins kill off gift-giving and other socially embedded forms of exchange; these had already long survived in parallel with commercial trade and would continue to do so, even when the ubiquity and flexibility of coinage eroded the range of their remit. Coinage began as one of several ways of marking and thereby underwriting modest denominations of metal; it had clear precursors in 8th-century BC Levantine experiments with inscribing weight units.[261] True coins started to be minted within a decade or two on either side of 600 BC, by Lydia to judge by their emblem of lion's head and paws, and the first known were found alongside stamped weights at Lydia's maritime outlet of Ephesus, a city-state where Anatolian and Greek traditions mingled around a famous shrine to Artemis.[262] They were made from electrum, an unassayable alloy that forced users to accept their face value rather than unknowable metallic worth. One plausible hypothesis is that these coins were intended for issuing pay to mercenaries, and for spending internally.

An electrum currency worked well for internal payments or taxes, but silver was more widely available and, as a longstanding exchange medium, offered better scope for external deployment. By the early 6th century BC, the east Aegean Greek towns bordering Lydia were issuing their own mainly silver coins, as was maritime Aegina.[263] City-states in southern Italy were soon active too, and in the late 6th century some on Cyprus and coastal, metal-rich Populonia in Etruria followed suit, the latter with large units rather than small change.[264] Yet set against this are thought-provoking instances of indifference that speak volumes about the non-necessity of coinage for sophisticated trading and statecraft, notably Sparta in the Aegean, and even more so the entire Phoenician sphere, up until the 5th century BC in the case of the Levant and Carthage, where it certainly did pay mercenaries, and two centuries later in Iberia.[265] And while coins minted by others might be used as money elsewhere, they could equally be treated as bullion, as was long the case in Egypt and most of the empires active in the east Mediterranean.[266] In fact, the observation that early minting mapped not only onto major hubs of trade (most devoid of their own source of silver), but also onto the exceptionally competitive world of Greek city-states, hints that the issuing of coins with polity-specific emblems was a major symbolic means of projecting civic identity. Hence the distinctive sea turtles stamped onto coins of Aegina, Phocaea's equally marine seal, Athena's owl or Metapontion's ear of grain, as well as subtler messages of dual affiliation, such as among the cluster of 'Ionian' city-states in the east Aegean that sometimes shared a common design on one face, asserting their individuality on the other. The origins and spread of coinage are embedded in the Mediterranean's past, just as much as they presage its future.

Temples and triremes

The last two crystallizations and up-scalings of earlier phenomena can be dealt with swiftly, but to ignore them entirely would be to overlook prominent features of the coalescing Mediterranean's cultural and agonistic landscapes. The role of shrines as integrating and negotiating spaces under divine jurisdiction had been on the rise for a long time. In addition to those in emerging towns and interregional centres, we have just encountered them in a new generation of emporia. In the 6th century this process reached its physical acme, as enormous, unmissable temples of increasingly stand-ard appearance sprang up across the Mediterranean, especially in the Greek world, where they were now mainly stone-built, with forests of columns and embellished by sculptures that loomed over the pedimented entrances and projected myth-encoded messages about local or wider Greek identity [**10.36**].[267] Over much of the 6th century BC, a new temple was begun on average every two years; Sicilian Selinous had nine by shortly after the century's close [PL. XLVI].[268] Some 270 tonnes of marble moved by sea each year to meet the sculptural demands alone.[269] The scale and cost signal the growing wealth of Greek city-states, the sharpening competition between them, witnessed in races to build ever more grandiose edifices by neighbours like Samos and Ephesus, and, last but not least, a strident assertiveness on such emergent ethnic interfaces as the east Aegean and southern Italy and Sicily, where the giants concen-trated (in this respect the great temples of Athens are anomalous, both those on the acropolis later destroyed by Persian assault, and the gargantuan temple of Zeus below,

10.36 Two pairs of vying colossal temples, in each case erected by neighbouring polities within a few decades of each other: (a) plans of the temple of Artemis at Ephesus (560 BC) and of Hera on Samos (530 BC); (b) end elevations of temple GT at Selinous (520 BC) and that to Olympian Zeus at Akragas (510 BC), both in Sicily. To underscore their gigantism, compare with the size of a typical treasury building at Delphi (c), similar to that shown in fig. 10.32.

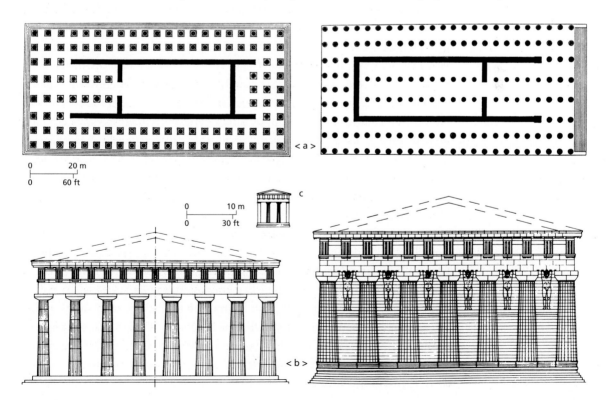

a project so ambitious that it was only finished in Roman times).[270] Most temples served similar roles to the smaller shrines that preceded them, but special opportunities arose at the great interregional sanctuaries of Delphi and Olympia. These were crammed with dedications by rich individuals and city-states that used their arenas to exhibit and compare their status before a cosmopolitan Mediterranean audience – we noted lucky Siphnos's exquisite 'treasury' earlier [PL. XLVIII].[271] For elites, these places simultaneously offered a perfect venue in which to establish civic credentials at home while letting off competitive steam among their wider peer group, by making offerings and other honourable acts in the city-state's name, especially once sporting events demanding leisure and wealth (notably chariot-racing) became part of the sacred festivals.[272] Nor, despite strictures on participation in the games, were all the dedicants at such places Greek. At Delphi, an Egyptian king part-sponsored the rebuild of Apollo's temple, a king of Lydia offered spectacular precious metal gifts, and in addition to the abundant Etruscan dedications, Caere erected its own treasury.[273]

Elsewhere, temples in an indigenous style that sprouted ridge-line sculptures arose by the late 6th century in Etruria and Rome, sometimes close to the cemeteries that they had begun to replace as foci of ritual. With its augurs and cults of water and wild beasts (not least as the sucklers of those destined to be future leaders), central Italian religion had deep local prehistoric roots.[274] Monumental shrines whose forms can only be vaguely grasped from ancient descriptions of them had cast their shadows over Levantine and derivative towns for centuries, and Egypt remained a venerable source of holy gigantism. Not until well after this book's end-date, and under empire, did secular architecture again rival the abodes of the Mediterranean's so dramatically upgraded gods.

The final feature concerns the face of battle. Fighting on land and sea had been widespread for millennia, and already reached formidable proportions in the east by the later 2nd millennia BC, with a further leap following the Neo-Assyrian reforms. Only in the 7th to 6th centuries BC, however, with city-state territories and rivalries coming to the fore, did it attain the guise familiar in Classical times. On land, the heavily armoured warrior was nothing new, especially in the Aegean, where eastern and European bronze traditions were melded to this end. What made the new hoplite version, with his closed 'Corinthian' helmet and round 7-kg (15-lb) shield, so effective was the association of soldiery with citizenship, of an oligarchical kind given the expense of the kit that each man provided, and the superseding of solo combat or fighting in loose ranks by dense, well-drilled bodies of men whose mutual reliance, down to their overlapping shields, reified ideals of civic cohesion.[275] We catch a glimpse of this around 650 BC on a Corinthian export to Veii, which depicts such troops clashing to the syncopation of pipes, surrounded by other evocations of elite lifestyles, and with less immediacy in a marked switch in the deposition of weaponry and armour from individual wealthy graves to civic dedications at sanctuaries [10.37]. Hoplite tactics spread over the east Mediterranean via mercenaries hired from the Aegean and adjacent areas, some fortune-hunters but others citizens out of favour in their home town. Earlier, we explored the

10.37 The changing face of battle on land: on the Chigi vase, a mid-7th-century BC Corinthian product excavated near Veii. For several centuries, such closely integrated ranks of heavily equipped hoplites would prove the most effective combat formations within, and as mercenaries, beyond, the Mediterranean.

upshot at both ends of this martial centrifuge in the case of Egypt, where manpower was manifestly not the problem so much as tactics effective against tough Mesopotamian field armies. Naturally, Egypt's monopoly did not last, as is revealed by a brother of the poet Alcaeus of Lesbos, who fought in the pay of Babylon during the siege of Ashkelon.[276] Still in the Levant, the Biblical Goliath's armour apparently hints at a late, pseudo-hoplite-derived interpolation in the description of David's adversary.[277] Piecemeal usage was probably also the reality in central Italy, where elements of the hoplite kit were popular, but so mingled with native weapons, such as the double battle-axe, as to cast doubt over whether tactics translated with the gear.[278] The exception could well be Rome, where the later memory of a 'centuriate reform' may explain why this city-state enjoyed a fighting edge in years to come.[279] Further west and at Carthage our ignorance is complete, but land warfare may have remained less sophisticated for longer than was possible in the closely packed cockpits of vying polities elsewhere.

At sea the critical shift came over a century later. Apart from capacious sailed 'tubs' for large cargos and open-sea traffic, pentekonters remained the workhorses of maritime mobility and naval fighting all over the basin for much of the 6th century, and effective ones too, if we consider their parts in tales of trade, population transfer, naval fighting and raiding recorded by Herodotus.[280] Reputedly just two pentekonters brought one initial nucleus of people from the Aegean to Africa, in a venture to which we shall return.[281] The pentekonters' eclipse came in the form of a much

10.38 The changing face of battle at sea: an ambitious experiment in the replication of an Athenian trireme, seen here underway. Note the ample space for troops used in land as well as sea combat, making such ships extremely effective exporters of violence under Mediterranean conditions.

larger sailed galley, the trireme, half as long again and typically with three times as many oarsmen in its triple banks [**10.38**].[282] Triremes were not decisively faster, but their ram packed a terrible punch and at the beachhead they could disgorge large numbers of soldiers, triggering a sudden leap in the scale of violence that could be unleashed from the sea with little warning on distant shores – a reminder, if one is needed, of the darker side of connectivity and the coercive impacts of marine technology. Their time and place of invention is disputed, although against the traditional consensus of a gradual spread from the 8th or 7th century BC Levant into the Aegean, a persuasive case can be made for a more rapid inception close to 540 BC, perhaps at Sidon under its latest imperial master, or maybe Carthage, both places where we shall see that transporting armies across to islands was becoming a military priority.[283] On highly connected seas the trireme, like the early 20th-century AD dreadnought, rendered previous fighting ships swiftly obsolete, and within a decade of 540 BC the leading east Aegean maritime city-states had adopted the new superships. Polycrates of Samos, for example, soon mustered forty to support his overseas ambitions. By the start of the following century, Aegina, Corinth and younger maritime polities such as Athens and Syracuse were building them on an equivalent scale, initially to fight each other. Triremes resembled dreadnoughts in their crippling cost as well, which exceeded the means of all but the very wealthiest individuals and restricted the naval scope of many entire city-states, thus accelerating the appearance of state navies as opposed to flotillas of elite-owned fighting vessels, and concentrating such formations in a few exceptionally rich cities. The political consequences would become ruthlessly clear within half a century.

The last great intakes

So far we have concentrated on the long, undulating belt of networks and converging lifestyles established along the axis of the Mediterranean early in the Iron Age. But escalating activities and demands ensured that over the later 7th and 6th centuries BC, most of the rest of the basin was drawn in too, bringing the geographical and cultural Mediterranean into ever closer alignment. As in the Late Bronze Age of the east, a few bypassed or resistant areas would still stand out. We shall come across examples in the central Adriatic, Liguria and parts of North Africa; others may have lingered on behind the barely explored wilder shores of southern Turkey. The slow intake of such backwaters would continue over the next few centuries, to peak temporarily in Roman times. By 500 BC, however, these places were already merely internal isolates within a framework that embraced and criss-crossed an entire Middle Sea. Nor did expansion halt at the physical edge of the basin, for from the 7th century BC the Mediterranean's people and practices began to spill over into neighbouring areas as never before, heralding the onset of a rolling big bang in global history that before long penetrated temperate Europe, western Asia and the Indian Ocean, and eventually leapt the Atlantic to the Americas.

The beginnings of this integration, which concern us here, sometimes involved quite modest areas of the basin. Indeed, we can imagine processes at work on many scales, down to innumerable microcosms of valleys, bays or islands hitherto on the fringes of the action. Highlands became increasingly integrated too, and although the impact of newly prosperous and sometimes predatory upland societies (famously the Samnite polity of the southern Apennines, and equivalents on the Meseta) was felt most keenly well after 500 BC, the roots lie somewhat further back, tangled in their landscapes' now steadily growing engagement with wider Mediterranean culture and markets (not least for the products of large-scale pastoralism on the part of new towns in the lowlands). Sometimes, too, there had been a previous but interrupted history of engagement. This was the case around the heads of two of the sub-basins. The north Aegean had barely lost its earlier thread of external ties, but only in the 7th century, as its metals, wine and slaves flowed south in quantity, did city-states start to carve out holds on its peninsulas and islands, alongside the large but loose indigenous communities of the Macedonian and Thracian interior, which had their own overland links into the Balkans and over to the Adriatic.[284] Offshore, gold-rich Thasos became a magnet for what were primly dismissed further south as the entrepreneurial dregs of the Aegean.[285]

Revival of contacts with the inner Adriatic, beyond Corinth's enclaves around its approaches, began later still, towards the end of the 6th century BC. Until then, the Adriatic had enjoyed a vigorously independent trade. Verucchio, inland from

modern Rimini, circulated masses of Baltic amber, while the earthwork builders of Arpi were among those sending painted pottery handmade in the Tavoliere
all over north and central Dalmatia.[286] It is tempting to interpret this enclosed
sea, with its easily closed-off access, maze of islands along the eastern side from
which to launch ambuscades on exposed shipping, coasts studded with little hillforts and fierce images of mounted warriors in the Tavoliere,[287] as actively inimical
to Mediterranean interlopers, and for some centuries successfully so. The recon-
nection, when it came, started in the north, exactly as in the late 2nd millennium
BC. Metal-trading Etruria and Venetic groups at later Padua and Este turned to this
alternative outlet on the sea as competition in the Tyrrhenian theatre stiffened and
the rich, steady harvest of the Po plain began to offer the prospect of a profitable
grain trade.[288] The equivalent of Frattesina as a maritime gateway to and from the Po
and its Alpine hinterland lay 50 km (30 miles) to the southeast, at Spina, near today's
coastal lagoons, and like Venice a place of canals and diverse people, its cemeteries soon full of Athenian pots.[289] Inland, a vibrant style of metal vessels combined
Etruscan, east Mediterranean and trans-Alpine art; depictions of the missionary
position, largely alien to eastern art, hint at undreamt of ramifications of connectivity.[290] Again as in the Bronze Age, the intervening Adriatic coasts and islands were
excluded from this connection. There was hardly a ripple of change in the local hillforts,[291] and no intrusive enclaves took hold until as late as the 4th century BC, when,
supported by Syracuse, Greek foundations arrived on islands such as Vis and Hvar
(the latter, incidentally, preserving the best landscape of pre-Roman field divisions
in the Mediterranean).[292] But there was one tiny, telling exception. Palagruža has
repeatedly acted as a mid-Adriatic barometer of seafaring trends, from its first hints
of Mesolithic exploration and role as a stepping stone for expanding farmers, to its
popularity as a destination for long-range canoe voyagers and converse emptiness
as the first sailing ships sped past it in a shrinking central Mediterranean. In the late
6th century BC, Palagruža was reinvented yet again, this time as a sea-shrine to the
legendary wandering hero Diomedes, whose name was scratched on Greek potsherds that link this barren scrap of now sacred rock to places far away.[293]

Not all newly incorporated regions were so limited, however, nor mediated by
previous cycles of contact. Two stand out in particular for their strategic significance
and almost unbroken previous indifference to external connections. In both cases, the
process of integration began, not surprisingly, with external interventions, and led to
swift changes in native societies, with ebullient new beginnings as fresh sectors of the
coast turned actively maritime, matched by severe disruption and losses on the part of
those at the receiving end.[294] One lay around the arc of the Mediterranean's third great
northern embayment, in southern France, extending into Catalonia and the islands
athwart its approaches. The other stretched along the immense African flank, a place
with a hitherto utterly different, largely self-contained history, whose incorporation
at this late juncture would soon lend a new dimension to Mediterranean history.

We begin in southern France [**10.39**]. Some time in the early 5th century BC, a
lead tablet inscribed in Greek on one side and Etruscan on the other was deposited at

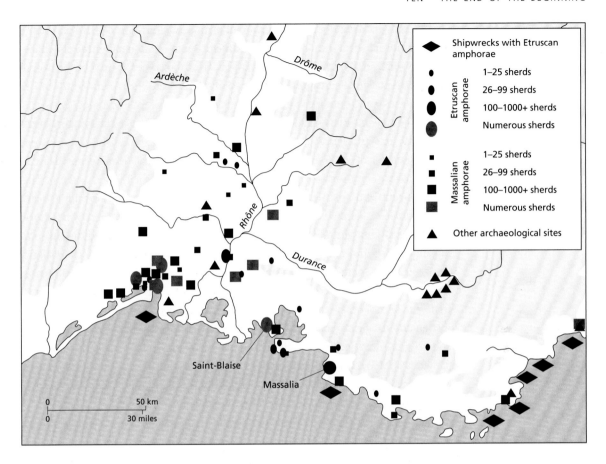

10.39 The opening up of the lower Rhône Valley to Mediterranean trade, before and after the establishment of Massalia, as represented by shipwrecks and the distribution of sites with known quantities of amphorae.

a modest indigenous trading post between the mouth of the Aude and the Pyrenean foothills, today known as Pech Maho.[295] The Greek side records the purchase of a boat from a port on the other side of the Pyrenees known as Emporion; the witnesses to the details of profit-sharing and debt (perhaps local dignitaries) bear Iberian names, while on the Etruscan face the place name Mataliai (Massalia) can be discerned. The only outstanding feature of this unexceptional vignette of Mediterranean maritime business, whose generics would have been at home in Late Bronze Age Ugarit, is that it would have been unthinkable just a few generations earlier in the part of the world in which it was embedded. Southern France's switch to front-line status came after several millennia during which relatively clement environments, minimal endowment with desirable resources and semi-enclosure by mountains and open sea had created a Mediterranean backwater in which life carried on at a low key, with only occasional blips, one in the 3rd millennium BC associated with beakers and megalithic tombs, when links up the Rhône and round Iberia briefly plugged it in, and a few of a muted kind in the opening centuries of the 1st millennium BC, as a trickle of Atlantic goods short-circuited Iberia across the Aude–Garonne isthmus, boosting a few settlements along the way. Even in the 8th and early 7th centuries BC, most inhabitants still lived in villages and farms set in half-wooded landscapes, farming, hunting and exploiting the aquatic plants and animals of the coastal *étangs*.[296] Naive as it would be to paint this lifestyle as idyllic, we can certainly surmise that, in comparative terms, this part of the Mediterranean had so far avoided many of the highs and lows experienced elsewhere.

The wider world's irruption began in the later 7th century, as part of the overall Tyrrhenian push by Etruscan traders, especially from Caere and Vulci, though others quickly joined in.[297] One approach route is delineated by a veritable marine graveyard of ships between Antibes and the Rhône delta, a grim testimony to the savagery of the Provençal coast and a credit to the intensity of underwater exploration, rivalled in the Mediterranean only off southern Turkey and northern Israel.[298] As a target of Etruscan trade, France soon overtook the older markets of Sardinia, Sicily and Carthage. This trade concentrated on exports of wine to the hitherto beer- or mead-drinking locals, accompanied by elaborate serving and drinking vessels in metal or *bucchero* pottery, with Greek amphorae and fine painted pots, plus a few Phoenician items, riding upon this or arriving in other hulls.[299] The big coastal village of Saint-Blaise, overlooking the watery world of the eastern Rhône delta, received exceptional amounts. Although caution is advisable in projecting later testimonies onto this first phase of the Gallic trade, the lack of other goods with which to reciprocate this influx, aside from some Iberian and Atlantic metalwork, suggests that the reverse flow, out to Etruscan ports and beyond, already consisted of local people sold into slavery to feed the insatiable demands of Mediterranean production – indeed this was probably the motivation for redirecting Etruscan energies towards a populous new region with little else to offer.[300] If so, as soon as a desirable Mediterranean intoxicant was injected, even sub-idyllic lifestyles began to unravel, to the advantage of some and ruination of others.

For several decades contact took the form of ship-to-shore encounters, which limited its social impact and reach inland.[301] Then, around 600 BC, a permanent enclave of traders began to coalesce on a promontory thrusting into a superb sheltered bay on the rocky flank of the Rhône delta, a day or two's walk, or half a day's sail, east of Saint-Blaise – closer than Gadir was to Huelva.[302] The archaeology of early Massalia (Marseilles) is a victim of this well-sited city's success ever since, but the community clearly began on a modest scale and, despite the story of its exclusive foundation by Phocaeans from the east Aegean, there are hints of Etruscan activity, as well as feasting and drinking areas of indigenous character – indeed 'Phocaeans' perhaps covered a multiplicity of characters circulating in the west [**10.40**]. Massalia grew quickly, if in a less orderly fashion than Carthage. At 30–40 ha (75–100 acres) by the later 6th century, it ranked as the largest town west of the Tyrrhenian Sea, with a quayside, a fortification wall of stone shipped from 25 km (15 miles) away, pottery workshops churning out amphorae and emulations of both local and east Aegean fine grey and painted wares, and a more stridently Greek identity as naval conflicts with an ethnic tinge flared up to its south.[303] Unlike equivalent Sicilian and south Italian towns, however, it secured only a modest territory, hemmed in by likewise fortified native villages, just enough to feed itself and, crucially, to cultivate its own vintages as a cash crop; the sea and shipping were still its lifeline. Massaliote wine, locally bottled and dispatched into the interior or back to Italy, first substituted and then broke the trade of the Etruscan city-states by mid-century, arrogating the profits of slaving with it.[304] This initiative,

10.40 Large-scale excavations near the Marseille Bourse delineate the first harbour of Massalia and the structures that grew up around it. As so often with silting Mediterranean conditions, the anchorage has since migrated seaward, and the current Vieux Port is visible beyond the prominent row of large buildings.

so Mediterranean in its agricultural and mercantile strategies working in concert, brought domesticated vines to a land where only the wild variety had existed before, and they flourished. In contrast, olive oil production only began after 500 BC, indicating the more immediate economic incentives and opportunities for social intercourse between the constituent groups in southern France that were offered by the grape.[305]

The impact on native societies was immense, if closely focused and leaving other parts of their culture unaffected.[306] Trade with the interior stayed in indigenous hands, and mediated by native customs and connections, but it was revolutionized in scale and intent. Strategically situated communities, mostly on the coast but a few inland at locations that would enjoy a long life thereafter (for example Arles, Nîmes and Carcassonne), sprouted extensive ditches and ramparts around sometimes orderly, rectilinear houses, mingling local traits with adoptions from wider Mediterranean culture.[307] This marked the emergence of the French oppida, quasi-urban hillforts that, unlike the situation in Etruria a few centuries earlier, were unknown until the region joined the mainstream – closer parallels lie in contemporary Iberia, although the latter had also generated earlier locally driven cycles of complexity, for example in the Argaric. Woodland clearance expanded the land for crops, and soon cereals would become a stored bulk commodity for the first time.[308] But for the present, wine and slaves dominated the economy. The former's consumption etiquette, even in local versions that ignored the niceties of straining and mixing, required vast numbers of Greek-style cups.[309] Whether due to the number of overlapping local networks or cunning handling on the part of Massalia, there is only scanty sign of prominent native winners; the losers, however, snared between competing hillforts and shipped off into the Mediterranean stripped of everything, were undoubtedly many. As the demand for slaves grew, southern French middlemen deploying the lure of Mediterranean wine began to tap populations further north, reopening for the first time in two millennia, with a new kind of traffic, the passage through the Rhône gap into temperate France.[310]

In addition to Massalia, smaller trading communities emerged at the lagoonal mouths of other rivers that offered communications with the interior, creating further instances of the classic transect from coast to hinterland, with capillary effects on land and sea. Pech Maho, whose tablet introduced us to radical change in southern France, goes back to the early 6th century, and by this time Saint-Blaise was a fortified plateau with a heterogeneous culture.[311] Late Etruscan-led efforts seem to have lain behind the appearance in the 520s BC of Lattara (Lattes, near Montpellier in Languedoc), while Massalia promoted Agathe (Agde) and outposts further west, in the shadow of the Pyrenees, at Roda and the aptly named Emporion, initially on a river-mouth island (a rather 'Phoenician' choice of location).[312] Both the last were tiny dots on the edge of a landscape of powerful Iberian communities, upon which Phoenician initiatives were also encroaching from the southwest.[313] One upshot of this proliferation of mini-Massalias was to draw more local people towards the maritime world and to revitalize coastwise traffic, which had been in abeyance since the disintegration of the beaker phase, thereby forging a new network that embraced locals, Phoenicians and Greeks alike in southwest France and Catalonia, and brought these areas closer together than at any time since the 3rd millennium BC, or even the Neolithic climax. Wine grown in coastal Iberia was shipped to Languedoc, and all over this region native people drew on Phoenician or, rarely, Greek scripts to perform local writing.[314] One fruit of this link may be the earliest written *periplous*, or sailing sequence, to survive from the Mediterranean. Badly garbled by late Roman interventions, it still retains a taste of 6th-century BC travel between Massalia and Iberia's Atlantic coast, past the variously decaying or thriving Phoenician enclaves along the peninsula's southern shore.[315] In contrast, the Alpine coast east of Marseilles into Liguria remained untouched, one of the last inaccessible fastnesses of the Mediterranean.

Further out to sea, the incorporation of two islands perennially very far from the stream owed everything to the amplified links now surrounding them. Corsica has so far presented a picture of almost uninterrupted remoteness, all the more surprising by the late 2nd millennium BC, from when it lay midway on the metal route between Etruria and Sardinia. Subsequently Corsica would revert to its isolated, archaic aspect, but in between came a bright flash of engagement in the 6th century at one point on the island's perimeter, intriguingly close to the find of an earlier oxhide ingot. This was Alalia, the implant started by Phocaeans (the same group implicated at Massalia) and provocatively located to intervene in the northern Tyrrhenian Sea and its routes to France.[316] When forced to abandon this enclave after a too-costly defence in the later 6th century, the survivors elected to transfer to Massalia; Alalia carried on in a much lower key, and with a less predominantly Greek mixture of inhabitants.[317]

The second island lay further west, among the Balearics. The mid- and late 1st millennium BC brought more contacts with the wider world on all these late-settled, previously remote islands. In this most faunally impoverished spot in the basin, what better measure of this than the influx of snakes, mice, other rodents, weasels, horses, red and fallow deer, all as intentional introductions or stowaways?[318] But interesting patterns can be observed among the islands' human inhabitants, too. The populous islands of Mallorca and Menorca retained a wary stance, their tower-like *talayots* replaced by fortified villages that imply ongoing predations from the sea.[319] Suspicion of outsiders only faded in the 4th and 3rd centuries BC, after the end point of this book, when many of their men were drawn to a labour market as paid slingers in the armies of Carthage. This coincided with the first substantial inflow of precious, exotic goods, as well as rituals on Menorca around *taulas*, T-shaped edifices made of hulking stone slabs, both the last gasp of the megalithic tradition and a crude echo of contemporary constructions seen for the first time by island-ers abroad.[320] Mallorca and Menorca both contrast with conifer-shrouded Ibiza, which lay deserted as late as 650 BC save, we might hazard, for the odd castaway, its total span of occupation to date amounting to the 2nd millennium BC. But as west Mediterranean economies and interaction grew to a scale at which Balearic cen-trality finally became potentially viable, Ibiza offered a rare opportunity to launch a new venture with excellent prospects for slave-worked cash-cropping, and no locals to complicate matters – rather like Madeira and the Azores 2000 years later, as Mediterranean societies took over the Atlantic's islands.[321] Phoenicians from Iberia set up Sa Caleta in the late 7th century BC, to process passing silver and iron.[322] Then, roughly at the same time as Massalia's foundation, a bigger operation took off at Ebesus (modern Ibiza town; both names stem from the Semitic Ibshim, meaning 'Island of Pines'), best known for its cemetery at Puig des Molins. Ibiza proved so effective as a trading hub between Iberia, France and routes eastward, as well as a wine exporter, that before long it attracted the attention of Carthage.

Mention of Carthage brings us to our second major realm of expansion within the Mediterranean. Whatever its prior seclusion, southern France shared several of its fundamentals with most other parts of the basin, not least agriculture, sedentism and metalworking. In Mediterranean North Africa west of the Nile, none of these can be taken for granted even at this date, and we can hardly imagine the consequent wrench and trauma for indigenous societies as novelties and foreign people began to pour in. Frustratingly, although we know quite a lot about the overseas ventures that effected the rapid integration of parts of the African Mediterranean, Herodotus and informed guesswork are almost the only options concerning the receiving end. Herodotus was writing at a time when North Africa had already been so changed that his assertions about past ways of life there are hard to evaluate. For what it is worth, he described a Cyrenaica roamed by seasonal pastoralists.[323] Perhaps these sowed grain in wadis after the autumn rains, as they headed south to graze their herds on the desert edges during the winter, returning to the coast for the summer and reaping a crop in the spring along their way, a plausible pattern with parallels in the recent past, when Cyrenaica sustained a substantial populace in a similar way, but entirely archaeologically unverified.[324] Haua Fteah cave experienced a long hiatus in visits before the first Greek items appeared, and elsewhere handmade pots and stone tools changed so little over the millennia that their dating remains very broad, to put it charitably.[325] The spread of cereals into the oases of the Libyan interior early in the 1st millennium BC, as noted at the start of this chapter, coupled with the presence of Libyan groups in the Nile Delta, perhaps encouraged a percolation of crops north or west into Cyrenaica too – but only perhaps, in our present state of knowledge.

10.41 The multitude of dolmens that dot the eastern Maghreb, sometimes in sizeable concentrations, are extremely poorly dated and explored, though they remain the most visible aspect of indigenous culture. Here, the Bou Nouara dolmen, situated in the upland interior near Constantine.

Until a few years ago there was nothing more than ongoing rituals at crudely dated dolmens to help evaluate Herodotus' altogether more startling statement that sedentary farmers already occupied the land west of Sirte, in the Maghreb [**10.41**].[326] But thanks to a trailblazing excavation beneath the later Carthaginian and Roman town of Althiburos, 100 km (60 miles) from the coast and 750 m (2450 ft) up in the well-watered valleys of the tell country close to Tunisia's border with Algeria, this parlous state of affairs has just begun to change.[327] At the bottom of the sequence, and preceding the first appearance of a few 8th-century BC red, wheel-made Phoenician plates, cultivated olive pips and scraps of iron and slag, lay a series of 10th- or 9th-century BC stone structures, along with handmade pottery, bones of sheep, goats, cattle and pigs, and, crucially, cultivated barley, wheat, legumes, millet and a few (wild?) grape pips. At this date, so distant from the coast and in this cultural milieu, such a signature is impossible to explain as escaped Carthaginian agriculture. Clearly, some inhabitants of the eastern Maghreb in the early 1st millennium BC were indeed already mixed farmers, though even this breakthrough barely nibbles from the younger end at the yawning gap of over 4000 years during which we know nothing about the fate of Neolithic agriculture in northwest Africa. As a possible alternative to invisible continuity in this respect, the spread of dolmens into the eastern Maghreb via southern Italy and Malta, some time around or shortly after the end of the 3rd millennium BC (as described in Chapter 8), could hint at a much more recent influx of farmers, one that slipped across the Sicilian narrows at a time when our antennae are ill-attuned to detect such kinds of movement.

Clearly, much remains to be resolved, but in the meantime, what of contacts across the sea more generally? A smattering of overseas visitors had been touching on North African shores and meeting their inhabitants intermittently for millennia. After Neolithic crossings at Gibraltar and the Sicilian narrows came a second horizon in the former sector during the 3rd millennium BC, associated with long-range voyaging, much of it on the Atlantic side of the strait, followed possibly by the connection just alluded to across the Mediterranean's waist, and, by the later 2nd millennium BC, a mixed Cypriot, Aegean and local signature where ships stopped for water and ostrich eggs en route to Egypt. After these come less solid hints, of interaction between Libyan pastoralists and sea people, archaeologically unverified legends of early Phoenician enclaves, at Utica and on the Cyrenaican coast, and even the *Odyssey*'s African interludes.[328] The North African shore had therefore never been hermetically sealed (an unlikely scenario anywhere in the basin), nor its people entirely unaccustomed to strangers from the sea; and conversely, some degree of navigational knowledge of its coasts must have built up among these visiting strangers over time. Yet most such encounters had little lasting or broader impact, and none tied North Africans firmly or permanently into the rest of the Mediterranean. People's priorities on either side of the sea seem to have been just too different, and in most places the distances too great for more regular contacts to yet wear this difference down. The same, in fact, holds true for the earliest centuries of settlement at Carthage, from the late 9th century to at least the end of the 8th century BC. Beyond its immediate productive hinterland, early Carthage faced resolutely seaward, largely ignoring the land mass at its back, with its presence in North Africa accidental to the maritime logic of its location. Save for a handful of extraneous items and practices, Althiburos, away in the hills, remained a separate world.

From the later 7th and 6th centuries, this began to change. Carthage, by now a massive trading city not readily supplied by cultivators walking out from it each day, and long a food importer itself, began to engage with local hinterland communities in the 6th century BC, though not until a century later did its towers bristle on Cape Bon, the great promontory to its east that it turned into an agricultural paradise, and the climax of Carthaginian rural settlement lay later still.[329] Native settlement at Althiburos resumed in the early 6th century after a short hiatus, much as before but with more imported pots (mostly associated with wine-drinking, as elsewhere in the Mediterranean), stronger signs of ironworking, and a cistern built after a blueprint from Carthage; shortly after 500 BC it lay on the fast-expanding frontier of Carthaginian territory.[330] To the east, where the rain-inducing mountains created a Mediterranean micro-ecology in the southeast corner of the Gulf of Gabès, fresh Phoenician enclaves appeared in the late 7th and 6th centuries, maybe prompted by Carthage. They were stone-built at Lepcis but at Sabratha flimsier and with layers of wind-blown sand suggestive of initially temporary residence.[331]

Where Africa bowed north again and its contours reared up to create the great green mountain of Cyrenaica, Greek-led ventures began to stud the rocky shores from the late 7th century, and soon thrust into the interior highlands.[332] Their foundation tales evoke a plausible medley of seasonal murex divers, pioneers marooned on an offshore rock, a passing Samian merchant bound for Egypt (reputedly Kolaios himself, shortly before he was blown west to Tartessos, and his fortune), small-island farmers fleeing a drought at home and, for good measure, the Delphic oracle.[333] Text and archaeology alike confirm that the main actors came from Sparta, Crete and Thera, the last by now resettled over the blanket of ash from the 2nd-millennium BC eruption. These origin points in the far south of the Aegean stand out from the usual suspects engaged in such activity, and hint at a distinctive set of links between the Aegean and the facing coast of Africa. Atypical Aegean participants, superficial prior contacts and vast differences between incomers and locals combine to shed light on what followed. Confidence and impunity are both implicit in the rapid Greek move inland to found Cyrene, in an ecological sweet spot once described in modern terms as 'twelve miles from its port, and two thousand feet above it', and by local people 2600 years earlier as lying beneath a gaping rent in the sky – just possibly a genuine scrap of a native description of a place with abundant rainfall, fossilized in Herodotus [PL. XLIX].[334] Local people and town-dwelling newcomers lived parallel existences that interacted, but only merged to significant degree after 500 BC.[335] Herodotus reported intermarriage, right at the top on the strength of one ruler's non-Greek name (Alizir), while imposing tumuli appealed to funerary expectations on both sides of the Mediterranean, and a few urban elites chose to be depicted with African clothes and hairstyles. On the other side of the balance stood enduring native food taboos about cows (previously kept only for dairying and blood?), and violently resolved flare-ups as towns swelled and impeded their neighbours' way of life. The northeast African ideological trappings that Greek rulers adopted included at least nominal kingship, and intermarriage with Egyptian royalty, but these reflected the dictates of political power games more than any wider cultural hybridity.

In spatial as well as social terms the integration of Mediterranean Africa was still far from complete in 500 BC. Long stretches remained untouched, notably most of the Maghreb between Carthage and Oran (due to a lack of desirable resources and poor harbours on a rugged and dangerous coast), as well as the arid Gulf of Sirte; the situation in the coastal corridor between Cyrenaica and the Nile is unknown. Inland, the Maghreb would be economically and politically transformed through its relations with Carthage over coming centuries, but only in Roman times were the drier tracts to the east greened by Libyan farmers who learned to first harvest the sporadic rains in order to harvest crops from it as well.[336] However, the momentous difference made to Mediterranean history by a string of urban, agricultural and trading polities along the African shore, engaged in production and consumption of a kind already generalized elsewhere, was already apparent.[337] Whatever the truth about the extent of indigenous farming, the practices introduced at Carthage and in Cyrenaica represented a dramatic change, well beyond such obvious introductions as the olive and vine. Carthaginian agronomy was later famed as the most sophisticated in the Mediterranean, a reputation that owed much to its 9000-year inheritance of experience and experiment in the heartland of farming back in the

Levant.[338] This was probably transferred intact, down to seeds and stocks, in the opening centuries of Carthage's existence, and once adapted to local conditions it gradually transformed the Tunisian plains into a gigantic agro-business. The Cyrenaican farms focused more straightforwardly on grain, which was sent over to the Aegean in vast amounts, while native knowledge contributed an endemic fennel-like plant, known in Greek as *silphion*, that became so prized across the Mediterranean for its flavour and medicinal properties that it was emblazoned on Cyrene's coins and overexploited to extinction [**10.42**].[339] Nor was the exchange all botanical. West African guinea fowl percolated in from the Maghreb at roughly the same time that Asian chickens spread westward via the Aegean [**10.43**].[340] Furthermore, it was only at this late stage that domesticated horses achieved a circum-Mediterranean distribution, taking to North African plains largely depleted of big game with consequences for the growth of cavalry that would be felt by the Roman legions at Cannae a few centuries later. Quadrigas, four-horse chariots invented under Assyria and widely copied as symbols of power and prowess, escaped via Egypt, Cyrene or Carthage into the Sahara, where they appeared, careering wildly, on pastoral rock art far out in the desert [**10.44**].[341] And one final unknown is whether Mediterranean

10.42 The now extinct fennel-like plant *silphion*, endemic to the Green Mountain, seen on Cyrene's coinage and probably the substance shown being weighed and packaged under the supervision of Cyrene's king in this mid-6th-century BC Peloponnesian cup.

10.43 A 5th-century BC Greek cartoon of a guinea fowl, a less-established exotic arrival than the ultimately South Asian chicken.

10.44 Horses and chariots (here two-horse models) took easily to the landscapes of North Africa, and offered new openings for displaying status and prowess far out in the Sahara. Here, in a composite reconstruction created in the 1960s of several images from the Tardrart Acacus, the chariots are juxtaposed with potentially much earlier figures of giraffes, barbary sheep and cattle.

metallurgy, for example the early ironworking practised in Carthage, Lixus or Egypt, had anything to do with the indigenous iron- and copper-based practices that sprang up in sub-Saharan Africa and Mauretania respectively around the same time.[342]

The inclusion of Africa also profoundly altered the Mediterranean's networks. Still wrapped in obscurity are the origins of those that from Roman times ran south out of the basin and brought Saharan and Sahelian goods, including gold, semi-precious stones, slaves and exotic animals (alive or reduced to their pelts or tusks) into the Mediterranean, penetrating the southern barrier that a hyper-arid Sahara had erected west of the Nile for the previous 3000 years.[343] The ground conditions for such connections were certainly already falling into place, even if Arabian dromedaries did not enter the Sahara until the early centuries AD.[344] In the eastern and central oases – where we plotted the rise of pastoral confederacies, the uptake of date cultivation, metallurgy and, when the rains increased, domestic cereals, grapes and figs – heralded a peak in social complexity from about 500 BC, in the form of the irrigating, hillfort-dwelling, partly literate communities known as the Garamantes, which were later indeed famed for trans-Saharan trade.[345] Meanwhile, back in the coastal zone, pastoralists with ties to these deep Saharan experts in desert transit coexisted with Mediterranean traders in Cyrenaica and surely other areas besides.

Ironically, we are on firmer ground at sea. The virtually total absence of evidence for North African seafaring west of the Nile has often been underlined in preceding chapters, and attributed to smooth coasts, scarcity of offshore islands and adverse navigational conditions, combined in the earlier Holocene with the magnetic pull of an inhabited Sahara. One minor exception is the filigreed coastline of Tunisia, where 6th-millennium BC transport of Pantellerian obsidian into the eastern Maghreb could have been effected by African mariners. Activity in the Sicilian strait may have continued intermittently over the millennia that separated this blip from Carthage and any immediate predecessor, whose establishment along the same stretch of coast was assuredly no coincidence, and which had created the first North African ship imagery west of Egypt by the 6th century BC. Aside from this, indigenous maritime interconnections in all likelihood simply did not exist along much of the southern, African shore. Even an earlier Egypt that was so active in the east Mediterranean and Red Sea had displayed no apparent interest in sending ships west along the coast. Instead, the integration of points on the African coast took the form (as during earlier, tentative manifestations) of north–south routes dovetailed to hubs of seafaring on the northern side of the Mediterranean. Hence the intimate ties between Carthage, Sicily, Sardinia and, later, the mid-strait Maltese islands, and Cyrenaica's strong Aegean connection, which lasted until Crete and Cyrene were merged into a single Roman trans-marine province, governed from the south Cretan Mesara plain.[346] As with France and Catalonia, only after the establishment of a series of North African trading centres did coastwise traffic start to string them together, and voyages along the African flank of the basin become a reality. Travel along the segment between the Nile and Cyrenaica extended westward a 2nd-millennium BC seaway that had formerly only reached as far as the landfall at Marsa Matruh. But entirely new at this juncture was the segment across, or gingerly into, the treacherous gulfs of Sirte and Gabès, which tied together Carthage, Cyrenaica and intervening outposts. Even the offshore island of Djerba, with its scraps of native pottery and tumuli, and its perilous approach through shoal-water, received a few Greek pots by the 6th century.[347] The last segment to be activated on a regular basis, perhaps well after 500 BC, lay to the west of Carthage, and the delay there was due less to any incremental east-to-west unfolding of connections, than to the lack of motivation to create enclaves in the central Maghreb, the adverse sailing conditions offshore, and the fact that an easier run to the west lay across the open sea, via an Ibiza now fully equipped to welcome shipping.

The Mediterranean's big bang begins

The bounds of the Mediterranean were burst open before the intake of the last internal isolates. We shall explore the movement of people, practices and trading connections, but there was a cosmological dimension too. For despite jealous guarding of the local associations of particular myths throughout antiquity, the shrinking sea and closer acquaintance with its surrounding inhabitants by growing numbers of highly mobile individuals inexorably banished exotic or mythic realms from simply the next sub-basin over, or (an old favourite) the Nile Valley, to more distant parts of Asia, Africa, Europe or an *ultima thule* in the Atlantic. The vagueness of the *Odyssey*'s fabulous physical and cultural geography west of the Aegean reflects a transitional moment in this process, and in a sense marked a Mediterranean ending.

We can start our more prosaic, if no less intriguing, exploration in the Atlantic extension of Mediterranean Africa (a region regarded as only partly linked-in even as the Roman province of Mauretania Tingitana),[348] and its reflection on the other side of the Strait of Gibraltar, where the Iberian coast starts to swing north. The key was Gadir, which we have so far treated as an only nominally Atlantic offshoot of the Mediterranean, and of Tyre in particular. By the 7th century BC, however, Gadir had evolved another face, as the hub of an independent maritime circuit centred on the strait, both sides of which were peppered with Phoenician outposts.[349] This reached back through the Pillars of Melqart to the Alboran Sea, but equally out into the tidal reaches of the inner Atlantic. Such shifts in the Phoenician west tend to be explained as reactions to the mounting woes of Tyre, but were more a result of the new regional dynamics that ensued once a new participant had been set up in a favourable position. In this case, Gadir's outposts extended along the Atlantic facade for a staggering total of 1400 km (870 miles) north and south of Gibraltar.[350] Those in Morocco contrast with the dearth in parts of the Mediterranean Maghreb, and attest to the abundance of goods obtained from a lusher interior (especially pelts, and ivory to be carved at Gadir). Rich Atlantic fisheries and the easy evaporation of fish-preserving salt on a tidal shore were another attraction, harking back to the glimpses of a developing eastern taste for preserved, amphora-bottled fish in the late 2nd to early 1st millennia BC, although the true mass production of salted fish (apparently mainly tuna chunks), and highly flavoured fish sauces, for a pan-Mediterranean market only took off at Gadir well after 500 BC.[351] Lixus, just 50 km (30 miles) south of the strait, at the mouth of a river that wound inland to the foothills of the Atlas mountains, began in the 8th century BC as a mixed endeavour by groups native to the strait and Phoenician entrepreneurs, with unusually little sign of wine-drinking.[352] In the following century it became monumentalized as a Phoenician centre of operations. Over 700 km (435 miles) further down the coast lay Mogador, in a sense the Atlantic equivalent of Marsa Matruh, with no permanent houses, but a probable ritual stele, plenty of fish and whale bones, Attic amphorae, and sherds inscribed with the name 'Magon', in all likelihood a Phoenician merchant – a man by the same name was richly buried back in Andalusia.[353] Mogador feels very far indeed from the Mediterranean, but in the 5th century BC it in turn acted as the jump-off point for a Carthage-sponsored voyage that plausibly reached much further round the West African coast.[354] As usual, we have no reliable knowledge of the local people with whom such Phoenician merchants traded, according to Herodotus by silent exchange on the beach.[355]

North of the strait, the situation was quite different. Gadir tapped into the pre-existing Atlantic metals trade, especially in tin, which had long been handled by big indigenous villages, with an especially powerful cluster around the Tagus. As far as the Mondego estuary in central Portugal, these began to receive large quantities of Phoenician goods manufactured in the west.[356] Only two actual 7th-century BC enclaves are known, a small, defended one at Abul on the Sado and another at Santa Olaia, while other Phoenician finds far inland – most famously the Aliseda treasure of gold jewelry and bronze and silver jugs – hint at parallel efforts to cultivate alternative overland access to northern Iberian metal sources.[357] What with Atlantic metals, fish and salt, African animal products, plus Mediterranean oil, wine and superlative craft skills, Gadir was clearly a place with a brilliant future.

Before we turn away from this 'Mediterranean Atlantic', there is an enigmatic codicil. The Canary Islands, about 1000 km (600 miles) from Gibraltar and 100 km (60 miles) off the nearest African shore, were certainly known by Roman times.[358] Pliny the Elder described them, and relics from Roman landfalls have been found. We cannot accurately date the arrival of the ancestors of the Guanche people who first farmed this archipelago, without metals, until their slaughter by European adventurers halfway through the transition from crusading to trans-Atlantic conquest. But the circumstantial evidence points to some time in the 1st millennium BC and a northwest African origin – the Guanche language and genes have Berber links, and a 'Neolithic' technology could reflect conditions in parts of coastal Morocco even this late, if not a post-arrival loss of metallurgy in an island environment entirely without ores. Even Canarian house mice match with the wider contemporary invasion of the west Mediterranean by this species.[359] Although the exact scenario may never be known, one likely context for the transfer of a mainly northwest African founding nucleus to the Canaries is the Atlantic seafaring exploits of 7th- to 6th-century Gadir. When and how a hoard of 4th- to 3rd-century BC Carthaginian and Cyrenaican coins, reputedly found vastly further out to sea in the Azores in AD 1749,

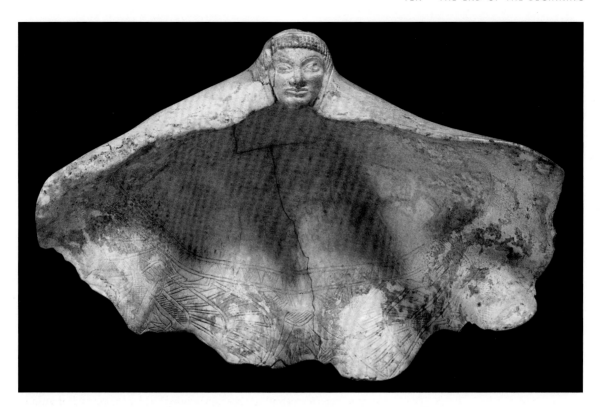

10.45 Giant clam shell with carved head and incised floral design, found on Rhodes. The production centre for these distinctive objects is unknown, but probably lay in the Levant, which enjoyed good connections to the Red Sea by this time.

had crossed 1500 km (900 miles) of open ocean, is a matter for happy speculation, though the limits of the possible for misadventures by experienced mariners in robust vessels are fairly generous.[360]

As we have seen in the west, the Mediterranean's maritime frontiers tended to be the fuzziest and most easily negotiable. Meanwhile, from the southeast end, Red Sea giant clam shells, often carved, travelled as far as the Aegean and Etruria [**10.45**].[361] The Red Sea had long been Egypt's other maritime outlet, and by no means a secondary one thanks to the lack (until recently) of internal competition and the cherished access it gave to subtropical goods. Necho's canal project highlighted the desire to link these two seas efficiently, but athwart them lay not only a substantial intervening isthmus but also, as we saw at Naukratis and Sais, a highly centralized state apparatus that operated as a brake and filter on mercantile expansion in this direction. The kind of union of seas and sea trades presided over by Gadir was not so easily achievable here, however successful (as earlier at Avaris) that between the Mediterranean and the Nile.

More propitious was the link to the Black Sea via the Dardanelles, the Sea of Marmara and the Bosphorus. The south and east shores of the Black Sea provided access to Anatolian and Caucasian metals, the mouth of the Danube opened up the Balkan interior, the Crimea offered a mini-Mediterranean climate and the steppic perimeter to the north gave onto a potentially vast grain-growing and slaving belt, while the sea itself teemed with little fish that could be salted and exported in huge, flavoursome quantities – far more so than the Mediterranean, thanks to the nutrients injected by so many great rivers.[362] Moreover, at least since Troy became a far-sung ruin, the connecting corridor had not been subject to political or economic controls. The start date for direct travel between the two seas is uncertain, but should go back to the 2nd, if not sporadically the 3rd, millennium BC, when eastern tin began to trickle along this axis. Near the end of the Bronze Age, a hoard on the Marmara coast contained oxhide ingot fragments plus an Aegean sword and double axes.[363] During the later 7th century connections took off.[364] The instigators came from the Mediterranean, with geography and timing guaranteeing the priority of ventures from the Aegean, itself almost half the size of the Black Sea, but far more island-studded, densely populated and networked. For once there is not a trace of a Phoenician presence, although more local activities probably wait to be revealed. The Black Sea became in effect a marine extension of Aegean Greece. East Aegean people, particularly from Miletus, took the lead, perhaps aiming to compensate themselves for losses of land and metal access to the expanding power of Lydia.[365] As the wealth to be gained became apparent, and city-state identities and interests more sharply delineated, the long, slender gateway to the Black Sea became the scene of a fast and fierce scramble for advantage. Megara gained an early foothold with the foundation of Byzantium, but during the 6th century Athens achieved a decisive hegemony that it would doggedly maintain until eventual naval catastrophe there in 405 BC spelt its defeat in the Peloponnesian War.

The Mediterranean's terrestrial edges often proved harder to open up, thanks to the physical, cultural and economic friction effects on overland expansion, which commonly endured in the guise of connections run by intervening middlemen. We saw this in North Africa, where the Nile Valley remained the only artery for direct movement far from the coast (recall the mercenaries' graffiti at Abu Simbel). The ancient, if ever-fluctuating engagement of the Mediterranean with the lands of the Jazira, Anatolia and Mesopotamia continued under successive eastern empires, with much of the human traffic out of the basin now taking the form of forced transfers of populations, although some Mediterranean merchants and other wealthy individuals still travelled freely inland. Greek mercenaries arrived in Mesopotamia later than in Egypt, mainly from the 4th century BC, and as harbingers of the victorious progress of much larger numbers in a Mediterranean conqueror's pay a few decades later, under Alexander the Great.

Along the northern edges of the basin, contacts up the river valleys and over the mountain passes with a shifting spectrum of chiefly societies in temperate Europe had been on the rise since the second half of the previous millennium, operating within different kinds of frameworks from those increasingly taken for granted in the Mediterranean. The original stimulus had been metals, but we saw how this extended to wine and slaves in France, while the growth of Etruria, especially its activities in the Po plain and around the head of the Adriatic, similarly boosted and diversified trans-Alpine trade.[366] North of the Alps, a cluster of Hallstatt centres emerged in response, the most elaborate at Heuneberg near Munich.[367] In return for the human and other merchandise dispatched south came by now time-honoured classes of Mediterranean

10.46 The general premise that only a minuscule fraction of ancient metalwork has survived into modern times, and much of that not at the original centres, but on the margins of ancient production and consumption, is dramatically borne out by the discovery of this enormous bronze wine-mixing vessel, probably made in the Peloponnese but discovered at Vix, in northern Burgundy, to where it was transported along the Rhône, as part of the Gallic slave trade.

trade goods, some of which found distant resting places: wine amphorae, fine Greek pots (mainly Athenian), carved ivory, and elaborately decorated Etruscan and Greek metal vessels for wine-drinking ceremonies, some so huge that they had to be transported in pieces.[368] Several of the last survive thanks to their rapid consumption in bombastic displays at local elite funerals. Indeed, if we seek a northerly equivalent to the deracinated, redeployed quadrigas by now galloping around the Sahara, it would be the Vix krater, a gargantuan bronze wine-mixing vessel, 1.64 m (5 ft 5 in.) tall, made in the Peloponnese, and yet buried in the last decades of the 6th century BC at a point along the Seine known also for its abundant amphora finds, precisely where the river became unnavigable and carriage from the Rhône, and then the headwaters of the Saône, switched to overland portage [**10.46**].[369]

As yet, the two ends of this particular chain stayed segregated worlds, but the first direct large-scale movements were underway further east, and in contrast to the impressive levels of mobility displayed by Mediterranean people within their basin, these instead took the form of incursions from the temperate north. Phrygia's early 7th-century *coup de grâce* had come, with Assyrian complicity, at the hands of a thrust around the Black Sea into Anatolia by the first great nomadic confederacy of horse-mounted archers to come together north of the Black Sea – an entity known to us as the 'Cimmerians'. These were both the descendants of three millennia of increasingly adept horse-riding there, and precursors of the better-known Scythians.[370] In political terms they were not unlike the late 2nd-millennium BC Libyan pastoral formations that had coalesced as raiders, fighters and settlers at another rich interface on the other side of the Mediterranean, along the margins of Egypt. Lydia later absorbed or expelled the Cimmerians, but the basin's growing wealth encouraged such formations and would start to draw them in with accelerating frequency. Soon not all were pastoral: in the 5th century BC the Po plain was flooded by 'Celtic' farming migrants as the eastern Hallstatt complex fell apart.[371] Both vortex and centrifuge, the pull and reach of this Middle Sea was becoming long indeed.

Into the familiar

Polybius, a high-born Greek intellectual of the 2nd century BC, held not unpleasantly as a hostage in Rome for his compatriots' good behaviour, opined in the great work he wrote there that only since about 220 BC had history (by which he meant political history, and of the Mediterranean basin and its neighbours) possessed a truly woven-together, interactive unity.[372] His choice of date signified the moment when Rome's drive to conquer really took off beyond Italy and the Tyrrhenian Sea, reaching swiftly to the Balkans and Spain. In fact, as we have seen, long before its political history drew together, the Mediterranean was already an integrated, dynamic nexus of culturally convergent societies and economies, politically independent yet in every other sense interdependent,[373] structured around a set of increasingly shared or easily convertible standards (citizens, coins, alphabets and Greek-style drinking vessels, to mention but a recent few), and all operating within an even older ecological whole.

Things would certainly get bigger on most fronts after 500 BC.[374] Major states, cities and the battles between them became more massive and complex operations; by the 3rd century BC the populations of Carthage, Rome and younger foundations at Alexandria and Antioch had all breached the six-figure barrier, with imperial Rome eventually approaching a million people.[375] At its ancient, and probably pre-modern, peak during the 2nd century AD the total population of the basin reached 35–50 million, roughly doubling the figure at 800 BC and a hefty advance, too, on the likely total some three centuries later, with astronomically faster growth in formerly thinly inhabited areas such as most of North Africa.[376] 'Carrying capacity' is a somewhat misleading term in as unstable a region as the Mediterranean,[377] but this

10.47 The up-scaling of artificial port facilities during the last few centuries BC, as well as the superior showing of Roman-period economic installations relative to their successors, is dramatically apparent in this aerial view of Caesarea, on the coast of modern Israel. Above water, the modest Crusader to modern harbour; below, as dark shadows, massive remains of breakwaters built by Herod the Great, in honour of the emperor Augustus, jut out into open sea.

population total, and other indices relating to production and consumption, seem to represent, in effect, a ceiling until the changed conditions of the last few centuries.[378] The Mediterranean's economy continued to grow, with an estimated rise of 25–50 per cent in per capita consumption in the thousand years after 800 BC.[379] This left strong marks on the productive landscape all over the basin, as countrysides became more thickly settled, entire regions optimally, and sometimes ruthlessly zoned, existing cash crops further ratcheted up or entirely new ones introduced, additional extraction techniques intensified (from mining to new water-mills), and market-driven pastoralism at last unleashed on a grand scale in the mountains.[380] At sea, wrecks and written testimony plot a gathering crescendo in the size and amount of shipping,[381] and to receive this on exposed coasts, huge hydraulic concrete harbours began to be built from around 300 BC [**10.47**].[382] Yet we have encountered earlier up-scalings and refinements of these and comparable phenomena throughout the course of this book, most often in the previous three millennia, but sometimes much earlier. To force a basic segregation now would be as unhelpful as to impose a divide between (for instance) the 3rd and 2nd millennia BC, or to dismiss the climax of growth under Rome on the grounds that the imperial state's income, when pegged against grain prices, can be calculated as equivalent to no more than that of a well-off university in the United States today.[383]

The final chapter of this book will summarize and draw together the principal strands that contributed to the emergence of this Middle Sea, starting millennia before Polybius and already complete several centuries before his birth. The present one ends with a brief bridging epilogue between the latest phases of the past we have explored and the ensuing 5th century BC, already an age of fewer, yet bigger principal players, most if not all more heavily investing in state infrastructure, and hotly engaged in what were by now in effect bi- or tri-polar contests for hegemony within and beyond their sector of the basin. This should further erase any false sense of an abrupt caesura between our largely archaeologically informed 'prehistory' and the 'ancient history' that followed (not that either term is very helpful). In violation of our ideal of balanced exploration, it selects a handful of large-scale phenomena and trusts that, in the closing moments, this will be forgiven in light of the ease with which it enables us to dovetail the past with some of the best-known phenomena of the new century.

We start in the central Mediterranean, where it is striking how, relatively soon after the 9th-century BC re-establishment of a scalar symmetry in the basin's maritime spaces, the physical centre of the basin began to sprout cities ambitious on the widest of Mediterranean stages. Two out of the three that eventually gained the mantle of more than regional significance, and finally fought each other to the death, only shook clear of the local competition after 500 BC, and so need only briefly detain us. One of these was Syracuse, the closest of all contenders to the absolute geographical centre of the basin, and equally close several times during the 5th and 4th centuries BC to consolidating a political dominance to match its economic and cultural prominence.[384] Another, of course, was Rome, whose ultimate win in the sweepstakes would at this stage be very hard to predict.[385] Rome in the 6th century BC was a large, populous city-state with a respectable territory of 800 sq. km (310 sq. miles), but so was Veii, its Tiber Valley neighbour and rival, and wider leaderships were coming together elsewhere in Etruria. True, over the next two centuries Rome grew fast and evolved effective means of incorporation, such as the political intake of its common people, the *plebs*, and the institution within Italy of colonies (its own term, connoting far more dependency than the Greek *apoikia*). In conjunction with earlier centuriate reform of the army, this boded very well for mobilizing citizens and holding captured ground. Yet it only defeated and annexed Veii in 396 BC, and the conquest of the peninsula's diverse other, and in some cases still barely urban, polities took more than another century.[386] Only from about 270 BC did Rome's rise towards lone superpower status accelerate, slightly before Polybius' onset of historical unity and for most of the time dominated by a protracted tussle against Carthage across the central and west Mediterranean. That feud ended in 146 BC, the year in which Rome also sacked another iconic city on the sea at Corinth, and after Rome had offered Carthage the option of relocating 15 km (10 miles) inland (in short, mercantile instead of military suicide).[387] These timescales seem to flash by after those we have dealt with, and could barely be detected before the Holocene, but they still left plenty of potential for specific events of this kind to pan out differently.

The third superpower in the central Mediterranean was Carthage itself, and in Braudel's words, 'a very special voice'.[388] Carthage had no immediately neighbouring competition and was certainly on an exceptional trajectory before 500 BC, one that in consequence demands a slightly fuller exploration here. As suggested earlier, it is likely to have become the largest city in the basin once Babylon had finished its work in the Levant;[389] if we had more than a few trenches dug into its early strata, uncertain inferences concerning its impact abroad and rare textual scraps embedded in hostile sources, parts of the history of the 6th and 5th centuries BC might appear in a different light (in fact, not unlike the situation with Hyksos Avaris a thousand years before). As with Gadir, too much weight can be placed on the fall of Tyre as the occasion for Carthage's ascent. Of course, the cessation of formal Tyrian activity in the centre and west opened up new opportunities, but, long before that, Carthage was already large, critical to diasporic Phoenician demography and active on its own account in the central Mediterranean. Other aspects of the transition from Phoenician to Punic can be overpainted, too – even the latter term is simply a Latin derivative of the former. While the rise of alternative gods to Tyrian Melqart did signify conscious separation, it also reflected an oligarchical distancing from Melqart's royal ties; when the house of Hamilcar Barca later began to pretend to a kingly aura, Melqart swiftly returned to favour.[390] Moreover, worship of Tanit and rituals at tophets were already established Carthaginian traits in Phoenician centres across the central Mediterranean when Tyre still thrived, while, conversely, the custom of elite suicide *in extremis*, enshrined in the story of Elissa's death, was maintained by Carthaginian military and other leaders up until the bitter end.[391] In terms of broader identities there is an impressive, even poignant continuity, as well; Tyre received its symbolic tithe long after it was in a position to demand it, and in the 5th century AD, St Augustine knew North Africans who spoke Punic and considered themselves to be Chanani – Canaanites.[392] More generally, historians may well have set the transition from an early trading hub to the territorial, military empire that confronted Rome too far back in time. Between these two stages in Carthage's life, during the 6th and early 5th centuries BC, there plausibly existed instead a supreme network node, a huge city-state powerful at sea, where it deployed slave-propelled galleys to extract tribute from distant ports (themselves intensifying extraction from their hinterlands), but whose later explicit terrestrial militarism, much of it dependent on mercenary armies, was in part a subsequent response to aggression by others, and in the first instance heavily armed, probing Greeks.[393] The 5th-century BC fortification of Cape Bon was surely in part a defensive reaction to prior challenges, decisively repulsed, such as the Spartan effort to force an enclave near Lepcis, or a Sicilian Greek attempt to do the same at Lilybaion, at the southern end of Motya's lagoon and right opposite Carthage itself.[394]

This would make sense of the wider picture, such as it is. In terms of gains on land, Carthage continued to make an only moderate showing in North Africa outside its own sizeable core territory until the 4th and especially 3rd centuries BC, when rural and slave communities began to stud the Maghreb, stimulating the formation of the first indigenous 'Numidian' polities in response.[395] Even nearby Utica held onto its independence as late as 500 BC. Abroad, 6th-century Carthage did begin to annex and sporadically settle land in southern Sardinia, an island that would find itself midway between North Africa and central Italy in the worst of senses over coming centuries.[396] The Campidano plain in the southwest of the island, much of which had lain fallow since the drying of the 'long' 3rd millennium BC, began to be opened up as a grain belt, perhaps employing the same agronomic expertise that operated in Carthage's immediate hinterland. Around this time, too, horses were introduced to Sardinia, probably via a circuitous route out of Africa, where they were virtually as recent arrivals.[397] But the takeover of the island was protracted and never complete, with reversals against dogged local resistance, and while it created a hybrid society in the south of the island, often using old nuraghi as dwellings or places of ritual, it left most of the uplands and all of the north still untouched.[398]

In contrast, Carthage had little trouble dominating by sea. In the central Mediterranean it had long been the major attractor for other Phoenician interests. In the west, where a few successful locations were already reordering connections to their own advantage during the 7th century, its increasing prominence correlated with further realignments as much as any formal imposed authority. Ongoing shifts there were inevitable given the emergence of a new zone of production and consumption further north in Catalonia and France, as well as a sharp decline in silver production in southwest Iberia, whether due to exhaustion of the lodes that could be accessed by existing technology, depletion of the woodland required for charcoal, or the crisis in local power attested (as cause or consequence) by the disappearance of elites from the lower Guadalquivir and the rise of less cooperative indigenous societies inland.[399] The fast-growing populations and uptake of Carthaginian burial customs and ideology at the select roster of major maritime towns of Phoenician

10.48 The 'Tyrannicides', Harmodius and Aristogeiton, in the act of striking at the younger brother of the Athenian tyrant Hippias, in a failed coup as much to do with aristocratic honour and sexual jealousy as political reform, but taken up by the soon-ensuing Athenian democracy as an heroic founding sacrifice. This Roman version copies a lost early 5th-century BC Greek original, which itself replaced a bronze sculpture commissioned at public expense in 509 BC and subsequently taken off to Susa by Persian troops some thirty years later.

origin that still prospered, notably Motya, Gadir, Malaka and Ebesus, reflected both their mercantile success and the influx of traders and maybe monitoring officials from Carthage.[400] In at least one instance Carthage even founded a new enclave, at Tingis under modern Tangier.[401] All in all, it looks very much as if we may be witnessing the informal genesis of the first truly extensive intra-Mediterranean empire.[402] If so, it was taking a very different guise from those that we have grown accustomed to see emanating overland from the east, with islands no longer seen as intractable overseas trouble spots, but as the vital articulating points, ancestors of what Braudel would memorably describe as 'la flotte immobile de Venise'.[403]

Nothing even remotely comparable to this Carthaginian network emerged in the Aegean until well into the 5th century BC, at the climax of its dramatically last-minute thrust into a truly decisive position within early Mediterranean history.[404] But profound changes were afoot by the end of the 6th century in Athens, later the almost-insular ruler of an even more archipelagic empire,[405] and equally emblematic of the combination of factors that propelled certain Greek city-states so rapidly forward: a newly advantageous geopolitical and networking position within pan-Mediterranean economies, the culturally and constitutionally creative fallout from fractious power politics, and a long tradition of value-added production and its marketing, to which Athens added the rarer benefit of a significant domestic source of precious metal, and hence exceptional wealth. At its peak in the 430s BC, Classical Athens was a walled city of 150–215 ha (370–530 acres) inhabited by 30,000–45,000 people (including the port of Piraeus), with some six to nine times that number living across the remainder of Attica.[406] This overall population represented roughly 1 per cent of estimated contemporary Mediterranean humanity in just over 0.1 per cent of Mediterranean terrestrial space, or, in other words, the most densely crammed landscape anywhere in the basin (including the Nile Delta), an achievement whose sustenance (literally and loosely) was a tribute to connectivity writ large. Athens already had some 20,000 inhabitants by about 500 BC, a marked improvement from its low profile in a 7th century dominated by Corinth and the east Aegean towns, and one that it owed to silver and shifting trade.[407] During most of the intervening period it had been presided over by an unexceptional mixture of kouros-erecting oligarchs and temple-sponsoring tyrants.[408] But in the last decade of the 6th century, Athens deviated from this past in a way that has lent immortality to its name ever since.

It is hard to look dispassionately at what would soon become known as the Athenian democracy. In tactical terms its institution in 508–507 BC was an only partly intended consequence of old rivalries between tyrants and other elite factions, one of which favoured popular enfranchisement as a counterbalance against its enemies [**10.48**].[409] Looked at another way, the expansion of the middling, sub-elite sort, identified in Athens itself by archaeology as early as the 8th century and later in Solonic writing, was a widespread feature across the Mediterranean, in some regions from even earlier times; where coupled with weak elite authority it made power-sharing solutions more or less inevitable. In this sense the creation of several tens of thousands of adult male citizens throughout Athens and Attica (at best a fifth of the total population, and, of course, excluding all women, slaves and foreigners) simply represented one end of a spectrum that ran through large, inclusive oligarchies such as Sparta's. Moreover, it is estimated that even under democracy as little as a tenth or twentieth of all Athenians retained the ownership of nearly a third of the land.[410] It is likewise unclear to what extent similar arrangements may have sprung up elsewhere at an early stage, for our sources come overwhelmingly from Athens, which as a major polity set the subsequent standard.[411] As with the Roman republic, whose inception lies around the same time,[412] we are quickly caught in circular reasoning: did such reforms make these city-states genuinely exceptionally successful and thereby lead to preferential survival of their records, or did later serendipities ensure the latter, and make these places appear more unusual than they once were? And yet for all these misgivings, and even setting aside its symbolic potency today, the Athenian democracy and its cultural hothouse environment offered something qualitatively, and in its eventual form, radically, new – a different course from most of the remainder of the basin, where the deeply rooted 'Archaic' world evolved seamlessly into its successors.[413]

Athens's near-nemesis, the Persian empire, presents a similar mixture of older roots and new directions.[414] A product of rapid conquests in the later 6th century, it built upon thousands of years of consolidating states and empires in Mesopotamia, but at the same time, with its heartland further east on the Iranian plateau, represented an eclipse of Mesopotamian political pre-eminence. It was bigger, more integrated and in consequence even more vastly wealthy than its Assyrian and Babylonian precursors, comprising at its height 6.2 million sq. km (2.4 million sq. miles) and 20–26 million people, the first figure larger than the entire Mediterranean basin (sea and land), and the second comparable to its total population at that time. Most of the enlargement lay to the east, as far as the Hindu Kush, but in the west it reached Cyrene, Cyprus and, through the former lands of Lydia, which it quickly crushed, into the east Aegean, with an ephemeral hold over tracts of European Thrace. Peninsular Greece found itself in a not dissimilar situation to Phoenicia with respect to Assyria a few centuries earlier, if with more immediately surrounding sea-room for manoeuvre.

Persia's engagement with the Mediterranean was more extensive than that of any previous empire, itself a tribute not least to the latter's rapidly growing riches.

Its hegemony extended over 20–25 per cent of the basin's entire coastline, including several of its most dynamic sectors, and it was the first outside power to establish real authority over islands, including Cyprus and most of those in the eastern Aegean, with Persian influence extending westward into the Cyclades. Thanks to the number of its coastal vassals, Persia conjured up war-fleets of unparalleled size – indeed the first triremes may have been built to its specifications.[415] In 525 BC the Persian call for Egyptian surrender at Memphis was made from the deck of a ship of Lesbos; slightly later, a coastal geography of the Aegean, presumably a *periplous* of some description, was written to imperial order by a team cruising around it in Sidonian ships.[416] Persian kings' determination to surpass decisively the Upper Sea bounds of Mesopotamian lordship may also cast light, alongside more prosaic rationales, on their persistent amphibious operations in the Aegean.[417] And despite its resort to overwhelming force when it met resistance (which drove some east Aegean dwellers, including another generation of Phocaeans, to relocate far to the west), and its unexceptional policy of forced relocation (which saw others re-employed at Persepolis), the Persian empire reverted in its Mediterranean territories to the light touch that had served Assyria so well.[418] It adapted its tribute and taxation arrangements to maritime realities, fostered recovery in the Levant and encouraged coastal towns in general to prosper, albeit with the teeth drawn from their politics under local rulers chosen from their own elite and responsible to provincial satraps. Greek pots returned in force to the Levant, as ever betraying other normally invisible flows, such as a vast consignment of purple cloth from the Argolid still stored in the palace at Susa when Alexander got there in 331 BC, and said to have been delivered 190 years earlier.[419] Quite unlike the explicitly thalassocentric projects already emerging at Carthage and soon at Athens, the Persian empire remained typical of the pragmatic, if often grudging, cohabitation between major land powers and the Mediterranean's maritime cities for centuries to come.

What went wrong in 500–499 BC in the east Aegean, where reconciling the demands of overbearing terrestrial polities with the call of the sea had proved tricky since the late 2nd millennium BC, is veiled in obscurity, though the young Athenian democracy, with its trading interests there and further north, assuredly had a hand in inciting opposition.[420] The resultant 'Ionian Revolt' caught up Caria and Cyprus too, and ended disastrously for its instigators in 494 BC, when nearly 1000 ships fought off the islet of Lade, today a hillock landlocked by alluvial mud a short stroll from Miletus.[421] Just fourteen years later the comparably sized navies of the Persian empire and a different alliance of Greek city-states would clash again, more famously, and with the inverse result, at Salamis.

XXXVI (*previous page*) The heavily trenched mound of Hissarlik, Bronze Age Troy, overlooks its still largely unexplored lower town and the plain that in antiquity would have been a slowly alluviating inlet of the sea; beyond, the maritime corridor of the Dardanelles. A site of both destruction and repeated myth construction from the Bronze Age to Schliemann, Troy remains one of the few substantially investigated centres along the interface between the Aegean and Anatolia.

XXXVII (*left*) The limestone gorges surrounding the southeast Sicilian settlement of Pantalica are riddled with rock-cut tombs dating to the late 2nd and early 1st millennia BC. Such places in the rugged interior long acted as redoubts for indigenous ways of doing things, but finds from them also reveal extensive contacts with the wider Mediterranean world.

XXXVIII Italian metalworking burgeoned in quality and quantity in the late 2nd and early 1st millennia BC, combining abundant local sources, technological know-how derived from the east Mediterranean and transalpine connections. This distinctive form of helmet, from Tarquinia in ore-rich Etruria, reveals a blend of eastern sheet-metalworking traditions and local fighting styles.

XXXIX (*below*) The fortified city of Tyre on its rocky offshore island, as depicted during the reign of the widely campaigning mid-9th-century BC Neo-Assyrian monarch Shalmaneser III on the bronze gates of Balawat in northern Mesopotamia. Horse-headed boats and a procession of bearers bring out of Tyre a tribute of metal vessels, ingots, bales of cloth, and possibly trays of pointed scrimshaw (whale ivory). Back on the island, a high-status man and woman appear to perform a libation ritual with metal dishes.

XL (*right*) Bronze boat model from Sardinia, dating to the early 1st millennium BC. While the basic form reflects the expansion of broad-hulled, masted and sail-driven designs to the central Mediterranean by this time, the stag-headed prow and open-work cabin suggest a local input too. Most such models derive from native nuragic ritual contexts or from mainland Italy at a time of impressive maritime interaction on the part of the island's coastal communities.

XLI (*below*) The royal tombs of Tanis, one of the principal Delta capitals of a fragmented Egypt during the early 1st millennium BC, were architecturally modest compared to earlier pharaonic burials and, like the city as a whole, relied heavily on reused stonework taken from earlier nearby cities such as Piramesse. Once a river-port close to the sea, the shifting branches of the Nile have now left the site high and dry.

XLII (*right*) Gilt silver 7th-century BC bowl with a mixture of east Mediterranean imagery from the Bernardini Tomb at Praeneste, modern Palestrina, east of Rome.

XLIII (*below*) Aerial view of a still sea-girt but no longer insular Cadiz, where the modern town entirely smothers those parts of the Phoenician and later ancient city that are not inundated by localized submergence. The core of the Phoenician settlement occupied the semi-submerged reefs in the foreground, divided by a sheltering channel faintly visible as deeper water, and extended onto higher ground on the main island.

XLIV (*left*) Replica of a 6th-century BC Attic funerary *kore*, slightly over life-size and known from its accompanying inscription to commemorate one Phrasikleia. Painted after surviving traces on the marble original, it illuminates both the high status of elite women at the time, and the largely lost world of richly decorated textiles.

XLV (*above*) Relations between pottery and largely lost metal vessels, as well as between Aegean and Italian ceramics, are evident in this pair of late 6th-century BC products: (*left*) Etruscan bucchero, in which the lustrous surface, ridged seams and strap-like handles faithfully evoke metalwork; (*right*) variant made in the Nikosthenic workshop of Athens to target an Etruscan market, with the basic form (alien to Greek tradition) retained but the surface allure now created by intricately painted decoration.

XLVI (*above*) Temple C, a massive construction in the Doric style, erected around 550 BC as one in a spate of such buildings in the Sicilian town of Selinous, typifies in particularly grandiose form the sacred architecture that dominated urban centres across the Mediterranean.

XLVII (*right*) Three inscribed gold tablets from Pyrgi, the coastal emporion of the Etruscan town of Caere, recording a dedication made around 500 BC in Phoenician and Etruscan.

591

XLVIII Gold and ivory head from Delphi, probably representing Apollo and possibly a Corinthian or east Greek dedication. This rare survival of large-scale work in such media, preserved as fire destruction debris alongside other fragments, including those of an almost life-size gilt silver bull, underscores the growing wealth of certain Greek cities at this time.

XLIX (*below*) Cyrene, set amidst the fully Mediterranean environment of the uplands of the Jebel Akhdar ('green mountain'), between Benghazi and Tobruk in present-day northeast coastal Libya. The Classical ruins largely obscure the remains of the first, late 7th-century BC southern Aegean foundation.

De profundis

The nature of early Mediterranean history

Out of the depths of its many and varied pasts the world of the Middle Sea, so famous and influential in its Classical and later forms, came together over millennia, starting long – sometimes very long – ago. To return to a metaphor suggested in Chapter 1, in order to trace its rise with least danger of back-projecting its final properties onto the diverse, lively trajectories of earlier times, we have had to explore a multitude of streams, and trace their courses over time, as some headed elsewhere or ran dry, while others began to flow in parallel, converge and finally blend into a stronger current. This history has been primarily one of the Mediterranean's people, but of necessity it became a natural history too, of the basin's physical fabric, of water (falling, flowing, undulating, fresh and salt), of changing bestiaries and flora, and not least the impacts of climatic turbulence on all of these. If it has been a history of change, transition and innovation, sometimes spectacular, arguably even revolutionary, in its consequences, it has also been one of deep-lying, endlessly modulated continuities over impressive time spans, and even the grandest transformations can in almost every case be traced back to smaller-scale, often surprisingly early beginnings.[1] Nor has all of this been a one-way, uninterrupted flow; right across the Mediterranean, independent cycles of initiative and growth have sprung up, flourished and fallen back repeatedly, some of a kind later reiterated, others to go extinct. Larger-scale abatements or fragmentations after dramatic spikes and periods of convergence, whether due to climate fluctuation, socio-economic change or both, have also been regular and often locally catastrophic features, though outright collapses have proven rare and tend to disguise a reversion to more flexible, resilient ways of doing things, usually exactly the sort of regrouping needed before further spurts of growth. Such apparent downturns should, at least for us, be entirely unmysterious, anticipatable and indeed informative; characteristically Mediterranean ways of life emerged from adversity and busts as well as boom times.

As expected, the formation of the Mediterranean world has turned out to be a far from closed-off history. At several markedly uncoordinated junctures, the African and European flanks, as well as neighbouring seas, injected new elements into the basin's mix, or found themselves at the receiving end of its expansion. Dwarfing all of these, however, was engagement with areas to the east and southeast. Yet before we write off early Mediterranean history as simply an appendage of the Near East (a big mistake), it is worth stressing how different each principal phase of engagement actually was. The first, which operated episodically over most of the last million-plus years, focused on the Suez isthmus and Levant as a periodically open passage from which pulses of African hominins and humans could percolate north of the basin, and more widely. For the second, associated with the rise in sedentism, plant and animal manipulation and ritual elaboration around the turn of the Holocene that gave us west Eurasian farming, the framework was the Fertile Crescent, a good proportion of which lay inside the basin. In neither instance was the Mediterranean beholden to a broader Near East as such. In the former case, the ultimate debt, shared with the rest of the globe, was to Africa. In the latter, whatever the complex interplays around the Fertile Crescent as a whole during the run-up to established farming, quite enough was going on in the Levantine sector alone to argue that, at an imaginative pinch, something like the Neolithic would have emerged there anyway, and spread across the basin (though, to add a note of contingency, the prior absence of such trends over its remainder meant that without that Levantine overlap, Mediterranean farming would have been vastly tardier and differently constituted, without, at the very least, wheat, sheep and goats).

Only in the third phase of decisive impact from this quarter did the Near East as a whole play a key role, led by Mesopotamia and Egypt. This comprised the rise of urban, state-level societies, economies and culture over the later 4th and 3rd millennia BC, and their expansion into adjacent parts of the Mediterranean, followed by major resurgences in the 2nd and early 1st millennia, as well as an underlying hum of lower-level ongoing interaction. That this last engagement gave a huge succession of boosts to the Mediterranean's economies, as well as instilling long-lasting cultural practices in eastern parts of the basin, some of which would later be taken up more widely, is axiomatic. Had the Mediterranean somehow been cataclysmically sundered from the Nile Valley and the lands along the Tigris and Euphrates around 3500–3000 BC, the upshot would indeed have been slower Mediterranean acceleration, at a guess to the tune of a millennium or two (depending on whereabouts in the basin, and with the likely pacesetters concentrated in the Levant, Aegean and southern Iberia), as well as intriguing differences from subsequent Mediterranean culture as we know it. And yet, as we have seen, and will now recapitulate, by the time Mesopotamia and Egypt had emerged, let alone the time that ripples of consequence reached the centre and west, most fundamental Mediterranean ways of doing things were already evident within the basin in an emergent form, and bearing their first fruit (albeit, in terms of political formations, initially more sustainably in the east, where tried-and-tested strategies for entrenching power could be more easily accessed). These emergent internal properties subtly reworked Near Eastern inputs, leading to fresh outcomes, and time and again confounded uni-directionality of influence in a welter of reticulate connections that further fostered ongoing growth on the basin's own account. To an increasing degree, the Mediterranean, the Near East and other neighbours began to coevolve, with the basin starting to act back decisively, even towards the east. Avaris in the age of the Hyksos was a start, as unenvisaged by the earliest river-kings as was the prospect, less than two centuries off by the close of this book, of Alexander the Great in Babylon.

Three common denominators revisited

Back, then, to the Mediterranean as our justifiably central theme. At the risk of oversimplification, of reducing fluid processes and incremental alterations in scale to a crude stadial sequence, we can now outline roughly how the Mediterranean changed from being, at the outset, a geographical expression devoid of cultural existence, into a dynamic, interactive, converging and, last but not least, widely recognized entity. As good a place to start as any is with the triad of common denominators underpinning Mediterranean life identified by Horden and Purcell in *The Corrupting Sea*, revisited in their order of historical appearance: fragmented micro-ecologies, connectivity, and uncertainty plus its attendant aspects of risk and opportunity.

The first of these turned out to be as old as the Mediterranean itself, hard-wired by the basin's tortured tectonics and shaping its fauna and flora for at least as long as it has influenced human, or indeed hominin, life. Within such mosaic-like conditions, people had learned the advantages of a mix and match approach, viable when stitched together over even modest distances, well before our own ancestors entered the basin. However, what actually filled each tessera of the mosaic was far from constant. True, fragmentation sometimes enabled a remarkable degree of survival for Mediterranean-type ecologies even when surrounding conditions were dire (for example, at Ohalo II, in Galilee, during the Last Glacial Maximum), or too lush. Yet it could just as easily create utterly different patterns of diversity from unfamiliar components (colonies of great auks near Cosquer Cave, off Marseilles, for instance), which presented their own extractive and adaptive challenges for the basin's people. Moreover, the fillings of the tesserae became increasingly subject to human intervention over time. The origins of this must go back, if with fugitive visibility on our part, to the controlled use of fire as a landscape modifier. With modern humans on the loose, skilful hunting began to depress preferred quarry species one by one – later, on certain islands, to the point of extinction for their bizarre endemic creatures. Then, over the millennia on either side of the start of the Holocene (the abrupt warming that really changed the playing field for humanity), assertive management of select plants and animals in the Levant and elsewhere in the Fertile Crescent culminated in farming, itself, at one level, a kind of micro-ecological niche construction.[2] The spread of farming unleashed the greatest rolling transformation of the Mediterranean's ecologies seen during the Holocene, one still unfolding today. It created, initially in tiny patches, a basic combination of fields, pasture and fringing wilderness resources that would prove hugely successful,[3] and by the time this reached Iberia, the Levant was putting together a more ambitious variant, including olives and vines as well as wider uses of animals, that could be deployed in all kinds of ways, from a bolster for subsistence to industrial-level extraction. As this, in turn, expanded during the 4th to 1st millennia BC, with fresh cultivars and breeds multiplying faster than new species were introduced (today there are 600 varieties of olives in the Mediterranean), and as specialized pastoralism took off in marginal lands, in certain regions together with investments in simple terracing or irrigation, an ever-shifting artificial mosaic spread out to complement or displace that of nature. Within our time frame, substitution and mutual accommodation of ecologies are more plausible than generalized overexploitation; we have in fact encountered relatively few human-induced eco-disasters – possible exceptions being the end of the Pre-Pottery Neolithic in the Levant and the later Iberian Argaric, plus several island wipeouts of endemic animals.

Connectivity was, of course, fundamental to the making of the Middle Sea. Beyond the universal need for interaction of some kind in order for any hominin to survive and reproduce, a sequence of new behaviours can be identified once modern humans had spread around the basin. Overland movements over impressive ranges rapidly become visible, transporting ornamental shells across hundreds of kilometres well before 50,000 BC on the African flank and not long after that on the European one – and although much of this could be due to the mobility of individual hunter-gatherer wearers (itself an index of extensive social interaction), it is perhaps unwise to rule out exchange of items, too, from an early date. Such terrestrial distances would have impressed a 2nd-millennium BC merchant, and although in the interim there were major changes (downward as well as upward) in the regularity of long-range transfers, a surge in volumes on the move with the coming of pack animals, and land routes that proved resilient to competition from the sea, overland connections would necessarily play second fiddle to maritime ones in terms of defining a marine basin as a theatre of interaction. To reiterate: no maritime links, no Middle Sea.

Whatever the truth about occasional ultra-early Pleistocene efforts at seagoing, there is no sign that the sea had yet become anything but a divider, and for even the first 35,000-odd years during which modern humans lived around it, the picture stayed one of tentative, short-range crossings, restricted to a few encouraging areas. The decisive shift from such, in this respect, 'pre-Mediterranean' conditions to a purposeful, medium-range and proficient practice came just before the start of the Holocene, and appears again to have taken place in a few favourable places, notably the Aegean and the waters between Cyprus and its mainland neighbours. Later, some Mesolithic hunter-gatherers followed suit in the central sub-basins, but the breakthrough was only generalized by the expansion of farmers, which, together with their subsequent infilling of the smaller islands, ensured modest degrees of maritime linkage over most littoral and insular zones by 5000 BC at the latest. The next phase began in the 'long' 3rd millennium BC, with the rise of long-range voyaging, much of it driven by new ideological preoccupations and wider social networks on land as well as sea (none of which lessened the ubiquity of humdrum short-range activity, now or later; indeed, for quite different reasons, this was simultaneously on the rise, as we shall be shortly reminded). In most areas, voyaging was at first prosecuted in bigger versions of the canoes that must have plied the seas since at least the start of the Neolithic, but in the east it meshed with a separate initiative made possible thanks to capital investments on the part of the first emergent states: those marvellous, distance-eating, bulk-shifting machines known as sailing ships. Over the 2nd millennium BC, sailing ships penetrated ever further west, being adopted as local maritime and social circumstances made it propitious, until, by around 1000 BC, the preconditions for a regular, closely knit Mediterranean-wide network were in place, and this reality was swiftly realized over the next few centuries. If we plot the infilling of the basin's blue parts by human traffic over time, the cumulative rise of the sea as the real centre of the Mediterranean stands out clearly [**11.1**]. Intriguingly, when we compare this with the administrative units into which Rome would later divide the Mediterranean's waters (an imposition itself redolent of supreme bureaucratic confidence on the empire's part), we see that the latter reflected not just physical geography, but also the phantom outlines and evolutionary histories of older maritime connections that we have traced, in a few cases right back to the end of the Pleistocene.

11.1 (*Above*) The overall expansion of zones of active seafaring across the Mediterranean, from before 6000 BC to 1300 BC, with arrows showing the additional direct linkages forged shortly thereafter, leading by about 500 BC to the infilling of the remaining maritime areas; (*below*) for comparison, the maritime administrative units of the Roman empire.

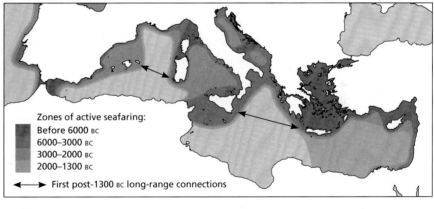

Zones of active seafaring:
Before 6000 BC
6000–3000 BC
3000–2000 BC
2000–1300 BC

◄——► First post-1300 BC long-range connections

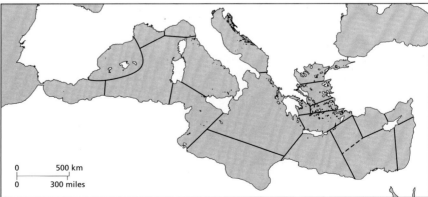

0   500 km
0   300 miles

Two other aspects of the overall growth of connectivity deserve mention, one positive, the other negative, at least in network terms. Starting with the positive, it is remarkable how early a combination of the Mediterranean's 'provocative' geography (as described in Chapter 2) and the changing play of human interactions across it created central places that then drew further connections towards them, and how often these locations shifted as conditions moved on. A concentration of prestige finds well before the Last Glacial Maximum at the intensely occupied Balzi Rossi caves in east Liguria could already hint at the benefits accruing to people at a major choke-point of connections under the, for us, unfamiliar conditions of a cold, overwhelmingly land-bound Mediterranean; after sea travel took off, this rugged and now tucked-away area has barely featured, and remained remote even in 500 BC. Regardless, the corridor of the Jordan Valley clearly worked to the connective advantage of Pre-Pottery Neolithic mega-sites located on well-watered soils along its length, and by the 5th millennium BC, if not earlier, the first true maritime hub that we can currently identify had arisen on Lipari in the Tyrrhenian Sea. In the 3rd millennium BC, often modestly sized but highly energetic networking centres became common throughout the basin, including, allowing for intervening vicissitudes, the ancestors of later Tyre, Aegina and perhaps Cadiz and Seville (the latter at Valencina de la Concepción), and their numbers and scales subsequently continued to proliferate, all long before Carthage, Pithekoussai or Corinth. Following on from early Ebla, which occupied a north Levantine regional hotspot with good access east to Mesopotamia and north into Anatolia, there was an increasing tendency during the 2nd and earlier 1st millennia BC for additional hubs to materialize where Mediterranean circuits met with arteries in and out of the basin, for example at Avaris in the Nile Delta, Troy on the Dardanelles, Fratessina at the head of the Adriatic, Cadiz in the form we know it, and latterly Massalia near the mouth of the Rhône. Moreover, what worked for specific locations could also apply to regions as a whole, and indeed this was one of the main ways in which entire new areas of the Mediterranean emerged into the limelight. Although the Levant's overland routes are some of the oldest in the basin, its maritime prominence was largely a later function of macro-conditions only existent from the later 4th and 3rd millennia BC, namely two superpowers at either end of it, plus sailing ships to run its length. Likewise, Etruria's moment came when its arable and metallurgical wealth were coupled with a position between the growing Tyrrhenian, Adriatic and Alpine spheres, while Sicily, at the geographical centre of the basin, rose rapidly once Mediterranean-wide connections took off. The Adriatic exhibited an unusually sharply syncopated series of extensions and retreats from engagement with the wider Mediterranean, correlated with changing circumstances in the neighbouring Aegean and Tyrrhenian sub-basins (premonitions of the later relative fortunes of Adriatic Venice and Tyrrhenian Genoa?). In a sense, much of the history of an emergent Middle Sea is the history of evolving connections.

The negative aspect, however, injects a note of caution, without which we too easily universalize mobility and high degrees of linkage, forget their hard-won status, particularly at sea, and as a result undermine their explanatory power. A trenchant question by Purcell serves as a good introduction: 'How many native Greek-speakers travelled more than 20 km (12 miles) from where they were born in the 7th century? 2 per cent, 25 per cent, 50 per cent?'[4] Answer: we do not know (my guess falls around the middle, but is as much a product of faith as analysis), and if we cannot tell for such a late, well-known group of actors, what hope have we for earlier periods? In fact, the accumulated, smoothed-out evidence of the last few chapters leaves no doubt that overall, in both relative and absolute terms, connections and mobility rose sharply in intensity and scale from the 3rd to 1st millennia BC, after stabilizing or even locally declining following the initial spread of farming. The timing and gradient of this take-off makes the Mediterranean exceptional on a global scale. But even allowing for the fact that all Mediterranean people relied on some kind of local or medium-range interconnections to survive (and ever more so as the basin began to dry out), certain areas manifestly remained much less widely tied in than others, especially by sea.[5] The most interesting example is North Africa west of the Nile. As in previous interglacials, stretching back almost 2 million years, people here were in fact well linked-in while the Sahara lay open, but their connections ran overwhelmingly south, away from the Mediterranean; even for much of the Holocene, links across Gibraltar and the Sicilian narrows were patchy in time and limited in impact. With a few minor exceptions, seafaring appears to have been eschewed along this coast, for a variety of geographical and cultural reasons, and with ultimately huge consequences for North Africa's inhabitants when it finally burst in on them. Smaller parallels include Liguria, as we have just seen, plus Corsica, its offshore extension in this sense, which has barely figured in the wider story compared to its metalliferous neighbour, Sardinia. Even Cyprus, a precociously sea-connected island just before and during the early Holocene, and again from the 2nd millennium BC onward, experienced over 4000 years of intervening parochialism, as it became internally self-sufficient, and until the outside world learned of its copper. Malta, a smaller island with a shorter history, swung repeatedly between wider integration and insular obscurity (in the temple period with spectacular results), while the still more recently settled Balearics were only just entering the mainstream as this history drew to a close. Given that the connecting sea could bring danger, disruption and loss as well as gain, reclusivity could be no bad thing in its own terms; life for many people in southern France (a further area that had turned its back to the sea for long periods) was assuredly safer, if maybe less exciting, before about 650–600 BC than afterwards. As expressed in Chapter 1, if the early history of the Mediterranean is in part that of how such seclusion was overcome, it is one often tinged with darkness.

Returning to the pursuit of the three common denominators, while the shifting ecological mosaic was aeons-old and starting to become more recognizable during the earlier Holocene, when competent seafaring, that prerequisite for connectivity, also became broadly distributed, the third element, uncertainty and its consequences, was rather younger. Of course, a seismic and volcanic hotspot swept by changeable winds and waves, one subjected over the long-term to climates ranging from the bucolic to the frigid, was never going to be a predictable place to live in, although it is easy to forget that the Mediterranean's role as a human refuge during the Pleistocene's coldest spells implies that under certain conditions it could, in fact, be regarded as less challenging than the lands to its north and south. However, the establishment of a less overtly dramatic regime of recurrent short-term uncertainty, notably in rainfall, within a climatic envelope that just permitted farming in most places most of the time (in short, Mediterranean conditions as we define them today as well as, crucially, risk over time spans that people could understand, and mitigate or exploit) was broadly a result of changes concentrated in the 'long' 3rd millennium BC, with slightly earlier episodes in drier areas like the southern Levant, and a later start (if ever to a severe degree) in the most clement spots. The widespread social response of farming groups, namely to spread out and intensify their short- and medium-range networks for mutual survival, encouraged an investment in quotidian connections far beyond that required in earlier times, thereby creating that endless 'Brownian motion' so vital to ensuring that Mediterranean life continued to tick over, plus a new breed of central places and ambitious people nicely located to gain by such movements. As this third fundamental slotted in with its two partners, it created the regime of interdependency that has dominated the basin ever since – one that, however transitory it may seem when held against the yardstick of the timescales explored in this book's earlier chapters, has had an enormous impact on the shape of subsequent Mediterranean history.

Acceleration towards the Middle Sea

From this juncture, the strands of the Mediterranean's history began to braid and combine ever more frequently, and we get an inkling of how a true Middle Sea might form, and what it might look like, with its sea-traders and other seekers after resources or glory, its specialized producers and discerning consumers, its striving, often competitive elites, its well-networked centres, its ships, suites of cash crops, bright metals and other minerals, and soon its labile deities. During the 3rd millennium BC, most manifestations of this integrated way of life were microcosmic (as many would always remain), and their intensity varied across the basin (another enduring feature), with the earliest pockets widely scattered. The little Cyclades – risky, sea-connected and thoroughly interdependent fragments – and other parts of the southern Aegean furnish excellent examples, as do several areas in southern Iberia, probably southern Italy and certainly the Levant. Underlining the fact that such microsystems emerged bottom-up, only the Levant furnishes a substantial overlap with that other contemporary development, the rise and expansion of Mesopotamia and Egypt, whose onset can be taken as ultimately coincidental or not, mainly depending on how much influence one accords the common reality of climate change. The swift upshot in the Levant was places like Ebla, a palatial town with a huge archive and long reach into the interior, as well as Byblos, the small, wealthy coastal community that traded by sea with the pharaohs. Yet even Ebla and Byblos behaved in a way that differed more in scale and sophistication than underlying essentials (the mobilization of a diverse Mediterranean resource base, plus trade in exotics) from leading communities further west. Copper Age Iberia, in particular, demonstrates how much could happen outside the reach of Near Eastern contacts. Indeed, if the Levant has been affirmed over the course of this book as a consistently interesting place in terms of what was cumulatively achievable within an extremely, if changeably, connected part of the Mediterranean, Iberia has proven how much could also be done in relative solitude.

In parallel with this, and yet largely segregated from it, Mediterranean Africa west of the Nile suffered a quite different fate. With its panoramic window on a more verdant and aqueous Sahara (filled first with sophisticated hunter-gatherers and then mobile pastoralists focused upon cattle), its paucity of domesticable crops, its slim and not always operational conduits for inflows of exogenous farmers, and its largely uninviting maritime facade, Mediterranean Africa had in fact been tracing different, and in their own terms, successful trajectories throughout the earlier Holocene. While the basin remained a relatively lush and unintegrated place, tolerant of a wild-growth of diversity, this was of little consequence, and is certainly not a matter for adverse judgment on our part – *vive la différence*, in North Africa, just as elsewhere. The climatic transition of the 'long' 3rd millennium BC altered all that, turning the Sahara into, to all intents and purposes, a permanent desert, and cutting off people in the Maghreb and Cyrenaica from their demographic, cultural and ideological heartland to the south. While a few signs of subsequent links across the Mediterranean have been picked up, most if not all appear to have been driven from the European side; the dynamo of North African developments shifted east, to the ribbon of the Nile, and across most of the remainder we more or less lose the archaeological signal for several thousand years. The 'long' 3rd millennium, which in so many ways laid the foundations of the Mediterranean as we know it, was a disaster for most of Mediterranean Africa, and therein lie the seeds of much that would eventually follow on this other, southern flank of the Middle Sea when Iron Age people from across the sea began to break in.

A great deal was decisively set in motion, or decisively lost, during the 'long' 3rd millennium BC, but over a thousand more years would elapse before the last major parts of the basin were integrated, or entrapped (depending on one's viewpoint). Over that time span, many of the developments were extensions of older, mainly 'long' 3rd-millennium BC trajectories (the rise of elites of varying power and reach over much of the basin, the new roles for metals, and increasing maritime connections between regions, to cite but a few), but the period is far from without interest, and glamour, in its own right, and spawned further contributions to the final outcome. The process of expansion was, moreover, anything but smooth, with one potentially widespread interruption at the end of the 3rd millennium BC, triggered by an arid spell (in which a few privileged regions like insular

Crete and rainy Dalmatia actually flourished), and another disruption in the east on either side of 1200 BC, which appears to have been a strictly human affair, and again had its relative winners as well as losers. The Levant enjoyed two great peaks, in the earlier 2nd and earlier 1st millennia BC (to complement a unique record of four prior spikes of complexity since the Natufian), with a mixed intervening experience under outside proto-empires. The Aegean likewise witnessed two differently staggered flourishings, in the 2nd and mid-1st millennia BC, separated by a deep trough in between. Far to the west, in Iberia, the Argaric rose in a slightly different zone from the Copper Age foci and crashed out of synchrony with anything outside the peninsula, to be then followed by shrouded new shoots further west, along the Guadalquivir. In the east, the decisive development was the incorporation, around the transition from the 3rd to 2nd millennia BC, of Cyprus, southern coastal Anatolia and the Aegean into a wider east Mediterranean world. This tied in to pre-existent circuits in the central Mediterranean during the middle of the 2nd millennium. In turn, the upshot, once sailing ships went native (especially in Sardinia) was that while the east underwent a phase of drastic restructuring in the centuries around 1200 BC, strong connections between the centre and west were forged for the first time. This series of extensive, overlapping networks across a sail-shrunk sea at last created the maritime preconditions necessary for regular pan-Mediterranean travel. 'Phoenician' trade, which hides a multiplicity of participants beyond Tyre and the central Levant, was the almost instantaneous result. Given the constant propensity for ambitious bottom-up growth in well-placed parts of the basin (most recently Etruria), the outcome once eastern demand also recovered and populations burgeoned during a clement 8th century was predictable, if not always plain, interpretative sailing. From start to finish, this process of integration had been self-ordering, effected by the complex interactions of countless mainly independent players, with only relatively fleeting, partial moments of centralized direction. It must surely rank as one of the most extraordinary creations of its age on the planet.

Three new traits came to the fore over the 2nd and earlier 1st millennia BC, in tandem with this expansion. Exchange was itself nothing new, and both 'utilitarian', short-range variants and prestige-seeking, typically longer-range activities may well be as ancient as we are in the Mediterranean. It is probably equally unwise to exclude broadly profit- and advantage-oriented attitudes to some of it by at least the Neolithic, just as it is naive to omit the thick social wrapping of many transactions much later; certainly by the 3rd millennium BC both metal-based proto-currencies and elaborate 'gift exchanges' were widely operating in the east. Mediterranean trade therefore had extensive roots; it coevolved with social and economic circumstances, and versions such as 'palatial trade' were less discrete stages than accentuations of particular features of longer overall duration, in this case centralized control and formalized circulation. But what was truly novel and transformative in the 2nd and earlier 1st millennia BC was the low cost of bulk movement by sea, as sailing ships spread, which allowed vastly more goods and materials to circulate, and enabled a genuinely interactive market to emerge, characterized by fluctuating consumer demands, profits sufficient to more than offset the outlay and risk of long-range ventures, specialist production niches and import substitution. Such markets, it has been observed, could act just as aggressively, in their own way, as the most aggrandizing polities.[6] Equally important was the definition of a core set of commodified trade goods, mainly metals, textiles, oil and wine, plus the latters' containers, alongside a suite of apex luxuries (precious metalwork, finely crafted rare stones, ivory and suchlike) and also, to an increasing degree, minor, sub-elite alternatives, such as painted pots, various vitreous goods and later iron. One measure of the impressively rapid growth in this field is the fact that well before 500 BC even cereals, one of the bulkiest and most mundane, if vital, of Mediterranean commodities, could be transported in quantity by sea over substantial distances. The myriad new towns that easier mobility and rising numbers of people would encourage in the first half of the 1st millennium BC could feed themselves from far away if necessary. Central to all this was, of course, the figure of the merchant in all his rich – and not-so-rich – variety, a persona whose ancestry lay among older traders, but that came into its own during the 2nd millennium BC. As the ultimate go-betweens, merchants contributed far beyond their numbers to bringing the Middle Sea into being; in a way, they were the Mediterranean's midwives.

Also coalescing over the same period, and engaging with the same conditions, was the Mediterranean polity. Plato placed his ideal city a wary 15 km (10 miles) inland,[7] but in fact most of those we have encountered had their focal point advantageously nearer the shore, if seldom right on it until the comparatively late growth of towns out of intrusive enclaves in the centre and west. Typically such polities combined a maritime outlet with surrounding lowland fields and a rugged hinterland for forest-derived products, orchards, pastoralism or mining, a cross section through Mediterranean ecological variation; and while a few of the locations that we have seen flourish over the 2nd and early 1st millennia BC were tiny islands with minimal adjacent farmland (Tyre being the ultimate example), most combined an advantageous maritime location with the arable wealth and ample labour that a decent, if rarely enormous, nearby territory provided.[8] Although sacred kingship never seems to have been much of a starter in the Mediterranean, the first major polities to arise in the east were focused on a royal palace with a tentacular reach through society and economy. Such palace organizations survived for just over a thousand years in the Levant, where they first arose in touch with Mesopotamian models, but their duration became progressively shorter as they were taken up elsewhere, and they never extended beyond the Aegean. In their place less formally structured elite groups pressed forward, often with strong mercantile interests, and a more flexible, freelance approach to economic activity – both reflections of the fluid openness of Mediterranean conditions, and the growing difficulty in controlling flows and sustaining a fixed advantage within such an unruly maritime world. Both are detectable at Ugarit and on Cyprus in the last centuries of the 2nd millennium BC, well before their pan-Mediterranean Iron Age heyday, when formerly modest local elites would swell their numbers and distribution immensely, getting rich, brokering power with each other and other social groups in new towns all over the basin, and devising fresh kinds of political structures in the process.

The Mediterranean gradually began to impact on established order beyond the basin, too, specifically along the Nile. The Delta, that hyper-populous triangle within the Mediterranean, but not of it in environmental terms, had been quiescent in the 3rd millennium BC under upriver kings, much in line with its relatively secluded earlier history. Thereafter, it turned into one of the most dynamic places in the Mediterranean, a gateway to prospects of wealth and foreign conquest for pharaohs, yet equally an entrance for Mediterranean people, activities and customs that threatened Egyptian traditional culture. Whether in the guise of the excoriated Levantine-derived Hyksos kings and their Mediterranean super-polity at Avaris, the still more gargantuan Ramessid capital at nearby Qantir, its architecturally cannibalizing successor at Tanis, or the later westward shift to Sais, the fulcra of power in Egypt were tugged relentlessly northward and forced to engage, with variable success, a sea whose corrupting effects they certainly recognized – and all this long before Alexander and Alexandria. One subversive message of this book has been the need for an alternative narrative of Nilotic history, viewed from the Delta, with the Ways of Horus curving off to the east across northern Sinai, and the Mediterranean shimmering just beyond.

The final trait is the spread of shared things, practices and identities over long distances, in other words, the cultural mediterraneanization of the basin's people. In fact, even this has its premonitions back in the 3rd millennium BC, in the form of the far-flung distribution of accoutrements of a shared way of life, interestingly already focused on alcoholic drinks, with beaker connections extending from the Atlantic to France, the coastal Maghreb, Sardinia and Sicily, and only slightly less impressive equivalents in the Adriatic and Aegean. The later 3rd millennium BC also witnessed the sharp cessation of two idiosyncratic island societies, on Malta and Cyprus. But, at least in the west and centre, the shared traits fizzled out shortly after 2000 BC, and long after that the Mediterranean retained a multitude of ways of life. Instead, a more direct lineage runs from the suite of 'international styles', designed from around the mid-2nd millennium BC for east Mediterranean elites keen to assert their cosmopolitan participation in a rarefied, far-flung world, exemplified by Aegean-style wall-paintings, carved ivories and decorated gold or silver bowls. More modest variants were coming into existence even before the paroxysms near the end of the 2nd millennium BC, due largely to initiatives in the Levant and Cyprus, where some of the burials stand out as extremely culturally eclectic, and it was these regions, too, that saw the repertoire as a whole through the transition to the Iron Age, when growing mobility, interaction and ritual dedications at widely visited sanctuaries spread the latest variants all over the basin, among a less restricted and more heterogeneous range of people. Comparable lineages can be traced for alphabetical writing, and the formalized wine-imbibing ceremonies of the eastern Mediterranean, though the latter blended with all kinds of local forms of group intoxication. How much all of this involved conscious imitation, as opposed to reinterpretation, subversion or simply mutual convergence is a matter for debate, and important underlying differences certainly remained.[9] But overall, a sea change had taken place. If a visitor from another part of the planet had been set down in the Mediterranean around 5000 BC, or even 2000 years later, and left to wander invisibly through it, he or she would have come across enormous diversity, and quite likely sooner or later found something with tolerable points of comparison to home. By, say, 600 BC the experience would have been utterly different. Common practices, looks, tastes, smells and presumably sounds would have been apparent all over the basin, alongside convergent ways of organizing, interacting, fighting, loving, worshipping and much more besides, with only a few lingering redoubts of sharply defined indifference. The stranger from across the planet would probably have felt at home nowhere in this now consciously distinctive world. In this both inclusive and exclusive sense, something that we might call a Mediterranean civilization had come into existence.[10]

Four questions for the later Mediterranean

To conclude that the remainder of Mediterranean history was just a 'post-prehistoric' epilogue would be trite, and misleading given the significant swerves of later times, not least renewed, more powerful drives towards greater centralization under Rome and subsequent empires, and the associated far from trivial challenge (overcome in full only once, by Rome) of politically uniting the entire basin. Mediterranean history had no more directional 'lock-ins' than that of any other part of the world.[11] My hope is that those primarily interested in the later past will have gained something from looking at the Mediterranean from an unfamiliar perspective, as a much longer-term creation, and by witnessing its early history the right way round – the way it actually unfolded. But just because most of the Mediterranean's fundamental natural and cultural components have a demonstrably, if variably, deep ancestry and had largely evolved significantly before 500 BC in no sense denies the benefit of continuing to analyse them in their typically even better-documented, ever-shifting later manifestations, in the same way that patterns first glimpsed in the 3rd millennium BC have yielded fresh insights when tracked over the next two millennia. Such analyses remain essential if we are to reveal the complete phylogenies of particular phenomena, and indeed of the very concept of the Mediterranean itself, from their inception to the present, and, equally, if proper sense is to be made of the interplay between Mediterranean life's enduring underpinnings and the endless contingencies of specific historical circumstance.

But one consequence of our affirmation of the high antiquity of so much in the Mediterranean is that later historians may need to search elsewhere to find themes that are substantially new to their periods, or at least previously insignificant, just as each chronological chapter of this book identified further threads to braid in with the twists and turns of pre-existing ones. Looking forward a few centuries from the vantage point of what we can now more fully appreciate is a convenient, emblematic and yet ultimately arbitrary end-date around 500 BC, several questions come to mind, whose definitive answers lie beyond this book's remit, but which can nonetheless be briefly outlined.

First, how and why did empires ruled from within the Mediterranean first arise? Before 500 BC, empire-scale integration had been pretty well entirely imposed from outside the basin, if we set aside the uncertain, spatially modest case of Minoan Crete (well within the scale of an ambitious territorial state in the contemporary east), and potential 6th-century BC moves in this direction by Carthage. Shortly afterwards, however, new kinds of empires superbly adapted to, and successfully exploitative of, the Mediterranean's attributes and rhythms begin to be seen, first in the guises of an explicit hegemony on the part of Carthage and the shorter-lived but highly centralized and truly colony-establishing 5th-century Athenian empire,[12] and in its most extensive, durable form under Rome, the vast majority of whose subjects lived within the basin [11.2]. In common with most empires, expansion was driven by a mixture of suitable internal incentives and surrounding opportunities, while Rome's impressive survival owed much to more recent efforts to create (beyond a super-rich state and elite) substantial numbers of participating and benefiting citizens, as well as exploited victims, out of the

11.2 The growth of empires from within the Mediterranean basin after 500 BC.

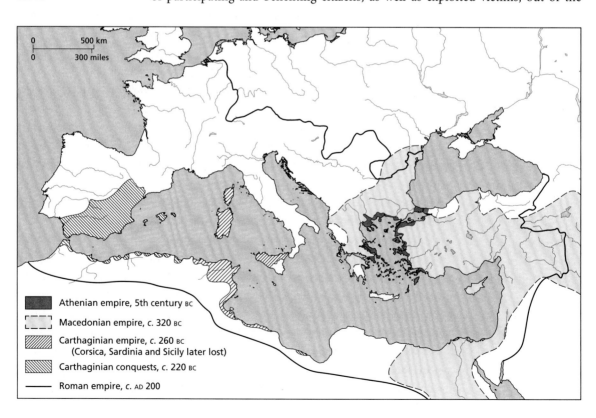

0   500 km
0   300 miles

▬ Athenian empire, 5th century BC

⌐ ̄ ̄⌐ Macedonian empire, *c.* 320 BC

▨ Carthaginian empire, *c.* 260 BC
(Corsica, Sardinia and Sicily later lost)

▧ Carthaginian conquests, *c.* 220 BC

— Roman empire, *c.* AD 200

roll call of subjects. Much of this eventually involved the abandonment of more exclusionary, and ultimately growth-limiting, forms of city-state political association.[13] But, in addition, the growth of empires within the Mediterranean resulted in large part from determined thalassocratic efforts to regulate the sea's traffic and legislate behaviour on it. These, if still never entirely successful, were decisively more so than in the past, thanks primarily to ever-larger resources to throw at the problem. Freya Stark's 'law-encircled sea' was gradually established,[14] as well as its inverse, at least if we define piracy by its widely acknowledged illegality rather than the time-honoured practice of maritime predation as such, with Etruscans on the losing side in the Tyrrhenian Sea among the first true 'pirates'. In the late 6th century, Polycrates of Samos fingered the thalassocratic mantle, and it may have been at his court that a poet first coined 'Aegean' (a term of obscure, non-Greek derivation, possibly from a long-lost, ancient sea god) for the patchwork of sea and islands that his ships sought to dominate.[15] Further great strides in this direction were made by 5th-century Athens, Carthage relied upon its warships for projecting power abroad and Rome, for all its land-based conquests, represented the acme of thalassocracy, finally killing off the most blatant forms of piracy and entirely eliminating enemy fleets from the Mediterranean. With at least this disruptive facet of the marine realm coerced, the long-dormant yet enormous potential for a central sea to facilitate the fast, reliable communications and huge redistributions essential for sustaining an internal empire was at last unleashed.[16] A compelling case can in fact be made that the gradual shift from the first riverine corridors of power to the surroundings of a massively larger sea, and the lack of a similarly extensive and centrally placed watery zone further east, helped to keep the core zone at the western end of Eurasia ahead of that in the east (based around China), until the 6th or 7th centuries AD, when the Mediterranean fell apart again.[17]

Second, why were Mediterranean polities over the coming few centuries so outstandingly successful at political expansion beyond the basin, a process that further hastened the Mediterranean on its way to becoming a crossroads of interaction not simply between its constituent shores (as we have seen over this book's time span), but between much more extensive continental hinterlands? This success was entirely unpredictable on the basis of what we have seen so far, and the answers are clearly connected to our first theme. To venture a stage further, why was so much of traditional 'core' Mesopotamian culture, after millennia of accommodating and reshaping previous conquerors and political changes at the top, in the long term either extinguished or heavily compromised by the introduction of Greek customs under Alexander and his successors [**11.3**]?[18] Much the same question might be asked of Egyptian traditions and equally Mediterranean Christianity. And what does this tell us about shifting constitutions of identity and civilization in each of these areas?

Third, stemming from the above, why did so many of the material and other traits practised and brought together by Greek people (often from foreign origins) start to be so widely adopted as a common vocabulary across the basin? Greeks had

11.3 Detail of the Alexander mosaic from Pompeii, composed after a lost earlier Greek painting of this close encounter between Alexander of Macedon and Darius III of Persia. The setting is probably the battle of Issus, near the Gulf of İskenderun, a long-significant region where, on that day in 333 BC, the potential for large-scale imperial expansion beyond the Mediterranean was first realized.

never before stood out as the Mediterranean's strongest voices, and even now they remained in political and economic terms just one among several assertive leading players. In Chapter 10, some doubt was cast on what broader messages, beyond an aesthetic preference, travelled with Greek painted pottery, and even later it is not at all self-evident what 'Hellenization' (if this is indeed an accurate term) actually meant in places like Carthage, how random or directed its increasingly viral expansion really was, and, incidentally, how it is implicated in the reduction of written languages to merely four by the time of the Roman empire (Greek, Latin, Punic and Aramaic). Moreover, this needs to be squared with the fact that, in the face of mortal external danger, 5th-century Aegean city-states evolved more chauvinist definitions of what it meant to be, and not to be, Greek – *barbaros* is barely attested before 500 BC.[19]

Fourth, if surely far from finally, why did the Classical Mediterranean witness so many world-changing conceptual and religious breakthroughs concerning relations between the individual, society, politics and the transcendent? A few hints have been offered in this book, notably the increasingly non-sacral nature of political authority in several regions, its frequently fragmented and contested basis, and the early lead established by areas on the interacting yet also resistant edges of the old Near Eastern heartland of power and knowledge, in the southern Levant and Aegean. But much has not been explained. Fuller answers lie in the direction of seeing the Mediterranean as a prominent case within the broader contemporary rise of such 'axial age' thought, in response to new forms of political reality, across widely separated parts of Eurasia.[20]

The view from Salamis

Naturally, these four themes overlap, and raise further issues that lie well beyond this book's scope. We can conclude, instead, on a less portentous note, with an attempt to portray the far deeper and often humbler pasts, as well as the fractal qualities, that lie behind even one of the most famous, conventionally epochal days in Mediterranean history. This book undertook to avoid writing the kind of early Mediterranean history that culminates in the Parthenon and its associated glories, but I hope will be forgiven for closing within sight of the flames of the Parthenon's predecessors on an acropolis torched by Persian fire. For Salamis, another scruffy little island set in a sapphire sea, its coast still full of ancient and modern nautical installations and today encroached by Athenian suburbs and the petrol refinery at Eleusis, is a quintessential Mediterranean place with which to close [**11.4**]. Its fractal properties are exceptionally pronounced, for the enclosed bay with its islets mimics in microcosm the surrounding Saronic Gulf, whose form in turn presents a minor version of the Aegean, which is itself a miniaturization in intensified form of the entire Middle Sea. The ships and sailors that fought there in 480 BC were the outcome of more than ten millennia of experience in seafaring, while the sheer chanciness of Mediterranean life is chillingly apparent in the brutal fact that on paper the result should have gone the other way, and probably would have done but for a few significant details of local coastlines, plus a lucky silver strike at Lavrio, which had enabled Athens to build a fleet of over 200 ships a few years before the battle.[21] According to a Greek tradition with rather too much pan-Mediterranean symmetry to be strictly plausible,

11.4 Salamis, almost enclosing its inner bay, at the eastern (right-hand) opening of which the famous sea battle unfolded in 480 BC. On the far right of this final, history-drenched Mediterranean microcosm, sits the modern Piraeus, its harbour and suburbs, while beyond, in the far distance, lie Euboea and the narrow sea-passage past Lefkandi, Chalkis and Eretria.

the very day of the fight was balanced by a Greek victory in western Sicily, where forces led by Syracuse routed those of Carthage.[22] A temporal, or historical, fractal is almost certainly operating too. We know relatively little about early Salamis, which only became an island during the Holocene, as rising seas crept into the Pleistocene valleys joining it to the mainland. In the 5th millennium BC, however, one of its caves was occupied, and by the 3rd millennium it had several settlements, all participants in the local interactions around the Saronic Gulf that kept this small world going, to the advantage of some more than others, and none more so than the nearby island of Aegina, a place of wider horizons that, as we saw in Chapter 7, had managed to capture late in the 3rd millennium BC a few carnelian beads, probably carved in the Indus Valley, a place so distant that it still lay on the frontier of Persia two millennia later (when Aegina was, incidentally, the original intended target of the newly constructed Athenian navy). There are likely to have been earlier Salaminian battles, too, smaller affairs but with a higher proportion of its own islanders as fighters, and not necessarily fought in its lee – all well before the island's 6th-century BC annexation by Athens. The attributes of the local epic hero Ajax echo fighting styles glorified in Mycenae's shaft graves, while earlier pots on Aegina carried some of the first images of seaborne warriors in the basin. Recent excavations at Kanakia, the principal late 2nd-millennium BC site on Salamis, have even discovered, along with a chunk of oxhide ingot, a fragment of scale armour stamped for Ramesses II, whether testimony to a roving fighter or passing scrap merchant.[23]

The moral is not that Salamis was always at the centre of things; it was not, and its few hours of glory on the world stage contrast with the repeated salience of Aegina. It is rather that even the most spectacular events and processes seen in the later Mediterranean were embedded in practices whose deeper antiquity has too often gone unrecognized. Just like the musters of ships that converged at Salamis, the innumerable strands of early history that came together to create the Mediterranean had diverse origins of unequal significance, traced various approach routes, bunched and combined at different times, and need to be measured against others (hundreds of vessels in the case of the Persian fleet) that were driven elsewhere or otherwise lost before the great merging. When the Persian king Xerxes, enthroned above the battle, looked down on the melee of metal, wood and humanity, he was staring unknowingly through the defeat of a day, and deep into the Mediterranean's past.

Notes

CHAPTER ONE (pp. 15–53)

1 Fieldwork by Kythera Island Project: Broodbank 2004: 73–81; Broodbank and Kiriatzi 2007; Krahtopoulou and Frederick 2008; http://www.ucl.ac.uk/kip.
2 Sakellarakis 1996.
3 Coldstream and Huxley 1972.
4 Sakellarakis 1996: 91, fn. 96.
5 Diamond 1997; Mithen 2003; Morris, I., 2010; Shryock and Smail (eds) 2011.
6 Braudel 1972a.
7 Alcock 2005.
8 Abulafia 2011, (ed.) 2003; Carpentier and Lebrun 1998; Norwich 2006.
9 Matvejević 1999, published in English as *Mediterranean: A Cultural Landscape* (Berkeley and London: University of California Press, 1999); Theroux 1995; on Matvejević, Horden and Purcell 2006: 731.
10 Horden and Purcell 2000; debated in *Mediterranean Historical Review* 18(2) 2003; Harris, W. V., (ed.) 2005a; Shaw, I., 2001; van Dommelen 2000; further reflections in Horden 2005.
11 Finley 1985.
12 Lévi-Strauss 1963: 77, cited in Horden and Purcell 2000: 51.
13 Castells, M., 2010; Knappett 2011, (ed.) 2013; Malkin 2011: 3–64.
14 Cañete 2010; Horden 2005: 27.
15 Burr 1932.
16 E.g. Horden and Purcell 2000: 133–34; Morris, I., 2003: 44.
17 For premonitions of this issue, Sherratt, A., 1994.
18 Papaconstantinou 2007.
19 Childe 1957; Herodotus, *The Histories*; Montelius 1899; Mosso 1910.
20 Renfrew 1972.
21 Antoniadou and Pace (eds) 2007; Blake and Knapp (eds) 2005; van Dommelen and Knapp (eds) 2010; Knapp and van Dommelen (eds) in press.
22 Trump 1980.
23 Braudel 2001; editorial quip by Oswyn Murray on p. xx; Broodbank 2010a.
24 Guilaine 1994. Demand (2011) offers an empirical survey of select aspects.
25 Norwich 2006: xiii; Abulafia 2011, especially 3–59.
26 Cunliffe 2001: 554.
27 Sherratt, A., and S. Sherratt 1991; Sherratt, A., 1993, 1994, 1995a; Sherratt, S., 2010a; also Beaugard 2011; cf. Broodbank 2011 for evaluation in a Mediterranean context; for a provocatively couched assertion of Near Eastern primacy, see Bernal 1987.
28 Rowlands 2010.
29 Rowlands 2010: 242–45; Wengrow 2010a.
30 Harris, W. V., 2005b: 2.
31 Sherratt, A., 1995a: 27.
32 Hall, J., 1997, 2002.

33 O'Connor, D., 2009: 89–91; Reese 1975: 29–30.
34 Schnapp 1996: 122–324.
35 Caylus 1752–67; Skeates 2005a: 305–8; 2007.
36 Jeffreys (ed.) 2003; El Daly 2005.
37 Wengrow 2006b.
38 Silberman 1998.
39 Kletter and De-Groot 2001: 79–80.
40 Chapman, R., 2003, 20–26; Guidi 1996; Lemonnier (ed.) 1993b.
41 Clarke, D., 1973: 10.
42 Killen 1964 for a classic study of Knossos and textiles; Michel 1992; Moran 1992.
43 This far from exhausts the investigative options; others include ethnographic insights, e.g. Forbes 2007; Halstead 1987.
44 Tringham 2003.
45 Bietak 1996; Doumas 1983; Stager et al. (eds) 2008.
46 Yon 2006.
47 Díaz-del-Río 2004; Pappa and Besios 1999; Vaquer 1990: 11, 231–65.
48 Alcock and Cherry (eds) 2004; Cherry 2003.
49 Bintliff 2004; Hamilton et al. 2006.
50 Bass, G. F., 1967; Yalçın et al. (eds) 2005.
51 Ballard (ed.) 2008.
52 Galili and Rosen 2011; Guilaine et al. (eds) 1984.
53 Marriner 2009.
54 Clottes et al. 2005.
55 Wachsmann 1998; Westerdahl 1992.
56 Knapp and Cherry 1994.
57 E.g. Tykot 1996.
58 Haskell et al. 2011: 123–31; Tite 2008.
59 Recently Pollard 2009 (with response by N. H. Gale, 2009).
60 Sillar and Tite 2000; Shortland (ed.) 2001.
61 Barnard and Eerkens (eds) 2007 for a range of worldwide examples.
62 Evans, J. G., and O'Connor 2005 for general introduction.
63 Brown, T., and Brown 2011 for general introduction.
64 Mays 2010 for general introduction.
65 Braudel 1972b: 450.
66 Blake and Knapp (eds) 2005: 4–5; Trump 1980 devoted about two-and-a-half pages out of 200 to North Africa west of Egypt in this time span, and is typical in this respect; most subsequent studies have drawn a veil or thrown up their hands with expressions of regret.
67 Ludwig 1942: x.
68 Camps, G., 1974.
69 McBurney 1967; Barker, Hunt and Reynolds 2007.
70 Sheppard 1990.
71 Mahjoubi 1997.
72 Stone 2004.
73 Mitchell 2005: 56–57; Shaw, B., 2003.
74 Close 2009; Shaw, B., 2003, 2006.
75 Van den Brink (ed.) 1988.
76 Borghouts 1988: 4.
77 Renfrew 1973.
78 Barker (ed.) 1996; Barker, Gilbertson and Mattingly (eds) 2007; Castro et al. 2000; Mithen and Black (eds) 2011; van der Leeuw

(ed.) 1998, especially 115–72.
79 Burroughs 2005; Finné et al. 2011; Roberts, N., and Reed 2009; Rosen, A., 2007; Tzedakis 2009; Woodward 2009a.
80 Staubwasser and Weiss 2006: 375–77; Tzedakis 2009: 99.
81 Alley et al. 2003.
82 Jalut et al. 2009; Roberts, N., 1998.
83 Braudel 1980: 194 on Toynbee 1934; Hassan 2002b: 21; Rosen, A., 2007: 8–16.
84 McAnany and Yoffee 2010, in reponse to Diamond 2005.
85 Abulafia 2011: 631–38, 726–27 with further references; Melotti 2007.
86 Dardis and Smith 1997; Grenon and Batisse (eds) 1989, especially 203–61.
87 King 1997; Williams, A., 1997.
88 Cherry 2003: 157.
89 Gaffney et al. 1997: 41–49.
90 Naccache 1998.
91 Papadopoulos, J., 1997a; Pace (ed.) 2000.
92 Hodder and Doughty 2007; Stanley-Price 2003.
93 Cilia (ed.) 2004: 428–29; Theuma and Grima 2006.
94 Brodie et al. 2000; Gill and Chippindale 1993.
95 Marthari 2001: 166; Perticarari and Giuntani 1986.
96 Bisheh 2001: 115.
97 Lowenthal 2007.
98 Futures: Blondel et al. 2010: 262–312; Grenon and Batisse (eds) 1989; Grove and Rackham 2001: 361–65; King et al. (ed.) 2001; several papers in Woodward (ed.) 2009: 561–650.
99 Anonymous 1996.
100 Given 1998; Naccache 1998: 147–49.
101 Hamilakis and Yalouri 1996: 125–27.
102 Greece: Hamilakis 2007; Spain: Gilman 2000: 265; Israel: Greenberg 2009; overall east Mediterranean: Meskell (ed.) 1998.
103 Hamilakis 1999.
104 Herzfeld 1984, 2005.
105 Horden and Purcell 2000: 28–29; Jirat-Wasiutynski 2007; Woolf 2003: 126–29.
106 Horden 2005: 26.
107 Driessen, H., 2001.
108 Fischer, J., 2005.
109 Davis 2000: 92.
110 O'Connor, D., and Quirke (eds) 2003.
111 On ancient globalization: LaBianca and Scham (eds) 2006; Jennings 2011.
112 Morris, I., 2003: 46–50.

CHAPTER TWO (pp. 54–81)

1 Quoted in Matvejević 1999: 130–31, 216.
2 Trump 1980: 3; Horden and Purcell 2005: 348.
3 Durrell 1958: 15.
4 Braudel 1972a: 363, 370.
5 Doonan 2009.
6 Chaunu 1978: 106.
7 As cited by Purcell 2005a: 211, 232.
8 Braudel 1972a: 168–230; Horden and Purcell 2000: 9–25; 2006: 734; Driessen, H., 1999.

9   Blondel *et al.* 2010: 16–21; Bolle 2003; Purcell 2003.
10 Durrell 1945: 10; Huxley 1936: 295; both discussed in Matvejević 1999: 176.
11 Knapp 1991: 46; Waelkens *et al.* 1999.
12 Clarke, A., and Frederick 2006: 116.
13 Horden and Purcell 2006: 736–37.
14 Grenon and Batisse (eds) 1989: 19, fig. 2.4.
15 Hassan 1997.
16 Horden and Purcell 2006: 734.
17 Blondel *et al.* 2010: 19, table 1.2.
18 Purcell 2003: 24.
19 Greaves 2007a.
20 Hassan 1997: 62.
21 Sherratt, A., 1996: 133–37.
22 Myres 1943, especially 6–7.
23 Blondel *et al.* 2010: 159–64.
24 As noted by Horden and Purcell 2006: 726.
25 Cf. Diamond 1997: 176–91 on the advantages of an east–west latitudinal alignment.
26 Broodbank 2000: 38–43, fig. 3.
27 Abulafia 2005; Fuller, Boivin *et al.* 2011 for the initial stages around the Indian Ocean.
28 Blondel *et al.* 2010: 72–76; Grove and Rackham 2001: 11; see also papers in *The Holocene* 11(6) (2001).
29 Allen 2009; Blondel *et al.* 2010: 17–18, 32–38; Grove and Rackham 2001: 45–71, 151–89.
30 For a 'new thalassology' see Peters 2003.
31 Wilson, S. M., 2007.
32 Habu 2010.
33 Cunliffe 2001: 213–310; Rönnby (ed.) 2003; van der Noort 2011.
34 Carter, R. A., 2010.
35 Anderson, A., 2010: 7–10; Glover and Bellwood (eds) 2004.
36 Falabella *et al.* 2008; Scott, L., and Lee-Thorp 2004.
37 McCorriston 1994 for the classic Californian comparison.
38 Horden and Purcell 2006: 738–40; Purcell 2003: 12–13.
39 Gamble, L., 2008; Kennett 2005.
40 Braudel 2001: 8 for this term; Mather 2009.
41 McNeill 1992: 12.
42 Oppenheimer and Pyle 2009; Stiros 2009; on responses, Balmuth *et al.* (ed.) 2005.
43 Blake 2005: 113–20.
44 Pilbeam and Young 2004.
45 Van der Geer *et al.* 2006: 120.
46 Braudel 2001: 23.
47 Grove and Rackham 2001: 11
48 On Mediterranean fractals, Malkin 2003: 57; for the fractal properties of Aegean islands, Korcak 1938.
49 Gilman and Thornes 1985.
50 Thornes *et al.* 2009.
51 Black *et al.* 2011; Grove and Rackham 2001: 24–28, 30–36.
52 Braudel 2001: 128.
53 McNeill 1992: 35.
54 Close 2009; Horden and Purcell 2000: 65–74.
55 Morris, I., 2010: 29–30.
56 The former is an oft-repeated cliché; for the latter, Cunliffe 1995: 9.

57 Janković and Petraschek 1987.
58 Bevan 2007: 172–79; Ruffell 1997: 17–19.
59 Ingold 1993 on the concept of 'taskscapes'.
60 Bevan 2007 for the east; Higgins and Higgins 1996 gives a detailed view of the Aegean.
61 Kassianidou and Knapp 2005: 218–30.
62 Blondel *et al.* 2010: 23–98, 235–85.
63 Rackham and Moody 1996: 54–57.
64 Bonhomme *et al.* 2004.
65 Blondel *et al.* 2010: 237–39; Marra 2005.
66 Blondel 2006.
67 Attenborough 1987; Blondel 2006; Grove and Rackham 2001.
68 On 'accretional' landscape: Fuller 2010: 11.
69 Braudel 2001: 24; 1972b: 452; also Gell 1985; Horden and Purcell 2000: 124–30.
70 Bairoch 1988: 11.
71 Rohling *et al.* 2009.
72 Blondel *et al.* 2010: 78–98, 186–201; Frantzis *et al.* 2003.
73 Margalef (ed.) 1985: 2.
74 Gallant 1985; Horden and Purcell 2000: 190–97.
75 Chapman, J., *et al.* 1996: 2, fig. 3; Forenbaher (ed.) 2009a: iii–v.
76 Matvejević 1999: 202.
77 Fabre 2004–5: 12–13.
78 Morton 2001; Pryor 1988: 12–24; Rohling *et al.* 2009.
79 Pryor 1988: 87–101.
80 Broodbank 2000: 92–96; Horden and Purcell 2000: 123–43.
81 Anderson, A., 2010: 5; Grenon and Batisse 1989: 31–33.
82 Adapted from McEvedy 2002: 11, fig. 6.2.
83 McEvedy 2002: 11; Snodgrass 2000: 173–74; see also Chapter 4 and Broodbank 2006: 219, fig. 3.
84 Dardis and Smith 1997: 275–80.
85 Erdoğu 2003; Matvejević 1999: 130.
86 Blondel *et al.* 2010: 127–33; Horden and Purcell 2000: 186–90, 196–97; Roberts, N., and Reed 2009.
87 Grove and Rackham 2001: 328–50; Stewart, I., and Morhange 2009.
88 Aksu *et al.* 1987.
89 Grove and Rackham 2001: 335.
90 Butzer 2002; Goedicke 1988: 165–66.
91 On types of anchorages: Blue 1997: 31–34, figs 1–2.
92 Broodbank 2000; Cherry 2004; Vigne 1994: 19, fig. 1; Vogiatzakis *et al.* (eds) 2008.
93 Broodbank 2000: 16–27, 36–43; Horden and Purcell 2000: 74–77, 133–35, 224–30; Knapp 2008: 1–30, 298–389.
94 Robb and Farr 2005: 26.

CHAPTER THREE (pp. 82–108)

1   Mather 2009: 14–16.
2   Bover and Alcover 2003.
3   Sahnouni 1998; for doubts, Geraads *et al.* 2004 and reply by Sahnouni *et al.* 2004.
4   Klein 2009: 241–434.
5   Dennell 2009: 98–113 for a recent summary.
6   Kohn and Mithen 1999; Lepre *et al.* 2011.

7   Dennell 2003: 2009: 77–80.
8   Dennell 2009: 84–98; Stringer 2011: 77–83.
9   Dennell 2003.
10 Hublin 2001; Raynal *et al.* 2001.
11 Alperson-Afil and Goren-Inbar 2010; Goren-Inbar *et al.* 2002.
12 Plato, *Phaedo* 109b.
13 Lewthwaite 1987.
14 Mussi 2001: 15–18.
15 Grove and Rackham 2001: 151–66 on approaches to the early formation of Mediterranean plant communities.
16 Williams, M., *et al.* 1998; useful summary in Klein 2009: 56–63; also EPICA 2004 for new data.
17 Taylor, K. C., *et al.* 1993.
18 Hetherington and Reid 2010.
19 Smith, J. R., 2012; Staubwasser and Weiss 2006.
20 Sherratt, A., 1996: 133.
21 Tzedakis 2009.
22 Blondel *et al.* 2010: 25–31; Médail and Diadema 2009.
23 Shackleton *et al.* 1984; Stewart, I., and Morhange 2009: 388–406; van Andel 1989; for a global perspective, Lambeck *et al.* 2002.
24 Bailey and Flemming 2008.
25 Mussi 2001: 86–90.
26 Bonfiglio *et al.* 2002; Marra 2005.
27 Schule 1993: 404.
28 Roebroeks 2006.
29 Klein 2009: 330–43; Stringer 2011: 25–26.
30 Mussi 2001: 80–84.
31 Stiner and Kuhn 2006: 695.
32 Alperson-Afil and Goren-Inbar 2010.
33 Parfitt *et al.* 2010.
34 Parés *et al.* 2006; Martinez-Navarro *et al.* 2005.
35 Mussi 2001: 19–53; see recently Carbonell *et al.* 2008 for earlier possibilities in Italy and also France.
36 Bermúdez de Castro *et al.* 1997.
37 For rare finds from southern Iberia dating to about 900,000 years ago, Scott, G. R., and Gilbert 2009.
38 Arribas and Palmqvist 1999; Turner 1992.
39 O'Regan 2008: 2140.
40 Kuhn 2010; Tourloukis 2010, including 38–44 for a broader treatment.
41 Broodbank 2006.
42 Cherry 1990: 201.
43 E.g. Bar-Yosef and Belfer-Cohen 2001; Dennell 2003; Bednarik 2003 for zealous advocacy; Derricourt 2005 for a trenchantly sceptical response.
44 Morwood *et al.* 1998; but see Bailey and Flemming 2008: 2158 and Dennell 2009: 432.
45 Mellars 1999: 354.
46 Bailey and Flemming 2008: 2161; Straus 2001.
47 O'Regan 2008.
48 For possible technological parallels, Sharon 2011.
49 Mussi 2001: 19–53, 86–90; Villa 2001.
50 Broodbank 2006: 200–5; Cherry 1990: 192–97; Simmons and associates 1999: 20–25.
51 Strasser *et al.* 2010, 2011.

52 Lykousis 2009; Reese 1990.
53 Bednarik 2003: 47–50.
54 Hublin 2000, 2001.
55 Stringer 2011: 32–33, 192–94.
56 Klein 2009: 308–11, 330–43, 435–64, 638–43.
57 Mussi 2001: 76.
58 Barham and Mitchell 2008: 159–259; Fleagle and Gilbert 2008; Klein 2009: 464–81, 615–43.
59 Hublin and McPherron (eds) 2012; Stringer and Barton 2008; for Taramsa, Vermeersch 2010.
60 Shea 2010.
61 Klein 2009: 435–614.
62 Boëda et al. 1999, 2008.
63 Stiner 2005: 192–93.
64 Stiner et al. 2011: 229–30 for recent discussion of this development.
65 Gamble, C., 1999a: 174–267; Stiner and Kuhn 2006: 706.
66 Klein 2009: 536–38, 571–73.
67 D'Errico and Nowell 2000.
68 Henshilwood et al. 2002; Klein 2009: 532–35.
69 Bouzouggar et al. 2007.
70 For recent discussions, see Renfrew and Morley (eds) 2009.
71 Barham and Mitchell 2008: 201–5, 238–40; Mattingly et al. 2003: 327–31.
72 Ramos et al. 2008.
73 Barham and Mitchell 2008: 238–44; Garcea 2009, 2010b.
74 Bouzouggar and Barton 2012.
75 Ambrose 1998.
76 Powell et al. 2009.
77 Klein 2009: 436–43.
78 Klein 2009: 639–43.
79 Stiner and Kuhn 2006: 706 on Neanderthal proneness to local extinction.
80 Karavanić and Janković 2006: 24–30.
81 Van Andel and Davies (eds) 2003.
82 Finlayson, C., 2008; Mussi 2001: 101–65; Runnels 2001: 237–40; Runnels et al. 2004.
83 Shea 2010.
84 Finlayson, C., 2009.
85 Woodward 2009b: 210–19.
86 Van Andel and Davies (eds) 2003.
87 Carrión et al. 2008; Finlayson, C., 2009: 143–48.
88 Stewart et al. 2003b.
89 Mussi 2001: 116–18, 125–28.
90 On this ecology, see Guthrie 1990.
91 Briggs et al. 2009; Shea 2007: 224–26.
92 Stiner 2005: 219–33; Stiner and Kuhn 2006: 702–3.
93 Gamble, C., 1999a: 260–67.
94 Pastó et al. 2000.
95 Gamble, C., 1999a: 204–10, 239–43; Mussi 2001: 140–42.
96 Darlas 1999: 298; Warren 1992.
97 Stiner and Kuhn 2006: 696–97.
98 Shea 2003: 320; Stringer et al. (eds) 2000.
99 Henry (ed.) 2003: 33–34; Runnels 2001: 239.
100 Karavanić and Janković 2006: 37–39.
101 Stiner and Kuhn 2006: 697.
102 Gale, R., and Carruthers 2000; Klein 1999: 549–51, table 6.11.

103 Stiner and Kuhn 2006: 698–703.
104 Barton 2000.
105 Barton 2000; Sánchez 2000: 131.
106 Currant et al. 2012; Stiner 1994: 133.
107 Cleyet-Merle and Madelaine 1995: 304.
108 Erlandson 2001; Henshilwood et al. 2001.
109 Davidson and Noble 1992; Erlandson 2010 for a global recent survey.
110 Mussi 2001: 101–65.
111 Ferentinos et al. 2012.
112 Kourtessi-Philippakis 1999; Vujević 2009.
113 Chelidonio 2001.
114 Pastó et al. 2000.

CHAPTER FOUR (pp. 109–47)

1 Camps, M., and Szmidt (eds) 2009 provide the only overall coverage.
2 Reimer et al. 2009.
3 Klein 2009: 647–60; Mellars and Stringer (eds) 1989; Mithen 1996.
4 Sherratt, A., 1997; van Peer and Vermeersch 2007.
5 Henshilwood and Marean 2003; McBrearty and Brooks 2000; several papers in Mellars et al. (eds) 2007; useful short summary in Barham and Mitchell 2008: 255–59.
6 Powell et al. 2009.
7 Close 2009; Garcea 2010b; Barton et al. 2005: 94; Linstädter, Eiwanger et al. 2012: 166–69.
8 Garcea 2009, 2010b; McBurney 1967: 135–84.
9 Olivieri et al. 2006.
10 Garcea 2004; Straus 2001.
11 Gamble, C., et al. 2004.
12 Recently O'Connell et al. 2010; O'Connor, S., 2010; Habu 2010: 161–62 for Japan.
13 Bailey 2009; Bulbeck 2007; Stringer 2000.
14 Vermeersch 2009.
15 Goring-Morris and Belfer-Cohen (eds) 2003; Shea 2008.
16 Otte and Yalçinkaya 2009; Papagianni 2009; Runnels 2001: 240–42, 258.
17 Mellars 2006.
18 Papagianni 2009: 130–33.
19 Otte 2010.
20 Pike et al. 2012.
21 Clottes (ed.) 2003; but see Bahn et al. 2009 for a sceptical response.
22 Mussi 2001: 167–217; Runnels 2001: 240–42; Zilhão 2009.
23 Chilardi et al. 1996.
24 Fedele et al. 2007; Mussi 2001: 191–94; Oppenheimer and Pyle 2009: 436, 443–44, fig. 15.4.
25 E.g. Finlayson, C., 2009: 121–75; Mellars 2004.
26 Mussi 2001: 221; Stewart, J. R., et al. 2003a.
27 Stiner and Kuhn 2006: 706.
28 Conard (ed.) 2006; Green et al. 2010; Stringer 2011: 192–95.
29 Gamble, C., 1999a: 377–83; Klein 2009: 590–95, 654–56.
30 Karavanić and Janković 2006: 30–34, 43.
31 Harvati et al. 2003; Runnels 2001: 240–42.
32 Bietti and Negrino 2007; Mussi 2001: 169–72.

33 Finlayson, C., 2008; Zilhão 2000a, 2009.
34 Duarte et al. 1999; Klein 2009: 589–90.
35 Finlayson, C., et al. 2006; for a cautionary note, Zilhão and Petitt 2006.
36 Aiello and Wheeler 2003; Stringer 2011: 101–2 for shoes.
37 Stiner and Kuhn 2006.
38 Gamble, C., 1999a: 268–416.
39 Rodseth et al. 1991.
40 Gamble, C., 1999a: 329–33; Mussi 2001: 258–64; on technologies of enchantment, see Gell 1992.
41 Gamble, C., 1999a: 319; Vanhaeren and d'Errico 2006, especially fig. 5.
42 Kuhn and Stiner 2007.
43 Runnels and van Andel 1988: 90–95; Gamble, C., 2007: 212–14 suggests much earlier hand-to-hand transfer of stone.
44 Roebroeks et al (eds) 2000; Davies and Gollop 2003.
45 Runnels 2001: 240–45.
46 Straus et al. 2000; Bicho et al. 2007: 123–31.
47 Mussi 2001: 264–66.
48 Mussi 2000, 2001: 225–29, 250–51, 254–64.
49 Clark, P. U., et al. 2009; Robinson, S., et al. 2006, especially 1533–35; Smith, J. R., 2010 for North Africa.
50 Leighton 1999: 16; Lucchi 2008; Mussi 2001: 221.
51 Terral et al. 2004.
52 Clottes et al. 2005: 24, 185–87.
53 Grove and Rackham 2001: 155.
54 Martin et al. 2010.
55 Lambeck 1996; Petit-Maire and Vrielynck 2005; van Andel 1989.
56 Stiner 1999.
57 Van Andel 1989: 737.
58 Clottes et al. 2005; Lambeck 1996.
59 Compare Miracle 2007 and Mussi 2001: 309–11, 312.
60 Churchill et al. 2000.
61 Bocquet-Appel and Demars 2000.
62 Mithen 2003: 11 for an informed guess.
63 E.g. Mussi 2001: 270–74.
64 Bar-Yosef and Belfer-Cohen 2010; Otte and Yalçinkaya 2009; Perlès 2000.
65 Close 2009.
66 Barker et al. 2008: 216; 2009: 81–82; Garcea 2009: 56–57.
67 Garcea 2010c: 59–60; Lubell 1984.
68 Hublin and McPherron (eds) 2012: viii; Linstädter, Eiwanger et al. 2012: 169–70; Barton et al. 2005.
69 Barton et al. 2005: 94–97.
70 Straus et al. 2000: 561–63.
71 Bicho et al. 2007: 101–5.
72 Schild and Wendorf 2010.
73 Nadel (ed.) 2002.
74 Klein 2009: 679–80.
75 Fuller, Willcox and Allaby, 2011: 642–43; Stringer 2011: 145–46.
76 Garcea 2009; Piperno et al. 2004; Wright, K. I., 1994.
77 Mussi 2001: 125–26.
78 Cleyet-Merle and Madelaine 1995: 305–6.
79 Clottes et al. 2005.
80 Dams 1987.

81 Morales-Muñiz and Roselló-Izquierdo 2008; Straus 2001: 98–99.
82 Broodbank 2008: 273–75; Facchini and Giusberti 1992.
83 Vigne 1999: 301–6.
84 Cherry 1992; Costa 2004: 17–19; Mussi 2001: 332, 342, fig. 7.30.
85 Sondaar et al. 1995.
86 Klein Hofmeijer 1997.
87 Melis and Mussi 2002.
88 Habu 2010: 161; Spriggs 1997: 58–59.
89 Barron et al. 2003: 65–67, figs 5.7, 5.9.
90 Vigne 2005a: 142.
91 Jalut et al. 2009; Robinson, S., et al. 2006.
92 Fagan 2004: 1–96 and Mithen 2003 for excellent global exploration of the opening phases of this transformation.
93 Farr 2010: 180, fig. 14.2.
94 Grove and Rackham 2001: 156–61; Tzedakis 2009: 114–19.
95 Hillman 1996.
96 For the Sahara, Hoelzmann et al. 2004: 234.
97 Mussi 2001: 324, fig. 7.23, 326–27.
98 Mussi 2001: 304; Uerpmann 1995.
99 Gamble, C., et al. 2004: 251; Walker 2008.
100 Stiner and Munro 2011.
101 Mussi 2001: 327–32, 341–44; Pluciennik 2002.
102 Bahn and Couraud 1984; d'Errico 1995; Mussi 2001: 344, 357–59.
103 Gamble, C., et al. 2005; Hillman 1996; Miller 2012.
104 Garcea 2010c: 62; Lubell 1984.
105 Yalçinkaya et al. (eds) 2002.
106 Watkins 1996.
107 Chataigner et al. 1998: 525, 533.
108 Whallon 2007b.
109 Ammerman 2010: 83; Bass, B., 1998: 172; Mussi 2001: 327–32.
110 Maher 2010; Martin et al. 2010.
111 Hachi 1996; Hachi et al. 2002.
112 Shipman 2009; Tchernov and Valla 1997; Vigne 2005b.
113 Arbuckle and Erek 2010; Phoca-Cosmetatou 2009.
114 Bailey 1999; Gamble, C., 1999b.
115 Peresani et al. 2008.
116 Mussi 2001: 313–24.
117 Fiore and Tagliacozzo 2008.
118 Colonese et al 2011: 92–94; on cockles and deer, Bailey 1978: 39.
119 Mannino and Thomas 2009.
120 Morales-Muñiz and Roselló-Izquierdo 2008.
121 Roche 1963: fig. 34.2; Straus 2001: 98.
122 Hansen, J. M., 1991: 109–27.
123 Blumler 1996; Diamond 1997: 134–38.
124 For the Maghreb, Barker 2006: 285.
125 Goring-Morris and Belfer-Cohen 2011.
126 Hillman 2000.
127 Barker 2006: 125.
128 Barker 2006: 116–28; Bar-Yosef 1998; Bar-Yosef and Valla (eds) 1991.
129 Woodburn 1982.
130 Auffray et al. 1988.
131 Lieberman 1993.
132 Munro 2004.

133 Wright, K. I., 2000: 92–98.
134 Bar-Yosef Mayer 1991.
135 Wengrow 2006a: 66–68.
136 E.g. Mussi 2001: 366.
137 Eshed et al. 2006; Mussi 2001: 362–66.
138 Roberts, N., 1998: 70–76; Robinson, S., et al. 2006: 1536.
139 Mithen 2003: 46–55 for a compelling portrayal; Munro 2004,
140 Grosman et al. 2008.
141 Bailey 1999: 162, 164.
142 Barker et al. 2009: 87; Linstädter, Eiwanger et al. 2012: 169–71.
143 Mussi 2001: 296, 305.

CHAPTER FIVE (pp. 148–201)

1 Simmons and associates 1999.
2 Hadjisterkotis and Reese 2008.
3 Summarized in Knapp 2010: 82–94.
4 Ammerman 2010: 86–90; Knapp 2010: 95–100.
5 Simmons 2004: 9.
6 Vigne 1999.
7 Cucchi et al. 2006; Vigne 1999.
8 Vigne 1999: 303–4.
9 Vigne 1999: 310–14 on this 'banalization'.
10 Perlès 1987: 142–45.
11 Habu 2010: 161; Spriggs 1997: 58–59.
12 Perlès 1999: 313–14, table 29.I; though modified by Stiner and Munro 2011.
13 Lambeck 1996: 603–4, figs 6–7.
14 Cherry 1981: 45.
15 Broodbank 2000: 101–5.
16 Tzala 1989.
17 Leavesley 2006: 191–93.
18 Broodbank 2006: 208–11, 217–20.
19 Laskaris et al. 2011 claim a slightly earlier date for obsidian in the Schisto Cave in Attica, but with a large error margin and still trialling technique.
20 Lernau and Lernau 1994: 118.
21 Broodbank 2006: 218–20; Irwin 1992: 5, 31 for the 'nursery' concept.
22 Broodbank 1999: 22–24, with earlier application.
23 Roberts, N., 1998.
24 Roberts, N., 1998: 87–126.
25 Rohling et al. 2009: 55–57; Rosen, A., 2007: 70–80.
26 Mithen and Black (eds) 2011 address this explicitly in a south Levantine context.
27 Grove and Rackham 2001: 151–61; Jalut et al. 2009: 5–10.
28 Grove and Rackham 2001: 144–45.
29 Roberts, N., 2002.
30 Brooks et al. 2003; Leblanc et al. 2006; Rohling et al. 2009: 55–57.
31 Shrine et al. 2001.
32 Barham and Mitchell 2008: 313.
33 Lambeck and Chappell 2001.
34 Desse and Desse-Berset 2003: 288–89.
35 Horowitz 1998.
36 Ryan and Pitman 1998; cf. among others Kotthoff et al. 2011.
37 Grove and Rackham 2001: 328–50; Stewart, I., and Morhange 2009.

38 Müllenhoff 2005.
39 Shackleton 1988: 37–41.
40 Berger and Guilaine 2009; Thomas et al. 2007.
41 Groube 1996.
42 For varied perspectives, Barker 2006; Bocquet-Appel and Bar-Yosef (eds) 2008; Hodder 1990; Renfrew 2007: 135–59.
43 For excellent overviews, Barker 2006: 104–48; Sherratt, A., 2007.
44 Diamond 2002.
45 Diamond 1997: 132–46, 157–75; Garrard 1984; Zohary et al. 2012.
46 Kislev et al. 2006.
47 Barker 2006: 128–30; Wright, K. I., 1994: 254–55.
48 Hillman et al. 2001.
49 Diamond 1997: 168–75.
50 Flannery 1969.
51 Munro 2004: 20–21.
52 Cauvin 2000, especially 123–25.
53 Sherratt, A., 1981; for a critical update, Halstead and Isaakidou 2011.
54 Richerson et al. 2001.
55 Fuller, Willcox and Allaby 2011.
56 Fuller, Willcox and Allaby 2011: 635–37.
57 Vigne et al. 2011; Zeder 2008.
58 Cauvin 2000; Hodder 2006: 233–58; Kuijt (ed.) 2000a.
59 Sherratt, A., 2007: 4–6.
60 Kuijt and Goring-Morris 2002: 369–82; Simmons 2007: 86–120.
61 Schmidt, K., 2006.
62 Sherratt, A., 2007: 3–4.
63 Sherratt, A., 1996: 133–37.
64 Sherratt, A., 2007: 6–9.
65 Kuijt and Goring-Morris 2002: 371–76; Simmons 2007: 106–7.
66 On recent discoveries of the latter, Kuijt and Finlayson 2009.
67 Rosen, A., 1986; Kotsakis 1999 in an Aegean context; Rosen, A., 1986.
68 Kuijt and Goring-Morris 2002: 373–74; Simmons 2007: 99.
69 Kuijt and Goring-Morris 2002: 377–78.
70 Sherratt, A., 2004: 57–60; 2007: 9–13.
71 Barker 2006: 137–46; Fuller, Willcox and Allaby 2011: 641.
72 Sherratt, A., 2007: 6–9.
73 Bogaard 2005.
74 Simmons 2007: 146–50.
75 Robb 2007: 36.
76 Simmons 2007: 114–15, 150.
77 Molleson 1994.
78 Byrd 2000.
79 Byrd 2005; Flannery 1972.
80 For earlier hunter-gatherer possibilities, Zubrow et al. (eds) 2010.
81 Sahlins 1974: 41–148; recently, Kuijt 2008.
82 Kuijt 2000b; Rollefson 2000.
83 For a recent discovery at Kfar HaHoresh, Goring-Morris 2005.
84 Kuijt and Goring-Morris 2002: 382–87.
85 Runnels and van Andel 1988; Sherratt, A., 2006: 57–58; Kuijt and Goring-Morris 2002: 380–82, 403–4.
86 Schmandt-Besserat 1992: 161–70, 197–98.

87   Kuijt and Goring-Morris 2002: 387–404.
88   Kuijt and Goring-Morris 2002: 394–98.
89   Bar-Yosef Mayer 2005: 181.
90   Kuijt and Goring-Morris 2002: 404–13;
     Simmons 2007: 175–84.
91   De Contenson 1992.
92   Helms, S., and Betts 1987.
93   Bar-Yosef and Alon 1988.
94   Kuijt and Goring-Morris 2002: 413–18.
95   Gamble, C., 2007: 198–203; Wengrow 1998.
96   Kuzmin 2006; now also Boaretto et al. 2009.
97   Evershed et al. 2008.
98   Sherratt, A., 2007: 13–14; Simmons 2007:
     184–94.
99   Rollefson 1996, but cf. now Campbell 2010.
100 Weniger et al. 2006; Maher et al. 2011 for a
     sceptical response.
101 Garrard et al. 1996; Wasse 2007: 54–55.
102 Caneva 1999; Sherratt, A., 2007: 13.
103 Galili et al. 2002, 2004.
104 Lernau and Lernau 1994: 118–21.
105 Simmons 2007: 198–228.
106 Akkermans and Schwartz 2003: 99–153;
     Caneva 1999: 84, fig. 10.
107 Galili and Rosen 2011: 273–74.
108 Simmons 2007: 217–21.
109 Wengrow 2008: 12–16.
110 Özbaşaran 2011; Sherratt, A., 2007: 11–12.
111 Binder 2002.
112 Esin and Harmankaya 1999.
113 Kassianidou and Knapp 2005: 216; Roberts,
     B. W., et al. 2009: 1012–14.
114 Hodder 2006.
115 Roberts, N., and Rosen 2009.
116 Özdoğan 2011: 419–20.
117 Schoop 2011.
118 Hodder 2006: 78, 251–55.
119 Yalçinkaya et al. (eds) 2002: 382.
120 Knapp 2010; Vigne et al. 2011.
121 Cherry 1985: 24–26.
122 Vigne et al. 2011: 258–59.
123 Guilaine and Le Brun (eds) 2003.
124 Vigne et al. 2011.
125 Peltenburg et al. 2001; Vigne et al. 2011.
126 For the first two, Vigne et al. 2011; Vigne
     and Cucchi 2005.
127 Sevketoğlu 2002.
128 Broodbank 2000: 20–21; McCartney 2007.
129 Peltenburg 2004: 84–85; Wasse 2007:
     60–63.
130 Gamble, C., 1986; Pluciennik 2008.
131 Runnels 2009.
132 Shennan and Edinborough 2007 for
     a similar conclusion further north.
133 Pluciennik 2008: 353.
134 Bouville 1987.
135 Taçon et al. 1996.
136 Lubell 2004.
137 Silvana et al. 1985.
138 Mussi 2001: 321–22.
139 Binder 2000.
140 Geddes et al. 1989.
141 Miracle 2002.
142 Mannino et al. 2007.
143 Komšo 2006: 73–74; Runnels 2001: 248–49;
     Runnels et al. 2004.
144 Straus 2008.

145 Zilhão 2000b: 144–45.
146 Runnels 2009.
147 Gatsov and Özdoğan 1994; Özdoğan 1999:
     210.
148 Perlès 2003; Stiner and Munro 2011.
149 Sampson (ed.) 2008; Sampson et al. 2002.
150 Strasser et al. 2010.
151 Trantalidou 2003.
152 Mylona 2003.
153 Costa 2004: 17–41.
154 Vigne and Desse-Berset 1995.
155 Barker 2005: 47–51.
156 Radić 2009: 13–15.
157 Tykot 1999: 69.
158 Rowley-Conwy 2011; Halstead 1996a: 303;
     2006; Halstead and Isaakidou 2011: 67.
159 Guilaine 1987.
160 Kotsakis 2008: 62–63, 67.
161 E.g. Ammerman and Biagi (eds) 2003;
     Price (ed.) 2000; Robb and Miracle 2007
     for a refreshingly new approach.
162 E.g. Barker 1985: 251–56.
163 Rowley-Conwy 2011; Zeder 2008.
164 Larson et al. 2007.
165 Zvelebil 2000.
166 Recently, Shennan 2007.
167 Renfrew 1987; more recently also Bellwood
     and Renfrew (eds) 2002: 369–466;
     Anthony 2007: 75–81.
168 Ammerman and Cavalli-Sforza 1984.
169 Van Andel and Runnels 1995; Zilhão
     2000b: 166–82; 2003.
170 Shennan 2007: 144–47.
171 Renfrew and Boyle (eds) 2000; Rowley-
     Conwy 2011: S433–34.
172 Chikhi et al. 2002.
173 Vigne 1999: 311–12, fig. 7.
174 Gkiasta et al. 2003.
175 Guilaine et al. 1984.
176 Robb 2007: 122–24.
177 Özdoğan 2007.
178 Özdoğan 2011: 419–25.
179 Krauss 2011; Özdoğan and Başgelen
     1999.
180 Perlès 2001.
181 Perlès 2001: 38–63; van Andel and Runnels
     1995.
182 Halstead 1996a; Perlès 2001: 20–51.
183 Perlès 2003.
184 Isaakidou and Tomkins (eds) 2008.
185 Broodbank and Strasser 1991.
186 Perlès 2001: 64–199.
187 Pyke and Yiouni 1996.
188 Broodbank 1999; Cavanagh 2004.
189 Broodbank 2008: 277–79.
190 Forenbaher and Miracle 2005.
191 Forenbaher and Kaiser 2011.
192 Rowley-Conwy et al. 2013.
193 Brown, K., 2004; Skeates 2000.
194 Fugazzola Delpino et al. (eds) 2002; Manen
     and Perrin 2009.
195 Barnett 2000: 106–16.
196 Spataro et al. 2005.
197 Spataro 2002: 23.
198 Rowley-Conwy et al. 2013.
199 Rottoli and Pessina 2007.
200 Perrin 2008.

201 Fontana et al. 2009; Rowley-Conwy et al.
     2013.
202 Malone and Stoddart 1992.
203 Binder 2000.
204 Zilhão 2003.
205 Ammerman 1985.
206 Rowley-Conwy 2000.
207 Binder 2000: 134–35.
208 Binder 2000; Rowley-Conwy et al. 2013.
209 Maggi 1999.
210 Costa 2004: 43–71.
211 Guilaine and Manen 2007; Zilhão 2000b.
212 Guilaine et al. 2007.
213 Guilaine and Manen 2007: 33, 36.
214 Bernabeu et al. 2009.
215 Bernabeu et al. 2008.
216 Martí 1977; Pérez 1980.
217 McClure et al. 2008: 332, 334.
218 Zilhão 2000b: 150–66.
219 Perrin 2003.
220 Zilhao 2000b: 145–48.
221 Calado and Rocha 2008.
222 Cunliffe 2008, 124–25; Rojo Guerra and
     Kunst 1999.
223 Berger and Guilaine 2009.
224 Ammerman 2011.
225 Zilhão 2003: 216–18.
226 Barker 2006: 273–83; van der Veen (ed.)
     1999.
227 Barham and Mitchell 2008: 334–44.
228 Di Lernia and Gallinaro 2010: 956.
229 Breunig et al. 1996.
230 Sutton 1977.
231 Huysecom et al. 2009.
232 Di Lernia (ed.) 1999a.
233 Marshall and Weissbrod 2011: 400–2.
234 Marshall and Hildebrand 2002.
235 Linstädter 2008; Lubell et al. 1984.
236 Linstädter 2008.
237 Lubell 2001: 133–37; Rahmani 2004; on
     changes in the later Capsian, Jackes and
     Lubell 2008.
238 Barker et al. 2010: 78.
239 Lubell 2001: 134; Mulazzani 2013.
240 Barker 2006: 288–94; Wengrow 2006a:
     18–21.
241 Butzer 2002; Stanley and Warne 2003.
242 Bellwood 2004: 101.
243 Close 2002.
244 Garrard et al. 1996: 218–19.
245 Gilman 1975.
246 Ballouche and Marinval 2003.
247 Linstädter 2008; Linstädter, Medved et al.
     2012.
248 Manen et al. 2007.

CHAPTER SIX   (pp. 202–48)

1   Roberts, N., et al. 2011.
2   Rosen, A., 2007: 80–88; Kuper and Kröpelin
    2006.
3   Stewart, I., and Morhange 2009: 393–97,
    fig. 13.8.
4   Domergue and Rico 2002; Grove and
    Rackham 2001: 328–50; Stewart, I., and
    Morhange 2009: 402–6.

5 Ammerman *et al.* 1995.
6 Di Lernia 1999b for the new Pastoral phases.
7 Marshall and Hillebrand 2002; Marshall and Weissbrod 2011.
8 Marshall and Hillebrand 2002.
9 Dunne *et al.* 2012.
10 Di Lernia 1999b: 151.
11 Di Lernia and Gallinaro 2010.
12 Hassan 2002c.
13 Camps 1982: 616.
14 Mattingly *et al.* 2003: 340.
15 Di Lernia 2002, 2006; Wengrow 2006a: 54–59.
16 Wengrow 2001a.
17 Wilson, P., 2006.
18 Holdaway *et al.* 2010; Phillips, R., *et al.* 2012.
19 Barker 2006: 292–93; Hassan 1997: 62; Wengrow 2006a: 29–30, 44–49.
20 Barker 2006: 293; Wetterstrom 1993.
21 Wengrow 2006a: 30.
22 van den Brink 2011: 63; Wengrow 2006a: 29–30, 34–35, 39, 83–87.
23 Hassan 1984, 1997; Wengrow 2006a: 44–47.
24 Hassan 1997: 55–56; Wengrow 2006a: 33–34.
25 Wengrow 2006a.
26 Wengrow 2010a: 42.
27 Butzer 1976: 83, table 4.
28 Wengrow 2006a: 84–86.
29 Rojo Guerra *et al.* 2010: 131–45; on Maghrebian genetics and the sharp differences across the Strait of Gibraltar, see Bosch *et al.* 2001.
30 Bensimon and Martineau 1987; Daugas 2002; Lubell 1984: 47; Nespoulet *et al.* 2008.
31 Rojo Guerra *et al.* 2010.
32 Linstädter 2008; Linstädter, Medved *et al.* 2012.
33 Weninger *et al.* 2006: 58–59.
34 Roubet 1979.
35 Rahmani 2004: 61, 98–99.
36 Klein and Scott 1986; McBurney 1967: 289, 303.
37 Mulazzani 2010.
38 Mulazzani 2013.
39 A model sporadically floated: Guilaine 1994: 49, 426; Lewthwaite 1989.
40 Mulazzani 2010: 2535.
41 Slim *et al.* 2004 for the exceptional density of later Punic and Roman remains along this stretch of coast.
42 Dawson 2011.
43 Sampson (ed.) 2008.
44 Dawson 2011; also Broodbank 1999 and Stoddart 2000.
45 Forenbaher 2009b: 78–79.
46 Forenbaher 2009b: 79–83.
47 Broodbank 2000: 149–56; Holloway and Lukesh 1995.
48 Fentress *et al.* 2009: 73; Vigne 1988.
49 Alcover 2008.
50 Bonino 1990.
51 Fugazzola Delpino and Mineo 1995.
52 Tichy 2000.
53 For a case study in the Cyclades: Broodbank 2000: 81–85, 126–33; Phoca-Cosmetatou 2011b.
54 Cherry and Torrence 1982.

55 As first proposed by Cherry 1981: 58–61.
56 Broodbank 2000: 129–43; Keegan and Diamond 1987: 58–59, 67–68.
57 Clarke, J., *et al.* 2007.
58 Wasse 2007: 60–63.
59 Clarke, J., *et al.* 2007.
60 Isaakidou and Tomkins (eds) 2008.
61 Costa 2004: 73–95; Melis 2009; Tykot 1999.
62 Vigne 1999: 313, fig. 8.
63 Perlès 1992.
64 Robb 2007: 275–81.
65 Robb 2007: 281–85.
66 Perrin 2003; Rowley-Conwy *et al.* 2013; Tresset and Vigne 2007: 189–210; Zilhão 2000b: 145–48.
67 Bentley 2007.
68 Guilaine 1976; 2003: 135–62; against 'peasants', Horden and Purcell 2000: 270–78 and Halstead 1987.
69 Robb 2007; Skeates 2005b: 87–119; Whitehouse 1992a; several papers in Whitehouse (ed.) 1998.
70 Guilaine *et al.* 1984: 221.
71 Tarrús 2008.
72 Buxó *et al.* 2000; Palomo *et al.* 2005.
73 Cf. papers in Halstead (ed.) 1999a with Robb 2007 and Whitehouse 1992a.
74 Halstead 2000: 115–17; Rowley-Conwy *et al.* 2013.
75 Rottoli and Pessina 2007: 146–47; Chapman, R., 2008: 225 for the honeypot.
76 Robb 2007: 120–58 for Italy.
77 Robb 2007: 144–49.
78 Pappa *et al.* 2004.
79 Whitehouse 1992a: 40–42, 44–45.
80 Robb 2007: 123–24; Tarrús 2008: 31.
81 Isaakidou 2008: 96–104.
82 Costa 2004: 77–78; Isaakidou 2008: 204–10; Robb 2007: 146–47; Vaquer 1990: 292.
83 Delhon *et al.* 2009.
84 Isaakidou 2011.
85 Barber 1991: 79–113; Perlès 2001: 251–52.
86 Sherratt, A., 1995b: 24–26.
87 McGovern 2003: 1–2, 7.
88 McGovern 2003: 40–84, 301–2; Areshian *et al.* 2012 for the Areni Cave.
89 McGovern 2003: 38–39.
90 Valamoti 2004: 29–30, 117; Valamoti *et al.* 2007.
91 Lillios 2008a: 127–28; Peña-Chocarro 2007: 181.
92 Halstead 2000: 115–17; Robb 2007: 261–64; Robb and Hove 2003.
93 Halstead 2008: 230–31; Malone and Stoddart 1992; Robb 2007: 33–34, 264–65.
94 Chapman, R., 2008: 199.
95 Robb 2007: 113–15.
96 Halstead 1991.
97 Forenbaher 2011.
98 Chapman, R., 2008: 237.
99 Braudel 1989–90: 27; see also Beeching *et al.* (eds) 1991; Vaquer 1990.
100 Vaquer 1990: 231–65.
101 Colliga 1998: 768, 782–86; Vaquer 1990: 221–31.
102 Brown, K., 2004; Skeates 2000; the tally of sites identified by all means still rises.

103 Hamilton *et al.* 2006; Morter and Robb 1998.
104 Whittle 1996: 294–99.
105 Leighton 1999: 66–72.
106 Halstead 1981: 312–13.
107 Pappa and Besios 1999; Valamoti 2004: 131–32.
108 Halstead 1999b; Kotsakis 1999.
109 Kotsakis 2006.
110 Halstead 1995a; Gallis 1985 for Platia Magoula Zarkou.
111 Demoule and Perlès 1993: 390–91; Halstead 1995a: 14–15, 18.
112 Forge 1972; Robb 1999; 2007: 70–73.
113 Robb 2007: 46–65.
114 Beyneix 1997; Robb 2007: 38–39.
115 Runnels *et al.* 2009.
116 Robb 2007: 39–40.
117 Robb 1993: 749–52.
118 Demoule and Perlès 1993: 376–82, 391–93; Malone 2003: 273–80; Robb 2007: 161–86.
119 Chapman, J., 1988: 13–14.
120 Perlès and Vitelli 1999; Robb 2007: 162.
121 Broodbank 2000: 160–65.
122 Guilaine 1994: 375, 390.
123 Bernabeu 2002; Cruz Beroccal and Vicent García 2007; McClure *et al.* 2008.
124 Webster 1996: 47.
125 Robb 2007: 55.
126 Whitehouse 1992a: 40–41, 49, 87–124; for the late wild asses, see Rowley-Conwy *et al.* 2013.
127 For a recent survey, Robb and Farr 2005; also Perlès 1992.
128 Cazella 2003; Perlès 1992: 137, 146; Spataro 2002: 179–92, 198, 202.
129 Robb and Farr 2005: 27–35.
130 Pétrequin *et al.* (eds) 2012.
131 Most recently, Ifantidis and Nikolaidou (eds) 2011.
132 Leighton 1999: 74–78; the Maltese find, Cilia (ed.) 2004: 239.
133 Galiberti 2005.
134 Guilaine 1994: 126–27; Weller 2002.
135 For the slightly earlier Franchthi finds, Perlès 2001: 223–26.
136 Pétrequin *et al.* (eds) 2012: 21, fig. 3.
137 Perlès 1992; Robb and Farr 2005.
138 Farr 2010: 184–88.
139 Costa 2007; Robb and Farr 2005: 34–38.
140 Farr 2010: 184–87, fig. 14.8; Robb 2007: 192–204.
141 Torrence 1986; for the Balkan interface, Kilikoglou *et al.* 1996.
142 Tykot 1996.
143 Tykot 1996.
144 Perlès 1992: 146; Robb and Farr 2005: 34–38, table 2.1.
145 Robb and Farr 2005: 36–37.
146 Farr 2010: 184–88.
147 Tykot 1996: 54–56.
148 Robb 2007: 286–341; Sherratt, A., and Sherratt 2008: 295–97.
149 Robb 2007: 300–5.
150 Demoule and Perlès 1993: 399–400; Halstead 2008: 229–35.

151 Skeates 1993a: 113–14; Tomkins 2008: 33–40; Webster 1996: 47–52.
152 Halstead 2008: 231; Robb 2007: 304.
153 Broodbank 2000: 149–56; Halstead 2008; Maggi 1999; Robb 2007: 304.
154 Demoule and Perlès 1993: 404–5; Robb 2007: 305–11, 314; less clearly in Iberia, Chapman, R., 2008.
155 Beyneix 2007; Cavanagh and Mee 1998: 6–10; Guilaine 2003: 184–95, 197–226.
156 Robb 1994: 50–51.
157 Webster 1996: 49–52.
158 Malone et al. 1995; Pace 2004.
159 Cunliffe 2001: 143; Guilaine 2003: 184–95, 197–226.
160 Chapman, R., 2008: 223–36.
161 Guilaine 2003: 186 for this phrase.
162 Broodbank 2000: 156–70; Demoule and Perlès 1993: 403; Robb 2007: 295–300.
163 Demoule and Perlès 1993: 398–401.
164 Robb 2007: 171–72, 295–28.
165 Demoule and Perlès 1993: 401.
166 Robb 2007: 298.
167 Skeates 1993: 113.
168 Broodbank 2000: 161–63, fig. 46.
169 Kassianidou and Knapp 2005: 215–30; Roberts, B. W., et al. 2009, though their conclusion is contentious.
170 For recent discoveries at Belovode, see Radivojević et al. 2010.
171 Higham et al. 2007; Ivanov and Avramova 2000; Renfrew 1986.
172 Nakou 1995: 3–7; Zachos 2007.
173 Coleman 1977: 3–4, 157–58; Mina 2008: 41, 122.
174 Kassianidou and Knapp 2005: 217–18; Skeates 1993b.
175 Pearce 2007: 48–50.
176 Ruiz-Taboada and Montero-Ruiz 1999; Roberts, B. W., 2008 for a more sceptical view.
177 Gérard 2002: 108; on this period in Anatolia more generally, Schoop 2011.
178 Takaoglu 2005.
179 Wilkinson, T. J., 2003: 72–74.
180 Pollock 1999: 65–67, 81–92; Wengrow 1998: 790–93.
181 Wengrow 1998, 2001b.
182 Algaze 2008: 102; Liverani 2006; Ur et al. 2007.
183 Sherratt, A., 1995a: 17–19.
184 Kennett and Kennett 2007.
185 Carter, R. A., 2010.
186 Akkermans and Schwartz 2003: 154–80; Steadman 1996.
187 Akkermans and Schwartz 2003: 162–63.
188 Garstang 1953: 130–53; Steadman 1996: 148–49.
189 Steadman 1996.
190 Akkermans and Schwartz 2003: 154–57, 163, 169–73.
191 Rowan and Golden 2009.
192 Bourke 2001, much of which focuses on Tuleilat Ghassul.
193 Levy (ed.) 1987; Levy et al. 1991.
194 Levy 2007: 57–68.
195 Rowan and Golden 2009: 59–60.

196 Rowan and Golden 2009: 50–56.
197 Schick (ed.) 1998.
198 Rowan and Golden 2009: 66–69; Levy 1995b for the chiefdom model.
199 Rowan and Golden 2009: 56–62, 65–66; for Gilat in particular, see Levy (ed.) 2006.
200 Commenge 2006: 443–45.
201 Burton and Levy 2006.
202 Neef 1990: 298–300.
203 Seaton 2008; Sherratt, A., 1999.
204 Rosen, A., and Weiner 1994.
205 Finlayson, W., et al. 2011: 200–6.
206 Fuller, Willcox and Allaby 2011: 631.
207 Lovell 2008; Rowan and Golden 2009: 23–24; van den Brink 2011: 65.
208 Genz 2003: 66–67.
209 Rowan and Golden 2009: 24.
210 Rowan and Golden 2009: 34–35; Seaton 2008: 148.
211 Grigson 1995: 267.
212 Sherratt, A., 1981: 282–83; 1999: 25–26; for a recent evaluation, Halstead and Isaakidou 2011: 63–64, 67–68.
213 Barber 1991: 20–30.
214 Bar-Adon 1980: 177–85.
215 Foxhall 2007: 97–129 for recent discussion of the challenges of olive cultivation.
216 Yener 2000: 26.
217 Yener 2000: 26–44.
218 Anthony 1996; Chernykh 1992: 26–52.
219 Golden 2010.
220 Golden 2010: 35–47; Levy 2007: 40–43.
221 Golden 2010: 108–49, 156.
222 Bar-Adon 1980.
223 Rowan and Golden 2009: 12, 14.
224 Ussishkin 1971; also Moorey 1988; but see Rowan and Golden 2009: 45.
225 Golden 2010: 152–56.
226 Moorey 1988: 178–81.
227 Thalmann 2006.
228 Gopher et al. 1990.
229 Rowan and Golden 2009: 62–65; Braun and van den Brink 2008: 644–50.
230 Oren and Gilead 1981.

CHAPTER SEVEN (pp. 257–344)

1   Over this time span, average population densities of 2–5 people per sq. km (5–13 per sq. mile) have been independently arrived at for several regions, including parts of the southern Levant (Gophna 1995: 276, 280), Aegean (Broodbank 2000: 87–89), Italy (Robb 2007: 99–100) and Iberia (Chapman, R., 2003: 132); these are liable to be too high for much of North Africa, too low for parts of the northern Levant and far too low for the Nile Delta, where some 25–75 people per sq. km (65–194 per sq. mile) can be postulated (Butzer 1976: 83, table 4); the pan-Mediterranean figure suggested here is therefore an order-of-magnitude approximation.
2   Keller et al. 2012; Oeggl et al. 2007; Robb 2009; Vanzetti et al. 2010.

3   Kemp 2006: 83–84, 91–92; Wengrow 2006a: 41–43, 207–8.
4   Barker 2006: 346–52; Brooks 2010; Jalut et al. 2009; Robinson, S., et al. 2006.
5   Roberts, N., et al. 2004; Roberts, N., et al. 2011.
6   Rambeau and Black 2011; Roberts, N., et al. 2011 for a clear discussion of the debate.
7   Rackham 2008: 48.
8   Grove and Rackham 2001: 268–69; Lloret et al. 2009: 546 for fires.
9   Nocete et al. 2005.
10 Finné et al. 2011; Roberts, N., 1998: 159–206.
11 Tzedakis 2009; Yll et al. 1997.
12 Grove and Rackham 2001: 144–45.
13 Rohling et al. 2009; Rosen, A., 2007: 129–32.
14 Boenzi et al. 2002.
15 Rambeau and Black 2011; Roberts, N., et al. 2004: 351–53; also Lamb et al. 1989.
16 Halstead 1989; Rosen, A., 2007: 140–42.
17 Halstead and O'Shea 1982.
18 Horden and Purcell 2000: 302.
19 Renfrew 1972: 304–7, 386–90.
20 Halstead 2005b.
21 Shennan 2002: 239–61.
22 Shennan 2002: 52, 171; see also Glantz et al. 1998.
23 Brooks 2006 also pursues this association.
24 Rosen, A., 2007: 1–15.
25 Hoelzmann et al. 2004: Kröpelin 2008.
26 Cremaschi 1999: 29.
27 Cremaschi 2001.
28 Di Lernia and Merighi 2006; MacDonald 1998.
29 Barham and Mitchell 2008: 356–99.
30 Lubell et al. 1984: 143–47.
31 Schulz et al. 2009.
32 Hoelzmann et al. 2004: 234; Mattingly 1995: 12.
33 Mattingly 1995: 5–11, 14–16.
34 Bensimon and Martineau 1990; Bokbot 2005; Daugas 2002.
35 Harrison and Gilman 1977; Schuhmacher et al. 2009.
36 Guilaine 1994: 302–3.
37 Searight 2004: 34–35, 51–52, 170–71.
38 McIntosh and McIntosh 1988.
39 Daugas 2002.
40 Aumassip 1987.
41 Barker et al. 2009: 88; McBurney 1967: 306.
42 Mallory-Greenough 2002: 81.
43 For one recent discovery, Lubell et al. 2009.
44 Herodotus IV: 168–96.
45 Hassan 1997: 64–65.
46 Wengrow 2006a: 50–59.
47 Brett and Fentress 1996: 14–15.
48 Wilkinson, T. A. H., 1999: 143.
49 Baines 1996.
50 Kennett and Kennett 2007.
51 Sherratt, A., 1995a: 17–19.
52 Smith, A., 2003: 84–109; Yoffee 2005; see also Bang and Scheidel (eds) 2012.
53 Yoffee 1993: 69.
54 Chapman, R., 2003: 71–100.
55 Wengrow 2008; Yoffee 2005: 91–109.
56 Chapman, R., 2003: 95.

57 Kemp 2006: 60–160; Wengrow 2006a: 127–258.

58 Baines 2004; Wengrow 2006a: 198–207.

59 Wilkinson, T. A. H., 1999: 41.

60 Wengrow 2006a: 83–89, 159–64.

61 Butzer 1976: 83, table 4 suggests a population of 210,000 at about 3000 BC, growing to 540,000 by 2500 BC; for the Delta's expansion, Butzer 2002: 89–96.

62 Andres and Wunderlich 1992: 164, 166; Köhler 1992.

63 Levy and van den Brink 2002: 11–13; Wengrow 2006a: 83–89.

64 Kroeper 1992.

65 Wilkinson, T. A. H., 1999; on demography, Butzer 1976: 83, table 4; Trigger 2003: 297.

66 Wilkinson, T. A. H., 1999: 339; Yoffee 2005: 43, table 3.1.

67 Butzer 2002: 95.

68 Wilkinson, T. A. H., 1999: 117; for possibly earlier beginnings, see Wengrow 2006a: 159–60.

69 Butzer 2002: 93; Wenke and Brewer 1996.

70 Van Zeist 1988.

71 McGovern 2003: 85–102.

72 Wengrow 2006a: 191–94.

73 Wilkinson, T. A. H., 1999: 221.

74 Adams, M. J., 2009.

75 Bietak 2009: 220.

76 Algaze 2008: 111.

77 Breniquet 2008; McCorriston 1997; Wengrow 2008.

78 Radner and Robson (eds) 2011.

79 Collon 2005: 13–40.

80 Akkermans and Schwartz 2003: 233–77; Yoffee 2005: 53–59.

81 Akkermans and Schwartz 2003: 177–87; Liverani 1993; Yoffee 2005: 142.

82 Sherratt, A., 1995a: 13–17, 1999.

83 Greenfield 2010: 39–42; Halstead and Isaakidou 2011: 62, 65.

84 Anthony 1996.

85 Renfrew 1972: 3–14; Wengrow 2010a; Yoffee 2005: 15–19.

86 Baines and Yoffee 1998.

87 Wengrow 2001b.

88 McGovern 2003: 305; 2009: 95–101, 165–70, 241–50.

89 Greenberg 2011: 237–39; McGovern 2009: 165–70; Porat and Goren 2002; Wengrow 2006a: 202–4.

90 Bevan 2007: 8–18.

91 Feldman 2006: 117; Wengrow 2010a: 32–38.

92 Akkermans and Schwartz 2003: 284–85.

93 Cialowicz 2007.

94 Yener 2000: 13.

95 Halstead and Isaakidou 2011: 68–70.

96 Halstead 1995b.

97 Ur 2003.

98 Littauer and Crouwel 1990; on Canaanean blades, see Anderson, P. J., et al. 2004.

99 Sherratt, A., 1999.

100 Bevan 2010; Wengrow 2008.

101 Rahmstorf 2010a; 2011: 110–13.

102 Bevan 2010a; Marfoe 1987: 34; Röllig 1976.

103 Sherratt, A., and Sherratt 1991: 360–62.

104 Ross 1999: 13–15, 199–201.

105 Ross 1999: 191–92.

106 Ross 1999: 292.

107 Wengrow 2011.

108 Kassianidou and Knapp 2005: 220.

109 Philip and Rehren 1996.

110 Sherratt, S., 2007: 253–54.

111 Bevan 2007: 63–68; Nakou 2000.

112 Helms, M. W., 1988; Sherratt, A., 1993: 17–26; Wengrow 2010a: 109–49.

113 Sherratt, A., and Sherratt 1991.

114 Yoffee 2005: 35.

115 Sherratt, A., 1993: 14–18; Wengrow 2010a: 19–27.

116 Sherratt, A., 1993, 1995a; Sherratt, A., and Sherratt 1991; for further consideration, see Broodbank 2011; Stein 1999.

117 Algaze 1993, 2008; Rothman (ed.) 2001.

118 Frangipane 2003; (ed.) 2010.

119 Strommenger 1980.

120 Philip 2002; Steadman 1996.

121 Hendrickx and Bavay 2002: 61; Wengrow 2006a: 119, 135–38, 187–95.

122 Ratnagar 2004.

123 Marfoe 1987.

124 George 2004; Marfoe 1987.

125 Foster, B. R., 2001.

126 Malamat 1998.

127 Mitchell 2005: 73–81.

128 Gale, R., et al. 2000: 249–50, 367–68; Frost 2004: 327; Marfoe 1987: 27; Wengrow 2006a: 82, 148–49, 226.

129 Discussed in Wengrow 2006a: 255, fn. 39.

130 Sowada 2009: 197; Wilkinson, T. A. H. 1999: 134.

131 Shaw, I., 2000b: 321; Vinson 1994: 25.

132 Levy and van den Brink 2002.

133 Braun 2002, 2003.

134 Greenberg and Eisenberg 2002.

135 Marcus 2002: 406–7.

136 Jenkins 1980; Ward, C. A., 2006.

137 Marshall and Weissbrod 2011.

138 Grigson 2006: 223–34, 233.

139 Bell 2012: 182; Ross 1999: 292; Rossel et al. 2008.

140 Brodie 2008.

141 Broodbank 2010b.

142 Casson 1971: 292–96.

143 Marcus 2002a: 404, 2006.

144 Anderson, A., 2010: 7–10.

145 Carter, R. A., 2010.

146 Ratnagar 2004: 212–35.

147 Braudel 2001: 92; Fabre 2004–5: 89–129.

148 Bowen 1960: 130–31.

149 Ward, C. A., 2006.

150 Bowen 1960: 117–19; Broodbank 2010: 254–55.

151 Fabre 2004–5: 5.

152 Fabre 2004–5: 45–47, 50–73.

153 Fabre 2004–5: 89–129; Marcus 2002a: 407–8; Vinson 1994: 21–26; Wachsmann 1998: 12–18.

154 Bowen 1960: 130.

155 Marcus 2002a: 403–4, 408–9; Wachsmann 1998: 248–51.

156 My thanks to John-Vincent Gallagher for sharing the conclusions of his unpublished

Oxford DPhil thesis (2008, especially page 104 for the cost of ship parts).

157 Chesson and Philip 2003: Greenberg 2011.

158 Wilkinson, T. J., et al. 2004.

159 Philip 2003.

160 Akkermans and Schwartz 2003; Genz 2003.

161 Barker, Adams et al. 2007: 242–54, 268.

162 Akkermans and Schwartz 2003: 267–68, 319; Whitehead et al. 2011.

163 Rosen, S., 2011.

164 Finkelstein 1995: 354–60.

165 Wilkinson, T. J., 2003: 135; cf. Frederick and Krahtopoulou 2000.

166 Mazzoni 2003; Philip 2003.

167 Matthiae 1980: 2003; Milano 1995.

168 For the nearest stretch of the Euphrates at this time, Cooper, L., 2006.

169 Archi 1990.

170 Milano 1995; Porter 2010: 75–76; Yoffee 2005: 111 on assemblies.

171 Archi 1990.

172 Matthiae 2003; Bevan 2004: 115–19.

173 Mazzoni 2003.

174 Ross 1999: 237–60.

175 Akkermans and Schwartz 2003: 268–70; Schwartz et al. 2000.

176 Greenberg 2002, 2003; Philip 2003.

177 Recently, Genz 2010: 49–51.

178 Chesson 2003; Philip 2003.

179 Chesson and Philip 2003; Greenberg 2011.

180 Greenberg 2011; Levy and van den Brink 2002.

181 Genz 2003.

182 Barker, Adams et al. 2007: 267–70; Levy 2007; Levy et al. 2002.

183 Hestrin and Tadmor 1963: 284–85, where they are less plausibly interpreted as scale armour.

184 Frank 1966.

185 Greenberg and Paz 2005; Levy and van den Brink 2002: 23–25.

186 Marcus 2002a: 406–7; Sharvit et al. 2002.

187 Artin 2009.

188 Roth 1991; Sowada 2009: 128, 134; also Bevan 2007: 77–78.

189 Fabre 2004–5: 92.

190 Saghieh 1983.

191 Bevan 2007: 73.

192 Bevan 2004: 119.

193 Bikai 1978: 5–6, 72.

194 Aubet 2001: 166; Herodotus II: 44.

195 Doumet-Serhal 2006; 2008: 5–7.

196 Rosenberg and Golani 2012; Yon 2006: 15.

197 Marcus 2002a: 409–11; similar developed along the Nile, see Wengrow 2006a: 138–40.

198 Greenberg 2011: 237–39; Marcus 2002a: 410.

199 Frost 2004.

200 Sagona and Zimansky 2009: 199–200.

201 Wilkinson, T. J., 2003: 202–3; Yener 2000: 71–110.

202 Çevik 2007; Sagona and Zimansky 2009: 172–224.

203 Frangipane et al. 2001.

204 Antonova et al. 1996; Yener 2000: 68–70.

205 Kassianidou and Knapp 2005: 224; Pare 2000b.

206 On Iberia, Murillo-Barroso and Montero-Ruiz 2012.
207 Kassianidou and Knapp 2005: 220.
208 Ambert 1996; Broodbank 2000: 292–97; Chapman, R., 2008: 241–42; Pearce 2007: 54, 73–76.
209 Karimali 2005: 201–4.
210 Chapman, R., 2008: 247–48; Pearce 2007: 51–52.
211 Wengrow 2011.
212 Robb 2007: 286–329.
213 Lillios 2008a.
214 Broodbank 2000: 247–49; Robb 2007: 221–22.
215 Robb 1994.
216 Nakou 1995: 9–15.
217 Whitehouse 1992b.
218 Barfield 1998; Guilaine 1994: 342–49.
219 Barker 2005: 55–57.
220 Cauliez 2011; Guilaine et al. 1995; Vaquer 1998: 437–64.
221 Trément 1989: 444.
222 Mills 1984: 119–24.
223 Chapman, R., 1990: 118–24; Nowicki 2008; Finkelstein 1995.
224 Broodbank 2000: 41, 88–89, 150–55; Vigne 1994.
225 Broodbank 2000: 81–91, 175–210.
226 Chapman, R., 2003: 124–25.
227 Bradley, R., et al. 2001: 503–16; Chapman, R., 1990: 132, 190; Chippindale 1998; Menéndez Iglesias 2008.
228 Whitelaw 2000 on such erosional processes, at a slightly lower altitude.
229 Maggi and de Pascale 2011.
230 Blondel et al. 2010: 225–27.
231 Braudel 1972a: 85–94; Garnsey 1988.
232 Cherry 1988; Halstead 1996b, 2008.
233 Malone et al. 2003.
234 Valamoti 2004: 115.
235 Margaritis 2013.
236 McGovern 2003: 247–51, 254–57.
237 Holloway 1975: 79–80; compare Barker 2005.
238 Chapman, R., 2008: 241; Terral et al. 2004.
239 Garrido-Pena et al. 2011.
240 Chapman, R., 2003: 155–58 rejects earlier claims for southern Iberia.
241 Barker 2005: 57; Grove and Rackham 2001: 193.
242 Halstead 1996b.
243 Broodbank 2000: 83; Costa 2004: 100–2 for a brief discussion, where acorn-processing is raised as another possibility.
244 Halstead and Isaakidou 2011: 67–68; Harding 2000: 254–64.
245 Eiroa García 1987.
246 De Saulieu and Serres 2006; Harding 2000: 124–28; Pullen 1992; Robb 2007: 302.
247 Lomba Maraundi et al. 2009; for France see Chambon 2000.
248 Guilaine 2003: 257–60.
249 Chapman, R., 1990: 178–96; Guilaine 2003: 334–35.
250 Guilaine 1994: 215–17.
251 Guilaine 1994: 213–17.
252 Harding 2000: 100–3; Maran 2007: 8–9.

253 Cavanagh and Mee 1998: 15–22; Legarra Herrero 2009.
254 Sagona and Zimansky 2009: 212–13.
255 Pétrequin 1993 for elegant analysis of fluctuating northern and southern influences.
256 Delhon et al. 2009.
257 Halstead 2008.
258 Renfrew 1972.
259 Halstead 1988, 1989.
260 Robb 1999 for Italy.
261 Broodbank 2000: 211–46 for a Cycladic example.
262 Lillios 2008b: 235; Monks 1997: 22–25.
263 Keeley 1997: 83–97.
264 Monks 1997 for Iberia.
265 Chapman, R., 1990: 18–34, 220–67 on the paucity of external contacts; Schuhmacher 2004: 150–63 fails to persuade otherwise.
266 Maran 2007: 10–11; Primas 1996.
267 Malone et al. 1994: 188.
268 Holloway 1975.
269 Canet and Roudil 1978; Vaquer et al. 1995.
270 Mille and Carozza 2009.
271 Guilaine 1994: 165, 168–69.
272 Chapman, R., 2008 for a recent overview.
273 Castro et al. 1999; also Carrión et al. 2010.
274 Chapman, R., 1990: 75–79; 2003: 126–29; Micó Pérez 1995.
275 Clark, G., and Piggott 1965: 257; Whittle 1996: 293–96.
276 Chapman, R., 2008: 201–5, 218–19.
277 Chapman, R., 1990: 152; Molina González and Cámara Serrano 2010.
278 Monks 1997.
279 Chapman, R., 1990: 176–95.
280 Chapman, R., 2005; Renfrew 1994: 8.
281 Kunst 1995.
282 Chapman, R., 2003: 168–72; Díaz-del-Río 2004; Hurtado 1997.
283 Nocete et al. 2010.
284 Nocete et al. 2008: 717–32; cf. Costa Caramé et al. 2010 for a sceptical assessment.
285 Nocete 2006; Nocete et al. 2010.
286 Nocete et al. 2010.
287 Aubet 2001: 270.
288 Cherry 1983; Renfrew 1972; Schoep et al. (eds) 2012.
289 Rutter 2001: 108–24.
290 Sampson 1985.
291 Rutter 2001: 111–13.
292 Efe and Fidan 2008; Erkanal 2008; Ünlüsoy 2006.
293 Antonova et al. 1996; Bachhuber 2009.
294 Broodbank 2000: 211–46.
295 Broodbank 2000: 279–83; Broodbank and Kiriatzi 2007; Doumas and La Rosa (eds) 1997; Gauss 2010.
296 Broodbank 2000: 63–64.
297 Broodbank 2000: 262–72; Doumas 1977; Renfrew 1972: 417–39.
298 Broodbank 2000: 212–16, 242–44.
299 Broodbank 2000: 223–36, 259–60; Renfrew, Philaniotou et al. 2007; Renfrew, Doumas et al. (eds) 2007.
300 Broodbank 2007.

301 Branigan 1991.
302 Day and Doonan (eds) 2007.
303 Legarra Herrero 2009.
304 Whitelaw 2012.
305 Guilaine 1994: 320–21.
306 For instance, Johnson and Earle 2000: 134–35, 277–79.
307 Chapman, R., 2000.
308 De Saulieu 2007.
309 Robb 1999.
310 Blanton 1998; Feinman 2001.
311 Antonova et al. 1996; Ünlüsoy 2006.
312 Gilman 1981; Shennan 2002: 206–61.
313 Robb 1994.
314 For example, Gimbutas 1973; compare Renfrew 1987: 9–41, 75–98.
315 Anthony 2007: 39–150; contrast Renfrew 1987: 145–77.
316 Robb 1993.
317 Anthony 2007: 340–70; Robb 1993; Sherratt, A., and Sherratt 1988.
318 Morter and Robb 1998.
319 Brodie 2008.
320 Uerpmann 1990, 1995.
321 Anthony and Brown 2011; Outram et al. 2009.
322 Anthony 2007: 412–17; Benzel 2008: 155; Kelekna 2009: 41–66; Littauer and Crouwel 1979: 45–46.
323 Chapman, R., 1990: 134–38; Nocete et al. 2010: 3.
324 Manfredini (ed.) 2002.
325 Broodbank 2010b: 254–55.
326 Castagnino Berlinghieri 2003: 74–78; Papathanasopoulos 1990.
327 Broodbank 2000: 96–101; Soles 2012.
328 Televantou 2008.
329 Pace 2004: 73–75; Woolner 1957.
330 Broodbank 2000: 100–1.
331 McGrail 1993.
332 Drakidès et al. 2010: 94–95.
333 Broodbank 2000: 101–2, 258–62.
334 Broodbank 2010b: 253.
335 Broodbank 1989; 2000: 256–58.
336 Broodbank 1993; 2000: 258–62, 287–91; Rahmstorf 2010b.
337 Broodbank 2000: 87–90, 175–319.
338 Broodbank 2000: 95–96.
339 Leighton 1999: 98, 112.
340 Bover and Alcover 2003.
341 Ramis et al. 2002: 16.
342 Guerrero Ayuso 2001; Waldren 1982.
343 Alcover 2008; Ramis et al. 2002; Ramis 2010.
344 Alcover 2008: 65; Bellard 1995.
345 Alcover 2008.
346 Bevan and Conolly 2013; Kyrou 1990: 72–76; Stoddart 2000.
347 Forenbaher 2009b: 80–83.
348 Maran 2007: 9–10; Reinholdt 2008.
349 Wengrow 2010a: 33–41.
350 Batiuk and Mitchell 2007; several papers in Lyonnet (ed.) 2007; Philip 1999.
351 For earlier comments on the approximately synchronous nature of several of these networks, Maran 2007: 13 and Rahmstorf 2008.

352 Vander Linden 2006a.
353 On the last, Murillo-Barroso and Martinón-Torres 2012.
354 Chenery and Evans 2011; Heyd 2007; Price et al. 2004.
355 Lemercier 2004, 2012; Müller and van Willigen 2001; vander Linden 2006b.
356 Guilaine et al. 2001; Vaquer 1998: 462–65.
357 Bokbot 2005; Nicolis and Mottes (eds) 1998; Ramis 2010: 73–74; Tusa 1999.
358 Cunliffe 2001: 213–46.
359 Bokbot 2005; Cunliffe 2001: 230.
360 Harrison and Gilman 1977.
361 Stoddart 2000: 65–68.
362 Giardino 2000b.
363 Maran 2007: 13–14 and Rahmstorf 2008: 162–63, fig. 7, both also suggest possible slight extensions into the Aegean.
364 Bernardini et al. 2009; Cazzella 2003.
365 Maran 2007: 8–11.
366 Broodbank 2000: 276–319; Renfrew 1972: 451–55.
367 Agouridis 1997; Broodbank 2000: 287–91.
368 Broodbank 2000: 292–99; several papers in Day and Doonan (eds) 2007.
369 Broodbank 2000: 283–87; Cherry 2010: 116–20; for the Black Sea, Bauer 2011 and Chernykh 1992: 54–97, 140–71.
370 Broodbank 2000: 309–19; Efe 2007; Şahoğlu 2005.
371 Spencer 2010: 673–76, 669–81; slightly later, Rutter 1983: 335–43.
372 Zimmermann 2005.
373 Rahmstorf 2011: 107–10; Soles 2005.
374 Rahmstorf 2010a; 2011: 110–13.
375 Bevan 2007: 93–99; Peltenburg 1996: 20–21, fig. 2.
376 Politis 2001: 180, 184.
377 Nakou 1995: 19; Sherratt, S., 2007: 251–60.
378 Kassianidou and Knapp 2005: 224; Pare 2000b: 6–7.
379 Ross 1999: 246–47.
380 Kassianidou and Knapp 2005: 223–25; Pare 2000b.
381 Maran 2007: 12; Rahmstorf 2011: 104–6.
382 Yener 1995; 2000: 71–123.
383 Valamoti and Jones 2010.
384 Efe 2007; Şahoğlu 2005.
385 Bachhuber 2009; Wengrow 2011: 142.
386 My thanks to John-Vincent Gallagher for sharing the conclusions of his unpublished Oxford DPhil thesis (2008, especially pages 23–25 and 49–56).
387 Bevan 2004: 113–19.
388 Broodbank 2000: 317–18.
389 Broodbank 2000: 283–87; Sherratt, A., and Sherratt 1991: 367–68.
390 Robb 2001; 2007: 329–34.
391 Costa 2004: 139–43.
392 Guilaine 1994: 338–39; Tinè 1990.
393 Pace 2004; Skeates 2010, especially 157–207, 224–37.
394 Robb and van Hove 2003: 252; compare Malone 1999 and Renfrew 1973: 169–70.
395 Pace 2004: 44–92.
396 Malone and Stoddart 2009.
397 See several contributions to Cilia (ed.) 2004.
398 Malone et al. 1988.
399 Evans, J. D., 1973; Sahlins 1955.
400 Skeates 2010: 88–90; Trump 2004b.
401 Robb 2001; Skeates 2010: 104–7.
402 Broodbank 2000: 19–21; Robb 2001.
403 Grima 2004.
404 Robb 2001.
405 Peltenburg 1993.
406 Peltenburg 1991.
407 Malone, Stoddart and Cook 2009; Skeates 2010: 24–25, 108–15.
408 Pace 2004: 211–27; Skeates 2010: 109–10.
409 Richards et al. 2001.
410 Steel 2004: 106–18.
411 Summarized by Knapp 2008: 103–30.
412 Frankel 2000; Peltenburg 2007; Webb and Frankel 2007.
413 Knapp 2008: 74–78.
414 Webb et al. 2006.

CHAPTER EIGHT (pp. 345–444)

1 Sanmartí et al. 2012.
2 Braudel 2001: 181.
3 Rosen, A., 2007: 80–88, 99–101, 129–32; Staubwasser and Weiss 2006; Weiss et al. 1993.
4 Cullen, H. M., et al. 2000; Dalfes et al. 1997; Matthews 2002; Rambeau and Black 2011; Rosen, A., 2007: 88, 144.
5 Drysdale et al. 2006; Jalut et al. 2009; Finné et al. 2011 are more sceptical.
6 McAnany and Yoffee (eds) 2010; Schwartz and Nichols (eds) 2006; Yoffee 2005: 131–60.
7 Rosen, A., 2007: 144–49.
8 Morris, E., 2006; Seidlmayer 2000.
9 Adams, M. J., 2009: 175–94.
10 Ward, W. A., 1978.
11 Yoffee 2005: 142–44.
12 Cooper, L., 2006b.
13 Kuzucuoğlu and Marro (eds) 2007.
14 Akkermans and Schwartz 2003: 244–46; Yon 2006: 16; Doumet-Serhal 2006.
15 Lichtheim 1975.
16 Gophna and Portugali 1988: 16; Rosen, A., 2007: 142–43.
17 Akkermans and Schwartz 2003: 278, 288–91; Ilan 1995: 297, 300–1.
18 Broodbank 2000: 320–26; Weiberg 2007: 93–96, 100.
19 Chapman, R., 2003: 130–32; Nocete et al. 2010.
20 Guilaine 2003: 250–51; Webster 1996: 62.
21 Rosen, A., 2007: 143–45.
22 Dever 1995; Wilkinson, T. J., 2003: 169.
23 Maran 1998: 18–24, 277, 323–30, 369–72, 404–10, 445–46; 2007: 14–18; Kaiser and Forenbaher 1999; Tomas 2010: 190–92.
24 Borgna and Guida 2009; Maran 2007: 14–18.
25 Pace 2004: 68–71, 210–19; Cutajar et al. 2009 for Xaghra on Gozo.
26 Heurtley 1934–35: 24.
27 Cazzella et al. 2007.
28 Maran 2007: 16–17.
29 Tomas 2010.
30 Cherry 1984, 2010; Schoep et al. (eds) 2012; Whitelaw 2004.
31 Watrous 2001: 196–99.
32 Whitelaw 2012: 136–44, 150, table 4.1.
33 Manning 1994, 2008; Watrous 2001: 193–96.
34 Schoep 1999.
35 Broodbank 2010: 255–56; Wedde 2000: 331–33.
36 Efe 2007: 60.
37 Knapp 1994: 281, fig. 9.4; 2008: 76–77; Merrillees 2003; Watrous 2001: 197–98.
38 Bevan 2004; Legarra Herrero 2011; Watrous 1998.
39 Tufnell and Ward 1966; Wengrow 2010b: 151–56.
40 Legarra Herrero 2011; Wengrow 2010b.
41 Wilkinson, T. J., 2003: 207.
42 Trigger 2003: 123–25.
43 Bennet 2007: 184; Ilan 1995: 305.
44 Bennet 2007: 188–90; Sherratt, A., and Sherratt 1991: 365–67.
45 Liverani 2000: 18; Schloen 2001; Sherratt, A., and Sherratt 1991: 376.
46 Halstead 1994: 208–11; on debt see McGeough 2007: 337, 368–69.
47 Halstead 1992; Sherratt, A., and Sherratt 1991: 365–66, 385, fig. 1.
48 Bevan 2010a: 42–47; Halstead 1992; McGeough 2007.
49 Blue 1997; Raban 1991.
50 My thanks to Ezra Marcus for pointing out this last possibility.
51 Marriner 2009; Marriner et al. 2006: 1525; Monroe 2009: 90.
52 Bard et al. 2007; Fattovich 2005.
53 Shaw, J., 1990; Wachsmann 1998: 42–45.
54 Stager 2001; also Monroe 2011; on the duties certainly levied at this time by river-ports and terrestrial stations on the caravan trade, see Cooper, E. N., 1992.
55 Bevan 2010b; on such 'micro-states', see Wright, J. C., 2010a: 250–53.
56 For example, Keswani 1996; Fleming 2004 for wider discussion of collective governance; the case of Crete is further considered below.
57 Compare Ilan 1995: 306, fig. 6; Marcus 2002b: 250.
58 Morris, I., 2006: 80 estimates about 1 million people for the southern Aegean by mid-millennium, by which time Deltaic Egypt was approaching another million (Butzer 1976: 83, table 4); ranges of 140,000–200,000 are estimated for the southern Levant alone just before this time (Ilan 1995: 305), to which must be added the lusher, larger north and the Mediterranean fringes of Anatolia. As discussed later, densities in the remaining expanses of the centre and west were little changed from the previous millennium, and the rest of North Africa remained apparently thinly populated.
59 For Minoan Crete, Branigan 2001b; Broodbank 2004: 77–81 for a remarkable spike on the island of Kythera.
60 Killebrew 2005: 93–96.

61 Sherratt, S., 2005: 25–30.
62 Callender 2000; Morris, E., 2006.
63 Altenmüller and Moussa 1991; Marcus 2007.
64 Bisson de la Roque *et al.* 1953; Pierrat-Bonnefois 2008: 65–66.
65 Butzer 2002: 92; Trigger 2003: 297.
66 El Beialy *et al.* 2001.
67 Baines 1996: 375–76; Butzer 1976: 83, table 4, estimates already 750,000 by 1800 BC.
68 Kemp 2006: 126–28; for forts, 25–26, 231–41.
69 Cited in Arnold 2010: 184.
70 Baines 1996: 376; Bietak 1996: 10–48; Sparks 2004.
71 Oren 1997b: 273–79; Sparks 2004: 29–33.
72 Bietak 1996, 2009, 2010.
73 Bietak 1996: 22–26, 36, 40; 2009; 2010: 153–56, 159.
74 Bietak 1996: 26–29, 59, 63; Maguire 2009.
75 Akkermans and Schwartz 2003: 288–326; Ilan 1995; Kempinski 1992.
76 Ilan 1995: 297.
77 Kemp 2006: 21; Philip 1989; Wengrow 2010b: 153–54.
78 Akkermans and Schwartz 2003: 290, 305, 318–19; Ilan 1995: 301.
79 Akkermans and Schwartz 2003: 301–2; Ilan 1995: 313–14.
80 Jidejian 1968: 35–39; Magness-Gardiner and Falconer 1994.
81 Ilan 1995: 301–5.
82 Kempinski 1992: 159–61, 171.
83 Marcus 2002b; Stager 2002.
84 Artzy 1995.
85 Ilan 1995: 306–8.
86 Ilan 1995: 308; Marcus 2002b.
87 Finkelstein 1995: 360–61; Ilan 1995: 304–5.
88 Falconer and Fall 2006.
89 For slightly later container production in this corridor, see Bourriau, A., *et al.* 2001.
90 Marcus 2007: 167–69.
91 Akkermans and Schwartz 2003: 306.
92 Akkermans and Schwartz 2003: 298–305; Gonnella *et al.* 2005; Feldman 2007 for the regeneration of the north more generally.
93 Woolley 1955; Yener 2007: 153–54.
94 Nichols and Weber 2006.
95 Akkermans and Schwartz 2003: 313–16 for an overview; Dalley 1984; Parrot 1958.
96 Malamat 1998: 45–47.
97 Sasson 2008: 95, 99–100.
98 Dalley 1984.
99 Cooper, E. N., 1992.
100 Joannès 1991.
101 Cline 2009: 126.
102 Cline 2009: 32; Sherratt, A., and Sherratt 1998: 339.
103 Sagona and Zimansky 2009: 225–44.
104 Bryce 2005: 27–30; Larsen 1987; Veenhof 1972; Dercksen 2004 on Assur.
105 Weisgerber and Cierny 2002.
106 Hallo 1992.
107 Bryce 2005: 41–95; Yoffee 2010: 184–87.
108 Weeks 2003.
109 Knapp (ed.) 1996: 3–11, 17–19; Merrillees 1984.
110 Knapp 2003.

111 Knapp 2008: 76–78.
112 Knapp 2008: 144–50, 186–99, 250.
113 Crewe 2007.
114 Knapp 2008: 133, 159–60; Maguire 2009; Ferrara 2012.
115 Bevan 2010b; Driessen, J., *et al.* (eds) 2002; Graham 1987.
116 Driessen, J., *et al.* (eds) 2002; Hägg and Marinatos (eds) 1987.
117 Adams, E., 2004; Bevan 2010b; Cadogan *et al.* (eds) 2004; Wiener 2007a.
118 Betancourt 2007.
119 Branigan 2001b; Whitelaw 2001; 2012: 150, table 4.1.
120 Branigan 2001b: 45–48; Driessen, J., 2010; Morris, I., 2007: 226–29: Whitelaw 2001: 17–21.
121 McEnroe 2010: 69–77; on the central court's capacity, Gesell 1987: 125–26.
122 Driessen, J., 2002, 2012.
123 Adams, E., 2006; Hamilakis 2002.
124 Broodbank 2004; Knappett and Nikolakopoulou 2005.
125 For example, Davis and Gorogianni 2008; Wiener 1990.
126 Aruz 2009; Kilian-Dirlmeier 1997.
127 Wright, J. C., 2010b.
128 Graziadio 1998; Sherratt, A., 1987.
129 Dickinson 1997; Karo 1930–33; Voutsaki 1998, 1999.
130 Bennet 2004: 96–98; Maran 2011.
131 Doumas 1983; for partial updates, Doumas 1992; Palyvou 2005.
132 Friedrich 2000; Oppenheimer and Pyle 2009: 460; Papadopoulos, G., 2009: 499–501.
133 Driessen, J., and MacDonald 1997, 2000.
134 Friedrich *et al.* 2006; Warburton (ed.) 2009; exhaustively up to the late 1990s, Manning 1999.
135 Balter 2006; Pearson *et al.* 2009.
136 Bonn-Muller 2010.
137 Goedicke 2000.
138 Morgan, L., 1988: 121–46, 150–54, 159–65; Wachsmann 1998: 86–99.
139 Bowen 1960; Roberts, O. T. P., 1987.
140 Wachsmann 1998: 241–43.
141 Monroe 2007.
142 Parkinson, R. B., 1997.
143 Marcus 2007.
144 Braudel 1972a: 123.
145 Broodbank 2000: 341–47; Marcus 2006: 188.
146 Marcus 2007: 145–46, fn. 23.
147 Wachsmann 1998: 297–99.
148 Odyssey XIV: 252–58.
149 Manning and Hulin 2005: 278; Morgan, L., 1988: 146–50; Morris, S., 1992: 92–94.
150 Knapp 1998.
151 Bevan 2007: 19–26.
152 Brysbaert 2008: 189–95; Cutler 2012; Moorey 2001: 11–12.
153 Moorey 2001: 11.
154 Ferrara 2012; Finkelberg 1998.
155 Bietak 1996: 35.
156 Bietak 1996: 35–36; see also Scheidel 2007: 62.

157 For thoughtful analyses of the problems, see Sherratt, A., and Sherratt 1991; recently also Bevan 2010a; Manning and Hulin 2005.
158 Cline 2009; on Tawaret, see Weingarten 1991.
159 Bevan 2010a: 48–57.
160 Hauptmann *et al.* 1999: 2–5.
161 Barker, Adams *et al.* 2007: 269–70; Bassiakos and Tselios 2012.
162 Bevan 2010a: 51–54; Gale, N. H., 1991b.
163 For last point, Bell 2012: 182.
164 Gale, N. H., 2001: 119.
165 Cierny and Weisgerber 2003.
166 Kassianidou and Knapp 2005: 233–36; Knapp *et al.* (eds) 1998; Shennan 1999 for temperate Europe.
167 Bevan 2007: 34.
168 Barber 1991; Bevan 2010a: 57–61.
169 Schneider, J., 2011: 299–301.
170 Barber 1998: 17.
171 Barber 1991: 311, 338–51; 1998.
172 Schneider, J., 2011: 296–98; also Burke 1999: 79–81.
173 James *et al.* 2009; Reifarth and Baccelli 2009.
174 Burke 1999.
175 Panagiotakopulu 2000.
176 Good 2011.
177 Knapp 1991; Bevan 2007: 115 for rock-crystal lump.
178 Asouti 2003.
179 Doumas 1992; on animals in Neopalatial Crete see also Shapland 2010.
180 Kislev *et al.* 1993.
181 Bevan 2007 extensively; 2010a: 62; Serpico 2004.
182 Bevan 2010a: 61–72; Sherratt, A., 1995b: 17–20; 1999; also Horden and Purcell 2000: 259–60.
183 McGovern 2003: 102–3, 118–19, 170, 181.
184 Serpico 2004.
185 Kelder 2009: 343–44; Newton *et al.* 2006.
186 Bourriau, A., *et al.* 2001; Sherratt, A, and Sherratt 1991: 362–63.
187 Marcus 2002a: 410.
188 Grace 1956; Bevan in preparation.
189 Bushnell 2012; Maguire 2009.
190 Manning and Hulin 2005: 286; Steel 2004: 154, 161–64.
191 Haskell 1985.
192 Nakou 2007 for slightly earlier beginnings; Vickers and Gill 1994 for the overall principle.
193 Merrillees 2003; see Marcus 2007: 162–64 for plainer Cretan exported products.
194 Barrett, C. E., 2009.
195 Braudel 2001: 256 already recognized this; more recently, Sherratt, S., 2010a: 95.
196 Morris, S., 1992: 93–94.
197 Bevan 2003; Wengrow 2010b: 146.
198 Anthony 2007: 65–75; compare Renfrew 1972: 355–56.
199 Steel 2004: 132.
200 Bevan 2007.
201 For example, Pare 2000b: 8 for tin; Newton *et al.* 2006: 406–7 for olives; Barber 1991: 83 for the horizontal ground-loom.

202 Moorey 2001: 8.
203 Anthony 2007: 397–405; Littauer and Crouwel 1979: 50–55.
204 Shaw, I., 2001: 65.
205 Oren (ed.) 1997a; Redmount 1995: 63–66.
206 Bietak 1996: 7; estimates for slightly larger upriver cities at Thebes and Amarna vary from 30,000 to 50,000 people (Yoffee 2005: 43, table 3.1).
207 Bourriau, J., 2000: 195–203.
208 Ben-Tor, D., 2007: 190–93.
209 Akkermans and Schwartz 2003: 324; Bietak 1997: 114; Bourriau, J., 2000: 208–10 on Kush.
210 Bourriau, J., 2000: 201.
211 Bietak 2008: 110 for Nubian soldiers.
212 Bietak 2008: 112; Marcus 2006.
213 Redford 1997: 14.
214 Bietak 1996: 20; Stager 2002: 361.
215 Redmount 1995.
216 Hassan 1997: 56 for an overall Egyptian population during the later 2nd millennium BC of 2.1 million.
217 Redford 1997: 14.
218 Bourriau, J., 2000: 207.
219 Baines 1996; Kemp 2006: 34–36.
220 Variously, Bourriau, J., 2004; Newton et al. 2006; Sparks 2004: 42–43.
221 Bietak 2005.
222 Kemp 2006: 40–41.
223 McGovern 2003: 120–23, 140.
224 Tallet 1998.
225 Bourriau, J., 2000: 215; Bryan 2000: 218.
226 Bryan 2000: 234, 245–47.
227 Akkermans and Schwartz 2003: 354.
228 Glatz 2009.
229 Akkermans and Schwartz 2003: 327–29, 346–48.
230 Bietak et al. 2007.
231 Feldman 2007.
232 Collon 1994.
233 Feldman 2007: 59; Knapp 1998: 198–202.
234 Feldman 2006.
235 Heltzer 1978: 102, 108–11; Kassianidou 2003.
236 Braudel 2001: 121; van de Mieroop 2007: 170–74.
237 Discussed in Feldman 2006: 118–19.
238 Callot 1987.
239 McGovern 2009: 178-79.
240 For example, Wright, J. C., 2004.
241 Serpico 2004.
242 Bisset et al. 1996; Merrillees 1962; Knapp 1991: 25–26; Mitchell 2005: 78–79; Sherratt, A., 1995b: 15–17 for the inappropriateness of the term 'drug'.
243 Krzyzskowska 1990: 16–18.
244 Caubet and Poplin 1987.
245 Bevan 2010a: 67–68; Eriksson 1991; Knappett et al. 2005.
246 Akkermans and Schwartz 2003: 331–33; Shortland et al. 2006.
247 Shortland 2012; Foster, K. P., 2008.
248 Akkermans and Schwartz 2003: 335–40; Calvet 2007; Calvet and Castel 2004; McGeough 2007; much of Monroe 2009; Schloen 2001; Yon 2006.

249 Calvet 2007: 101–3; Yon 2006: 9–14.
250 McGeough 2007: 191–93, 273–96, 311–22; Schloen 2001: 335.
251 Margueron 2008; Monroe 2009.
252 Knapp 1991: 36.
253 Singer 1999: 715–19.
254 Feldman 2006: 63–64; Schaeffer 1939: 30–32; Yon 2006: 8, 143.
255 Akkermans and Schwartz 2003: 340–41; Bounni et al. 1998.
256 Monroe 2009.
257 Monroe 2007.
258 Needham 2009 on 'maritories'; Knapp 1993 against Bronze Age thalassocracies; Malamat 1998: 48–49 on the Ugaritic sea god.
259 Bell 2012; Monroe 2009.
260 Cline 2009: 120–21; Monroe 2009: 164–67.
261 Bell 2012; Monroe 2009.
262 Bell 2012: 182–83; Bevan 2007: 149–50, 178–79; Courtois 1990; Yon 2006: 51–54.
263 Bell 2012: 183–84; Calvet 2000.
264 Bell 2012: 184, table 19.1.
265 Bryce 2002: 88–90; Monroe 2009: 175–78.
266 Monroe 2009: 203, 216–21.
267 Monroe 2009: 192–96.
268 Bickel 1998; Kemp 2006: 302–35; Monroe 2009: 181–92; Zingarelli 2010.
269 Kemp 2006: 324–26; Monroe 2009: 214–15; Zingarelli 2010: 39.
270 Monroe 2009: 196–99.
271 Moran 1992.
272 Cohen and Westbrook (eds) 2000; Feldman 2006; Liverani 2001.
273 Liverani 2000.
274 Moran 1992: 12–16, EA 7.
275 Feldman 2006: 68–70.
276 Meier 2007; van de Mieroop 2007: 215–21.
277 Feldman 2006.
278 Liverani 2000: 23–25.
279 Feldman 2006: 111; Liverani 2001: 141–95; Panagiotopoulos 2001: 27–72.
280 Moran 1992: 1–5, 8–10, EA 1, EA 4; discussed in Feldman 2006: 20, 174.
281 Moran 1992: 160–62, 188–90, 236–37, EA 88, EA 114, EA 149.
282 Moran 1992: 120–21, EA 49.
283 Knapp 2008: 307–16; Moran 1992: 104–13, EA 33–40.
284 Moran 1993: 103, EA 32; discussed in Feldman 2006: 130, 140, 149–51.
285 Feldman 2006: 17.
286 Feldman 2006.
287 Feldman 2002.
288 Pulak 1998; 2008a: 289–310; Yalçın et al. (eds) 2005; cargo summarized usefully in Monroe 2009: 10–12.
289 Pulak 1999.
290 Monroe 2010.
291 In a later context, see Horden and Purcell 2000: 368–70, 612–15, table 7.
292 A similar function as drinking-water reservoirs may explain earlier terrestrial finds, from the first half of the 2nd millennium BC, of massive Egyptian pottery containers offloaded at Sidon; see Doumet-Serhal 2008: 58.

293 Monroe 2009: 39–63 for wider discussion.
294 Monroe 2009: 13–15; 2011: 91–95.
295 Pulak 2008b.
296 Cucchi 2008.
297 Bachhuber 2006; Pulak 2005; 2008a: 299–304.
298 Bass, G. F., 1991: 70.
299 Wachsmann 1998: 10–11.
300 Monroe 2009: 14–15; Pulak 1998: 220.
301 White (ed.) 2002; White and White 1996.
302 For instance, Sakellarakis, Y., 1990.
303 Panagiotopoulos 2001; Wachsmann 1987: 27–77.
304 Habu 2010: 159.
305 Cline 2009: 111–20; Haider 2001.
306 Burns 2010: 20–25; Cline 1998.
307 Bates 1927: 137–40; White (ed.) 2002.
308 Curtin 1984: 12–13 for discussion of this.
309 Barjomovic 2012: 12–37; from a comparative perspective, d'Altroy 2001 and Smith, M., 2001.
310 Sherratt, A., and Sherratt 1991: 361, 386, fig. 2; on this campaign, Bryan 2000: 245–46.
311 Bryce 2005: 230–33.
312 Glatz 2009, 2013.
313 Gonen 1992; Heinz (ed.) 2010.
314 Wachsmann 1998: 10.
315 Bunimovitz 1995; Gonen 1992.
316 Akkermans and Schwartz 2003: 333–34; Liverani 2005: 24–29.
317 Moran 1992: 307.
318 Akkermans and Schwartz 2003: 334; Biran 1993; Pfälzner 2009; Richter 2009.
319 Akkermans and Schwartz 2003: 333; Gonen 1992: 236–40, 247–49.
320 Gonen 1992: 249–51; Kempinski 1992: 199; Pitard 1999.
321 Knapp 2008: 131–280.
322 Knapp 2008: 331–32.
323 Knapp 2008: 335–41; on the tablets, Goren et al. 2004.
324 Knapp 2008: 324.
325 Knapp 2008: 324–41, though with differing conclusions.
326 Keswani 1996.
327 Knapp 1986; 2008: 159–73; Steel 2004: 158–71.
328 Knapp 1986; 2008: 138–41; Webb and Frankel 1994.
329 Ferrara 2012: 132–45.
330 Bevan 2010a: 55–56.
331 Bevan 2010a: 53–54; Hirschfeld 1993: 312–13; Kassianidou 2003.
332 Sherratt, S., 2003a: 42, mainly on the ensuing centuries.
333 Mee 1982; Sherratt, S., 2010a: 89–91.
334 Platon 1971: 59–66, 115–221.
335 Preston 2008: 311–12.
336 Bennet 1985.
337 Chadwick 1992.
338 Preston 2008.
339 Shaw, J., 2006: 16–39.
340 Rutter 1999, 2004.
341 Shelmerdine 2001; Voutsaki and Killen (eds) 2001.
342 Tartaron 2010: 175–79.

343 Maran 2011; Sherratt, S., 2001.

344 Bennet 2007: 181–82.

345 Bennet 2007: 192–201; Halstead 1992.

346 Cline 2009: 128–31.

347 Sherratt, S., 2001.

348 Ventris and Chadwick 1973: 332–48;
     Krzyzskowska 1996.

349 Leonard 1994; Sherratt, S., 1999; van
     Wijngaarden 2002.

350 Vermeule and Karageorghis 1982.

351 Bell 2006: 30–60; Manning and Hulin 2005:
     282–85; van Wijngaarden 2002.

352 Steel 2002.

353 Manning and Hulin 2005: 284; Sherratt, S.,
     1999; van Wijngaaarden 2002: 125–202.

354 Bryce 2005: 123–26, 129–38, 193–97; 2006:
     73–74, 107–8; Glatz 2009: 137–38.

355 Singer 2008; Bryce 2006: 101–2.

356 Bryce 2005: 147–48, 193–97; 2006: 78,
     83–84.

357 Bryce 2006: 100–6.

358 Niemeier 2005: 203; Bryce 2006: 83.

359 Bryce 2006.

360 Becks 2006; Jablonka 2006; Pavuk 2005:
     271–72.

361 Günel 1999; Hawkins 1998; Mee 1998;
     Mountjoy 1998.

362 Bryce 2005: 54–55.

363 Moran 1992: 111–12, EA 38.

364 Davis and Bennet 1991.

365 Halstead 1994: 200.

366 Andreou et al. 2001: 299–304;
     Margomenou 2009.

367 Jones, G., 1987: 118–22; Jones et al. 1986.

368 Kiriatzi et al. 1997.

369 Van Wijngaarden 2002.

370 Bevan 2010a; Manning and Hulin 2005:
     282–91; Shaw, B., 2001 for the extension of
     these conditions into later times.

371 Bevan 2010a: 45; Zaccagnini 2000: 147.

372 Sherratt, A., and Sherratt 2001: 23; also
     Shennan 2002: 165–68.

373 Manning and Hulin 2005: 282.

374 Monroe 2009: 151–205, 284–87, 290–92.

375 Bevan 2007: 135

376 Bevan 2004: 37; Feldman 2006; Monroe
     2009: 281–83.

377 Sherratt, S., 2010a.

378 Sherratt, S., 1999; 2010a.

379 Pare 2000b.

380 Webster 1996: 97; compare Rowland 2001:
     40–41.

381 Whitelaw 2012: 150, table 4.1; see also
     Branigan 2001b: 46–48.

382 For the southern Levant, Ilan 1995: 305.

383 Baines 1983: 584 on literacy.

384 Barker 2005: 65; Chapman, R., 2003:
     156–57.

385 Rottoli and Pessina 2007: 149 for the
     botanical evidence.

386 Chapman, R., 1990: 122.

387 Broodbank 2010b: 255–58; for the Filicudi
     find, Martinelli et al. 2010: 308–12.

388 Guilaine 2003: 253–67, 306–7; Sherratt, A.,
     1990: 148 for the idea of a 'neo-megalithic'
     in a northwest European context.

389 Despite Iberian claims, based on Marxist

390 definitions of the state; discussed in
     Chapman, R., 2003: 59–64, 95–99, 159–63.
     For a critical appraisal, Gilman 2013.

390 Montero Ruiz 1993; Rovira and Montero
     2003.

391 Chapman, R., 1990: 163–65.

392 Chapman, R., 1990: 33–34; Harrison and
     Gilman 1977; Schuhmacher 2004, but with
     some caution.

393 Costa Caramé et al 2010: 92; Martín de la
     Cruz 2008: 290.

394 Aubet 2001: 201–4; Martín de la Cruz 2008:
     291–92.

395 Chapman, R., 2003: 131–58; 2008: 205–10;
     Lull et al. 2010.

396 Castro et al. 1999; Gilman and Thornes
     1985.

397 Aranda Jiménez and Molina 2006; Lull
     et al. 2010.

398 Castro et al. 1999.

399 Aranda Jiménez and Esquivel Guerrero
     2006, 2007.

400 Lull 2000: 590.

401 Chapman, R., 2003: 139–42; Murillo-
     Barroso and Montero-Ruiz 2012: 66–67.

402 Castro et al. 1999: 853–55.

403 Risch 2002.

404 Castro et al. 1999; Chapman, R., 2003:
     135, 137.

405 Gilman 1991 for a classic early discussion.

406 Lull et al. 2010: 18.

407 Castro et al. 2000.

408 Chapman, R., 2003: 116.

409 Chapman, R., 2008: 22–35; Gilman et al.
     1997; Martín et al. 1993.

410 Lillios 1997.

411 Chapman, R., 2008: 243–46; Nocete et al.
     2010; Sanjuán 1999.

412 Lull et al. 2002; Ramis 2010: 72–76.

413 Bellard 1995; Fernández-Miranda 1997:
     60–62.

414 Ramis 2010: 76.

415 Berger et al. 2007; Vital 2008.

416 Gascó 1994: 118.

417 Mille and Carozza 2009: 156–59, 168.

418 Costa 2004: 112–18, 139–43, 167–68.

419 Webster 1996: 85–107; Blake 1998.

420 Webster 1996: 62–84; Demurtas and
     Demurtas 1992.

421 Webster 1996, 87–98; 2001: 1, 4.

422 Blake 2001.

423 Skeates 2012: 175–79.

424 Webster 1996: 96–100.

425 Barfield 1994; Bietti Sestieri 2010: 210–78.

426 Bietti Sestieri 2010: 21–63; Pearce 2007:
     87–107.

427 Sherratt, A., 1987; 1993: 24–29.

428 Bietti Sestieri 2010: 21–26, 51, fig. 22.

429 Harding 2000: 132 for gnocchi.

430 Bernabò Brea 2011.

431 Bernabò Brea et al. (eds) 1997; Bietti
     Sestieri 2010: 63–78; Pearce 1998;
     Provenzano 2008.

432 Borgna and Guida 2009.

433 Hänsel 2007; Tomas 2010: 194–97.

434 Chapman, J., et al. 1996: 67–73, 130–33,
     220–27.

435 Barker 2005: 59–60; Bietti Sestieri 2010:
     79–169.

436 Cornell 1995: 48.

437 Albore Livadie 2002, 2008.

438 Barker 1995: 132–58.

439 Tafuri 2005.

440 Cazzella and Recchia 2008; Malone et al.
     1994: 171, 188–89.

441 Bietti Sestieri 2010: 106–26, 138–69;
     Skeates 2005b: 160–64, 170–72.

442 Bietti Sestieri 2010: 112–13, 122–23,
     138–43; Cazzella and Moscoloni 1999;
     Guglielmino 2004–6.

443 Bietti Sestieri 2010: 140–49, 163–65; Peroni
     2000; Vianello 2005 108–10, 150–53.

444 Leighton 1999: 113–86.

445 Leighton 1999: 150–54, 162–67; compare
     Bennet and Shelmerdine 2001 for Pylos.

446 Giardino and Pepe 2005; Leighton 1999:
     132–38, 157–62; Rizio 2005.

447 Castagnino Berlinghieri 2003: 74–78.

448 Martinelli (ed.) 2005.

449 Marazzi and Tusa 2005.

450 Holloway and Lukesh 1995.

451 Marazzi and Tusa 2005.

452 Guilaine 1994: 263–66; Sanmartí et al.
     2012: 23.

453 Pace 2004: 219–27.

454 Trump 2004a.

455 Doonan 2001; Leighton 1999: 157–62.

456 Tanasi and Vella (eds) 2011.

457 Blake 2008; Cazzella and Recchia 2009;
     Vagnetti 1999; Vianello 2005.

458 Harding 1984; Kristiansen and Larsen
     2005: 108–250; Sherratt, A., 1993.

459 Extensive discussion in Harding 2000.

460 Rahmstorf 2010b: 686–88.

461 Harding 1984: 68–87; 2007.

462 Harding 1984; Sherratt, A., 1993: 30–38; for
     Sicilian Leighton 1999: 104.

463 Harding 1984: 74–82; Sherratt, A., and
     Sherratt 2001: 19 for Tutankhamun.

464 Bennet 2004: 97.

465 Sherratt, A., 1987; 1993: 26–29.

466 Kristiansen and Larsen 2005: 184, fig. 79;
     Valamoti 2007: 286–88.

467 Sherratt, A., and Sherratt 2001: 26–27.

468 Özbaşaran 1995.

469 Sherratt, A., 1993.

470 Kassianidou 2003; Pare 2000b.

471 Kristianen and Larsen 2005: 132–38; Pare
     2000b: 29; Shennan 1993; Treherne 1995;
     Wengrow 2011: 137–39.

472 Discussed in Harding 2000: 211–12;
     Shennan 1995: 300–8.

473 Bryan 2000: 252 for Amenhotep II's claim.

474 Sherratt, A., and Sherratt 2001: 19.

475 Pare 2000b: 8.

476 Braudel 1972a: 203; Casson 1971: 270–96
     for a general discussion.

477 Sherratt, A., 1993, especially figs 6 and 12.

478 Cazzella and Recchia 2009: 29–32; Jones,
     R. E., and Vagnetti 1991; Jones, R. E., et al.
     2005; Vagnetti 1999.

479 Tartaron 2004.

480 Cazzella and Recchia 2009: 35–36.

481 Cazzella and Recchia 2009: 32–36;

Guglielmino 2004–6: 93; Vianello 2005: 52–53, 55–58.

482 Blake 2008: 9–21; van Wijngaarden 2002: 203–73; Vianello 2005.

483 Blake 2008: 10; Pace 2004: 211–12.

484 Guilaine 1994: 237–38.

485 Webster 1996: 103.

486 Alberti 2005.

487 Leighton 1999: 150–52.

488 Jones, R. E., et al. 2005.

489 Peroni 2000; Vagnetti 1999: 142–49; Cazzella and Recchia 2009: 27–28 suggest a possible earlier 2nd-millennium BC start to olive and murex exploitation, but the evidence is slender.

CHAPTER NINE (pp. 445–505)

1 Galán 2005: 134–73; see also Baines 1999.

2 Raban 1998: 428–30.

3 Akkermans and Schwartz 2003: 360–61; Markoe 2000: 110.

4 For a range of views on these changes: Gitin et al. (eds) 1998; Ward, W. A., and Joukowsky (eds) 1992. On the coming of the age of iron, see Stig Sørensen and Thomas (eds) 1989; Wertime and Muhly (eds) 1980.

5 Bell 2006: 99–100, 110; Sherratt, S., 2003b: 50–51.

6 Aubet 2001: 1–17; Sherratt, S., 2005: 35–36.

7 Aubet 2001: 29–31.

8 Akkermans and Schwartz 2003: 358–59, 361.

9 Bell 2006: 108–9; Singer 1999: 704–31.

10 Knapp 2008: 131–372; Sherratt, S., 2003b: 42–53.

11 Knapp 1986.

12 Knapp 2008: 331–32.

13 Iacovou 2005a.

14 Sherratt, S., 2003b: 42–51; on Nile perch, Reese 2008: 196.

15 Iacovou 2005b; Knapp 2009: 249–97.

16 Knapp 2008: 321–22.

17 Hirschfeld 1996.

18 Several papers in Bonfante and Karageorghis (eds) 2001; Sherratt, S., 2003b: 42–43, 51; Vagnetti and Lo Schiavo 1989.

19 Karageorghis (ed.) 1994; Sherratt, S., 2003b: 51–53.

20 Muhly 2006; Sherratt, S., 1994.

21 Khakhutaishvili 2009, though the earliest production here is still fuzzily dated.

22 Sherratt, S., 1994.

23 Childe 1942: 183, drawing on the work of Engels.

24 Hasel 1998; Killebrew 2005: 51–92.

25 Dever 1992.

26 Killebrew 2005: 154–55; Zuckerman 2009.

27 Compare Killebrew 2005: 197–245 and Yasur-Landau 2010 with Bauer 1998 and Sherratt, S., 1998; 2005: 32–35.

28 Yasur-Landau 2010: 282–87, 289–94, 307–8, 312–13.

29 Finkelstein 2007a, 2007b (summarizing a lifetime's publications); Finkelstein and Silberman 2001: 27–122; Liverani 2005: 52–76; Mazar 2007a, 2007b for an alternative

perspective and Killebrew 2005: 149–96 for potential ways forward.

30 Finkelstein 1995.

31 Yasur-Landau 2010: 296.

32 Finkelstein 2007b: 77–78; Wengrow 1996.

33 Barako 2000: 513–30; Bauer 1998; Sherratt, S., 2003b: 44–49.

34 Gonen 1992: 247; Rothenberg 1972: 63–111.

35 Levy and Najjar 2006.

36 Mazar 2007b: 97.

37 Artzy 1994; Sherratt, S., 2003b: 48–49.

38 Artzy 1994: 134–35; Bell 2006: 212–13.

39 Van de Mieroop 2011: 240–82.

40 On the last, Kemp 2006: 313–15.

41 Janssen 1975: 551–58.

42 Van de Mieroop 2011: 213–39.

43 Bryce 2005: 234–41; van de Mieroop 2007: 36–40, 129–30.

44 Edel 1997.

45 Bickel 1998.

46 Bietak 2010: 169.

47 Pusch and Herold 1999; van de Mieroop 2007: 73–74, 178–79, 218.

48 Rehren et al. 2001; Shortland 2012: 169–73.

49 Bietak 2010; van de Mieroop 2007: 216–18.

50 Van de Mieroop 2011: 145–46.

51 Morris, S., 1998: 285.

52 Schofield and Parkinson 1994.

53 O'Connor, D., 1972: 689–96, fig. 3; elaborated in Kemp 2006: 31–32, fig. 8.

54 Leahy (ed.) 1990.

55 For contrasting interpretations, O'Connor, D., 1990 and Ritner 2009.

56 Di Lernia and Merighi 2006; Mattingly et al. 2003: 342–48.

57 Wachsmann 1998: 203–4.

58 Snape 2003: 100–5; Snape and Wilson 2007.

59 Bryce 2005: 45–46, 221–325.

60 Glatz and Matthews 2005.

61 Seeher 2001.

62 Akkermans and Schwartz 2003: 348–50; van de Mieroop 2004: 169–74.

63 Bryce 2005: 343–44; Harmanşah 2011.

64 Akkermans and Schwartz 2003: 366–77; Sagona and Zimansky 2009: 291–315.

65 Bryce 2005: 348; Postgate and Thomas (eds) 2007.

66 Aubet 2001: 30; van de Mieroop 2004: 169–74; Yoffee 2010: 188–89.

67 Cohen and Westbrook (eds) 2000: 235.

68 Liverani 2000: 22.

69 Akkermans and Schwartz 2003: 348–51; compare Glatz 2009.

70 Dickinson 2006: 24–78; Morris, I., 2006; for a spectrum of recent ideas, Deger-Jalkotzy and Lemos (eds) 2006.

71 Morris, S., 1992: 101–49, and more generally.

72 Wallace 2010: 49–166.

73 Phillips, J., 2005; Rutter 1992; Sherratt, S., 2001: 219–24.

74 Maran 2006; Sherratt, S., 2001.

75 Sherratt, S., 1990; Wiener 2007b: 21–26.

76 Korfmann (ed.) 2006 for multiple perspectives on later 2nd-millennium BC Troy.

77 Dickinson 2006: 73, 178–83; Sherratt, S., 2000.

78 Morris, I., 2007: 213–31; on external contacts, Kourou 2009.

79 Zangger et al. 1997.

80 Morris, I., 2007: 220–26.

81 Divon 2008; Singer 1999: 715–19.

82 Knapp 2009 for a recent succinct survey.

83 Sandars 1978 is the foundational text; also Dothan and Dothan 1992, Oren (ed.) 2000 and most recently Yasur-Landau 2010.

84 Breasted 1906: 33–49, sections 59–82.

85 Singer 1999: 719–25.

86 Dothan and Dothan 1992; Oren (ed.) 2000; Sandars 1978.

87 Yasur-Landau 2010: 34–193 for one recent effort to do so.

88 Sherratt, S., 1998: 307.

89 Morris, I., 2010: 215–20, for whom it reflects the first substantial narrowing of the developmental gap between the western and eastern ends of Eurasia.

90 Wallace 2010: 54–68.

91 Drews 1993: 135–225, without necessarily the wider explanatory inference; Sherratt, S., 1990: 810–12, 819–20.

92 Bryce 2002: 259.

93 Bryce 2005: 224–26, 290–93.

94 Iacono 2012; Jung 2009; Sherratt, S., 2000.

95 Recently, Boileau et al. 2010.

96 Anthony and Brown 2011: 154–56.

97 On fodder crops, Blondel et al. 2010: 209–10.

98 Wachsmann 1998: 123–212.

99 Palaima 1991: 284.

100 Artzy 1997: 5.

101 Bryce 2005: 335.

102 Roberts, O. T. P., 1991; Wachsmann 1998: 251–54; my thanks to John-Vincent Gallagher for sharing the conclusions of his unpublished Oxford DPhil thesis (2008, especially page 192 for the first Aegean evidence).

103 As illustrated by Wachsmann 1998: 166–73, 179–81.

104 Wachsmann 1998: 130–58; Wedde 1991, 2005.

105 Further on new fighting ships, Artzy 1988.

106 Bass, G. F., 1967; 2010.

107 Phelps et al. (eds) 1999; Ward, C. A., 2010: 157.

108 Aubet 2001: 168–70; Pryor 1988: 14, fig. 2, 91–95 for the medieval Mediterranean.

109 Vagnetti and Lo Schiavo 1989; Sherratt, S., 2003a: 42–43; 51.

110 Artzy 1997.

111 Braudel 1972a: 296–98; Horden and Purcell 2000: 154–59, 387–88.

112 Artzy 1997; Sherratt, A., and Sherratt 1991: 373.

113 Braudel 1972a: 107.

114 Sherratt, S., 1998.

115 Renfrew 1985: 361–91.

116 Artzy 1998.

117 Basch and Artzy 1985.

118 Sherratt, A., 1995a: 4–5, 16–17, 24–25; on Mediterranean abatement, Horden and Purcell 2000: 154, 263–70, 567–69, 589–90.

119 Morris, I., 2010: 33–34, 223–26.

120 As argued in a series of classic papers:

121 Monroe 2009: 284–92.

122 Sherratt, S., 2000.

123 Morris, S., 1992.

124 Bevan 2010a: 59, 65; Sherratt, S., 2010a: 97, 99, table 4.1; also noted by Shaw, I., 2001 as a feature of the later Mediterranean.

125 Sherratt, S., 1999; for the central Mediterranean, Blake 2008: 21–25.

126 Liverani 1987; Sherratt, S., 2003a.

127 Bell 2006: 95–100, 110.

128 Sherratt, S., 2001.

129 Bickel 1998; Kemp 2006: 313–17, 319–26.

130 For this lack of critical self-awareness, Monroe 2009: 297.

131 Bryce 2005: 309–10.

132 Sherratt, S., 1998: 307.

133 Vagnetti and Lo Schiavo 1989; Bonfante and Karageorghis (eds) 2001.

134 Watrous 1998.

135 Broodbank 2010b: 256–57; Giardino 1995: 336.

136 Sherratt, A., 1993: 33–38; Horden and Purcell 2000: 143–52, 298–341.

137 Sherratt, A., 1993: 33–38.

138 Andreou et al. 2000: 317–18; Bietti Sestieri 1997: 377–78; Pearce 2007: 99–101.

139 Harding 2000: 144–50.

140 Barfield 1994: 140–41; Harding 2000: 112, 400–4 on the urnfield mortuary ritual more generally.

141 Harding 2000: 322; Wachsmann 1998: 177–97.

142 Bietti Sestieri 2010: 318–48; Blake 2008: 24.

143 Vanzetti 2000.

144 Taylour 1958: 108–9, 131, pl. 14.

145 Guglielmino 2004.

146 Vanzetti 2000.

147 Franco 1999; Lafe and Galaty 2009: 107–8.

148 Guglielmino 2004–6: 99–101, figs 16.1–16.2.

149 Militello 2005; Vianello 2005, 54–55, 77–80.

150 Leighton 1999: 155–57.

151 E.g. Stoddart 2000: 68–69.

152 Leighton 1999: 188.

153 Cilia (ed.) 2004: 219–27.

154 Webster 1996: 108–52.

155 Webster 1996: 116.

156 Webster 1996: 143–49.

157 Russell 2010.

158 Lo Schiavo et al. (eds) 2005 for a survey of Sardinian metals and metallurgy.

159 Lo Schiavo et al. (eds) 2009.

160 Lo Schiavo et al. (eds) 2009.

161 Matthäus 2001 argues for a tenuous connection with the east Mediterranean right through to the resumption of indisputably visible contacts in the 9th century BC, though this is disputable given the presently rough dating of metal types and contexts.

162 Lo Schiavo 2012; Lo Schiavo et al. 1985; Ridgway and Ridgway 1992.

163 Lo Schiavo et al. (eds) 2005: 313–15, 401–5 on the first iron.

164 Yalçın et al. 2005: 349.

165 Karageorghis 2012.

166 Russell 2010: 113–21.

167 Bietti Sestieri 1997: 390–96; Rahmstorf 2005; Sherratt, S., 2000: 84–87.

168 Iacono 2012.

169 Forenbaher 2009b: 80, 83–84.

170 Tomas 2010: 198–211.

171 Pearce 2007: 89, 103.

172 Pearce 2007: 76–77.

173 Pearce 2007: 89–90.

174 Pearce 2007: 99–101.

175 Bietti Sestieri 1997: 375–77; Cremaschi et al. 2006.

176 Rahmstorf 2005: 669.

177 Pearce 2007: 103–6.

178 Bietti Sestieri 1997: 392–96; 2010: 186–98; Pearce 2000; 2007: 102–3.

179 Cunliffe 2008: 44.

180 Vianello 2005: 60.

181 Jung 2009: 82–83.

182 Bietti Sestieri 1997: 376–80, 386.

183 Giardino 1995: 109–29.

184 Pearce 2007: 106–7.

185 Barker and Rasmussen 1998: 53–60; Bietti Sestieri 1997: 380–85; 2010: 225–42.

186 Barker 2005: 59.

187 Bietti Sestieri 1992: 45–62; Cornell 1995: 48–57.

188 Chapman, R., 1990: 254; Sherratt, A., 1993: 39–41.

189 Blake 2008: 6–7.

190 Costa 2004: 114–18, 139–47.

191 Harding 2000: 289–91; Kristiansen and Larsen 2005: 330–33, fig. 155.

192 Gascó 2009; Guilaine and Verger 2008: 219–229; Vital 2008.

193 Martín de la Cruz 2008; Rowland 2001: 53.

194 Domergue and Rico 2002; Parker 1992: 181.

195 Giardino 2000b; Lo Schiavo 2008.

196 Guerrero Ayuso 2008; Lull et al. 2002.

197 Bellard 1995.

198 Garcia 2005: 169–70, 181–82; Zapatero 1997: 158–74.

199 Sanjuán 1999; recently also Delgado 2013: 316–19.

200 Soler 1965; Vives-Ferrándiz 2008: 244 for a recent dating estimate.

201 This extraordinary material is strangely under-discussed; see Cunliffe 2001: 282; Delgado 2008: 352–53; Giardino 1995: 298.

202 Delgado 2008: 355–63; Gonzáles de Canales Cerisola et al. 2004, 2006; Nijboer and van der Plicht 2006.

203 Aubet 2001: 26–29.

204 Book of Isaiah 23: 8.

205 Aubet 2001: 97–143.

206 Braudel 2001: 214–15 for an early recognition of the role of capital in Phoenician long-range voyages.

207 Markoe 2000: 143–69.

208 Aubet 2001: 30–31; Porada 1973.

209 Leroux et al. 2003.

210 Marriner 2009; Raban 1998: 430–36.

211 Aubet 2001: 31–43.

212 Marriner 2009: 103–57.

213 Curtis 2009.

214 Aubet (eds) 2004.

215 Aubet 2001: 150–58 196–97; Malkin 2011: 119–41.

216 Aubet 2001: 43–51, 85–88.

217 For more optimistic viewpoints: Aubet 2001: 43–46; Sherratt, S., and Sherratt 1993: 364.

218 Kourou 2009; Sherratt, S., 2010b; Stampolidis and Kotsonas 2006; for Calabria, Pacciarelli 1999.

219 Sherratt, S., 2010b.

220 Aubet 2001: 43–46, 68–69.

221 Horden and Purcell 2000: 115–22.

222 Aubet 2001: 68–69.

223 Aubet 2001: 51–54; Karageorghis 1976: 95–172.

224 Sherratt, S., 2003b: 234–36.

225 Aubet 2001: 52.

226 Aubet 2001: 194–206; Sherratt, S., and Sherratt 1993: 364–65.

227 Aubet 2001: 201–4.

228 Zamora López et al. 2010.

229 Aubet 2001, 204–9; Sherratt, S., and Sherratt 1993: 364

230 Bafico et al. 1997.

231 Aubet 2001: 161–63, 219; Blake 2008: 1, fn. 3.

232 Aubet 2001: 214–18.

233 Niemeyer et al. 2007; Docter et al. 2007.

234 Docter 2005, et al. 2008; on the wider chronological controversy, Brandherm and Trachsel (eds) 2008; Delgado 2008: 375–77; Guidi and Whitehouse 1996.

235 González-Ruibal 2004: 288–89; for the Scilly Isles find, see Current Archaeology 272 (2012) p.10.

236 Frankenstein 1979; also Aubet 2001: 54–60.

237 Stronach 1975: 175.

238 Bedford 2009: 40–41, 47–52.

239 Aubet 2001: 54–55; Curtis 2008: 434.

240 Giardino 1995, 2000.

241 Cunliffe 2001: 275–89.

242 Celestino et al. (eds) 2008; Karageorghis and Lo Schiavo 1989.

243 Giardino 2000: 102–3.

244 Morel 1984: 150.

245 Van Dommelen 2005: 150–51; Webster 1996: 154–94.

246 Lilliu 1966; Webster 1996: 198–206.

247 Webster 1996: 115–16.

248 Lo Schiavo 2000.

249 Guerrero Ayuso 2006: 31–35, fig. 15; Parker 1992: 146, fn. 365.

250 Lo Schiavo 2000: 143–44, 155–56; Ridgway and Ridgway 1992; Botto 2007.

251 For the west, Botto 2004–5: 19–26; González de Canales Cerisola et al. 2011.

252 Bauer 1998: 162.

253 Bafico et al. 1997; Ridgway 2000: 182–83; Hayne 2010: 154–57 for a recent summary.

254 Bonhomme et al. 2011; Cucchi et al. 2005.

255 Aubet 2001: 204–6, 257; Delgado 2013.

256 Marzoli et al. 2010.

257 Arruda 2008; Aubet 2001: 292–94.

258 Rey da Silva 2009: 19–30.

259 Lull et al. 2002: 121–24.

260 Lull *et al.* 1999.
261 Iacovou 2005a; Knapp 2008: 290–97; Sherratt, S., 2003b: 235.
262 van de Mieroop 2011: 270–72.
263 van de Mieroop 2011: 267–69.
264 Liverani 2005: 101–3; compare interpretations in Finkelstein 2007c: 148–49 and Mazar 2007c: 123–24.
265 Montet 1947–60; Stierlin and Ziegler 1987.
266 Gubel 2006: 87.
267 Schneider, J., 2011: 298–302.
268 Shaw, I., 2000b: 327.
269 Akkermans and Schwartz 2003: 366–77.
270 Akkermans and Schwartz 2003: 388, 392; Waldbaum 1997.
271 Holladay 1995: 383–87.
272 Among many discussions, Schniedewind 1996.
273 Finkelstein and Silberman 2006; Liverani 2005: 88–101; for a less sceptical view, Mazar 2007c.
274 Morris, I., 2010: 234–35 for the wider implications.
275 Liverani 2005: 104–27; Finkelstein and Silberman 2001: 169–95.
276 Popham 1994: fig. 2.12, with additional finds now in the centre and west; Ridgway 2000: 182–83.
277 Lemos 2002: 140–46, 161–68; 2006: 519–27; Sherratt, S., 2010b.
278 Papadopoulos, J. K., 1997b for a revisionist perspective; Dickinson 2006: 212–15 for an overall evaluation.
279 Papadopoulos, J. K., 1997b: 192; Popham and Lemos 1995; recently Kroll 2008.
280 Akurgal 1983.
281 Osborne 2009a: 55–65; Whitley 2001: 84–90.
282 Hall 2007: 120–27; Mazarakis Ainian 2006; Morris, I., 2007: 232–33.
283 Whitley 1991.
284 Morgan, C., 1990; 1994: 109–24; Whitley 2001: 137–38, 142–43.
285 Kotsonas *et al.* in press; Wallace 2010: 231–326; Wengrow 2010b: 141 on the earlier resonances of the Europa myth.
286 Barker and Rasmussen 1998: 60–84; Bietti Sestieri 1997: 380–85; 2010: 293–300; Riva 2010a: 13–18.
287 Bietti Sestieri 1997: 379, 396–98; 2010: 301–17; Leighton 1999: 187–217.
288 Barker and Rasmussen 1998: 65–68, fig. 26.
289 Barker and Rasmussen 1998: 69–70.
290 Bietti Sestieri 1992; Riva 2010a: 29–38, though the emphasis falls chronologically later.
291 Smith, C., 2005: 91–99.
292 Bietti Sestieri 1992.
293 Bietti Sestieri 1997: 385–92.
294 Riva 2010a: 19–21, 29.
295 Bietti Sestieri 1997: 397.
296 Pearce 2007: 102.
297 Bispham 2007: 183–91.
298 Snodgrass 2000: 175.
299 Gascó 2009: 318–19; Guilaine *et al.* 1986; Guilaine and Verger 2008: 229–35.
300 Irwin 1992: 31–100.
301 Aubet 2001: 172.

CHAPTER TEN (pp. 506–84)

1 For an excellent collection of studies on the interstitial 7th century BC, see Étienne (ed.) 2010.
2 Sallares 2007: 19–20 for a summary; more sceptically, Finné *et al.* 2011.
3 Morris, I., *et al.* 2007: 9; Morris, I., 2007: 219 for the Aegean; Bedford 2007: 310–11 for the Levant.
4 Mattingly *et al.* 2007.
5 Herring 2007: 281–82, 286–89.
6 Van der Veen 2006.
7 Bedford 2009; Parpola 2003; Yoffee 2005: 153.
8 Aubet 2001: 54–59.
9 Taylor, J., 2000: 352–59.
10 Oded 1979.
11 Aubet 2001: 54–57.
12 Markoe 2000: 163–64; Wilkinson, T. J., 2003: 29.
13 Gitin 1997; Faust and Weiss 2011; for Ekron see Gitin 1990.
14 Faust and Weiss 2011.
15 Mattingly *et al.* 2007.
16 Finkelstein and Silberman 2001: 267–70.
17 Boardman 1980: 69–70, fig. 56.
18 Haubold 2012; Malamat 1998: 46.
19 Iacovou 2005a: 28, 34; Radner 2010.
20 Cited in Morris, S., 2006: 67; see also Muhly 2009.
21 Faust and Weiss 2011.
22 Aubet 2001: 90–95; Frankenstein 1979.
23 Buchner and Ridgway 1993; Osborne 1996: 40–41; 2009a: 106–10; Ridgway 2000.
24 Albore Livadie and Cicirelli 2003; Cuozzo 2007: 244–55.
25 Becker 1995; Docter and Niemeyer 1994; Kelly 2012; Osborne 2009a: 108–10.
26 Connors 2004.
27 Aubet 2001: 177–78; Wallinga 1993: 33–65.
28 Ballard *et al.* 2002.
29 Dietler 2007: 267–69; Osborne 1996: 41.
30 Dougherty 2003.
31 Morrison *et al.* 2000: 25–34; Wallinga 1993: 45–65.
32 Aubet 2001: 177–78; Wallinga 1993: 13–15, 23–32.
33 Purcell 1990.
34 Sherratt, S., and Sherratt 1993: 364–69.
35 Aubet 2001: 157, 257–62, 273–79; 2006: 106–7.
36 Aubet 2001: 285–91; Sherratt, S., and Sherratt 1993; Sherratt, S., 2010b: 119–20, 130–31.
37 Neville 2007: 140.
38 Gill 1988.
39 Kostoglou 2010; Ridgway 2000: 187.
40 Aubet 2001: 82.
41 Barker 2005: 65.
42 Buxó 2008.
43 Dietler 2007: 255–56; 2010; Hodos 2000; Vives-Ferrándiz 2008.
44 Bevan in preparation.
45 Van Zeist *et al.* 2001.
46 Whitley 2001: 102–3.
47 Croissant and d'Ercole 2010.
48 Barker and Rasmussen 1998: 132–34, 203–5.

49 A distinction noted in Braudel 2001: 212; recently, Vives-Ferrándiz 2008.
50 Discussed from many viewpoints in Riva and Vella (eds) 2006.
51 Feldman 2006: 195; Onnis 2008.
52 Boardman 1980: 64–71; Cunliffe 2008: 292; Riva 2006.
53 Morris, S., 1992, 2006.
54 Cunliffe 2001: 272; Whitley 2001: 120–21.
55 Riva and Vella (eds) 2006.
56 Burkert 1992; West 1997; on the image from Tenos, Osborne 2009a: 156–58.
57 Griffiths 2005; Wengrow 2010a: 32–38.
58 Barker and Rasmussen 1998: 227–32, 242.
59 Barker and Rasmussen 1998: 94–99; Sherratt, S., 2003b; Whitley 2001: 128–33.
60 Sherratt, S., 2003b.
61 Cornell 1995: 41–44; Robb 1993: 756–57.
62 Dietler 2007: 243–45.
63 Morris, I., 1987, especially 129–41, 183–89, 205–10; Iacovou 2005a: 26–27; Karageorghis 1969: 23–164; Riva 2005, 2010a.
64 Morris, I., 2000: 195–256.
65 D'Agostino 1977.
66 Riva 2005, 2006.
67 Sams 1995.
68 Iacovou 2005: 28–31.
69 Robb 2007: 340 for Italy.
70 Morris, I., 1987; 2000: 109–91.
71 Bedford 2007: 313–14.
72 Finkelstein and Silberman 2001: 229–50; Liverani 2005: 143–82.
73 Niemeyer *et al.* 2007; Docter 2004; Docter *et al.* 2007.
74 Van Dommelen 2005: 148–51, 155–58.
75 De Polignac 2005; Hall 2007: 74–79; Rasmussen 2005; Smith, C., 2005; Whitley 2001: 165–74; for the west see Dietler 2007: 261.
76 Smith, C., 2005: 93–99; Whitley 2001: 169–71.
77 Malkin 2003; 2011; Purcell 1990: 44–49.
78 Purcell 2005b: 122–30 is particularly instructive.
79 Morris, I., 2007: 219.
80 Cambitoglou *et al.* 1971, 1988; Whitley 2001: 171–73.
81 For recent discussion see Dietler 2010: 27–74; Hurst and Owen (eds) 2005; Gosden 2004; Lyons and Papadopoulos (eds) 2002; Osborne 2008; Tsetskhladze and de Angelis (eds) 1994; van Dommelen 1998. Hall 2007: 93–118 and Whitley 2001: 124–27 provide good evaluations for southern Italy and Sicily.
82 McEvedy 2002: 11, figs 6.2–6.3; Snodgrass 2000: 173–74.
83 Aubet 2001; Malkin 2011: 97–118; Purcell 1990.
84 For example, de Angelis 2003: 43–44.
85 Malkin 2003: 62 for this term.
86 Aubet 2001: 257–79; Delgado 2008: 384–94.
87 Gener Basallote *et al.* 2012; Zamora López *et al.* 2010.
88 Aubet 2001: 279–91; Delgado 2008: 394–417; Neville 2007: 140–42.
89 Belén Deamos 2009; Delgado 2008: 348–49, 354.

90   Aubet 2001: 305–37; 2006; Delgado 2008: 441–59.
91   Aubet 2001: 332–37.
92   Delgado and Ferrer 2007: 23–29.
93   Aubet 2001: 317–21; 2006; Schubart 2003.
94   Aubet 2001: 305–37.
95   Aubet 2001: 321–26.
96   Aubet 2001: 326–27.
97   Aubet 2001: 297–301; Cañete and Vives-Ferrándiz 2011; Villada et al. 2007.
98   Delgado 2008: 429–41; Vives-Ferrándiz 2008.
99   Aubet 2001: 235–43; van Dommelen 1998: 69–113; 2006: 144–49.
100 Van Dommelen 2006: 146–47.
101 Aubet 2001: 231–35; Giammellaro et al. 2008: 129–46, 151–56; Leighton 1999: 219–22, 225–32; on west Sicilian population growth see Earle and Kristiansen (eds) 2010: 78.
102 Aubet 2001: 231–34; Delgado and Ferrer 2007: 31–34.
103 De Angelis 2003: 10–14; Leighton 1999: 219–25, 232–37.
104 De Angelis 2003: 17–97; de Polignac 2005: 51.
105 Van Dommelen 2005: 147.
106 de Angelis 2003: 54; Morris, I., 2012.
107 Leighton 1999: 219–22, 232–68; Morris, I., 2003: 47–49; Morris, I., et al. 2001.
108 Leighton 1999: 212–15.
109 Attema 2005, 2008.
110 Carter 2009: 51–89.
111 Osborne 2009a: 122.
112 Morris, I., 2012: 294–95 explores later ramifications of this in a Greek context.
113 Aubet 2001: 277 summarizes these roles nicely in the context of shrines at Cadiz.
114 Vella 2004.
115 Brody 1998; Meier 2007.
116 Pace 2004: 101; López-Bertran 2011; Shaw, J., 1989.
117 Aubet 2001: 273–79.
118 Morgan 1990; Whitley 2001: 134–50; on Delphi compare Malkin 2011: 112–17 and Osborne 2009a: 190–94.
119 Whitley 2001: 156–64.
120 Riva 2005.
121 Osborne 2009b: 86–89; Morris, S., 2006: 71–74.
122 Morris, S., 2006: 67–68, 76.
123 Sherratt, S., 2005.
124 Sherratt, S., 2003b; 2010b: 125.
125 Malkin 2011: 14 and Maran 2011: 283 in a Mediterranean context.
126 Sherratt, S., 2005, 2010b.
127 For example, Leighton 1999: 215–17.
128 Aubet 2001: 245–56; van Dommelen 2005: 148–51.
129 Malkin 1998, 2011; Sherratt, S., 2003b.
130 Hall 2002; Sherratt, S., 2005.
131 Monroe 2009 on the Bronze Age origins of this phenomenon.
132 Hall 2002.
133 Radner 2010; Sherratt, S., 2003b.
134 García Sanjuán 2005.
135 Finkelstein and Silberman 2001: 222–95.

136 Bennet 1997; Finkelstein and Silberman 2001; Morris and Laffineur (eds) 2007; Sherratt, S., 1990.
137 Finkelstein and Silberman 2001: 229–313; Morris, I., 1986.
138 Sherratt, S., 2003b.
139 Bedford 2007: 313–14.
140 Bedford 2007: 310–12.
141 Barkay 1992: 372–73; Liverani 2005: 182–98, and for subsequent patterns, 231–307, with Stern 1995.
142 Markoe 2000: 47–49.
143 Stern 1995: 436–37.
144 Aubet 2001: 59–60, 94.
145 Abulafia 2011: 354–69 and onward.
146 Roosevelt 2009; also Osborne 2009a: 256–57.
147 Horden and Purcell 2000: 89–122; Purcell 2005c.
148 Osborne and Cunliffe (eds) 2005; Scheidel 2007: 77–79.
149 Horden and Purcell 2000: 89–122; Shaw, B., 2001: 427–28 on congealed dynamics.
150 Hansen, M. H., 2012; Morris, I., 1997.
151 Osborne 2005; also Foxhall 2005.
152 Van Dommelen 2005: 143–44.
153 Aubet 2001: 326–29; Belarte 2009; Sanmartí 2009b; Dietler 2007.
154 Aubet 2001: 233.
155 Reese 2005.
156 Aubet 2001: 240–41; van Dommelen and Finocchi 2008.
157 Attema 2005; de Angelis 2003: 122–99; Carter, J. C., 2006: 91–132, 195–237; Morris, I., 2003: 46–50; Osborne 2007: 286–87.
158 Carter, J. C., 2006: 91–132; Horden and Purcell 2000: 284–87; Osborne 2009a: 186–87, 224–27.
159 Herring 2007: 286–90; Lomas 1994; Whitehouse and Wilkins 1989.
160 Morris, I., 2003: 46–49.
161 Whitehouse and Wilkins 1989.
162 Barker and Rasmussen 1998: 140 for Pompeii; Herring 2000; Lomas 2000.
163 Dietler 2007: 245; Whitehouse and Wilkins 1989.
164 Barker and Rasmussen 1998: 167–74, 195–98; Rasmussen 2005; Riva 2010a: 177–92; Smith, C., 2005.
165 Barker and Rasmussen 1998: 141–78, 219–24.
166 Hall 2007: 67–92; Hansen, M. H., 2012; Morris, I., 1997; Scheidel 2007: 74–78; Whitley 2001: 165–94.
167 Hall 2007: 231; Whitley 2001: 169.
168 Hall 2007: 231.
169 Hansen, M. H., 2012: 260; Morris, I., 2012: 282–84.
170 Hansen, M. H., 2012; Snodgrass 1986.
171 Runciman 1990; Whitley 2001: 179–88; Hall 2007: 119–44.
172 Morgan, C. 2003.
173 Cornell 1995: 1–26, 119–72; Smith, C., 1996.
174 Hall 2007: 137–43; Osborne 2009a: 180–85, 258–65.

175 Barker and Rasmussen 1998: 87–91; Cornell 1995: 119–50; Hall 2007: 120–27; Riva 2006; Smith, C., 1996: 173–78, 185–86.
176 Hansen, M. H., 2012: 260; Morris, I., 2012.
177 Spivey 1990.
178 Foxhall 2005: 235–36, 239; Osborne 2009a: 214–20.
179 Osborne 1994.
180 Barker and Rasmussen 1998: 86–87, 135–36.
181 Gschnitzer 1993.
182 Aubet 2001: 157; Ameling 2012: 363–71, 375–80.
183 Wallace 2010; Whitley 2010.
184 Morris, I., 2000: 109–91; 2007: 236–40; Smith, C., 2005: 102–8, especially on similarities between the Aegean and Italy. On Iberia: Ruiz and Molinos 2013; Wagner 2013.
185 D'Agostino 1990.
186 Osborne 2009a: 178–80.
187 Robb 2007: 334–41 explores this.
188 Osborne 2009a: 202–13.
189 Cornell 1995: 175–97; Smith, C., 1997.
190 Carter, J. C., 2006: 204–6; Whitley 2001: 190–91 for Athens.
191 Barker and Rasmussen 1998: 232–57; Riva 2010a.
192 Cornell 1995: 13, 166; Osborne 2009a: 292.
193 Osborne 2009a: 174–78; Whitley 2001: 188–90.
194 Cornell 1995: 130–41, 156–59.
195 Hall 2007: 270–75; Osborne 2009a: 229–30, 257–58; Snodgrass 1986.
196 Bron et al. 1984; Whitley 2001: 195–230.
197 Foxhall 2005: 244–46.
198 Foxhall 2005; Morris, S., 2006: 69, 74.
199 Hall 2007: 261.
200 Whitley 2001: 213–23.
201 Tronchetti and van Dommelen 2005; for hints of Phoenician statuary, see Belén Deamos and Chapa Brunet 2012.
202 Foxhall 1998, 2005; Osborne 1996, 1998.
203 Aubet 2001: 257–341; 2005; Delgado 2008: 459–65
204 Barker and Rasmussen 1998: 193–99, 205–15; Malkin 2002: 159–72 on 'Odysseus'; Riva 2010b.
205 Drakidès et al. 2010: 96–109.
206 Morris, I., 2007: 212; Osborne 2007.
207 Sherratt, S., and Sherratt 1993: 369–74.
208 On this term, Delgado and Ferrer 2007: 30.
209 Van Dommelen and Goméz Bellard 2008: 9.
210 McGovern 2009: 192.
211 Buxó 2008.
212 Purcell 2006: 23.
213 Shortland 2012: 169–73.
214 Osborne 1996; Whitley 2001: 174–79.
215 Whitley 2001: 177–78.
216 Vickers and Gill 1994; Whitley 2001: 175–76, 204–13, 286–92.
217 Osborne 1996.
218 Osborne 2009b: 84.
219 Osborne 2009b.
220 Buxó 2008; Stika 2008.

221 Hall 2007: 247; Möller 2007: 363–64.
222 Hall 2007: 242, 247; Figueira 1981; Purcell 1990: 51.
223 Horden and Purcell 2000: 115–22; Purcell 2005b.
224 Stika 2008.
225 Purcell 1990: 48; Sherratt, S., and Sherratt 1993: 363.
226 Scheidel 2007: 62–63; Sherratt, S., and Sherratt 1993: 371; but this is a topic about which much of the literature is reprehensibly coy.
227 Hall 2007: 196.
228 Sherratt, A., 2006.
229 Figueira 1981.
230 Malkin 2011: 143–52; Sherratt, S., and Sherratt 1993: 374.
231 Boardman 1980: 178–79; Braudel 2001; 252.
232 Barker and Rasmussen 1998: 210–15; Hall 2007: 247–48; Osborne 2009a: 213.
233 Gibson and Edelstein 1985: 144–46; Whitley 2001: 392–94; Morris, S., and Papadopoulos 2005 for slightly later Greek towers as secure accommodation for slaves.
234 For the latter two, Herodotus IV: 152.
235 Extensive discussion in Morris, S., 1992.
236 Osborne 1996: 31–32.
237 Treister 1996: 232.
238 Osborne 2009a: 256–65.
239 Morris, I., 2007: 238; Osborne 2009a: 259–65.
240 Herodotus III: 57.
241 Purcell 2005a: 217 on harbour dues as a 'levy on inter-dependence'.
242 Morel 1984: 150 on the fragility of these places.
243 Morris, I., 2007: 239.
244 Cornell 1995: 112, 120, 321; Smith, C., 1996: 179–81.
245 Riva 2010b; Serra Ridgway 1990.
246 Serra Ridgway 1990: 519.
247 Butzer 2002: 83–85; Hassan 1997: 66–69.
248 Fabre 2004–5: 60–63.
249 Lloyd 2000: 369–83; Ritner 2009 for the preceding situation.
250 Herodotus II: 158.
251 Herodotus IV: 42.
252 Boardman 1980: 114–17, 133–35; Lloyd 2000: 372–73.
253 On the artistic and architectural dimensions of this, Tanner 2003.
254 Herodotus II: 154.
255 Braudel 2001: 247 for this analogy.
256 Boardman 1980: 118–33; Hall 2007: 243–47; Möller 2000.
257 Herodotus II: 178–79.
258 Osborne 2007: 290–91; Morris, S., 2006: 68.
259 Malkin 2011: 65–85 for Rhodians at Naukratis.
260 Whitley 2001: 124.
261 Sherratt, S., and Sherratt 1993: 374.
262 Osborne 2007: 292–94; 2009a: 237–45; Morris, S., 2006: 70–71 on Ephesus.
263 Osborne 2009a: 237–44.
264 Dietler 2007: 270–72.

265 Ameling 2012: 377; Dietler 2007: 270–72; Osborne 2007: 278, 290–91.
266 For instance, Osborne 2007: 290.
267 Osborne 2009a: 246–57; Whitley 2001: 223–30.
268 Osborne 2007: 287–88.
269 Snodgrass 1983.
270 Osborne 2009a: 248–53; Snodgrass 1986: 55–56.
271 Neer 2001; Whitley 2001: 228–30.
272 Hall 2007: 270–73; Snodgrass 1986: 53–55.
273 Herodotus I: 46–52; II: 180; also Boardman 1980: 208.
274 As exemplified in Barker and Rasmussen 1998: 224–57; Whitehouse 1995.
275 Hall 2007: 155–77; Whitley 2001: 179–85.
276 Fantalkin 2011: 103–4.
277 Finkelstein and Silberman 2006: 196–98.
278 D'Agostino 1990.
279 Cornell 1995: 179–97.
280 Wallinga 1993: 66–83.
281 Herodotus IV: 153.
282 Wallinga 1993: 103–85; Morrison et al. 2000.
283 Aubet 2001: 176 and Morrison et al. 2000: 25–46 for the standard view; Wallinga 1993: 103–29 makes the revisionist case.
284 Whitley 2001: 252–55.
285 Osborne 2009a: 220–24.
286 Colonna 2003; Riva 2007.
287 Croissant and d'Ercole 2010: 352–54.
288 Lomas 2007.
289 Barker and Rasmussen 1998: 140, 158.
290 Barfield 1998: 150, fig. 6, 154.
291 Chapman, J., and Shiel 1993: 287–91.
292 Gaffney et al. 1997.
293 Kirigin et al. 2009.
294 Purcell 2005b: 122.
295 Rodríguez Somolinos 1996.
296 Py 1993: 48–82; 2009: 11–17.
297 Dietler 2010: 94–103.
298 Dietler 2010: 133–38; Long et al. (eds) 2002.
299 Dietler 2005: 41–52; 2010: 95–97.
300 Riva 2010b; Sallares 2007: 30.
301 Dietler 2010: 95–97.
302 Dietler 2010: 104–11.
303 Dietler 2005: 69–102; 2010: 308–16.
304 Dietler 2005: 161–80; 2010: 120–22, 196–98, 216–19.
305 Dietler 2007: 255–56; 2010: 230; Terral et al. 2004.
306 Dietler 2005: 155–61, 173–81; 2010.
307 Garcia 2005; Dietler 2005: 125–43; 2010: 259–308.
308 Garcia 2005: 176–78.
309 Dietler 2005: 52–61; 2010: 203–6.
310 Dietler 2010: 210–11.
311 Garcia 2005: 170–72; Dietler 2010: 145–55.
312 Dietler 2010: 114–20; Py 2009.
313 Sanmartí 2009a, 2009b.
314 Dietler 2007: 256, 262–66.
315 Murphy 1977.
316 Malkin 2011: 143–52.
317 Malkin 2011: 150.
318 Alcover 2010; Vigne 1999: 307, fig. 5.
319 Fernández-Miranda 1997.

320 Lull et al. 2002.
321 Goméz Bellard 2008; Horden and Purcell 2000: 224–30 on such island economies.
322 Aubet 2001: 337–39; Goméz Bellard 2008: 44–48.
323 Herodotus IV: 168–81.
324 Barker 2006: 277; Close 2009: 48.
325 Barker et al. 2009: 88; Hodos 2006: 164–69.
326 Herodotus IV: 187, 191; on dolmens see Guilaine 1994: 263–66.
327 Kallala and Sanmartí (eds) 2011; Sanmartí et al. 2012.
328 Aubet 2001: 46–47, 162–63, 208 for Phoenician possibilities.
329 Fentress and Docter 2008: 107–13.
330 Sanmartí et al. 2012.
331 Hodos 2006: 159.
332 Hodos 2006: 159–60.
333 Herodotus IV: 150–59; Osborne 2009a: 8–16.
334 Myres 1943: 25; Herodotus IV: 158.
335 Hodos 2006: 158–99.
336 Barker (ed.) 1996; Fentress and Docter 2008: 122–27.
337 Shaw, B., 2003.
338 Krings 2008, though perhaps excessively sceptical of the surviving ancient sources.
339 Horden and Purcell 2000: 65.
340 Donkin 1991: 8–27 for guinea fowl.
341 Mattingly et al. 2003: 345–46.
342 Deme and McIntosh 2006; Mitchell 2005: 138–40.
343 Mitchell 2005: 137–71.
344 Mitchell 2005: 145–47.
345 Mattingly et al. 2003: 346–72; 2006.
346 On the last, see Horden and Purcell 2000: 65–74 on the Green Mountain.
347 Fentress 2009: 73.
348 Shaw, B., 2006.
349 On this ambit, see Shaw, B., 2006.
350 Aubet 2001: 291–304; Cunliffe 2001: 297–310; 2008: 299.
351 Morales-Muñiz and Roselló-Izquierdo 2008.
352 Cañete and Vives-Ferrándiz 2011.
353 Aubet 2001: 297–304.
354 Cunliffe 2001: 89–91; López Pardo 1996.
355 Herodotus IV: 196.
356 Vilaça 2008 for earlier phases; Arruda 2009; Delgado 2008: 417–29.
357 Cunliffe 2001: 271–72.
358 Mitchell 2005: 175–78; Mercer 1980: 17–24; Atoche Peña 2002.
359 Bonhomme et al. 2011: 1038.
360 Cunliffe 2001: 302; Mitchell 2005: 175.
361 Boardman 1980: 71.
362 Gabrielsen and Lund (eds) 2007; Sherratt, S., 1993: 42.
363 Harding 2007: 51.
364 Doonan 2009.
365 Greaves 2007b.
366 Sherratt, A., 1993: 39–43.
367 Cunliffe 2008: 309–12; Sherratt, A., 1993: 42.
368 Cunliffe 2008: 309–15.
369 Brun and Chaume 1997.
370 Lebedynsky 2004.

371 Häussler 2007.
372 Polybius I: 3.
373 Osborne 2008 for this nice distinction.
374 Morris, I., 2010: 263–91 for a summary; 2012 for the Greek experience.
375 Scheidel 2007: 77–79.
376 Morris, I., et al. 2007: 9; Scheidel 2007: 42–48, table 3.1; Braudel 1972a: 394–418 implies 25–30 million people in the basin itself during the 16th century AD; by the mid-19th century that figure had climbed to 60–70 million.
377 Horden and Purcell 2000: 267.
378 Morris, I., 2010: 157.
379 Morris, I., et al. 2007: 11.
380 Barker 2005: 65–66; Foxhall 2003; Sallares 2007: 29 and many other contributions to Scheidel et al. (eds) 2007; Whittaker (ed.) 1988.
381 Parker 1992: figs 3–4; Schneider, H., 2007: 163.
382 Wilson, A. I., et al. 2013.
383 Morris, I., et al. 2007: 10.
384 Morris, I., 2009: 125–26, 159–63; 2012: 284–86, 291–93, 296–99.
385 Cornell 1995: 198–214; Smith, C., 1996: 184–232; 2005.
386 Bradley, G., 2007; Cornell 1995: 293–402.
387 On the demand for Carthaginian relocation, Horden and Purcell 2006: 736–37.
388 Braudel 2001: 223; Ameling 2012 for a recent overview.
389 Docter et al. 2007.
390 Aubet 2001: 157.
391 Numerous examples of the latter are provided in Lancel 1995.
392 Aubet 2001: 11.
393 Van Dommelen and Goméz Bellard (eds) 2008: 8–12, 231–40.
394 Boardman 1980: 189.
395 Brett and Fentress 1996: 24–43; Fentress and Docter 2008.
396 Van Dommelen 1998: 115–59; 2005: 147–51; van Dommelen and Finocchi 2008.
397 Vigne 1999: 302, fig. 3 for Sardinia.
398 Blake 1998; van Dommelen 1998: 115–59, continued into Roman times, 161–209; Hayne 2010.
399 Aubet 2001: 341–46; Celestino Pérez 2009; Cunliffe and Keay 1995: 19–23; Sanmartí 2008.
400 Aubet 2001: 341–46.
401 Aubet 2001: 191.
402 Van Dommelen and Goméz Bellard (eds) 2008: 8–12, 236–40; the extent is far greater than that of any hegemony over off-island regions that may have been established by one or more polities of Bronze Age Crete.
403 In the French original; translated less lyrically as 'Venice's stationary fleet' in Braudel 1972a: 149.
404 Morris, I., 2012: 292–93, 298 is brief but interesting on this theme.
405 Meiggs 1972; Morris, I., 2009.
406 Morris, I., 2007: 95; 2009: 114–15; Whitley 2001: 236.
407 Morris, I., 2006: 74–75, 80; Whitley 2001: 233–43.
408 Hall 2007: 178–202; Osborne 2009a: 202–13; Whitley 2001: 255–65.
409 On the early Athenian democracy: Hall 2007: 210–34; Osborne 2009a: 276–97; Morris, I., 1997: 95–98.
410 Morris, I., 1997: 95.
411 On other early democracies, Zimmerman 1975; Robinson, E. W., 1997 for subsequent Classical democracies.
412 Cornell 1995: 215–41; Smith, C., 1997.
413 For instance, Osborne 2009a: 330.
414 Bedford 2007; Briant 2002; Scheidel 2007: 45.
415 Wallinga 1993: 103–29.
416 Herodotus III: 13, 136.
417 Haubold 2012.
418 Bedford 2007: 311; Osborne 2009a: 330–34; Purcell 2005a.
419 Plutarch Alexander 36; Schneider, J., 2011: 296–97.
420 Morris, S., 2006: 78–79.
421 Herodotus VI: 7–18; Osborne 2009a: 304–7.

CHAPTER ELEVEN (pp. 593–610)

1 For a similar perspective, Robb 2007: 320–26.
2 Smith, B. D., 2007.
3 Blondel 2006: 720–25.
4 Purcell 1990: 37.
5 On areas repelled from sea, and their later rarity: Horden and Purcell 2005: 364–66; 2006: 739–40.
6 Knapp 1993: 342.
7 Plato Laws 704–5, discussed in Horden and Purcell 2006: 736.
8 Compare Sherratt, A., 1995a: 18–19.
9 Jiménez 2010 for a recent discussion in a later, Roman context.
10 Compare Rowlands 2010: 242–45.
11 Morris, I., 2010.
12 Constantakopoulou 2007; Meiggs 1972; Morris, I., 2009; Osborne 1999.
13 Runciman 1990.
14 Stark 1956: 155.
15 Ceccarelli 2012.
16 Horden and Purcell 2000: 24–25, 134–35.
17 Morris, I., 2010: 35, 267–70, 280–330; also Hodges and Whitehouse 1983; McCormick 2001: 25–119.
18 Rempel and Yoffee 1999; Yoffee 2005: 141, 153–60.
19 Hall 2002; 2007: 259, 270–75.
20 Jaspers 1949 for the original thesis; Wolf 1967, cited in Rowlands 2010: 245; Morris, I., 2010: 254–63, 669 for thoughtful recent analysis.
21 Herodotus VII: 144; see also Cawkwell 2005: 263–64 and more generally on the battle of Salamis.
22 Herodotus VII: 165–66.
23 Lolos 2009; for earlier battle-boat depictions on Aegina, Siedentopf 1991, pls 35–38.

Bibliography

ABBREVIATIONS USED
CNRS = Centre National de la Recherche Scientifique
MIAR = McDonald Institute for Archaeological Research
UP = University Press
AAR = *African Archaeological Review*
ABSA = *Annual of the British School at Athens*
AJA = *American Journal of Archaeology*
ARP = *Accordia Research Papers*
ÄL = *Ägypten und Levante*
AS = *Anatolian Studies*
BASOR = *Bulletin of the American Schools of Oriental Research*
BSPF = *Bulletin de la Société Préhistorique Française*
CA = *Current Anthropology*
CAJ = *Cambridge Archaeological Journal*
EA = *Evolutionary Anthropology*
EJA = *European Journal of Archaeology*
JAA = *Journal of Anthropological Archaeology*
JAS = *Journal of Archaeological Science*
JB = *Journal of Biogeography*
JEA = *Journal of European Archaeology*
JHE = *Journal of Human Evolution*
JMA = *Journal of Mediterranean Archaeology*
JQS = *Journal of Quaternary Science*
JWP = *Journal of World Prehistory*
LS = *Libyan Studies*
MHR = *Mediterranean Historical Review*
OJA = *Oxford Journal of Archaeology*
PCPS =*Proceedings of the Cambridge Philological Society*
PNAS = *Proceedings of the National Academy of Sciences*
PPS = *Proceedings of the Prehistoric Society*
QI = *Quaternary International*
QR = *Quaternary Research*
QSR = *Quaternary Science Reviews*
WA = *World Archaeology*

Abate, D., M. Faka, C. Keleshis *et al.*, 2023. 'Aerial Image-based Documentation and Monitoring of Illegal Archaeological Excavations.' *Heritage* 6: 4302–19.

Abulafia, D., (ed.) 2003. *The Mediterranean in History*. London: Thames & Hudson. Los Angeles: J. Paul Getty Museum.

— 2005. 'Mediterraneans' in W. V. Harris 2005a, 64–93.

— 2011. *The Great Sea: A Human History of the Mediterranean*. London: Allen Lane. New York: Oxford UP.

Adams, E., 2004. 'Power Relations in Minoan Palatial Towns: An Analysis of Neopalatial Knossos and Malia.' *JMA* 17: 191–222.

— 2006. 'Social Strategies and Spatial Dynamics in Neopalatial Crete: An Analysis of the North-central Area.' *AJA* 110: 1–36.

Adams, M. J., 2009. 'An Interim Report on the Naqada III – First Intermediate Period Stratification at Mendes 1999–2005' in D. Redford (ed.), 2009. *Delta Reports*. Vol. I: *Research in Lower Egypt*. Oxford and Oakville: Oxbow. 121–206.

Agouridis, C., 1997. 'Sea Routes and Navigation in the Third Millennium Aegean.' *OJA* 16: 1–24.

Aiello, L., and P. Wheeler, 2003. 'Neanderthal Thermoregulation and the Glacial Climate' in van Andel and Davies 2003, 147–66.

Akkermans, P. M. M. G., and G. M. Schwartz, 2003. *The Archaeology of Syria: From Complex Hunter-gatherers to Early Urban Societies (ca. 16,000–300 BC)*. Cambridge and New York: Cambridge UP.

Aksu, A. E., D. J. W. Piper and T. Konuk, 1987. 'Late Quaternary Tectonic and Sedimentation History of Outer Izmir Bay and Çandarlı Basin, Western Turkey.' *Marine Geology* 76: 89–104.

Akurgal, E., 1983. *Alt-Smyrna*. Ankara: Türk Tarih Kurumu Basımevi.

Alberti, G., 2005. 'Earliest Contacts between Southeastern Sicily and Cyprus in the Late Bronze Age' in Laffineur and Greco 2005, 343–51.

Albore Livadie, C., 2002. 'A First Pompeii: The Early Bronze Age Village of Nola–Croce del Papa (Palma Campania phase).' *Antiquity* 76: 941–42.

— 2008. 'Sites et Campagnes de l'Âge due Bronze sous les Cendres de Vésuve' in Guilaine 2008, 126–41.

— and C. Cicirelli, 2003. 'L'Insediamento Protistorico in Località Longola di Poggiomarino: Nota Preliminare.' *La Parola del Passato* LVIII: 88–128.

Alcock, S. E., 2005. 'Alphabet Soup in the Mediterranean Basin: The Emergence of the Mediterranean Serial' in W. V. Harris 2005a, 314–336.

— and J. F. Cherry, (eds) 2004. *Side-by-Side Survey: Comparative Regional Studies in the Mediterranean World*. Oxford: Oxbow.

—, T. N. D'Altroy, K. D. Morrison and C. M. Sinopoli, (eds) 2001. *Empires: Perspectives from Archaeology and History*. Cambridge and New York: Cambridge UP.

Alcover, J. A., 2008. 'The First Mallorcans: Prehistoric Colonization in the Western Mediterranean.' *JWP* 21: 19–84.

— 2010. 'Introduccions de Mamífers a les Balears: L'Establiment d'un Nou Ordre' in C. Álvarez (ed.), *Seminari Sobre Espècies Introduïdes i Invasores a les Illes Balears*. Palma: Govern de les Illes Balears. 175–86.

Algaze, G., 1993. *The Uruk World System: The Dynamics of Expansion of Early Mesopotamian Civilization*. Chicago: Chicago UP.

— 2008. *Ancient Mesopotamia at the Dawn of Civilization: The Evolution of an Urban Landscape*. Chicago and London: Chicago UP.

Allen, H., 2009. 'Vegetation and Ecosystem Dynamics' in Woodward 2009a, 203–28.

Alley, R. B., J. Marotzke, W. D. Nordhaus *et al.*, 2003. 'Abrupt Climate Change.' *Science* 299: 2005–10.

al-Maqdissi, M., D. M. Banacossi and P. Pfältzer, (eds) 2009. *Schätze des Alten Syrien: Die Entdeckung des Königreichs Qatna*. Stuttgart: Konrad Theiss.

Alperson-Afil, N., and N. Goren-Inbar, 2010. *The Acheulian Site of Gesher Benot Ya'aqov*. Vol. II: *Ancient and Controlled Use of Fire*. New York: Springer. Oxford: Oxbow.

Altenmüller, H., and A. M. Moussa, 1991. 'Die Inschrift Amenemhets II aus dem Ptah-Tempel von Memphis: Ein Vorbericht.' *Studien zur Altägyptischen Kultur* 18: 1–48.

Ambert, P., 1996. 'Cabrières (France): Mines et Métallurgie au IIIème Millénaire B.C. Apports de la Métallurgie Expérimentale.' in B. Bagolini and F. Lo Schiavo (eds), *The Copper Age in the Near East and Europe*. Vol. 10 of *Colloquium XIX. Metallurgy: Origins and Technology*. Forlì: Abaco. 41–50.

Ambrose, S. H., 1998. 'Late Pleistocene Human Population Bottlenecks, Volcanic Winter, and Differentiation of Modern Humans.' *JHE* 34: 623–51.

Ameling, W., 2012. 'Carthage' in Bang and Scheidel 2012, 361–82.

Ammerman, A. J., 1985. *The Acconia Survey: Neolithic Settlement and the Obsidian Trade*. London: Institute of Archaeology.

— 2010. 'The First Argonauts: Toward the Study of the Earliest Seafaring in the Mediterranean' in A. Anderson *et al.* 2010, 81–92.

— 2011. 'The Paradox of Early Voyaging in the Mediterranean and the Slowness of the Neolithic Transition between Cyprus and Italy' in G. Vavouranakis (ed.), *The Seascape in Aegean Prehistory*. Aarhus: Aarhus UP. 31–50.

— and P. Biagi, (eds) 2003. *The Widening Harvest: The Neolithic Transition in Europe. Looking Back, Looking Forward*. Boston: Archaeological Institute of America. Oxford: Oxbow.

— and L. L. Cavalli-Sforza, 1984. *The Neolithic Transition and the Genetics of Populations*. Princeton and Guildford: Princeton UP.

—, M. de Min, R. Housely and C. E. McClennen, 1995. 'More on the Origins of Venice.' *Antiquity* 69: 501–10.

—, D. H. Marshall, J. Benjamin and T. Turnbull, 2011. 'Underwater Investigations at the Early Sites of Aspros and Nissi Beach on Cyprus' in Benjamin *et al.* 2011, 263–71.

Anderson, A., 2010. 'The Origins and Development of Seafaring: Towards a Global Approach' in A. Anderson *et al.* 2010, 3–16.

—, J. H. Barrett and K. V. Boyle, (eds) 2010. *The Global Origins and Development of Seafaring*. Cambridge: MIAR.

Anderson, P. C., J. Chabot and A. van Gijn, 2004. '*The Functional Riddle* of "Glossy" Canaanean Blades and the Near Eastern Threshing Sledge.' *JMA* 17: 87–129.

Andreou, S., M. Fotiadis and K. Kotsakis, 2001. 'Review of Aegean Prehistory V: The Neolithic and Bronze Age of Northern Greece' in T. Cullen 2001, 259–327.

Andres, W., and J. Wunderlich, 1992. 'Environmental Conditions for Early Settlement at Minshat Abu Omar' in van den Brink 1992, 157–66.

Anonymous, 1996. 'Regional National Historic Peace Park of Troy and Urban Development.' *International Journal of Cultural Property* 5: 315–17.

Anthony, D., 1996. 'V. G. Childe's World System and the Daggers of the Early Bronze Age' in B. Wailes (ed.), *Craft Specialization and Social Evolution. In Memory of V. Gordon Childe*. Philadelphia: Pennsylvania UP. 47–66.

— 2007. *The Horse, the Wheel, and Language: How Bronze-Age Riders from the Eurasian Steppes Shaped the Modern World*. Princeton and Woodstock: Princeton UP.

— and D. Brown, 2011. 'The Secondary Products Revolution, Horse-riding, and Mounted Warfare.' *JWP* 24: 131–60.

Antoniadou, S., and A. Pace, (eds) 2007. *Mediterranean Crossroads*. Athens: Pierides Foundation.

Antonova, I., V. Tolstikov and M. Treister, 1996. *The Gold of Troy: Searching for Homer's Fabled City*. London: Thames & Hudson. New York: Ministry of Culture of the Russian Federation.

Aranda Jiménez, G., and J. A. Esquivel Guerrero, 2006. 'Ritual Funerario y Comensalidad en las Sociedades de la Edad del Bronce del Sureste Peninsular: La Cultura de El Argar.' *Trabajos de Prehistoria* 63: 117–33.

— and — 2007. 'Poder y Prestigio en las Sociedades de la Cultura de El Argar: El Consumo Comunal de Bóvidos y Ovicápridos en los Rituales de Enterramiento.' *Trabajos de Prehistoria* 64: 95–118.

— and F. Molina, 2006. 'Wealth and Power in the Bronze Age of the South-east of the Iberian Peninsula: The Funerary Record of Cerro de la Encina.' *OJA* 25: 47–59.

Arbuckle, B. S., and C. M. Erek, 2010. 'Late Epipaleolithic Hunters of the Central Taurus: Faunal Remains from Direkli Cave, Kahramanmaraş, Turkey.' *International Journal of Osteoarchaeology*. DOI: 10.1002/oa.1230. (Online journal.)

Archi, A., 1990. 'The City of Ebla and the Organization of the Rural Territory' in E. Aerts and H. Klengel (eds), *The Town as Regional Economic Centre in the Ancient Near East*. Leuven: Leuven UP. 15–19.

Areshian, G. E., B. Gasparyan, P. S. Avetisyan *et al.*, 2012. 'The Chalcolithic of the Near East and South-eastern Europe: Discoveries and New Perspectives from the Cave Complex Areni-1, Armenia.' *Antiquity* 86: 115–30.

Arnold, D., 2010. 'Image and Identity: Egypt's Eastern Neighbours, East Delta People and the Hyksos' in Marée 2010, 183–222.

Arribas, A., and P. Palmqvist, 1999. 'On the Ecological Connection between Sabre-tooths and Hominids: Faunal Dispersal Events in the Lower Pleistocene and a Review of the Evidence for the First Human Arrival in Europe.' *JAS* 26: 571–85.

Arruda, A. M., 2008. 'Estranhos Numa Terra (Quase) Estranha: Os Contactos Pré-coloniais no Sul do Território Actualmente Português' in Celestino *et al.* 2008, 355–70.

— 2009. 'Phoenician Colonization on the Atlantic Coast of the Iberian Peninsula' in Dietler and López-Ruiz 2009, 113–30.

Artin, G., 2009. *La 'Nécropole Énéolithique' de Byblos: Nouvelle Interprétations*. Oxford: Archaeopress.

Artzy, M., 1988. 'Development of War/Fighting Boats of the IInd Millennium BC in the Eastern Mediterranean.' *Report of the Department of Antiquities, Cyprus*, 1988: 181–86.

— 1994. 'Incense, Camels and Collared Rim Jars: Desert Trade Routes and Maritime Outlets in the Second Millennium.' *OJA* 13: 121–47.

— 1995. 'Nami: A Second Millennium International Maritime Trading Center in the Mediterranean' in S. Gitin (ed.), *Recent Excavations in Israel: A View to the West*. Dubuque: Kendall/Hunt. 17–40.

— 1997. 'Nomads of the Sea' in Swiny *et al.* 1997, 1–16.

— 1998. 'Routes, Trade, Boats and "Nomads of the Sea"' in Gitin *et al.* 1998, 439–49.

Aruz, J., 2009. 'The Aegean or the Near East: Another Look at the "Master of Animals" Pendant in the Aegina Treasure' in J. L. Fitton (ed.), *The Aigina Treasure: Aegean Bronze Age Jewellery and a Mystery Revisited*. London: British Museum. 46–50.

—, K. Benzel and J. M. Evans, (eds) 2008. *Beyond Babylon: Art, Trade, and Diplomacy in the Second Millennium BC*. New Haven: Yale UP.

Aslan, C. C., 2009. 'End or Beginning? The Late Bronze Age to Iron Age Transformation at Troia' in Bachhuber and Roberts 2009, 144–51.

Asouti, E., 2003. 'Wood Charcoal from Santorini (Thera): New Evidence for Climate, Vegetation and Timber Imports in the Aegean Bronze Age.' *Antiquity* 77: 471–84.

Aston, A., 2020. 'How the Cycladic Islanders Found Their Marbles: Material Engagement, Social Cognition and the Emergence of Keros.' *Cambridge Archaeological Journal* 30: 1–24.

Atoche Peña, P., 2002. 'La Colonización de Archiépelago Canario: Un Proceso Mediterráneo?' in Waldren and Ensenyat 2002, 337–54.

Attema, P., 2005. 'Early Urbanization between 800 and 600 BC in the Pontine Region (South Lazio), the Salento Isthmus (Apulia), and the Sibaritide (Northern Calabria)' in Osborne and Cunliffe 2005, 113–42.

— 2008. 'Conflict or Coexistence? Remarks on Indigenous Settlement and Greek Colonization in the Foothills and Hinterland of the Sibaritide (Northern Calabria, Italy)' in P. Bilde and J. Petesen (eds), *Meeting of Cultures in the Black Sea Region: Between Conflict and Coexistence*. Aarhus: Aarhus UP. 67–100.

Attenborough, D., 1987. *The First Eden: The Mediterranean World and Man*. London: Collins. Boston: Little, Brown.

Aubet, M., 2001. *The Phoenicians and the West: Politics, Colonies and Trade*. 2nd edn. Cambridge and New York: Cambridge UP.

— (ed.) 2004. *The Phoenician Cemetery of Tyre-Al Bass: Excavations 1997–1999*. Beirut: Direction Général des Antiquités, Musée National.

— 2005. 'Mainake: The Legend and the New Archaeological Evidence' in Osborne and Cunliffe 2005, 187–202.

— 2006. 'On the Organization of the Phoenician Colonial System in Iberia' in Riva and Vella 2006, 94–109.

Auffray, J.-C., E. Tchernov and E. Nevo, 1988. 'Origine du Commensalisme de la Souris Domestique (*Mus musculus domesticus*) Vis-à-vis de l'Homme.' *Comptes Rendus de l'Académie des Sciences de Paris Sér. III: Sciences de la Vie* 307: 517–22.

Aumassip, G., 1987. 'Le Néolithique en Algérie: État de la Question.' *L'Anthropologie* 91: 585–621.

Bachhuber, C., 2006. 'Aegean Interest on the Uluburun Ship.' *AJA* 110: 345–63.

— 2009. 'The Treasure Deposits of Troy: Rethinking Crisis and Agency on the Early Bronze Age Citadel.' *AS* 59: 1–18.

— and R. G. Roberts, (eds) 2009. *Forces of Transformation: The End of the Bronze Age in the Mediterranean*. Oxford and Oakville: Oxbow.

Bafico, S., I. Oggiano, D. Ridgway and G. Garbini, 1997. 'Fenici e Indigeni a Sant'Imbenia (Alghero)' in P. Bernardini, R. D'Oriano and P. G. Spanu (eds), *Phoinikes B Shrdn – I Fenici in Sardegna: Nuove Acquisizioni*. Cagliari: La Memoria Storica. 45–53.

Bahn, P., and C. Couraud, 1984. 'Azilian Pebbles: An Unsolved Mystery.' *Endeavour* 8: 156–58.

—, P. Pettitt and C. Züchner, 2009. 'The Chauvet Conundrum: Are Claims for the "Birthplace of Art" Premature?' in P. Bahn (ed.), *An Enquiring Mind*. Oxford and Oakville: Oxbow. 253–78.

Bailey, G. N., 1978. 'Shell Middens as Indicators of Postglacial Economies: A Territorial Perspective' in P. Mellars (ed.), *The Early Postglacial Settlement of Northern Europe: An Ecological Perspective*. London: Duckworth. 1979, Pittsburgh: Pittsburgh UP. 37–64.

— 1999. 'The Palaeolithic Archaeology and Palaeogeography of Epirus with Particular Reference to the Investigations of the Klithi Rockshelter' in Bailey *et al.* 1999, 159–69.

— 2010. 'Earliest Coastal Settlement, Marine Palaeoeconomies and Human Dispersal: The Africa-Arabia Connection' in A. Anderson *et al.* 2010, 29–40.

—, E. Adam, E. Panagopoulou, C. Perlès and K. Zachos, (eds) 1999. *The Palaeolithic Archaeology of Greece and Adjacent Areas*. London: British School at Athens.

— and N. Flemming, 2008. 'Archaeology of the Continental Shelf: Marine Resources, Submerged Landscapes and Underwater Archaeology.' *QSR* 27: 2153–65.

— and P. Spikins, (eds) 2008. *Mesolithic Europe*. New York and Cambridge: Cambridge UP.

Baines, J., 1983. 'Literacy and Ancient Egyptian Society.' *Man* 18: 572–99.

— 1996. 'Contextualizing Egyptian Representations of Society and Ethnicity' in J. S. Cooper and G. M. Schwartz (eds), *The Study of the Ancient Near East in the Twenty-First Century*. Winona Lake: Eisenbrauns. 339–84.

— 1999. 'On Wenamun as a Literary Text' in J. Assmann and E. Blumenthal (eds), *Literatur und Politik im Pharaonischen und Ptolemäischen Ägypten*. Cairo: Institut Français d'Archéologie Orientale. 209–33.

— 2004. 'The Earliest Egyptian Writing: Development, Context, Purpose' in S. D. Houston (ed.), *The First Writing: Script Invention as History and Process*. Cambridge and New York: Cambridge UP. 150–89.

— and N. Yoffee, 1998. 'Order, Legitimacy, and Wealth in Ancient Egypt and Mesopotamia' in Feinman and Marcus 1998, 199–260.

Bairoch, P., 1988. *Cities and Economic Development: From the Dawn of History to the Present*. English translation. Chicago: Chicago UP.

Ballard, R. D., (ed.) 2008. *Archaeological Oceanography*. Princeton and Woodstock: Princeton UP.

—, L. Stager, D. Master *et al.*, 2002. 'Iron-Age Shipwrecks in Deep Water off Ashkelon, Israel.' *AJA* 106: 151–68.

Ballouche, A., and P. Marinval, 2003. 'Données Palynologiques et Carpologiques sur la Domestication des Plantes et l'Agriculture dans le Néolithique Ancien de Maroc Septentrional. (Site de Kaf That el-Ghar).' *Revue d'Archéometrie* 27: 49–54.

Balmuth, M. S., D. K. Chester and P. A. Johnston, 2005. *Cultural Responses to the Volcanic Landscape: The Mediterranean and Beyond*. Boston: Archaeological Institute of America. Oxford: Oxbow.

—, A. Gilman and L. Prados-Torreira, (eds) 1997. *Encounters and Transformations: The Archaeology of Iberia in Transition*. Sheffield: Sheffield Academic.

Balter, M., 2006. 'New Carbon Dates Support Revised History of Ancient Mediterranean.' *Science* 312: 508–9.

Bang, P., and W. Scheidel, (eds) 2012. *The Oxford Handbook of the State in the Ancient Near East and Mediterranean*. Oxford and New York: Oxford UP.

Bar-Adon, P., 1980. *The Cave of the Treasure: The Finds from the Caves in Naḥal Mishmar*. Jerusalem: Israel Exploration Society.

Barako, T. J., 2000. 'The Philistine Settlement as Mercantile Phenomenon?' *AJA* 104: 513–30.

Barbaza, M., N. Valdeyron, J. Andre *et al.*, (eds) 2009. *De Méditerranée et d'Ailleurs...: Mélanges Offerts à Jean Guilaine*. Toulouse: Archives d'Écologie Préhistorique.

Barber, E. J. W., 1991. *Prehistoric Textiles: The Development of Cloth in the Neolithic and Bronze Ages with Special Reference to the Aegean*. Princeton and Oxford: Princeton UP.

— 1998. 'Aegean Ornaments and Designs in Egypt' in Cline and Harris-Cline 1998, 13–17.

Bard, K., R. Fattovich and C. Ward, 2007. 'Sea Port to Punt: New Evidence from Marsa Gawasis, Red Sea (Egypt)' in J. Starkey, P. Starkey and T. Wilkinson (eds), *Natural Resources and Cultural Connections of the Red Sea*. Oxford: Archaeopress. 143–48.

Barfield, L., 1994. 'The Bronze Age of Northern Italy: Recent Work and Social Interpretation' in Mathers and Stoddart 1994, 129–44.

— 1998. 'Gender Issues in North Italian Prehistory' in Whitehouse 1998, 143–56.

Barjomovic, G., 2012. 'Mesopotamian Empires' in Bang and Scheidel 2012, 120–61.

Barham, L., and P. Mitchell, 2008. *The First Africans: African Archaeology from the Earliest Toolmakers to Most Recent Foragers*. Cambridge and New York: Cambridge UP.

Barkay, G., 1992. 'The Iron Age II–III' in A. Ben-Tor 1992, 302–73.

Barker, G., 1985. *Prehistoric Farming in Europe*. Cambridge and New York: Cambridge UP.

— 1995. *A Mediterranean Valley: Landscape Archaeology and Annales History in the Biferno Valley*. London and New York: Leicester UP.

— (ed.) 1996. *Farming the Desert: The UNESCO Libyan Valleys Archaeological Survey*. London: Society for Libyan Studies.

— 2005. 'Agriculture, Pastoralism, and Mediterranean Landscapes in Prehistory' in Blake and Knapp 2005, 46–76.

— 2006. *The Agricultural Revolution in Prehistory: Why Did Foragers Become Farmers?* Oxford and New York: Oxford UP.

—, R. Adams, O. Creighton *et al.*, 2007. 'Chalcolithic (*c.* 5000–3600 cal BC) and Bronze Age (*c.* 3600–1200 cal BC) Settlement in Wadi Faynan: Metallurgy and Social Complexity' in Barker, Gilbertson and Mattingly 2007, 227–70.

—, D. Gilbertson and D. Mattingly, (eds) 2007. *Archaeology and Desertification: The Wadi Faynan Landscape Survey, Southern Jordan*. Oxford: Council for British Research in the Levant.

—, C. Hunt, S. McLaren *et al.*, 2007. 'Early Holocene Environments and Early Farming *c.* 11,000–7,000 cal. BP, *c.* 9500–5000 cal. BC' in Barker, Gilbertson and Mattingly 2007, 199–226.

—, — and T. Reynolds, 2007. 'The Haua Fteah, Cyrenaica (Northeast Libya): Renewed Investigations of the Cave and Its Landscape, 2007.' *LS* 38: 93–114.

—, L. Basell, I. Brooks *et al.*, 2008. 'The Cyrenaican Prehistory Project 2008: The Second Season of Investigations of the Haua Fteah Cave and Its Landscape, and Further Results from the Initial 2007 Fieldwork.' *LS* 39: 175–222.

—, A. Antoniadou, H. Barton *et al.*, 2009. 'The Cyrenaican Prehistory Project 2009: The Third Season of Excavations of the Haua Fteah Cave and Its Landscapes, and Further Results from the 2007–2008 Fieldwork.' *LS* 40: 55–94.

—, —, S. Armitage *et al.*, 2010. 'The Cyrenaican Prehistory Project 2010: The Fourth Season of Investigations of the Haua Fteah Cave and Its Landscape, and Further Results from the 2007–2009 Fieldwork.' *LS* 41: 63–88.

— and T. Rasmussen, 1998. *The Etruscans*. Oxford and Malden: Blackwell.

Barnard, H., and J. W. Eerkens, (eds) 2007. *Theory and Practice of Archaeological Residue Analysis*. Oxford: Archaeopress.

Barnett, W. K., 2000. 'Cardial Pottery and the Agricultural Transition in Mediterranean Europe' in Price 2000, 93–116.

Barrett, C. E., 2009. 'The Perceived Value of Minoan and Minoanizing Pottery in Egypt.' *JMA* 22: 211–34.

Barrett, J. C., and P. Halstead, (eds) 2004. *The Emergence of Civilisation Revisited*. Oxford: Oxbow.

Barron, E., T. H. van Andel and D. Pollard, 2003. 'Glacial Environments II: Reconstructing the Climate of Europe in the Last Glaciation' in van Andel and Davies 2003, 57–78.

Barton, R. N. E., 2000. 'Mousterian Hearths and Shellfish: Late Neanderthal Activities on Gibraltar' in Stringer *et al.* 2000, 211–20.

—, J. Bouzouggar, S. N. Collcutt *et al.*, *2005*. 'The Late Upper Palaeolithic Occupation of the Moroccan Northwest Maghreb during the Late Glacial Maximum.' *AAR* 22: 77–100.

Bar-Yosef, O., 1998. 'The Natufian Culture in the Levant: Threshold to the Origins of Agriculture.' *EA* 6: 159–77.

— 2002. 'The Natufian Culture and the Early Neolithic: Social and Economic Trends in Southwestern Asia' in Bellwood and Renfrew 2002, 113–26.

— and D. Alon, 1988. 'Excavations in Nahal Hemar Cave.' *'Atiqot* 18: 1–30.

— and A. Belfer-Cohen, 2001. 'From Africa to Eurasia – Early Dispersals.' *QI* 75: 19–28.

— and —, 2010. 'The Levantine Upper Palaeolithic and Epipalaeolithic' in Garcea 2010a, 144–67.

— and F. Valla, (eds) 1991. *The Natufian Culture in the Levant*. Ann Arbor: Michigan UP.

Bar-Yosef Mayer, D., 1991. 'Changes in the Selection of Marine Shells from the Natufian to the Neolithic' in Bar-Yosef and Valla 1991, 629–36.

— 2005. 'The Exploitation of Shell Beads in the Palaeolithic and Neolithic of the Levant.' *Paléorient* 31: 176–85.

Basch, L., and M. Artzy, 1985. 'Appendix 2: Ship Graffito at Kition' in V. Karageorghis and M. Demas (eds), *Excavations at Kition V: I. The Pre-Phoenician Levels, Areas I and II*. Nicosia: Department of Antiquities. 322–36.

Bass, B., 1998. 'Early Neolithic Offshore Accounts: Remote Islands, Maritime Exploitation, and the Trans-Adriatic Cultural Network.' *JMA* 11: 165–90.

Bass, G. F., (ed.) 1967. *Cape Gelidonya: A Bronze Age Shipwreck*. Philadelphia: American Philosophical Society.

— 1991. 'Evidence of Trade from Bronze Age Shipwrecks' in N. H. Gale 1991a, 69–82.

— 2010. 'Cape Gelidonya Shipwreck' in Cline 2010, 797–803.

Bassiakos, Y., and T. Tselios, 2012. 'On the Cessation of Local Copper Production in the Aegean in the 2nd Millennium BC' in Kassianidou and Papasavvas 2012, 151–61.

Bates, O., 1927. 'Excavations at Marsa Matruh.' *Harvard African Studies* 8: 125–97.

Batiuk, S., and S. R. Mitchell, 2007. 'Early Transcaucasian Cultures and Their Neighbors: Unravelling Migration, Trade, and Assimilation.' *Expedition* 49: 7–17.

Battarbee, R. W., F. Gasse and C. E. Stickley, (eds) 2004. *Past Climate Variability through Europe and Africa*. Dordrecht: Springer.

Bauer, A. A., 1998. 'Cities of the Sea: Maritime Trade and the Origin of Philistine Settlement in the Early Iron Age Southern Levant.' *OJA* 17: 149–68.

Beaujard, P., 2011. 'Evolutions and Temporal Delimitations of Bronze Age World-systems in Western Asia and the Mediterranean' in T. C. Wilkinson *et al.* 2011, 7–26.

Becker, M. J., 1995. 'Human Skeletal Remains from the Pre-Colonial Greek Emporium of Pithekoussai on Ischia (NA): Culture Contact in Italy from the Early VIII to the II Century BC' in Christie 1995, 273–81.

Becks, R., 2006. 'Troia in der späten Bronzezeit – Troia VI und Troia VIIa' in Korfmann 2006, 155–66.

Bedford, P. R., 2007. 'The Persian Near East' in Scheidel *et al.* 2007, 302–30.

— 2009. 'The Neo-Assyrian Empire' in I. Morris and Scheidel 2009, 30–65.

Bednarik, R. G., 2003. 'Seafaring in the Pleistocene.' *CAJ* 13: 41–66.

Beeching, A., D. Binder, J.-C. Blanchet *et al.*, 1991. *Identité du Chasséen*. Nemours: A.P.R.A.I.F.

Belarte, M., 2009. 'Colonial Contacts and Protohistoric Indigenous Urbanism on the Mediterranean Coast of the Iberian Peninsula' in Dietler and López-Ruiz 2009, 91–113.

Belén Deamos, M., 2009. 'Phoenicians in Tartessos' in Dietler and López-Ruiz 2009, 193–228.

— and T. Chapa Brunet, 2012. 'De sog. Krieger von Cadiz: Zur Steinskulptur im Phönizischen Kontext der Iberischen Halbinsel.' *Madrider Mitteilungen* 53: 220–38.

Belhouchet, L., 2008. 'Les Gravures sur Coquilles d'Oeufs d'Autruche en Afrique du Nord: Interprétation des Décors Géometriques.' *Sahara* 19: 77–84.

Bell, C., 2006. *The Evolution of Long Distance Trading Relationships across the LBA/Iron Age Transition on the Northern Levantine Coast: Crisis, Continuity and Change, a Study Based on Imported Ceramics, Bronze and Its Constituent Metals*. Oxford: Archaeopress.

— 2012. 'The Merchants of Ugarit: Oligarchs of the Late Bronze Age Trade in Metals?' in Kassianidou and Papasavvas 2012, 180–87.

Bellard, C. G., 1995. 'The First Colonization of Ibiza and Formentera (Balearic Islands, Spain): Some More Islands out of the Stream?' *WA* 26: 442–55.

Bellwood, P., 2004. *First Farmers: The Origins of Agricultural Societies*. Malden and Oxford: Blackwell.

— and C. Renfrew, (eds) 2002. *Examining the Farming/ Language Dispersal Hypothesis*. Cambridge: MIAR.

Benjamin, J., C. Bonsall, C. Pickard and A. Fischer, (eds) 2011. *Submerged Prehistory*. Oxford and Oakville: Oxbow.

Bennet, J., 1985. 'The Structure of the Linear B Administration at Knossos.' *AJA* 89: 231–49.
— 1997. 'Homer and the Bronze Age' in I. Morris and B. Powell (eds), *A New Companion to Homer*. Leiden and New York: Brill. 511–34.
— 2004. 'Iconographies of Value: Words, People and Things in the Late Bronze Age Aegean' in J. C. Barrett and Halstead 2004, 90–106.
— 2007. 'The Aegean Bronze Age' in Scheidel *et al.* 2007, 175–210.
— and C. Shelmerdine, 2001. 'Not the Palace of Nestor: The Development of the "Lower Town" and Other Non-palatial Settlements in LBA Messenia' in Branigan 2001a, 135–40.
Bensimon, Y., and M. Martineau, 1987. 'Le Néolithique Marocain en 1986.' *L'Anthropologie* 91: 623–52.
— and —, 1990. 'Deux Nouvelles Poteries Néolithiques sur le Littoral du Sahara Marocain.' *L'Anthropologie* 94: 591–601.
Bentley, A., 2007. 'Mobility, Specialisation and Community Diversity in the Linearbandkeramik: Isotopic Evidence from the Skeletons' in Whittle and Cummings 2007, 117–40.
Ben-Tor, A., (ed.) 1992. *The Archaeology of Ancient Israel*. New Haven: Yale UP.
Ben-Tor, D., 2007. *Scarabs, Chronology, and Interconnections: Egypt and Palestine in the Second Intermediate Period*. Friborg: Academic.
Benzel, K., 2008. 'The Horse in the Ancient Near East' in Aruz *et al.* 2008, 155–60.
Berger, J.-F., J.-L. Brochier, J. Vital *et al.*, 2007. 'Nouveau Regard sur la Dynamique des Paysages et l'Occupation Humaine à l'Âge du Bronze en Moyenne Vallée du Rhône' in H. Richard, M. Magny and C. Mordant (eds), *Environnements et Cultures à l'Âge du Bronze en Europe Occidentale*. Besançon: Editions du CTHS. 259–83.
— and J. Guilaine, 2009. 'The 8200 cal BP Abrupt Environmental Change and the Neolithic Transition: A Mediterranean Perspective.' *QI* 200: 31–49.
Bermúdez de Castro, J. M., J. L. Arsuaga, E. Carbonell *et al.*, 1997. 'A Hominid from the Lower Pleistocene of Atapuerca, Spain: Possible Ancestor to Neandertals and Modern Humans.' *Science* 276: 1392–95.
Bernabeu, J., 2002. 'The Social and Symbolic Context of Neolithization' in E. Badal, J. Bernabeu and B. Marti (eds), *El Paisaje en el Neolítico Mediterráneo*. 209–33.
—, L. Molina Balaguer, M. A. Esquembre *et al.*, 2009. 'La Cerámica Impresa Mediterránea en el Origen Neolítico de la Península Ibérica?' in Barbaza *et al.* 2009, 83–95.
—, —, T. Orozco Kohler *et al.*, 2008. 'Early Neolithic at the Serpis Valley, Alicante, Spain' in Diniz 2008, 53–60.
Bernabò Brea, M., A. Cardarelli and M. Cremaschi, (eds) 1997. *La Terramare: La Più Antica Civiltà Padana*. Milan: Electa.
—, M. Cremaschi, L. Bronzoni *et al.*, 2011. 'Soil Use from the Late Chalcolithic to the Early Middle Bronze Age in the Central Po Plain' in van Leusen *et al.* 2011, 207–14.
Bernal, M., 1987. *Black Athena: The Afroasiatic Roots of Classical Civilization*. Vol. 1: *The Fabrication of Ancient Greece 1785–1985*. London: Free Association Books. New Brunswick: Rutgers UP.
Bernáldez-Sánchez, E., E. García-Viñas, F. Sanguino *et al.*, 2024. 'Equids (Equus sp.) in Southern Spain from the Palaeolithic to the Bronze Age.' *JQS* 39: 261–76.
Bernardini, F., E. Montagnari and A. Velušček, 2009. 'Prehistoric Cultural Connections in Northeastern Adriatic Regions Identified by Archaeometric Analyses of Stone Axes' in Forenbaher 2009a, 47–58.
Betancourt, P. P., 2007. *Introduction to Aegean Art*. Philadelphia: INSTAP Academic. Oxford: Oxbow.
Bevan, A., 2003. 'Reconstructing the Role of Egyptian Culture in the Value Regimes of the Bronze Age Aegean: Stone Vessels and Their Social Contexts' in Matthews and Roemer 2003, 57–73.
— 2004. 'Emerging Civilized Values? The Consumption and Imitation of Egyptian Stone Vessels in EMII-MMI Crete and Its Wider Eastern Mediterranean Context' in J. C. Barrett and Halstead 2004, 107–26.
— 2007. *Stone Vessels and Values in the Bronze Age Mediterranean*. Cambridge and New York: Cambridge UP.
— 2010a. 'Making and Marking Relationships: Bronze Age Brandings and Mediterranean Commodities' in A. Bevan and D. Wengrow (eds), *Cultures of Commodity Branding*. Walnut Creek: Left Coast. 35–85.
— 2010b. Political Geography and Palatial Crete.' *JMA* 23: 27–54.
— 2014. 'Mediterranean Containerization.' *CA* 55:387–418.
— and J. Conolly, 2013. *Mediterranean Islands, Fragile Communities and Persistent Landscapes: Antikythera in Long-term Perspective*. Cambridge and New York: Cambridge UP.
Beyneix, A., 1997. 'Les Sépultures Chasséennes du Sud de la France.' *Zephyrus* 50: 125–78.
Bicho, N., A. F. Carvalho, C. González-Sainz *et al.*, 2007. 'The Upper Paleolithic Rock Art of Iberia.' *Journal of Archaeological Method and Theory* 14: 81–151.
Bickel, S., 1998. 'Commercants et Bateliers au Nouvel Empire: Mode de Vie et Statut d'un Groupe Social' in Grimal and Benu 1998, 157–72.
Bietak, M., 1996. *Avaris the Capital of the Hyksos: Recent Excavations at Tell el-Dab'a*. London: British Museum.
— 1997. 'Avaris, Capital of the Hyksos Kingdom: New Results of Excavations' in Oren 1997a, 87–139.
— 2005. 'The Tuthmoside Stronghold of Perunefer.' *Egyptian Archaeology* 26: 13–17.
— 2008. 'Tell el-Dab'a in the Nile Valley' in Aruz *et al.* 2008, 110–12.
— 2009. 'Near Eastern Sanctuaries in the Eastern Nile Delta' in Maila-Afeiche 2009, 209–28.
— 2010. 'From Where Came the Hyksos and Where Did They Go?' in Marée 2010, 139–82.
—, N. Marinatos and C. Palyvou, (eds) 2007. *Taureador Scenes in Tell el-Dab'a (Avaris) and Knossos*. Vienna: Österreichischen Akademie der Wissenschaften.
Bietti, A., and F. Negrino, 2007. '"Transitional" Industries from Neandertals to Anatomically Modern Humans in Continental Italy: Present State of Knowledge' in J. Riel-Salvatore and G. A. Clark (eds), *New Approaches to the Study of Early Upper Paleolithic 'Transitional' Industries in Western Eurasia: Transitions Great and Small*. Oxford: Archaeopress. 41–60.
Bietti Sestieri, A. M., 1992. *The Iron Age Community of Osteria dell'Osa: A Study of Socio-political Development in Central Tyrrhenian Italy*. Cambridge and New York: Cambridge UP.
— 1997. 'Italy in Europe in the Early Iron Age.' *PPS* 63: 371–402.
— 2010. *L'Italia nell'Età del Bronzo e del Ferro: Dalle Palafitte a Romolo (2200–700 a.C.)*. Rome: Carocci.
—, A. Cazzella and A. Schnapp, 2002. 'The Mediterranean' in B. Cunliffe, W. Davies and A. Renfrew (eds), *Archaeology: The Widening Debate*. Oxford: British Academy. 411–38.
Bikai, P. M., 1978. *The Pottery of Tyre*. Warminster: Aris & Phillips.
Binder, D., 2000. 'Mesolithic and Neolithic Interaction in Southern France and Northern Italy: New Data and Current Hypotheses' in Price 2000, 117–43.
— 2002. 'Stones Making Sense: What Obsidian Could Tell about the Origins of the Central Anatolian Neolithic' in Gérard and Thissen 2002, 79–92.
Bintliff, J., 2004. 'Time, Structure and Agency: The Annales, Emergent Complexity and Archaeology' in J. Bintliff (ed.), *A Companion to Archaeology*. Malden and Oxford: Blackwell. 174–94.
Biran, A., 1993. 'Tel Dan' in E. Stern (ed.), *The New Encyclopedia of Archaeological Excavations in the Holy Land*. Vol. 1. Jerusalem: Israel Exploration Society & Carta. New York: Simon & Schuster. 323–32.
Bisheh, G., 2001. 'One Damn Illicit Excavation after Another: The Destruction of the *Archaeological* Heritage of Jordan' in Brodie *et al. 2001, 115–18.*
Bispham, E., 2007. 'The Samnites' in G. Bradley *et al.* 2007, 179–223.
Bisset, N. G., J. G. Bruhn and M. H. Zenk, 1996. 'The Presence of Opium in a 3,500 Year Old Cypriote Base-ring Juglet.' *ÄL* 6: 203–4.
Bisson de la Roque, F., G. Contenau and F. Chapouthier, 1953. 'Le Trésor de Tôd.' *Documents de Fouilles de l'Institut Français d'Archéologie Oriental du Cairo 11*.
Black, E., B. Hoskins, J. Slingo and D. Brayshaw, 2011. 'The Present-day Climate of the Middle East' in Mithen and Black 2011, 13–24.
Blake, E., 1998. 'Sardinia's Nuraghi: Four Millennia of Becoming.' *WA* 30: 59–71.
— 2001. 'Constructing a Nuragic Locale: The Spatial Relationship between Tombs and Towers in Bronze Age Sardinia.' *AJA* 105: 145–61.
— 2005. 'The Material Expression of Cult, Ritual, and Feasting' in Blake and Knapp 2005, 102–29.
— 2008. 'The Mycenaeans in Italy: A Minimalist Position.' *Papers of the British School at Rome* 76: 1–34.
— and A. B. Knapp, (eds) 2005. *The Archaeology of Mediterranean Prehistory*. Oxford and Malden: Blackwell.
Blanton, R. E., 1998. 'Beyond Centralization: Steps toward a Theory of Egalitarian Behavior in Archaic States' in Feinman and Marcus 1998, 135–71.
Blondel, J., 2006. 'The "Design" of Mediterranean Landscapes: A Millennial Story of Humans and Ecological Systems during the Historic Period.' *Human Ecology* 34: 713–29.
—, J. Aronson, J.-Y. Bodiou and G. Boeuf, 2010. *The Mediterranean Region: Biological Diversity in Time and Space*. 2nd edn. Oxford and New York: Oxford UP.
Blue, L., 1997. 'Cyprus and Cilicia: Typology and Palaeogeography of Second Millennium Harbours' in Swiny *et al.* 1997, 31–43.
Blumler, M., 1996. 'Ecology, Evolutionary Theory and Agricultural Origins' in D. R. Harris 1996, 25–50.
Boardman, J., 1980. *The Greeks Overseas: Their Early Colonies and Trade*. Rev edn. London and New York: Thames & Hudson.
Boaretto, E., W. Xiaohong, Y. Jiarong *et al.*, 2009. 'Radiocarbon Dating of Charcoal and Bone Collagen Associated with Early Pottery at Yuchanyan Cave, Hunan Province, China.' *PNAS* 106: 9595–600.
Bocquet-Appel, J.-P., and O. Bar-Yosef, (eds) 2008. *The Neolithic Demographic Transition and Its Consequences*. New York: Springer.
— and P. Y. Demars, 2000. 'Population Kinetics in the Upper Palaeolithic in Western Europe.' *JAS* 27: 551–70.
Boëda, E., S. Bonilauri, J. Connan *et al.*, 2008. 'Middle Palaeolithic Bitumen Use at Umm el Tlel around 70,000 BP.' *Antiquity* 82: 853–61.
—, J. M. Geneste and C. Griggo, 1999. 'A Levallois Point Embedded in the Vertebra of a Wild Ass (*Equus africanus*): Hafting, Projectiles and Mousterian Hunting Weapons.' *Antiquity* 73: 394–402.
Boenzi, F., M. Caldara, M. Moresi and L. Pennetta, 2002. 'History of the Salpi Lagoon-sabhka (Manfredonia Gulf, Italy).' *Il Quaternario* 14: 93–104.
Bogaard, A., 2005. '"Garden Agriculture" and the Nature of Early Farming in Europe and the Near East.' *WA* 37: 177–96.
Boileau, M.-C., L. Badre, E. Capet *et al.*, 2010. 'Foreign Ceramic Tradition, Local Clays: The Handmade Burnished Ware of Tell Kazel (Syria).' *JAS* 37: 1678–89.
Bokbot, Y., 2005. 'La Civilizacion del Vaso Campaniforme en Marruecos y la Cuestion del Sustrato Calcolitico Precampaniforme' in M. Rojo Guerra, R. Garrido-Pena and I. García-Martínez de Lagrán (eds), *El Campaniforme en la Peninsula Ibérica y su Contexto Europeo*. Valladolid: Universidad de Valladolid. 137–59.
Bolger, D., and L. C. Maguire, (eds) 2010. *The Development of Pre-state Communities in the Ancient Near East*. Oxford and Oakville: Oxbow.
Bolle, H.-J., 2003. 'Climate, Climate Variability, and Impacts in the Mediterranean Area: An Overview' in H.-J. Bolle (ed.), *Mediterranean Climate: Variability and Trends*. London and New York: Springer. 5–86.
Bonfante, L., and V. Karageorghis, (eds) 2001. *Italy and Cyprus in Antiquity 1500–450 BC*. Nicosia: The Costakis and Leto Severis Foundation.
Bonfiglio, L., A. C. Marra, F. Masini *et al.*, 2002. 'Pleistocene Faunas of Sicily: A Review' in Waldren and Ensenyat 2002, 428–36.
Bonhomme, F., A. Orth, T. Cucchi *et al.*, 2004. 'A New Species of Wild Mice on the Island of Cyprus.' *Comptes Rendus Biologiques* 327: 501–7.
—, —, — *et al.*, 2011. 'Genetic Differentiation of the House Mouse around the Mediterranean Basin: Matrilineal Footprints of Early and Late Colonization.' *Proceedings of the Royal Society B* 278: 1034–43.
Bonino, M., 1990. 'A Neolithic Boat in the Adriatic.' *Mariner's Mirror* 76: 113–15.
Bonn-Muller, E., 2010. 'First Minoan Shipwreck.' *Archaeology* 63: 44–7.
Bonsall, C., (ed.) 1989. *The Mesolithic in Europe*. Edinburgh: J. Donald.
Borghouts, J. F., 1988. 'Surveying the Delta: Some Retrospects and Prospects' in van den Brink 1988, 3–8.
Borgna, E., and P. C. Guida, 2009. 'Seafarers and Land-travellers in the Bronze Age of the Northern Adriatic' in Forenbaher 2009a, 89–104.
Bosch, E., F. Calafell, D. Comas *et al.*, 2001. 'High-resolution Analysis of Human Y-chromosome Variation Shows a Sharp Discontinuity and Limited Gene Flow between Northwestern Africa and the Iberian Peninsula.' *American Journal of Human Genetics* 68: 1019–29.
Botto, M., 2004–5. 'Da "Sulky" a Huelva: Considerazioni sui Commerci Fenici nel Mediterraneo Antico.' *Annali di Archeologia e Storia Antica* 11–12: 9–27.
— 2007. 'I Rapporti fra la Sardegna e le Coste Medio-Tirreniche della Penisola Italiana: La Prima Metà del I Millennio aC' in G. M. Della Fina (ed.), *Etruschi, Greci, Fenici e Cartaginesi nel Mediterraneo Centrale*. Rome: Quasar. 75–136.
Bounni, A., E. Lagarce and J. Lagarce, 1998. *Ras Ibn Hani I: Le Palais Nord du Bronze Récent*. Beirut: Institut Français du Proche-Orient.
Bourke, S., 2001. 'The Chalcolithic Period' in B. MacDonald, R. Adams and P. Bienkowski (eds), *The Archaeology of Jordan*. Sheffield: Sheffield Academic. 107–62.
Bourriau, A., L. Smith and M. Serpico, 2001. 'The Provenance of Canaanite Amphorae Found at Memphis and Amarna in the New Kingdom' in Shortland 2001, 113–46.

Bourriau, J., 2000. 'The Second Intermediate Period (*c.* 1650–1550 BC)' in I. Shaw 2000a, 184–217.
— 2004. 'The Beginnings of Amphora Production in Egypt' in J. Bourriau and Phillips 2004, 78–95.
— and J. Phillips, 2004. *Invention and Innovation: The Social Context of Technological Change 2: Egypt, The Aegean and the Near East, 1650–1150 BC.* Oxford: Oxbow.
Bouville, C., 1987. 'Les Restes Humains de la Baume Fontbregoua a Salernes (Var)' in J. Guilaine (ed.), *Premières Communautés Paysannes en Mèditerranèe Occidentale.* Paris: CNRS. 501–5.
Bouzouggar, A., and R. N. E. Barton, 2012. 'The Identity and Timing of the Aterian in Morocco' in Hublin and McPherron 2012, 93–106.
—, —, M. Vanhaeren *et al.*, 2007. '82,000-year-old Shell Beads from North Africa and Implications for the Origins of Modern Human Behavior.' *PNAS* 104: 9964–69.
Bover, P., and J. A. Alcover, 2003. 'Understanding Late Quaternary Extinctions: The Case of *Myotragus balearicus* (Bate 1909).' *JB* 30: 771–81.
Bowen, R. L., 1960. 'Egypt's Earliest Sailing Ships.' *Antiquity* 34: 117–31.
Bradley, G., 2007. 'Romanization: The End of the Peoples of Italy?' in G. Bradley *et al.* 2007, 295–322.
—, E. Isayev and C. Riva, (eds) 2007. *Ancient Italy: Regions without Boundaries.* Exeter: Exeter UP.
Bradley, R., C. Chippindale and K. Helskog, 2001. 'Post-Paleolithic Europe' in D. S. Whitley (ed.), *Handbook of Rock Art Research.* Oxford and Walnut Creek: AltaMira. 482–529.
Brandherm, D., and M. Trachsel, (eds) 2008. *A New Dawn for the Dark Age? Shifting Paradigms in Mediterranean Iron Age Chronology.* Oxford: Archaeopress.
Branigan, K., 1991. 'Mochlos – An Early Aegean "Gateway Community"?' in Laffineur and Basch 1991, 97–105.
— (ed.) 2001a. *Urbanism in the Aegean Bronze Age.* London: Sheffield Academic.
— 2001b. 'Aspects of Minoan Urbanism' in Branigan 2001a, 38–50.
Braudel, F., 1972a. *The Mediterranean and the Mediterranean World in the Age of Philip II.* 2 vols. English translation. Berkeley and London: California UP.
— 1972b. 'Personal Testimony.' *Journal of Modern History* 44: 448–67.
— 1980. *On History.* English translation. London: Weidenfeld & Nicolson. Chicago: Chicago UP.
— 1982–84. *Civilization and Capitalism.* 3 vols. English translation. London: Collins. New York: Harper & Row.
— 1989–90. *The Identity of France.* 2 vols. English translation. London: Fontana.
— 2001. *The Mediterranean in the Ancient World.* English translation. London and New York: Allen Lane.
Braun, E., 2002. 'Egypt's First Sojourn in Canaan' in van den Brink and Levy 2002, 173–89.
— 2003. 'South Levantine Encounters with Ancient Egypt at the Beginning of the Third Millennium' in Matthews and Roemer 2003, 21–38.
— and E. C. M. van den Brink, 2008. 'Appraising South Levantine–Egyptian Interaction: Recent Discoveries from Israel and Egypt' in Midant-Reynes and Tristant 2008, 643–88.
Breasted, J. H., 1906. *Ancient Records of Egypt: Historical Documents from the Earliest Times to the Persian Conquest.* Vol. IV. Chicago: Chicago UP.
Breniquet, C., 2008. *Essai sur le Tissage en Mésopotamie: Des Premières Communautés Sédentaires au Milieu du IIIe Millénaire avant J.-C.* Paris: De Boccard.
Brett, M., and E. Fentress, 1996. *The Berbers.* Oxford and Cambridge: Blackwell.
Breunig, P., K. Neumann and W. van Neer, 1996. 'New Research on the Holocene Settlement and Environment of the Chad Basin in Nigeria.' *AAR* 13: 111–45.
Briant, P., 2002. *From Cyrus to Alexander: A History of the Persian Empire.* English translation. Winona Lake: Eisenbrauns.
Briggs, A. W., J. M. Good, R. E. Green *et al.*, 2009. 'Targeted Retrieval and Analysis of Five Neandertal mtDNA Genomes.' *Science* 325: 318–31.
Brodie, N., 2008. 'The Donkey: An Appropriate Technology for Early Bronze Age Land Transport and Traction' in Brodie *et al.* 2008, 299–304.
—, J. Doole and C. Renfrew, (eds) 2001. *Trade in Illicit Antiquities: The Destruction of the World's Archaeological Heritage.* Cambridge: MIAR.
—, —, G. Gavalas and C. Renfrew, (eds) 2008. *Horizon: A Colloquium on the Prehistory of the Cyclades.* Cambridge and Oakville: MIAR.
—, — and P. Watson, 2000. *Stealing History: The Illicit Trade in Cultural Material.* Cambridge: MIAR.
Brody, A., 1998. *'Each Man Cried to His God': The Specialized Religion of Canaanite and Phoenician Seafarers.* Atlanta: Scholars.
Bron, C., F. Lissarrague, C. Bérard *et al.*, (eds) 1984. *La Cité des Images: Religion et Société en Grèce Antique.* Paris: F. Nathan.
Broodbank, C., 1989. 'The Longboat and Society in the Cyclades in the Keros-Syros Culture.' *AJA* 93: 319–37.
— 1993. 'Ulysses without Sails: Trade, Distance, Knowledge and Power in the Early Cyclades.' *WA* 24: 315–31.
— 1999. 'Colonization and Configuration in the Insular Neolithic of the Aegean' in Halstead 1999a, 15–41.
— 2000. *An Island Archaeology of the Early Cyclades.* Cambridge and New York: Cambridge UP.
— 2004. 'Minoanisation.' *PCPS* 50: 46–91.
— 2006. 'The Origins and Early Development of Mediterranean Maritime Activity.' *JMA* 19, 199–230.
— 2007. 'The Pottery' in Renfrew, Doumas *et al.* 2007, 115–237.
— 2008. 'Long after Hippos, Well before Palaces: A Commentary on the Cultures and Contexts of Neolithic Crete' in Isaakidou and Tomkins 2008, 273–90.
— 2010a. 'Braudel's Bronze Age' in O. Krzyszkowska (ed.) *Cretan Offerings: Studies in Honour of Peter Warren.* London: British School at Athens. 33–40.
— 2010b. '"Ships A-sail from over the Rim of the Sea": Voyaging, Sailing and the Making of Mediterranean Societies *c.* 3500–800 BC' in Anderson *et al.* 2010, 249–64.
— 2011. 'The Mediterranean and the Mediterranean World in the Age of Andrew Sherratt' in T. C. Wilkinson *et al.* 2011, 27–36.
— and E. Kiriatzi, 2007. 'The First "Minoans" of Kythera Re-visited: Technology, Demography, and Landscape in the Prepalatial Aegean.' *AJA* 111: 241–74.
— and T. F. Strasser, 1991. 'Migrant Farmers and the Neolithic Colonization of Crete.' *Antiquity* 65: 233–45.
— and G. Lucarini, 2019. 'The Dynamics of Mediterranean Africa, ca. 9600–1000 BC: An Interpretative Synthesis of Knowns and Unknowns.' *JMA* 32: 195–267.
—, —, Y. Bokbot *et al.*, 2024. 'Oued Beht, Morocco: A New Complex Early Farming Society in Northwest Africa and its Implications for Western Mediterranean Interaction During Later Prehistory.' *Antiquity* 98.
Brooks, N., 2006. 'Cultural Responses to Aridity in the Middle Holocene and Increased Social Complexity.' *QI* 151: 29–49.
— 2010. 'Human Responses to Climatically-driven Landscape Change and Resource Scarcity: Learning from the Past and Planning for the Future' in I. P. Martini and W. Chesworth (eds), *Landscapes and Societies: Selected Cases.* London: Springer. 43–66.
—, N. Drake, S. McLaren and K. White, 2003. 'Studies in Geography, Geomorphology, Environment and Climate' in Mattingly 2003, 37–74.
Brown, K., 2004. 'Aerial Archaeology of the Tavoliere: The Italian Air Photographic Record and the Riley Archive.' *ARP* 9: 123–46.
Brown, T., and K. Brown, 2011, *Biomolecular Archaeology: An Introduction.* Chichester and Malden: Wiley-Blackwell.
Brun, P., and B. Chaume, 1997. *Vix et les Éphémères Principautés Celtiques. Paris: Errance.*
Bryan, B. M., 2000. 'The Eighteenth Dynasty before the Amarna Period (*c.* 1550–1352 BC)' in I. Shaw 2000a, 218–71.
Bryce, T., 2002. *Life and Society in the Hittite World.* Oxford and New York: Oxford UP.
— 2005. *The Kingdom of the Hittites.* New edn. Oxford and New York: Oxford UP.
— 2006. *The Trojans and Their Neighbours.* London and New York: Routledge.
Brysbaert, A., 2008. *The Power of Technology in the Bronze Age Eastern Mediterranean: The Case of the Painted Plaster.* London and Oakville: Equinox.
Buchner, G., and D. Ridgway, 1993. *Pithekoussai I: La Necropoli.* Rome: Giorgio Bretschneider.
Bulbeck, D., 2007. 'Where River Meets Sea.' *CA* 48: 315–21.
Bunimovitz, S., 1995. 'On the Edge of Empires – Late Bronze Age (1500–1200 BCE)' in Levy 1995a, 320–31.
Burke, B., 1999. 'Purple and the Aegean Textile Trade of the Early Second Millennium BC' in P. Betancourt, V. Karageorghis, R. Laffineur and W. D. Niemeier (eds), *MELETEMATA: Studies in Aegean Archaeology.* Liège: Université de Liège. 75–82.
Burkert, W., 1992. *The Orientalizing Revolution: Near Eastern Influence on Greek Culture in the Early Archaic Age.* Cambridge and London: Harvard UP.
Burns, B. E., 2010. *Mycenaean Greece, Mediterranean Commerce, and the Formation of Identity.* Cambridge and New York: Cambridge UP.
Burr, V., 1932. *Nostrum Mare: Ursprung und Geschichte der Namen des Mittelmeeres und seiner Teilmeere in Altertum.* Stuttgart: W. Kohlhammer.
Burroughs, W. J., 2005. *Climate Change in Prehistory: The End of the Reign of Chaos.* Cambridge and New York: Cambridge UP.
Burton, M., and T. E. Levy, 2006. 'Appendix 1: Organic Residue Analysis of Selected Vessels from Gilat. Gilat Torpedo Jars' in Levy 2006, 849–62.
Bushnell, L., 2012. 'Fragrant Copying? Mycenaean Perfumed Oil and the Role of Cyprus' in A. Georgiou (ed.), *Cyprus: An Island Culture. Society and Social Relations from the Bronze Age to the Venetian Period.* Oxford and Oakville: Oxbow. 196–209.
Butzer, K. W., 1976. *Early Hydraulic Civilization in Egypt: A Study in Cultural Ecology.* Chicago and London: Chicago UP.
— 1997. 'Late Quaternary Problems of the Egyptian Nile: Stratigraphy, Environments, Prehistory.' *Paléorient* 23: 151–73.
— 2002. 'Geoarchaeological Implications of Recent Research in the Nile Delta' in van den Brink and Levy 2002, 83–97.
Buxó, R., 2008. 'The Agricultural Consequences of Colonial Contacts on the Iberian Peninsula in the First Millennium BC.' *Vegetation History and Archaeobotany* 17: 235–36.
—, N. Rovira and C. Saüch, 2000. 'Les Restes Vegetals de Llavors i Fruits' in A. Bosch, J. Chinchilla and J. Tarrús (eds), *El Poblat Lacustre Neolitic de la Draga: Excavacions de 1990 a 1998.* Girona: Museu d'Arqueologia de Catalunya. 129–40.
Byrd, B. F., 2000. 'Households in Transition: Neolithic Social Organization within Southwest Asia' in Kuijt 2000a, 63–98.
— 2005. *Early Village Life at Beidha, Jordan: Neolithic Spatial Organization and Vernacular Architecture: The Excavations of Mrs Diana Kirkbride-Helbæk.* Oxford and New York: Oxford UP.
Cadogan, G., E. Hatzaki and A. Vasilakis, 2004. *Knossos: Palace, City, State.* London: British School at Athens.
Calado, M., and L. Rocha, 2008. 'Sources of Monumentality: Standing Stones in Context (Fontainhas, Alentejo Central, Portugal)' in Diniz 2008, 61–70.
Callender, G., 2000. 'The Middle Kingdom Renaissance (*c.* 2055–1650 BC)' in I. Shaw 2000a, 137–71.
Callot, O., 1987. 'Les Huileries du Bronze Récent à Ougarit: Premiers Éléments pour une Étudein' in Yon 1987, 197–212.
Calvet, Y., 2000. 'The House of Urtenu.' *Near Eastern Archaeology* 63: 210–13.
— 2007. 'Ugarit: The Kingdom and the City – Urban Features' in K. L. Younger (ed.), *Ugarit at Seventy-five.* Winona Lake: Eisenbrauns. 101–11.
— and Y. Castel, 2004. 'La Vie dans la Capitale d'Ougarit' in G. Galliano and Y. Castel (eds), *Le Royaume d'Ougarit aux Origines de l'Alphabet.* Paris: Somogy Éditions d'Art. 218–39.
Cambitoglou, A., J. M. Birmingham and J. R. Green, 1971. *Zagora 1: Excavations of a Geometric Settlement on the Island of Andros, Greece.* Sydney: Sydney UP.
—, —, J. J. Coulton, A. Birchall and J. R. Green, 1988. *Zagora 2: Excavation of a Geometric Town on the Island of Andros, Greece.* Athens: Archaeological Society.
Campbell, D., 2010. 'Modelling the Agricultural Impacts of the Earliest Large Villages at the Pre-pottery Neolithic-Pottery Neolithic Transition' in W. Finlayson and Warren 2010, 173–83.
Camps, G., 1974. *Les Civilisations Préhistoriques de l'Afrique du Nord.* Paris: Doin.
— 1982. 'Beginnings of Pastoralism and Cultivation in Northwest Africa and the Sahara: Origins of the Berbers' in J. D. Clark (ed.), *The Cambridge History of Africa*, Vol. 1: *From the Earliest Times to c.500 B.C.* Cambridge: Cambridge UP. 548–612.
Camps, M., and C. Szmidt, (eds) 2009. *The Mediterranean from 50,000 to 25,000 BP: Turning Points and New Directions.* Oxford and Oakville: Oxbow.
Canet, H., and J.-L. Roudil, 1978. 'Le Village Chalcolithique de Cambous à Viols-en-Laval (Hérault).' *Gallia Préhistoire* 21: 143–88.
Cañete, C., 2010. 'Classifying an Oxymoron: On Black-boxes, Materiality and Identity in the Scientific Representation of the Mediterranean' in van Dommelen and Knapp 2010, 19–37.
— and J. Vives-Ferrándiz, 2011. '"Almost the Same." Dynamic Domination and Hybrid Contexts in Iron Age Lixus, Larache, Morocco.' *WA* 43: 124–43.
Caneva, I., 1999. 'Mersin-Yumuktepe in the Seventh Millennium BC: An Updated View' in Özdoğan and Başgelen 1999, Vol. 3, 1–29.
Carbonell, E., and Z. Castro-Curel, 1992. 'Paleolithic Wooden Artefacts from the Abric Romaní (Capellades, Barcelona, Spain).' *JAS* 19: 707–19.
—, M. Mosquera, M. Rodríquez *et al.*, 2008. 'Eurasian Gates: The Earliest Human Dispersals.' *Journal of Anthropological Research* 64: 195–228.
Carpentier, J., and F. Lebrun, 1998. *Histoire de la Méditerranée.* Paris: Seuil.
Carrión, J. S., S. Fernández, G. Jiménez-Moreno *et al.*, 2010. 'The Historical Origins of Aridity and Vegetation Degradation in Southeastern Spain.' *Journal of Arid Environments* 74: 731–36.

—, C. Finlayson, S. Fernández *et al.*, 2008. 'A Coastal Reservoir of Biodiversity for Upper Pleistocene Human Populations: Palaeoecological Investigations in Gorham's Cave (Gibraltar) in the Context of the Iberian Peninsula.' *QSR* 27: 2118–35.

Carrión Marco, Y., G. Pérez-Jordà, F. Kherbouche and L. Peña-Chocarro, 2022. 'Plant Use and Vegetation Trends in Algeria from Late Glacial to Middle Holocene: Charcoal and Seeds from Gueldaman GLD 1 Cave (Babors d'Akbou).' *Review of Palaeobotany and Palynology* 297: 104562.

Carter, J. C., 2006. *Discovering the Greek Countryside at Metaponto*. Ann Arbor: Michigan UP. Bristol: Bristol UP.

Carter, R. A., 2010. 'The Social and Environmental Context of Neolithic Seafaring in the Persian Gulf' in A. Anderson *et al.* 2010, 191–202.

Carter T., D. A. Contreras, J. Holcomb *et al.*, 2019. 'Earliest Occupation of the Central Aegean (Naxos), Greece: Implica-tions for Hominin and *Homo sapiens*' Behavior and Dispersals.' *Science Advances* 5: eaax0997.

Casson, L., 1971. *Ships and Seamanship in the Ancient World*. Princeton: Princeton UP.

Castagnino Berlinghieri, E. F., 2003. *The Aeolian Islands, Crossroads of Mediterranean Maritime Routes: A Survey on Their Maritime Archaeology and Topography from the Prehistoric to the Roman Periods*. Oxford: Archaeopress.

Castells, M., 2010. *The Rise of the Network Society*. 2nd edn. Chichester and Malden: Wiley-Blackwell.

Castro, P. V., R. Chapman, S. Gili *et al.*, 1999. 'Agricultural Production and Social Change in the Bronze Age of Southeast Spain: The Gatas Project.' *Antiquity* 73: 846–56.

—, —, — *et al.*, 2000. 'Archaeology and Desertification in the Vera Basin (Almeria, South-east Spain).' *EJA* 3: 147–66.

Caubet, A., and F. Poplin, 1987. 'Matières Dures Animales: *Étude du* Matériau' in Yon 1997, 273–306.

Cauliez, J., 2011. 'Restitution des Aires Culturelles au Néolithique Final dans le Sud-est de la France: Dynamiques de Formation et d'Évolution des Styles Céramiques.' *Gallia Préhistoire* 53: 85–202.

Cauvin, J., 2000. *Birth of the Gods and the Origins of Agriculture*. English translation. Cambridge and New York: Cambridge UP.

Cavanagh, W. G., 2004. 'WYSIWYG: Settlement and Territoriality in Southern. Greece during the Early and Middle Neolithic Periods.' *JMA* 17: 165–89.

— and C. Mee, 1998. *A Private Place: Death in Prehistoric Greece*. Jonsered: Paul Åströms.

Cavazzuti, C., R. Skeates, A. R. Millard *et al.*, 2019. 'Flows of People in Villages and Large Centres in Bronze Age Italy through Strontium and Oxygen Isotopes.' *PLOS ONE* 14: 1–43.

Cawkwell, G., 2005. *The Greek Wars: The Failure of Persia*. New York and Oxford: OUP.

Caylus, A. C. F. de, 1752–67. *Recueil d'Antiquités Égyptiennes, Étrusques, Grecques, Gauloises. Paris.*

Cazzella, A., 2003. 'L'Adriatico nel Neolitico e nell'Eneolitico' in Lenzi 2003, 38–48.

— and M. Moscoloni, 1999. 'The Walled Bronze Age Settlement of Coppa Nevigata, Manfredonia and the Development of Craft Specialisation in Southeastern Italy' in Tykot *et al.* 1999, 205–16.

—, A. Pace and G. Recchia, 2007. 'Cultural Contacts and Mobility between the South Central Mediterranean and the Aegean during the Second Half of the 3rd Millennium BC' in Antoniadou and Pace 2007, 243–60.

— and G. Recchia, 2008. 'A View from the Apennines: The Role of the Inland Sites in Southern Italy during the Bronze Age' in Grimaldi *et al.* 2008, 137–43.

— and — 2009. 'The "Mycenaeans" in the Central Mediterranean: A Comparison between the Adriatic and the Tyrrhenian Seaways.' *Pasiphae* 3: 27–40.

Ceccarelli, P., 2012. 'Naming the Aegean Sea.' *MHR* 27: 25–49.

Celestino, S., N. Rafel and X.-L. Armada, (eds) 2008. *Contacto Cultural entre el Mediterráneo y el Atlántico (Siglos XII-VIII Ane): La Precolonización a Debate*. Madrid: Consejo Superior de Investigaciones Científicas.

Celestino Pérez, S., 2009 'Precolonization and Colonisation in the Interior of Tartessos' in Dietler and López-Ruiz 2009, 229–353.

Çevik, Ö., 2007. 'Emergence of Different Social Systems in the EBA Anatolia: Urbanization versus Centralization.' *AS* 57: 131–40.

Chadwick, J., 1992. *The Decipherment of Linear B*. Rev. 2nd edn. Cambridge: Cambridge UP.

Chambon, P., 2000. 'Les Pratiques Funéraires dans les Tombes Collectives de la France Néolithique.' *BSPF* 97: 265–74.

Chapman, J., 1988. 'Ceramic Production and Social Differentiation: The Dalmatian Neolithic and the Western Mediterranean.' *JMA* 1: 3–25.

— and R. Shiel, 1993. 'Social Change and Land Use in Dalmatia.' *PPS* 59: 61–104.

—, — and Š. Batović, 1996. *The Changing Face of Dalmatia: Archaeological and Ecological Studies in a Mediterranean Landscape*. London and New York: Leicester UP.

Chapman, R., 1990. *Emerging Complexity: The Later Prehistory of South-east Spain, Iberia and the West Mediterranean* Cambridge and New York: Cambridge UP.

— 2000. 'Review of Germán Delibes de Castro, ed., Minerales y Metales en la Prehistoria Reciente. Algunos Testimonios de Su Explotación y Laboreo en la Peninsula Ibérica. (Studia Archaeológica 88, Universidad de Valladolid, Valladolid, 1998).' *EJA* 3: 273–75.

— 2003. *Archaeologies of Complexity*. London and New York: Routledge.

— 2005: 'Changing Social Relations in the Mediterranean Copper and Bronze Ages' in Blake and Knapp 2005, 77–101.

— 2008. 'Producing Inequalities: Regional Sequences in Later Prehistoric Southern Spain.' *JWP* 21: 195–260.

Charvát, P., 2002. *Mesopotamia before History*. London and New York: Routledge.

Chataigner, C., J. L Poidevin and N. O Arnaud, 1998. 'Turkish Occurrences of Obsidian and Use by Prehistoric Peoples in the Near East from 14,000 to 6000 BP.' *Journal of Vulcanology and Geothermal Research* 85: 517–37.

Chaunu, P., 1978. *European Expansion in the Later Middle Ages*. English translation. Oxford and New York: North Holland.

Chelidonio, G., 2001. 'Manufatti Litici su Ciottolo da Milos (Isole Cicladi) (Nota Preliminare).' *Pegaso* 1: 116–44.

Chenery, C. A., and J. A. Evans, 2011. 'A Summary of the Strontium and Oxygen Isotope Evidence for the Origins of Bell Beaker Individuals Found near Stonehenge' in A. Fitzpatrick (ed.), *The Amesbury Archer and the Boscombe Bowmen: Bell Beakers Burials on Boscombe Down, Amesbury, Wiltshire*. Salisbury: Wessex Archaeology. 185–91.

Chernykh, E. N., 1992. *Ancient Metallurgy in the USSR: The Early Metal Age*. Cambridge and New York: Cambridge UP.

Cherry, J. F., 1981. 'Pattern and Process in the Earliest Colonization of the Mediterranean Islands.' *PPS* 47: 41–68.

— 1983. 'Evolution, Revolution, and the Origins of Complex Society in Minoan Crete' in O. Krzyszkowska and L. Nixon (eds), *Minoan Society*. Bristol: Bristol Classical. 19–45.

— 1984. 'The Emergence of the State in the Prehistoric Aegean.' *PCPS* 30: 18–48.

— 1985. 'Islands out of the Stream: Isolation and Interaction in Early East Mediterranean Insular Prehistory' in A. B. Knapp and T. Stech (eds), *Prehistoric Production and Exchange: The Aegean and Eastern Mediterranean*. Los Angeles: Institute of Archaeology. 12–29.

— 1988. 'Pastoralism and the Role of Animals in the Pre- and Protohistoric Economies of the Aegean' in Whittaker 1988, 4–34.

— 1990. 'The First Colonization of the Mediterranean Islands: A Review of Recent Research.' *JMA* 3: 145–221.

— 1992. 'Palaeolithic Sardinians? Some Questions of Evidence and Method' in Tykot and Andrews 1992, 28–39.

— 2003. 'Archaeology beyond the Site: Regional Survey and Its Future' in J. K. Papadopoulos and Leventhal 2003, 137–60.

— 2004. 'Mediterranean Island Prehistory: What's Different and What's New?' in S. M. Fitzpatrick (ed.), *Voyages of Discovery: The Archaeology of Islands*. Westport: Praeger. Oxford: Harcourt Education. 233–48.

— 2010. 'Sorting out Crete's Prepalatial Off-island Interactions' in W. A. Parkinson and Galaty 2010, 107–40.

— and T. Leppard, 2025. *Human Dispersal, Human Evolution, and the Sea: The Palaeolithic Seafaring Debate*. Boulder: Colorado UP.

— and R. Torrence, 1982. 'The Earliest Prehistory of Melos' in C. Renfrew and M. Wagstaff (eds), *An Island Polity: The Archaeology of Exploitation in Melos*. Cambridge and New York: Cambridge UP. 24–34.

Chesson, M. S., 2003. 'Households, Houses, Neighborhoods and Corporate Villages: Modelling the Early Bronze Age as a House Society.' *JMA* 16: 79–102.

— and G. Philip, 2003. 'Tales of the City? "Urbanism" in the Early Bronze Age Levant from Mediterranean and Levantine Perspectives.' *JMA* 16: 3–16.

Chikhi, L., R. A. Nichols, G. Barbujani and M. A. Beaumont, 2002. 'Y Genetic Data Support the Neolithic Demic Diffusion Model.' *PNAS* 99: 11008–13.

Chilardi, S., D. W. Frayer, P. Gioia *et al.*, 1996. 'Fontana Nuova di Ragusa (Sicily, Italy): Southernmost Aurignacian Site in Europe.' *Antiquity* 70: 553–63.

Childe, V. G., 1942. *What Happened in History*. Harmondsworth: Penguin.

— 1957. *The Dawn of European Civilization*. 6th rev. edn. London: Routledge & Kegan Paul.

Chippindale, C., 1998. *A High Way to Heaven: Clarence Bicknell and the 'Vallée des Merveilles'*. Tende: Conseil Général des Alpes-Maritimes.

Christie, N., (ed.) 1995. *Settlement and Economy in Italy, 1500 BC to AD 1500*. Oxford: Oxbow.

Churchill, S., V. Formicola, T. Holliday *et al.*, 2000. 'The Upper Palaeolithic Population of Europe in an Evolutionary Perspective' in Roebroeks *et al.* 2000, 31–58.

Cialowicz, K. M., 2007. *Ivory and Gold: Beginnings of Egyptian Art*. Poznan: Poznan Prehistoric Society.

Cierny, J., and G. Weisgerber, 2003. 'Bronze Age Tin Mines in Central Asia' in Giumlia-Mair and Lo Schiavo 2003, 23–31.

Cilia, D., (ed.) 2004. *Malta before History: The World's Oldest Free-standing Stone Architecture*. Sliema: Miranda.

Cintas-Peña, M., and L. García Sanjuán, 2022. 'Women, Residential Patterns and Early Social Complexity: From Theory to Practice in Copper Age Iberia.' *JAA* 67: 101422.

—, M. Luciañez-Triviño, R. Montero Artús *et al.*, 2023. 'Amelogenin Peptide Analyses Reveal Female Leadership in Copper Age Iberia (*c.* 2900–2650 BC).' *Scientific Reports* 13: 9594.

Clark, G., and S. Piggott, 1965. *Prehistoric Societies*. London: Hutchinson. New York: Knopf.

Clark, J. D., and S. A. Brandt, (eds) 1984. *From Hunters to Farmers: Considerations of the Causes and Consequences of Food Production in Africa*. Berkeley and London: California UP.

Clark, P. U., A. S. Dyke, J. D. Shakun *et al.*, 2009. 'The Last Glacial Maximum.' *Science* 325: 710–14.

Clarke, A., and U. Frederick, 2006. 'Closing the Distance: Interpreting Cross-cultural Engagements through Indigenous Rock Art' in Lilley 2006, 116–34.

Clarke, D., 1973. 'Archaeology: The Loss of Innocence.' *Antiquity* 47: 6–18.

Clarke, J., (ed.) 2005. *Archaeological Perspectives on the Transmission and Transformation of Culture in the Eastern Mediterranean*. Oxford: Oxbow.

— with contributions by C. McCartney and A. Wasse, 2007. *On the Margins of Southwest Asia: Cyprus during the 6th to 4th Millennia BC*. Oxford and Oakville: Oxbow.

Clarkson, C., Z. Jacobs, B. Marwick *et al.*, 2017. 'Human Occupation of Northern Australia by 65,000 Years Ago.' *Nature* 547: 306–10.

Clemente, F., M. Unterländer, O. Dolgova *et al.*, 2021. 'The Genomic History of the Aegean Palatial Civilizations.' *Cell* 184: 2565–86.e21.

Cleyet-Merle, J.-J., 1990. *La Préhistoire de la Peche*. Paris: Errance.

— and S. Madelaine, 1995. 'Inland Evidence of Human Sea Coast Exploitation in Palaeolithic France' in A. Fischer 1995, 303–8.

Cline, E. H., 1998. 'Amenhotep III, the Aegean, and Anatolia' in D. O'Connor and E. H. Cline (eds), *Amenhotep III: Perspectives on His Reign*. Ann Arbor: Michigan UP. 236–50.

— 2009. *Sailing the Wine-dark Sea: International Trade and the Late Bronze Age Aegean*. Rev. edn. Oxford: Archaeopress.

— (ed.) 2010. *The Oxford Handbook of the Bronze Age Aegean (ca. 3000-1000 BC)*. Oxford and New York: Oxford UP.

— and D. Harris-Cline, (eds) 1998. *The Aegean and the Orient in the Second Millennium*. Liège: Université de Liège. Austin: Texas UP.

Close, A. E., 2002. 'Sinai, Sahara, Sahel: The Introduction of Domestic Caprines to Africa' in T. Lenssen-Erz, U. Tegtmeier and S. Kröpelin *et al.*, *Tides of the Desert: Contributions to the Archaeology and Environmental History of Africa in Honour of Rudolph Kuper*. Köln: Heinrich-Barth-Institut. 459–70.

— 2009. 'The Middle-Upper Palaeolithic Hiatus of Insular North Africa' in M. Camps and Szmidt 2009, 35–50.

Clottes, J., (ed.) 2000. 'Art between 30,000 and 20,000 BP' in Roebroeks *et al.* 2000, 87–104.

— (ed.) 2003. *Return to Chauvet Cave: Excavating the Birthplace of Art: The First Full Report*. London: Thames & Hudson.

—, J. Courtin and L. Vanrell, 2005. *Cosquer Redécouvert*. Paris: Seuil.

Cohen, R., and R. Westbrook, (eds) 2000. *Amarna Diplomacy: The Beginnings of International Relations*. Baltimore: Johns Hopkins UP.

Coldstream, J. N., and G. L. Huxley, 1972. *Kythera: Excavations and Studies Conducted by the University of Pennsylvania Museum and the British School at Athens*. London: Faber & Faber. 1973, Park Ridge: Noyes.

Coleman, J. E., 1977. *Kephala: A Late Neolithic Settlement and Cemetery*. Princeton: American School of Classical Studies.

Colledge, S., and J. Conolly, (eds) 2007. *The Origins and Spread of Domestic Plants in Southwest Asia and Europe*. Walnut Creek: Left Coast. London: Institute of Archaeology.

Colliga, A. M., 1998. 'Le Nord-est de la Peninsule Ibérique (et la *Baléares*)' in J. Guilaine (ed.), *Atlas du Neolithique Europeen*. Vol. 2B: *L'Europe Occidentale*. Liège, Université de Liège. 763–824.

Collon, D., 1994. 'Bull-leaping in Syria.' *ÄL* 4: 81–88.
— 2005. *First Impressions: Cylinder Seals in the Ancient Near East*. Rev. edn. London: British Museum.
Colonese, A. C., M. A. Mannino, D. E. Bar-Yosef Mayer *et al.*, 2011. 'Marine Mollusc Exploitation in Mediterranean Prehistory: An Overview.' *QI* 239: 86–103.
Colonna, G., 2003. 'L'Adriatico tra VIII e Inizio V Secolo A.C. con Particolare Riguardo a Ruolo di Adria' in Lenzi 2003, 146–75.
Commenge, C., 2006. 'Gilat's Ceramics: Cognitive Dimensions of Pottery Production' in Levy 2006, 394–506.
Conard, N. J., (ed.) 2006. *When Neanderthals and Modern Humans Met*. Tübingen: Kerns.
Connors, C., 2004. 'Monkey Business: Imitation, Authenticity, and Identity from Pithekoussai to Plautus.' *Classical Antiquity* 23: 179–207.
Constantakopoulou, C., 2007. *The Dance of the Islands: Insularity, Networks, the Athenian Empire and the Aegean World*. Oxford and New York: OUP.
Cooper, E. N., 1992. 'Trade, Trouble and Taxation along the Caravan Roads of the Mari Period' in S. E. Orel (ed.), *Death and Taxes in the Ancient Near East*. Lewiston and Lampeter: E. Mellen. 1–15.
Cooper, L., 2006a. *Early Urbanism on the Syrian Euphrates*. New York and London: Routledge.
— 2006b. 'The Demise and Regeneration of Bronze Age Urban Centers in the Euphrates Valley of Syria' in Schwartz and Nichols 2006, 18–37.
Cornell, T. J., 1995. *The Beginnings of Rome: Italy and Rome from the Bronze Age to the Punic Wars (c. 1000–264 BC)*. London and New York: Routledge.
Costa, L. J., 2004. *Corse Préhistorique: Peuplement d'une Île et Modes de Vie des Sociétés Insulaires (IXe – IIe Millénaires av. J.-C.)*. Paris: Errance.
— 2007. *L'Obsidienne: Un Témoin d'Échanges en Mediterranee Prehistorique*. Paris: Errance.
Costa Caramé, M. E., M. Díaz-Zorita Bonilla, L. García Sanjuán and D. W. Wheatley, 2010. 'The Copper Age Settlement of Valencina de la Concepción (Seville, Spain): Demography, Metallurgy and Spatial Organization.' *Trabajos de Prehistoria* 67: 85–117.
Courtois, J.-C., 1990. 'Yabninu et le Palais Sud d'Ougarit.' *Syria* 67: 103–41.
Cremaschi, M., 1999. 'Late Quaternary Geological Evidence for Environmental Changes in South-western Fezzan (Lybian Sahara)' in Cremaschi and di Lernia 1999, 13–48.
— 2001. 'Holocene Climatic Changes in an Archaeological Landscape: The Case Study of Wadi Tanezzuft and Its Drainage Basin (SW Fezzan, Libyan Sahara).' *LS* 32: 3–27.
— and S. di Lernia, (eds) 1999. *Wadi Teshuinat: Palaeoenvironment and Prehistory in South-western Fezzan (Libyan Sahara)*. Florence: All'Insegna del Giglio.
—, C. Pizzi and V. Valsecchi, 2006. 'Water Management and Land Use in the Terramare and a Possible Climatic Co-factor in Their Abandonment: The Case Study of the Terramara of Poviglio Santa Rosa (Northern Italy).' *QI* 151: 87–98.
Crewe, L., 2007. *Early Enkomi: Regionalism, Trade and Society at the Beginning of the Late Bronze Age on Cyprus*. Oxford: Archaeopress.
Crielaard, J. P., V. Stissi and G. J. van Wijngaarden, (eds) 1999. *The Complex Past of Pottery: Production, Circulation and Consumption of Mycenaean and Greek Pottery (Sixteenth to Early Fifth Centuries BC)*. Amsterdam: J. C. Gieben.
Croissant, F., and C. d'Ercole, 2010. 'Sociétés, Styles et Identités' in Étienne 2010, 311–68.
Cruz Berrocal, M., L. García Sanjuán and A. Gilman, (eds) 2013. *The Prehistory of Iberia: Debating Early Social Stratification and the State*. London and New York: Routledge.
— and J. Vicent García, 2007. 'Rock Art as an Archaeological and Social Indicator: The Neolithisation of the Iberian Peninsula.' *JAA* 26: 676–97.
Cucchi, T., 2008. 'Uluburun Shipwreck Stowaway House Mouse: Molar Shape Analysis and Indirect Clues about the Vessel's Last Journey.' *JAS 35*: 2953–59.
—, A. Bălăşescu, C. Bem *et al.*, 2005. 'First Occurrence of the House Mouse (*Mus musculus domesticus* Schwarz & Schwarz, 1943) in the Western Mediterranean: A Zooarchaeological Revision of Subfossil Occurrences.' *Biological Journal of the Linnean Society* 84: 429–45.
—, A. Orth, J.-C. Auffray *et al.*, 2006. 'A New Endemic Species of the Subgenus Mus (*Rodentia, Mammalia*) on the Island of Cyprus.' *Zootaxa* 1241: 1–36.
Cullen, H. M., P. B. deMenocal, S. Hemming *et al.*, 2000. 'Climate Change and the Collapse of the Akkadian Empire: Evidence from the Deep Sea.' *Geology* 28: 379–82.
Cullen, T., (ed.) 2001. *Aegean Prehistory: A Review*. Boston: Archaeological Institute of America.
Cunliffe, B., 1995. 'Diversity in the Landscape: The Geographical Background to Urbanism in Iberia' in Cunliffe and Keay 1995a, 5–28.
— 2001. *Facing the Ocean: The Atlantic and Its Peoples*. Oxford and New York: Oxford UP.
— 2008. *Europe between the Oceans: Themes and Variations, 9000 BC–AD 1000*. New Haven and London: Yale UP.
— and S. Keay, (eds) 1995a. *Social Complexity and the Development of Towns in Iberia: From the Copper Age to the Second Century AD*. Oxford and New York: Oxford UP.
— and — 1995b. 'Introduction' in Cunliffe and Keay 1995a, 1–4.
Cuozzo, M., 2007. 'Ancient Campania: Cultural Interaction, Political Borders and Geographical Boundaries' in G. Bradley *et al.* 2007, 224–67.
Currant, A. P., Y. Fernández-Jalvo and C. Price, 2012. 'The Large Mammal Remains from Vanguard Cave' in R. N. E. Barton, C. Stringer and J. C. Finlayson (eds), *Neanderthals in Context: A Report of the 1995–1998 Excavations at Gorham's and Vanguard Caves, Gibraltar*. Oxford: Oxford University School of Archaeology. 236–39.
Curtin, P. D., 1984. *Cross-cultural Trade in World History*. Cambridge and New York: Cambridge UP.
Curtis, J., 2009. 'Phoenicians on the Balawat Gates' in Maila-Afeiche 2009, 427–38.
Cutajar, N., R. Grima, A. Pace *et al.*, 2009. 'Spatial and Stratagraphic Analysis of Tarxien Cemetery Levels' in Malone *et al.* 2009, 207–18.
Cutler, J., 2012. 'Ariadne's Thread: The Adoption of Cretan Weaving Technology in the Wider Southern Aegean in the Mid-Second Millennium BC' in M.-L. Nosch and R. Laffineur (eds) *Kosmos: Jewellery, Adornment and Textiles in the Aegean Bronze Age*. Leuven: Peeters. 145–54.
D'Agostino, B., 1977. 'Grecs et "Indigènes" sur la Côte Tyrrhénienne au VII Siècle: La Transmission des Ideologies entre Élites Sociales.' *Annales: Économies, Sociétés, Civilisations* 32: 3–20.
— 1990. 'Military Organization and Social Structure in Archaic Etruria' in Murray and Price 1990, 59–82.
Dalfes, H. N., G. Kukla and H. Weiss, (eds) 1997. *Third Millennium BC Climate Change and Old World Collapse*. London and New York: Springer.
Dalley, S., 1984. *Mari and Karana: Two Old Babylonian Cities*. Piscataway: Gorgias.
D'Altroy, T. N., 2001. 'Politics, Resources, and Blood in the Inka Empire' in Alcock *et al.* 2001, 201–26.
Dams, L., 1987. 'Fish Images in Palaeolithic Cave Art.' *Archaeology Today* 8: 16–20.
Dardis, G., and B. Smith, 1997. 'Coastal Zone Management' in King *et al.* 1997, 273–99.
Darlas, A., 1999. 'Palaeolithic Research in Kalamakia Cave, Areopolis, Peloponnese' in Bailey *et al.* 1999, 293–302.
Daugas, J.-P., 2002. 'Le Néolithique du Maroc: Pour un Modèle d'Évolution Chronologique et Culturelle.' *Bulletin d'Archéologie Marocaine* 19: 135–75.
Davidson, I., and W. Noble, 1992. 'Why the First Colonisation of the Australian Region Is the Earliest Evidence of Modern Human Behaviour.' *Archaeology in Oceania* 27: 135–42.
Davies, W., and P. Gollop, 2003. 'The Human Presence in Europe during the Last Glacial Period II: Climate Tolerance and Climate Preferences of Mid- and Late Glacial Hominids' in van Andel and Davies 2003, 131–46.
—, P. Valdes, C. Ross and T. H. van Andel, 2003. 'The Human Presence in Europe during the Last Glacial Period III: Site Clusters, Regional Climates and Resource Attractions' in van Andel and Davies 2003, 191–220.
Davis, J. L., 2000. 'Warriors for the Fatherland: National Consciousness and Archaeology in Barbarian Epirus and Verdant Ionia, 1912–22.' *JMA* 13: 76–98.
-- 2022. *A Greek State in Formation: The Origins of Civilization in Mycenaean Pylos*. Berkeley and London: California UP.
— and J. Bennet, 1991. 'Making Mycenaeans: Warfare, Territorial Expansion, and Representations of the Other in the Pylian Kingdom' in Laffineur 1991, 105–19.
— and E. Gorogianni, 2008. 'Potsherds from the Edge: The Construction of Identities and the Limits of Minoanized Areas of the Aegean' in Brodie *et al.* 2008, 339–48.
Dawson, H., 2011. 'Island Colonisation: Settling the Neolithic Question' in Phoca-Cosmetatou 2011a, 31–54.
Day, P. M., and R. C. P. Doonan, (eds) 2007. *Metallurgy in the Early Bronze Age Aegean*. Oxford and Oakville: Oxbow.
De Angelis, F., 2003. *Megara Hyblaia and Selinous: Two Greek City-states in Archaic Sicily*. Oxford: University of Oxford Committee for Archaeology.
De Contenson, H., 1992. *Préhistoire de Ras Shamra*. 2 vols. Paris: Erc.
Deger-Jalkotzy, S., and I. S. Lemos, (eds) 2006. *Ancient Greece: From the Mycenaean Palaces to the Age of Homer*. Edinburgh: Edinburgh UP.
Delgado, A., 2008. 'Fenicios en Iberia' in F. Gracia Alonso (ed.), *De Iberia a Hispania*. Barcelona: Ariel. 347–474.
— 2013. 'Households, Merchants, and Feasting: Socioeconomic Dynamics and Commoners' Agency in the Emergence of the Tartessian World (Eleventh to Eighth Centuries B.C.)' in Cruz Berrocal *et al.* 2013, 311–36.
— and M. Ferrer, 2007. 'Cultural Contacts in Colonial Settings: The Construction of New Identities in Phoenician Settlements of the Western Mediterranean.' *Stanford Journal of Archaeology* 5: 18–42.
Delhon, C., S. Thiébault and J.-F. Berger, 2009. 'Environment and Landscape Management during the Middle Neolithic in Southern France: Evidence for Agro-sylvo-pastoral Systems in the Middle Rhone Valley.' *QI* 200: 50–65.
Demand, N. H., 2011. *The Mediterranean Context of Early Greek History*. Chichester and Malden: Wiley-Blackwell.
Deme, A., and S. K. McIntosh, 2006. 'Excavations at Walaldé: New Light on the Settlement of the Middle Senegal Valley by Iron-using Peoples.' *Journal of African Archaeology* 4: 317–47.
Demoule, J.-P., and C. Perlès, 1993. 'The Greek Neolithic: A New Review.' *JWP* 7: 355–416.
Demurtas, L. M., and S. Demurtas, 1992. 'Tipologie Nuraghiche: I Protonuraghi con Corridio Passante' in Tykot and Andrews 1992, 176–84.
Dennell, R., 2003. 'Dispersal and Colonization, Long and Short Chronologies: How Continuous Is the Early Pleistocene Record for Hominids outside East Africa?' *JHE* 45: 421–40.
— 2009. *The Palaeolithic Settlement of Asia*. Cambridge and New York: Cambridge UP.
De Polignac, F., 2005. 'Forms and Processes: Some Thoughts on the Meaning of Urbanization in Early Archaic Greece' in Osborne and Cunliffe 2005, 45–70.
Dercksen, J. G., 2004. *Old Assyrian Institutions*. Leiden: Nederlands Instituut voor het Nabije Oosten.
D'Errico, F., 1995. 'A New Model and Its Implications for the Origins of Writing: The La Marche Antler Revisited.' *CAJ* 5: 163–206.
— and A. Nowell, 2000. 'A New Look at the Berekhat Ram Figurine: Implications for the Origins of Symbolism.' *CAJ* 10: 123–67.
Derricourt, R., 2005. 'Getting "Out of Africa": Sea Crossings, Land Crossings and Culture in the Hominin Migrations.' *JWP* 19: 119–32.
De Saulieu, G., 2007. 'Hiérarchisation Sociale et Art Rupestre dans les Alpes: La Figure Solaire dans l'Art Gravé du Chalcolithique et du Debut de l'Age du Bronze' in J. Guilaine (ed), *Le Chalcolithique et la Construction des Inégalités*. Vol. I: *Le Continent Européen*. Paris: Errance. 123–50.
— and T. Serres, 2006. 'Les Représentations de la Traction Animale dans la Région du Mont Bego (Alpes-Maritimes, France)' in P. Pétrequin, R. M. Arbogast, A. M. Pétrequin *et al.* (eds), *Premiers Chariots, Premiers Araires: La Diffusion de la Traction Animale en Europe pendant les IVe et IIIe Millénaires avant Notre Ère*. Paris: CNRS. 73–86.
Desse, J., and N. Desse-Berset, 2003. 'Les Premiers Pêcheurs de Chypre' in Guilaine and Le Brun 2003, 279–91.
Dever, W. G., 1992. 'The Late Bronze-Early Iron I Horizon in Syria-Palestine: Egyptians, Canaanites, "Sea Peoples", and Proto-Israelites' in W. A. Ward and Joukowsky 1992, 99–110.
— 1995. 'Social Structure in the Early Bronze IV Period in Palestine' in Levy 1995a, 282–96.
— and S. Gitin, (eds) 2003. *Symbiosis, Symbolism, and the Power of the Past: Canaan, Ancient Israel, and their Neighbors from the Late Bronze Age through Roman Palaestina*. Winona Lake: Eisenbrauns.
Diamond, J., 1997. *Guns, Germs and Steel: The Fates of Human Societies*. New York: W. W. Norton. London: Jonathan Cape.
— 2002. 'Evolution, Consequences and Future of Plant and Animal Domestication.' *Nature* 418: 700–7.
— 2005. *Collapse: How Societies Choose to Fail or Succeed*. New York and London: Penguin.
Díaz-Andreu, M., and S. Keay (eds), 1997. *The Archaeology of Iberia: The Dynamics of Change*. London and New York: Routledge.
Díaz-Del-Río, P., 2004. 'Copper Age Ditched Enclosures in Central Iberia.' *OJA* 23: 107–21.
— and L. García Sanjuán, (eds) 2006. *Social Inequality in Iberian Late Prehistory*. Oxford: Archaeopress.
Dickinson, O. T. P. K., 1997. 'Arts and Artefacts in the Shaft Graves: Some Observations' in Laffineur and Betancourt 1997, 46–49.
— 2006. *The Aegean from Bronze Age to Iron Age: Continuity and Change between the Twelfth and Eighth Centuries BC*. London and New York: Routledge.
Dietler, M., 2005. *Consumption and Colonial Encounters in the Rhône Basin of France: A Study of Early Iron Age Political Economy*. Paris: CNRS.

— 2007. 'The Early Iron Age in the Western Mediterranean' in Scheidel *et al.* 2007, 242–76.

— 2010. *Archaeologies of Colonialism: Consumption, Entanglement, and Violence in Ancient Mediterranean France*. Berkeley and London: California UP.

— and C. López-Ruiz, (eds) 2009. *Colonial Encounters in Ancient Iberia: Phoenician, Greek and Indigenous Relations*. Chicago and London: Chicago UP.

Diffey C., R. Neef, J. Seeher and A. Bogaard, 2020. 'The Agroecology of an Early State: New Results from Hattusha.' *Antiquity* 94: 1204–23.

Di Lernia, S., (ed.) 1999a. *The Uan Afuda Cave: Hunter-gatherer Societies of Central Sahara*. Florence: All'Insegna del Giglio.

— 1999b. 'Discussing Pastoralism: The Case of the Acacus and Surroundings (Libyan *Sahara*).' *Sahara* 11: 7–20.

— 1999c. 'Early Holocene Pre-pastoral Cultures in the Uan Afuda Cave, Wadi Kessan, Tadrart Acacus (Libyan Sahara)' in Cremaschi and di Lernia 1999, 123–54.

— 2002. 'Dry Climatic Events and Cultural Trajectories: Adjusting Middle Holocene Pastoral Economy of the Libyan Sahara' in Hassan 2002a, 225–50.

— 2006. 'Building Monuments, Creating Identity: Cattle Cult as a Social Response to Rapid Environmental Changes in the Holocene Sahara.' *QI* 151: 50–62.

— and S. Gallinaro, 2010. 'The Date and Context of Neolithic Rock Art in the Sahara: Engravings and Ceremonial Monuments from Messak Settafet (South-west Libya).' *Antiquity* 84: 954–75.

— and F. Merighi, 2006. 'Transitions in the Later Prehistory of the Libyan Sahara, as Seen from the Acacus Mountains' in Mattingly *et al.* 2006, 111–21.

Di Maida, G., 2022. 'The Earliest Human Occupation of Sicily: A Review.' *Journal of Island and Coastal Archaeology* 17: 402–19.

Diniz, M., (ed.) 2008. *The Early Neolithic in the Iberian Peninsula: Regional and Transregional Components*. Oxford: Archaeopress.

Divon, S. A., 2008. 'A Survey of the Textual Evidence for "Food Shortage" from the Late Hittite Empire' in L. d'Alfonso, Y. Cohen, and D. Sürenhagen (eds), *The City of Emar among the Late Bronze Age Empires: History, Landscape, and Society*. Münster: Ugarit-Verlag. 101–9.

Docter, R., 2004. 'The Topography of Ancient Carthage: *Preliminary Results of Recent Excavations and Some Prospects*.' *Talanta* 34–35: 113–33.

—, F. Chelbi, B. Maraoni Telmini *et al.*, 2007. 'Punic Carthage: Two Decades of Archaeological Investigations' in J. L. López Castro (ed.), *La Ciudades Fenicio-púnicas en el Mediterráneo Occidental*. Almería: Editorial Universidad de Almería. 85–104.

—, —, — *et al.*, 2008. 'New Radiocarbon Dates from Carthage: Bridging the Gap between History and Archaeology?' in C. Sagona (ed.), *Beyond the Homeland: Markers in Phoenician Chronology*. Leuven and Dudley: Peeters. 379–422.

— and H. G. Niemeyer, 1994. 'Pithekoussai: The Carthaginian Connection. On the Archaeological Evidence of Euboeo-Phoenician Partnership in the 8th and 7th Centuries BC' in B. d'Agostino and D. Ridgway, *Apoikia: I Più Antichi Insediamenti Greci in Occidente. Funzioni e Modi dell'Organizzazione Politica e Sociale*. Naples: Istituto Universitario Orientale. 101–15.

—, —, A. Nijboer and J. van der Plicht, 2005. 'Radiocarbon Dates of Animal Bones in the Earliest Levels of Carthage' in G. Bartoloni and F. Delpino (eds), *Oriente e Occidente: Metodi e Discipline a Confronto. Rifflessioni sulla Cronologia dell'Età del Ferro Italiana*. Pisa: Istituti Editoriali e Poligrafici Internazionali. 557–77.

Domergue, C., and C. Rico, 2002. 'À Propos de Deux Lingots de Cuivre Antiques Trouvés en Mer sur la Côte Languedocienne' in L. Rivet and M. Sciallano, *Vivre, Produire et Échanger: Reflets Méditerrannéens*. Montagnac: Monique Mergoil. 141–52.

Donkin, R. A., 1991. *Meleagrides: An Historical and Ethnographical Study of the Guinea Fowl*. London: Ethnographica.

Doonan, O., 2001. 'Domestic Architecture and Settlement Planning in Early and Middle Bronze Age Sicily: Thoughts on Innovation and Social Process.' *JMA* 14: 159–88.

— 2009. 'The Corrupting Sea and the Hospitable Sea: Some Early Thoughts toward a Regional History of the Black Sea' in D. B. Counts and A. S. Tuck, *Koine: Mediterranean Studies in Honor of R. Ross Holloway*. Oxford and Oakville: Oxbow. 68–74.

Dothan, T., and M. Dothan, 1992. *People of the Sea: The Search for the Philistines*. New York and Oxford: Macmillan.

Dougherty, C., 2003. 'The Aristonothos Krater: Competing Stories of Conflict and Collaboration' in C. Dougherty and L. Kurke (eds), *The Cultures within Ancient Greek Culture: Contact, Conflict, Collaboration*. 35–56.

Doumas, C., 1977. *Early Bronze Age Burial Habits in the Cyclades*. Göteborg: Paul Åströms.

— 1983. *Thera: Pompeii of the Ancient Aegean: Excavations at Akrotiri 1967–79*. London and New York: Thames & Hudson.

— 1992. *The Wall-Paintings of Thera*. Athens and London: Thera Foundation.

— and V. La Rosa, (eds) 1997. *I Poliochni kai i Proimi Epochi tou Chalkou sto Voreio Aigaio*. Athens: Panepistimio Athinon Tomeas Archaiologias kai Istorias tis Technis.

Doumet-Serhal, C., (ed.) 2004. *Decade: A Decade of Archaeology and History in the Lebanon*. Beirut: The Lebanese British Friends of the National Museum.

— (ed.) 2006. *The Early Bronze Age in Sidon*. Beirut: Institut Français du Proche-Orient.

— 2008. 'The Kingdom of Sidon and Its Mediterranean Connections' in C. Doumet-Serhal (ed.), *Networking Patterns of the Bronze and Iron Age Levant: The Lebanon and Its Mediterranean Connections*. London: Lebanese British Friends of the National Museum. 1–70.

Drakidès, D., E. Nantet, M. Gras and A. Esposito, 2010. 'Échanges et Circulations' in Étienne 2010, 91–146.

Drews, R., 1993. *The End of the Bronze Age: Changes in Warfare and the Catastrophe ca. 1200 BC*. Princeton and Chichester: Princeton UP.

Driessen, H., 1999. 'Pre- and Post-Braudelian Conceptions of the Mediterranean Area: The Puzzle of Boundaries.' *Narodna Umjetnost: Croatian Journal of Ethnology and Folklore Research* 36: 53–63.

— 2001. 'People, Boundaries and the Anthropologist's Mediterranean.' *Anthropological Journal on European Cultures* 10: 11–25.

Driessen, J., 2002. 'The King Must Die: Some Observations on the Use of Minoan Court Compounds' in J. Driessen *et al.* 2002, 1–13.

— 2010. 'Spirit of Place: Minoan *Houses* as Major Actors' in Pullen 2010, 35–65.

— 2012. 'A Matrilocal House Society in Pre- and Protopalatial Crete?' in Schoep *et al.* 2012, 358–83.

— and C. F. MacDonald, 1997. *The Troubled Island: Minoan Crete before and after the Santorini Eruption*. Liège: Université de Liège. Austin: Texas UP.

— and — 2000. 'The Eruption of the Santorini Volcano and Its Effects on Minoan Crete' in W. J. McGuire, D. R. Griffiths, P. L. Hancock and I. Stewart (eds), *The Archaeology of Geological Catastrophes*. London and Tulsa: Geological Society. 81–93.

—, I. Schoep and R. Laffineur, 2002. *Monuments of Minos: Rethinking the Minoan Palaces*. Liège: Université de Liège.

Drysdale, R., G. Zanchetta, J. Hellstrom *et al.*, 2006. 'Late Holocene Drought Responsible for the Collapse of Old World Civilizations Is Recorded in an Italian Cave Flowstone.' *Geology* 34: 101–4.

Duarte, C., J. Maurício, P. B. Pettitt *et al.*, 1999. 'The Early Upper Paleolithic Human Skeleton from the Abrigo do Lagar Velho (Portugal) and Modern Human Emergence in Iberia.' *PNAS* 96: 7604–9.

Dunne, J., R. P. Evershed, M. Salque *et al.*, 2012. 'First Dairying in Green Saharan Africa in the Fifth Millennium BC.' *Nature* 486: 390–94.

Durrell, L., 1945. *Prospero's Cell: A Guide to the Landscape and Manners of the Island of Corfu*. London: Faber & Faber. 1960, New York: E. P. Dutton.

— 1958. *Balthazar*. London: Faber & Faber. New York: E. P. Dutton.

Earle, T., and K. Kristiansen, (eds) 2010. *Organising Bronze Age Societies: The Mediterranean, Central Europe, and Scandinavia Compared*. Cambridge and New York: Cambridge UP.

Edel, E., 1997. *Der Vertrag zwischen Ramses II von Ägypten und Hattušili III von Hatti*. Berlin: Mann.

Efe, T., 2007. 'The Theories of the "Great Caravan Route" between Cilicia and Troy: The Early Bronze Age III Period in Inland Western Anatolia.' *AS* 57: 47–64.

— and E. Fidan, 2008. 'Complex Two in the Early Bronze II Upper Town of Küllüoba near Eskiş ehir.' *Anatolica* 34: 67–102.

Eiroa García, J. J., 1987. 'Noticia Preliminar de la Primera Campaña de Excavaciones Arqueológicas en el Poblado de La Salud y en Vueva Sagrada I (Lorca), Murcia.' *Anales de Prehistoria y Arqueología* 3: 53–76.

El Beialy, S. Y., K. J. Edwards and A. S. El-Mahmoudi, 2001. 'Geophysical and Palynological Investigations of the Tell El Dabaa Archaeological Site, Nile Delta, Egypt.' *Antiquity* 75: 735–44.

El Daly, O., 2005. *Egyptology: The Missing Millennium: Ancient Egypt in Medieval Arabic Writings*. London: UCL.

EPICA Community Members, 2004. 'Eight Glacial Cycles from an Antarctic Ice Core.' *Nature* 429: 623–28.

Erdoğu, B., 2003. 'Visualizing Neolithic Landscape: The Early Settled Communities in Western Anatolia and Eastern Aegean Islands.' *EJA* 6: 7–25.

Eriksson, K., 1991. 'Red Lustrous Wheelmade Ware: A Product of Late Bronze Age Cyprus' in J. A. Barlow, D. Bolger and B. Kling (eds), *Cypriot Ceramics: Reading the Prehistoric Record*. Philadelphia: University Museum of Archaeology and Anthropology. 81–96.

Erkanal, H., 2008. 'Liman Tepe: A New Light on the Prehistoric Aegean Cultures' in H. Erkanal, H. Hauptmann, V. Sahoglou and R. Tuncel (eds), *The Aegean in the Neolithic, Chalcolithic and the Early Bronze Age*. Ankara: Ankara UP. 179–90.

Erlandson, J. M., 2001. 'The Archaeology of Aquatic Adaptations: Paradigms for a New Millennium.' *Journal of Archaeological Research* 9: 287–350.

— 2010. 'Neptune's Children: The Evolution of Human Seafaring' in A. Anderson *et al.* 2010, 19–27.

Eshed, V., A. Gopher and I. Hershkovitz, 2006. 'Tooth Wear and Dental Pathology at the Advent of Agriculture: New Evidence from the Levant.' *American Journal of Physical Anthropology* 130: 145–59.

Esin, U., and S. Harmankaya, 1999. 'Aş ıklı' in Özdoğan and Baş gelen 1999, 115–32.

Étienne, R., (ed.) 2010. *La Méditerranée au VIIe Siècle av. J.-C: Essais d'Analyses Archéologiques*. Paris: De Boccard.

Evans, J. D., 1973. 'Islands as Laboratories for the Study of Cultural Process' in C. Renfrew (ed.), *The Explanation of Culture Change: Models in Prehistory*. London: Duckworth. 517–20.

Evans, J. G., and T. P. O'Connor, 2005. *Environmental Archaeology: Principles and Methods*. 2nd edn. Stroud: Sutton.

Evershed, R. P., S. Payne and A. G. Sherratt, 2008. 'Earliest Date for Milk Use in the Near East and Southeastern Europe Linked to Cattle Herding.' *Nature* 455: 528–31.

Fabre, D., 2004–5. *Seafaring in Ancient Egypt*. London: Periplus.

Facchini, F., and G. Giusberti, 1992. '*Homo sapiens sapiens* Remains from the Island of Crete' in G. Bräuer and F. H. Smith (eds), *Continuity or Replacement: Controversies in Homo sapiens Evolution*. Rotterdam and Brookfield: A. A. Balkema. 189–208.

Fagan, B., 2004. *The Long Summer: How Climate Changed Civilization*. London: Granta.

Falabella, F., M. T. Planella and R. H. Tykot, 2008. 'El Maíz (*Zea mays*) en el Mundo Prehispánico de Chile Central.' *Latin American Antiquity* 19: 25–46.

Falconer, S. E., and P. L. Fall, 2006. *Bronze Age Rural Ecology and Village Life at Tell el-Hayyat, Jordan*. Oxford: Archaeopress.

Fantalkin, A., 2011. 'Why Did Nebuchadnezzar II Destroy Ashkelon in Kislev 606 B.C.E.?' in I. Finkelstein and N. Na'aman (eds), *The Fire Signals of Lachish: Studies in the Archaeology and History of Israel in the Late Bronze Age, Iron Age, and Persian Period*. Winona Lake: Eisenbrauns. 87–111.

Farr, R. H., 2010. 'Island Colonization and Trade in the Mediterranean' in A. Anderson *et al.* 2010, 179–89.

Fattovich, R., 2005. 'Marsa Gawasis: A Pharaonic Coastal Settlement by the Red Sea in Egypt' in J. C. M. Starkey (ed.), *People of the Red Sea*. Oxford: Archaeopress. 15–22.

Faust, A., and E. Weiss, 2011. 'Between Assyria and the Mediterranean World: The Prosperity of Judah and Philistia in the Seventh Century BCE in Context' in T. C. Wilkinson *et al.* 2011, 189–204.

Fedele, F. G., B. Giaccio, R. Isaia *et al.*, 2007. 'The Campanian Ignimbrite Factor: Towards a Reappraisal of the Middle to Upper Palaeolithic "Transition" in J. Grattan and R. Torrence (eds), *Living under the Shadow: Cultural Impacts of Volcanic Eruptions*. Walnut Creek: Left Coast.

Feinman, G. M., 2001. 'Mesoamerican Political Complexity: The Corporate-network Dimension' in J. Haas (ed.), *From Leaders to Rulers*. New York and London: Kluwer Academic/ Plenum. 151–75.

— and J. Marcus, (eds) 1998. *Archaic States*. Santa Fe: School of American Research.

Feldman, M. H., 2002. 'Ambiguous Identities: The "Marriage" Vase of Niqmaddu II and the Elusive Egyptian Princess.' *JMA* 15: 75–99.

— 2006. *Diplomacy by Design: Luxury Arts and an "International Style" in the Ancient Near East, 1400-1200 BCE*. Chicago and London: Chicago UP.

— 2007. 'Frescoes, Exotica, and the Reinvention of the Northern Levantine Kingdoms during the Second Millennium B.C.E.' in M. Heinz and M. H. Feldman (eds), *Representations of Political Power: Case Histories from Times of Change and Dissolving Order in the Ancient Near East*. Winona Lake: Eisenbrauns. 39–66.

Fentress, E., 2009 'The Classical and Early Punic Periods' in Fentress *et al.* 2009, 72–74.

— and R. Docter, 2008. 'North Africa: Rural Settlement and Agricultural Production' in van Dommelen and Goméz Bellard 2008, 101–28.
—, A. Drine and R. Holod, (eds) 2009. *An Island through Time: Jerba Studies*. Journal of Roman Archaeology Supp. Monograph 71.
Ferentinos, G., M. Gkioni, M. Geraga and G. Papatheodorou, 2012. 'Early Seafaring Activity in the Southern Ionian Islands, Mediterranean Sea.' *JAS* 39: 2167–76.
Fernandes, D. M., A. Mittnik, I. Olalde *et al*., 2020. 'The Spread of Steppe and Iranian-related Ancestry in the Islands of the Western Mediterranean.' *Nature Ecology & Evolution* 4: 334–45.
Fernández Flores, A., L. García Sanjuán and M. Díaz-Zorita Bonilla, (eds) 2016. *Montelirio: Un Gran Monumento Megalítico de la Edad del Cobre*. Seville: Junta de Andalucía. 503–53.
Fernández-Miranda, M., 1997. 'Aspects of Talayotic Culture' in Balmuth *et al*. 1997, 59–68.
Ferrara, S., 2012. *Cypro-Minoan Inscriptions*. Oxford: Oxford UP.
Figueira, T. J., 1981. *Aegina: Society and Politics*. New York: Arno.
Finkelberg, M., 1998. 'Bronze Age Writing: Contacts between East and West' in Cline and Harris-Cline 1998, 265–72.
Finkelstein, I., 1995. 'The Great Transformation: The "Conquest" of the Highlands Frontiers and the Rise of the Territorial States' in Levy 1995a, 349–65.
— 2007a. 'Patriarchs, Exodus, Conquest: Fact or Fiction?' in B. B. Schmidt 2007, 41–55.
— 2007b. 'When and How Did the Israelites Emerge?' in B. B. Schmidt 2007, 73–83.
— 2007c. 'The Two Kingdoms: Israel and Judah' in B. B. Schmidt 2007, 147–57.
— and N. A. Silberman, 2001. *The Bible Unearthed: Archaeology's New Vision of Ancient Israel and the Origin of Its Sacred Texts*. New York and London: Free Press.
— and — 2006. *David and Solomon: In Search of the Bible's Sacred Kings and the Roots of Western Tradition*. New York: Free Press. London: Simon & Schuster.
Finlayson, C., 2008. 'On the Importance of Coastal Areas in the Survival of Neanderthal Populations during the Late Pleistocene.' *QSR* 27: 2246–52.
— 2009. *The Humans Who Went Extinct: Why Neanderthals Died out and We Survived*. Oxford and New York: Oxford UP.
—, F. G. Pacheco and J. Rodríguez-Vidal, 2006. 'Late Survival of Neanderthals at the Southernmost Extreme of Europe.' *Nature* 443: 850–53.
Finlayson, W., J. Lovell, S. Smith and S. Mithen, 2011. 'The Archaeology of Water Management in the Jordan Valley from the Epipalaeolithic to the Nabataean, 21,000 BP (19,000 BC) to AD 106' in Mithen and Black 2011, 191–217.
—, and G. Warren, (eds) 2010. *Landscapes in Transition: Understanding Hunter-gatherer and Farmer Landscapes in the Early Holocene of Europe and the Levant*. Oxford and Oakville: Oxbow.
Finley, M. I., 1985. *The Ancient Economy*. 2nd edn. London: Hogarth. Berkeley: California UP.
Finné, M., K. Holmgren, H. S. Sundqvist *et al*., 2011. 'Climate in the Eastern Mediterranean, and Adjacent Regions, during the Past 6,000 Years - A Review.' *JAS* 38: 3153–73.
Fiore, I., and A. Tagliacozzo, 2008. 'La Caccia a Riparo Dalmeri nel Tardiglaciale dell'Italia Nord-orientale' in Mussi 2008, 55–65.
Fischer, A., (ed.), 1995. *Man and Sea in the Mesolithic: Coastal Settlement above and below Present Sea Level*. Oxford: Oxbow.
Fischer, J., 2005. *Die Rückkehr de Geschichte: Die Welt nach dem 11. September und die Erneuerung des Westens*. Köln: Kiepenheuer & Witsch.
Fischer, N., and H. van Wees, (eds) 1998. *Archaic Greece: New Approaches and New Evidence. London:* Duckworth.
Flannery, K., 1969. 'Origins and Ecological Effects of Early Domestication in Iran and the Near East' in P. J. Ucko and G. W. Dimbleby (eds), *The Domestication and Exploitation of Plants and Animals*. Chicago: Aldine. London: Duckworth. 73–100.
— 1972. 'The Origins of the Village as a Settlement Type in Mesoamerica and the Near East' in Ucko *et al*. 1972, 23–54.
Fleagle, J. C., and C. C. Gilbert, 2008. 'Modern Human Origins in Africa.' *EA* 17: 1–2.
Fleming, D. E., 2004. *Democracy's Ancient Ancestors: Mari and Early Collective Governance*. Cambridge and New York: Cambridge UP.
Fontana, F., M. G. Cremona, E. Ferrari *et al*., 2009. 'People and Their Land at the Southern Margins of the Central Po Plain in the Early Mesolithic in McCartan *et al*. 2009, 296–302.
Forbes, H., 2007. *Meaning and Identity in a Greek Landscape: An Archaeological Ethnography*. Cambridge and New York: Cambridge UP.
Forenbaher, S., 2008. 'Archaeological Record of the Adriatic Offshore Islands as an Indicator of Long-distance Interaction in Prehistory.' *EJA* 11: 223–44.
— (ed.) 2009a. *A Connecting Sea: Maritime Interaction in Adriatic Prehistory*. Oxford: Archaeopress.
— 2009b. 'Adriatic Offshore Islands and Long-distance Interaction in Prehistory' in Forenbaher 2009a, 73–88.
— 2011. 'Shepherds of a Coastal Range: The Archaeological Potential of the Velebit Mountain Range (Eastern Adriatic)' in van Leusen *et al*. 2011, 113–21.
— 2018. *Special Place, Interesting Times: The Island of Palagruža and Transitional Periods in Adriatic Prehistory*. Oxford: Archaeopress.
— and T. Kaiser, 2011. 'Palagruža and the Spread of Farming in the Adriatic' in Phoca-Cosmetatou 2011a, 99–111.
— and P. Miracle, 2005. 'The Spread of Farming in the Eastern Adriatic.' *Antiquity* 79: 514–28.
Forge, A., 1972. 'Normative Factors in the Settlement Size of Neolithic Cultivators (New Guinea)' in Ucko *et al*. 1972, 363–76.
Foster, B. R., 2001. *The Epic of Gilgamesh: A New Translation, Analogues, Criticism*. New York: Norton.
Foster, K. P., 2008. 'Minoan Faience Revisited' in C. M. Jackson and E. C. Wager (eds), *Vitreous Materials in the Late Bronze Age Aegean*. Oxford and Oakville: Oxbow. 173–86.
Foxhall, L., 1998. 'Cargoes of the Heart's Desire: The Character of Trade in the Archaic Mediterranean World' in N. Fischer and van Wees 1998, 295–309.
— 2003. 'Cultures, Landscapes, and Identities in the Mediterranean World.' *MHR* 18: 75–92.
— 2005. 'Village to City: Staples and Luxuries? Exchange Networks and Urbanization' in Osborne and Cunliffe 2005, 233–48.
— 2007. *Olive Cultivation in Ancient Greece: Seeking the Ancient Economy*. Oxford and New York: Oxford UP.
— (ed.) 2021. *Interrogating Networks: Investigating Networks of Knowledge in Antiquity*. Oxford: Oxbow Books.
Franco, M. C., 1999. 'Antiche Relazioni Transmarine nel Salento' in C. Giardino (ed.), *Culture Marinare nel Mediterraneo Centrale e Occidentale fra il XVII e il XV Secolo aC*. Rome: Bagatto. 189–202.
Frangipane, M., 2003. 'Developments in Fourth Millennium Public Architecture in the Malatya Plain: From Simple Tripartite to Complex and Bipartite Pattern' in M. Özdoğan, H. Hauptmann and N. Başgelen (eds), *From Villages to Cities*. Istanbul: Arkeoloji ve Sanat Yayınları. 147–69.
— (ed.) 2010. *Economic Centralisation in Formative States: The Archaeological Reconstruction of the Economic System in 4th Millennium Arslantepe*. Rome: Sapienza UP.
—, G. M. Di Nocera, A. Hauptmann *et al*., 2001. 'New Symbols of a New Power in a "Royal" Tomb from 3000 BC Arslantepe, Malatya (Turkey).' *Paléorient* 27: 105–39.
Frank, A. G., 1966. 'The Development of Underdevelopment.' *Monthly Review* 18: 17–31.
Frankel, D., 2000. 'Migration and Ethnicity in Prehistoric Cyprus: Technology as Habitus.' *EJA* 3: 167–87.
Frankenstein, S., 1979. 'The Phoenicians in the far west: A function of neo-Assyrian imperialism' in M. T. Larsen (ed.), *Power and Propaganda: A Symposium on Ancient Empires*. Copenhagen: Akademisk. 263–94.
Frantzis, A., P. Alexiadou, G. Paximadis *et al*., 2003. 'Current Knowledge of the Cetacean Fauna of the Greek Seas.' *Journal of Cetacean Research Management* 5: 219–32.
Frederick, C. D., and A. Krahtopoulou, 2000. 'Deconstructing Agricultural Terraces: Examining the Influence of Construction Method on Stratigraphy, Dating and Archaeological Visibility' in Halstead and Frederick 2000, 79–94.
Fregel, R., F. L. Méndez, Y. Bokbot *et al*., 2018. 'Ancient Genomes from North Africa Evidence Prehistoric Migrations to the Maghreb from both the Levant and Europe.' *PNAS* 115: 6774–79.
Friedrich, W. L., 2000. *Fire in the Sea: The Santorini Volcano, Natural History and the Legend of Atlantis*. Cambridge and New York: Cambridge UP.
—, B. Kromer, M. Friedrich *et al*., 2006. 'Santorini Eruption Radiocarbon Dated to 1627–1600 B.C.' *Science* 312: 548.
Frost, H., 2004. 'Byblos and the Sea' in Doumet-Serhal 2004, 316–47.
Fugazzola Delpino, M. A., and M. Mineo, 1995. 'La Piroga Neolitica del Lago di Bracciano, La Marmotta.' *Bullettino di Paletnologia Italiano* 86: 197–266.
—, A. Pessina and V. Tiné, (eds) 2002. *La Ceramiche Impresse Nel Neolitico Antico: Italia E Mediterraneo*. Rome: Istituto Poligrafico e Zecca dello Stato.
Fuller, D. Q., 2010. 'An Emerging Paradigm Shift in the Origins of Agriculture.' *General Anthropology* 17: 8–12.
—, N. Boivin, T. Hoogervorst and R. Allaby, 2011. 'Across the Indian Ocean: The Prehistoric Movement of Plants and Animals.' *Antiquity* 85: 544–58.
—, G. Willcox and R. G. Allaby, 2011. 'Cultivation and Domestication Had Multiple Origins: Arguments against the Core Area Hypothesis for the Origins of Agriculture in the Near East.' *WA* 43: 628–52.
Furholt, M., 2021. 'Mobility and Social Change: Understanding the European Neolithic Period after the Archaeogenetic Revolution.' *Journal of Archaeological Research* 29: 481–535.
Gabrielsen, V., and J. Lund, (eds) 2007. *The Black Sea in Antiquity: Regional and Interregional Economic Exchanges*. Aarhus and Lancaster: Aarhus UP.
Gaffney, D., 2021. 'Pleistocene Water Crossings and Adaptive Flexibility within the *Homo* Genus.' *Journal Of Archaeological Research* 29: 255–326.
Gaffney, V., B. Kirigin, M. Petric and N. Vujnovic, 1997. *Adriatic Islands Project: Contact, Commerce and Colonialism, 6000 BC–AD 600*. Vol. 1: *The Archaeological Heritage of Hvar, Croatia*. Oxford: Archaeopress.
Galán, J. M., 2005. *Four Journeys in Ancient Egyptian Literature*. Göttingen: Seminar für Ägyptologie und Koptologie.
Galanaki, I., Y. Galanakis, R. Laffineur and H. Tomas, (eds) 2007. *Between the Aegean and Baltic Seas: Prehistory Across Borders*. Liège: Université de Liège.
Galanidou, N., and C. Perlès, (eds) 2003. *The Greek Mesolithic: Problems and Perspectives*. London: British School at Athens.
Gale, N. H., (ed.) 1991a. *Bronze Age Trade in the Mediterranean*. Jonsered: Paul Åströms.
— 1991b. 'Copper Oxhide Ingots: Their Origin and Their Place in the Bronze Age Metals Trade in the Mediterranean' in N. H. Gale 1991a, 197–239.
— 2001. 'Archaeology, Science-based Archaeology and the Mediterranean Bronze Age Metals Trade: A Contribution to the Debate.' *EJA* 4: 113–30.
— 2009. 'A Response to the Paper of A.M. Pollard: What a Long, Strange Trip It's Been: Lead Isotopes and Archaeology' in Shortland *et al*. 2009, 191–96.
Gale, R., and W. Carruthers, 2000. 'Charcoal and Charred Seed Remains from Middle Palaeolithic Levels at Gorham's and Vanguard Caves' in Stringer *et al*. 2000, 207–10.
—, P. Gasson, N. Hepper and G. Killen, 2000. 'Wood' in P. T. Nicholson and I. Shaw (eds), *Ancient Egyptian Materials and Technologies*. Cambridge and New York: Cambridge UP. 335–71.
Galiberti, A., (ed.) 2005 *Defensola: Una Miniera di Selce di 7000 Anni Fa*. Siena: Protagon Editori Toscani.
Galili, E., O. Lernau and I. Zohar, 2004. 'Fishing and Marine Adaptations at Atlit-Yam, a Submerged Neolithic Village off the Carmel Coast, Israel.' *'Atiqot* 48: 1–34.
— and B. Rosen, 2011. 'Submerged Neolithic Settlements off the Carmel Coast, Israel: Cultural and Environmental Insights' in Benjamin *et al*. 2011, 272–86.
—, —, A. Gopher and L. Kolska-Horwitz, 2002. 'The Emergence and Dispersion of the Eastern Mediterranean Fishing Village: Evidence from Submerged Neolithic Settlements off the Carmel Coast, Israel.' *JMA* 15: 167–98.
Gallant, T. W., 1985. *A Fisherman's Tale*. Gent: Belgian Archaeological Mission in Greece.
Gallis, K., 1985. 'A Late Neolithic Foundation Offering from Thessaly.' *Antiquity* 59: 20–24.
Gamble, C., 1986. 'The Mesolithic Sandwich: Ecological Approaches and the Archaeological Record of the Early Post-Glacial' in M. Zvelebil (ed.), *Hunters in Transition: Mesolithic Societies of Temperate Eurasia and Their Transition to Farming*. Cambridge and New York: Cambridge UP. 33–42.
— 1999a. *Palaeolithic Societies of Europe*. Cambridge and New York: Cambridge UP.
— 1999b. 'Faunal Exploitation at Klithi: A Late Glacial Rockshelter in Epirus, Northwestern Greece' in Bailey *et al*. 1999, 179–87.
— 2007. *Origins and Revolutions: Human Identity in Earliest Prehistory*. Cambridge and New York: Cambridge UP.
—, W. Davies, P. Pettitt and M. Richards, 2004. 'Climate Change and Evolving Human Diversity in Europe during the Last Glacial.' *Philosophical Transactions of the Royal Society of London* 359: 243–54.
—, —, M. Richards *et al*., 2005. 'Archaeological and Genetic Foundations of the European Population during the Lateglacial: Implications for "Agricultural Thinking".' *CAJ* 15: 55–85.
Gamble, L., 2008. *The Chumash World at European Contact: Power, Trade, and Feasting among Complex Hunter-gatherers*. Berkeley and London: California UP.
Garcea, E. A. A., 2004. 'Crossing Deserts and Avoiding Seas: Aterian North African-European Relations.' *Journal of Anthropological Research* 60: 27–53.

— 2009. 'The Evolutions and Revolutions of the Late Middle Stone Age and Lower Later Stone Age in North-west Africa' in M. Camps and Szmidt 2009, 51–66.
— (ed.) 2010a. *South-eastern Mediterranean Peoples between 130,000 and 10,000 Years Ago*. Oxford and Oakville: Oxbow.
— 2010b. 'The Spread of Aterian Peoples in North Africa' in Garcea 2010a, 37–53.
— 2010c. 'The Lower and Upper Later Stone Age of North Africa' in Garcea 2010a, 54–65.
Garcia, D., 2005. 'Urbanization and Spatial Organization in Southern France and North-eastern Spain during the Iron Age' in Osborne and Cunliffe 2005, 169–86.
García Sanjuán, L., 2005: 'Grandes Piedras Viejas, Memoria y Pasado: Reutilizaciones del Dolmen de Palacio III (Almadén de la Plata, Sevilla) durante la Edad del Hierro' in S. Celestino Pérez and J. Jiménez Ávila (eds), *El Periodo Orientalizante*. Mérida. CSIC. 595–604.
—, R. Montero Artús, S. Emslie *et al.*, 2023. 'Beautiful, Magic, Lethal: A Social Perspective of Cinnabar Use and Mercury Exposure at the Valencina Copper Age Mega-site (Spain).' *Journal of Archaeological Method and Theory*. https://doi.org/10.1007/s10816-023-09631-8.
—, M. L. Triviño, T. X. Schuhmacher *et al.*, 2013. 'Ivory Craftsmanship, Trade and Social Significance in the Southern Iberian Copper Age: The Evidence from the PP4-Montelirio Sector of Valencina de la Concepción (Seville, Spain).' *EJA* 16: 610–35.
Garnsey, P., 1988. 'Mountain Economies in Southern Europe: Thoughts on the Early History, Continuity and Individuality of Mediterranean Upland Pastoralism' in Whittaker 1988, 196–209.
Garrard, A., 1984. 'The Selection of South-west Asian Animal Domesticates' in J. Clutton-Brock and C. Grigson (eds), *Animals and Archaeology*. Vol. 3: *Early Herders and Their Flocks*. Oxford: Archaeopress. 117–32.
—, S. Colledge and L. Martin, 1996. 'The Emergence of Crop Cultivation and Caprine Herding in the "Marginal" Zone of the Southern Levant' in D. R. Harris 1996, 204–26.
Garrido-Pena, R., M. A. Rojo-Guerra, I. García-Martínez de Lagrán and C. Tejedor-Rodríguez, 2011. 'Drinking and Eating Together: The Social and Symbolic Context of Commensality Rituals in the Bell Beakers of the Interior of Iberia (2500–2000 cal BC)' in G. Aranda Jiménez, S. Montón-Subías and M. Sánchez Romero (eds), *Guess Who's Coming to Dinner: Feasting Rituals in the Prehistoric Societies of Europe and the Near East*. Oxford and Oakville: Oxbow. 109–29.
Garstang, J., 1953. *Prehistoric Mersin: Yümük Tepe in Southern Turkey. The Neilson Expedition in Cilicia*. Oxford: Clarendon.
Gascó, J., 1994. 'Development and Decline in the Bronze Age of Southern France: Languedoc and Provence' in Mathers and Stoddart 1994, 99–128.
— 2009. 'Les "Insensibles Transformations" de la Fin de l'Âge du Bronze dans le Sud de la France' in Barbaza *et al.* 2009, 311–22.
Gatsov, I., and M. Özdoğan, 1994. 'Some Epi-palaeolithic Sites from Northwest Turkey: Ağaçlı, Domalı and Gümüş dere.' *Anatolica* 20: 97–120.
Gauss, W., 2010. 'Aegina Kolonna' in Cline 2010, 737–51.
Geddes, D., J. Guilaine and J. Coulerou, 1989. 'Post-Glacial Environments, Settlement, and Subsistence in the Pyrenees: The Balma Margineda, Andorra' in Bonsall 1989, 561–71.
Gell, A., 1985. 'How to Read a Map: Remarks on the Practical Logic of Navigation.' *Man* 20: 271–86.
— 1992. 'The Technology of Enchantment and the Enchantment of Technology' in J. Coote and A. Shelton (eds), *Anthropology, Art and Aesthetics*. Oxford and New York: Clarendon. 40–66.
Gener Basallote, J. M., A. Navarro García, J. M. Pajuelo Sáez *et al.*, 2012. 'Las Crétulas del Siglio VIII A.C. de las Excavaciones del Solar del Cine Cómico (Cádiz).' *Madrider Mitteilungen* 53: 134–86.
Genz, H., 2003. 'Cash Crop Production and Storage in the Early Bronze Age Southern Levant.' *JMA* 16: 59–78.
— 2010. 'Thoughts on the Function of "Public Buildings" in the Early Bronze Age Southern Levant' in Bolger and Maguire 2010, 46–52.
George, A., 2004. 'Gilgamesh and the Cedars of Lebanon' in Doumet-Serhal 2004, 450–55.
Geraads, D., J.-P. Raynal and V. Eisenmann, 2004. 'The Earliest Human Occupation of North Africa: A Reply to Sahnouni *et al.* (2002).' *JHE* 46: 751–61.
Gérard, F., 2002. 'Transformation and Societies in the Neolithic of Central Anatolia' in Gérard and Thissen 2002, 105–17.
— and L. Thissen, (eds) 2002. *The Neolithic of Central Anatolia: Internal Developments and External Relations during the 9th–6th millennia CAL BC*. Istanbul: Ege Yayınları.
Gesell, G. C., 1987. 'The Minoan Palace and Public Cult' in Hägg and Marinatos 1987, 123–27.
Giammellaro, A. S., F. Spatafora and P. van Dommelen, 2008. 'Sicily and Malta: between Sea and Countryside' in van Dommelen and Goméz Bellard 2008, 129–58.
Giardino, C., 1995. *The West Mediterranean between the 14th and 8th Centuries BC: Mining and Metallurgical Spheres*. Oxford: Archaeopress.
— 2000a. 'Sicilian Hoards and Protohistoric Metal Trade in the Central West Mediterranean' in Pare 2000a, 99–107.
— 2000b. 'The Beginning of Metallurgy in Tyrrhenian South-central Italy' in Ridgway *et al.* 2000, 49–73.
— and C. Pepe, 2005. 'The Island of Vivara: An International Port of Trade of the Middle of the Second Millennium BC in a Volcanic Landscape' in Balmuth *et al.* 2005, 149–63.
Gibson, S., and G. Edelstein, 1985. 'Investigating Jerusalem's Rural Landscape.' *Levant* 17: 139–55.
Gill, D. W., 1988. 'Silver Anchors and Cargoes of Oil: Some Observations on Phoenician Trade in the Mediterranean.' *Papers of the British School at Rome* 56: 1–12.
— and C. Chippindale, 1993. 'Material and Intellectual Consequences of Esteem for Cycladic Figures.' *AJA* 97: 601–59.
Gilman, A., 1975. *The Later Prehistory of Tangier, Morocco*. American School of Prehistoric Research Bulletin 29. Cambridge: Peabody Museum.
— 1981. 'The Development of Social Stratification in Bronze Age Europe.' *CA* 22: 1–23.
— 1991. 'Trajectories towards Social Complexity in the Later Prehistory of the Mediterranean' in T. Earle (ed.), *Chiefdoms: Power, Economy and Ideology*. Cambridge and New York: Cambridge UP. 146–68.
— 2000. '*Book Review: Book Marks - Guest Editorial.' EJA 3: 265–67.*
— 2013. 'Were There States during the Late Prehistory of Southern Iberia?' in Cruz Berrocal *et al.* 2013, 10–28.
—, M. Fernández-Miranda, M. D. Fernández-Posse and C. Martín, 1997. 'Preliminary Report on a Survey Program of the Bronze Age of Northern Albacete Province, Spain' in Balmuth *et al.* 1997, 33–50.
— and B. Thornes, 1985. *Land-use and Prehistory in South-east Spain*. London and Boston: Allen & Unwin.
Gimbutas, M. A., 1973. 'The Beginnings of the Bronze Age in Europe and the Indo-Europeans: 3500–2500 B.C.' *Journal of Indo-European Studies* 1: 163–214.
Gitin, S., 1990. '*Ekron* of the Philistines Part II: Olive-oil Suppliers to the World.' *Biblical Archaeology Review* 46: 33–42.
— 1997. 'The Neo Assyrian Empire and Its Western Periphery: The Levant with a Focus on Philistine Ekron' in S. Parpola and R. M. Whiting (eds), *Assyria 1995*. Helsinki: University of Helsinki. 77–104.
—, A. Mazar and E. Stern, (eds) 1998. *Mediterranean Peoples in Transition*. Jerusalem: Israel Exploration Society.
Giumlia-Mair, A., and F. Lo Schiavo, (eds) 2003. *The Problem of Early Tin*. Oxford: Archaeopress.
Given, M., 1998. 'Inventing the Eteocypriots: Imperialist Archaeology and the Manipulation of Ethnic Identity.' *JMA* 11: 3–29.
Gkiasta, M. T., T. Russell, S. J. Shennan and J. Steele, 2003 'Neolithic Transition in Europe: The Radiocarbon Record Revisited.' *Antiquity* 77: 45–62.
Glantz, M. H., D. G. Streets, T. R. Stewart *et al.*, 1998. *Exploring the Concept of Climate Surprises: A Review of the Literature on the Concept of Surprise and How It Is Related to Climate Change*. Boulder: Environmental and Societal Impacts Group.
Glatz, C., 2009. 'Empire as Network: Spheres of Material Interaction in Late Bronze Age Anatolia.' *JAA* 28: 127–41.
— 2013. 'Negotiating Empire – A Comparative Investigation into the Responses to Hittite Imperialism by the Vassal State of Ugarit and the Kaska Peoples of the Anatolian Black Sea Region' in G. Areshian (ed.), *Empires and Diversity: On the Crossroads of Archaeology, History and Anthropology*. Los Angeles: Cotsen Institute of Archaeology.
— and R. Matthews, 2005. 'Anthropology of a Frontier Zone: Hittite-Kaska Relations in Late Bronze Age North-central Anatolia.' *BASOR* 339: 47–65.
Glover, I., and P. Bellwood, (eds) 2004. *Southeast Asia: From Prehistory to History*. London and New York: RoutledgeCurzon.
Goedicke, H., 1988. 'The Northeastern Delta and the Mediterranean' in van den Brink 1988, 165–75.
— 2000. 'An Ancient Naval Finial of the Middle Kingdom.' *ÄL* 10: 77–82.
Golden, J. M., 2010. *Dawn of the Metal Age: Technology and Society during the Levantine Chalcolithic*. London and Oakville: Equinox.
Goméz Bellard, C., 2008. 'Ibiza: The Making of New Landscapes' in van Dommelen and Goméz Bellard 2008, 44–75.
Gonen, R., 1992. 'The Late Bronze Age' in A. Ben-Tor 1992, 211–57.
Gonnella, J., W. Khayyata and K. Kohlmeyer, 2005. *Die Zitadelle von Aleppo und der Tempel des Wettergottes: Neue Forschungen und Entdeckungen*. Münster: Rhema.
González de Canales Cerisola, F., L. Serrano Pichardo and J. Llompart Gómez, 2004. *El Emporio Fenicio Precolonial de Huelva (ca. 900–770 BC)*. Madrid: Biblioteca Nueva.
—, — and — 2006. 'The Pre-colonial Phoenician Emporium of Huelva ca. 900–770 BC.' *Bulletin Antieke Beschaving* 81: 13–29.
—, — and — 2011. 'Reflexiones sobre la Conexión Cerdeña-Huelva con Motivo de un Nuevo Jarro Ascoide Sardo.' *Madrider Mitteilungen* 52: 238–65.
González-Ruibal, A., 2004. 'Facing Two Seas: Mediterranean and Atlantic Contacts in the North-west of Iberia in the First Millennium BC.' *OJA* 23: 287–317.
— and M. Ruiz-Gálvez, 2016. 'House Societies in the Ancient Mediterranean (2000–500 BC).' *JWP* 29: 383–437.
Good, I., 2011. 'Strands of Connectivity: Assessing the Evidence for Long Distance Exchange of Silk in Later Prehistoric Eurasia' in T. C. Wilkinson *et al.* 2011, 218–30.
Gopher, A., Z. Tsuk, S. Shalev and R. Gophna, 1990. 'Earliest Gold Artifacts in the Levant.' *CA* 31: 436–43.
Gophna, R., 1995. 'Early Bronze Age Canaan: Some Spatial and Demographic Observations' in Levy 1995a, 269–80.
— and J. Portugali, 1988. 'Settlement and Demographic Processes in Israel's Coastal Plain from the Chalcolithic to the Middle Bronze Age.' *BASOR* 269: 11–28.
Goren, Y., S. Bunimovitz, I. Finkelstein and N. Na'aman, 2004. 'VI. Alashiya' in Y. Goren, I. Finkelstein and N. Na'aman (eds), *Inscribed in Clay: Provenance Studies of the Amarna Tablets and Other Ancient Near Eastern Texts*. Tel Aviv: Emery and Claire Yass Publications in Archaeology. 48–75.
Goren-Inbar, N., E. Werker and C. S. Feibel, 2002. *The Acheulian Site of Gesher Benot Ya'aqov, Israel*. Vol. 1: *The Wood Assemblage*. Oxford: Oxbow.
Goring-Morris, A. N., 2005. 'Life, Death and the Emergence of Differential Status in the Near Eastern Neolithic: Evidence from Kfar HaHoresh, Lower Galilee, Israel' in J. Clarke 2005, 89–105.
— and A. Belfer-Cohen, (eds) 2003. *More than Meets the Eye: Studies on Upper Palaeolithic Diversity in the Near East*. Oxford and Oakville: Oxbow.
— and — 2011. 'Neolithicization Processes in the Levant: The Outer Envelope.' *CA* 52 (S4): S195–S208.
Gosden, C., 2004. *Archaeology and Colonialism: Cultural Contact from 5000 B.C. to the Present*. Cambridge and New York: Cambridge UP.
Goudie, A., 2009. 'Aeolian Processes and Landforms' in Woodward 2009a, 415–31.
Grace, V. R., 1956. 'The Canaanite Jar' in S. S. Weinberg (ed.), *The Aegean and the Near East*. Locust Valley: J. J. Augustin. 80–109.
Graham, J. W., 1987. *The Palaces of Crete*. Rev. edn. Princeton: Princeton UP.
Graziadio, G., 1998. 'Trade Circuits and Trade-routes in the Shaft Grave Period.' *Studi Micenei ed Egeo-Anatolici* 40: 29–76.
Greaves, A., 2007a. 'Trans-Anatolia: Examining Turkey as a Bridge between East and West.' *AS* 57: 1–15.
— 2007b. 'Milesians in the Black Sea: Trade, Settlement and Religion' in Gabrielsen and Lund 2007, 9–22.
Green, R. E., J. Krause, A. W. Briggs *et al.*, 2010. 'A Draft Sequence of the Neandertal Genome.' *Science* 328: 710–22.
Greenbaum, G., D. E. Friesem, E. Hovers *et al.*, 2019. 'Was Inter-population Connectivity of Neanderthals and Modern Humans the Driver of the Upper Paleolithic Transition rather than its Product?' *QSR* 217: 316–29.
Greenberg, R., 2002. *Early Urbanizations in the Levant: A Regional Narrative*. London and New York: Leicester UP.
— 2003. 'Early Bronze Age Megiddo and Bet Shean: Discontinuous Settlement in Sociopolitical Context.' *JMA* 16: 17–31.
— 2009. 'Extreme Exposure: Archaeology in Jerusalem 1967–2007.' *Conservation and Management of Archaeological Sites* 11: 262–81.
— 2011. 'Traveling in (World) Time: Transformation, Commoditization, and the Beginnings of Urbanism in the Southern Levant' in T. C. Wilkinson *et al.* 2011, 231–42.
— and E. Eisenberg, 2002. 'Egypt, Bet Yerah and Early Canaanite Urbanization' in Levy and van den Brink 2002, 213–22.
— and Y. Paz, 2005. 'The Early Bronze Age Fortifications of Tel Bet Yerah.' *Levant* 37: 81–103.
Greenfield, H. J., 2010. 'The Secondary Products Revolution: The Past, the Present and the Future.' *WA* 42: 29–54.

Grenon, M., and M. Batisse, (eds) 1989. *Futures for the Mediterranean Basin: The Blue Plan*. Oxford and New York: Oxford UP.

Griffiths, R. D., 2005. 'Gods' Blue Hair in Homer and in Eighteenth-Dynasty Egypt' *Classical Quarterly* 55: 329–34.

Grigson, C., 1995. 'Plough and Pasture in the Early Economy of the Southern Levant' in Levy 1995a, 245–68.

— 2006. 'Farming? Feasting? Herding? Large Mammals from the Chalcolithic of Gilat' in Levy 2006, 215–319.

Grima, R., 2004. 'The Landscape Context of Megalithic Architecture' in Cilia 2004, 326–46.

Grimal, N., and B. Benu, (eds) 1998. *Le Commerce en Égypte Ancienne*. Cairo: Institut Français d'Archéologie Orientale.

Grimaldi, S., T. Perrin and J. Guilaine, (eds) 2008. *Mountain Environments in Prehistoric Europe: Settlement and Mobility Strategies from the Palaeolithic to the Early Bronze Age*. Oxford: Archaeopress.

Grosman, L., N. D. Munro and A. Belfer-Cohen, 2008. 'A 12,000-year-old Shaman Burial from the Southern Levant (Israel).' *PNAS* 105: 17665–69.

Groube, L., 1996. 'The Impact of Diseases upon the Emergence of Agriculture' in D. R. Harris 1996, 101–29.

Groucutt, H. S., W. C. Carleton, K. Fenech *et al.*, 2022. 'The 4.2 ka Event and the End of the Maltese "Temple Period".' *Frontiers in Earth Science* 9: 771683.

Grove, A. T., and O. Rackham, 2001. *The Nature of Mediterranean Europe: An Ecological History*. London and New Haven: Yale UP.

Gschnitzer, F., 1993. 'Phoinikisch-Karthagisches Verfassungsdenken' in K. Raaflaub (ed.), *Anfänge Politischen Denkens in der Antike*. Munich: R. Oldenbourg. 87–198.

Gubel, E., 2006. 'Notes on the Phoenician Component of the Orientalizing Horizon' in Riva and Vella 2006, 85–93.

Guerrero Ayuso, V. M., 2001. 'The Balearic Islands: Prehistoric Colonization of the Furthest Mediterranean Islands from the Mainland.' *JMA* 14: 136–58.

— 2006. 'Nautas Baleáricos durante la Prehistoria (Parte II): De la Iconografía Naval a las Fuentes Históricas.' *Pyrenae* 37: 7–45.

— 2008. 'El Bronce Final en las Baleares: Intercambios en la Antesala de la Colonización Fenicia del Archipélago' in Celestino *et al.* 2008, 183–217.

Guglielmino, R., 2004–6. 'Roca Vecchia (Lecce): New Evidence for Aegean Contacts with Apulia during the Late Bronze Age.' *ARP* 10: 87–102.

Guidi, A., 1996. 'Processual and Post-processual Trends in Italian Archaeology' in A. Bietti, A. Cazella, A. Johnson and A. Voorrips (eds), *Theoretical and Methodological Problems*. Forlì: A.B.A.C.O. 29–36.

— and R. Whitehouse, 1996. 'A Radiocarbon Chronology for the Bronze Age: The Italian Situation' in K. Randsborg (ed.), *Absolute Chronology: Archaeological Europe 2500–500 BC*. Copenhagen: Munksgaard. 271–82.

Guilaine, J., 1976. *Premiers Bergers et Paysans de l'Occident Méditerranéen*. Paris: Mouton.

— 1987. 'Les Néolithiques Européens: Colons et/ou Créateurs.' *L'Anthropologie* 91: 343–50.

— 1994. *La Mer Partagée: La Méditerranée avant l'Écriture, 7000–2000 avant Jésus-Christ*. Paris, Hachette.

— 2003. *De la Vague à la Tombe: La Conquête Néolithique de la Méditerranée (8000–2000 avant J.-C.)*. Paris: Seuil.

— (ed.) 2008. *Villes, Villages, Campagnes de l'Âge du Bronze*. Paris: Errance.

—, P. Barthès, J. Vaquer and P. Lambert, 1995. *Temps et Espace dans le Bassin de l'Aude du Néolithique à l'Age du Fer*. Toulouse: Centre d'Archéologie.

—, F. Claustre, O. Lemercier and P. Sabatier, 2001. 'Campaniformes et Environnement Culturel en France Mediterranéenne' in Nicolis 2001, 229–75.

—, A. Freises, R. Montjardin *et al.*, (eds) 1984. *Leucate-Corrège: Habitat Noyé du Néolithique Cardial*. Toulouse: Centre d'Anthropologie des Sociétés Rurales.

— and A. Le Brun, (eds) 2003. *Le Néolithique de Chypre*. Athens: École Française d'Athènes.

— and C. Manen, 2007. 'From Mesolithic to Early Neolithic in the Western Mediterranean' in Whittle and Cummings 2007, 21–51.

—, C. Manen and J.-D. Vigne, 2007. *Pont de Roque-Haute: Nouveaux Regards sur la Néolithisation de la France Méditerranéenne*. Toulouse: Centre de Recherche sur la Préhistoire et la Protohistoire de la Méditerranée.

—, G. Rancoule, J. Vaquer *et al.*, (eds) 1986. *Carsac: Une Agglomération Protohistorique en Languedoc*. Toulouse: Centre d'Anthropologie des Sociétés Rurales.

— and S. Verger, 2008. 'La Gaule et la Méditerranée (13e–8e Siècles avant Notre Ère)' in Celestino *et al.* 2008, 219–37.

Günel, S., 1999. *Panaztepe II: M.Ö. 2. Bine Tarihlendirilen Panaztepe Seramiğinin Batı Anadolu ve Ege Arkeolojisindeki Yeri ve Önemi*. Ankara: Türk Tarih Kurumu Yayınları.

Guthrie, R. D., 1990. *Frozen Fauna of the Mammoth Steppe: The Story of Blue Babe*. Chicago: Chicago UP.

Habu, J., 2010. 'Seafaring and the Development of Cultural Complexity in Northeast Asia: Evidence from the Japanese Archipelago' in A. Anderson *et al.* 2010, 159–70.

Hachi, H., 1996. 'L'Ibéromaurisian, Découverte des Fouilees d'Afalou (Bédjaïa, Algérie).' *L'Anthropologie* 100: 55–76.

—, F. Fröhlich, A. Gendron-Badou *et al.*, 2002. 'Figurines du Paléolithique Supérieur en Matière Minérale Plastique Cuite d'Afalou Bou Rhummel (Babors, Algérie). Premières Analyses par Spectroscopie d'Absorption Infrarouge.' *L'Anthropologie* 106: 57–97.

Hadjisterkotis, E., and D. S. Reese, 2008. 'Considerations on the Potential Use of Cliffs and Caves by the Extinct Endemic Late Pleistocene Hippopotami and Elephants of Cyprus.' *European Journal of Wildlife Research* 54: 122–33.

Hägg, R., and N. Marinatos, (eds) 1987. *The Function of the Minoan Palaces*. Stockholm: Svenska institutet i Athen.

Haider, P., 2001. 'Minoan Deities in an Egyptian Medical Text' in R. Laffineur and R. Hägg (eds), *Potnia: Deities and Religion in the Aegean Bronze Age*. Liège: Université de Liège. 479–82.

Hall, J. M., 1997. *Ethnic Identity in Greek Antiquity*. Cambridge and New York: Cambridge UP.

— 2002. *Hellenicity: Between Ethnicity and Culture*. Chicago and London: Chicago UP.

— 2007. *A History of the Archaic Greek World ca. 1200–479 BC*. Oxford and Malden: Blackwell.

Hallo, W. W., 1992. 'Trade and Traders in the Ancient Near East' in C. Charpin and F. Joannès (eds), *La Circulation des Biens, des Personnes et des Idèes dans le Proche-Orient Ancien*. Paris: Editions Recherche sur les Civilisations. 351–56.

Halstead, P., 1981. 'Counting Sheep in Neolithic and Bronze Age Greece' in Hodder *et al.* 1981, 307–39.

— 1987. 'Traditional and Ancient Rural Economy in Mediterranean Europe: Plus ça Change?' *Journal of Hellenic Studies* 107: 77–87.

— 1988. 'On Redistribution and the Origin of Minoan-Mycenaean Palatial Economies' in E. French and K. Wardle (eds), *Problems in Greek Prehistory*. Bristol: Bristol Classical. 519–30.

— 1989. 'The Economy Has a Normal Surplus: Economic Stability and Social Change among Early Farming Communities of Thessaly, Greece' in P. Halstead and J. O'Shea (eds), *Bad Year Economics: Cultural Responses to Risk and Uncertainty*. Cambridge and New York: Cambridge UP. 68–80.

— 1991. 'Present to Past in the Pindhos: Specialisation and Diversification in Mountain Economies.' *Rivista di Studi Liguri* 56: 61–80.

— 1992. 'The Mycenaean Palatial Economy: Making the Most of the Gaps in the Evidence.' *PCPS* 38: 57–86.

— 1994. 'The North-South Divide: Regional Paths to Complexity in Prehistoric Greece' in Mathers and Stoddart 1994, 195–219.

— 1995a. 'From Sharing to Hoarding: The Neolithic Foundations of Aegean Bronze Age Society' in R. Laffineur and W.-D. Niemeier (eds), *Politeia: Society and State in the Aegean Bronze Age*. Liège: Université de Liège. Austin: Texas UP. 11–21.

— 1995b. 'Plough and Power: The Economic and Social Significance of Cultivation with the Ox-drawn Ard in the Mediterranean.' *Bulletin on Sumerian Agriculture* 8: 11–22.

— 1996a. 'The Development of Agriculture and Pastoralism in Greece: When, How, Who and What?' in D. R. Harris 1996, 296–309.

— 1996b. 'Pastoralism or Household Herding? Problems of Scale and Specialization in Early Greek Animal Husbandry.' *WA* 28: 20–42.

— (ed.) 1999a. *Neolithic Society in Greece*. Sheffield: Sheffield Academic.

— 1999b. 'Neighbours from Hell? The Household in Neolithic Greece' in Halstead 1999a, 77–95.

— 2000. 'Land Use in Postglacial Greece: Cultural Causes and Environmental Effects' in Halstead and Frederick 2000, 110–28.

— 2006. 'Sheep in the Garden: The Integration of Crop and Livestock Husbandry in Early Farming Regimes of Greece and Southern Europe' in D. Serjeantson and D. Field (eds), *Animals in the Neolithic of Britain and Europe*. Oxford: Oxbow. 42–55.

— 2008. 'Between a Rock and a Hard Place: Coping with Marginal Colonisation in the Later Neolithic and Early Bronze Age of Crete and the Aegean' in Isaakidou and Tomkins 2008, 229–57.

— and C. D. Frederick, (eds) 2000. *Landscape and Land Use in Postglacial Greece*. Sheffield: Sheffield Academic.

— and V. Isaakidou, 2011. 'Revolutionary Secondary Products: The Development and Significance of Milking, Animal-traction and Wool-gathering in Later Prehistoric Europe and the Near East' in T. C. Wilkinson *et al.* 2011, 61–76.

— and J. O'Shea, 1982. 'A Friend in Need Is a Friend Indeed: Social Storage and the Origins of Social Ranking' in C. Renfrew and S. Stephen (eds), *Ranking, Resource and Exchange: Aspects of the Archaeology of Early European Society*. Cambridge and New York: Cambridge UP. 92–99.

Hamilakis, Y., 1999. 'La Trahison des Archéologues? Archaeological Practice as Intellectual Activity in Post-modernity.' *JMA* 12: 60–72.

— 2002. 'Too Many Chiefs: Factional Competition in Neopalatial Crete' in J. Driessen *et al.* 2002, 179–99.

— 2007. *The Nation and Its Ruins: Antiquity, Archaeology, and National Imagination in Greece*. Oxford and New York: Oxford UP.

— and E. Yalouri, 1996. 'Antiquities as Symbolic Capital in Modern Greek Society' *Antiquity* 70: 117–29.

Hamilton, S., R. Whitehouse, K. Brown *et al.*, 2006. 'Phenomenology in Practice: Towards a Methodology for a "Subjective" Approach.' *EJA* 9: 31–71.

Hänsel, B., 2007. 'Agaische Siedlungsstrukturen in Monkodonja/Istrien?' in Galanaki *et al.* 2007, 149–56.

Hansen, J. M., 1991. *The Palaeoethnobotany of Franchthi Cave*. Bloomington and Indianapolis: Indiana UP.

Hansen, M. H., 2012. 'Greek City-states' in Bang and Scheidel 2012, 259–78.

Harding, A. F., 1984. *The Mycenaeans and Europe*. London and Orlando: Academic.

— 2000. *European Societies in the Bronze Age*. Cambridge and New York: Cambridge UP.

— 2007. 'Interconnections between the Aegean and Continental Europe in the Bronze and Early Iron Ages: Moving beyond Scepticism' in Galanaki *et al.* 2007, 47–56.

Hardy, D. A., C. G. Doumas, J. A. Sakellarakis and P. M. Warren, (eds) 1990. *Thera and the Aegean World III*. Vol. 1: *Archaeology*. London: Thera Foundation.

Harmanşah, Ö., 2011. 'Moving Landscapes, Making Place: Cities, Monuments and Commemoration at Malizi/Melid.' *JMA* 24: 55–83.

Harper, K., 2017. *The Fate of Rome: Climate, Disease, and the End of an Empire*. Princeton: Princeton UP.

Harris, D. R., (ed.) 1996. *The Origins and Spread of Agriculture and Pastoralism in Eurasia*. Washington DC: Smithsonian Institution. London: UCL.

Harris, W. V., (ed.) 2005a. *Rethinking the Mediterranean*. Oxford and New York: Oxford UP.

— 2005b. 'The Mediterranean and Ancient History' in W. V. Harris 2005a, 1–44.

Harrison, R. J., and A. Gilman, 1977. 'Trade in the Second and Third Millennia BC between the Maghreb and Iberia' in V. Markotic (ed.), *Ancient Europe and the Mediterranean*. Warminster: Aris & Phillips. 90–104.

Harvati, K., and R. R. Ackerman, 2022. 'Merging Morphological and Genetic Evidence to Assess Hybridization in Western Eurasian Late Pleistocene Hominins.' *Nature Ecology & Evolution* 6: 1573–85.

—, K., E. Panagopoulou and P. Karkanas, 2003. 'First Neanderthal Remains from Greece: The Evidence from Lakonis.' *JHE* 45: 465–73.

—, C. Röding, A. M. Bosman *et al.*, 2019. 'Apidima Cave Fossils Provide Earliest Evidence of *Homo sapiens* in Eurasia.' *Nature* 571: 500–504.

Hasel, M. G., 1998. *Domination and Resistance: Egyptian Military Activity in the Southern Levant, ca. 1300–1185 BC*. Leiden and Boston: Brill.

Haskell, H. W., 1985. 'The Origin of the Aegean Stirrup Jar and Its Earliest Evolution and Distribution (MB III–LBI).' *AJA* 89: 221–29.

—, R. E. Jones, P. M. Day and J. T. Killen, 2011. *Transport Stirrup Jars of the Bronze Age Aegean and East Mediterranean*. Philadelphia: INSTAP Academic.

Hassan, F., 1984. 'Environment and Subsistence in Predynastic Egypt' in J. D. Clark and Brandt 1984, 57–64.

— 1997. 'The Dynamics of a Riverine Civilization: A Geoarchaeological Perspective on the Nile Valley, Egypt.' *WA* 29: 51–74.

— (ed.) 2002a, *Droughts, Food, and Culture: Ecological Change and Food Security in Africa's Later Prehistory*. New York and London: Kluwer Academic/Plenum.

— 2002b. 'Palaeoclimate, Food and Culture Change in Africa: An Overview' in Hassan 2002a, 11–26.

— 2002c. 'Archaeology and Linguistic Diversity in North Africa' in Bellwood and Renfrew 2002, 127–33.

Haubold, J., 2012. 'The Achaemenid Empire and the Sea.' *MHR* 27: 5–24.

Hauptmann, A., F. Begemann and S. Schmitt-Strecker, 1999. 'Copper Objects from Arad: Their Composition and Provenance.' *BASOR* 314: 1–17.

Häussler, R., 2007. 'At the Margins of Italy: Celts and Ligurians in North-West Italy' in G. Bradley *et al.* 2007, 45–78.

Hawkins, J. D., 1998. 'Tarkasnawa King of Mira "Tarkondemos": Boğazköy Sealings and Karabel.' *AS 48*: 1–31.

Hayne, J., 2010. 'Entangled Identities on Iron Age Sardinia?' in van Dommelen and Knapp 2010, 147–69.

Heinz, M., (ed.) 2010. *Kamid el-Loz: Intermediary between Cultures*. Beirut: Bulletin d'Archéologie et d'Architecture Libanaises.

Helms, M. W., 1988. *Ulysses' Sail: An Ethnographic Odyssey of Power, Knowledge, and Geographical Distance*. Princeton: Princeton UP.

Helms, S., and A. V. G. Betts, 1987. 'The Desert "Kites" of the Badiyat Esh-Sham and North Arabia.' *Paléorient* 13: 41–67.

Heltzer, M., 1978. *Goods, Prices and the Organisation of Trade at Ugarit: Marketing and Transportation in the Eastern Mediterranean in the Second Half of the II Millennium B.C.E.* Wiesbaden: Reichert.

Hendrickx, S., and L. Bavay, 2002. 'Relative Chronological Position of Egyptian Predynastic and Early Dynastic Tombs with Objects Imported from the Near East and the Nature of Interregional Contacts' in van den Brink and Levy 2002, 58–80.

Henry, D. O., (ed.) 2003. *Neanderthals in the Levant: Behavioral Organization and the Beginnings of Human Modernity*. London and New York: Continuum.

Henshilwood, C. S., F. d'Errico, C. W. Marean *et al.*, 2001. 'An Early Bone Tool Industry from the Middle Stone Age at Blombos Cave, South Africa: Implications for the Origins of Modern Human Behaviour, Symbolism and Language.' *JHE* 41: 631–78.

—, —, R. Yates *et al.*, 2002. 'Emergence of Modern Human Behavior: Middle Stone Age Engravings from South Africa.' *Science* 295: 1278–80.

— and C. W. Marean, 2003. 'The Origin of Modern Human Behavior.' *CA* 44: 627–51.

Herodotus, *The Histories*. Transl. A. de Sélincourt, rev. edn 2003. London and New York: Penguin. In the original: *Herodoti Historiae* Vols 1–2, ed. K. Hude, 1963. Oxford and New York: Clarendon.

Herring, E., 2000. '"To See Ourselves as Others See Us!": Construction of Native Identities in Southern Italy' in Herring and Lomas 2000, 45–77.

— 2007. 'Daunians, Peucetians and Messapians? Societies and Settlements in South-east Italy' in G. Bradley *et al.* 2007, 268–94.

— and K. Lomas, (eds) 2000. *The Emergence of State Identities in Italy in the First Millennium BC*. London: Accordia Research Institute.

Hershkovitz, I., H. May, R. Sarig *et al.*, 2021. 'A Middle Pleistocene *Homo* from Nesher Ramla, Israel.' *Science* 372: 1424–28.

—, G. W. Weber, R. Quam *et al.*, 2018. 'The Earliest Modern Humans Outside Africa.' *Science* 359: 456–59.

Herzfeld, M., 1984. 'The Horns of the Mediterraneanist Dilemma.' *American Ethnologist* 11: 439–54.

— 2005. 'Practical Mediterraneanism: Excuses for Everything, from Epistemology to Eating' in W. V. Harris 2005a.

Hestrin, R., and M. Tadmor, 1963. 'A Hoard of Tools and Weapons from Kfar Monash.' *Israel Exploration Journal* 13: 265–88.

Hetherington, R., and R. G. Reid, 2010. *The Climate Connection: Climate Change and Modern Human Evolution*. Cambridge and New York: Cambridge UP.

Heurtley, W. A., 1934–35. 'Excavations in Ithaca, II.' *ABSA* 35: 1–44.

Heyd, V., 2007. 'Families, Prestige Goods, Warriors and Complex Societies: Beaker Groups of the 3rd Millennium cal BC along the Upper and Middle Danube.' *PPS* 73: 321–70.

Higgins, M. D., and R. Higgins, 1996. *A Geological Companion to Greece and the Aegean*. Ithaca: Cornell UP. London: Duckworth.

Higham, T., J. Chapman and V. Slachev, 2007. 'New Perspectives on the Varna Cemetery (Bulgaria) – AMS Dates and Social Implications.' *Antiquity* 81: 640–54.

Hillman, G., 1996. 'Late Pleistocene Changes in Wild Plant-foods Available to Hunter-gatherers of the Northern Fertile Crescent: Possible Preludes to Cereal Cultivation' in D. R. Harris 1996, 159–203.

— 2000. 'The Plant Food Economy of Abu Hureyra 1 and 2. Abu Hureyra 1: The Epipalaeolithic' in A. M. T. Moore, G. C. Hillman and A. J. Legge, *Village on the Euphrates: From Foraging to Farming at Abu Hureyra*. London and New York: Oxford UP. 327–99.

—, R. Hedges, A. Moore *et al.*, 2001. 'New Evidence of Late Glacial Cereal Cultivation at Abu Hureyra on the Euphrates.' *The Holocene* 11: 383–93.

Hirschfeld, N., 1993. 'Incised Marks (Post-firing) on Aegean Wares' in C. Zerner, P. Zerner and J. Winder (eds), *Pottery as Evidence for Trade in the Aegean Bronze Age 1939–1989*. Amsterdam: J. C. Gieben. 311–18.

— 1996. 'Cypriots in the Mycenaean Aegean' in E. De Miro, L. Godart and A. Sacconi (eds), *Atti e Memorie del Secondo Congresso Internazionale di Micenologia*. Rome: Gruppo Editoriale Internazionale. 289–97.

Hodder, I., 1990. *The Domestication of Europe: Structure and Contingency in Neolithic Societies*. Oxford and Cambridge: Basil Blackwell.

— 2006. *Çatalhöyük: The Leopard's Tale: Revealing the Mysteries of Çatalhöyük*. London and New York: Thames & Hudson.

— and L. Doughty, (eds) 2007. *Mediterranean Prehistoric Heritage: Training, Education and Management*. Cambridge: MIAR.

—, G. Isaac and N. Hammond, (eds) 1981. *Pattern of the Past: Studies in Honour of David Clarke*. Cambridge and New York: Cambridge UP.

Hodges, R., and D. Whitehouse, 1983. *Mohammed, Charlemagne and the Origins of Europe*. Ithaca: Cornell UP. London: Duckworth.

Hodos, T., 2000. 'Wine Wares in Protohistoric Eastern *Sicily*' in C. Smith and J. Serrati, *Sicily from Aeneas to Augustus*. Edinburgh: Edinburgh UP. 41–54.

— 2006. *Local Responses to Colonization in the Iron Age Mediterranean*. London and New York: Routledge.

— 2020. *The Archaeology of the Mediterranean Iron Age: A Globalising World c.1100–600 BCE*. Cambridge and New York: Cambridge UP.

Hoelzmann, P., F. Gasse, L. M. Dupont *et al.*, 2004. 'Palaeoenvironmental Changes in the Arid and Subarid Belt (Sahara-Sahel-Arabian Peninsula) from 150 kyr to Present' in Battarbee *et al.* 2004, 219–56.

Holdaway, S., W. Wendrich and R. Phillipps, 2010. 'Identifying Low-level Food Producers: Detecting Mobility from Lithics.' *Antiquity* 84: 185–94.

Holladay, J. S., 1995. 'The Kingdoms of Israel and Judah: Political and Economic Centralization in the Iron IIA–B (ca. 1000–750 BCE)' in Levy 1995a, 368–98.

Holloway, R. R., 1975. 'Buccino: The Early Bronze Age Village of Tufariello.' *Journal of Field Archaeology* 2: 11–81.

— and S. Lukesh, 1995. *Ustica: The Results of the Excavations of the Regione Siciliana*. Vol. 1. Louvain-la-Neuve: Département d'Archéologie et d'Histoire de l'Art.

Homer, *The Odyssey*. Transl. E. V. Rieu, rev. edn 2003. London and New York: Penguin. In the original: *Homeri Opera*, Vols 3 and 4, ed. T. W. Allen, 1917. Oxford and New York: Clarendon.

Horden, P., 2005. 'Mediterranean Excuses: Historical Writing on the Mediterranean since Braudel.' *History and Anthropology* 16: 25–30.

— and N. Purcell, 2000. *The Corrupting Sea: A Study of Mediterranean History*. Oxford and Malden: Blackwell.

— and — 2005. 'Four Years of Corruption: A Response to Critics' in W. V. Harris 2005a, 348–75.

— and — 2006. 'The Mediterranean and "the New Thalassology".' *American Historical Review* 111: 722–40.

Horowitz, A., 1998. 'The First Mediterranean Navigators – Possible Role of Climate in the Neolithic Settlement of the Islands' in A. Demaison (ed.), *Navigation, Échanges et Environnement en Mediterranée*. Montpellier. 112–16.

Hublin, J.-J., 2000. 'Modern-Nonmodern Hominid Interactions: A Mediterranean Perspective' in O. Bar-Yosef and D. Pilbeam (eds), *The Geography of Neandertals and Modern Humans in Europe and the Greater Mediterranean*. Cambridge: Peabody Museum. 157–82.

— 2001. 'Northwestern African Middle Pleistocene Hominids and Their Bearing on the Emergence of *Homo sapiens*' in L. Barham and K. Robson-Brown (eds), *Human Roots: Africa and Asia in the Middle Pleistocene*. Bristol: Centre for Human Evolutionary Research. 99–121.

—, A. Ben-Ncer, S. Bailey *et al.*, 2017. 'New Fossils from Jebel Irhoud, Morocco and the Pan-African Origin of *Homo sapiens*.' *Nature* 546: 289–92.

— and S. P. McPherron, (eds) 2012. *Modern Origins: A North African Perspective*. New York: Springer.

Hurst, H., and S. Owen, (eds) 2005. *Ancient Colonizations: Analogy, Similarity and Difference*. London: Duckworth.

Hurtado, V., 1997. 'The Dynamics of the Occupation of the Middle Basin of the River Guadiana between the Fourth and Second Millennia BC' in Díaz-Andreu and Keay 1997, 98–127.

Huxley, A., 1936. *The Olive Tree and Other Essays*. London: Chatto & Windus.

Huysecom, E., M. Rasse, L. Lespez *et al.*, 2009. 'The Emergence of Pottery in Africa during the 10th Millennium cal. BC: New Evidence from Ounjougou (Mali).' *Antiquity* 83: 905–17.

Iacono, F., 2012. 'Westernizing Aegean of LH III C' in M. E. Alberti and S. Sabatini (eds), *Exchange Networks and Local Transformation*. Oxford: Oxbow. 60–79.

—, E. Borgna, M. Cattani *et al.*, 2022. 'Establishing the Middle Sea: The Late Bronze Age of Mediterranean Europe (1700–900 BC).' *Journal of Archaeological Research* 30: 371–445.

Iacovou, M., 2005a. 'The Early Iron Age Urban Forms of Cyprus' in Osborne and Cunliffe 2005, 17–43.

— 2005b. 'Cyprus at the Dawn of the First Millennium BC: Cultural Homogenisation versus the Tyranny of Ethnic Identifications' in J. Clarke 2005, 125–34.

— 2006. 'From the Myceanaen qa-si-re-u to the Cypriote pa-si-le-wo-se: The Basileus in the Kingdoms of Cyprus' in Deger-Jalkotzy and Lemos 2006, 315–36.

Ifantidis, F., and M. Nikolaidou, (eds) 2011. *Spondylus in Prehistory: New Data and Approaches: Contributions to the Archaeology of Shell Technologies*. Oxford: Archaeopress.

Ilan, D., 1995. 'The Dawn of Internationalism – the Middle Bronze Age' in Levy 1995a, 297–319.

Ingold, T., 1993. 'The Temporality of the Landscape.' *WA* 25: 24–174.

Irwin, G., 1992. *The Prehistoric Exploration and Colonisation of the Pacific*. Cambridge and New York: Cambridge UP.

Isaakidou, V., 2008. '"The Fauna and Economy of Neolithic Knossos" Revisited' in Isaakidou and Tomkins 2008, 90–114.

— 2011. 'Farming Regimes in Neolithic Europe: Gardening with Cows and Other Models' in A. Hadjikoumis, E. Robinson and S. Viner (eds), *The Dynamics of Neolithisation: Studies in Honour of Andrew Sherratt*. Oxford and Oakville: Oxbow. 90–112.

— and P. D. Tomkins (eds) 2008. *Escaping the Labyrinth: The Cretan Neolithic in Context*. Oxford and Oakville: Oxbow.

Ivanov, I., and M. Avramova, 2000. *Varna Necropolis: The Dawn of European Civilization*. Sofia: Agató.

Jablonka, P., 2006. 'Leben außerhalb der Burg – Die Unterstadt von Troia' in Korfmann 2006, 167–80.

Jackes, M., and D. Lubell, 2008. 'Environmental and Cultural Change in the Early and Mid Holocene: Evidence from the Telidjene Basin, Algeria.' *AAR* 25: 41–55.

Jalut, G., J. J. Dedoubat, M. Fontugne and T. Otto, 2009. 'Holocene Circum-Mediterranean Vegetation Changes: Climate Forcing and Human Impact.' *QI* 200: 4–18.

James, M. A., N. Reifarth, A. J. Mukherjee *et al.*, 2009. 'High Prestige Royal Purple Dyed Textiles from the Bronze Age Tomb at Qatna, Syria.' *Antiquity* 83: 1109–18.

Janković, S., and W. E. Petraschek, 1987. 'Tectonics and Metallogeny of the Alpine Himalayan Belt in the Mediterranean Area and Western Asia.' *Episodes* 10: 169–75.

Janssen, J. J., 1975. *Commodity Prices from the Ramessid Period: An Economic Study of the Village of Necropolis Workmen at Thebes*. Leiden: Brill.

Jarriel, K., 2018. 'Across the Surface of the Sea: Maritime Interaction in the Cycladic Early Bronze Age.' *JMA* 31: 52–76.

Jaspers, K., 1953. *The Origin and Goal of History*. English translation. London: Routledge & K. Paul. New Haven: Yale UP.

Jeffreys, D., (ed.) 2003. *Views of Ancient Egypt since Napoleon Bonaparte: Imperialism, Colonialism and Modern Appropriations*. London: UCL. Portland: Cavendish.

Jenkins, N., 1980. *The Boat beneath the Pyramid: King Cheops' Royal Ship*. London: Thames & Hudson. New York: Holt, Rinehart & Winston.

Jennings, J., 2011. *Globalizations and the Ancient World*. Cambridge and New York: Cambridge UP.

Jidejian, N., 1968. *Byblos through the Ages*. Beirut: Dar el-Machreq.

Jiménez, A., 2010. 'Reproducing Difference: Mimesis and Colonialism in Roman *Hispania*' in van Dommelen and Knapp 2010, 38–63.

Jirat-Wasiutynski, V., 2007. *Modern Art and the Idea of the Mediterranean*. Toronto and London: Toronto UP.

Joannès, F., 1991. 'Létain de l'Elam à Mari' in L. De Meyer and H. Gasche (eds), *Mesopotamie et Elam*. Gent: Universiteit Gent. 65–76.

Johnson, A. W., and T. K. Earle, 2000. *The Evolution of Human Societies: From Foraging Group to Agrarian State*. 2nd edn. Stanford: Stanford UP.

Jones, G., 1987. 'Agricultural Practice in Greek Prehistory.' *ABSA* 82: 115–23.

—, K. Wardle, P. Halstead and D. Wardle, 1986. 'Crop Storage at Assiros.' *Scientific American* 254: 96–103.

Jones, R. E., S. T. Levi and M. Bettelli, 2005. 'Mycenaean Pottery in the Central Mediterranean: Imports, Imitations and Derivatives' in Laffineur and Greco 2005, 539–45.

— and L. Vagnetti, 1991. 'Traders and Craftsmen in the Central Mediterranean: Archaeological Evidence and Archaeometric Research' in N. H. Gale 1991a, 127–47.

Jung, R., 2009. 'Pirates of the Aegean: Italy – the East Aegean – Cyprus at the End of the Second Millennium BC' in Karageorghis and Kouka 2009, 72–93.

Kaiser, T., and S. Forenbaher, 1999. 'Adriatic Sailors and Stone Knappers: Palagruža in the 3rd Millennium BC.' *Antiquity* 73: 313–24.

Kallala, N., and J. Sanmartí, (eds) 2011. *Althiburos I. La Fouille dans l'Aire du Capitole et la Nécropole Méridionale.* Tarragona: Institut Català d'Arqueologia Clàssica.

Karageorghis, V., 1969. *Salamis in Cyprus: Homeric, Hellenistic and Roman.* London: Thames & Hudson.

—1976. *Kition: Mycenaean and Phoenician Discoveries in Cyprus.* London: Thames & Hudson.

— (ed.) 1994. *Cyprus in the 11th Century BC.* Nicosia: A. G. Leventis Foundation.

— 2012. 'Postscriptum' to Lo Schiavo 'Cyprus and Sardinia, beyond the Oxhide Ingots' in Kassianidou and Papasavvas 2012, 148.

— and O. Kouka, (eds) 2009. *Cyprus and the East Aegean: Intercultural Contacts from 3000 to 500 BC.* Nicosia: A. G. Leventis Foundation.

— and F. Lo Schiavo, 1989. 'A West Mediterranean Obelos from Amathus.' *Rivista di Studi Fenici* 17: 15–29.

Karavanić, I., and I. Janković, 2006. 'The Middle and Early Upper Paleolithic in Croatia.' *Opuscula Archaeologica* 30: 21–54.

Karimali, E., 2005. 'Lithic Technologies and Use' in Blake and Knapp 2005, 180–214.

Karo, G., 1930–33. *Die Schachtgräber von Mykenai.* Munich: Bruckmann.

Kassianidou, V., 2003. 'The Trade of Tin and the Island of Copper' in Giumlia-Mair and Lo Schiavo 2003, 109–20.

— and A. B. Knapp, 2005. 'Archaeometallurgy in the Mediterranean: The Social Context of Mining, Technology, and Trade' in Blake and Knapp 2005, 220–56.

— and G. Papasavvas, (eds) 2012. *Eastern Mediterranean Metallurgy and Metalwork in the Second Millennium BC.* Oxford: Oxbow.

Keegan, W. F., and J. M. Diamond, 1987. 'Colonization of Islands by Humans: A Biogeographical Perspective.' *Advances in Archaeological Method and Theory* 10: 49–92.

Keeley, L. H., 1997. *War before Civilization.* New York and Oxford: Oxford UP.

Kelder, J., 2009. 'Royal Gift Exchange between Mycenae and Egypt: Olives as "Greeting Gifts" in the Late Bronze Age Eastern Mediterranean.' *AJA* 113: 339–52.

Kelekna, P., 2009. *The Horse in Human History.* Cambridge and New York: Cambridge UP.

Keller, A., A. Graefen, M. Ball *et al.*, 2012. 'New Insights into the Tyrolean Iceman's Origin and Phenotype as Inferred by Whole-genome Sequencing.' *Nature Communications* 3: 698.

Kelly, O., 2012. 'Beyond Intermarriage: The Role of the Indigenous Italic Population at Pithekoussai.' *OJA* 31: 245–60.

Kemp, B. J., 2006. *Ancient Egypt: Anatomy of a Civilization.* 2nd edn. London and New York: Routledge.

Kempinski, A., 1992. 'The Middle Bronze Age' in A. Ben-Tor 1992, 159–210.

Kennett, D., 2005. *The Island Chumash: Behavioral Ecology of a Maritime Society.* Berkeley and London: California UP.

— and J. P. Kennett, 2007. 'Influence of Holocene Marine Transgression and Climate Change on Cultural Evolution in Southern Mesopotamia' in D. Anderson, D. Sandweiss and K. A. Maasch (eds), *Climate Change and Cultural Dynamics: A Global Perspective on Mid-Holocene Transitions.* London and Boston: Elsevier/Academic. 229–64.

Keswani, P. S., 1996. 'Hierarchies, Heterarchies, and Urbanization Processes: The View from Bronze Age Cyprus.' *JMA* 9: 211–50.

Khakhutaishvili, D. A., 2009. *The Manufacture of Iron in Ancient Colchis.* Oxford: Archaeopress.

Kilian-Dirlmeier, I., 1997. *Das Mittelbronzezeitliche Schachtgrab von Ägina.* Mainz: Philipp von Zabern.

Kilikoglou, V., Y. Bassiakos, A. P. Grimanis *et al.*, 1996. 'Carpathian Obsidian in Macedonia, Greece.' *JAS* 23: 343–49.

Killebrew, A., 2005. *Biblical Peoples and Ethnicity.* Leiden and Boston: Brill.

Killen, J. T., 1964. 'The Wool Industry of Crete in the Late Bronze Age.' *ABSA* 59: 1–15.

King, R., 1997. 'Population Growth: An Avoidable Crisis' in King *et al.* 1997, 164–80.

—, P. de Mas and J. Mansvelt Beck, (eds) 2001. *Geography, Environment and Development in the Mediterranean.* Brighton and Portland: Sussex Academic.

—, L. Proudfoot and B. Smith, (eds) 1997. *The Mediterranean: Environment and Society.* London and New York: Arnold.

Kirch, P. V., 2000. *On the Road of the Winds: An Archaeological History of the Pacific Islands before European Contact.* Berkeley and London: California UP.

Kiriatzi, E., S. Andreou, S. Dimitrias and K. Kostakis, 1997. 'Coexisting Traditions: Handmade and Wheelmade Pottery in Late Bronze Age Central Macedonia' in Laffineur and Betancourt 1997, 361–67.

— and C. Broodbank, 2021. 'Social Places and Spaces on and beyond Kythera during the Second Palace Period: Exploring the Island's Landscape and Connectivity' in B. Eder and M. Zavadil (eds), *(Social) Place and Space in Early Mycenaean Greece.* Vienna: Austrian Academy of Sciences Press. 365–82.

Kirigin, B., A. Johnston, M. Vučetić and Z. Lušić, 2009. 'Palagruža – the Island of Diomedes – and Notes on Ancient Greek Navigation in the Adriatic' in Forenbaher 2009a, 137–55.

Kislev, M. E., M. Artz and E. Marcus, 1993. 'Import of an Aegean Food Plant to a Middle Bronze IIA Coastal Site in Israel.' *Levant* 25: 145–54.

—, A. Hartmann and O. Bar-Yosef, 2006. 'Early Domesticated Fig in the Jordan Valley.' *Science* 312: 1372–74.

Klein, R. G., 2009. *The Human Career: Human Biological and Cultural Origins.* 3rd edn. Chicago: Chicago UP.

— and K. Scott, 1986. 'Re-analysis of Faunal Assemblages from the Haua Fteah and Other Late Quaternary Archaeological Sites in Cyrenaican Libya.' *JAS* 13: 515–42.

Klein Hofmeijer, G. K., 1997. *Late Pleistocene Deer Fossils from Corbeddu Cave: Implications for Human Colonization of the Island of Sardinia.* Oxford: Archaeopress.

Kletter, R., and A. De-Groot, 2001. 'Excavating to Excess? Implications of the Last Decade of Archaeology in Israel.' *JMA* 14: 76–85.

Knapp, A. B., 1986. *Copper Production and Divine Protection: Archaeology, Ideology and Social Complexity on Bronze Age Cyprus.* Göteborg: Paul Åströms.

— 1991. 'Spice, Drugs, Grain and Grog: Organic Goods in Bronze Age East Mediterranean Trade' in N. H. Gale 1991a, 21–68.

— 1993. 'Thalassocracies in Bronze Age Eastern Mediterranean Trade: Making and Breaking a Myth.' *WA* 24: 332–47.

— 1994. 'Emergence, Development and Decline on Bronze Age Cyprus' in Mathers and Stoddart 1994, 271–304.

— (ed.) 1996. *Sources for the History of Cyprus.* Vol. II: *Near Eastern and Aegean Texts from the Third to the First Millennia BC.* Altamont: Greece and Cyprus Research Center.

— 1998. 'Mediterranean Bronze Age Trade: Distance, Power and Place' in Cline and Harris-Cline 1998, 193–207.

— 2003. 'The Archaeology of Community on Bronze Age Cyprus: Politiko *Phorades* in Context.' *AJA* 107: 559–80.

— 2008. *Prehistoric and Protohistoric Cyprus: Identity, Insularity, and Connectivity.* Oxford and New York: Oxford UP.

— 2009. 'Migration, Hybridisation and Collapse: Bronze Age Cyprus and the Eastern Mediterranean.' *Scienze dell'Antichità* 15: 219–39.

— 2010. 'Cyprus's Earliest Prehistory: Seafarers, Foragers and Settlers.' *JWP* 23: 79–120.

— and E. Blake, 2005. 'Prehistory in the Mediterranean: The Corrupting and Connecting Sea' in Blake and Knapp 2005, 1–23.

— and J. F. Cherry, 1994. *Provenience Studies and Bronze Age Cyprus: Production, Exchange and Politico-economic Change.* Madison: Prehistory.

—, V. C. Pigott and E. W. Herbert, (eds) 1998. *Social Approaches to an Industrial Past: The Archaeology and Anthropology of Mining.* London and New York: Routledge.

— and P. van Dommelen, (eds) in press. *Cambridge Handbook of the Mediterranean World in the Bronze–Iron Ages.* Cambridge and New York: Cambridge UP.

Knappett, C., 2011. *Archaeology of Interaction: Network Perspectives on Material Culture and Society.* Oxford and New York: Oxford UP.

— (ed.) 2013. *Network Analysis in Archaeology: New Approaches to Regional Interaction.* Oxford and New York: Oxford UP.

—, V. Kilikoglou, V. Steele and B. Stern, 2005. 'The Circulation and Consumption of Red Lustrous Wheelmade Ware: Petrographic, Chemical and Residue Analysis.' *AS* 25: 25–59.

— and C. Broodbank, 2021. 'Social Places and Spaces on and beyond Kythera during the Second Palace Period: Exploring the Island's Landscape and Connectivity' in B. Eder and M. Zavadil (eds), *(Social) Place and Space in Early Mycenaean Greece.* Vienna: Austrian Academy of Sciences Press. 365–82.

— and I. Nikolakopoulou, 2005. 'Exchange and Affiliation Networks in the MBA Southern Aegean: Crete, Akrotiri and Miletus' in Laffineur and Greco 2005, 175–85.

— and J. Leidwanger, (eds) 2018. *Maritime Networks in the Ancient Mediterranean World.* Cambridge and New York: Cambridge UP.

—, R. Rivers and T. Evans, 2011. 'Modelling Maritime Interaction in the Aegean Bronze Age, II: The Eruption of Thera and the Burning of the Palaces.' *Antiquity* 85: 1008–23.

Knodell, A. R., D. Athanasoulis, Ž. Tankosić *et al.*, 2022. 'An Island Archaeology of Uninhabited Landscapes: Offshore Islets Near Paros, Greece (The Small Cycladic Islands Project).' *Journal of Island and Coastal Archaeology* 17: 475–511.

Köhler, C., 1992. 'The Pre- and Early Dynastic Pottery of Tell el-Fara'in (Buto)' in van den Brink 1992, 11–20.

Kohn, M., and S. Mithen, 1999. 'Handaxes: Products of Sexual Selection?' *Antiquity* 73: 518–26.

Komšo, D., 2006. 'Mezolitik u Hrvatskoj.' *Opuscula Archaeologica* 30: 55–92.

Korcak, J., 1938. 'Deux Types Fondamontaux de Distribution Statistique.' *Bulletin de l'Institut International de Statistique* 3, 295–99.

Korfmann, M. O., (ed.) 2006. *Troia: Archäologie eines Siedlungshügels und seiner Landschaft.* Mainz: Philipp von Zabern.

Kostoglou, M., 2010. 'Iron, Connectivity and Local Identities in the Iron Age to Classical Mediterranean' in van Dommelen and Knapp 2010, 170–89.

Kotsakis, K., 1999. 'What Tells Can Tell: Social Space and Settlement in the Greek Neolithic' in Halstead 1999a, 66–76.

— 2006. 'Settlement of Discord: Sesklo and the Emerging Household' in N. Tasić and C. Grozdanov (eds), *Homage to Milutin Garašanin.* Belgrade: Serbian Academy of Sciences and Arts. 207–20.

— 2008. 'A Sea of Agency: Crete in the Context of the Earliest Neolithic in Greece' in Isaakidou and Tomkins 2008, 49–72.

Kotsonas, A., T. Whitelaw, A. Vasilakis and M. Bredaki, in press. 'Early Iron Age Knossos: An Overview Based on the Surface Investigations of the Knossos Urban Landscape Project (KULP)' in *Proceedings of the 11th International Cretological Conference.* Rethymnon: Association for History and Folklore Studies in Rethymnon.

Kotthoff, U., A. Koutsodendris, J. Pross *et al.*, 2011. 'Impact of Lateglacial Cold Events on the Northern Aegean Region Reconstructed from Marine and Terrestrial Proxy Data.' *JQS* 26: 86–96.

Kourou, N., 2009. 'The Aegean and the Levant in the Early Iron Age: Recent Developments' in Maila-Afeiche 2009, 361–73.

Kourtessi-Philippakis, G., 1999. 'The Lower and Middle Palaeolithic in the Ionian Islands: New Finds' in Bailey *et al.* 1999, 282–87.

Krahtopoulou, A., and C. Frederick, 2008. 'The Stratigraphic Implications of Long-term Terrace Agriculture in Dynamic Landscapes: Polycyclic Terracing from Kythera Island, Greece.' *Geoarchaeology* 23: 550–85.

Krause, J., L. Orlando, D. Serre *et al.*, 2007. 'Neanderthals in Central Asia and Siberia.' *Nature* 449: 902–4.

Krauss, R., (ed.) 2011. *Beginnings: New Research in the Appearance of the Neolithic between Northwest Anatolia and the Carpathian Basin.* Rahden/Westfalen: Marie Leidorf.

Krings,V., 2008. 'Rereading Punic Agriculture: Representation, Analogy and Ideology in the Classical Sources' in van Dommelen and Goméz Bellard 2008, 22–43.

Kristiansen, K., 2014. 'Towards a New Paradigm? The Third Science Revolution and Its Possible Consequences in Archaeology.' *Current Swedish Archaeology* 22: 11–34.

—, G. Kroonen and E. Willerslev, (eds) 2023. *The Indo-European Puzzle Revisited: Integrating Archaeology, Genetics, and Linguistics.* Cambridge and New York: Cambridge UP.

—, and T. B. Larsen, 2005. *Rise of Bronze Age Society: Travels, Transmissions and Transformations.* Cambridge and New York: Cambridge UP.

Kroeper, K., 1992. 'Tombs of the Elite in the Minshat Abu Omar' in van den Brink 1992, 127–50.

Kroll, J. H., 2008. 'Early Iron Age Balance Weights at Lefkandi, Euboea.' *OJA* 27: 37–48.

Kröpelin, S., D. Verschuren, A.-M. Lezine *et al.*, 2008. 'Climate-driven Ecosystem Succession in the Sahara: The Past 6000 Years.' *Science* 320: 765–68.

Krzyszkowska, O., 1990. *Ivory and Related Materials: An Illustrated Guide.* London: Institute of Classical Studies.

— 1996. 'Furniture in the Aegean Bronze Age' in G. Herrmann (ed.), *The Furniture of Western Asia: Ancient and Traditional.* Mainz: Philipp von Zabern. 85–103.

Kuhn, S. L., 2010. 'Was Anatolia a Bridge or a Barrier to Early Hominin Dispersals?' *QI* 223–24: 434–35.
— and M. C. Stiner, 2007. 'Body Ornamentation as Information Technology: Towards an Understanding of the Significance of Early Beads' in Mellars *et al.* 2007, 45–54.
Kuijt, I., (ed.) 2000a. *Life in Neolithic Farming Communities: Social Organization, Identity, and Differentiation.* New York: Kluwer Academic/Plenum.
— 2000b. 'Keeping the Peace: Ritual, Skull Caching and Community Integration in the Levantine Neolithic' in Kuijt 2000a, 137–62.
— 2008. 'Demography and Storage Systems during the Southern Levantine Neolithic Demographic Transition' in Bocquet-Appel and Bar-Yosef 2008, 287–314.
— and C. Finlayson, 2009. 'Evidence for Food Storage and Predomestication Granaries 11,000 Years Ago in the Jordan Valley.' *PNAS* 106: 10873–74.
— and A. N. Goring-Morris, 2002. 'Foraging, Farming and Social Complexity in the Pre-Pottery Neolithic of the South-Central Levant: A Review and Synthesis.' *JWP* 16: 361–440.
Kunst, M., 1995. 'Central Places and Social Complexity in the Iberian Copper Age' in Lillios 1995, 32–43.
Kuper, R., and S. Kröpelin, 2006. 'Climate-controlled Holocene Occupation in the Sahara: Motor of Africa's Evolution.' *Science* 313: 803–7.
Kuzmin, Y. V., 2006. 'Chronology of the Earliest Pottery in East Asia: Progress and Pitfalls.' *Antiquity* 80: 362–71.
Kuzucuoğlu, C., and C. Marro, (eds) 2007. *Sociétés Humaines et Changement Climatique à la Fin du Troisième Millénaire: Une Crise a-t-elle eu Lieu en Haute Mésopotamie?* Paris: De Boccard.
Kyrou, A. K., 1990. *Sto Stavrodromi tou Argolikou: Istoriko kai Archaiologiko odoiporiko s'ena Choro tis Thalassas tou Aigaiou.* Vol. 1. Athens: Photosyn Abee.
LaBianca, Ø., and S. A. Scham, (eds) 2006. *Connectivity in Antiquity: Globalization as a Long-term Historical Process.* London and Oakville: Equinox.
Lafe, O., and M. L. Galaty, 2009. 'Albanian Coastal Settlement from Prehistory to the Iron Age' in Forenbaher 2009a, 105–11.
Laffineur, R., (ed.) 1991. *Polemos: Le Contexte Huerrier en Égée à l'Âge du Bronze.* Liège: Université de Liège.
— and L. Basch, (eds) 1991. *Thalassa: L'Egée Préhistorique et la Mer.* Liège: Université de Liège.
— and P. P. Betancourt, (eds) 1997. *Techne: Craftsmen, Craftswomen and Craftsmanship in the Aegean Bronze Age.* Liège: Université de Liège. Austin: Texas UP.
— and E. Greco, (eds) 2005. *Emporia: Mycenaeans and Minoans in the Central and Eastern Mediterranean.* Liège: Université de Liège. Austin: Texas UP.
Lamb, H. F., U. Eicher and V. R. Switsur, 1989. 'An 18,000-year Record of Vegetation, Lake-level and Climatic Change from Tigalmamine, Middle Atlas, Morocco.' *JB* 16: 65–74.
Lambeck, K., 1996. 'Sea-level Change and Shoreline Evolution in Aegean Greece since Upper Palaeolithic Time.' *Antiquity* 70: 588–611.
— and J. Chappell, 2001. 'Sea Level Change through the Last Glacial Cycle.' *Science* 292: 679–86.
—, T. M. Esat and E. K. Potter, 2002. 'Links between Climate and Sea Levels for the Past Three Million Years.' *Nature* 419: 199–206.
Lancel, S., 1995. *Carthage: A History.* English translation. Oxford and Cambridge: Blackwell.
Larsen, M. T., 1987. 'Commercial Networks in the Ancient Near East' in Rowlands *et al.* 1987, 47–56.
Larson, G., U. Albarella, K. Dobney *et al.*, 2007. 'Ancient DNA, Pig Domestication, and the Spread of the Neolithic into Europe.' *PNAS* 104: 15276–81.
Laskaris, N., A. Sampson, F. Mavridis and I. Liritzis, 2011. 'Late Pleistocene/ Holocene Seafaring in the Aegean: New Obsidian *Hydration Dates* with the *Early* SIMS-SS Method.' *JAS* 38: 2475–79.
Lazaridis, I., A. Mittnik, N. Patterson *et al.*, 2017. 'Genetic Origins of the Minoans and Mycenaeans.' *Nature* 548: 214–18.
Leahy, A., (ed.) 1990. *Libya and Egypt c. 1300–750 BC.* London: SOAS Centre of Near and Middle Eastern Studies and the Society for Libyan Studies.
Leavesley, M., 2006. 'Late Pleistocene Complexities in the Bismarck Archipelago' in Lilley 2006, 189–204.
Lebedynsky, I., 2004. *Les Cimmériens: Les Premiers Nomades des Steppes Européennes, IXe-VIIe Siècles av. J.-C.* Paris: Errance.
Leblanc, M., G. Favreau, J. Maley *et al.*, 2006. 'Reconstruction of Megalake Chad Using Shuttle Radar Topographic Mission Data.' *Palaeogeography, Palaeoclimatology, Palaeoecology* 239: 16–27.
Legarra Herrero, B., 2009. 'The Minoan Fallacy: Cultural Diversity on Crete at the Beginning of the Bronze Age as Assessed through the Mortuary Behavior.' *OJA* 28: 29–57.
— 2011. 'New Kid on the Block: The Nature of the First Systemic Contacts between Crete and the Eastern Mediterranean around 2000 BC' in T. C. Wilkinson *et al.* 2011, 266–81.
— and Marcos Martinón-Torres, 2021. 'Heterogeneous Production and Enchained Consumption: Minoan Gold in a Changing World (ca. 2000 BCE).' *AJA* 125: 333–60.
Leighton, R., 1999. *Sicily before History: An Archaeological Survey from the Palaeolithic to the Iron Age.* London: Duckworth. Ithaca: Cornell UP.
Lemercier, O., 2004. 'Historical Model of Settling and Spread of Bell Beaker Culture in Mediterranean France' in J. Czebrezuk (ed.), *Similar but Different: Bell Beakers in Europe.* Poznan: Adam Mickiewicz UP. 193–203.
— 2012. 'The Beaker Transition in Mediterranean France' in H. Fokkens and F. Nicolis (eds), *Background to Beakers: Inquiries in Regional Cultural Backgrounds of the Bell Beaker Complex.* Leiden: Sidestone. 117–56.
Lemonnier, P., (ed.) 1993a. *Technological Choices: Transformation in Material Cultures since the Neolithic.* London and New York: Routledge.
— 1993b. 'Introduction' in Lemonnier 1993a, 1–35.
Lemos, I. S., 2002. *The Protogeometric Aegean: The Archaeology of the Late Eleventh and Tenth Centuries BC.* Oxford and New York: Oxford UP.
— 2006. 'Athens and Lefkandi: A Tale of Two Sites' in Deger-Jalkotzy and Lemos 2006, 505–30.
Lenzi, F., (ed.) 2003. *L'Archeologia dell'Adriatico dalla Preistoria al Medioevo.* Florence: All'Insegna del Giglio.
Leonard, A., 1994. *An Index to the Late Bronze Age: Aegean Pottery from Syro-Palestine.* Jonsered: Paul Åströms.
Leppard, T. P., 2019. 'Social Complexity and Social Inequality in the Prehistoric Mediterranean.' *CA* 60: 283–308.
— and J. F. Cherry, 2024. 'Connectivity and Demography in the Insular and Coastal Mediterranean: Perspectives from Palaeogenomics and Radiocarbon Probability Distributions' in S. M. Fitzpatrick and J. M. Erlandson (eds), *The Oxford Handbook of Island & Coastal Archaeology.* Oxford: Oxford UP.
Lepre, C. J., H. Roche, D. V. Kent *et al.*, 2011. 'An Earlier Origin for the Acheulian.' *Nature* 477: 82–85.
Lernau, H., and O. Lernau, 1994. 'The Fish Remains' in M. Lechevallier and A. Ronen (eds), *Le Gisement de Hatoula en Judée Occidentale, Israël: Rapport des Fouilles 1980–1988.* Paris: Association Paléorient. 111–21.
Leroux, G., A. Véron and C. Morhange, 2003. 'Geochemical Evidences of Early Anthropogenic Activity in Harbour Sediments from Sidon.' *Archaeology and History in the Lebanon* 18: 115–19.
Lévi-Strauss, C., 1963. *Totemism.* English translation. Boston: Beacon. 1964 London: Merlin.
Levy, T. E., (ed.) 1987. *Shiqmim I: Studies Concerning Chalcolithic Societies in the Northern Negev Desert, Israel (1982–1984).* Oxford: Archaeopress.
— (ed.) 1995a. *The Archaeology of Society in the Holy Land.* 2nd edn. London: Leicester UP. New York: Continuum.
— 1995b. 'Cult, Metallurgy and Rank Societies – Chalcolithic Period (ca. 4500–3500 BCE)' in Levy 1995a, 226–44.
— (ed.) 2006. *Archaeology, Anthropology and Cult: The Sanctuary at Gilat, Israel.* London and Oakville: Equinox.
— 2007. *Journey to the Copper Age: Archaeology of the Holy Land.* San Diego: San Diego Museum of Man.
—, R. B. Adams, A. Hauptmann *et al.*, 2002. 'Early Bronze Age Metallurgy: A Newly Discovered Copper Manufactory in Southern Jordan.' *Antiquity* 76, 425–37.
—, D. Alon, C. Grigson *et al.*, 1991. 'Subterranean Settlement and Adaptation in the Negev Desert, ca. 4500–3700 B.C.' *National Geographic Research and Exploration* 7: 394–413.
— and M. Najjar, 2006. 'Edom and Copper: The Emergence of Ancient Israel's Rival.' *Biblical Archaeology Review* 32: 24–35.
— and E. C. M. van den Brink, 2002. 'Interaction Models, Egypt and the Levantine Periphery' in van den Brink and Levy 2002, 3–38.
Lewthwaite, J., 1987. 'The Braudelian Beaker: A Chalcolithic Conjoncture in Western Mediterranean Prehistory' in William H. Waldren and Rex C. Kennard (eds), *Bell Beakers of the Western Mediterranean: Definition, Interpretation, Theory and New Site Data.* Oxford: Archaeopress. 31–60.
— 1989. 'Isolating the Residuals: The Mesolithic Basis of Man-Animal Relationships on the Mediterranean Islands' in Bonsall 1989, 541–55.
Lichtheim, M., 1975. 'The Admonitions of Ipuwer' in M. Lichtheim, *Ancient Egyptian Literature.* Vol. I: *The Old and Middle Kingdoms.* Berkeley and London: California UP. 149–63.
Lieberman, D. E., 1993. 'Variability in Hunter-gatherer Seasonal Mobility in the Southern Levant: From the Mousterian to the Natufian.' *Archaeological Papers of the American Anthropological Association* 4: 207–19.
Lilley, I., (ed.) 2006. *Archaeology in Oceania: Australia and the Pacific Islands.* Oxford and Malden: Blackwell.
Lillios, K. T., (ed.) 1995. *The Origins of Complex Societies in Late Prehistoric Iberia.* Ann Arbor: International Monographs in Prehistory.
— 1997. 'Groundstone Tools, Competition, and Fission: The Transition from the Copper to the Bronze Age in the Portuguese Lowlands' in Balmuth *et al.* 1997, 25–32.
— 2008a. *Heraldry for the Dead: Memory, Identity, and the Engraved Stone Plaques of Neolithic Iberia.* Austin: Texas UP.
— 2008b. 'Engaging Memories of European Prehistory' in A. Jones (ed.), *Prehistoric Europe: Theory and Practice.* Chichester and Malden: Wiley-Blackwell. 228–54.
Lilliu, G., 1966. *Sculture della Sardegna Nuragica.* Cagliari: Edizioni della Zattera.
Linstädter, J., 2008. 'The Epipalaeolithic–Neolithic Transition in the Mediterranean Region of Northwest Africa.' *Quartär* 55: 33–54.
—, 2016. 'Climate Induced Mobility and the Missing Middle Neolithic of Morocco' in M. Reindel, K. Bartl, F. Lüth and N. Benecke (eds), *Palaeoenvironment and the Development of Early Settlements.* Rahden: Verlag Marie Leidorf. 63–80.
—, J. Eiwanger, A. Mikdad and G.-C. Weniger, 2012. 'Human Occupation of Northwest Africa: A Review of Middle Palaeolithic to Epipalaeolithic Sites in Morocco.' *QI* 274: 158–74.
—, I. Medved, M. Solich and G.-C. Weniger, 2012. 'Neolithicisation Process within the Alboran Territory: Models and Possible African Impact.' *QI* 274: 219–32.
Littauer, M. A., and J. H. Crouwel, 1979. *Wheeled Vehicles and Ridden Animals in the Ancient Near East.* Leiden: Brill.
— and — 1990. 'Ceremonial Threshing in the Ancient Near East.' *Iraq* 52: 19–23.
Liverani, M., 1987. 'The Collapse of the Near Eastern Regional System at the End of the Bronze Age: The Case of Syria' in Rowlands *et al.* 1987, 66–73.
— 1993. 'Model and Actualization: The Kings of Akkad in the Historical Tradition' in M. Liverani (ed.), *Akkad: The First World Empire: Structure, Ideology, Traditions.* Padova: Sargon. 41–68.
— 2000. 'The Great Powers' Club' in Cohen and Westbrook 2000, 15–27.
— 2001. *International Relations in the Ancient Near East, 1600–1100 B.C.* Basingstoke and New York: Palgrave.
— 2005. *Israel's History and the History of Israel.* London and Oakville: Equinox.
— 2006. *Uruk: The First City.* London and Oakville: Equinox.
Lloret, F., J. Piñol and M. Castellnou, 2009. 'Wildfires' in Woodward 2009a, 541–60.
Lloyd, A., 2000. 'The Late Period' in I. Shaw 2000a, 364–87.
Lolos, Y., 2009. 'Salamis ca. 1200 BC: Connections with Cyprus and the East' in E. Borgna and P. Càssola Guida (eds), *Dall'Egeo all'Adriatico: Organizzazioni Sociali, Modi di Scambio e Interazione in Età Postpalaziale (XII–XI Sec. a.C.).* Rome: Quasar. 29–46.
Lomas, K., 1994. 'The City in South-east Italy: Ancient Topography and the Evolution of Urban Settlement, 600–300 BC.' *ARP* 4: 63–77.
— 2000. 'Cities States and Ethnic Identity in Southeast Italy' in Herring and Lomas 2000, 79–90.
— 2007. 'Ethnicity and Statehood in Northern Italy: The Ancient Veneti' in G. Bradley *et al.* 2007, 21–24.
Lomba Maraundi, J., M. V. López Martínez, F. Ramos Martínez and A. Avilés Fernández, 2009. 'El Enterramiento Múltiple, Calcolítico, de Camino del Molino (Caravaca, Murcia): Metodología y Primeros Resultados de un Yacimiento Excepcional.' *Trabajos de Prehistoria* 66: 143–60.
Long, L., P. Pomey, J.-C. Sourisseau (eds), 2002. *Les Etrusques en Mer: Épaves d'Antibes à Marseille.* Marseille: Musées de Marseille.
López-Bertran, M., 2011. 'Practical Movements: Kinetic Rituals in the Ancient Western Mediterranean.' *JMA* 24: 85–109.
López Pardo, F., 1996. 'Los Enclaves Fenicioіs en el África Noroccidental: Del Modelo de las Escalas Náuticas al de Colonización con Implicaciones Productivas.' *Gérion* 14: 251–88.
López-Ruiz, C., 2021. *Phoenicians and the Making of the Mediterranean.* Cambridge and London: Harvard UP.
Lo Schiavo, F., 2000. 'Sea and Sardinia: Nuragic Bronze Boats' in Ridgway *et al.* 2000, 141–58.
— 2008. 'La Metallurgia Sarda: Relazioni fra Cipro, Italia e la Penisola Iberica. Un Modello Interpretativo' in Celestino *et al.* 2008, 417–36.
— 2012. 'Cyprus and Sardinia, beyond the Oxhide Ingots' in Kassianidou and Papasavvas 2012, 142–50.

—, A. Giumlia-Mair, U. Sanna and R. Valera, (eds) 2005. *Archaeometallurgy in Sardinia: From the Origins to the Beginning of the Early Iron Age*. Montagnac: Éditions Monique Mergoil.
—, E. Macnamara and L. Vagnetti, 1985. 'Late Cypriot Imports to Italy and Their Influence on Local Bronzework.' *Papers of the British School at Rome* 53: 1–71.
—, J. D. Muhly, R. Maddin and A. Giumlia-Mair, (eds) 2009. *Oxhide Ingots in the Central Mediterranean*. Rome: A. G. Leventis Foundation.
Lovell, J. L., 2008. 'Horticulture, Status and Long-range Trade in Chalcolithic Southern Levant: Early Connections with Egypt' in Midant-Reynes and Tristant 2008, 739–60.
Lowenthal, D., 2007. 'Mediterranean between History and Heritage' in Antoniadou and Pace 2007, 661–90.
Lubell, D., 1984. 'Palaeoenvironments and Epi-Palaeolithic Economies in the Maghreb (ca. 20,000 to 5,000 BP)' in J. D. Clark and Brandt 1984, 41–56.
— 2001. 'Late Pleistocene–Early Holocene Maghreb' in P. N. Peregrine and M. Ember (eds), *Encyclopedia of Prehistory*. Vol. 1: *Africa*. New York and London: Kluwer Academic/Plenum. 129–49.
— 2004. 'Are Land Snails a Signature for the Mesolithic–Neolithic Transition in the Circum-Mediterranean?' *Documenta Praehistorica* XXXI: 1–24.
—, P. Sheppard and M. Jackes, 1984. 'Continuities in the Epipalaeolithic of Northern Africa with Emphasis on the Maghreb' in F. Wendorf and A. E. Close (eds), *Advances in World Archaeology*. Vol. 3. Orlando: Academic. 143–91.
— with contributions by J. Feathers and J.-L. Schwenninger, 2009. 'Post-Capsian Settlement in the Eastern Maghreb: Implications of a Revised Chronological Assessment for the Adult Burial in Ain Misteheyia.' *Journal of African Archaeology* 7: 175–89.
Lucarini, G., Y. Bokbot and C. Broodbank, 2021. 'New Light on the Silent Millennia: Mediterranean Africa, ca. 4000–900 BC.' *AAR* 38: 17–64.
Lucchi, M. R., 2008. 'Vegetation Dynamics during the Last Interglacial–Glacial Cycle in the Arno Coastal Plain (Tuscany, Western Italy): Location of a New Tree Refuge.' *QSR* 27: 2456–66.
Ludwig, E., 1942. *The Mediterranean: Saga of a Sea*. New York and London: McGraw-Hill.
Lull, V., 2000. 'Argaric Society: Death at Home.' *Antiquity* 74: 581–90.
—, R. Micó, C. Rihuete and R. Risch, 1999. *La Cova des Càrritx y la Cova des Mussol: Ideología y Sociedad en la Prehistoria de Menorca*. Barcelona: Consell Insular de Menorca.
—, —, — and — 2002. 'Social and Ideological Changes in the Balearic Islands during the Later Prehistory' in Waldron and Ensenyat 2002, 117–26.
—, —, — and — 2010. 'Las Relaciones Políticas y Económicas de El Argar.' *Menga: Revista de Prehistoria de Andalucía* 1: 11–36.
—, C. Rihuete-Herrada, R. Risch *et al.*, 2021. 'Emblems and Spaces of Power during the Argaric Bronze Age at La Almoloya, Murcia.' *Antiquity* 95: 329–48.
Lykousis, V., 2009. 'Sea-level Changes and Shelf Break Prograding Sequences during the Last 400 ka in the Aegean Margins: Subsidence Rates and Palaeogeographic Implications.' *Continental Shelf Research* 29: 2037–44.
Lyonnet, B., (ed.) 2007. *Les Cultures des Caucase (VIe-IIIe Millénaires avant Notre Ère) Leurs Relations avec le Proche-Orient*. Paris: CNRS.
Lyons, C. L., and J. K. Papadopoulos, (eds) 2002. *The Archaeology of Colonialism*. Los Angeles: Getty Research Institute.
MacDonald, K. C., 1998. 'Before the Empire of Ghana: Pastoralism and the Origins of Cultural Complexity in the Sahel' in G. Connah (ed.), *Transformations in Africa: Essays on Africa's Later Past*. London and Washington: Leicester UP. 71–103.
— 2003. 'Cheikh Anta Diop and Ancient Egypt in Africa' in D. O'Connor and D. A. M. Reid (eds), *Ancient Egypt in Africa*. London: UCL. 93–105.
Maggi, R., 1999. 'Coasts and Uplands in Liguria and Northern Tuscany from the Mesolithic to the Bronze Age' in Tykot *et al.* 1999, 47–65.
— and A. de Pascale, 2011. 'Fire Making Water on the Ligurian Apennines' in van Leusen *et al.* 2011, 105–12.
Magness-Gardiner, B., and S. E. Falconer, 1994. 'Community, Polity, and Temple in a Middle Bronze Age Levantine Village.' *JMA* 7: 127–64.
Maguire, L. C., 2009. *Tell el-Dab'a. XXI: The Cypriot Pottery and Its Circulation in the Levant*. Vienna: Österreichischen Akademie der Wissenschaften.
Maher, L. A., 2010. 'People and Their Places at the End of the Pleistocene: Evaluating Perspectives on Physical and Cultural Landscape Change' in W. Finlayson and Warren 2010, 34–45.
—, E. B. Banning and M. Chazan, 2011. 'Oasis or Mirage? Assessing the Role of Abrupt Climate Change in the Prehistory of the Southern Levant.' *CAJ* 21: 1–29.
Mahjoubi, A., 1997. 'Reflections on the Historiography of the Ancient Maghrib' in Michel Le Gall and Kenneth Perkins (eds), *The Maghrib in Question: Essays in History and Historiography*. Austin: Texas UP. 17–34.
Maila-Afeiche, A.-M., (ed.) 2009. *Interconnections in the Eastern Mediterranean: Lebanon in the Bronze and Iron Ages*. Beirut: Ministry of Culture of Lebanon.
Malamat, A., 1998. 'The Sacred Sea' in B. Z. Kedar and R. J. Z. Werblowsky (eds), *Sacred Space: Shrine, City, Land*. Basingstoke: Macmillan. New York: New York UP. 45–54.
Malkin, I., 1998. *The Returns of Odysseus: Colonization and Ethnicity*. Berkeley and London: California UP.
— 2002. 'A Colonial Middle Ground: Greek, Etruscan, and Local Elites in the Bay of Naples' in Lyons and Papadopoulos 2002, 151–81.
— 2003. 'Mediterranean Paradigms and Classical Antiquity.' *MHR* 18.
— 2011. *A Small Greek World: Networks in the Ancient Mediterranean*. New York and Oxford: Oxford UP.
Mallory-Greenough, L. M., 2002. 'The Geographical, Spatial, and Temporal Distribution of Predynastic and First Dynasty Basalt Vessels.' *JEA* 88: 67–93.
Malone, C., 1999. 'Processes of Colonisation in the Central Mediterranean.' *ARP* 7: 37–57.
— 2003. 'The Italian Neolithic: A Synthesis of Research.' *JWP* 17: 235–312.
—, G. Ayala, M. Fitzjohn and S. Stoddart, 2003. 'Under the Volcano.' *ARP* 9: 7–22.
—, C. Brogan, R. Grima *et al.*, 2020. 'Conclusions' in C. Malone, R. Grima, R. McLaughlin *et al.* (eds), *Temple Places: Excavating Cultural Sustainability in Prehistoric Malta*. Cambridge: MIAR. 457–82.
— and S. Stoddart, 1992. 'The Neolithic site of San Marco, Gubbio (Perugia), Umbria: Survey and Excavation 1985–7.' *Papers of the British School at Rome* 60: 1–69.
— and — 2009. 'Conclusions' in Malone *et al.* 2009, 361–84.
—, —, A. Bonnano, *et al.*, 1995. 'Mortuary Ritual of Fourth Millennium BC Malta: The Zebbug Tomb from the Brochtorff Circle (Gozo).' *PPS* 61: 303–45.
—, —, — and D. Trump, (eds) 2009. *Mortuary Customs in Prehistoric Malta*. Cambridge: MIAR.
—, — and G. Cook, 2009. 'Dating Maltese Prehistory' in Malone *et al.* 2009, 341–46.
—, — and D. Trump, (eds) 1988. 'A House for the Temple Builders: Recent Investigations on Gozo, Malta.' *Antiquity* 62: 297–301.
—, — and R. Whitehouse, 1994. 'The Bronze Age of S. Italy, Sicily and Malta' in Mathers and Stoddart 1994, 167–94.
Manen, C., G. Marchand and A. Faustino Carvalho, 2007. 'Le Néolithique Ancien de la Péninsule Ibérique: Vers une Nouvelle Évaluation du Mirage Africain?' in J. Evin (ed.), *Un Siècle de Construction du Discours Scientifique en Préhistoire*. Vol. 3: *Aux Conceptions d'Aujourd'hui*. Paris: *BSPF*. 133–51.
— and T. Perrin, 2009. 'Réflexions sur la Genèse du Cardial «Franco-Ibérique»' in Barbaza *et al.* 2009, 427–43.
Manfredini, A., (ed.) 2002. *Le Dune, il Lago, il Mare: Una Comunità di Villaggio dell'Età del Rame a Maccarese*. Florence: Insituto Italiano di Preistoria e Protostoria.
Manning, S. W., 1994. 'The Emergence of Divergence: Development and Decline on Bronze Age Crete and the Cyclades' in Mathers and Stoddart 1994, 221–70.
— 1999. *A Test of Time: The Volcano of Thera and the Chronology and History of the Aegean and East Mediterranean in the Mid Second Millennium BC*. Oxford: Oxbow.
— 2008. 'Formation of the Palaces' in Shelmerdine 2008, 105–20.
— and L. Hulin, 2005. 'Maritime Commerce and Geographies of Mobility in the Late Bronze Age of the Eastern Mediterranean: Problematizations' in Blake and Knapp 2005, 270–302.
—, C. Kocik, B. Lorentzen *et al.*, 2023. 'Severe Multi-year Drought Coincident with Hittite Collapse around 1198–1196 BC.' *Nature* 614: 719–24.
Mannino, M. A., and K. D. Thomas, 2009. 'Current Research on Prehistoric Human Coastal Ecology: Late Pleistocene and Early Holocene Hunter-gatherer Transitions in North-west Sicily' in McCartan *et al.* 2009, 140–45.
—, —, M. J. Leng *et al.*, 2007. 'Marine Resources in the Mesolithic and Neolithic at the Grotta Dell'Uzzo (Sicily): Evidence from Isotope Analyses of Marine Shells.' *Archaeometry* 49: 117–33.
Maran, J., 1998. *Kulturwandel auf dem Griechischen Festland und den Kykladen im Späten 3. Jahrtausend v. Chr*. Bonn: Habelt.
— 2006. 'Coming to Terms with the Past: Ideology and Power in Late Helladic IIIC' in Deger-Jalkotzy and Lemos 2006, 123–50.
— 2007. 'Seaborne Contacts between the Aegean, the Balkans and the Central Mediterranean in the 3rd Millennium BC – The Unfolding of the Mediterranean World' in Galanaki *et al.* 2007, 3–21.
— 2011. 'Lost in Translation: The Emergence of Mycenaean Culture as a Phenomenon of Glocalization' in T. C. Wilkinson *et al.* 2011, 282–94.
Marazzi, M., and S. Tusa, 2005. 'Egei in Occidente: Le Più Antiche Vie Marittime alla Luce dei Nuovi Scavi sull'Isola di Pantelleria' in Laffineur and Greco 2005, 599–609.
Marcus, E. S., 2002a. 'Early Seafaring and Maritime Activity in the Southern Levant from Prehistory through the Third Millennium BCE' in van den Brink and Levy 2002, 403–17.
— 2002b. 'The Southern Levant and Maritime Trade during the Middle Bronze IIa Period' in E. Oren and S. Ahituv (eds), *Aharon Kempinski Memorial Volume: Studies in Archaeology and Related Disciplines*. Beer Sheva: Ben-Gurion UP. 241–63.
— 2006. 'Venice on the Nile? On the Maritime Character of Tell Dab'a/Avaris' in E. Czerny, I. Hein, H. Hunger *et al.* (eds), *Timelines: Studies in Honour of Manfred Bietak*. Vol. I. Leuven and Dudley: Peters. 187–90.
— 2007. 'Amenemhet II and the Sea: Maritime Aspects of the Mit Rahina (Memphis) Inscription.' *ÄL* 17: 137–90.
Marcus, J. H., C. Posth, H. Ringbauer *et al.*, 2020. 'Genetic History from the Middle Neolithic to Present on the Mediterranean Island of Sardinia.' *Nature Communications* 11: 939.
Marée, M., (ed.) 2010. *The Second Intermediate Period (Thirteenth-Seventeenth Dynasties): Current Research, Future Prospects*. Leuven: Peeters.
Marfoe, L. 1987. 'Cedar Forest to Silver Mountain: Social Change and the Development of Long-distance Trade in Early Near Eastern Societies' in Rowlands *et al.* 1987, 25–35.
Margalef, R., (ed.) 1985. *The Western Mediterranean*. Oxford and New York: Pergamon.
Margaritis, E., 2013. 'Distinguishing Exploitation, Domestication, Cultivation and Production: The Olive in the Third Millennium Aegean.' *Antiquity* 87.
Margomenou, D., 2009. 'Food Storage in Prehistoric Northern Greece: Interrogating Complexity at the Margins of the "Mycenaean World".' *JMA* 21: 191–212.
Margueron, J.-C., 2008. 'Ugarit: Gateway to the Mediterranean' in Aruz *et al.* 2008, 236–38.
Markoe, G. E., 2000. *Phoenicians*. London: British Museum. Berkeley: California UP.
Marra, A. C., 2005. 'Pleistocene Mammals of Mediterranean Islands.' *QI* 129: 5–14.
Marriner, N., 2009. *Geoarchaeology of Lebanon's Ancient Harbours*. Oxford: Archaeopress.
—, C. Morhange and C. Doumet-Serhal, 2006. 'Geoarchaeology of Sidon's Ancient Harbours, Phoenicia.' *JAS* 33: 1514–35.
Marshall, F., and E. Hildebrand, 2002. 'Cattle before Crops: The Beginnings of Food Production in Africa.' *JWP* 16: 99–143.
— and L. Weissbrod, 2011. 'Domestication Processes and Morphological Change: Through the Lens of the Donkey and African Pastoralism.' *CA* 52 (S4): S397–S413.
Marthari, M. E., 2001. 'Altering Information from the Past: Illegal Excavations in Greece and the Case of the Early Bronze Age Cyclades' in Brodie *et al.* 2001, 161–72.
Martí, B., 1977. *Cova de l'Or (Beniarrés, Alicante)*. Vol. 1. Valencia: Servicio de Investigacion Prehistorica.
Martín, C., M. Fernández-Miranda, M. D. Fernández-Posse and A. Gilman, 1993. 'The Bronze Age of La Mancha.' *Antiquity* 67: 23–45.
Martin, L., Y. Edwards and A. N. Garrard, 2010. 'Hunting Practices at an Eastern Jordanian Epipalaeolithic Aggregation Site: The Case of Kharaneh IV.' *Levant* 42: 107–35.
Martín de la Cruz, J. C., 2008. 'El Valle Medio del Guadalquivir' in Celestino *et al.* 2008, 289–99.
Martinelli, M. C., (ed.) 2005. *Il Villaggio dell'Età del Bronzo Medio di Portella a Salina nelle Isole Eolie*. Florence: Istituto Italiano di Preistoria e Protostoria.
—, G. Fiorentino, B. Prosdocimi *et al.*, 2010. 'Nuove Ricerche nell'Insediamento sull'Istmo di Filo Braccio a Filicudi: Nota Preliminare Sugli Scavi 2009.' *Origini* 32: 285–314.
Martinez-Navarro, B., I. Toro and J. Agisti, 2005. 'Early Pleistocene Faunal and Human Dispersals into Europe: The Large Mammal Assemblages from Venta Micena, Fuente Nueva-3 and Barranco Leon-5 (Orec, Spain)' in N. Molines, M.-H. Moncel and J.-L. Monnier (eds), *Les Premiers Peuplements en Europe: Certitudes et Hypotheses?* Oxford: Archaeopress. 125–33.

Martinón-Torres, María, 2022. 'Human Evolution in Eurasia: The Fossils that Darwin Did Not Know' in J. Bertranpetit and J. Peretó (eds), *Illuminating Human Evolution: 150 Years after Darwin*. Springer Singapore. 93–105.
—, X. Wu, J. M. Bermúdez de Castro et al., 2017. '*Homo sapiens* in the Eastern Asian Late Pleistocene.' *CA* 58: 434–48.
Marzoli, D., F. López Pardo, J. Suárez Padilla *et al.*, 2010. 'Los Inicios del Urbanismo en las Sociedades Autóctonas Localizadas en el Entorno del Estrecho de Gibraltar: Investigaciones en los Castillejos de Alcorrín y su Territorio (Manilva, Málaga).' *Menga: Revista de Prehistoria de Andalucía* 1: 153–83.
Mather, A., 2009. 'Tectonic Setting and Landscape Development' in Woodward 2009a, 5–32.
Mathers, C., and S. Stoddart, (eds) 1994. *Development and Decline in the Mediterranean Bronze Age*. Sheffield: J. R. Collis.
Matthäus, H., 2001. 'Studies on the Interrelations of Cyprus and Italy during the 11th to 9th Centuries BC: A Pan-Mediterranean Perspective' in Bonfante and Karageorghis 2001, 153–214.
Matthews, R., 2002. 'Zebu: Harbingers of Doom in Bronze Age Western Asia?' *Antiquity* 76: 438–46.
— and C. Roemer, (eds) 2003. *Ancient Perspectives on Egypt*. London: UCL. Portland: Cavendish.
Matthiae, P., 1980. *Ebla: An Empire Rediscovered*. London: Hodder and Stoughton. 1981, Garden City: Doubleday.
— 2003. 'Ebla and the Early Urbanization of Syria' in J. Aruz (ed.), *Art of the First Cities: The Third Millennium B.C. from the Mediterranean to the Indus*. New York: Metropolitan Museum of Art. 165–78.
Mattingly, D. J., (ed.) 2003. *The Archaeology of Fazzān*. Vol. 1: *Synthesis*. London: Society for Libyan Studies.
— 1995. *Tripolitania*. Ann Arbor: Michigan UP. London: Batsford.
— 2006. 'The Garamantes: The First Libyan State' in Mattingly *et al.* 2006, 189–204.
—, S. McLaren, E. Savage *et al.*, (eds) 2006. *The Libyan Desert: Natural Resources and Cultural Heritage*. London: Society for Libyan Studies.
—, P. Newson, J. Grattan *et al.*, 2007. 'The Making of Early States: The Iron Age and Nabataean Periods' in Barker, Gilbertson and Mattingly 2007, 271–304.
—, T. Reynolds and J. Dore, 2003. 'Synthesis of Human Activities in Fazzan' in Mattingly 2003, 327–73.
Matvejević, P., 1999. *Mediterranean: A Cultural Landscape*. English translation. Berkeley: California UP.
Mays, S., 2010. *The Archaeology of Human Bones*. 2nd edn. London and New York: Routledge.
Mazar, A., 2007a. 'The Patriarchs, Exodus, and Conquest Narratives in Light of Archaeology' in B. B. Schmidt 2007, 57–65.
— 2007b. 'The Israelite Settlement' in B. B. Schmidt 2007, 85–98.
— 2007c. 'The Search for David and Solomon: An Archaeological Perspective' in B. B. Schmidt 2007, 117–39.
Mazarakis Ainian, A., 2006. 'The Archaeology of *Basileis*' in Deger-Jalkotzy and Lemos 2006, 181–211.
Mazzoni, S., 2003. 'Ebla: Crafts and Power in an Emergent State of Third Millennium BC Syria.' *JMA* 16: 173–91.
McAnany, P. A., and N. Yoffee, (eds) 2010. *Questioning Collapse: Human Resilience, Ecological Vulnerability, and the Aftermath of Empire*. Cambridge and New York: Cambridge UP.
McBrearty, S., and A. S. Brooks, 2000. 'The Revolution that Wasn't: A New Interpretation of the Origin of Modern Human Behavior.' *JHE* 39: 453–563.
McBurney, C. B. M., 1967. *The Haua Fteah (Cyrenaica) and the Stone Age of the South-east Mediterranean*. Cambridge: Cambridge UP.
McCartan, S., R. Schulting, G. Warren and P. Woodman, (eds) 2009. *Mesolithic Horizons*. Vol. 1. Oxford and Oakville: Oxbow.
McCartney, C., 2007. 'Lithics' in J. Clarke *et al.* 2007, 72–90.
McClure, S. B., Ll. Molina and J. Bernabeu, 2008. 'Neolithic Rock Art in Context: Landscape History and the Transition to Agriculture in Mediterranean Spain.' *JAA* 27: 326–27.
McCormick, M., 2001. *Origins of the European Economy: Communications and Commerce, AD 300–900*. Cambridge and New York: Cambridge UP.
—, 2019. 'Climates of History, Histories of Climate: From History to Archaeoscience.' *The Journal of Interdisciplinary History* 50: 3–30.
McCorriston, J., 1994. 'Acorn-eating and Agricultural Origins: California Ethnographies as Analogies for the Ancient Near East.' *Antiquity* 68: 97–107.
— 1997. 'The Fiber Revolution: Textile Extensification, Alienation, and Social Stratification in Ancient Mesopotamia.' *CA* 38: 517–49.
McEnroe, J. C., 2010. *Architecture of Minoan Crete: Constructing Identity in the Aegean Bronze Age*. Austin: Texas UP.
McEvedy, C., 2002. *The New Penguin Atlas of Ancient History*. 2nd edn. London and New York: Penguin.
McGeough, K. M., 2007. *Exchange Relationships at Ugarit*. Leuven and Dudley: Peeters.
McGovern, P. E., 2003. *Ancient Wine: The Search for the Origins of Viticulture*. Princeton and Oxford: Princeton UP.
— 2009. *Uncorking the Past: The Quest for Wine, Beer, and Other Alcoholic Beverages*. Berkeley and London: California UP.
McGrail, S., 1993. 'Prehistoric Seafaring in the Channel' in Scarre and Healy 1993, 199–210.
McIntosh, S. K., and R. J. McIntosh, 1988. 'From Stone to Metal: New Perspectives on the Later Prehistory of West Africa.' *JWP* 2: 89–133.
McNeill, J. R., 1992. *Mountains of the Mediterranean World: An Environmental History*. Cambridge and New York: Cambridge UP.
Médail, F., and K. Diadema, 2009. 'Glacial Refugia Influence Plant Diversity Patterns in the Mediterranean Basin.' *JB* 36: 1333–45.
Mee, C., 1982. *Rhodes in the Bronze Age: An Archaeological Survey*. Warminster: Aris & Phillips.
— 1998. 'Anatolia and the Aegean in the Late Bronze Age' in Cline and Harris-Cline 1998, 137–48.
Meier, S., 2007. 'Granting God a Passport: Transporting Gods across International Boundaries" in P. Kousoulis and K. Magliveras (eds), *Moving across Borders: Foreign Relations, Religion, and Cultural Interactions in the Ancient Mediterranean*. Leuven and Dudley: Peeters. 185–208.
Meiggs, R., 1972. *The Athenian Empire*. Oxford: Clarendon. 1979 New York: Oxford UP.
Melis, R., 2009. 'La Sardaigne et ses Relations Méditerranéennes entre les Ve et IIe Millénaires av. J.-C.: Quelques Observations' in Barbaza *et al.* 2009, 509–20.
— and M. Mussi, 2002. 'S. Maria is Acquas, a New Pre-Neolithic Site: South-western Sardinia' in Waldren and Ensenyat 2002, 454–61.
Mellars, P., 1999. 'The Neanderthal Problem Continued.' *CA* 40: 341–64.
— 2004. 'Neanderthals and the Modern Human Colonization of Europe.' *Nature* 432: 461–65.
— 2006. 'Archaeology and the Dispersal of Modern Humans in Europe: Deconstructing the Aurignacian.' *EA* 15: 167–82.
—, K. Boyle, O. Bar-Yosef and C. Stringer, (eds) 2007. *Rethinking the Human Revolution: New Behavioural and Biological Perspectives on the Origin and Dispersal of Modern Humans*. Cambridge: MIAR.
— and C. Stringer, (eds) 1989. *The Human Revolution: Behavioural and Biological Perspectives on the Origins of Modern Humans*. Princeton: Princeton UP. Edinburgh: Edinburgh UP.
Melotti, M., 2007. *Mediterraneo tra Miti e Turismo: Per una Sociologia del Turismo Archeologico*. Milano: CUEM.
Menéndez Iglesias, B., 2008. 'The Chalcolithic and Ancient Bronze Age Engravings of the Mont Bego Region.' *Annali dell'Università degli Studi di Ferrara Special Volume 2008*. 123–28.
Mercer, J., 1980. *The Canary Islanders: Their Prehistory, Conquest, and Survival*. London: Collings.
Merrillees, R. S., 1962. 'Opium Trade in the Bronze Age Levant.' *Antiquity* 36: 287–92.
— 1984. 'Ambelikou-*Aletri*: A Preliminary Report.' *Report of the Department of Antiquities, Cyprus, 1984*. 1–13.
— 2003. 'The First Appearances of Kamares Ware in the Levant.' *ÄL* 13: 127–52.
Meskell, L., (ed.) 1998. *Archaeology under Fire: Nationalism, Politics and Heritage in the Eastern Mediterranean and Middle East*. London and New York: Routledge.
Michel, C., 1992. 'Les "Diamants" du Roi de Mari' in J. M. Durand (ed.), *Florilegium Marianum: Recueil d'Études en l'Honneur de Michel Fleury*. Vol 1. Paris: NABU. 127–36.
Micó Pérez, R., 1995. 'Los Millares and the Copper Age of the Iberian Southeast' in Lillios 1995, 169–76.
Midant-Reynes, B., and Y. Tristant, (eds) 2008. *Egypt at Its Origins 2*. Leuven: Peeters.
Milano, L., 1995. 'Ebla: A Third Millennium City-state in Ancient Syria' in Sasson 1995, 1219–30.
Militello, P., 2005. 'Mycenaean Palaces and Western Trade: A Problematic Relationship' in Laffineur and Greco 2005, 585–98.
Mille, B., and L. Carozza, 2009. 'Moving into the Metal Ages: The Social Importance of Metal at the End of the Neolithic Period in France' in T. L. Kienlin and B. W. Roberts (eds), *Metals and Societies*. Bonn: Habelt. 143–71.
Miller, R., 2012. 'Mapping the Expansion of the Northwest Magdalenian.' *QI* 272–73: 209–30.
Mills, N., 1984. 'The Neolithic of Southern France' in C. Scarre (ed.), *Ancient France: Neolithic Societies and Their Landscapes 6000–2000 BC*. Edinburgh: Edinburgh UP. 91–145.
Mina, M., 2008. *Anthropomorphic Figurines: From the Neolithic and Early Bronze Age Aegean. Gender Dynamics and Implications for the Understanding of Early Aegean Prehistory*. Oxford: Archaeopress.
Miracle, P., 2002. 'Mesolithic Meals from Mesolithic Middens' in P. Miracle and N. Milner (eds), *Consuming Passions and Patterns of Consumption*. Cambridge: MIAR. 65–88.
— 2007. 'The Late Glacial "Great Adriatic Plain": "Garden of Eden" or "No Man's Land" during the Epipalaeolithic? A View from Istria (Croatia)' in Whallon 2007a, 41–51.
Mitchell, P., 2005. *African Connections: Archaeological Perspectives on Africa and the Wider World*. Oxford and Lanham: AltaMira.
Mithen, S., 1996. *The Prehistory of the Mind: A Search for the Origins of Art, Religion and Science*. London and New York: Thames & Hudson.
— 2003. *After the Ice: A Global Human History, 20,000–5000 BC*. Cambridge: Harvard UP. London: Phoenix.
— and E. Black, (eds) 2011. *Water, Life and Civilisation: Climate, Environment and Society in the Jordan Valley*. Cambridge and New York: Cambridge UP.
Molina González, F., and J. A. Cámara Serrano, 2010. 'Los Millares y su Dominio Sobre el Valle del Andarax.' *PH: Boletín del Instituto Andaluz del Patrimonio Histórico* 73: 60–65.
Möller, A., 2000. *Naukratis: Trade in Archaic Greece*. Oxford and New York: Oxford UP.
— 2007. 'Classical Greece: Distribution' in Scheidel *et al.* 2007, 362–84.
Molleson, T., 1994. 'The Eloquent Bones of Abu Hureyra.' *Scientific American* 271: 70–75.
Monks, S. J., 1997. 'Conflict and Competition in Spanish Prehistory: The Role of Warfare in Societal Development from the Late Fourth to the Third Millennium B.C.' *JMA* 10: 3–32.
Monroe, C. M., 2007. 'Vessel Volumetrics and the Myth of the Cyclopean Bronze Age Ship.' *Journal of the Economic and Social History of the Orient* 50: 1–18.
— 2009. *Scales of Fate: Trade, Tradition, and Transformation in the Eastern Mediterranean, ca. 1350–1175 BCE*. Münster: Ugarit-Verlag.
— 2010. 'Sunk Costs at Late Bronze Age Uluburun.' *BASOR* 357: 19–33.
— 2011. 'From Luxuries to Anxieties: A Liminal View of the Late Bronze Age World-system' in T. C. Wilkinson *et al.* 2011, 87–99.
Montelius, O., 1899. *Der Orient und Europe: Einfluss der Orientalischen Cultur auf Europa bis zur Mitte des Letzten Jahrtausends V. Chr.* Stockholm: K. Akademie.
Montero-Ruiz, I., 1993. 'Bronze Age Metallurgy in Southeast Spain.' *Antiquity* 67: 46–57.
Montet, P., 1947–60. *La Nécropole Royale de Tanis*. Vols I–III. Paris: Pierre Montet.
Moorey, P. R. S., 1988. 'The Chalcolithic Hoard from Nahal Mishmar, Israel, in Context.' *WA* 20: 171–89.
— 2001. 'The Mobility of Artisans and Opportunities for Technology Transfer between Western Asia and Egypt in the Late Bronze Age' in Shortland 2001, 1–14.
Moots, H. M., M. Antonio, S. Sawyer *et al.*, 2023. 'A Genetic History of Continuity and Mobility in the Iron Age Central Mediterranean.' *Nature Ecology & Evolution* 7: 1515–24.
Morales-Muñiz, A., and E. Roselló-Izquierdo, 2008. 'Twenty Thousand Years of Fishing in the Strait: Archaeological Fish and Shellfish Assemblages from Southern Iberia' in T. C. Rick and J. M. Erlandson (eds), *Human Impacts on Ancient Marine Ecosystems: A Global Perspective*. Berkeley and London: California UP. 243–78.
Moran, W. L., 1992. *The Amarna Letters*. Baltimore and London: Johns Hopkins UP.
Morel, J.-P., 1984. 'Greek Colonization in Italy and the West (Problems of Evidence and Interpretation)' in T. Hackens, N. D. Holloway and R. R. Holloway (eds), *Crossroads of the Mediterranean*. Providence: Brown University Center for Old World Archaeology and Art. 123–61.
Moreno García, J. C., 2020. 'Egyptology and Global History: Between Geocultural Power and the Crisis of the Humanities.' *Journal of Egyptian History* 13: 29–76.
Morgan, C., 1990. *Athletes and Oracles: The Transformation of Olympia and Delphi in the Eighth Century BC*. Cambridge and New York: Cambridge UP.
Morgado, A., E. García-Alfonso, L. F. García del Moral *et al.*, 2018. 'Embarcaciones Prehistóricas y Representaciones Rupestres: Nuevos Datos del Abrigo de Laja Alta (Jimena de la Frontera, Cádiz).' *Complutum* 29: 239–65.

— 1994. 'The Evolution of a Sacral "Landscape": Isthmia, Perachora, and the Early Corinthian State' in S. E. Alcock and R. Osborne (eds), *Placing the Gods: Sanctuaries and Sacred Space in Ancient Greece*. Oxford and New York: Clarendon. 105–42.

— 2003. *Early Greek States beyond the Polis*. London and New York: Routledge.

Morgan, L., 1988. *The Miniature Wall Paintings of Thera: A Study in Aegean Culture and Iconography*. Cambridge and New York: Cambridge UP.

Morris, E., 2006. '"Lo, Nobles Lament, the Poor Rejoice": State Formation in the Wake of Social Flux' in Schwartz and Nichols 2006, 72–84.

Morris, I., 1986. 'The Use and Abuse of Homer.' *Classical Antiquity* 5: 81–136.

— 1987. *Burial and Ancient Society: The Rise of the Greek City-state*. Cambridge and New York: Cambridge UP.

— 1992. *Death-ritual and Social Structure in Classical Antiquity*. Cambridge and New York: Cambridge UP.

— 1997. 'An Archaeology of Inequalities? The Greek City-states' in D. L. Nichols and T. H. Charlton (eds), *The Archaeology of City-states: Cross-cultural Approaches*. Washington and London: Smithsonian Institution.

— 2000. *Archaeology as Cultural History: Words and Things in Iron Age Greece*. Malden and Oxford: Blackwell.

— 2003. 'Mediterraneanization.' *MHR* 18: 30–55.

— 2006. 'The Collapse and Regeneration of Complex Society in Greece 1500–500 BC' in Schwartz and Nichols 2006, 72–84.

— 2007. 'Early Iron Age Greece' in Scheidel *et al.* 2007, 211–41.

— 2009. 'The Greater Athenian State (478–404 BC)' in I. Morris and Scheidel 2009, 99–177.

— 2010. *Why the West Rules – For Now: The Patterns of History, and What They Reveal about the Future*. New York: Farrar, Straus and Giroux. London: Profile.

— 2012. 'Greek Multi-city States' in Bang and Scheidel 2012, 279–303.

—, T. Jackman, E. Blake and S. Tusa, 2001. 'Stanford University Excavations on the Acropolis of Monte Polizzo, Sicily, I: Preliminary Report on the 2000 Season.' *Memoirs of the American Academy in Rome* 46: 253–71.

—, R. P. Saller and W. Scheidel, 2007. 'Introduction' in Scheidel *et al.* 2007, 1–12.

— and W. Scheidel, (eds) 2009. *The Dynamics of Ancient Empires: State Power from Assyria to Byzantium*. Oxford and New York: Oxford UP.

Morris, S., 1992. *Daidalos and the Origins of Greek Art*. Princeton and Chichester: Princeton UP.

— 1998. 'Daidalos and Kothar: The Future of Their Relationship' in Cline and Harris-Cline 1998, 281–89.

— 2006. 'The View from East Greece: Miletus, Samos and Ephesus' in Riva and Vella 2006, 66–84.

— and R. Laffineur, (eds) 2007. *Epos: Reconsidering Greek Epic and Aegean Bronze Age Archaeology*. Liège: Université de Liège.

— and J. Papadopoulos, 2005. 'Greek Towers and Slaves.' *AJA* 109: 155–225.

Morrison, J., J. Coates and N. Rankov, 2000. *The Athenian Trireme: The History and Reconstruction of an Ancient Greek Warship*. 2nd edn. New York and Cambridge: Cambridge UP.

Morter, J., and J. E. Robb, 1998. 'Space, Gender, and Architecture in the Southern Italian Neolithic' in Whitehouse 1998, 83–94.

Morton, J., 2001. *The Role of the Physical Environment in Ancient Greek Seafaring*. Leiden and Boston: Brill.

Morwood, M. J., P. B. O'Sullivan, F. Aziz and A. Raza, 1998. 'Fission-track Ages of Stone Tools and Fossils on the East Indonesian Island of Flores.' *Nature* 392: 173–76.

Mosso, A., 1910. *The Dawn of Mediterranean Civilization*. London: Unwin.

Mountjoy, P. A., 1998. 'The East Aegean–West Anatolian Interface in the Late Bronze Age: Mycenaeans and the Kingdom of Ahhiyawa.' *AS* 48: 33–67.

Mourad, A.-L., 2021. *The Enigma of the Hyksos, Volume II: Transforming Egypt into the New Kingdom. The Impact of the Hyksos and Egyptian Near Eastern Relations*. Wiesbaden: Harrassowitz.

Muhly, J. D., 2006. 'Texts and Technology: The Beginnings of Iron Metallurgy in the Eastern Mediterranean' in T. P. Tassios and C. Polyvou (eds), *Ancient Greek Technology*. Athens: Technical Chamber of Commerce. 19–31.

— 2009. 'The Origin of the Name "Ionian"' in Karageorghis and Kouka 2009, 23–30.

Mulazzani, S., 2010. 'Obsidian from the Epipalaeolithic and Neolithic Eastern Maghreb: A View from the Hergla Context (Tunisia).' *JAS* 37: 2529–37.

— (ed.) 2013. *Le Capsien de Hergla (Tunisie): Culture, Environnement et Économie*. Frankfurt: Africa Magna.

Müllenhoff, M., 2005. *Geoarchäologische, Sedimentologische und Morphodynamische Untersuchungen im Mündungsgebiet des Büyük Menderes (Mäander), Westtürkei*. Marburg: Marburger Geographische Gesellschaft e.V.

Müller, J., and S. van Willigen, 2001. 'New Radiocarbon Evidence for European Bell Beakers and the Consequences for the Diffusion of the Bell Beaker Phenomenon' in Nicolis 2001, 59–80.

Munro, N., 2004. 'Zooarchaeological Measures of Hunting Pressure and Occupation Intensity in the Natufian.' *CA* 45 (S4): S7–S33.

Murillo-Barroso, M., and Marcos Martinón-Torres, 2012. 'Amber Sources and Trade in the Prehistory of the Iberian Peninsula.' *EJA* 15: 187–216.

— and I. Montero-Ruiz, 2012. 'Copper Ornaments in the Iberian Chalcolithic: Technology versus Social Demand.' *JMA* 25: 53–73.

—, E. Peñalver, P. Bueno *et al.*, 2018. 'Amber in Prehistoric Iberia: New Data and a Review.' *PLOS ONE* 13: e0202235.

Murphy, J. P., (ed.) 1977. *Rufius Festus Avienus. Ora Maritima: Or, Description of the Seacoast from Brittany Round to Massilia*. Chicago: Ares.

Murray, O., and S. Price, (eds) 1990. *The Greek City From Homer to Alexander*. Oxford and New York: Oxford UP.

Mussi, M., 2000. 'Heading South: The Gravettian Colonisation of Italy' in Roebroeks *et al.* 2000, 355–74.

— 2001. *Earliest Italy: An Overview of the Italian Paleolithic and Mesolithic*. New York and London: Kluwer Academic/Plenum.

— (ed.) 2008. *Il Tardiglaciale in Italia: Lavori in Corso*. Oxford: Archaeopress.

Mylona, D., 2003. 'The Exploitation of Fish Resources in Mesolithic Sporades: Fish Remains from the Cave of Cyclops, Yioura' in Galanidou and Perlès 2003, 181–88.

Myres, J. L., 1943. *Mediterranean Culture*. Cambridge: Cambridge UP.

Naccache, A. F. H., 1998. 'Beirut's Memorycide: Hear No Evil, See No Evil' in Meskell 1998, 140–58.

Nadel, D., (ed.) 2002. *Ohalo II: A 23,000-year-old Fisher-hunter-gatherers' Camp on the Shore of the Sea of Galilee*. Haifa: Hecht Museum.

Nakou, G., 1995. 'The Cutting Edge: A New Look at Early Aegean Metallurgy.' *JMA* 8: 1–32.

— 2000. 'Metalwork, Basketry and Pottery in the Aegean Early Bronze Age' in A. Serghidou (*ed.*), *Dorema: A Tribute to the A. G. Leventis Foundation on the Occasion of Its 20th Anniversary*. Nicosia: A. G. Leventis Foundation. 27–57.

— 2007. 'Absent Presences' in Day and Doonan 2007, 224–44.

Needham, S., 2009. 'Encompassing the Sea: "Maritories" and Bronze Age Maritime Interactions' in P. Clark (ed.), *Bronze Age Connections: Cultural Contact in Prehistoric Europe*. Oxford and Oakville: Oxbow. 12–37.

Neef, R., 1990. 'Introduction, Development and Environmental Implications of Olive Culture: The Evidence from Jordan' in S. Bottema, G. Entjes-Nieborg and W. van Zeist (eds), *Man's Role in the Shaping of the Eastern Mediterranean Landscape*. Rotterdam: A. A. Balkema. 295–306.

Neer, R. T., 2001. 'Framing the Gift: The Politics of the Siphnian Treasury at Delphi.' *Classical Antiquity* 20: 273–344.

Nespoulet, R., M. Hajraoui and F. Amani, 2008. 'Palaeolithic and Neolithic Occupations in the Témara Region (Rabat, Morocco): Recent Data on Hominin Contexts and Behavior.' *AAR* 25: 21–39.

Neumann, G. U., E. Skourtanioti, M. Burri *et al.*, 2022. 'Ancient *Yersinia pestis* and *Salmonella enterica* Genomes from Bronze Age Crete.' *Current Biology* 32: 3641–49.e8.

Neville, A., 2007. *Mountains of Silver and Rivers of Gold: The Phoenicians in Iberia*. Oxford: Oxbow.

Newton, C., J.-F. Terral and S. Ivorra, 2006. 'The Egyptian Olive (*Olea europaea* subsp. *europaea*) in the Later First Millennium BC: Origins and History Using the Morphometric Analysis of Olive Stones.' *Antiquity* 80: 405–14.

Nichols, J. J., and J. A. Weber, 2006. 'Amorites, Onagers, and Social Reorganization in Middle Bronze Age Syria' in Schwartz and Nichols 2006, 38–57.

Nicolis, F., (ed.) 2001. *Bell Beakers Today: Pottery, People, Culture, Symbols in Prehistoric Europe*. Vol. 1. Trento: Ufficio Beni Archeologici.

— and E. Mottes, (eds) 1998. *Simbolo ed Enigma: Il Bicchiere Campaniforme e l'Italia nella Preistoria Europea dell III Millennio A.C.* Trento: Ufficio Beni Archeologici.

Niemeyer, H. G., R. F. Docter and K. Schmidt, 2007. *Karthago: Die Ergebnisse der Hamburger Grabung unter dem Decumanus Maximus*. Mainz: Philipp von Zabern.

Niemeier, W. D., 2005. 'The Minoans and Mycenaeans in Western Asia Minor: Settlement, Emporia or Acculturation?' in Laffineur and Greco 2005, 199–204.

Nijboer, A. J., and J. van der Plicht, 2006. 'An Interpretation of the Radiocarbon Determinations of the Oldest Indigenous-Phoenician Stratum Thus far, Excavated at Huelva, Tartessos (South-west Spain).' *Bulletin Antieke Beschaving* 81: 31–36.

Nocete, F., 2006. 'The First Specialised Copper Industry in the Iberian Peninsula: Cabezo Juré (2900–2200 BC).' *Antiquity* 80: 646–57.

—, E. Álex, J. M. Nieto *et al.*, 2005. 'An Archaeological Approach to Regional Environmental Pollution in the South-western Iberian Peninsula Related to Third Millennium BC Mining and Metallurgy.' *JAS* 32: 1566–76.

—, R. Lizcano, A. Peramo and E. Gómez, 2010. 'Emergence, Collapse and Continuity of the First Political System in the Guadalquivir Basin from the Fourth to the Second Millennium BC: The Long-term Sequence of Úbeda (Spain).' *JAA* 29: 219–37.

—, G. Queipo, R. Sáez *et al.*, 2008. 'The Smelting Quarter of Valencina de la Concepción (Seville, Spain): The Specialised Copper Industry in a Political Centre of the Guadalquivir Valley during the Third Millennium BC (2750–2500 BC).' *JAS* 35: 717–32.

Norwich, J. J., 2006. *The Middle Sea: A History of the Mediterranean*. New York: Doubleday. 2007 London: Chatto & Windus.

Nowicki, K., 2008. 'The Final Neolithic (Late Chalcolithic) to Early Bronze Age Transition in Crete and the South-east Aegean Islands: Changes in Settlement Patterns and Pottery' in Isaakidou and Tomkins 2008, 201–28.

O'Connell, J. F., J. Allen and K. Hawkes, 2010. 'Pleistocene Sahul and the Origins of Seafaring' in A. Anderson *et al.* 2010, 57–68.

O'Connor, D., 1972. 'The Geography of Settlement in Ancient Egypt' in Ucko *et al.* 1972, 681–98.

—1990. 'The Nature of Tjemhu (Libyan) Society in the Later New Kingdom' in Leahy 1990, 29–113.

— 2009. *Abydos: Egypt's First Pharaohs and the Cult of Osiris*. London and New York: Thames & Hudson.

— and S. Quirke, (eds) 2003. *Mysterious Lands*. London: UCL. Portland: Cavendish.

O'Connor, S., 2010. 'Pleistocene Migration and Colonization in the Indo-Pacific Region' in A. Anderson *et al.* 2010, 41–55.

Oded, B., 1979. *Mass Deportations and Deportees in the Neo-Assyrian Empire*. Wiesbaden: Reichert.

Oeggl, K., W. Kofler, A. Schmidl *et al.*, 2007. 'The Reconstruction of the Last Itinerary of "Ötzi", the Neolithic Iceman, by Pollen Analyses from Sequentially Sampled Gut Extracts.' *QSR* 26: 853–61.

Olalde, I., S. Brace, M. E. Allentoft *et al.*, 2018. 'The Beaker Phenomenon and the Genetic Transformation of Northwest Europe.' *Nature* 555: 190–96.

—, S. Mallick, N. Patterson *et al.*, 2019. 'The Genomic History of the Iberian Peninsula over the Past 8000 Years.' *Science* 363: 1230–34.

Olivieri, A., A. Achilli, M. Pala *et al.*, 2006. 'The mtDNA Legacy of the Levantine Early Upper Palaeolithic in Africa.' *Science* 314: 1767–70.

Onnis, F., 2009. 'Levantine Iconology: Was There a Conscious Figurative Programme in the Decoration of the "Phoenician" Metal Bowl?' *Bulletin d'Archéologie et d'Architecture Libanaises* Hors-Série VI: 499–514.

Oppenheimer, C., and D. Pyle, 2009. 'Volcanoes' in Woodward 2009a, 435–68.

O'Regan, H. J., 2008. 'The Iberian Peninsula – Corridor or Cul-de-sac? Mammalian Faunal Change and Possible Routes of Dispersal in the Last 2 Million Years.' *QSR* 27: 2136–44.

Oren, E. D., (ed.) 1997a. *The Hyksos: New Historical and Archaeological Perspectives*. Philadelphia: Pennsylvania University Museum.

— 1997b. 'The "Kingdom of Sharuhen" and the Hyksos Kingdom' in Oren 1997a, 253–83.

— (ed.) 2000. *The Sea Peoples and Their World: A Reassessment*. Philadelphia: Pennsylvania University Museum.

— and I. Gilead, 1981. 'Chalcolithic Sites in Northeastern Sinai.' *Tel Aviv* 8: 25–44.

Orengo, H. A., and A. Garcia-Molsosa, 2019. 'A Brave New World for Archaeological Survey: Automated Machine Learning-based Potsherd Detection Using High-Resolution Drone Imagery.' *JAS* 112: 105013.

Osborne, J. F., and J. M. Hall, (eds) 2022. *The Connected Iron Age: Interregional Networks in the Eastern Mediterranean, 900–600 BCE*. Chicago: Chicago UP.

Osborne, R., 1994. 'Looking on – Greek Style. Does the Sculpted Girl Speak to Women Too ?' in I. Morris (ed.), *Classical Greece: Ancient Histories and Modern Archaeologies*. Cambridge and New York: Cambridge UP. 81–96.

— 1996. 'Pots, Trade and the Archaic Greek Economy.' *Antiquity* 70: 31–44.
— 1998. 'Early Greek Colonisation? The Nature of Greek Settlement in the West' in N. Fischer and van Wees 1998, 251–70.
— 1999. 'Archaeology and the Athenian Empire.' *Transactions of the American Philological Association* 129: 319–32.
— 2005. 'Urban Sprawl: What Is Urbanization and Why Does It Matter?' in Osborne and Cunliffe 2005, 1–16.
— 2007. 'Archaic Greece' in Scheidel *et al.* 2007, 277–301.
— 2008. 'Colonial Cancer.' *JMA* 21: 281–84.
— 2009a. *Greece in the Making 1200–479 BC.* 2nd edn. London and New York: Routledge.
— 2009b. 'What Travelled with Greek Pottery?' in I. Malkin, C. Constantakopoulou and K. Panagopoulou (eds), *Greek and Roman Networks in the Mediterranean.* London: Routledge. 83–93.
— and B. Cunliffe, (eds) 2005. *Mediterranean Urbanization 800–600 BC.* Oxford: Oxford UP.
Otte, M., (ed.) 2010. *Les Aurignaciens.* Paris: Errance.
— and I. Yalçinkaya, 2009. 'The Palaeolithic of Turkey' in M. Camps and Szmidt 2009, 101–14.
Outram, A. K., N. A. Stear, R. Bendrey *et al.*, 2009. 'The Earliest Horse Harnessing and Milking.' *Science* 323: 1332–35.
Özbaşaran, M., 1995. 'The Historical Background of Researches at the Caves of Yarımburgaz' in *Readings in Prehistory: Studies Presented to Halet Çambel.* Istanbul: Graphis Yayınları. 27–39.
— 2011. 'The Neolithic on the Plateau' in Steadman and McMahon 2011, 99–124.
Özdoğan, M., 1999. 'Northwestern Turkey: Neolithic Cultures in between the Balkans and Anatolia' in M. Özdoğan and N. Başgelen (eds), *The Neolithic in Turkey: The Cradle of Civilization: New Discoveries.* Istanbul: Arkeoloji ve Sanat Yayınları. 202–24.
— 2007. 'Amidst Mesopotamia-centric and Euro-centric Approaches: The Changing Role of the Anatolian Peninsula between the East and the West.' *AS* 57: 17–24.
— 2011. 'Archaeological Evidence on the Westward Expansion of Farming Communities from Eastern Anatolia to the Aegean and the Balkans.' *CA* 52 (S4): S415–S430.
— and N. Başgelen, (eds) 1999. *The Neolithic in Turkey: New Excavations and New Research.* 4 vols. Galatasaray: Archaeology & Art Publications.
Pacciarelli, M., 1999. *Torre Galli: La Necropoli della Prima Età del Ferro.* Soveria Mannelli: Rubbettino.
Pace, A., (ed.) 2000. *The Hal Saflieni Hypogaeum 4000 BC–2000 AD.* Malta: Museums Department.
— 2004. 'The Sites' in Cilia 2004, 42–227.
Pacheco-Ruiz, R., J. Adams, F. Pedrotti *et al.*, 2019. 'Deep Sea Archaeological Survey in the Black Sea – Robotic Documentation of 2,500 Years of Human Seafaring.' *Deep Sea Research Part I: Oceanographic Research Papers* 152: 103087.
Palaima, T., 1991. 'Maritime Matters in the Linear B Texts' in Laffineur and Basch 1991, 273–310.
Palomo, A., J. F. Gibaja, R. Piqué *et al.*, 2005. 'La Caza en el Yacimiento Neolítico Lacustre de La Draga (Banyoles, Girona)' in P. Arias Cabal, R. Otañón Peredo and C. García-Moncó Piñiero (eds), *III Congreso del Neolítico en la Península Ibérica.* Santander: Universidad de Cantabria. 135–43.
Palyvou, C., 2005. *Akrotiri Thera: An Architecture of Affluence 3500 Years Old.* Philadelphia: INSTAP Academic.
Panagiotakopulu, E., 2000. 'Butterflies, Flowers and Aegean Iconography: A Story about Silk and Cotton' in S. Sherratt (ed.), *The Wall Paintings of Thera.* Athens: Thera Foundation. 585–92.
Panagiotopoulos, D., 2001. 'Keftiu in Context: Theban Tomb-paintings as a Historical Source.' *OJA* 20: 263–83.
Papaconstantinou, D., 2007. 'Mediterranean Archaeologies: A Comment on the Structure of Archaeological Communities in the Mediterranean Region' in Antoniadou and Pace 2007, 85–108.
Papadopoulos, G., 2009. 'Tsunamis' in Woodward 2009a, 493–512.
Papadopoulos, J. K., 1997a. 'Knossos' in M. de la Torre (ed.), *Conservation of Archaeological Sites in the Mediterranean Region.* Los Angeles: Getty Conservation Institute. 93–126.
— 1997b. 'Phantom Euboians.' *JMA* 10: 191–219.
— and R. M. Leventhal, (eds) 2003. *Theory and Practice in Mediterranean Archaeology: Old World and New World Perspectives.* Los Angeles: Institute of Archaeology.
Papagianni, D., 2009. 'Mediterranean Southeastern Europe in the Late Middle and Early Upper Palaeolithic: Modern Human Route to Europe or Neanderthal Refugium?' in M. Camps and Szmidt 2009, 115–36.
Papathanasopoulos, G. A., 1990. 'Dokos Excavation 1989: The Early Helladic Wreck and the Prehistoric Settlement.' *Enalia* 1: 34–37.
Pappa, M., and M. Besios, 1999. 'The Makriyalos Project: Rescue Excavations at the Neolithic Site of Makriyalos, Pierra, Northern Greece' in Halstead 1999a, 108–20.
—, P. Halstead, K. Kotsakis and D. Urem-Kotsou, 2004. 'Evidence for Large-scale Feasting at Late Neolithic Makriyalos, N. Greece' in P. Halstead and J. C. Barrett (eds), *Food, Cuisine and Society in Prehistoric Greece.* Oxford: Oxbow. 16–44.
Pare, C. F. E., (ed.) 2000a. *Metals Make the World Go Round: The Supply and Circulation of Metals in Bronze Age Europe.* Oxford: Oxbow.
— 2000b. 'Bronze and the Bronze Age' in Pare 2000a, 1–38.
Parés, J. M., A. Pérez-González, A. Rosas *et al.*, 2006, 'Matuyama-age Lithic Tools from the Sima del Elefante Site, Atapuerca (Northern Spain).' *JHE* 50: 163–69.
Parfitt, S. A., N. M. Ashton, S. G. Lewis *et al.*, 2010, 'Early Pleistocene Human Occupation at the Edge of the Boreal Zone in Northwest Europe.' *Nature* 466: 229–33.
Parker, A. J., 1992. *Ancient Shipwrecks of the Mediterranean and the Roman Provinces.* Oxford: Tempvs Reparatvm.
Parkinson, R. B., 1997. *The Tale of Sinuhe and Other Ancient Egyptian Poems 1940–1640 BC.* Oxford: Oxford UP.
Parkinson, W. A., and M. L. Galaty, (eds) 2010. *Archaic State Interaction: The Eastern Mediterranean in the Bronze Age.* Santa Fe: School for Advanced Research.
Parpola, S., 2003. 'Assyria's Expansion in the 8th and 7th Centuries and Its Long-term Repercussions in the West' in Dever and Gitin 2003, 99–111.
Parrot, A., 1958. *Le Palais.* Vol. 1: *Architecture.* Paris: Geuthner.
Pastó, I., E. Allue and J. Vallverdu, 2000. 'Mousterian Hearths at Abric Romaní, Catalonia (Spain)' in Stringer *et al.* 2000, 59–67.
Pavuk, P., 2005. 'Aegeans and Anatolians: A Trojan Perspective' in Laffineur and Greco 2005, 269–77.
Pearce, M., 1998. 'New Research on the Terramare of Northern Italy.' *Antiquity* 72: 743–46.
— 2000. 'Metals Make the World Go Round: The Copper Supply for Frattesina' in Pare 2000a, 108–15.
— 2007. *Bright Blades and Red Metal: Essays on North Italian Prehistoric Metalwork.* London: Accordia Research Institute.
Pearson, C. L., D. S. Dale, P. W. Brewer *et al.*, 2009. 'Dendrochemical Analysis of a Tree-ring Growth Anomaly Associated with the Late Bronze Age Eruption of Thera.' *JAS* 36: 1206–14.
Peltenburg, E., 1991. 'Kissonerga-Mosphilia: A Major Chalcolithic Site in Cyprus.' *BASOR* 282–83: 17–35.
— 1993. 'Settlement Discontinuity and Resistance to Complexity in Cyprus, ca. 4500–2500 B. C. E.' *BASOR* 292: 9–23.
— 1996. 'From Isolation to State Formation in Cyprus, *c.* 3500–1500 BC' in V. Karageorghis and D. Michaelides (eds), *The Development of the Cypriot Economy: From the Prehistoric Period to the Present Day.* Nicosia: Panepistemio Kyprou. 17–44.
— 2004. 'Introduction: A Revised Cypriot Prehistory and Some Implications for the Study of the Neolithic' in Peltenburg and Wasse 2004, xi–xx.
— 2007. 'East Mediterranean Interaction in the 3rd Millennium BC' in Antoniadou and Pace 2007, 139–59.
—, S. Colledge, P. Croft *et al.*, 2001. 'Neolithic Dispersals from the Levantine Corridor: A Mediterranean Perspective.' *Levant* 33: 35–64.
— and A. Wasse, (eds) 2004. *Neolithic Revolution: New Perspectives on Southwest Asia in Light of Recent Discoveries on Cyprus.* Oxford and Oakville: Oxbow.
Peña-Chocarro, L., 2007. 'Early Agriculture in Central and Southern Spain' in Colledge and Conolly 2007, 173–87.
Peresani, M., O. De Curtis, R. Duches *et al.*, 2008. 'Grotta del Clusantin, un Sito Inusuale nel Sistema Insediativo Epigravettiano delle Alpi Italiane' in Mussi 2008, 67–79.
Pérez, M., 1980. 'La Fauna de Vertebrados' in B. Martí, V. Pascual, M. D. Gallart *et al.* (eds), *Cova de l'Or (Beniarrés, Alicante).* Vol. 2. Valencia: Servicio de Investigacion Prehistorica. 193–255.
Perlès, C., 1987. *Les Industries Lithiques Taillées de Franchthi (Argolide, Grèce).* Vol. I. *Présentation Générale et Industries Paléolithiques.* Bloomington and Indianapolis: Indiana UP.
— 1992. 'Systems of Exchange and Organization of Production in Neolithic Greece.' *JMA* 5: 115–64.
— 1999. 'Long-term Perspectives on the Occupation of the Franchthi Cave: Continuity and Discontinuity' in Bailey *et al.* 1999, 311–18.
— 2000. 'Greece, 30,000–20,000 BP' in Roebroeks *et al.* 2000, 375–411.
— 2001. *The Early Neolithic of Greece: The First Farming Communities in Europe.* Cambridge and New York: Cambridge UP.
— 2003. 'The Mesolithic at Franchthi: An Overview of Data and Problems' in Galanidou and Perlès 2003, 79–88.
— and K. D. Vitelli, 1999. 'Craft Specialization in the Neolithic of Greece' in Halstead 1999a, 96–107.
Peroni, R., 2000. 'In Calabria Prima dei Greci: Cent-Anni de Saci à Broglio de Trebisacce.' *Archeo: Attualità del Passato* 16: 57–83.
Perrin, T., 2003. 'Mesolithic and Neolithic Cultures Co-existing in the Upper Rhône Valley.' *Antiquity* 77: 732–39.
— 2008. 'La Néolithisation de la Vallée du Rhône et de ses Marges' in Grimaldi *et al.* 2008, 121–30.
Perticarari, L., and A. Giuntani, 1986. *I Segreti di un Tombarolo.* Milan: Rusconi.
Peters, E., 2003. 'Quid Nobis cum Pelago? The New Thalassalogy and the Economic History of Europe.' *Journal of Interdisciplinary History* 34: 49–61.
Petit-Maire, N., and B. Vrielynck, 2005. *The Mediterranean Basin: The Last Two Climatic Extremes.* Châtenay-Malabry: ANDRA.
Pétrequin, P., 1993. 'North Wind, South Wind: Neolithic Technical Choices in the Jura Mountains, 3700–2400 BC' in Lemonnier 1993a, 36–76.
—, S. Cassen, M. Errera *et al.*, (eds) 2012. *Jade: Grandes Haches Alpines du Néolithique Européen. Ve au IVe millénaires av. J.-C.* Besançon: Franche-Comté UP.
Pfälzner, P., 2009. 'Residenz der Toten Herrscher – Die Köningsgruft' in al-Maqdissi *et al.* 2009, 200–3.
Phelps, W., Y. Lolos and Y. Vichos, (eds) 1999. *The Point Iria Wreck: Interconnections in the Mediterranean, ca. 1200 BC.* Athens: Hellenic Institute of Marine Archaeology.
Philip, G., 1989. *Metal Weapons of the Early and Middle Bronze Ages in Syria-Palestine.* Oxford: Archaeopress.
— 1999. 'Complexity and Diversity in the Southern Levant during the Third Millennium BC: The Evidence of Khirbet Kerak Ware.' *JMA* 12: 26–57.
— 2002. 'Contacts between the "Uruk" World and the Levant during the Fourth Millennium BC: Evidence and Interpretation' in J. N. Postgate (ed.), *Artefacts of Complexity: Tracking the Uruk in the Near East.* Oxford: Aris & Phillips. 207–35.
— 2003. 'The Early Bronze Age of the Southern Levant. A Landscape Approach.' *JMA* 16: 103–32.
— and T. Rehren, 1996. 'Fourth Millennium BC Silver from Tell esh-Shuna, Jordan: Archaeometallurgical Investigation and Some Thoughts on Ceramic Skeuomorphs.' *OJA* 15: 129–50.
Philippa-Touchais, A., G. Touchais, S. Voutsaki and J. C. Wright, (eds) 2010. *Mesohelladika. The Greek Mainland in the Middle Bronze Age.* Athens: École Française d'Athènes.
Phillips, J., 2005. 'The Last Pharaohs on Crete: Old Contexts and Old Readings Reconsidered' in Laffineur and Greco 2005, 455–61.
Phillips, R., S. Holdaway, W. Wendrich and R. Cappers, 2012. 'Mid-Holocene Occupation of Egypt and Global Climatic Change.' *QI* 251: 64–76.
Phoca-Cosmetatou, N., 2009. 'Specialisation and Diversification: A Tale of Two Subsistence Strategies from Late Glacial Italy.' *Before Farming* 2009/3: 1–29. (Online journal.)
— (ed.) 2011a. *The First Mediterranean Islanders: Initial Occupation and Survival Strategies.* Oxford: School of Archaeology.
— 2011b. 'Initial Occupation of the Cycladic Islands in the Neolithic: Strategies for Survival' in Phoca-Cosmetatou 2011a, 77–97.
Pierrat-Bonnefois, G., 2008. 'The Tôd Treasure' in Aruz *et al.* 2008, 65–67.
Pike, A. W. G., D. L. Hoffmann, M. Garcia-Diez *et al.*, 2012. 'U-series Dating of Paleolithic Art in 11 Caves in Spain.' *Science* 336: 1409–13.
Pilbeam, D., and N. Young, 2004. 'Hominoid Evolution: Synthesising Disparate Data.' *Comptes Rendus Palévol* 3: 305–21.
Piperno, D. R., E. Weiss, I. Hoist and D. Nadel, 2004. 'Processing of Wild Cereal Grains in the Upper Paleolithic Revealed by Starch Grain Analysis.' *Nature* 430: 670–73.
Pitard, W., 1999. 'The Alphabetic Ugaritic Tablets' in Watson and Wyatt 1999, 46–57.
Pitron, G. 2023. Published in English as *The Dark Cloud: How the Digital World is Costing the Earth.* London: Scribe.
Plato, *Phaedo.* In *The Last Days of Socrates.* Transl. H. Tredennick, rev. edn 2003. London and New York: Penguin. In the original: *Platonis Opera* Vol. 1, ed. E. A. Duke, W. F. Hicken, W. S. M. Nicoll *et al.*, 1995. Oxford and New York: Clarendon.
Plato, *Laws.* Transl. T. Saunders, rev. edn 2004. London and New York: Penguin. In the original: *Platonis Opera* Vol. 5, ed. J. Burnet, 1922. Oxford and New York: Clarendon.
Platon, N., 1971. *Zakros: The Discovery of a Lost Palace of Ancient Crete.* New York: Scribner.

Plucіennik, M., 2002. 'Art, Artefact, Metaphor' in Y. Hamilakis, M. Pluciennik and S. Tarlow (eds), *Thinking through the Body: Archaeologies of Corporeality*. New York and London: Kluwer Academic/Plenum.
— 2008. 'The Coastal Mesolithic of the European Mediterranean' in Bailey and Spikins 2008, 328–56.
Plutarch, *Alexander*. In the original and transl. by B. Perrin in *Plutarch Lives*. Vol. VII: *Demosthenes and Cicero. Alexander and Caesar*, 1919. Cambridge and London: Harvard UP.
Politis, T., 2001. 'Gold and Granulation: Exploring the Social Implications of a Prestige Technology in the Bronze Age Mediterranean' in Shortland 2001, 161–93.
Pollard, A. M., 2009. 'What a Long, Strange Trip It's Been: Lead Isotopes and Archaeology' in Shortland *et al.* 2009, 181–89.
Pollock, S., 1999. *Ancient Mesopotamia: The Eden that Never Was*. Cambridge: Cambridge UP.
Polybius, *The Histories*. 6 vols. In the original and transl. by W. Paton, rev. edn 2011. Cambridge and London: Harvard UP.
Popham, M. R., 1994. 'Precolonization: Early Greek Contact with the East' in Tsetskhladze and de Angelis 1994, 11–34.
— and I. S. Lemos, 1995. 'A Euboean Warrior Trader.' *OJA* 14: 151–57.
— and — 1996. *Lefkandi III: The Toumba Cemetery. The Excavations of 1981, 1984, 1986 and 1992–4*. Athens: British School at Athens.
Porada, E., 1973. 'Notes on the Sarcophagus of Ahiram.' *Journal of the Ancient Near Eastern Society* 5: 355–72.
Porat, N., and Y. Goren, 2002. 'Petrography of the Naqada IIIa Canaanite Pottery from Tomb U-j in Abydos' in van den Brink and Levy 2002, 252–70.
Porter, A., 2010. 'From Kin to Class – and Back Again! Changing Paradigms of the Early Polity' in Bolger and Maguire 2010, 72–78.
Postgate, J. N., and D. Thomas, (eds) 2007. *Excavations at Kilise Tepe 1994–1998: From Bronze Age to Byzantine in Western Cilicia*. Cambridge and Oakville: MIAR.
Powell, A., S. Shennan and M. G. Thomas, 2009. 'Late Pleistocene Demography and the Appearance of Modern Human Behavior.' *Science* 324: 1298–1301.
Preston, L., 2008. 'Late Minoan II to IIIB Crete' in Shelmerdine 2008, 310–26.
Price, T. D., (ed.) 2000. *Europe's First Farmers: An Introduction*. New York and Cambridge: Cambridge UP.
—, C. Knipper, G. Grupe *et al.*, 2004. 'Strontium Isotopes and Prehistoric Human Migration: The Bell Beaker Period in Central Europe.' *EJA* 7: 9–40.
Primas, M., 1996. *Velika Gruda*. Vol. I: *Hügelgräber des Frühen*. Bonn: Habelt.
Provenzano, N., 2008. 'Les Terramares: Entre Urope et Méditerranée' in Guilaine 2008, 144–58.
Pryor, J., 1988. *Geography, Technology and War: Studies in the Maritime History of the Mediterranean, 649–1571*. Cambridge and New York: Cambridge UP.
Pulak, C., 1998. 'The Uluburun Shipwreck: An Overview.' *International Journal of Nautical Archaeology* 27: 188–224.
— 1999. 'The Late Bronze Age Shipwreck at Uluburun' in Phelps *et al.* 1999, 209–38.
— 2005. 'Who Were the Mycenaeans Aboard the Uluburun Ship?' in Laffineur and Greco 2005, 295–310.
— 2008a. 'The Uluburun Shipwreck and Late Bronze Age Trade' in Aruz *et al.* 2008, 289–310.
— 2008b. '190a, b: Canaanite Jars' in Aruz *et al.* 2008: 317–20.
Pullen, D. J., 1992. 'Ox and Plow in the Early Bronze Age Aegean.' *AJA* 96: 45–54.
— (ed.) 2010. *Political Economies of the Aegean Bronze Age*. Oxford and Oakville: Oxbow.
Purcell, N., 1990. 'Mobility and the Polis' in Murray and Price 1990, 29–58.
— 2003. 'The Boundless Sea of Unlikeness? On Defining the Mediterranean.' *MHR* 18: 9–29.
— 2005a. 'The Ancient Mediterranean: The View from the Customs House' in W. V. Harris 2005a, 200–33.
— 2005b. '*Colonization* and Mediterranean History' in Hurst and Owen 2005, 115–39.
— 2005c. 'Statics and Dynamics: Ancient Mediterranean Urbanism' in Osborne and Cunliffe 2005, 249–72.
— 2006. 'Orientalizing: Five Historical Questions' in Riva and Vella 2006, 21–30.
Pusch, E. B., and A. Herold, 1999. 'Qantir/Pi-Ramesses' in K. A. Bard (ed.), *Encyclopedia of the Archaeology of Ancient Egypt*. London and New York: Routledge. 647–49.
Py, M., 1993. *Les Gaulois du Midi: De la Fin de l'Âge du Bronze à la Conquête Romaine*. Paris: Hachette.
— 2009. *Lattara: Lattes; Hérault; Comptoir Gaulois Méditerranéen entre Etrusques, Grecs et Romains*. Paris: Errance.
Pyke, G., and P. Yiouni, 1996. *Nea Nikomedeia: The Excavation of an Early Neolithic Village in Northern Greece, 1961–1964*. Vol. 1: *The Excavation and the Ceramic Assemblage*. London: British School at Athens.
Quinn, J., 2018. *In Search of the Phoenicians: Who Were the Ancient Phoenicians, and Did They Actually Exist?* Princeton: Princeton UP.
Raban, A., 1991. 'Minoan and Canaanite Harbours' in Laffineur and Basch 1991, 129–46.
— 1998. 'Near Eastern Harbors: Thirteenth–Seventh Centuries BCE' in Gitin *et al.* 1998, 428–38.
Racimo, F., M. Sikora, M. Vander Linden *et al.*, 2020. 'Beyond Broad Strokes: Sociocultural Insights from the Study of Ancient Genomes.' *Nature Reviews: Genetics* 21: 355–66.
Rackham, O., 2008. 'Holocene History of Mediterranean Island Landscapes' in Vogiatzakis *et al.* 2008, 36–60.
— and J. Moody, 1996. *Making of the Cretan Landscape*. Manchester and New York: Manchester UP.
Radić, D., 2009. 'The Beginnings of Trans-Adriatic Navigation: A View from Vela Spila Cave (Korcula Island)' in Forenbaher 2009a, 13–24.
Radivojević, M., T. Rehren, E. Pernicka *et al.*, 2010. 'On the Origins of Extractive Metallurgy: New Evidence from Europe.' *JAS* 37: 2775–87.
Radner, K., 2010. 'The Stele of Sargon II of Assyria at Kition: A Focus for an Emerging Cypriot Identity?' in R. Rollinger, B. Gufler, M. Lang and I. Madreiter (eds), *Interkulturalität in der Alten Welt: Vorderasien, Hellas, Ägypten und die Vielfältigen Ebenen des Kontakts*. Wiesbaden: Harrassowitz. 429–49.
— and E. Robson, (eds) 2011. *The Oxford Handbook of Cuneiform*. Oxford and New York: Oxford UP.
Rahmani, N., 2004. 'Technological and Cultural Change among the Last Hunter-gatherers of the Maghreb: The Capsian (10,000 B.P. to 6000 B.P.).' *JWP* 18: 57–105.
Rahmstorf, L., 2005. '*Terramare* and Faience: Mycenaean Influence in Northern Italy during the Late Bronze Age' in Laffineur and Greco 2005, 663–72.
— 2008. 'The Bell Beaker Phenomenon and the Interaction Spheres of the EBA East Mediterranean: Similarities and Differences' in A. Lehoërff (ed.), *Construire le Temps: Histoire et Méthods des Chronologies et Calendriers des Derniers Millénaires avant Notre Ère en Europe Occidentale*. Glux-en-Glenne: Centre Archéologique Européen. 149–70.
— 2010a. 'The Concept of Weighing during the Bronze Age in the Aegean, the Near East and Europe' in I. Morley and C. Renfrew (eds), *The Archaeology of Measurement: Comprehending Heaven, Earth and Time in Ancient Societies*. Cambridge and New York: Cambridge UP. 88–105.
— 2010b. 'Die Nutzung von Booten und Schiffen in der Bronzezeitlichen Ägäis und die Fernkontakte der Frühbronzezeit' in F. Bertemes and H. Meller (eds), *Der Griff nach den Sternen: Wie Europas Eliten zu Macht und Reichtum Kamen*. Halle: Landesamt für Denkmalpflege und Archäologie Sachsen-Anhalt. 675–97.
— 2011. 'Re-integrating "Diffusion": The Spread of Innovations among the Neolithic and Bronze Age Societies of Europe and the Near East' in T. C. Wilkinson *et al.* 2011, 100–19.
Rambeau, C., and S. Black, 2011. 'Palaeoenvironments of the Southern Levant 5,000 BP to Present: Linking the Geological and Archaeological Records' in Mithen and Black 2011, 94–104.
Ramis, D., 2010. 'From Colonisation to Habitation: Early Cultural Adaptation in the Balearic Bronze Age' in van Dommelen and Knapp 2010, 64–85.
—, J. A. Alcover, J. Coll and M. Trias, 2002. 'The Chronology of the First Settlement of the Balearic Islands.' *JMA* 15: 3–24.
Ramos, J., D. Bernal, S. Dominguez-Bella *et al.*, 2008. 'The Benzú Rockshelter: A Middle Palaeolithic Site on the North African Coast.' *QSR* 27: 2210–18.
Rasmussen, T., 2005. 'Urbanization in Etruria' in Osborne and Cunliffe 2005, 71–90.
Ratnagar, S., 2004. *Trading Encounters: From the Euphrates to the Indus in the Bronze Age*. 2nd edn. Delhi and Oxford: Oxford UP.
Raynal, J. P., F. Z. Sbihi Alaoui, L. Magoga *et al.*, 2001. 'The Earliest Occupation of North-Africa: The Moroccan.' *QI* 75: 65–75.
Redford, D. B., 1997. 'Textual Sources for the Hyksos Period' in Oren 1997a, 1–44.
Redmount, C. A., 1995. 'Pots and Peoples in the Egyptian Delta: Tel El-Maskhuta and the Hyksos.' *JMA* 8: 61–89.
Reese, D., 1975. 'Men, Saints, or Dragons?' *Expedition* 17: 26–30.
— (ed.) 1990. *Pleistocene and Holocene Fauna of Crete and Its First Settlers*. Madison: Prehistory.
— 2005. 'Whale Bones and Shell Purple-dye at Motya (Western Sicily, Italy).' *OJA* 24: 107–14.
— 2008. 'Organic Imports from Late Bronze Age Cyprus.' *Opuscula Atheniensia* 31–32: 191–209.
Rehren, T., E. Pusch and A. Herold, 2001. 'Problems and Possibilities in Workshop Reconstruction: Qantir and the Organisation of LBA Glass Working Sites' in Shortland 2001, 223–38.
Reich, D., 2018. *Who We Are and How We Got Here: Ancient DNA and the New Science of the Human Past*. Oxford: Oxford UP.
Reifarth, N., and G. Baccelli, 2009. 'Königsornat in Purpur und Gold – Die Textilfunde' in al-Maqdissi *et al.* 2009, 216–19.
Reimer, P. J., M. G. L. Baillie, E. Bard *et al.*, 2009. 'IntCal09 and Marine09 Radiocarbon Age Calibration Curves, 0–50,000 years cal BP.' *Radiocarbon* 51: 1111–50.
Reinberger, K. L., L. J. Reitsema, B. Kyle *et al.*, 2021. 'Isotopic Evidence for Geographic Heterogeneity in Ancient Greek Military Forces.' *PLOS ONE* 16: e0248803.
Reinholdt, C., 2008. *Der Frühbronzezeitliche Schmuckhortfund von Kap Kolonna: Ägina und die Ägäis im Goldzeitalter des 3. Jahrtausends v. Chr.* Vienna: Österreichischen Akademie der Wissenschaften.
Reitsema, L. J., A. Mittnik, B. Kyle *et al.*, 2022. 'The Diverse Genetic Origins of a Classical Period Greek Army.' *PNAS* 119: e2205272119.
Rempel, J., and N. Yoffee, 1999. 'The End of the Cycle? Assessing the Impact of Hellenization on Mesopotamian Civilization' in B. Böck, E. Cancik-Kirschbaum and T. Richter (eds), *Munuscula Mesopotamica: Festschrift für Johannes Renger*. Münster: Ugarit-Verlag. 385–98.
Renfrew, C., 1972. *The Emergence of Civilisation: The Cyclades and the Aegean in the Third Millennium BC*. London: Methuen.
— 1973. *Before Civilization: The Radiocarbon Revolution and Prehistoric Europe*. New York: Knopf. London: Jonathan Cape.
— 1985. *The Archaeology of Cult: The Sanctuary at Phylakopi*. London: Thames & Hudson.
— 1986. 'Varna and the Emergence of Wealth in Prehistoric Europe' in A. Appadurai (ed.), *The Social Life of Things: Commodities in Cultural Perspective*. Cambridge and New York: Cambridge UP.
— 1987. *Archaeology and Language: The Puzzle of Indo-European Origins*. London: J. Cape.
— 1994. 'Preface' in Mathers and Stoddart 1994, 5–12.
— 2007. *Prehistory: The Making of the Human Mind*. London: Weidenfeld & Nicolson. New York: Random House.
— and K. Boyle, (eds) 2000. *Archaeogenetics: DNA and the Population Prehistory of Europe*. Cambridge: MIAR.
—, C. Doumas, L. Marangou and G. Gavalas, (eds) 2007. *Keros, Dhaskalio Kavos: The Investigations of 1987–88*. Cambridge and Oakville: MIAR.
— and I. Morley, (eds) 2009. *Becoming Human: Innovation in Prehistoric Material and Spiritual Culture*. Cambridge and New York: Cambridge UP.
—, O. Philaniotou, N. Brodie *et al.*, 2007. 'Keros: Dhaskalio and Kavos, Early Cycladic Stronghold and Ritual Centre. Preliminary Report of the 2006 and 2007 Excavation Seasons.' *ABSA* 102: 103–36.
—, —, — *et al.*, (eds) 2018. *The Marble Finds from Kavos and the Archaeology of Ritual*. Cambridge: MIAR.
Rey da Silva, A., 2009. *Iconografía Náutica de la Península Ibérica en la Protohistoria*. Oxford: Archaeopress.
Richards, M. P., R. E. M. Hedges, I. Walton *et al.*, 2001. 'Neolithic Diet at the Brochtorff Circle, Malta.' *EJA* 4: 253–62.
Richerson, P. J., R. Boyd and R. L. Bettinger, 2001. 'Was Agriculture Impossible during the Pleistocene but Mandatory during the Holocene? A Climate Change Hypothesis.' *American Antiquity* 66: 387–411.
Richter, D., R. Grün, R. Joannes-Boyau *et al.*, 2017. 'The Age of the Hominin Fossils from Jebel Irhoud, Morocco, and the Origins of the Middle Stone Age.' *Nature* 546: 293–96.
Richter, T., 2009. 'Aus den Schreibstuben der Könige – Textfunde aus Qatna' in al-Maqdissi *et al.* 2009, 108–13.
Ridgway, D., 2000. 'The First Western Greeks Revisited' in Ridgway *et al.* 2000, 179–91.
— and F. R. S. Ridgway, 1992. 'Sardinia and History' in Tykot and Andrews 1992, 355–63.
—, —, M. Pearce *et al.*, (eds) 2000. *Ancient Italy in Its Mediterranean Setting: Studies in Honour of Ellen Macnamara*. London: Accordia Research Institute.
Risch, R., 2002. *Recursos Naturales, Medios de Producción y Explotación Social: Un Análisis Económico de la Industria Lítica de Fuente Álamo (Almería), 2250–1400 antes de Nuestra Era*. Mainz: Philipp von Zabern.
Ritner, R., 2009. 'Fragmentation and Re-integration in the Third Intermediate Period' in G. P. F. Broekman, R. J. Demarée and O. E. Kaper (eds), *The Libyan Period in Egypt: Historical and Cultural Studies into the 21st–24th Dynasties*. Leuven: Peeters. 327–40.
Riva, C., 2005. 'The Culture of Urbanization in the Mediterranean *c.* 800–600 BC' in Osborne and Cunliffe 2005, 203–32.

— and I. Grau Mira, 2022. 'Global Archaeology and Microhistorical Analysis: Connecting Scales in the 1st-Millennium B.C. Mediterranean.' *Archaeological Dialogues* 29: 1–14.
— 2006. 'The Orientalizing Period in Etruria: Sophisticated Communities' in Riva and Vella 2006, 110–34.
— 2007. 'The Archaeology of Picenum: The Last Decade' in G. Bradley *et al.* 2007, 79–113.
— 2010a. *The Urbanisation of Etruria: Funerary Practices and Social Change, 700–600 BC*. Cambridge and New York: Cambridge UP.
— 2010b. 'Trading Settlements and the Materiality of Wine Consumption in the North Tyrrhenian Sea Region' in van Dommelen and Knapp 2010, 210–32.
— and N. C. Vella, (eds) 2006. *Debating Orientalization: Multidisciplinary Approaches to Processes of Change in the Ancient Mediterranean*. London and Oakville: Equinox.
Rizio, A., 2005. 'Vivara: An "International" Port in the Bronze Age' in Laffineur and Greco 2005, 623–27.
Robb, J. E., 1993. 'A Social Prehistory of European Languages.' *Antiquity* 67: 747–60.
— 1994. 'Gender Contradictions, Moral Coalitions and Inequality in Prehistoric Italy.' *JEA* 2: 20–49.
— 1999. 'Great Persons and Big Men in the Italian Neolithic' in Tykot *et al.* 1999, 111–20.
— 2001. 'Island Identities: Ritual, Travel, and the Creation of Difference in Neolithic Malta.' *EJA* 4: 175–202.
— 2007. *The Early Mediterranean Village: Agency, Material Culture, and Social Change in Neolithic Italy*. Cambridge and New York: Cambridge UP.
— 2009. 'Towards a Critical Ötziography: Inventing Prehistoric Bodies' in H. Lambert and M. McDonald (eds), *Social Bodies*. New York and Oxford: Berghahn. 100–28.
— and R. H. Farr, 2005. 'Substances in Motion: Neolithic Mediterranean "Trade"' in Blake and Knapp 2005, 24–45.
—, S. A. Inskip, C. Cessford *et al.*, 2019. 'Osteobiography: The History of the Body as Real Bottom-line History.' *Bioarchaeology International* 3: 16–31.
— and P. Miracle, 2007. 'Beyond "Migration" versus "Acculturation": New Models for the Spread of Agriculture' in Whittle and Cummings 2007, 99–116.
— and D. Van Hove, 2003. 'Gardening, Foraging and Herding: Neolithic Land Use and Social Territories in Southern Italy.' *Antiquity* 77: 241–54.
Roberts, B. W., 2008. 'Creating Traditions and Shaping Technologies: Understanding the Emergence of Metallurgy in Western Europe *c.* 3500–2000 BC.' *WA* 40: 354–72.
—, C. P. Thornton and V. C. Pigott, 2009. 'Development of Metallurgy in Eurasia.' *Antiquity* 83: 1012–22.
Roberts, C. N., J. Woodbridge, A. Palmisano *et al.*, 2019. 'Mediterranean Landscape Change during the Holocene: Synthesis, Comparison and Regional Trends in Population, Land Cover and Climate.' *The Holocene* 29: 923–37.
Roberts, N., 1998. *The Holocene: An Environmental History*. 2nd edn. Oxford and New York: Blackwell.
— 2002. 'Did Prehistoric Landscape Management Retard the Post-Glacial Spread of Woodland in Southwest Asia?' *Antiquity* 76: 1002–10.
—, D. Brayshaw, C. Kuzucuoğlu *et al.*, 2011. 'The Mid-Holocene Climatic Transition in the Mediterranean: Causes and Consequences.' *The Holocene* 21: 3–13.
— and J. Reed, 2009. 'River Systems and Environmental Change' in Woodward 2009a, 255–86.
— and A. Rosen, 2009. 'Diversity and Complexity in Early Farming Communities of Southwest Asia: New Insights into the Economic and Environmental Basis of Neolithic Catalhoyuk.' *CA* 50: 393–402.
—, T. Stevenson, B. Davis *et al.*, 2004. 'Holocene Climate, Environment and Cultural Change in the Circum-Mediterranean Region' in Battarbee *et al.* 2004, 343–62.
Roberts, O. T. P., 1987. 'Wind-power and the Boats from the Cyclades.' *International Journal of Nautical Archaeology* 16: 309–11.
— 1991. 'The Development of the Brail into a Viable Sail Control for Aegean Boats of the Bronze Age' in Laffineur and Basch 1991, 55–60.
Robinson, E. W., 1997. *The First Democracies: Early Popular Government outside Athens*. Stuttgart: F. Steiner.
Robinson, S. A., S. Black, B. W. Sellwood and P. J. Valdes, 2006. 'A Review of Palaeoclimates and Palaeoenvironments in the Levant and Eastern Mediterranean from 25,000 to 5000 years BP: Setting the Environmental Background for the Evolution of Human Civilisation.' *QSR* 25: 1517–41.
Roche, J., 1963. *L'Epipaléolithique Marocain*. Lisbon: Fondation Calouste Gulbenkian.
Rodrigue, A., 2012. 'Nador Klalcha (Gharb): Nouvelle Station du Campaniforme au Maroc.' *Bulletin du Musée d'Anthropologie Préhistorique de Monaco* 52: 69–79.
Rodríguez Somolinos, H., 1996. 'The Commercial Transaction of the Pech Maho Lead: A New Interpretation.' *Zeitschrift für Papyrologie und Epigraphik* 111: 74–78.
Rodseth L., R. W. Wrangham and A. M. Harrigan, 1991. 'The Human Community as a Primate Society.' *CA* 32: 221–54.
Roebroeks, W., 2006. 'The Human Colonisation of Europe: Where Are We?' *JQS* 21: 425–35.
—, M. Mussi and J. Svoboda, (eds) 2000. *Hunters of the Golden Age: The Mid-Upper Palaeolithic of Eurasia, 30,000–20,000 BP*. Leiden: Leiden UP.
Rohling, E., R. Abu-Zied, J. Casford *et al.*, 2009. 'The Marine Environment: Present and Past' in Woodward 2009a, 33–67.
Rojo Guerra, M., R. Garrido Pena and J. A. Bellver Garrido, 2010. *Zafrín: Un Asentamiento del Neolítico Antiguo en las Islas Chafarinas (Norte de África, España)*. Valladolid: Universidad de Valladolid.
— and M. Kunst, 1999. 'Zur Neolithisierung des Inneren der Iberischen Halbinsen: Erste Ergebnisse des Interdisziplinären, Spanisch–Deutschen Forschungsprojekts zur Entwicklung einer Prähistorischen Siedlungskammer in der Umgebung von Ambrona (Soria, Spanien).' *Madrider Mitteilungen* 40: 1–52.
Rollefson, G., 1996. 'The Neolithic Devolution: Ecological Impact and Cultural Compensation at 'Ain Ghazal, Jordan' in Joe D. Seger (ed.), *Retrieving the Past: Essays on Archaeological Research and Methodology in Honor of Gus W. van Beek*. Winona Lake: Eisenbrauns. 219–30.
— 2000. 'Ritual and Social Structure at Neolithic Ain Ghazal' in Kuijt 2000a, 165–90.
Röllig, W., 1976. 'Der Altmesopotamische Markt.' *Die Welt des Orients* 8: 286–95.
Rönnby, J., (ed.) 2003. *By the Water: Archaeological Perspectives on Human Strategies around the Baltic Sea*. Flemingsberg: Södertörns Högskola.
Roosevelt, C. H., 2009. *The Archaeology of Lydia: From Gyges to Alexander*. Cambridge and New York: Cambridge UP.
— and C. Luke, 2017. 'The Story of a Forgotten Kingdom? Survey Archaeology and the Historical Geography of Central Western Anatolia in the Second Millennium BC.' *EJA* 20: 120–47.
Rosas, A., and M. Bastir, 2020. 'An Assessment of the Late Middle Pleistocene Occipital from Apidima 1 Skull (Greece).' *L'Anthropologie* 124: 102745.
Rosen, A., 1986. *Cities of Clay: The Geoarcheology of Tells*. Chicago and London: Chicago UP.
— 2007. *Civilizing Climate: Social Responses to Climate Change in the Ancient Near East*. Lanham and Plymouth: AltaMira.
— and S. Weiner, 1994. 'Identifying Ancient Irrigation: A New Method Using Opaline Phytoliths from Emmer Wheat.' *JAS* 21: 125–32.
Rosen, S., 2011. *An Investigation into Early Desert Pastoralism: Excavations at the Camel Site, Negev*. Los Angeles: Cotsen Institute of Archaeology.
Rosenberg, D., and A. Golani, 2012. 'Groundstone Tools of a Copper-smiths' Community: Understanding Stone-related Aspects of the Early Bronze Age Site of Asqelon Barnea.' *JMA* 25: 25–57.
Ross, J. C., 1999. *The Golden Ruler: Precious Metals and Political Development in the Third Millennium B.C. Near East*. Ann Arbor: UMI Dissertation Services. (PhD thesis.)
Rossel, S., F. Marshall, J. Peters *et al.*, 2008. 'Domestication of the Donkey: Timing, Processes, and Indicators.' *PNAS* 105: 3715–20.
Roth, A. M., 1991. *Egyptian Phyles in the Old Kingdom: The Evolution of a System of Social Organization*. Chicago: Oriental Institute.
Rothenberg, B., 1972. *Timna: Valley of the Biblical Copper Mines*. London: Thames & Hudson.
Rothman, M. S., (ed.) 2001. *Uruk Mesopotamia and Its Neighbors: Cross-cultural Interactions in the Era of State Formation*. Santa Fe and Oxford: School of American Research.
Rottoli, M., and A. Pessina, 2007. 'Neolithic Agriculture in Italy: An Update of Archaeobotanical Data with Particular Emphasis on Northern Settlements' in Colledge and Conolly 2007, 141–54.
Roubet, C., 1979. *Économie Pastorale Préagricole: En Algérie Orientale. Le Néolithique de Tradition Capsienne, Exemple: L'Aurès*. Paris: CNRS.
Rovira, S., and I. Montero, 2003. 'Natural Tin–Bronze Alloy in Iberian Peninsula Metallurgy: Potentiality and Reality' in Giumlia-Mair and Lo Schiavo 2003, 15–22.
Rowan, Y., and J. Golden, 2009. 'The Chalcolithic Period of the Southern Levant: A Synthetic Review.' *JWP* 22: 1–92.
Rowland, R. J., 2001. *The Periphery in the Center: Sardinia in the Ancient and Medieval Worlds*. Oxford: Archaeopress.
Rowlands, M., 1984. 'Conceptualizing the European Bronze and Early Iron Age' in J. Bintliff (ed.), *European Social Evolution: Archaeological Perspectives*. Bradford: Bradford UP. 147–56.
— 2010. 'Concluding Thoughts' in van Dommelen and Knapp 2010, 233–47.
—, M. Larsen and K. Kristiansen, (eds) 1987. *Centre and Periphery in the Ancient World*. Cambridge and New York: Cambridge UP.
Rowley-Conwy, P., 2000. 'Milking Caprines, Hunting Pigs: The Neolithic Economy of Arene Candide in Its West Mediterranean Context' in P. Rowley-Conwy (ed.), *Animal Bones, Human Societies*. Oxford and Oakville: Oxbow. 124–32.
— 2011. 'Westward Ho! The Spread of Agriculture from Central Europe to the Atlantic.' *CA* 52 (S4): S431–S451.
—, L. Gourichon, D. Helmer and J.-D. Vigne, 2013. 'Early Domestic Animals in Italy, Istria, the Tyrrhenian Islands and Southern France' in S. Colledge, J. Conolly, K. Dobney and K. Manning (eds), *The Origins and Spread of Domestic Animals in Southwest Asia and Europe*. Walnut Creek: Left Coast. London: Institute of Archaeology. 161–94.
Ruffell, A., 1997. 'Geological Evolution of the Mediterranean Basin' in King *et al.* 1997, 12–29.
Ruiz, A. and M. Molinos, 2013. 'Oppida, Lineages, and Heroes in the Society of Princes: The Iberians of the Upper Guadalquivir' in Cruz Berrocal *et al.* 2013, 357–77.
Ruiz-Taboada, A., and I. Montero-Ruiz, 1999. 'The Oldest Metallurgy in Western Europe.' *Antiquity* 73: 897–903.
Runciman, W. G., 1990. 'Doomed to Extinction: The *Polis* as an Evolutionary Dead-end' in Murray and Price 1990, 347–67.
Runnels, C., 2001. 'The Stone Age of Greece from the Palaeolithic to the Advent of the Neolithic' in T. Cullen 2001, 225–58.
— 2009. 'Mesolithic Sites and Surveys in Greece: A Case Study from the Southern Argolid.' *JMA* 22: 57–73.
—, M. Korkuti, M. L. Galaty *et al.*, 2004. 'The Palaeolithic and Mesolithic of Albania: Survey and Excavation at the Site of Kryegjata B (Fier District).' *JMA* 17: 3–29.
—, C. Payne, N. V. Rifkind *et al.*, 2009. 'Warfare in Neolithic Thessaly: A Case Study.' *Hesperia* 78: 165–94.
— and T. van Andel, 1988. 'Trade and the Origins of Agriculture in the Eastern Mediterranean.' *JMA* 1: 83–109.
Russell, A., 2010. 'Foreign Materials, Islander Mobility and Elite Identity in Late Bronze Age Sardinia' in van Dommelen and Knapp 2010, 106–26.
Rutter, J. B., 1983. 'Fine Gray-burnished Pottery of the EH III Period: The Ancestry of Gray Minyan.' *Hesperia* 52: 327–55.
— 1992. 'Cultural Novelties in the Post-palatial Aegean World: Indices of Vitality or Decline?' in W. A. Ward and Joukowsky 1992, 61–78.
— 1999. 'Cretan External Relations during LM IIIA2-B (ca. 1370–1200 B.C.): A View from the Mesara' in Phelps *et al.* 1999, 139–86.
— 2001. 'The Prepalatial Bronze Age of the Southern and Central Greek Mainland' in T. Cullen 2001, 19–76.
— 2004. 'Off-island Ceramic Imports to Kommos, Crete: New Discoveries and Identifications; Old Problems Unresolved.' *Bulletin of the Institute of Classical Studies* 47: 189–90.
Ryan, W., and W. Pitman, 1998. *Noah's Flood: The New Scientific Discoveries about the Event that Changed History*. New York: Simon & Schuster. 2000, London: Touchstone.
Safadi, C., and F. Sturt, 2019. 'The Warped Sea of Sailing: Maritime Topographies of Space and Time for the Bronze Age Eastern Mediterranean.' *JAS* 103: 1–15.
Saghieh, M., 1983. *Byblos in the Third Millennium BC: A Reconstruction of the Stratigraphy and a Study of the Cultural Connections*. Warminster: Aris & Phillips.
Sagona, A., and P. Zimansky, 2009. *Ancient Turkey*. London and New York: Routledge.
Sahlins, M., 1955. 'Esoteric Efflorescence in Easter Island.' *American Anthropologist* 57: 1045–52.
— 1974. *Stone Age Economics*. London: Tavistock.
Sahnouni, M., 1998. *The Lower Palaeolithic of the Maghreb: Excavations and Analyses at Ain Hanech, Algeria*. Oxford: Archaeopress.
—, D. Hadjouis, J. van der Made *et al.*, 2004. 'On the Earliest Human Occupation in North Africa: A Response to Geraads *et al.*' *JHE* 46: 763–75.
—, J. M. Parés, M. Duval *et al.*, 2018. '1.9-million- and 2.4-million-year-old Artifacts and Stone Tool-cutmarked Bones from Ain Boucherit, Algeria.' *Science* 362: 1297–301.
Şahoğlu, V., 2005. 'The Anatolian Trade Network and the Izmir Region during the Early Bronze Age.' *OJA* 24: 339–61.
—, J. H. Sterba, T. Katz *et al.*, 2022. 'Volcanic Ash, Victims, and Tsunami Debris from the Late Bronze Age Thera Eruption Discovered at Çeşme-Bağlararası (Turkey).' *PNAS* 119: e2114213118.
Sakellarakis, Y., 1990. 'The Fashioning of Ostrich-egg Rhyta in the Creto-Mycenaean Aegean' in Hardy *et al.* 1990, 285–308.
— 1996. 'Minoan Religious Influence in the Aegean: The Case of Kythera.' *ABSA* 91: 81–99.

Sallares, R., 2007. 'Ecology' in Scheidel *et al.* 2007, 15–37.
Sampson, A., 1985. *Manika: Mia Protoelladiki Poli sti Halkida I.* Athens: Society for Euboean Studies.
— (ed.) 2008. *The Cave of the Cyclops: Mesolithic and Neolithic Networks in the Northern Aegean, Greece.* Philadelphia: INSTAP Academic.
—, J. K. Kozlowski, M. Kaszanowska and B. Giannouli, 2002. 'The Mesolithic Settlement at Maroulas, Kythnos.' *Mediterranean Archaeology and Archaeometry* 2: 45–67.
Sams, G., 1995. 'Midas of Gordion and the Anatolian Kingdom of Phrygia' in Sasson 1995, 1147–59.
Sánchez, M. C., 2000. 'Bajondillo Cave (Torremolinos, Malaga, Andalucia) and the Middle-Upper Palaeolithic Transition in Southern Spain' in Stringer *et al.* 2000, 123–32.
Sandars, N. K., 1978. *The Sea Peoples: Warriors of the Ancient Mediterranean 1250–1150 BC.* London: Thames & Hudson.
Sanjuán, L. G., 1999. 'Expressions of Inequality: Settlement Patterns, Economy and Social Organization in the Southwest Iberian Bronze Age (*c.*1700–1100 BC).' *Antiquity* 73: 337–51.
Sanmartí, J., 2009a. 'Colonial Activities and Iberian Origins.' *JMA* 21: 277–80.
— 2009b. 'Colonial Relations and Social Change in Iberia (Seventh to Third Centuries BC) in Dietler and López-Ruiz 2009, 49–88.
—, N. Kallala, M. C. Belarte *et al.*, 2012. 'Filling Gaps in the Protohistory of the Eastern Maghreb: The Althiburos Archaeological Project (el Kef, Tunisia).' *Journal of African Archaeology* 10: 21–44.
Sasson, J. M., (ed.) 1995. *Civilizations of the Ancient Near East.* Vol. II. New York: Scribner. London: Simon & Schuster.
— 2008. 'Texts, Trade, and Travelers' in Aruz *et al.* 2008, 95–101.
Scarre, C., and F. Healy, (eds) 1993. *Trade and Exchange in Prehistoric Europe.* Oxford: Oxbow.
Schaeffer, C. F. A., 1939. *Ugaritica I: Études Relatives aux Decouvertes de Ras Shamra.* Paris: P. Guethner.
Scheidel, W., 2007. 'Demography' in Scheidel *et al.* 2007, 38–86.
—, I. Morris and R. Saller, (eds) 2007. *The Cambridge Economic History of the Greco-Roman World.* Cambridge and New York: Cambridge UP.
Schick, T., (ed.) 1998. *The Cave of the Warrior: A Fourth Millennium Burial in the Judean Desert.* Jerusalem: Israel Antiquities Authority.
Schild, R., and F. Wendorf, 2010. 'Late Palaeolithic Hunter-gatherers in the Nile Valley of Nubia and Upper Egypt' in Garcea 2010a, 89–125.
Schloen, J. D., 2001. *The House of the Father as Fact and Symbol: Patrimonialism in Ugarit and the Ancient Near East.* Winona Lake: Eisenbrauns.
Schmandt-Besserat, D., 1992. *Before Writing.* Austin: Texas UP.
Schmidt, B. B., (ed.) 2007. *The Quest for the Historical Israel: Debating Archaeology and the History of Early Israel.* Atlanta: Society of Biblical Literature.
Schmidt, K., 2006. *Sie Bauten die Ersten Tempel: Das Rätselhafte Heiligtum der Steinzeitjäger. Die Archäologische Entdeckung am Göbekli Tepe.* Munich: C. H. Beck.
Schnapp, A., 1996. *The Discovery of the Past: The Origins of Archaeology.* English translation. London: British Museum. 1997, New York: Harry N. Abrams.
Schneider, H., 2007. 'Technology' in Scheidel *et al.* 2007, 144–71.
Schneider, J., 2011. 'Anticipating the Silk Road: Some Thoughts on the Wool–Murex Connection in Tyre' in T. C. Wilkinson *et al.* 2011, 295–302.
Schniedewind, W. M., 1996. 'Tel Dan Stela: New Light on Aramaic and Jehu's Revolt.' *BASOR* 302: 75–90.
Schoep, I., 1999. 'The Origins of Writing and Administration on Crete.' *OJA* 18: 265–76.
—, P. Tomkins and J. Driessen, (eds) 2012. *Back to the Beginning: Reassessing Social and Political Complexity on Crete during the Early and Middle Bronze Age.* Oxford and Oakville: Oxbow.
Schofield, L., and R. B. Parkinson, 1994. 'Of Helmets and Heretics: A Possible Egyptian Representation of Mycenaean Warriors on a Papyrus from El-Amarna.' *ABSA* 89: 157–70.
Schoop, U., 2011. 'The Chalcolithic on the Plateau' in Steadman and McMahon 2011, 150–73.
Schubart, H., 2003. *Toscanos y Alarcón: El Asentamiento Fenicio en la Desembocadura del Río de Vélez.* Barcelona: Bellaterra.
Schuhmacher, T. X., 2004. 'Frühbronzezeitliche Kontakte im Westlichen und Zentralen Mittelmeerraum und die Rolle der Iberischen Halbinsel.' *Madrider Mitteilungen* 45: 147–80.
—, J. L. Cardoso and A. Banerjee, 2009. 'Sourcing African Ivory in Chalcolithic Portugal.' *Antiquity* 83: 983–97.
Schule, W., 1993. 'Mammals, Vegetation and the Initial Human Settlement of the Mediterranean Islands: A Palaeoecological Approach.' *JB* 20: 399–411.
Schulz, E., A. Adamou, A. Abichou *et al.*, 2009. 'The Desert in the Sahara: Transitions and Boundaries' in R. Baumhauer and J. Runge (eds), *Holocene Palaeoenvironmental History of the Central Sahara.* Boca Raton: CRC. 64–89.
Schwartz, G. M., H. H. Curvers and B. Stuart, 2000. 'A 3rd-millennium BC Élite Tomb from Tell Umm el-Marra, Syria.' *Antiquity* 74: 771–72.
— and J. J. Nichols, (eds) 2006. *After Collapse: The Regeneration of Complex Societies.* Tucson: Arizona UP.
Scott, A., R. C. Power, V. Altmann-Wendling *et al.*, 2021. 'Exotic Foods Reveal Contact Between South Asia and the Near East during the Second Millennium BCE.' *PNAS* 118: e2014956117.
Scott, G. R., and L. Gibert, 2009. 'The Oldest Hand-axes in Europe.' *Nature* 461: 82–85.
Scott, L., and J. A. Lee-Thorp, 2004. 'Holocene Climatic Trends and Rhythms in Southern Africa' in Battarbee *et al.* 2004, 69–92.
Searight, S., 2004. *The Prehistoric Rock Art of Morocco: A Study of Its Extension, Environment and Meaning.* Oxford: Archaeopress.
Seaton, P., 2008. *Chalcolithic Cult and Risk Management at Teleilat Ghassul: The Area E Sanctuary.* Oxford: Archaeopress.
Seeher, J., 2001. 'Die Zerstörung der Stadt Hattuša' in G. Wilhelm (ed.), *Akten des IV. Internationalen Kongresses für Hethitologie.* Wiesbaden: Harrassowitz. 623–34.
Seidlmayer, S., 2000. 'The First Intermediate Period (*c.* 2160–2055 BC)' in I. Shaw 2000a, 118–47.
Serpico, M., 2004. 'Natural Product Technology in New Kingdom Egypt' in J. Bourriau and Phillips 2004, 96–120.
Serrano, J. G., A. C. Ordóñez, J. Santana *et al.*, 2023. 'The Genomic History of the Indigenous People of the Canary Islands.' *Nature Communications* 14: 4641.
Serra Ridgway, F. R., 1990. 'Etruscans, Greeks, Carthaginians: The Sanctuary at Pyrgi' in J.-P. Descoeudres (ed.), *Greek Colonists and Native Populations.* Oxford and New York: Oxford UP. 511–30.
Sevketog˘lu, M., 2002. 'Akanthou-Arkosyko (Tatlısu-Çiftlikdüzü): The Anatolian Connections in the 9th Millennium BC' in Waldren and Ensenyat 2002, 98–106.
Shackleton, J. C., 1998. *Marine Molluscan Remains from Franchthi Cave.* Bloomington: Indiana UP.
—, T. H. van Andel and C. N. Runnels, 1984. 'Coastal Palaeogeography of the Central and Western Mediterranean *during* the Last 125,000 Years and Its *Archaeological* Implications.' *Journal of Field Archaeology* 11: 307–14.
Shapland, A., 2010. 'Wild Nature: Human-Animal Relations on Neopalatial Crete' in *CAJ* 20: 109–27.
—, 2022. *Human-Animal Relations in Bronze Age Crete: A History through Objects.* Cambridge and New York: Cambridge UP.
Sharon, G., 2011. 'Flakes Crossing the Straits? Entame Flakes and Northern Africa-Iberia Contact during the Acheulean.' *AAR* 28: 125–40.
Sharvit, J., E. Galili, B. Rosen and E. C. M. van den Brink, 2002. 'Predynastic Maritime Traffic along the Carmel Coast of Israel: A Submerged Find from North Atlit Bay' in van den Brink and Levy 2002, 159–66.
Shaw, B., 2001. 'Challenging Braudel: A New Vision of the Mediterranean.' *Journal of Roman Archaeology* 14: 419–53.
— 2003. 'A Peculiar Island: Maghrib and Mediterranean.' *MHR* 18: 93–125.
— 2006. *At the Edge of the Corrupting Sea: A Lecture Delivered at New College, Oxford, on 9th May 2005.* Oxford: University of Oxford.
Shaw, I., (ed.) 2000a. *The Oxford History of Ancient Egypt.* Oxford and New York: Oxford UP.
— 2000b. 'Egypt and the outside World' in I. Shaw 2000a, 314–29.
— 2001. 'Egyptians, Hyksos and Military Hardware: Causes, Effects or Catalysts?' in Shortland 2001, 59–71.
Shaw, J., 1989. 'Phoenicians in Southern Crete.' *AJA* 93: 165–83.
—1990. 'Bronze Age Aegean Harboursides' in Hardy *et al.* 1990, 420–36.
— 2006. *Kommos: A Minoan Harbor Town and Greek Sanctuary in Southern Crete.* Athens: American School of Classical Studies.
Shea, J. J., 2003. 'The Middle Paleolithic of the East Mediterranean Levant.' *JWP* 17: 313–94.
— 2007. 'The Boulevard of Broken Dreams: Evolutionary Discontinuity in the Late Pleistocene Levant' in Mellars *et al.* 2007, 219–34.
— 2008. 'Transitions or Turnovers? Climatically Forced Extinctions of *Homo sapiens* and Neanderthals in the East Mediterranean Levant.' *QSR* 27: 2253–70.
— 2010. 'Neanderthals and Early *Homo sapiens* in the Levant' in Garcea 2010a, 126–43.
Shelmerdine, C. W., 2001. 'Review of Aegean Prehistory VI: The Palatial Bronze Age of the Central and Southern Greek Mainland' in T. Cullen 2001, 329–81.
— (ed.) 2008. *The Cambridge Companion to the Aegean Bronze Age.* Cambridge and New York: Cambridge UP.
Shennan, S., 1993. '*Commodities*, Transactions and Growth in the Central-European Early Bronze Age.' *JEA 1: 59–72.*
— (ed.) 1995. *Bronze Age Copper Producers of the Eastern Alps: Excavations at St. Veit-Klinglberg.* Bonn: Habelt.
— 1999. 'Cost, Benefit and Value in the Organization of Early European Copper Production.' *Antiquity* 73: 352–63.
— 2002. *Genes, Memes and Human History: Darwinian Archaeology and Cultural Evolution.* London and New York: Thames & Hudson.
— 2007. 'The Spread of Farming into Central Europe and Its Consequences: Evolutionary Models' in T. Kohler and S. van der Leeuw (eds), *The Model-based Archaeology of Socionatural Systems.* Santa Fe: School for Advanced Research.
— and K. Edinborough, 2007. 'Prehistoric Population History: From the Late Glacial to the Late Neolithic in Central and Northern Europe.' *JAS* 34: 1339–45.
Sheppard, P., 1990. 'Soldiers and Bureaucrats: The Early History of Prehistoric Archaeology in the Maghreb' in Peter Robertshaw (ed.), *A History of African Archaeology.* London: J. Currey. New York: Heinemann.
Sherratt, A. S., 1981. 'Plough and Pastoralism: Aspects of the Secondary Products Revolution' in Hodder *et al.* 1981, 261–305.
— 1987. '*Warriors and Traders*: Bronze Age Chiefdoms in Central Europe' in B. Cunliffe (ed.), *Origins: The Roots of European Civilisation.* London: BBC. 1988, Chicago: Dorsey.
— 1990. 'The Genesis of Megaliths: Monumentality, Ethnicity and Social Complexity in Neolithic North-west Europe.' *WA* 22: 147–67.
— 1993. 'What Would a Bronze-Age World System Look Like? Relations between Temperate Europe and the Mediterranean in Later Prehistory.' *JEA* 1: 1–58.
— 1994. 'Core, Periphery and Margin: Perspectives on the Bronze Age' in Mathers and Stoddart 1994, 335–45.
— 1995a. 'Reviving the Grand Narrative: Archaeology and Long-term Change: The Second David L. Clarke Memorial Lecture.' *JEA* 3: 1–32.
— 1995b. 'Alcohol and Its Alternatives: Symbol and Substance in Pre-industrial Cultures' in J. Goodman, P. E. Lovejoy and A. Sherratt (eds), *Consuming Habits: Global and Historical Perspectives on How Cultures Define Drugs.* London and New York: Routledge. 11–46.
— 1996. 'Plate Tectonics and Imaginary Prehistories: Structure and Contingency in Agricultural Origins' in D. R. Harris 1996, 130–40.
— 1997. 'Climatic Cycles and Behavioural Revolutions.' *Antiquity* 71: 271–87.
— 1999. 'Cash-crops before Cash: Organic Consumables and Trade' in C. Gosden and J. Hather (eds), *The Prehistory of Food: Appetites for Change.* London and New York: Routledge. 13–34.
— 2004. 'Fractal Farmers: Patterns of Neolithic Origin and Dispersal' in J. Cherry, C. Scarre and S. Shennan (eds), *Explaining Social Change: Studies in Honour of Colin Renfrew.* Cambridge: MIAR. 53–64.
— 2006. 'Portages: A Simple but Powerful Idea in Understanding Human History' in C. Westerdahl (ed.), *The Significance of Portages.* Oxford: Archaeopress. 1–13.
— 2007. 'Diverse Origins: Regional Contributions to the Genesis of Farming' in Colledge and Conolly 2007, 1–20.
— and S. Sherratt, 1988. 'The Archaeology of Indo-European: An Alternative View.' *Antiquity* 62: 584–95.
— and — 1991. 'From Luxuries to Commodities: The Nature of Mediterranean Bronze Age Trading Systems' in N. H. Gale 1991a, 351–86.
— and — 1998. 'Small Worlds: Interaction and Identity in the Ancient Mediterranean' in Cline and Harris-Cline 1998, 329–43.
— and — 2001. 'Technological Change in the East Mediterranean Bronze Age: Capital, Resources and Marketing' in Shortland 2001, 15–38.
— and — 2008. 'The Neolithic of Crete, as Seen from Outside' in Isaakidou and Tomkins 2008, 291–302.
Sherratt, S., 1990. '"Reading the Texts": Archaeology and the Homeric Question.' *Antiquity* 64: 807–24.
— 1994. 'Commerce, Iron and Ideology: Metallurgical Innovation in 12th–11th Century Cyprus' in Karageorghis 1994, 59–106.
— 1998. '"Sea Peoples" and the Economic Structure of the Late Second Millennium in the Eastern Mediterranean' in Gitin *et al.* 1998, 292–313.
— 1999. 'E Pur si Muove: Pots, Markets and Values in the Second Millennium Mediterranean' in Crielaard *et al.* 1999, 163–211.

— 2000. 'Circulation of Metals and the End of the Bronze Age in the Eastern Mediterranean' in Pare 2000a, 82–98.
— 2001. 'Potemkin Palaces and Route-based Economies' in Voutsaki and Killen 2001, 214–28.
— 2003a. 'The Mediterranean Economy: "Globalization" at the End of the Second Millennium BCE' in Dever and Gitin 2003, 37–62.
— 2003b. 'Visible Writing: Questions of Script and Identity in Early Iron Age Greece and Cyprus.' *OJA* 22: 225–42.
— 2005. '"Ethnicities", "Ethnonyms" and Archaeological Labels: Whose Ideologies and Whose Identities?' in J. Clarke 2005, 25–38.
— 2007. 'The Archaeology of Metal Use in the Early Bronze Age Aegean: A Review' in Day and Doonan 2007, 245–63.
— 2010a. 'The Aegean and the Wider World: Some Thoughts on a World-systems Perspective' in W. A. Parkinson and Galaty 2010, 81–106.
— 2010b. 'Greeks and Phoenicians: Perceptions of Trade and Traders in the Early First Millennium BC' in A. A. Bauer and A. S. Agbe-Davies (eds), *Social Archaeologies of Trade and Exchange: Exploring Relationships among People, Places, and Things*. Walnut Creek: Left Coast. 119–42.
— and A. Sherratt, 1993. 'The Growth of the Mediterranean Economy in the Early First Millennium BC.' *WA* 24: 361–78.
Shipman, P., 2009. 'The Woof at the Door.' *American Scientist* 97: 286–89.
Shortland, A. J., (ed.) 2001. *The Social Context of Technological Change: Egypt and the Near East, 1650–1550 BC*. Oxford: Oxbow.
— 2012. *Lapis Lazuli from the Kiln: Glass and Glassmaking in the Late Bronze Age*. Leuven: Leuven UP.
—, I. C. Freestone and T. Rehren, (eds) 2009. *From Mine to Microscope: Advances in the Study of Ancient Technology*. Oxford and Oakville: Oxbow.
—, C. A. Hope and M. S. Tite, 2006. 'Cobalt Blue Painted Pottery from 18th Dynasty Egypt.' *Geological Society, London, Special Publications* 257: 91–99.
Shrine, T., W. Böhme, H. Nickel *et al.*, 2001. 'Rediscovery of Relict Populations of the Nile Crocodile *Crocodylus niloticus* in South-eastern Mauretania, with Observations on Their Natural History.' *Oryx* 35: 260–62.
Shryock, A., and D. L. Smail, (eds) 2011. *Deep History: The Architecture of Past and Present*. Berkeley and London: California UP.
Siedentopf, H. B., 1991. *Alt-Ägina*. Vol. IV.2: *Mattbemalte Keramik der Mittleren Bronzezeit*. Mainz: Philipp von Zabern.
Silberman, N. A., 1998. 'The Sea Peoples, the Victorians, and Us' in Gitin *et al.* 1998, 268–75.
Sillar, B., and M. S. Tite, 2000. 'The Challenge of "Technological Choices" for Materials Science Approaches in Archaeology.' *Archaeometry* 42: 2–20.
Silvana, M., T. Borgognini and R. Elen, 1985. 'Dietary Patterns in the Mesolithic Samples from Uzzo and Molara Caves (Sicily): The Evidence of Teeth.' *JHE* 14: 241–54.
Simmons, A. H., 2004. 'Bitter Hippos of Cyprus: The Island's First Occupants and Last Endemic Animals – Setting the Stage for Colonization' in Peltenburg and Wasse 2004, 1–14.
— 2007. *The Neolithic Revolution in the Near East: Transforming the Human Landscape*. Tucson: Arizona UP.
— and associates, 1999. *Faunal Extinctions in an Island Society: Pygmy Hippopotamus Hunters of Cyprus*. New York and London: Kluwer Academic/Plenum.
Simões L. G., T. Günther, R. M. Martínez-Sánchez *et al.*, 2023. 'Northwest African Neolithic Initiated by Migrants from Iberia and Levant.' *Nature* 618: 550–56.
Singer, I., 1999. 'A Political History of Ugarit' in Watson and Wyatt 1999, 603–733.
— 2008. 'Purple-dyers in Lazpa' in B. J. Collins, M. R. Bachvarova and I. C. Rutherford (eds), *Anatolian Interfaces: Hittites, Greeks and Their Neighbours*. Oxford: Oxbow. 21–43.
Skeates, R., 1993a. 'Neolithic Exchange in Central and Southern Italy' in Scarre and Healy 1993, 109–14.
— 1993b. 'Early Metal Use in the Central Mediterranean.' *ARP* 4: 5–48.
— 1997. 'Copper Age Settlement and Economy in Le Marche, Central Italy: A Social Perspective.' *JMA* 10: 49–72.
— 2000. 'The Social Dynamics of Enclosure in the Neolithic of the Tavoliere, South-east Italy.' *JMA* 13: 155–88.
— 2005a. 'Museum Archaeology and the Mediterranean Cultural Heritage' in Blake and Knapp 2005, 303–20.
— 2005b. *Visual Culture and Archaeology: Art and Social Life in Prehistoric South-east Italy*. London: Duckworth.
— 2007. 'Italian Prehistory Collections as Mediterranean Cultural Heritage' in Antoniadou and Pace 2007, 691–714.
— 2010. *An Archaeology of the Senses: Prehistoric Malta*. Oxford and New York: Oxford UP.
— 2012. 'Caves in Need of Context: Prehistoric Sardinia' in K. A. Bergsvik and R. Skeates (eds), *Caves in Context: The Cultural Significance of Caves and Rockshelters in Europe*. Oxford and Oakville: Oxbow. 166–87.
Skourtanioti, E., H. Ringbauer, G. A. Gnecchi Ruscone *et al.*, 2023. 'Ancient DNA Reveals Admixture History and Endogamy in the Prehistoric Aegean.' *Nature Ecology & Evolution* 7: 290–303.
Slim, H., P. Trousset, R. Paskoff and A. Oueslati, 2004. *La Littoral de la Tunisie: Étude Géoarchéologique et Historique*. Paris: CNRS.
Slimak, L., 2023. 'The Three Waves: Rethinking the Structure of the First Upper Paleolithic in Western Eurasia.' *PLOS ONE* 18: e0277444.
—, C. Zanolli, T. Higham *et al.*, 2022. 'Modern Human Incursion into Neanderthal Territories 54,000 Years Ago at Mandrin, France.' *Science Advances* 8: eabj9496.
Smith, A. T., 2003. *The Political Landscape: Constellations of Authority in Early Complex Societies*. Berkeley and London: California UP.
Smith, B. D., 2007. 'Niche Construction and the Behavioural Context of Plant and Animal Domestication.' *EA* 16: 188–99.
Smith, C., 1996. *Early Rome and Latium: Economy and Society c. 1000 to 500 BC*. Oxford and New York: Oxford UP.
— 1997. 'Servius Tullius, Cleisthenes and the Emergence of the *Polis* in Central Italy' in L. G. Mitchell and P. J. Rhodes (eds), *The Development of the* Polis *in Archaic Greece*. London and New York: Routledge. 208–16.
— 2005. 'The Beginnings of Urbanization in Rome' in Osborne and Cunliffe 2005, 91–111.
Smith, J. R., 2010. 'Palaeoenvironments of Eastern North Africa and the Levant in the Late Pleistocene' in Garcea 2010a, 6–17.
— 2012. 'Spatial and Temporal Variation in the Nature of Pleistocene Pluvial Phase Environment across North Africa' in Hublin and McPherron 2012, 35–48.
Smith, M., 2001. 'The Aztec Empire and the Mesoamerican World System' in Alcock *et al.* 2001, 128–54.
Snape, S., 2003. 'The Emergence of Libya on the Horizon of Egypt' in D. O'Connor and Quirke 2003, 93–106.
— and P. Wilson, 2007. *Zawiyet Umm el-Rakham I: The Temple and Chapels*. Bolton: Rutherford.
Snodgrass, A. M., 1983. 'Heavy Freight in Archaic Greece' in P. Garnsey, K. Hopkins and C. R. Whittaker (eds), *Trade in the Ancient Economy*. Berkeley: University of California. London: Chatto & Windus. 16–26.
— 1986. 'Interaction by Design: The Greek City State' in A. C. Renfrew and J. F. Cherry (eds) *Peer Polity Interaction and Socio-political Change*. Cambridge and New York: Cambridge UP. 47–58.
— 2000. 'Prehistoric Italy: A View from the Sea' in Ridgway *et al.* 2000, 171–78.
Soler, J. M., 1965. *El Tesoro de Villena*. Madrid: Ministerio de Educación Nacional.
Soles, J. S., 2005. 'From Ugarit to Mochlos – Remnants of an Ancient Voyage' in Laffineur and Greco 2005, 429–39.
— 2012. 'Mochlos Boats' in E. Matzourani and P. Betancourt (eds), *Philistor: Studies in Honor of Costis Davaras*. Philadelphia: INSTAP Academic. 187–200.
Sondaar, P. Y., R. Elburg, G. Klein Hofmeijer *et al.*, 1995. 'The Human Colonisation of Sardinia: A Late Pleistocene Human Fossil from Corbeddu Cave.' *Comptes Rendus de l'Academie des Sciences* 320 (IIa): 145–50.
Sowada, K. N., 2009. *Egypt in the Eastern Mediterranean during the Old Kingdom: An Archaeological Perspective*. Fribourg: Academic.
Sparks, R. T., 2004. 'Canaan in Egypt: Archaeological Evidence for a Social Phenomenon' in J. Bourriau and Phillips 2004, 25–54.
Spataro, M., 2002. *The First Farming Communities of the Adriatic: Pottery Production and Circulation in the Early and Middle Neolithic*. Trieste: Italo Svevo.
—, P. Biagi and S. J. Shennan, 2005. 'Rapid Rivers and Slow Seas? New Data for the Radiocarbon Chronology of the Balkan Peninsula' in L. Nikolova and J. Higgins (eds), *Prehistoric Archaeology and Anthropological Theory and Education*. Salt Lake City: International Institute of Anthropology. 43–51.
Spencer, L., 2010. 'The Regional Specialization of Ceramic Production in the EH III through MH II Period' in Philippa-Touchais *et al.* 2010, 669–81.
Spivey, N., 1990. 'The Power of Women in Etruscan Society' *ARP* 2: 55–67.
Spriggs, M., 1997. *The Island Melanesians*. Oxford and Cambridge: Blackwell.
Stager, L. E., 2001. 'Port Power in the Early and the Middle Bronze Age: The Organization of Maritime Trade and Hinterland Production' in S. R. Wolff (ed.), *Studies in the Archaeology of Israel and Neighboring Lands*. Chicago: Oriental Institute. 625–38.
— 2002. 'The MB IIA Ceramic Sequence at Tel Ashkelon and Its Implications for the "Port Power" Model of Trade' in M. Bietak (ed.), *The Middle Bronze Age in the Levant*. Vienna: Österreichischen Akademie der Wissenschaften. 353–62.
—, J. D. Schloen and D. M. Master, 2008. *Ashkelon I: Introduction and Overview*. Winona Lake: Eisenbrauns.
Stampolidis, N., and A. Kotsonas, 2006. 'Phoenicians in Crete' in Deger-Jalkotzy and Lemos 2006, 337–60.
Stanley, D. J., and A. G. Warne, 2003. 'Sea Level and Initiation of Predynastic Culture in the Nile Delta.' *Nature* 363: 435–38.
Stanley-Price, N., 2003. 'Site Preservation and Archaeology in the Mediterranean Region' in J. K. Papadopoulos and Leventhal 2003, 269–84.
Stark, F., 1956. *The Lycian Shore*. London: John Murray. New York: Harcourt.
Staubwasser, M., and H. Weiss, 2006. 'Holocene Climate and Cultural Evolution in Late Prehistoric–Early Historic West Asia.' *QR* 66: 372–87.
Steadman, S., 1996. 'Isolation or Interaction: Prehistoric Cilicia and the Fourth Millennium Uruk Expansion.' *JMA* 9: 131–65.
— and G. McMahon, (eds) 2011. *Oxford Handbook of Ancient Anatolia, 10,000–323 B.C.E.* Oxford and New York: Oxford UP.
Steel, L., 2002. 'Consuming Passions: A Contextual Study of the Local Consumption of Mycenaean Pottery at Tell el-Ajjul.' *JMA* 15: 25–51.
— 2004. *Cyprus before History: From the Earliest Settlers to the End of the Bronze Age*. London: Duckworth.
Stein, G. J., 1999. *Rethinking World-systems: Diasporas, Colonies, and Interaction in Uruk Mesopotamia*. Tucson: Arizona UP.
Stern, E., 1995. 'Between Persia and Greece: Trade, Administration and Warfare in the Persian and Hellenistic Periods (539–63 BC)' in Levy 1995a, 432–45.
Stewart, I., and C. Morhange, 2009. 'Coastal Geomorphology and Sea-level Change' in Woodward 2009a, 385–414.
Stewart, J. R., T. van Kolfschoten, A. Markova and R. Musil, 2003a. 'Neanderthals as Part of the Broader Late Pleistocene Megafaunal Extinctions?' in van Andel and Davies 2003, 221–32.
—, —, — and — 2003b. 'The Mammalian Faunas of Europe during Oxygen Isotope Stage Three' in van Andel and Davies 2003, 103–30.
Stierlin, H., and C. Ziegler, 1987. *Tanis: Trésors des Pharaons*. Fribourg: Seuil.
Stig Sørensen, M. L., and R. Thomas, (eds) 1989. *The Bronze Age-Iron Age Transition in Europe: Aspects of Continuity and Change in European Societies* c. *1200 to 500 B.C.* Vol. 1. Oxford: Archaeopress.
Stika, H., 2008. 'Plant Remains from the Early Iron Age in Western Sicily: Differences in Subsistence Strategies of Greek and Elymian Sites.' *Vegetation History and Archaeobotany* 17: 139–48.
Stiner, M. C., 1994. *Honor among Thieves: A Zooarchaeological Study of Neandertal Ecology*. Princeton and Chichester: Princeton UP.
— 1999. 'Palaeolithic Mollusc Exploitation at Riparo Mochi (Balzi Rossi, Italy): Food and Ornaments from the Aurignacian through Epigravettian.' *Antiquity* 73: 735–54.
— 2005. *The Faunas of Hayonim Cave (Israel): A 200,000-year Record of Paleolithic Diet, Demography, and Society*. Cambridge: Peabody Museum.
—, A. Gopher and R. Barkai, 2011. 'Hearth-side Socioeconomics, Hunting and Paleoecology during the Late Lower Paleolithic at Qesem Cave, Israel.' *JHE* 60: 213–33.
— and S. L. Kuhn, 2006. 'Changes in the "Connectedness" and Resilience of Paleolithic Societies in Mediterranean Ecosystems.' *Human Ecology* 34: 693–712.
— and N. D. Munro, 2011. 'On the Evolution of Diet and Landscape during the Upper Paleolithic through Mesolithic at Franchthi Cave (Peloponnese, Greece).' *JHE* 60: 618–36.
Stiros, S., 2009. 'Earthquakes' in Woodward 2009a, 469–92.
Stocker, S. R., and J. L. Davis, 2017. 'The Combat Agate from the Grave of the Griffin Warrior at Pylos.' *Hesperia: The Journal of the American School of Classical Studies at Athens* 86: 583–605.
Stoddart, S. K. F., 2000. 'Contrasting Political Strategies in the Islands of the Southern Central Mediterranean.' *ARP* 7: 59–73.
Stone, D. L., 2004. 'Problems and Possibilities in Comparative Survey: A North African Perspective' in Alcock and Cherry 2004, 132–43.
Strasser, T. F., E. Panagopoulou, C. N. Runnels *et al.*, 2010. 'Stone Age Seafaring in the Mediterranean: Evidence from the Plakias Region for Lower Palaeolithic and Mesolithic Habitation of Crete.' *Hesperia* 79: 145–90.

—, C. Runnels, K. Wegmann *et al.*, 2011. 'Dating Palaeolithic Sites in Southwestern Crete, Greece.' *JQS* 26: 553–56.
Straus, L. G., 2001. 'Africa and Iberia in the Pleistocene.' *QI* 75: 91–102.
— 2008. 'The Mesolithic of Atlantic Iberia' in Bailey and Spikins 2008, 302–37.
—, N. Bicho and A. C. Winegardner, 2000. 'The Upper Palaeolithic Settlement of Iberia: First-generation Maps.' *Antiquity* 74: 553–66.
Stringer, C., 2000. 'Coasting out of Africa.' *Nature* 405: 24–27.
— 2011. *The Origin of Our Species*. London: Allen Lane. Published in 2012 in the United States as *Lone Survivors: How We Came to Be the Only Humans on Earth*. New York: Times Books.
— and R. N. E. Barton, 2008. 'Putting North Africa on the Map of Modern Human Origins.' *EA* 17: 5–7.
—, — and J. C. Finlayson, (eds) 2000. *Neanderthals on the Edge: Papers from a Conference Marking the 150th Anniversary of the Forbes' Quarry Discovery, Gibraltar*. Oxford: Oxbow.
Strommenger, E., 1980. *Habuba Kabira: eine Stadt vor 5000 Jahren*. Mainz: Philipp von Zabern.
Stronach, D., 1995. 'The Imagery of the Wine Bowl: Wine in Assyria in the Early First Millennium BC' in P. E. McGovern, S. J. Fleming and S. H. Katz (eds), *The Origins and Ancient History of Wine*. Luxembourg: Gordon and Breach. 175–95.
Sutton, J. E. G., 1977. 'The African Aqualithic.' *Antiquity* 51: 25–34.
Swiny, S., R. Hohlfelder and H. W. Swiny, (eds) 1997. *Res Maritimae: Cyprus and the Eastern Mediterranean from Prehistory to Late Antiquity*. Atlanta: Scholars.
Taçon, P., M. Wilson and C. Chippindale, 1996. 'Birth of the Rainbow Serpent in Arnhem Land Rock Art and Oral History.' *Archaeology in Oceania* 31: 103–24.
Tafuri, M. A., 2005. *Tracing Mobility and Identity: Bioarchaeology and Bone Chemistry of the Bronze Age Sant'Abbondio Cemetery (Pompeii, Italy)*. Oxford: Archaeopress.
—, S. Soncin, S. Panella *et al.*, 2023. 'Regional Long-term Analysis of Dietary Isotopes in Neolithic Southeastern Italy: New Patterns and Research Directions.' *Scientific Reports* 13: 7914.
Takaoglu, T., 2005. *A Chalcolithic Marble Workshop at Kulaksizlar in Western Anatolia: An Analysis of Production and Craft Specialization*. Oxford: Archaeopress.
Tallet, P., 1998. 'Quelques Aspects de l'Économie du Vin en Égypte Ancienne, au Nouvel Empire' in Grimal and Benu 1998, 241–63.
Tanasi, D., and N. C. Vella, (eds) 2011. *Site, Artefacts and Landscape: Prehistoric Borġ in-Nadur, Malta*. Monza: Polimetrica.
Tanner, J. T., 2003. 'Finding the Egyptian in Early Greek Art' in Matthews and Roemer 2003, 115–43.
Tarrús, J., 2008. 'La Draga (Banyoles, Catalonia), an Early Neolithic Lakeside Village in Mediterranean Europe.' *Catalonian Historical Review* 1: 17–33.
Tartaron, T., 2004. *Bronze Age Landscape and Society in Southern Epirus*. Oxford: Archaeopress.
— 2010. 'Between and Beyond: Political Economy in Non-Palatial Mycenaean Worlds' in Pullen 2010, 161–83.
— 2013. *Maritime Networks in the Mycenaean World*. Cambridge and New York: Cambridge UP.
Taylor, K. C., G. W. Lamorey, G. A. Doyle *et al.*, 1993. 'The "Flickering Switch" of Late Pleistocene Climate Change.' *Nature* 361: 432–36.
Taylor, J., 2000. 'The Third Intermediate Period (1069–664 BC)' in I. Shaw 2000, 352–59.
Taylour, W., 1958. *Mycenaean Pottery in Italy and Adjacent Areas*. Cambridge: Cambridge UP.
Tchernov, E., and F. Valla, 1997. 'Two New Dogs, and Other Natufian Dogs, from the Southern Levant.' *JAS* 24: 65–95.
Televantou, C. A., 2008. 'Strofilas: A Neolithic Settlement on Andros' in Brodie *et al.* 2008, 43–53.
Terral, J.-F., N. Alonso, R. B. I. Capdevila *et al.*, 2004. 'Historical Biogeography of Olive Domestication (*Olea europaea* L.) as Revealed by Geometrical Morphometry Applied to Biological and Archaeological Material.' *JB* 31: 63–77.
Terrenato, N., 2019. *The Early Roman Expansion into Italy: Elite Negotiation and Family Agendas*. Cambridge and New York: Cambridge UP.
Thalmann, J.-P., 2006. 'Obsidian at Tell Arqa, North Lebanon: A Stopover Point on a Trade Route?' *Baghdader Mitteilungen* 37: 575–92.
Theroux, P., 1995. *Pillars of Hercules: A Grand Tour of the Mediterranean*. New York: G. P. Putnam's Sons. 1996, London: Penguin.
Theuma, N., and R. Grima, 2006. 'The Neolithic Temples of Malta: Towards a Re-evaluation of Heritage' in A. Leask and A. Fyall (eds), *Managing World Heritage Sites*. Amsterdam and London: Elsevier. 263–72.
Thomas, E. R., E. W. Wolff, R. Mulvaney *et al.*, 2007. 'The 8.2 ka Event from Greenland Ice Cores.' *QSR* 26: 70–81.
Thornes, J., F. López-Bermúdez and J. Woodward, 2009. 'Hydrology, River Regimes and Sediment Yield' in Woodward 2009a, 229–54.
Tichy, R., 2000. *L'Expedition Monoxylon: Une Pirogue Monoxyle en Mediterranée Occidentale*. Privately circulated booklet.
Tinè, S., 1990. *Relazione Preliminare al Colloquio sul Santuario di Monte d'Accoddi: 10 Anni di Nuovi Scavi*. Sassari: Ciclostilato.
Tite, M. S., 2008. 'Ceramic Production, Provenance and Use – A Review.' *Archaeometry* 50: 216–31.
Tomas, H., 2010. 'The World beyond the Northern Margin: The Bronze Age Aegean and the East Adriatic Coast' in W. A. Parkinson and Galaty 2010, 181–212.
Tomkins, P. D., 2008. 'Time, Space and the Reinvention of the Cretan Neolithic' in Isaakidou and Tomkins 2008, 21–48.
Torrence, R., 1986. *Production and Exchange of Stone Tools: Prehistoric Obsidian in the Aegean*. Cambridge and New York: Cambridge UP.
— and J. Grattan, (eds) 2002. *Natural Disasters and Cultural Change*. London and New York: Routledge.
Tourloukis, E., 2010. *Early and Middle Pleistocene Archaeological Record of Greece: Current Status and Future Prospects*. Leiden: Leiden UP.
Toynbee, A., 1934. *A Study of History*. London: Oxford UP.
Trantalidou, K., 2003. 'Faunal Remains from the Earliest Strata of the Cave of the Cyclops, Youra' in Galanidou and Perlès 2003, 143–72.
Treherne, P., 1995. 'The Warrior's Beauty: The Masculine Body and Self-identity in Bronze-Age Europe.' *JEA* 3: 105–44.
Treister, M., 1996. 'The Trojan Treasures: Description, Chronology, Historical Context' in Antonova *et al.* 1996, 197–234.
Trément, F., 1989. 'La Région des Étangs de Saint-Blaise: Pour une Approche Archéologique et Paléo-Écologique d'un Milieu de Vie.' *BSPF* 10/12: 441–50.
Tresset, A., and J.-D. Vigne, 2007. 'Substitution of Species, Techniques and Symbols at the Mesolithic/Neolithic Transition in Western Europe' in Whittle and Cummings 2007, 189–210.
Trigger, B. G., 2003. *Understanding Early Civilizations. A Comparative Study*. Cambridge and New York: Cambridge UP.
Tringham, R., 2003. '(Re-)digging the Site at the End of the Twentieth Century: Large-scale Archaeological Fieldwork in a New Millennium' in J. K. Papadopoulos and Levanthal 2003, 89–108.
Tronchetti, C., and P. van Dommelen, 2005. 'Entangled Objects and Hybrid Practices: Colonial Contacts and Elite Connection at Monte Prama, Sardinia.' *JMA* 18: 183–208.
Trump, D. H., 1980. *Prehistory of the Mediterranean*. New Haven: Yale UP. London: Allen Lane.
— 2004a. 'The Enigma of the Cart-ruts' in Cilia 2004, 378–97.
— 2004b. 'The Prehistoric Pottery' in Cilia 2004, 242–67.
Tsetskhladze, G., and F. de Angelis, (eds) 1994. *Archaeology of Greek Colonisation: Historical Interpretation of Archaeology*. Stuttgart: F. Steiner.
Tufnell, O., and W. A. Ward, 1966. 'Relations between Byblos, Egypt, and Mesopotamia at the End of the Third Millennium BC: A Study of the Montet Jar.' *Syria* 43: 165–241.
Turner, A., 1992. 'Large Carnivores and Earliest European Hominids: Changing Determinants of Resource Availability during the Lower and Middle Pleistocene.' *JHE* 22: 109–26.
Tusa, S., 1999. 'Short-term Cultural Dynamics within the Mediterranean Cultural Landscape' in Tykot *et al.* 1999, 149–83.
Tykot, R., 1996. 'Obsidian Procurement and Distribution in the Central and Western Mediterranean.' *JMA* 9: 39–82.
— 1999. 'Islands in the Stream: Stone Age Cultural Dynamics in Sardinia and Corsica' in Tykot *et al.* 1999, 67–82.
— and T. K. Andrews, (eds) 1992. *Sardinia in the Mediterranean: A Footprint in the Sea*. Sheffield: Sheffield Academic.
—, J. Morter and J. E. Robb, (eds) 1999. *Social Dynamics in the Prehistoric Central Mediterranean*. London: Accordia Research Institute.
Tzala, C., 1989. 'O Dromos tou Obsidianou me ena Papyrenio Skaphos stis Kyklades.' *Archaiologia* 32: 11–20.
Tzedakis, C., 2009. 'Cenozoic Climate and Vegetation Change' in Woodward 2009a, 89–137.
Ucko, P. J., R. Tringham and G. W. Dimbleby, (eds) 1972. *Man, Settlement and Urbanism*. London: Duckworth.
Uerpmann, H.-P., 1990. 'Die Domestikation des Pferdes im Chalkolithikum West-und Mitteleuropas.' *Madrider Mitteilungen* 31: 109–53.
— 1995. 'Domestication of the Horse: When, Where, and Why?' in L. Bodson (ed.), *Le Cheval et les Autres Équidées: Aspects de l'Histoire de Leur Insertion dans les Activités Humaines*. Liège: Université de Liège. 15–29.
Ünlüsoy, S., 2006. 'Vom Reihenhaus zum Megaron – Troia I bis Troia III' in Korfmann 2006, 133–44.
Ur, J., 2003. 'CORONA Satellite Photography and Ancient Road Networks: A Northern Mesopotamian Case Study.' *Antiquity* 77: 102–15.
—, P. Karsgaard and J. Oates, 2007. 'Early Urban Development in the Near East.' *Science* 317: 1188.
Ussishkin, D., 1971. 'The "Ghassulian" Temple in Ein Gedi and the Origin of the Hoard from Nahal Mishmar.' *Biblical Archaeologist* 34: 23–29.
Vagnetti, L., 1999. 'Mycenaean *Pottery* in the Central Mediterranean' in Crielaard *et al.* 1999, 137–61.
— and F. Lo Schiavo, 1989. 'Late Bronze Age Long Distance Trade in the Mediterranean: The Role of the Cypriots' in E. Peltenburg (ed.), *Early Society in Cyprus*. Edinburgh: Edinburgh UP. 217–43.
Valamoti, S., 2004. *Plants and People in Late Neolithic and Early Bronze Age Northern Greece: An Archaeobotanical Investigation*. Oxford: Archaeopress.
— 2007. 'Food across Borders: A Consideration of the Neolithic and Bronze Age Archaeobotanical Evidence from Northern Greece' in Galanaki *et al.* 2007, 281–93.
— and G. Jones, 2010. 'Bronze and Oil: A Possible Link between the Introduction of Tin and Lallemantia to Northern Greece.' *ABSA* 105: 83–96.
—, M. Mangafa, C. Koukouli-Chrysanthaki and D. Malamidou, 2007. 'Grape-pressings from Northern Greece: The Earliest Wine in the Aegean.' *Antiquity* 81: 54–61.
Van Andel, T. H., 1989. 'Late Quaternary Sea Level Change and Archaeology.' *Antiquity* 63: 733–45.
— and W. Davies, (eds) 2003. *Neanderthals and Modern Humans in the European Landscape during the Last Glaciation: Archaeological Results of the Stage 3 Project*. Cambridge: MIAR.
— and C. Runnels, 1995. 'The Earliest Farmers in Europe.' *Antiquity* 69: 481–500.
Van de Loosdrecht, M., A. Bouzouggar, L. Humphrey *et al.*, 2018. 'Pleistocene North African Genomes Link Near Eastern and Sub-Saharan African Human Populations.' *Science* 360: 548–52.
Van de Mieroop, M., 2004. *A History of the Ancient Near East ca. 3000–323 BC*. Oxford and Malden: Blackwell.
— 2007. *The Eastern Mediterranean in the Age of Ramesses II*. Oxford and Malden: Blackwell.
— 2011. *A History of Ancient Egypt*. Chichester and Malden: Wiley-Blackwell.
Van den Brink, E. C. M., (ed.) 1988. *The Archaeology of the Nile Delta, Egypt: Problems and Priorities*. Amsterdam: Netherlands Foundation for Archaeological Research in Egypt.
— (ed.) 1992. *The Nile Delta in Transition: 4th–3rd Millennium BC*. Tel Aviv: Edwin C. M. van den Brink.
— 2011. 'Continuity and Change – Cultural Transmission in the Late Chalcolithic–Early Bronze Age I: A View from Early Modi'in, a Late Prehistoric Site in Central Israel' in J. L. Lovell and Y. M. Rowan (eds), *Culture, Chronology and the Chalcolithic: Theory and Transition*. Oxford and Oakville: Oxbow. 61–70.
— and T. E. Levy, (eds) 2002. *Egypt and the Levant: Interrelations from the 4th through the Early 3rd millennium B.C.E.* London and New York: Leicester UP.
Van de Noort, R., 2011. *North Sea Archaeologies: A Maritime Biography, 10,000 BC–AD 1500*. New York and Oxford: Oxford UP.
Van der Geer, A. A. E., M. Dermitzakis and J. de Vos, 2006. 'Crete before the Cretans: The Reign of Dwarfs.' *Pharos* 13: 121–32.
Van der Leeuw, S., (ed.) 1998. *The Archaeomedes Project: Understanding the Natural and Anthropogenic Causes of Land Degradation and Desertification in the Mediterranean*. Luxemburg: Office for Official Publications of the European Union.
Vander Linden, M., 2006a. *Le Phénomène Campaniforme dans l'Europe du 3ème Millénaire: Synthèse et Perspectives*. Oxford: Archaeopress.
— 2006b. 'For Whom the Bell Tolls: Social Hierarchy vs Social Integration in the Bell Beaker Culture of Southern France.' *CAJ* 16: 317–32.
Van der Veen, M., (ed.) 1999. *The Exploitation of Plant Resources in Ancient Africa*. New York and London: Kluwer Academic/Plenum.
— 2006. 'Food and Farming in the Libyan Sahara' in Mattingly *et al.* 2006, 171–78.
Van Dommelen, P., 1998. *On Colonial Grounds: A Comparative Study of Colonialism and Rural Settlement in First Millennium BC West Central Sardinia*. Leiden: Faculty of Archaeology.
— 2000. 'Writing Ancient Mediterranean Landscapes.' *JMA* 13: 230–36.

— 2005. 'Urban Foundations? Colonial Settlement and Urbanization in the Western Mediterranean' in Osborne and Cunliffe 2005, 143–67.
— 2006. '*The Orientalizing Phenomenon: Hybridity and Material Culture in the Western Mediterranean*' in Riva and Vella 2006, 135–52.
— and S. Finocchi, 2008. 'Sardinia: Diverging Landscapes' in van Dommelen and Goméz Bellard 2008, 159–201.
— and C. Goméz Bellard, 2008. *Rural Landscapes of the Punic World*. London and Oakville: Equinox.
— and A. B. Knapp, (eds) 2010. *Material Connections in the Ancient Mediterranean: Mobility, Materiality, and Mediterranean Identities*. Abingdon and New York: Routledge.
— 2017. 'Classical Connections and Mediterranean Practices: Exploring Connectivity and Local Interactions' in T. Hodos (ed.), *The Routledge Handbook of Archaeology and Globalization*. Abingdon: Routledge. 618–33.
Vanhaeren, M., and F. d'Errico, 2006. 'Aurignacian Ethno-linguistic Geography of Europe Revealed by Personal Ornaments.' *JAS* 33: 1105–28.
Van Leusen, M., G. Pizziolo and L. Sarti, (eds) 2011. *Hidden Landscapes of Mediterranean Europe: Cultural and Methodological Biases in Pre- and Protohistoric Landscape Studies*. Oxford: Archaeopress.
Van Peer, P., and P. M. Vermeersch, 2007. 'The Place of Northeast Africa in the Early History of Modern Humans: New Data and Interpretations on the Middle Stone Age' in Mellars *et al.* 2007, 187–98.
Van Wijngaarden, G. J., 2002. *Use and Appreciation of Mycenaean Pottery in the Levant, Cyprus and Italy (1600–1200 BC)*. Amsterdam: Amsterdam UP.
Van Zeist, W., 1988. 'Plant Remains from a First Dynasty Burial at Tell Ibrahim Awad' in van den Brink 1988, 111–14.
—, S. Bottema and M. van der Veen, 2001. *Diet and Vegetation at Ancient Carthage: The Archaeobotanical Evidence*. Groningen: Institute of Archaeology.
Vanzetti, A., 2000. 'Broglio di Trebisacce nel Quadro dell'Italia Meridionale' in M. Harari and M. Pearce (eds), *Il Protovillanoviano al di qua e al di là dell'Appennino*. Como: New Press. 133–71.
—, M. Vidale, M. Gallinaro *et al.*, 2010. 'The Iceman as a Burial.' *Antiquity* 84: 681–92.
Vaquer, J., 1990. *Le Neolithique en Languedoc Occidental*. Paris: CNRS.
— 1998. 'Le Midi Méditerranéen de la France' in J. Guilaine (ed.), *Atlas du Néolithique Europeen*. Vol. 2A: *L'Europe Occidentale*. Liège: Université de Liège. 413–500.
—, J. Guilaine and J. Coularou, 1995. 'Carsac (Carcassonne)' in Guilaine *et al.* 1995, 41–46.
Veenhof, K. R., 1972. *Aspects of Old Assyrian Trade and Its Terminology*. Leiden: Brill.
Vella, N., 2004. 'A Maritime Perspective: Looking for Hermes in an Ancient Seascape' in J. Chrysostomides, C. Dendrinos and J. Harris (eds), *The Greek Islands and the Sea*. Camberley: Porphyrogenitus. 33–57.
Ventris, M., and J. Chadwick, 1973. *Documents in Mycenaean Greek*. 2nd edn. Cambridge and New York: Cambridge UP.
Vermeersch, P. M., 2009. 'Egypt from 50 to 25 ka BP: A Scarcely Inhabited Region?' in M. Camps and Szmidt 2009, 67–88.
— 2010. 'Middle and Upper Palaeolithic in the Egyptian Nile Valley' in Garcea 2010a, 66–88.
Vermeule, E., and V. Karageorghis, 1982. *Mycenaean Pictorial Vase Painting*. Cambridge and London: Harvard UP.
Vianello, A., 2005. *Late Bronze Age Mycenaean and Italic Products in the West Mediterranean: A Social and Economic Analysis*. Oxford: Archaeopress.
Vickers, M., and D. Gill, 1994. *Artful Crafts: Ancient Greek Silverware and Pottery*. Oxford and New York: Oxford UP.
Vigne, J.-D., 1988. 'Données Préliminaries sur l'Histoire du Peuplement Mammalien de l'Ilot de Zembra (Tunisie).' *Mammalia* 52: 567–74.
— 1994. *L'Ile Lavezzi: Hommes, Animaux, Archéologie et Marginalité (XIIIe–XXe Siècles, Bonifacio, Corse)*. Paris: CNRS.
— 1999. 'The Large "True" Mediterranean Islands as a Model for the Holocene Human Impact on the European Vertebrate Fauna? Recent Data and New Reflections' in N. Benecke (ed.), *The Holocene History of the European Vertebrate Faunas*. Rahden: Marie Leidorf. 295–322.
— 2005a. 'Premières Manifestations de l'Homme Moderne en Corse et en Sardaigne: Nouvelles Données et Réflexions' in A. Tuffreau (ed.), *Peuplements Humains et Variations Environnementales au Quaternaire*. Oxford: Archaeopress. 139–45.
— 2005b. 'L'Humérus de Chien Magdalénien de Erralla (Gipuzkoa, Espagne) et la Domestication Tardiglaciaire du Loup en Europe.' *Munibe* 57: 279–87.
—, I. Carrère, F. Briois and J. Guilaine, 2011. 'The Early Process of Mammal Domestication in the Near East: New Evidence from the Pre-Neolithic and Pre-Pottery Neolithic in Cyprus.' *CA* 52 (S4): S255–S271.
— and T. Cucchi, 2005. 'Premiéres Navigations au Proche-Orient: Les Informations Indirects de Chypre.' *Paléorient* 31: 186–94.
— and N. Desse-Berset, 1995. 'The Exploitation of Animal Resources in the Mediterranean during the Pre-Neolithic: The Example of Corsica' in A. Fischer 1995, 309–18.
Vilaça, R., 2008. 'Reflexões em Torno da «Presença Mediterrânea» no Centro Doterritório Português, na Charneira do Bronze para o Ferro' in Celestino *et al.* 2008, 371–402.
Villa, P., 2001. 'Early Italy and the Colonization of Western Europe.' *QI* 75: 113–30.
Villada, F., J. Ramón and I. Suárez Padilla, 2007. 'Nuevos Datos en Torno a los Incisios del Poblamiento de la Ciudad de Ceuta: Avance Preliminar de la Excavación de la Plaza de la Catedral.' *Akros* 6: 125–34.
Villalba-Mouco, V., C. Oliart, C. Rihuete-Herrada *et al.*, 2021. 'Genomic Transformation and Social Organization during the Copper Age-Bronze Age Transition in Southern Iberia.' *Science Advances* 7: eabi7038.
Vinson, S., 1994. *Egyptian Boats and Ships*. Princes Risborough: Shire.
Vital, J., 2008. 'Architectures, Societés, Espaces durant l'Âge du Bronze: Quelques Exemples dans la Basin Rhodanien' in Guilaine 2008, 179–201.
Vives-Ferrándiz, J., 2008. 'Negotiating Colonial Encounters: Hybrid Practices and Consumption in Eastern Iberia (8th–6th Centuries BC).' *JMA* 21: 241–72.
Vogiatzakis, I. N., G. Pungetti and A. M. Mannion, (eds) 2008. *Mediterranean Island Landscapes: Natural and Cultural Approaches*. Berlin and New York: Springer.
Voutsaki, S., 1998. 'Mortuary Evidence, Symbolic Meanings and Social Change: A Comparison between Messenia and the Argolid in the Mycenaean Period' in K. Branigan, *Cemetery and Society in the Aegean Bronze Age*. Sheffield: Sheffield Academic. 41–58.
— 1999. 'Mortuary Display, Prestige and Identity in the Shaft Grave Era' in I. Kilian-Dirlmeier and M. Egg (eds), *Eliten in der Bronzezeit*. Mainz: Habelt. 103–18.
— and J. Killen, (eds) 2001. *Economy and Politics in the Mycenaean Palace States*. Cambridge: Cambridge Philological Society.
Vujević, D., 2009. 'The Relationship between the Middle Palaeolithic Sites in the Zadar Hinterland and the Zadar Islands' in Forenbaher 2009a, 1–12.
Wachsmann, S., 1987. *Aegeans in the Theban Tombs*. Leuven: Peeters.
— 1998. *Seagoing Ships and Seamanship in the Bronze Age Levant*. College Station: Texas A&M UP. London: Chatham.
Waelkens, M., E. Paulissen, M. Vermoere *et al.*, 1999. 'Man and Environment in the Territory of Sagalassos, a Classical City in SW Turkey.' *QSR* 18: 697–709.
Wagner, C. G., 2013. 'Tartessos and the Orientalizing Elites' in Cruz Berrocal *et al.* 2013, 337–56.
Waldbaum, J. C., 1997. 'Greeks *in* the East or Greeks *and* the East? Problems in the Definition and Recognition of Presence.' *BASOR* 305: 1–17.
Waldren, W. H., 1982. *Balearic Prehistoric Ecology and Culture: The Excavation and Study of Certain Caves, Rock Shelters and Settlements*. Oxford: Archaeopress.
— and J. A. Ensenyat, (eds) 2002. *World Islands in Prehistory: International Insular Investigations*. Oxford: Archaeopress.
Walker, N., 2008. 'Locating Micro-refugia in Periglacial Environments during the LGM' in Grimaldi *et al* 2008, 47–54.
Wallace, S., 2010. *Ancient Crete: From Successful Collapse to Democracy's Alternatives, Twelfth to Fifth Centuries BC*. Cambridge: Cambridge UP.
Wallinga, H. T., 1993. *Ships and Sea-power before the Great Persian War*. Leiden and New York: Brill.
Warburton, D. A., (ed.) 2009. *Time's up! Dating the Minoan Eruption of Santorini*. Athens: Danish Institute at Athens.
Ward, C. A., 2006. 'Boat-building and Its Social Context in Early Egypt: Interpretations from the First Dynasty Boat-grave Cemetery at Abydos.' *Antiquity* 80: 118–29.
— 2010. 'Seafaring in the Bronze Age Aegean: Evidence and Speculation' in Pullen 2010, 149–60.
Ward, W. A., 1978. *Studies on Scarab Seals*. Vol. I: *Pre-12th Dynasty Scarab Amulets*. Warminster: Aris & Phillips.
— and M. S. Joukowsky, (eds) 1992. *The Crisis Years: The 12th Century BC from beyond the Danube to the Tigris*. Dubuque: Kendall/Hunt.
Warren, P. M., 1992. 'Lapis Lacedaemonius' in J. M. Sanders (ed.), *Philolakon: Lakonian Studies in Honour of Hector Catling*. London: British School at Athens. 285–96.
Wasse, A., 2007. 'Climate, Economy and Change: Cyprus and the Levant during the Late Pleistocene–Mid Holocene' in J. Clarke *et al.* 2007, 43–63.
Watkins, T., 1996. 'Excavations at Pınarbaşı: The Early Stages' in Ian Hodder (ed.), *On the Surface: Çatalhöyük 1993–95*. Cambridge: MIAR. 57–58.
Watrous, L. V., 1998. 'Egypt and Crete in the Early Middle Bronze Age: A Case of Trade and Cultural Diffusion' in Cline and Harris-Cline 1998, 19–28.
— 2001. 'Crete from Earliest Prehistory through the Protopalatial Period' in T. Cullen 2001, 157–224.
—, P. M. Day and R. E. Jones, 1998. 'The Sardinian Pottery from the Late Bronze Age Site of Kommos in Crete: Description, Chemical and Petrographic Analysis, and Historical Context' in M. S. Balmuth and R. H. Tykot (eds), *Sardinian and Aegean Chronology: Towards the Resolution of Relative and Absolute Dating in the Mediterranean*. Oxford: Oxbow. 337–40.
Watson, W. G. E., and N. Wyatt, (eds) 1999. *Handbook of Ugaritic Studies*. Boston: Brill.
Webb, J., and D. Frankel, 1994. 'Making an Impression: Storage and Surplus Finance in Late Bronze Age Cyprus.' *JMA* 7: 5–26.
— and — 2007. 'Identifying Population Movements by Everyday Practice: The Case of Third Millennium Cyprus' in Antoniadou and Pace 2007, 189–216.
—, —, Z. A. Stos and N. Gale, 2006. 'Early Bronze Age Metal Trade in the Eastern Mediterranean: New Compositional and Lead Isotope Evidence from Cyprus.' *OJA* 25: 261–88.
Webster, G., 1996. *A Prehistory of Sardinia: 2300–500 BC*. Sheffield: Sheffield Academic.
— 2001. *Duos Nuraghes: A Bronze Age Settlement in Sardinia*. Oxford: Archaeopress.
Wedde, M., 1991. 'War at Sea: The Mycenaean and Early Iron Age Oared Galley' in Laffineur 1991, 465–78.
— 2000. *Towards a Hermeneutics of Aegean Bronze Age Ship Imagery*. Manheim: Bibliopolis.
— 2005. 'The Mycenaean Galley in Context: From Fact to Idée Fixe' in Laffineur and Greco 2005, 29–38.
Weeks, L. R., 2003. *Early Metallurgy of the Persian Gulf: Technology, Trade, and the Bronze Age World*. Leiden and Boston: Brill.
Weiberg, E., 2007. *Thinking the Bronze Age: Life and Death in Early Helladic Greece*. Uppsala: Uppsala UP.
Weide, A., 2021. 'Towards a Socio-Economic Model for Southwest Asian Cereal Domestication.' *Agronomy* 11: 2432.
Weingarten, J., 1991. *The Transformation of Egyptian Tawaret into the Minoan Genius: A Study in Cultural Transmission in the Middle Bronze Age*. Partille: Åström.
Weisgerber, G., and J. Cierny, 2002. 'Tin for Ancient Anatolia?' in Ü. Yalçin (ed.), *Anatolian Metal*. Vol. II. Bochum: Deutsches Bergbau-Museum. 179–86.
Weiss, H., M. A. Courty, W. Wetterstrom *et al.*, 1993. 'The Genesis and Collapse of Third Millennium North Mesopotamian Civilization.' *Science* 261: 995–1004.
Weller, O., 2002. 'The Earliest Rock Salt Exploitation in Europe: A Salt Mountain in the Spanish Neolithic.' *Antiquity* 76: 317–18.
Wengrow, D., 1996. 'Egyptian Taskmasters and Heavy Burdens: Highland Exploitation and the Collared-rim Pithos of the Bronze/Iron Age Levant.' *OJA* 15: 307–26.
— 1998. 'The Changing Face of Clay: Continuity and Change in the Transition from Village to Urban Life in the Near East.' *Antiquity* 72: 783–95.
— 2001a. 'Rethinking Cattle Cults in Early Egypt: Towards a Prehistoric Perspective on the Narmer Palette.' *CAJ* 11: 91–104.
— 2001b. 'The Evolution of Simplicity: Aesthetic Labour and Social Change in the Neolithic Near East.' *WA* 33: 168–88.
— 2006a. *The Archaeology of Early Egypt: Social Transformations in North-east Africa, 10,000–2,650 BC*. Cambridge and New York: Cambridge UP.
— 2006b. 'The Idea of Prehistory in the Middle East' in R. Layton, S. Shennan and P. Stone (eds), *A Future for Archaeology: The Past in the Present*. London: UCL. Walnut Creek: Left Coast. 187–97.
— 2008. 'Prehistories of Commodity Branding.' *CA* 49: 7–34.
— 2010a. *What Makes Civilization? The Ancient Near East and the Future of the West*. Oxford and New York: Oxford UP.
— 2010b. 'The Voyages of Europa: Ritual and Trade in the Eastern Mediterranean circa 2300–1850 BC' in W. A. Parkinson and Galaty 2010, 141–60.
— 2011. '"Archival" and "Sacrificial" Economies in Bronze Age Eurasia: An Interactionist Approach to the Hoarding of Metals' in T. C. Wilkinson *et al.* 2011, 135–44.
Weninger, B., E. Alram-Stern and E. Bauer *et al.*, 2006. 'Climate Forcing due to the 8200 cal yr BP Event Observed at Early Neolithic Sites in the Eastern Mediterranean.' *QR* 66: 401–20.

Wenke, R., and D. Brewer, 1996. 'The Archaic-Old Kingdom Delta: The Evidence from Mendes and Kom el-Hisn' in M. Bietak (ed.), *House and Palace in Ancient Egypt*. Vienna: Österreichischen Akademie der Wissenschaften. 265–85.

Wertime, T. A., and J. D. Muhly, (eds) 1980. *The Coming of the Age of Iron*. New Haven and London: Yale UP.

West, M. L., 1997. *The East Face of Helicon: West Asiatic Elements in Greek Poetry and Myth*. Oxford and New York: Clarendon.

Westerdahl, C., 1992. 'The Maritime Cultural Landscape.' *International Journal of Nautical Archaeology* 21: 5–14.

Wetterstrom, W., 1993. 'Foraging and Farming in Egypt: The Transition from Hunting and Gathering to Horticulture in the Nile Valley' in T. Shaw, P. Sinclair, B. Andah and A. Okpoko (eds), *The Archaeology of Africa: Food, Metals and Towns*. London and New York: Routledge. 165–226.

Whallon, R., (ed.) 2007a. *Late Palaeolithic Environments and Cultural Relations around the Adriatic*. Oxford: Archaeopress.

— 2007b. 'Social Territories around the Adriatic in the Late Pleistocene' in Whallon 2007a, 61–65.

White, D., (ed.) 2002. *Marsa Matruh*. Philadelphia: Institute for Aegean Prehistory Academic.

— and A. P. White, 1996. 'Coastal Sites of Northeast Africa: The Case against Bronze Age Ports.' *Journal of the American Research Center in Egypt* 33: 11–30.

Whitehead, P., S. Smith and A. Wade, 2011. 'Modelling Water Resources and Climate Change at the Bronze Age Site of Jawa in Northern Jordan: A New Approach Utilising Stochaistic Simulation Techniques' in Mithen and Black 2011, 289–301.

Whitehouse, R., 1992a. *Underground Religion: Cult and Culture in Prehistoric Italy*. London: Accordia Research Centre.

— 1992b. 'Tools the Manmaker: The Cultural Construction of Gender in Italian Prehistory.' *ARP* 3: 41–54.

— 1995. 'From Secret Society to State Religion: Ritual and Social Organization in Prehistoric and Protohistoric Italy' in Christie 1995, 83–88.

— (ed.) 1998. *Gender and Italian Archaeology: Challenging the Stereotypes*. London: Accordia Research Institute.

— and J. Wilkins, 1989. 'Greeks and Natives in South-east Italy: Approaches to the Archaeological Evidence' in T. Champion, *Centre and Periphery: Comparative Studies in Archaeology*. London and Boston: Unwin Hyman. 102–26.

Whitelaw, T. M., 2000. 'Settlement Instability and Landscape Degradation in the Southern Aegean in the Third Millennium BC' in Halstead and Frederick 2000, 135–61.

— 2001. 'From Sites to Communities: Defining the Human Dimensions of Minoan Urbanism' in Branigan 2001a, 15–37.

— 2004. 'Alternative Pathways to Complexity in the Southern Aegean' in J. C. Barrett and Halstead 2004, 232–56.

— 2012. 'The Urbanisation of Prehistoric Crete: Settlement Perspectives on Minoan State Formation' in Schoep et al. 2012, 114–76.

Whitley, J., 1991. 'Social Diversity in Dark Age Greece.' *ABSA* 86: 341–65.

— 2001. *The Archaeology of Ancient Greece*. Cambridge and New York: Cambridge UP.

— 2010. 'La Crète au VIIe S.' in Étienne 2010, 170–82.

Whittaker, C. R., (ed.) 1988. *Pastoral Economies in Classical Antiquity*. Cambridge: Cambridge Philological Society.

Whittle, A., 1996. *Europe in the Neolithic: The Creation of New Worlds*. Cambridge and New York: Cambridge UP.

— and V. Cummings, (eds) 2007. *Going over: The Mesolithic-Neolithic Transition in North-west Europe*. Proceedings of the British Academy 144. Oxford: Oxford UP.

Wiener, M. H., 1990. 'The Isles of Crete? The Minoan Thalassocracy Revisited' in Hardy et al. 1990, 128–55.

— 2007a. 'Neopalatial Knossos: Rule and Role' in P. Betancourt, M. Nelson, and H. Williams, *Krinoi kai Limenes: Studies in Honor of Joseph and Maria Shaw*. Philadelphia: INSTAP Academic. 231–42.

— 2007b. 'Homer and History: Old Questions, New Evidence' in S. Morris and Laffineur 2007, 3–33.

Wilkinson, T. A. H., 1999. *Early Dynastic Egypt*. London and New York: Routledge.

Wilkinson, T. C., S. Sherratt and J. Bennet, (eds) 2011. *Interweaving Worlds: Systemic Interactions in Eurasia, 7th to 1st Millennia BC*. Oxford and Oakville: Oxbow.

Wilkinson, T. J., 2003. *Archaeological Landscapes of the Near East*. Tucson: Arizona UP.

—, J. Ur and J. Casana, 2004. 'From Nucleation to Dispersal: Trends in Settlement Pattern in the Northern Fertile Crescent' in Alcock and Cherry 2004, 189–205.

Williams, A., 1997. 'Tourism and Uneven Development in the Mediterranean' in King et al. 1997, 208–26.

Williams, M., D. Dunkerley, P. De Deckker et al., 1998. *Quaternary Environments*. 2nd edn. New York and London: Arnold.

Wilson, A. I., K. Schörle and C. Rice, 2013. 'Roman Ports and Mediterranean Connectivity' in S. Keay (ed.), *Rome, Portus and the Mediterranean*. London: British School at Rome. 367–91.

Wilson, P., 2006. 'Prehistoric Settlement in the Western Delta: A Regional and Local View from Sais (Sa el-Hagar).' *Journal of Egyptian Archaeology* 92: 75–126.

Wilson, S. M., 2007. *The Archaeology of the Caribbean*. New York and Cambridge: Cambridge UP.

Wolf, E., 1967. 'Understanding Civilisations: A Review Article.' *Comparative Studies in Society and History* 9: 446–65.

Woodburn, J., 1982. 'Egalitarian Societies.' *Man* 17: 431–51.

Woodward, J. C., (ed.) 2009a. *The Physical Geography of the Mediterranean*. Oxford and New York: Oxford UP.

— 2009b. 'Quaternary Geography and the Human Past' in N. Castree, D. Demeritt, D. Liverman and B. Rhoads (eds), *A Companion to Environmental Geography*. Chichester and Malden: Wiley-Blackwell. 198–222.

Woolf, G., 2003. 'A Sea of Faith?' *MHR* 18: 126–43.

Woolley, C. L., 1955. *Alalakh: An Account of the Excavations at Tell Atchana in the Hatay, 1937–1949*. London: Society of Antiquaries.

Woolner, D., 1957. 'Graffiti of Ships at Tarxien, Malta.' *Antiquity* 31: 60–67.

Wright, H. T., 2001. 'Cultural Action in the Uruk World' in Rothman 2001, 123–48.

Wright, J. C., (ed.) 2004. *The Mycenaean Feast*. Princeton: American School of Classical Studies at Athens.

— 2010a. 'Political Economies in the Aegean Bronze Age: A Response' in Pullen 2010, 248–66.

— 2010b. 'Towards a Social Archaeology of Middle Helladic Greece' in Philippa-Touchais et al. 2010, 903–15.

Wright, K. I., 1994. 'Ground Stone Tools and Hunter-gatherer Subsistence in Southwest Asia: Implications for the Transition to Farming.' *American Antiquity* 59: 238–63.

— 2000. 'The Social Origins of Cooking and Dining in Early Villages of Western Asia.' *PPS* 66: 89–121.

Yalçın, U., C. Pulak and R. Slotta, 2005. *Das Schiff von Uluburun: Welthandel vor 3000 Jahren*. Bochum: Deutsches Bergbau-Museum.

Yalçinkaya, I., M. Otte, J. Kozlowski and O. Bar-Yosef, (eds) 2002. *La Grotte d'Ököüzini: Évolution du Paléolithique Final du Sud-ouest de l'Anatolie*. Liège: Université de Liège.

Yamada, S., 2000. *The Construction of the Assyrian Empire: A Historical Study of the Inscriptions of Shalmaneser III (859–824 BC) Relating to His Campaigns to the West*. Leiden and Boston: Brill.

Yasur-Landau, A., 2010. *The Philistines and Aegean Migration at the End of the Late Bronze Age*. Cambridge and New York: Cambridge UP.

Yener, K. A., 1995, 'Swords, Armor, and Figurines: A Metalliferous View from the Central Taurus.' *Biblical Archaeologist* 58: 41–47.

— 2000. *The Domestication of Metals: The Rise of Complex Metal Industries in Anatolia*. Leiden and Boston: Brill.

— 2007. 'The Anatolian Middle Bronze Age Kingdoms and Alalakh: Mukish, Kanesh and Trade.' *AS* 57: 151–60.

Yll, E. I., R. Pérez-Obiol, J. Pantaleón-Cano and J. Roure, 1997. 'Palynological Evidence for Climatic Change and Human Activity during the Holocene on Minorca (Balearic Islands).' *QR* 48: 339–47.

Yoffee, N., 1993. 'Too Many Chiefs? (or, Safe Texts for the '90s)' in N. Yoffee and A. G. Sherratt (eds), *Archaeological Theory: Who Sets the Agenda?* Cambridge and New York: Cambridge UP. 60–78.

— 2005. *Myths of the Archaic State: Evolution of the Earliest Cities, States and Civilizations*. Cambridge and New York: Cambridge UP.

— 2010. 'Collapse in Ancient Mesopotamia: What Happened, What Didn't' in Macanany and Yoffee 2010, 176–204.

Yon, M., (ed.) 1987. *Le Centre de la Ville (Ras Shamra-Ougarit III)*. Paris: Éditions Recherche sur les Civilisations.

— 2006. *The City of Ugarit at Tell Ras Shamra*. Winona Lake: Eisenbrauns.

Zaccagnini, C., 2000. 'The Interdependence of the Great Powers' in Cohen and Westbrook 2000, 141–53.

Zachos, K., 2007. 'The Neolithic Background: A Reassessment' in Day and Doonan 2007, 168–206.

Zaidner, Y., L. Centi, M. Prévost et al., 2021. 'Middle Pleistocene *Homo* Behavior and Culture at 140,000 to 120,000 Years Ago and Interactions with *Homo sapiens*.' *Science* 372: 1429–33.

Zamora López, J. A., J.-M. Gener Basallote, M.-Á. Navarro García et al., 2010. 'Epígrafes Fenicios Arcaicos en la Excavación del Teatro Cómico de Cádiz.' *Rivista di Studi Fenici* 38: 203–36.

Zangani, F., 2022. *Globalization and the Limits of Imperialism: Ancient Egypt, Syria, and the Amarna Diplomacy*. Prague: Charles University.

Zangger, E., M. E. Timpson, S. B. Yazvenko et al., 1997. 'The Pylos Regional Archaeological Project. Part II: Landscape Evolution and Site Preservation.' *Hesperia* 66: 549–641.

Zapatero, G. R., 1997. 'Migration Revisited: Urnfields in Iberia' in Diaz-Andreu and Keay 1997, 158–74.

Zeder, M., 2008. 'Domestication and Early Agriculture in the Mediterranean Basin: Origins, Diffusion, and Impact.' *PNAS* 105: 11597–604.

Zilhão, J., 2000a. 'The Ebro Frontier: A Model for the Late Extinction of Iberian Neanderthals' in Stringer et al. 2000, 111–21.

— 2000b. 'From the Mesolithic to the Neolithic in the Iberian Peninsula' in Price 2000, 144–82.

— 2003. 'The Neolithic Transition in Portugal and the Role of Demic Diffusion in the Spread of Agriculture across West Mediterranean Europe' in Ammerman and Biagi 2003, 207–23.

— 2009. 'The Ebro Frontier Revisited' in M. Camps and Szmidt 2009, 293–312.

— and P. Petitt, 2006. 'On the New Dates for Gorham's Cave and the Late Survival of Iberian Neanderthals.' *Before Farming* 2006/3: 95–122. (Online journal.)

Zimmerman, H.-D., 1975. 'Frühe Ansätze zur Demokratie in den Griechischen Poleis.' *Klio* 57: 293–99.

Zimmermann, T., 2005. 'Perfumes and Policies – A "Syrian Bottle" from Kinet Höyük and Anatolian Trade Patterns in the Advanced Third Millennium BC.' *Anatolica* 31: 161–69.

Zingarelli, A. P., 2010. *Trade and Market in New Kingdom Egypt: Internal Socio-economic Processes and Transformations*. Oxford: Archaeopress.

Zohary, D., M. Hopf and E. Weiss, 2012. *Domestication of Plants in the Old World: The Origin and Spread of Domesticated Plants in Southwest Asia, Europe, and the Mediterranean Basin*. 4th edn. Oxford and New York: Oxford UP.

Zubrow, E., F. Audouze and J. Enloe, (eds) 2010. *The Magdalenian Household: Unraveling Domesticity*. Albany: New York State UP.

Zuckerman, S., 2009. 'The Last Days of a Canaanite Kingdom: A View from Hazor' in Bachhuber and Roberts 2009, 100–7.

Zvelebil, M., 2000. 'The Social Context of the Agricultural Transition in Europe' in Renfrew and Boyle 2000, 57–80.

Sources of illustrations

p.2 Courtesy 360 Degree Historical Researches Association; pp.8–9 ML Design & Ben Plumridge © Thames & Hudson Ltd; pp.10–14 Geoff Penna © Thames & Hudson Ltd; 1.1 Georgios Alexandris/iStockphoto.com; 1.2 Louis Monier/Gamma-Rapho via Getty Images; 1.3 Thompson, J. O., 1948, *History of Ancient Geography*, Oxford, p.99; 1.4 Bibliothèque Nationale, Paris; 1.5 Schaeffer 1939; 1.6 Heritage Malta; 1.7 Courtesy Archaeological Museum of Banyoles; 1.8 Catherine Bibollet/akg-images; 1.9 Paolo Matthiae; 1.10 Drazen Tomic © Thames & Hudson Ltd (after Vaquer 1990, p.256, fig.132, p.258, fig.135); 1.11 Photo Cyprian Broodbank; 1.12 Bill Curtsinger/National Geographic Stock; 1.13 NASA/Goddard Space Flight Center, The SeaWiFS Project/GeoEye Satellite Image; 1.14 Photo D. Bainbridge; 1.15 Drazen Tomic © Thames & Hudson Ltd (after Tzedakis 2009, p.105, fig.4.6); 1.16 Jerónimo Alba/age fotostock/SuperStock; 1.17 Drazen Tomic © Thames & Hudson Ltd (after Naccache 1998, pp.142–43, figs.7.1–7.2); 1.18 Photo Daniel Cilia; 1.19 © Nicholas P. Goulandris Foundation – Museum of Cycladic Art, Athens; 1.20 Sipa Press/Rex Features; 1.21 Egyptian Museum, Cairo; 2.1 Drazen Tomic & Ben Plumridge © Thames & Hudson Ltd (after Grenon and Batisse 1989, p.8, fig.1.7, p.19, fig.2.4; Horden and Purcell 2000, p.14, Map 1; Woodward (ed.) 2009, p.72, fig.3.3a); 2.2 Drazen Tomic & Ben Plumridge © Thames & Hudson Ltd; 2.3 After Mitchell, W. I., (ed.) 2004, *The Geology of Northern Ireland*, Geological Survey of Northern Ireland, Belfast, p.149, fig.12.1; 2.4 Illustration by Pietro Fabris. From Hamilton, W., 1776-79, *Campi Phlegraei*, Naples; 2.5 Drazen Tomic © Thames & Hudson Ltd (after Grove and Rackham 2001, p.28, fig.2.4); 2.6 Drazen Tomic © Thames & Hudson Ltd (after Kassianidou and Knapp 2005, p.219, fig.9.1); 2.7 Artwork by Robert Nicholls (www.paleoceations.com); 2.8 Photo Cyprian Broodbank; 2.9 Drazen Tomic © Thames & Hudson Ltd (after Broodbank 2006, p.219, fig.3, adapted from McEvedy 1967, p.11, fig.6.2 by Andrew Bevan); 2.10 Drazen Tomic © Thames & Hudson Ltd; 2.11 © Elia Kahvedjian; 3.1 Illustration Richard Bonson. From Attenborough 1987, p.10; 3.2 Courtesy Mohamed Sahnouni; 3.3 Drazen Tomic & Ben Plumridge © Thames & Hudson Ltd (refugia after Médail and Diadema 2009, fig.1; snow distributions after Bradmöller *et al.* 2012, 'The Repeated Replacement Model – Rapid Climate Change and Population Dynamics in Late Pleistocene Europe', *QI* 247, pp.38–39, fig.2; insets after Bailey 2010, p.30, fig.3.1 and Mussi 2001, p.17, fig.2.3); 3.4 Courtesy Israel Antiquities Authority; 3.5 Duby Tal/age fotostock; 3.6 Richard Klein; 3.7 Javier Trueba/MSF/Science Photo Library; 3.8 Elisabet Díaz (after Boëda *et al.* 1999, pp.397–99, figs.3–5); 3.9 Elisabet Díaz (after Camps 1974); 3.10 Ira Block/National Geographic; 3.11 © John Sibbick; 4.1 Drazen Tomic & Ben Plumridge © Thames & Hudson Ltd; 4.2 © Kuhn and Stiner, 2003; 4.3 Ministère de la culture et de la communication, Direction régionale des affaires culturelles de Rhône-Alpes, Service regional de l'archéologie; 4.4 From Mussi 2001, p.255, fig.6.16(5–8); 4.5 Musée des Antiquités, Saint-German-en-Laye; 4.6 Prof. Daniel Nadel, University of Haifa; 4.7 After Clark, J. D., 1975–7, *Interpretation of Prehistoric Technology from Ancient Egypt and Other Sources*, Part 2, from *Paleorient* 3, pp.127–50 and Henry, D. O., 1989, *From Foraging to Agriculture: The Levant at the End of the Ice Age*, University of Pennsylvania Press, Philadelphia; 4.8 Illustration V. Feruglio. From Clottes, J. and J. Courtin 1994, *The Cave Beneath the Sea*, Éditions du Seuil, Paris; 4.9 (above) After Mithen 2003, p.12, (below) Drazen Tomic © Thames & Hudson Ltd (after Lambeck 1996, pp.602–3, fig.6; 4.10 After Bovio Marconi, J., 1953, *Incisioni rupestri all'Addaura*, BPI, Palermo 8.5: 5–22 and Graziosi, P., 1973, *L'arte preistorica in Italia*, Sansoni, Florence; 4.11 Photo Andrew Garrard; 4.12 Geoff Bailey; 4.13 From Roche 1963, Planches, fig.34-2; 4.14 Drawing Peter Bull Art Studio. From Scarre, C. (ed.), 2009, *The Human Past*, Thames & Hudson, London © Thames & Hudson Ltd, London; 4.15 Illustration Greg Harlin (wrh-illustration.com); 5.1 © Ian West; 5.2 Drazen Tomic & Ben Plumridge © Thames & Hudson Ltd; 5.3 (above) Drazen Tomic © Thames & Hudson Ltd (after Broodbank 2000, p.104, fig.25), (below) Photo Catherine Perles. Courtesy Hellenic Institute for the Preservation of Nautical Traditions; 5.4 Drazen Tomic © Thames & Hudson Ltd (boundaries adapted after Marshall and Hildebrand 2002, p.108, fig.1; inset after Smith 2010, p.11, fig.2.2); 5.5 Drazen Tomic © Thames & Hudson Ltd (after Weiss, E., and D. Zohary 2011 'The Neolithic Southwest Asian Founder Crops: Their Biology and Archaeobotany', *CA* 52, S4, pp.S242–49, figs.2–7); 5.6 Klaus Schmidt/DAI; 5.7 Drazen Tomic © Thames & Hudson Ltd (after Sherratt, A.G., 2005 'The Origins of Farming in South-West Asia', Archatlas (http://www.archatlas.org/OriginsFarming/Farming.php), figs.7–9); 5.8 Drawing Eric Carlson. From Kuijt and Finlayson 2009; 5.9 (above) From Byrd 2005, fig.454, (below) From Byrd 2005, fig.448(B); 5.10 Ashmolean Museum/The Art Archive; 5.11 Drazen Tomic © Thames & Hudson Ltd (after Helms and Betts 1987, p.44, fig.3); 5.12, 5.13 Courtesy Israel Antiquities Authority; 5.14 Illustration Oliver Rennert; 5.15 Excavations of Jean Guilaine. Computer graphics © Simple Past/Marc Azéma; 5.16 Drazen Tomic © Thames & Hudson Ltd (after Vigne, Carrère, Briois and Guilaine 2011, p.S257, fig.1); 5.17 Courtesy Pablo Arias - COASTTRAN archaeological project; 5.18 Photo Scala, Florence - courtesy of the Ministero Beni e Att. Culturali; 5.19 Courtesy A. Sampson; 5.20 Courtesy Jean-Denis Vigne; 5.21 Drazen Tomic © Thames & Hudson Ltd (adapted after Barbaza, Valdeyron, Andre *et al.*, (eds) 2009, p.67, fig.2); 5.22 (above) From Rodden, R. J., 1965, 'An Early Neolithic Village in Greece', *Scientific American* 212, no.4 April, (below) Drawing Peter Bull Art Studio. From Scarre, C. (ed.), 2009, *The Human Past*, Thames & Hudson, London. © Thames & Hudson Ltd, London; 5.23 Image processing by Mike Seager Thomas. Tavoliere-Gargano Prehistory Project; 5.24 After Marti, B. From Guilaine, J., 1994, p.375 fig.268; 5.25 Drazen Tomic © Thames & Hudson Ltd (after Guilaine, Manen and Vigne 2007, p.271, fig.125); 5.26 Drazen Tomic © Thames & Hudson Ltd (after Leighton 1999, p.58, fig.26); 5.27 Photo Jitka Soukopova; 5.28 Rahmani 2004, fig.1. Courtesy Dr. N. Rahmani; 6.1 Drazen Tomic & Ben Plumridge © Thames & Hudson Ltd; 6.2 From Di Lernia, S., and D. Zampetti (eds), 2008, *La Memoria dell'Arte. Le pitture rupestri dell'Acacus tra passato e futuro*, All'Insegna del Giglio, Florence; 6.3 From Caton-Thompson, G., and E. W. Gardner 1934, *The Desert Fayum*, Royal Anthropological Institute, London, Plate XXV (detail); 6.4 Luis Pascual Repiso. From Rojo Guerra *et al.*, 2010. Courtesy M. Rojo Guerra; 6.5 Photo Simone Mulazzani; 6.6 Drazen Tomic © Thames & Hudson Ltd; 6.7 (above) Courtesy JB Productions and Radomir Tichy, (below) from Fugazzola Delpino and Mineo 1995, pp.197–267. © S-MNPE, Luigi Pigorini Museum, Rome. Courtesy MiBAC; 6.8 Cyprus Museum, Nicosia. Courtesy Department of Antiquities, Cyprus; 6.9 Photo Cyprian Broodbank; 6.10, 6.11 Courtesy Archaeological Museum of Banyoles; 6.12 Museo Arqueológico Nacional, Madrid; 6.13 Ashmolean Museum, University of Oxford; 6.14 From Gallis, K., 1985, PL XV; 6.15 Drazen Tomic © Thames & Hudson Ltd (after Papathanassopoulos, G. A., (ed.) 1996 *Neolithic Culture in Greece*, p.56, fig.11; Athens: N. P. Goulandris Foundation); 6.16 Filiberto Scarpelli, Museo delle Origini, Sapienza Università di Roma; 6.17 (left) From Guilaine 1994, p.109, fig.75, (right) From Guilaine 1994, p.46, fig.26; 6.18 Photo E. Davanzo. Archive Prof. Santo Tiné. Courtesy Istituto per l'Archeologia Sperimentale Genova; 6.19 Museo Nazionale, Cagliari; 6.20 Drazen Tomic © Thames & Hudson Ltd (after Whitehouse 1992a, p.109, fig.5.17); 6.21 Drazen Tomic © Thames & Hudson Ltd (after Pétrequin *et al.* (eds) 2012, p.21, fig.3, p.696, fig.133); 6.22 Drazen Tomic © Thames & Hudson Ltd (after Cunliffe 2008, p.119, fig.5.6; Robb and Farr 2005, p.28. fig.2.1; Tykot 1996, p.69, fig.10); 6.23 Contu, E., 1964, *Tombe preistoriche dipinte e scolpite di Thiesi e Bessude (Sassari)*, Rivista di Scienze Preistoriche, vol.XIX, pl.V; 6.24 Photo Cyprian Broodbank; 6.25 Diros Neolithic Museum; 6.26 Photo Tilemahos Efthimiadis. Museum of Cycladic Art, Athens; 6.27 From Garstang, J., 1953, p.130; 6.28 © National Geographic; 6.29 Courtesy Israel Antiquities Authority; 6.30 Photo Werner Braun; 7.1 Drazen Tomic & Ben Plumridge © Thames & Hudson Ltd; 7.2 Austrian Police; 7.3 Drazen Tomic (after Tracy Wellman). From Scarre, C. (ed.), 2009, *The Human Past*, London: Thames & Hudson © Thames & Hudson Ltd, London; 7.4 Egyptian Museum, Cairo; 7.5 Drazen Tomic © Thames & Hudson Ltd; 7.6 © dk/Alamy; 7.7 DAI, Cairo; 7.8 Tips Images/Superstock; 7.9 (top) Drazen Tomic © Thames & Hudson Ltd (Butzer 2002, p.88, fig.4.5), (centre left) From Wilkinson 1999, p.318, fig.8.9(3), (centre right) After Ziermann, M., *MDAIK* 58 (2002), p.480, Abb.8. From Kemp 2006, p.87, fig.29, (bottom) Giraudon/Bridgeman Art Library; 7.10 From Amiet, P., 1961, *La Glyptique Mésopotamienne Archaïque*, Paris; 7.11 Ashmolean Museum/The Art Archive; 7.12 Illustration José-Manuel Benito; 7.13 After Strommenger 1980, fig.12 and Sürenhagen, D., 1974/75. 'Untersuchungen zur Keramikproduction innerhalb der Spät-Uruklichen siedlung Habuba Kabira-süd in Nord Syrien', *Acta Praehistorica et Archaeologica* 5/6: pp.43–164, map 2. From Algaze 1993; 7.14 Musée du Louvre, Paris; 7.15 Drazen Tomic © Thames & Hudson Ltd (after Van den Brink and Levy 2002, p.45, fig.2.4); 7.16 DAI, Cairo; 7.17 Photo John Ross; 7.18 Courtesy Israel Antiquities Authority; 7.19 Egyptian Museum, Cairo; 7.20 Williams, B. B., 1986, *Excavations Between Abu Simbel and the Sudan Frontier Part I*, University of Chicago, Oriental Institute Nubian Expedition, vol. III., plate 34; 7.21 from Borchardt, L. 1913, *Das Grabdenkmal des Königs S'ahu-Re*, Leipzig: Band II, Blatt 13; 7.22 Drazen Tomic © Thames & Hudson Ltd (left after Braemer, F., B. Geyer, C. Castel and M. Abdulkarim 2010 'Conquest of New Lands and Water Systems in the Western Fertile Crescent (Central and Southern Syria)', *Water History* 2: 91–114; this image p.105, fig.12); 7.23 Idlib Museum, Syria; 7.24 National Museum, Aleppo, Syria; 7.25 Photo Cyprian Broodbank; 7.26 Drazen Tomic © Thames & Hudson Ltd (after Ben-Tor (ed.) 1992, p.105, fig.4.18); 7.27 Vorderasiatisches Museum, Staatliche Museen zu Berlin; 7.28 © Roger Wood/Corbis; 7.29 Servizio Beni Culturali, Ufficio Beni Archeologici, Trento; 7.30 Alain Aigoin, Montpellier; 7.31 (a) Drazen Tomic © Thames & Hudson Ltd (after Robb 2001, p.178, fig.1), (b) after Broodbank, C., 2008, 'The Early Bronze Age in the Cyclades', in Shelmerdine, C., (ed.) *The Cambridge Companion to the Aegean Bronze Age*, p.67, fig.3.4; 7.32 (above) Drawing J. Pfaff. From Pullen 1992, p.50, fig.1, (below) Photo Ingi Paris/akg-images; 7.33 J. D. Dallet/age fotostock; 7.34 After P. Cazalis de Fondouce. From Guilaine 1994, p.213, fig.143; 7.35 After J. Porcar. From Guilane 1994, p.142, fig.92; 7.36 Museo Irpino, Avellino. Photo Giovanni Iannone; 7.37 © Miguel Salvatierra; 7.38 Drazen Tomic © Thames & Hudson Ltd (after Chapman 2003, p.170, fig.6.2; Costa Caramé, Díaz-Zorita Bonilla, García Sanjuán and Wheatley, 2010, p.94, fig.3; Díaz-Del-Río 2004, p.118, fig.5); 7.39 (below left) after M. Heath. From Guilaine 1994, p.430, fig.332, (below right) Drazen Tomic © Thames & Hudson Ltd (after Hägg, R., and D. Konsola (eds), 1986, *Early Helladic Architecture and Urbanization*, fig.32; Göteborg: Paul Åströms Förlag); 7.40 From Schliemann, H., 1874, *Atlas trojanischer Alterthümer*, Leipzig; 7.41 Pushkin State Museum of Fine Arts, Moscow; 7.42 National Museum, Copenhagen; 7.43 Photo Cyprian Broodbank; 7.44 After T. Ortego, E. Hernandez-Pacheco, M. Almagro et H. Breuil. From Guilaine 1994, p.111, fig.78; 7.45a Reproduced by the kind permission of The Fitzwilliam Museum, Cambridge; 7.45b Ben Plumridge © Thames & Hudson Ltd (after Broodbank 2000, p.98, fig.23); 7.45c Ben Plumridge © Thames & Hudson Ltd (after Televantou 2008, p.47 fig.6.8); 7.45d Drawing Douglas Faulmann; 7.46 Institut Català de Paleontologia Miquel Crusafont. Photo Meike Köhler; 7.47 © Andrej Crcek/Alamy; 7.48 Archaeological Museum of Aigina, Greece; 7.49 Excavations A. Müller and O. Lemercier. Photo O. Lemercier; 7.50 Drazen Tomic © Thames & Hudson Ltd (after Broodbank 2000, p.284, fig.93; Rahmstorf 2011, p.108, fig.9.2); 7.51 Pushkin State Museum of Fine Arts, Moscow; 7.52 Photo Pilar Torres; 7.53 DeAgostini/SuperStock; 7.54 Drawing by Gordon Thomas. Courtesy E. Peltenburg, Lemba Archaeological Project; 7.55 Gianni Dagli Orti/Cyprus Museum, Nicosia/The Art Archive; 8.1 Drazen Tomic & Ben Plumridge © Thames & Hudson Ltd; 8.3 (left) after Evans, J. D., 1956, 'Bossed bone plaques of the second millennium', *Antiquity* 30; Biancofiore, F., and Ponzetti, F. M., 1957, *Tomba di tipo siculo con nuovo osso a globuli nel territorio di Altamura (Bari)*, BPI, 66, (right) Drazen Tomic © Thames & Hudson Ltd (after Maran 1998, plate 71); 8.4 Drazen Tomic © Thames & Hudson Ltd (after Whitelaw 2012, p.151, fig.4.2, p.155, fig.4.14, p.157, fig.4.15); 8.5 Photo CMS (Corpus der minoischen und mykenischen Siegel); 8.6 The

Archaeological Museum of Archanes; 8.7 (below left) From Tufnell and Ward 1966, 43-3-4, fig.5, (below centre) From Tufnell and Ward 1966, 43-3-4, fig.2, (below right) From Tufnell and Ward 1966, 43-3-4, fig.10; 8.10 From Kemp 2005, p.226, fig.82; 8.11 From Kemp 2005, p.43, fig.13; 8.12 From Bietak, M. (ed.), 2007, *Egypt and the Levant*, XVII, 2007; 8.13 Beirut National Museum; 8.14 imagebroker.net/SuperStock; 8.15 © RØHR Productions Ltd; 8.16 Drazen Tomic © Thames & Hudson Ltd (after Roaf, M., 1990, *Cultural Atlas of Mesopotamia and the Ancient Near East*, p.119); 8.17 Troodos Archaeological and Environmental Survey Project (TAESP). Photo Michael Given; 8.18 From Myers, J. W., Myers, E. E., and Cadogan, G., 1992, *The Aerial Atlas of Ancient Crete*, © 1992 by the Regents of the University of California. Published by the University of California Press; 8.19 Courtesy The Department of Classics, University of Cincinnati; 8.20 National Archaeological Museum, Athens; 8.21 Drazen Tomic © Thames & Hudson Ltd (after Friedrich 2000 p.51, fig.4.6, p.80, fig.6.11); 8.22 John Hios/akg-images; 8.23 British Museum, London; 8.24 Drawing by Baroness von Bissing; 8.25 (below) Bodrum Museum of Underwater Archaeology, Turkey, (right) Schaeffer 1939, pl. IX; 8.26 (a) and (b) Trustees of the British Museum, London; 8.27 From Evans, A., 1921, *Palace of Minos I*, Macmillan, London. Supplementary plate IV; 8.28 From Bevan 2007, p.126, fig.6.16. Courtesy Andrew Bevan; 8.29 Luxor Museum; 8.30 Drazen Tomic © Thames & Hudson Ltd (after Bietak 1996, p.4. fig.2 and Bourriau 2000, p.187, with updates from Bietak 2009 'Perunefer: The Principal New Kiongdom Naval Base', *Egyptian Archaeology* 34: 15–17); 8.31 Drazen Tomic © Thames & Hudson Ltd; 8.32 Drawing William Schenk; 8.33 Griffith Institute, University of Oxford; 8.34 Schaeffer, C. F. A, 1939, pl.VIII; 8.35 Drazen Tomic © Thames & Hudson Ltd (adapted after Yalçın, Pulak and Slotta, 2005, p.409, fig.10); 8.36 (a) Schimmel Collection, New York/Werner Forman Archive, (b) Drawing by William Schenck after Callot 1987, p.208, fig.10, (c) Courtesy The Department of Classics, University of Cincinnati; 8.37 (a) Drazen Tomic © Thames & Hudson Ltd (after Yon 2006, p.11, fig.6), (b) RSO, archives of the mission. From Kassianidou and Papasavvas 2012, p.170, fig.18.2, (c) Drazen Tomic © Thames & Hudson Ltd (after Yon 2006, p.37. fig.20), (d) (after Yon 2006, p.35, fig.19), (e) Drazen Tomic © Thames & Hudson Ltd (after Yon 2006, p.52, fig.28), 8.38 Musée du Louvre, Paris; 8.39 Drazen Tomic © Thames & Hudson Ltd (data from Bell 2012, p.184, table 19.1); 8.40 British Museum, London; 8.41 After Schaeffer 1939, vol.III, fig.118; 8.42 Cemal Pulak/Wendy van Duivenvoorde; 8.43 Photo Donald Frey, INA; 8.44 Bill Curtsinger/National Geographic Stock; 8.45 Courtesy Donald White; 8.46 Rogers Fund, 1933 (33.8.1). Metropolitan Museum of Art, New York/Art Resource/Scala, Florence; 8.47 After Wreszinski, W., 1923–42, *Atlas zur Altaegyptischen Kulturgeschichte*, Leipzig; 8.48 Oriental Institute of Chicago, adapted by Sherratt and Sherratt 1991, p.386, fig.2; 8.49 Trustees of the British Museum, London; 8.50 Drazen Tomic © Thames & Hudson Ltd (after Shaw 2006, p.37, fig.26); 8.51 Cyprus Museum, Nicosia. Courtesy Department of Antiquities, Cyprus; 8.52 Photo G. H. Norrie. Courtesy Assiros archive; 8.53 British Museum, London; 8.54 (after Broodbank 2010, p.259, fig.20.3); 8.55 Siret & Siret, 1887, *Les Premières âges du métal dans le sud-est de l'Espagne*, pl.68. Haddon Library, Faculty of Archaeology and Anthropology, University of Cambridge; 8.56 Photo Cyprian Broodbank; 8.57 Gonzalo Aranda/Departmento de Prehistoria y Arqueología Universidad de Granada; 8.58 Associació d'Amics del Museu de Manacor; 8.59 Photo Cyprian Broodbank; 8.60 DeA Picture Library/The Art Archive; 8.61 imagebroker.net/SuperStock; 8.62 Archaeological Museum of Istria, Pula. Photo Fran Hrži , 2004; 8.63 Drazen Tomic © Thames & Hudson Ltd (after Chapman, Shiel and Batovi 1996, p.131, fig.102); 8.64 Giovanni Lattanzi; 8.65 Marka/SuperStock; 8.66 National Archaeological Museum, Athens; 8.67 Drazen Tomic © Thames & Hudson Ltd (distribution courtesy of Francesco Iacono); 8.68 (top) After Voza, G., 1973, *Thapsos*, Centre Jean Bérard Napoli, Siracusa 1973. From Leighton 1999, fig.75, p.151, (centre) After Leighton 1999, fig.90, p.171, (below) After Voza, G., 1973, *Thapsos*, Centre Jean Bérard Napoli, Siracusa 1973. From Leighton, R., 1999, p.151, fig.75; 8.69 National Museum, Athens; 9.1 Drazen Tomic & Ben Plumridge © Thames & Hudson Ltd; 9.2 From Wreszinski, W., 1923, *Atlas zur Altaegyptischen Kulturgeschichte*, Hinrichs, Leipzig, vol. 2, pl.67; 9.3 Cyprus Museum, Nicosia. Courtesy Department of Antiquities, Cyprus; 9.4, 9.5 Trustees of the British Museum, London; 9.6 Photograph courtesy of UCSD Levantine Archaeology Laboratory; 9.7 K. A. Kitchen; 9.8 Ägyptisches Museum und Papyrussamlung, Staatliche Museen zu Berlin, 21826; 9.9 From Kemp 2005, p.32, fig.8; 9.10 After Bates, O., *The Eastern Libyans*, London, 1914; 9.11 After Basch, L. 1994, 'Un navire grec en Égypte à L'époque de Ulysse', *Neptunia* 195, p.24, fig.14; 9.12 JTB Photo/SuperStock; 9.13 Photo F. Dakoronia; 9.14 After Champollion, 1835, 'Monuments de l'Egypte…', Paris; 9.15 (below) Archaeological Museum of Eretria, (right) Drazen Tomic © Thames & Hudson Ltd (after Boileau, Badre, Capet *et al.*, 2010, Harding 2000, p.191, fig.5.12, Iacono 2012, p.64, fig.5.2, Sherratt 2000, p.86, fig.5.1, with additions); 9.16 Drazen Tomic © Thames & Hudson Ltd (after Karageorghis 1976, pp.62–63, fig.11); 9.17 Francis Dzikowski © Theban Mapping Project; 9.18 Courtesy R. Guglielmino; 9.19 © Giorgio Todde - Sardonic Studio; 9.21 Drazen Tomic © Thames & Hudson Ltd (left) after Barker and Rasmussen 1998, p.55, fig.22) (right) after Cornell 1995, p.49, Map 3; 9.22 age fotostock/SuperStock; 9.23 Photo Cyprian Broodbank; 9.24 Museo Arqueológico "José María Soler" de Villena. Photo trazovillena.com; 9.25 Album/Oronoz/akg-images; 9.26 Drazen Tomic © Thames & Hudson Ltd (after Cunliffe 2001, p.279, fig.7.13, Cunliffe 2008, p.290; 9.27 (above left) González de Canales Cerisola, Serrano Pichardo and Llompart Gómez 2004, pl.13, (above right) Courtesy Dr. Fernando Gonzalez de Canales Cerisola; 9.28 Erich Lessing/akg-images; 9.29 © Georg Gerster/Panos Pictures; 9.30 Armée de l'Air, *c.*1934; 9.31 Trustees of the British Museum, London; 9.32 Museo archeologico nazionale, Cagliari; 9.33 Drazen Tomic © Thames & Hudson Ltd (after Aubet 2001, p.221, fig.48, Docter 2004, p.123, fig.5, with additions from Docter, Chelbi, Maraoni Telmini *et al.*, 2007); 9.34 Drazen Tomic © Thames & Hudson Ltd (after Giardino 1995, p.196, fig.90, p.239, fig.118, Celestino (ed.) 2008, p.436, fig.13); 9.35 (above left) Museo archeologico nazionale, Cagliari, (above right) G. Dagli Orti/De Agostini Picture Library/akg-images; 9.36 Drazen Tomic © Thames & Hudson Ltd; (after Cucchi, Bălăşescu, Bem *et al.*, 2005, p.433, fig.2); 9.37 Drazen Tomic © Thames & Hudson Ltd (after Rey da Silva 2009, p.19, fig.5, p.24, fig.13); 9.38 Photo Cyprian Broodbank; 9.39 Photo Ruth Whitehouse; 9.40 Musée du Louvre, Paris; 9.41, 9.42 Israel Museum, Jerusalem; 9.43 (a) after H. Sackett, British School at Athens, (b) Ben Plumridge © Thames & Hudson Ltd (after Popham, M., P. Calligas and H. Sackett (eds), 1990, *Lefkandi II: The Protogeometric Building at Toumba*, pls.13, 22) (c) Ben Plumridge © Thames & Hudson Ltd (after Popham, M., E. Touloupa and H. Sackett 1982, 'The Hero of Lefkandi', *Antiquity* 56, pl.XXIII:b) (d) Ben Plumridge © Thames & Hudson Ltd (after Popham and Lemos 1996, pl.135); 9.44, 9.45 Museo Archeologico, Florence; 10.1 British Museum, London; 10.2 Drazen Tomic & Ben Plumridge © Thames & Hudson Ltd; 10.3 Balage Balogh/ArchaeologyIllustrated.com; 10.4 Vorderasiatisches Museum, Staatliche Museen zu Berlin. Photo Scala, Florence/BPK, Bildagentur für Kunst, Kultur und Geschichte, Berlin; 10.5 Drazen Tomic © Thames & Hudson Ltd; 10.6 Museo Archeologico, Pithecusa; 10.7 Courtesy H. Singh, J. Howland © WHOI, IFE, Ashkelon Expeditions; 10.9 (top) District Museum, Limassol. RCS Libri and Grandi Opere, Milan, (centre) Antikensammlung, Pergamon Museum, Staatliche Museen zu Berlin, (bottom) Trustees of the British Museum, London; 10.10 From Boardman 1980, p.67, fig.46; 10.11 Drazen Tomic © Thames & Hudson Ltd (after J. Haywood, 1997, *Ancient Civilizations of the Near East and Mediterranean*, p.80); 10.12 Drazen Tomic © Thames & Hudson Ltd (after Cornell 1995, p.42, map 2); 10.13 Marka/SuperStock; 10.14 Zev Radovan/Bible Land Pictures/Alamy; 10.15 Ministero della Pubblica Istruzione, Rome; 10.16 Drazen Tomic © Thames & Hudson Ltd (after Morris 1992, p.175, fig.40, Whitley 2001, p.172, fig.8.2); 10.17a–c Drazen Tomic © Thames & Hudson Ltd (after H. G. Niemeyer 1995 'Phoenician Toscanos as a settlement model? Its urbanistic character in the context of Phoenician expansion and Iberian acculturation', in Cunliffe and Keay (eds), 67–88 [this image p.73, fig.3], Zamora *et al.*, 2010, p.208, fig.4); 10.17d Reconstruction by Gener, J. M., Navarro, M. & Pajuelo, J.M. From Zamora *et al.*, 2010, p.209, fig.5; 10.18 Photo Cyprian Broodbank; 10.19 Drazen Tomic © Thames & Hudson Ltd (after Étienne 2010, p.9, fig.2, Hall 2007, p.109, map 5.2); 10.20 P. Amandry/École Française d'Athènes; 10.21 Photo Gösta Hellner, DAI, Athens, 1984/371; 10.22 JTB Photo/SuperStock; 10.23 After Buchner, G. and Ridgway, D., 1993; 10.24 Drazen Tomic © Thames & Hudson Ltd (after Carter 2006, p.203, fig.5.9); 10.26 Museo delle Antichità Etrusche e Italiche, Sapienza Università di Roma; 10.27 Collection Dagli Orti/The Art Archive; 10.28 Tips Images/SuperStock; 10.29 National Archaeological Museum, Athens; 10.30 Numismatic Museum, Athens; 10.31 © Erin Babnik/Alamy; 10.32 After Fouilles de Delphes (Trésor des Siphniens) fig.133; 10.33 Photo Cyprian Broodbank; 10.34 Photo Hervé Lewandowski/RMN-Grand Palais (Musée du Louvre, Paris); 10.35 Numismatic Museum, Athens; 10.36 From Snodgrass 1986, p.56, fig.3.7 (Ephesos and Samos) and fig.3.9 (Selinous and Delphi); 10.37 Museo Nazionale di Villa Giula, Rome. Photo Hirmer; 10.38 © Paul Lipke, The Trireme Trust; 10.39 Drazen Tomic © Thames & Hudson Ltd (after Dietler 2005, p.43, fig.9, p.45, fig.11, Dietler 2010, p.201, fig.7.4); 10.40 Photothèque Centre Camille Jullian/LAMM MMSH – CNRS; 10.41 G. Camps; 10.42 (above left) Cabinet des Médailles, Bibliothèque Nationale, Paris, (above right) British Museum, London; 10.43 From Morin, J. A. J., 1912, *Dessin des Animaux en Grèce d'aprèsles Vases Peints*, Paris; 10.44 From Di Lernia, S., and D. Zampetti (eds), 2008, *La Memoria dell'Arte. Le pitture rupestri dell'Acacus tra passato e futuro*, All'Insegna del Giglio, Florence, p.169, fig.7-17-6; 10.45 Trustees of the British Museum, London; 10.46 Musée du Châtillonnais, Châtillon-sur-Seine; 10.47 Bill Curtsinger/National Geographic Stock; 10.48 Musée Archéologique, Naples; 11.1 Drazen Tomic © Thames & Hudson Ltd; 11.2 Drazen Tomic © Thames & Hudson Ltd (after Bang and Scheidel (eds) 2012, p.362, map 13.1, Morris 2009, p.100. fig.4); 11.3 Musée Archéologique, Naples; 11.4 Photo Brian McMorrow (www.pbase.com/bmcmorrow).

Colour plates:
I © Laws1964/Dreamstime.com; II Gordon Gahan/National Geographic/Getty Images; III Robert Polidori; IV NASA/GSFC/LaRC/JPL, MISR Team; V Johnson Space Center, NASA; VI Javier Trueba/MSF/Science Photo Library; VII © Gibraltar Museum 2006; VIII Photo H. Foster, Private Collection © Pierre Bolduc; IX A. Chene, CNRS, Centre Camille-Jullian; X Israel Museum, Jerusalem/Bridgeman Art Library; XI Philip Edwards, La Trobe University; XII Israelimages/akg-images; XIII Bible Land Pictures/akg-images; XIV Courtesy Israel Antiquities Authority; XV Ian Todd; XVI Tips Images/SuperStock; XVII © David Mattingly; XVIII After S. J. Mallon, S. J. Koeppel, R. Neuville. From Guilaine 1994, p.132, fig.90; XIX © Kenneth Garrett; XX Photo Cyprian Broodbank; XXI Courtesy Israel Antiquities Authority; XXII Israel Museum, Jerusalem/Collection of the Israel Antiquities Authority/Bridgeman Art Library; XXIII DeAgostini/SuperStock; XXIV Courtesy Polish Expedition to Eastern Nile Delta; XXV © Georg Gerster/Panos Pictures; XXVI, XXVII © Kenneth Garrett; XXVIII Flirt/SuperStock; XXIX Musée du Louvre, Paris; XXX John Hios/akg-images; XXXI AFP/Getty Images; XXXII © M. Bietak, N. Marinatos, C. Palyvou and Austrian Academy of Sciences, Vienna; XXXIII Gordon Gahan/National Geographic; XXXIV Bodrum Museum of Underwater Archaeology, Turkey; XXXV age fotostock/SuperStock; XXXVI © Hakan Öge; XXXVII Cubo Images/SuperStock; XXXVIII G. Nimatallah/DeA Picture Library/The Art Archive; XXXIX Trustees of the British Museum, London; XL G. Dagli Orti/De Agostini Picture Library/akg-images; XLI age fotostock/SuperStock; XLII Museo di Villa Giulia, Rome; XLIII Paisajes Espanoles, S.A; XLIV Colour reconstruction by V. Brinkmann *et al.*; XLV (above left) Ashmolean Museum, University of Oxford, (above right) Museo di Villa Giulia, Rome; XLVI Hervé Champollion/akg-images; XLVII Museo di Villa Giulia, Rome; XLVIII Archaeological Museum, Delphi; XLIX Photo Susan Kane.

Index

Page numbers in *italics* indicate illustrations.

Aborigines 57
Abric Romaní *84*, 105, 108
Abruzzi 66
Abruzzo-Marche 236
Abu Hawam *347*, 411
Abu Hureyra *111*, 136, *151*, 161
Abu Simbel *508*, *509*, 554, 576
Abul *508*, 574
Abydos 26, *205*, 208, *258*, *274*, 289, *346*: ivory handle *287*; Tomb U-j 270, *271*, 277, 286
Abyla 487
acacia 290
Acacus mountains 266
achabs 266
Achaea 411: people 462, 463
Achaemenid empire *508*. See also Persian empire
Acheron delta 443
Acheulian 84: 'cleavers' 94; tools 91, 95
Acinipo *508*, 538
acorns 106, 174, 179, 181, 210, 224: charred 362
Acqua Fredda *446*, 477
Acquarossa 540
Acre. See Akko
acropolis: Athens 410, 557; Lipari 217, 218, *218*, 475
Addaura Cave *110*, 131, *131*
Adige Valley 135, 227, 261, 478
Adonis River 301
Adriatic 122, 193, 196, 215, 217, 230, 233, 312, 332, 335, 415, 425, 431, 441–42, 444, 463, 473, 477, 576, 598: brooches 472; coast 180, 562; farming 190; Final Neolithic 203; independent trade 561; islands 121, 212, 562; Italy 75, 79; metalwork 460; mountains 63, 66–67, 190, 192; Neolithic expansion 187; obsidian 232; plain 132; pottery 464; Sea 29, 36, 55, 57, 73, 78, 90, 91, 108; seafarers 352; trading centres 504
Aegean 57, 73–78, 121–23, 127, 132, 146, 181, 188, 215, 217, 223, *259*, 306, 310–16, 333, 352, 372, 407, 412, 442, 502, 512, 596: amphorae *xxviii*, xxvi, xxix, 517; beads 118; boat images 327; break up of villages 306; Bronze Age 16, 537; cave sites 309; cist graves 235; city-states 540–41, 543–45, 555, 561; Cypriot pottery 368; Early Bronze Age 304, 305, 320; eastern influence 520; elite houses 541; exports 32, 472; figurines 228; Final Neolithic 234; galleys 465, 514; geography 65; geology 64; gold mines 551; goods 561; growth of towns 539; harbours 357; islands xxiv–xxv, 212, 214, 227, 370; large-scale shipping 550; Late Neolithic 224; limestone uplands 67; long-range trading 532; marble beakers 236, 238; maritime exploration 154; maritime trade 322; mercenaries 554; merchants 402, 555; metals 305, 336, *336*, 561; MIS 3 103; Neanderthal collapse 116; Neolithic 224; Neolithic 203; obsidian 232; olive oil 310; opium poppies 223; painted pottery 382, 413, 443, 469, 476, 477, 478, 481; palatial elites 462; political collapse 459; population 507, 553; population growth 538; population movements 523; pottery 216, 235, 402, 431, 458, 489, 490, 500, 517, 548; scripts 31; Sea 90, 93, 102; sea levels *129*; seaboard 335; seafaring 155, 183; seal-stone 474; seals (artifact) 336; ships 465, 569; shrines 531; silver 353, 378, 381, 582; social interaction 235; southern 600; standard measurements 477; -style vessels 360; -style wall-paintings, Egypt 403; sword 576; texts 536; tin 337; towers 551; trade 339, 410, 411; traits in the Levant 363; tree cover 157; tribute 323; triremes 560; and Tyrrhenian 502; volcanoes 68
Aegina 303, 322, 333, 371, 410, *509*, 548, 553, 556, 598, 610: people 555; triremes 560
Aenaria. See Ischia
Aeneas (hero) 513, 533
Aeolian islands 68, 212, 417, 429, 430, 443, 533
aerial: archaeology 33; photography 190, 224
Aetokremnos 148–49, *148*, *151*, 152, 154, 175, 177
Afalou bou Rhummel Cave *110*, 132
Afghanistan 278, 402
Africa(n) xv–xx, 18, 35, 36–40, 46, 58, 59, *63*, 64, 73, 75, 147, 234, 265–68, 456–58, 490, 494–95, 505, 527, 562, 594, 601: animal migrations 83; archaeologists 38;

Chanani 581; circumnavigation 554; climate change 157; coastal 57, 75, 107, 156, 523; Dabban sites 125; desert sands *37*; desiccation 270; domestication 198; donkeys 289; drop in water-level 263; early hominins 109, 111, 115; geography 57; growing connections 567–73; hominin expansion 84–87, 89, 91; islands 78, 128; lack of farming 179; landscapes 130; Mediterranean *xvi*, 196–201; Middle Stone Age 98; mobility 229; molluscs 90; Neanderthals 102; 19th-century archaeology 28; pastoralism 204–12; pastoralists 203; political independence 39; pottery 227; prevailing winds *37*; savannah 85; sea-crossing 320; seafarers 211, 212; shell ornaments 118; stone points *101*; sub-Saharan 572; tectonics 63, 64, 82
Afro-Asiatic languages 205
Agathe. See Agde
Agde *508*, 546, 566
Agia Irini 308, *347*, 371
Agios Georgios 16, *17*
agoras 544
Agrigento 443, 474
Aha *274*
Ahhiyawa. See Achaea
Ahmose 383–84, 386–87
Ai Bunar *204*, 236
Ain Boucherit xiii
'Ain Ghazal *151*, 168–70, 186, *xiii*
Ain Hanech 83–86, *84*: chopping tool *83*
Ain Mallaha *111*, 145, *145*
Ajax 610
Akhenaten 396, 408
Akhetaten *346*, *347*, 396. See also Amarna
Akkad 280, 285–86, 295, 388, 398–99, 409, 441, 511: hegemony 349; kings *285*, 304, 350, 366; language 393, 396; seals (artifact) 327; texts 285, 289, 295
Akko *347*, 363, 411, *447*
Akragas *508*, 538, 548
Akrotiri (Cyprus) 148, *148*
Akrotiri (Thera/Santorini) 29, *30*, 32, *347*, 371, 378: wall-paintings 357, 373–74, 388, 401, *xxx*
alabaster 68
Alacahöyük *259*, 304, 451
Alalakh *347*, 365, 367, 388
Alalia *508*, 550, 567
Alashiya, king of 407
Alassa *347*, 408
Alban Hills 479, 503
Albania 76, 180, 190, 474: obsidian 184
Alboran Sea 74, 127, 209, 573
Alcaeus of Lesbos 479
alcohol 36, 222, 273, 277, 333, 515, 516, 604. See also beer; fermentation; mead; wine
Alcorrín *446*, 496
alder 157
Alentejo upland 235
Alepotrypa *204*: jewelry *237*
Aleppo 294, 297, 365, 406, *447*, 487, *xxxi*. See also Yamhad
Alexander the Great 50, 486, 576, 584, 595
Alexandria 38, 40, 57, *509*, 525, 553, 578
alfalfa 464
Algeria 37, 39, 83, 86, 100, 101, 199, 210, 268, 568: climate 66; eastern 211; landscapes 209
Algiers 267
Alicante 194, 227
Alicudi 78, 212
Aliseda 574
alloying 246, 281, 304, 321, 336, 418
alluvium 238, 267
Almería 66, 312, 316, 334, 419
Al-Mina *447*, 499, 500
almonds 121, 157: Uluburun shipwreck 401
alphabets 407, 448, 485, 512, 513, 518, 532, 604
Altai mountains 432
Altamira *110*, 132

Altamura *85*, 96
altars 242, 297, 351, 362, 499
Althiburos *508*, 568, 569
alum 68, 442
Amanus mountains 285, 304
Amarna *346*, *347*, 398, 407–9, 411, 454, 456, 463, 466, 468: archive 396; diplomacy 448; letters 397, 399, 401–2, 412, 444–45, 449, 459
Amathus *447*, 492, *509*, 520
Ambelikou *347*, 367
amber 318, 333, 338, 423, 431–32, 442, 481, 504: Baltic 401, 562; beads *463*, 482; Italy 478, 512; Uluburun shipwreck 401
Amenemhat II 360, 441
Amenhotep III 396, 404
Amesbury 333
amethyst 68
Ammishtamru 394
Ammon 507
Amorites 349, 350, 499: names 363; tribal polities 366
amphorae xxvi–xxix, *xxviii*, 303, 379, 386, 387, 484, 494, 513: Attic, in Morocco 574; Canaanite *34*, 385, 405; central Europe 577; display 547; Gadir 527; Greek, in France 564; Greek, in Sicily 539; Iberia 484; Italy 516; Marseilles 564
amulets 230, 354
Amun 445, 446, 448, 454
Amuq plain 33, 64, 171, 188, 240, 241, 246, 284, 365, 499
Amurru kingdom 471
Anatolia(n) xii, 58, 68, 74, 75–77, 93–94, 102, 113, 123, 162–63, 184, 186, 196, 204, 216, 223, 237, 245, 277, 279, 283–84, 297, 315, 326, 338, 459, 488, 495, 576–77, 598: axes 236; beads 236; chariots 383; coast 181, 500; Copper Age 203, 219; cremation 460, 474; daggers 246, 333, 451; early farming 178; elites 520; empire 537; farming expansion 187; figurines *238*; Hatti 387, 388; lake district 175; massif 327; merchants 396; metalworkers 239; metals 69; monoliths 163; mountains 120; names 450; Neolithic 173; obsidian 145, 229, 248; palaces 366; passages into 294; plateau 57, 69, 105, 130, 132; pottery 333, *336*, 360, 391; precious metals 367; sea-crossings 155, 156; silver 376; tin 337; trade 343, 399; traits in the Levant 363; uplands 178, 507; west 304, 320; woodland 157. *See also* Turkey
anatomically modern humans 97–100, 102, 107, 109–16, 131. *See also* early modern humans
anchorages *17*, 75, 268, 477, 486, 487, 525: Cyprus 368; Egypt 403
anchors 363, 373: stone 291, 303, 330, 393, 553; Ugarit 393; Uluburun shipwreck 401
Ancona 477
Andalusia 93, 574: coast 194, 526, 527
Andarax River 317, 318
andesite 105
Andorran Pyrenees 180
Andros 153, 327, 523: boats 328, *328*
animals 70: as wealth 206; domestic, Libya 507; domesticated 161, 166, 169, 177, *193*, 289; dung 266; exotic 572; extinctions 92, 595, 596; fat 379, 549; figurines 165; game 90; Holocene *176*; husbandry 198, 215, 220, 343; images *131*, 163, 197; migrations 83, 95, 145; totems 247; wild 194, 221. *See also under names of individual species*
annaliste movement 18
Antarctica 42, *63*, 88
antelopes 104
Antequera *258*, 312, *312*, 318
Antibes 564
Antidragonera 16
Antigori *446*, 477
Antikythera 331
Anti-Lebanon mountains 64
Antioch 365, *509*, 578
antiquities: Greek and Roman 26; trade in illegal 48, 49
Anti-Taurus mountains 63
antler artifacts 105: picks 230
Apasa 411
Apennines *63*, 87, 105, 120, 180, 192–93, 427–28, 478, 561
Aphrodite 18, 450, 487, 512
Apidima Cave xiv

apoikia 524, 580
Apollo 522, 553, 558, *XLVIII*
Apulia 79, 87, 104, 119, 147, 190, 228, 351, 474, 507: obsidian 184
'Aqualithic' 198
aqueducts 540
aquifers 157
Arab Spring 49
Arabia(n) 59, 201, 390: camel trail 554; castle 365; dromedaries 572; exotics 487; imports 521; incense 499, 510; pottery 522; script 510; tectonics 63, 64
Arad *259*, 298, *298*, 299
Araguina-Sennola 183
Aral Sea 63
Aramaeans 499
archaeological: phases 203; science 35
archaeology: absorption into mainstream 29; aerial 33; colonial 94; environmental 36; Hellenic 50; maritime 34–35; Mediterranean 22–24; 19th-century 28; prehistoric 27; 21st century 29; underwater 34–35, 402, 564
archers: horse-mounted 577; images 315, *315*
archery gear 333, 335, 351
Archi *110*, 126
archipelagos. *See* islands
Arco *258*: stele *306*
arctic foxes 104
Ardèche 114
Arene Candide *110*, *150*, 192, 193, *204*, 230, 232: body ornaments *119*; leapfrogging *192*
Areni Cave 222
Areopagus hill 502
Argaric culture 566, 602: communities 419, 422; elites 421; sword 481
Argolid 444, 465, 584
Argonauts 329
Argos *447*, 460, 502, *509*, 540: population 522
aridity 88, 146, 163, 348, 350
Arkhangelos Mikhail 149
Arkosyko *151*, 175, 178
Arles 312, 316, *508*, 565
Armenia 222
armies 456, 558, 580: Assyrian 464, 507, 508; camel-borne 511; Carthaginian 567; Greek 581; Mesopotamian 559; Roman 571; Spartan 541; transport of 560
armour 462, 473, 547, 558, 610
Arno River 120, 539
aromatics 285
Arpi *508*, 539, 562
arrows/arrowheads 125, *125*, 146, 163, 172, 189, 207, 219, 242, 261, *261*, 305, 332: injuries 260, 315; Neolithic 16, 26
Arrubiu 446, *475*
Arslantepe *205*, 246, *259*, 279, *279*, 283, 304
art 109, 221: Egyptian 261, 273, 284; market 48, 322; representational 32. *See also* rock art
Artemis 556
arthritis 260
Arwad *447*, 449, 459, 485, *509*, 525
aryballos 517
Arzawa 399, 411
Asfaka *151*
ash, volcanic *30*, 372, *372*
Ashdod *447*, 452
Ashkelon *151*, 171, *259*, *286*, 303, *347*, 363, *447*, 452, *509*, 511, 513, 521: sack of 536, 559
Ashur-Dan II 446
Asia 112: animals 94; central *63*; early hominins 93; East 62, 78; exports, 32; hunter-gatherers 170; onagers 130; savannah 85; southeast *63*; southwest, climate 348; steppes 432; tin 70, 337, 366, 377
Asiago plateau 135
Asıklı Höyük *151*, 173
asses: steppe 104, 326; wild 99, *99*, 130, 197, 289
Assiros *347*, 412
Assiut *347*, *377*
Assur *347*, 367, *446*, *447*, 458, 459, 488
Assurnasirpal II 491
Assyria(n) *446*, 464, 470, 499, 507, *508*, 514, 542, 553, 571, 583–84: army 508; assault on Israel 534; demands on Tyre 511; economic growth 510; governor 523; hunters 104; images 486; imperial policy 508–12, 520;

kings 484; palaces 515; people 20; reliefs 513; replaced by Babylon 536, 537; slave labour 549; tribute 491
Astarte 455, 464, 467, 488, 490, 527, 530–31, 553
astral aids 341
astronomical events 41
Aswan 124, 200, *346*, 381
Atapuerca *84*, 92–93, 96, *97*, *VI*
Atatürk, Mustafa Kemal 51
Aterian industry 101, 103, 123: point *101*; sites 112
Athenian Panathenaia 544
Athens 44, 50, 67, 225, 373, 410, *447*, 460, 479, 502, *509*, 540, 547–48, 550, 552, 576, 582: acropolis 18; cemeteries 521; coins 556; democracy 583–84; empire 606, *606*, 607, 610; navy 15; population 522; temples 557; triremes 560; tumuli 519; workshops 551
Atlantic 482, 494, 573: coast 194, 566; connections 421; Europe 334; facade 61, 62, 235, 334, 483; fish 127; fisheries 573; Galicia 490; goods 563, 574; islands 567; metals trade 574; Morocco 263, 267, 334; Ocean 38, 63, 66, 72, 73, 82, 89, 90, 126, 146, 159, 184, 187, 209, 304; sea-cores 265; seafaring 574; tides 180; traders 492; traditions 311; weather 43, 66
Atlas mountains 66, 120, 121, 266, 267, 418, 574
atlatls 125
Atlit-Yam *151*, 171–72, *171*, 178, 219, *447*, 485
Attica *vi*, viii, 69, 152–54, *153*, 237, 321, 460, 487, 541, 552, 582, 583: amphora, in Morocco 574
Aude River 58, 195, 224, 504, 563
Aude Valley 180, 223, 307, 316, 334
Aude-Garonne isthmus 563
augurs 397
Aurès mountains 210
Aurignacian 114, 116, 118, 127, 152, 233: Sicily 155
aurochs 104, 105, 119, 124, 126, 130, 131, 136, 147, 161, 174, 179, 185, 197, 199, 201, *xv*
Aurora Bed (Atapuerca) 92
Ausonians 533
autarky 167, 397
authority 226, 314, 358, 454: pharaonic 553–54; political 608; Rome 541; sacral 375. *See also* elites; power; status
Avaris 32, 40, *347*, 362, 364, 371, 383–86, 388, 403, 407, *447*, 452, 471, 523, 575, 580, 595, 598, 604, *XXXII*: demography 416; palaces 455. *See also* Tell el-Dab'a
Avlemonas 15, 16, 17, *17*
awls 173: copper 237
axes 218: Alpine 230, *231*; basalt *84*, 230; battle 321, *321*, 559; bronze 363, 385; copper 260, 305, 351; double 576; flanged 425; greenstone 230, 342; images *306*; Morocco 267; moulds 236; polished 190, 230; shaft-hole 246; Sicilian 492; stone 165, 184, 197, 210, 215, 217, 246, 341; Uluburun shipwreck 401
Azor 289
Azores 567, 574
Azraq lake 121, 132, *133*

Ba'alat Gebal 302, 354
Baal 394, 534
Baal Hammon 543
Baal-Zephon 362, 455
Bab-el-Mandeb strait 63, 87, 112
Babylon *346*, 366–67, 397–98, *508*, 538, 559, 580, 583, 595: rule 536–37, 553
Badajoz 318
Badarian societies 203, 206
Bademağacı *151*, 175
Bafa Gölü 77, 159
balance scales: images 396, 411; model 371
balance weights: Iberia 484; Italy 477; Levant 502, 505; Phoenician 526; Uluburun shipwreck 401
Balawat *XXXIX*
Balearics 78, 90, *151*, 156, 213, 263, 331, 422, 481, 491, 493, 495–96, 498, 546, 567: isolation of 599; preservation conditions 29
Bali 94
Balkans 37, 58, 77, 93, 132, 188, 192, 230–31, 236, 277, 338, 431, 442, 459, 561, 575: coast 156; daggers 246; interior 116; metal 69, 351; mountains 120; Neolithic 190; precious metals 236, 237; and Rome 578; Vinča traditions 238
Balma Margineda *150*, 180

Baltic 402: amber 401, 431, 432, 562; beaker network 333; Sea 60, *61*, 73
Balzi Rossi Caves *110*, 119, 121, *VIII*: body ornaments *119*
banners 290
barbarian ware 463–64, 472
barbary sheep 123, 130, 197, 198, 199, 210
Barcelona 223
Barcelona Declaration (1995) 51
barge, royal 288
Bari 444
barley 125, 135, 160, *161*, 165, 193, 194, 201, 309, 420, 549: Egypt 206; Libya 507; Menorca 422; North Africa 568; Spain 223; wild 181, 189, 196
basalt 68: axes *84*, 230; bowls 242; pillars 241; vessels 208, 268
basket(s)/basketry 117, 169, 170, 179, 198, 242: Africa 198; grass *222*; imitations on pottery 191, *191*; Italy 428; -lined pits *207*; La Draga 219, *219*; painted *222*; Uluburun shipwreck 401
Basque country 195, 315: language 519
Basta *151*, 168
Bates, Oric 403, 404
Bates's Island *347*, 403, 404, *447*
Batsalis, Angelos 48
battle axes. *See* axes, battle
Baudelaire, Charles 18
Bay of Akko 449, 488
Bay of Biscay 334
Bay of Haifa *286*, 411
Bay of Kotor 335
Bay of Malaga 526
Bay of Naples *64*, 180, 335, 428, 512, *512*, 513
Bayraklı *447*, 502
beaches 74, 91, 92: fossil 90
beads 118, 120, 173, *199*, 206, 219, 236, 351, 354, 399, 432: Aetokremnos 149; amber 463, 482; carnelian *332*, 333; faience 41, 336, 343; Morocco 267; ostrich eggshell 199; picrolite 216; shell 113, *113*, 114, 184; stone 226
beaker network *258*, 333–35, 350, 417, 492, 528, 566, 604
beakers *334*, 563: marble 236, 238
bears 378
beavers 135
beds, gilt, Cyprus 399
beech 378
beehives 227
beer 273, 276–77, *278*, 310, 333, 378–79, 511: France 564; jars, 287
Beersheba 241, 246, 248, 293, 453, 510: crops 243
beetles 43, 348
Beidha *151*, 166
Beirut 46, 46, 303, *347*, 365
Beldibi Cave *111*, 132
Belgrade 236
Bellerophon 518
bellow muzzles 525
Belovode *204*, 236
Benghazi 38
Beni Hasan *347*, 361
Benzú rockshelter 100
Beqaa Valley 64, 365, 406
Berbers 51, 154: languages 205, 268
Berekhat Ram *85*, 99
Bering Sea 61
berries 124, 174, 179, 181, 220
Beth Shean *447*, 451
Beth Yerah *259*, *286*, 287, 298: silos *299*
Beycesultan *204*, 238
Bible 27, 452, 487, 498, 499, 510, 535, 559
Biferno Valley 192, 428, 477
big men 324, 325, 441, 502, 520
Bir el Ater *84*, 101
Bir es-Safadi *205*, 241
Bir Nasib *347*, 376
birch 120, 121, 130
birds 104, 106, 136, 182, 183: Aetokremnos 148; beaks 131; and boat symbolism 474; consumption *193*; flightless 70, 126; game 117; images 504; water 124. *See also under names of individual species*
Birket Habu 396
Biruti. *See* Ras ibn Hani
bison 93, 104, 105, *114*

bitter vetch 160
bitumen 99, *99*, 168, 239
Bizmoune Cave xiii
Black Sea ix, 55, 58, 60, *61*, 63, 73, 102, 113, 121, 159, 188, 222, 236, 306, 325–26, 335, 337, 412, 431–32, 442, 464, 575–77: battle axes 321; marble beakers 238
blackwood 410: Cyprus 399; Egypt 397; Uluburun shipwreck 401
blades 98, 101, 109, 232, 233: flint 26, 190, 242; sickle 393; stone 332
Blombos Cave 100, 106, 110
blood-group signatures 195
boars 100, 104, 124, 130, 136, 147, 161, 174, *176*, 179, 180, 181, 201: Aetokremnos 148; feasts 180; wild 182, 185, 193, 197, 210. *See also* pig(s)
boat images 291–92, *291*, *292*, 301, 327, 329, 334, 342, 373–74, 399, 416–17, 467, 474, 496, 513–14, *xxxix*: Africa 457; models 207, 338, 363, 472, 493, *xl*; Tarxien 351
boat(s) 66, 152, 172, 213, 214–15, 290, 328, 374, 444: of Amun 445, 446; -building 327; lack of evidence 154; papyrus 200; reed *153*, 177, 239, 290; small 466; solar boat of Khufu 288, *288*, *xxiii*; technology 75, 472–73. *See also* canoes; galleys; seafaring; ship(s); shipwrecks
Bòbila Madurell *204*, 224
body ornaments 145
Boğazköy. *See* Hattusa
Bohemia 70, 415
Boker Tachtit *111*, 113
Bolkardag mountains 240
Bølling-Allerød interstadial *129*, 130–31, 133, 136, 146, 149, 156
Bologna 504, 540
Bonaparte, Napoleon 26, 51, 68
bone: artifacts 105, 109, *199*; -boxes 241; chemistry 180; gaming pieces 401; harpoons 135; needles 117; plaques 351; -working, Italy 512
bonito 182
Bono Ighinu figurines 228, *228*
Book of Kings 498
booty 404, 405, 509
Borg in-Nadur *346*, 431
Bosphorus 55, 90, 113, 575
bottlenecks 185: communication 120; genetic 97, 101
bottles 335; gold and silver 482
Bou Nouara 508
Boussargues *258*, *307*, 316
bow(s) 125, 219, 242, 261, *261*, 464: composite 383; -driven drill 276
bowls 484, 517: basalt 242; bevel-rimmed 283, 284; bronze 472, 487; chlorite 168; copper 472; Corsica 217; Dalmatia 332; Egyptian 338; France 217; gilt silver *xlii*; handmade 463; house-shaped 343; pedestalled 243; stone 248, 296, 301; Uluburun shipwreck 401; wood 219, 242
boxwood 330, 366, 385
Boyd Hawes, Harriet 28
Brač 132, 212
bracelets 219, 230: gold 482; Morocco 267; serpentine 217; shell 268
brain size 98
Brancusi, Constantin 48
Braudel, Fernand 18, *18*, 19, 21, 23–24, 33, 37, 41, 43, 51, 54–55, 59, 64–65, 72, 73, 224, 257, 345, 466, 580, 582
bread 276: moulds 272, 283, 287; ovens 170, 526
bride-price 397
Britain 92, 94, 132, 158, 441: beaker network 333; Empire 28
Brittany 70, 235, 334, 415: axes *231*
broad beans 219
Brodsky, Joseph 54, 62
Broglio di Trebisacce *346*, 428, *442*, 444, *446*, 474, 529
bronze 69, 281, 282, 305, 336, 337, 343, 360, 410, 451: axes 363, 385; bowls 472, 487, 517; bull heads 493; daggers 360; drinking vessels 411, 520; figurines 26, *26*, 48, 493, 517; goddess, Uluburun shipwreck 401; Iberia 483; ingots 465; Italy 478; jugs 574; model, ridden camel 511; Mycenae 371; pre-alloyed for export 479; production 473; smiting gods 525; tools, Uluburun shipwreck 401; vessels 485; wine-mixing vessel 577; -working, large-scale 455
Bronze Age 70, 80, 242, 269, 343, 427, 500, 502, 505:

Aegean 537; art 32; central and west Mediterranean 415–23; climax 386; cloth industry 31; hoards 576; to Iron Age transition 417; juglets 517; kingship 470; Kythera 16; landscape 372; palace 188; palatial states 353, 355, 461, 468, 469; polities 540; towers 50; town 30; trading 377; Vivara 512; volcanic eruptions 29
brooches 472, 479
brown bears 104
Bubastis *259*, 270
buffalos 157: images 197, *xxxii*
Bulgaria 236
bull heads: bronze 493; libation vessel 371; relief 235
bull-leaping 370: images 388
bullion 280, 305, 515, 523, 556
burial(s) *ii*, 99, 105, 120, 124, 145, *145*, 147, 181–82, 268, 299, 317, 335, 351, 504: Africa 206; beaker 333; cairns 430; caves 248, 481, 498; children 207; Crete 409; Cueva Sagrada 311; customs, Carthaginian 581; Cueva de los Murciélagos *222*; Cyprus 343; donkey 289; elite 291; Etruria 493; founder 179; France 312; gender-distinguished 420; gravegoods viii, 235; high-status women 297; human 165, 167, 177, 247; Iberia *xx*, *xxi*, xxii, *xxiii*, 222, *222*; Italy 425, 428, 540; Levant 241, 342; Los Millares 318; Malta 235; miners 323; monuments 270, 275; more prominent 234; mounds, Spain 418; Mycenae 371; neo-megalithic, France 417; Neolithic 223; northern Mediterranean 223; Old Kingdom 349; Palagruža 332; rituals 482; royal 281, 498; Sardinia 340, 424; shell-decorated 131; Sicily 474; Ur 336. *See also* cemeteries; grave(s); funerary activity; human remains; tomb(s)
burins 109
Burnaburiash II 397
burning, controlled 136
Busiris 274
bustards 147, 148
butchery 99, 106, 149
Buto *259*, 270, 271, *271*, 274, 275, 286
Byblos *259*, 286, 301, *302*, 303, 330, *347*, 349, 354, 357, 363, 365, 398, 445–50, *447*, 467, 484–85, 499, 601: route 333; ships 303–4, 328, 338, 353, 505
Byrsa (Carthage) 490
Byzantium *509*, 576

Ca Na Costa *258*, 331
Cabezo Juré *258*, 318, 327
cabinets of curiosities 26
caboteur 473
Cabrières *258*, 316
Cadiz *258*, *446*, 487, 489, *508*, 598, *xliii*: archipelago 320, 329; rainfall 66. *See also* Gadir
Caere *479*, 503, *508*, 514, 553, 564: population 522; treasury at Delphi 558
Cairo 57, 83, 206, 445
Calabria 79, 87, 91, 191, 192, 218, 223, 233, 234, 475, 487, 550: greenstone axes 232; obsidian 232
California 61, *61*, 62, 64, 96: canoes 329
Calpe 487
Cambous *258*, 311
camels 157, 511: caravans 510; images 511; trail 554
Camino del Molino *258*, 311
Camp de Laure *346*, 422
Campania 64, 69, 316, 351, 428–29, 503, 512–13, 524: cremations 520; obsidian 232
Campiano plain 128, 217, 475, 581
camps 180
Can Tintorer *204*, 230, *258*, 323
Canaanean blades 279
Canaanites 359, 403, 449, 485, 532, 581: amphorae *34*, 385, 405; clothing, images 377; communities 363; donkey sacrifices 362; jars 379, 390, 393, 401, 402, 458; names 363; traditions 452; vintners in Egypt 387
canal system 554, 575
Canary Islands v, 56, 334, 574
canids 70, 127, 128, 183. *See also* dogs; foxes; wolves
Cannae 571
Cannatello *346*, *442*, 444, *446*, 474, 475, 476
cannibalism 349
canoes x, *xi*, 178–79, 182, 191, 290, 327, 328–29, 350, 374, 465, 477, 495, 597: dugout 198, 214–15, *214*, 217, 219; images 327, *328*, 329, 417; Neolithic 328
Canopic branch (of Nile) 274, 553, 555
Cantabrian mountains 195

Cape Bon 73, 211, 430, 490, 547, 581
Cape Gelidonya 34, *72*, *389*, *447*, 465, 468, 476: shipwreck 546
Cape Iria *447*, 465
Cape Maleas 16
Cape Matapan 73
Cape of Good Hope 266
Cape Province 61, *61*, 62, 70
Capéletti Cave *204*, 210, *258*, 268
Capitoline deities 540
Capri 95
Capsian groups 39, 199, 205, 210
captives 279, 287, 360, 361, 549. *See also* slaves
Capua *446*, 503, *512*
caravans 287, 289, 361, 373, 379, 407, 454, 464: camel 510; cities 365; donkey 367
carburization 451
Carcassonne 24, *508*, 565
Carchemish 379, 406, *446*, *447*, 459, 471
Cardial pottery *191*, 201, 210, 227
cargoes 35, 75, 373–74, 381, 442, 465, 472, 514, 546, 548, 550, 559: growing 549; sea-borne 327; transport by boat 329; Uluburun shipwreck 399–402
Caria 584: mercenaries 554
Caribbean 61, *61*, 62, 78, 204
Carmel range 76, 102, *103*, 105, 171, 172, 402: coast 364, 467: peninsula 286
carnelian beads *332*, 333
carnivores 93, 151
Carolingians 51
Carpathian: basin 325; communities 432; copper 442; mountains 69, 231
Carsac *258*, 316, *446*, 504
Carthage 39, 211, 383, *446*, 489–90, 494, 500, 505, *508*, 515–17, 520–25, 528, 533, 538, 542–43, 547, 552, 559, 564, 567, 569–73, 578, 580–82, 584, 598, 606–8, 610: armies 567; burial customs 581; chariots 571; coins 574; currency 556; elite women 542; empire *606*; on Etruscan coast 553; ironworking 571; ships 550; triremes 560
cartouches 287, 296
carts 355, 373, 393, 464: model 416; -wheels 416
carvings, stone 333, 496
Casablanca *84*, 85, 267
cash-cropping 407, 416, 488, 510, 516, 523, 539, 547, 549, 551, 564, 579: Cyprus 408; Ibiza 567
Caspian mountains 222, 337
Caspian Sea 56, 58, 60, *61*, 63, 464
'Castelnovian' Mesolithic 193
Castillo de Doña Blanca *508*, 525
casting 236, 335, 337
Catalans 51
Çatalhöyük *151*, 173–75, *174*, 186, *205*, 227, 269, *xv*
Catalonia *30*, 105, 219, 223–24, 230, 331, 422, 481, 504, 562, 566, 572, 581: dolmens 235; tombs 234
Catania 74
catfish 124, 206: sign of 261
cats 177: sabre-tooth 92
cattle 161, 166, 177, 201, 224, 309, 330, 343: absence of 175; Algeria 268; bone lesions 221, 244; Corsica 193; Cyprus *176*, 178; domestication 198; Egypt 273; haulage 311; herding 201, 204; hobbles 205; Iberia 421; images *206*, 289, 309, *311*; Italy 428; Jordan 363 lack of on Cyprus 216; Levantine in Africa 207; milk 162; North Africa 266, 568; pastoralism 205, 267; relative value to donkeys 289; Sardinia 476; shrine 343; traction 277; wild 210
Caucasian: metalworkers 451; pottery 333
Caucasus ii, 63, 85, 125, 222, 304, 326, 327, 337, 507
cauldrons 517: wine-mixing 531
cavalry 571. *See also* horses
cave(s) 90, 92, 96–97, 102, 127, 189, 193–94, 216, 219, 234, 241, 248, 330: Aegean 309; art 114, *114*, 118, 132, *ix*; Balearics 29, 498; burial 481; ceremonial 228; climate change 43; Israel 29; Italy 105; Judaean hills 244; Levant 245; occupations 205, 267; painted 35, 496; as ritual places 212; Sardinia 424; Spain 29
cave bears 106
Cave of the Warrior *205*, 241, 242, 246
Cayla de Mailhac *446*, 504
Çayönü *151*, 173

cedar 121, 168, 266, 285–86, 288, *288*, 294, 302, 360, 366, 378, 385, 445, 459, 470, 510: Egypt 397; imports 287
Celtic: beans 309; farming 578; people 51
cemeteries 49, 234–36, 267, 301, 502: Aegean 321; Athens 521; Carthage 522; Crete 323: desecrated 349; Egypt 271; Iberia 527; Ibiza 567; Iron Age 378; Italy 428, 479; Malta 343: as means of asserting land rights 311; Sardinia 546; Spain 318; Syracuse 28; Ur *278*; Venice 562. *See also* burial(s); funerary activity; grave(s); human remains; tomb(s)
Ceprano *85*, 93
cereals xxvi, *xxvii*, 125, 135, 160, 166, 169, 207, 220, 221, 245, 209, 296, 356: Africa 572; bulk crops 293, 393, 566; domesticated 177, 189, 199; Italy 428; La Draga 522; large-scale accumulations 240; Levantine in Africa 207; Libya 568; pollen 209; storage 264; wild 130, 160, 162, 163, 185. *See also* grain *and under names of individual species*
ceremonies 165, 544: Crete 370; drinking 390; feasting 243; royal 270, 277, 290; space 343; structures, Africa 206
Cerro de la Encina *258*, 327, *346*, 419, 420
Cerro de la Virgen *258*, 317
Cerro del Villar *508*, 527
Cerro Salomón *508*, 525
Cerro Virtud *204*, 237, 238
Cerveteri. *See* Caere
Cetina culture *347*, 351, 428: connections 477; expansion 431, 472
Ceuta 38, 100, *446*, 487, *508*, 527
Cévennes mountains 306
Chad 205: language 205
Chafarinas Islands 209
Chalandriani-Kastri *259*, *308*, 322, 327, *328*
Chalcolithic 175
chalices 416: Spain 420
Chalkis *509*, 522
chamber tombs 343
chamoix 104, 105, 130, 131, 134
Chanani 581
Chania vii
Channel Islands 62
chapparal 62
charcoal 36, 120, 121
chariots 383, 387, 389, 425, 454, 455, 500, 517: Cyprus 399; Egypt 397; horse harness 432; images 388, 411, 471, 571; North Africa 571; racing 558
charnel houses 299
Charybdis (whirlpool) 74
Chasséen culture 224, 232: landscape 310; pottery 236; villages 306
Châtelperronian 116
Chauvet Cave *110*, 114, *114*
check dams 244, 245, 293
cheese 170, 264, 412
Cheops. *See* Khufu
chert *xiv*, xv, 184: Cyprus 149
chickens 386: Asian 571
chickpeas 160, *161*
chiefdoms 242, 431
child survival rates 115
Childe, Gordon 23, 43, 316, 451
Chile 61, *61*, 62
China *63*, 96, 262: bows 464; silk 378
Chios 212
chisels 246: sign of 261
chlorite bowls 168
choppers 83, *83*
Chotts Megalake *158*
churns 243
Cilicia(n) 171, 188, 240, 241, 246, 405, 449, 458, 461, 470: Gates 68, 304; pottery 391
Cimmerians 577
cinnabar 68, 229
cinnamon 360
cist(s) 267: graves 234, 235, 312
cistern 569
citadel 321: Avaris 383, 386
cities: coastal 290, 488, 491; Crete 370; destruction by Babylon 536, 537; first 239; Harappan 284; Levant 394, 521; on the sea 303
citizenship 549
city-states 547, 549, 551–52, 556, 580, 583, 607: Aegean

540–41, 543–45, 555, 561; Etruscan 553, 564; Greek 582, 584; identities 576; Italy 540; rise of 537, 538; warfare 559, 560
civilization 314
civilizing processes 276–82
clam shells 575
Clarke, David 29
Classical period 20, 62, 87, 290, 309, 370, 442, 489, 490, 558, 608
Classics 25
clay 68, 170: boat models 327, 338; bone-boxes 241; bread moulds 272; coffins 451; Egyptian 301; imitation sistrum 354; low value of 380; pellets 172; potting 218; provenance 243; seal impressions 240; sealings 239; tablets 31, *31*, 276, 397, 448; tokens 168, 190, 239; vessels, ritual 16; wagon model *279*; weights 221
clematis 219
climate ix–xii, 56–57, 61, 88–89, 113, 120, 129–30, 146, 156–58, 202, 348, 506, 600: Africa 601; change 41–44, *42*, 100, 151, 265, 313–14; deterioration 196; fluctuations 90, 104; Levant 263; maritime 102; reconstruction 154; uncertain 245; zones *61*
cloth 10: industry 31; purple 509, 584; Tyre 509. *See also* dye; linen; wool
clothing 117, 118, 221, 275, 322, 463: Aegean 403; African 570; Canaanite, images 377; Greek 545; Levantine in paintings 357, 361; Libyan 457; patterned 306, 310
clover 273
Clusantin. *See* Grotta del Clusantin
Côa Valley *110*, 119
coasts 75–76, *76*, 77, 121, 200: communities 524–25, 527; geography 193; landscapes 35, 78, *1*; Levant 315; navigation 72–79; plains 306; routes 334; tourism *45*; wetlands 203
cockles 135, 181: impressed into pottery 191
cod 127
Coddu Vecchiu *346*, 425
coffins 288, 451: wood 297
cognitive development 87, 89, 111
coins 280, 555–56, 571, 574
Colline Metallifere *446*, 478–79
colonies 521, 524
Colosseum 157
colourants. *See* dye
combs 206: ivory 478
commerce. *See* economies; merchants; trade
composite tools 98–99, 125
Comte de Caylus 26, *26*
conduits 540
conflict 270, 315. *See also* warfare
Congo 107
conifers 157
connections 19, 230, 232, 307, 311, 323, 325, 596, 598, 599: African 567–73; Atlantic 421; Cetina culture 477; island 307, *308*; maritime 303, 338, *346–47*, 351, *446–47*, *508–9*, 596, *597*; social 115; urban *346–47*
Constantine I 24, 37
Constantinople 105
Contrada di Diana *204*, 218, 220
convoys 402
Cook, Thomas 45
cooking 190, 219, 225, 227, 296, 343
cooking pots 36, 465: handmade 526; Sardinia 217
Coppa Nevigata *346*, 428, 444
copper 69, 173, 207, 237, 246–48, 280–81, 287, 299, *299*, 304, 318–19, 336–37, 360, 441, *xxii*, *xxvii*: Aegean 411; arsenical 246, 281, 305; awls 237; axes 260, 305, 351; beads 206; bowls 472; Carpathian 442; chests 360; Cyprus 343, 367–68, 399, 401–2, 408–9, 476, 599; daggers 316, 351; diminishing importance of 515; Egypt 208; Iberia 482, 484; ingots 465; javelin heads 418; Levant 239, 453; Menorca 422; mines 236, 286, 316, 423, 488, 510; Omani 239, 284, 376; ores 218, 342; oxhide ingots *34*, 376, 377, 389, 393, 401, 403, 409, 431, 450, 477, 481, 567, 576, 610; oxide ores 305; production 300, 449; salts 441; sheets 299; Sinai 285, 360; smelting 238, 451; sources 69; sulphide 305; tools 267, 321; torcs 431; Ugarit 393; weapons 305
Copper Age 80, 175, 203, 216, 219, 236, 238, 239, 245–47, 269, 287, 293, 299, 300, 483, 505, 602: artifacts 26; Cilicia 241; communities 318; demise of 421; farming

243; fortified sites 317; Iberia 310, 601; Levant 244, 246, 289, 386; Los Millares 419; rock art xxiv, 308–9; sea traffic 301; settlements 306; temples 531; tombs 534
coral 168, 173
Corbeddu Cave *110*, 128
Cordoba mountains 222
cores: Greenland 42, *42*; Kythera 16; lake 88, 372; Persian Gulf 348; seabed 83, 88, 158, 263, 265, 372
cores (stone) 98, 232, 233
Corfu 45, 108, 180, 190, 514, 529
coriander 360, 401
Corinth *447*, 465, 487, *509*, 512, 514, 517, 529, 547, 550, 582, 598: enclaves 561; helmet 558; imports 532; perfume flasks 546; people 522, 529, 548; seafarers 524; shrines 531, 532; temples 540; triremes 560; walls 540
corn, grinding 296
cornets 243, 244
Cornwall 70, 415, 490
corralling 198, 226, 330
Corsardinia 121, 126–28, 152, 155
Corsica 36, 46, 70, 73, 78, 107, 120–21, 155–56, 182, 187, 192–93, 233, 307, 310, 334, 423–25, 476, 495, 504, 550: bracelets 217; cattle 193; as a gateway 480; isolation of 566–67, 599; leapfrogging *192*; Neolithic 216; obsidian 232; Roman 151
cosmetic pots 302, 354
cosmic order 262, 277
cosmologies: eastern 518; Egyptian 301; royal 333
Cosquer Cave 35, *110*, 121, 126–27, *126*, 202, 595, *ix*
Costa del Sol 65
cothon 486
Cova de l'Or *150*, 194, *204*, 227: leapfrogging *192*; pottery *191*
Cova des Carritx *446*, 496, 498
cowrie shells 168, *168*: headdress 341
craftspeople 276, 295–96, 356, 375, 388, 397, 551: mobile 517
creativity 110, 111
cremations 351, 500, 502, 533: Anatolia 460, cemeteries 234, 479; Italy 479, 512; ritual 473, 474; Spain 520; urns 351, 526
Cretaceous period *63*
Crete/Cretans iv, 28, 35, 50, 64, 70, 78, 96, 120–21, 127, 156, 183, 188, 196, 234, 307, 309, 320, 323–24, 335, 352, 358, 366, 368, 369, 370, 372–74, 381, 462, 487, 494–95, 502, 543, 572, 602, *i*, *ii*: in Africa 570; boat images 327, *328*; bronze axes as a symbol 363; cart model 416; deities 531; demography 416; eastern imports 354; Egyptian artifacts 336, 374; goblets 336; gold viii, 337; harbours 410; influence on others 371; lily 388; Mesolithic 182, 189; Minoan 16, 25, 31, 606; Neolithic 216; palaces 409, 432, 441; palatial collapse 459; polities 381; ports 472; scripts 518; seals (artifact) 353, 373; shell middens 378; shrews 150; stirrup jars 465; tectonics 65; trees 157; votive metalwork 517; wall-paintings 388; wheels 382
Crimea 575
Crkvice 66
Croatia 46, 102, 105, 108, 116, 180: arctic fauna 104
Croce del Papa, Nola 29, *346*, 427, *512*
crocodiles 65, 157, 532
Cro-Magnon rockshelter 109
crops 164, 166, 173, 194, 200: Aegean 413; Beersheba 243; Maghreb, absence of 205; Neolithic xxvi, 215; overproduction 264; spread of, North Africa 210; transport of 279
Croton *509*, 551
crowns 247
crucibles 493, 525
crustaceans 180
Cueta 201
Cueva de los Murciélagos *204*, 222, *222*, 223
Cueva del Romeral 312, *312*
Cueva Sagrada *258*, 311
cult(s): offerings 243; sites 243; water *228*, 424
cultivation, floodwater 165, 196
culture: elite 276, 277, 278; symbolic 219; transformation of 160
Cumae *508*, 512, 524
cumin 410
cuneiform 24, 276, 407, 448, 518: literacy 362; tablets 295
Cunliffe, Barry 24

cups 335, 444: Athenian 548; Greek-style, in France 566; handled 416; ivory, Morocco 267; Nuzi ware 391; painted 227, *227*; patterned 381; Rhodian 512
currencies 515, 555–56: metal-based 375; proto- 280, 305, 376, 413, 431, 602
currents 74
Cyclades 16, 28, 48, 108, 125, 152–53, 182, 213, 217, 234, 237, 320, 322–24, 331, 350, 370, 430, 431, 460, 467, 500, 518, 523, 531, 541, 552, 584, 600: boat images 327, *328*; marble figurines 25, 48, *48*, 322–23, *322*, 335; networks 307–8, *308*; sea-trading 335; ships 329; trade 339; volcanic eruptions 29
Cyclopes 26
Cyclops Cave *151*, 182, *182*, *204*, 212
cylinder seals 276, 283, 294, 336, 415: demise of 518; Egypt 362; Uluburun shipwreck 400–1
Cypro-Minoan script 368, 393, 409
Cyprus 28, 31, 46, 49–50, 74, 76, 78, 90, 95, 148–49, *148*, 152–53, 162, 171, 173, 183–84, 186–88, 248, 304, 342–43, 354, 360, 367–68, 396, 399, 405, 407–9, 431, 445, 450, 452, 477, 487, 490, 492, 494, 498, 511–12, 523, 534, 542, 554, 556, 583–84, 596, 604: adoption of Greek identity 533; Aegean painted pottery 411; animals 70, *176*; artifacts, Uluburun shipwreck 401; ascendancy of 470; attacks on 462; boat buying 394; copper 402; exports 450; farming 495; figurines 215–16, *216*; geography 64, 65; 'house societies' iii; influence on Sardinia 476; ironware 460; isolation of 599; juglets 380, 390, 391; letter from 398; links with Egypt 384; links with Sardinia 465; literacy 518; maritime trade 404; merchants 468, 555; metals 69, 377; migrations to 463; Neolithic 175, 178; Phoenician inscriptions 488; pithoi 465; ports 466; pottery 444; roundhouses *176*; scripts 375; sea-crossings 154, 156; seclusion 343; sheep 382; ships 489, 569; shipwrecks 35; tombs 414, 519, 520; traders 488; traits in the Levant 363; venison 382; Wenamun on 449
Cyrenaica 38, 40, 73, 76, 101, 112, 123, 157, 210, 266, 268, 568–70, 572–73, 601: coins 574
Cyrene *509*, 570–72, 583, *xlix*: chariots 571

Dabban 112, 123, 125
Dafuna 198
Dagan 295
daggers 246, 247, 277, 306, 351, 363, 371, 480: Anatolia 451; bronze 360; copper 316, 351; flint 305, 316; gold 333; Iberia 418, 483; images *306*, 308, 324; iron 304
Dahkla 200, *447*, 457
dairy products 279, 293, 310
Dalmatia 58, 65, 74–75, 87, 108, 123, 155, 159, 183, 190, 223, 227, 230, 305, 310, 312, 351, 425, 426, 474, 477, 504, 562, 602: bowls 332; islands 79; mountains 316; Neanderthals 102
dam-building 37
Damascus 163–64, *347*, 363, *447*, 499, 500
Damietta branch (of Nile) 553
Danaans 462
dance 545
Danilo phase 227
Danube River 58, 326, 335, 401, 575: basin 113; plain 425
Dar es Sultan *84*, 98
Dardanelles 50, 55, 73, 90, 113, 121, 181, 188, 322, 575, 598
date palm 174, 244, 457
dates (fruit) 244
de Nerval, Gérard 18
Dead Sea 64, 68, 77, 121, 146, 163, 241–42, 246: Scrolls 246
death rituals, Malta 341
dedications 536
deer 65, 70, 91, 94–95, 105, 128, 131, 136, 151, 157, 161, 174, 177, 179, 181–83, 215, 247, 567: Cyprus 216; extinct 127; hunting 178; images 221, 228; Italy 93; teeth 118
deforestation 71
Değirmentepe *205*, 246
dehesa 310
deities 275, 295, 376, 486, 493, 530, 534, 538, 543, 553, 556, 558, 580: Italy 540; politically neutral 467
Delos 213, *509*, 531, 545
Delphi *509*, 531, 532, 552, 558, *xlviii*
Demaratos of Corinth 542, 543, 551
democracy 583, 584

demography 160, 358, 416, 506–7, 582
Denyen 462
depas cups 335
desertification 42, 207, 363
'desert kites' 169, *169*
deserts 89, 93, 202, 262, 265–68. *See also* Negev; Sahara
desiccation 29, 265, 270
Dhar Tichitt 266
Dhaskalio Kavos *259*, *308*, 322, *322*, 323
Dhimini *204*, 225, *225*
Dhra' *151*, *165*
dialects 226
Diana-Bellavista pottery 236
Dido 490
Didyma 159
diet 36, 117, 146, 166, 179, 180, 194, 325: donkey 289; vegetarian 220
diffusionism 24
digging sticks 219
Dikili Tash *204*, 222
Dimitra 222
Dinarics 63, 66, 190, 192
dinosaurs 63
Diomedes 562
Dionysios of Halikarnassos 542
diseases 159, 160, 166, 376: animal 150; human 261
Dispilio *204*, 219
ditches 224, 226, 316, 318
diversification 264
divinities. *See* deities
Djebaut, shrine of *271*
Djerba 39, 78, 213, 266, 573
Djoser, pyramid of 273
Dmanisi 85
DNA iv, xii, xviii, xxii, 112, 116, 186: ancient 92; mitochondrial vi, 36, 96, 97; vines 222. *See also* genetics
Dodecanese 212, 460
Dog River 68, *iii*
Doganella 540
dogs 133, 161, 175, *176*, 316, *316*, 330, 428
dogwood arrows 219
dolmens 235, 241, 311, 312, 349, 424, 444, 568: Corsica 423; Menorca 422
Dolomites 114
dolphins 106, 180, 183
domestication 160, 184, 186, 193–94, 196, 198, 221: Egypt 206; exogenous 185
donkey(s) 130, 289, 297, 326, 327, 343, 355, 377, 444, 473: caravans 361, 367, 464; figurines 289, *289*; Italy 479; sacrificed 362; trail 550
Dor 445, *447*, 451, 467
Dordogne 105
dormice 330. *See also* mice
doves, Ugarit 395
dowries 397
drainage 226
dress pins 306, 473
drills, bow-driven 276
drinking: ceremonies 336, 390; cups 227, 443; customs 545; events 482; goblets 294; horns 243, 247; vessels 278, 333, *334*, 335, 343, 351, 411, 416, 431, 500, 517, 520, 539, 547, 564
dromedaries 453, 464, 572
drought(s) 44, 67, 92, 124, 161, 264, 313, 348, 361: -free areas 352
drying 264
Dugi 108
Durrell, Lawrence 55, 56
Dursunlu *85*, 94
dusky grouper 158
dwarf elephants 70, *71*, 91, 149
dwarf hippopotami 95
dwarfism 70
dye 125, 244–45, 296, 306, 485, 499, 515: Carthage 490; purple 377–78, 393, 444, 527

eagles 147
Eanna temple (Uruk) 275
ear pathology 171
early modern humans 97, 108, 595, 596: expansion 110–11, 594
Early Stone Age 91, 100

earrings 383
earthquakes 64
East Anglia 92
Easter Island 342
Ebesus *508*, 567, 582
Ebla *259*, 294–96, 301–4, 315, 336–38, *347*, 349, 355, 365, 367, 472, 598, 600, 601, *xxv*: clay tablets *31*; kings 323; limestone inlay *295*; tin 337
Ebro River 58, 195, 230, 331, 481, 527
eclogite 230
ecology 42, 71, 122, 262, 595
economies/economic(s): capital-based 323, 375; growth 579; inequities 416, 441, 470, 515; interregional 283; large-scale 172, 276; life 315; mercantile 491; networks 306; palace-based 295, 296; production 167; reorganization 282; security 359; transformations 160, 279
Edera Cave 191
Edom 453, 507, 510
eels 183
egalitarian societies 226, 242, 260
Egypt/Egyptian 18, 27, 40, 77, 198, 203, 238–39, 245, 248, 269–75, 297, 304–5, 312, 314–16, 349, 362, 383–86, 397, 404–5, 407, 455, 470–71, 491, 553–55, 570, 572, 575, 594, 604: Amarna age 468; anchorages 403; art 52, 261, *261*, 284; artifacts on Crete 374; basalt vessels 268; boat images 292, 303, 327, 373, 374; bowls 248, 296, 338; bulk movements of cereals 393; Canaanite clothing, images of 377; cattle herding 205; cedar imports 286; chariots 571; clay 301; cosmology 301; Cretan pottery 380; Cypriot pottery 368, 385; deities 532; diminished stature 448, 454; domesticates 206; 18th dynasty 386, 387, 455; elites 268; expeditions 333; exports 32; farming xxvi, 200; grain harvest 67; graves 381; hieroglyphs 354; horses 383, 464; imports 360; influence on Levant 451; king at Delphi 558; kings 386, 388; languages 205, 268, 290, 393; large-scale societies 262; and the Levant 52, *259*, 286, 488; Levantine vines 379; Libyans in art 52; linen 499; links to Cyprus 384; looms 221; Mamluk rulers 537; mercenaries 559; merchants 396; monuments 31; New Kingdom *346*, 383, 387, 396, 406, 454, 457, 471, 498; New Kingdom pharaohs 68, 386; Nile Delta 37; and nomadic seafarers 466; Nubian in art 52; olive oil 379; pharaohs 41, 59, 74; pottery 287; Predynastic 207; preservation conditions 29; propaganda 461, 462; rise of 258, 600; rituals 271; rulers 261, 262; sacred buildings 329; seaborne attacks on Levant 326; ships 402; stone vessels 243, 336, 343, 381, 382, 394, 526; -style faience 517; temples 360; tin 337; tombs 26, 270, 271, 286; tourism 45; trade 374, 378; traits in the Levant 363; 12th dynasty 359, 361; 26th dynasty 553; war on 508, 509, 511; writing 276
Ein Gedi *205*, 242, 243, 247, *xx*
einkorn wheat 160, *161*
Ekron *447*, 452, *509*, 510
Ekwesh 462
El Argar 419, 420
El Castillo Cave *110*, 113
El Malagón *258*, 317
Elba 127, 155, 212, 504, 527: iron 512, 546, 550; obsidian 232
elders 226, 242, 276
electrum 248, *xix*: currency 556
Elephantine *258*, 302, 360
elephants 70, 92, 104, 151, 157, 387: fossil 26; images 197; Italy 93; ivory 267, 365, 390, 391, 401, 403, 409, 414. *See also* dwarf elephants
Elgin marbles 18
Elissa 490, 580
elite(s) 264, 280, 333, 349, 358, 603–4: Aegean 338; burials 291; coastal 388; competitive 411; culture 276–78; Egyptian 268; funerals 577; Greek 558; houses, Aegean 541; intermarriage, description in texts 295; Iron Age 463, 519, 521, 523, 530, 534; landed 245; lifestyles 517, 558; lifestyles, demise of 411; male seafarers 329; power-sharing 541–43; rising 503–4; suicide 580; urban 542, 570; women 370, 541–42
elk 122
El-Kiffen *258*, 267
el-Lisht 359
elm 120
el-Mekta *150*, 199

Elymian language 519
emery 360
emmer wheat 160, *161*
Empedocles of Akragas 26
empires 269, 404–15, *508–9*, 578, 606–7, *606*
emporia 552, 553, 557
Emporion *508*, 563, 566
En Besor *259*, 287
encampments 206
enclosures 194, 318, 538
endemics 91, 95, 104, 150, 152
English Channel 492
Enkomi *347*, 407–9, 415, *447*, 449, 450, 462, 478, 523
Enlightenment 26
entrepôts 428, 473, 474, 478, 499, 529, 538
environment 61, 66–67, 100, 108, 132, 133, 262: Levant 293
environmental: archaeology 36; challenges 115, 117; change 41–44, 149, 262–65; conditions, changing 233; developments 103; diversity 89; mediterraneanization 313; sustainability 45
Epée de Roland *258*, 312, *313*
Ephesus 77, *347*, 411, *509*, 556, 531, 557
Ephyra 443
Epigravettian 123
Epipalaeolithic 131, 136
Epirus 119, 443, 473
equids 130, 311. *See also* donkeys; horses
Eretria *509*, 520, 522
Eridu *204*, 239
Eritrea 285
erosion 71, 263, 421
Erzgebirge 70
Es Coll de Cala Morell *346*, *422*
Es Tudons *446*
escargotières 210, *211*
esparto grass 222, *222*, 311
Este *508*, 562
estuaries 106, 188, 195
Étang de Berre *258*, 307
Eteocypriot 50
Ethiopia 69
ethnic: cleansing 50; distinctions 547; self-awareness 532–34
ethnographic parallels 203–4
Etna 38, 342, 529
Etruria 26, 28, 31, 33, 68–69, 478–80, 482, 492–93, 503–4, 512, 514, 517, 524, 534, 566, 580, 598: amphorae 516; *bucchero* pottery 546, *xlv*; cremations 520; currency 556; deities 540; elite women 541–42; grapes 515; growth of towns 539; imported pottery 548; language 519; lineages 543; metal trade 527, 562, 567; metal vessels 577; people 532, 607; ports 553; pottery inscriptions 542; sea trade 546; ships 550; temples 558; texts 553; tombs 48, 544; traders 564
Euboea 78, 79, *153*, 460, 500; 512, 515, 520, 550: seafarers 524
Euphrates River 59, 132, 136, 161, 165, 170, 177, 283, 284, 294, 295, 349, 365, 395, 406
Eurasia 63, 89: early hominins 109; farming 594; Neolithic 165
Euripos Strait 321, 487, 550
Europa 503
Europe 58, *63*, 230, 245, 335: animal migrations 83; beaker network 333; central 576, 577; early hominins 109, 115; hunter-gatherer population 122; imperialism 62; intermarriage 219; landscapes 223; lions 94; megalithic tombs 41; metallurgy 236; Middle Palaeolithic 98; Neolithic 204; Neolithicization 184–88; 19th century 102; plains 113; river valleys 222; societies 442; southern, cremation 460; Upper Palaeolithic 114. *See also under names of individual countries*
European Union 51
Evans, Sir Arthur 28, 352
evaporites 82
evolutionary anthropology xiii–xiv, 242
Evros River 188
exchange 162, 168, 172, 229, 230, 233, 243, 337, 359, 596, 602: arenas 230; cross-cultural 398; Maghreb 267; networks 441; rates 556; standards 425; values, differences 413, 414. *See also* currencies; gift-exchange; trade

Exodus 452
exotics 145: fruits 244; goods 243, 329, 567; pottery 342
extinctions 89, 150, 151, 595, 596
Ezekiel 536

Fabris, Pietro *64*
faience 388, 391, 423, 430, 441, 487, 517, 555: beads 41, 336, 343; Crete 369; cylinder seals 415; Mycenae 371; necklaces 351; plaques 404
fallow deer 104, 216, 567: antlers 100; Cyprus *176*, 342
famines 349
farmers iv; deported to Mesopotamia 510; France 195; Jordan 48; Libyan 570; migrant 193; Nile Delta 360; reduced to peasants 270; sedentary 268
farming 43, 62, 162, 165, 168–69, 172, 175, 178, 220, 299: capital-intensive 296; Celtic 578; Cyprus 177, 189, 495; Cyrenaica 571; demise of 293; diversified 292; early 160; as entrapment 166; Etruria 503; Eurasian 594; France 422; Holocene 265; Istria 191; large-scale 356; Levant 241, 243, 244; Maghreb v, xix, 205; mixed 166, 205, 309, 310, 355, 452, 568; modern 44; North Africa 568; Sardinia 476; settlements 224; small-scale 350; spread of *150–51*, 184, *185*, *192*, 193, 196, 200, 227, 238, 332, 595–96, 599, 600; sustainable 421; techniques, Cyprus 368; transition to 184–88; triumph of 219
fatty acids 170
fava beans 549
Fayum 206, 207, 384, 456: storage pits *207*
feasting 168, 218, 220, 324, 390, 420, 482, 502, 519, 542
feathers 461: headdresses 478
Feinan 246, 453
fermentation 221, 272, 276, 333, 310, 416, 515. *See also* alcohol; beer; mead; wine
Fertile Crescent 59, 135, *151*, 160–64, *161*, 173, 185–86, 244, 594–95. *See also* Levant
fertility, Neolithic obsession with 195
Fezzan 100, 198, 265
Fiavé *346*, 426
fig(s) 160, 220, 278, 363: Africa 572; Libya 507; trees 360; Uluburun shipwreck 401
figureheads 493
figurines 32, 118–19, 128, 132, 219, 227, 237, 296, 333, 335, 343, 443, 450, 493: 'Ain Ghazal 168, *xiii*; animal 165; Bono Ighinu 228, *228*; bronze 26, *26*, 517; cruciform 216, *216*, 342; Cycladic 48, *322*, 335; Cyprus 216, *216*; donkey 289, *289*; fat 340; female 165, 172, 188, *189*, 190, 228, 341, *xxi*; frog-like 190; horse 327; human, varied 306; ivory 241, *viii*, 'Kilia' type 238, *238*; Kythera 16; Levantine 530; marble 25, 48, 238, 322, 323; obsidian 173; Phoenician 531; Phylakopi 467; Sardinia 217; Uluburun 401, *xxxiv*; violin-shaped 241, 243. *See also* sculptures; statues
Fikirtepe phase 188
Filicudi 212, 417
filigree 278
Filitosa *346*, 423, *446*, 480
Final Neolithic 203, 237
finger cymbals, Uluburun shipwreck 401
Finley, Moses 19
fir 130
fire 86, 92, 99, 102, 149: -lighting equipment 261
firedogs 513
Fischer, Joschka 51
fish 70, 73–74, 106, 118, 124, 126–28, 131, 158–59, 171–72, 180, 199, 209, 211, 215, 248, 307, 351, 450, 574: amphora-bottled 573; Black Sea 575; consumption 193; Egypt 206; inland 155; hooks 178, *182*; images 127; Italy 221; lake 135; preserved, Iberia 484; processing, Gadir 527; processing tools 182; salted 573; sauces 573; totem 327; Ugarit 395
fisheries, Atlantic 573
fishing 107, 178, 181, 290: Africa 205; gear, Uluburun shipwreck 401
flakes 98
flasks 336, 343, 485, 502, 517: oil 487, 512; perfume 546; zoomorphic 343
flatbreads 167, 220
flatfish 106: images 127
flax 160: cords 125
Les Fleurs du Mal 18
Flinders Petrie, William Matthew 286

flint 68, 105, 114, 125, 135, 229, 237, 318, 334, 342: arrowhead, in shoulder 260; blades 190, 242; daggers 316; fine 305; grey 230; -knapping 318; La Draga 219; Levant 242; mine 230; Morocco 267; mounted 136; sickle blades 393; on sledges 279; tools 26, 83; trade 218
floods/flooding 67, 159, 164, 174, 264, 553: flash- 264, 348; legends 239; Nile 349
floodwater 244, 245: cultivation 196, 207
Florence 217
Flores 85, 94, 95
flour, Italy 428
Fontbouisse 307, 316, 331
Forcalquier-La Fare *258*, *334*
Formentera 78, 331, 422, 481
fortifications 240, *240*, 294, 300, *307*, 315, 319, 321–22, 425, 430, 481, 504: Aegean 459; Avaris 383, 384; Balearics 567; Copper Age 317; Hattusa 458; Iberia 421; Italy 474; Marseilles 564; Mycenaean centres 410; Phylakopi 467; Tyre 486
Forum Boarium (Rome) 427
Forum Romanum (Rome) 479
foxes 104, *176*, 177
France 58, 75, 105–6, 116, 119, 121–23, 127, 180, 187, 194–95, 230–31, 233, 259, 306, 310, 316, 331, 415, 481, 483, 495, 550, 572, 581: arctic fauna 104; axes *231*; beaker network 333–34; bowls 217; break up of villages 306; burials 417; cave art 114; coastal traffic 566; copper 69; empire 28; harpoons 135; isolation of 423, 599; lead tablet 562; leapfrogging 201; limestone uplands 67; lowland plains 64; Magdalenian 123; Mediterranean 192, 422; metals 237, 305, Middle Neolithic 224; MIS 3 103; Neanderthals 102; Neolithic 203; obsidian 232; oppida 566; Riviera 308; shipwrecks 546–48; slaves 576; southern 480, 504, 562–65; tombs 311; underwater archaeology 35; Upper Palaeolithic 39; violent death 179; western 492; wine 576
Franchthi Cave *111*, 119, 131, 135, *151*, 152–53, 159, 181–82, 187–89, *204*, 230
Franco, Francisco 29
frankincense 390
Fratessina *446*, 478, 504, 562, 598
Freud, Sigmund 23
Friuli 425, 477
Friuli-Ljubljana gap 58
fruits 169, 210, 219, 280, 285: fermentation 222; Italy 428. *See also* grapes; wine
Fuente Álamo *346*, 419
Fumane. *See* Grotta di Fumane
funerary activity 277, 306, 324, 338, 420, 502: contexts 177; customs, Egypt 271; elite 577; monuments 291, 297, 481, 519; practices, Menorca 496, 498; rites 247. *See also* burial(s); cemeteries; grave(s); human remains; tomb(s)
fungi 179
Funtana *446*, 476, 493
fur 261
furniture 410, 520: decorated 399; Egypt 397; stone 296

Gaban rockshelter *204*, 227
Gadir 515, 525, 527, 538, 546, 548, 573–75, 582. *See also* Cadiz
galena 173
Galicia 334, 490
Galilee 147, 241, 287, 363–64, 488, 499, 500, 595: basin 363
Galite islands 213
galleys 465, 514, 560, 581
Gallipoli 50
game animals 181: Rhafas Cave 210; wild 205
gaming pieces, Uluburun shipwreck 401
Garamantes 572
Gargano 79, 229, 230
Garonne River 58, 195, 223, 224
Garrigues 306–8, 316
Gatas *346*, 419
Gath *447*, 452
Gaudo culture *258*, 335, 428, 512
Gaul: pre-Roman 442; trade 564
Gavdos 410
Gazel 46, 74, 384, 387, *447*, 510, 523
Gazel *192*

gazelle(s) 83, 101, 121, 124, 130, 136, 145, 157, 161, 163, 169–71, 199, 247, 268, 378: bone sickle 145, *x*; images *289*
Gebal. *See* Byblos
Gediz River 412
Gela 508, 546
Gelidonya. *See* Cape Gelidonya
gender: distinctions 145; labour divisions 166–67; roles 117, 306, 341
genetics iv, vii, viii, xix, 70, 96, 97, 105, 186, 195: analyses 219; mutation 109; of olives 310; research 198; shift 162
Genoa 120
genocide 115
geography: Cretaceous 63; Mediterranean 54–81; North Africa 40
geology 63–71, 82, 83, 88
geopolitics 51, 386: Mesopotamia 285
Germany 92, 101, 576
Gesher Benot Ya'aqov 85, 86, 92
Gezer 447, 452
Ggantija temple *258*, 341
Ghab depression 77, 387
Giali 68
giant owls 91
giant tortoises 71, 94
giants' tombs 424
Gibraltar 55, 73–74, 75, 83, 100, 102, 109, 116, 121, 127, 155, 182, 201, 209, 327, 334, 482, 487, 489, 491, 496, 527, 531, 569, 574, 599, *VII*: Neanderthals 104–6, *107*
Gibraltar Strait. See Strait of Gibraltar
gift(s) 397, 403: exchange 398, 459, 602; -giving 118, 324, 356, 399, 556
Giglio 192, 212, 546
Gilat *205*, 242, 243, *XXI*: ram 244
Gilgal *151*, 164
Gilgamesh 278, 285, 511
gilt-bronze figurines 363
Gioura 182, *182*, 212
Giovinazzo dolmen *347*, 444
giraffes 157: images 197, 205
Giza (Egypt) *259*, 272, 304
glacial: aridity 163; conditions 146; cycles 93, 100; plains 158
glaciers 42, 89, 116, 120, 128
glass 410, 443, 547: Egypt 397, 455; -making 455; moulded 415; production 391, 405
global: population 123; warming 44, 50
globalization 53
glocalization 532
Glykys Limin (Epirus) *347*, *442*, 443
gneiss 338
gnocchi 426
goat(s) 124, 130, 136, 161, 166, 169–73, 177, 187, 189, 190, 201, 206, 209, 220–21, 310, 330, 343: Cyprus *176*, 342; Cyrenaica 268; domesticated 200; herding 201, 223, 245, 268, 309; hunting 133; images *289*; Italy 309, 428; Jordan 363; Lampedusa 212; large-scale herding 279, 293; Levantine in Africa 205, 207; Menorca 422; milk 162; North Africa 266, 568; Rhafas Cave 210; Tremiti islands 212; Tunisia 210; wild 152; wool 244; Zembra 213
goat-antelopes 83, 151, 330–31
Göbekli Tepe *151*, 163, *163*, 177, *259*
goblets 294, 336
gods/goddesses 277, 278, 302, 530: bronze from Uluburun 401, *XXXIV*; city 276; Egyptian 261; Phoenician 244; Roman 540; tutelary 538. *See also* deities *and under names of individual gods/goddesses*
Goethe, Johann Wolfang von 56
Göksu River 459
Golan Heights 241, 244, 311, 364
gold 69, 207–8, 236–37, 248, 277, 281, 285, 296–97, 305, 318, 336, 385, 388, 410, 441–42, *XIX*: Anatolia 367; balance scale model 371; beads 206; bottles 482; bowls 482, 517; bracelets 482; Cretan 337; Cyprus 343; dagger 333; Egypt 397, 537, 555; flask 336; granulation 551; handles 304; ingots 360; jewelry 323, 527, 574; pin *337*; mines, Aegean 551; Mycenae 371; Nubia 359, 384, 386; rings 383; Saharan 572; sheets 278, 553, *XLVII*; sources 69; symbolism of 280; throne 532; tools 321; as tribute 389, 509; Uluburun shipwreck 401; vessels 485; Wenamun's 445

Goliath 559
Göllü Dag *151*, 173, 174
Göltepe 304
Gordion *509*, 520
Gorham's Cave *84*, 106, *110*, *127*, *150*, 182, *508*, 531
Gozo 78, 235, 340–42, 343, 430, 475: obsidian 351; shrews 150
graffiti 68, 308, 490, 576: Iberia 484; ship images 464
grafting 244
grain 310: African to Aegean 571; bulk transport 548, 549; as a commodity 281; Egyptian 555; fermentation 222; images 556; shortages 387; silos 207, 224, 428; storage 240, 527; trade 562; trade profits 552; Ugarit 395. *See also* cereals *and under names of individual species*
Granada 66, 316, 419
granaries 219, 240, 298, 321: Hattusa xxvi, 461; model 502
Grand Tour 26
Grands Causses 67, 306
granite: menhirs 340; red 68
granulation 278, 336, 551
grape(s) 125, 350, 381, 515: Africa 572; -crushing, models 343; cultivation 244; France 565; Libya 507; pips 273, 484, 568; Uluburun shipwreck 401; vines 210, 222, 547; wild 220. *See also* vine(s); viticulture; wine
grasses 106, 130: for clothing 221, 261, *261*; wild 210
grassland 83, 89, 103, 224
grave(s) 325: chiefly 323; cist 234; communal 376; corridor 311; Cyclades 322; Egyptian 381; goods 110, 235; Pithekoussai 521; shaft 371, 376, 410, 432, 610. *See also* burial(s); cemeteries; funerary activity; human remains; tomb(s)
Gravettian 118, 119, 123, 125: body ornaments *119*
Gravina *509*, 538
Gravisca *508*, 553
great auks 126, 147, 595: images 126, 127, *IX*
Great Pyramid 288
Great Rift Valley 64, 84, 109
Greece 37, 134, 180, 188, 219, 221, 266, 320, 350, 371, 404, 410, 443–44, 474: amphorae in France 564; art 382; city-states 541, 582, 584; Classical 87; climate 66; core 42; drinking parties 390; farming 190; geography 63; goods in Sicily 539; *Homo heidelbergensis* 92; identity 534–35, 539, 557; influence 607–8; *Lallemantia* plants 337; language 25, 409, 459, 518, 519; lowland plains 64; mercenaries 554, 576; metals 237; mythology 63, 548; Neolithic communities 189; 19th-century archaeology 28; obsidian 184; palaces 35; poets 484; population growth 582; pottery 536, 577, 584; priestesses 542; sanctuaries 558; scripts 566; seafarers 524; settlers, North Africa 38; shrines 555; statues, inspired by Egypt 545; symposium 545; temples 545, 557–58; towns 544, 545; Upper Palaeolithic 119; western 351; wine making 222; writing 515
greenhouse gases 88
Greenland 42, *63*: ice cores 372; ice sheet *42*, 88
greenstone axes 230, 342
griffins 376, 388: images 517
Grimaldi Caves. See Balzi Rossi Caves
grinding stones 125, 136, *145*, 161, 209, 212, 218, 229
Grotta-Aplomata 322
Grotta dei Cervi *204*, 221, *228*
Grotta del Clusantin *110*, 135
Grotta dell'Uzzo *150*, 179, 180, 182, 192: meat and mollusc consumption 193
Grotta di Fumane *110*, 113, 113
Grotta di Sant'Agostino *85*, 106
Grotta Paglicci *110*, 119, 125, 130
Grotta Patrizi *204*, 226
Grotta Romanelli *85*, 106, *111*, 127, 147
Grotta Scaloria *204*, 228, *228*
Grotte Cosquer. See Cosquer Cave
Grotte des Pigeons. See Taforalt Cave
Grotte Mandrin xiv
Grotte Vaufrey *84*, 105
gruel 167, 220
Guadalhorce delta 527
Guadalquivir River 78, 82, 194, 318–20, 339, 421, 481–82, *483*, 488, 520, 525, 527, 581, 602
Guadiana River 318
Guanche people 574
Gubbio 192, 223

Guernica 49
guest friendship 515, 542
Guilaine, Jean 24, 323
guinea fowl 571
gulet 72
Gulf of Antalya 132, 175
Gulf of Aqaba 102, 510
Gulf of Cadiz 263, 305, 319, 482–83, *483*, 485, 496
Gulf of Cagliari 477
Gulf of Corinth 64, 335, 351, 531, 532, 550
Gulf of Gabès 73, 122, 268, 569, 573
Gulf of Iskenderun 75, 155, 177, 195, 240, 285, 301, 487
Gulf of Mexico 60, *61*
Gulf of Sirte 55, 66, 73, 210, 266, 268, 490, 568, 570, 573
Gulf of Suez 201
Gulf of Taranto 474
Gulf of the Lion 74, 83, 209
Gulf War 48

Habuba Kebira *258*, *259*, 283–84, *284*, 295
Hacılar *151*, 175, 238
haddock 127
hairpins 306
hairstyles 457: Aegean 403; African 570; images 361
hake 178
Hal Saflieni 47, *47*, *258*, 340, *341*
Hala Sultan Tekke *347*, 408, 411, *447*, 450
halberds: Iberia 418; images *306*, 308
Halk en Menjel lagoon 211
Hallstatt 442: centres 576; complex 578
hallucinogens 223, 310
Hama 241, *259*, 284, 297, *347*, 349
Hamilcar Barca 580
Hamilton, William 64
Hammam *259*: wagon model *279*
Hammamet Gulf 211
Hanahal *111*, x
hand axes 84, *84*, 92, 93, 98
handprints 228
Hannibal 308
hapiru 469
Harappan cities 284
harbours 35, 217, 291, 357, *357*, 396, 447, 486: Athens 552; Carthage 490; concrete 579; Crete 410; dry 203; Egypt 396, 553; Italy 553; moles 551; Ugarit 393. *See also* anchorages; ports
hares 104, 117, 135, 199
harnesses 432, 464
harpoon(s) 107, 125, 155, 197: Iberian 135, *135*, 184; images 272; tip, iron 538
hartebeest 199
harvesting 227, 265, 266, 549
Hathor 302, 354
Hatoula *151*, 155
Hatti 367, 387–88, 396, 398–99, 404–5, 407, 411, 454–55, 458, 468, 470–71. See also Hattusa; Hittites
Hattusa xxvi, *xxvii*, 367, 384, 391, 405, 411–12, *447*, 450, 455, 458, 461, 463–64, 466. See also Hatti; Hittites
Haua Fteah 38, *38*, 85, 98, 101, 107, *111*, 112, 147, *151*, 199, *204*, 210, *259*, 268, *509*, 568
Hazael 499
hazel 157, 219: -nuts 220
Hazor *259*, 297, *347*, 364, 369, 375, 406
headdresses 120, 169, *228*: feather 478
headhunting 179
hearths *32*, 99, 105, 106, *145*, 148, 224
Hecataeus *21*, 536
Heinrich events 90, 146
Hejaz 59
Heliopolis 40
Hellenization 608
helmets 480, 558: horned 450, 461, 493; Italian 532, *XXXVIII*; Mesopotamian 483
hematite 246
Hengistbury Head 492
Hephaestus 529
Hera 532
Herakles 487
Heraklion 50
herbs 220
Herculaneum 26
Hergla *204*, 211, *211*
Herodotus 23, 24, 54, 268, 303, 536, 559, 568, 570, 574

herons, images *271*
Hesiod 518
Heuneberg *508*, 576
hides 162, 221, 572
Hierakonpolis *204*, 208, *258*, 270, 272
hieroglyphs 354, 407
High Atlas mountains 63
Hilazon Tachtit Cave *111*, 147, *147*
hillforts 418, 426, 441, 503, 504: Adriatic 562; Dalmatia 426, 477; France 566; Iberia 538
Himalayas 63, 68
Himera *ii*
Hindu Kush 583
hippopotami 70, 83, 95, 104, 151, 154, 157, 175, 261: ivory 247, 248, 335, 391, 401, 474
hippopotamoid deity 376
Hissarlik. *See* Troy
Hittites 346, 367, 456: language 393, 399; political collapse 458. *See also* Hatti; Hattusa
hoards *247*, 281, 333, 425, 441, 449, 473–74, 482–83, 493, 496, 504, 576
hobbles, cattle 205
Hoca Çeşme *151*, 188
hoes 210
holly 120
holm 62
Holocene 41, 43, 89, 90, 104, 149, 155–56, 158–59, *164*, 171, 173, 177, 182, 199, 200, 209, 229, 330, 348, 580, 594, 599, 601, 610: climate 128, *129*; demographic growth 160; early 178, 196; end of 263; farming 265; 'foraging seascapes' 183; lakes *158*; Levant 160–69; Sahara xvi–vii, 326
Holy Land 49
Homer 27, 278, 322, 335, 412, 518, 535. *See also* Iliad; Odyssey
hominins 97: early expansion 83–87, 89, 91–116, 594. *See also* anatomically modern humans; early modern humans
Homo antecessor 93
Homo erectus 83
Homo ergaster 83, 86, 93
Homo habilis 83
Homo heidelbergensis 91, 92, 92, 96, 98, 100
Homo sapiens 96, 113: Levant xiii, 160
honey 220, 227, *227*, 333, 385, 411
hooks 182
hoplites 558, 559
Hoplitomeryx 91
Horden, Peregrine 19, 20, 21, 54, 57, 65, 264, 307, 537, 595
Horn of Africa 285
horse(s) 65, 83, 93, 104, 119, 126, 130, 147, 326, 343, 373, 383, 405, 425, 455, 500, 567: Africa 457, 571; Cyprus 399; Egypt 397; gear 502; Iberia 327, *327*, 421; images *327*, 464; Malta 343; -mounted archers 577; Sardinia 581; Ugarit 395
horticulture 166, 189, 220, 243, 275
Horus 272
house mice 136, 178, 402, 494–95, *495*, 574. *See also* mice
House of David 499
'House of the Tiles' (Lerna) *320*, 321, 324
houses: Çatalhöyük *174*; circular 342; Cyprus 216; Iberia 526; Levant 362; megaron 234; models *225*; mud-brick 220, 271; Natufian 164, 167; Neolithic *189*, 223, 225; painted 235; round *176*, 178; subterranean 216, 241; Tremiti islands 212; Ugarit 32; wattle-and-daub 192, 304; wooden 219
Hudson Bay 60, *61*
Huelva mountains 421, *446*, 482–83, *483*, 487–88, 492, 496, 500, *508*, 525, 538
Hula basin 363
human remains 128, 132, 161, 178–80, 223, 226, 247, 260–61: Malta 340; sacrifices 304; skull 127; teeth 136; violent death 124, 226. *See also* burial(s); cemeteries; funerary activity; grave(s); tomb(s)
Humbaba 285
humidity 159, 160
Hungary 187
hunter-gatherers 43, 116–20, 122, 136, 163, 167: Africa 601; art 163, *163*; California 62; contact with farmers 191; Corsardinia 128; France 195; Greece 16, 188; language 227; last in Mediterranean 178–84, 219; lifestyles 229; Mesolithic enclaves *150–51*; mobility

596; Morocco 209; Neolithic 218, 223; North Africa 39–40; retaining traditional lands 194; Sahara 204; seafaring 62, 184, 187; sedentary 200; spirit worlds 196, 197; villages 204
hunting 87, 104–6, 114, 133, 136, 145, 167, 172, 202, 326, 595: efficiency 115; France 422; gazelle 268; images *228*, 272, 388; Levant 161; Neolithic 215; resurgence of 310; technologies 126; Tunisia 210
Hurrian: language 393; names 363, 450
Huxley, Aldous 57
Hvar 46, 212, 213, 562
Hyblaean massif 229
hybridity, human 116
hyenas 92, 102, 104
Hyksos 383–86, *385*, 388, 452, 455–56, 471, 523, 535, 580, 595: kings 604
hymns 295
hypogea 235, 312, 340–41, 342

I Faraglioni 346, 430, 431
Iberia(n) 55, 58, 69, 74, 77, 101, 124, 195, 237, 258, 306, 307, 316, 352, 422, 480, 490, 492, 494, 548, 563: alcohol 515–16; amphorae 516, 517; arctic fauna 104; Argaric iv, 596; arrow injuries 315; Atlantic coast 566; Aurignacian 114; beakers 334; coast 106, 194, 573; communities 566; Copper Age *v*, *xx*, *xxi*, *xxii*, *xxiii*, 310; currency 556; *dehesa* ecologies 221; early hominins 93, 116; eastern influence 520; farming 179; harpoons 135, 184; hunter-gatherers 122, 218; imports 481, 483, 484; inequalities 418; isolation of 419, 515, 601; ivory 267; language 519; leapfrogging 201; Magdalenian 123; Meseta 63, 326; metal extraction 238; metals 421, 482, 483, 574; MIS 3 103; Neandethals 102; Neolithic 39, 183; opium poppies 222; ornaments 229; ostrich egg 267; peninsula 57; Phoenician enclaves 525–26; pottery 236, 308; refugia 121; rock art 315; scripts 519; silver 537, 551, 581; southern 600; tectonics 82; tin 415; tombs 311, 531; towns 524; tree cover 157; tribute 323; use of metal 305; viticulture 546; weapons 418; wine 566
Iberomaurusian hunter-gatherers 39, 123, 132, 135, 197, 199: tools 128
ibexes 91, 104–5, 119–20, 126, 130–31, 134–35, 180, 247: images 126
Ibiza 78, 331, 422, 481, 567, 573: as a trading hub 567
ice: ages 88; -bergs 90, 120, 146, 153; caps 88, 202; cores *42*, 372; sheets 121, 129, 159
Iceman 29, *258*, 260–61, *260*, *261*, 308, 310
identity 534–35, 539, 557, 604, 607: collective 544
Iliad 535
Ilıpınar 188, 238
illicit antiquities 48
incense 385, 390, 453, 499, 510: burner *291*
Incoronata 529
India 63
Indian Ocean 63, 87, 89
Indo-European languages 186, 519: speakers 325, 326
Indonesia 94, 101
Indus Valley 262, 284, 290, 333, 336–37
Ineb-hedj. *See* Memphis
inequality 264, 277, 319, 323
infections 159
ingots 281, 338, 343, 360, 425, 494: images 449; pick 477, *477*, 479; possible gold/electrum 248, *xix*; Sicily 529; silver 337. *See also* oxhide ingots
inhumations. *See* burial(s)
innovation(s) 108, 168, 170, 202, 239, 245, 265, 275–76, 312, 328, 338, 356, 383, 407, 415, 478, 504: Menorca 422; sails 464; in transportation 288–92
inscriptions 360, 553, 562: Phoenician 488; textual 268
insecurity 315, 417, 461, 515
interglacial periods 41, 89, 92, 98, 100–3, 129–30, 156, 599
intermarriage 186, 219, 226, 375, 512, 542, 570: description in texts 295
Ionia(n) 335: city-states 556; islands 460, 474; Revolt 584
Ipogeo Manfredi 221
Iran: plateau 583; pottery 33
Iraq 63, 238
Ireland 483
Irniba 296
iron 69: daggers 304; Elba 512, 546, 550; harpoon tip 538; Iberia 482, 484; Italy 478; meteoric 321; North

Africa 568; ore 246; regular production 451; Tyre 509; -working 490, 569, 572
Iron Age 20, 53, 80, 201, 234, 238, 245, 268, 412, 422, 441, 449, 486, 503, 505: Aegean 460; cemeteries 378; Egypt 519, 521, 523, 530, 534; resurgence 468; shrines 530, 531; societies 461; trade 513
irrigation 207, 238, 244, 275, 310, 349, 359, 363, 596
Isaiah 484
Ischia 115, 429, *512*, 513
Isernia la Pineta *85*, 93
Ishar-Damu 295
Isidore of Seville 21
Islam 51: empires 62; monuments 39
island(s) 66, 74, 78–79, 87, 90–91, 94–96, 121, 128, 158, 183, 187–88, 204, 223, 230, 322, 339–44: Adriatic 562; animals, unusual *71*; burials 182; connections 307, *308*; endemics 150; geography 193; Greek 107; landscapes 181, 217, *iv*; mammals 152; Neolithic expansion , 212–18, *213*; societies 604; volcanic 68. *See also under names of individual islands*
Island of the Moon 527
Island Southeast Asia 85, 94, 95
Isles of the Blest 554
isolation 89, 342, 419, 423, 476, 515, 566–67, 599, 601
isotope analyses 36, 106
Israel 46, 74, 99, 102, 105, 113, 219, 248, 287, 293, 297, 303, 365, 411, 445, 470, 485, 487, 505, 507, 510, 535: archaeology 29; Assyrian assault on 534; fish 155; Nesher Ramla xiii; polities 488; preservation conditions 29; prophets 390, 484, 521; rivers *81*; shipwrecks 35
Isthmia 502
Istria 79, 122, 147, 180, 426: farming 191
Italy 28–29, *37*, 57, 63, 73, 75, 78, 91, 119, 155, 180, 187, 190, 195, 223, 226–27, 230–31, 305, 310, 351, 425, 477, 478–80, 500, 503–4, 512, 562: adoption of Greek identity 533; arctic fauna 104; armour 473; axes *231*; beads 118; beakers 334; break up of villages 306; cist graves 235; city-states 556; coastal sites 106; cremation 474; early hominins 93; eastern influence 520; Epigravettian 123; enclosures 538; exports 484; Final Neolithic 203; flint daggers 305; geography 63, 87; growth of towns 538, 539; handmade pottery 464; heel of 156, 233; helmets 532; hoplite kit 559; Lake Monticchio core 103; language 518; Late Neolithic 234; leapfrogging *192*; liver-divination 518; lowland plains 64; maritime expansion 194; metals 237, 305; MIS 3 103; Neanderthal 116, 102; Neolithic 104, 214, 224; 19th-century archaeology 28; northeast 191; obsidian 184, 232; oil and wine industry 546; olives 57, 515; Pliocene *85*; ritual sites 221; Samnites 561; Serro d'Alto-style pottery *227*; southeast 416; southern 600; tectonics 70; tombs 234; towns 522, 524, 552; volcanoes 29, 65, 115; wine-drinking customs 545
Ithobaal 500
Ittireddu 476, 493
ivory 118, 120, 248, 318, 323, 334, 360, 363, 410, 443, 459, 572: carved 485, 500, 517, *viii*; combs 478; Crete 369; cups, Morocco 267; Cyprus 399; Egypt 397; elephant 390, 391, 403, 409, 414; figurines 241, 444; handles 286, *287*; hippopotamus 247, 335, 391, 474, *xxii*; Iberia 421; inlays 517; Phoenician 487; Tyre 509; Ugarit 389, 393; Uluburun shipwreck 401
Izmir 175, 238, 502

Jabbul plain 297
jadeite 230
Jaén 318
Japan 112, 128, 152
jar(s) 247, 272, 278, 286: beer 287; for bulk transport 303; burials 301, 312; Canaanite 379, 390, 393, 401–2, 458; handmade 463; large 310; Levantine 287; painted 303; perfume 547; piriform 391; Sardinia 472; Sicily 474; Spain 420; stirrup 380, 391, 401, 458, 465, 490; storage 309, 518
Java 94
javelins 219, 462: copper 418; images 450
Jawa *151*, *169*, *259*, 293
Jazira 59, 160, 172, 241, 276, 278, 348, 349, 387–88, 391, 405, 459, 470, 507, 511, 576: wagon model 279, *279*
Jazirat al-Maghreb. *See* Maghreb
Jebel Akhdar 66, *xlix*
Jebel Aruda 284

Jebel el Gharbi 66, 101, 123, 266
Jebel Irhoud xiii, xiv–xv, 84, 98
jellyfish 126
Jericho 27, 151, 164, 164, 168, 177, 205, 241, 347, 363, XII
Jerusalem 244, 347, 363, 398, 447, 487, 498–99, 507, 509, 510, 521, 534, 536, 551
jet 318
jewelry 237, 278, 296, 305–6, 321, 336, 371, 376: gold 323, 574; Greek 545; Iberia 420; -makers 517; Sardinia 527; Troy 324
Jezebel 500
Jezreel Valley 363–65, 379, 488
Johnson, Samuel 26
joinery 292
Jordan 184, 194, 241, 244, 246, 293, 350, 365, 452: copper 173; farmers 48; population 507; PPNB houses 166; Valley 64, 84, 86, 121, 124, 130, 133, 163–64, 164, 170, 240, 241, 258, 363, 364, 598; water management 168, 169
Judah, kingdom of 507, 510, 520–21, 534
Judaean: desert 448; hills 164, 169, 244, 246
juglets 380: Bronze Age 517; Cypriot 390, 391; Uluburun shipwreck 401
jugs 291, 335, 484: bronze 574; handmade 463; silver 574; zoomorphic 343
juniper 104, 106, 121, 266, 286, 294
Juno. See Uni
Jupiter (Roman god) 540

Kaf Taht el-Ghar 150, 201
Kalamakia 85, 105
Kalavasos 347, 408
Kaletepe 85, 94, 151, 173
Kamares painted pottery 369
Kamid el-Loz. See Kumidi
Kamose 384, 386
Kanakia 610
Kandinsky, Wassily 80
Kanesh 367, 373, 375, 389, 394
Kaptara 366. See also Keftiu
Karaburun Peninsula 321
Karnab mine 377
Karnak 405, 446, 545
Karpass peninsula 178
Kaska groups 458
Kastoria 219
Kastri 16, 259, 322, 347, 370
Katanda 107
Kea 153, 237, 237, 371
Keats, John 87
Kebara Cave 85, 102, 103, 106, 147: tool types 124
Kebibat 84, 98
keels 374, 399
Kefalonia 108
Keftiu 366, 403, 414: bean 378
Kehf el Hammar Cave 110, 123
Kenamun, tomb of 357, 396, 401
Kenyon, Kathleen 28
Kephala 204, 237, 237
Kerkennah islands 78, 213
Keros 322, 322, 329: marble figurines 48
Kestel mine 259, 304, 337
Kfar Monash 299
Kfar Samir 151, 172
Khiam 163
Khirbet en-Nahas 447, 453
Khirbet Umbashi 259, 293, 294
Khirokitia 175, 178, 205, 216
Khoisan pastoralists 62
Khufu 288, 288, 291, XXIII
'Kilia' type figurines 238, 238
Kilise Tepe 447, 459
King of the Four Quarters 285
kings 272, 304, 358, 406: Akkad 350, 366; Assyrian 484; communication with merchants 404; Ebla 295; Egypt 386–88, 397; foreign at Delphi 558; Hyksos 604; Levantine 405; Neo-Assyrian 491, 507
kingship 261, 262, 276, 520, 544: Aegean 541; Bronze Age 470; Egyptian 52
Kition 347, 408, 447, 450, 467, 488, 509, 511, 518, 525, 534
Kizzuwatna 405
Klimonas 151, 175
Klithi 111, 134, 134

knives 136, 261, 463
Knossos 16, 27, 151, 188–89, 216, 221, 234, 259, 321, 323, 335, 336, 338, 353, 369–71, 384, 404, 409, 415–16, 447, 460, 487, 503, 509, 522, II
Kolaios of Samos 551, 570
Kolonna 259, 322
Kommos 347, 410, 447, 472, 477, 487, 495, 509, 531
komodos 94
Konya plain 174, 175, 189
Korčula 180, 212
korai 546, XLIV
Korphi t'Aroniou 328
Kos 412
Kourion 347, 408, 447, 450
kouroi 545–46
Krakatoa 372
Krapina Cave 85, 102
kraters 411, 577
Ksar Akil 111, 113
Kulaksızlar 238
Küllüoba 259, 321, 338
Kültepe. See Kanesh
Kumidi 347, 406
Kurunta 458
Kush, kingdom of 386
Kushmashusha 407
Kvarner Gulf 122
Kynos 447, 460
Kyrenia 64
Kythera viii, 15, 16, 17, 18, 33, 39, 68, 213, 322, 370, 487
Kythnos 153, 182

L'Arbreda Cave 110, 113
La Bastida 346, 419
La Defensola 204, 230
La Draga 30, 204, 219–21, 219, 220
La Galite 78
La Marmotta 204, 214–15, 219, 220, 223, 228: dugout canoe 214
La Mer Partagée 24
La Muntanya de Sal 204, 230
La Papúa 346, 421
La Pastora 346, 418. See also Valencina de la Concepción
La Pijotilla 258, 318, 319
La Pileta 110, 127
La Starza 346, 428
La Tène 442
Labayu 407
Lachish 507, 509
Lade island 77, 584
ladles 219
Lady of Byblos. See Ba'alat Gebal
Lagar Velho 110, 116
lagoons 73, 76–77, 87, 92, 147, 159, 187, 200, 203, 211, 211, 219, 306–7, 428: coastal 263; Italy 478
Lagozza pottery 236
Laja Alta 446, 496
lake(s) 42, 83, 89, 157, 198, 205, 219, 348: cores 372; dwellings 426; Egypt 207; Tunisia 210; villages 310, 477
Lake Banyoles 219
Lake Bracciano 219
Lake Garda 477
Lake Hula 145
Lake Ioannina 42, 111, 134
Lake Iznik 188
Lake Lisan 121, 124, 146
Lake Mega-Chad 157, 158, 198
Lake Megafezzan 158
Lake Monticchio 85, 105
Lake Tigalmamine 263
Lallemantia plants 337
Lampedusa 49, 49, 78, 211, 212, 216
Lampione 78
lamps 401, 525
land snails 131, 199
land-bridges 39, 58, 70, 90–91, 94–95, 336
landscapes 33, 87: Algeria 209; ancient 47; coastal 78; European 223; North Africa 130; over-exploitation 461; symbolic meaning 117
languages 92, 100, 190, 195, 226, 295, 325–26, 393, 518–19: Egyptian 289; Indo-European 186; of Italy 519; Nilo-Saharan 197; trade 359
Languedoc 64, 76, 194, 306, 504, 566

Lanzarote 265
lapis lacedaemonius 105
lapis lazuli 278, 282, 284, 288, 296–97, 321, 321, 333, 336–38, 360, 385, 391, 397, 441
Lapithos 259, 343
Larnaca 488
Las Pilas 258, 317
Lascaux Cave 110, 132
Last Glacial Maximum 90, 116–28, 126, 129, 131, 133, 135–36, 146, 152, 154–55, 158, 160–61, 182, 229, 239, 244, 266, 595, 598: coastline 110–11
Late Neolithic 241
Late Pastoral phase 266
Late Stone Age 112
Latin language 519
Latium 106
Latmian Gulf 159
Lattara 508, 566
Lattes. See Lattara
Laurasia 63
laurel 120
Lavazzo island 307
Lavrio 69, 204, 237, 370, 509: silver 552, 609
laws 536, 544: against illegal antiquities trade 48
lead 69, 237, 360: Iberia 482, 484; ingots 546; -rich bronzes 492; sources 69; tablet, France 562
leapfrogging 186, 188–96, 192, 201
Lear, Edward 45
leather 261: bag, painted 311; clothing 117; industry, Turkey 365; Mari 366; ox-yoke 476; rolls 448; sandals 242; shoe 222
Lebanon 35, 37, 50, 63, 64, 68, 113, 145, 248, 285–87, 293, 301, 303, 363, 364, 404, 406, 447, 510: cedar 360; geography 65; mountains 120; trade 378; war 49
Ledro 311
Lefkada 108, 335
Lefkandi 447, 502, 504, 509, 520
legumes 135, 185, 199, 220, 568
Lelantine plain 522
Lemnos 132, 322
lentils 160, 181
Lentini 508, 529
lentisk 106
leopards 147, 174
Lepanto, battle of 454
Lepcis 508, 569, 581
Lerna 259, 320, 321, 351
Lesbos 78, 584
Leucate 150, 187, 204, 219
Levallois technique 98
Levant 20, 27, 31, 33, 55, 57–59, 68, 74, 75, 79, 89, 123, 132–33, 135, 146, 152, 170–73, 186, 196, 204, 208, 210, 216, 238–48, 292–300, 305, 312, 324, 338–39, 348, 350, 361–62, 396, 404–5, 449, 494, 580, 595, 600, 602–3: amphorae 516; balance weights 484, 502, 505; boat images 327; boats 374; bulk movements of cereals 393; camel trail 554; captives 286; chariots 383; cities 521; cities, destruction by Babylon 536, 537; domesticates 207; climate 263; clothing in art 287, 357, 361; coastal 303, 315, 470, 487; copper 69, 285, 453; Copper Age 203, 289, 386; corridor 294; craftsmen 517; Cretan pottery 380; cross-cultural exchange 398; culture 363; currency 556; cylinder seals 336; Cypriot pottery 368; diet 146; early hominins 85–87, 89, 91, 93, 109, 111, 113, 115; early humans 101, 594; and Egypt 259, 270, 286, 326, 451, 454, 488, 554; grave goods 110; Greek pottery 584; hill country 307; as intermediary 375; jars 278, 287; javelin heads in Iberia 418; juglets 380; lakes 121; looms 221; maritime 300–4; mega-sites 323; merchants 407, 468, 518; Middle Palaeolithic 98; MIS 3 103; Neanderthals 105; Neolithic 160–69, 178, 495; phases 203; pigs in Africa 206; plants 161; political collapse 462; population 52, 112, 507, 524; ports 357, 484, 485; pottery 227, 236, 261; rainfall 156; as refugia 121; rift valley lakes 77; sailing ships 493; sea trade 511; sea-crossings 154; sheep and goats 205; shell ornaments 118; ships 406, 498; silver 284; societies 62, 362; southern, settlements 365; supremacy over Egypt 448; tin 337; trade 374; tree cover 157; uplands 130; Upper Palaeolithic xiii, 117; vassals 455; vines 273, 379; war on 387; wine trade 514; wooden artifacts 92; woodland 130

levees 200
Lévi-Strauss, Claude iii, 20
libation vessel, bull's head 371
Libya(n) 28, 39, 46, 66, 123, 198, 268, 404, 456, 457, 507, 554: cattle herding 205; and Egypt 461, 568; in Egyptian art 52, 457; farmers 570; lakes 157; names 498; palette 289; pastoralists 569; politics 553; wadis 158
Liguria 58, 65, 120–21, 193, 230, 234, 309, 566, 598: isolation of 599; obsidian 184
Ligurian: coast 105, 119; language 519; tradition 191
lily, Cretan 388
Lilybaion 581
Limantepe 321
lime trees 157
lime-plaster 168, 169, 170
limestone 65, 157, 307, 426: choppers 83; landscapes 63, 67, 103; plateaux 195, 306
limpets 181
linden 219
lineages 168, 543
Linear A 369
Linear B 409, 410, 502
'Linearbandkeramik' dispersal 187
linen 169, 169, 221, 241, 247, 291–92, 310: cloth 160; Cyprus 399; Egyptian 261, 377, 499, 555; garments 275; textiles, large-scale production 410; tunic 311
Linosa 78
lions 94, 104, 289: images 114, 205, 517, 545, 556
Lipari 68, 78, 212, 214–15, 217, 218, 230, 232, 232, 236–37, 315, 346, 428, 430, 475–76, 598
lipids 36
literacy 410, 459, 518, 519. See also alphabets; writing
Little Ice Age 41
liver-divination 518
Lixus 508, 527, 572, 574
Llanete de los Moros 446, 481
localism 422
Lombok 94
longhouses 241, 307, 307, 316, 321: boat-shaped 330, 422
looms 221, 245, 343, 382, 386, 420, 539
looting 48: Egyptian tombs 381, 471
Lorca 311, 317, 346, 419
Los Dogues 258, 315
Los Millares 258, 312, 317–18, 317, 319, 321, 323, 324, 346, 350, 419
lost-wax technique 247, 493
lotus 388
Ludwig, Emil 38
Lukka. See Lycia
Luwian language 393
luxury goods 380, 385, 415, 517
Lycia 412, 459, 462, 518: sea-raiders 469
Lydia 508, 537, 541, 545, 552, 556, 576, 583: offering at Delphi 558
Lyell, Charles 88
lyre, Uluburun shipwreck 401

Maadi 203, 205, 208, 248, 259, 289
Maccarese 258, 327
macchia 62
Macedonia 64, 66, 188, 223, 225, 426, 500, 502, 561, 606
maceheads 207, 247
mackerel 182
Madeira 78
Madione mountains 120
Madriolo 446, 477, 477
Magdalenian 123, 126, 132, 135, 181
Maghreb 38–40, 57, 63, 65–66, 73, 96, 101, 107, 110, 112, 123, 132, 135, 147, 157, 184, 196–97, 199, 203, 208, 210, 212, 231–33, 260, 266–68, 334, 339, 418, 430, 495, 568, 570, 571, 573, 581, 601: beakers 334; farming 201, 205
Mahadu 393, 394, 395
Mahmatlar 259, 304
Majorca iv
Mainake. See Cerro del Villar
Makriyalos 204, 221, 225
Mala Gruda 259, 316, 333, 335
Mala Palagruža 332
Malaga 74, 104, 106, 127. See also Malaka
Malaga Bay 546

Malaka 508, 546, 582. See also Malaga
Maleas. See Cape Maleas
Malia 259, 323, 369
Mallorca 45, 64, 78, 83, 259, 330, 331, 481, 496, 567: beakers 334
Malta 28, 36, 78, 121, 211–12, 214, 230, 236, 258, 335, 340–43, 351, 409, 430, 431, 444, 465, 475, 531, 604: animals, unusual 71; boat images 327, 328; burial complex 46–47, 47; figurines 341; islands xxiv, 343, 572; isolation of 599; obsidian 232; sacred buildings 329; temples 41, XXVIII; tombs 235
Mamluk rulers 537
mammoths 95, 104, 127: ivory 118, 120
Mandate period 50
Mandra Antine 204, 235
Mani Peninsula 105
Manika 259, 321, 322, 550
Manus island 154
mapping 72–79
maquis 316
marble 68, 69, 318, 557: beakers 236; figurines 25, 48, 238, 322, 323; vessels 219
Mari 258, 259, 295–96, 347, 349, 365–66, 375, 377–79, 391, 393
marine: activity 171; foods 127, 180; life 73; shells 106, 113, 113, 118, 180; -style painted pottery 369; temperature 42
Marine Isotope Stages (MIS) 88, 89: MIS 3 103–4, 115; MIS 4 101, 103, 111
maritime: archaeology 34–35; cargo transport 290; climates 102; connections 303, 338, 346–47, 351, 446–47, 508–9, 596, 597; contact zones 58; culture 330; expansion 194; exploration 154–56; history 329; hunter-gatherers 187; interaction 304, 465–66, 502; Levant 300–304; mobility 187, 230; networks 248, 258–59; proficiency 188; routes 301; technology 215, 464, 491, 494, 560; trade 322, 362, 370; warrior cult 332
market(s) 377–78, 443, 544, 552, 556, 603: -driven pastoralism 579; eastern 460, 491; Levant 395, 452; mechanisms 375; Near Eastern 510; palatial 402; scenes, images 396
marl landscapes 65
marmots 135, 135
Maroni 50, 347, 408
Maroulas 151, 182
Marrakesh 66
Marroquíes Bajos 258, 318, 319
Marsa Gawasis 357
Marsa Matruh 259, 268, 347, 403, 404, 411, 447, 450, 457, 490, 572
Marseilles 35, 74, 121–22, 126, 508, 525, 550, 563–64, 566–67, 595, 598
marshes 76, 77, 192, 200, 206, 291
martens 147
Mas d'Azil 110, 126
Mas d'Is 150, 194
masculinity, celebrations of 306
masks 197, 199, 199: stone 169, XIV
masons 526
mass production 269, 277
massacre victims 349
Massalia. See Marseilles
Matalaiai. See Marseilles
mathematics 536, 545
matorral 62, 104
mats 169: esparto 311; papyrus 200; reed 241, 247
Matvejevic, Predrag 19
Mauretania 157, 572
Mauretania Tingitana 573
Mauritania 266
mead 310, 333, 515, 564
Meander: River 77, 238: delta 77
measurement standards 221, 269, 280, 376, 401, 477, 556. See also standardization; weight(s)
meat 99, 161–62, 168, 174, 180, 184, 273, 309: cooking 219; preserved, Italy 428; stone-boiling 125
medicine 261
medieval period 20: mosaics 105
Medinet Habu 461, 462, 464
Mediterranean: archaeology, 22–24, 27, 29, 44–53; as a barrier 87, 94, 112; boundaries 56; central 472–82;

centrality of 20; climate zones 61; defining 54–60; as a desert 82; as a divider 596; east, trade 373–83, 391–404; east vs west 339; as a field of study 18, 19, 22; geography of 54–81, I, II, III, IV; landscapes 357; as a natural crossroads 60; northern 304–14; palaeo-87–91; as a refuge 600
Mediterranean Breviary 19
mediterraneanization 53, 388, 518, 528, 604
mediterraneoids 60–62
megalithic: buildings 340; tombs 267, 311, 318, 330, 331, 422, 563
megaliths 235, 267, 567. See also menhirs
Megara 509, 576
Megara Hyblaea 508, 523, 529
megaron houses 225, 234
mega-sites 169–70, 173, 175, 186, 226, 238, 242, 318, 321, 323, 550, 598
Megiddo 259, 286, 297, 298, 301, 347, 405, 407, 521, 523
Melanesia 112, 128, 152, 154
Melos 16, 68, 108, 151, 152–55, 153, 182, 215, 231: obsidian 154–55, 189, 238
Melqart 20, 488, 490, 543, 580: Pillars of 487, 489, 573; temple 486, 525
Les Mémoires de la Méditerranée 23–24
Memphis 59, 259, 272, 275, 286, 347, 359, 384, 387, 396, 509, 555, 584
menageries 378
Mendes 259, 274, 275, 347, 349
Mendesian branch (of Nile) 274
Mendolito 508, 529
Menerva 540
menhirs 195, 267, 267, 340. See also megaliths
Menorca iv, 78, 83, 330, 331, 422, 424, 481, 496, 567
Menton Caves. See Balzi Rossi Caves
Mentor 17–18
Mercati, Michele 26
mercenaries 469, 554, 558, 581: in Egypt 461, 576; Greek 576
merchants 404–15, 464, 498, 551–52, 576, 603: Aegean 402, 555; Anatolia 396; communication with kings 404; Cyprus 398, 450, 555; Egypt 396, 397; Iberia 526; Levant 394–95, 398, 407, 487, 518; Mesopotamia 367; oligarchs 484; Phoenician 574; Samian 570; Tyre 511; Ugarit 407, 414
Merenptah 452
Merimde Beni Salame 205, 206–7, 274
Mersin (Yumuktepe) 151, 171–72, 189, 205, 240–41, 240, 248
Mesara plain 35, 323, 326, 339, 572
Meseta 104, 121, 123, 130, 180, 220, 235, 421
Mesolithic 80, 180, 183, 189, 192, 596: Crete 182; enclaves 150–51; Europe 179
Mesopotamia 59, 160, 238–39, 241, 246, 269, 275–76, 294, 297, 305, 312, 314–16, 326, 333, 337–38, 355, 366, 454, 491, 499, 507, 536, 553, 576, 594, 603: armies 559; chariots 290; coastal cities 290; farmers deported to 510; feasting 278; gold 389; helmet 483; innovations 239; large-scale societies 262; merchants 367; olive oil 379; people 403, 511; rise of 258, 600; tin 336; traits in the Levant 363
Messapic language 519
Messina Strait. See Strait of Messina
Messinian: event 159, 330; land-bridge 95; Salinity Crisis 82–83, 82, 87
metal(s)/metallurgy 35, 69–70, 170, 202, 236, 246, 276, 280, 296–97, 299, 306, 324, 330, 335, 338, 465, 504: Aegean 305, 336, 336, 561; Africa 571; Anatolian 288; artifacts 35, 203, 420; Balearics 496; Balkans 351; cauldrons 517; Cyprus 377, 451; decorated 517; early 204–5; Etruria 479, 480; extraction, Spain 263; firedogs 513; flasks 336; Iberia 334, 418, 421, 482–83, 525, 574; ingots 494; Italy 425, 477, XXXVIII; lack of 239, 341; Levant 248, 292; meteoric 451; Near Eastern 354; ores 68; places of origin 237; precious 281, 300, 399; production 321, 322; Sardinia 217, 442, 476, 500, 527; Sicily 477; social pre-eminence 305; sources 69, 285; Spain 318; tools 328; trade 370, 376, 431, 515, 527, 567, 574; tribute 405; Turkey 240–41; Tuscany 442, 500; vessels 366, 380, 403, 562, 577; votives 475; weapons 277, 363; -workers 239, 362, 487, 492; -working 260, 278, 333, 393, 457, 512, 552, 567. See also copper; gold; iron; lead; silver
Metaponton 509, 529, 538, 544: coins 556

metoikic status 552
mice 70, *176*, 183, 567: Cypriot 150; dor- 330; house 136, 178, 402, 494–95, *495*, 574; wood- 330, 495
micro-ecologies 179
microliths 174, 179, 199: arrowheads 189; knives 136; products 125, *125*; projectile points 133
Midas of Phrygia 532
middens 135, *180*, 181, 194, 509
Middle Assyrian *446*, 459
Middle Bronze Age 452
Middle Copper Age 342
Middle Kingdom Egypt 359, 360–61, 374, 377, 385: boats 373; demise of 381; rise of 362; statues 384; tin-bronze 382
Middle Palaeolithic 98, 101, 108: stone tools xiv–xv, *99*
Middle Pastoral 205
Middle Stone Age 98, 100, 112
Midi 218, 311, 423, 480
migration(s): Aegean 469; fish 73; mass 452; tales 533; tunny 182
Miletus *77*, *347*, 412, *509*, 536, 576, 584: people 555
military: actions 406; innovations 383
milk 162, 184, 198, 210, 244, 273, 279: Iberia 421; products 170, *206*, 243, 264, 412, *xxi*; Ugarit 395
milking 172, 221, 310, 326, *xvii*: models 343
Millawanda. *See* Miletus
millet 173, 432, 473, 568
mines/mining 223, 236, 281, 286, 299, 304, 305, 335, 337, 361, 579: Aegean 336; communities 318; copper 246, 316, 367–68, 488, 510; Egypt 376; Etruria 480; flint 230; gold, Aegean 551; Iberia 421, 525; Italy 478, 504; Neolithic 230; Sinai 288; Spain 420; sulphur 429; turquoise 407
Minet el-Beida. *See* Mahadu
Minoan 16, 25, 31, 503, 606: artifacts 50; palaces 352, 470; scripts 190; seals 105; society 320; state formation 353; traditions 432
Minoanization 371
Minshat Abu Omar *259*, 271, 272, *274*
Miocene 65, 82
Mirabella Eclano *258*, 316, *316*
mirrors 472, 532: obsidian 173
MIS. *See* Marine Isotope Stages
Mit Rahina 361: inscription 360, 401; shipwreck 374, 378
Mitanni *346*, 388, 391, 458, 470
mitochondrial DNA. *See* DNA, mitochondrial
Mitterberg mine *346*, 441
Mnajdra 47, *258*, *xxviii*
Moab 507
mobility 118, 120, 124, 132–33, 135, 147, 229, 264, 289, 376, 462–64, 492, 509, 523–24, 528, 573, 598–99, 603–4: becoming institutionalized 333; hunter-gatherer 596
Mochlos *259*, 323, 327, *328*, 329, 336, *336*, 338
models: balance scale 371; boat 207, 327, 338, 363, 472, 493; cart 416; granary 502; milking 343; ploughing 343, *344*; ridden camel 511; rivercraft 290; temple 341; wagon 279, *279*
Modi'in *205*, 244
Mogador *508*, 574
Molise 93
molluscs 90, 126, 152, 157, 159, 179–81, 183, 199, 211, 301, 307: consumption *193*; Cyprus 149; for dye 377–78, 401, 484, 509, 538, 570
Monaco 46
Mondego estuary 574
monk seal 106
monkeys 104, 378
Monkodonja *346*, 426
monoculture 420
monoliths 163, *163*
monsoon(s) 43, 130, 157, 197: belts 89, *153*, 265
Mont Bégo *258*, 308, *311*, *xxvi*
Monte Arci 69, *204*, 232, *232*
Monte Avena *110*, 114
Monte Baranta *258*, 316
Monte Beigua *231*
Monte d'Accoddi *258*, 340, *340*, *346*, 424
Monte Gargano 87, 91, 130
Monte Grande *346*, 429, 430, *442*, *446*, 474
Monte Iudica *110*, 114
Monte Leone rockshelter *150*, 183
Monte Pellegrino 131

Monte Poggiolo *85*, 93
Monte Polizzo *508*, 529, 539, 549
Monte Prama *508*, 546
Monte Sirai *508*, 538
Monte Viso 231
Montelius, Oscar 23
Montenegro 66, 333
Montpellier 566
Montu, temple 360
monument(s): Akkadian 285; -building 544; burial 270, 275; Egypt 31, 208; funerary 291, 297; North Africa; Portugal 181
Moore, Henry 48
moringa oil 385
Morocco 38, 39, 55, 78, 100, 104, 107, 123, 135, 155, 201, 209–10, 267, 334, 517, 527, 573, 574: Atlantic 263
mortars 136, *145*, *xi*
mosaics, medieval 105
Mosphilia *259*, 342, *342*
Mosso, Angelo 23
motilla 421
Motya *508*, 528, 538, 581, 582
mouflons 152, 213
moulds 236, 246, 336, 441, 493: bread 272, 283, 287; copper *299*, 393; for metal 430
mountains 63, 130: as impediments 230; as a shield 89
Mousterian 98
mud-brick 164, 190
Mugharet el 'Aliya *84*, 107
Mujina Peć ina Cave *85*, 105
multilingualism 325
Munich 576
mural painters 551
Murcia 311, 316; La Almoloya xxii, *xxiii*
murex 377, 378, 401, 484, 509, 538, 570
Mureybet *151*, 170
Murlo 540
Mursia *346*, 430
museums 47, 48, 50
music 375, 545: instruments 277, 401, 546
mussels 106, *107*, 221
Mut 532
Mycenae 16, 281, *347*, 371, 376, 404, 410, 415, 431–32, *447*, 462, 477, 610, *xxxiii*: drinking vessels 413; palaces 459, 547; shaft graves 610; territorial states 550
Mylouthkia *151*, 175, 177
Myotragus balearicus 83, 151, 330–31, *331*
Myres, John 60
myrrh 390, 453, 499, 510
Myrtos *259*, 309
myths 118, 174, 179, 295, 503, 573: Greek 548; Ugaritic 381, 394. *See also* deities; gods/goddesses
M'zora *258*, 267, *267*

Nabta Playa 198, 200
Nagar 239
Nahal Hemar Cave *151*, 169, *169*, *xiv*
Nahal Mishmar Cave *205*, 246–48, *247*
Nahal Qana Cave *205*, 241, 248, *xix*
Nahr Ibrahim River 301
Naples 115, 180
Naqada *205*, 208
Naram-Sin 276, 285, *285*, 295
Narbonne 219
narcotics 36
Narmer 272, 287: palette 261, *261*, 270
national identity 50, 53. *See also* identity
Natufian culture 136, 145, 161, 163, 495, 602: burial *147*; communities *145*, 146–47; Early 179; Late 155; teeth 146
Naukratis *509*, 553–55, 575
Nausikaä 447
naval: engagements 406, 529; flotillas 514, 584; forces 547; warfare 559, 560. *See also* ship(s), for war
navetas 422, 481, 496
navigation 35, 62, 107, 152, 158, 212, 214, 233, 331, 491: coastal 72–79; long-range 329; marks 393
Naxos (Greece) *xiv*, xv, 328
Naxos (Sicily) *508*, 528
Nea Nikomedeia *151*, 189, *189*
Neander Valley 101
Neanderthalization 96
Neanderthals 92, 96, 98–109, *107*, 112–13, 115, 117,

125–27, 152, 155: collapse 116; genome 97, 102; landscapes *103*; refugia 110–11; societies 118
Near East 24, 27: impact on Mediterranean 594–95; influence 545; languages 205; markets 510
Nebuchadnezzar 536
Necho 554, 575
necklaces: faience 351; images *306*
necropoleis 272, 488
needles 117, *199*
Negev 66, 102, 113, 136, 158, 172, 178, 241, 243, 293, 298, 510
Neith 275
Nemea *259*, 311, *311*
Neo-Assyrian *446*: kings 507; reforms 558
Neo-Babylonia *508*
Neo-Classical doctrines 26
Neolithic 24, 80, 104, 202, 216, 318, 505, 566, 594: Africa xv–xvi, 206; agriculture 568; Anatolian plateau 173; animal husbandry 215; arrowheads 16, 26; boundaries 333; canoes 328, 597; changes from 306; communities 189, 192; cup, painted *227*; diet 194; expansion 195; France 36; houses *30*, 223; Iberia 39, 184; Levant 160–69, 238, 495; as a low-altitude phenomenon 223; maritime 193; Middle 190; networks 236; package 184, 196, 200, 211–12, 215; pottery 228; Rabat 209; sea-crossings 569; settlement 187, *191*, *225*, 226, 327; societies 178, 218; tells, decline of 320; terminals 305; trade 217; villages *32*, 35, 214, 219, *220*, 221, 269, 313
Neolithicization 184–88
Nerja Cave *110*, 127, *150*, 194
Netiv Hagdud *151*, 164
nets 117, 135, 136, *169*, 179, 182, 197, 198
networks 67, 118, 122, 163, 170, 233, 306, 314, 315, 332–33, 335, 337, 350, 491, 494, 547, 597, 602: Carthaginian 581–82; expansion of 532; maritime 248, *258–59*, *308*; Mediterranean 20; survival 265
New York, museums 50
New Zealand, canoes 329
Nigeria 198
Nikosthenes 551
Nile River 59, 67–68, 73–74, 77, 124, 130, 132, 145, 158, 197, 203, 239, 244–45, 259, 261–62, 265, 267–71, *274*, 279, 290, 306, 339, 357, 381, 404, 601: compared to Grand Canyon 82; corridor 59, 268, 272; Delta 32, 37, 40, 46, 57, 75, 204, 206, 208, 210, 238, 257–58, 266, 268, 272, *274*, 285, 291, 310, 325, 354, 361, 364, 374, 383–86, 405, 413, 426, 490, 541, 553, 598: demography 416; First Cataract 302; floods 349; harbour, image 396; juglets 380; molluscs 301; perch 450; pottery trade 391; shells 248; towns 523; Valley 40, 68, 200, 205–6, 234, 266, 345, 359, 594
Nîmes *508*, 565
Nimrud *446*, *447*, 491
Nineveh 507, *508*, 515
Niqmaddu II 399
Niqmepa 394
Nora *446*, 489, *489*
nomadism 205, 266, 464
North America 63, 159
North Sea 73
Norwich, John Julius 24
Nubia 69, 101, 276, 285, 291, 339, 359, 360, 376, *508*, 554: gold 386, 389; people 52, *52*, 403
numerical system 554
Numidia 39: polities 581
nuraghi 50, 424–25, 477, 493–94, 496, 527–28, 581, *xxxv*
nutrition 170
nuts 124–25, 179, 181, 210, 219, 247, 428
Nuzi ware cups 391

oak(s) 103–4, 120–21, 124, 130, 219, 221, 224, 262, 310: broadleaf 263; forests 157
oases 59, *164*, 200, 208, 242, 265–66, 268, 350, 457, 507, 554: route 384; theory 43
oats 181, 189, 196, 464
'Obelisk temple' (Byblos) 363
obsidian 35, 68, 105, 108, 132, 145, 152–54, 163, 168, 173–74, 178, 181–82, 184, 194, 211–12, 217, 229, 236, 428–30, 476: Anatolia 229, 238, 248; dispersal 231–33, *232*; Kythera 16; Lipari 215, 218, 230; Melos 153, 189, 215; Pantelleria 213, 230–32, *231*, 351, 572; Sardinia 216; sources *69*, *153*; trade 248; Tyrrhenian 305

Oceanos 63
ochre 99, 218, 229–30, 242, 342: carved 100, 110; drawings 135; -painted chambers 340
octopus, images 444
Odiel River 482
Odysseus 329, 351
Odyssey 74, 374, 447, 535, 549, 569, 573
offerings 363, 502, 531–32, 558: Kythera 16; Sardinia 528; vessels 241. *See also* sacrifices
Ognina 346, 429, 430
Ohalo II *111, 124*, 125–26, 135, 244, 595
oil 35, 36, 268, 285, 287–88, 296, 356, 360, 411, 414, 443: Aegean 555; cash-cropping 510; cedar 286; Cyprus 399; flasks 485, 487, 502, 512; flax 160; Gadir 527; growing markets for 507; industry, Italy 546; Levant 452, 511; perfumed 277, 336, 381, 397, 410, 517; -pressing installations 393; receipts for 500; trade profits 552; Ugarit 395; vessels 303. *See also* olive(s), oil
Öküzini *111, 132, 151*, 175, 188
Old Kingdom Egypt 272, 287, 359, 378, 396, 499: boats 373; disintegration 349; monuments 303; pottery 277; stone vessels 381, 382; texts 291; tombs *274*
Old Testament 295, 452, 486, 499, 535, 536
Olduvai Gorge 83, *83*
oligarchy 451, 542–44, 558, 580
olive(s) viii, 56–57, 62, 104, 121, 125, 157, 172, 245, 247, 280, 293, 296, 313, 316, 339, 343, 350, 381, 386, 444, 473–74, 547, 549, 596: cash-cropping 355; Cyprus 449; domestic 309, 310; genetics 121; groves 416; Iberia 516; Italy 515; North Africa 570; pips, North Africa 568; pollen 88; trees 372; Uluburun shipwreck 401; wild 262
Olmedo 316
Olympia *347*, 351, 502, *509*, 531, 532, 558
Oman 239: copper 284, 367, 376
onagers 130, 136, 365
onions, wild 199
opium 222, 223, 230, 390
Oran 527, 570
Oranian 'Neolithic' 210
Orce *84*, 93
orchards 386, 500
Ore Mountains. *See* Erzgebirge
ores 236, 245, 304, 308: Alpine 423, 441; Iberia 482; Italy 512. *See also* metal(s)/metallurgy
orientalization 518
ornaments 145, 179, 229: body *119*, 208; Greek, in Sicily 539
Orontes: River 241, 295, 463, 499; Valley 297, 363
Oropos *509*, 515
orpiment, Uluburun shipwreck 401
Orsi, Paolo 28
Ortygia 529
Oscan language 519
Osiris 26
Osorkon 498
Osteria dell'Osa *446*, 504
Ostia *508*, 553
ostrich eggs/eggshell 106, 199, *199*, 209, 318, 323, 334, 351, 371, 478, 569: beads, Morocco 267; carved 132; decorated 199; Iberia 484; Uluburun shipwreck 401
ostriches: feathers 457; images 205
Otomani culture 425, 442: copper 441
Otranto Strait. *See* Strait of Otranto
Ottoman empire 28, 37
Oued Beht *xvii, xviii, xix, xxii*
Oued Djebbana *84*, 100
Oujda 210
outriggers 327
ovens 526: bread 170; earth 218, 219, 220; France 221; Italy 221
owls 91: images 556
oxen 279, 296, 311, 426: carts 464; images 309, *311*; yokes *311*, 476. *See also* cattle
oxhide ingots 376–77, 389, 403, 409, 431, 450, 477, 481, 567, 576, 610: images 471; Ugarit 393; Uluburun shipwreck *34*, 401
oxygen isotope ratios 88
oysters 181
Ozieri phase 217, 235, 340: pottery styles 236; villages 234

Pacific Northwest, canoes 329
Pacific Ocean 42, 85, 154
paddles 108
Padua *508, 562*
Paestum. *See* Poseidonia
pageants 544. *See also* ceremonies; festivals
Paglicci. *See* Grotta Paglicci
paint: bat-dung 221; gold 236; on pebbles 179
paintings: cave *114*, 228, *IX*; Palaeolithic 202; tomb 361. *See also* wall-paintings
Pakefield 94
Pakistan 262, 278
palace(s) 276, 294–96, 302, 338, 356, 358–59, 413, 415, 484: Aegean 459; Amathus 520; Anatolia 366; Assyrian 515; Avaris 384, 386, 388, 403, 455; Bronze Age 188; challenges faced by 414; Crete 369, 370–71, 409; design 500; economies 366, 472; elites, Aegean 462; Greece 35; markets 402; Minoan 352–53; Mycenaean 443, 547; states 353, 355, 468, 469; systems 532, 548, 602–3; towns 323; Ugarit 32, 391, 393
Palaeolithic 38, 80, 91–92, 101, 187: art 127; caves 127; Cyprus 148; figurines 228; Greece 119; Lower 91, 92; Middle 98, 101, 108; paintings 202; seafaring xv; tools 99, 128; Turkey 36–37; Upper 39, 109, 111–12, 114, 117, 119, 229
Palaghju 346, 423, *446*, 480
Palagruža 78–79, 184, 190, 213, *258, 331–32, 335*, 477, 562
Palatine 504
Palermo 105, 131, 213
Palermo Stone 291
palettes 272: pigment-grinding 206
Paliokastritsa 45
Paliopaphos *347*, 408, *447*, 450
palisades 224, 226, 318
palm trees 121, 290
Palmarola 69, 184, 212, 215: obsidian 232, *232*
palmettes 388
Palmyra. *See* Tadmor
Panarea 212, *218*, 429
Panaztepe 412
Pantalica *446*, 474, *508*, 529, *XXXVII*
Pantelleria 69, 78, 184, 211–13, 215, 230–32, 430, 572, *XVI*
Papuan villages 203
papyrus 273, 275, 301, 388, 445–46, 448, 456, 484: Egyptian 555; medical 403; reed 200
Parapola 331
Paris basin 187
Paris, museums 50
Parpalló Cave *110*, 124
Passo di Corvo *204*, 224, 233
Pastoral phases 203
pastoralism 202, 204–12, 266, 268, 293, 299, 361, 406, 561, 596: Africa 457, 568, 601; cattle *206*; expansion *204–5*; market-driven 579; mobile 40, 601; sheep/goat 150–51. *See also* pastoralists
pastoralists 62, 241, 264, 289, 309, 326, 432, 499, 569: Africa 572; Sudan 203. *See also* pastoralism
peak-top sanctuaries 353, 355
pear 181
pearl millet 196
peas 106, 160, *161*, 219
pebbles, incised 131
Pech Maho *508*, 563, 566
Peiro Signado *150*, 194
Peisistratids 541
Peisistratos of Athens 551
Pelagie islands 78
Peleset 461, 462. *See also* Philistines; Sea People
Pella *347*, 365
Peloponnese 16, 33, 73, 79, 105, 119, 152, 223, 234, 311, 331, 371, 409, 412–13, 432, 460, 465, 502, 529, 531, 532: war 576
Pelusiac branch (of Nile) *274*, 360, 361, 383, 553
pendants 351, 501: ivory *VIII*; jadeite 230
Pendimoun rockshelter 193
penis sheaths 131, 457
Penitenzeria *204*, 223
pentekonters 559
Pepi I 302
Peqi'in *205*, 241
Perachora 532
perch 450

Perdigoes *258, 319*
perfume 378: flasks 546; Greek 545; jars *297*, 547; oil 410, 485
Periander of Corinth 541
periplous 72–79
Perpignan 219
Persepolis *508*, 584
Persian empire 583, 584, 610: wars 25
Persian Gulf 60, *61*, 62, 239, 269, 284–85, 290, 348, 511
Perunefer 387, 396, 411
Peschiera 446, 477
pestles *145*, 183, *XI*
Petralona *85*, 92
Petrie, Flinders 28
Phaedo 87
Phaiakia 535
Phaistos 259, 323, *347*, 369, 381
Phaleron 552
Phanourios minutus. See pigmy hippopotami
pharaohs 41, 68, 78, 205, 261, 269, 272, 275, 278, 291, 323, 349, 359, 362, 365, 386, 397, 403, 406–7, 452, 454, 456–57, 461, 471, 498, 604: gifts 338; prestige 553–54
Philip II of Macedon 24, 37
Philistines 461, 462, 463, 470: polities 499; towns 452
philosophy 536, 545
Phlegraean Fields 115
Phocaea *509*, 550: coins 556; people 564, 567, 584
Phoenicia(n) i, 449, 450, 484, 583: activity 547; alphabet 518; amphorae 516, 517; communities 542; demography 580; enclaves 500, 522, 525, 527–29, 566, 569; on Etruscan coast 553; expansion 511; expedition around Africa 554; exports to France 564; goddesses 244; Iberia's resemblance to 526; language 519; necropolis 488; network 546; North Africa 38; outposts 573; people 20, 50, 266–67, 301, 319, 343, 485, 487, 512, 514, 530, 533–34, 556, 567; plates, in Africa 568; ports 459; pottery 489; seafarers 494; ships 515; towns 470, 582; traders 419, 481, 555, 574; zone 551
Phorades *347*, 367
phrygana 62
Phrygia 520, 532, 577: polities 537
Phylakopi *447*, 467
physicians 397
phytoliths 36
Piazza della Signoria, Florence 217
Picasso, Pablo 49
pick ingots 477, *477*, 479
picks 230, 525
picrolite 149, 216, *216*, 342
Pi-emrôye. *See* Naukratis
pig(s) 131, 161, 166, *176*, 177, 185, 189, 201, 309, 330: bone, carved 227; Cyprus 342; fat 57; Italy 428; Jordan 363; Lampedusa 212; Levant 452; Levantine in Africa 206, 207; North Africa 568; wild 175
pigments 99, 105, 205–6, 229, 237. *See also* dye; ochre; paint
pigmy hippopotami 148–49
Pillars of Hercules 20. *See also* Melqart, pillars of
Pindos mountains 63, *134*, 223, 412
pine 62, 103–4, 120–22, 130, 294
pine nuts 106, 199
pins 173, 306, 336, *337*, 473
Piombino 479
piracy 466, 552, 607
Piraeus 18, 552, 582
Piramesse *447*, 455, 456, 498. *See also* Qantir
piriform jars 391
pistachio 106, 157, 181, 262
Pithekoussai *508*, 512–13, *512*, 515, 518, 522, 524, 530, 532, 548, 598: amphorae 517; graves 521
pithoi 244, 401, 402, 465
Pitiusic islands 78
Piyamaradu 463
Placard Cave *110*: spearhead *123*
plains 64, 66: coastal 306; Europe 113. *See also under names of individual plains*
plant(s) 56, *56*, 61, 70, 136, 210: aquatic 124; domestication 160, *161*, 165, 173, 177, 201; management, early 595; North Africa 196; paucity of 193; processing 125; shift in dominant 262; wild 181. *See also under names of individual species*

plaques 124: bone 351; bossed 428; faience 404; sandstone 226

plate tectonics 63–71, 82, 90

plates: Phoenician 526, 568; wheelmade 484

Platia Magoula Zarkou *204*, 225, *225*

Plato 55, 87, 603

playas 200

Pleistocene 83, 87–91, 95, 108, 125, 128, 133, 146, 151, 155, 160, 199, 205, 217, 300, 326, 597, 600, 610: animals 104; climate 41, 100, *129*; coastal plains 130; Cyprus 149; evaporation 159; glaciations 116; ice caps 202; postglacial 179; refugia *84–85*; sea 94; seafaring 596

Pliny the Elder 151, 574

Pliocene 82, 85: Italy *85*

ploughs/ploughing 221, 244, 273, 276, 279, 287, 293, 313, 339, 426: images 309, 311, *311*; models 343, *344*

Po: plain vii, 3, 192, 218, 308, 519, 562, 576, 578; river 73, 230, 232, 425, 426; steppes 104; Valley 64, 113, 120, 135, 194–96; wetlands 478

poetry 459, 519, 536, 542–43, 545: epic 535; Greek 484

Poggiomarino *508*, 512, *512*

Poland, wheels 382

Poliochni *259*, 322, 336, *336*

politics/political 51: change 468, 469, 470; collapses 449–60; culture 234, 408; description in texts 295; expansion, Egypt 270; legitimacy 375; structure 276

polities 269, 358, 519, 603, 607: Aegean 381–82; Bronze Age 547; Crete 359, 385; Cyprus 408; Etruscan 479; Iron Age 471, 522, 534; Israel 488; Levant 363–64, 395, 398, 507, 542; Mycenaean 412; Numidian 581; palatial 375; Philistine 499; Phrygian 537

pollen 36, 88, 120–21, 128, 157, 201, 209, 360: analysis, Iceman 261; cores 103; records 43; Kythera 16

pollock 127

pollution 45

Polybius 151, 578, 579

Polycrates of Samos 541, 545, 551, 560, 607

pomegranates 244, 247, 401

Pompeii 26, 428, 512, *512*, 539

ponds 206

Pont de Roque-Haute *150*, 194: leapfrogging *192*

Pontevedra 416

Pontic mountains 246, 277, 338, 458

poplar 219

poppies 222, *223*

population 33, 358: Aegean 460; collapse 172, 216; growth 132, 238, 241, 506–7, 538, 582, 603; Iron Age 522; migrations 186; redistributions 179; Vera Basin 419

Populonia 446, 504, *508*, 552, 556

portable art 132

Portella *346*, 430

Porto Badisco 221, *228*

ports 357, 358, 552: communities 524; Crete 472; Cyprus 466; Etruscan 553; Levant 484, 485; Phoenician 459. *See also* anchorages; harbours

Portugal 56, 116, 119, 181, 195, 235, 318, 574: core *42*

Portus 553

Poseidonia *508*, 550

pottery 170, 184, 190, 197, 219, 227, 246, 283, 376: absence of 175, 178; Aegean 394, 402–3, 431, *442*, 443, 465, 489, 548; Aegean in Ugarit 394; Africa 198, 199; African pastoralist 205; Anatolia *336*; Arabian 454; Athenian in Venice 562; barbarian ware 463–64; black-and-white 517; black-figure 548, 551, *XLV*; boat images 329; *bucchero*, Etruscan, in France 564; Capsian 210; Cardial *191*, 201, 210; Carthage 490; central Mediterranean 430; chaff-tempered 241; composition of 35, 36; Copper Age 319; Corinthian 547; for cosmetics 302, 354; Cretan style in Egypt 362; Crete 380; Cyclades 308; Cypriot 216, 343, 368, 403, 444; Cypriot in Egypt 362, 385; Cyrenaica 268; decorated 194, 226, 235, 236, 267, 306, 318, 322, 329; decorated, decline of 239; demise of local styles 235; drinking and serving, Crete 370; Egypt 206, 207, 271, 287, 397; Egyptian-style 208; elaborate 341; Etruscan 26, 542, 546, *XLV*; flasks 336; Fontbouisse 307; France 306, 308; Greek 189, 536; Greek in Africa 573; Greek in central Europe 577; Greek in the Levant 584; handmade 472, 568; Iberia 308, 310, 483; Ilıpınar 238; images on 213; imported, Egypt 555; impressed 191,

191, 192, 195, 209, 227; incised 189; Italy 428; Knossos-style 216; Kythera 16; Lampedusa 212; Levantine 247, 261, 303, 403; Makriyalos 221; Malta 341–42; mass produced 236, 409; Mesopotamia 284; monochrome 485; Morocco 267; Mycenaean 411, 413; Neolithic 229; North Africa 268, 568; painted 212, 218, 333–34, 429, 472, 513; painted, Aegean 382, 411, 413–15, 469, 476–78, 481, 500; painted, Arpi 562; painted, Crete 369; painted, Egypt 270; painted, Greek 608; perforated 310; Phoenician 487, 489, 526; plain 239, 420; polychrome figural style 517; pot-marks 430; red-figure 548; residues in 205; ritual 327; Sardinian 217, 493, 502; Sardinian styles 330; Serro d'Alto-style *227*; sherd with copper slag 237–38; ship images 464; standardization 275; styles 41, 185, 194; technology 338, 353; Tell el-Hayyat 365; as a trade item 391; for transporting liquids 34, 379, 411, 516; uniformity 235; wheel-made 275, 276, 294, 336, 362, 380, 444, 473–74, 481

pouring vessels 381. *See also* flasks; juglets; jugs

power 270, 271, 306, 314, 323, 329, 352, 358. *See also* authority; elite(s); status

PPN. *See* Pre-Pottery Neolithic

PPNA. *See* Pre-Pottery Neolithic A (PPNA)

PPNB. *See* Pre-Pottery Neolithic B (PPNB)

PPNC. *See* Pre-Pottery Neolithic C (PPNC)

Praeneste *508*, *XLIII*

precipitation. *See* rainfall

pre-Neolithic languages 519

Pre-Pottery Neolithic (PPN) *151*, 163, 178, 225, 596, 598

Pre-Pottery Neolithic A (PPNA) 164–65, 167–68, 170, 175

Pre-Pottery Neolithic B (PPNB) 165, *166*, 167–69, 173, 175, 179, 189, 216, 226, 244, 323: animals *176*; decorated skull *168*; mega-sites 238, 242

Pre-Pottery Neolithic C (PPNC) 170

preservation conditions 29

prestige 306: goods 287, 321–24, 321, 350, 375, 598

prickly oak 62, 262

Priene 77, *77*

priestesses 542

priesthood 543

Prince Albert I of Monaco 119

privacy 167

profit 413, 484, 511, 523, 552, 602, 603: from grain trade 562

projectile points 101, 124, 125, 133

Prolagus sardus 127, 128, 150–51, 183, *183*

propaganda, Egyptian 461, 462

prophets, Israelite 390, 521

proto-Berbers 205

proto-empires *346*, 468

Provence 58, 119, 121–22, *191*, 193, 306, 564: leapfrogging *192*

pueblos 204

Puig des Molins 567

Pula 122

pulses 160, 169, 177, 309, 310

Pumay 489

Pumayyaton 490

pumice 427

punch 333

Punic 484, 580: language 581; towns 486; wars 490

Punt 285, 357

Punta Milazzese *346*, 429

Pupicina Cave *150*, 180

Purcell, Nicholas 19, 20, 21, 54, 57, 65, 264, 307, 537, 547, 595

Pylos *xxv*, *347*, 410, 412, 418, 429, *447*, 464: palaces 459, 460

pyramids 41, 272, *273*, 424

Pyrenees 51, 63, 105, 120, 180, 195, 224, 230, 481–82, 566: foothills 563

Pyrgi *508*, 553, *553*, *XLVII*

Qadesh 31, *447*, 454, 456, 458

Qafzeh *85*, 98, 100

Qantir *447*, 455, 604. *See also* Piramesse

Qarthadasht 488. *See also* Carthage

Qatna *259*, 297, *347*, 365, 366, 375, 387: royal tomb 407; textiles 378

quadrigas 571, 577

quarries 113, 114, 232, 268: obsidian 230

quartz 318

quays 393, 485

Qustul *258*, 291: incense burner *291*

Rabat *204*, 209, 267

rabbits 104, 117, 213: actually *Prolagus sardus* 151

radiocarbon dating 41, 109, 154

rafts, vegetation 95, 96

Ragusa *346*, 444

raiding 552: by sea 329, 359, 462, 466, 469

Rainbow Serpent myths 179

rainfall 56, 66–67, 66, 72, 89, 121, 130, 136, 156–57, 166, 263, 265, 313, 348, 350, 600: Egypt 207; unpredictable 264

Ramesses II 24, 31, 455, 610: images *52*; statues 554

Ramesses III 464: mortuary temple 461

Ramessid Egypt 454, 471, 537, 604

rams (animal). *See* sheep

rams: battering 362; ship-mounted 514, 560

Ras ed-Drek 490

Ras ibn Hani 393, 449

Ras Shamra 27, *151*, 169, 171, *259*, 303. *See also* Ugarit

Rasm Harbush 205, 244

rats, black 213

razors 305–6

reaping tools *125*

reciprocity 168

red deer 104, 114, 120, 130, 135, 567

Red Sea 59, 60, *61*, 62–64, 68, 87, 112, 145, 163, 200–1, 205, 261, 285, 357, 453, 500, 554, 572, 575: saga 374; shell beads 206; shells 169; voyages 390, 487

Red Skorba wares 236

reed(s) 168, 275: boats 239, 290; mats 241, 247; Ugarit 395

refugia 12, *84–85*, 89, 104, *110–11*, 112, 115, 121, 123, 130, 131, 146, 196

reindeer 104, 120

religious festivals 277, 544, 558

Renfrew, Colin 23, 314

reptiles 150

rescue archaeology 29, *32*

reservoirs 265

Reshef 530

resins 36, 70, 277, 285, 288, 303, 360

Rhafas Cave *204*, 210

Rhine River 118, 333

rhinoceroses 104, 157

Rhodes 78, 188, 212, 338, 409, 412, 487, 512, 523

Rhône River 58, 73, 77, 193–95, 223–24, 230, 232, 306, 312, 331, 334, 422, 563, 566, 577, 598: compared to Grand Canyon 82; corridor 316; delta 203, 564; Valley 74, 119, 221

Ricardo, David 414

riding 326, 511, 577

Rif mountains 63, 64, 82, 267

Rift Valley. *See* Great Rift Valley

Rimini 562

ring-idols 237

rings, gold 383

Río Tinto 263, 482, 515

Riparo Dalmeri *110*, 135

Riparo di Fontana Nuova *110*, 114

Riparo Mochi 121

Ripoli *204*, 234

ritual(s) *131*, 172, 199, 218–19, 247, 276, 323, 390: ancestor 519; arenas 235; buildings 168; centres 224, 558; Egypt 271; enclosure 533; experts 397; Fertile Crescent 164; games 531; Malta 341, 342; Menorca 567; objects 226; offerings, Sardinia 528; places 223, 227, 493; power 308; Sardinia 424, 528; stands 472; stele 574; structures 340

rivercraft 289, 290: adaptation to seacraft 291

riveting 278

Roaix *258*, 312

Roca Vecchia *347*, 428, *442*, 443, *447*, 474

Rochelongue 546

rock art 119, 157, 179, *315*, 324: Africa 197, 198, 205, 571; Alps 311; Atlas mountains 267; boat images 329; carvings 131, *131*, 412; Copper Age xxiv, 308–9; France *114*, *IX*; Iberia 315; Levantine-style *227*; Maghreb 418; Sahara *197*; ship images 464; tradition 227

rock crystal 31, 318, 321, 378
rock-cut tombs 42, 217, 340, *422*, 424, *XXXVII*
Roda *508*, 566
rodents 123, 567: giant 70
roe deer 104, 130
Roman period 262, 266, 321, 465, 515, 525, 538, 547, 558, 561, 570, 572, 574: authors 484; Corsica 151; empire 33, 39, 77, 378, 383, 467, 578, *606*; legions 571; olives 57; republic 583; sack of Carthage 522; tourism 45; towns 210, 412; Zembra 213. See also Rome
Romanelli. See Grotta Romanelli
Rome 28, 33, 92–93, 214, 327, *346*, 427, *446*, 479, *479*, 503–4, *508*, 540, 541, 547–48, 553, 578–81, 597, 606–7: centralization of Mediterranean 605; *mare nostrum* 20; population 522; temples 558. See also Roman period
Ronda 538
roof-tiles 531
rope 292, 401
Rosetta branch (of Nile) 553
Rosetta Stone 554
roundhouses 175, 177, 342, *342*, 474
'route of the isles' *446–47*, 465, 491, 496, 504
rowing 292
Rudna Glava *204*, 236
'ruined landscape' theory 71
Russia 102, 113, 132: steppes 58, 66, 73, 119, 373, 383, 432
rye 161, 464

Sa Caleta *508*, 567
Sabratha *508*, 569
sacrifice(s) 483, 511: human 533; in water 477
Sado River 194, 574
safflower, Uluburun shipwreck 401
saffron 378
Sahara 51, 58, 66, 87, 89, 100–1, 112, 120, 196–204, 210, 265–68, 577, 599, 601: Aterian 103; Atlantic shore 209; environments and societies 40; goods 572; Holocene *158*, 326; lakes 43, 130, *158*; oasis 507; pastoralism *204–5*, *206*, 208, 210; rainfall 156; rock art *197*; watershed 157
Sahel 158: fauna 197
Sahure 291
saiga antelopes 104
sailing 327, 338, 464: images 362; invention of 290, 330; latitude *446–47*, 465, 466; ships 81, 292, 300, 301, 329, 331, 343, 353–54, 373, 393, 416, 422, 442, 477, 492–93, 537, 548, 597, 602; technology 55, 303, 472–73
St Augustine 581
Saint-Blaise *508*, 564, 566
Saint-Michel-du-Touch *204*, 224, 226, 234
Saint-Véran *346*, 423
Saïs *205*, 206, *259*, *274*, 275, *509*, 553–55, 575, 604
Salamis (Cyprus) 450, *509*, 519, 520, 523
Salamis (Greece) 584, 609–10
Salé *84*, 98
Salento 104
Saliagos *204*, 215
Salina 212, 430
salinity 42
salmon, images 127
salt 220, 230, 393, 573, 574: marshes 159; pots 227; preservation 264
'saltwater country' 57
Samaria 241, 407, *447*, 500, *509*: Assyria's elimination of 521; elites 521
Samnite: polities 561; territory 504
Samos *509*, 531, 532, 554, 557: people 555
Samothrace 412
San Fernando, rainfall *66*
San Juan ante Portam Latinam 315
San Marco 150, 192, *204*, 223
sanctuaries 476: Crete 353, 355; Greek 558. See also temples
sandals 242: papyrus 200. See also shoes
sandstone plaques 226
Sant'Abbondio cemetery *346*, 428
Sant'Agostino. See Grotta di Sant'Agostino
Sant'Angelo Muxaro *508*, 529
Sant'Antioco 527
Sant'Imbenia *446*, 494, 489
Sant'Iroxi Decimoputzu *346*, 424

Santa Maria is Acquas *110*, 128
Santa Olaia 508, 574
Santiago de Compostela 105
Santorini. See Thera
Saône River 577
Sappho 542, 545
Saqqara *259*, *272*, *273*, *347*, 348
sarcophagi 485, 488
Sard language 519
Sardis *509*, 537
sardines 135, 183
Sardinia iii, iv, vii, 35, 69, 73, 76, 78, 95, 107, 121, 127–28, 155–56, 182, 187, 192–93, 234, 237, 305, 307, 310, 316, 330–31, 335, 340, 350, 431, 443–44, 462, 480, 488–89, 491–93, 504, 512, 517, 528, 533, 543, 572: amphorae 516; Argaric sword 481; beakers 334; boom 476; canids 70; Corsican bracelets 217; Cypriot influence 476; demography 476; exports 484; figurines 26, *26*, 48, 228, *228*; grapes 515; horses 581; isolation 476; links with Cyprus 465; metals 442, 500, 527, 567; Neolithic 216; nuraghi 496; obsidian 184, 232; pottery 217, 236, *463*; *Prolagus sardus* 151; stone statues 546; stone towers 424; tin 415; tombs 234, *235*, 312, 524
Sarepta *447*, 449
Sargon II 511, 534
Sargon of Akkad 276, 285, 295
Saronic Gulf 371, 410, 550, 609, 610
sauceboats 335
Sauveterrian 180
savannah(s) 83, 85, 104, 121, 157–58, 164, 262, 310, 421: animals, images 556
Sawaw. See Marsa Gawasis
saws 328
scalping 179
Scandinavia 334
scarabs 354, 360, 362, 376, 384, 432, 465: Sardinia 527; seal *xxv*, 349; Uluburun shipwreck 402
scarification 231
Schliemann, Heinrich 27, 324, 335
Schöningen 92
Sciacca 489
Scilly Isles 490
Scoglio del Tonno *347*, 428, *442*, 443, *447*, 529
scoops 219
Scorpion king 270
Scotland 230
scrapers 109, 133
scribes 407, 469
scripts 393–94, 409, 510, 518: alphabetical 448; Greek 566; Iberia 519; syllabic 534. See also writing(s)
scrub 104, 157, 262, 266
sculptures 48: Greek 557. See also figurines; statues
Scythians 326, 577
sea: contacts 287; cores 372; -crossings 49, 72, 94, 95, 112, 115, 122, 128, 152–54, 180, 182, 211, 213–14, 231, *308*, 320, *346–47*, 374, 403, 465–66, 596–97; -fishing 126–28; inland 61; levels 42, 82, 84, 90, 129–30, 158–59, 171, 376; level rise 146, 181–82, 187, 193, 202; mammals 126, 180; -moats 486, 525; raids 329, 359, 462, 466, 469; -routes 338, 362, 470; shells, Red Sea 163; temperatures 42, 120; trade 52, 239, 322, 327, 357, 359, 373, 386, 443, 492, 511, 546; trade, long-range 330–39, 478, 491
Sea of Galilee 125, 183, 209, *209*: images 126, 556
Sea of Japan 61, *61*, 62
Sea of Marmara 159, 181, 188, 194, 195, 432, 575–76
Sea of Okhotsk 61
Sea People 462, 464, 466, 468–69, 478, 480, 484, 494: networks 470. See also Shardana
sea turtles, images 556
seabirds 180
seafaring *x*, 62, 108, 113, 127, 147, 154–56, 178, 183–84, 212, 301, 319, 329, 441, 477, 599, 609: abilities 152; absence of, in North Africa *xix–xx*, 572; Adriatic 352; expansion *597*; hunter-gatherer 187; knowledge 195; Neolithic 211, 212; nomadic 466; technology 177. See also boats; canoes; galleys; ship(s); shipwrecks
seafood 135, 188, 221
sealings 239, 275, 287, *336*, 338
seals (animal) 183, 209, *209*: images 126, 556
seals (artifact) *xxv*, 188, 276, *278*, 279, 287, 299, 327, 336, 354, 360, 363, 373, 376, 517–18: Cretan 353; impressions in clay 240; Minoan 105; Sardinia 527
seal-stone 474

seasonality 124, 160
seaweed 106
Second World War. See World War II
sedentism 124, 136, 145, 166, 208, 567, 594
sedimentation rates 43
seeds 36, 124, 125, 169
Segesta *508*, 539
Segura River 527
Seine River 577
Selinous *508*, 538, 548–49, 557, *XLVI*
Semitic: languages 205, 295; loanwords 410; names 450
Sennacherib 507
Serbia 236
serekhs *286*, 287
Seriphos 153
serpentine bracelets 217
Serpis basin 227
serving vessels 411, 500, 517: Etruscan, in France 564
Servius Tullius 544
Sesklo *204*, 225
Sète 481
Setefilla *446*, 482
Seth 455
settlement(s): changing landscapes 234; Corsica 221; Crete 221; demise of large 298, 349; ditch-enclosed 190; drowned 29, 35; Egypt 361; farming 184; fortified 258, 496; France 221; growth 217; Italy 221; Levant 168, 172, 298, 300; Neolithic 187, *225*, 226, 327; Sardinia 221; small-scale 320
Seville 78, 318, 319, 418, 598
Sexi *508*, 526
shaft graves. See grave(s), shaft
Shalmaneser III 446
shamans 131
Shardana 456, 461–62, 464, 473. See also Sea People
sharks 178
Sharuhen. See Tell el-Ajjul
shashu 469
Shechem *347*, 407
sheep 136, 161, 166, 169–74, 187, 189–90, 194, 201, 206, 209, 220–21, 296, 310, 330: cave-based 223; Cyprus *176*, 342, 382; domesticated 200; figurines *243*, 244; herding 201, 245, 268, 309; herding, large-scale 279, 293; Jordan 363; Lampedusa 212; Levantine in Africa 205, 207; Menorca 422; milk 162; North Africa 266, 568; Rhafas Cave 210; shells, Red Sea 169; Tremiti islands 212; Tunisia 210; wild 185; wool 244
Shekelesh 461, 462. See also Sea People
shekels 394
shell(s) 106, 121, 132, 135, 145, 158, 168, 173–74, *180*, 207, 211, 229: Aetokremnos 148; artifacts 105, *199*; beads 184, 206; bracelets 268; clam 575; decorated 199; as decoration 168–69, *168*, 596; middens 181, 194, 378, 509; Nile 248; ornaments 100, 101, 126, 180; perforated 113, *113*, 114, 118; Red Sea 169
shellfish 180, 209, 221
Sherratt, Andrew 24
Sherratt, Susan 24
shields 462, 496, 558: images 450
Shillourokambos 151, 175, *176*, 177
ship(s) *ix*, 290, 328, 338, 343, 394, 456: Aegean 416; Athenian 15; -building 35, 464–65, 527; Byblos 301, 450, 505; Cypriot 489; Egyptian 300, 301, 402; images 303, 353, 354, *357*, 362, 373–74, 432, 461, 464, 490, 572, *xxx*; Levantine 357, 406, 447; North Africa 569; Phoenician 515; sailing 300, 301, 373, 393, 422, 442, 493, 537, 548, 597, 602; symbolism of 329; technology 327, 477; timbers, Iberia 484; for war 514, 550, 559–60, 584, 607, 609. See also boat(s); canoes; galleys; seafaring; shipwrecks
shipwrecks 17–18, 29, 34–35, 46, 75, 281, 327, 374, 378, 394, 399–402, 409, 444, 465–66, 481, 495, 546, 579: France 548, 564; Iberia 483–84
Shiqmim *205*, 241, *242*, 244, 246
shoes 117, 222: sandals 200, 242
shovels 476
shrews 150
shrines 242–43, 247, 275, 297, 353, 355, 360, 450, 452, 502, 534, 557–58: Balearics 493; Carthage 522; cattle 343; Corinth 522; Cyprus 408; Ephesus 556; Greek 555; Iberia 525; Iron Age 530, 531; Italy 553; Kythera 16; Levant 363; Motya 538; Sardinia 476; sea 562

Šibenik 190
Siberia *63*
Sicily *ii*, 27, 35, *37*, 68–69, 73–74, 78–79, 87–88, 91, 107, 114–15, 120, 131, 135, 155, 179, 187, 190–93, 211–12, 214–15, 223, 225–26, 230, 305, 309, 330–31, 333, 342, 428, 430, 442–44, 462, 465, 474–75, 479, 490, 492–93, 500, 503, 513, 548, 598: narrows 90, 94–95, 121, 568–69, 572, 599: adoption of Greek identity 533; amphorae 517; bone plaques 351; cist graves 235; climate 66; flint 229; fossil elephants 26; grapes 515; Greek goods in 539; growth of towns 538–39; hunter-gatherers 186; meat and mollusc consumption *193*; metals 237; obsidian 184, 232; Phoenician presence 528–29; shipwrecks 546; shrews 150; temples 557; towns 523–24, 552
sickles 125, 136, 199, *199*, 219, 279: blades 212; flint 393; handle 145, *x*; images *227*
Sidari *151*, 180, 190
Sidon 35, *259*, 303, *347*, 349, 357, 363, 365, 445, *447*, 449, 485, 488, 503, 509, *509*, 511, 536: cup 381; ships 584; triremes 560
sieges 398, 486
Sierra Morena 420, 482, 525
Sierra Nevada 63, 65, 66, 123, 194
Siginu 394
Silifke 396
silk 378
silos *32*, 165, 224, *299*, 310
silphion 571, *571*
silver 69, 246, 280–81, 285, 296–97, 301, 305, 337–38, 354, 360, 385, 388, 441, 515, 556: Aegean 353, 376, 381, 411, 555, 582; Anatolia 367, 376; Attica 487; bottles 482; bowls 517; Canaanite amphorae 405; Cyprus 343, 399; extraction 284; Iberia 418, 484, 551; Iberia, devalued 537, 581; ingots 304; inlay 283; jewelry 237, *237*; jugs 574; Lavrio 370, 552, 609; Levantine 284; Mesopotamia 389; Mycenae 371; shekels 394; sources 69; tools 321; trade, Gadir 525; Tyre 509; Ugarit 394; Uluburun shipwreck *401*; vessels 485; Wenamun's 445
silver-gold alloy 248, 297
silver-lead working 485
Sima de los Huesos (Atapuerca) 96, *97*
Sima del Elephante (Atapuerca) 92–93
Simonelli Cave *111*, 127
Sinai 66, 109, 132, 158, 163, 201, 241, 248, 286–87, 289, 360–61, 376, 407, 453, 604: copper 69, 285; Egyptian outposts 298; mines 288; ores, Egyptian monopoly 299; turquoise 68, 282
Sinaranu 394, 402
sinkholes 92
Sinuhe 361
Siphnos *153*, 552, 558
sistrum, clay imitations 354
6200 event 159, 179, 181, 196, 198–99, 201, 205, 238
Skarkos *308*
Skerki Bank 35
skeuomorphism *227*, 282, 380, 381
Skhirat *258*, 267
Skhul *85*, 98, 100
Sks. *See* Sexi
skulls: *Homo heidelbergensis 92*; human 165, 177; manipulation 172; masks 199; plastered 168, *168*, 169
slag 238, 299, 376, 477
slaves 549, 564: Aegean 561; as a commodity 281; France 566, 576; Saharan 572
sledgehammers 476
sledges, threshing 279, *279*
sleds 221
Slovenia 425
smelting 218, 236, 238, 246, 299, 304–5, 335, 420, 451, 476–77, 512
Smendes 445, 447, 450, 455
Smilčić *151*, 190
smithing 476
smoking (for preservation) 264
snails 152, 179, 210
snakes 567
snares 117, 136
Sneferu 291
soap 378
social: affiliations 118; alliances 333; change 44, 352; complexity 62, 269, 350; connections 115; debt/

obligation 265; hierarchies 418; inequality 264, 277, 316, 319; interaction, Neolithic 235; life 315; networks 122, 236, 306, 597; order 277, 324, 380; organization 242; power 320; reorganization 282; structures 92, 233, 424, 425; transformations 160, 269–76
societies: Aegean 350; consumer 280; cooperative 341; egalitarian 242, 260; European 442; large-scale 172, 262, 283; Levantine 293
Socrates 87
soldiery 278, 454, 558. *See also* armies; mercenaries
Solomon 499
Solon 543, 549, 583
Solutrean 123, 126, 181: spearheads 123, *123*; tools 128
Son Mercer de Baix 346, 422
Sorgenti della Nova *446*, 479
sorghum 196, 198
Sorrentine peninsula 180
Sostratos of Aegina 551, 553
South Africa 61, 62, 100
South America *63*
South China Sea 61, *61*, 62
South Pole 88
Soviet Union, collapse 29
Spain *63*, 75, 96, 116, 127, 194, 219, 223, 227, 305, 311, 418, 420, 495, 546: caves 92, 114; chalices 416; climate 42; drop in water-level 263; early hominins 92; geography 65; growth of towns 538; islands 209; metals 263, 305; 19th-century archaeology 28; olives 57; preservation conditions 29; rainfall 66; and Rome 578; tombs 311, 520; tourism 45; war 49
Spanish vetchling 378
sparrows 136
Sparta *509*, 541, 550, 581, 583: in Africa 570; currency 556; people 15, 522, 529
spears 92, 98, 277, 363: -heads 123, *123*, 283, 432; Iberia 418; throwing 125
specialization 414, 546
speech, divergence of 226
spelt wheat 473
sperm whales 73, 459, 538: engraved 126
sphinxes 388
spices 360
Spina *508*, 562
spindle(s) 219: whorls 243
spinning 310
spiny oyster (*Spondylus gaederopus*) 230
spook masks 241
Sporades 108, 182, 212
sportfishing, images 272
springs 157, 363, 476
squirrels 135
stamp seals 172, 336, 518
standardization 247, 269, 275, 281: bronze production 473; in trade 413, 556. *See also* measurement standards; weight(s)
starch grains 125
Stark, Freya 607
states 269, 270, 358: formation 287, 353. *See also* city-states
statues: Egyptian 554; Greek, inspired by Egypt 545; Middle Kingdom 384; sheet-gold 278, *XXIV*; stone 517, 545–46. *See also* figurines; sculptures
steatite 118
stegadonts 94
stele *285*, *306*, 455, 534, 574: Kamose 384; Sardinia 489; stone 511
Stelida *xiv*, *xv*
Stentinello 192, *204*, 225, 226: styles 191
steppe(s) iv, 58, 62, 66, 73, 89, 93, 103, 120, 130, 163, 171, 262, 289, 350, 355, 406, 432, 464: asses 124, 130, 131, 147; -desert 293; Po 104; Russia 113, 119, 373, 383
stirrup jars 380, 391, 401, 458, 465, 490
stockades 177
stockpiling 414, 468
stone(s): Alpine 230; anchors 291, 303, 330, 393, 401, 553; arrowheads *125*, 332; artifacts 105; axes 165, 184, 197, 210, 215, 217, 236, 246, 267, 341, 401; battle axes 321; beads 206, 226; blades 332; bowls 248, 296, 301; burnt 199; carvings 333, 496; chopper 83, *83*; coloured 205, 206; grinding 125, 136, *145*, 161, 209, 212, 218, 229; high-quality 308; Iberia 308; lack of 239; longhouses

241, 307, *307*; masks 169; ornaments 148, 208; perforated, as hobbles 205; plaques 124; points, hafted 98–99, *99*, *101*; provenance 243; quarrying 268; rare 68, 288; ritual structures 340; slabs, ochre drawings on 135; spearheads 123, *123*; standing 306; statues 517, 545–46; stele 511; tombs 312; tools 83–84, *83*, 94–95, 98, 101, 109, 123, 148, 179, 198, 268, 568; towers 423–25; tumuli 266; vase 399; vessels 175, 208, 275, 278, 302, 381, 382, 517; vessels, Crete 323, 369, 409; vessels, Egypt 243, 336, 394, 526; vessels, Egyptian, on Cyprus 343; vessels, Morocco 267; weights 221. *See also under individual types of stone*
storage 145, 162, 227, 244, 264, 295, 310, 321, 412: jars 309, 420, 518; large-scale 356; magazines 240; pits 136, 181, *207*, 318; silos *32*, *165*, 224, *299*, 310
Strabo 54
Strait of Bonifacio 423
Strait of Gibraltar 90, 94–96, 112, 128, 135, 320, 430, 527, 573
Strait of Messina 74, 91, 114, 219, 233, 443, 528, 529
Strait of Otranto 156, 190, 351, 428, 443, 474, 504, 519, 524, 529, 533
Stromboli 212, *218*
Strophylas *259*, 327, *328*
Struma River 58
sturgeon 127
Su Nuraxi *346*, *XXXV*
Sudan 40, 69, 196, 198, 205, 402: pastoralists 203
Suez isthmus 59, 87, 112, 594
Sulcis *508*, 527, 538
Suleiman the Magnificent 37
sulphide ores 281, 343, 367
sulphur 68, 442: mine 429
Sultan Mehmet II 50
Sumer 59
Sumerian language 295, 393
sun-disc images 474
surplus 19, 264, 296, 420. *See also* cash-cropping; stockpiling
Susa *204*, 239, *258*, 275, *285*, 290, *508*, 584
Sušac 79, 190, 212
swans, flightless *71*
swordfish 74, 219
swords 277, 283, 371, 480: Aegean 576; Argaric 481; Iberia 418; Sardinia 424; slashing 462–63, 472, 492; votive 493
Sybaris *509*, 529, 550
sycamore 290
symbolism 100, 109, 110, 131, 219, *228*, 280
Syracuse 429–30, *508*, 529, 538, 548, 562, 579: cemeteries 28; triremes 560
Syria 77, 99, 136, 164, 283, 285, 293, 297, 363: elephants 104; wagon model 279, *279*
Syros 322, 327, *328*

Tabaqat Fahr. *See* Pella
tablets 366, 393, 397, 409, 410, 448: clay *31*, 276; cuneiform 295; lead, France 562; Ugarit 394; writing 546
taboos 452, 570
Tadmor *347*, 350, 366
Tadrart Acacus 198: rock art *206*
Taforalt Cave *84*, 100, *110*, 123, 132, *150*, 184: harpoon 135, *135*
Tagus River 180, 194, 235, 320, 334, 421, 496, 574: sites *150*
Tajikistan 377
Tale of Sinuhe 360, 363
Tamar Hat *110*, 123
tamarisk 124, 290, 421
Tamassos *447*, 488
Tanaja 404
Tangier 201, *508*, 582: megaliths 267, *267*
Tanis *447*, 455, 456, 464, 471, 604, *XLI*
Tanit 533, 543, 580
Tanitic branch (of Nile) *274*
Taramsa *85*, 98
Taranto 428, 443, 529. *See also* Taras
Taras *509*, 529. *See also* Taranto
Tarfaya *204*, 209
Tarquinia *446*, 479, *508*, 540, 542, 551, 553, 553, *XXXVIII*
Tarsus *259*, 304, 338, 343, *447*, 459, 507
Tartessos 570: elite 525; language 519

Tarxien *258*, 327, *328*, *346*, 351, 430
Tas-Silg *508*, 531
tattoos *119*, 237, 260, 322, 457: needles 306
taulas 567
Taurus mountains 63, 130, 133, 174, 239, 246, 285, 337, 405: foothills 132; passes 178
Tavertet tombs 234
Tavoliere 64, 195, 212, 223–24, 230, 233–34, 239, 306, 313, 428, 507, 539, 562: cist graves 235; plain 190; settlements *191*, 220
Tawaret 376
taxes 270, 280, 298, 349, 356, 396, 463, 484, 500, 511, 552, 556, 584
tectonics. *See* plate tectonics
teeth: children's 135; decay 166; deer 118; deliberately removed 219; human 136, 179
Tehran 56
Tel Aviv 287
Tel Dan *259*, 297, *347*, 364, 407, *447*, 499
Tel Dor *447*
Tel Erani *259*, *286*, 287, 301
Tel Haror *347*, 375
Tel Kabri *205*, 248, *347*, 388
Tel Masos *447*, 453
Tel Nami *347*, 364, 371, 378, *447*, 467, 468
Tel Yarmouth *259*, *286*, 298
Tell Arqa *205*, 248
Tell Aswad *151*, 164
Tell Atchana 365
Tell Brak *204*, 239, *258*, *259*, 275, *347*, 349
Tell el-Ajjul *347*, 384, 411, 523
Tell el-Dab'a 32, *274*, 345, *347*, 361, 362, 376, 381
Tell el-Fara'in. *See* Buto
Tell el-Farkha *259*, 278, *xxiv*
Tell el-Hayyat *347*, 363, 365, 406
Tell el-Maskhuta *347*, 385
Tell el-Sakan *259*, *286*, 287
Tell esh-Shuna *259*, 281
Tell Ibrahim Awad *259*, *274*, 275, *347*, 360
Tell Iktanu *347*, 350
Tell Jemmeh *509*, 510
Tell Judaidah 337
Tell Kurdu *205*, 240
Tell Mardikh. *See* Ebla
Tell Sakka 363
Tellian 'Neolithic' 210
tell(s) 164, 168, 188, 190, 356, 412, 536: Africa 20; communities, decline of 320; Thessaly 220, 225, 234
temperature rises 130, 156. *See also* climate
tempering 451
temple(s) 239, 275, 281, 283, 284, 295, 302: Aphrodite 450; Byblos 363; Copper Age 531; Corinth 540; Egypt 360, 363, 471; Etruria 558; Greek 545, 557–58, *xlvi*; Hattusa 458; Karnak 405; Levant 362; Malta 41, 47, 327, 340–43, 351; of Melqart 486, 525; Mesopotamia 363; officials 276; politically neutral 467; Ramesses III 461; Rome 558; Sicily 557; Thebes 404; Ugarit 32, 393; urban 540; workshops 276
Temple Mount (Jerusalem) 534
temporality, concept of 18
Tenos 518
terebinth 121, 157, 277–78, 390, 401
terracing 16, 310, 507, 596: walls 293
terracotta, architectural 531, 551
terramare villages 426: demise of 478
Tethys ocean 63, *63*, 88
Tétouan 201
textile(s) 125, 221, 241–44, 275–76, 279, 306, 321, 377, 381, 414: Egypt 397; images 377; industries 296, 449; manufacturing 371; Mari 366; Mesopotamian 367; Uluburun shipwreck 401
Thapsos 27, *346*, 417, 429, *442*, 443–44, *446*, 476, *508*, 529
Tharros *508*, 527
Thasos 212, *258*, 474, 487, *509*
Thebes (Egypt) 59, *346*, 357, 383–87, 396, 403–5, 445–46, *447*, 454–55, 461, 471, 508, *508*, *509*
Thebes (Greece) *259*, 321, *347*, 410, 459
Theognis of Megara 543
Thera 29, *30*, 32, 372, *372*, 388, 409: and Africa 570; volcano 371
Theroux, Paul 19
Theseus 67

Thessaloniki 188, 225, 412
Thessaly 28, 64, 188, 190, 195–96, 212, 220, 223–27, 234, 239, 240, 412
Thrace 561, 583
throne, gold 532
Thucydides 528, 536
Thutmose I 387
Thutmose III 387, 389, 391, 403, 405, 406
Tiber River 427, 503, 539, 553: Valley 540, 580
tide, lack of 73
Tighenif *84*, 86
Tiglath-Pileser I *446*, 459
Tiglath-Pileser III 507
Tigris River 59, 367, 458, 507, 594
Tiksatin *204*, *xvii*
timber 174, 175, 291, 301, 491
Timgad 210
Timna *447*, 453
tin 70, 305, 336–37, 367, 389, 451, 515, 574: Aegean 411; -bronzes 337, 362, 382, 415, 441, 482; central Asia 366, 377; -copper bronzes 281; Cornish 492; eastern 576; Egypt 397; Europe 415, 442; Iberia 418, 482; ingots 401; Italy 479; sources 69; Ugarit 394; Uluburun shipwreck 401
Tinetnit 447
Tingis. *See* Tangier
Tiryns *259*, 321, *347*, 410, *447*, 450, 460: amber beads 463; palaces 459
Tjehenu 268
Tlos 412
Toba supervolcano 101, 103, 111
Tod *346*, 360, 376, *xxix*
tokens 239: clay 168, 190; pottery 430
tomb(s) 268, 284, 304, 311, 316, 324, 362, 429: Africa 206; collective 420; Copper Age 534; corbelled 317, 410; Crete 337; Cyprus 368, 408, 414, 519, 520; curses 519; Dan 407; Egypt 26, 270, 271, *274*, 286, 377, 396, 403, 471; Etruscan 48, 544; Europe 41; France 563; giants' 424; goods 334; Iberia 531; Lefkandi 502; Levant 363; looting 381, 471; Los Millares 318; megalithic 41, 267, 330, 457; Menorca 422; paintings 361; Qatna 407; rock-cut 217, 234, 340, *422*, 429, *xxxvii*; royal 281, 284; Sardinia 235, *235*; Spain 318, 520; stone 312; tholos-like 444; Tutankhamun 345; Ugarit 32, 393, 415; wealthy 474. *See also* burial(s); cemeteries; funerary activity; grave(s), human remains
Tomb U-j, Abydos 270, *271*, 277, 286
tongs 476
tophets 533, 538, 580
Toppo Daguzzo *346*, 428
Torcello 478
Torremolinos 45
torcs, copper 431
Torralba *84*, 92
tortoise(s) 106, *107*, 117, 147: -shell lyre 401. *See also* giant tortoises
Toscanos *508*, 526, 538
totems 221, 247
Toulouse *32*, 224
tourism 44, *45*, 46
towers 423–25, 551: Bronze Age 50
towns 355, 358: Aegean 582; central and west Mediterranean 521–23; Crete 370; Cyprus 408; Greece 544, 545; grid-planned 361, 523; growth of 537–39, 548; Italy 552; Nile Delta 523; Phoenician 582; Roman 412; Sicily 552
Toynbee, Arnold 43
traction 221, 276, 277, 287, 293, 311, 421, 476: images 279, *279*, 311
trade 62, 168, 178, 218–19, 226, 229–30, 239, 281–87, 297, 304, 318, 329, 332, 338, 343, 350, 356–57, 361, 492, 546: Aegean 459; Anatolia 367; Arabian 510; collapse of 349; copper 368; Cyprus 408; description in texts 295; east Mediterranean 373–83, 391–404; freelance 468, 470, 514; Gallic 564; growing volume of 549; hubs 352; in illegal antiquities 48; inter-island 323; Iron Age 513; long-distance 326, 380, 395; maritime 322; metals 236; Neolithic 217; networks 370, 413, 441, 515, 547; obsidian 248; patterns 299; Phoenician 487, 488; profits 511; routes 35, 363, 405, 431, 453, 487; shell bracelets 268. *See also* exchange
traders 404–15, 470: Cypriot 488; eastern 494; Etruscan 564; Levant 496, 502; Phoenician 555; Sardinian 493

trading posts. *See* entrepôts
Tramontana 64
transportation 67: innovations 288–92
traps 116, 179
tree-ring dating 41, 43, 72
trees 89, 103–4, 120, 146, 172, 262, 263: crops 293; felling 170
Tremiti Islands 79, 190, 212
Trianda *347*, 371
tribute 287, 290, 323, 389, 398, 403–7, 420, 459, 468, 491, 511, 581, 584
Trieste 191: karst 122, 180, 351, 426
tripod stands 219
Tripoli (Lebanon) *347*, 365
Tripoli (Libya) 42, 66, 101
triremes 560, 584
Trogir 105
Troina *258*, 309
Troodos mountains 65, 368, 407
trout 70, 159, 180: images 127
Troy 27, 50, *259*, 304, 306, 321–22, 324–25, 335–36, *336*, 338, *347*, 350, 412, 428, 432, *447*, 460, 533, 535, 576, 598, *xxxvi*: fall of 489; silver 337
Trump, David 23, 55
trumpets, Uluburun shipwreck 401
tsetse fly belt 266
Tsountas, Christos 28
tsunamis 372
tubers 83, 198
Tufariello *258*, 310, 316
Tuleilat Ghassul *205*, 241–45, *xviii*
tumuli 234, 266–68, 312, 316, 333, 335, 349–51, 426, 430, 520, 570: Athens 519; Etruria 519, 544; Levant 241
tundra 102, 104, 120
Tunisia vii, 38, 39, 69, 73, 75, 78, 122, 199, 210, *211*, 213, 547, 568, 572: coastal 211; plains 571; vegetation change 263
tunny 73, 178, 181, *181*, 182, 215, 573
Turkey 51, 58, 74, 77, 94, 132, 152, 159, 188, 366–67, 372, 412: climate 66; coast 194; drop in water-level 263; geography 65; lowland plains 64; Neolithic communities 189; phases 203; sea-crossings 72, 154, 156; south coast 374; tectonics 65; tourism 45; volcanoes 65. *See also* Anatolia
turpentine resins 390
turquoise 68, 248, 282, 286, 336, 385, 391: mines 407; Siniatic 360
Tuscany 26, 104, 155, 192, 212, 232, 234: metals 442, 500; mines 504; tin 415
Tutankhamun 281, 345, 386, 387, 432, 498: chariot gear 389; tomb 196
Tyre 35, *259*, 303, 323, 329, *347*, 349, 365, 394, 398, 445, *447*, 449, 486–88, 490, 498–99, 507, 509, 511, 515, 525, 527, 531, 573, 598, *xxxix*: elites 521; fall of 536, 543, 547, 580; people 524; warships 514
Tyrolese Alps 260
Tyrrhenian 73, 75, 192, 215, 217, 220, 230, 415–16, 425–26, 442–44, 463, 473, 480, 562: and Aegean 502; brooches 472; communities 492; Final Neolithic 203; islands 429; metallurgy 237; Neolithic expansion 187; obsidian 305; region 135, 216, 534, 546; Sea 73, 88, 114, *192*, 193–94, 312, 430, 513, 524, 529, 567, 598; seafarers 502; social interaction 235; trade 335, 481, 542; tradition 191

Uan Afuda Cave 198
Ubaid period *204*, 241, 246, 284: villages 238, 239
Ubeidiya 84–86, *85*, *86*, 89: basalt hand axe *84*
Üçağızlı *111*, 113, 127: perforated shells 113
Ugarit 27, *27*, 32, *151*, 169, *259*, 303, *347*, 349, 357, 365–66, 368, 384, 388, 391, *392*, 393, *395*, 396, 399, 401–2, 405–7, 409, 411, 441, *447*, 449, 461–62, 464, 484, 518, 548, 604: Aegean pottery 394; Egyptian artifacts 394; ivory 389; language 393; merchants 414; mythology 381, 394; palace 391; texts 390; tombs 415; trade 390. *See also* Ras Shamra
Uluburun 34, *34*, 74, *347*, 389, 399, 411, 466, *xxxiv*: shipwreck 399–402, 409–10, 412, 441, 444, 446, 465, 495
Ulucak *151*, 175
Ulysses. *See* Utuzte
Umbria 223: language 519
Umm el Tlel *85*, 99: stone point *99*